...AND INSTRUCTORS!

Test Delivery

- Tests or quizzes created from the test bank are automatically graded and linked into the grade book. This saves instructors a great amount of time.
- Select test bank questions have algorithmic functionality and are easily identified.

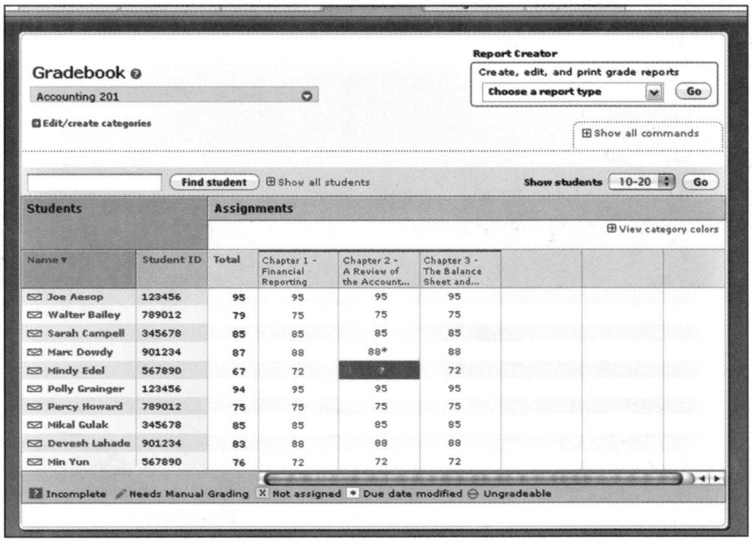

Assessment Options

- In an effort to help institutions and faculty meet AACSB & CMA accreditation standards, Thomson South-Western has tagged all ThomsonNOW content against AACSB & CMA standards.
- A custom report measures student success against specific assessment standards, allowing instructors to track progress.

Course Management

- An instructor grade book includes grades for algorithmically-generated questions.
- Options for points or percentage grading are available, and instructors have the ability to overwrite and weight grades. This grading flexibility is particularly helpful for managing a student with special needs.
- ThomsonNOW operates seamlessly with the popular WebCT® / Blackboard® technology platforms.

WebCT
A Blackboard® Company

Blackboard

Hansen & Mowen

Managerial Accounting

8TH EDITION

DON R. HANSEN
Oklahoma State University

MARYANNE M. MOWEN
Oklahoma State University

THOMSON
SOUTH-WESTERN

Australia · Brazil · Canada · Mexico · Singapore · Spain · United Kingdom · United States

THOMSON

SOUTH-WESTERN

Managerial Accounting, Eighth Edition

Don R. Hansen, Maryanne M. Mowen

VP/Editorial Director:
Jack W. Calhoun

Publisher:
Rob Dewey

Acquisitions Editor:
Keith Chassé

Developmental Editor:
Allison Rolfes

Sponsoring Editor:
Amanda Wolfe

Marketing Manager:
Kristen Hurd

Sr. Content Project Manager:
Heather Mann

Technology Project Editor:
Sally Nieman

Manufacturing Coordinator:
Doug Wilke

Production House:
Lachina Publishing Services

Printer:
Quebecor World
Dubuque, IA

Art Director:
Linda Helcher

Internal Designer:
Lou Ann Thesing

Cover Designer:
Lou Ann Thesing

Cover Images:
© Flying Colours Ltd/
Digital Vision/Getty Images

Photography Manager:
John Hill

Photo Researcher:
Darren Wright

Printed in the United States of America
1 2 3 4 5 09 08 07 06

Student Edition ISBN 13:
978-0-324-37600-5
Student Edition ISBN 10:
0-324-37600-6
Instructor's Edition ISBN 13:
978-0-324-37605-0
Instructor's Edition ISBN 10:
0-324-37605-7

Library of Congress Control Number:
2006934291

For more information about our products, contact us at:
Thomson Learning Academic Resource Center
1-800-423-0563

Thomson Higher Education
5191 Natorp Boulevard
Mason, OH 45040
USA

Preface

The eighth edition of Hansen & Mowen's *Managerial Accounting* introduces students to the fundamentals of management accounting. Though it is assumed that students have been introduced to the basics of financial accounting, extensive knowledge of financial accounting is not needed. The emphasis is on the use of accounting information in today's business environment, so this text provides coverage of the most cutting edge topics and developments in the field. Thus, the text should be of value to students with a variety of backgrounds. Although written to serve undergraduates, the text has been used successfully at the graduate level. There is sufficient variety in the assignment material to accommodate both undergraduate and graduate students.

Many business school students who are required to take a course in management accounting are not accounting majors. For these students, it is often difficult to appreciate the value of the concepts being taught. *Managerial Accounting, 8e*, overcomes this attitude by using introductory chapter scenarios based on real-world settings, photos illustrating practical applications of management accounting concepts, and realistic examples illustrating the concepts within the chapters. Seeing that effective management requires a sound understanding of how to use accounting information should pique the interests of both accounting and nonaccounting majors.

One major area of improvement for this edition has been to enhance the quality and quantity of end-of-chapter material. As a result of extensive focused reviewing and analysis, the end-of-chapter material now offers several activities by level of difficulty for each learning objective to ensure that students will have plenty of opportunity to practice the concepts they learn in the chapter. The end-of-chapter activities are unmatched by any text on the market.

We are confident that this innovative managerial accounting text will prepare your students to perform at their best. The new edition will ensure stronger student performance and ongoing satisfaction with your managerial accounting course.

NEW Features of the Eighth Edition

The eighth edition now offers even more to ensure you and your students experience a higher level of performance in managerial accounting, including:

The Most Current Coverage of Contemporary Topics. A new entire chapter on Activity-Based Management (Chapter 5), a new chapter covering Lean Accounting (Chapter 16), and a new appendix on Joint Product Costing (after Chapter 7) in this edition dedicate significant attention to the most current issues in managerial accounting today. New materials on simplifying ABC are also introduced in Chapter 4.

Streamlined, Reorganized Table of Contents. We have streamlined, reorganized, and carefully tailored this edition's contents to reflect the way your students best learn contemporary and traditional managerial accounting topics. Special topics are now grouped together in the last part of the text to enhance understanding.

Variety and Strength in End-of-Chapter Problems and Exercises. Based on detailed reviewer feedback, exercises and problems now offer more variety and are clearly classified both by level of difficulty and by corresponding learning objectives for your ease in selecting appropriate assignments for each class. All end-of-chapter materials directly correspond to AACSB and CMA standards to ensure student comprehension and positive outcomes. Furthermore, there are a significant number of new and revised exercises and problems in each chapter.

Connection throughout Chapter-Opening Scenarios. New chapter-opener cases now introduce a fictional company that is referenced throughout each chapter to connect and illustrate major chapter concepts. These cases provide a focused look at how each chapter's managerial accounting concepts apply to today's business world.

New! Ethical Insights Boxes. Important ethical concepts capture student interest, assist in retaining critical managerial accounting topics, and show students how to learn from ethical dilemmas as they prepare for CPA and CMA exams. These are identified by a marginal icon.

New! Managers Decide Decision-Making Boxes. This edition's new emphasis on decision-making throughout each chapter challenges students to apply what they learn in a decision context and shows the relevance of managerial accounting concepts to the real business world.

NEW! ThomsonNOW™ for Managerial Accounting. This outcomes-driven, integrated online learning and course management system provides the ultimate in flexibility and ease of use with the results you want NOW to support your course goals and ensure positive student performance. You'll save time as you efficiently teach and reinforce content with an integrated eBook, interactive learning tools, and personalized study plans; test with an algorithmic test bank; and grade results based on AACSB and CMA accreditation standards.

Hallmark Features

We have also retained those features that have made this text successful through seven editions:

Integrated Strategic Cost Management Concepts. An emphasis on budgeting, ABM, and decentralization keeps materials relevant and prepares today's students for situations they will encounter.

Unique Environmental Cost Management Chapter. Introduce your students to the emerging field of environmental cost management with new, actual examples that demonstrate the value of environmental cost management as they show how managers can reduce costs by implementing environmentally conscious processes.

New E-Commerce Coverage in First Chapter. A new section presented early in this edition (within Chapter 1) overviews the impact of e-commerce on today's management accounting issues.

Integrated Strategic Cost Management Concepts. An emphasis throughout this edition on budgeting, ABM, and decentralization keeps the materials relevant to situations encountered in the business world.

Integrated Coverage of Contemporary and Traditional Topics. This edition introduces the latest costing techniques alongside more traditional topics to help students see the advantages and disadvantages of a traditional cost management system versus cost management systems that include practices such as ABC, ABM, target costing, and the Balanced Scorecard. Coverage of both traditional and contemporary topics helps ensure that students are well prepared to work in a variety of business environments.

Integrated Use of Spreadsheets. To accurately reflect industry practice, this edition illustrates key managerial techniques, such as regression, using spreadsheets rather than cumbersome manual calculations.

International Coverage. A full chapter (Chapter 18) highlighting international issues, as well as numerous international examples integrated throughout the text, emphasizes the critical importance of this topic.

Simplified Budgeting Coverage. A simpler example more clearly illustrates important budgeting concepts in this edition.

Least Squares Regression Manual Computation. Coverage of manual computation of regression coefficients helps students understand the technical and theoretical concepts underlying ordinary least squares analysis.

Ethics Coverage. As with previous editions, the eigthth edition emphasizes the study of ethical conduct for management accountants. The role of ethics is discussed in Chapter 1, and the Statement of Ethical Professional Conduct developed by the Institute of Management Accountants is introduced. The impact of the Sarbanes-Oxley Act and its ethics requirements for publicly traded companies is discussed. Chapter 1 has several substantive problems on ethics, and subsequent chapters have at least one problem or case involving an ethical dilemma. These problems allow the instructor to introduce value judgments into management accounting decision making. Chapter 14, dealing with international issues in management accounting, also has a section that discusses ethics in the international environment.

Real-World Emphasis. The eighth edition incorporates real-world applications of management accounting concepts, making the study of these concepts more familiar and interesting to the student. Real-company examples are incorporated throughout. Names of real companies are highlighted throughout the text for easy identification and are listed in a company index at the back of the text. Photos are included to help students relate to the real-world nature of management accounting.

Increased Coverage of Service Industry. Service businesses are experiencing unprecedented growth in today's economy. Managers of service businesses often use the same management accounting models as manufacturers, but they must adapt them to their own unique situations of providing intangibles to consumers. To address this need, many service industry applications are included in the eighth edition. In addition, many real-company examples of service businesses are given.

Chapter Organization and Structure

Each chapter is carefully structured to help students focus on important concepts and retain them. Components found in each chapter include:

Learning Objectives. Each chapter begins with a set of learning objectives to guide students in their study of the chapter. These objectives outline the organizational flow of the chapter and serve as points of comprehension and evaluation. Learning objectives are tied to specific sections of topic coverage within the chapter. They are repeated in the margin at the beginning of the corresponding chapter coverage and are summarized at the end of the chapter.

Summary of Learning Objectives. Each chapter concludes with a comprehensive summary of the learning objectives. Students can review and test their knowledge of key concepts and evaluate their ability to complete chapter objectives.

Scenario. An interesting, real-world scenario opens each chapter. The scenario ties directly to concepts covered in the chapter and helps students relate chapter topics to actual business happenings. "Questions to Think About," critical-thinking questions that appear at the end of each scenario, are designed to pique student interest in the chapter and stimulate class discussion.

Key Terms. Throughout each chapter, key terms appear in bold font for quick identification. A list of key terms, with page references, is presented at the end of each chapter to provide additional reinforcement. All key terms are defined in a comprehensive glossary at the end of the text.

Review Problems. Each chapter contains at least one review problem with the accompanying solution provided. These review problems demonstrate the application of major concepts and procedures covered in the chapter.

Questions for Writing and Discussion. Approximately 15 to 25 short-answer questions appear at the end of each chapter to test students' knowledge of chapter concepts. Many of the questions call for students to use critical thinking and written and oral communication skills. Several questions can be used to stimulate class participation and discussion.

Exercises and Problems. Exercises and problems are correlated by learning objectives, listed in the margin below the exercise and problem titles. A document showing correlations of each end of chapter activity by level of difficulty, learning objective, and AACSB and CMA learning outcomes standards is available on the free website. Exercises and problems adapted from past CMA exams are designated with a margin icon.

Exercises. Exercises usually emphasize one or two chapter concepts and can be completed fairly quickly (30 minutes maximum). Exercises require basic application and computation and often ask students to interpret and explain their results.

Problems. Each chapter contains many end-of-chapter problems, with varying degrees of length and difficulty. Problems usually have more than one issue and present challenging situations, complex computations, and interpretations.

Managerial Decision Cases. Most chapters contain at least two cases. Cases have greater depth and complexity than problems. They are designed to help students integrate multiple concepts and further develop their analytical skills. Several cases deal with ethical behavior.

Research Assignments. Research assignments appear in all chapters (except Chapter 1), allowing students to expand their research and communication skills beyond the classroom. One research assignment in each chapter, labeled "Cybercase," requires the student to research information on the Internet.

Check Figures. Key figures for solutions to selected problems and cases are provided at the end of the text as an aid to students as they prepare their answers.

Chapter by Chapter Changes

Chapter 1 Added material on Sarbanes-Oxley (SOX) and ethics requirements for publicly-traded companies. Added section on corporate codes of conduct mandated by SOX.

Chapter 4 New materials on simplifying ABC have been added.

Chapter 5 This is a newly named and formed chapter with some new material and some elements previously found in other chapters; consolidating materials pertaining to activity-based management (ABM).

Chapter 6 Major revision due to the combining of two previous chapters on job-order costing and process costing.

Chapter 7 Added appendix on joint product costing.

Chapter 10 Combines two previous chapters into one. Includes absorption and variable costing, segmented reporting, investment center performance evaluation, and transfer pricing.

Chapter 16 Half of this chapter is brand-new material focusing on lean manufacturing and lean accounting. Value streams, pull manufacturing, lead times, forms and sources of waste, value stream costing, value stream reporting, value stream reporting, and value-stream performance measurement are examples of topics discussed.

Ancillaries

Instructor's Manual, 0-324-37717-7 (Prepared by Scott Colvin, Naugatuck Valley Community Technical College). The instructor's manual contains a complete set of lecture notes for each chapter and a transition guide for the seventh edition of Management Accounting, as well as other widely used management accounting texts.

Solutions Manual, 0-324-64499-X (Prepared by Don Hansen and Maryanne Mowen, Oklahoma State University). The solutions manual contains the solutions for all end-of-chapter questions, exercises, problems, and cases. Solutions have been verified multiple times to ensure their accuracy and reliability.

Test Bank, 0-324-37622-7 (Prepared by Jane Stoneback, Central Connecticut State University). Revised for the eighth edition, the test bank offers multiple-choice problems, short problems, and essay problems. Designed to make exam preparation as convenient as possible for the instructor, each test bank chapter contains enough questions and problems to permit the preparation of several exams without repetition of material. All questions are identified by level of difficulty, learning objective, and AACSB and CMA learning outcomes standards.

ExamView® Testing Software. This supplement, included on the Instructor's Resource CD-ROM, contains all of the questions in the printed test bank. This program is an easy-to-use test creation software compatible with Microsoft Windows. Instructors can add or edit questions, instructions, answers, and select questions (randomly or numerically) by previewing them on the screen. Instructors can also create and administer quizzes online, whether over the Internet, a local area network (LAN), or a wide area network (WAN).

Spreadsheet Templates. Spreadsheet templates using Microsoft Excel are available for downloading from the product support website. These templates provide outlined formats of solutions for selected end-of-chapter exercises and problems. These exercises and problems are identified with a margin symbol. The templates allow students to develop spreadsheet and "what-if" analysis skills.

PowerPoint Slides (Prepared by Gail Wright, Bryant University). Selected transparencies of key concepts and exhibits from the text are available in PowerPoint presentation software. Available on the Instructor's Resource CD-ROM or the product support website.

Instructor's Resource CD-ROM, 0-324-23493-7. Key instructor ancillaries (solutions manual, instructor's manual, test bank, ExamView®, and PowerPoint® slides) are provided on CD-ROM, giving instructors the ultimate tool for customizing lectures and presentations.

Product Website (http://thomsonedu.com/accounting/hansen). A website designed specifically for *Managerial Accounting, 8e* includes online and downloadable instructor and student resources. The website features an interactive study center organized by chapter, with learning objectives, Web links, glossaries, and online quizzes with automatic feedback.

ThomsonNOW™ Make the most of your course with **ThomsonNOW™ for Hansen & Mowen** *Managerial Accounting, 8e.* This integrated, online learning and course management system provides the ultimate in flexibility and ease of use with the results you want NOW. ThomsonNOW supports your course goals and ensures positive student performance. You'll save time as you efficiently teach and reinforce content with an integrated eBook, Experience Managerial Accounting videos, interactive learning tools, and personalized study plans; test with an algorithmic test bank; and grade results based on AACSB and CMA accreditation standards. For more information visit http://www.thomsonedu.com

JoinIn™ on TurningPoint® JoinIn™ on TurningPoint® is a unique Microsoft® PowerPoint®-based, interactive student response system and lecture tool that merges the instructor's PowerPoint presentation with interactive questions that assess students' understanding of material on the spot. As students are quizzed using clicker technology, instructors can use the instant feedback to lecture more efficiently.

JoinIn on TurningPoint is the right solution to help you:

- Boost students' interaction and engagement.
- Assist students who lack confidence to participate by interacting anonymously.
- Illustrate the relevance of lecture topics with polls, data slicing, and ranking the popularity of answers.
- Check attendance.
- Improve retention.
- Assess students' understanding of a concept instantaneously and identify the "Teachable Moment."
- Manage your lecture, make assessments, collect student responses, and post results to your gradebook, all in one tool.

WebTutor™ Toolbox on WebCT® and on Blackboard® WebTutor Toolbox complements *Managerial Accounting, 8e* by providing interactive reinforcement. WebTutor's online teaching and learning environment brings together content management, assessment, communication, and collaboration capabilities for enhancing in-class instruction or as a study resource for students. Access certificates for WebTutor can be bundled with the textbook or sold separately. For more information, including a demo, visit http://e.thomsonlearning.com

Business & Company Resource Center. The power to answer all types of business queries is at your fingertips with **Business & Company Resource Center (BCRC)**. Unlike other available online business resources, this comprehensive database offers a dynamic research opportunity, providing accurate, up-to-date company and industry intelligence for thousands of firms. BCRC provides access to a wide variety of global business information including competitive intelligence, career and investment opportunities, business rankings, company histories and much more. To learn more visit http://www.gale.com/BusinessRC/

Experience Managerial Accounting Video Series. A series of 14 videos illustrating key management accounting concepts including job order, cost volume profit, activity based costing, Pricing, cost behavior, budgeting, process costing and more. These videos feature companies such as Washburn Guitar, BP, Hard Rock Café, Cold Stone Creamery, and more. Access to these videos can be included at no additional cost with a **new** book or can be purchased separately at the bookstore or purchased directly online. See your Thomson South-Western sales representative for more details or visit http://thomsonedu.com/accounting/hansen

Acknowledgments

We would like to express our appreciation for all who have provided helpful comments and suggestions. The reviewers of the prior editions helped make it a successful product. Many valuable comments from instructors and students have helped us make significant improvements in the text. We would particularly like to thank the following reviewers, who provided in-depth reviews:

Reviewers

Alex Ampadu
University at Buffalo

James Aselta
Sacred Heart University

Professor Rowland Atiase
University of Texas at Austin

Kashi R. Balachandran
New York University

H. Francis Bush
Virginia Military Institute

Michael Flores
Wichita State University

Professor Ananda R. Ganguly
Purdue University

Liming Guan
University of Hawaii at Manoa

Pamela Z. Jackson
Augusta State University

Gordon Klein
UCLA

Cathy X. Larson
Middlesex Community College

J. Mike Metzcar, CPA
Indiana Wesleyan University

Theodora L. Moten
LeTourneau University

Cynthia Nye
Bellevue University

Kathy F. Otero
University of Texas at El Paso

Frederick W. Rankin
Colorado State University

Juan M. Rivera
University of Notre Dame

Richard Schmidt
LeTourneau University Online

E. Daniel Shim
Sacred Heart University

Dr. John J. Surdick
Xavier University

Lynda Thoman
Purdue University

Wendy Tietz
Kent State University

Bill Wempe
Texas Christian University

Scott White
Lindenwood University

James E. Williamson
San Diego State University

George R. Wilson
University of Georgia

Priscilla S. Wisner
Montana State University

Zoomerang Survey Participants

Wagdy M. Abdallah
Seton Hall University

Joseph Adamo
Cazenovia College

Sue Aman
Kaskaskia College

Douglas M. Asbury
University of Findlay

Sandra Bailey
Oregon Tech

Kashi Balachandran
New York University

Carroll Barnes
Minneapolis Community & Technical College

Nancy E. Coulmas
Bloomsburg University

Kevin Devine
Xavier University

Maggie Houston
Wright State University

Celina Jozsi
University of South Florida

Patti Lopez
Valencia Community College

Lowell Mooney
Georgia Southern University

Abbie Gail Parham
Georgia Southern University

Angela Sandberg
Jacksonville State University

Akili J. Sanyika
Georgia Perimeter College

Ramgopal Venkataraman
University of Minnesota - Twin Cities

Priscilla Wisner
Montana State University

We also would like to thank our verifiers for the text and solutions manual—Scott Butterfield, Clayton State University; and Ann Martel, Marquette University. Their careful editing helped us produce a text and ancillary package of high quality and accuracy.

We also want to express our gratitude to the Institute of Management Accountants for its permission to use adapted problems from past CMA examinations. The IMA has also given us permission to reprint the ethical standards of conduct for management accountants.

Finally, we should offer special thanks to the staffs of Thomson Publishing and Lachina Publishing Services. They have been helpful and have carried out their tasks with impressive expertise and professionalism.

Don R. Hansen
Maryanne M. Mowen

About the Authors

Don R. Hansen

Dr. Don R. Hansen is Professor of Accounting at Oklahoma State University. He received his Ph.D. from the University of Arizona in 1977. He has an undergraduate degree in mathematics from Brigham Young University. His research interests include activity-based costing and mathematical modeling. He has published articles in both accounting and engineering journals including *The Accounting Review, The Journal of Management Accounting Research, Accounting Horizons,* and *IIE Transactions.* He has served on the editorial board of *The Accounting Review.* His outside interests include family, church activities, reading, movies, watching sports, and studying Spanish.

Maryanne M. Mowen

Dr. Maryanne M. Mowen is Associate Professor of Accounting at Oklahoma State University. She received her Ph.D. from Arizona State University in 1979. Dr. Mowen brings an interdisciplinary perspective to teaching and writing in cost and management accounting, with degrees in history and economics. In addition, she does scholarly research in behavioral decision theory. She has published articles in journals such as *Decision Science, The Journal of Economics and Psychology,* and *The Journal of Management Accounting Research.* Dr. Mowen's interests outside the classroom include reading, playing golf, traveling, and working crossword puzzles.

Brief Contents

Contents

PART 4 PLANNING AND CONTROL

© Jupiter Images

PART 1

Basic Management Accounting Concepts

chapter 1

Introduction: The Role, History, and Direction of Management Accounting

learning objectives

After studying this chapter, you should be able to:

1. Discuss the need for management accounting information.
2. Differentiate between management accounting and financial accounting.
3. Provide a brief historical description of management accounting.
4. Identify the current focus of management accounting.
5. Describe the role of management accountants in an organization.
6. Explain the importance of ethical behavior for managers and management accountants.
7. List three forms of certification available to management accountants.

Scenario

Consider the following comments made by individuals from several different organizations:

A. Partner of a Legal Firm: The managing partner of Collins, Ling, and Jefferson, a large regional law firm, just received a request to bid on a potential job from MegaProducts, Inc. (MPI). MPI had decided to outsource most of its legal work. Its request for proposals provided each law firm with a record of the hours of legal service and the types of services provided by MPI's internal legal staff for the past five years. The bid was to take the form of a flat hourly billing rate. Competition for this job was intense. In order to generate a competitive bid, the partner needed an accurate assessment of cost per hour for each type of legal service that would be performed. Then she could obtain the weighted-average cost per hour based on the expected hours of each type of service. Finally, she could calculate an hourly billing rate that would provide the law firm with a reasonable dollar return. (Product costing and pricing decision)

B. Plant Manager: Jeff Rand, plant manager, identified three projects that could improve quality and decrease the factory's production time. First, only suppliers who provide components with a defect rate of less than one per thousand would be selected. Second, die-making operations could be automated. Third, manufacturing cells would be formed for each major product. Jeff knew that once the alternatives were implemented he would need to know if and by how much the number of defective units dropped and if cycle time actually decreased. He also needed a way to track those changes to the resulting production costs to see if they decreased—to see if cost improvement actually occurred. (Continuous improvement)

C. Chief Executive Officer of a Cruise Line: The recession had resulted in decreased profits; the CEO wondered if the cruise line should consider reducing costs and services. The controller suggested that profit would increase if current passenger volume was maintained but variable costs were reduced by $10 per passenger. The marketing vice president suggested that reducing fares could increase overall profit. She claimed that reducing fares by 20 percent and increasing advertising by $500,000 would increase the number of passengers by 20 percent. A combination of the two approaches might change the strategic position of the cruise line. Therefore, the CEO asked for revised budgets to see which approach (or a combination of the two) offered the most profit—in both the short run and the long run. (Planning and cost-volume-profit analysis)

D. Hospital Administrator: After reading the latest monthly performance report for subunits of the hospital, the administrator was very pleased with the performance of the laboratory. Last month, the laboratory had reduced costs even while the number of tests run had increased. As a result, the laboratory attracted more business by charging lower rates that were justified by the lower costs. The lab manager had told the administrator that the activity-based management approach that had been installed had resulted in significant waste reduction. The administrator felt that this management system could be profitably used by other subunits, such as radiology and physical therapy. (Managerial control)

Questions to Think About

1. Who uses management accounting information?
2. For what purposes is management accounting information used?
3. Should a management accounting system provide both financial and nonfinancial information?
4. What organizations need a management accounting information system?

Management Accounting Information System

Objective 1

Discuss the need for management accounting information.

The **management accounting information system** provides information needed to satisfy specific management objectives. At the heart of a management accounting information system are processes; they are described by activities such as collecting, measuring, storing, analyzing, reporting, and managing information. Information on economic events is processed into outputs that satisfy the system's objectives. Outputs may include special reports, product costs, customer costs, budgets, performance reports, and even personal communication. The operational model of a management accounting information system is illustrated in Exhibit 1-1.

The management accounting information system is not bound by any formal criteria that define the nature of the processes, inputs, or outputs. The criteria are flexible and based on management objectives. The management accounting system has three broad objectives:

1. To provide information for costing out services, products, and other objects of interest to management.
2. To provide information for planning, controlling, evaluation, and continuous improvement.
3. To provide information for decision making.

These three objectives show that managers and other users need access to management accounting information and need to know how to use it. It can help them identify and solve problems and evaluate performance. Accounting information is used in all phases of management, including planning, controlling, and decision making. Furthermore, the need for such information is not limited to manufacturing organizations; it is used in manufacturing, merchandising, service, and nonprofit organizations as well.

Information Needs of Managers and Other Users

The opening scenarios can be used to illustrate each of the management accounting system objectives. Scenario A (bidding by a legal firm) shows the importance of determining the cost of products (objective 1). Scenario B emphasizes the importance of tracking costs and nonfinancial measures of performance over time. Thus, Scenario A emphasizes the importance of accuracy in product costing, while Scenario B underscores the importance of tracking efficiency measures—using both financial and nonfinancial measures (objective 2). Trends in these measures allow

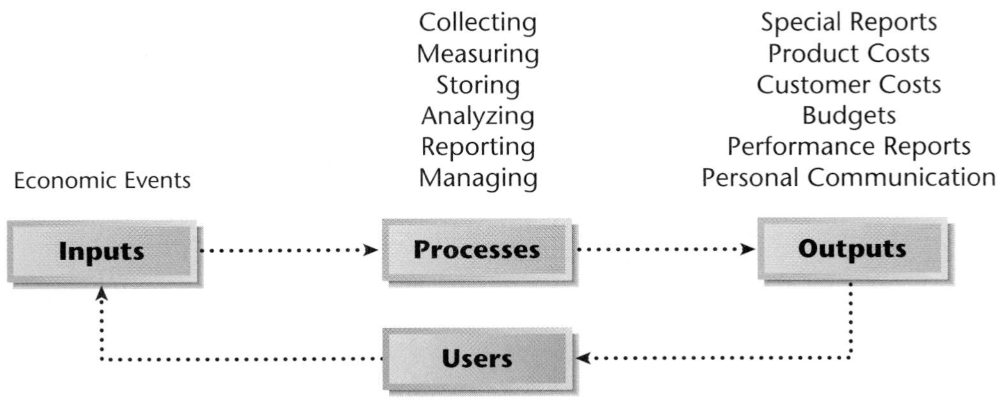

Exhibit 1-1 Operational Model: Management Accounting Information System

managers to evaluate the soundness of decisions designed to improve productivity, lower costs, increase market share, and improve profitability. For example, **Huffman Corporation**, a manufacturer of machine tools, tracks cycle-time changes for producing its products. The cycle time for producing the latest version of its computerized grinding machine dropped from 2,400 hours to 800 hours within a five-year period. These productivity gains have created a 35 percent compound growth rate in earnings.[1] Accuracy in cost assignments and the use of nonfinancial information by both managers and nonmanagers have emerged as fundamental requirements for many organizations. These and other related issues have led to the development of an improved management accounting information system known as an *activity-based cost management information system.*

Scenarios B, C, and D illustrate planning, controlling, evaluation, and continuous improvement (objective 2). Managers, executives, and workers need an information system that will identify problems, such as the possibility of cost overruns, or benefits, such as the ability of a subunit manager to innovate and increase efficiency (Scenario C). Once problems are known, actions can be taken to identify and implement solutions. Scenario B also illustrates that both financial and nonfinancial information is needed so that workers can evaluate and monitor the effects of decisions that are intended to improve operational and unit performance. Operational and financial performance information allows workers to assess the effectiveness of their efforts to improve. Workers and managers should be committed to continuously improving the activities they perform. **Continuous improvement** means searching for ways to increase the overall efficiency and productivity of activities by reducing waste, increasing quality, and reducing costs. Thus, information is needed to help identify opportunities for improvement and to evaluate the progress made in implementing actions designed to create improvement.

The third objective, providing information for decision making, is intertwined with the first two. For example, information on the costs of products, customers, processes, and other objects of interest to management can be the basis for identifying problems and alternative solutions. Similar observations can be made about information pertaining to planning, controlling, and evaluation. Examples include using product costs to prepare a bid (Scenario A), helping a manager decide whether to increase profits by reducing prices and increasing advertising or decreasing variable costs or both, or helping a manager decide whether to change the organization's strategic position (Scenario C). This last scenario also underscores the importance of **strategic decision making**, which is defined as the process of choosing among alternative strategies with the goal of selecting one or more strategies that provide a company with a reasonable assurance of long-term growth and survival.

The Management Process

The management process is defined by the following activities: (1) planning, (2) controlling, and (3) decision making. The management process describes the functions carried out by managers and empowered workers. Empowering workers to participate in the management process means giving them a greater say in how the company operates. Thus, **employee empowerment** is the authorizing of operational personnel to plan, control, and make decisions without explicit authorization from middle- and higher-level management.

Employee empowerment rests on the belief that employees closest to the work can provide valuable input in terms of ideas, plans, and problem solving. Workers are allowed to shut down production and identify and correct problems. Their input

1 Steve Liesman, "High-Tech Devices Speed Manufacturing and May Play Larger Role in Economy," *Wall Street Journal Interactive Edition* (February 15, 2001). Access the referenced article in the chapter web links at the Interactive Study Center at http://www.thomsonedu.com/accounting/hansen.

Direct labor workers are very closely connected to products and services. They are often able to see opportunities for improved efficiency and quality that managers cannot. Employee empowerment recognizes this and affords employees the power to make beneficial changes.

© Getty Images/PhotoDisc

is sought and used to improve production processes. Two examples illustrate the power of this concept. First, empowered workers at **Duffy Tool and Stamping** saved $14,300 per year by redesigning a press operation.[2] In one department, completed parts (made by a press) came down a chute and fell into a parts tub. When the tub became full, press operators had to stop operation while the stock operator removed the full tub and replaced it with an empty one. Empowered workers redesigned the operation so that each press had a chute with two branches—each leading to a different tub. Now completed parts are routed into one branch of the chute. When the tub associated with the active branch becomes full, the completed parts are routed to the other branch and its tub while the full tub is being removed and replaced with an empty tub. This new design avoids machine downtime and produces significant savings. Second, **GR Spring and Stamping** implemented an employee empowerment program, and within a four-year period, the number of ideas implemented increased from 0.67 per employee to 11.22 per employee.[3] Increased involvement in managing the company through employee empowerment is a key element in enhancing continuous improvement efforts.

Planning The managerial activity called **planning** is the detailed formulation of action to achieve a particular end; it requires setting objectives and identifying methods to achieve those objectives. For example, a firm's objective may be to increase its profitability by improving the overall quality of its products. By improving product quality, the firm should be able to reduce scrap and rework, decrease the number of customer complaints and warranty work, reduce the cost of inspection, and so on, thus increasing profitability. But how can this be accomplished? Managers must develop a plan that, when implemented, will lead to the achievement of the desired objective. A plant manager, for example, may start a supplier evaluation program to identify and select suppliers who are willing and able to supply defect-free parts. In another example, empowered workers might identify production causes of defects and create new methods for producing a product that will reduce scrap and rework and the need for inspection. The new methods should be clearly specified and detailed in the plan.

2 George F. Hanks, "Excellence Teams in Action," *Management Accounting* (February 1995): p. 35.

3 Joseph F. Castellano, Donald Klein, and Harper Roehm, "Minicompanies: The Next Generation of Employee Empowerment," *Management Accounting* (March 1998): pp. 22–30.

Controlling Planning is only half the battle. Once a plan is created, it must be implemented and monitored by managers and workers to ensure that the plan is being carried out as intended. **Controlling** is the managerial activity of monitoring a plan's implementation and taking corrective action as needed. Control is usually achieved with the use of feedback. **Feedback** is information that can be used to evaluate or correct the steps being taken to implement a plan. Based on feedback, a manager (or worker) may decide to let the implementation continue as is, take corrective action of some type to put the actions back in harmony with the original plan, or do some midstream replanning.

Feedback is a critical part of the control function. Feedback can be financial or nonfinancial. For example, the chute redesign at Duffy Tool and Stamping saved more than $14,000 per year (financial feedback). Moreover, the redesign eliminated machine downtime and increased the number of units produced per hour (operational feedback). Both measures are part of the management accounting information system and convey important information. Often financial and nonfinancial feedback is in the form of formal reports, called **performance reports**, that compare actual data with planned data or benchmarks.

Decision Making The process of choosing among competing alternatives is **decision making**. This managerial function is intertwined with planning and controlling. A manager cannot plan without making decisions. Managers must choose among competing objectives and methods to carry out the chosen objectives. Only one of numerous competing plans can be chosen. Similar comments can be made concerning the control function.

A major role of the management accounting information system is to supply information for decision making. For example, the partner in the legal firm in Scenario A was faced with the prospect of submitting a bid on a contract for legal services. A large number of bids are possible, but the partner must choose just one to submit to the prospective customer. The partner requested information concerning the expected hourly cost for each type of legal service. This cost information, along with the partner's knowledge of competitive conditions, should improve his or her ability to select a bid price. Imagine having to submit a bid without some idea of the cost of providing the legal services.

Organization Type

The use of accounting information by managers is not limited to manufacturing. Regardless of the organizational form, managers must be proficient in using accounting information. The basic concepts taught in this text apply to a variety of settings. The four scenarios at the beginning of this chapter involved legal services, manufacturing, health care, leisure services, profit, and nonprofit organizations. Hospital administrators, presidents of corporations, dentists, educational administrators, and city managers can all improve their managerial skills by being well grounded in the basic concepts and use of accounting information.

Management Accounting and Financial Accounting

Objective 2

Differentiate between management accounting and financial accounting.

An organization's accounting information system has two major subsystems: a management accounting system and a financial accounting system. The two accounting subsystems differ in their objectives, the nature of their inputs, and the type of processes used to transform inputs into outputs. The **financial accounting information system** is primarily concerned with producing outputs for external users, using well-specified economic events as inputs and processes that meet certain rules and conventions. For financial accounting, the nature of the inputs and the rules and conventions governing processes are defined by the Securities and Exchange Commission (SEC), the Financial Accounting Standards Board (FASB), and for public companies, the Public Company Accounting Oversight Board (PCAOB). The overall objective is the preparation of external reports (financial statements) for investors, creditors, government agencies, and other outside users. This information is used for such things as investment decisions, stewardship evaluation, monitoring activities, and regulatory measures. Financial accounting could be called external accounting.

Because the management accounting system produces information for internal users, such as managers, executives, and workers, it could be properly called internal accounting. Management accounting identifies, collects, measures, classifies, and reports information that is useful to internal users in planning, controlling, and decision making.

When management accounting is compared with financial accounting, several differences can be identified. Some of the more important differences are summarized in Exhibit 1-2.

- *Targeted users.* Management accounting focuses on the information needs of internal users, while financial accounting focuses on information for external users.
- *Restrictions on inputs and processes.* Management accounting is not subject to the requirements of generally accepted accounting principles. The Securities and Exchange Commission (SEC), the Public Company Accounting Oversight Board (PCAOB), and the Financial Accounting Standards Board (FASB) set the accounting procedures that must be followed for financial reporting. The inputs and processes of financial accounting are well-defined and restricted. Only certain kinds of economic events qualify as inputs, and processes must follow generally accepted methods. Unlike financial accounting, management accounting has no official body that prescribes the format, content, and rules for selecting inputs and processes and preparing financial reports. Managers are free to choose whatever information they want—provided it can be justified on a cost-benefit basis.
- *Type of information.* The restrictions imposed by financial accounting tend to produce objective and verifiable financial information. For management accounting, information may be financial or nonfinancial and may be more subjective in nature.
- *Time orientation.* Financial accounting has a historical orientation. It records and reports events that have already happened. Although management accounting also records and reports events that have already occurred, it strongly emphasizes providing information about future events. Management, for example, may not only want to know what it costs to produce a product, it may also want to know what it *will* cost to produce a product. Knowing what it will cost helps in planning material purchases and making pricing decisions, among other things. This future orientation is demanded to support the managerial planning and decision making.
- *Degree of aggregation.* Management accounting provides measures and internal reports used to evaluate the performance of entities, product lines, departments, and managers. Very detailed information is needed and provided. Financial accounting, on the other hand, focuses on overall firm performance, providing a more aggregated viewpoint.
- *Breadth.* Management accounting is much broader than financial accounting. It includes aspects of managerial economics, industrial engineering, and management science, as well as numerous other areas.

It should be emphasized, however, that both management accounting and financial accounting information systems are part of the total accounting information system. Unfortunately, the content of the management accounting system is often driven by the needs of the financial accounting system. The reports of management and financial accounting are frequently derived from the same database, which

Management Accounting	Financial Accounting
1. Internally focused	1. Externally focused
2. No mandatory rules	2. Must follow externally imposed rules
3. Financial and nonfinancial information; subjective information possible	3. Objective financial information
4. Emphasis on the future	4. Historical orientation
5. Internal evaluation and decisions based on very detailed information	5. Information about the firm as a whole
6. Broad, multidisciplinary	6. More self-contained

Exhibit 1-2 Comparison of Management and Financial Accounting

may have been established to support the reporting requirements of financial accounting. Many organizations need to redesign this database in order to satisfy more fully the needs of the internal users. For example, while overall firm profitability is of interest to investors, managers need to know the profitability of individual products. The accounting system should be designed to provide total profits *and* profits for individual products. The key is flexibility—the accounting system should be able to supply different information for different purposes.

A Brief Historical Perspective of Management Accounting

Objective 3

Provide a brief historical description of management accounting.

Most of the product-costing and management accounting procedures used in the 20th century were developed between 1880 and 1925.[4] Prior to 1914, many of the early developments concerned product costing—tracing a firm's profitability to individual products and using this information for strategic decision making. By 1925,

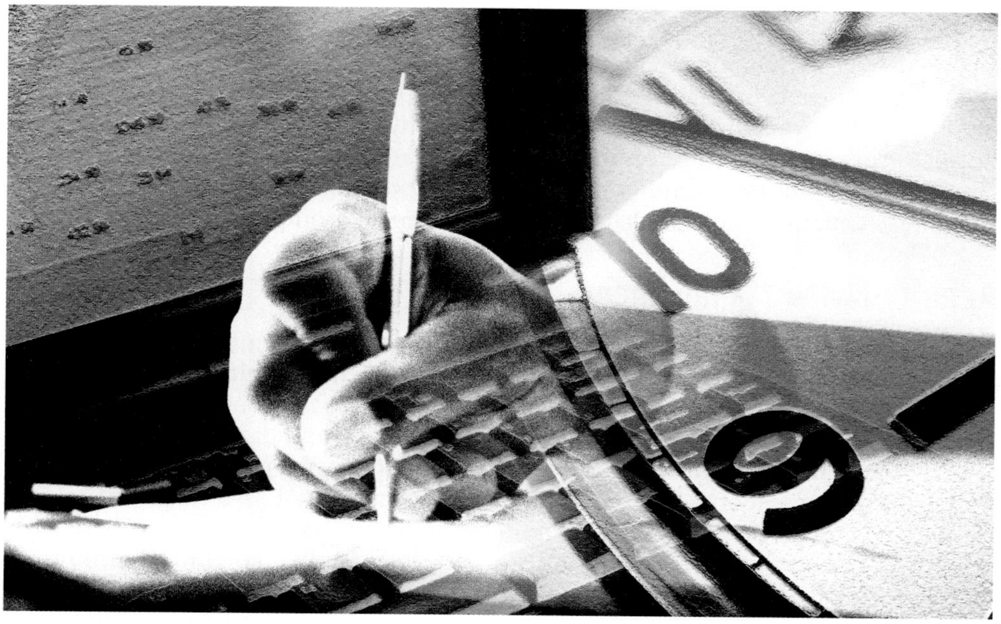

© Getty Images/PhotoDisc

The development of sophisticated tools of analysis mirrors the growth in the demands placed on management accountants. Where once paper and pencil sufficed for simple product costing, now complex decisions, in a global marketplace, require the use of high-powered computers and servers.

4 The information in this section is based on H. Thomas Johnson and Robert Kaplan, *Relevance Lost: The Rise and Fall of Management Accounting* (Boston: Harvard Business School Press, 1987).

most of this emphasis had been abandoned in favor of inventory costing—assigning manufacturing costs to products so that the cost of inventories could be reported to external users of a firm's financial statements.

Financial reporting became the driving force for the design of cost accounting systems. Managers and firms were willing to accept aggregated average cost information about individual products, as they did not feel the need for more detailed and accurate cost information about individual products. As long as a company had relatively homogeneous products that consumed resources at about the same rate, the average cost information supplied by a financially driven cost system was good enough. Furthermore, for some firms, even as product diversity increased, the need to have more accurate cost information was offset by the high cost of the processing required to provide such information. For many firms, the cost of a more detailed cost system apparently exceeded its benefits.

Some effort to improve the managerial usefulness of conventional cost systems took place in the 1950s and 1960s. Users discussed the shortcomings of information supplied by a system designed to prepare financial reports. Efforts to improve the system, however, essentially centered on making the financial accounting information more useful to users rather than on producing an entirely new set of information and procedures apart from the external reporting system.

In the 1980s and 1990s, many recognized that the traditional management accounting practices no longer served managerial needs. Some claimed that existing management accounting systems were obsolete and virtually useless. More accurate product and resource costing were needed for managers to improve quality and productivity and to reduce costs. In response to the perceived failure of the traditional management accounting system, efforts were made to develop a new management accounting system that would satisfy the demands of the current economic environment.

Current Focus of Management Accounting

Objective 4

Identify the current focus of management accounting.

The economic environment has required the development of innovative and relevant management accounting practices. Consequently, activity-based management accounting systems have been developed and implemented in many organizations. Additionally, the focus of management accounting systems has been broadened to enable managers to better serve the needs of customers and manage the firm's value chain. Furthermore, to secure and maintain a competitive advantage, managers must emphasize time, quality, and efficiency, and accounting information must be produced to support these three fundamental organizational goals. More recently, the emergence of e-business requires management accounting systems to provide information that enables managers to deal with this new environment.

Activity-Based Management

The demand for more accurate and relevant management accounting information has led to the development of activity-based management. **Activity-based management** is a systemwide, integrated approach that focuses management's attention on activities with the objective of improving customer value and the resulting profit. Activity-based management emphasizes activity-based costing (ABC) and process value analysis. Activity-based costing improves the accuracy of assigning costs by first tracing costs to activities and then to products or customers that consume these activities. Process value analysis emphasizes activity analysis—trying to determine why activities are performed and how well they are performed. The objective is to find ways to perform necessary activities more efficiently and to eliminate those that do not create customer value.

Customer Orientation

Activity-based management has the objective of increasing customer value by managing activities. Customer value is a key focus because a firm can establish a competitive advantage by creating better customer value for the same or lower cost than that of its competitors or creating equivalent value for a lower cost than that of its competitors. **Customer value** is the difference between what a customer receives (customer realization) and what the customer gives up (customer sacrifice). What is received is called the total product. The **total product** is the complete range of tangible and intangible benefits that a customer receives from a purchased product. Thus, customer realization includes basic and special product features, service, quality, instructions for use, reputation, brand name, and any other factors deemed important by customers. Customer sacrifice includes the cost of purchasing the product, the time and effort spent acquiring and learning to use the product, and **postpurchase costs**, which are defined as the costs of using, maintaining, and disposing of the product. Increasing customer value means increasing customer realization, decreasing customer sacrifice, or both.

Strategic Positioning Increasing customer value to create a sustainable competitive advantage is achieved through judicious selection of strategies. Cost information plays a critical role in this process through a process called *strategic cost management*. **Strategic cost management** is the use of cost data to develop and identify superior strategies that will produce a sustainable competitive advantage. Generally, firms choose a strategic position that corresponds to one of two general strategies: (1) cost leadership and (2) superior products through differentiation.[5] The objective of the cost leadership strategy is to provide the same or better value to customers at a *lower* cost than competitors; its objective is to increase customer value by reducing sacrifice. For example, reducing the cost of making a product by improving a process would allow the firm to reduce the product's selling price, thus reducing customer sacrifice. A differentiation strategy, on the other hand, increases customer value by increasing realization. Providing customers with something not provided by competitors creates a competitive advantage. For example, a computer retailer could offer on-site repair service, a feature not offered by other rivals in the local market. Of course, a viable differentiation strategy must ensure that the value added to the customer by differentiation exceeds the firm's cost of providing the differentiation. Typically, different strategies require different cost information, implying that cost systems may differ according to the strategy adopted by a firm.

Value-Chain Framework A focus on customer value means that the management accounting system should produce information about both realization and sacrifice. Collecting information about customer sacrifice means gathering information outside the firm. But there are even deeper implications. Successful pursuit of cost leadership and/or differentiation strategies requires an understanding of a firm's internal and industrial value chains. Effective management of the internal value chain is fundamental to increasing customer value, especially if maximizing customer realization at the lowest possible cost (to the firm) is a goal. The **internal value chain** is the set of activities required to design, develop, produce, market, and deliver products and services to customers. Thus, emphasizing customer value forces managers to determine which activities in the value chain are important to customers. A management accounting system should track information about a wide variety of activities that span the internal value chain. Consider, for example, the

5 Japanese firms have also shown that it is possible to pursue a strategy that combines the two: a differentiation with cost advantage strategy.

delivery segment. Timely delivery of a product or service is part of the total product and, thus, of value to the customer. Customer value can be increased by increasing the speed of delivery and response. **Federal Express** exploited this part of the value chain and successfully developed a service that was not being offered by the **U.S. Postal Service**. Today, many customers believe that a delivery delayed is a delivery denied. This seems to indicate that a good management accounting system ought to develop and measure indicators of customer satisfaction.

The industrial value chain is also critical for strategic cost management. The **industrial value chain** is the linked set of value-creating activities from basic raw materials to the disposal of the final product by end-use customers. Exhibit 1-3 illustrates a possible value chain for the apple industry. A given firm operating within the industry may not span the entire value chain. The exhibit illustrates that different firms participate in different segments of the chain. Breaking down a firm's value chain into its strategically important activities is basic to successful implementation of cost leadership and differentiation strategies. Fundamental to a value-chain framework is the recognition of the complex linkages and interrelationships among activities both within and external to the firm. There are two types of linkages: *internal* and *external*. **Internal linkages** are relationships among activities that are performed within a firm's portion of the industrial value chain (the internal value chain). **External linkages** are activity relationships between the firm and the firm's suppliers and customers. Thus, we can talk about *supplier linkages* and *customer linkages*. Using these

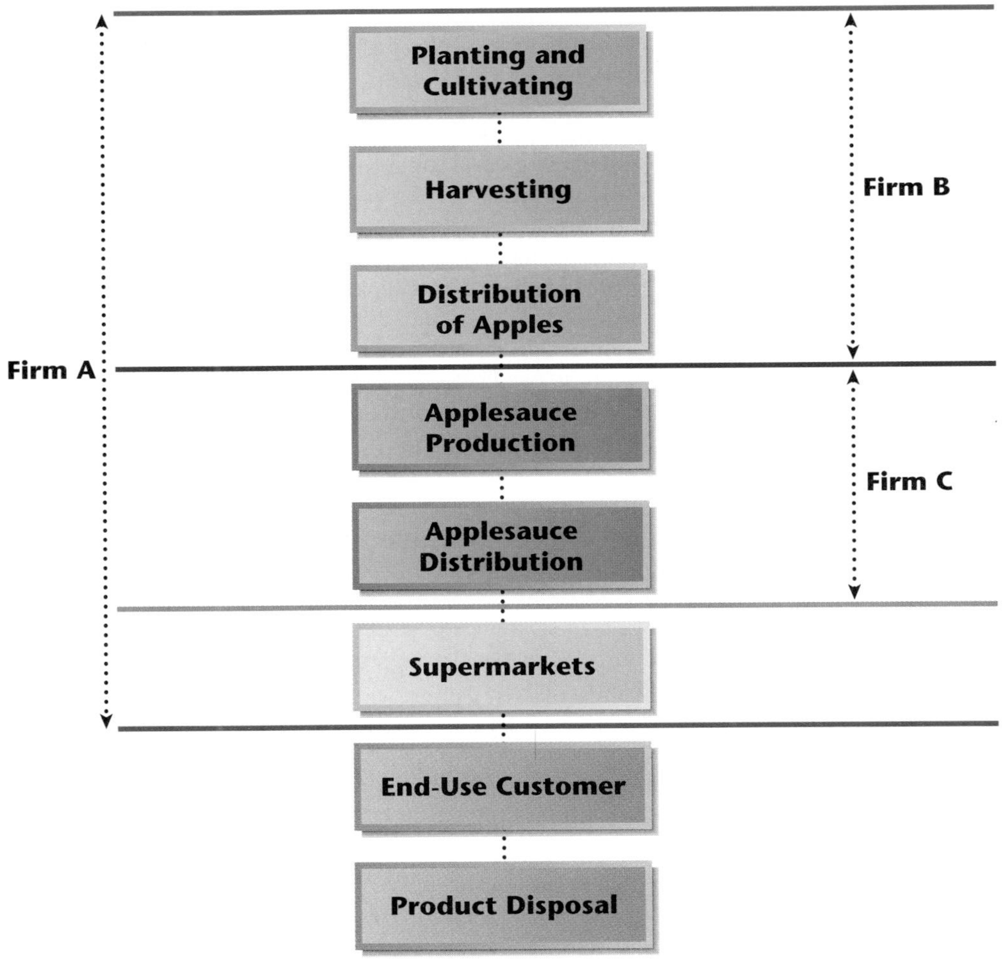

Exhibit 1-3 Value Chain: Apple Industry

linkages to bring about a win-win outcome for the firm, its suppliers, and its customers is the key to successful strategic cost management. It is also the key feature of what is now called *supply chain management.* **Supply chain management** is the management of material flows beginning with suppliers and their upstream suppliers, moving to the transformation of materials into finished goods, and finishing with the distribution of finished goods to customers and their downstream customers. Understanding the industrial value chain and going beyond immediate suppliers and customers may reveal hidden benefits. Of course, the firm's objective is to manage these linkages better than its competitors, thus creating a competitive advantage.

Companies have internal customers as well. For example, the procurement process acquires and delivers parts and materials to producing departments. Providing high-quality parts on a timely basis to managers of producing departments is just as vital for procurement as it is for the company as a whole to provide high-quality goods to external customers. The emphasis on managing the internal value chain and servicing internal customers reveals the importance of a cross-functional perspective.

Cross-Functional Perspective

Managing the value chain means that a management accountant must understand many functions of the business, from manufacturing to marketing to distribution to customer service. This need is magnified when the company is involved in international trade. We see this in the varying definitions of product cost. Activity-based management has moved beyond the traditional manufacturing cost definition of product cost to more inclusive definitions. These product costs may include initial design and engineering costs, manufacturing costs, and the costs of distribution, sales, and service. An individual who understands the shifting definitions of cost from the short run to the long run can be invaluable in determining what information is relevant in decision making. For example, strategic decisions may require a product cost definition that assigns the costs of all value-chain activities, whereas a short-run decision that is concerned with whether a special order should be accepted or rejected may require a product cost that assigns only marginal or incremental costs.

Why try to relate management accounting to marketing, management, engineering, finance, and other business functions? When a value-chain approach is taken and customer value is emphasized, we see that these disciplines are interrelated; a decision affecting one affects the others. For example, many manufacturing companies engage in frequent trade loading, the practice of encouraging (often by offering huge discounts) wholesalers and retailers to buy more product than they can quickly resell. As a result, inventories become bloated, and the wholesalers and retailers stop purchasing for a time. This looks like a marketing problem, but it is not—at least not entirely. When selling stops, so does production. Thus, trade-loading companies experience wild swings in production. Sometimes, their factories produce around the clock to meet demand for the heavily discounted product; other times, their factories are idle, and workers are laid off. In effect, the sales end up costing the companies millions of dollars of added production cost. A cross-functional perspective lets us see the big picture. This broader vision allows managers to increase quality, reduce the time required to service customers (both internal and external), and improve efficiency.

Total Quality Management

Continuous improvement is crucial to establishing manufacturing excellence. Making products with little waste that actually perform according to specifications are the twin objectives of world-class firms; they are the keys to survival in today's world-class competitive environment. A philosophy of **total quality management**, in which manufacturers strive to create an environment that will enable workers to manufacture perfect (zero-defect) products, has replaced the "acceptable quality" attitudes of the past. This total emphasis on quality has also created a demand for a management accounting system that provides financial and nonfinancial information about quality.

Service industries are also dedicated to improving quality. Service firms present special problems because quality may differ from employee to employee. As a result, service firms are emphasizing consistency through the development of systems to support employee efforts. For example, **Park Place Lexus** of Plano, Texas, is a 2005 Malcolm Baldridge Quality Award winner. Park Place Lexus measures client satisfaction with new vehicles (99.8 percent), with pre-owned vehicles (98 percent), and with vehicle maintenance and service (near 98 percent). Park Place Lexus is also improving in profitability; its gross profit increased by 51.3 percent from 2000 to 2004. Clearly, quality initiatives are paying off.[6]

Quality cost measurement and reporting are key features of a management accounting system for manufacturing and service industries. In both cases, the system should be able to provide both operational and financial information about quality, including information such as the number of defects, quality cost reports, quality cost trend reports, and quality cost performance reports.

Time as a Competitive Element

Time is a crucial element in all phases of the value chain.[7] World-class firms reduce time to market by compressing design, implementation, and production cycles. These firms deliver products or services quickly by eliminating non-value-added time, that is, time of no value to the customer (for example, the time a product spends on the loading dock). Interestingly, decreasing non-value-added time appears to go hand in hand with increasing quality. The overall objective, of course, is to increase customer responsiveness.

The rate of technological innovation has increased for many industries, and the life of a particular product can be quite short. Managers must be able to respond quickly and decisively to changing market conditions. Information to allow them to accomplish this must be available. For example, **Hewlett-Packard** has found that it is better to be 50 percent over budget in new product development than to be six months late. This correlation between cost and time is the kind of information that should be available from a management accounting information system.

Efficiency

While quality and time are important, improving these dimensions without corresponding improvements in profit performance may be futile, if not fatal. Improving efficiency is also a vital concern. Both financial and nonfinancial measures of efficiency are needed. Cost is a critical measure of efficiency. Trends in costs over time and measures of productivity changes can provide important measures of the efficacy of continuous improvement decisions. For these efficiency measures to be of value, costs must be properly defined, measured, and assigned; furthermore, production of output must be related to the inputs required, and the overall financial effect of productivity changes should be calculated.

6 As reported in the Baldridge Award Recipient profile, http://www.nist.gov/public_affairs/baldrige_2005/parkplacelexus.htm.

7 An excellent analysis of time as a competitive element is contained in A. Faye Borthick and Harold P. Roth, "Accounting for Time: Reengineering Business Processes to Improve Responsiveness," *Journal of Cost Management* (Fall 1993): pp. 4–14.

E-business

Electronic business (e-business) is any business transaction or information exchange that is executed using information and communication technology. E-business is expected to grow significantly over the coming years. It provides opportunities for a company to expand sales throughout the world and may lower costs significantly relative to paper-based transactions. It also facilitates value-chain (supply) management. Management accountants need to understand the benefits and risks of e-business as well as its opportunities. They also play a vital role in providing relevant cost information concerning e-business. For example, managers may need to know the cost per electronic transaction versus the cost per paper transaction.

The Role of the Management Accountant

Objective 5

Describe the role of management accountants in an organization.

Business today is moving faster than ever before. Changes in technology, communications, economic conditions, and the legal environment are affecting firms and their management accountants in new ways. Management accountants must support management in all phases of business decision making. As specialists in accounting, they must be intelligent, well prepared, up to date with new developments, and familiar with the customs and practices of all countries in which their firms operate. They are expected to be knowledgable about the legal environment of business and, in particular, about the Sarbanes-Oxley Act of 2002.

Structure of the Company

The role of management accountants in an organization is one of support. They assist those individuals who are responsible for carrying out an organization's basic objectives. Positions that have direct responsibility for the basic objectives of an organization are referred to as **line positions**. Positions that are supportive in nature and have only indirect responsibility for an organization's basic objectives are called **staff positions**.

For example, assume that the basic mission of an organization is to produce and sell laser printers. The vice presidents of manufacturing and marketing, the factory manager, and the assemblers are all line positions. The vice presidents of finance and human resources, the cost accountant, and the purchasing manager are all staff positions.

The partial organization chart shown in Exhibit 1-4 illustrates the organizational positions for production and finance. Because one of the basic objectives of the organization is to produce, those directly involved in production hold line positions. Although management accountants, such as controllers and cost accounting managers, may wield considerable influence in the organization, they have no authority over the managers in the production area. The managers in line positions are the ones who set policy and make the decisions that impact production. However, by supplying and interpreting accounting information, management accountants can have significant input into policies and decisions.

The **controller**, the chief accounting officer, supervises all accounting departments. Because of the critical role that management accounting plays in the operation of an organization, the controller is often viewed as a member of the top management team and is encouraged to participate in planning, controlling, and decision-making activities. As the chief accounting officer, the controller has responsibility for both internal and external accounting requirements. This charge may include direct responsibility for internal auditing, cost accounting, financial accounting (including SEC reports and financial statements), systems accounting (including

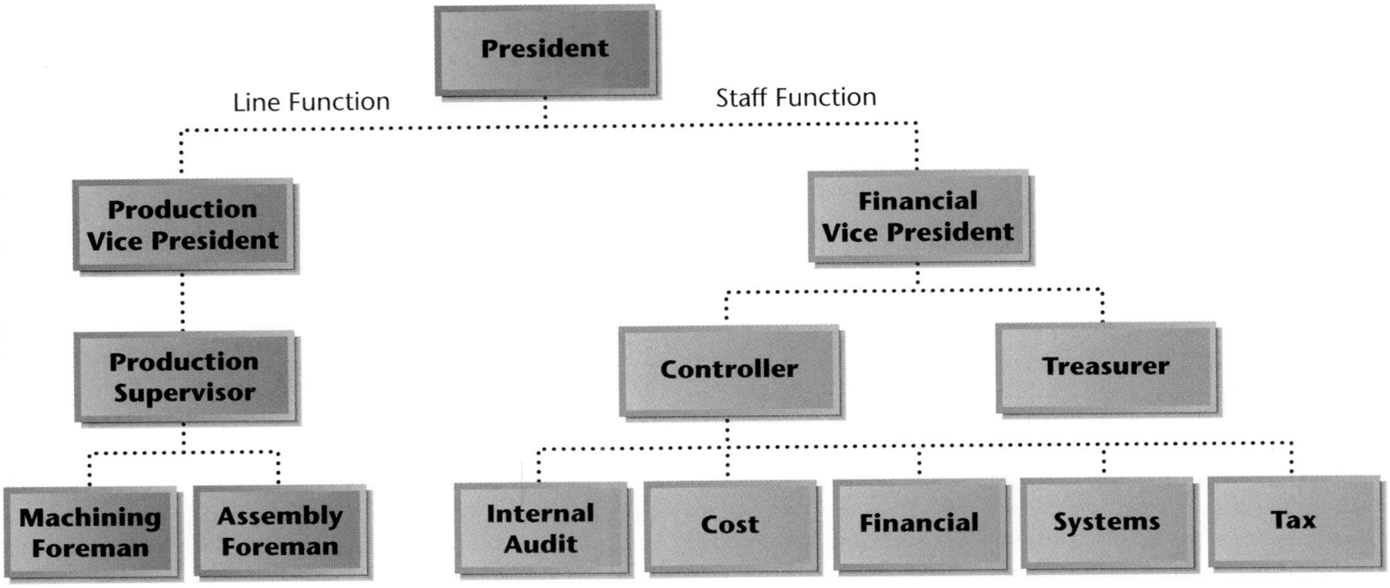

Exhibit 1-4 Partial Organization Chart, Manufacturing Company

analysis, design, and internal controls), and taxes. The duties and organization of the controller's office vary from firm to firm. For example, in some firms, the internal audit department may report directly to the financial vice president; similarly, the systems department may report directly to the financial vice president or some other vice president. One possible organization of a controller's office is also shown in Exhibit 1-4.

The **treasurer** is responsible for the finance function. Specifically, the treasurer raises capital and manages cash and investments. The treasurer may also be in charge of credit, collection, and insurance. As shown in Exhibit 1-4, the treasurer reports to the financial vice president.

Sarbanes-Oxley Act of 2002

In June 2002, Congress passed the Sarbanes-Oxley Act. This legislation was passed in response to the collapse of Enron and the revelations of securities fraud and accounting misconduct associated with companies such as WorldCom, Adelphia, and HealthSouth. The **Sarbanes-Oxley Act (SOX)** established stronger government control and regulation of public companies in the United States. SOX applies to **publicly traded companies**, companies that issue stock traded on U.S. stock exchanges. Major sections of SOX include establishment of the Public Company Accounting Oversight Board (PCAOB), enhanced auditor independence, tightened regulation of corporate governance, control over management, and management/auditor assessment of the firm's internal controls. SOX also led to increased attention to corporate ethics, and this is discussed in the next section.

Importantly, private companies, nonprofit entities, and governmental agencies or entities are not covered by SOX and not subject to PCAOB control. However, these entities have been affected by SOX through their dealings with constituents and their boards of directors. In particular, the intense scrutiny of internal control under SOX is a feature that many would like to see applied to nonprofit entities. Internal control is a process put into place by management and the board of directors to ensure that objectives are achieved in the areas of effectiveness and efficiency of operations, reliability of financial reporting, and compliance with applicable laws and regulations.[8] All entities should achieve their legitimate objectivies, and good internal control can help to ensure that. Management accountants, through the offices of internal auditing or the chief financial officer (CFO), are the people in the organization who are expected to help their organizations comply with SOX.

Management Accounting and Ethical Conduct

Objective 6

Explain the importance of ethical behavior for managers and management accountants.

Virtually all management accounting practices were developed to assist managers in maximizing profits. Traditionally, the economic performance of the firm has been the overriding concern. Yet managers and management accountants should not become so focused on profits that they develop a belief that the only goal of a business is maximizing its net worth. The objective of profit maximization should be constrained by the requirement that profits be achieved through legal and ethical means. While this has always been an implicit assumption of management accounting, the assumption should be made explicit. To help achieve this objective, many of the problems in this text force explicit consideration of ethical issues.

Ethical Behavior

ETHICS

Ethical behavior involves choosing actions that are "right," "proper," and "just." Our behavior can be right or wrong; it can be proper or improper; and the decisions we make can be just or unjust. Though people often differ in their views of the meaning of the ethical terms cited, a common principle seems to underlie all ethical systems. This principle is expressed by the belief that each member of a group bears some responsibility for the well-being of other members. Willingness to sacrifice one's self-interest for the well-being of the group is the heart of ethical action.

This notion of sacrificing one's self-interest for the well-being of others produces some core values—values that describe what is meant by right and wrong in more concrete terms. James W. Brackner, writing for the "Ethics Column" in *Management Accounting,* made the following observation:

> For moral or ethical education to have meaning, there must be agreement on the values that are considered "right." Ten of these values are identified and described by Michael Josephson in "Teaching Ethical Decision Making and Principled Reasoning." The study of history, philosophy, and religion reveals a strong consensus as to certain universal and timeless values essential to the ethical life.
>
> These ten core values yield a series of principles that delineate right and wrong in general terms. Therefore, they provide a guide to behavior.[9]

The ten core values referred to in the quotation follow:

1. Honesty
2. Integrity
3. Promise keeping
4. Fidelity
5. Fairness
6. Caring for others
7. Respect for others
8. Responsible citizenship
9. Pursuit of excellence
10. Accountability

Although it may seem contradictory, sacrificing one's self-interest for the collective good may not only be right and bring a sense of individual worth but may also

8 Definition taken from COSO Internal Control Integrated Framework, http://www.coso.org/publications/executive_summary_integrated_framework.htm.

9 James W. Brackner, "Consensus Values Should Be Taught," *Management Accounting* (August 1992): p. 19. For a more complete discussion of the ten core values, see also Michael Josephson, "Teaching Ethical Decision Making and Principled Reasoning," *Ethics: Easier Said Than Done* (Winter 1988): pp. 29–30.

be good business sense. Companies with a strong code of ethics can create strong customer and employee loyalty. While liars and cheats may win on occasion, their victories are often short term. Companies in business for the long term find that it pays to treat all of their clients honestly and loyally.

Company Codes of Conduct and SOX

The Sarbanes-Oxley Act requires that a company's senior financial officers be subject to a code of ethics *or* that the company must disclose publicly that they are not. Since no company wants to say publicly that its CEO or CFO is not subject to a code of ethics, companies not only have codes of ethics, those codes do apply to the top corporate officers. In practice, companies have developed codes of ethics, often called codes of conduct, that are applicable to all their employees. The codes can, and do, differ from company to company. Some are lengthy, with ample guidance for particular circumstances. Others are briefer and more general; they expect employees to internalize the ethical guidelines and to apply them in a variety of circumstances. A number of companies, including GlaxoSmithKline, John Deere, Nike, and Pixar, have posted their codes of conduct on their websites. This is now standard practice for public companies.

http://www.gsk.com/responsibility/cr_issues/business_ethics.htm
http://www.deere.com/en_US/investinfo/corpgov/ethics.html
http://www.nike.com/nikebiz/nikebiz.jhtml?page=25&cat=code
http://corporate.pixar.com/downloads/Code_of_Conduct.pdf

Management accountants and all employees are expected to be knowledgeable about their company's code of ethics. Along with other employees, they may be asked to sign a document stating that they have read and understand the code. They should also be aware of provisions for whistle-blower assistance. SOX gives protection to those who blow the whistle on financial misconduct or fraudulent financial reporting. Companies must establish mechanisms through which employees and other stakeholders can report suspected misconduct. The company is required, then, to follow up on all such reports. Many public companies have outsourced their ethics hotlines to reputable outside companies in order to provide assurance that employee complaints and tips can be made anonymously.

Managers Decide

Gifts and Conflicts of Interest

Joseph Menardi,* a new graduate of the Culinary Institute of America, was hired as head chef of a popular local restaurant. Several months after Joseph started work, the restaurant's meat supplier offered him six choice steaks—worth about $100—as a gift for "being such a great customer." Joseph was surprised and pleased by the offer; he looked forward to treating his friends to a special dinner. Is is all right for Joseph to accept the gift? A new chef may think that it is—but this is wrong! The purpose of the gift is to make Joseph less objective in his choice of supplier. He could be fired for such behavior. In fact, many corporate codes of conduct explicitly prohibit such behavior. ■

*This is a real situation, but the name has been changed.

Standards of Ethical Conduct for Management Accountants

Organizations commonly establish standards of conduct for their managers and employees. Professional associations also establish ethical standards. For example, the Institute of Management Accountants has established ethical standards for management accountants. In 2005, the IMA issued a revised statement outlining standards of ethical conduct for management accountants. Called the "Statement of Ethical Professional Practice," the revised statement was designed to accord with the provisions of the Sarbanes-Oxley Act of 2002 and to meet the global needs of IMA's international members. The revised statement is based on the principles of honesty, fairness, objectivity, and responsibility. The Statement of Ethical Professional Practice and the recommended resolution of ethical conflicts are presented in Exhibit 1-5.

To illustrate an application of the statement, suppose a manager's bonus increases as reported profits increase. The manager has an incentive to find ways to increase profits, including unethical approaches. For example, he or she could delay promoting deserving employees or use cheaper parts to make a product. In either case, if the motive is simply to increase the reported income, and the bonus, the behavior could be unethical. Neither action is in the best interest of the company or its employees.

Members of IMA shall behave ethically. A commitment to ethical professional practice includes overarching principles that express our values, and standards that guide our conduct.

Principles

IMA's overarching ethical principles include: Honesty, Fairness, Objectivity, and Responsibility. Members shall act in accordance with these principles and shall encourage others within their organizations to adhere to them.

Standards

A member's failure to comply with the following standards may result in disciplinary action.

I. Competence

Each member has a responsibility to:
1. Maintain an appropriate level of professional expertise by continually developing knowledge and skills.
2. Perform professional duties in accordance with relevant laws, regulations, and technical standards.
3. Provide decision support information and recommendations that are accurate, clear, concise, and timely.
4. Recognize and communicate professional limitations or other constraints that would preclude responsible judgment or successful performance of an activity.

II. Confidentiality

Each member has a responsibility to:
1. Keep information confidential except when disclosure is authorized or legally required.
2. Inform all relevant parties regarding appropriate use of confidential information. Monitor subordinates' activities to ensure compliance.
3. Refrain from using confidential information for unethical or illegal advantage.

Exhibit 1-5 IMA Statement of Ethical Professional Practice

III. Integrity

Each member has a responsibility to:

1. Mitigate actual conflicts of interest; regularly communicate with business associates to avoid apparent conflicts of interest. Advise all parties of any potential conflicts.
2. Refrain from engaging in any conduct that would prejudice carrying out duties ethically.
3. Abstain from engaging in or supporting any activity that might discredit the profession.

IV. Credibility

Each member has a responsibility to:

1. Communicate information fairly and objectively.
2. Disclose all relevant information that could reasonably be expected to influence an intended user's understanding of the reports, analyses, or recommendations.
3. Disclose delays or deficiencies in information, timeliness, processing, or internal controls in conformance with organization policy and/or applicable law.

Resolution of Ethical Conflict

In applying the Standards of Ethical Professional Practice, you may encounter problems identifying unethical behavior or resolving an ethical conflict. When faced with ethical issues, you should follow your organization's established policies on the resolution of such conflict. If these policies do not resolve the ethical conflict, you should consider the following courses of action:

1. Discuss the issue with your immediate supervisor except when it appears that the supervisor is involved. In that case, present the issue to the next level. If you cannot achieve a satisfactory resolution, submit the issue to the next management level. If your immediate superior is the chief executive officer or equivalent, the acceptable reviewing authority may be a group such as the audit committee, executive committee, board of directors, board of trustees, or owners. Contact with levels above the immediate superior should be initiated only with your superior's knowledge, assuming he or she is not involved. Communication of such problems to authorities or individuals not employed or engaged by the organization is not considered appropriate, unless you believe there is a clear violation of the law.
2. Clarify relevant ethical issues by initiating a confidential discussion with an IMA Ethics Counselor or other impartial advisor to obtain a better understanding of possible courses of action.
3. Consult your own attorney as to legal obligations and rights concerning the ethical conflict.

Source: http://www.imanet.org/about_ethics_statement.asp

Exhibit 1-5 concluded

Yet where should the blame be assigned? After all, the reward system strongly encourages the manager to increase profits. Is the reward system at fault, or is the manager who chooses to increase profits at fault? Or both?

In reality, both are probably at fault. It is important to design evaluation and reward systems to minimize the incentives to pursue undesirable behavior. Yet designing a perfect reward system is not a realistic expectation. Managers have an obligation to avoid abusing the system. Standards III-1 and III-2 state that management accountants should "mitigate actual conflicts of interest" and "refrain from engaging in any conduct that would prejudice carrying out duties ethically." Manipulating income to increase a bonus can be interpreted as a violation of this standard. Basically, the prospect of an increased bonus (for example, a favor) should not influence a manager to engage in unethical actions.

Certification

Objective 7

List three forms of certification available to management accountants.

Numerous forms of certification are available to management accountants. We will briefly describe three of the major types: a Certificate in Management Accounting, a Certificate in Public Accounting, and a Certificate in Internal Auditing. Each certification offers particular advantages to a management accountant. In each case, an applicant must meet specific educational and experience requirements and pass a qualifying examination to become certified. Thus, all three certifications offer evidence that the holder has achieved a minimum level of professional competence.

Furthermore, all three certifications require the holders to engage in continuing professional education in order to maintain certification. Because certification reveals a commitment to professional competency, most organizations encourage their management accountants to become certified.

The CMA

In 1974, the Institute of Management Accountants (IMA) sponsored a new certification called the Certificate in Management Accounting. This certificate was designed to meet the specific needs of management accountants. A **certified management accountant (CMA)** has passed a rigorous qualifying examination, has met an experience requirement, and participates in continuing education.

One of the key requirements for obtaining the CMA is passing a qualifying examination. Four areas are emphasized: (1) economics, finance, and management; (2) financial accounting and reporting; (3) management reporting, analysis, and behavioral issues; and (4) decision analysis and information systems. The parts to the examination reflect the needs of management accounting and underscore the earlier observation that management accounting has more of an interdisciplinary flavor than other areas of accounting.

One of the main purposes of the CMA was to establish management accounting as a recognized, professional discipline, separate from the profession of public accounting. Since its inception, the CMA program has been very successful. Many firms now sponsor and pay for classes that prepare their management accountants for the qualifying examination, as well as provide other financial incentives to encourage acquisition of the CMA.

The CPA

The Certificate in Public Accounting is the oldest and best-known certification in accounting. Its purpose is to provide minimal professional qualification for external auditors. The responsibility of external auditors is to provide assurance concerning the reliability of a firm's financial statements. A **certified public accountant (CPA)** is permitted (by law) to serve as an external auditor. CPAs must pass a national examination and be licensed by the state in which they practice. Although the Certificate in Public Accounting does not have a management accounting orientation, it is held by many management accountants.

Standardized tests are used for a number of certification programs. These help to ensure that candidates meet a minimum standard for accounting knowledge, and help to assure public trust.

The CIA

The other certification available to internal accountants is the Certificate in Internal Auditing. The forces that led to the creation of this certification in 1974 are similar to those that resulted in the CMA. Internal auditing differs from external auditing and management accounting, and many internal auditors felt a need for a specialized certification. The **certified internal auditor (CIA)** has passed a comprehensive examination designed to ensure technical competence and has gained two years of experience.

Summary of Learning Objectives

1. Discuss the need for management accounting information.

Managers, workers, and executives use management accounting information to identify and solve problems and to evaluate performance. Essentially, management accounting information helps managers carry out their roles of planning, controlling, and decision making. Planning is the detailed formulation of action to achieve a particular end. Controlling is the monitoring of a plan's implementation. Decision making is choosing among competing alternatives.

2. Differentiate between management accounting and financial accounting.

Management accounting differs from financial accounting in several ways. Management accounting information is intended for internal users, whereas financial accounting information is directed toward external users. Management accounting is not bound by the externally imposed rules of financial reporting. Furthermore, it tends to be more subjective and uses both financial and nonfinancial measures, whereas financial accounting provides audited, objective financial information. Finally, management accounting provides more detail than financial accounting, and it tends to be broader and multidisciplinary.

3. Provide a brief historical description of management accounting.

Most of the product costing and internal accounting procedures used today were developed between 1880 and 1925. By 1925, the emphasis of management accounting procedures had become inventory costing, stemming from the emphasis on external reporting. In the 1950s and 1960s, some effort was made to improve the managerial usefulness of traditional cost systems. In recent years, significant action has been taken to radically change the nature and practice of management accounting, largely in response to some dramatic changes in the competitive environment.

4. Identify the current focus of management accounting.

Management accounting must provide information that allows managers to focus on customer value, total quality management, and time-based competition. This implies that information about value-chain activities and customer sacrifice (such as postpurchase costs) must be collected and made available. Activity-based management is a major innovative response to the demand for more accurate and relevant management accounting information. Additionally, managers must decide on the strategic position of the firm. One of two positions is usually emphasized, either cost leadership or product differentiation. Which position is chosen can affect the nature of the management accounting information system.

5. Describe the role of management accountants in an organization.

Management accountants are responsible for identifying, collecting, measuring, analyzing, preparing, interpreting, and communicating information used by management to achieve the basic objectives of the organization. Management accountants need to be sensitive to the information needs of managers. Management accountants serve as staff members of the organization and are responsible for providing information; they are usually intimately involved in the management process as valued members of the management team.

6. Explain the importance of ethical behavior for managers and management accountants.

Management accounting aids managers in their efforts to improve the economic performance of the firm. Unfortunately, some managers have overemphasized the economic dimension and have engaged in unethical and illegal actions. Many of these actions have relied on the management accounting system to bring about and even support that unethical behavior. To emphasize the importance of the ever-present constraint of ethical behavior on profit-maximizing behavior, this text presents ethical issues in many of the problems appearing at the end of each chapter.

7. List three forms of certification available to management accountants.

Three of the major types of certification are the CMA, the CPA, and the CIA. The CMA is a certification designed especially for management accountants. The prestige of the CMA has increased significantly over the years and it is now well regarded by the industrial world. The CPA is primarily intended for those practicing public accounting; however, because this certification is highly regarded, many management accountants also hold it. The CIA serves internal auditors and is also greatly respected.

Key Terms

Activity-based management, 10
Certified internal auditor (CIA), 22
Certified management accountant (CMA), 21
Certified public accountant (CPA), 21
Continuous improvement, 5
Controller, 15
Controlling, 7
Customer value, 11
Decision making, 7
Electronic business (e-business), 15
Employee empowerment, 5
Ethical behavior, 17
External linkages, 12
Feedback, 7
Financial accounting information system, 7
Industrial value chain, 12
Internal linkages, 12
Internal value chain, 11
Line positions, 15
Management accounting information system, 4
Performance reports, 7
Planning, 6
Postpurchase costs, 11
Publicly traded companies, 16
Sarbanes-Oxley Act (SOX), 16
Staff positions, 15
Strategic cost management, 11
Strategic decision making, 5
Supply chain management, 13
Total product, 11
Total quality management, 13
Treasurer, 16

Questions for Writing and Discussion

1. What is a management accounting information system?
2. Describe the inputs, processes, and outputs of a management accounting information system.
3. What are the three objectives of a management accounting information system?
4. What types of organizations need management accounting information systems?
5. Who are the users of management accounting information?
6. For what purpose is management accounting information used?
7. Should a management accounting system provide both financial and nonfinancial information? Explain.
8. What is meant by continuous improvement?
9. Describe what is meant by employee empowerment.
10. Explain why operational workers need management accounting information.
11. Describe the connection between planning, feedback, and controlling.
12. What role do performance reports play with respect to the control function?
13. How do management accounting and financial accounting differ?
14. Explain the role of financial reporting in the development of management accounting. Why has this changed in recent years?
15. What is activity-based management? Why is it important?
16. Explain the meaning of customer value. How is focusing on customer value changing management accounting?
17. What is the internal value chain? Why is it important?
18. What is the industrial value chain? Why is it important?
19. What is supply chain management? Explain its relationship to the industrial value chain.
20. What is e-business? Explain why it is important for a management accountant to understand e-business.
21. Explain why today's management accountant must have a cross-functional perspective.
22. Discuss the relationship of time-based competition and management accounting information.

23. What is the difference between a staff position and a line position?
24. The controller should be a member of the top management staff. Do you agree or disagree? Explain.
25. What is the role of the controller in an organization? Describe some of the activities over which he or she has control.
26. What is ethical behavior? Is it possible to teach ethical behavior in a management accounting course?
27. Firms with higher ethical standards will experience a higher level of economic performance than firms with lower or poor ethical standards. Do you agree? Why or why not?
28. Review the code of ethical conduct for management accountants. Do you believe that the code will have an effect on the ethical behavior of management accountants? Explain.
29. Identify the three forms of accounting certification discussed. Which form of certification do you believe is best for a management accountant? Why?
30. What is the Sarbanes-Oxley Act of 2002? What are its major provisions?

Exercises

1-1

Management Accounting Information System
LO1

The items that follow are associated with a management accounting information system.

a. Incurrence of environmental costs
b. Preparing a report that summarizes environmental costs
c. A statement of the cost of goods manufactured
d. Usage of direct labor
e. Providing information for decision making
f. Incurrence of quality costs
g. Measuring the cost of design
h. Providing information for planning and control
i. A report showing the trend in quality costs
j. Using power for manufacturing a product
k. Costing out products and customers
l. A report that compares actual costs of materials with expected costs
m. Measuring the costs of lost sales due to defective products
n. Providing cost information for decision making

Required

Classify the items into one of the following categories:

1. Inputs
2. Processes
3. Outputs
4. System objectives

1-2

Management Accounting versus Financial Accounting
LO2

The actions that follow are associated with a firm's accounting information system.

a. Preparing a report that details profit by customer
b. Preparing an income statement that complies with generally accepted accounting principles
c. Preparing a monthly cash budget
d. Voluntarily reporting safety costs to potential and existing investors
e. Research to determine how to report an uninsured facility destroyed by flood
f. Reporting on the trends in defect rates to the plant manager
g. Determining the cost of dropping a product
h. Determining the cost of producing a new product
i. Determining the cost of bad debts for the balance sheet
j. Assessing postpurchase costs
k. A report that shows a trend in warranty costs

l. Reporting the value of marketable securities
m. Determining how to consolidate the financial reports of two subsidiaries
n. A report comparing the activity-based product costs with traditional product costs

Required

Classify the above actions as belonging either to management accounting or financial accounting.

1-3

Historical Perspective
LO3

Choose the best answer for each of the following:

1. Most of the product costing and management accounting procedures used in the twentieth century were developed
   a. between 1929 and 1940.
   b. between 1880 and 1925.
   c. between 1950 and 1970.
   d. by the FASB in 1905.
2. After 1925, the driving force for the design of cost accounting systems was
   a. the stock market crash of 1929.
   b. the need for strategic planning.
   c. financial reporting.
   d. the need for sound cost information for internal decision making.
   e. None of the above.
3. In the 1980s and 1990s, many recognized that
   a. the efforts in the 1950s and 1960s to improve the managerial usefulness of conventional cost systems were entirely successful.
   b. the cost of more detailed cost systems exceeded their benefits.
   c. the traditional management accounting system was obsolete.
   d. more accurate product costing was needed.
   e. All of the above are true.
   f. Only c and d are true.

1-4

Management versus Financial Accounting; Historical versus Current Focus
LO2, LO3, LO4

Choose the best answer for each of the following:

1. Management accounting is best characterized by which of the following statements?
   a. It produces (principally) objective and verifiable financial information.
   b. It has a historical orientation.
   c. It focuses on overall firm performance, providing an aggregated viewpoint.
   d. It is subject to generally accepted accounting principles.
   e. None of the above.
2. The current focus of management accounting can best be described as
   a. a system that achieves relevance by making financial accounting information more useful to internal users.
   b. having emphasis on activity-based costing and process value analysis.
   c. lacking a customer orientation.
   d. having emphasis on assigning manufacturing costs to products so that inventory cost can be reported to external users.
   e. All of the above.
3. Which of the following is *not* part of the current focus of management accounting?
   a. It emphasizes the use of cost information for strategic decision making.
   b. It measures and reports quality costs as well as nonfinancial measures of quality such as defect rates.
   c. It emphasizes the use of aggregated average cost information for individual products.

d. It tries to determine why activities are performed and how well they are performed.
e. None of the above.

1-5

Current Focus of Management Accounting
LO4

Match the following items:

1. Continuous reduction in cost
2. Linked set of value-creating activities
3. Using cost data to identify superior strategies
4. Selling over the Internet
5. A product's total tangible and intangible benefits
6. Suppliers and customers
7. Flow of materials from upstream to downstream
8. Internal value chain
9. Zero defects
10. Realization of less sacrifice
11. Activity-based costing and process value analysis

a. Strategic cost management
b. Total quality management
c. Internal linkages
d. Activity-based management
e. Customer value
f. E-business
g. Industrial value chain
h. External linkages
i. Total product
j. Supply chain management
k. Efficiency

1-6

Line versus Staff
LO5

The job responsibilities of four employees of Jamison, Inc., follow.

Penny Reynolds, Cost Accounting Manager. Penny is responsible for measuring and collecting costs associated with the manufacture of the small appliance product line. She is also responsible for preparing periodic reports comparing the actual costs with planned costs. These reports are provided to the production line managers and the plant manager. Penny helps explain and interpret the reports.

Karol Jeffers, Sales Manager. Karol is responsible for coordinating the sales team for Jamison's small appliance products group. Karol hires, trains, and supervises the sales staff. She is also responsible for sales in the northeast region, and spends about 25 percent of her time on the road, selling Jamison's consumer products to retailers. She is responsible for seeing that sales quotas are met as well as for controlling selling costs for the consumer products line.

Porter Elbart, Industrial Engineer. Porter is based in the small appliance manufacturing plant. He and his two engineering colleagues are responsible for the smooth running of the production equipment. When a new product is developed, Porter designs and implements the production process, adapting manufacturing equipment as necessary or ordering new equipment and getting it up and running

Joe Jespers, Production Manager. Joe is responsible for the manufacture of the coffeemaker line. He supervises the line workers, helps develop the production schedule, and is responsible for seeing that production quotas are met. He is also held accountable for controlling manufacturing costs.

Required

Identify Penny, Karol, Porter, and Joe as line or staff, and explain your reasons.

1-7

Ethical Behavior
LO6

ETHICS

Consider the following scenario:

Manager: If I can reduce my costs by $40,000 during this last quarter, my division will show a profit that is 10 percent above the planned level, and I will receive a $10,000 bonus. However, given the projections for the fourth quarter, it does not look promising. I really need that $10,000. I know one way I can qualify. All I have to do is lay off my three most expensive salespeople. After all, most of the orders are in for the fourth quarter, and I can always hire new sales personnel at the beginning of the next year.

Required

What is the right choice for the manager to make? Why did the ethical dilemma arise? Is there any way to redesign the accounting reporting system to discourage the type of behavior the manager is contemplating?

1-8

Ethical Issues
LO6

ETHICS

Assess and comment on each of the following statements that have appeared in newspaper editorials:

a. Business students come from all segments of society. If they have not been taught ethics by their families and by their elementary and secondary schools, a business school can have little effect on them.
b. Sacrificing self-interest for the collective good won't happen unless a majority of Americans also accept this premise.
c. Competent executives manage people and resources for the good of society. Monetary benefits and titles are simply the by-products of doing a good job.
d. Unethical firms and individuals, like high rollers in Las Vegas, are eventually wiped out financially.

1-9

Ethics
LO6

ETHICS

Consider the following conversation between Dave, a printer, and Steve, an assistant in the local university's athletic department.

Steve: Dave, our department needs to have 10,000 posters printed for the basketball team for next year. Here's the mock-up; we'll need them in a month. How much will you charge?

Dave: Well, given the costs I have for ink and paper, I can come in around $5,000.

Steve: Great, here's what I want you to do. Print me up an invoice for $7,500, that's our budget. Then, when they pay you, you give me a check for $2,500. I'll make sure you get the job.

Required

Is this ethical? What should Dave do?

1-10

Certifications
LO7

Classify the following as pertaining to the CMA, CPA, or CIA:

a. The oldest and best-known certification
b. Is concerned with internal auditing only
c. Qualifying exam covers economics, finance, and management
d. Must be licensed by the state to practice
e. The only certification that allows the holder to engage in external auditing
f. Sponsored by the Institute of Management Accountants
g. Must meet certain experience requirements
h. Must pass a qualifying examination

Problems

1-11

Employee Empowerment
LO1

Duffy Tool and Stamping has formed "excellence teams" made up of production line employees. These teams have been given the charge to improve production processes and enhance employee safety. They follow a very structured problem-solving methodology and have managed to make numerous improvements in production as well as safety. During a six-year period, pretax profits increased each year. Duffy's management largely credits the excellence teams for the cost reductions and increased profits.

Another company, **Grand Rapids Spring and Wire Products**, has formed minicompanies within its factory. The objective of minicompanies is to have each employee assume ownership of his or her work. Each minicompany has its own suppliers and customers (all within the factory). Furthermore, each minicompany is assigned its own support people: accountants, engineers, marketing people, and so on. The individuals within the minicompany are given responsibility for developing and maintaining good relations with their suppliers and customers, identifying problems, and developing and implementing solutions to those problems. The focus of each minicompany is on quality, cost, delivery, safety, and morale. The company has successfully created a quality culture, achieved a reputation for being a competitive, world-class manufacturer, and has become a "learning" organization.

Required

1. What are the objectives of excellence teams and minicompanies? Did the companies achieve these objectives?
2. Do you think that employee empowerment is a good idea? Explain your answer. If yes, do you see any disadvantages? Explain.
3. What role, if any, does management accounting information have in employee empowerment?
4. What do you suppose is meant by the phrase "quality culture"? What is meant by a learning organization?

1-12

The Managerial Process
LO1

Each of the following scenarios requires the use of accounting information to carry out one or more of the following managerial activities: planning, controlling (including performance evaluation), or decision making. Identify the managerial activity or activities that are applicable for each scenario, and indicate the role of accounting information in the activity.

A. **Laboratory Manager:** An HMO approached me recently and offered us its business on an entire range of blood tests. It provided a price list of the amount it is willing to pay for each test. In many cases, the prices are below what we normally charge. I need to know our costs of the individual tests to assess the feasibility of accepting its offer and perhaps suggest some price adjustments on some of the tests.

B. **Operating Manager:** This report indicates that we have 30 percent more defects than originally targeted. An investigation into the cause has revealed the problem. We were using a lower-quality material than expected, and the waste has been higher than normal. By switching to the quality level originally specified, we can reduce the defects to the planned level.

C. **Divisional Manager:** Our market share has increased because of higher-quality products. Current projections indicate that we should sell 25 percent more units than last year. I want a projection of the effect this increase in sales will have on profits. I also want to know our expected cash receipts and cash expenditures on a month-by-month basis. I have a feeling that some short-term borrowing may be necessary.

D. **Plant Manager:** Foreign competitors are producing goods with lower costs and delivering them more rapidly than we can to customers in our markets. We need to decrease the cycle time and increase the efficiency of our manufacturing process. There are two proposals that should help us accomplish these goals, both of which involve investing in computer-aided manufacturing. I need to know the future cash flows associated with each system and the effect each system has on unit costs and cycle time.

E. **Manager:** At the last board meeting, we established an objective of earning a 25 percent return on sales. I need to know how many units of our product we need to sell to meet this objective. Once I have the estimated sales in units, we need to outline a promotional campaign that will take us where we want to be. However, in order to compute the targeted sales in units, I need to know the expected unit price and a lot of cost information.

F. **Manager:** Perhaps the Harrison Medical Clinic should not offer a full range of medical services. Some services seem to be having a difficult time showing any kind of profit. I am particularly concerned about the mental health service. It has not shown a profit since the clinic opened. I want to know what costs can be avoided if I drop the service. I also want some assessment of the impact on the other services we offer. Some of our patients may choose this clinic because we offer a full range of services.

1-13

Customer Value; Strategic Positioning
LO4

Adriana Alvarado has decided to purchase a personal computer. She has narrowed the choices to two: Drantex and Confiar. Both brands have the same processing speed, 6.4 gigabytes of hard-disk capacity, a 3.5-inch disk drive, and a CD-ROM drive, and each comes with the same basic software support package. Both come from mail-order companies with good reputations. The selling price for each is identical. After some review, Adriana discovers that the cost of operating and maintaining Drantex over a three-year period is estimated to be $300. For Confiar, the operating and maintenance cost is $600. The sales agent for Drantex emphasized the lower operating and maintenance costs. The agent for Confiar, however, emphasized the service reputation of the product and the faster delivery time. (Confiar can be purchased and delivered one week sooner than Drantex.) Based on all the available information, Adriana has decided to buy Confiar.

Required

1. What is the total product purchased by Adriana?
2. How does the strategic positioning differ for the two companies?
3. When asked why she decided to buy Confiar, Adriana responded, "I think that Confiar offers more value than Drantex." What are the possible sources of this greater value? What implications does this have for the management accounting information system?
4. Suppose that Adriana's decision was prompted mostly by the desire to receive the computer quickly. Informed that it was losing sales because of the longer time to produce and deliver its products, the management of the company producing Drantex decided to improve delivery performance by improving its internal processes. These improvements decreased the number of defective units and the time required to produce its product. Consequently, delivery time and costs both decreased, and the company was able to lower its prices on Drantex. Explain how these actions translate into strengthening the competitive position of the Drantex PC relative to the Confiar PC. Also discuss the implications for the management accounting information system.

1-14

Role of Management Accountants
LO5

CMA

Management accountants are actively involved in the process of managing the entity. This process includes making strategic, tactical, and operating decisions while helping to coordinate the efforts of the entire organization. To fulfill these objectives, the management accountant accepts certain responsibilities that can be identified as (1) planning, (2) controlling, (3) evaluating performance, (4) ensuring accountability of resources, and (5) external reporting.

Required

Describe each of these responsibilities of the management accountant, and identify examples of practices and techniques. **(CMA adapted)**

1-15

Ethical Issues
LO6

ETHICS

CMA

The Alert Company is a closely held investment service group that has been very successful over the past five years, consistently providing most members of the top management group with 50 percent bonuses. In addition, both the chief financial officer and the chief executive officer have received 100 percent bonuses. Alert expects this trend to continue.

Recently, Alert's top management group, which holds 35 percent of the outstanding shares of common stock, has learned that a major corporation is interested in acquiring Alert. Alert's management is concerned that this corporation may make an attractive offer to the other shareholders and management would be unable to prevent the takeover. If the acquisition occurs, this executive group is uncertain about continued employment in the new corporate structure. As a consequence, the management group is considering changes to several accounting policies and practices that, although not in accordance with generally accepted accounting principles, would make the company a less attractive acquisition. Management has told Roger Deerling, Alert's controller, to implement some of these changes. Roger has also been informed that Alert's management does not intend to disclose these changes immediately to anyone outside the top management group.

Required

Using the code of ethics for management accountants, evaluate the changes that Alert's management is considering, and discuss the specific steps that Roger should take to resolve the situation. **(CMA adapted)**

1-16

Ethical Issues
LO6

ETHICS

CMA

Webson Manufacturing Company produces component parts for the airline industry and has recently undergone a major computer system conversion. Michael Darwin, the controller, has established a troubleshooting team to alleviate accounting problems that have occurred since the conversion. Michael has chosen Maureen Hughes, assistant controller, to head the team that will include Bob Randolph, cost accountant; Cynthia Wells, financial analyst; Marjorie Park, general accounting supervisor; and George Crandall, financial accountant.

The team has been meeting weekly for the last month. Maureen insists on being part of all the team conversations in order to gather information, make the final decision on any ideas or actions that the team develops, and prepare a weekly report for Michael. She has also used this team as a forum to discuss issues and disputes about him and other members of Webson's top management team. At last week's meeting, Maureen told the team that she thought a competitor might purchase Webson's common stock because she had overheard Michael talking about this on the telephone. As a result, most of Webson's employees now informally discuss the sale of Webson's common stock and how it will affect their jobs.

Required

Is Maureen Hughes's discussion with the team about the prospective sale of Webson's common stock unethical? Discuss, citing specific standards from the code of ethical conduct to support your position. **(CMA adapted)**

1-17

Ethical Responsibilities
LO6

ETHICS

CMA

Universal Air Inc. supplies instrumentation components to airplane manufacturers. Although there are only a few competitors in this market, the competition is fierce.

Universal uses a traditional performance incentive plan that awards bonuses on the basis of divisional profit. Recently, Charles Gross, chief executive officer, concluded that Universal's objectives may be better served with new performance measures. On January 1, 2005, Charles charged his top-level managers to be part of an executive team to develop new measures for Universal.

The executive team conducted a customer survey. Universal has always prided itself on being on the technological forefront; the survey results had indicated technology to be a low priority, and customers were more concerned with product quality and customer service. As a result, the executive team developed 30 new indicators to measure middle-management performance. The executive team directed the controller to develop the necessary new monthly reports and graphs to report on these new measures. The executive team then told the middle managers that their performance would be evaluated using these new indicators. The middle managers were not enthusiastic and felt that some of the measures were influenced by the performance of several other departments outside their control. Over the next few months, customer complaints increased, and a major customer chose a competitor over Universal.

Upon seeing the results, Charles decided to review the new process. Last week in a meeting with executive and middle managers, Charles emphasized that new measures should help balance the company's performance between increased customer value and improved operating efficiency. Charles set up two cross-functional teams that include executive and middle managers, one for new product development and one for the customer order and fulfillment process. The objectives of these cross-functional teams are to develop a second set of new measures and to evaluate the impact of these new measures on each team's individual performance. Both teams are to focus on cost, quality, and scheduling time.

Richard Strong, quality inspection manager, is the brother-in-law of John Brogan, cost accumulation manager. On June 1, John telephoned Sara Wiley, the purchasing manager at Magic Aircraft Manufacturing Inc., one of Universal's major customers. John said, "Listen, Sara, we're going through all these hoops over here to measure performance, and management seems to be changing these measures every day. It was so easy before, getting a bonus on the bottom line; now we have to worry about things out of our control based on how the customer perceives our performance. Would you do me a favor? If you have any complaints, please have your people call me directly so I can forward the complaint to the right person. All that really matters is if all of us can make money." In actuality, Richard was the only person to whom John reported the customer complaints offered by Sara.

Required

Referring to the Standards of Ethical Conduct for Management Accountants, discuss whether or not John Brogan's behavior is unethical. **(CMA adapted)**

Research Assignment

1-18

Code of Ethics, Internet Research
LO6

ETHICS

Using the Internet, find three companies that have posted their code of ethics or code of conduct. Write a brief description of each code. Do the codes differ due to the business in which each company operates? Discuss.

chapter 2

Basic Management Accounting Concepts

learning objectives

After studying this chapter, you should be able to:

1. Describe the cost assignment process.
2. Define tangible and intangible products, and explain why there are different product cost definitions.
3. Prepare income statements for manufacturing and service organizations.
4. Outline the differences between functional-based and activity-based management accounting systems.

Scenario

Carol Anne Barrow's mother was known throughout the county for her pies and pastries. She was the odds-on favorite to win blue ribbons at every county fair. Carol Anne shared her mother's love for baking, and turned it into a multimillion-dollar baking company—Blue Ribbon Baking, Inc. Founded in 1967, Blue Ribbon Baking produces a wide variety of fruit and cream pies, as well as coffee cakes and tarts. The pies are frozen and sold through grocery stores in a five-state region. For years, Carol Anne felt that the business model was working. However, increased competition and decreasing margins in grocery stores led her to search for other areas in which the firm could expand.

The executive group at Blue Ribbon Baking searched for months for additional product and service opportunities. The group had narrowed down the expansion opportunities to two. The first was a proposal to open freestanding Blue Ribbon Cafes. The second was the opportunity for Blue Ribbon Baking to serve as the exclusive provider of mini coffee cakes to a fast-food chain.

In looking at these possibilities, Carol Anne realized that it was crucial to understand the costs of each. She had a good understanding of the manufacturing and selling costs of the basic pie line—making dough; rolling out and cutting individual pie shells; filling the shells with fruits, chocolate, coconut, pumpkin, etc.; and freezing and packaging. She also understood the costs of selling the pies to distributors and grocery stores. Now she needed to develop just as good an understanding of the potential costs and revenues of the new businesses under consideration. What were the costs of opening freestanding restaurants? What would they provide in addition to pies and pastries? Did Blue Ribbon Baking have the necessary expertise? For the fast-food chain, what quantities would be necessary? What special processing equipment would be needed? Would a new factory be needed? Would more specialized equipment be required? What about the labor—could her current employees handle the new process? How would Blue Ribbon Baking get the breakfast cakes to the chain's outlets? Carol Anne directed her executive team to develop a comprehensive assessment of the costs and potential revenues of each opportunity.

Two days later, the executive team met again. At that time, the controller, Luis Acevedo, reported that Blue Ribbon's current cost accounting system did not provide much guidance for the projection of costs to the potential product and service lines. The pie and tart manufacturing lines used many of the same activities. However, restaurants would have very different activities, and provide services as well as products. The mini coffee cakes would have very different packaging and distribution activities. If Blue Ribbon Baking expanded into these areas, the cost accounting system would require significant upgrading and refinement—one that could handle the assignment of different activities to the various product and service lines. The group agreed to consider the impact of potential expansion on production, marketing, and administrative costs, and to start pilot projects in each area so that supporting information could be gathered before the company was fully committed to either opportunity.

Questions to Think About

1. What is the difference between products and services? How might that affect accounting?
2. Why wouldn't the current product cost accounting provide useful information for the expansion into the two new product lines?
3. How would the pilot projects allow Blue Ribbon Baking to gather new accounting information?
4. Is assigning costs accurately as important for services as it is for products?

Cost Assignment: Direct Tracing, Driver Tracing, and Allocation

Objective 1

Describe the cost assignment process.

To study management accounting, it is necessary to understand the meaning of cost and the associated cost terminology. Assigning costs to products, services, customers, and other objects of managerial interest is one of the principal objectives of a management accounting information system. Increasing the accuracy of cost assignments produces higher-quality information, which can then be used to make better decisions. For example, the lubricant affiliates of **Mobil Oil Corporation**'s downstream division found that more accurate cost assignments resulted in better product mix decisions and significant increases in profits. One notable example of the importance of cost accuracy comes from the company's Korean affiliate. Its existing cost accounting system indicated that a marine lubricant, representing 20 percent of the total volume, was losing money. After changing to a more accurate cost accounting system, it discovered that this high-volume product was among the least expensive of its products to produce. Its existing cost accounting system was overstating the cost of the marine lubricant by 300 percent.[1] In the service sector, the **United States Postal Service** used more accurate cost assignments to justify offering customers credit/debit card service, thus increasing customer satisfaction while simultaneously producing projected annual savings of $28.8 million by the year 2001.[2] The experiences of Mobil and the United States Postal Service illustrate the importance of accurate cost assignments. However, before discussing the cost assignment process, we first need to define what we mean by "cost" and more fully describe its managerial importance.

The cost of a gallon of gasoline includes much more than the cost of refining crude oil into gasoline. There are also the costs of: distribution to get the gasoline to retail outlets, pumps, and outlet stores; labor to staff the outlets and keep the area clean and supplied; and so on.

© Getty Images/PhotoDisc

1 Tom Kang, "ABC Gathers Speed at Mobil," a June 14, 2001, article located in the activity-based costing category, which can be accessed via the chapter web links at the Interactive Study Center at http://www.thomsonedu.com/acconting/hansen.

2 Terrell L. Carter, "How ABC Changed the Post Office," *Management Accounting* (February 1998): pp. 28–36.

Cost

Cost is the cash or cash-equivalent value sacrificed for goods and services that is expected to bring a current or future benefit to the organization. We say cash equivalent because noncash resources can be exchanged for the desired goods or services. For example, equipment may be traded for materials used in production. Cost can be thought of as a dollar measure of the resources used to achieve a given benefit. Minimizing the cost required to achieve the benefit means that a firm is becoming more efficient. However, costs must be managed strategically. For example, managers should have the objective of providing the same (or greater) customer value for a lower cost than their competitors. In this way, the strategic position of the firm is increased, and a competitive advantage created.

Managers must also understand the meaning of *opportunity cost*. **Opportunity cost** is the benefit given up or sacrificed when one alternative is chosen over another. For example, a firm may invest $100,000 in inventory for a year instead of investing the capital in a productive investment that would yield a 12 percent rate of return. The opportunity cost of the capital tied up in inventory is $12,000 (0.12 × $100,000) and is part of the cost of carrying the inventory.

Costs are incurred to produce future benefits. In a profit-making firm, future benefits usually mean revenues. As costs are used up in the production of revenues, they are said to expire. Expired costs are called **expenses**. In each period, expenses are deducted from revenues in the income statement to determine the period's profit. For a company to remain in business, revenues must consistently exceed expenses; moreover, the income earned must be large enough to satisfy the owners of the firm. Thus, cost and price are related in the sense that price must exceed cost so that sufficient income is earned. Furthermore, lowering prices increases customer value by lowering customer sacrifice, and the ability to lower prices is connected to the ability to lower costs. Hence, managers need to know cost and trends in cost. Usually, however, knowing cost really means knowing what something or some object costs. Assigning costs to determine the cost of this object is therefore critical in providing this information to managers.

Cost Objects

Management accounting systems are structured to measure and assign costs to entities, called *cost objects*. A **cost object** is any item such as a product, customer, department, project, activity, and so on, for which costs are measured and assigned. For example, if Blue Ribbon Baking wants to determine the cost of adding mini coffee cakes, then the cost object is the mini coffee cake line. If a hospital wants to determine the cost of an operating department, then the cost object is the operating department. If a toy manufacturer wants to determine the cost of developing a new toy, then the cost object is the new toy development project.

In recent years, *activities* have emerged as important cost objects. An **activity** is a basic unit of work performed within an organization and can also be described as an aggregation of actions within an organization useful to managers for purposes of planning, controlling, and decision making. Activities not only act as cost objects but also play a prominent role in assigning costs to other cost objects. Examples of activities include setting up equipment for production, moving materials and goods, purchasing parts, billing customers, paying bills, maintaining equipment, expediting orders, designing products, and inspecting products. Notice that an activity is described by an action verb (for example, paying and designing) joined with an object (for example, bills and products) that receives the action. Notice also that the action verb and object reveal very specific goals. Blue Ribbon Baking's executive team felt that the packing activity for mini coffee cakes would be different—and cost a different amount—than the packaging activity for the individually boxed pies.

Managers Decide

Real-Time Accounting Information Helps Companies Thrive

When Jim Kilts took over as chairman and CEO of Gillette in early 2001, the company was in deep trouble. Its market share for most product lines was falling, sales were stagnant or declining, and the share value had dropped by 30 percent over the past three years. Kilts knew that the first step in turning the company around was to instill financial discipline through more detailed management accounting. Sales and income by product line were calculated and tracked. This allowed Kilts to see that Gillette's razor blades were very profitable, but Duracell batteries were not. Previously, the company tallied up its sales results at the end of the quarter—too late to take quick action on problems. Now, Kilts and his senior management team receive a morning report detailing the number of razors, batteries, and toothbrushes the company sold the day before.

We can see that Jim Kilts needed detailed financial information by product line. The product line, and individual products within the product line, became important cost objects. ■

Source: Katrina Brooker, "Jim Kilts Is an Old-School Curmudgeon," *Fortune* (December 30, 2002): 94–102.

Accuracy of Assignments

Assigning costs accurately to cost objects is crucial. Accuracy is not evaluated based on knowledge of some underlying "true" cost. Rather, it is a relative concept and has to do with the reasonableness and logic of the cost assignment methods used. The objective is to measure and assign, as well as possible, the cost of the resources consumed by a cost object. The intuitive and somewhat tongue-in-cheek guideline is expressed as follows: "It is better to be approximately correct than precisely inaccurate." Some cost assignment methods are clearly more accurate than others. For example, suppose you want to determine the cost of lunch for Ryan Chesser, a student who frequents Hideaway, an off-campus pizza parlor. One cost assignment approach is to count the number of customers Hideaway has between 12:00 p.m. and 1:00 p.m. and then divide the total receipts earned during this period by this number of customers. Suppose that this comes out to $5.175 per lunchtime customer (note the three-decimal precision). Thus, based on this approach, we would conclude that Ryan spends $5.175 per day for lunch. Another approach is to go with Ryan and observe how much he spends. Suppose that he has a small pizza, salad, and a medium drink each day, costing $6.50. It is not difficult to see which cost assignment is more accurate. The $5.175 cost assignment is distorted (in spite of its three-decimal precision) by the consumption patterns of other customers (cost objects). As it turns out, most lunchtime clients order the luncheon special for $4.99 (a minipizza, salad, and medium drink).

Distorted cost assignments can produce erroneous decisions and bad evaluations. For example, if a plant manager is trying to decide whether to continue producing power internally or to buy it from a local utility company, then an accurate assessment of how much it is costing to produce the power is fundamental to the analysis. An overstatement of the cost of power production could suggest to the manager that the internal power department should be shut down in favor of external purchase, whereas a more accurate cost assignment might reveal the opposite. It is easy to see that bad cost assignments can prove to be costly. As the pizza example suggests, establishing a cause-and-effect relationship between the cost to be assigned and the cost object is the key to creating a reasonably accurate cost assignment.

Traceability The relationship of costs to cost objects should be exploited to increase the accuracy of cost assignments. Costs are directly or indirectly associated with cost objects. **Indirect costs** are costs that cannot be easily and accurately traced to a cost object. **Direct costs** are those costs that can be easily and accurately traced to a cost object.[3] "Easily traced" means that the costs can be assigned in an economically feasible way, while "accurately traced" means that the costs are assigned using a cause-and-effect relationship. Thus, **traceability** is simply the ability to assign a cost to a cost object in an economically feasible way by means of a cause-and-effect relationship. The more costs that can be traced to the object, the greater the accuracy of the cost assignments. Establishing traceability is fundamental in building accurate cost assignments.

It is possible for a particular cost item to be classified as both a direct cost and an indirect cost. Management accounting systems typically deal with many cost objects. It all depends on which cost object is the point of reference. For example, if a hospital is the cost object, then the cost of heating and cooling the hospital is a direct cost. However, if the cost object is a surgical procedure performed in the hospital, then this utility cost is an indirect cost.

Methods of Tracing Traceability means that costs can be assigned easily and accurately, whereas **tracing** is the actual assignment of costs to a cost object using an observable measure of the resources consumed by the cost object. Tracing costs to cost objects can occur in one of two ways: (1) direct tracing or (2) driver tracing. **Direct tracing** is the process of identifying and assigning costs that are exclusively and physically associated with a cost object. This is most often accomplished by *physical observation*. Consider the pizza example. The cost object is Ryan Chesser's lunch. By observing that he has a small pizza, salad, and medium drink, we can assign the cost of $6.50. The cost is directly traceable to him. As a second example, let the cost object be a product: bicycles. The product uses both materials and labor. It is easy to observe how many wheels, other parts, and hours of labor are required to produce each bicycle. Both material and labor usages are physically observable, and therefore, their costs can be directly charged to a bicycle. In both examples, the cost objects are the *exclusive* consumers of the resources in question. Ideally, all costs should be charged to cost objects using direct tracing. Unfortunately, it is often the case that cost objects are not the exclusive consumers of resources. In this case, we appeal to driver tracing to assign costs.

Driver tracing is the use of drivers to assign costs to cost objects. In a cost assignment context, **drivers** are observable causal factors that *measure* a cost object's resource consumption. They are factors that cause changes in resource usage and thus have a cause-and-effect relationship with the costs associated with a cost object. For example, assume that Ryan Chesser and Shana Parker go to lunch together. Shana and Ryan agree to share the cost of the lunch. They order a medium pizza (divided into 10 slices) for $9, a pitcher of root beer for $2 (five glasses of content), and Shana orders a small salad for $1. How much cost should be assigned to each person? Note that the two share the pizza and root beer, whereas the salad is a "resource" exclusive to Shana. The cost of the salad, then, is assigned by direct tracing ($1 to Shana and $0 to Ryan). To assign the costs of the pizza and root beer,

3 This definition of direct costs is based on the glossary of terms prepared by Computer-Aided Manufacturing-International, Inc. (CAM-I). *See* Norm Raffish and Peter B. B. Turney, "Glossary of Activity-Based Management," *Journal of Cost Management* (Fall 1991): pp. 53–63. Other terms defined in this chapter and in the text also follow the CAM-I glossary.

drivers are chosen: slices of pizza and glasses of root beer, respectively. A rate is calculated per unit of resource (as measured by the drivers): $0.90 per slice of pizza ($9/10) and $0.40 per glass of root beer ($2/5). Next, usage of the driver is observed for each person (cost object). Assume that Ryan eats seven slices of pizza and drinks three glasses of root beer, with Shana consuming the remainder. Thus, the cost per person is calculated as follows:

	Shana	**Ryan**
Salad (direct tracing)	$1.00	$0.00
Pizza (driver tracing):		
$0.90 × 3 slices	2.70	—
$0.90 × 7 slices	—	6.30
Root beer (driver tracing):		
$0.40 × 2 glasses	0.80	—
$0.40 × 3 glasses	—	1.20
Totals	$4.50	$7.50

This simple pizza example of a shared resource extends into more complex business settings. Inspecting products may be the "pizza" shared by precision surgical instruments produced in a plant. The cost of inspection can be assigned to individual instruments (the cost objects) using number of inspection hours ("slices of pizza") consumed by each type of instrument. Consider, as a second example, the cost of a heart monitor used by cardiac patients (the cost object). The heart monitor is the "pizza," and monitoring hours used could be the "slices of pizza" chosen to assign the costs to cardiac patients. Thus, the tracing principles described by the pizza example relate directly to costing within realistic business environments.

Driver tracing is usually less precise than direct tracing. However, if the cause-and-effect relationship is sound, then a high degree of accuracy can be expected. Consider, for example, the driver: number of slices of pizza. Suppose that the slices are not exactly equal in size and that Shana chose to eat three of the smaller slices. Thus, her cost for pizza is really less than $2.70. Even so, if the difference in the size of slices is not great, then we can still say that the cost is accurate. Nonetheless, this illustrates the importance of how we select, specify, and measure drivers. These more detailed issues are explored in greater depth in Chapters 3 and 4. For now, it is sufficient to understand their role in cost assignment and that they can produce somewhat less accurate assignments than direct tracing. Of more immediate concern is the situation where cost objects are not exclusive consumers of resources and where no cause-and-effect relationship can be defined (or where using a causal relationship is cost-prohibitive).

Assigning Indirect Costs Indirect costs are those costs that cannot be assigned to cost objects using either direct or driver tracing. That is, no causal relationship exists between the cost and the cost object or that tracing is not economically feasible. Assignment of indirect costs to cost objects is called **allocation**. Since no causal relationship exists, allocating indirect costs is based on convenience or some assumed linkage. For example, suppose that Blue Ribbon Baking Company installed the mini coffee cake line in its existing factory building. Consider the cost of heating and lighting this plant in which the two different product lines are manufactured. Suppose that this utility cost is to be assigned to the two product lines. Clearly, it is difficult to see any causal relationship. A convenient way to allocate this cost is simply to assign it in proportion to the direct labor hours used by each product. Arbitrarily assigning indirect costs to cost objects reduces the overall accuracy of the cost assignments. Accordingly, the best costing policy may be assigning only direct (traceable) costs to cost objects. However, allocations of indirect costs may serve other purposes besides accuracy. For example, allocating indirect costs to products (a cost object) may be required to satisfy external reporting conventions. Nonetheless, most managerial uses of cost assignments are better served by accuracy; thus, at the very least, tracing and allocation cost assignments should be reported separately.

Cost Assignment Summarized The foregoing discussion reveals three methods of assigning costs to cost objects: direct tracing, driver tracing, and allocation. These methods are illustrated in Exhibit 2-1. Of the three methods, direct tracing is the most accurate; it relies on physically observable, exclusive causal relationships. Driver tracing relies on causal factors, or drivers, to assign costs to cost objects. The accuracy of driver tracing depends on the quality of the causal relationship. Identifying drivers and assessing the quality of the causal relationship is much more costly than either direct tracing or allocation. In fact, one advantage of allocation is its simplicity and low cost of implementation. However, allocation is the least accurate cost assignment method, and its use should be avoided where possible. In many cases, the benefits of increased accuracy outweigh the additional measurement cost associated with driver tracing. This cost-benefit issue is discussed more fully later in the chapter. What it really entails is choosing among competing management accounting information systems.

Product and Service Costs

Objective 2

Define tangible and intangible products, and explain why there are different product cost definitions.

An organization's output represents one of its most important cost objects. There are two types of output: tangible products and services. **Tangible products** are goods produced by converting raw materials through the use of labor and capital inputs, such as plant, land, and machinery. Televisions, hamburgers, automobiles, computers, clothes, and furniture are examples of tangible products. **Services** are tasks or activities performed for a customer or an activity performed by a customer using an organization's products or facilities. Services are also produced using materials, labor, and capital inputs. Insurance coverage, medical care, dental care, funeral care, and accounting are examples of service activities performed for customers. The Blue Ribbon Cafes, considered by Blue Ribbon Baking, would provide services. Car rental, video rental, and skiing are examples of services where the customer uses an organization's products or facilities.

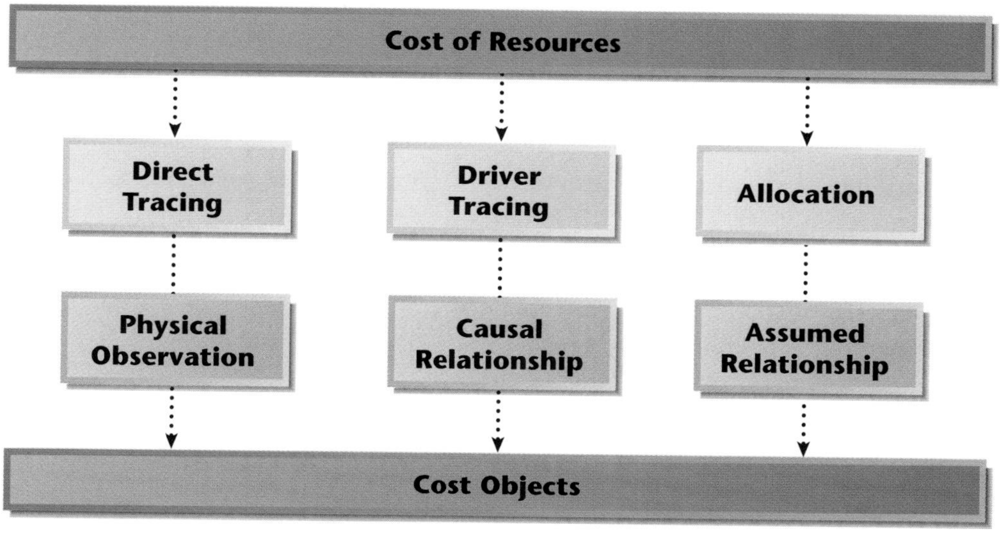

Exhibit 2-1 Cost Assignment Methods

Services differ from tangible products on four important dimensions: intangibility, perishability, inseparability, and heterogeneity. **Intangibility** means that buyers of services cannot see, feel, hear, or taste a service before it is bought. Thus, services are intangible products. **Perishability** means that services cannot be stored for future use by a consumer (there are a few unusual cases where tangible goods cannot be stored) but must be consumed when performed. Although services cannot be stored, some services, like plastic surgery, have long-term effects and need not be repeated for a given customer. Other services have short-term effects and generate repeat customers. Examples of repetitive services are checking account services, janitorial services, and dry cleaning. **Inseparability** means that producers of services and buyers of services must usually be in direct contact for an exchange to take place. In effect, services are often inseparable from their producers. For example, an eye examination requires both the patient and the optometrist to be present. However, producers of tangible products need not have direct contact with the buyers of their goods. Thus, buyers of automobiles never need to have contact with the engineers and assembly line workers who produced their automobiles. **Heterogeneity** means that there is a greater chance of variation in the performance of services than in the production of products. Service workers can be affected by the job undertaken, the mix of other individuals with whom they work, their education and experience, and personal factors such as home life. These factors make providing a consistent level of service more difficult. The measurement of productivity and quality in a service company must be ongoing and sensitive to these factors. These differences affect the types of information needed for planning, controlling, and decision making. Exhibit 2-2 illustrates the features associated with services, some of their derived properties, and how they interface with the management accounting system. Notice that accurate cost assignments, quality, and productivity are concerns shared by producers of services with producers of tangible products.

Feature	Derived Properties	Impact on Management Accounting
Intangibility	Services cannot be stored. No patent protection. Cannot display or communicate services. Price difficult to set.	No inventories. Strong ethical code.* Demand for more accurate cost assignment.*
Perishability	Service benefits expire quickly. Services may be repeated often for one customer.	No inventories. Need for standards and consistent high quality.*
Inseparability	Customer directly involved with production of service. Centralized mass production of services difficult.	Costs often accounted for by customer type.* Demand for measurement and control of quality to maintain consistency.*
Heterogeneity	Wide variation in service product possible.	Productivity and quality measurement and control must be ongoing.* Total quality management critical.*

*Many of these effects are also true of tangible products.

Exhibit 2-2 Interface of Services with Management Accounting

Organizations that produce tangible products are called *manufacturing* organizations. Those that produce intangible products are called *service* organizations. Managers of both types of organizations need to know how much individual products cost. Accurate product costs are vital for profitability analysis and strategic decisions concerning product design, pricing, and product mix. Individual product cost can refer to either a tangible or an intangible product. Thus, when we discuss product costs, we are referring to both intangible and tangible products.

Different Costs for Different Purposes

Product cost is a cost assignment that supports a well-specified managerial objective. The meaning of "product cost" depends on the managerial objective being served. This illustrates a fundamental cost management principle: "Different costs for different purposes." As a first example, suppose that management is interested in strategic profitability analysis. To support this objective, management needs information about all the revenues and costs associated with a product. In this case, a value-chain product cost is appropriate because it accounts for all the costs necessary to assess strategic profitability. A firm's **internal value chain** is the set of all activities required to design, develop, produce, market, distribute, and service a product. The internal value chain is illustrated in Exhibit 2-3. A value-chain product cost is obtained by first assigning costs to the set of activities that define the value chain and then assigning the cost of those activities to products. As a second example, suppose that the managerial objective is short-run or tactical profitability analysis. In this case, the costs of designing and developing may not be relevant—especially for existing products. A decision, for example, to accept or reject an order for an existing product would depend on the price offered by the potential customer and the costs of producing, marketing, distributing, and servicing the special order. Thus, only the operating activities within the value chain (production, marketing, and customer service) would be important, and the assignment of the costs of these activities to the product defines an operating product cost. As a third example, suppose that the managerial objective is external financial reporting. In this case, traditional product

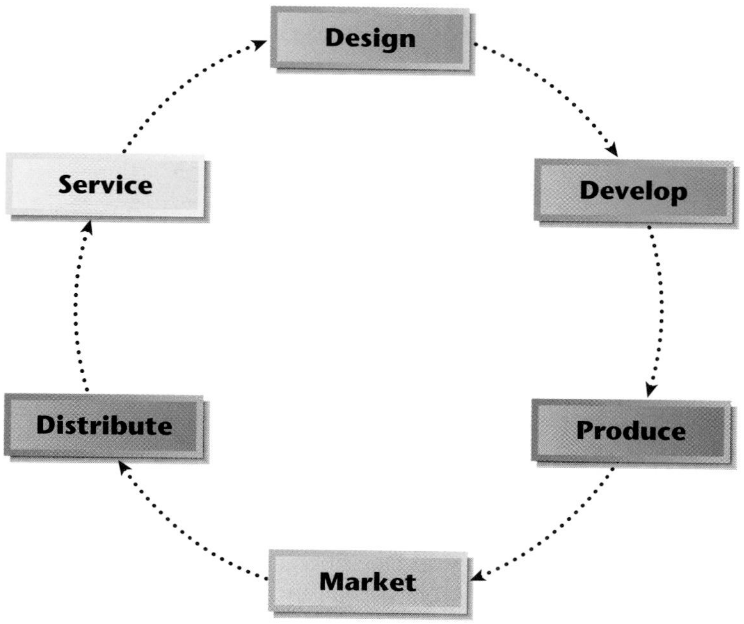

Exhibit 2-3 The Internal Value Chain Activities

costs are needed. The rules and conventions that govern external financial reporting mandate that only production costs can be used in calculating product costs. Exhibit 2-4 summarizes the three product cost examples. Other objectives may use still other product cost definitions.

Product Costs and External Financial Reporting

One of the central objectives of a cost management system is the calculation of product costs for external financial reporting. For product-costing purposes, externally imposed conventions dictate that costs be classified in terms of the special purposes, or functions, they serve. Costs are subdivided into two major functional categories: production and nonproduction. **Production costs** are those costs associated with the manufacture of goods or the provision of services. **Nonproduction costs** are those costs associated with the functions of designing, developing, marketing, distribution, customer service, and general administration. Nonproduction costs are often divided into two general categories: selling costs, which are the costs of marketing, distribution, and customer service; and administrative costs, which are the costs of designing, developing, and general administration.

For tangible goods, production and nonproduction costs are often referred to as *manufacturing costs* and *nonmanufacturing costs*, respectively. Production costs can be further classified as direct materials, direct labor, and overhead. Only these three cost elements can be assigned to products for external financial reporting.

Direct Materials

Direct materials are those materials that are directly traceable to the goods or services being produced. The cost of these materials can be directly charged to products because physical observation can be used to measure the quantity consumed by each product. Materials that become part of a tangible product or those that are used in providing a service are usually classified as direct materials. For example, steel in an automobile, wood in furniture, alcohol in cologne, denim in jeans, braces for correcting teeth, surgical gauze and anesthesia for an operation, a casket for a funeral service, and food on an airline are all direct materials. The pies manufactured by Blue Ribbon Baking have direct materials of flour, shortening, fruit, sugar, and thickener.

Direct Labor

Direct labor is labor that is directly traceable to the goods or services being produced. As with direct materials, physical observation can be used to measure the quantity of labor used to produce a product or service. Those employ-

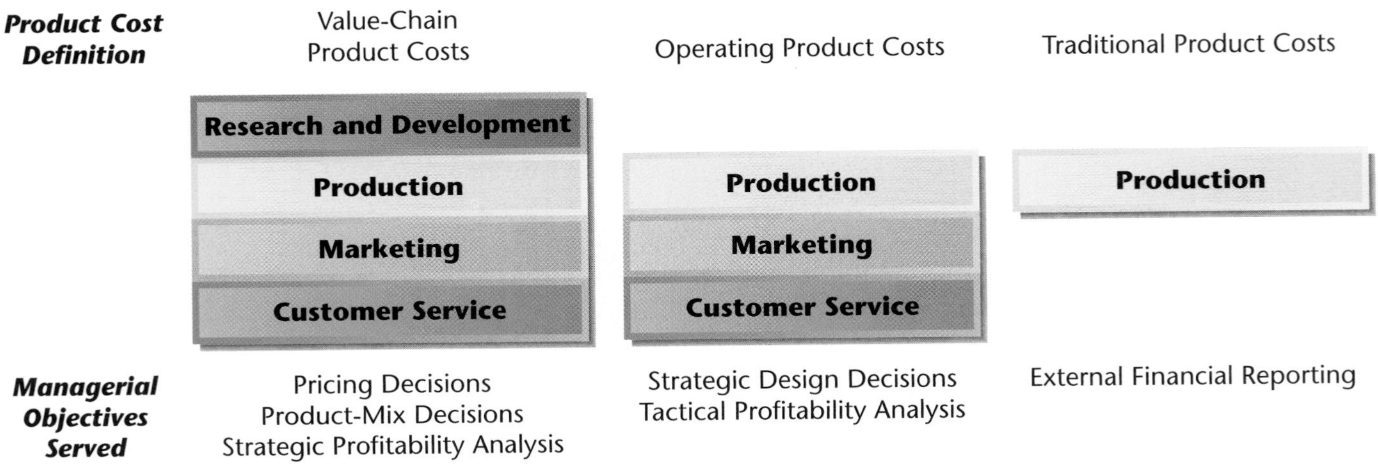

Exhibit 2-4 Examples of Product Cost Definitions

ees who convert raw materials into a product or who provide a service to customers are classified as direct labor. Workers on an assembly line at **DaimlerChrysler**, a chef in a restaurant, a surgical nurse attending an open heart operation, and a pilot for **Southwest Airlines** are all examples of direct labor. The Blue Ribbon Baking employees who mix and roll the dough, make the pie filling, fill the pies, and so on, are direct labor.

© Getty Images/PhotoDisc

Here we can see the direct materials (in the loaf of bread), direct labor, and overhead (the oven, the electricity to heat the oven, and the paddle to move the loaves into and out of the oven).

Overhead All production costs other than direct materials and direct labor are lumped into one category called **overhead**. In a manufacturing firm, overhead is also known as *factory burden* or *manufacturing overhead.* The overhead cost category contains a wide variety of items. Many inputs other than direct labor and direct materials are needed to produce products. Examples at Blue Ribbon Baking include depreciation on buildings and equipment, maintenance, supplies, supervision, material handling, power, property taxes, landscaping of factory grounds, and plant security. **Supplies** are generally those materials necessary for production that do not become part of the finished product or are not used in providing a service. Dishwasher detergent in a fast-food restaurant and oil for production equipment are examples of supplies.

Direct materials that form an insignificant part of the final product are usually lumped into the overhead category as a special kind of indirect material. This is justified on the basis of cost and convenience. The cost of the tracing exceeds the benefit of increased accuracy. The glue used in furniture or toys is an example.

The cost of overtime for direct laborers is usually assigned to overhead as well. The rationale is that typically no particular production run can be identified as the cause of the overtime. Accordingly, overtime cost is common to all production runs and is therefore an indirect manufacturing cost. Note that only the overtime cost is treated this way. If workers are paid an $8 per hour regular rate and a $4 per hour overtime premium, then only the $4 overtime premium is assigned to overhead. The $8 regular rate is still regarded as a direct labor cost. In certain cases, however, overtime is associated with a particular production run; for example, a special order is taken when production is at 100 percent capacity. In these special cases, it is appropriate to treat overtime premiums as a direct labor cost for that special order.

Prime and Conversion Costs Combinations of different production costs lead to the concepts of conversion costs and prime costs. **Prime cost** is the sum of direct materials cost and direct labor cost. **Conversion cost** is the sum of direct labor cost and overhead cost. For a manufacturing firm, conversion cost can be interpreted as the cost of converting raw materials into a final product.

Selling and Administrative Costs There are two broad categories of nonproduction costs: selling costs and administrative costs. For external financial reporting, selling and administrative costs are *noninventoriable* or *period costs.* **Noninventoriable (period) costs** are expensed in the period in which they are incurred. Thus, none of these costs are assigned to products or appear as part of the reported values of inventories on the balance sheet. In a manufacturing organization, the level of these costs can be significant (often greater than 25 percent of sales revenue), and controlling them may bring greater cost savings than the same effort exercised in controlling production costs. For service organizations, the relative importance of selling and administrative costs depends on the nature of the service produced. Physicians and dentists, for example, do very little marketing and thus have very low selling costs. On the other hand, a grocery chain experimenting with special services such as alternative shopping and delivery technologies may incur substantial marketing costs.

Those costs necessary to market, distribute, and service a product or service are **marketing (selling) costs**. They are often referred to as *order-getting* and *order-filling* costs. Examples of selling costs include salaries and commissions of sales personnel, advertising, warehousing, shipping, and customer service. The first two items are examples of order-getting costs; the last three are order-filling costs.

All costs associated with research, development, and general administration of the organization that cannot reasonably be assigned to either marketing or production are **administrative costs**. General administration has the responsibility of ensuring that the various activities of the organization are properly integrated so that the overall mission of the firm is realized. The president of the firm, for example, is concerned with the efficiency of selling, production, and research and development activities. Proper integration of these activities is essential to maximizing the overall profits of a firm. Examples, then, of general administrative costs are top executive salaries, legal fees, printing the annual report, and general accounting. Research and development costs are the costs associated with designing and developing new products.

External Financial Statements

Objective 3

Prepare income statements for manufacturing and service organizations.

To meet external reporting requirements, costs are classified according to function. In preparing an income statement, production costs and selling and administrative costs are segregated. They are segregated because production costs are viewed as product costs, and selling and administrative costs are viewed as period costs. Thus, production costs attached to the products sold are recognized as an expense (cost of goods sold) on the income statement. Production costs that are attached to products not sold are reported as inventory on the balance sheet. Selling and administrative expenses are viewed as costs of the period and must be deducted each and every period as expenses; these costs do not appear on the balance sheet.

Income Statement: Manufacturing Firm

The income statement based on a functional classification for a manufacturing firm is displayed in Exhibit 2-5. This income statement follows the traditional format taught in an introductory financial accounting course. Income computed by following a functional classification is frequently referred to as **absorption-costing (full-costing) income** because all manufacturing costs are fully assigned to the product.

Under the absorption-costing approach, expenses are segregated according to function and then deducted from sales to arrive at income before income taxes. As can be seen in Exhibit 2-5, there are two major functional categories of expenses: cost of goods sold and operating expenses. These categories correspond, respectively, to a firm's manufacturing and nonmanufacturing expenses. **Cost of goods sold** is the cost of direct materials, direct labor, and overhead attached to the units sold. To compute the cost of goods sold, it is first necessary to determine the cost of goods manufactured.

Cost of Goods Manufactured The **cost of goods manufactured** represents the total cost of goods *completed* during the current period. The only costs assigned to goods completed are the manufacturing costs of direct materials, direct labor, and overhead. The details of this cost assignment are given in a supporting schedule, called the *statement of cost of goods manufactured.* An example of this supporting schedule for the income statement in Exhibit 2-5 is shown in Exhibit 2-6.

Manufacturing Organization
Income Statement
For the Year Ended December 31, 2008

Sales		$2,800,000
Less cost of goods sold:		
Beginning finished goods inventory	$ 500,000	
Add: Cost of goods manufactured	1,200,000	
Cost of goods available for sale	$1,700,000	
Less: Ending finished goods inventory	300,000	1,400,000
Gross Margin		$1,400,000
Less operating expenses:		
Selling expenses	$ 600,000	
Administrative expenses	300,000	900,000
Income before income taxes		$ 500,000

Exhibit 2-5 Income Statement for a Manufacturing Organization

Notice in Exhibit 2-6 that the total manufacturing costs added during the period are added to the manufacturing costs found in beginning work in process, yielding total manufacturing costs. The costs found in ending work in process are then deducted from total manufacturing costs to arrive at the cost of goods manufactured. If the cost of goods manufactured is for a single product, then the average unit cost can be computed by dividing the cost of goods manufactured by the units produced. For example, assume that the statement in Exhibit 2-6 was prepared for the production of bottles of perfume and that 480,000 bottles were completed during the period. The average unit cost is $2.50 per bottle ($1,200,000/480,000).

Manufacturing Organization
Income Statement
For the Year Ended December 31, 2008

Direct materials:		
Beginning inventory	$200,000	
Add: Purchases	450,000	
Materials available	$650,000	
Less: Ending inventory	50,000	
Direct materials used		$ 600,000
Direct labor		350,000
Manufacturing overhead:		
Indirect labor	$122,500	
Depreciation	177,500	
Rent	50,000	
Utilities	37,500	
Property taxes	12,500	
Maintenance	50,000	450,000
Total manufacturing costs added		$1,400,000
Add: Beginning work in process		200,000
Total manufacturing costs		$1,600,000
Less: Ending work in process		400,000
Cost of goods manufactured		$1,200,000

Exhibit 2-6 Statement of Cost of Goods Manufactured

Work in process consists of all partially completed units found in production at a given point in time. Beginning work in process consists of the partially completed units on hand at the beginning of a period. Ending work in process consists of those on hand at the period's end. In the statement of cost of goods manufactured, the cost of these partially completed units is reported as the cost of beginning work in process and the cost of ending work in process. The cost of beginning work in process represents the manufacturing costs carried over from the prior period; the cost of ending work in process represents the manufacturing costs that will be carried over to the next period. In both cases, additional manufacturing costs must be incurred to complete the units in work in process.

Income Statement: Service Organization

An income statement for a service firm is shown in Exhibit 2-7. In a service organization, the cost of services sold is computed differently from the cost of goods sold in a manufacturing firm. As the income statement reveals, there are no beginning or ending finished goods inventories. Unlike a manufacturing firm, the service firm has no finished goods inventories—it is not possible to store services. Thus, in a direct comparison with manufacturing firms, cost of services sold would always correspond to cost of goods manufactured. Furthermore, as Exhibit 2-7 reveals, the cost of services sold during a period (equivalent to cost of goods manufactured) can be computed following the same format shown in Exhibit 2-6. Exhibit 2-7 reveals that it is possible to have work in process for services. For example, an architect may have drawings in process, and an orthodontist may have numerous patients in various stages of process for braces.

Types of Management Accounting Systems: A Brief Overview

Objective 4

Outline the differences between functional-based and activity-based management accounting systems.

Management accounting systems can be broadly classified as functional-based systems and activity-based systems. Both functional-based and activity-based approaches are found in practice. **Functional-based management (FBM) accounting systems** were in existence throughout the 1900s and are still widely used in

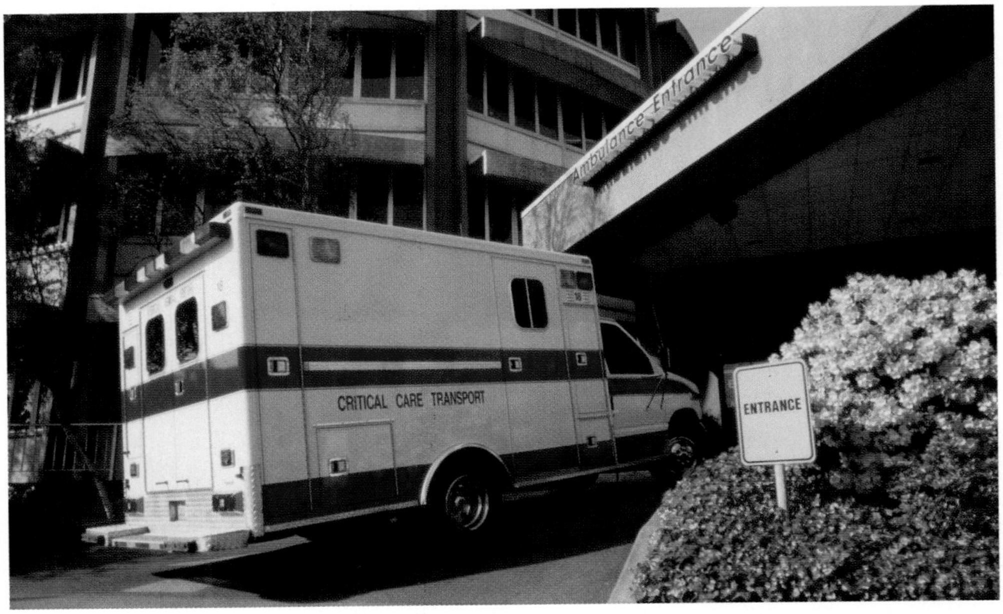

Service firms, like ambulance companies, must calculate the cost of services rendered. We can see overhead cost implied by the cost of the ambulance and fuel. Direct labor includes the driver and the EMT. Materials include any intravenous solutions, oxygen and breathing masks, gauze, and bandages.

Income Statement:
Service Organization
For the Year Ended December 31, 2008

Sales			$300,000
Less expenses:			
Cost of services sold:			
Beginning work in process		$ 5,000	
Service costs added:			
Direct materials	$ 40,000		
Direct labor	80,000		
Overhead	100,000	220,000	
Total		$225,000	
Less: Ending work in process		10,000	215,000
Gross margin			$ 85,000
Less operating expenses:			
Selling expenses		$ 8,000	
Administrative expenses		22,000	30,000
Income before income taxes			$ 55,000

Exhibit 2-7 Income Statement for a Service Organization

both manufacturing and service sectors. **Activity-based management (ABM) accounting systems** are much newer (developed within the last three decades). Activity-based cost management systems are also used extensively, and their use is increasing—particularly among organizations faced with product and customer diversity, more product complexity, shorter product life cycles, increased quality requirements, and intense competitive pressures. Examples of activity-based systems are found within the medical industry (e.g., hospitals and medical laboratories), the finance industry (e.g., banks and brokerage firms), the transportation industry (e.g., airlines and railroads), and in manufacturers of all types (e.g., electronics and automobile firms).

FBM versus ABM Accounting Systems

The general models for functional-based and activity-based management accounting systems are displayed in Exhibits 2-8 and 2-9. Notice that both models have two dimensions. The vertical dimension of each describes how costs are assigned to cost objects like products and customers, while the horizontal dimension is concerned with how the systems try to improve operational efficiency and control costs. The heart of the FBM model is functions, while the corresponding element of the ABM model is activities. Functions are usually grouped into organizational units such as departments and plants (for example, engineering, quality control, and assembly are functions organized as departments). Activities with a common objective group together to form **processes**. For example, purchasing goods, receiving goods, and paying for goods received are major activities that define the procurement process. Comparing each dimension provides significant insight into how the two management accounting models differ.

FBM Cost View In an FBM accounting system, resource costs are assigned to functional units and then to products. In assigning costs, direct tracing and driver tracing are used, but in an FMB system driver tracing uses only **production (unit-level) drivers**, measures of consumption that are highly correlated with production output. Thus, units of product or drivers that are highly correlated with units

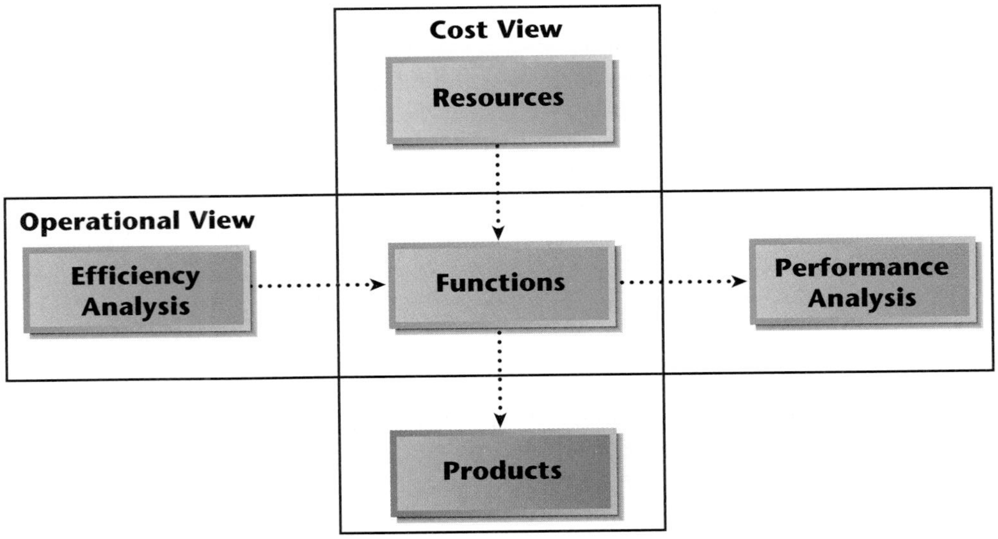

Exhibit 2-8 Functional-Based Management Model

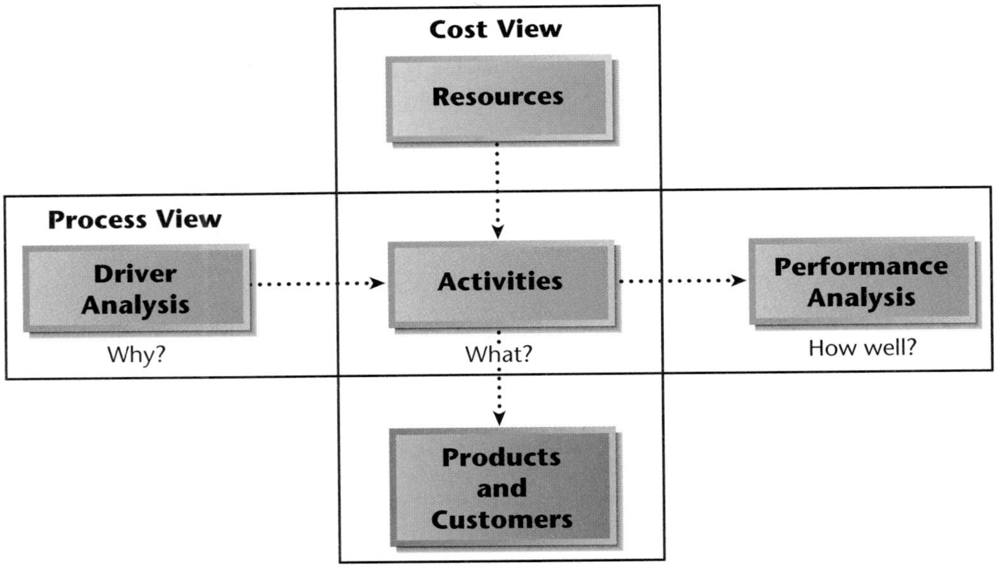

Exhibit 2-9 Activity-Based Management Model

produced, such as direct labor hours, direct materials, and machine-hours, are the only drivers assumed to be of importance. Because FBM systems use only drivers related to the production function to assign costs, this cost assignment approach is referred to as production- or **functional-based costing (FBC)**. The production or unit-level drivers on which FBC relies often are not the only drivers that explain cause-and-effect relationships. Drivers other than production drivers that describe cause-and-effect relationships are referred to as **non-unit-level drivers**. For example, production drivers such as units produced or direct labor hours may have nothing to do with the cost of purchasing raw materials. In reality, the number of purchase orders might be the appropriate measure of consumption by each product. Yet, in an FBC system, purchasing costs would be assigned using a measure like units produced or direct labor hours. Cost assignments made in these cases must be classified as allocation (recall that allocation is cost assignment based on assumed linkages or convenience). Furthermore, if non-unit-level costs such as purchasing are significant, functional-based costing can be described as allocation-intensive.

The product-costing objective of functional-based costing is typically satisfied by assigning production costs to inventories and cost of goods sold for purposes of external financial reporting. More comprehensive product cost definitions, such as the value-chain and operating cost definitions illustrated in Exhibit 2-4, are not available for management use. However, production-based costing systems often furnish useful variants of the traditional product cost definition. For example, prime costs and variable manufacturing costs per unit may be reported (variable costs are discussed in Chapter 3).

ABM Cost View In **activity-based costing (ABC)**, costs are traced to activities and then to products. As with functional-based costing, both direct tracing and driver tracing are used; however, the role of driver tracing is significantly expanded by identifying and using drivers unrelated to the volume of product produced (non-unit-based drivers). Thus, activity-based cost assignments emphasize tracing over allocation; in fact, it could be called tracing-intensive. The use of both unit-based and non-unit-based drivers increases the accuracy of cost assignments and the overall quality and relevance of cost information. For example, consider assigning the costs of the activity "moving raw materials and partially finished goods from one point to another within a factory." The number of moves required for a product is a much better measure of the product's demand for the material-handling activity than the number of units produced. In fact, the number of units produced may have nothing to do with measuring products' demands for material handling. (A batch of 10 units could require as much material-handling activity as a batch of 100 units.)

Activity-based product costing tends to be flexible. Cost information is produced to support a variety of managerial objectives, including the financial reporting objective. More comprehensive product costing definitions are emphasized for better planning, controlling, and decision making. For example, a more flexible accounting system, with its wealth of information on costs, activities, and drivers, could act as an early warning system of ethical problems. **Metropolitan Life Insurance Company** was dismayed to learn that some of its agents were selling policies as retirement plans. This practice is illegal, and it cost the company more than $20 million in fines as well as $50 million in refunds to policyholders.[4] Comprehensive data on sales, individual agents, types of policies, and policyholders could have alerted Metropolitan Life to a potential problem. Thus, the maxim of "different costs for different purposes" takes on real meaning.

FBM's Operational Efficiency View Providing information for planning and control is another objective of management accounting. The **functional-based management** approach to control assigns costs to organizational units and then holds the organizational unit manager responsible for controlling the assigned costs. Performance is measured by comparing actual outcomes with standard or budgeted outcomes. The emphasis is on financial measures of performance (nonfinancial measures are usually ignored). Managers are rewarded based on their ability to control costs. Thus, the functional-based approach traces costs to individuals who are responsible for incurring costs. The reward system is used to motivate these individuals to manage costs by increasing the operating efficiency of their organizational units. This approach assumes that maximizing the performance of the overall organization is achieved by maximizing the performance of individual organizational subunits (referred to as *responsibility centers*).

4 Chris Roush, "Fields of Green—and Disaster Areas," *Business Week* (9 January 1995): p. 94.

ABM's Operational Efficiency View Activity-based control subsystems differ significantly from functional-based systems. The functional-based emphasis is on managing costs. The emerging consensus, however, is that management of activities, not costs, is the key to successful control. **Activity-based management** focuses on the management of activities with the objective of improving the value received by the customer and the profit received by providing this value.[5] It includes driver analysis, activity analysis, and performance evaluation and draws on activity-based costing as a major source of information. The process view is concerned with identifying factors that cause an activity's cost (explains why costs are incurred), assessing what work is done (identifies activities), and evaluating the work performed and the results achieved (how well the activity is performed). Thus, activity-based control requires detailed information on activities.

This new approach focuses on accountability for activities rather than costs and emphasizes the maximization of systemwide performance instead of individual performance. Activities cut across functional and departmental lines, are systemwide in focus, and require a global approach to control. Essentially, this form of control admits that maximizing the efficiency of individual subunits does not necessarily lead to maximum efficiency for the system as a whole. Another significant difference also should be mentioned. In an activity-based management accounting information system, both financial and nonfinancial measures of performance are important. Exhibit 2-10 compares the characteristics of functional- and activity-based cost management systems.

Choice of a Management Accounting System

Activity-based management accounting offers significant benefits, including improved product costing accuracy, improved decision making, enhanced strategic planning, and better ability to manage activities. Furthermore, the activity-based system is particularly suited for supporting the goal of continuous improvement—an objective that is critical for firms competing on a global basis. These benefits, however, are not obtained without costs. An activity-based management accounting system is more complex, and it requires a significant increase in measurement activity—and measurement can be costly. However, with the advances in information technology, the

Functional-Based	Activity-Based
1. Unit-based drivers	1. Unit-based and non-unit-based drivers
2. Allocation intensive	2. Tracing intensive
3. Narrow and rigid product costing	3. Broad and flexible product costing
4. Focus on managing costs	4. Focus on managing activities
5. Sparse activity information	5. Detailed activity information
6. Maximization of individual unit performance	6. Systemwide performance maximization
7. Use of financial measures of performance	7. Use of both financial and nonfinancial measures of performance

Exhibit 2-10 Comparison of Functional- and Activity-Based Cost Management Systems

5 This definition of activity-based management and the illustrative model in Exhibit 2-9 are based on Norm Raffish and Peter B. B. Turney, "Glossary of Activity-Based Management," *Journal of Cost Management* (Fall 1991): pp. 53–63. Many other terms throughout the text relating to activity-based management are also drawn from this source.

costs of measurement have declined, making activity-based systems more attractive. Simultaneously, the cost of making bad decisions has increased (because of more intense competition resulting from the emergence of a worldwide economy, deregulation of services, and so on). The need to improve the quality of decision making has also increased the appeal of activity-based approaches. For many firms, the benefits of replacing an FBM system with an ABM system outweigh the costs. Thus, the use of activity-based costing and activity-based management is spreading, and the interest in activity-based management accounting is high.

Summary of Learning Objectives

1. Describe the cost assignment process.

Costs are assigned to cost objects such as products, projects, plants, and customers. There are three methods of cost assignment: direct tracing, driver tracing, and allocation. Direct tracing and driver tracing offer more accuracy because they are based on cause-and-effect relationships. Direct tracing relies on physical observation to assign costs. Driver tracing relies on the use of causal factors called drivers to assign costs. Allocation relies on assumed relationships and convenience to assign costs. Allocation is essentially an arbitrary assignment and should be avoided as much as possible.

2. Define tangible and intangible products, and explain why there are different product cost definitions.

There are two types of output: tangible products and services. Tangible products are goods that are produced by converting raw materials through the use of labor and capital inputs such as plant, land, and machinery. Services are tasks or activities performed for a customer or an activity performed by a customer using an organization's products or facilities. Product cost is defined as cost assigned to a product that satisfies a particular managerial objective. Since managerial objectives can differ, product cost definitions can differ—each depending on the managerial objective being served.

3. Prepare income statements for manufacturing and service organizations.

If expenses are grouped according to function and then deducted from revenues, the result is an absorption-costing income statement. Absorption-costing income statements are required for external financial reporting. For manufacturing firms, the major functional classifications are manufacturing and nonmanufacturing; for service organizations, the categories are production and nonproduction. For manufacturing firms, the cost of goods manufactured must be calculated. No such requirement exists for a service firm.

4. Outline the differences between functional-based and activity-based management accounting systems.

A functional-based management system uses unit-based drivers only, tends to be more allocation-intensive, uses narrow product cost definitions, focuses on managing costs, provides little activity information, emphasizes individual organizational unit performance, and uses financial measures of performance. An activity-based management system uses both unit-level and non-unit-level drivers, is tracing-intensive, allows flexible product costing definitions, focuses on managing activities, provides detailed activity information, emphasizes systemwide performance, and uses both financial and nonfinancial measures of performance.

Key Terms

Functional-based management (FBM) accounting systems, 46
Heterogeneity, 40
Indirect costs, 37
Inseparability, 40
Intangibility, 40
Internal value chain, 41
Marketing (selling) costs, 44
Noninventoriable (period) costs, 43
Nonproduction costs, 42
Non-unit-level drivers, 48
Opportunity cost, 35
Overhead, 43
Perishability, 40
Prime cost, 43
Processes, 47
Product cost, 41
Production costs, 42
Production (unit-level) drivers, 47
Services, 39
Supplies, 43
Tangible products, 39
Traceability, 37
Tracing, 37
Work in process, 46

Review Problems

1. Manufacturing, Cost Classification, Cost Tracing, and the Income Statement

Pop's Burger Heaven produces and sells quarter-pound hamburgers. Each burger sells for $1.50. During December, Pop's sold 10,000 burgers (the average amount sold each month). The restaurant employs cooks, servers, and one supervisor (the owner, John Peterson). All cooks and servers are part-time employees. Pop's maintains a pool of part-time employees so that the number of employees scheduled can be adjusted to the changes in demand. Demand varies on a weekly as well as a monthly basis.

A janitor is hired to clean the building on a weekly basis. The building is leased from a local real estate company. The building has no seating capabilities. All orders are filled on a drive-through basis.

The supervisor schedules work, opens the building, counts the cash, advertises, and is responsible for hiring and firing. The following costs were incurred during December:

Hamburger meat	$1,600	Utilities	$500
Lettuce	300	Depreciation:	
Tomatoes	250	Cooking equipment	200
Buns	300	Cash register	50
Other ingredients	20	Advertising	100
Cooks' wages	2,550	Janitor's wages	120
Servers' wages	2,032	Janitorial supplies	50
Supervisor's salary	2,000	Rent	800

Required

1. Classify each cost for Pop's December operations into one of the following categories: direct materials, direct labor, overhead, or selling and administrative expenses.
2. Prepare an absorption-costing income statement for the month of December.
3. Suppose Pop's also produces a grilled chicken sandwich and you want to determine the cost of producing both hamburgers and grilled chicken sandwiches. How would you assign the shared cost of depreciation for the cooking equipment to each product? Is this direct tracing, driver tracing, or allocation? Explain.

Solution

1. Direct materials: Hamburger meat, lettuce, tomatoes, and buns
   Direct labor: Cooks' wages

Overhead: Other ingredients, utilities, depreciation on the cooking equipment, janitor's wages, janitorial supplies, and rent
Selling and administrative expenses: Servers' wages, supervisor's salary, depreciation on the cash register, and advertising

Explanation of Classification Cooks are direct laborers because they make the hamburgers. "Other ingredients" are overhead because of cost and convenience, even though technically they are direct materials. Because the primary purpose of the building is production (cooking hamburgers), all of the rent and building-related costs are classified as indirect production costs. (An argument could be made that the building also supports the selling and administrative functions and, consequently, a portion of the rent and building-related costs should be classified as selling and administrative costs.) Servers are responsible for taking and filling orders and are, therefore, classified as sales personnel. The cash register is used to support the sales function. The supervisor is responsible for overseeing the business as a whole and coordinating the sales and production functions. Thus, his salary is an administrative cost.

2.

Sales ($1.50 × 10,000)		$15,000
Less cost of goods sold:		
Direct materials	$2,450	
Direct labor	2,550	
Overhead	1,690	6,690
Gross margin		$ 8,310
Less operating expenses:		
Selling expenses	$2,182	
Administrative expenses	2,000	4,182
Income before income taxes		$ 4,128

3. Depreciation on equipment could be assigned using equipment hours or percentage of space used by each product. This would be driver tracing. Direct tracing is not appropriate because the equipment is not used exclusively by any product.

2. Services, Cost Systems, and the Income Statement

Celestial Funeral Home offers a full range of services. Based on past experience, Celestial uses the following formula to describe its total overhead costs: $Y = \$200,000 + \$50X$, where Y = total overhead costs and X = number of funerals. Overhead costs are assigned by dividing total overhead costs by the number of funerals. For a given funeral, the cost of direct materials ranges from $1,500 to $10,000, depending on the family's selection of a coffin. The average cost is $4,000. Direct labor averages $1,000 per funeral. During 2008, Celestial conducted 1,000 funerals. The average price charged for each funeral is $7,000. Celestial incurs annual selling expenses of $50,000 and administrative expenses of $150,000.

Required

1. Does Celestial sell a tangible or an intangible product? Explain.
2. Does Celestial use a functional-based or an activity-based management accounting system? Explain. Do you think this is a good choice? Explain.
3. What is the total overhead cost incurred by Celestial for the year?
4. What is the overhead cost per funeral for the year?
5. Calculate the unit product cost for the year.
6. Prepare an income statement for Celestial.

Solution

1. Funerals are intangible products. They are services, cannot be stored, and are connected to the producer (inseparability).
2. The use of a unit-based driver (number of funerals) to assign overhead costs (and apparently direct materials and direct labor) suggests a functional-based system. A functional-based system probably will work quite well for a local funeral home business. There is very little product diversity; selling and administrative expenses represent a small portion of total costs; and there are virtually no preproduction costs (research and development costs are absent). Thus, product cost is essentially defined by production costs. Furthermore, the absence of a great variety of products, coupled with the fact that overhead costs represent a small percentage of product costs, makes driver tracing much less important (direct materials and direct labor can be assigned using direct tracing).
3. Y = \$100,000 + \$25(1,000)
   = \$250,000
4. \$250,000/1,000 = \$250
5. Unit product cost:

Direct materials	$4,000
Direct labor	1,000
Overhead	250
Total	$5,250

6. **Celestial Funeral Home Income Statement**
For the Year Ended December 31, 2008

Sales		$7,000,000
Less cost of services sold:		
Direct materials	$4,000,000	
Direct labor	1,000,000	
Overhead	250,000	5,250,000
Gross margin		$1,750,000
Less operating expenses:		
Selling expenses	$ 50,000	
Administrative expenses	150,000	200,000
Income before income taxes		$1,550,000

Questions for Writing and Discussion

1. What is meant by "product costing accuracy"?
2. What is a cost object? Give some examples.
3. What is an activity? Give some examples of activities within a manufacturing firm.
4. What is a direct cost? An indirect cost?
5. What does traceability mean? What is tracing?
6. What is allocation?
7. What are drivers? Give an example of a driver.
8. Explain the difference between direct tracing and driver tracing.
9. Explain how driver tracing works.
10. What is a tangible product?
11. What is a service?
12. Explain how services differ from tangible products.
13. Give three examples of product cost definitions. Why do we need different product cost definitions?
14. Identify the three cost elements that determine the cost of making a product (for external reporting).
15. How do the income statements of a manufacturing firm and a service firm differ?
16. Describe some of the major differences between a functional-based cost management system and an activity-based cost management system.
17. When would a company choose an activity-based cost management system over a functional-based system? What forces are moving firms to implement activity-based cost management systems?

Exercises

2-1

Direct Tracing and Driver Tracing
LO1

For each of the following situations, tell whether the cost would be directly traced, driver traced, or allocated to the cost object.

a. Company reimbursement of salespersons for the use of their personal cars to travel in selling the product. Reimbursement is at the rate of $0.49 per mile driven.
b. A job candidate for a position at a university is taken out to lunch by a member of the faculty. The entire cost of the meal is considered a legitimate expense of the hiring process.
c. Mandy Burton is the secretary-treasurer for her sorority alum group. This is a volunteer position. Mandy recently sent a meeting reminder out to all members. To do so, she paid for stamps and photocopying.
d. Jed Washington, a junior in college, runs a lawn-mowing service in the summers. Jed wants to know the cost of mowing a lawn so that he can price the service appropriately. He decides that the relevant costs are depreciation on the mower and edger, gas to run both, and the gas to run his truck to get from job to job.

2-2

Driver Tracing
LO1

Listed below are costs that are to be assigned to certain cost objects. For each case, identify possible drivers that could be used for the cost assignment. For example, Cost: Setting up equipment; Cost Object: Products; Driver: Number of setups used by each product.

Cost	Cost Object
a. Preparing credit card statements in a bank	Customer accounts
b. Laundering bed sheets and clothing in a hospital	Departments
c. Filling orders	Customers
d. Ordering supplies	Departments
e. Inspecting products	Products
f. Assembling components	Products
g. Nursing care	Patients
h. Preparing tax returns	Clients
i. Purchasing parts	Products
j. Physical therapy in a hospital	Patients

2-3

Cost Assignment Methods
LO1

TropicalSpa is a full-service spa offering tanning, massages, and hair and nail care services. The tanning area provides only tanning services and consists of three tanning booths, a waiting area with several chairs, and a desk for the tanning supervisor. Suppose that the tanning area is the cost object. Assume that all or a portion of the following costs must be assigned to the tanning area.

a. Salary of the tanning supervisor
b. Electricity for the TropicalSpa building in which the tanning area is located
c. Disinfectant spray and wipes to clean the tanning equipment after each client use
d. Maintenance for the tanning equipment, arranged through a monthly maintenance contract with the equipment manufacturer's local representative
e. Cost of the weekly custodial services arranged by TropicalSpa for the building
f. Salary of the receptionist at the entrance to TropicalSpa
g. Purchase of flowers given to employees on their birthday
h. Depreciation on tanning equipment
i. Cost of insurance rider taken to cover increased liability due to tanning services
j. Cost of advertising on local radio stations for TropicalSpa services
k. Cost of telephone equipment and services for TropicalSpa
l. Plastic pump bottles and aloe lotion that are provided in each tanning booth
m. Property tax on the TropicalSpa building and land

Required

Identify which cost assignment method would most likely be used to assign the costs of each activity to the tanning area: direct tracing, driver tracing, or allocation. When driver tracing is selected, identify a potential driver that could be used for the tracing.

2-4

Value-Chain Activity LO2

The following activities are performed within a manufacturing firm. Classify each activity according to its value-chain activity category (for example, activity: grinding parts; value-chain activity category: producing).

a. Advertising products
b. Repairing goods under warranty
c. Designing a new process
d. Assembling parts
e. Shipping goods to a wholesaler
f. Inspecting incoming raw materials and parts
g. Storing finished goods in a warehouse
h. Creating a new computer chip
i. Answering product-use questions using a customer hotline
j. Moving partially finished goods from one department to another
k. Building a prototype of a new product
l. Creating plans for a new model of an automobile
m. Conducting a phone-sales campaign
n. Picking goods from a warehouse
o. Setting up equipment

2-5

Product Cost Definitions LO2

Three possible product cost definitions were introduced: value-chain, operating, and traditional. Identify which of the three best fits the following situations (justify your choice):

a. Setting the price for a new product
b. Valuation of finished goods inventories for external reporting
c. Choosing among different products in order to maintain a product mix that will provide the company with a long-term sustainable competitive advantage
d. Choosing among competing product designs
e. Calculating cost of goods sold for external reporting
f. Deciding whether to increase the price of an existing product
g. Deciding whether to accept or reject a special order, where the price offered is lower than the normal selling price
h. Determining which of several potential new products should be developed, produced, and sold

2-6

Tangible and Intangible Product, Cost Definitions LO2

Holmes Company produces wooden playhouses. When a customer orders a playhouse, it is delivered in pieces with detailed instructions on how to put it together. Some customers prefer that Holmes put the playhouse together, and they purchase the playhouse plus the installation package. Holmes then pulls two workers off the production line and sends them to construct the playhouse on site.

Required

1. What two products does Holmes sell? Classify each one as a tangible product or a service.
2. Do you think Holmes would assign costs to each individual product? Why or why not?
3. Describe the opportunity cost of the installation process.

2-7

Product and Period Costs
LO2

Loring Company incurred the following costs last year:

Direct materials	$216,000
Factory rent	24,000
Direct labor	120,000
Factory utilities	6,300
Supervision in the factory	50,000
Indirect labor in the factory	30,000
Depreciation on factory equipment	9,000
Sales commissions	27,000
Sales salaries	65,000
Advertising	37,000
Depreciation on the headquarters building	10,000
Salary of the corporate receptionist	30,000
Other administrative costs	175,000
Salary of the factory receptionist	28,000

Required

1. Classify each of the above costs using the table format given below. Be sure to total the amounts in each column.
   Example: Direct materials $216,000

	Product Cost			Period Cost	
Costs	Direct Materials	Direct Labor	Overhead	Selling Expense	Administrative Expense
Direct materials	$216,000				

2. What was the total product cost for last year?
3. What was the total period cost for last year?
4. If 30,000 units were produced last year, what was the unit product cost?

2-8

Product Costs
LO2

Kyoto Company manufactures digital cameras. In January, Kyoto produced 10,000 cameras with the following costs:

Direct materials	$560,000
Direct labor	96,000
Overhead	220,000

There were no beginning or ending inventories of work in process (WIP).

Required

1 What was total product cost in January?
2. What was product cost per unit in January?
3. What was total prime cost in January?
4. What was prime cost per unit in January?
5. What was total conversion cost in January?
6. What was conversion cost per unit in January?

2-9

Product Costs
LO2

Colbyville Insurance Company sells automobile and life insurance policies. As a service to its agents, the manager provides complimentary calendars that agents can give as gifts to clients and prospective clients. The calendars cost $0.50 each. Early in February, the manager wanted to know how many calendars had been given out in January. Sue Ellen, the office assistant, gathered the following information:

a. On January 1, there were 150 calendars on hand.
b. An order for 1,000 additional calendars was placed on January 3. It arrived on January 10.
c. On January 31, there were 614 calendars on hand.

Required

1. How many calendars did agents take to give to clients during January?
2. What is the cost of the calendars given out?
3. What is the cost of the ending inventory of calendars on hand?

2-10

Cost of Goods Manufactured
LO3

EXCEL

Sterling Company manufactures laundry detergent. At the beginning of February, the following information was supplied by its accountant:

Raw materials inventory	$73,000
Work-in-process inventory	80,400
Finished goods inventory	62,000

During February, direct labor cost was $210,400, raw materials' purchases were $301,800, and the total overhead cost was $478,590. The inventories at the end of February were

Raw materials inventory	$ 56,000
Work-in-process inventory	103,000
Finished goods inventory	95,240

Required

1. Prepare a statement of cost of goods manufactured for February.
2. Prepare a statement of cost of goods sold for February.

2-11

Preparation of Income Statement: Manufacturing Firm
LO3

EXCEL

Asher, Inc. manufactures desk lamps. Last year 800,000 lamps were made and sold for $32 each. The actual unit cost for a desk lamp follows:

Direct materials	$15.00
Direct labor	4.00
Overhead	8.00
Total unit cost	$27.00

The only selling expenses were a commission of $1.60 per unit sold and advertising totaling $90,000. Administrative expenses, all fixed, equaled $500,000. There were no beginning or ending finished goods inventories. There were no beginning or ending work-in-process inventories.

Required

1. Prepare an income statement for external users. Do you need to prepare a supporting statement of cost of goods manufactured? Explain.
2. Suppose that there were 800,000 desk lamps produced (and 800,000 sold) but that the company had a beginning finished goods inventory of 50,000 lamps produced in the prior year at $25 per unit. The company follows a first-in, first-out policy for its inventory (meaning that the units produced first are sold first for purposes of cost flow). What effect does this have on the income statement? Show the new statement.

2-12

Cost of Goods Manufactured and Sold
LO3

Mellon Company, a manufacturing firm, has supplied the following information from its accounting records for the year 2008 (in thousands of dollars):

Purchases of raw materials	$76,000
Direct labor cost	52,500
Supplies used	5,300
Factory insurance	1,050
Commissions paid	7,500
Factory supervision	9,675
Advertising	2,400
Material handling	11,000
Work-in-process inventory, December 31, 2007	47,500
Work-in-process inventory, December 31, 2008	42,000
Materials inventory, December 31, 2007	10,400
Materials inventory, December 31, 2008	28,500
Finished goods inventory, December 31, 2007	20,055
Finished goods inventory, December 31, 2008	10,750

EXCEL

Required

1. Prepare a statement of cost of goods manufactured.
2. Prepare a statement of cost of goods sold.
3. What was total prime cost for 2008? Total conversion cost?

2-13

Income Statement; Cost Concepts; Service Company
LO2, LO3

Garrett Peckam owns and operates three Muffle-Man outlets in Fort Worth, Texas. Muffle-Man specializes in replacing mufflers with mufflers that have a lifetime guarantee. Muffle-Man is a franchise popular throughout the Southwest. In April, purchases of materials equaled $175,000, the beginning inventory of materials was $14,000, and the ending inventory of materials was $17,300. Payments to direct labor during the month totaled $30,960. Overhead incurred was $145,000. The Fort Worth outlets also spent $25,000 on advertising and selling expenses during the month. A franchise fee of $3,000 per outlet is paid every month. Revenues for April were $410,000.

Required

1. What was the cost of materials used for muffler-changing services during April?
2. What was the prime cost for April?
3. What was the conversion cost for April?
4. What was the total service cost for April?
5. Prepare an income statement for the month of April.
6. Muffle-Man purchases all its mufflers from Remington Company, a manufacturer of mufflers. Discuss the differences between the products offered by Remington and Muffle-Man.

2-14

Cost Assignment; Product Cost Definitions
LO1, LO2

Gallagher Company produces chemicals used in the mining industry. Each plant is dedicated to producing a single industrial chemical. One of its plants produces an electrolyte used in the copper industry's solvent extraction process. During the most recent year, the electrolyte plant produced and sold 3,000,000 pounds of electrolyte. No inventories of the chemical are carried. The chemical sells for $2.70 per pound. Annual manufacturing costs for the electrolyte plant totaled $3,615,000. The plant is also responsible for packaging and shipping its products. Distribution and packaging costs for the electrolyte plant were $300,000. Research and development costs are incurred centrally and assigned to each plant in proportion to their sales revenues. The revenues of the electrolyte plant were 25 percent of the total revenues of the company. For the year just completed, the company reported $1.8 million for research and development. The company also reported $360,000 in sales commissions. Commissions are also assigned to plants in proportion to sales.

Required

1. Compute the unit product cost that must be used for external financial reporting purposes (cost per pound of electrolyte). How would the other costs be treated for external financial reporting?
2. Compute the unit operating product cost. What purpose might this cost serve?
3. Compute the unit value-chain product cost. Why would management want to know this product cost?
4. Classify the cost assignments for the value-chain product cost as direct tracing, driver tracing, or allocation. For any cost classified as allocation, is it possible to change this assignment to driver tracing or direct tracing? Explain.

2-15

Cost Assignment; Functional-Based versus Activity-Based Management Accounting Systems LO1, LO4

Cariari Manufacturing produces two different models of cameras. One model has an automatic focus; the other requires the user to focus manually. The two products are produced in batches (an equal number of batches is used for each product). Each time a batch is produced, the equipment must be configured (set up) for the specifications of the camera model being produced. The machine configuration required for the automatic focus model is more complex and consumes more of the setup activity resources than the manual focus camera does. Total setup costs are $100,000 per year. Total setup hours are 10,000, with 7,000 hours needed for the automatic focus camera and 3,000 hours needed for the manual focus camera.

The manual focus model is more labor-intensive and requires much more assembly time and less machine time. Total direct labor hours used for both products are 100,000, with 70,000 hours used for the manual model and 30,000 used for the automatic model. There are 40,000 units of the manual model and 60,000 units of the automatic model produced each year. Cariari currently assigns only manufacturing costs to the two products. Overhead costs are assigned to the two products in proportion to the direct labor hours used by each product. All other costs are viewed as period costs.

Cariari budgets costs for all departments within the plant—support departments like maintenance and purchasing as well as production departments like machining and assembly. Departmental managers are evaluated and rewarded based on their ability to control costs. Individual managerial performance is assessed by comparing actual costs with budgeted costs.

Required

1. Is Cariari using a functional-based or an activity-based management accounting system? Explain.
2. Setup costs are overhead costs. What is the setup cost assigned per unit for each model using Cariari's current method of assigning overhead costs to products? Would you classify this cost assignment as direct tracing, driver tracing, or allocation? Explain.
3. Can you suggest a better way of assigning setup costs? Provide calculations, and explain why you think this method is better. Is this method compatible with production-based costing or with activity-based costing? Explain.

2-16

Various Topics; Multiple Choice LO1, LO2, LO3, LO4

Choose the best answer for each of the following questions:

1. An example of driver tracing is

   a. assigning the cost of raw materials to a product.
   b. assigning the cost of grounds maintenance to products using direct labor hours.
   c. assigning the cost of assembly labor to products.
   d. assigning the cost of inspection to products using inspection hours.
   e. Only b and d.

2. Services differ from tangible products in that
   a. services cannot be stored for future use.
   b. producers and buyers of services must be in direct contact for an exchange.
   c. there is less variation in the performance of services.
   d. buyers cannot see, feel, hear, or taste a product before it is bought.
   e. Only a and b.

3. Kolaser Company has the following production data for the month of July:

Direct labor	$250,000
Actual overhead	350,000
Direct materials used	400,000
Warehousing	40,000

   Kolaser's conversion cost for July is

   a. $600,000.
   b. $640,000.
   c. $650,000.
   d. $750,000.

4. Refer to the data in Question 3. Kolaser's prime cost for July is

   a. $600,000.
   b. $640,000.
   c. $650,000.
   d. $750,000.

5. Activity-based management differs from functional-based management on which of the following dimensions?

   a. It is more tracing intensive.
   b. It provides detailed activity information.
   c. It uses both unit-level and non-unit-level drivers.
   d. It focuses on managing activities.
   e. All of the above.

Problems

2-17

Direct Tracing and Driver Tracing
LO1, LO2

Limon Hospital has two types of patients: normal care and intensive care. On a daily basis, both types of patients consume resources necessary for their care. For example, they occupy beds, receive nursing help, use care supplies (lotion, gauze, tissues, etc.), have bedding, towels, and clothes laundered, eat meals, etc. Bill Simons, the hospital administrator, wants to calculate the cost per patient day for each type of patient.

To illustrate how daily care costs can be assigned to each type of patient, information has been gathered for nursing care. There are always four nurses on duty. There are three shifts, each lasting eight hours. Nurses work 40 hours per week and are paid an average of $45,000 per year, including benefits. Full-time nurses work 50 weeks per year. The hospital employs only one part-time nurse, who is paid $22,500 for the hours worked during the year (only the amount needed to ensure that the four-nurse coverage policy is satisfied). Assume that a year is exactly 52 weeks. During the year, normal-care patients accounted for 8,000 patient days, and intensive-care patients accounted for 2,000 patient days. Intensive-care patients use half of the nursing care hours.

Required

1. Calculate the nursing cost per patient day for each patient type using patient days to assign the cost.

2. Calculate the nursing cost per patient day for each patient type using nursing hours used to assign the cost. Is this cost assignment more accurate than the one using patient days? Explain your reasoning.
3. Suppose that one nurse on each shift is dedicated to the intensive care unit and that the other three nurses provide additional help as needed. What additional information would you like to have to assign nursing costs so that a cost per patient day can be calculated for each patient type? Which of the three assignment methods are you using?
4. Suppose that the hospital administrator asks you to calculate the cost of laundry per patient day for each patient type. Describe how you would assign laundry cost, and specify the information that would be needed to do so. Did you use direct tracing or driver tracing? Explain.

2-18

Cost Identification
LO2

Following is a list of cost items described in the chapter and a list of brief descriptive settings. Match the items with the settings. More than one cost classification may be associated with each setting; however, select the setting that *best* seems to fit the item.

Cost terms

a. Opportunity cost
b. Period cost
c. Product cost
d. Direct labor cost
e. Selling cost
f. Conversion cost
g. Prime cost
h. Direct materials cost
i. Manufacturing overhead cost
j. Administrative cost

Settings

1. Marcus Armstrong, manager of Timmins Optical, estimated that the cost of plastic, wages of the technician producing the lenses, and overhead totaled $30 per pair of single-vision lenses.
2. Linda was having a hard time deciding whether to return to school. She was concerned about the salary she would have to give up for the next four years.
3. Randy Harris is the finished goods warehouse manager for a medium-size manufacturing firm. He is paid a salary of $90,000 per year. As he studied the financial statements prepared by the local CPA firm, he wondered how his salary was treated.
4. Jamie Young is in charge of the legal department at company headquarters. Her salary is $95,000 per year. She reports to the chief executive officer.
5. All factory costs that are not classified as direct materials or direct labor.
6. The new product required machining, assembly, and painting. The design engineer requested the accounting department to estimate the labor cost of each of the three operations. The engineer supplied the estimated labor hours for each operation.
7. After obtaining the estimate of direct labor cost, the design engineer estimated the cost of the materials that would be used for the new product.
8. The design engineer totaled the costs of direct materials and direct labor for the new product.
9. The design engineer also estimated the cost of converting the raw materials into their final form.

10. The auditor pointed out that the depreciation on the corporate jet had been incorrectly assigned to finished goods inventory (the jet was primarily used to fly the CEO and other staff to various company sites). Accordingly, the depreciation charge was reallocated to the income statement.

2-19

Various Topics; Matching
LO1, LO2, LO3, LO4

Match the following items (by definition or example):

1. Direct costs
2. Drivers
3. Tracing
4. Intangibility
5. Overhead cost
6. Heterogeneity
7. Perishability
8. Absorption-costing income
9. Functional-based costing
10. Activity-based costing
11. Inseparability
12. Prime cost
13. Opportunity cost
14. Work in process
15. Cost object

a. Customers
b. Attending college instead of working
c. Measures of a cost object's resource usage
d. Variation in performance of services
e. Producers and buyers in direct contact
f. Uses only unit-level drivers
g. Assigning costs using causal relationships
h. Uses unit-level and non-unit-level drivers to assign costs
i. Partially finished goods
j. Direct materials plus direct labor
k. Inability to store services
l. Cannot see, hear, taste, or feel before buying
m. Costs traceable to a cost object
n. Functional, full-costing income
o. Production costs not directly traceable

2-20

Functional-Based versus Activity-Based Management Accounting Systems
LO4

The following actions are associated with either activity-based management accounting or functional-based management accounting.

a. Budgeted costs are compared with the actual costs of the Maintenance Department.
b. The Maintenance Department manager receives a bonus for "beating" the budget.
c. The costs of resources are traced to activities and then to products.
d. The Purchasing Department is evaluated on a departmental basis.
e. Activities are identified and listed.
f. Activities are categorized as adding value or not adding value to the organization.
g. A standard for a product's material usage cost is set and compared against the product's actual material usage cost.
h. The cost of performing an activity is tracked over time.
i. The distance between moves is identified as the cause of material-handling costs.
j. A purchasing agent is rewarded for buying parts below the standard price set by the company.
k. The cost of the material-handling activity is reduced dramatically by redesigning the plant layout.

l. An investigation is undertaken to find out why the actual labor cost for the production of 1,000 units is greater than the labor standard allowed.
m. The percentage of defective units is calculated and tracked over time.
n. Engineering has been given the charge to find a way to reduce setup time by 75 percent.
o. The manager of the Receiving Department lays off two receiving clerks so that the fourth-quarter budget can be met.

Required

Classify these actions as belonging to either an activity-based management accounting system or a functional-based management accounting system. Explain your classification.

2-21

Income Statement; Cost of Services Provided; Service Attributes
LO2, LO3

Lebowski and Associates is an architectural firm that employs 100 professionals and 15 staff. The firm does design work for small and medium-size companies. The following data are provided for the year ended June 30, 2008:

Designs processed	9,400
Designs in process, June 30, 2007	$ 900,000
Designs in process, June 30, 2008	1,400,000
Cost of services added	13,550,000
Beginning direct materials inventory	200,000
Purchases, direct materials	400,000
Direct labor	12,000,000
Overhead	1,100,000
Administrative	500,000
Selling	600,000

Required

1. Calculate the direct materials used in the production of services.
2. Prepare a statement of cost of services sold.
3. Refer to the statement prepared in Requirement 1. What is the dominant cost? Will this always be true of service organizations? If not, provide an example of an exception.
4. Assume that the average fee for a design is $1,950. Prepare an income statement for Lebowski and Associates.
5. Discuss four differences between services and tangible products. How do these differences affect the computations in Requirement 1?

2-22

Income Statement; Cost of Goods Manufactured
LO3

EXCEL

Kimmelman Company produced 5,000 loveseats during the year. The loveseats sell for $650 each. Kimmelman had 600 loveseats in finished goods inventory at the beginning of the year. At the end of the year, there were 800 loveseats in finished goods inventory. Kimmelman's accounting records provide the following information:

Purchases of materials	$675,000
Direct materials inventory, December 31, 2007	93,600
Direct materials inventory, December 31, 2008	133,600
Direct labor	400,000
Indirect labor	80,000
Rent, factory building	84,000
Supplies used in production	14,600
Depreciation, factory equipment	120,000

(continued)

Utilities, factory	$ 23,912
Salary, sales supervisor	180,000
Commissions, salespersons	360,000
General administration	600,000
Work-in-process inventory, December 31, 2007	26,082
Work-in-process inventory, December 31, 2008	29,992
Finished goods inventory, December 31, 2007	160,000
Finished goods inventory, December 31, 2008	228,200

Required

1. Prepare a statement of cost of goods manufactured.
2. Compute the average cost of producing one unit of product in 2008 (rounded to the nearest dollar).
3. Prepare an income statement for external users.

2-23

Cost Identification and Analysis; Cost Assignment; Income Statement
LO1, LO2, LO3

Melissa Vassar has decided to open a printing shop. She has secured two contracts. One is a five-year contract to print a popular regional magazine. This contract calls for 5,000 copies each month. The second contract is a three-year agreement to print tourist brochures for the state. The state tourist office requires 10,000 brochures per month.

Melissa has rented a building for $1,400 per month. Her printing equipment was purchased for $40,000 and has a life expectancy of 20,000 hours with no salvage value. Depreciation is assigned to a period based on the hours of usage. Melissa has scheduled the delivery of the products so that two production runs are needed. In the first run, the equipment is prepared for the magazine printing. In the second run, the equipment is reconfigured for brochure printing. It takes twice as long to configure the equipment for the magazine setup as it does for the brochure setup. The total setup costs per month are $600.

Insurance costs for the building and equipment are $140 per month. Power to operate the printing equipment is strongly related to machine usage. The printing equipment causes virtually all the power costs. Power costs will run $350 per month. Printing materials will cost $0.40 per copy for the magazine and $0.08 per copy for the brochure. Melissa will hire workers to run the presses as needed (part-time workers are easy to hire). She must pay $10 per hour. Each worker can produce 20 copies of the magazine per printing hour or 100 copies of the brochure. Distribution costs are $500 per month. Melissa will pay herself a salary of $1,500 per month. She is responsible for personnel, accounting, sales, and production—in effect, she is responsible for coordinating and managing all aspects of the business.

Required

1. What are the total monthly manufacturing costs?
2. What are the total monthly prime costs? Total monthly prime costs for the regional magazine? For the brochure? Did you use direct tracing, driver tracing, or allocation to assign costs to each product?
3. What are the total monthly conversion costs? Suppose that Melissa wants to determine monthly conversion costs for each product. Assign monthly conversion costs to each product using direct tracing and driver tracing whenever possible. For those costs that cannot be assigned using a tracing approach, you may assign them using direct labor hours.
4. If Melissa receives $1.80 per copy of the magazine and $0.45 per brochure, how much will her income before income taxes be for the first month of operations? (Prepare an income statement.)

Managerial Decision Cases

2-24

Cost Classification; Income Statement; Unit-Based Cost Behavior; Service Organization
LO2, LO3

Gateway Construction Company is a family-operated business that was founded in 1950 by Samuel Gateway. In the beginning, the company consisted of Gateway and three employees laying gas, water, and sewage pipelines as subcontractors. Currently, the company employs 25 to 30 people; Jack Gateway, Samuel's son, directs it. The main line of business continues to be laying pipeline.

Most of Gateway's work comes from contracts with city and state agencies. All of the company's work is located in Nebraska. The company's sales volume averages $3 million, and profits vary between 0 and 10 percent of sales.

Sales and profits have been somewhat below average for the past three years due to a recession and intense competition. Because of this competition, Jack Gateway is constantly reviewing the prices that other companies bid for jobs; when a bid is lost, he makes every attempt to analyze the reasons for the differences between his bid and that of his competitors. He uses this information to increase the competitiveness of future bids.

Jack has become convinced that Gateway's current accounting system is deficient. Currently, all expenses are simply deducted from revenues to arrive at net income. No effort is made to distinguish among the costs of laying pipe, obtaining contracts, and administering the company. Yet all bids are based on the costs of laying pipe.

With these thoughts in mind, Jack began a careful review of the income statement for the previous year (see below). First, he noted that jobs were priced on the basis of equipment hours, with an average price of $165 per equipment hour. However, when it came to classifying and assigning costs, he decided that he needed some help. One thing that really puzzled him was how to classify his own salary of $114,000. About half of his time was spent in bidding and securing contracts, and the other half was spent in general administrative matters.

Gateway Construction
Income Statement
For the Year Ended December 31, 2008

Sales (18,200 equipment hours) @ $165 per hour ...		$3,003,000
Less expenses:		
Utilities ...	$ 24,000	
Machine operators ...	218,000	
Rent, office building ...	24,000	
CPA fees ...	20,000	
Other direct labor ...	265,700	
Administrative salaries ...	114,000	
Supervisory salaries ...	70,000	
Pipe ...	1,401,340	
Tires and fuel ...	418,600	
Depreciation, equipment ...	198,000	
Salaries of mechanics ...	50,000	
Advertising ...	15,000	
Total expenses ...		2,818,640
Income before income taxes ...		$ 184,360

Required

1. Classify the costs in the income statement as (1) costs of laying pipe (production costs), (2) costs of securing contracts (selling costs), or (3) costs of general

administration. For production costs, identify direct materials, direct labor, and overhead costs. The company never has significant work in process (most jobs are started and completed within a day).

2. Using the functional classification developed in Requirement 1, prepare an absorption-costing income statement. What is the average cost per equipment hour for laying pipe?
3. Assume that a significant driver is equipment hours. Identify the costs that would likely be traced to jobs using this driver. Explain why you feel these costs are traceable using equipment hours. What is the cost per equipment hour for these traceable costs?

2-25

Cost Information and Ethical Behavior; Service Organization
LO1

ETHICS

Jean Erickson, owner and manager of an advertising company in Charlotte, North Carolina, had arranged a meeting with Leroy Gee, the chief accountant of a large, local competitor. The two are lifelong friends. They grew up together in a small town and attended the same university. Leroy was a competent, successful accountant but currently was experiencing some personal financial difficulties. The problems were created by some investments that had turned sour, leaving him with a $15,000 personal loan to pay off—just at the time that his oldest son was scheduled to enter college.

Jean, on the other hand, was struggling to establish a successful advertising business. She had recently acquired the rights to open a branch office of a large regional advertising firm headquartered in Atlanta, Georgia. During her first two years, she had managed to build a small, profitable practice; however, the chance to gain a significant foothold in the Charlotte advertising community hinged on the success of winning a bid to represent the state of North Carolina in a major campaign to attract new industry and tourism. The meeting she had scheduled with Leroy concerned the bid she planned to submit.

Jean: Leroy, I'm at a critical point in my business venture. If I can win the bid for the state's advertising dollars, I'll be set. Winning the bid will bring $600,000 to $700,000 of revenues into the firm. On top of that, I estimate that the publicity will bring another $200,000 to $300,000 of new business.

Leroy: I understand. My boss is anxious to win that business as well. It would mean a huge increase in profits for my firm. It's a competitive business, though. As new as you are, I doubt that you'll have much chance of winning.

Jean: You may be wrong. You're forgetting two very important considerations. First, I have the backing of all the resources and talent of a regional firm. Second, I have some political connections. Last year, I was hired to run the publicity side of the governor's campaign. He was impressed with my work and would like me to have this business. I am confident that the proposals I submit will be very competitive. My only concern is to submit a bid that beats your firm. If I come in with a lower bid and good proposals, the governor can see to it that I get the work.

Leroy: Sounds promising. If you do win, however, there will be a lot of upset people. After all, they are going to claim that the business should have been given to local advertisers, not to some out-of-state firm. Given the size of your office, you'll have to get support from Atlanta. You could take a lot of heat.

Jean: True. But I am the owner of the branch office. That fact alone should blunt most of the criticism. Who can argue that I'm not a local? Listen, with your help, I think I can win this bid. Furthermore, if I do win it, you can reap some direct benefits. With that kind of business, I can afford to hire an accountant, and I'll make it worthwhile for you to transfer jobs. I can offer you an up-front bonus of $15,000. On top of that, I'll increase your annual salary by 20 percent. That should solve most of your financial difficulties. After all, we have been friends since day one—and what are friends for?

Leroy: Jean, my wife would be ecstatic if I were able to improve our financial position as quickly as this opportunity affords. I certainly hope that you win the bid. What kind of help can I provide?

Jean: Simple. To win, all I have to do is beat the bid of your firm. Before I submit my bid, I would like you to review it. With the financial skills you have, it should be easy for you to spot any excessive costs that I may have included. Or perhaps I included the wrong kind of costs. By cutting excessive costs and eliminating costs that may not be directly related to the project, my bid should be competitive enough to meet or beat your firm's bid.

Required

1. What would you do if you were Leroy? Fully explain the reasons for your decision.
2. What is the likely outcome if Leroy agrees to review the bid? Is there much risk to him personally if he reviews the bid? Should the degree of risk have any bearing on his decision?
3. Apply the code of ethics for management accountants to the proposal given to Leroy (see Chapter 1). What standards would be violated if he agrees to review the bid? Assume that Leroy is a member of the IMA and holds a CMA.

Research Assignments

2-26

Cybercase
LO1, LO2, LO3

On the Internet, access the SEC home page, via the chapter web links at the Interactive Study Center at http://www.thomsonedu.com/accounting/hansen. Next, access the EDGAR database. Obtain copies of financial statements for a manufacturing firm and a service firm (e.g., **Texas Instruments** and **Chase Manhattan Bank**). Write a memo discussing the differences and similarities of the two statements.

2-27

Research Assignment
LO1, LO2, LO4

Interview an accountant who works for a manufacturing or service firm (preferably one who works in cost accounting). Ask that person the following questions, and write up his or her responses:

a. What product(s) does your firm produce?
b. What costs are assigned to the product(s) produced?
c. For a particular product, what direct materials are used?
d. What percentage of total manufacturing costs is direct labor? Direct materials? Overhead?
e. How is overhead assigned to the products?
f. Do you now use or plan to use an activity-based management system? Why or why not?

© Getty Images

PART 2

Activity-Based Accounting

chapter 3

Activity Cost Behavior

learning objectives

After studying this chapter, you should be able to:

1. Define cost behavior for fixed, variable, and mixed costs.
2. Explain the role of the resource usage model in understanding cost behavior.
3. Separate mixed costs into their fixed and variable components using the high-low method, the scatterplot method, and the method of least squares.
4. Evaluate the reliability of a cost equation.
5. Discuss the role of multiple regression in assessing cost behavior.
6. Describe the use of managerial judgment in determining cost behavior.

Scenario

Reddy Heaters, a producer of insert heaters for coffeepots, had recently begun the implementation of an activity-based costing system. Jamie Weathers, CEO, appointed Rick Anderson to head up a team to examine the feasibility of simultaneously implementing an activity-based budgeting (ABB) system. Rick Anderson began searching for experiences of others who had experimented with ABB and came across an article discussing the experience of Scottish Courage Brewing.[1] He first discovered that Scottish Courage Brewing was a pioneer of ABB in the United Kingdom. Next, he noted that a key factor in the development of the ABB system was the identification of activities, resources, and the relationship between activities and resources as the volume of activity changed. Scottish Courage Brewing *assumed* that a linear relationship existed between measures of activity consumption and resources. Based on this assumption, the ABB model predicted that activity cost would change as the activity volume changed. In reality, many activity costs did not follow a linear relationship but instead followed a stepped path. Consequently, Scottish Courage Brewing had significant difficulties with managing costs because the underlying actual cost behavior was more complicated than the simple assumed variable relationship.

After reading of this experience, Rick realized that managing costs and improving efficiency required an understanding of how the costs of activities change as activity output changes. To drive this home to the members of his team, he had the team carefully study the cost behavior of a rework activity. They discovered that when a bad product is detected, it is analyzed to determine the problem and then reworked so that the product functions as it should. Some costs, such as depreciation on the equipment used and supervision, do not change as the number of reworked products increases. Other costs, such as materials and power, do increase with the number of units reworked. However, some costs will change only with fairly large changes in activity output.

Rick began to realize that knowing how cost behaves was vital information. If, for example, some costs of the rework activity vary with the number of units reworked, then these costs can be managed by reducing the number of reworked units. Finding ways to reduce the number of defective units will allow the cost of the rework activity to decrease, increasing overall efficiency. On the other hand, some rework costs may be more fixed in nature and reduction of these costs may only follow step reductions in the number of units reworked.

Questions to Think About

1. Suppose that the division reduces the demand for the rework activity. Will resource spending be reduced by the same proportion for this activity? Is there a difference between resource spending and resource usage?
2. Suppose the total cost of rework activity and the total number of units reworked are known. Given this information, is it possible to determine how much of this total cost is variable? How much is fixed? Is knowing fixed- and variable-cost behavior important?
3. What role does management play in determining cost behavior?
4. Can you think of reasons other than those suggested by the scenario that make it important for managers to understand cost behavior?

1 Activity-based accounting promises a better understanding of costs, increased accuracy in costing assignments, and an increase in economic efficiency. How these promises can be realized is explored in the next three chapters.

The Basics of Cost Behavior

Objective 1

Define cost behavior for fixed, variable, and mixed costs.

In Chapter 2, we looked at the way costs could be used to determine the cost of goods sold and the value of ending inventory. These costs are important for preparing external financial reports, namely, the income statement and the balance sheet. The costs that are reported on these statements are organized by function. That is, all costs of the company are put into one of three categories: production or manufacturing (in the cost of goods sold account), marketing expenses, and administrative expenses. This organization is fine for external reporting; in fact, it is required. However, the functional groupings are not helpful at all for budgeting, control, and decision making. For these purposes, we need to understand cost behavior.

Suppose that Reddy Heaters has a plant that is expanding rapidly. Last year, the plant made and sold 10,000 units; in the coming year, it expects to sell 20,000 units. Could we say that costs in the coming year will double? No, probably not. In fact, we would expect that the cost of making 20,000 units would be less than twice the cost of making 10,000 units. The reason is that, while some costs are *variable* and will double as output doubles, other costs are *fixed* and will not change as output doubles. In order to answer what will happen to costs as output doubles, we need to know about cost behavior.

Cost behavior is the general term for describing whether costs change as output changes. Costs react to output changes in many different ways. We will begin by looking at the simplest possibilities—fixed costs, variable costs, and mixed costs.

Fixed Costs

A cost that stays the same as output changes is a **fixed cost**. More formally, a fixed cost is a cost that, in total, remains constant within a relevant range as the level of activity output changes. To illustrate fixed-cost behavior, consider once again Reddy Heaters, a company that produces insert heaters for coffeepots. Although numerous activities are performed within the plant, we will look at only one: the pipe-cutting activity. Here, machines are used to cut thin metal pipe into 3-inch segments. Since one 3-inch segment is used in each insert heater, we can use the number of heaters as the output measure for the cutting activity.

For simplicity, assume that the cutting activity uses two inputs: (1) cutting machines and (2) the power to operate the cutting machines. Consider the cutting machines: They are leased for $60,000 per year and have the capacity to produce up to 240,000 3-inch segments in a year. The cost of leasing the cutting machines is a fixed cost, since it stays at $60,000 per year no matter how many segments are cut. This behavior is illustrated by the following example:

Lease of Machines	Number of 3-Inch Segments	Unit Cost
$60,000	0	N/A
60,000	60,000	$1.00
60,000	120,000	0.50
60,000	180,000	0.33
60,000	240,000	0.25

Two parts of the fixed-cost definition need further discussion: relevant range and the phrase "in total." **Relevant range** is the range of output over which the assumed cost/output relationship is valid. For the cutting activity, the cutting machines currently leased can produce up to 240,000 units of 3-inch pipe per year. Thus, the relevant range is from zero to 240,000 units—the output for which the total cost of leasing remains constant. Reddy Heaters pays $60,000 per year for leasing the equipment, regardless of whether it produces 0, 60,000, 120,000, or 240,000 units.

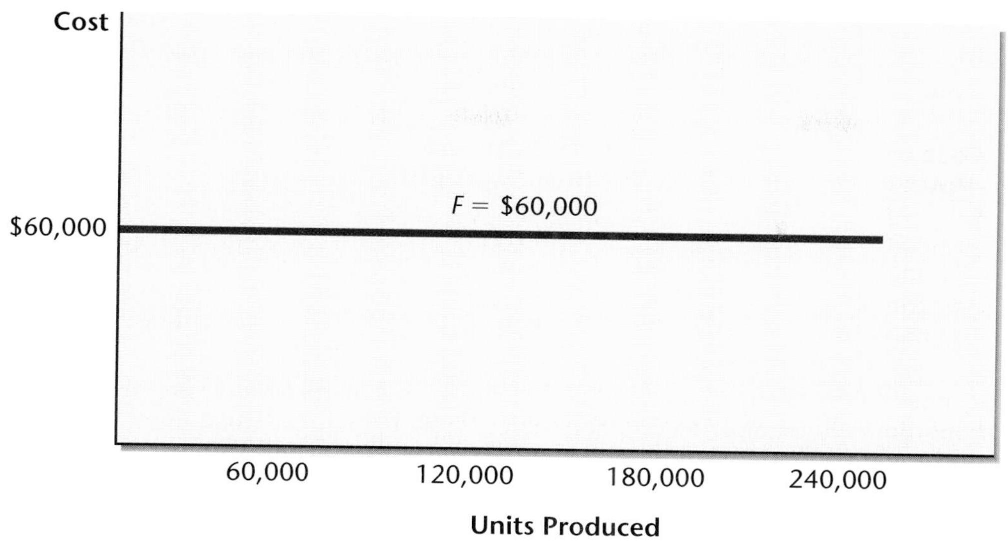

Exhibit 3-1 Fixed-Cost Behavior: Cutting Activity, Reddy Heaters

Let's look at a graph of fixed costs in Exhibit 3-1. For the relevant range, fixed-cost behavior is illustrated by a horizontal line. Notice that at 120,000 units produced, the leasing cost is \$60,000; at 240,000 units produced, the leasing cost is still \$60,000. This line visually demonstrates that cost remains unchanged as the level of the output varies. Total fixed costs can be represented by the following equation:

$$\text{Total fixed costs} = \$60,000$$

Notice that total fixed cost does not depend on the output measure (number of heaters). It is \$60,000 no matter what the output.

While the total cost of leasing remains unchanged, the cost per segment (the unit cost) does change as more segments are produced. As the table shows, within the range of 60,000 to 240,000 units, the unit cost of leasing the pipe-cutting machines decreases from \$1.00 to \$0.25. Thus, while total fixed cost remains unchanged in total as output increases, the unit fixed cost will change because the fixed costs are being spread out over more output.

A final note on fixed costs is that they can change—but that change does not depend on changes in output. For example, suppose that the company leasing the cutting machines to Reddy Heaters increases the lease payment from \$60,000 to \$65,000 per year. The cost of the machines would still be fixed, but at the new higher amount. In the graph, the entire fixed-cost curve would shift up to \$65,000. The relevant range would still be 0 to 240,000 units. Thus, at 120,000 units produced, the leasing cost is \$65,000; at 240,000 units produced, the leasing cost is still \$65,000. Again, the cost remains unchanged as the level of output (number of segments) varies.

Variable Costs

While fixed costs remain unchanged as output varies, variable costs do change as output changes. A **variable cost** is a cost that, in total, varies in direct proportion to changes in output. That is, a variable cost goes up as output goes up, and it goes down as output goes down.

Let's expand the Reddy Heaters example to include the other resource used by the cutting activity: power. Power cost, however, behaves differently from the cost of the cutting machines. Power is consumed only if output is produced, and as more output is produced, more power is used. Assume that each time a segment is cut, the machines use 0.1 kilowatt-hour at $2.00 per kilowatt-hour. The cost of power per 3-inch segment is $0.20 ($2.00 × × 0.1). The cost of power for various levels of activity output follows:

Cost of Power	Number of 3-Inch Segments	Unit Cost
$ 0	0	$ 0
12,000	60,000	0.20
24,000	120,000	0.20
36,000	180,000	0.20
48,000	240,000	0.20

As more 3-inch segments are produced, the total cost of power increases in direct proportion. For example, as output doubles from 60,000 to 120,000 units, the total cost of power doubles from $12,000 to $24,000. Notice also that the unit cost of power is constant.

Variable costs can also be represented by a linear equation. Here, total variable cost depends on the level of the driver. This relationship can be described by the following:

Total variable cost = Variable cost per unit × Number of units

In the Reddy Heaters example, the cost of power is described by the following equation:

Total variable cost = $0.20 × Number of segments

Exhibit 3-2 graphically illustrates a variable cost. Notice that the variable cost curve is a straight line starting at the origin. At zero units produced, total variable cost is zero. However, as units produced increase, the total variable cost also increases. For example, at 120,000 units, the total variable cost is $24,000. It can be seen here that total cost increases in direct proportion to increases in the number of segments produced; the rate of increase is measured by the slope of the line. Here, the slope of the line is 0.20.

Mixed Costs

A **mixed cost** is a cost that has both a fixed and a variable component. For example, sales representatives are often paid a salary plus a commission on sales. Suppose that Reddy Heaters has three sales representatives, each earning a salary of $10,000 per year plus a commission of $0.50 for every insert heater they sell. The activity is

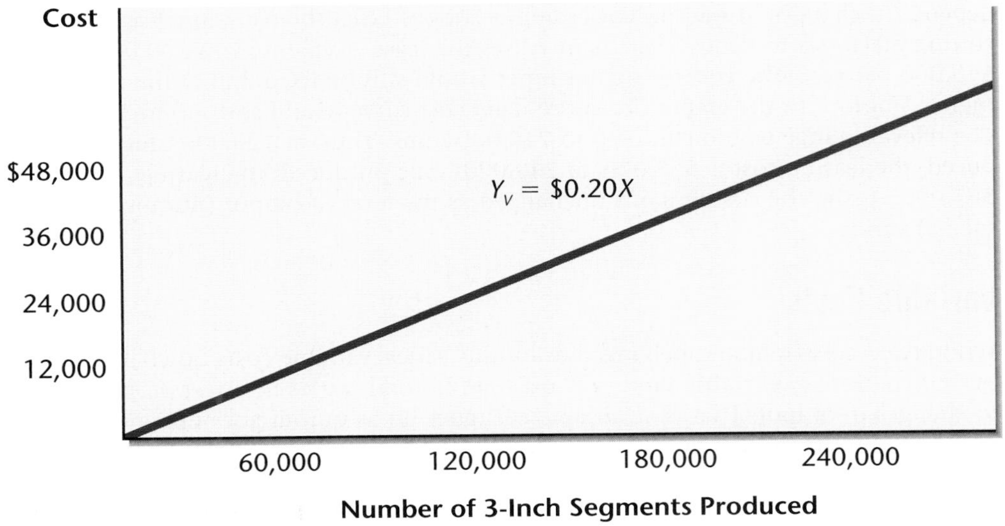

Exhibit 3-2 Variable-Cost Behavior: Cutting Activity, Reddy Heaters

selling inserts, and the driver is units sold. If 100,000 insert heaters are sold, then the total selling cost is $80,000—the sum of the fixed salary cost of $30,000 (3 × $10,000) and the variable cost of $50,000 ($0.50 × 100,000). The linear equation for a mixed cost is given by:

$$\text{Total cost} = \text{Fixed cost} + \text{Total variable cost}$$

For Reddy Heaters, the selling cost is represented by the following equation:

$$\text{Total cost} = \$30{,}000 + (\$0.50 \times \text{Units sold})$$

The following table shows the selling cost for different levels of sales activity:

Inserts Sold	Variable Cost of Selling	Fixed Cost of Selling	Total Selling Cost	Selling Cost per Unit*
40,000	$ 20,000	$30,000	$ 50,000	$1.25
80,000	40,000	30,000	70,000	0.88
120,000	60,000	30,000	90,000	0.75
160,000	80,000	30,000	110,000	0.69
200,000	100,000	30,000	130,000	0.65

*Rounded

The graph for our mixed-cost example given in Exhibit 3-3 assumes that the relevant range is 0 to 200,000 units. Mixed costs are represented by a line that intercepts the vertical axis (at $30,000 for this example). The intercept corresponds to the fixed-cost component, and the slope of the line gives the variable cost per unit of cost driver (slope is 0.50 for this example).

Classifying Costs According to Behavior

In our discussion of fixed, variable, and mixed costs, we concentrated on the definitions and took for granted a number of factors that are important for determining whether a cost is fixed or variable. Now it is time to look more closely at the way we can classify costs according to behavior. To assess cost behavior, we must first consider the time horizon. Then, we must identify the resources needed and the output of the activity. Finally, we must measure the inputs and outputs and determine the impact of output changes on the activity cost.

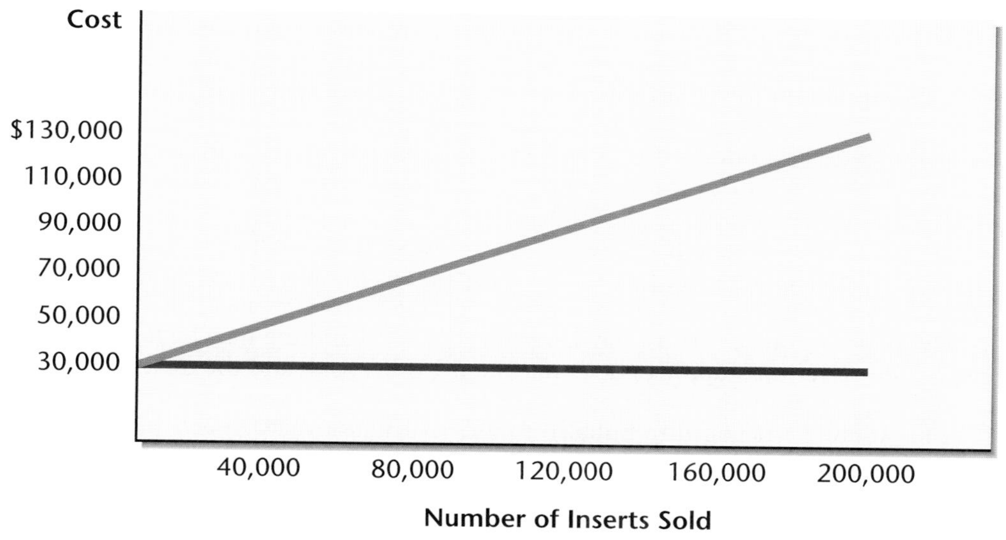

Exhibit 3-3 Mixed-Cost Behavior: Cutting Activity, Reddy Heaters

Time Horizon Determining whether a cost is fixed or variable depends on the time horizon. According to economics, in the **long run**, all costs are variable; in the **short run**, at least one cost is fixed. But how long is the short run? In the Reddy Heaters example, the leasing cost of the cutting machines was fixed for a year, so a year was the length of the short run for that cost. The length of the short run may differ from one cost to another.

Consider a process that takes materials and molds them into the shape of a garden hose. The output is the number of feet of hose. As the amount of hose changes, the direct materials used are relatively easy to adjust (acquiring more as the output increases and less as it decreases). For all practical purposes, the firm may treat direct materials as strictly variable even though for the next few hours (or days) the amount of materials already purchased may be fixed.

What about direct labor? In some settings, a company may be able to hire and lay off its labor relatively quickly—in which case labor could be treated as a variable cost. In other cases, a company may not lay off labor for short-term drops in production. For example, there may be contracts with labor unions that prohibit layoffs. Such a contract may make layoffs impossible in the short run even when there have been permanent changes in the need for labor. Only when the contract is renegotiated can the level of labor be adjusted. In this case, direct labor is a fixed cost rather than a variable cost. The same observation can be made for other forms of labor. For example, salaries of production line supervisors are also difficult to adjust as the activity output fluctuates. It could take months, or even a year or two, to determine whether a drop in production is permanent and the number of supervisory jobs needs to be reduced. Accordingly, this cost is typically seen as fixed.

The length of the short-run period depends to some extent on management judgment and the purpose for which cost behavior is being estimated. For example, submitting a bid on a one-time, special order may span only a month, long enough to create a bid and produce the order. Other types of decisions, such as dropping a product line or adjusting the product mix, will affect a much longer period of time. In this case, the costs that must be considered are long-run variable costs, including product design and development, market development, and market penetration.

Resources and Output Measures Every activity needs resources to accomplish the task it has to do. Resources might include materials, energy or fuel, labor, and capital. These inputs are combined to produce an output. For example, if the activity is moving materials, the inputs could include crates (materials), fuel (energy), a forklift operator (labor), and a forklift (capital). The output would be moved materials. But how do we measure this output? One measure is the number of times the activity is performed. For example, suppose that the activity is moving materials from the storeroom to the assembly line. A good measure of output is the number of moves. The more moves that are made, the higher the cost of moving. Therefore, we could say that the number of moves is a good output measure for the activity of moving materials. Exhibit 3-4 illustrates the relationship between inputs, activities, output, and cost behavior.

Another term for output measure is driver. Recall from Chapter 2 that activity drivers are observable causal factors that measure the amount of resources a cost object uses. Activity drivers explain changes in activity costs by measuring changes in activity use or output. Thus, the driver for material handling may be number of moves; the driver for shipping goods may be the units sold; and the driver for laundering hospital bedding may be pounds of laundry. The choice of driver is tailored not only to the particular firm but also to the particular activity or cost being measured. Therefore, in order to understand the behavior of costs, we must first determine the underlying activities and the associated drivers that measure activity capacity and usage. The need to understand this cost-activity relationship leads us to the determination of an appropriate measure of activity output, or activity driver.

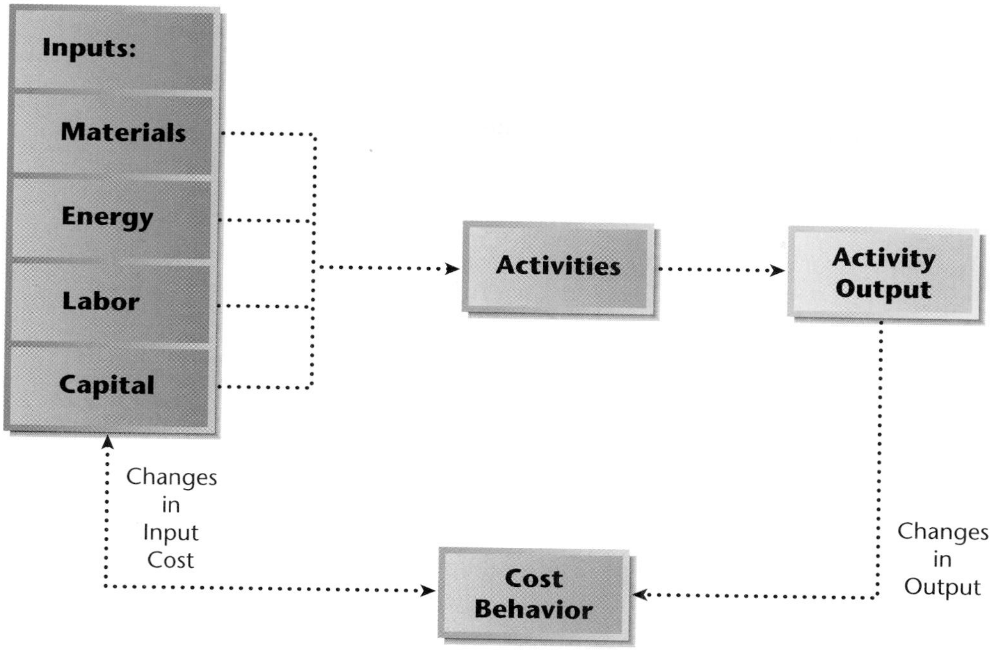

Exhibit 3-4 Activity Cost Behavior Model

Activity drivers are divided into two general categories: production (or unit-level) drivers and non-unit-level drivers. Production drivers explain changes in cost as units produced change. Pounds of direct materials, kilowatt-hours used to run production machinery, and direct labor hours are examples of production drivers. In other words, as pounds of materials used, kilowatt-hours, and direct labor hours increase, output also increases.

© Getty Images/PhotoDisc

The preparation needed to produce a batch of cookies is a good example of a non-unit level activity. It is an activity performed each time a batch is produced, whether one dozen or two dozen cookies are baked.

Non-Unit-Level Drivers Non-unit-level drivers explain changes in cost as factors other than units change. For example, setups are a non-unit-level activity. Every time the factory has to stop producing one product in order to set up the production line to produce another product, setup costs are incurred. No matter how many units are in the new batch, the cost to set up remains the same. You have probably run into this type of activity in your personal life. Let's consider a common household production activity—making chocolate chip cookies. Suppose that you decide to make two dozen cookies. First, you will have to set up for the cookie baking by taking out a bowl, spoon, baking sheet, and the relevant ingredients. On another occasion, you might decide to make four dozen cookies. You still have to set up, and it will probably take the same amount of time as it took you to set up for two dozen cookies. The point is that setting up is not related to the number of units (cookies). Instead, it is a non-unit-level activity. Other examples of non-unit-level costs include depreciation on the factory, the salary of the factory manager, and the cost of running the purchasing department.

In a functional-based cost system, cost behavior is assumed to be described by unit-level drivers only. In an activity-based system, both unit-level and non-unit-level drivers are used. Thus, the ABC system produces a much richer view of cost behavior than a functional-based system.

Activities, Resource Usage, and Cost Behavior

Objective 2

Explain the role of the resource usage model in understanding cost behavior.

Short-run costs often do not adequately reflect all the costs necessary to design, produce, market, distribute, and support a product. Long-run and short-run cost behaviors are related to activities and the resources needed to perform them. Capacity is simply the actual or potential ability to do something. So, when we talk about capacity for an activity, we are describing the amount of the activity that the company can perform. How much capacity is needed depends on the level of performance required. Usually, we can assume that the capacity needed corresponds to the level where the activity is performed efficiently. This efficient level of activity performance is called **practical capacity**. On occasion, there is excess capacity. To see how that happens and how it affects cost behavior, we need to look at flexible and committed resources.

Flexible Resources

It would be nice if a company could purchase only those resources it needed at precisely the time the resources were needed. Sometimes that happens. For example, direct materials are frequently purchased at the time and in the amount needed. This kind of resource is called a *flexible resource.* **Flexible resources** are supplied as used and needed; they are acquired from outside sources, where the terms of acquisition do not require any long-term commitment for any given amount of the resource. Thus, the organization is free to buy only the amount needed. As a result, the quantity of the resource supplied equals the quantity demanded. Materials and energy are examples. There is no unused capacity for this category of resources, since the amount of resource used just equals the amount purchased.

Since the cost of the resources supplied as needed equals the cost of resources used, the total cost of the resource increases as demand for the resource increases. Thus, the cost of flexible resources is a variable cost.

Committed Resources

Other resources must be purchased before they are needed. A factory building is a good example. The building must be planned and built before production takes place. **Committed resources** are resources that are supplied in advance of usage; they are acquired by the use of either an explicit or implicit contract to obtain a given quantity of resource, regardless of whether the amount of the resource available is fully used or not. Committed resources may have unused capacity, since more may be available than is actually used.

Let's look further at committed resources. Many resources are acquired before the actual demands for the resource are realized. For example, organizations acquire many multiperiod service capacities by paying cash up front or by entering into an explicit contract that requires periodic cash payments. Buying or leasing buildings and equipment is an example of this form of advance resource acquisition. The annual expense associated with the multiperiod category is independent of actual usage of the resource; thus, these expenses can be defined as **committed fixed costs**, and they provide long-term activity capacity.

A second and more important example of committed resources concerns organizations that acquire resources in advance through implicit contracts, usually with their salaried and hourly employees. The implicit understanding is that the organization will maintain employment levels even though there may be temporary downturns in the quantity of activity used. As a result, the expense associated with this category of resources is independent of the quantity used—at least in the short run. Thus, in the short run, the amount of resource expense remains unchanged even though the quantity used may vary, and this resource cost category can be treated (cautiously) as a fixed expense. We may call these shorter-term committed resources **discretionary fixed costs**. They are costs incurred for the acquisition of short-term activity capacity.

Consider Reddy Heaters' receiving activity, which has the objective of bringing purchased materials into the organization. Hiring three receiving clerks who can supply the capacity of processing 9,000 receiving orders for $90,000 is an example of implicit contracting ("receiving orders" is the driver used to measure the receiving activity's capacity and usage). Certainly, none of the three clerks would expect to be laid off if only 6,000 orders were actually processed—unless, of course, the downturn in demand is viewed as permanent. Suppose that the drop is permanent. In this case, we have an activity with too much capacity, and until we reduce the capacity, resource spending will not be reduced. Thus, resource spending changes lag changes in permanent activity output demands.

Step-Cost Behavior

In our discussion of cost behavior, we have assumed that the cost function is continuous. In reality, some cost functions are discontinuous, as shown in Exhibit 3-5. This type of cost function is known as a step function. A **step cost** displays a constant level of cost for a range of output and then at some point jumps to a higher level of cost, where it remains for a similar range of output. In Exhibit 3-5, the cost is $100 as long as activity output is between 0 and 10 units. If the output is between 10 and 20 units, the cost jumps to $200.

Items that display step-cost behavior must be purchased in chunks. The width of the step defines the range of output for which that amount of resource must be acquired. The width of the step in Exhibit 3-5 is 10 units. If the width of the step is narrow, as in Exhibit 3-5, the cost of the resource changes in response to fairly small changes in usage. Some step costs display narrow steps. For example, let's examine Reddy Heaters' use of copier paper. The paper is not purchased sheet by sheet. Instead, it is purchased in boxes of 10 reams (5,000 sheets) each. Reddy uses many

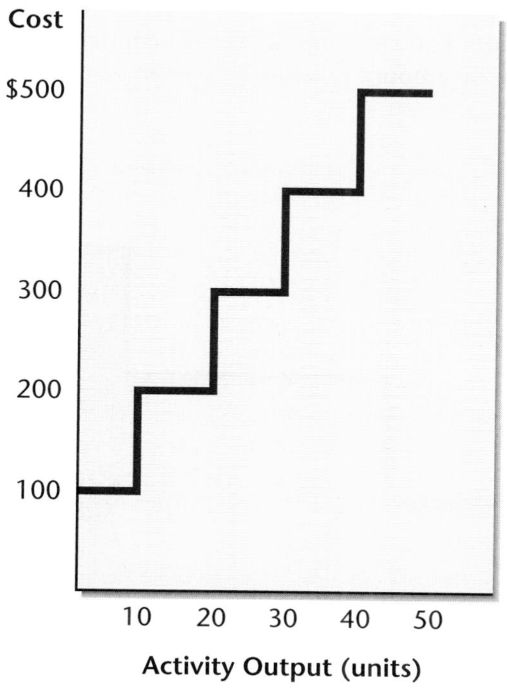

Exhibit 3-5 Step-Cost Function: Copier Activity, Reddy Heaters

boxes a year, so the step is narrow. If the width of the step is narrow, we can approximate this cost with a strictly variable-cost assumption.

Other types of step costs have fairly wide steps. In reality, many so-called fixed costs probably are best described by a step-cost function. Many committed resources, particularly those that involve implicit contracting, follow a step-cost function. For example, Reddy Heaters has hired three sustaining engineers for one of its largest plants; these engineers are responsible for redesigning existing products to meet changing customer needs. Each engineer is paid $70,000 per year and is capable of processing 2,500 engineering change orders per year. Then, the company could process as many as 7,500 (3 × 2,500) change orders per year at a total cost of $210,000 (3 × $70,000). The nature of the resource requires that the capacity be acquired in chunks (one engineer hired at a time). The cost function for this example is displayed in Exhibit 3-6. Notice that the width of the step is 2,500 units, a much wider step than the cost function in Exhibit 3-5.

Step costs with wide steps are assigned to the fixed-cost category. Most of these costs are fixed over the normal operating range of a firm. If that range is 5,000 to 7,500 change orders (as shown in Exhibit 3-6), then the firm will spend $210,000 on engineering resources. Only if Reddy Heaters wants to increase its capacity for engineering above the 7,500 order level will it increase spending on engineers. Of course, if the use of engineering services is not at the maximum of 7,500 orders—perhaps 6,000 orders are actually being processed per year—then there is excess capacity for this service. Frequently, there is excess capacity for activities that are characterized by this type of step-cost behavior.

For example, during the year Reddy Heaters may not actually process 7,500 change orders; that is, all of the available change order-processing capacity may not be used. Assume that 6,000 change orders were processed during the year. We can see that 80 percent (6,000/7,500) of the possible engineering capacity is actually being used. The Engineering Department has 20 percent (1,500/7,500) unused or excess capacity. The cost of this unused capacity is $42,000 (0.20 × $210,000). Note that the cost of unused activity occurs because the resource (engineers) must be acquired in lumpy amounts. Even if Reddy Heaters had anticipated the need for only 6,000 change orders, it would have been difficult to hire the equivalent of 2.4 engineers (6,000/2,500).

The example illustrates that when resources are acquired in advance, there may be a difference between the amount purchased and the amount actually used. This

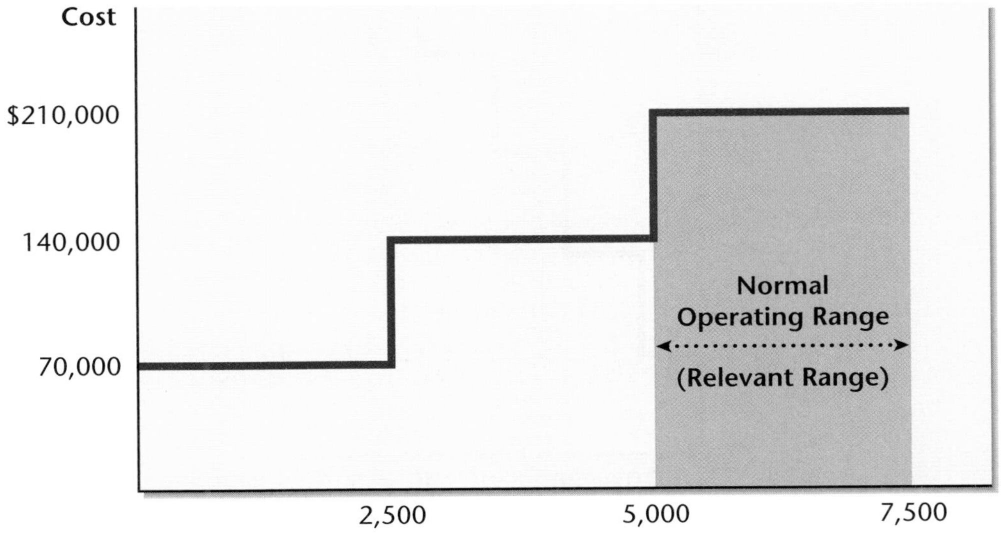

Exhibit 3-6 Step-Fixed Costs: Sustaining Engineering, Reddy Heaters

can occur only for activities that require committed resources, with costs that display a fixed-cost behavior. To see that this is so, let's expand our engineering example to include both flexible and committed resources. Recall that there are three engineers, each paid \$70,000 and each capable of processing 2,500 change orders. Further assume that Reddy Heaters spent \$90,000 on supplies for the engineering activity and that these supplies are a flexible resource. What is the total cost of one change order?

The cost of a single change order is a combination of its fixed cost (the committed resource—engineers) and its variable cost (the flexible resource—supplies). To calculate the fixed cost per unit, we need to calculate the fixed activity rate. The **fixed activity rate** is simply the total committed cost divided by the *total capacity* available.

$$\text{Fixed engineering rate} = \$210{,}000/7{,}500 = \$28 \text{ per change order}$$

Of course, the **variable activity rate** is the total cost of flexible resources divided by the *capacity* used.

$$\text{Variable engineering rate} = \$90{,}000/6{,}000 = \$15 \text{ per change order}$$

Therefore, the total cost of one change order is \$43. Notice the difference between the 7,500 change orders used to compute the fixed activity rate and the 6,000 change orders used to compute the variable activity. Because the fixed rate is based on committed resources, we use the capacity available. After all, the three engineers could have processed as many as 7,500 orders. For the variable activity rate, we use the actual capacity used. This is because the flexible resources are purchased as necessary, so the \$90,000 of supplies relate to the 6,000 change orders actually processed.

Typically, the functional-based costing system provides information only about the cost of the resources purchased. An activity-based management system, on the other hand, tells us how much of the activity is used and the cost of its usage. Furthermore, the relationship between total resources available and resources used is expressed by the following equation:

$$\text{Resources available} = \text{Resources used} + \text{Unused capacity} \qquad (3.1)$$

This equation can be expressed in both physical and financial terms.

For the engineering change order example, equation 3.1 takes the following form when expressed in physical terms.

$$\begin{aligned} \text{Available orders} &= \text{Orders used} + \text{Orders unused} \\ 7{,}500 \text{ orders} &= 6{,}000 \text{ orders} + 1{,}500 \text{ orders} \end{aligned}$$

When equation 3.1 is expressed in financial terms, we simply attach dollar amounts. For the engineering example, this takes the following form:

$$\begin{aligned} \text{Cost of orders supplied} &= \text{Cost of orders used} + \text{Cost of unused orders} \\ &= [(\$28 + \$15) \times 6{,}000] + (\$28 \times 1{,}500) \\ &= \$258{,}000 + \$42{,}000 \\ &= \$300{,}000 \end{aligned}$$

Of course, the \$300,000 is precisely equal to the \$210,000 spent on engineers and the \$90,000 spent on supplies.

Why is this formulation important? It is important because it gives managers crucial information about their ability to expand or contract production. The \$42,000 of excess engineering capacity means that, for example, a new product could be introduced without increasing current spending on engineers.

Implications for Control and Decision Making

The activity-based model just described can improve both managerial control and decision making. Operational control systems encourage managers to pay more attention to controlling resource usage and spending. For example, a well-designed

Careful analysis and thought must be invested in managing activity capacity. Unused activity capacity provides resources that can be used to increase profitability.

operational control system allows managers to assess the changes in resource demands that will occur from new product-mix decisions. Adding new, customized products may increase the demands for various overhead activities. If sufficient unused activity capacity does not exist, then resource spending must increase. Similarly, if activity management brings about excess capacity (by finding ways to reduce resource usage), managers must carefully consider what is to be done with the excess capacity. Eliminating the excess capacity may decrease resource spending and thus improve overall profits. Alternatively, the excess capacity could be used to increase the number and type of products, thereby increasing revenues without increasing spending. The way in which resource usage and spending are affected by managing activities is more fully explored in Chapter 5.

The activity-based resource usage model also allows managers to calculate the changes in resource supply and demand resulting from implementing such decisions as whether to make or buy a part, to accept or reject special orders, and to keep or drop product lines. Additionally, the model increases the power of a number of traditional management accounting decision-making models. The impact on decision making is explored in the decision-making chapters found in Part 5 (Chapters 11 through 14). Most of the decision-making models in those chapters depend heavily on knowledge of cost behavior.

Methods for Separating Mixed Costs into Fixed and Variable Components

Objective 3

Separate mixed costs into their fixed and variable components using the high-low method, the scatter-plot method, and the method of least squares.

While some costs can be fairly easy to classify as strictly variable, fixed, or step-fixed, others fall into the mixed-cost category. In these cases, it is necessary to separate them into fixed and variable components.

Often the only information available is the total cost of an activity and a measure of activity usage. For example, the accounting system will usually record both the total cost of the maintenance activity for a given period and the number of maintenance hours provided during that period. How much of the total maintenance cost represents a fixed charge and how much represents a variable charge is *not* revealed by the accounting records. Often, the total cost is simply recorded with no attempt to separate the fixed and variable costs.

Since accounting records may reveal only the total cost and the associated usage of a mixed-cost item, it is necessary to separate the total cost into its fixed and variable components. Only through a formal effort to separate costs can all costs be classified into the appropriate cost behavior categories.

There are three widely used methods of separating a mixed cost into its fixed and variable components: the high-low method, the scatterplot method, and the method of least squares. Each method requires us to make the simplifying assumption of a linear cost relationship. Therefore, before we examine each of these methods more closely, let's review the concept of linearity.

Linearity Assumption

The definition of variable cost assumes a linear relationship between the cost of an activity and its associated driver. For example, Reddy Heaters uses one 3-inch segment of pipe in each insert heater. Each 3-inch segment costs \$4. The total variable cost of 3-inch segments can be expressed as:

$$\text{Total variable cost} = \$4 \times \text{Units produced}$$

If 100 insert heaters are produced, the total cost of pipe segments is \$400 (\$4 × 100). If 200 insert heaters are produced, the total cost is \$800 (\$4 × 200). As production doubles, the cost of the 3-inch segments doubles. In other words, cost increases in direct proportion to the number of units produced. The linear relationship for the pipe-segments example is shown in Exhibit 3-7. How reasonable is this assumption that costs are linear? Do variable activity costs really increase in direct proportion to increases in the level of the activity driver? If not, then how closely does this assumed linear cost function approximate the underlying cost function?

Economists usually argue that variable costs increase at a decreasing rate up to a certain volume, at which point they increase at an increasing rate. This type of nonlinear behavior is displayed in Exhibit 3-8. Here, variable costs increase as the number of units increases, but not in direct proportion. For example, a power supplier that initially has ample capacity may set prices that decrease per kilowatt-hour to encourage consumption; yet once the power plant capacity has been met, any further demands may produce higher prices to ration a now-scarce resource among users. What if the nonlinear view more accurately portrays reality? What do we do

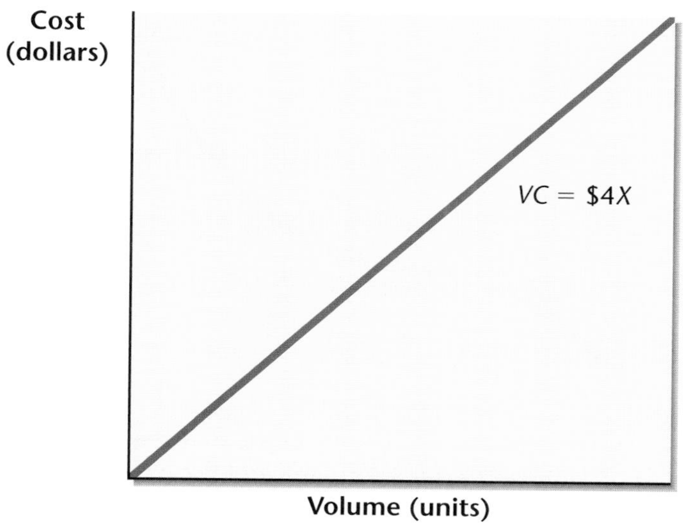

Exhibit 3-7 Linearity of Variable Costs: 3-Inch Segments, Reddy Heaters

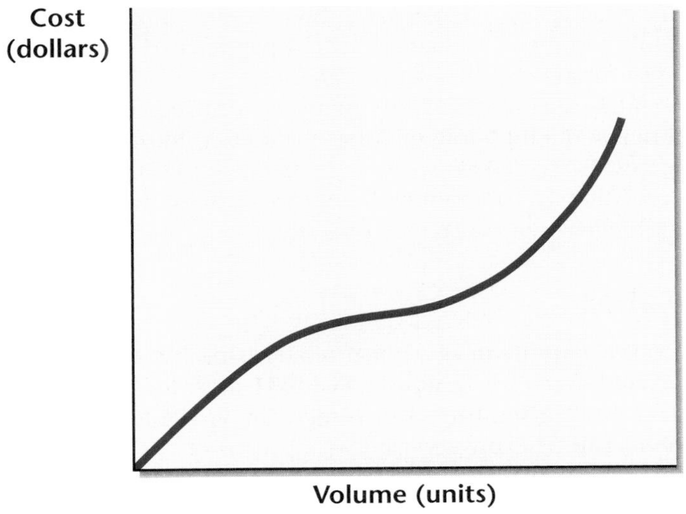

Exhibit 3-8 Nonlinearity of Variable Costs

then? One possibility is to determine the actual cost function. But every activity could have a different cost function, and this approach could be very time consuming and expensive (if it can even be done). It is much simpler to assume a linear relationship.

If the linear relationship is assumed, then the main concern is how well this assumption approximates the underlying cost function. Exhibit 3-9 gives us some idea of the consequences of assuming a linear cost function. Recall that the relevant range is the range of output for which the assumed cost relationships are valid. Here, validity refers to how closely the linear cost function approximates the underlying cost function. Note that for units of the activity driver beyond X_1 the approximation appears to break down.

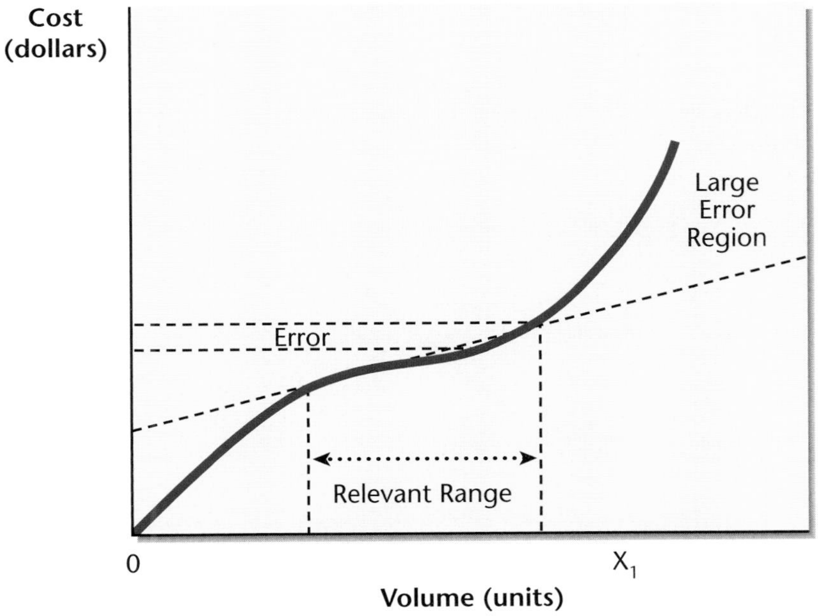

Exhibit 3-9 Linear Approximation

The equation for a straight line is

Total cost = Fixed cost + (Variable rate × Output)

This equation is a **cost formula**. Let's take a closer look at each term in the cost formula. The *dependent variable* is the cost we are trying to predict, or "Total cost." In this equation, total cost depends on only one variable, "Output." Output is the measure of activity; it is the *independent variable.* "Fixed cost" is the *intercept parameter,* and it is the fixed cost portion of total cost. Finally, "Variable rate" is the cost per unit of activity; it is also called the *slope parameter.* Exhibit 3-10 shows this graphically.

The **dependent variable** is a variable whose value depends on the value of another variable. It is easy to see that we are trying to find the "Total cost"—and that its value depends on the values of the parameters and variable on the right-hand side of the equation. The **independent variable** is a variable that measures output and explains changes in the cost. It is an activity driver. The choice of an independent variable is related to its economic plausibility. That is, the manager will attempt to find an independent variable that causes or is closely associated with the dependent variable. The **intercept parameter** corresponds to fixed cost. Graphically, the intercept parameter is the point at which the mixed-cost line intercepts the cost (vertical) axis. The **slope parameter** corresponds to the variable cost per unit of activity. Graphically, this represents the slope of the mixed-cost line.

Since accounting records reveal only the amount of activity output and the total cost, those values must be used to estimate the intercept and slope parameters (the fixed cost and the variable rate). With estimates of fixed cost and variable rate, the fixed and variable components can be estimated, and the behavior of the mixed cost can be predicted as activity usage changes.

Three methods will be described for estimating the fixed cost and the variable rate. These methods are the high-low method, the scatterplot method, and the method of least squares. The same data will be used with each method so that comparisons among them can be made. The data have been accumulated for the setup activity of Reddy Heaters' Newark, New Jersey, plant. The plant manager believes that setup hours are a good driver for the activity setting up the production line. Assume that the accounting records of the plant disclose the following setup costs and setup hours for the past five months:

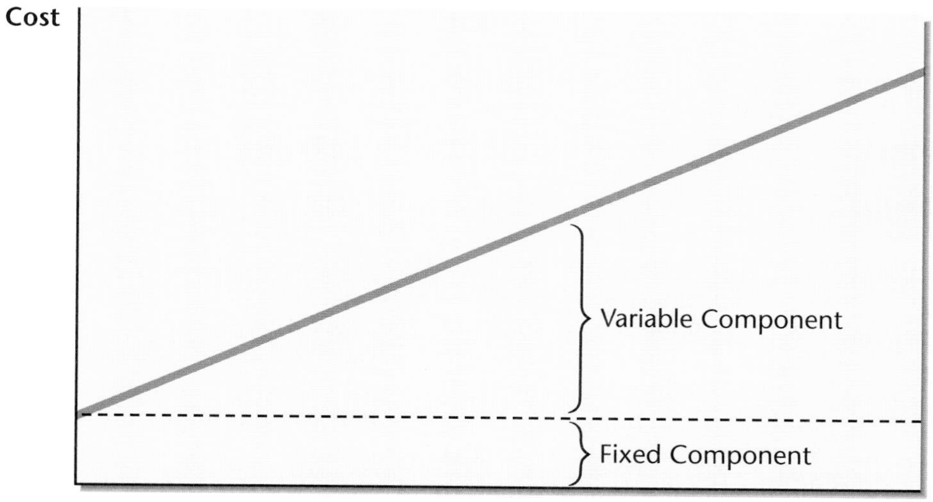

Exhibit 3-10 Mixed-Cost Behavior

Month	Setup Costs	Setup Hours
January	$1,000	100
February	1,250	200
March	2,250	300
April	2,500	400
May	3,750	500

The High-Low Method

From basic geometry, we know that two points are needed to determine a line. Once we know two points on a line, then we can determine its equation. Given two points, the intercept (fixed cost) and the slope (variable rate) can be determined. The **high-low method** is a method of determining the equation of a straight line by preselecting two points (the high and low points) that will be used to compute the intercept and slope parameters. The *high point* is defined as the point with the highest output or activity level. The *low point* is defined as the point with the lowest output or activity level. Notice that both the high and the low point are determined by the high amount and the low amount for the independent variable.

The equations for determining the variable rate and fixed cost are, respectively:

Variable rate = Change in cost/Change in output
Variable rate = (High cost − Low cost)/(High output − Low output)

and

Fixed cost = Total cost for high point − (Variable rate × High output)

or

Fixed cost = Total cost for low point − (Variable rate × Low output)

Notice that the fixed-cost component is computed using the total cost at either the high point or the low point.

For Reddy Heaters, the high point is 500 setup hours at a cost of $3,750, or (500, $3,750). The low point is 100 setup hours at a cost of $1,000, or (100, $1,000). Once the high and low points are defined, the values for the fixed cost and the variable rate can be computed:

Variable rate = ($3,750 − $1,000)/(500 − 100)
= $2,750/400
= $6.875

Fixed cost = Total cost for high point − (Variable rate × High output)
= $3,750 − ($6.875 × 500)
= $312.50

Finally, the cost formula using the high-low method is:

Total cost = $312.50 + ($6.875 × Setup hours)

The key point about the total cost formula determined above is that it is the formula used to predict setup costs based on the number of setup hours. If the number of setup hours for June is expected to be 350, this cost formula will predict a total cost of $2,718.75, with fixed costs of $312.50 and variable costs of $2,406.25.

The high-low method has the advantage of objectivity. That is, any two people using the high-low method on a particular data set will arrive at the same answer. In addition, the high-low method allows a manager to get a quick fix on a cost relationship using only two data points. For example, a manager may have only two years of data. Sometimes, this will be enough to get a crude approximation of the cost relationship.

The high-low method is usually not as accurate as the other methods. Why? First, the high and low points may be outliers. Outliers represent atypical cost-activity relationships. If so, the cost formula computed using these two points will not represent what usually takes place. The scatterplot method can help a manager avoid this trap by selecting two points that appear to be representative of the general activity cost pattern. Second, even if these points are not outliers, other pairs of points clearly may be more representative. Again, the scatterplot method allows the choice of the more representative points.

The Scatterplot Method

The **scatterplot method** is a method of determining the equation of a line by plotting the data on a graph. The first step in applying the scatterplot method is to plot the data points so that the relationship between setup costs and activity level can be seen. This plot is referred to as a **scattergraph** and is shown in Exhibit 3-11. The vertical axis is total setup cost, and the horizontal axis is number of setup hours. Inspecting Exhibit 3-11 gives us increased confidence that the assumption of a linear relationship between setup costs and setup hours is reasonable for the indicated range of activity. Thus, one purpose of a scattergraph is to see whether or not an assumed linear relationship is reasonable. Additionally, inspecting the scattergraph may reveal several points that do not seem to fit the general pattern of behavior. Upon investigation, it may be discovered that these points (the outliers) were due to some unusual occurrences. This knowledge may justify their elimination and perhaps lead to a better estimate of the underlying cost function.

A scattergraph can help provide insight concerning the relationship between cost and activity usage. In fact, a scattergraph allows one to visually fit a line to the points on the scattergraph. In doing so, the line chosen should be the one that appears to best fit the points. In making that choice, a manager or cost analyst is free to use past experience with the behavior of the cost item. Experience may provide a good intuitive sense of how setup costs behave; the scattergraph then becomes a useful tool to quantify this intuition. Fitting a line to the points in this

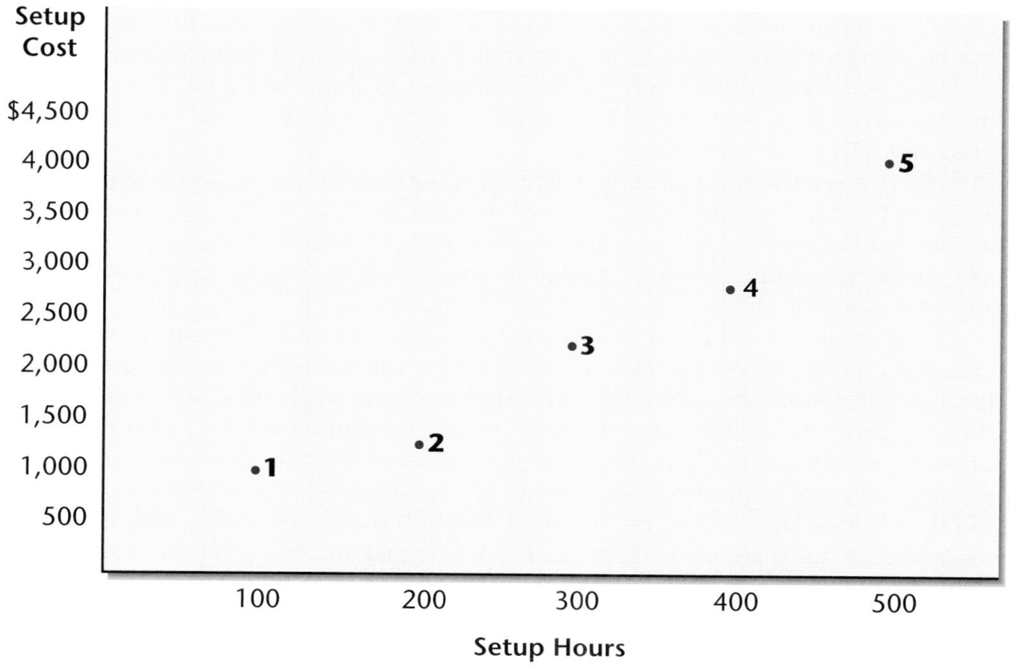

Exhibit 3-11 Scattergraph for Reddy Heaters, New Jersey Plant

way is how the scatterplot method works. Keep in mind that the scattergraph and other statistical aids are tools that can help managers improve their judgment. Using the tools does not restrict the manager from using judgment to alter any of the estimates produced by formal methods.

Examine Exhibit 3-11 carefully. Based only on the information contained in the graph, how would you fit a line to the points in it? Suppose that you decide that a line passing through points 1 and 3 provides the best fit. If so, how could this decision be used to compute the fixed cost and variable rate so that the fixed- and variable-cost components can be estimated?

Assuming your choice of the best-fitting line is the one passing through points 1 and 3, the variable cost per unit can be computed in the following way. First, let point 1 be designated by (100, \$1,000) and point 3 by (300, \$2,250). Next, use these two points to compute the slope:

$$\begin{aligned}\text{Variable rate} &= (\$2{,}250 - \$1{,}000)/(300 - 100)\\ &= \$1{,}250/200\\ &= \$6.25\end{aligned}$$

Thus, the variable cost per setup hour is \$6.25. Given the variable cost per unit, the final step is to compute the fixed-cost component. If we use point 3, the following equation results:

$$\begin{aligned}\text{Fixed cost} &= \$2{,}250 - (\$6.25 \times 300)\\ &= \$375\end{aligned}$$

Of course, the fixed-cost component can also be computed using point 1, which produces the same result.

$$\begin{aligned}\text{Fixed cost} &= \$1{,}000 - (\$6.25 \times 100)\\ &= \$375\end{aligned}$$

The fixed and variable components of setup cost have now been identified. The cost formula for the setup activity can be expressed as:

$$\text{Total cost} = \$375 + (\$6.25 \times \text{Setup hours})$$

Using this formula, the total cost of setting up for between 100 and 500 setup hours can be predicted and then broken down into fixed and variable components. For example, assume that 350 setup hours are planned for June. Using the cost formula, the predicted cost is \$2,562.50 [\$375 + (\$6.25 × 350)]. Of this total cost, \$375 is fixed and \$2,187.50 is variable.

The cost formula for the setup activity was obtained by fitting a line to points 1 and 3 in Exhibit 3-11. Judgment was used to select the line. While one person may decide that the best-fitting line is the one that passes through points 1 and 3, others, using their own judgment, may decide that the line should pass through points 2 and 4, or points 1 and 5.

A significant advantage of the scatterplot method is that it allows us to see the data. Exhibit 3-12 gives examples of cost behavior situations that are not appropriate for a simple application of the high-low method. Graph A shows a nonlinear relationship between activity cost and activity usage. An example of this might be a volume discount given on direct materials or evidence of learning by workers (for example, as more hours are worked, the total cost increases at a decreasing rate due to the increased efficiency of the workers). Graph B shows an upward shift in cost if more than X_1 units are made. Perhaps this means that an additional supervisor must be hired or a second shift run. Graph C shows outliers that are not representative of the overall cost relationship.

The scatterplot method suffers from the lack of any objective criterion for choosing the best-fitting line. The quality of the cost formula depends on the quality of the subjective judgment of the analyst. The high-low method removes the subjectivity in the choice of the line. Regardless of who uses the method, the same line will result.

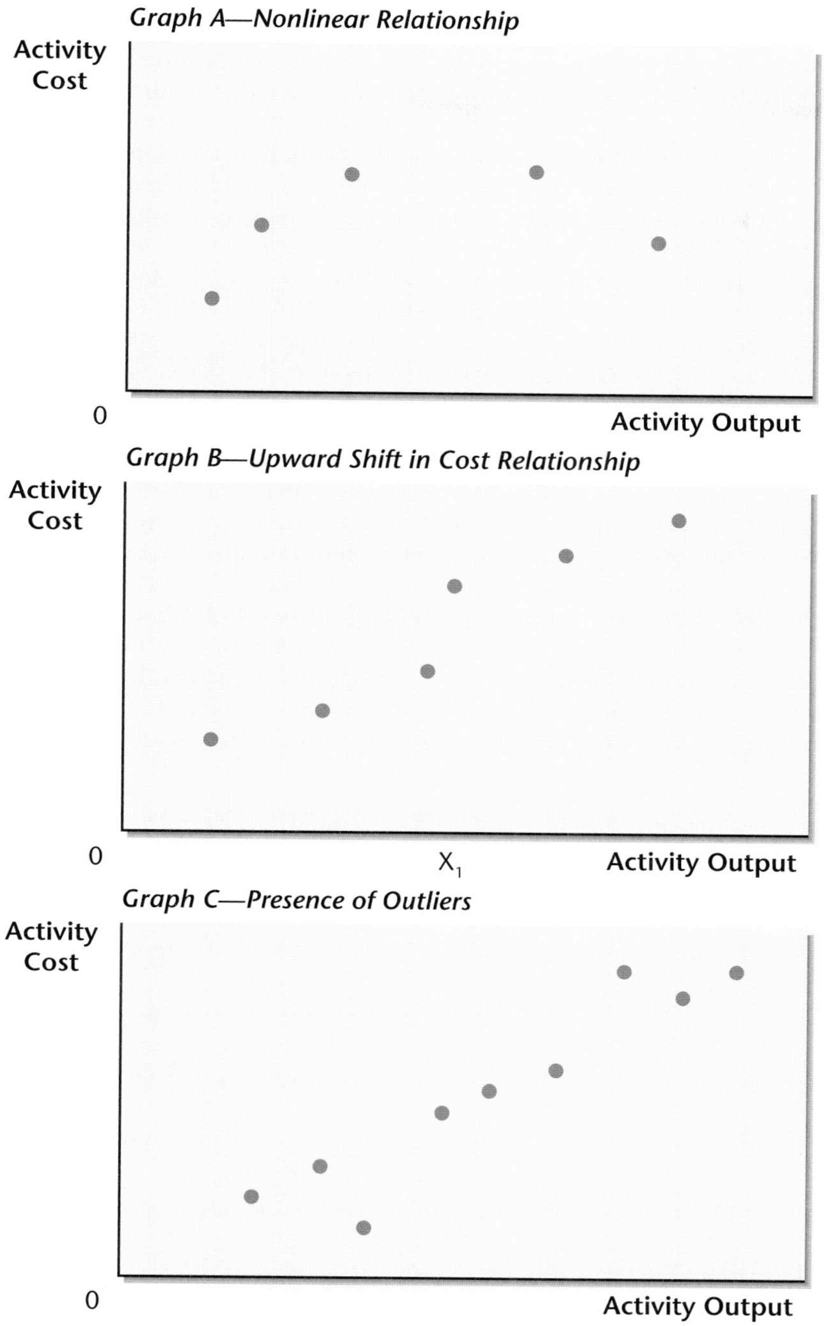

Exhibit 3-12 Cost Behavior Patterns

The scatterplot and high-low methods produce equations with a large difference in fixed and variable components. Using these equations, the predicted setup cost for 350 setup hours is $2,562.50 according to the scatterplot method and $2,718.75 according to the high-low method. Which is "right"? Since the two methods can produce significantly different cost formulas, the question of which method is better naturally arises. Ideally, a method that is objective and, at the same time, produces the best-fitting line is needed. The method of least squares defines best fitting and is objective in the sense that using the method for a given set of data will produce the same cost formula.

The Method of Least Squares

Up to this point, we have alluded to the concept of a line that best fits the points shown on a scattergraph. What do we mean by best-fitting line? Intuitively, it is the line to which the data points are closest. But what is meant by closest?

Recall that we are looking for a straight line that is the best predictor of total cost for some activity. Consider Exhibit 3-13. Here, an arbitrary line has been drawn. The closeness of each point to the line can be measured by the vertical distance of the point from the line. This vertical distance is the difference between the actual cost and the cost predicted by the line. For point 5, the predicted cost is 5*, and the deviation is the distance between points 5 and 5* (the distance from the point to the line).

The vertical distance measures the closeness of a single point to the line, but we need a measure of how close all the points are to the line. One possibility is to measure the deviations of all points to the line and add all the single measures to obtain an overall measure. However, this overall measure may be misleading. For example, the sum of small positive deviations could result in an overall measure greater than the sum of large positive deviations and large negative deviations because of the canceling effect of positive and negative numbers. To correct for this problem, the **method of least squares** first squares each single deviation and then sums these squared deviations as the overall measure of closeness. Squaring the deviations avoids the cancellation problem caused by a mix of positive and negative numbers.

Since the measure of closeness is the sum of the squared deviations of the points from the line, the smaller the measure, the better the line fits the points. For example, the scatterplot method line has a closeness measure of 343,750. A similar calculation produces a closeness measure of 523,438 for the high-low line. Thus, the scatterplot line fits the points better than the high-low line. This outcome supports

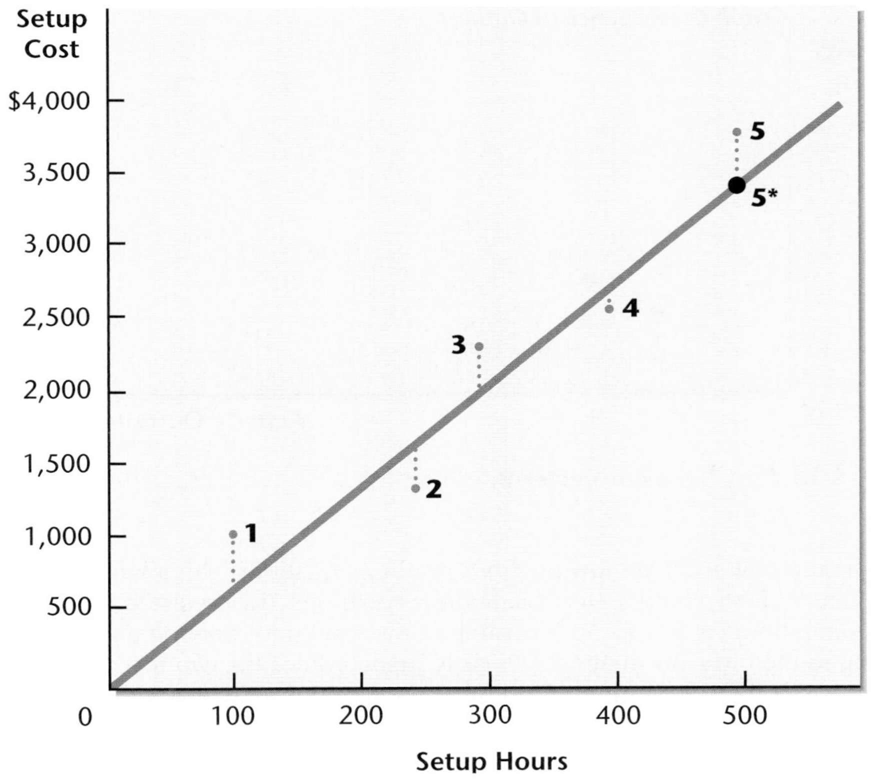

Exhibit 3-13 Line Deviations

the earlier claim that the use of judgment in the scatterplot method is superior to the high-low method.

In principle, comparing closeness measures can produce a ranking of all lines from best to worst. The line that fits the points better than any other line is called the **best-fitting line**. It is the line with the smallest (least) sum of squared deviations. The method of least squares identifies the best-fitting line. You can learn the manual computation of the least squares formulas in a statistics class. For our purposes, we can let a computer regression program do the computations for us.

Using the Regression Programs

Spreadsheet packages facilitate regression analysis for large data sets and multiple variables.

© Getty Images/PhotoDisc

Computing the regression formula manually is tedious, even with only five data points. As the number of data points increases, manual computation becomes impractical. (Instructions for the manual computation of simple regression are provided on the text's website under Alternative Coverage. When multiple regression is used, manual computation is virtually impossible.) Fortunately, spreadsheet packages such as Lotus 1-2-3, Quattro Pro, and Microsoft Excel[2] have regression routines that will perform the computations. All you need to do is input the data. The spreadsheet regression program supplies more than the estimates of the coefficients. It also provides information that can be used to see how reliable the cost equation is—a feature that is not available for the scatterplot and high-low methods.

The first step in using the computer to calculate regression coefficients is to enter the data. Exhibit 3-14 shows the computer screen you would see if you entered the Reddy Heaters data on setups into a spreadsheet. It is a good idea to label your variables as is done here. That is, the months are labeled, as is column B for setup costs and column C for number of setup hours. The next step is to run the regression. In Excel (ver. 7) and Quattro Pro (ver. 8), the regression routine is located under the "tools" menu (located toward the top right of the screen). When you pull down the "tools" menu, you will see other menu possibilities. In Quattro Pro, choose "numeric tools" and then "regression." In Excel, choose "add in" and then add the "data analysis tools." When the data analysis tools have been added, "data analysis" will appear at the bottom of the "tools" menu; click on "data analysis," and then click on "regression."

When the "regression" screen pops up, you can tell the program where the dependent and independent variables are located. It is easy to simply place the cursor at the beginning of the "independent" rectangle and then (again using the cursor) block the values under the independent variable column, in this case, cells C2 through C6. Then, move the cursor to the beginning of the "dependent" rectangle and block the values in cells B2 through B6. Finally, you need to tell the computer where to place the output. Block a nice-sized rectangle, say cells A9 through F16, and click on "OK." In less than the blink of an eye, the regression output is complete. The regression output is shown in Exhibit 3-15.

Now, let's take a look at the output in Exhibit 3-15. First, let's locate the fixed cost and variable rate coefficients. These are highlighted in the exhibit. The fixed cost is the constant, in this case, 125. The variable rate is the X coefficient, here, 6.75. Now, we can construct the cost formula for setup costs. It is:

$$\text{Setup costs} = \$125 + (\$6.75 \times \text{Setup hours})$$

2 Quattro Pro is a registered trademark of **Novell, Inc.** Excel is a registered trademark of **Microsoft Corporation.** Any reference to Quattro Pro or Excel refers to this footnote.

Spreadsheet Data for Reddy Heaters.xls

Month	Setup Costs	Setup Hours
Jan	1,000	100
Feb	1,250	200
Mar	2,250	300
Apr	2,500	400
May	3,750	500

Exhibit 3-14 Spreadsheet Data for Reddy Heaters

We can use this formula to predict setup costs for future months as we did with the formulas for the high-low and scatterplot methods.

Since the regression cost formula is the best-fitting line, it should produce better predictions of setup costs. For 350 setup hours, the setup cost predicted by the least-squares line is \$2,487.50 [\$125 + (\$6.75 × 350)], with a fixed component of \$125 plus a variable component of \$2,362.50. Using this prediction as a standard, the scatterplot line most closely approximates the least-squares line.

Regression Output for Reddy Heaters.xls

	Regression Output:		
Constant			125
Std Err of Y Est			299.304749934466
R Squared			0.944300518134715
No. of Observation			5
Degrees of Freedom			3
X Coefficient(s)		6.75	
Std Err of Coef.		0.9464847243	

Exhibit 3-15 Regression Output for Reddy Heaters

Reliability of Cost Formulas

Objective 4

Evaluate the reliability of a cost equation.

While the computer output in Exhibit 3-15 can give us the fixed and variable cost coefficients, its major usefulness lies in its ability to provide information about how reliable the estimated cost formula is. This is a feature not provided by either the scatterplot or high-low methods. We will use the output in Exhibit 3-15 as the basis for discussing a statistical assessment of a cost formula's reliability: **goodness of fit**. Although the output provides other useful information for assessing statistical reliability, we will just look at goodness of fit. This measure is important because the method of least squares identifies the best-fitting line, but it does not reveal how good the fit is. The best-fitting line may not be a good-fitting line. It may perform miserably when it comes to predicting costs.

R^2—The Coefficient of Determination

Initially, we assume that a single activity driver explains changes (variability) in activity cost. Our experience with the Reddy Heaters example suggests that setup hours can explain changes in setup costs. The scattergraph shown in Exhibit 3-11 confirms this belief because it reveals that setup costs and setup hours seem to move together. Thus, it seems reasonable that setup hours would explain much of the variability in setup costs. We can determine statistically just how much variability is explained by looking at the *coefficient of determination*, or R^2. R^2, or the **coefficient of determination**, is the percentage of variability in the dependent variable that is explained by an independent variable. This percentage is a goodness-of-fit measure. The higher the percentage of cost variability explained, the better the fit. Since the coefficient of determination is the proportion of variability explained, it always has a value between 0 and 1.0. In Exhibit 3-15, the coefficient of determination is labeled "R Squared" and is highlighted. The value given is 0.944301, which means that about 94 percent of the variability in setup costs is explained by the number of setup hours. This result tells us that the least-squares line is a good-fitting line.

There is no cutoff point for a good versus a bad coefficient of determination. Clearly, the closer R^2 is to 1, the better. However, is 89 percent good enough? How about 73 percent? Or even 46 percent? The answer is that it depends. If your cost formula yields a coefficient of determination of 75 percent, you know that your independent variable explains three-fourths of the variability in cost. You also know that some other factor or combination of factors explains the remaining one-fourth. Depending on your tolerance for error, you may want to improve the equation by trying different independent variables (for example, number of setups rather than setup hours) or by trying multiple regression (which is explained in a succeeding section of this chapter).

Coefficient of Correlation

Another measure of goodness of fit is the **coefficient of correlation**, which is the square root of the coefficient of determination. Since square roots can be negative, the value of the coefficient of correlation can range between -1 and $+1$. If the coefficient of correlation is positive, then the two variables (in this example, cost and activity) move together in the same direction, and positive correlation exists. Perfect positive correlation would yield a value of 1.00 for the coefficient of correlation. If, on the other hand, the coefficient of correlation is negative, then the two variables move in a predictable fashion but in opposite directions. Perfect negative correlation would yield a coefficient of correlation of -1.00. A coefficient of correlation value close to zero indicates no correlation. That is, knowledge of the movement of one variable gives us no clue as to the movement of the other variable. Exhibit 3-16 illustrates the concept of correlation.

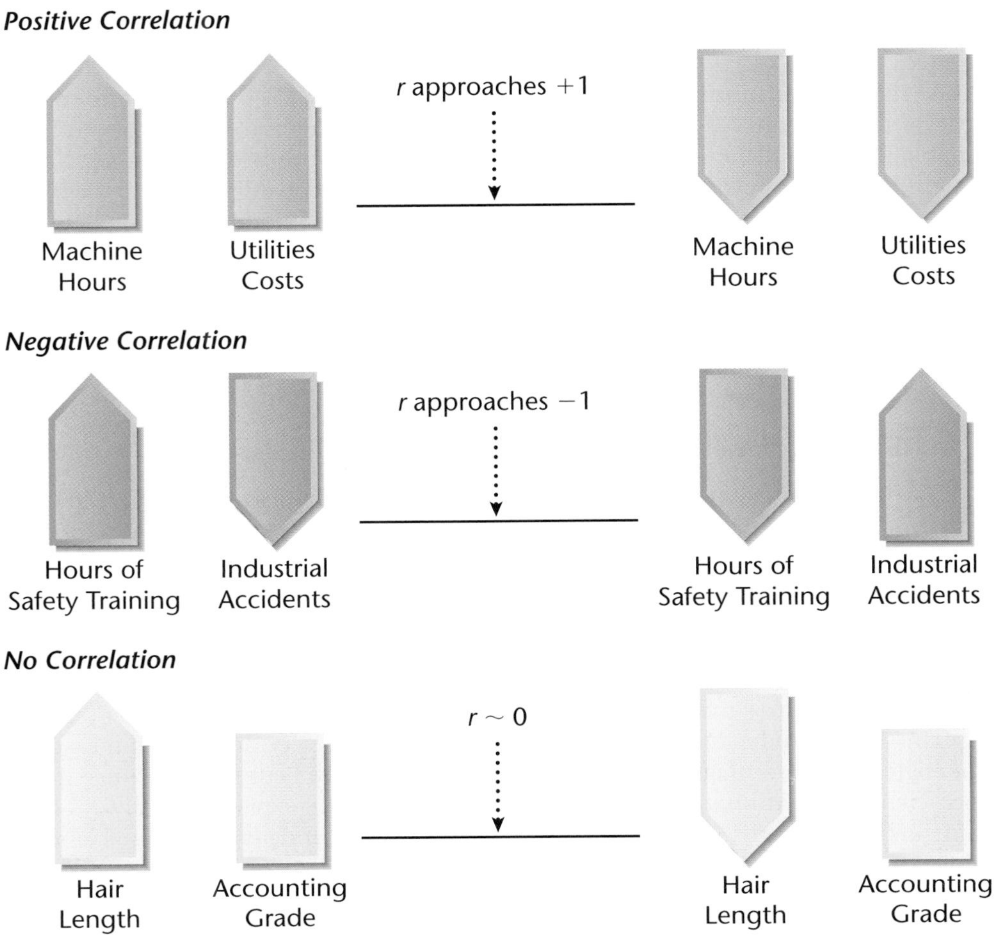

Exhibit 3-16 Correlation Illustrated

For the Reddy Heaters example, the coefficient of correlation (r) is simply the square root of R^2, or $0.97 = \sqrt{.094}$. However, square roots can be either positive or negative. What is the sign for Reddy Heaters? The square root here is positive because the correlation between setup hours and setup cost is positive. In other words, as the number of setup hours worked increases, the total setup cost also increases. This positive correlation is reflected by a positive sign on the X coefficient shown in Exhibit 3-15. If cost decreases as activity usage increases, then the coefficient of correlation (and the value of the X coefficient) is negative. The sign of the coefficient reveals the sign of the coefficient of correlation. The very high positive correlation between setup costs and setup hours indicates that setup hours is a good choice for a cost driver.

Multiple Regression

Objective 5

Discuss the role of multiple regression in assessing cost behavior.

Sometimes, obtaining the best cost formula is more complicated than simply identifying one activity driver and regressing activity cost on this driver. The outcome may not produce a cost formula that is good enough for managerial use. For Reddy Heaters, 94 percent of the variability in setup cost was explained by changes in activity output (setup hours), and that is an excellent result. In other cases, however, a single independent variable may explain much less of the variability in the dependent variable. Then, one possible solution is to search for additional explanatory variables.

In the case of two or more explanatory variables, the linear equation is expanded to include the additional variables:

$$\text{Total cost} = b_0 + (b_1 \times X_1) + (b_2 \times X_2) + \ldots.$$

Where:

b_0 = the fixed cost or intercept
b_1 = the variable rate for the first independent variable
X_1 = the first independent variable
b_2 = the variable rate for the second independent variable
X_2 = the second independent variable

When there are two or more independent variables, the high-low and scatterplot methods cannot be used. Fortunately, the extension of the method of least squares is straightforward. Whenever least squares is used to fit an equation involving two or more explanatory variables, the method is called **multiple regression**. Because the computations required for multiple regression are so complex, a computer is required.

For example, suppose that the accounting supervisor for the Reddy Heaters New Jersey plant is analyzing the plant's utilities cost. The accounting supervisor knows that electricity is used to power the machines and suspects that machine hours would be a good driver. In addition, utilities are also used to power the air conditioning, and the cost of utilities in the summer rises significantly for this reason. Thus, utilities cost is explained by more than one variable and produces a more complex cost equation.

$$\text{Utilities cost} = \text{Fixed cost} + (b_1 \times \text{Machine hours}) + (b_2 \times \text{Summer})$$

In this equation, machine hours is a continuous variable that takes on values much like those for setup hours. The variable "Summer" requires further explanation. "Summer" is a dichotomous or dummy variable; it takes on the values 0 and 1. That is, a particular month either is in the summer or it is not. In New Jersey, there are five hot months in the year, May through September. These will be defined as summer months for purposes of our regression. Exhibit 3-17 illustrates 12 months of data for the utilities regression.

Let's take a closer look at the data in Exhibit 3-17. In January, there were 1,340 machine hours, total utilities cost was $1,740, and January is not a summer month—hence, the variable "Summer" takes the value 0. In May, there were 1,500 machine hours, it is a summer month (so "Summer" takes the value 1), and total utilities cost was $2,390. The other 10 months of data can be interpreted in the same manner.

When multiple regression is run on these data, the results in Exhibit 3-18 are obtained. These results give rise to the following equation:

$$\text{Utilities cost} = \$291.58 + (\$1.068 \times \text{Machine hours}) + (\$501.88 \times \text{Summer})$$

This equation can be used to predict utilities for future months. Suppose that the accountant wants to predict the cost of utilities for the following April and anticipates 1,350 machine hours. The budgeted cost would be $1,733.38 [$291.58 + ($1.068 × 1,350) + ($501.88 × 0)]. If, instead, the cost of utilities for May were to be predicted based on 1,350 machine hours, budgeted cost would be $2,235.26 [$291.58 + ($1.068 × 1,350) + ($501.88 × 1)].

Notice that the R^2 is 0.99, or 99 percent. You might try running the above regression using just machine hours as the independent variable. The R^2 for that regression is much lower, clearly indicating the value of adding the second driver.

Month	Mhrs	Summer	Utilities Cost
Jan	1340	0	$1,740
Feb	1298	0	1,636
Mar	1376	0	1,788
April	1405	0	1,770
May	1500	1	2,390
June	1432	1	2,304
July	1322	1	2,250
Aug	1416	1	2,284
Sept	1370	1	2,260
Oct	1580	0	1,991
Nov	1460	0	1,840
Dec	1455	0	1,867

Exhibit 3-17 Data for Reddy Heaters Utilities Cost Regression

Constant		291.5792
Std Err of Y Est		27.57531
R Squared		0.991396
No. of Observation		12
Degrees of Freedom		9
X Coefficient(s)	1.068282	501.88
Std Err of Coef.	0.104435868	16.16961742

Exhibit 3-18 Multiple Regression Results for Reddy Heaters Utilities Cost

Managerial Judgment

Objective 6

Describe the use of managerial judgment in determining cost behavior.

Managerial judgment is critically important in determining cost behavior, and it is a widely used method in practice. Many managers simply use their experience and past observation of cost relationships to determine fixed and variable costs. This method, however, may take a number of forms. Some managers simply assign particular activity costs to the fixed category and others to the variable category, ignoring the possibility of mixed costs. Thus, a chemical firm may regard materials and utilities as strictly variable with respect to pounds of chemical produced and all

Managers Decide

Variable Costing Income

In Germany and other European countries, many companies are now providing variable costing income statements to investors. For example, Andreas STIHL, Inc., a manufacturer of leaf blowers, chain saws, trimmers, and other assorted landscaping products, requires all of its European subsidiaries to report both absorption costing income (following typical U.S. Generally Accepted Accounting Principles (GAAP)) and variable costing income. Variable costing income classifies expenses by their cost behavior. First, all expenses that vary with production volume are subtracted from sales to yield the firm's contribution margin. Next, fixed costs are subtracted from contribution margin to yield operating income. The objective of the dual reporting is to facilitate decision making on various issues such as pricing and make-or-buy decisions. This reporting requirement means that all manufacturing costs must be broken out into fixed and variable components. ■

Source: Carl S. Smith, "Going for GPK," *Strategic Finance*, Apr. 2005; 86, 10, pp. 36-39.

other costs as fixed. Even labor, a traditional and common example of a unit-based variable cost, may be fixed for this firm. The appeal of this method is simplicity. Before opting for this course, management would do well to make sure that each cost is predominantly fixed or variable and that the decisions being made are not highly sensitive to errors in classifying costs. To illustrate the use of judgment in assessing cost behavior, Reddy Heater, before implementing its ABC system, used production volume as a driver and used its chart of accounts to organize costs into fixed and variable components. Reddy's accountants used their knowledge of the company to assign expenses, using a decision rule that categorized an expense as fixed if it were fixed 75 percent of the time and variable if it were variable 75 percent of the time.

Management may instead identify mixed costs and divide these costs into fixed and variable components by deciding just what the fixed and variable parts are—that is, using experience to say that a certain amount of a cost is fixed and that, therefore, the rest must be variable. For example, a factory may put the lease payments for a photocopier into one account and the cost of paper and toner into another. The result is that it is easy to group the lease account with other fixed cost accounts and to treat the variable costs separately. Then, the variable component can be computed using one or more cost/volume data points. This has the advantage of accounting for mixed costs but is subject to a similar type of error as the strict fixed/variable dichotomy. That is, management may be wrong in its assessment.

Finally, management may use experience and judgment to refine statistical estimation results. Perhaps the experienced manager might "eyeball" the data and throw out several points as being highly unusual or might revise results of estimation to take into account projected changes in cost structure or technology. Statistical techniques are highly accurate in depicting the past, but they cannot foresee the future, which is, of course, what management really wants.

The advantage of using managerial judgment to separate fixed and variable costs is its simplicity. In situations in which the manager has a deep understanding of the firm and its cost patterns, this method can give good results. However, if the manager does not have good judgment, errors will occur. Therefore, it is important to consider the experience of the manager, the potential for error, and the effect that the error could have on related decisions.

Summary of Learning Objectives

1. Define cost behavior for fixed, variable, and mixed costs.

Cost behavior is the way in which a cost changes in relation to changes in activity usage. The time horizon is important in determining cost behavior because costs can change from fixed to variable depending on whether the decision takes place over the short run or the long run. Variable costs are those that change in total as activity usage changes. Usually, we assume that variable costs increase in direct proportion to increases in activity usage. Fixed costs are those that do not change in total as activity usage changes. Mixed costs have both a variable and a fixed component.

2. Explain the role of the resource usage model in understanding cost behavior.

The resource usage model adds to our understanding of cost behavior. Resources acquired in advance of usage are categorized as committed resources. Resources acquired as used and needed are flexible resources. Some costs, especially discretionary fixed costs, tend to follow a step-cost function. These resources are acquired in lumpy amounts. If the width of the step is sufficiently large, then the costs are viewed as fixed; otherwise, they are approximated by a variable cost function.

3. Separate mixed costs into their fixed and variable components using the high-low method, the scatterplot method, and the method of least squares.

There are three formal methods of decomposing mixed costs: the high-low method, the scatterplot method, and the method of least squares. In the high-low method, the two points chosen from the scattergraph are the high and low points with respect to activity level. These two points are then used to compute the intercept and the slope of the line on which they lie. The high-low method is objective and easy. However, if either the high or low point is not representative of the true cost relationship, the relationship will be estimated incorrectly.

The scatterplot method involves inspecting a scattergraph (a plot showing total mixed cost at various activity levels) and selecting two points that seem best to represent the relationship between cost and activity. Since two points determine a line, the two selected points can be used to determine the intercept and the slope of the line on which they lie. The intercept gives an estimate of the fixed-cost component, and the slope gives an estimate of the variable cost per unit of activity. The scatterplot method is a good way to identify nonlinearity, the presence of outliers, and the presence of a shift in the cost relationship. Its disadvantage is that it is subjective.

The method of least squares uses all of the data points (except outliers) on the scattergraph and produces a line that best fits all of the points. The line is best fitting in the sense that it is closest to all the points as measured by the sum of the squared deviations of the points from the line. The method of least squares produces the line that best fits the data points and is, therefore, recommended over the high-low and scatterplot methods.

4. Evaluate the reliability of a cost equation.

The least-squares method has the advantage of offering methods to assess the reliability of cost equations. The coefficient of determination allows an analyst to compute the amount of cost variability explained by a particular cost driver. The correlation coefficient also measures the strength of the association but has the additional advantage of indicating the direction of the relationship.

5. Discuss the role of multiple regression in assessing cost behavior.

One driver may not be sufficient in explaining enough of the variability in activity cost behavior. In this case, adding additional variables to the equation may increase its ability to predict activity costs as well as provide insights on how activity cost can be managed.

6. Describe the use of managerial judgment in determining cost behavior.

Managerial judgment can be used alone or in conjunction with the high-low, scatterplot, or least-squares methods. Managers use their experience and knowledge of cost and activity-level relationships to identify outliers, understand structural shifts, and adjust parameters due to anticipated changing conditions.

Key Terms

Review Problems

1. Resource Usage and Cost Behavior

Kaylin Manufacturing Company has three salaried accounts payable clerks responsible for processing purchase invoices. Each clerk is paid a salary of $30,000 and is capable of processing 5,000 invoices per year (working efficiently). In addition to the salaries, Kaylin spends $9,000 per year for forms, postage, checks, and so on (assuming 15,000 invoices are processed). During the year, 12,500 invoices were processed.

Required

1. Calculate the activity rate for the purchase order activity. Break the activity into fixed and variable components.
2. Compute the total activity availability, and break this into activity usage and unused activity.
3. Calculate the total cost of resources supplied, and break this into activity usage and unused activity.

Solution

1. Activity rate = [(3 × $30,000) + $9,000]/15,000
= $6.60 per invoice
Fixed activity rate = $90,000/15,000 = $6.00 per invoice
Variable activity rate = $9,000/15,000 = $0.60 per invoice

2. Activity availability = Activity usage + Unused activity
15,000 invoices = 12,500 invoices + 2,500 invoices

3. Cost of resources supplied = Cost of activity used + Cost of unused activity
$90,000 + ($0.60 × 12,500) = ($6.60 × 12,500) + ($6.00 × 2,500)
$97,500 = $82,500 + $15,000

2. High-Low and Least-Squares Methods

Kim Wilson, controller for Max Enterprises, has decided to estimate the fixed and variable components associated with the company's shipping activity. She has collected the following data for the past six months:

Packages Shipped	Total Shipping Costs
10	$ 800
20	1,100
15	900
12	900
18	1,050
25	1,250

Required

1. Estimate the fixed and variable components for the shipping costs using the high-low method. Using the cost formula, predict the total cost of shipping if 14 packages are shipped.
2. Estimate the fixed and variable components using the method of least squares. Using the cost formula, predict the total cost of shipping if 14 packages are shipped.
3. For the method of least squares, explain what the coefficient of determination tells us. Compute the coefficient of correlation.

Solution

1. The estimate of fixed and variable costs using the high-low method is as follows:

$$\begin{aligned}
\text{Variable rate} &= (\$1{,}250 - \$800)/(25 - 10) \\
&= \$450/15 \\
&= \$30 \text{ per package} \\
\text{Fixed amount} &= \$1{,}250 - \$30(25) = \$500 \\
\text{Total cost} &= \$500 + \$30X \\
&= \$500 + \$30(14) \\
&= \$920
\end{aligned}$$

2. The output of a spreadsheet regression routine is as follows:

Regression Output:		
Constant		509.911894273125
Std Err of Y Est		32.1965672507378
R Squared		0.96928536465981
		4
No. of Observations		6
Degrees of Freedom		4
X Coefficient(s)	29.4052863436125	
Std Err of Coef.	2.61723229918858	

Y = \$509.91 + \$29.41(14) = \$921.65

3. The coefficient of determination (R^2) tells us that about 96.9 percent of total shipping cost is explained by the number of packages shipped. The correlation coefficient (r) equals the square root of the coefficient of determination, or 0.984.

Questions for Writing and Discussion

1. Why is knowledge of cost behavior important for managerial decision making? Give an example to illustrate your answer.
2. How does the length of the time horizon affect the classification of a cost as fixed or variable? What is the meaning of short run? Long run?
3. Explain the difference between resource spending and resource usage.
4. What is the relationship between flexible resources and cost behavior?
5. What is the relationship between committed resources and cost behavior?
6. Explain the difference between committed and discretionary fixed costs. Give examples of each.
7. Describe the difference between a variable cost and a step cost with narrow steps. When is it reasonable to treat these step costs as if they were variable costs?
8. What is the difference between a step cost with narrow steps and a step cost with wide steps?
9. What is an activity rate?
10. Why do mixed costs pose a problem when it comes to classifying costs into fixed and variable categories?

11. Why is a scattergraph a good first step in decomposing mixed costs into their fixed and variable components?
12. Describe how the scatterplot method breaks out the fixed and variable costs from a mixed cost. Now describe how the high-low method works. How do the two methods differ?
13. What are the advantages of the scatterplot method over the high-low method? The high-low method over the scatterplot method?
14. Describe the method of least squares. Why is this method better than either the high-low method or the scatterplot method?
15. What is meant by the "best-fitting line"?
16. Is the best-fitting line necessarily a good-fitting line? Explain.
17. Describe what is meant by "goodness of fit." Explain the meaning of the coefficient of determination.
18. What is the difference between the coefficient of determination and the coefficient of correlation? Which of the two measures of goodness of fit do you prefer? Why?
19. When is multiple regression required to explain cost behavior?
20. Some firms assign mixed costs to either the fixed or variable cost categories without using any formal methodology to separate them. Explain how this practice can be defended.

Exercises

3-1

Cost Behavior
LO1

The salary for a plant supervisor for a manufacturing facility is $120,000 per year. The plant's capacity is 300,000 units per year.

Required

1. Prepare a table that shows how the cost of supervision behaves in total and on a per-unit basis as production increases from 0 to 250,000 units per year, using 50,000-unit increments.
2. How would you classify the behavior of the cost of supervision?

3-2

Cost Behavior
LO1

Rico Food Company sells and delivers various specialty foods to homes. Rico believes that the best driver for its delivery activity is "miles traveled." Not surprisingly, it discovered that the cost of fuel for delivery trucks doubled as the miles traveled doubled. The fuel cost for 4,000 miles was $1,200 and for 10,000 miles was $3,000.

Required

1. Prepare a table that shows the total cost of fuel and unit cost for miles traveled ranging from 0 to 10,000 miles, using increments of 2,000 miles.
2. How would you describe the behavior of the cost of fuel for delivery trucks?

3-3

Cost Behavior
LO1

Smith Concrete Company owns enough ready-mix trucks to deliver up to 100,000 cubic yards of concrete per year (considering each truck's capacity, weather, and distance to each job). Total truck depreciation is $200,000 per year. Raw materials (cement, gravel, and so on) cost about $25 per cubic yard of cement.

Required

1. Prepare a graph for truck depreciation. Use the vertical axis for cost and the horizontal axis for cubic yards of cement.
2. Prepare a graph for raw materials. Use the vertical axis for cost and the horizontal axis for cubic yards of cement.
3. Assume that the normal operating range for the company is 90,000 to 96,000 cubic yards per year. Classify truck depreciation and raw materials as variable or fixed costs.

3-4

Cost Behavior
LO1

Lorberg Company produces a variety of products, including some that require the use of a specialized forming machine. Lorberg can rent forming machines for $10,000 per year. Each machine can produce as many as 20,000 units per year.

Required

1. Prepare a table that shows the total cost of forming equipment rental and unit cost for units ranging from 0 to 50,000, using increments of 10,000 units.
2. How would you describe the behavior of the forming equipment rental cost?

3-5

Step Costs, Relevant Range
LO1

Mallory, Inc., produces large industrial machinery. Mallory has a machining department and a group of direct laborers called machinists. Each machinist is paid $50,000 and can machine up to 500 units per year. Mallory also hires supervisors to develop machine specification plans and to oversee production within the machining department. Given the planning and supervisory work, a supervisor can oversee at most three machinists. Mallory's accounting and production history shows the following relationships between number of units produced and the costs of materials handling and supervision (measured on an annual basis):

Units Produced	Direct Labor	Supervision
0–500	$ 50,000	$ 40,000
501–1,000	72,000	40,000
1,001–1,500	108,000	40,000
1,501–2,000	144,000	80,000
2,001–2,500	180,000	80,000
2,501–3,000	216,000	80,000
3,001–3,500	252,000	120,000
3,501–4,000	288,000	120,000

Required

1. Prepare a graph that illustrates the relationship between direct labor cost and number of units produced in the machining department. (Let cost be the vertical axis and number of units produced the horizontal axis.) Would you classify this cost as a strictly variable cost, a fixed cost, or a step cost?
2. Prepare a graph that illustrates the relationship between the cost of supervision and the number of units produced. (Let cost be the vertical axis and number of units produced the horizontal axis.) Would you classify this cost as a strictly variable cost, a fixed cost, or a step cost?
3. Suppose that the normal range of activity is between 1,400 and 1,500 units and that the exact number of machinists is currently hired to support this level of activity. Further suppose that production for the next year is expected to increase by an additional 500 units. By how much will the cost of direct labor increase? Cost of supervision?

3-6

Cost Behavior in a Service Organization
LO1, LO2

Morrison Community Hospital has five laboratory technicians who are responsible for doing a series of standard blood tests. Each technician is paid a salary of $30,000. The lab facility represents a recent addition to the hospital and cost $300,000. It is expected to last 20 years. Equipment used for the testing cost $10,000 and has a life expectancy of five years. In addition to the salaries, facility, and equipment, the hospital expects to spend $200,000 for chemicals, forms, power, and other supplies. This $200,000 is enough for 200,000 blood tests.

Required

Assuming that the driver (measure of output) for each type of cost is the number of blood tests run, classify the costs by completing the following table. Put a check mark in the appropriate box for variable cost, discretionary fixed cost, or committed fixed cost.

Cost Category	Variable Cost	Discretionary Fixed Cost	Committed Fixed Cost
Technician salaries			
Laboratory facility			
Laboratory equipment			
Chemicals and other supplies			

3-7

Cost Behavior in a Service Organization
LO1, LO2

State University's football team just received a bowl game invitation, and the students and alumni are excited. Holiday Travel Agency, located close to campus, decided to put together a bowl game package. For $50,000, a 737 jet could be chartered to take up to 170 people to and from the bowl city. A block of 85 hotel rooms could be confirmed for $400 each (a three-night commitment); Holiday Travel must pay for all the rooms in advance and cannot cancel any of them. The day of the game, a pregame buffet will be catered at $20 per person, and each person will receive a game favor package (consisting of a sweatshirt, a T-shirt, a commemorative pin with the school and bowl logos, and two pom-poms in the school's colors). All items in the favor package can be purchased by Holiday Travel on December 21 and will cost the agency $25 per set. Buses will be chartered in the bowl city to transport participants to and from the airport and the game. Each bus holds 50 people and can be chartered for $500. The bowl game is scheduled for December 28, and the trip will span three nights—December 26, 27, and 28. Purchasers must reserve their package and pay in full by December 20.

Required

List the resources that are mentioned in the above scenario. Then, for each resource, determine: (1) whether it is a flexible or committed resource and (2) the type of cost behavior displayed (variable, fixed, mixed, step cost).

3-8

Cost Behavior
LO1, LO2

EXCEL

Custom-Molding, Inc., is a manufacturer of molded plastic action figures that fast-food restaurants purchase to include in children's meal packs. Each action figure takes about 0.90 ounces of plastic costing $0.03 per ounce and is molded in a mold. Custom-Molding contracts with an outside supplier to develop new molds based on current movie and cartoon characters. Each set of molds costs $5,000 and could be used indefinitely but, practically speaking, lasts for three months and makes 100,000 action figures. (After that, the children are tired of those figures and want to move on to others.) Direct labor and variable overhead cost $0.02 per unit and other facility costs total $10,000 per year. Custom-Molding, Inc., produces 400,000 action figures over the course of the year.

Required

1. What is the total cost of producing action figures for the year? The per unit cost?
2. Categorize each resource as flexible or committed. What is the cost behavior of each resource?

3-9

Cost Behavior
LO1

Colby Company manufactures digital thermometers. Based on past experience, Colby has found that its total maintenance costs can be represented by the following formula: Maintenance cost = $24,000 + $0.30X, where X = Number of digital thermometers. Last year, Colby produced 200,000 thermometers. Actual maintenance costs for the year were as expected.

Required

1. What is the total maintenance cost incurred by Colby last year?
2. What is the total fixed maintenance cost incurred by Colby last year?
3. What is the total variable maintenance cost incurred by Colby last year?
4. What is the maintenance cost per unit produced?
5. What is the fixed maintenance cost per unit?
6. What is the variable maintenance cost per unit?
7. Recalculate Requirements 1 to 6 assuming that only 100,000 thermometers were produced.

3-10

Resource Supply and Usage; Activity Rates; Service Organization
LO2

Enid Communications provides cable television service to a number of communities in a midwestern state, including the town of Helena. In the Helena operation, there are 20 service technicians who install cable service and provide repairs. Each technician is salaried at $24,000 per year and works one of two daily eight-hour shifts. Each technician can perform an average of eight service calls per day. There are 250 working days per year.

Enid uses 12 trucks for the Helena operation, each fully equipped to perform installations and repairs on site. Each truck has a depreciation cost of $10,000 per year. (The 12 trucks allow each technician to have a truck for his or her shift, with two extra trucks in case of breakdown or scheduled maintenance.)

Last year, supplies, small tools, and fuel cost approximately $420,000; these seem to be highly correlated with the number of service calls. A total of 35,000 service calls were made last year.

Required

1. Classify the resources associated with the cable repair and installation activity into one of the following: (1) committed resources and (2) flexible resources.
2. Calculate the variable activity rate and the fixed activity rate for the repair and installation activity. What is the total cost of one service call?
3. Using the average data given above, what is the largest number of service calls that could be completed per year? This is the total activity availability. Break this total activity availability into activity usage (number of service calls actually made) and unused capacity (calls that could have been made but were not).
4. Calculate the total cost of committed resources used last year, and break this into the cost of service calls made and the cost of unused service call capacity.

3-11

Flexible and Committed Resources; Capacity Usage for a Service Organization
LO2

Jana Morgan is about to sign up for cellular telephone service. She is primarily interested in the safety aspect of the phone—that is, she wants to have one available for emergencies. She does not want to use it as her primary phone. Jana has narrowed her options down to two plans:

	Plan 1	Plan 2
Monthly fee	$ 20	$ 30
Free local minutes	60	120
Additional charges per minute:		
Airtime	$0.40	$0.30
Long distance	0.15	—
Regional roaming	0.60	—
National roaming	0.60	0.60

Both plans are subject to a $25 activation fee and a $120 cancellation fee if the service is cancelled before one year. Jana's brother will give her a cell phone that he no longer needs. It is not the latest version (and is not Internet capable), but will work well with both plans.

Required

1. Classify the charges associated with the cellular phone service as (1) committed resources or (2) flexible resources.
2. Assume that Jana will use, on average, 45 minutes per month in local calling. For each plan, split her minute allotment into used and unused capacity. Which plan would be more cost effective? Why?
3. Assume that Jana loves her cell phone and ends up talking frequently with friends while traveling within her region. On average, she uses 60 local minutes a month and 30 regional minutes. For each plan, split her minute allotment into used and unused capacity. Which plan would be more cost effective? Why?

3-12

Mixed Costs, Scattergraph, Service Organization
LO1, LO3

Ben Hanson owns an art gallery. He accepts paintings and sculpture on consignment and then receives 20 percent of the price of each piece as his fee. Space is limited, and there are costs involved, so Ben is careful about accepting artists. When he does accept one, he arranges for an opening show (usually for three hours on a weekend night) and sends out invitations to his customer list. At the opening, he serves soft drinks and casual munchies to create a comfortable environment for prospective customers to view the new works and chat with the artist. On average, each opening costs $500. Ben has given as many as 20 opening shows in a year. The total cost of running the gallery, including rent, furniture and fixtures, utilities, and a part-time assistant, amounts to $80,000 per year.

Required

1. Prepare a graph that illustrates the relationship between the cost of giving opening shows and the number of opening shows given. (Let opening show cost be the vertical axis and number of opening shows given the horizontal axis.) Would you classify this cost as a strictly variable cost, a fixed cost, or a mixed cost?
2. Prepare a graph that illustrates the relationship between the cost of running the gallery and the number of opening shows given. (Let gallery cost be the vertical axis and number of opening shows given the horizontal axis.) Would you classify this cost as a strictly variable cost, a fixed cost, or a mixed cost?
3. Prepare a graph that illustrates the relationship between Ben's total costs (the sum of the costs of giving opening shows and running the gallery) and the number of opening shows given. Let the cost be the vertical axis and number of opening shows given the horizontal axis. Would you classify this cost as a strictly variable cost, a fixed cost, or a mixed cost?
4. Assume that the cost driver is number of opening shows. Develop the cost formula for the gallery's costs for a year.

5. Using the formula developed in Requirement 1, what is the total cost for Ben in a year with 12 opening shows? With 14 opening shows?

3-13

High-Low Method, Service Organization
LO3

Kylie Hepworth has been operating a beauty shop in a college town for the past 10 years. Recently, Kylie rented space next to her shop and opened a tanning salon. She anticipated that the costs for the tanning service would be primarily fixed but found that tanning salon costs increased with the number of appointments. Costs for this service over the past eight months are as follows:

Month	Tanning Appointments	Total Cost
January	700	$1,758
February	2,000	2,140
March	3,100	2,790
April	2,500	2,400
May	1,500	1,800
June	2,300	2,275
July	2,150	2,200
August	3,000	2,640

Required

1. Which month represents the high point? The low point?
2. Using the high-low method, compute the variable rate for tanning. Compute the fixed cost per month.
3. Using your answers to Requirement 2, write the cost formula for tanning services.
4. Calculate the total predicted cost of tanning services for September for 2,500 appointments using the formula found in Requirement 3. Of that total cost, how much is the total fixed cost for September? How much is the total predicted variable cost for September?

3-14

Scattergraph Method, Service Organization
LO3, LO4

Refer to Exercise 3-13 for data on Kylie Hepworth's tanning salon. Assume that Kylie's accountant used an Excel spreadsheet program to run ordinary least squares on the data the following results were produced.

Intercept	1,290
X Variable	0.45

Required

1. Prepare a scattergraph based on Kylie's data. Use cost for the vertical axis and number of tanning appointments for the horizontal. Based on an examination of the scattergraph, does there appear to be a linear relationship between the cost of tanning services and the number of appointments?
2. Identify the cost formula for tanning services using the results from the method of least squares.
3. Using the formula computed in Requirement 1, what is the predicted cost of tanning services for September for 2,500 appointments?

3-15

Separating Fixed and Variable Costs; Service Setting
LO3, LO4

EXCEL

Jim Beaumont, the owner of Lube 'n' Go, is interested in determining the fixed and variable costs of performing a standard oil change. Since the oil changes are fairly standard, each one taking about the same amount of time and using about the same amount of grease, paper towels, etc., Jim thinks the number of oil changes would be a good independent variable. The total monthly cost includes the salaries of the two service persons, depreciation on the facility and equipment, utilities, and supplies such as grease and wipes. (The cost of oil is not included, as it differs from car to car and is charged to each customer based on the number of quarts actually used.) Data for the past eight months are as follows:

Month	Number of Oil Changes	Total Cost
May	1,100	$7,150
June	1,400	7,950
July	1,380	8,350
August	1,250	7,425
September	890	5,730
October	900	5,730
November	850	5,450
December	700	5,150

Required

1. Prepare a scattergraph based on these data. Use cost for the vertical axis and number of oil changes for the horizontal. Based on an examination of the scattergraph, does there appear to be a linear relationship between the cost of oil changes and the number of oil changes performed?
2. Compute the cost formula for oil changing services using the high-low method. Calculate the predicted cost for January for 1,000 oil changes using the high-low formula.
3. Compute the cost formula for oil change services using the method of least squares. Using the regression cost formula, what is the predicted cost for January for 1,000 oil changes? What does the coefficient of determination tell you about the cost formula computed by regression?
4. Which cost formula—the one computed using the high-low method or the one using the least-squares coefficients—do you think is better? Explain.

3-16

Separating Fixed and Variable Costs; Service Setting
LO3, LO4

EXCEL

Louise McDermott, controller for the Galvin plant of Veromar, Inc., wanted to determine the cost behavior of moving materials throughout the plant. She accumulated the following data on the number of moves (from 100 to 800, in increments of 100) and the total cost of moving materials at those levels of moves.

Number of Moves	Total Cost
100	$ 3,000
200	4,650
300	3,400
400	8,500
500	10,000
600	12,600
700	13,600
800	14,560

Required

1. Prepare a scattergraph based on these data. Use cost for the vertical axis and number of moves for the horizontal axis. Based on an examination of the scattergraph, does there appear to be a linear relationship between the total cost of moving materials and the number of moves?
2. Compute the cost formula for moving materials using the high-low method. Calculate the predicted cost per month with 550 moves using the high-low formula.
3. Compute the cost formula for moving materials using the method of least squares. Using the regression cost formula, what is the predicted cost for a month with 550 moves? What does the coefficient of determination tell you about the cost formula computed by regression?
4. Evaluate the cost formula using the least-squares coefficients. Could it be improved? Try dropping the third data point (300, $3,400) and rerunning the regression.

3-17

Method of Least Squares; Evaluation of Cost Equation
LO3, LO4

The method of least squares was used to develop a cost equation to predict the cost of maintenance. Monthly data for the past four years were used for the regression. The following computer output was received:

Intercept	\$5,750
Slope	16
Coefficient of correlation	0.89
Standard error	\$168

The driver used was "number of maintenance hours."

Required

1. What is the cost formula?
2. Using the cost formula, predict the cost of maintenance if 650 maintenance hours are to be worked next month.
3. What percentage of the variability in maintenance cost is explained by number of maintenance hours? Do you think the equation will predict well? Why or why not?
4. Using the results from the regression equation, predict the cost of maintenance for next year if 8,400 maintenance hours are predicted.

3-18

Multiple Regression
LO5

Velman Company wants to determine the factors that are associated with overhead. The controller for Velman constructed a multiple regression equation using the following independent variables: direct labor hours, number of setups, and number of purchase orders. The analysis was run using the past 60 months of data. The following printout is obtained:

Parameter	Estimate	t for H_o Parameter = 0	Pr > t	Standard Error of Parameter
Intercept	2,130	65.00	0.0001	225.000
Direct labor hours	17	3.17	0.0050	3.256
Number of setups	810	4.90	0.0050	108.256
Number of purchase orders	26	7.96	0.0250	5.103

$R^2 = 0.95$
$S_e = 150$
Observations 60

Required

1. Write out the cost formula for monthly overhead for Velman Company.
2. If Velman budgets the following for next month, what is the budgeted overhead cost?

Direct labor hours	600
Number of setups	50
Number of purchase orders	120

3. Suppose that Velman's engineers found a way to reduce the number of setups by 50 percent. How much would be saved in overhead cost for the following month?

3-19

Multiple Regression
LO5

Materhorn, a manufacturer of VCRs, is interested in determining the cost of its warranty repair activity. Two cost drivers have been identified that are believed to be important in explaining the cost of this activity: the number of defective products produced and the hours of inspection. To see if the belief is valid, the company's cost analysts have gathered 100 weeks of data and run a multiple regression analysis. The following printout is obtained:

Parameter	Estimate	t for H_o Parameter = 0	Pr > t	Standard Error of Parameter
Intercept	2,000	80.00	0.0001	25.000
Number of defects	60	2.58	0.0050	23.256
Inspection hours	–10	21.96	0.0250	5.103

$R^2 = 0.88$
$S_e = 150$
Observations 100

Required

1. Write out the cost formula for Materhorn's warranty repair activity.
2. If Materhorn expects to have 100 defects per week and to spend 150 hours on inspection, what are the anticipated warranty repair costs?
3. Is the number of defects positively or negatively correlated with warranty repair costs? Are inspection hours positively or negatively correlated with warranty repair costs?
4. What does R^2 mean in this equation? Overall, what is your evaluation of the cost formula that was developed for the warranty repair activity?

Problems

3-20

Identifying Variable Costs, Committed Fixed Costs, and Discretionary Fixed Costs
LO1, LO2

Required

Classify each of the following costs for a jeans manufacturing company as a variable cost, committed fixed cost, or discretionary fixed cost.

a. The cost of buttons.
b. The cost to lease warehouse space for completed jeans. The lease contract runs for two years at $5,000 per year.
c. The salary of a summer intern.
d. The cost of landscaping and mowing the grass. The contract with a local mowing company runs from month to month.
e. Advertising in a national magazine for teenage girls.
f. Electricity to run the sewing machines.
g. Oil and spare needles for the sewing machines.
h. Quality training for employees—typically given for four hours at a time, every six months.
i. Food and beverages for the company 4th of July picnic.
j. Natural gas to heat the factory during the winter.

3-21

Scattergraph; High-Low Method; Predicting Cost

Shaw Company has gathered data on its overhead activities and associated costs for the past 10 months. Joseph Booth, a member of the controller's department, has convinced management that overhead costs can be better estimated and controlled if the fixed and variable components of each overhead activity are known. One such activity is receiving raw materials (unloading incoming goods, counting goods, and inspecting goods), which he believes is driven by the number of receiving orders. Ten months of data have been gathered for the receiving activity and are as follows:

Month	Receiving Orders	Receiving Cost
1	1,000	$18,000
2	700	15,000
3	1,500	28,000

Month	Receiving Orders	Receiving Cost
4	1,200	$17,000
5	1,300	25,000
6	1,100	21,000
7	1,600	29,000
8	1,400	24,000
9	1,700	27,000
10	900	16,000

Required

1. Prepare a scattergraph based on the 10 months of data. Does the relationship appear to be linear?
2. Using the high-low method, prepare a cost formula for the receiving activity. Using this formula, what is the predicted cost of receiving for a month in which 1,475 receiving orders are processed?
3. Prepare a cost formula for the receiving activity for a quarter. Based on this formula, what is the predicted cost of receiving for a quarter in which 4,650 receiving orders are anticipated? Prepare a cost formula for the receiving activity for a year. Based on this formula, what is the predicted cost of receiving for a year in which 18,000 receiving orders are anticipated?
4. Now assume that Joseph used the method of least squares on the receiving data and obtained the following results:

Intercept	3,212
Slope	15.15

Using the results from the method of least squares, repeat Requirements 2 and 3 (round your answers to the nearest dollar).

3-22

Method of Least Squares

Refer to Problem 3-21 for the first 10 months of data on receiving orders and receiving cost. Now suppose that Joseph has gathered two more months of data:

Month	Receiving Orders	Receiving Cost
11	1,200	$28,000
12	950	17,500

Required

1. Run two regressions using a computer spreadsheet program such as Excel. First, use the method of least squares on the 10 months of data from Problem 3-21. Then, use the method of least squares on the 12 months of data (10 months from Problem 3-21 and the additional two months given in this problem). Write down the results for the intercept, slope, and R^2 for each regression. Compare the results.
2. Prepare a scattergraph using all 12 months of data. Do any points appear to be outliers? Suppose Joseph has learned that the factory suffered severe storm damage during month 11 that required extensive repairs to the receiving area—including major repairs on a forklift. These expenses, included in month 11 receiving costs, are not expected to recur. What step might Joseph, using his judgment, take to amend the results from the method of least squares?
3. Rerun the method of least squares, using all the data except for month 11. (You should now have 11 months of data.) Prepare a cost formula for receiving based on these results and calculate the predicted receiving cost for a month with 1,475 receiving orders. Discuss the results from this regression versus those from the regression for 12 months of data.

3-23

Cost Behavior; High-Low Method; Pricing Decision
LO1, LO3

EXCEL

Fonseca, Ruiz, and Dunn is a large, local accounting firm that is located in a southwestern city. Carlos Ruiz, one of the firm's founders, appreciates the success his firm has enjoyed and wants to give something back to his community. He believes that an inexpensive accounting services clinic could provide basic accounting services for small businesses located in the barrio. He wants to price the services at cost.

Since the clinic is brand new, it has no experience to go on. Carlos decided to operate the clinic for two months before determining how much to charge per hour on an ongoing basis. As a temporary measure, the clinic adopted an hourly charge of $25, half the amount charged by Fonseca, Ruiz, and Dunn for professional services.

The accounting services clinic opened on January 1. During January, the clinic had 120 hours of professional service. During February, the activity was 150 hours. Costs for these two levels of activity usage are as follows:

	120 Professional Hours	150 Professional Hours
Salaries:		
Senior accountant	$2,500	$2,500
Office assistant	1,200	1,200
Internet and software subscriptions	700	850
Consulting by senior partner	1,200	1,500
Depreciation (equipment)	2,400	2,400
Supplies	905	1,100
Administration	500	500
Rent (offices)	2,000	2,000
Utilities	332	365

Required

1. Classify each cost as fixed, variable, or mixed, using hours of professional service as the activity driver.
2. Use the high-low method to separate the mixed costs into their fixed and variable components.
3. Luz Mondragon, the chief paraprofessional of the clinic, has estimated that the clinic will average 140 professional hours per month. If the clinic is to be operated as a nonprofit organization, how much will it need to charge per professional hour? How much of this charge is variable? How much is fixed?
4. Suppose the clinic averages 170 professional hours per month. How much would need to be charged per hour for the clinic to cover its costs? Explain why the per-hour charge decreased as the activity output increased.

3-24

High-Low Method; Method of Least Squares; Correlation
LO3, LO4, LO5

Livingston Company has gathered data on its overhead activities and associated costs for the past 10 months. Brett Wilkinson, a member of the controller's department, has convinced management that overhead costs can be better estimated and controlled if the fixed and variable components of each overhead activity are known. Brett has identified 150 different activities and has grouped them into sets based on her belief that they share a common driver. (This classification process has reduced the number of cost formulas needed from 150 to 25.) For example, she has decided that processing sales orders, scheduling, and setups can be grouped together (as a general order-filling activity) based on her belief that the costs of the three related activities are all driven by the same driver, number of setups. To confirm her activity classification and driver assignment, she has gathered 10 months of data on the cost of filling sales orders and on the number of setups. Just in case the number of setups is not a good driver, she also collected data on setup hours.

Month	Setups	Setup Hours	Order-Filling Cost
1	1,000	3,000	$18,000
2	700	2,500	15,000
3	1,500	4,500	28,000
4	1,200	3,200	17,000
5	1,300	4,400	25,000
6	1,100	2,800	18,000
7	1,600	5,500	30,000
8	1,400	3,900	24,000
9	1,700	2,300	21,000
10	900	2,300	15,000

Required

1. Using the high-low method, prepare a cost formula for the order filling activity using number of setups as the driver.
2. Using the method of least squares, prepare a cost formula for the order filling activity using number of setups as the driver. What does the coefficient of determination tell us about the use of receiving orders as the independent variable?
3. Using the method of least squares, prepare a cost formula for the order filling activity using setup hours as the driver. What does the coefficient of determination tell us about the use of setup hours as the independent variable?
4. Run a multiple regression using both the number of setups and setup hours as the independent variables. Which of the three regression equations do you think is best? Why?

3-25

Cost Formulas; Single and Multiple Cost Drivers; Coefficient of Correlation
LO3, LO4, LO5

For the past five years, Garner Company has had a policy of producing to meet customer demand. As a result, finished goods inventory is minimal, and, for the most part, units produced equal units sold.

Recently, Garner's industry entered a recession, and the company is producing well below capacity (and expects to continue doing so for the coming year). The president is willing to accept orders that at least cover their variable costs so that the company can keep its employees and avoid layoffs. Also, any orders above variable costs will increase overall profitability of the company. Toward that end, the president of Garner Company implemented a policy that any special orders will be accepted if they cover the costs that the orders cause.

To help implement the policy, Garner's controller developed the following cost formulas:

Direct material usage = $94X, r = 0.95
Direct labor usage = $16X, r = 0.96
Overhead = $350,000 + $80X, r = 0.75
Selling costs = $50,000 + $7X, r = 0.93

where X = direct labor hours

Required

1. Compute the total unit variable cost. Suppose that Garner has an opportunity to accept an order for 20,000 units at $212 per unit. Each unit uses one direct labor hour for production. Should Garner accept the order? (The order would not displace any of Garner's regular orders.)
2. Explain the significance of the coefficient of correlation measures for the cost formulas. Did these measures have a bearing on your answer in Requirement 1? Should they have a bearing? Why?

3. Suppose that a multiple regression equation is developed for overhead costs: $Y = \$100{,}000 + \$85X_1 + \$5{,}000X_2 + \$300X_3$, where X_1 = direct labor hours, X_2 = number of setups, and X_3 = engineering hours. The correlation coefficient for the equation is 0.94. Assume that the order of 20,000 units requires 12 setups and 600 engineering hours. Given this new information, should the company accept the special order referred to in Requirement 1? Is there any other information about cost behavior that you would like to have? Explain.

3-26

High-Low Method; Regression; Multiple Regression; Service Organization
LO3, LO4, LO5

West Valley Regional Hospital has collected data on all of its activities for the past 14 months. Data for cardiac nursing care follow:

Month	Cost	Hours of Nursing Care
May 2008	$ 66,000	1,600
June 2008	76,500	1,900
July 2008	78,100	1,950
August 2008	73,180	1,800
September 2008	69,500	1,700
October 2008	64,250	1,550
November 2008	52,000	1,200
December 2008	66,000	1,600
January 2009	110,000	1,800
February 2009	86,485	1,330
March 2009	105,022	1,700
April 2009	100,000	1,600
May 2009	120,000	2,000
June 2009	109,500	1,790

Required

1. Using the high-low method, calculate the variable rate per hour and the fixed cost for the nursing care activity. Comment on your results.
2. Upon looking into the events that happened at the end of 2008, you find that the cardiology ward bought a cardiac-monitoring machine for the nursing station. A decision was also made to add a new supervisory position for the evening shift. Monthly depreciation on the monitor and the salary of the new supervisor total $10,000. In addition, the rest of the nursing staff received a raise, and the cost of supplies had increased. Run the following regressions:

   a. Create a dummy variable called "changes" that takes the value 0 for observations in 2008 and the value 1 for observations in 2009. Run multiple regression on these data.
   b. Run a regression on the 2008 data, using nursing hours as the single independent variable.
   c. Run a regression on the 2009 data, using nursing hours as the single independent variable.

   Which of the above three regressions should be used to budget the cost of the cardiac nursing care activity for the remainder of 2009? Discuss your findings. Which cost formula should be used to budget the cost of the cardiac nursing care activity for the remainder of 2009?

3-27

Comparison of Regression Equations
LO1, LO3, LO4, LO5

Goldsmith Company is attempting to determine cost behavior of its overhead activities for its Dallas plant. One of the major activities is receiving. Two possible drivers have been mentioned: number of orders and material pounds. The plant controller has accumulated the following data for the setup activity:

Month	Receiving Costs	Pounds	Orders
February	$15,400	4,000	140
March	15,300	4,200	100
April	20,104	6,000	100
May	18,800	5,400	120
June	19,168	6,000	40
July	16,960	5,000	80
August	17,100	4,800	120
September	19,470	5,800	100
October	21,000	6,000	180

Required

1. Estimate a cost formula with pounds as the driver and only independent variable. If the Dallas plant forecasts 5,200 pounds for the next month, what will the budgeted receiving cost be?
2. Estimate a cost formula with number of orders as the cost driver and only independent variable. If the Dallas plant forecasts 160 orders for the next month, what will the budgeted setup cost be?
3. Which of the two regression equations do you think does a better job of predicting receiving costs? Explain.
4. The multiple regression equation using both pounds and number of orders as independent variables follows:

$$Y = \$1{,}493.27 + \$2.61\ (\text{pounds}) + \$13.71\ (\text{orders}),\ R^2 = 0.998$$

Using Excel, verify the above formula and then calculate the budgeted cost using the multiple regression equation. Would you recommend using a multiple-driver equation over a single-driver equation? Explain.

Managerial Decision Case

3-28

Suspicious Acquisition of Data; Ethical Issues
LO1

ETHICS

Bill Lewis, manager of the Thomas Electronics Division, called a meeting with his controller, Brindon Peterson, CMA, and his marketing manager, Patty Fritz. The following is a transcript of the conversation that took place during the meeting.

Bill: Brindon, the variable-costing system that you developed has proved to be a big plus for our division. Our success in winning bids has increased, and as a result, our revenues have increased by 25 percent. However, if we intend to meet this year's profit targets, we are going to need something extra—am I right, Patty?

Patty: Absolutely. While we have been able to win more bids, we still are losing too many, particularly to our major competitor, Kilborn Electronics. If I knew more about their bidding strategy, I think we could be more successful in competing with them.

Bill: Would knowing their variable costs help?

Patty: Certainly. It would give me their minimum price. With that knowledge, I'm sure we could find a way to beat them on several jobs, particularly for those jobs where we are at least as efficient. It would also help us identify where we are not cost-competitive. With this information, we might be able to find ways to increase our efficiency.

Bill: Well, I have good news. I have some data here in these handouts that reveal bids that Kilborn made on several jobs. I have also been able to obtain the direct labor hours worked for many of these jobs. But that's not all. I have monthly totals for manufacturing costs and direct labor hours for all their jobs for the past 10 months. Brindon, with this information, can you estimate what the variable manufacturing cost per hour is? If you can, we can compute the variable costs for each job and the markup that Kilborn is using.

Brindon: Yes, an analysis of the data you're requesting is possible. I have a question, though, before I do this. How did you manage to acquire these data? I can't imagine that Kilborn would willingly release this information.

Bill: What does it matter how the data were acquired? The fact is, we have this information, and we have an opportunity to gain a tremendous competitive advantage. With that advantage, we can meet our profit targets, and we will all end the year with a big bonus.

After the meeting, in a conversation with Patty, Brindon learned that Bill was dating Jackie Wilson, a cost accountant (and CMA) who happened to work for Kilborn. Patty speculated that Jackie might be the source of the Kilborn data. Upon learning this, Brindon expressed some strong reservations to Patty about analyzing the data.

Required

1. Assume that Bill did acquire the data from Jackie Wilson. Comment on Jackie's behavior. Which standards of ethical conduct did she violate? (See Chapter 1 for a listing of the ethical code.)
2. Were Brindon's instincts correct? Should he have felt some reservations about analyzing the data? Would it be ethical to analyze the data? Do any of the IMA standards of ethical conduct apply? What would you do if you were Brindon? Explain.

Research Assignment

3-29

Cybercase
LO2, LO6

Use the Internet to gather information on one of the theme parks at Disney World—the Magic Kingdom, Epcot Center, MGM Studios, or the Animal Kingdom. Access this information in the chapter web links at the Interactive Study Center at http://www.thomsonedu.com/accounting/hansen.

Once you have selected your park, list as many resources as possible and classify them as flexible or committed. Discuss the cost behavior of each. How do you think cost behavior affected the planning for the theme park?

chapter 4

Activity-Based Product Costing

learning objectives

After studying this chapter, you should be able to:

1. Discuss the importance of unit costs.
2. Describe functional-based costing approaches.
3. Tell why functional-based costing approaches may produce distorted costs.
4. Explain how an activity-based costing system works for product costing.
5. Explain how the number of activity rates can be reduced.

Scenario

Makenzie Hepworth, president and owner of SpringBanc, a full-service bank located in Springdale, Arkansas, had just returned from lunch with her brother-in-law, Cameron Hepworth. Cameron was the controller of the Springdale BelRing plant, a producer of telephones. Cameron had described how Henderson Associates, a regional consulting firm, had replaced BelRing's direct-labor-based costing system with an activity-based costing system, providing more accurate cost assignments. The more accurate cost assignments had produced some decisions that had significantly improved the profitability of the BelRing plant. That afternoon, after reviewing SpringBanc's most recent financial reports, Makenzie decided to call Jan Booth, the partner at Henderson Associates who had led the BelRing project. Makenzie was hopeful that more accurate costing might help her improve the profitability of SpringBanc.

Makenzie asked Jan Booth to evaluate the operations, procedures, and policies of the credit department of the bank to see what effect activity-based costing would have on the costs of the department's products. Nine weeks after Jan agreed to undertake the engagement, Makenzie received the following memo:

MEMO

To: Makenzie Hepworth, President
From: Jan Booth, Partner, Henderson Associates
Subject: Causes of Lackluster Performance
Date: August 15, 2008

Our preliminary analysis reveals that many of your problems are related to the use of average-cost information to assess product profitability. Differentiation of services is increasing in all financial institutions, including your bank. With differentiation comes increased complexity and product diversity, making average costing an entirely inappropriate approach to costing out your products. Your choices of types of products and services offered are rooted in the way you are currently assigning costs to products. You are using a traditional, functional-based costing system, and our analysis shows that it is causing distortions in product costs. The functional-based system is indicating that your low-volume products—which typically require more complex procedures and more special handling—are earning a higher margin than your high-volume, less-complex-to-produce products. Using a more accurate cost assignment approach, we obtain opposite results. In fact, it appears that 20 percent of your products are earning 80 percent of your profits. The under-costing of low-volume products and over-costing of high-volume products are affecting your bids and your ability to compete successfully in your markets. Under-costing of low-volume products and the over-costing of high-volume products affect more than just decisions.

Questions to Think About

1. What are product costs?
2. What role do product costs play in bids?
3. What is meant by a traditional, functional-based costing system? Why might it cause distortions in product costs?
4. Assuming SpringBanc's problems are founded in the way costs are assigned to products, what can SpringBanc do to solve the problem?

Unit Costs

Objective 1

Discuss the importance of unit costs.

Functional-based and activity-based costing assigns costs to cost objects such as products, customers, suppliers, materials, and marketing channels. Once costs are assigned to the cost object, a unit cost is computed by dividing the total cost assigned by the units of the particular cost object. Because of their importance, calculation of unit product costs will be discussed first. We discuss customer and supplier costing in Chapter 5. Conceptually, computing a unit product cost is simple. The **unit cost** is the total cost associated with the units produced divided by the number of units produced. For example, if BelRing produces 100 phones of the same model and the total cost for these phones is $6,000, then the cost of each phone is $60 ($6,000/100)). Similarly, for the credit department of SpringBanc, if the total cost of servicing 1,000 platinum credit cards is $50,000 per year, then the servicing cost per card is $50 ($50,000/1,000). Although the concept is simple, the practical reality of the computation can be somewhat more complex. First, what is meant by "total cost"? Does this mean only production costs? Or production costs plus marketing costs? Or all costs of the organization? Second, how do we measure the costs to be assigned? Do we use actual costs incurred or estimated costs? Third, how do we assign costs to the product?

The first question is answered by defining what is meant by "product cost." Recall that the product cost definition depends on the managerial objective being served. For example, product cost is often defined as production costs: the sum of direct materials, direct labor, and manufacturing overhead. This product cost definition is mandated for external financial reporting and, therefore, plays a key role in valuing inventories and determining income. It is also useful for making certain decisions. For example, it can serve as a critical input for establishing bid prices. Furthermore, this product cost definition is useful for illustrating the differences between functional- and activity-based cost assignment approaches (for simplicity and consistency, this definition will be used throughout this chapter). The second and third questions are concerned with how costs are measured and assigned to products. Total production costs must be measured, and then these costs must be associated with the units produced. **Cost measurement** consists of determining the dollar amounts of direct materials, direct labor, and overhead used in production. The dollar amounts may be the actual amounts expended for the manufacturing inputs or they may be *estimated* amounts. Often, estimated amounts are used to ensure timeliness of cost information or to control costs. The process of associating the costs, once measured, with the units produced is called **cost assignment**. Functional- and activity-based approaches are two competing ways of assigning costs to products.

© Getty Images/PhotoDisc

Calculating the unit servicing cost for credit cards is just as important for a bank as calculating the unit cost of producing a phone is for a manufacturing company.

Importance of Unit Product Costs

A cost accounting system measures and assigns costs so that the unit cost of a product or service can be determined. Unit cost is a critical piece of information for both manufacturing and service firms. For example, bidding is a common requirement in the markets for specialized products and services (consider bids for special tools, audits, and medical tests and procedures). It is virtually impossible to submit a meaningful bid without knowing the unit costs of the products or services to be produced. Other examples can be cited. Decisions concerning product and service design and introduction of new products and services are affected by expected unit costs. Decisions to make or buy a product or service, to accept or reject a special order, or to keep or drop a product or service require unit cost information. Because unit cost information is so vital, its accuracy is essential. Distorted unit product costs are not acceptable.

Production of Unit Cost Information

To produce unit cost information, a product cost definition, cost measurement, and cost assignment are required. As already mentioned, this chapter uses the traditional product cost definition. There are also a number of different ways to measure and assign costs. Two possible measurement systems are *actual* costing and *normal* costing. **Actual costing** assigns the actual costs of direct materials, direct labor, and overhead to products. In practice, strict actual costing systems are rarely used, because they cannot provide accurate unit cost information on a timely basis. **Normal costing** assigns the actual costs of direct materials and direct labor to products; however, overhead costs are assigned to products using *predetermined rates.* A **predetermined overhead rate** is a rate based on estimated data and computed using the following formula:

Predetermined overhead rate = Budgeted (estimated) cost/Estimated activity usage

How overhead rates are used to assign costs to products will become clear as the specifics of functional- and activity-based costing are discussed. Since functional-based costing can be viewed as a special case of activity-based costing, we will discuss it first. Furthermore, by discussing functional-based costing first, the potential advantages of activity-based costing become much clearer.

Functional-Based Product Costing

Objective 2

Describe functional-based costing approaches.

Functional-based product costing assigns the cost of direct materials and direct labor to products using direct tracing. Overhead costs, on the other hand, are assigned using driver tracing and allocation. Specifically, functional-based costing uses *unit-level activity drivers* to assign overhead costs to products. **Unit-level activity drivers** are factors that cause changes in cost as the units produced change. The use of only unit-based drivers to assign overhead costs to products assumes that the overhead consumed by products is highly correlated with the number of units produced. For those overhead costs for which this assumption is valid, the unit-based assignment corresponds to driver tracing; for those overhead costs that violate the assumption, the cost assignment is an allocation.

A functional-based predetermined overhead rate requires specification of a unit-level driver, an estimation of the capacity measured by the driver, and an estimation of the expected overhead. Examples of unit-level drivers commonly used to assign overhead include

1. Units produced
2. Direct labor hours

3. Direct labor dollars
4. Machine hours
5. Direct material dollars

After choosing a unit-level driver, the next step is to determine the activity capacity that the driver measures. Although any reasonable capacity level could be chosen, the four usual candidates are expected capacity, normal capacity, theoretical capacity, and practical capacity. **Expected activity capacity** is the activity output the firm expects to attain for the coming year. **Normal activity capacity** is the average activity output that a firm experiences in the long term (normal volume is computed over more than one period). **Theoretical activity capacity** is the absolute maximum activity output that can be realized assuming everything operates perfectly. **Practical activity capacity** is the maximum output that can be realized if everything operates efficiently. Of the four choices, the last three share the advantage of using the same activity level period after period. As a result, they each produce less period-to-period fluctuation of the per-unit overhead cost than a rate based on expected actual capacity. Using practical or theoretical capacity is often recommended because it avoids assigning unused capacity costs to products and encourages management of the excess capacity. Exhibit 4-1 illustrates these four measures of activity capacity.

Plantwide Rates

Exhibit 4-2 illustrates how plantwide overhead rates are computed. This calculation consists of two stages. First, budgeted overhead costs are accumulated in one large plantwide pool (first-stage cost assignment). Overhead costs are directly assigned to the pool by simply adding all the overhead costs expected to be incurred within the plant for a year. In a sense, we could argue that these costs are assigned to a very broad macroactivity: production. Once costs are accumulated in this pool, a plantwide rate is computed using a unit-level driver (usually direct labor hours). Finally, over-

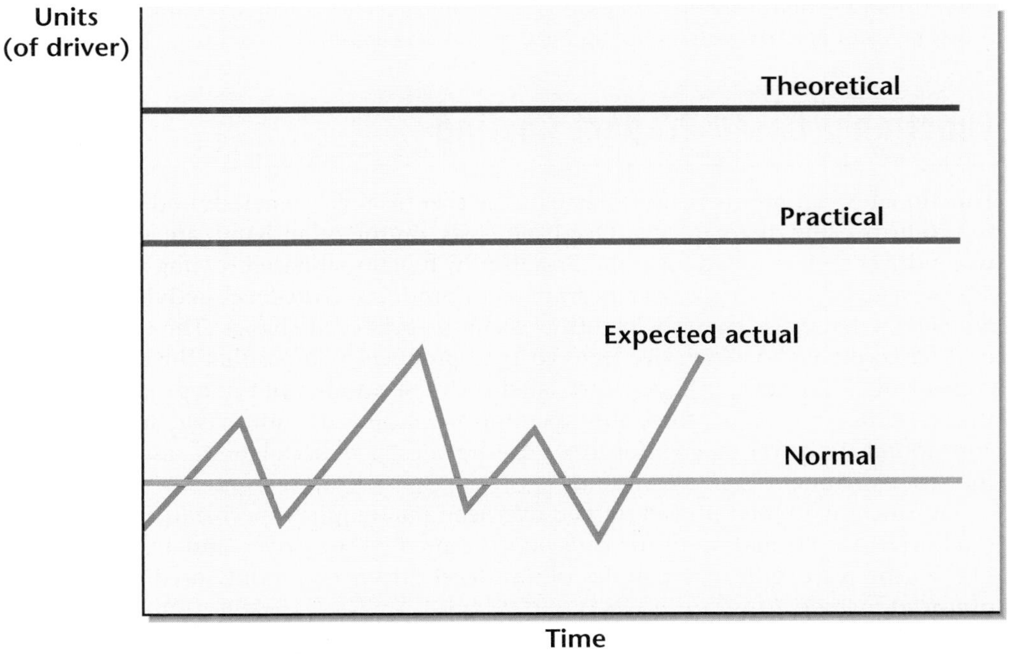

Exhibit 4-1 Activity Capacity Measures

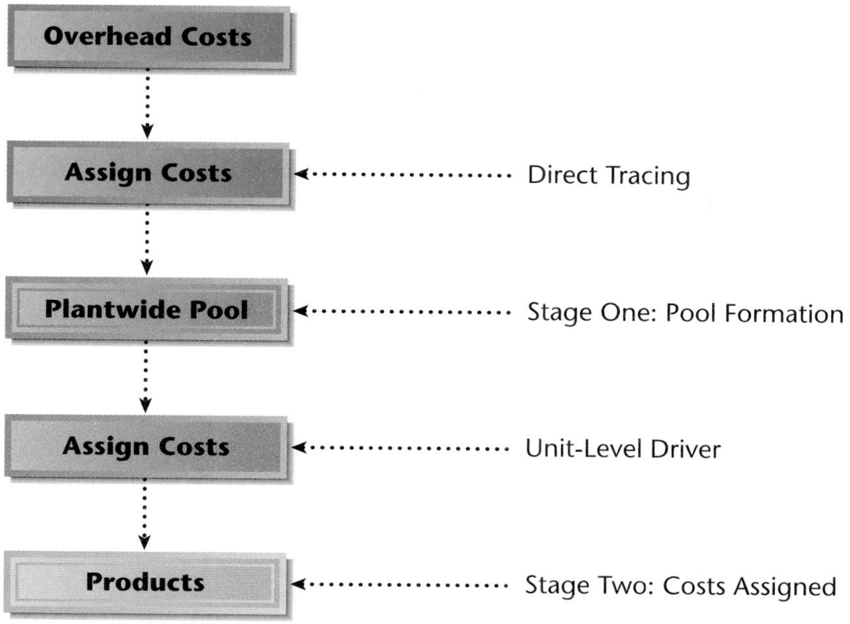

Exhibit 4-2 Functional-Based Costing: Plantwide Rate

head costs are assigned to products, multiplying the rate by the actual total direct labor hours used by each product.

Computation of a Plantwide Rate The computation of a plantwide rate is best illustrated with the costing approach used by BelRing before Henderson Associates changed its costing system. In its Springdale plant, BelRing produces two telephones: a cordless phone and a regular model. The company has the following estimated and actual data for the year 2008:

Budgeted overhead	$360,000
Expected activity (in direct labor hours)	100,000
Actual activity (in direct labor hours)	100,000
Actual overhead	$380,000

Thus, for 2008, a rate based on expected direct labor hours is computed as follows:

Predetermined overhead rate = Budgeted overhead/Expected activity
= $360,000/100,000 direct labor hours (DLH)
= $3.60 per DLH

Applied Overhead The total overhead assigned to actual production at any point in time is called **applied overhead** and is computed using the following formula:

Applied overhead = Overhead rate × Actual activity output

Using the overhead rate, applied overhead for the year is

Applied overhead = Overhead rate × Actual activity
= $3.60 × 100,000 DLH
= $360,000

The difference between the actual overhead and the applied overhead is called an **overhead variance**. For BelRing, the overhead variance is $20,000 ($380,000 − $360,000). If the actual overhead is greater than the applied overhead, the variance is called **underapplied overhead**. For the BelRing example, the overhead is $20,000 underapplied. If the actual overhead is less than the applied overhead, the variance is called **overapplied overhead**. Usually, at the end of the year, underapplied overhead is added to cost of goods sold, and overapplied overhead is subtracted from cost of goods sold.

Per-Unit Cost The unit cost of a product is computed by adding the total prime costs for a product to its assigned overhead costs and then dividing this total cost by the units produced. To illustrate unit-cost computation, assume the following actual data were collected for each product:

	Cordless	Regular
Units produced	10,000	100,000
Prime costs	$78,000	$738,000
Direct labor hours	10,000	90,000

The unit-cost calculations are summarized in Exhibit 4-3. Notice the role that the predetermined plantwide rate ($3.60 per DLH) plays in calculating the unit manufacturing cost.

Departmental Rates

Exhibit 4-4 illustrates a two-stage conceptual framework for departmental overhead rates. In the first stage, the plantwide overhead costs are divided up and assigned to individual production departments, creating departmental overhead cost pools. We describe in detail in Chapter 7 how this is done. Once costs are assigned to individual production departments, then unit-based drivers such as direct labor hours (for labor-intensive departments) and machine hours (for machine-intensive departments) are used to compute departmental rates. Products passing through the departments are assumed to consume overhead resources in proportion to the department's unit-based drivers (such as machine hours or direct labor hours used). Thus, in the second stage, overhead is assigned to products by multiplying the departmental rates by the amount of the driver used in the respective departments. The total overhead assigned to products is simply the sum of the amounts applied in each department.

The rationale for departmental rates is simple. Some producing departments may be more "overhead-intensive" than other producing departments. Thus, products spending more time in overhead-intensive departments should be assigned more overhead cost than those spending less time. Departmental rates pick up these possible effects, while plantwide rates lose them through averaging.

Computation of Departmental Rates Shortly before the Henderson Associates visit, the BelRing's Springdale plant moved from the use of a plantwide rate to departmental rates. The Springdale plant has two production departments: fabrica-

	Cordless	Regular
Prime costs	$ 78,000	$ 738,000
Overhead costs:		
$3.60 × 10,000	36,000	—
$3.60 × 90,000	—	324,000
Total manufacturing costs	$114,000	$1,062,000
Units produced	÷ 10,000	÷ 100,000
Unit cost (total costs/units)	$ 11.40	$ 10.62

Exhibit 4-3 Unit-Cost Computation: Plantwide Rate—BelRing Springdale Plant

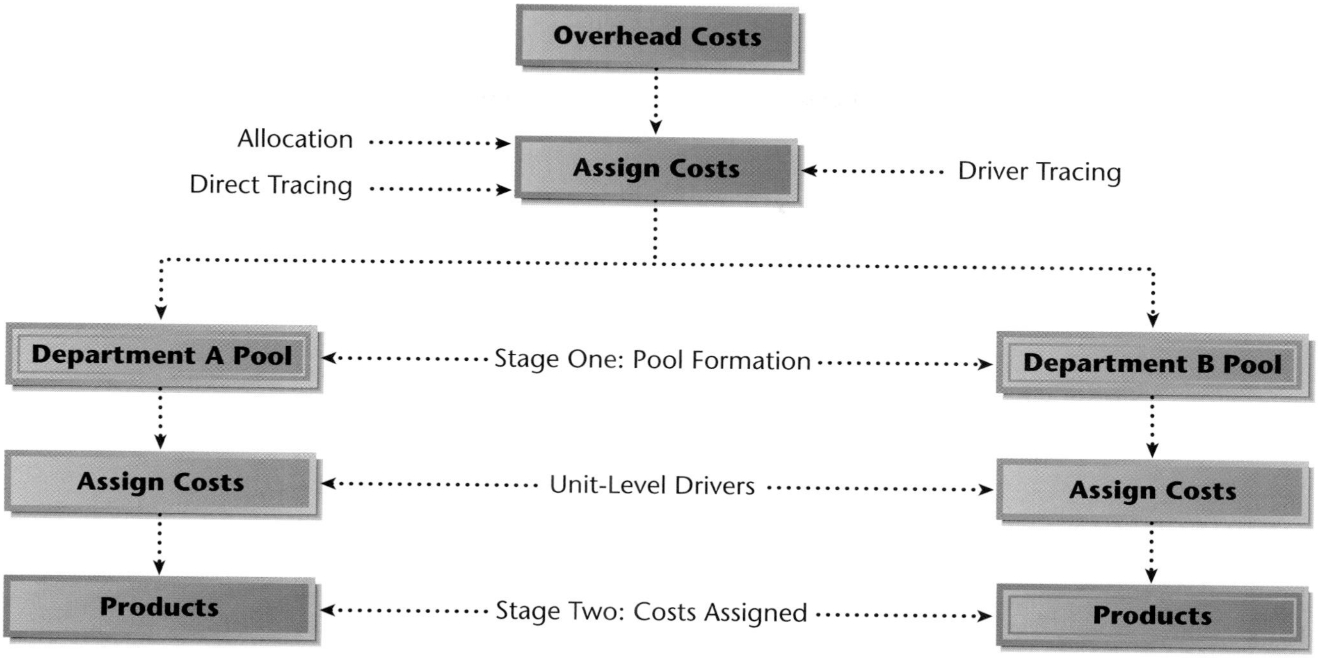

Exhibit 4-4 Functional-Based Costing: Departmental Rates

tion and assembly. In fabrication, a major electronic component is made. Other parts are purchased from suppliers and sister divisions. Data relating to the departments for the year 2006 are given in Exhibit 4-5. Notice that fabrication is machine intensive (compare expected machine hours), while assembly tends to be labor intensive. Observing this, BelRing based its departmental overhead rates on machine hours in fabrication and on direct labor hours in assembly. Two overhead rates are calculated as follows:

Fabrication rate = Budgeted overhead/Expected machine hours
= \$252,000/40,000
= \$6.30 per MHr

Assembly rate = Budgeted overhead/Expected direct labor hours
= \$108,000/80,000
= \$1.35 per DLH

	Fabrication	Assembly
Budgeted overhead	\$252,000	\$108,000
Expected and actual usage (direct labor hours):		
Cordless	7,000	3,000
Regular	13,000	77,000
	20,000	80,000
Expected and actual usage (machine hours):		
Cordless	4,000	1,000
Regular	36,000	9,000
	40,000	10,000

Exhibit 4-5 Departmental Data—BelRing Springdale Plant

Applied Overhead Total applied overhead for the year is simply the sum of the amounts applied in each department:

$$\begin{aligned}\text{Applied overhead} &= (\$6.30 \times \text{Actual machine hours}) + (\$1.35 \times \text{Actual direct labor hours}) \\ &= (\$6.30 \times 40{,}000) + (\$1.35 \times 80{,}000) \\ &= \$252{,}000 + \$108{,}000 \\ &= \$360{,}000\end{aligned}$$

Per-Unit Cost Using the departmental rates, the data from Exhibit 4-5, and the earlier information on prime costs and units produced, the computation of the unit cost is shown in Exhibit 4-6.

Limitations of Functional-Based Cost Accounting Systems

Objective 3

Tell why functional-based costing approaches may produce distorted costs.

Plantwide and departmental rates have been used for decades and continue to be used successfully by many organizations. In some settings, however, they do not work well and may actually cause severe product cost distortions. For some companies, product cost distortions can be damaging, particularly for those characterized by intense or increasing competitive pressures (often on a worldwide level), continuous improvement, total quality management, total customer satisfaction, and sophisticated technology. As firms operating in this competitive environment adopt new strategies to achieve competitive excellence, their cost accounting systems often must change to keep pace. Specifically, the need for more accurate product costs has forced many companies to take a serious look at their costing procedures. Cost accounting systems that worked reasonably well in the past may no longer be acceptable.

Often organizations experience certain symptoms indicating that their cost accounting system is outdated. For example, if costs are distorted and severe overcosting of a major, high-volume product is the outcome, then bids will be systematically lost, even when the company feels it is pursuing an aggressive bidding strategy. This can be especially puzzling when the company is confident that it is operating as efficiently as its competitors. Thus, one symptom of an outdated costing system is the inability to explain the outcome of bids. On the flip side, if competitors' prices seem unrealistically low, it should cause managers to wonder about the accuracy of their costing systems. Similarly, if somehow an organization's costing system is systematically understating the cost of low-volume, specialty products—products that require special processes and handling—then the organization may find that it has a seemingly profitable niche all to itself. Yet, it may find operational managers want-

	Cordless	Regular
Prime costs	$ 78,000	$ 738,000
Overhead costs:		
($6.30 × 4,000) + ($1.35 × 3,000)	29,250	—
($6.30 × 36,000) + ($1.35 × 77,000)	—	330,750
Total manufacturing costs	$107,250	$1,068,750
Units produced	÷ 10,000	÷ 100,000
Unit cost (total costs/units)	$ 10.73*	$ 10.69*

*Rounded

Exhibit 4-6 Unit-Cost Computation: Departmental Rates BelRing Springdale Plant ing to drop some of these "niche" products. These symptoms of an outdated cost accounting system along with several others are listed in Exhibit 4-7.[1]

Organizations that have experienced some or all of these symptoms have found that their plantwide or departmental rates are simply no longer capable of accurately assigning overhead costs to individual products. At least two major factors impair the ability of unit-based plantwide and departmental rates to assign overhead costs accurately: (1) the proportion of non-unit-related overhead costs to total overhead costs is large, and (2) the degree of product diversity is great.

Non-Unit-Related Overhead Costs

The use of either plantwide rates or departmental rates assumes that a product's consumption of overhead resources is related strictly to the units produced. For activities that are performed each time a unit is produced, this assumption makes sense. But what if there are *non-unit-level activities*—activities that are not performed each time a unit of product is produced? Consider, for example, two activities: setting up equipment and reengineering products. Setup costs are incurred each time a batch of products is produced. A batch may consist of 1,000 or 10,000 units, and the cost of setup is the same. Yet, as more setups are done, setup costs increase. The number of setups, not the number of units produced, is a much better measure of the consumption of the setup activity. Similarly, product reengineering costs may depend on the number of different engineering work orders rather than the units produced of any given product. Thus, *non-unit-level drivers* such as setups and engineering orders are needed for accurate cost assignment of non-unit-level activities. **Non-unit-level activity drivers** are factors that measure the consumption of non-unit-level activities by products and other cost objects. **Activity drivers**, then, are factors that measure the consumption of activities by products and other cost objects; furthermore, activity drivers can be classified as *unit-level* and *non-unit-level*.

Using only unit-level activity drivers to assign non-unit-related overhead costs can create distorted product costs. The severity of this distortion depends on whether overhead costs are large enough to significantly affect product costs. One study suggests that overhead costs should be at least 15 percent of total manufacturing costs for ABC to produce significant decision benefits.[2] Of course, if non-unit-based overhead

1. The outcome of bids is difficult to explain.
2. Competitors' prices appear unrealistically low.
3. Products that are difficult to produce show high profits.
4. Operational managers want to drop products that appear profitable.
5. Profit margins are difficult to explain.
6. The company has a highly profitable niche all to itself.
7. Customers do not complain about price increases.
8. The accounting department spends a lot of time supplying cost data for special projects.
9. Some departments are using their own cost accounting system.
10. Product costs change because of changes in financial reporting regulations.

Exhibit 4-7 Symptoms of an Outdated Functional Costing System

1 The list of warning signals is based on Robin Cooper, "You Need a New Cost System When," *Harvard Business Review* (January–February, 1989): pp. 77–82.

2 See Robert Vokurka and Rhonda R. Lummus, "At What Overhead Level Does Activity-Based Costing Pay Off?" *Production and Inventory Management Journal* (First Quarter, 2001): pp. 40–48.

costs are only a small percentage of total overhead costs, then the distortion of product costs would be quite small. In such a case, using unit-based activity drivers to assign overhead costs would be acceptable.

Product Diversity

The presence of significant non-unit overhead costs is a necessary but not sufficient condition for plantwide and departmental rate failure. For example, if products consume the non-unit-level overhead activities in the same proportion as the unit-level overhead activities, then no product costing distortion will occur (with the use of traditional overhead assignment methods). The presence of product diversity is also necessary. **Product diversity** simply means that products consume overhead activities in systematically different proportions. Products might consume overhead in different proportions for several reasons. For example, differences in product size, product complexity, setup time, and size of batches all can cause products to consume overhead at different rates. Regardless of the nature of the product diversity, product cost will be distorted whenever the quantity of unit-based overhead that a product consumes does not vary in direct proportion to the quantity consumed of non-unit-based overhead. The proportion of each activity consumed by a product is defined as the **consumption ratio**. How non-unit-level overhead costs and product diversity can produce distorted product costs is best illustrated with an example.

An Example Illustrating the Failure of Unit-Based Overhead Rates

To illustrate how traditional unit-based overhead rates can distort product costs, we will return to BelRing, this time providing more detailed information about the overhead activities that define total overhead cost. The detailed data are provided in Exhibit 4-8 (assume that the measures are expected and actual outcomes). Because the quantity of regular phones produced is ten times greater than that of cordless phones, we can label the regular phones a high-volume product and the cordless phones a low-volume product. The phones are produced in batches.

For simplicity, only four types of overhead activities, performed by four distinct support departments, are assumed: setting up the equipment for each batch (different configurations are needed for the electronic components associated with each

Activity Usage Measures

	Cordless	Regular	Total
Units produced per year	10,000	100,000	110,000
Prime costs	$78,000	$738,000	$816,000
Direct labor hours	10,000	90,000	100,000
Machine hours	5,000	45,000	50,000
Production runs	20	10	30
Number of moves	60	30	90

Activity Cost Data (Overhead Activities)

Activity	Activity Cost
Setups	$120,000
Material handling	60,000
Machining	100,000
Testing	80,000
Total	$360,000

Exhibit 4-8 Product-Costing Data—BelRing Springdale Plant

phone), moving a batch, machining, and testing. Testing is performed after each department's operations. After fabrication, each component is tested to ensure functionality. After assembly, the entire unit is tested to ensure that it is operational.

Problems with Costing Accuracy The activity usage data in Exhibit 4-8 reveal some serious problems with either plantwide or departmental rates for assigning overhead costs. The main problem with either procedure is the assumption that machine hours or direct labor hours drive or cause all overhead costs.

From Exhibit 4-8, we know that producing regular phones, the high-volume product, uses nine times as many direct labor hours as producing cordless phones, the low-volume product (90,000 hours versus 10,000 hours). Thus, if a plantwide rate is used, the regular phones will be assigned nine times more overhead cost than the cordless phones. But is this reasonable? Do unit-based drivers explain the consumption of all overhead activities? In particular, can we reasonably assume that each product's consumption of overhead increases in direct proportion to the direct labor hours used? Let's look at the four overhead activities and see if unit-based drivers accurately reflect the demands of regular and cordless phone production.

Examination of the data in Exhibit 4-8 suggests that a significant portion of overhead costs is not driven or caused by direct labor hours. For example, each product's demands for setup and material-handling activities are more logically related to the number of production runs and the number of moves, respectively. These non-unit activities represent 50 percent ($180,000/$360,000) of the total overhead costs—a significant percentage. Notice that the low-volume product, cordless phones, uses twice as many runs as the regular phones (20/10) and twice as many moves (60/30). However, use of direct labor hours, a unit-based activity driver, and a plantwide rate assigns nine times more setup and material-handling costs to the regular phones than to the cordless. Thus, product diversity exists, and we should expect product cost distortion because the quantity of unit-based overhead that each product consumes does not vary in direct proportion to the quantity consumed of non-unit-based overhead.

The consumption ratios for the two products are illustrated in Exhibit 4-9. Consumption ratios are simply the proportion of each activity consumed by a product. The consumption ratios suggest that a plantwide rate based on direct labor hours will overcost the regular phones and undercost the cordless phones.

The problem is only aggravated when departmental rates are used (refer to Exhibit 4-5). In the Assembly Department, regular phones consume 25.67 times as many direct labor hours as the cordless phones (77,000/3,000). In the Fabrication Department, regular phones consume nine times as many machine hours as the cordless phones (36,000/4,000). Thus, the regular phones receive about 25.67 times more overhead than the cordless phones in the Assembly Department, and in the

Overhead Activity	Cordless Phone	Regular Phone	Activity Driver
Setups	0.67[a]	0.33[a]	Production runs
Material handling	0.67[b]	0.33[b]	Number of moves
Machining	0.10[c]	0.90[c]	Machine hours
Testing	0.10[d]	0.90[d]	Direct labor hours

[a]20/30 (cordless) and 10/30 (regular)
[b]60/90 (cordless) and 30/90 (regular)
[c]5,000/50,000 (cordless) and 45,000/50,000 (regular)
[d]10,000/100,000 (cordless) and 90,000/100,000 (regular)

Exhibit 4-9 Product Diversity: Consumption Ratios—BelRing Springdale Plant

Fabrication Department they receive nine times more overhead. As Exhibit 4-6 shows, with departmental rates, the unit cost of the cordless phones decreases to $10.73, and the unit cost of the regular phones increases to $10.69. This change is in the wrong direction, which emphasizes the failure of unit-based activity drivers at either the plant level or the departmental level to reflect accurately each product's demands for setup and material-handling costs.

Solving the Problem of Cost Distortion The cost distortion just described can be solved by the use of activity rates. That is, rather than assigning the overhead costs to departmental or plantwide pools, why not calculate a rate for each overhead activity and then use this activity rate to assign overhead costs? Using the drivers indicated in Exhibit 4-9 and the data provided in Exhibit 4-8, activity rates are computed below.

Setup rate:	$120,000/30 runs = $4,000 per run
Material-handling rate:	$60,000/90 moves = $666.67 per move
Machining rate:	$100,000/50,000 machine hours = $2 per machine hour
Testing rate:	$80,000/100,000 direct labor hours = $0.80 per direct labor hour

To assign overhead costs, the amount of activity consumed by each product is needed. These amounts are found in Exhibit 4-8. The calculation of the unit cost for each product using activity rates is given in Exhibit 4-10.

Comparison of Functional-Based and Activity-Based Product Costs

In Exhibit 4-11, the unit cost from activity-based costing is compared with the unit costs produced by functional-based costing using either a plantwide or a departmental rate. This comparison clearly illustrates the effects of using only unit-based activity drivers to assign overhead costs. The activity-based cost assignment reflects the pattern of overhead consumption and is, therefore, the most accurate of the three costs shown in Exhibit 4-11. Activity-based product costing reveals that functional-based costing undercosts the cordless phones and overcosts the regular phones. In fact, the ABC assignment almost doubles the cost of the cordless phones and

	Cordless	Regular
Prime costs	$ 78,000	$738,000
Overhead costs:		
Setups:		
$4,000 × 20	80,000	
$4,000 × 10		40,000
Material handling:		
$666.67 × 60	40,000	
$666.67 × 30		20,000
Machining:		
$2 × 5,000	10,000	
$2 × 45,000		90,000
Testing:		
$0.80 × 10,000	8,000	
$0.80 × 90,000		72,000
Total manufacturing costs	$ 216,000	$960,000
Units produced	÷ 410,000	÷ 100,000
Unit cost (total costs/units)	$ 21.60	$ 9.60

Exhibit 4-10 Unit Cost Calculation Using Activity Rates
BelRing Springdale Plant

Managers Decide

ABC and Dairy Products

ABC has been used to analyze the profitability of products in the dairy case of food retailers. Milk was found to be the most profitable item, taking up just 23 percent of the space in the dairy case yet providing 25 percent of the revenues and 34 percent of the profits. The activity-based unit cost for dairy items was calculated using distribution activities, handling activities, space, and time on the shelf. The average activity-based cost for a dairy-case item was $0.11, with juice costing $0.23 and milk less than $0.05. ABC also revealed that per-unit cost is affected by the type of handling activities used. Costs can be lowered by an appropriate choice of a stocking activity. For example, front-loading and hand-stocking costs 5.5 cents per item whereas using a roll-in cart for stocking costs only 2.7 cents per unit. ■

Source: Jerry Dryer, "ABC's of Milk Selling," *Dairy Foods* (May 1999): p. 31.

decreases the cost of the regular phones by almost $1.00 per unit—a movement in the right direction given the pattern of overhead consumption. In a diverse product environment, ABC promises greater accuracy, and given the importance of making decisions based on correct facts, a detailed look at ABC is certainly merited.

Activity-Based Product Costing: Detailed Description

Objective 4

Explain how an activity-based costing system works for product costing.

In Exhibits 4-1 and 4-2, we saw that functional-based overhead costing involves two major stages: first, overhead costs are assigned to an organizational unit (plant or department), and second, overhead costs are then assigned to products. As Exhibit 4-12 illustrates, an **activity-based costing (ABC) system** first traces costs to activities and then to products. The underlying assumption is that activities consume resources and that products, in turn, consume activities. Thus, the basic activity-based costing model is also a two-stage process. An ABC costing system, however, emphasizes direct tracing and driver tracing (exploiting cause-and-effect relationships), while a functional-based costing system tends to be allocation intensive (largely ignoring cause-and-effect relationships). As the Exhibit 4-12 model reveals, the focus of activity-based costing is activities. Thus, identifying activities must be the first step in designing an activity-based costing system.

Identifying Activities and Their Attributes

Since an activity is action taken or work performed by equipment or people for other people, identifying activities is usually accomplished by interviewing managers or representatives of functional work areas (departments). A set of key questions is

	Cordless	Regular	Source
Plantwide rate	$11.40	$738,000	Exhibit 4-3
Departmental rate	10.73	10.69	Exhibit 4-6
Activity rate	21.60	9.60	Exhibit 4-10

Exhibit 4-11 Comparison of Unit Costs

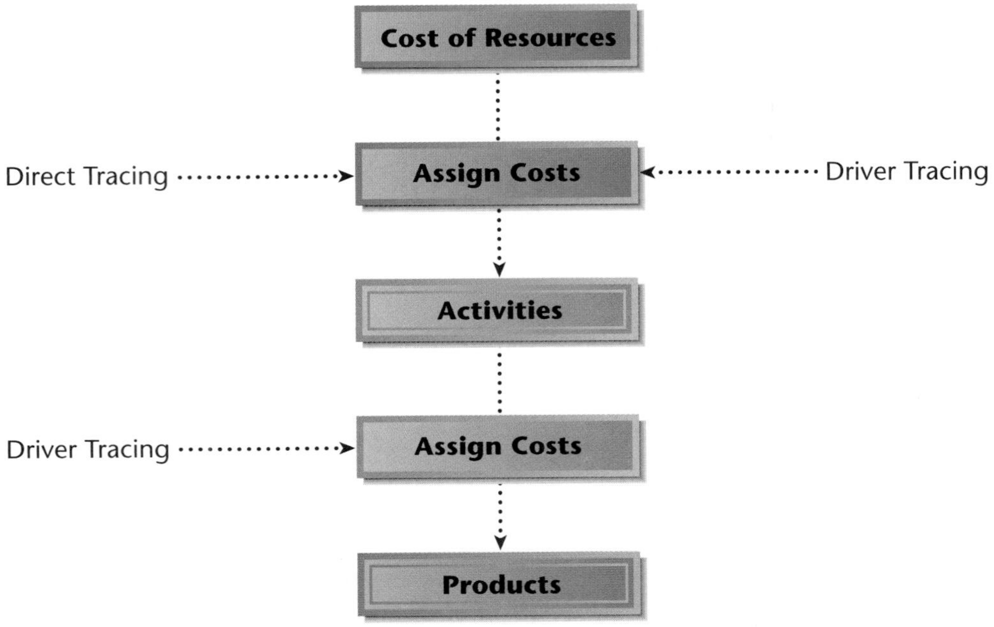

Exhibit 4-12 ABC: Two-Stage Assignment

asked whose answers provide much of the data needed for an activity-based costing system. This interview-derived data is used to prepare an *activity dictionary.* An **activity dictionary** lists the activities in an organization along with some critical activity attributes. **Activity attributes** are financial and nonfinancial information items that describe individual activities. What attributes are used depends on the purpose. Examples of activity attributes associated with a costing objective include types of resources consumed, amount (percentage) of time spent on an activity by workers, cost objects that consume the activity output (reason for performing the activity), a measure of the activity output (activity driver), and the activity name.

© Digital Vision

Interviewers are commonly used to identify activities and their attributes.

Key Set of Questions Interview questions can be used to identify activities and activity attributes needed for costing purposes. The information derived from these questions serves as the basis for constructing an activity dictionary as well as providing data helpful for assigning resource costs to individual activities. The list is not exhaustive but serves to illustrate the nature of the information-gathering process.

1. How many employees are in your department? (Activities consume labor.)
2. What do they do (please describe)? (Activities are people doing things for other people.)
3. Do customers outside your department use any equipment? (Activities also can be equipment doing work for other people.)
4. What resources are used by each activity (equipment, materials, energy)? (Activities consume resources in addition to labor.)

5. What are the outputs of each activity? (Helps identify activity drivers.)
6. Who or what uses the activity output? (Identifies the cost object: products, other activities, customers, etc.)
7. How much time do workers spend on each activity? By equipment? (Information needed to assign the cost of labor and equipment to activities.)

Illustrative Example Suppose, for example, that Jan Booth of Henderson Associates interviews the manager of SpringBanc's credit card department, asking the seven questions just listed. Consider the purpose of and response to each question, in the order indicated.

- *Question 1 (labor resource):* There are six employees, including me.
- *Question 2 (activity identification):* There are four major activities: supervising employees, processing credit card transactions, issuing customer statements, and answering customer questions.
- *Question 3 (activity identification):* Yes. Automatic bank tellers service customers who require cash advances.
- *Question 4 (resource identification):* We each have our own computer, printer, and desk. Paper and other supplies are needed to operate the printers. Of course, we each have a telephone as well.
- *Question 5 (potential activity drivers):* Well, for supervising, I manage employees' needs and try to ensure that they carry out their activities efficiently. Processing transactions produces a posting for each transaction in our computer system and serves as a source for preparing the monthly statements. The number of monthly customer statements has to be the product for the issuing activity, and I suppose that customers served is the output for the answering activity. And I guess that the number of cash advances would measure the product of the automatic teller activity, although the teller really generates more transactions for other products such as checking accounts. So, perhaps the number of teller transactions is the real output.
- *Question 6 (potential cost objects identified):* We have three products: classic, gold, and platinum credit cards. Transactions are processed for these three types of cards, and statements are sent to clients holding these cards. Similarly, answers to questions are all directed to clients who hold these cards. As far as supervising, I spend time ensuring the proper coordination and execution of all activities except for the automatic teller. I really have no role in managing that particular activity.
- *Question 7 (identifying resource drivers):* I just completed a work survey and have the percentage of time calculated for each worker. All five clerks work on each of the three departmental activities. About 40 percent of their time is spent processing transactions, with the rest of their time split evenly between preparing statements and answering questions. Phone time is used only for answering client questions, and computer time is 70 percent transaction processing, 20 percent statement preparation, and 10 percent answering questions. Furthermore, my own time and that of my computer are 100 percent administrative.

Activity Dictionary Based on the answers to the survey, an activity dictionary can now be prepared. Exhibit 4-13 illustrates the dictionary for the credit card department. The activity dictionary names the activity (usually by using an action verb and an object that receives the action), describes the tasks that make up the activity, classifies the activity as *primary* or *secondary,* lists the users (cost objects), and identifies a measure of activity output (activity driver). A **primary activity** is an activity that is consumed by a product or customer. A **secondary activity** is one that is consumed by other primary and secondary activities. Ultimately, secondary activities are consumed by primary activities. For example, the supervising activity is consumed by the following primary activities: processing transactions, preparing statements, and answering phones. The three products, classic, gold, and platinum credit

Activity Name	Activity Description	Activity Type	Cost Object(s)	Activity Driver
Supervising employees	Scheduling, coordinating, and evaluating performance	Secondary	Activities within department	Total labor time for each activity
Processing transactions	Sorting, keying, and verifying	Primary	Credit cards	Number of transactions
Preparing statements	Reviewing, printing, stuffing, and mailing	Primary	Credit cards	Number of statements
Answering questions	Answering, logging, reviewing database, and making call backs	Primary	Credit cards	Number of calls
Providing automatic tellers	Accessing accounts, withdrawing funds	Primary	Credit cards, checking and savings accounts	Number of teller transactions

Exhibit 4-13 Activity Dictionary: SpringBanc Credit Card Department

cards, in turn, consume the primary activities. It is not unusual for a typical organization to produce an activity dictionary containing 200 to 300 activities.

Assigning Costs to Activities

Once activities are identified and described, the next task is determining how much it costs to perform each activity. This requires identification of the resources being consumed by each activity. Activities consume resources such as labor, materials, energy, and capital. The cost of these resources is found in the general ledger, but how much is spent on each activity is not revealed. Thus, it becomes necessary to assign the resource costs to activities using direct and driver tracing. For labor resources, a *work distribution matrix* is often used. A work distribution matrix simply identifies the amount of labor consumed by each activity and is derived from the interview process (or a written survey). For example, the manager of SpringBanc's credit card department disclosed the following about labor usage by the individual activities (see Question 7):

	Percentage of Time on Each Activity	
Activity	**Supervisor**	**Clerks**
Supervising employees	100%	0%
Processing transactions	0	40
Preparing statements	0	30
Answering questions	0	30

The time spent on each activity is the basis for assigning the labor costs to the activity. If the time is 100 percent, then labor is exclusive to the activity and the assignment method is direct tracing (such would be the case for the labor cost of supervision). If the resource is shared by several activities (as is the case of the clerical resource), then the assignment is driver tracing, and the drivers are called *resource drivers.* **Resource drivers** are factors that measure the consumption of resources by activities. Once resource drivers are identified, then the costs of the resource can be assigned to the activity. Assume, for example, that the supervisor's salary is $50,000 and each clerk is paid a salary of $30,000 ($150,000 total clerical cost for five clerks). The amount of labor cost assigned to each activity is given below.

Supervising employees	\$50,000 (by direct tracing)
Processing transactions	\$60,000 (0.4 × \$150,000)
Preparing statements	\$45,000 (0.3 × \$150,000)
Answering questions	\$45,000 (0.3 × \$150,000)

Labor, of course, is not the only resource consumed by activities. Activities also consume materials, capital, and energy. The interview, for example, reveals that the activities within the credit card department use computers (capital), phones (capital), desks (capital), and paper (materials). The automatic teller activity uses the automatic teller (capital) and energy. The costs of these other resources must also be assigned to the various activities. They are assigned in the same way as was described for labor (using direct tracing and resource drivers). The cost of computers, for example, could be assigned using direct tracing (for the supervising activity) and hours of usage for the remaining activities. From the interview, we know the relative usage of computers by each activity. The general ledger reveals that the cost per computer is \$1,200 per year. Thus, an additional \$1,200 would be assigned to the supervising activity, and \$6,000 (5 × \$1,200) would be assigned to the other activities based on relative usage—70 percent to processing transactions (\$4,200), 20 percent to preparing statements (\$1,200), and 10 percent to answering questions (\$600). Repeating this process for all resources, the total cost of each activity can be calculated. Exhibit 4-14 gives the cost of the activities associated with the credit card department under the assumption that all resource costs have been assigned. (These numbers are assumed because all resource data are not given for their calculation.)

Assigning Activity Costs to Other Activities

Assigning costs to activities completes the first stage of activity-based costing. In this first stage, activities are classified as primary or secondary. If there are secondary activities, then intermediate stages exist. In an intermediate stage, the cost of secondary activities is assigned to those activities that consume their output. For example, supervising employees is a secondary activity. The output measure is the total employee time used by each activity (see the activity dictionary, Exhibit 4-13). From the work distribution matrix prepared earlier, we know that the three departmental activities (primary activities) use clerical labor in the proportions, 40 percent, 30 percent, and 30 percent. Thus, the cost of the supervising activity would be assigned to each consuming primary activity using these ratios (which now function as an activity driver). The new costs using the activity driver and the activity costs from Exhibit 4-14 are calculated and presented in Exhibit 4-15.

Assigning Costs to Products

Once the costs of primary activities are determined, they can be assigned to products in proportion to their usage of the activity, as measured by activity drivers. This assignment is accomplished by calculating a predetermined activity rate and multiplying

Supervising employees	\$ 75,000
Processing transactions	100,000
Preparing statements	79,500
Answering questions	69,900
Providing automatic tellers	250,000

Exhibit 4-14 Activity Costs: First Stage—SpringBanc Credit Card Department

Processing transactions	$130,000[a]
Preparing statements	102,000[b]
Answering questions	92,400[c]
Providing automatic tellers	250,000

[a]$100,000 + (0.4 × $75,000)
[b]$79,500 + (0.3 × $75,000)
[c]$69,900 + (0.3 × $75,000)

Exhibit 4-15 Activity Costs: Intermediate Stage
SpringBanc Credit Card Department

this rate by the actual usage of the activity. From Exhibit 4-13, the activity drivers are identified for each of the four primary activities: number of transactions for processing transactions, number of statements for preparing statements, number of calls for answering questions, and number of teller transactions for the activity of providing automatic tellers. To calculate an activity rate, the practical capacity of each activity must be determined. To assign costs, we also need the amount of each activity consumed by each product. For our purposes, we will assume that the practical activity capacity is equal to the total activity usage by all products. For the SpringBanc Credit Card Department, the following actual data have been collected:

	Classic Card	Gold Card	Platinum Card	Total
Number of cards	5,000	3,000	2,000	10,000
Transactions processed	600,000	300,000	100,000	1,000,000
Number of statements	60,000	36,000	24,000	120,000
Number of calls	10,000	12,000	8,000	30,000
Number of teller transactions*	15,000	3,000	2,000	20,000

*The number of teller transactions for the cards is 10 percent of the total transactions from all sources. Thus, teller transactions total 200,000 (10 × 20,000).

Using these data and the costs from Exhibit 4-15, the activity rates can be calculated:

Rate calculations:

Processing transactions:	$130,000/1,000,000 = $0.13 per transaction
Preparing statements:	$102,000/120,000 = $0.85 per statement
Answering questions:	$92,400/30,000 = $3.08 per call
Providing automatic tellers:	$250,000/200,000 = $1.25 per transaction

These rates provide the price charged for activity usage. Using these rates, costs are assigned as shown in Exhibit 4-16. As should be evident, the assignment process is the same as the one used for BelRing illustrated earlier in Exhibit 4-10. However, we now know the whole story behind the development of the activity rates and usage measures. Furthermore, the SpringBanc setting emphasizes the utility of activity-based costing in service organizations.

Detailed Classification of Activities

For product-costing purposes, activities can be classified into one of the following four general activity categories: (1) unit level, (2) batch level, (3) product level, and (4) facility level. Classifying activities into these general categories facilitates product costing because the costs of activities associated with the different levels respond to

	Classic	Gold	Platinum
Processing transactions:			
$0.13 × 600,000	$ 78,000		
$0.13 × 300,000		$39,000	
$0.13 × 100,000			$13,000
Preparing statements:			
$0.85 × 60,000	51,000		
$0.85 × 36,000		30,600	
$0.85 × 24,000			20,400
Answering questions:			
$3.08 × 10,000	30,800		
$3.08 × 12,000		36,960	
$3.08 × 8,000			24,640
Providing automatic tellers:			
$1.25 × 15,000	18,750		
$1.25 × 3,000		3,750	
$1.25 × 2,000			2,500
Total costs	$178,550	$110,310	$60,540
Units	÷ 5,000	÷ 3,000	÷ 2,000
Unit cost (total cost/units)	$ 35.71	$ 36.77	$ 30.27

Exhibit 4-16 Assigning Costs: Final Stage

different types of drivers (cost behavior differs by level). The definition of the activities belonging to each general category clearly illustrates this feature. **Unit-level activities** are those performed each time a unit is produced. For example, machining and assembly are activities performed each time a unit is produced. The costs of unit-level activities vary with the number of units produced. **Batch-level activities** are those performed each time a batch of goods is produced. The costs of batch-level activities vary with the number of batches, but they are fixed with respect to the number of units in each batch. Setups, inspections (unless each unit is inspected), production scheduling, and material handling are examples of batch-level activities. **Product-level (sustaining) activities** are those performed as needed to support the various products produced by a company. These activities consume inputs that develop products or allow products to be produced and sold. These activities and their costs tend to increase as the number of different products increases. Engineering changes, development of product-testing procedures, marketing a product, process engineering, and expediting are examples of product-level activities. **Facility-level activities** are those that sustain a factory's general manufacturing processes. These activities benefit the organization at some level but do not provide a benefit for any specific product. Examples include plant management, landscaping, support of community programs, security, property taxes, and plant depreciation.

Inspection and scheduling are examples of batch-level activities.

Of the four general levels, the first three—unit level, batch level, and product level—contain product-related activities. For these three levels, it is possible to measure the demands placed on the activities by individual products. Activities within these three levels can further be subdivided on the basis of consumption ratios. Activities with the same consumption ratios can use the same activity driver to assign costs. Thus, in effect, all activities within each of the first three levels that have the same activity driver are grouped together. This final grouping creates a homogeneous set of activities: a collection of activities that are at the same level and use the same activity driver.

The fourth general category, facility-level activities, poses a problem for the ABC philosophy of tracing costs to products. Tracing activity costs to individual products depends on the ability to identify the amount of each activity consumed by a product (product demands for activities must be measured). Facility-level activities (and their costs) are common to a variety of products, and it is not possible to identify how individual products consume these activities. A pure ABC system, therefore, would not assign these costs to products. They would be treated as period costs. In effect, these costs are fixed costs—costs that are not driven by any of the cost drivers found in any of the first three categories. In practice, companies adopting ABC systems usually implement a full-costing approach and allocate these facility-level costs to individual products. Unit-level, batch-level, or product-level cost drivers are often used for the allocation. As a practical matter, assigning these costs may not significantly distort product costs, because they are likely to be small relative to the total costs that are appropriately traced to individual products.

There is, however, a possible exception to this observation about facility-level costs and allocation. When a company has organized its production facilities around product lines, then it can be argued that space drivers measure the consumption of facility-level costs. This is because floor space within a plant is dedicated to the production of a single product or subassembly. In this case, square footage occupied can be viewed as a possible activity driver for facility costs. Assigning facility-level costs on the basis of space drivers can also serve to motivate managers to reduce the space needed for production, thus reducing facility-level costs over time.

Managers Decide

ABC in a Service Organization

Activity-based costing is useful for all types of organizations and businesses. For example, the Small Business Administration (SBA) uses Oros, an activity-based costing software, to determine the costs of its activities and cost objects. The SBA adopted an ABC system because it provides a more accurate revelation of the costs of programs and services. This enables the SBA to engage in improvements that produce a more efficient delivery of its programs and services. ABC is used to prepare the SBA's annual statement of net costs. It is also used to prepare other unit cost reports. To maintain the accuracy of the assignment of resources costs to the various activities, the SBA conducts a survey (at least annually) of its employees to assess the amount of time spent on activities. Thus, the SBA's ABC work distribution matrix is frequently updated to ensure accurate activity cost determination. ■

Source: "Activity Based Costing," Small Business Administration, http://www.sba.gov/cfo/abc.html, accessed July 16, 2004.

Reducing the Size and Complexity of the Activity-Based Costing System

Objective 5

Explain how the number of activity rates can be reduced.

In the first stage of activity-based costing, activities are identified, costs are associated with individual activities, and activities are classified as primary or secondary. In the intermediate stage, costs of secondary activities are reassigned to primary activities. In the final stage, costs of primary activities are assigned to products or customers. Assigning costs to other activities (intermediate stage) or assigning costs to products and customers (final stage) requires the use of activity rates. In principle, there is an activity rate calculated for each activity. An organization may have hundreds of different activities and, thus, hundreds of activity rates. Although information technology certainly is capable of handling this volume, there may be some merit to reducing the number of rates, if possible. For example, fewer rates may produce more readable and manageable product cost reports. Further, the ongoing data collection requirement is reduced as the number of rates is reduced. Fewer rates may also reduce the perceived complexity of an activity-based costing system, increasing the likelihood of managerial acceptance. One of the more frequently quoted reasons for refusing to implement an ABC system is the perceived complexity of the system.

Reducing Rates Using Consumption Ratios

One very straightforward way of reducing rates is to group all activities with the same consumption ratios into one cost pool. For example, suppose that a BelRing plant uses has seven activities, two of which are *testing products* and *packing products*, costing $44,000 and $36,000, respectively. Two models of telephones are produced. The activity data for these two activities are as follows:

		Consumption of Activity	
Activity	**Driver**	**Standard Model**	**Luxury Model**
Testing products	Testing hours	4,000	6,000
Packing products	Packing orders	7,200	10,800

The activity rates for each activity are $4.40 per testing hour ($44,000/10,000) and $2.00 per packing order ($36,000/18,000). The amount of cost assigned to the Standard Model is $32,000 [($4.40 × 4,000) + ($2.00 × 7,200)] and the amount assigned to the Luxury Model is $48,000 [$4.40 × 7,200) + ($2.00 × 10,800)]. Notice that the consumption ratios are equal for each activity: 0.40 and 0.60 (the Standard Model consumes 40 percent of each activity and the Luxury Model consumes 60 percent). Since the consumption ratios are the same, it is possible to combine the two activities into one pool with a total cost of $80,000. Either driver can be used to calculate the **pool rate**. For example, if testing hours are used, then the activity rate is $8.00 per testing hour ($80,000/10,000). The amount assigned to the Standard Model is $32,000 ($8.00 × 4,000) and the amount assigned to the Luxury Model is $48,000 ($8.00 × 6,000), exactly the same assignment as using the two separate rates. Thus, the first step in reducing the size of an ABC system is to combine all activities with the same rates into one single cost pool.

Reducing Rates by Approximating ABC

An approximately relevant ABC system may make an organization better off than a precisely useless one. One way to reduce the number of rates is to use only the most expensive activities and their drivers to assign costs to products.[3] The costs of the less

3 Tom Pryor, "Simplify Your ABC," *Cost Management Newsletter* (June 2004), Issue No. 152.

Activity	Activity Cost	Driver	Expected Consumption Ratios Quantity[a]	Standard	Luxury
1. Setting up batches	$ 200,000	Number of setups	1,000	0.25	0.75
2. Machining	250,000	Machine hours	100,000	0.50	0.50
3. Testing	80,000	Test hours	10,000	0.30	0.70
4. Purchasing materials	350,000	Purchase orders	3,500	0.20	0.80
5. Unloading materials	60,000	Receiving orders	3,000	0.35	0.65
6. Moving materials	60,000	Number of moves	1,500	0.40	0.60
Total activity cost	$1,000,000				
Unit-level (plantwide) cost assignment[b]				$500,000	$500,000
Activity-based cost assisgnment[c]				$314,000	$686,000

[a]Total amount of activity expected to be used by each product.
[b]Calculated using machine hours as the single unit-level driver: Standard = 0.50 × $1,000,000; Luxury = 0.50 × $1,000,000.
[c]Calculated using each activity cost and either the associated consumption ratios or activity rates. For example, the cost assigned to the standard model using the consumption ratio for setting up batches is 0.25 × $200,000 = $50,000. Repeating this calculation for each activity and summing yields a total of $323,000 assigned to the standard cell phone.

Exhibit 4-17 ABC Data—BelRing Denver Plant

expensive activities are allocated to the cost pools of the selected expensive activities. In this way, most costs are assigned to the products accurately. The costs of the most expensive activities are assigned using the appropriate cause-and-effect drivers, while the costs the less expensive activities are assigned somewhat arbitrarily. This approach is simple and easy to understand and often leads to a good approximation of the ABC assignments.

To illustrate the nature of this approximating approach, a data set for BelRing's Denver plant is used. The Denver plant produces two types of cell phones: standard and luxury. The ABC data for this plant is given in Exhibit 4-17. Notice that activities 1, 2, and 4 account for 80 percent of total activity cost. The cost assignments using the cost pools and the associated activity drivers of these three activities are shown in Exhibit 4-18. The costs of the three relatively inexpensive activities are allocated to the three expensive activities in proportion to their original cost.

Exhibit 4-18 illustrates that the ABC cost assignments are approximated quite well by the reduced system of three drivers. For the standard cell phone, the error is about 2.5 percent [($314,000 − $306,250)/$314,000], using the ABC assignment as the benchmark.

Activity	Activity Cost	Driver	Expected Consumption Ratios Quantity[a]	Standard	Luxury
1. Setting up batches	$ 250,000	Number of setups	1,000	0.25	0.75
2. Machining	312,500	Machine hours	100,000	0.50	0.50
4. Purchasing materials	437,500	Purchase orders	3,500	0.20	0.80
Total activity cost	$1,000,000				
Reduced system ABC assignment[b]				$306,250	$693,750

[a]Original activity cost plus share of the remaining less expensive activities. For example, the cost pool for setting up batches is $200,000 + [($200,000/$800,000) × $200,000].
[b]Costs are assigned to each product using the consumption ratios of the respective pools. For example, the cost assigned to the standard cell phone for setups is 0.25 × $250,000 = $62,500. Repeating this calculation for the other two activities and summing yields a total of $306,250.

Exhibit 4-18 Approximating ABC Assignments—BelRing Denver Plant

Comparison with Functional-Based Costing

In a functional-based system, the consumption of overhead by products is assumed to be explained only by unit-based activity drivers. For plantwide rates, only one driver is used to assign costs. In a more sophisticated functional system, overhead costs are classified as fixed or variable with respect to unit-based drivers. Unit-based costing systems allocate fixed overhead to individual products, using fixed overhead rates, and assign variable overhead, using variable overhead rates. From the perspective of activity-based costing, the variable overhead is appropriately traced to individual products (for this category, overhead consumption increases as units produced increases). However, assigning fixed overhead costs using unit-based activity drivers can be arbitrary and may not reflect the activities actually consumed by the products. Many of the costs assigned in the traditional fixed overhead category are, in reality, batch-level, product-level, and facility-level costs that vary with drivers other than unit-level drivers.

Activity-based costing systems improve product costing accuracy by recognizing that many of the so-called fixed overhead costs vary in proportion to changes other than production volume. By understanding what causes these costs to increase or decrease, managers can trace them to individual products. This cause-and-effect relationship allows managers to improve product costing accuracy, which can significantly improve decision making. Additionally, this large pool of fixed overhead costs is no longer so mysterious. Knowing the underlying behavior of many of these costs allows managers to exert more control over the activities that cause the costs. However, it is also true that this increased accuracy comes with increased complexity. Thus, it may be necessary to develop a simpler system than a full-blown ABC system, but one which still comes close to the accuracy of ABC.

Summary of Learning Objectives

1. Discuss the importance of unit costs.
Unit costs are important for valuing inventory, determining income, and providing input to a variety of decisions such as pricing, making or buying, and accepting or rejecting special orders. Because of their importance, their accuracy becomes a critical issue.

2. Describe functional-based costing approaches.
Functional-based costing assigns direct materials and direct labor using direct tracing; overhead is assigned using a two-stage process. In the first stage, overhead costs are collected in pools, either at the plant level or the departmental level. Once the pools are defined, the costs of the overhead pools are assigned to products using unit-level drivers, the most common being direct labor hours.

3. Tell why functional-based costing approaches may produce distorted costs.
Overhead costs have increased in significance over time and in many firms represent a much higher percentage of product costs than direct labor. At the same time, many overhead activities are unrelated to the units produced. Functional-based costing systems are not able to assign the costs of these non-unit-related overhead activities properly. These overhead activities are consumed by products in different proportions than unit-based overhead activities. Because of this, assigning overhead using only unit-based drivers can distort product costs. This can be a serious matter if the non-unit-based overhead costs are a significant proportion of total overhead costs.

4. Explain how an activity-based costing system works for product costing.
Activities are identified and defined through the use of interviews and surveys. This information allows an activity dictionary to be constructed. The activity dictionary lists activities and potential activity drivers, classifies activities as primary or secondary, and provides any other attributes deemed to be important. Resource costs are assigned to activities by using direct tracing and resource drivers. The costs of secondary activities are ultimately assigned to primary activities using activity drivers. Finally, the costs of primary activities are assigned to products, customers,

and other cost objects. Thus, the cost assignment process is described by the following general steps: (1) identifying the major activities and building an activity dictionary, (2) determining the cost of those activities, (3) identifying a measure of consumption for activity costs (activity drivers), (4) calculating an activity rate, (5) measuring the demands placed on activities by each product, and (6) calculating product costs.

5. Explain how the number of activity rates can be reduced.

Rates can be reduced by combining activities with the same consumption ratios into one cost pool. Rates can also be reduced with an approximating approach by selecting the most expensive activities and allocating the costs of the remaining activities to the reduced set in proportion to their original costs.

Key Terms

Activity attributes, 130
Activity-based costing (ABC) system, 129
Activity dictionary, 130
Activity drivers, 125
Actual costing, 119
Applied overhead, 121
Batch-level activities, 135
Consumption ratio, 126
Cost assignment, 118
Cost measurement, 118
Expected activity capacity, 120
Facility-level activities, 135
Non-unit-level activity drivers, 125
Normal activity capacity, 120
Normal costing, 119
Overapplied overhead, 122
Overhead variance, 121
Pool rate, 137
Practical activity capacity, 120
Predetermined overhead rate, 119
Primary activity, 131
Product diversity, 126
Product-level (sustaining) activities, 135
Resource drivers, 132
Secondary activity, 131
Theoretical activity capacity, 120
Underapplied overhead, 121
Unit cost, 118
Unit-level activities, 135
Unit-level activity drivers, 119

Review Problems

1. Plantwide Rates

Nabors Company produces two types of stereo units: deluxe and regular. For the most recent year, Nabors reports the following data:

Budgeted overhead	$180,000
Expected activity (in direct labor hours)	50,000
Actual activity (in direct labor hours)	51,000
Actual overhead	$200,000

	Deluxe	Regular
Units produced	5,000	50,000
Prime costs	$40,000	$300,000
Direct labor hours	5,000	46,000

Required

1. Calculate a predetermined overhead rate based on direct labor hours.
2. What is the applied overhead?
3. What is the under- or overapplied overhead?
4. Calculate the unit cost of each stereo unit.

Solution

1. Rate = $180,000/50,000 = $3.60 per direct labor hour
2. Applied overhead = $3.60 × 51,000 = $183,600

3. Overhead variance = $200,000 − $183,600 = $16,400 underapplied
4. Unit cost:

	Deluxe	Regular
Prime costs	$40,000	$300,000
Overhead costs:		
$3.60 × 5,000	18,000	
$3.60 × 46,000		165,600
Total manufacturing costs	$58,000	$465,600
Units produced	5,000	50,000
Unit cost (total costs/units)	$ 11.60	$ 9.31*

*Rounded

2. Departmental Rates

Nabors Company gathers the following departmental data for a second year. Two types of stereo units are produced: deluxe and regular.

	Fabrication	Assembly
Budgeted overhead	$120,000	$60,000
Expected and actual usage (direct labor hours):		
Deluxe	3,000	2,000
Regular	3,000	43,000
	6,000	45,000

	Fabrication	Assembly
Expected and actual usage (machine hours):		
Deluxe	2,000	5,000
Regular	18,000	5,000
	20,000	10,000

In addition to the departmental data, the following information is provided:

	Deluxe	Regular
Units produced	5,000	50,000
Prime costs	$40,000	$300,000

Required

1. Calculate departmental overhead rates, using machine hours for fabrication and direct labor hours for assembly.
2. Calculate the applied overhead by department.
3. Calculate the applied overhead by product.
4. Calculate unit costs.

Solution

1. Departmental rates:

   Fabrication: $120,000/20,000 = $6.00 per machine hour
   Assembly: $60,000/45,000 = $1.33* per direct labor hour

   *Rounded

2. Applied overhead (by department):

   Fabrication: $6.00 × 20,000 = $120,000
   Assembly: $1.33 × 45,000 = $59,850

3. Applied overhead (by product):

   Deluxe: ($6.00 × 2,000) + ($1.33 × 2,000) = $14,660
   Regular: ($6.00 × 18,000) + ($1.33 × 43,000) = $165,190

4. Unit cost (rounded to the nearest cent):

   Deluxe: ($40,000 + $14,660)/5,000 = $10.93
   Regular: ($300,000 + $165,190)/50,000 = $9.30

3. Activity-Based Rates

Nabors Company produces two types of stereo units: deluxe and regular. Activity data follow:

	Product-Costing Data		
Activity Usage Measures	**Deluxe**	**Regular**	**Total**
Units produced per year	5,000	50,000	55,000
Prime costs	$39,000	$369,000	$408,000
Direct labor hours	5,000	45,000	50,000
Machine hours	10,000	90,000	100,000
Production runs	10	5	15
Number of moves	120	60	180

	Activity Cost Data (Overhead Activities)
Activity	**Activity Cost**
Setups	$ 60,000
Material handling	30,000
Power	50,000
Testing	40,000
Total	$180,000

Required

1. Calculate the consumption ratios for each activity.
2. Group activities based on the consumption ratios and activity level.
3. Calculate a rate for each pooled group of activities.
4. Using the pool rates, calculate unit product costs.

Solution

1. Consumption ratios:

Overhead Activity	Deluxe	Regular	Activity Driver
Setups	0.67[a]	0.33[a]	Production runs
Material handling	0.67[b]	0.33[b]	Number of moves
Power	0.10[c]	0.90[c]	Machine hours
Testing	0.10[d]	0.90[d]	Direct labor hours

[a]10/15 (deluxe) and 5/15 (regular)
[b]120/180 (deluxe) and 60/180 (regular)
[c]10,000/100,000 (deluxe) and 90,000/100,000 (regular)
[d]5,000/50,000 (deluxe) and 45,000/50,000 (regular)

2. Batch-level: setups and material handling
Unit-level: power and testing

3.

Batch-Level Pool			Unit-Level Pool	
Setups	$60,000		Power	$ 50,000
Material handling	30,000		Testing	40,000
Total	$90,000		Total	$ 90,000
Runs	÷ 15		Machine hours	÷100,000
Pool rate	$ 6,000 per run		Pool rate	$ 0.90 per machine hour

4. Unit costs: activity-based costing

	Deluxe	Regular
Prime costs	$ 39,000	$369,000
Overhead costs:		
Batch-level pool:		
($6,000 × 10)	60,000	
($6,000 × 5)		30,000
Unit-level pool:		
($0.90 × 10,000)	9,000	
($0.90 × 90,000)		81,000
Total manufacturing costs	$108,000	$480,000
Units produced	÷ 5,000	÷ 50,000
Unit cost (total costs/units)	$ 21.60	$ 9.60

Questions for Writing and Discussion

1. Explain why knowing the unit cost of a product or service is important.
2. What is cost measurement? Cost assignment? What is the difference between the two?
3. Explain why an actual overhead rate is rarely used for product costing.
4. Describe the two-stage process associated with plantwide overhead rates.
5. Describe the two-stage process for departmental overhead rates.
6. Explain why departmental rates might be chosen over plantwide rates.
7. Explain how a plantwide overhead rate, using a unit-level cost driver, can produce distorted product costs. In your answer, identify two major factors that impair the ability of plantwide rates to assign cost accurately.
8. Explain how low-volume products can be undercosted and high-volume products overcosted if only unit-level cost drivers are used to assign overhead costs.
9. Explain how undercosting low-volume products and overcosting high-volume products can affect the competitive position of a firm.
10. What are non-unit-level overhead activities? Non-unit-level cost drivers? Give some examples.
11. What is meant by "product diversity"?
12. What is an overhead consumption ratio?
13. Explain how departmental overhead rates can produce product costs that are more distorted than those computed using a plantwide rate.
14. Overhead costs are the source of product cost distortions. Do you agree or disagree? Explain.
15. What is activity-based product costing?
16. What is an activity dictionary?
17. What is the difference between primary and secondary activities?
18. Explain how costs are assigned to activities.
19. What are unit-level activities? Batch-level activities? Product-level activities? Facility-level activities?
20. Explain how the number of activity rates can be reduced in an ABC system while maintaining a reasonable level of accuracy.

Exercises

4-1

Normal versus Actual Costing
LO1

Monte Company produces ski boots. At the beginning of the year, the cost manager estimated that overhead costs would be $11,640,000 and that the units produced would be 1,200,000. Actual data concerning production for the past year follow:

	Quarter 1	Quarter 2	Quarter 3	Quarter 4	Total
Units produced	400,000	160,000	80,000	560,000	1,200,000
Prime costs	$8,000,000	$3,200,000	$1,600,000	$11,200,000	$24,000,000
Overhead costs	$3,200,000	$2,400,000	$3,600,000	$2,800,000	$12,000,000

Required

1. Calculate the unit cost for each quarter and for the year using the following costs:
   a. Actual prime costs
   b. Actual overhead costs
   c. Actual total manufacturing costs
2. What do the calculations in Requirement 1 tell you about actual costing?
3. Using supporting calculations, describe how normal costing would work.

4-2

Plantwide Rates; Overhead Variance
LO1, LO2

Millison Manufacturing uses a normal costing system. Budgeted overhead for the coming year is $27,000,000. Expected actual activity is 90,000 direct labor hours. During the year, Millison worked a total of 91,000 direct labor hours and actual overhead totaled $27,200,000.

Required

1. Compute the predetermined overhead rate for Millison Manufacturing.
2. Compute the applied overhead.
3. Compute the overhead variance, and label the variance as underapplied or overapplied overhead.
4. Explain why predetermined rates are used.

4-3

Unit Cost; Plantwide Overhead Rate; Applied Overhead
LO1, LO2

EXCEL

Gandars Associates produces carburetors for small engines and uses a normal costing system. The following data are available for 2006:

Budgeted:	
Overhead	$4,500,000
Machine hours	187,500
Direct labor hours	600,000
Actual:	
Units produced	750,000
Overhead	$4,466,250
Prime costs	$6,750,000
Machine hours	187,875
Direct labor hours	585,000

Overhead is applied on the basis of direct labor hours.

Required

1. What is the predetermined overhead rate?
2. What is the applied overhead for 2006?

3. Was overhead overapplied or underapplied, and by how much?
4. What is the unit cost for the year?

4-4

Unit Overhead Cost; Predetermined Plant Overhead Rate; Applied Overhead
LO1, LO2

Using the information from **Exercise 4-3**, suppose Gandars Associates applies overhead to production on the basis of machine hours instead of direct labor hours.

Required

1. What is the predetermined overhead rate?
2. What is the applied overhead for 2006?
3. Is overhead overapplied or underapplied, and by how much?
4. What is the unit cost?
5. How can Gandars Associates decide whether to use direct labor hours or machine hours as the basis for applying overhead?

4-5

Unit Overhead Cost; Predetermined Departmental Overhead Rates; Overhead Variance
LO1, LO2

EXCEL

Romsen Manufacturing, Inc., a producer of precision machine parts, uses a predetermined overhead rate to apply overhead. Overhead is applied on the basis of machine hours in the Drilling Department and on the basis of direct hours in the Assembly Department. At the beginning of 2006, the following estimates are provided for the coming year:

	Drilling	Assembly
Direct labor hours	20,000	200,000
Machine hours	280,000	20,000
Inspection hours	4,000	8,000
Direct labor cost	$380,000	$1,800,000
Overhead cost	$600,000	$392,000

Actual results reported for 2006 are as follows:

	Drilling	Assembly
Direct labor hours	42,000	196,000
Machine hours	288,000	22,000
Inspection hours	4,000	8,000
Direct labor cost	$168,000	$882,400
Overhead cost	$602,000	$412,000

Required

1. Compute the predetermined overhead rates for each department.
2. Compute the applied overhead for the year 2006. What is the underapplied or overapplied overhead for each department? For the firm?
3. Suppose a job used 4,000 machine hours in drilling and 1,600 direct labor hours in assembly. If the job size is 8,000 units, what is the overhead cost per unit?

4-6

Predetermined Overhead Rates; Unit Product Costs
LO1, LO2

Refer to **Exercise 4-5**. Suppose that the overhead costs are divided between two activities as follows:

Machining	$632,000
Inspection	360,000

Required

1. Calculate predetermined overhead rates for the two activities, machining and inspection.

2. Suppose a job used 4,000 machine hours and 800 inspection hours. If the job size is 8,000 units, what is the overhead cost per unit?

4-7

Consumption Ratios
LO2

Welstar Company produces two types of get-well cards: scented and regular. Drivers for four activities are given below:

	Scented Cards	Regular Cards
Inspection hours	40	160
Setup hours	50	50
Machine hours	200	600
Number of moves	225	75

Required

1. Calculate the consumption ratios for the four drivers.
2. Is there evidence of product diversity? Explain.

4-8

Activity Rates
LO3

Refer to **Exercise 4-7**. The following activity data have been collected:

Inspecting products	$2,000
Setting up equipment	2,500
Machining	4,000
Moving materials	900

Required

1. Calculate the activity rates that would be used to assign costs to each product.
2. Suppose that the activity rate for inspecting products is $20 per inspection hour. How many hours of inspection are expected for the coming year?

4-9

Activity-Based Product Costing; Service organization
LO3

EXCEL

Suppose that a cardiology ward has gathered the following information for four nursing activities and two types of patients:

		Patient Category		
	Driver	Normal	Intensive	Activity Rate
Treating patients	Treatments	5,000	20,000	$4.00
Providing hygienic care	Hygienic hours	5,000	11,000	5.00
Responding to requests	Requests	30,000	50,000	2.00
Monitoring patients	Monitoring hours	20,000	180,000	0.75

Required

1. Determine the total nursing costs assigned to each patient category.
2. Output is measured in patient days. Assuming that the normal patient category uses 10,000 patient days and the intensive patient category uses 8,000 patient days, calculate the nursing cost per patient day for each type of patient.

4-10

Product Costing Accuracy; Consumption Ratios
LO3

Plata Company produces two products: a mostly handcrafted soft leather briefcase under the label Maletin Elegant and a leather briefcase produced largely through automation and sold under the label Maletin Fina. The two products use two overhead activities, with the following costs:

Setting up equipment	$ 3,000
Machining	18,000

The controller has collected the expected annual prime costs for each briefcase, the machine hours, the setup hours, and the expected production.

	Elegant	Fina
Direct labor	$9,000	$3,000
Direct materials	$3,000	$3,000
Units	3,000	3,000
Machine hours	500	4,500
Setup hours	100	100

Required

1. Do you think that the direct labor costs and direct materials costs are accurately traced to each briefcase? Explain.
2. Calculate the consumption ratios for each activity.
3. Calculate the overhead cost per unit for each briefcase, using a plantwide rate based on direct labor costs. Comment on this approach to assigning overhead.
4. Calculate the overhead cost per unit for each briefcase using overhead rates based on machine hours and setup hours. Explain why these assignments are more accurate than using direct labor costs.

4-11

Assigning Costs to Activities; Resource Drivers
LO4

Receiving has three activities: unloading, counting goods, and inspecting. Unloading uses a forklift that is leased for $12,000 per year. The forklift is used only for unloading. The fuel for the forklift is $2,400 per year. Other operating costs (maintenance) for the forklift total $1,000 per year. Inspection uses some special testing equipment that has a depreciation of $800 per year and an operating cost of $500. Receiving has three employees who have an average salary of $40,000 per year. The work distribution matrix for the receiving personnel is given below:

Activity	Percentage of time on each activity
Unloading	40%
Counting	25%
Inspecting	35%

There are no other resources used for these activities.

Required

1. Calculate the cost of each activity.
2. Explain the two methods used to assign costs to activities.

4-12

Formation of an Activity Dictionary
LO4

A hospital is in the process of implementing an ABC system. A pilot study is being done to assess the effects of the costing changes on specific products. Of particular interest is the cost of caring for patients who receive in-patient recovery treatment for illness, surgery (noncardiac), and injury. These patients are housed on the third and fourth floors of the hospital (the floors are dedicated to patient care and have only nursing stations and patient rooms). A partial transcript of an interview with the hospital's nursing supervisor is provided below.

1. How many nurses are in the hospital?
   There are 101 nurses, including me.
2. Of these 100 nurses, how many are assigned to the third and fourth floors?
   Fifty nurses are assigned to these two floors.
3. What do these nurses do (please describe)?
   Provide nursing care for patients, which, as you know, means answering questions, changing bandages, administering medicine, changing clothes, etc.

4. And what do you do?
   I supervise and coordinate all the nursing activity in the hospital. This includes surgery, maternity, the emergency room, and the two floors you mentioned.
5. What other lodging and care activities are done for the third and fourth floors by persons other than the nurses?
   The patients must be fed. The hospital cafeteria delivers meals. The laundry department picks up dirty clothing and bedding once each shift. The floors also have a physical therapist assigned to provide care on a physician-directed basis.
6. Do patients use any equipment?
   Yes. Mostly monitoring equipment.
7. Who or what uses the activity output?
   Patients. But there are different kinds of patients. On these two floors, we classify patients into three categories according to severity: intensive care, intermediate care, and normal care. The more severe the illness, the more activity used. Nurses spend much more time with intermediate care patients than with normal care. The more severe patients tend to use more of the laundry service as well. Their clothing and bedding need to be changed more frequently. On the other hand, severe patients use less food. They eat fewer meals. Typically, we measure each patient type by the number of days of hospital stay. And you have to realize that the same patient contributes to each type of product.

Required

Prepare an activity dictionary with four categories: activity name, activity description, primary or secondary classification, and activity driver.

4-13

Resource Drivers; Activity-based Costing; Approximately Relevant ABC Assignments
LO4, LO5

Milan Machining Company has identified the following overhead activities, costs, and activity drivers for the coming year:

Activity	Expected Cost	Activity Driver	Activity Capacity
Setup	$60,000	Number of setups	300
Inspecting	20,000	Inspection hours	2,000
Grinding	90,000	Machine hours	18,000
Receiving	?	Number of parts	60,000

The company produces two different machine subassemblies used by other manufacturers. Expected annual data for the two subassemblies follow:

	Subassembly A	Subassembly B
Direct materials	$340,000	$380,000
Direct labor	$240,000	$240,000
Units completed	40,000	50,000
Number of setups	150	150
Inspection hours	1,500	500
Machine hours	7,200	10,800
Parts used	20,000	40,000

Upon investigation, you discover that the Receiving Department employs one worker who spends 40 percent of his time on the receiving activity and 25 percent of his time on inspecting products. His salary is $50,000. Receiving also uses a forklift, at a cost of $10,000 per year for depreciation and fuel. The forklift is used only in receiving.

Required

1. Determine the cost of the Receiving activity
2. Assign the overhead costs to each product using ABC.

3. Now approximate the ABC assignments using the two most expensive activities to form cost pools (the cost of the less expensive activities are allocated to the expensive activities in proportion to their original cost).
4. What is the percentage error from using the approximation in Requirement 3 (for each product)? Explain why this simplification may be a good approach to use.

4-14

Activity-Based Costing; Approximately Relevant ABC Assignments LO4, LO5

Tristar Manufacturing produces two types of battery-operated toy soldiers: infantry and special forces. The soldiers are produced using one continuous process. Four activities have been identified: machining, setups, receiving, and packing. Resource drivers have been used to assign costs to each activity. The overhead activities, their costs, and the other related data are as follows:

Product	Machine Hours	Setups	Receiving Orders	Packing Orders
Infantry	20,000	300	200	2,400
Special forces	20,000	100	400	800
Costs	$80,000	$32,000	$18,000	$48,000

Required

1. Classify the overhead activities as unit-level, batch-level, product-level, or facility-level.
2. Assign the overhead costs to each product using ABC. Now combine the setup and packing activities into one cost pool and repeat the assignment using the number of setups as the driver. Explain why the cost assigned to each product remains the same.
3. Given the results of Requirement 2 (after combining and reducing to three pools), reduce the number of pools to two by using the two most expensive activities as only two cost pools and allocating the remaining activity costs to the other two pools based in proportion to their costs.
4. Calculate the percentage difference in the approximately relevant product cost and the ABC product cost. Now calculate the error if machine hours had been used as a single plantwide rate. Comment on the merits of the approximating approach.

4-15

Activity Classification LO4

Colbie Components produces two types of wafers: wafer A and wafer B. A wafer is a thin slice of silicon used as a base for integrated circuits or other electronic components. The dies on each wafer represent a particular configuration designed for use by a particular end product. Colbie produces wafers in batches, where each batch corresponds to a particular type of wafer (A or B). In the wafer inserting and sorting process, dies are inserted, and the wafers are tested to ensure that the dies are not defective. Materials are ordered and received just in time for production. Terms for payment of materials are 2/10, n/30. Discounts are always taken (payment occurs on the last date possible).

The following activities are listed in Colbie's activity dictionary:

1. Developing test programs
2. Making probe cards
3. Testing products
4. Setting up batches
5. Engineering design
6. Handling wafer lots
7. Inserting dies
8. Purchasing materials
9. Receiving materials
10. Paying suppliers

11. Providing utilities (heat, lighting, and so on)
12. Providing space

Required

1. Which activities are done each time a wafer is produced (unit-level activities)?
2. Which activities are done each time a batch is produced (batch-level activities)?
3. Which activities are done to enable production to take place (product-level activities)?
4. Which activities are done to sustain production processes (facility-level activities)?

Problems

4-16

Functional-Based versus Activity-Based Costing
LO2, LO3, LO4

Descout Company for years produced only one product: backpacks. Recently, the company decided to add a line of duffel bags. With this addition, the company began assigning overhead costs using departmental rates. (Prior to this, the company used a predetermined plantwide rate based on *units produced.*) Departmental rates meant that overhead costs had to be assigned to each producing department to create overhead pools so that predetermined departmental rates could be calculated. Surprisingly, after the addition of the duffel-bag line and the switch to departmental rates, the costs to produce the backpacks increased and their profitability dropped.

The marketing manager and the production manager both complained about the increase in the production cost of backpacks. The marketing manager was concerned because the increase in unit costs led to pressure to increase the unit price of backpacks. She was resisting this pressure because she was certain that the increase would harm the company's market share. The production manager was receiving pressure to cut costs also, yet he was convinced that nothing different was being done in the way the backpacks were produced. He was also convinced that further efficiency in the manufacture of the backpacks was unlikely. After some discussion, the two managers decided that the problem had to be connected to the addition of the duffel-bag line.

Upon investigation, they were informed that the only real change in product-costing procedures was in the way overhead costs are assigned. A two-stage procedure was now in use. First, overhead costs are assigned to the two producing departments, patterns and finishing. Some overhead costs are assigned to the producing departments using direct tracing, and some are assigned using driver tracing. For example, the salaries of the producing department's supervisors are assigned using direct tracing, whereas the costs of the factory's accounting department are assigned using driver tracing (the driver being the number of transactions processed for each department). Second, the costs accumulated in the producing departments are assigned to the two products using direct labor hours as a driver (the rate in each department is based on direct labor hours). The managers were assured that great care was taken to associate overhead costs with individual products. So that they could construct their own example of overhead cost assignment, the controller provided information necessary to show how accounting costs are assigned to products:

	Department		
	Patterns	**Finishing**	**Total**
Accounting cost	$48,000	$72,000	$120,000
Transactions processed	32,000	48,000	80,000
Total direct labor hours	10,000	20,000	30,000
Direct labor hours per backpack*	0.10	0.20	0.30
Direct labor hours per duffel bag*	0.40	0.80	1.20

*Hours required to produce one unit of each product.

The controller remarked that the cost of operating the accounting department had doubled with the addition of the new product line. The increase came because of the need to process additional transactions, which had also doubled in number.

During the first year of producing duffel bags, the company produced and sold 100,000 backpacks and 25,000 duffel bags. The 100,000 backpacks matched the prior year's output for that product.

Required

1. Compute the amount of accounting cost assigned to a backpack before the duffel-bag line was added using a plantwide rate approach based on units produced. Is this assignment accurate? Explain.
2. Suppose that the company decided to assign the accounting costs directly to the product lines using the number of transactions as the activity driver. What is the accounting cost per unit of backpacks? per unit of duffel bags?
3. Compute the amount of accounting cost assigned to each backpack and duffel bag using departmental rates based on direct labor hours.
4. Which way of assigning overhead does the best job, the functional-based approach using departmental rates or the activity-based approach using transactions processed for each product? Explain. Discuss the value of activity-based costing before the duffel-bag line was added.

4-17

Plantwide versus Departmental Rates; Product Costing Accuracy; Pool Rates
LO2, LO3, LO4, LO5

EXCEL

Tamarindo Company produces speakers (Model A and Model B). Both products pass through two producing departments. Model A's production is much more labor-intensive than Model B's. Model B is also the more popular of the two speakers. The following data have been gathered for the two products:

	Product Data	
	Model A	**Model B**
Units produced per year	30,000	300,000
Prime costs	$200,000	$2,000,000
Direct labor hours	140,000	300,000
Machine hours	20,000	200,000
Production runs	40	60
Inspection hours	800	1,200
Maintenance hours	10,000	90,000

Overhead Costs	
Setup costs	$ 360,000
Inspection costs	280,000
Machining	320,000
Maintenance	360,000
Total	$1,320,000

Required

1. Compute the overhead cost per unit for each product using a plantwide rate based on direct labor hours.
2. Compute the overhead cost per unit for each product using activity-based costing.
3. Suppose that Tamarindo decides to use departmental overhead rates. There are two departments: Department 1 (machine intensive) with a rate of $4.66 per machine hour, and Department 2 (labor intensive) with a rate of $1.20 per direct labor hour. The consumption of these two drivers is given below:

	Department 1	Department 2
Model A	10,000	130,000
Model B	170,000	270,000

Compute the overhead cost per unit for each product using departmental rates.

4. Using the activity-based product costs as the standard, comment on the ability of departmental rates to improve the accuracy of product costing. (Did the departmental rates do better than the plantwide rate?)

4-18

Production-Based Costing versus Activity-Based Costing; Assigning Costs to Activities; Resource Drivers
LO3, LO4

Wilson Company produces lawn mowers. One of its plants produces two versions of mowers: a basic model and a deluxe model. The deluxe model has a sturdier frame, a higher horsepower engine, a wider blade, and mulching capability. At the beginning of the year, the following data were prepared for this plant:

	Basic Model	Deluxe Model
Expected quantity	40,000	20,000
Selling price	$180	$360
Prime costs	$160	$320
Machine hours	5,000	5,000
Direct labor hours	10,000	10,000
Engineering support (hours)	1,500	4,500
Receiving (orders processed)	250	500
Material handling (number of moves)	1,200	4,800
Purchasing (number of requisitions)	100	200
Maintenance (hours used)	1,000	3,000
Paying suppliers (invoices processed)	250	500
Setting up equipment (number of setups)	16	64

Additionally, the following overhead activity costs are reported:

Maintaining equipment	$114,000
Engineering support	120,000
Material handling	?
Setting up equipment	96,000
Purchasing materials	60,000
Receiving goods	40,000
Paying suppliers	30,000
Providing space	20,000
Total	$?

Facility-level costs are allocated in proportion to machine hours (provides a measure of time the facility is used by each product). Material handling uses three inputs: two forklifts, gasoline to operate the forklift, and three operators. The three operators are paid a salary of $60,000 each. The operators spend 25 percent of their time on the receiving activity and 75 percent on moving goods (material handling). Gasoline costs $4.50 per move. Depreciation amounts to $9,000 per forklift per year.

Required

1. Calculate the cost of the material-handling activity. Label the cost assignments as driver tracing and direct tracing. Identify the resource drivers.
2. Calculate the cost per unit for each product using direct labor hours to assign all overhead costs.
3. Calculate activity rates and assign costs to each product. Calculate a unit cost for each product and compare these costs with those calculated in Requirement 2.
4. Calculate consumption ratios for each activity.

5. Explain how the consumption ratios calculated in Requirement 4 can be used to reduce the number of rates. Calculate the rates that would apply under this approach.

4-19

ABC Costing and Cost Behavior
LO4, LO5

Dulce Sound Company produces several different models of a compact disc player system. The company has recently adopted an ABC system. The unit cost expected for the deluxe model, Model FRX, follows:

Unit-level costs (includes materials and labor)	$120
Batch-level costs	80
Product-level costs	40
Facility-level costs	20
Total unit cost	$260

The unit cost is based on an expected volume of 20,000 units. These units will be produced in 20 equal batches. The product-level costs are all from engineering support. The product-level costs are driven by engineering orders. The $40 cost assignment is based on 10 orders. Facility-level costs are allocated on the basis of direct labor hours (one hour per unit produced).

Required

1. Calculate the total manufacturing cost to produce 20,000 units of the deluxe model. Present the total cost for each activity category.
2. Now assume that the company has revised its forecast for the deluxe model and expects to produce 30,000 units. A decision was made to handle the increased production by increasing batch size to 1,500 units. The increased production will not require an increase in engineering support. Calculate the total cost to produce the 30,000 units of the deluxe model. Present the total cost for each activity category. Explain the outcome.
3. Assume that the revised forecast of 30,000 units is made. Now, however, the decision is made to handle the extra production by increasing the number of batches from 20 to 30. Also, the sale of the extra 10,000 units is possible only if an engineering modification is made. This increases the expected engineering orders from 10 to 12. Explain why the costs changed from those predicted in Requirement 2.
4. Discuss the value of classifying and reporting costs by activity category.

4-20

Activity-Costing; Assigning Resource Costs; Primary and Secondary Activities
LO3, LO4

Trinity Clinic has identified three activities for daily maternity care: occupancy and feeding, nursing, and nursing supervision. The nursing supervisor oversees 150 nurses, 25 of whom are maternity nurses (the other nurses are located in other care areas such as the emergency room and intensive care). The nursing supervisor has three assistants, a secretary, several offices, computers, phones, and furniture. The three assistants spend 75 percent of their time on the supervising activity and 25 percent of their time as surgical nurses. They each receive a salary of $48,000. The nursing supervisor has a salary of $70,000. She spends 100 percent of her time supervising. The secretary receives a salary of $22,000 per year. Other costs directly traceable to the supervisory activity (depreciation, utilities, phone, etc.) average $100,000 per year.

Daily care output is measured as "patient days." The clinic has traditionally assigned the cost of daily care by using a daily rate (a rate per patient day). There are actually different kinds of daily care, and rates are structured to reflect these differences. For example, a higher daily rate is charged for an intensive care unit than for a maternity care unit. Within units, however, the daily rates are the same for all patients. Under the traditional, functional approach, the daily rate is computed by dividing the annual costs of occupancy and feeding, nursing, and a share of supervision by the unit's capacity expressed in patient days. The cost of supervision is assigned to each care area based on the number of nurses. A single driver (patient days) is used to assign the costs of daily care to each patient.

A pilot study has revealed that the demands for nursing care vary within the maternity unit, depending on the severity of a patient's case. Specifically, demand for nursing services per day increases with severity. Assume that within the maternity unit there are three levels of increasing severity: normal patients, cesarean patients, and patients with complications. The pilot study provided the following activity and cost information:

Activity	Annual Cost	Activity Driver	Annual Quantity
Occupancy and feeding	$1,000,000	Patient days	10,000
Nursing care (maternity)	950,000	Hours of nursing care	50,000
Nursing supervision	?	Number of nurses	150

The pilot study also revealed the following information concerning the three types of patients and their annual demands:

Patient Type	Patient Days Demanded	Nursing Hours Demanded
Normal	7,000	17,500
Cesarean	2,000	12,500
Complications	1,000	20,000
Total	10,000	50,000

Required

1. Calculate the cost per patient day using a functional-based approach.
2. Calculate the cost per patient day using an activity-based approach.
3. The hospital processes 1,000,000 pounds of laundry per year. The cost for the laundering activity is $500,000 per year. In a functional-based costing system, the cost of the Laundry Department is assigned to each user department in proportion to the pounds of laundry produced. Typically, maternity produces 200,000 pounds per year. How much would this change the cost per patient day calculated in Requirement 1? Now describe what information you would need to modify the calculation made in Requirement 2. Under what conditions would this activity calculation provide a more accurate cost assignment?

4-21

Reducing Number of Rates Using Consumption Ratios; Activity-Based Costing
LO4, LO5

Mendoza Company has recently decided to convert from conventional product costing to an activity-based system. The company produces two types of clocks: small and large. The clocks are produced in batches. Information concerning these two products follows:

	Small Clock	Large Clock
Quantity produced	100,000	200,000
Direct labor hours	100,000	100,000
Material handling (number of moves)	2,000	4,000
Engineering (hours)	10,000	5,000
Receiving (number of orders processed)	250	500
Setups	60	20
Maintenance (hours used)	4,000	2,000
Machining (machine hours)	50,000	50,000
Inspection (number of hours)	3,000	1,000

Additionally, the following overhead costs are reported for the activities associated with the two products:

Material handling	$120,000
Maintenance equipment	80,000
Machining	90,000
Engineering	100,000
Receiving*	30,000
Setups	96,000
Inspection	60,000

*Materials are ordered and received each time a batch is produced

Required

1. Classify activities as unit-level, batch-level, product-level, and facility-level.
2. Reduce the rates by grouping all activities with identical consumption ratios into homogeneous cost pools. Select an activity driver for each cost pool, and compute a pool rate.
3. Using the pool rates calculated in Requirement 2, assign all overhead costs to the two products, and compute the overhead cost per unit for each.

4-22

Product Costing Accuracy; Corporate Strategy; Activity-Based Costing
LO3, LO4, LO5

Pearson Manufacturing is engaged in the production of chemicals for industrial use. One plant specializes in the production of chemicals used in the copper industry. Two compounds are produced: compound X-12 and compound S-15. Compound X-12 was originally developed by Pearson's chemists and played a key role in copper extraction from low-grade ore. The patent for X-12 has expired, and competition in this market has intensified dramatically. Compound X-12 produced the highest volume of activity and for many years was the only chemical compound produced by the plant. Five years ago, S-15 was added. Compound S-15 was more difficult to manufacture and required special handling and setups. For the first three years after the addition of the new product, profits increased. In the last two years, however, the plant has faced intense competition, and its sales of X-12 have dropped. In fact, the plant showed a small loss in the most recent reporting period. The plant manager is convinced that competing producers have been guilty of selling X-12 below the cost to produce it—perhaps with the objective of expanding their market shares. The following conversation between Diane Woolridge, plant manager, and Rick Dixon, divisional marketing manager, reflects the concerns of the division about the future of the plant and its products.

Rick: You know, Diane, the divisional manager is very concerned about the plant's trend. He indicated that in this budgetary environment, we can't afford to carry plants that don't show a profit. We shut one down just last month because it couldn't handle the competition.

Diane: Rick, our compound X-12 has a reputation for quality and value—we have a very pure product. It has been a mainstay for years. I don't understand what's happening.

Rick: I just received a call from one of our major customers concerning X-12. He said that a sales representative from another firm had offered the chemical at $10 per kilogram—about $6 less than what we ask. It's hard to compete with a price like that. Perhaps the plant is simply obsolete.

Diane: No. I don't agree. We have good technology. I think that we are efficient. And it's costing a little more than $10 to produce X-12. I don't see how these companies can afford to sell it so cheaply. I'm not convinced that we should meet the price. Perhaps we should emphasize producing and selling more of S-15. Our margin is high on this product, and we have virtually no competition for it. We just recently raised the price per kilogram, and our customers didn't blink an eye.

Rick: You may be right. I think we can increase the price even more and not lose business. I called a few customers to see how they would react to a 25 percent increase in price, and they all said that they would still purchase the same quantity as before.

Diane: It sounds promising. However, before we make a major commitment to S-15, I think we had better explore other possible explanations. The market potential is much less than that for X-12. I want to know how our production costs compare to our competitors. Perhaps we could be more efficient and find a way to earn our normal return on X-12. Besides, my production people hate producing S-15. It's very difficult to produce.

After meeting with Rick, Diane requested an investigation of the production costs and comparative efficiency. Independent consultants were hired. After a three-month assessment, the consulting group provided the following information on the plant's production activities and costs associated with the two products:

	X-12	S-15
Production (kilograms)	1,000,000	200,000
Selling price	$15.93	$12.00
Overhead per unit*	$6.41	$2.89
Prime cost per kilogram	$4.27	$3.13
Number of production runs	100	200
Receiving orders	400	1,000
Machine hours	125,000	60,000
Direct labor hours	250,000	22,500
Engineering hours	5,000	5,000
Material handling (number of moves)	500	400

*Calculated using a plantwide rate based on direct labor hours, which is the current way of assigning the plant's overhead to its products.

The consulting group recommended switching the overhead assignment to an activity-based approach. It maintained that activity-based costing assignment is more accurate and will provide better information for decision making. To facilitate this recommendation, the plant's activities were grouped into homogeneous sets based on common consumption ratios. The costs of these pooled activities follow:

Overhead pool:*	
Setup costs	$ 240,000
Machine costs	1,750,000
Receiving costs	2,100,000
Engineering costs	2,000,000
Material-handling costs	900,000
Total	$6,990,000

*The pools are named for the major activities found within them. All overhead costs within each pool can be assigned using a single driver (based on the major activity after which the pool is named).

Required

1. Verify the overhead cost per unit reported by the consulting group using direct labor hours to assign overhead. Compute the per-unit gross margin for each product.
2. Recompute the unit cost of each product using activity-based costing. Compute the per-unit gross margin for each product.
3. Should the company switch its emphasis from the high-volume product to the low-volume product? Comment on the validity of the plant manager's concern that competitors are selling below the cost of producing compound X-12.
4. Explain the apparent lack of competition for S-15. Comment also on the willingness of customers to accept a 25 percent increase in price for this compound.
5. Describe what actions you would take based on the information provided by the activity-based unit costs.

4-23

Approximately Relevant ABC
LO5

EXCEL

Ellishawk Company has identified the following overhead activities, costs, and activity drivers for the coming year:

Activity	Expected Cost	Activity Driver	Activity Capacity
Testing products	$252,000	Number of tests	300
Purchasing materials	36,000	Number of orders	1,800
Machining	252,000	Machine hours	21,000
Receiving	60,000	Receiving hours	2,500

Ellishawk produces two models of electronic game computers with the following expected activity demands:

	Model A	Model B
Units completed	10,000	20,000
Number of tests	200	100
Number of orders	600	1,200
Machine hours	12,000	9,000
Receiving hours	750	1,750

Required

1. Determine the total overhead assigned to each product using the four activity drivers.
2. Determine the total overhead assigned to each model using the two most expensive activities. The costs of the two relatively inexpensive activities are allocated to the two expensive activities in proportion to their costs.
3. Using ABC as the benchmark, calculate the percentage error and comment on the accuracy of the reduced system. Explain why this approach may be desirable.

4-24

Approximately Relevant ABC
LO5

Airepart, Inc., produces two different types of subassemblies for the aircraft industry. Airepart produces a major component for the subassemblies in the cutting and welding department. Other parts and the manufactured component are then assembled in the assembly department. The activities, expected costs, and drivers associated with these two manufacturing processes are as follows:

Process	Activity	Cost	Activity Driver	Expected Quantity
Cutting and Welding	Welding	$ 2,000,000	Welding hours	4,000
	Machining	1,000,000	Machine hours	10,000
	Inspecting	70,000	No. of inspections	1,000
	Materials handling	52,000	No. of moves	12,000
	Setups	400,000	No. of batches	100
		$3,522,000		
Assembly	Changeover	$ 28,000	Changeover hours	1,000
	Rework	50,000	Rework orders	50
	Testing	40,000	No. of tests	750
	Materials handling	60,000	No. of parts	50,000
	Engineering support	70,000	Engineering hours	2,000
		$ 248,000		

Note: In the assembly process, the materials handling activity is a function of product characteristics rather than batch activity.

Other overhead activities, their costs, and drivers are as follows:

Activity	Cost	Activity Driver	Quantity
Purchasing	$50,000	Purchase requisitions	500
Receiving	70,000	Receiving orders	2,000
Paying suppliers	80,000	No. of invoices	1,000
Providing space and utilities	30,000	Machine hours	10,000
	$230,000		

Other production information concerning the two subassemblies is also provided as follows:

	Subassembly A	Subassembly B
Units produced	1,500	3,000
Welding hours	1,600	2,400
Machine hours	3,000	7,000
Inspections	500	500
Moves	7,200	4,800
Batches	45	55
Changeover hours	540	460
Rework orders	5	45
Tests	500	250
Parts	40,000	10,000
Engineering hours	1,500	500
Requisitions	425	75
Receiving orders	1,800	200
Invoices	650	350

The per-unit overhead costs using the 14 activity-based drivers are $1,108 and $779 for Subassemblies A and B, respectively.

Required

1. Determine the percentage of total costs represented by the three most expensive activities.
2. Allocate the costs of all other activities to the three activities identified in Requirement 1. Allocate the other activity costs to the three activities in proportion to their individual activity costs. Now assign these total costs to the products using the drivers of the three chosen activities.
3. Using the costs assigned in Requirement 1, calculate the percentage error using the ABC costs as a benchmark. Comment on the value and advantages of this ABC simplification.

Managerial Decision Cases

4-25

ABC; Distorted Product Costs
LO3, LO4

Sharp Paper, Inc., has three paper mills, one of which is located in Memphis, Tennessee. The Memphis mill produces 300 different types of coated and uncoated specialty printing papers. This large variety of products was the result of a full-line marketing strategy adopted by Sharp's management. Management was convinced that the value of variety more than offset the extra costs of the increased complexity.

During 2006, the Memphis mill produced 120,000 tons of coated paper and 80,000 tons of uncoated paper. Of the 200,000 tons produced, 180,000 were sold. Sixty products account for 80 percent of the tons sold. Thus, 240 products are classified as low-volume products.

Lightweight lime hopsack in cartons (LLHC) is one of the low-volume products. LLHC is produced in rolls, converted into sheets of paper, and then sold in cartons. In 2006, the cost to produce and sell one ton of LLHC was as follows:

Direct materials:		
Furnish (3 different pulps)	2,225 pounds	$ 450
Additives (11 different items)	200 pounds	500
Tub size	75 pounds	10
Recycled scrap paper	(296 pounds)	(20)
Total direct materials		$ 940
Direct labor		$ 450
Overhead:		
Paper machine ($100 per ton × 2,500 pounds)		$ 125
Finishing machine ($120 per ton × 2,500 pounds)		150
Total overhead		$ 275
Shipping and warehousing		$ 30
Total manufacturing and selling cost		$1,695

Overhead is applied using a two-stage process. First, overhead is allocated to the paper and finishing machines using the direct method of allocation with carefully selected cost drivers. Second, the overhead assigned to each machine is divided by the budgeted tons of output. These rates are then multiplied by the number of pounds required to produce one good ton.

In 2008, LLHC sold for $2,400 per ton, making it one of the most profitable products. A similar examination of some of the other low-volume products revealed that they also had very respectable profit margins. Unfortunately, the performance of the high-volume products was less impressive, with many showing losses or very low profit margins. This situation led Ryan Chesser to call a meeting with his marketing vice president, Jennifer Woodruff, and his controller, Kaylin Penn.

Ryan: The above-average profitability of our low-volume specialty products and the poor profit performance of our high-volume products make me believe that we should switch our marketing emphasis to the low-volume line. Perhaps we should drop some of our high-volume products, particularly those showing a loss.

Jennifer: I'm not convinced that the solution you are proposing is the right one. I know our high-volume products are of high quality, and I am convinced that we are as efficient in our production as other firms. I think that somehow our costs are not being assigned correctly. For example, the shipping and warehousing costs are assigned by dividing these costs by the total tons of paper sold. Yet . . .

Kaylin: Jennifer, I hate to disagree, but the $30-per-ton charge for shipping and warehousing seems reasonable. I know that our method to assign these costs is identical to a number of other paper companies.

Jennifer: Well, that may be true, but do these other companies have the variety of products that we have? Our low-volume products require special handling and processing, but when we assign shipping and warehousing costs, we average these special costs across our entire product line. Every ton produced in our mill passes through our mill shipping department and is either sent directly to the customer or to our distribution center and then eventually to customers. My records indicate quite clearly that virtually all the high-volume products are sent directly to customers, whereas most of the low-volume products are sent to the distribution center. Now, all the products passing through the mill shipping department should receive a share of the $2,000,000 annual shipping costs. I am not convinced, however, that all products should receive a share of the receiving and shipping costs of the distribution center as currently practiced.

Ryan: Kaylin, is this true? Does our system allocate our shipping and warehousing costs in this way?

Kaylin: Yes, I'm afraid it does. Jennifer may have a point. Perhaps we need to reevaluate our method to assign these costs to the product lines.

Ryan: Jennifer, do you have any suggestions concerning how the shipping and warehousing costs ought to be assigned?

Jennifer: It seems reasonable to make a distinction between products that spend time in the distribution center and those that do not. We should also distinguish between the receiving and shipping activities at the distribution center. All incoming shipments are packed on pallets and weigh one ton each (there are 14 cartons of paper per pallet). In 2008, Receiving processed 56,000 tons of paper. Receiving employs 15 people at an annual cost of $600,000. Other receiving costs total about $500,000. I would recommend that these costs be assigned using tons processed.

Shipping, however, is different. There are two activities associated with shipping: picking the order from inventory and loading the paper. We employ 30 people for picking and 10 for loading, at an annual cost of $1,200,000. Other shipping costs total $1,100,000. Picking and loading are more concerned with the number of shipping items than with tonnage. That is, a shipping item may consist of two or three cartons instead of pallets. Accordingly, the shipping costs of the distribution center should be assigned using the number of items shipped. In 2008, for example, we handled 190,000 shipping items.

Ryan: These suggestions have merit. Kaylin, I would like to see what effect Jennifer's suggestions have on the per-unit assignment of shipping and warehousing for LLHC. If the effect is significant, then we will expand the analysis to include all products.

Kaylin: I'm willing to compute the effect, but I'd like to suggest one additional feature. Currently, we have a policy to carry about 25 tons of LLHC in inventory. Our current costing system totally ignores the cost of carrying this inventory. Since it costs us $1,665 to produce each ton of this product, we are tying up a lot of money in inventory—money that could be invested in other productive opportunities. In fact, the return lost is about 16 percent per year. This cost should also be assigned to the units sold.

Ryan: Kaylin, this also sounds good to me. Go ahead and include the carrying cost in your computation.

To help in the analysis, Kaylin gathered the following data for LLHC for 2008:

Tons sold	10
Average cartons per shipment	2
Average shipments per ton	7

Required

1. Identify the flaws associated with the current method of assigning shipping and warehousing costs to Sharp's products.
2. Compute the shipping and warehousing cost per ton of LLHC sold using the new method suggested by Jennifer and Kaylin.
3. Using the new costs computed in Requirement 2, compute the profit per ton of LLHC. Compare this with the profit per ton computed using the old method.

Do you think that this same effect would be realized for other low-volume products? Explain.

4. Comment on Ryan's proposal to drop some high-volume products and place more emphasis on low-volume products. Discuss the role of the accounting system in supporting this type of decision making.
5. After receiving the analysis of LLHC, Ryan decided to expand the analysis to all products. He also had Kaylin reevaluate the way in which mill overhead was assigned to products. After the restructuring was completed, Ryan took the following actions: (a) the prices of most low-volume products were increased, (b) the prices of several high-volume products were decreased, and (c) some low-volume products were dropped. Explain why his strategy changed so dramatically.

4-26

Activity-Based Product Costing and Ethical Behavior
LO4, LO5, LO6

ETHICS

Consider the following conversation between Leonard Bryner, president and manager of a firm engaged in job manufacturing, and Chuck Davis, CMA, the firm's controller.

Leonard: Chuck, as you know, our firm has been losing market share over the past three years. We have been losing more and more bids, and I don't understand why. At first I thought other firms were undercutting simply to gain business, but after examining some of the public financial reports, I believe that they are making a reasonable rate of return. I am beginning to believe that our costs and costing methods are at fault.

Chuck: I can't agree with that. We have good control over our costs. Like most firms in our industry, we use a normal job-costing system. I really don't see any significant waste in the plant.

Leonard: After talking with some other managers at a recent industrial convention, I'm not so sure that waste by itself is the issue. They talked about activity-based management, activity-based costing, and continuous improvement. They mentioned the use of something called activity drivers to assign overhead. They claimed that these new procedures can help produce more efficiency in manufacturing, better control of overhead, and more accurate product costing. A big deal was made of eliminating activities that added no value. Maybe our bids are too high because these other firms have found ways to decrease their overhead costs and to increase the accuracy of their product costing.

Chuck: I doubt it. For one thing, I don't see how we can increase product costing accuracy. So many of our costs are indirect costs. Furthermore, everyone uses some measure of production activity to assign overhead costs. I imagine that what they are calling activity drivers is just some new buzzword for measures of production volume. Fads in costing come and go. I wouldn't worry about it. I'll bet that our problems with decreasing sales are temporary. You might recall that we experienced a similar problem about 12 years ago—it was two years before it straightened out.

Required

1. Do you agree or disagree with Chuck Davis and the advice that he gave Leonard Bryner? Explain.
2. Was there anything wrong or unethical in the behavior that Chuck Davis displayed? Explain your reasoning.
3. Do you think that Chuck was well informed—that he was aware of what the accounting implications of activity-based costing were and that he knew what was meant by cost drivers? Should he have been well informed? Review (in Chapter 1) the first category of the standards of ethical conduct for management accountants. Do any of these standards apply in Chuck's case?

Research Assignment

4-27

Cybercase
LO4, LO5, LO6

There are numerous examples of ABC applications in the real world. A good source of ABC case studies for various industries is found at the SAS website in the chapter web links at the Interactive Study Center on http://www.thomsonedu.com/accounting/hansen. Access that site and select *Success Stories.* Within the *Success by Solution* category, click on *Activity-Based Management.* Choose two firms and then read about their experience with ABC. Answer the following questions about the two cases:

1. What were the reasons offered for implementing ABC?
2. What implementation procedures were used?
3. How many activities were identified?
4. What types of benefits (results) were achieved by each company?
5. What problems were mentioned, if any?

chapter 5

Activity-Based Management

learning objectives

After studying this chapter, you should be able to:

1. Describe activity-based management and explain its relationship to activity-based costing
2. Explain process value analysis.
3. Describe activity performance measurement.
4. Describe activity-based customer and supplier costing.

Scenario

Rick Anderson, president and owner of Roberts Truck Products (RTP, Inc.), was both pleased and concerned. He was pleased because his company was the market leader in electronic instrument panels for heavy-duty trucks and had a respectable share of the market for hydraulic cylinders. He was concerned because his company was facing an increasingly competitive business environment. It had become more evident that his company must seek better ways of making strategic business decisions and collecting accurate, reliable information to facilitate this process. Moreover, Rick was convinced that greater efficiency was needed—that operating processes needed to be streamlined, waste needed to be eliminated, and quality and delivery performance needed to be improved. Rick expressed these concerns to Michele-Dawn Barker, the managing partner of the local office of a national consulting firm, who suggested that he consider implementing activity-based management (ABM). When Rick mentioned that RTP, Inc., was considering the implementation of an activity-based costing (ABC) system, Michele immediately noted that ABC was a key component of an ABM system. Michele-Dawn then offered to visit RTP, examine the operations, and prepare a formal proposal for implementing an ABM system.

Within two months, Rick received the proposal. He was intrigued by the following two excerpts from the proposal:

Excerpt 1:

"Following GAAP, Roberts Truck Products currently assigns the costs for selling, merchandising, and distribution to the period when these costs are incurred. No effort is made to trace these costs to individual customers or customer groups. We have done this tracing and have found that many of your customers are not profitable. We have found that a small percentage of your customers and a small percentage of your products are generating most of your profits. These results suggest that you need more accurate costing so that Roberts Truck Products can better manage products and customers. I will provide a more detailed report along with specific recommendations for changing your product and customer mixes so that your profits will increase. We are confident that our recommended changes will allow you to increase your reported net profit by at least 200 percent.[1] Furthermore, an accurate assessment of what your suppliers are costing may produce additional profitability increases."

Excerpt 2:

"Since processes are defined by activities, activity management is needed. Activity-based management identifies activities, their costs, their output, and their value to the organization. The outputs of an activity-based management system are critical inputs for the performance management system. Moreover, since activity-based management is all about the economics of an organization, it facilitates and supports the objective of waste reduction. It is fundamental to increasing efficiency and maintaining and improving your competitive position."

Convinced that better cost information would help him to reduce waste and increase profits, Rick immediately told Michele-Dawn that he would like to implement an ABM system.

Questions to Think About

1. Why is accurate cost information about customers and suppliers important?

2. What is wrong with the claim that all customers are good customers?

3. Will accurate cost information guarantee that a firm is competitive?

4. How can managing activities increase efficiency?

5. How can we determine whether activities are of value to a firm?

6. What role, if any, do cost reports play in managing activities?

1 Experience suggests that eliminating unprofitable customers, by making them profitable or dropping them, will increase net profits by at least 200 percent. In some cases, the increase has been greater than 1,000 percent. See Gary Cokins, "Are All of Your Customers Profitable (To You)?" an online article accessible via the chapter web links at the Interactive Study Center on this text's website, http://www.thomsonedu.com/accounting/hansen.

Activity-Based Management: A Conceptual Overview

Objective 1

Describe activity-based management and explain its relationship to activity-based costing.

Activity accounting is an essential factor for operationalizing continuous improvement. A company like RTP, Inc., that faces significant competition must continually seek ways to eliminate waste and increase efficiency. As Michele-Dawn strongly implied in her proposal, processes are the source of many of the improvement opportunities that exist within RTP and, for that matter, any organization. Processes are made up of activities that are linked to perform a specific objective. Improving processes means improving the way activities are performed. Thus, management of activities, not costs, is the key to successful control for firms operating in continuous improvement environments. The realization that activities are crucial to both improved costing and more effective control has led to a new view of business processes called *activity-based management.*

Activity-based management (ABM) is a systemwide, integrated approach that focuses management's attention on activities with the objective of improving customer value and the profit achieved by providing this value. ABC is a major source of information for activity-based management. Thus, the activity-based management model has two dimensions: a cost dimension and a process dimension. This two-dimensional model is presented in Exhibit 5-1. The cost dimension provides cost information about resources, activities, and cost objects of interests such as products, customers, suppliers, and distribution channels. The objective of the cost dimension is improving the accuracy of cost assignments. As the model suggests, the cost of resources is traced to activities, and then the cost of activities is assigned to cost objects. This activity-based costing dimension is useful for product costing, strategic cost management, and tactical analysis. The second dimension, the process dimension, provides information about what activities are performed, why they are performed, and how well they are performed. This dimension's objective is cost reduction. It is this dimension that provides the ability to engage in and measure continuous improvement.

A careful analysis of activities can lead to an understanding of how to reduce costs.

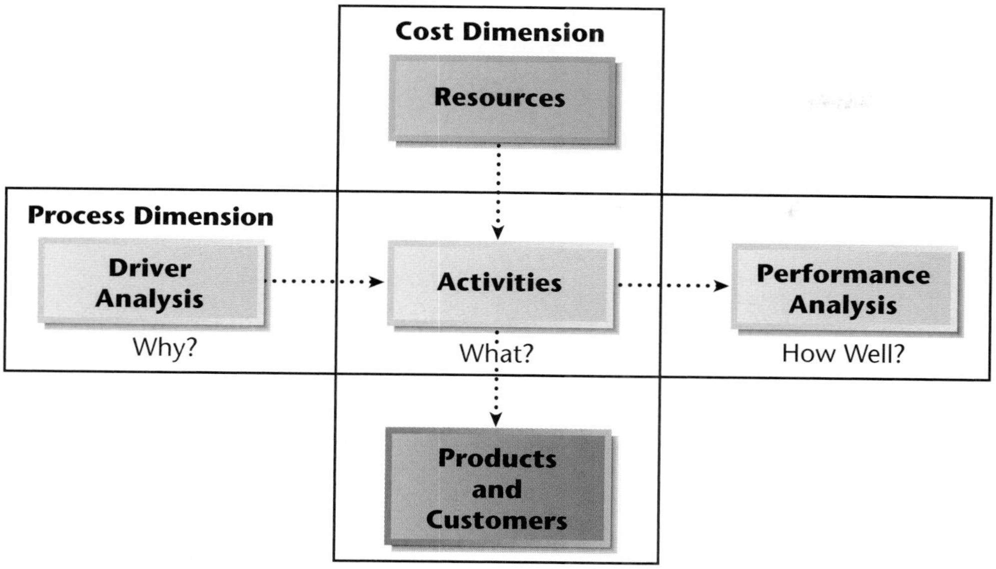

Exhibit 5-1 The Simple Two-Dimensional ABM Model

Implementing ABM

Activity-based management (ABM) is a more comprehensive system than an ABC system. ABM adds a process view to the cost view of ABC. ABM encompasses ABC and uses it as a major source of information. ABM can be viewed as an information system that has the broad objectives of (1) improving decision making by providing accurate cost information and (2) reducing costs by encouraging and supporting continuous improvement efforts. The first objective is the domain of ABC, while the second objective belongs to process value analysis. The second objective requires more detailed data than ABC's objective of improving the accuracy of costing assignments. If a company intends to use both ABC and process value analysis (PVA), then its approach to implementation must be carefully conceived. For example, if ABC creates aggregate cost pools based on homogeneity or approximating techniques, much of the detailed activity information may not be needed. Yet, for PVA, this detail must be retained. Clearly, how to implement an ABM system is a major consideration. Exhibit 5-2 provides a representation of an ABM implementation model.

The model in Exhibit 5-2 shows that the overall objective of ABM is to improve a firm's profitability, an objective achieved by identifying and selecting opportunities for improvement and using more accurate information to make better decisions. For example, root cause analysis (finding the real cause of the problems) reveals opportunities for improvement. By identifying costs caused by waste—which is an outcome of assessing the value of each activity—priorities can be established based on the initiatives that offer the most cost reduction. Furthermore, the potential cost reduction itself is measured by ABC calculations.

Exhibit 5-2 also show that 10 steps define an ABM implementation: four that are associated with ABC, four that are associated with PVA, and two common steps. The PVA steps will be discussed extensively in the next section of this chapter, whereas the ABC steps were discussed in Chapter 4 and should be quite familiar. However, one very important extension of ABC will be described in this chapter: the application of ABC to cost objects other than products—specifically, customers and suppliers. Of the 10 steps described in Exhibit 5-2, the two steps common to ABC and PVA are (1) systems planning and (2) activity identification, definition, and classification.

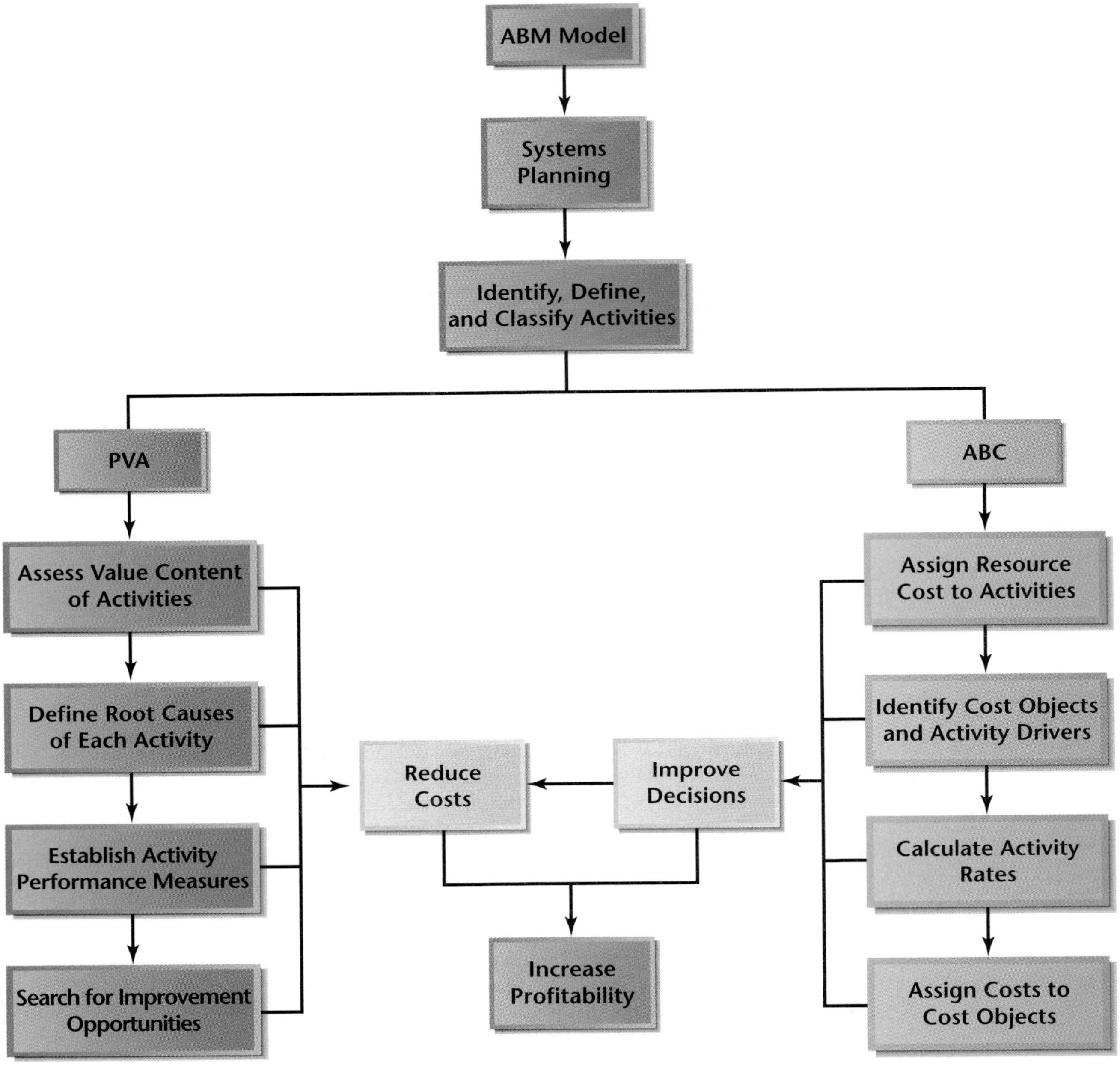

Exhibit 5-2 ABM Implementation Model

Systems Planning Systems planning provides the justification for implementing ABM and addresses the following issues:

1. The purpose and objectives of the ABM system
2. The organization's current and desired competitive position
3. The organization's business processes and product mix
4. The timeline, assigned responsibilities, and resources required for implementation
5. The ability of the organization to implement, learn, and use new information

To obtain buy-in by operating personnel, the objectives of an ABM system must be carefully identified and related to the firm's desired competitive position, business processes, and product mix. The broad objectives have already been mentioned (improving accuracy and continuous improvement); however, it is also necessary to develop specific desired outcomes associated with each of these two objectives. For example, one specific outcome is that of changing the product mix based on more accurate costs (with the expectation that profits will increase). Another specific outcome is that of improving the firm's competitive position by increasing process efficiency through elimination of non-value-added activities. Planning also entails establishing a timeline for the implementation project, assigning specific responsibilities to individuals or teams, and developing a detailed budget. Although all five issues listed are important, the information usage issue deserves special attention. Successful implementation is strongly dependent on the organization's ability to learn how to use the new information provided by ABM. Users must be convinced that this new information can solve specific problems. They also need to be trained to use activity-based costing information to produce better decisions, and they need to understand how ABM drives and supports continuous improvement.

Activity Identification, Definition, and Classification Identifying, defining, and classifying activities requires more attention for ABM than for ABC. The activity dictionary should include a detailed listing of the tasks that define each activity. Knowing the tasks that define an activity can be very helpful for improving the efficiency of value-added activities. Classification of activities also allows ABM to connect with other continuous improvement initiatives such as just-in-time (JIT) manufacturing, total quality management, and total environmental quality cost management. For example, identifying quality-related and environmental activities enables management to focus attention on the non-value-added activities of the quality and environmental categories. ABC also provides a more complete understanding of the effect that quality and environmental costs have on products, processes, and customers. It is important to realize that successful implementation requires time and patience. This is especially true when it comes to using the new information provided by an ABM system. For example, one survey revealed that it takes an average of 3.1 years for nonaccounting personnel to grow accustomed to using ABC information.[2]

Why ABM Implementations Fail ABM can fail as a system for a variety of reasons. One of the major reasons is the lack of support of higher-level management. Not only must this support be obtained before undertaking an implementation project, but it must also be maintained. Loss of support can occur if the implementation takes too long or the expected results do not materialize. Results may not occur as expected because operating and sales managers do not have the expertise to use the new activity information. Thus, significant efforts to train and educate need to be undertaken. Advantages of the new data need to be spelled out carefully, and managers must be taught how these data can be used to increase efficiency and productivity. Resistance to change should be expected; it is not unusual for managers to receive the new cost information with skepticism. Showing how this information can enable them to be better managers should help to overcome this resistance. Involving nonfinancial managers in the planning and implementation stages may also reduce resistance and secure the required support.

Failure to integrate the new system is another major reason for an ABM system breakdown. The probability of success is increased if the ABM system is not in competition with other improvement programs or the official accounting system. It is important to communicate the concept that ABM complements and enhances other improvement programs. Moreover, it is important that ABM be integrated to the point that activity costing outcomes are not in direct competition with the traditional accounting numbers. Managers may be tempted to continue using the traditional accounting numbers in lieu of the new data.

2 Kip R. Krumwiede, "ABC: Why It's Tried and How It Succeeds," *Management Accounting* (April 1998): 32–38.

ABM and Responsibility Accounting

Responsibility accounting is a fundamental tool of managerial control and is defined by four essential elements: (1) assigning responsibility, (2) establishing performance measures or benchmarks, (3) evaluating performance, and (4) assigning rewards. The objective of responsibility accounting is to influence behavior in such a way that individual and organizational initiatives are aligned to achieve a common goal or goals. Exhibit 5-3 illustrates the responsibility accounting model.

A particular responsibility accounting system is defined by how the four elements in Exhibit 5-3 are defined. Three types of responsibility accounting systems have evolved over time: *financial (functional)-based, activity-based,* and *strategic-based.* All three are found in practice today. Of the three, only financial-based and activity-based will be discussed in this chapter. The strategic-based responsibility accounting systems are discussed in Chapter 16.

A **financial (functional)-based responsibility accounting system** assigns responsibility to organizational units and expresses performance measures in financial terms. Essentially, firms choose the responsibility accounting system that is compatible with the requirements and economics of their particular operating environment. Firms that operate in a stable environment with standardized products and processes and low competitive pressures will likely find the less complex, financial-based responsibility accounting systems to be quite adequate. For example, a firm that produces concrete pipes and blocks has products and production processes that

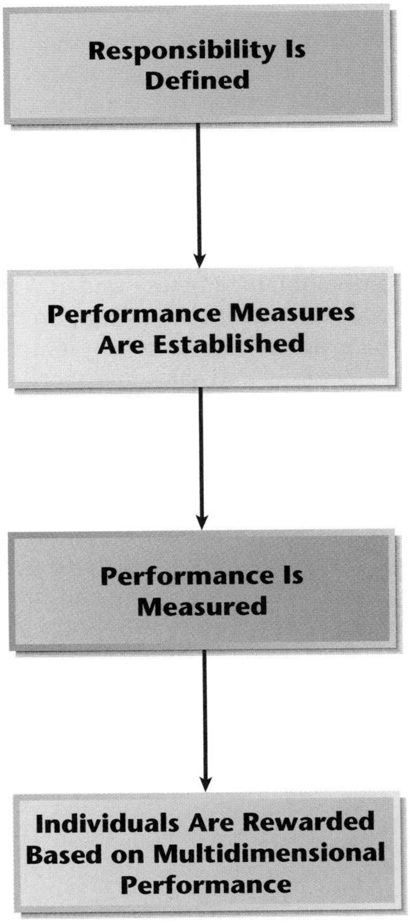

Exhibit 5-3 Elements of a Responsibility Accounting System

are well defined and relatively stable. Functional skills are specialized to gain operating efficiencies. Interactions with suppliers and customers are mostly limited to arm's-length transactions. Competition tends to be local or regional as opposed to national or international. A successful firm operating in this type of environment would tend to emphasize maintaining the status quo: preservation of market share, stable growth, and continuation of efficient production.

On the other hand, a firm like **Hewlett-Packard**, involved in producing computers and computer-related products, operates in an environment where change is rapid. Products and processes are constantly being redesigned and improved, and stiff national and international competitors are always present. The competitive environment demands that firms offer customized products and services to diverse customer segments. This, in turn, means that firms must find cost-efficient ways of producing high-variety, low-volume products. This usually means that more attention is paid to linkages between the firm and its suppliers and customers with the goal of improving cost, quality, and response times for all parties in the value chain. Furthermore, for many industries, product life cycles are shrinking, placing greater demands on the need for innovation. Thus, organizations operating in a dynamic, rapidly changing environment are finding that adaptation and change are essential to survival. To find ways to improve performance, firms operating in this kind of environment are forced to reevaluate how they do things. Improving performance translates into constantly searching for ways to eliminate waste—a process known as *continuous improvement.* Waste reduction, the theme of continuous improvement, is made possible through the use of various waste reduction tools such as JIT purchasing and manufacturing, reengineering, total quality management, employee empowerment, and computer-aided manufacturing. These tools or methods attempt to eliminate waste, which appears in the form of such things as inventories, unnecessary activities, defective products, rework, setup time, and underutilization of employee talents and skills. ABM with its cost and process views is ideal for dealing with a dynamic environment that emphasizes continuous improvement.

Thus **activity-based responsibility accounting** is the responsibility accounting system developed for firms operating in continuous-improvement environments. This accounting system assigns responsibility to processes and uses both financial and nonfinancial measures of performance, thus emphasizing both financial and process perspectives. A comparison of each of the four elements of the responsibility accounting model for each responsibility system reveals the key differences between the two approaches.

Financial-Based Responsibility Compared with Activity-Based Responsibility

Assigning Responsibility Exhibit 5-4 lists the differences in responsibility assignments between the two systems. Financial-based responsibility accounting focuses on *functional* organizational units and individuals. First, a responsibility center is identified. This center is typically an organizational unit such as a plant, department, or production line. Whatever the functional unit is, responsibility is

Financial-Based Responsibility	Activity-Based Responsibility
1. Organizational units	1. Processes
2. Local operating efficiency	2. Systemwide efficiency
3. Individual accountability	3. Team accountability
4. Financial outcomes	4. Financial outcomes

Exhibit 5-4 Responsibility Assignments Compared

Reducing the cost of surgical instruments is made possible by improving the efficiency of manufacturing processes.

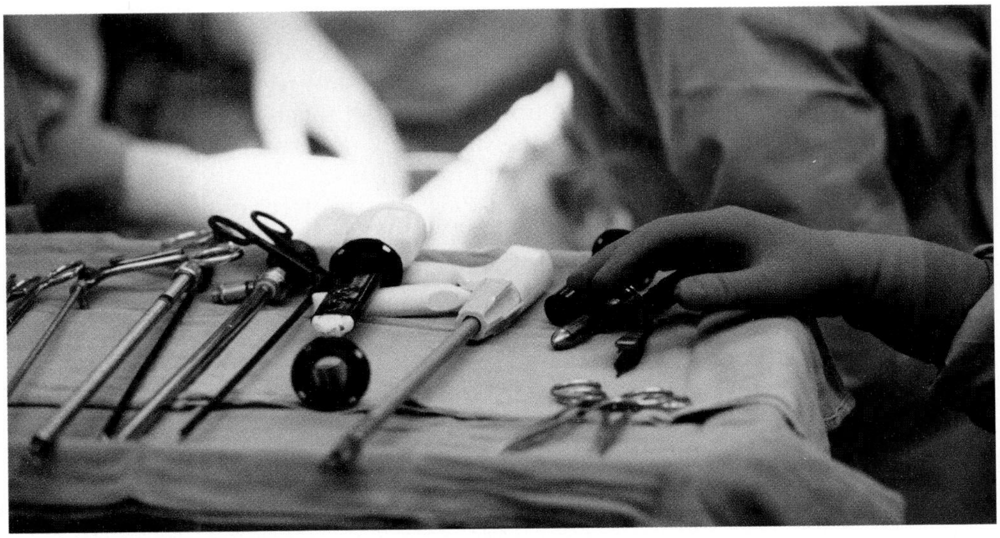

© Getty Images/PhotoDisc

assigned to the individual in charge. Responsibility is defined in financial terms (for example, costs). Emphasis is on achieving optimal financial results at the local level (i.e., organizational unit level). Exhibit 5-4 reveals that in an activity- or process-based responsibility system, the focal point changes from units and individuals to processes and teams. Systemwide optimization is the emphasis. Also, financial responsibility continues to be vital. The reasons for the change in focus are simple. In a continuous improvement environment, the financial perspective translates into continuously *enhancing revenues, reducing costs,* and *improving asset utilization.* Creating this continuous growth and improvement requires an organization to constantly improve its capabilities of delivering value to customers and shareholders. A process perspective is chosen instead of an organizational-unit perspective because processes are the *sources* of value for customers and shareholders and because they are the key to achieving an organization's financial objectives. The customer can be internal or external to the organization. Procurement, new product development, manufacturing, and customer service are examples of processes.

Since processes are the way things are done, changing the way things are done means changing processes. Three methods can change the way things are done: *process improvement, process innovation,* and *process creation.* **Process improvement** refers to incremental and constant increases in the efficiency of an existing process. For example, **Medtronic Xomed**, a manufacturer of surgical products (for ears, nose, and throat specialists), improved their processes by providing written instructions telling workers the best way to do their jobs. Over a three-year period, the company reduced rework by 57 percent, scrap by 85 percent, and the cost of its shipped products by 38 percent.[3] Activity-based management is particularly useful for bringing about process improvements. Processes are made up of activities that are linked by a common objective. Listing these activities and classifying them as value-added or non-value-added immediately suggests a way to make the process better: eliminate the non-value-added activities.

Process innovation (business reengineering) refers to the performance of a process in a radically new way with the objective of achieving dramatic improvements in response time, quality, and efficiency. **IBM Credit**, for example, radically redesigned its credit approval process and reduced its time for preparing a quote from seven days to one; similarly, **Federal-Mogul**, a parts manufacturer, used

3 William Leventon, "Manufacturers Get Lean to Trim Waste," *Medical Device & Diagnostic Industry* (September 2004), available at http://www.devicelink.com/mddi/archive/04/09/contents.html.

process innovation to reduce development time for part prototypes from 20 weeks to 20 days.[4] **Process creation** refers to the installation of an entirely new process with the objective of meeting customer and financial objectives. **Chemical Bank**, for example, identified three *new* internal processes: understanding customer segments, developing new products, and cross-selling the product line.[5] These new internal processes were viewed as critical by the bank's management for improving the customer and profit mix and creating an enabled organization. It should be mentioned that process creation does not mean that the process has to be *original* to the organization. It means that it is *new* to the organization. For example, developing new products is a process common to many organizations but evidently was new to Chemical Bank.

Establishing Performance Measures Once responsibility is defined, performance measures must be identified and standards set to serve as benchmarks for performance measurement. Exhibit 5-5 provides a comparison of the two systems' approaches to the task of defining performance measures. According to Exhibit 5-5, budgeting and standard costing are the cornerstones of the benchmark activity for a financial-based system. This, of course, implies that performance measures are objective and financial in nature. Furthermore, they tend to support the status quo and are relatively stable over time. Exhibit 5-5 reveals some striking differences for firms operating in a continuous improvement environment. First, performance measures are process-oriented and, thus, must be concerned with process attributes such as process time, quality, and efficiency. Second, performance measurement standards are structured to support change. Therefore, standards are dynamic in nature. They change to reflect new conditions and new goals and to help maintain any progress that has been realized. For example, standards can be set that reflect some desired level of improvement for a process. Once the desired level is achieved, the standard is changed to encourage an additional increment of improvement. In an environment where constant improvement is sought, standards cannot be static. Third, optimal standards assume a vital role. They set the ultimate achievement target and, thus, identify the potential for improvement. Finally, standards should reflect the value added by individual activities and processes. Identifying a value-added standard for each activity is much more ambitious than the traditional financial responsibility system. It expands control to include the entire organization.

Evaluating Performance Exhibit 5-6 compares performance evaluation under financial- and activity-based responsibility accounting systems. In a financial-based framework, performance is measured by comparing actual outcomes with budgeted outcomes. In principle, individuals are held accountable only for those items over which they have control. Financial performance, as measured by the ability to meet or beat a stable financial standard, is strongly emphasized. In the activity-based

Financial-Based Measures	Activity-Based Measures
1. Organizational unit budgets	1. Process-oriented standards
2. Standard costing	2. Value-added standards
3. Static standards	3. Dynamic standards
4. Currently attainable standards	4. Optimal standards

Exhibit 5-5 Performance Measures Compared

4 Thomas H. Davenport, *Process Innovation* (Boston: Harvard Business School Press, 1993): 2.

5 Norman Klein and Robert Kaplan, *Chemical Bank: Implementing the Balanced Scorecard* (Harvard Business School, Case 125-210, 1995): 5–6.

Financial-Based Performance Evaluation	Activity-Based Performance Evaluation
1. Financial efficiency	1. Time reductions
2. Controllable costs	2. Quality improvements
3. Actual versus standard	3. Cost reductions
4. Financial measures	4. Trend measurement

Exhibit 5-6 Performance Evaluation Compared

framework, performance is concerned with more than just the financial perspective. The process perspective adds time, quality, and efficiency as critical dimensions of performance. Decreasing the time a process takes to deliver its output to customers is viewed as a vital objective. Thus, nonfinancial, process-oriented measures such as cycletime and on-time deliveries become important. Performance is evaluated by gauging whether these measures are improving over time. The same is true for measures relating to quality and efficiency. Improving a process should translate into better financial results. Hence, measures of cost reductions achieved, trends in cost, and cost per unit of output are all useful indicators of whether a process has improved. Progress toward achieving optimal standards and interim standards needs to be measured. The objective is to provide low-cost, high-quality products, delivered on a timely basis.

Assigning Rewards In both systems, individuals are rewarded or penalized according to the policies and discretion of higher management. As Exhibit 5-7 shows, many of the same financial instruments (e.g., salary increases, bonuses, profit sharing, and promotions) are used to provide rewards for good performance. Of course, the nature of the incentive structure differs in each system. For example, the reward system in a financial-based responsibility accounting system is designed to encourage individuals to achieve or beat budgetary standards. In the activity-based responsibility system, the reward system is more complicated: Individuals are accountable for team as well as individual performance. Since process-related improvements are mostly achieved through team efforts, group-based rewards are more suitable than individual rewards. For example, standards can be set for unit costs, on-time delivery, quality, inventory turns, scrap, and cycle time. Bonuses can then be awarded to the team whenever performance is maintained on all measures and improves on at least one measure. Notice the multidimensional nature of this measurement and reward system. Another difference concerns the notion of gainsharing versus profit sharing. Profit sharing is a global incentive designed to encourage employees to contribute to the overall financial well-being of the organization. Gainsharing is more specific. Employees are allowed to share in gains related to specific improvement projects. Gainsharing helps obtain the necessary buy-in for specific improvement projects inherent to activity-based management.

Financial-Based Rewards	Activity-Based Rewards
1. Financial performance basis	1. Multidimensional performance basis
2. Individual rewards	2. Group rewards
3. Salary increases	3. Salary increases
4. Promotions	4. Promotions
5. Bonuses and profit sharing	5. Bonuses, profit sharing, and gainsharing

Exhibit 5-7 Rewards Compared

Managers Decide

ABM for Engine Maintenance

US Airways implemented an activity-based management (ABM) system to manage its in-house engine maintenance business unit. First, ABM helped determine the cost of engine maintenance with increased accuracy. Second, ABM provided operational and financial information that allowed work teams to identify opportunities for improvement. Thus, ABM provided accurate cost information and simultaneously revealed opportunities for improvement. ABM identified 410 activities—such as tear down, welding, waiting for tooling, and rework—of which 47 were identified as non-value-added. The non-value-added activities were rank-ordered on the basis of activity cost, which provided information about where the most significant process improvement opportunities were located. The various work teams then investigated the root causes of the efforts being expended on the non-value-added activities. Once the root causes were identified, the teams took action to reduce or eliminate the non-value-added activities. The net result was a process savings of $4.3 million per year. ■

Source: Joe Donnelly and Dave Buchanan, "Implementation Lands $4.3M in Process Improvement Savings," http://www.bettermanagement.com (accessed September 7, 2004).

Process Value Analysis

Objective 2

Explain process value analysis.

Process value analysis is fundamental to activity-based responsibility accounting; it focuses on accountability for activities rather than costs; and it emphasizes the maximization of systemwide performance instead of individual performance. Process value analysis helps convert the concepts of activity-based responsibility accounting from a conceptual basis to an operational basis. As the models in Exhibits 5-1 and 5-3 illustrate, process value analysis is concerned with (1) *driver analysis,* (2) *activity analysis,* and (3) *activity performance measurement.*

Driver Analysis: The Search for Root Causes

Managing activities requires an understanding of what causes activity costs. Every activity has inputs and outputs. **Activity inputs** are the resources consumed by the activity in producing its output. **Activity output** is the result or product of an activity. For example, if the activity is writing a computer program, the inputs would be such things as a programmer, a computer, a printer, computer paper, and disks. The output would be a computer program. An **activity output measure** is the number of times the activity is performed. It is the quantifiable measure of the output. For example, the number of programs is a possible output measure for writing programs.

The output measure effectively is a measure of the demands placed on an activity and is what we have been calling an *activity driver.* As the demands for an activity change, the cost of the activity can change. For example, as the number of programs written increases, the activity of writing programs may need to consume more inputs (labor, disks, paper, and so on). However, output measures, such as the number of programs, may not (and usually don't) correspond to the *root causes* of activity costs; rather, they are the consequences of the activity being performed. **Root causes** are the most basic causes for an activity being performed. The purpose of *driver analysis* is to reveal the root causes. Thus, **driver analysis** is the effort expended to identify those factors that are the root causes of activity costs. For instance, an analysis may reveal that the root cause of the cost of moving materials is plant layout. Once the root cause is known, then action can be taken to improve the activity. Specifically, reorganizing plant layout can reduce the cost of moving materials.

Often the root cause of the cost of an activity is also the root cause of other related activities. For example, poor supplier quality may be the root cause of both the costs of inspecting purchased parts (output measure × number of inspection hours) and reordering (output measure × number of reorders). By implementing total quality management and a supplier evaluation program, both activities and the procurement process itself may be improved.

Activity Analysis: Identifying and Assessing Value Content

The heart of process value analysis is activity analysis. **Activity analysis** is the process of identifying, describing, and evaluating the activities an organization performs. Activity analysis should produce four outcomes: (1) what activities are done, (2) how many people perform the activities, (3) the time and resources required to perform the activities, and (4) an assessment of the value of the activities to the organization, including a recommendation to select and keep only those that add value. Steps 1–3 have been described in Chapter 4. Those steps were critical for assigning costs. Step 4, determining the value-added content of activities, is concerned with cost reduction rather than cost assignment. Therefore, some feel that this is the most important part of activity analysis. Activities can be classified as *value-added* or *non-value-added.*

Value-Added Activities Those activities necessary to remain in business are called **value-added activities**. Some activities—required activities—are necessary to comply with legal mandates. For example, RTP, Inc., is a public company. All the activities that RTP must do to comply with the reporting requirements of the Securities and Exchange Commission and the filing requirements of the Internal Revenue Service are examples of mandated activities. These activities are value-added by *mandate.* The remaining activities in the firm are *discretionary.* A discretionary activity is classified as value-added provided it simultaneously satisfies three conditions: (1) the activity produces a change of state, (2) the change of state was not achievable by preceding activities, and (3) the activity enables other activities to be performed.

For example, recall that RTP, Inc., manufactures hydraulic cylinders. The first activity, cutting rods, cuts long rods into the correct lengths for the cylinders. Next, the cut rods are welded to cut plates. The cutting-rod activity is value-added because (1) it causes a change of state—uncut rods become cut rods, (2) no prior activity was supposed to create this change of state, and (3) it enables the welding activity to be performed. Though the value-added properties are easy to see for an operational activity like cutting rods, what about a more general activity like supervising production workers? A managerial activity is specifically designed to manage other value-added activities—to ensure that they are performed in an efficient and timely manner. Supervision certainly satisfies the enabling condition. Is there a change in state? There are two ways of answering in the affirmative. First, supervising can be viewed as an enabling resource that is consumed by the operational activities that do produce a change of state. Thus, supervising is a secondary activity that serves as an input that is needed to help bring about the change of state expected for value-added primary activities. Second, it could be argued that the supervision brings order by changing the state from uncoordinated activities to coordinated activities. Once value-added activities are identified, we can define value-added costs. **Value-added costs** are the costs to perform value-added activities with perfect efficiency.

Non-Value-Added Activities All activities other than those that are absolutely essential to remain in business, and therefore considered unnecessary, are referred to as *non-value-added activities.* A **non-value-added activity** can be identified by its failure to satisfy any one of the three previous defining conditions. Violation of the first two is the usual case for non-value-added activities. Inspecting cut rods (for correct length), for example, is a non-value-added activity. Inspection is a state-detection activity, not a state-changing activity (it tells us the state of the cut rod—whether it is the right length or not). For this reason, it fails the first condition. Consider the activity of reworking goods or subassemblies. Rework is designed to bring a good from a nonconforming state to a conforming state. In other words, a change of state occurs. Yet, the activity is non-value-added because it repeats work; it is doing something that should have been done by preceding activities (Condition 2 is violated). **Non-value-added costs** are costs that are caused either by non-value-added activities or the inefficient performance of valued-added activities. Due to increased competition, many firms are attempting to eliminate non-value-added activities because they add unnecessary cost and impede performance; firms are also striving to optimize value-added activities. Thus, activity analysis attempts to identify and eventually eliminate all unnecessary activities and, simultaneously, increase the efficiency of necessary activities.

The theme of activity analysis is waste elimination. As waste is eliminated, costs are reduced. The cost reduction *follows* the elimination of waste. Note the value of managing the *causes* of the costs rather than the costs themselves. Though managing costs may increase the efficiency of an activity, if the activity is unnecessary, what does it matter if it is performed efficiently? An unnecessary activity is wasteful and should be eliminated. For example, moving materials and partially finished goods is often cited as a non-value-added activity. Installing an automated material-handling system may increase the efficiency of this activity, but changing to cellular manufacturing with on-site, just-in-time delivery of materials could virtually eliminate the activity. It is easy to see which is preferable.

Examples of Non-Value-Added Activities Reordering parts, expediting production, and rework because of defective parts are examples of non-value-added activities. Other examples include warranty work, handling customer complaints, and reporting defects. Non-value-added activities can exist anywhere in the organization. In the manufacturing operation, five major activities are often cited as wasteful and unnecessary:

1. *Scheduling.* An activity that uses time and resources to determine when different products have access to processes (or when and how many setups must be done) and how much will be produced.
2. *Moving.* An activity that uses time and resources to move materials, work in process, and finished goods from one department to another.
3. *Waiting.* An activity in which materials or work in process use time and resources by waiting on the next process.
4. *Inspecting.* An activity in which time and resources are spent ensuring that the product meets specifications.
5. *Storing.* An activity that uses time and resources while a good or material is held in inventory.

None of these activities adds any value for the customer. (Note that inspection would not be necessary if the product were produced correctly the first time; it therefore adds no value for the customer.) The challenge of activity analysis is to find ways to produce the good without using any of these activities.

Cost Reduction Continuous improvement carries with it the objective of cost reduction. Efforts to reduce costs of existing products and processes is referred to as **kaizen costing**. Competitive conditions dictate that companies must deliver products the customers want, on time, and at the lowest possible cost. This means that an organization must continually strive for cost improvement. Kaizen costing is characterized by constant, incremental improvements to existing processes and products. Activity analysis is a key element of kaizen costing. Activity analysis can reduce costs in four ways:[6]

1. Activity elimination
2. Activity selection
3. Activity reduction
4. Activity sharing

Activity elimination focuses on non-value-added activities. Once activities that fail to add value are identified, measures must be taken to rid the organization of these activities. For example, the activity of inspecting incoming parts seems necessary to ensure that the product using the parts functions according to specifications. Use of a bad part can produce a bad final product. Yet, this activity is necessary only because of the poor-quality performance of the supplying firms. Selecting suppliers who are able to supply high-quality parts or who are willing to improve their quality performance to achieve this objective will eventually allow the elimination of incoming inspection. Cost reduction then follows.

Activity selection involves choosing among different sets of activities that are caused by competing strategies. Different strategies cause different activities. Different product design strategies, for example, can require significantly different activities. Activities, in turn, cause costs. Each product design strategy has its own set of activities and associated costs. All other things being equal, the lowest-cost design strategy should be chosen. In a kaizen cost framework, redesign of existing products and processes can lead to a different, cheaper set of activities. Thus, activity selection can have a significant effect on cost reduction.

Activity reduction decreases the time and resources required by an activity. This approach to cost reduction should be primarily aimed at improving the efficiency of necessary activities or be a short-term strategy for improving non-value-added activities until they can be eliminated. Setup activity is a necessary activity that is often cited as an example for which less time and fewer resources need to be used. Finding ways to reduce setup time—and thereby lower the cost of setups—is another example of the kaizen costing concept.

Activity sharing increases the efficiency of necessary activities by using economies of scale. Specifically, the quantity of the cost driver is increased without increasing the total cost of the activity itself. This lowers the per-unit cost of the cost driver and the amount of cost traceable to the products that consume the activity. For example, a new product can be designed to use components already being used by other products. By using existing components, the activities associated with these components already exist, and the company avoids the creation of a whole new set of activities.

Activity Performance Measurement

Assessing how well activities (and processes) are performed is fundamental to management's efforts to improve profitability. Activity performance measures exist in both financial and nonfinancial forms. These measures are designed to assess how well an activity was performed and the results achieved. They are also designed to

6 Peter B. B. Turney, "How Activity-Based Costing Helps Reduce Cost," *Journal of Cost Management* (Winter 1991): pp. 29–35.

reveal if constant improvement is being realized. Measures of activity performance center on three major dimensions: (1) efficiency, (2) quality, and (3) time.

Efficiency focuses on the relationship of activity inputs to activity outputs. For example, one way to improve activity efficiency is to produce the same activity output with lower cost for the inputs used. *Quality* is concerned with doing the activity right the first time it is performed. If the activity output is defective, then the activity may need to be repeated, causing unnecessary cost and reduction in efficiency. The *time* required to perform an activity is also critical. Longer times usually mean more resource consumption and less ability to respond to customer demands. Time measures of performance tend to be nonfinancial, whereas efficiency and quality measures are both financial and nonfinancial.

Measures of Activity Performance

Objective 3

Describe activity performance measurement.

Knowing how well we are currently performing an activity should disclose the potential for doing better. Since many of the nonfinancial measures that will be discussed for the process perspective of the *Balanced Scorecard* (strategic-based responsibility accounting system discussed in Chapter 16) also apply at the activity level, this section will emphasize financial measures of activity performance. Financial measures of performance should also provide specific information about the dollar effects of activity performance changes. Thus, financial measures should indicate both potential and actual savings. Financial measures of activity efficiency include (1) value- and non-value-added activity cost reports, (2) trends in activity cost reports, (3) kaizen standard setting, (4) benchmarking, and (5) life-cycle costing.

Value- and Non-Value-Added Cost Reporting

Reducing non-value-added costs is one way to increase activity efficiency. A company's accounting system should distinguish between value-added costs and non-value-added costs because improving activity performance requires eliminating non-value-added activities and optimizing value-added activities. Hence, a firm should identify and formally report the value-added and non-value-added costs of each activity. Highlighting non-value-added costs reveals the magnitude of the waste the company is currently experiencing, thus providing some information about the potential for improvement. This encourages managers to place more emphasis on controlling non-value-added activities. Progress can then be assessed by preparing trend and cost reduction reports. Tracking these costs over time permits managers to assess the effectiveness of their activity-management programs.

Knowing the amount of costs saved is important for strategic purposes. For example, if an activity is eliminated, then the costs saved should be traceable to individual products. These savings can produce price reductions for customers, making the firm more competitive. Changing the pricing strategy, however, requires knowledge of the cost reductions created by activity analysis. A cost-reporting system, therefore, is an important ingredient in an activity-based responsibility accounting system.

Value-added costs are the only costs that an organization should incur. The *value-added standard* calls for the complete elimination of non-value-added activities; for these activities, the optimal output is zero with zero cost. The value-added standard also calls for the complete elimination of the inefficiency of activities that are necessary but inefficiently carried out. Thus, value-added activities also have an optimal output level. A **value-added standard**, therefore, identifies the optimal activity output. Identifying the optimal activity output requires activity output measurement.

Setting value-added standards does not mean that they will be (or should be) achieved immediately. The idea of continuous improvement is to move toward the ideal, not to achieve it immediately. Workers (teams) can be rewarded for improvement.

Moreover, nonfinancial activity performance measures can be used to supplement and support the goal of eliminating non-value-added costs (these are discussed later in the chapter). Finally, measuring the efficiency of individual workers and supervisors is not the way to eliminate non-value-added activities. Remember, activities cut across departmental boundaries and are part of processes. Focusing on activities and providing incentives to improve processes is a more productive approach. Improving the process should lead to improved results.

By comparing actual activity costs with value-added activity costs, management can assess the level of activity inefficiency and determine the potential for improvement. To identify and calculate value-added and non-value-added costs, output measures for each activity must be defined. Once output measures are defined, then value-added standard quantities (*SQ*) for each activity can be defined. Value-added costs can be computed by multiplying the value-added standard quantities by the price standard (*SP*). Non-value-added costs can be calculated as the difference between the actual level of the activity's output (*AQ*) and the value-added level (*SQ*), multiplied by the unit standard cost. These formulas are presented in Exhibit 5-8. Some further explanation is needed.

For flexible resources (resources acquired as needed), *AQ* is the actual quantity of activity used. For committed resources (resources acquired in advance of usage), *AQ* represents the actual quantity of activity capacity acquired, as measured by the activity's practical capacity. This definition of *AQ* allows the computation of non-value-added costs for both variable and fixed activity costs. For fixed activity costs, *SP* is the budgeted activity costs divided by *AQ*, where *AQ* is practical activity capacity.

To illustrate the power of these concepts, consider the following four production activities for RTP, Inc.: welding, reworking defective products, setting up equipment, and inspecting purchased components. Setups and material usage are necessary activities; inspection and rework are unnecessary. The following data pertain to the four activities:

Activity	Activity Driver	SQ	AQ	SP
Welding	Welding hours	10,000	12,000	$40
Rework	Rework hours	0	10,000	9
Setups	Setup hours	0	6,000	60
Inspection	Number of inspections	0	4,000	15

Notice that the value-added standards (*SQ*) for rework and inspection call for their elimination; the value-added standard for setups calls for a zero setup time. Ideally, there should be no defective products; by improving quality, changing production processes, and so on, inspection can eventually be eliminated. Setups are necessary, but in a waste-free environment, efforts are made to drive setup times to zero.

Exhibit 5-9 classifies the costs for the four activities as value-added or non-value-added. For simplicity, and to show the relationship to actual costs, the actual price

Value-added costs = $SQ \times SP$

Non-value-added costs = $(AQ - SQ)SP$

Where

SQ = The value-added output level for an activity

SP = The standard price per unit of activity output measure

AQ = The actual quantity used of flexible resources or the practical activity capacity acquired for committed resources

Exhibit 5-8 Formulas for Value-Added and Non-Value-Added Costs

Activity	Value-Added Costs	Non-Value-Added Costs	Actual Costs
Welding	$400,000	$ 80,000	$480,000
Rework	0	90,000	90,000
Setups	0	360,000	360,000
Inspection	0	60,000	60,000
Total	$400,000	$590,000	$990,000

Exhibit 5-9 Value-Added and Non-Value-Added Cost Report for the Year Ended December 31, 2008

per unit of the activity driver is assumed to be equal to the standard price. In this case, the value-added cost plus the non-value-added cost equals actual cost.

The cost report in Exhibit 5-9 allows the managers of RTP, Inc., to see the non-value-added costs; as a consequence, it emphasizes the opportunity for improvement. By redesigning the products, welding time can be reduced. By training welders and improving labor skill, management can reduce rework. Reducing setup time and implementing a supplier evaluation program are actions that can be taken to improve performance for the setup and inspection activities. Thus, reporting value- and non-value-added costs at a point in time may trigger actions to manage activities more effectively. Seeing the amount of waste may induce managers to search for ways to improve activities and bring about cost reductions. Reporting these costs may also help managers improve planning, budgeting, and pricing decisions. For example, lowering the selling price to meet a competitor's price may be seen as possible if a manager can see the potential for reducing non-value-added costs to absorb the effect of the price reduction.

Trend Reporting

As RTP, Inc., takes actions to improve activities, do the cost reductions follow as expected? One way to answer this question is to compare the costs for each activity over time. The goal is activity improvement as measured by cost reduction, and so we should see a decline in non-value-added costs from one period to the next—provided the activity analysis is effective. Assume, for example, that at the beginning of 2008, four major activity-management decisions were implemented: the use of statistical process control, product redesign, a labor-training program, and a supplier evaluation program. How effective were these decisions? Did a cost reduction occur as expected? Exhibit 5-10 provides a cost report that compares the *non-value-added costs* of 2008 with those that occurred in 2007. The 2008 costs are assumed but would be computed the same way as shown for 2007. We assume that *SQ* is the same for both years. Comparing 2008 non-value-added costs directly with those in 2007 requires *SQ* to be the same for both years. If *SQ* changes, prior-year, non-value-added costs are

	Non-Value-Added Costs		
Activity	2007	2008	Change
Welding	$ 80,000	$ 50,000	$ 30,000
Rework	90,000	70,000	20,000
Setups	360,000	200,000	160,000
Inspection	60,000	35,000	25,000
Total	$590,000	$355,000	$235,000

Exhibit 5-10 Trend Report: Non-Value-Added Costs

adjusted by simply assuming the same percentage deviation from standard in the current year as was realized in the prior year.

The trend report reveals that cost reductions followed, as expected. RTP, Inc., managed to eliminate almost half of the non-value-added costs. There is still ample room for improvement, but activity improvement so far has been successful. As a note of interest, comparison of the actual costs of the two periods would have revealed the same reduction. Reporting non-value-added costs, however, reveals not only the reduction but also where it occurred; it provides managers with information on how much potential for cost reduction remains as well. Nevertheless, there is an important qualification. Value-added standards, like other standards, are not cast in stone. New technology, new designs, and other innovations can change the nature of activities performed. Value-added activities can be converted to non-value-added activities, and value-added levels can change as well. Thus, as new ways for improvement surface, value-added standards can change. Managers should not become content but should continually seek higher levels of efficiency.

The Role of Kaizen Standards

Kaizen costing is concerned with reducing the costs of existing products and processes. In operational terms, this translates into reducing non-value-added costs. Controlling this cost reduction process is accomplished through the repetitive use of two major subcycles: (1) the kaizen, or continuous improvement, cycle and (2) the maintenance cycle. The kaizen subcycle is defined by a Plan-Do-Check-Act sequence. If a company emphasizes reducing non-value-added costs, the amount of improvement planned for the coming period (month, quarter, etc.) is set (the *Plan* step). A **kaizen standard** reflects the planned improvement for the upcoming period. The planned improvement is assumed to be attainable, so kaizen standards are a type of currently attainable standard. Actions are taken to implement the planned improvements (the *Do* step). Next, actual results (e.g., costs) are compared with the kaizen standard to provide a measure of the level of improvement attained (the *Check* step). Setting this new level as a minimum standard for future performance locks in the realized improvements and initiates simultaneously the maintenance cycle and a search for additional improvement opportunities (the *Act* step). The maintenance cycle follows a Standard-Do-Check-Act sequence. A *standard* is set based on prior improvements (locking in these improvements). Next, actions are taken (the *Do* step) and the results checked to ensure that performance conforms to this new level (the *Check* step). If not, then corrective actions are taken to restore performance (the *Act* step). The kaizen cost-reduction process is summarized in Exhibit 5-11.

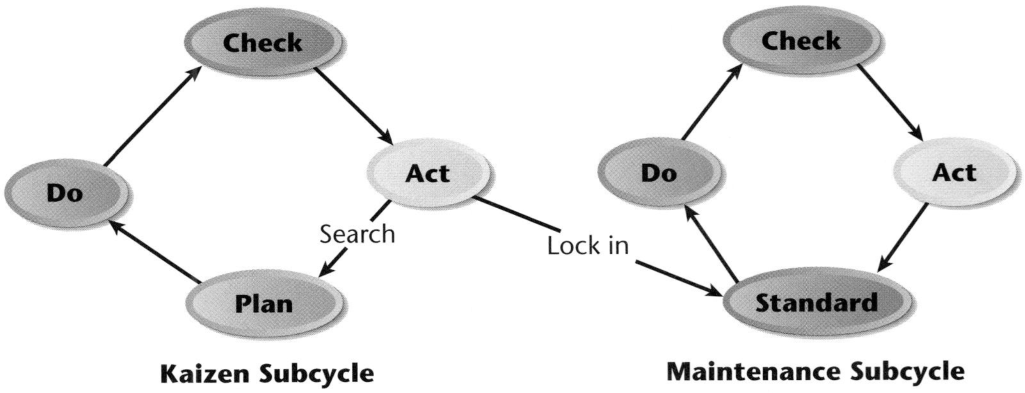

Exhibit 5-11 Kaizen Cost Reduction Process

For example, assume that RTP, Inc., tests every unit produced of its electronic instrument panels. The unit-level, value-added standard for this product calls for zero inspection hours per unit and a value-added inspection cost of $0 per unit. Assume that in the prior year, the company used 15 minutes to test each panel at a cost of $15 per testing hour. Thus, the actual testing cost per unit is $3.75 ($15 × 1/4 hr.). This is also the non-value-added cost. For the coming quarter, the company is installing a new production process that is expected to increase the reliability of the panels being produced. These changes are expected to reduce the testing time from 15 minutes to 10 minutes. Hence, the planned cost reduction is $1.25 per unit. The kaizen standard is defined as 10 minutes per unit with a standard testing cost of $2.50 per unit, the actual prior-year cost less the targeted reduction ($3.75 − $1.25). Now, suppose that the actual cost achieved after implementing the new production process is $2.50. The actual improvements expected did materialize, and the new minimum standard is $2.50, locking in the improvements. Until further improvements are achieved, testing costs should be no more than $2.50. For subsequent periods, additional improvements would be sought and a new kaizen standard defined. For example, in the third quarter, RPT, Inc., is planning to install a statistical process control system that will increase the reliability of the process even more so that inspection time can be further reduced. This will then produce a lower standard than the $2.50 per unit now in effect.

Benchmarking

Another approach to standard setting that is used to help identify opportunities for activity improvement is called *benchmarking*. **Benchmarking** uses best practices as the standard for evaluating activity performance. Within an organization, different units (for example, different plant sites) that perform the same activities are compared. The unit with the best performance for a given activity sets the standard. Other units then have a target to meet or exceed. Furthermore, the best practices unit can share information with other units on how it has achieved its superior results. For this process to work, it is necessary to ensure that activity definitions and activity output measures are consistent across units. Such things as activity rates, the cost per unit of activity output, or the amount of activity output per unit of process output can be used to rank activity performance and identify the best performer.

For example, assume the output of the purchasing activity is measured by the number of purchase orders. Suppose further that the cost of the purchasing activity for one plant is $90,000, and activity output is 4,500 purchase orders. Dividing the cost of the purchasing activity by the number of purchase orders prepared gives a unit cost of $20 per order. Now, if the best unit cost is $15 per purchase order, then the plant with the $20 per-unit cost knows it has the ability to improve activity efficiency by at least $5 per unit. By studying the purchasing practices of the best plant, activity efficiency should increase.

Internal benchmarking does not have to be restricted to cost management. For example, **Rank Xerox**, an 80-percent-owned subsidiary of **Xerox** operating mostly in Europe, used internal benchmarking to boost revenues.[7] The benchmarking project was assigned to a team. This team studied the sales data and made country-by-country comparisons. It discovered that the French Division sold five times more color copiers than its sister divisions and that the Swiss Division's sales of the top-of-the-line DocuPrint machines were 10 times greater than those of any other country. The team identified the best practices of the top performers and had other divisions implement them. By copying France's best practices, the Swiss Division

7 Thomas A. Stewart and Ed Brown, "Beat the Budget and Astound Your CFO," *Fortune* (October 28, 1996). Check the chapter web links at the Interactive Study Center on http://www.thomsonedu.com/accounting/hansen for access to this online article.

increased sales of color copiers by 328 percent, Holland by 300 percent, and Norway by 152 percent. At the end of the first year, Rank Xerox determined that overall sales increased by $65 million because of internal benchmarking. By the end of the second year, this figure increased to $200 million.

The objective of benchmarking is to become the best at performing activities and processes. Thus, benchmarking should also involve comparisons with competitors or other industries. However, it is often difficult to obtain the necessary data for external benchmarking to work. In some cases, it may be possible to study best practices of noncompetitors. There are certain activities and processes that are common to all organizations. If superior external best practices can be identified, then they can be used as standards to motivate internal improvements. The federal government has used best practices of private sector companies to improve its services. The U.S. Department of Agriculture (USDA), for example, sent a team to **Citicorp** to study how Citicorp serviced mortgages. As a result, the USDA consolidated its loan-servicing activities from 2,000 field offices into one central unit in St. Louis. This action, along with other changes, cut the cost of servicing the USDA's loan portfolio by $250 million over five years.[8]

Drivers and Behavioral Effects

Activity output measures are needed to compute and track non-value-added costs. Reducing a non-value-added activity should produce a reduction in the demand for the activity and, therefore, a reduction in the activity output measures. If a team's performance is affected by its ability to reduce non-value-added costs, then the selection of activity drivers (as output measures), and how they are used, can affect behavior. For example, if the output measure chosen for setup costs is setup time, an incentive is created for workers to reduce setup time. Since the value-added standard for setup costs calls for their complete elimination, the incentive to drive setup time to zero is compatible with the company's objectives, and the induced behavior is beneficial.

Suppose, however, that the objective is to reduce the number of unique parts a company processes, thus reducing the demand for activities such as purchasing and incoming inspection. If the costs of these activities are assigned to products based on the number of parts, the incentive created is to reduce the number of parts in a product. Yet, if too many parts are eliminated, the functionality of the product may be reduced to a point where the marketability of the product is adversely affected. Identifying the value-added standard number of parts for each product through the use of functional analysis can discourage this type of behavior.[9] Designers can then be encouraged to reduce the non-value-added costs by designing the product to reach the value-added standard number of parts. The standard has provided a concrete objective and defined the kind of behavior that the incentive allows.

Activity Capacity Management

Activity capacity is the number of times an activity can be performed. Activity drivers measure activity capacity. For example, consider the inspecting activity for batches of hydraulic cylinders produced by RTP, Inc. A sample from each batch is taken to determine the batch's overall quality. The demand for the inspection activity determines the amount of activity capacity that is required. For instance, suppose that the number of batches inspected measures activity output. Now, suppose that 60 batches are scheduled to be produced. Thus, the required capacity is 60 batches.

8 Al Gore, *Businesslike Government: Lessons Learned from America's Best Companies* (U.S. Government Information, 1997). For more information, visit the chapter web links at the Interactive Study Center on http://www.thomsonedu.com/accounting/hansen.

9 Functional analysis compares the price customers are willing to pay for a particular product function with the cost of providing that function.

Finally, assume that a single inspector can inspect 20 batches per year. Thus, RTP, Inc., must hire three inspectors to provide the necessary capacity. If each inspector is paid a salary of $40,000, the budgeted cost of the activity capacity is $120,000. This is the cost of the resources (labor) acquired in advance of usage. The budgeted activity rate is $2,000 per batch ($120,000/60).

There are several questions relating to activity capacity and its cost. First, *what* should the activity capacity be? The answer to this question provides the ability to measure the amount of improvement possible. Second, *how* much of the capacity acquired was actually used? The answer to this question signals a nonproductive cost and, at the same time, an opportunity for capacity reduction and cost savings.

Capacity Variances Exhibit 5-12 illustrates the calculation of two capacity variances: the *activity volume variance* and the *unused capacity variance.* The **activity volume variance** is the difference between the actual activity level acquired (practical capacity, *AQ*) and the value-added standard quantity of activity that should be used (*SQ*). Assuming that inspection is a non-value-added activity, $SQ = 0$ is the value-added standard. The volume variance in this framework has a useful economic interpretation: it is the non-value-added cost of the inspection activity. It measures the amount of improvement that is possible through analysis and management of activities ($120,000 in this example). However, since the supply of the activity in question (inspections) must be acquired in blocks (one inspector at a time), it is also important to measure the current demand for the activity (actual usage).

When supply exceeds demand by a large enough quantity, management can take action to reduce the quantity of the activity provided. Thus, the **unused capacity variance**, the difference between activity availability (*AQ*) and activity usage (*AU*), is important information that should be provided to management. The goal is to reduce the demand for the activity until such time as the unused capacity variance equals the activity volume variance. Why? Because the activity volume variance is a non-value-added cost, and the unused activity volume variance measures the progress made in reducing this non-value-added cost. The calculation of the unused capacity variance is also illustrated in Exhibit 5-12. Notice that the unused capacity is 20 batches valued at $40,000. Assume that this unused capacity exists because management has been engaged in a quality-improvement program that has reduced the need to inspect certain batches of products. This difference between the supply of the inspection resources and their usage should impact future spending plans. (Reduction of a non-value-added activity is labeled as favorable.)

For example, we know that the supply of inspection resources is greater than its usage. Furthermore, because of the quality-improvement program, we can expect this difference to persist and even become greater (with the ultimate goal of reducing the cost of inspection activity to zero). The management of RTP, Inc., now must be willing

AQ = The activity capacity acquired (practical capacity)
SQ = The activity capacity that should be used
AU = The actual usage of the activity
SP = The fixed activity rate

$SP \times SQ$	$SP \times AQ$	$SP \times AU$
$2,000 × 0	$2,000 × 60	$2,000 × 40
$0	$120,000	$80,000

Activity Volume Variance $120,000 U — Unused Capacity Variance $40,000 F

Exhibit 5-12 Activity Capacity Variances—Inspection Activity—RTP, Inc.

to exploit the unused capacity they have created. Essentially, activity availability can be reduced, and, thus, the spending on inspection can be decreased. A manager can use several options to achieve this outcome. Since the inspection demand has been reduced by 20 batches, the company needs only two full-time inspectors. The extra inspector could be permanently reassigned to an activity where resources are in short supply. If reassignment is not feasible, the company should lay off the extra inspector.

This example illustrates an important feature of activity capacity management. Activity improvement can create unused capacity, but managers must be willing and able to make the tough decisions to reduce resource spending on the redundant resources to gain the potential profit increase. Profits can be increased by reducing resource spending or by transferring the resources to other activities that will generate more revenues.

Activity-Based Customer and Supplier Costing

Objective 4

Describe activity-based customer and supplier costing.

In an activity-based costing system, product costing accuracy is improved by tracing activity costs to the products that consume the activities. ABC can also be used to accurately determine the costs of customers and suppliers. Knowing the costs of customers and suppliers can be vital information for improving a company's profitability. **LSI Logic**, a high-tech producer of semiconductors, implemented ABC customer costing and discovered that 10 percent of its customers were responsible for about 90 percent of its profits. It also discovered that it was actually losing money on about 50 percent of its customers. It worked to convert its unprofitable customers into profitable ones and invited those who would not provide a fair return to take their business elsewhere. As a consequence, its sales decreased but its profits tripled.[10]

Activity-Based Customer Costing

Customers are thus cost objects of fundamental interest. As the LSI Logic experience illustrates, customer management can produce significant gains in profit. It is possible to have customer diversity just as it is possible to have product diversity. Customers can consume customer-driven activities in different proportions. Sources of customer diversity include such things as order frequency, delivery frequency, geographic distance, sales and promotional support, and engineering support requirements. Knowing how much it costs to service different customers can be vital information for such purposes as pricing, determining customer mix, and improving profitability. Furthermore, because of diversity of customers, multiple drivers are needed to trace costs accurately. This outcome means that ABC can be useful to organizations that may have only one product, homogeneous products, or a JIT structure where direct tracing diminishes the value of ABC for product costing.

The cost of a supplier is usually much more than the purchase price of a component. ABC can improve the accuracy of determining the cost of a company's suppliers.

© Getty Images/PhotoDisc

10 Gary Cokins, "Are All of Your Customers Profitable (To You)?" an online article accessible via the chapter web links at the Interactive Study Center on this text's website, http://www.thomsonedu.com/accounting/hansen.

Customer Costing versus Product Costing Assigning the costs of customer service to customers is done in the same way that manufacturing costs are assigned to products. Customer-driven activities such as order entry, order picking, shipping, making sales calls, and evaluating a client's credit are identified and listed in an activity dictionary. The cost of the resources consumed is assigned to activities, and the cost of the activities is assigned to individual customers. The same model and procedures that apply to products apply to customers as well. A simple example will illustrate the basics of ABC customer costing.

Example Suppose that RTP, Inc., produces some small parts for 11 major buyers. ABC is used to assign production costs to products. Of the 11 customers, one accounts for 50 percent of the sales, with the remaining 10 accounting for the rest of the sales. The 10 smaller customers purchase parts in roughly equal quantities. Orders placed by the smaller customers are about the same size. Data concerning RTP's customer activity follow:

	Large Customer	Ten Smaller Customers
Units purchased	500,000	500,000
Orders placed	2	200
Number of sales calls	10	210
Manufacturing cost	$3,000,000	$3,000,000
Order-filling costs allocated*	$202,000	$202,000
Sales-force costs allocated*	$110,000	$110,000

*Allocated based on sales volume.

Currently, customer-driven costs are assigned to customers based on units sold, a unit-level driver. ABC improves the assignment by using drivers that better reflect the consumption of the activities by customers: number of orders and number of sales calls. The activity rates are $2,000 per order ($404,000/202 orders) for order filling and $1,000 per call ($220,000/220 calls) for the sales-force activity. Using this information, the customer-driven costs can be assigned to each group of customers as follows:

	Large Customer	Ten Smaller Customers
Order-filling costs	$ 4,000	$400,000
Sales-force costs	10,000	210,000

Managers Decide

ABC and Customer Profitability

In a 1998 survey conducted by the Ohio State University's Supply Chain Management Research Group, about one-fourth of the respondents said that the need to measure customer profitability was their primary motivation for implementing ABC. They also pointed out that measuring customer profitability has assumed more importance because customers are demanding more logistics services without commensurate increases in prices. Interest was also expressed in applying ABC across the entire supply chain to determine how activity costs are driven by the services requested by other supply chain members. ■

Source: Thomas A. Foster, "Time to Learn the ABC's of Logistics," *Logistics Management and Distribution Report* 38 (2): 67–70.

This reveals a much different picture of the cost of servicing each type of customer. The smaller customer is costing more, attributable to smaller, more frequent orders and the evident need of the sales force to engage in more negotiations to make a sale.

What does this tell the management of RPT that it didn't know before? First, the large customer costs much less to service than the smaller customers and perhaps should be charged less. Second, it raises some significant questions relative to the smaller customers. Is it possible, for example, to encourage larger, less frequent orders? Perhaps offering discounts for larger orders would be appropriate. Why is it more difficult to sell to the smaller customers? Why are more calls needed? Are they less informed than the large customer about the products? Can we improve profits by influencing our customers to change their buying behavior?

Activity-Based Supplier Costing

Activity-based costing can also help a manager identify the true cost of its suppliers. The cost of a supplier is much more than the purchase price of the components or materials acquired. Just like customers, suppliers can affect many internal activities of a firm and significantly increase the cost of purchasing. A more correct view is one where the costs associated with quality, reliability, and delivery timeliness are added to the purchase costs. Managers are then required to evaluate suppliers based on total cost, not just purchase price. Activity-based costing is the key to tracing costs relating to purchase, quality, reliability, and delivery performance to suppliers.

Supplier Costing Methodology Assigning the costs of supplier-related activities to suppliers follows the same pattern as ABC product and customer costing. Supplier-driven activities such as purchasing, receiving, inspecting incoming components, reworking products (because of defective components), expediting products (because of late deliveries of suppliers), and warranty work (due to defective supplier components) are identified and listed in an activity dictionary. The cost of the

	Murray Inc.		Plata Associates	
	Part A1	Part B2	Part A1	Part B2
Purchase cost:				
$20 × 80,000	$1,600,000			
$52 × 40,000		$2,080,000		
$24 × 10,000			$240,000	
$56 × 10,000				$560,000
Repairing products:				
$400 × 1,600	640,000			
$400 × 380		152,000		
$400 × 10			4,000	
$400 × 10				4,000
Expediting products:				
$2,000 × 60	120,000			
$2,000 × 40		80,000		
Total costs	$2,360,000	$2,312,000	$244,000	$564,000
Units	÷ 80,000	÷ 40,000	÷ 10,000	÷ 10,000
Total unit cost	$ 29.50	$ 57.80	$ 24.40	$ 56.40

Exhibit 5-13 Supplier Costing

resources consumed is assigned to these activities, and the cost of the activities is assigned to individual suppliers. A simple example will illustrate the basics of ABC supplier costing.

Example To illustrate activity-based supplier costing, consider a particular purchasing practice of RPT's purchasing manager. The RPT purchasing manager uses two suppliers, Murray Inc. and Plata Associates, as the source of two electronic components used in the production of its electronic panels (for large trucks): Part A1 and Part B2. The purchasing manager prefers to use Murray because it provides the parts at a lower price; however, the second supplier is used as well to ensure a reliable supply of the parts. Now consider two activities: *repairing products* (under warranty) and *expediting products*. Repairing products occurs because of part failure (bought from suppliers) or defective manufacturing, including assembly. Expediting products takes place due to late delivery of parts or process failure. Part failure and late delivery are attributable to suppliers, whereas defective manufacturing, assembly, and process failure costs are attributable to internal processes. Warranty repair costs attributable to supplier part failure are assigned to suppliers using the number of failed parts as the driver. The costs of expediting attributable to late deliveries are assigned using the number of late shipments as the driver. Activity cost information and other data needed for supplier costing follow:

I. Activity Costs Caused by Suppliers (e.g., failed parts or late delivery)

Activity	Costs
Repairing products	$800,000
Expediting products	200,000

II. Supplier Data

	Murray Inc.		Plata Associates	
	Part A1	**Part B2**	**Part A1**	**Part B2**
Unit purchase price	$20	$52	$24	$56
Units purchased	80,000	40,000	10,000	10,000
Failed units	1,600	380	10	10
Late shipments	60	40	0	0

Using the preceding data, the activity rates for assigning costs to suppliers are computed as follows:

$$\text{Repair rate} = \$800{,}000/2{,}000^*$$
$$= \$400 \text{ per failed part}$$

*(1,600 + 380 + 10 + 10)

$$\text{Expediting rate} = \$200{,}000/100^*$$
$$= \$2{,}000 \text{ per late delivery}$$

*(60 + 40)

Using these rates and the activity data, the total purchasing cost per unit of each component is computed and shown in Exhibit 5-13. The results show that the "low-cost" supplier actually costs more when the supplier-related activities of repairing and expediting are considered. If all costs are considered, then the choice becomes clear: Plata Associates is the better supplier with a higher quality product, more on-time deliveries, and, consequently, a lower overall cost per unit.

Summary of Learning Objectives

1. Describe activity-based management and explain its relationship to activity-based costing.

ABM focuses on activities with the objective of improving customer value and increasing firm profitability. It has both a cost view and a process view. The cost view is concerned with assigning costs accurately and the process view is concerned with reducing costs by eliminating waste.

2. Explain process value analysis.

Process value analysis provides information about why work is done and how well it is done. It involves cost driver analysis, activity analysis, and performance measurement. It is this dimension that connects process volume analysis to the concept of continuous improvement. A key element of activity-based control is activity analysis—the process of identifying and describing a firm's activities, assessing their value to the organization, and selecting only those that are of value. Cost reduction is realized by decreasing, eliminating, selecting, and sharing activities. Emphasis is placed on identifying non-value-added costs and eliminating them. These costs are the result of unnecessary activities and inefficiencies found in necessary activities.

3. Describe activity performance measurement.

Activity performance is evaluated on three dimensions: efficiency, quality, and time. Financial measures of efficiency allow managers to identify the dollar values for potential improvement and for improvements achieved. Value- and non-value-added cost reports, trends in costs, benchmarking, kaizen standards, capacity management, and life-cycle budgeting are examples of financial measures of activity efficiency.

4. Describe activity-based customer and supplier costing.

Tracing customer-driven costs to customers can provide significant information to managers. Accurate customer costs allow managers to make better pricing decisions, customer-mix decisions, and other customer-related decisions that improve profitability. Similarly, tracing supplier-driven costs to suppliers can enable managers to choose the true low-cost suppliers, producing a stronger competitive position and increased profitability.

Key Terms

Activity analysis, 176
Activity capacity, 184
Activity elimination, 178
Activity inputs, 175
Activity output, 175
Activity output measure, 175
Activity reduction, 178
Activity selection, 178
Activity sharing, 178
Activity volume variance, 185
Activity-based management (ABM), 166
Activity-based responsibility accounting, 171
Benchmarking, 183
Driver analysis, 175
Financial (functional)-based responsibility accounting system, 170
Kaizen costing, 178
Kaizen standard, 182
Non-value-added activities, 177
Non-value-added costs, 177
Process creation, 173
Process improvement, 172
Process innovation (business reengineering), 172
Process value analysis, 175
Responsibility accounting, 170
Root causes, 175
Unused capacity variance, 185
Value-added activities, 176
Value-added costs, 176
Value-added standard, 179

Review Problems

1. Functional-Based Responsibility Accounting versus Activity-Based Responsibility Accounting

The labor standard for a company is 2.0 hours per unit produced, which includes setup time. At the beginning of the last quarter, a total of 20,000 units had been produced and 44,000 hours used. The production manager was concerned about the prospect of reporting an unfavorable labor efficiency variance at the end of the year. Any unfavorable variance over 9 to 10 percent of the standard usually meant a negative performance rating. Bonuses were adversely affected by negative ratings. Accordingly, for the last quarter, the production manager decided to reduce the number of setups and use longer production runs. He knew that his production workers usually were within 5 percent of the standard. The real problem was with setup times. By reducing the setups, the actual hours used would be within 7 to 8 percent of the standard hours allowed.

Required

1. Explain why the behavior of the production manager is unacceptable for a continuous improvement environment.
2. Explain how an activity-based responsibility accounting approach would discourage the kind of behavior described.

Solution

1. In a continuous improvement environment, efforts are made to reduce inventories and eliminate non-value-added costs. The production manager is focusing on meeting the labor usage standard and is ignoring the impact on inventories that longer production runs may have.
2. Activity-based responsibility accounting focuses on activities and activity performance. For the setup activity, the value-added standard would be zero setup time and zero setup costs. Thus, avoiding setups would not save labor time, and it would not affect the labor variance. Of course, labor variances themselves would not be computed—at least not at the operational level.

2. Activity Volume Variance; Unused Activity Capacity; Value- and Non-Value-Added Cost Reports; Kaizen Standards

Pollard Manufacturing has developed value-added standards for its activities, among which are the following three: materials usage, purchasing, and inspecting. The value-added output levels for each of the activities, their actual levels achieved, and the standard prices are as follows:

Activity	Activity Driver	*SQ*	*AQ*	*SP*
Using lumber	Board feet	24,000	30,000	$10
Purchasing	Purchase orders	800	1,000	50
Inspection	Inspection hours	0	4,000	12

Assume that material usage and purchasing costs correspond to flexible resources (acquired as needed) and inspection uses resources that are acquired in blocks, or steps, of 2,000 hours. The actual prices paid for the inputs equal the standard prices.

Required

1. Assume that continuous improvement efforts reduce the demand for inspection by 30 percent during the year (actual activity usage drops by 30 percent). Calculate the activity volume and unused capacity variances for the inspection activity. Explain their meaning. Also, explain why there is no activity volume or unused capacity variance for the other two activities.
2. Prepare a cost report that details value-added and non-value-added costs.
3. Suppose that the company wants to reduce all non-value-added costs by 30 percent in the coming year. Prepare kaizen standards that can be used to evaluate the company's progress toward this goal. How much will this save in resource spending?

Solution

1.

$SP \times SQ$		$SP \times AQ$		$SP \times AU$
$12 × 0		$12 × 4,000		$12 × 2,800
$0		$48,000		$33,600
	Activity Volume Variance		Unused Capacity Variance	
	$48,000 U		$14,400 F	

The activity volume variance is the non-value-added cost. The unused capacity variance measures the cost of the unused activity capacity. The other two activities have no volume variance or capacity variance because they use only flexible resources. No activity capacity is acquired in advance of usage; thus, there cannot be an unused capacity variance or an activity volume variance.

2.

	Costs		
	Value-Added	**Non-Value-Added**	**Total**
Using lumber	$240,000	$ 60,000	$300,000
Purchasing	40,000	10,000	50,000
Inspection	0	48,000	48,000
Total	$280,000	$118,000	$398,000

3.

	Kaizen Standards	
	Quantity	**Cost**
Using lumber	28,200	$282,000
Purchasing	940	47,000
Inspection	2,800	33,600

If the standards are met, then the savings are as follows:

Using lumber:	$10 × 1,800 =	$ 18,000
Purchasing:	$50 × 60 =	3,000
Savings		$ 21,000

No reduction occurs in resource spending for inspection because it must be purchased in increments of 2,000 and only 1,200 hours were saved—another 800 hours must be reduced before any reduction in resource spending is possible. The unused capacity variance must reach $24,000 before resource spending can be reduced.

Questions for Writing and Discussion

1. What are the two dimensions of the activity-based management model? How do they differ?
2. Describe a financial (functional)-based responsibility accounting system.
3. Describe an activity-based responsibility accounting system. How does it differ from financial (functional)-based responsibility accounting?
4. What is driver analysis? What role does it play in process value analysis?
5. What is meant by "activity inputs"? By "activity output"? Explain what is meant by "activity output measurement."
6. What is activity analysis? Why is this approach compatible with the goal of continuous improvement?
7. What are value-added activities? Value-added costs?
8. What are non-value-added activities? Non-value-added costs? Give an example of each.
9. Identify and define four different ways to manage activities so that costs can be reduced.
10. Explain how value-added standards are used to identify value- and non-value-added costs.
11. Explain how trend reports of non-value-added costs can be used.

12. What is a kaizen standard? Describe the kaizen and maintenance subcycles.
13. Explain how benchmarking can be used to improve activity performance.
14. In controlling non-value-added costs, explain how activity output measures (activity drivers) can induce behavior that is either beneficial or harmful. How can value-added standards be used to reduce the possibility of dysfunctional behavior?
15. What is the meaning of the activity volume variance? Explain how the unused capacity variance is useful to managers.
16. Describe the value of activity-based customer costing.
17. Explain how activity-based costing can help a firm identify its true low-cost suppliers.

Exercises

5-1

ABC versus ABM
LO1

YoungerU, Inc., produces deluxe and regular home exercise equipment. Recently, YoungerU has been losing market share with its regular equipment because of competitors offering a product with the same quality and features but at a lower price. A careful market study revealed that if YoungerU could reduce its regular model price by $10 per unit, it would regain its former share of the market. Management, however, is convinced that any price reduction must be accompanied by a cost reduction of $10 so that per-unit profitability is not affected. Cameron Hepworth, controller believes that poor overhead costing assignments may be distorting management's view of each product's cost and therefore, the ability change selling prices. Cameron has identified the following three overhead activities: machining, testing, and rework. The three activities, their costs, and practical capacities are as follows:

Activity	Cost	Practical Capacity
Machining	$1,800,000	150,000 machine hours
Testing	1,200,000	40,000 testing hours
Rework	600,000	20,000 rework hours

Other information regarding the two products is also provided. The consumption patterns of the two products are as follows:

	Regular	Deluxe
Units	100,000	10,000
Machine hours	50,000	10,000
Testing hours	20,000	20,000
Rework hours	5,000	15,000

YoungerU assigns overhead costs to the two products using a plantwide rate based on machine hours.

Required

1. Calculate the unit overhead cost of the regular exercise equipment using machine hours to assign overhead costs. Now, repeat the calculation using ABC to assign overhead costs. Did improving the accuracy of cost assignments solve YoungerU's competitive problem? What did it reveal?
2. Now, assume that *in addition* to improving the accuracy of cost assignments, Cameron observes that defective supplier components is the root cause of both the testing and rework activities. Suppose further that YoungerU has found a new supplier that provides higher quality components that such that testing and rework costs are reduced by 50 percent. Now, calculate the cost of each product (assuming that testing and rework time are also reduced by 50 percent) using ABC. The relative consumption patterns also remain the same. Comment on the difference between ABC and ABM.

5-2

Functional-Based versus Activity-Based Responsibility Accounting
LO1

For each of the following situations, two scenarios are described, labeled *A* and *B*. Choose which scenario is descriptive of a setting corresponding to activity-based responsibility accounting and which is descriptive of functional-based responsibility accounting. Provide a brief commentary on the differences between the two systems for each situation, addressing the possible advantages of the activity-based view over the functional-based view.

Situation 1

A: The purchasing manager, receiving manager, and accounts payable manager are given joint responsibility for procurement. The charge given to the group of managers is to reduce costs of acquiring materials, decrease the time required to obtain materials from outside suppliers, and reduce the number of purchasing mistakes (e.g., wrong type of materials or the wrong quantities ordered).

B: The plant manager commended the manager of the Grinding Department for increasing his department's machine utilization rates—and doing so without exceeding the department's budget. The plant manager then asked other department managers to make an effort to obtain similar efficiency improvements.

Situation 2

A: Delivery mistakes had been reduced by 70 percent, saving over $40,000 per year. Furthermore, delivery time to customers had been cut by two days. According to company policy, the team responsible for the savings was given a bonus equal to 25 percent of the savings attributable to improving delivery quality. Company policy also provided a salary increase of 1 percent for every day saved in delivery time.

B: Bill Johnson, manager of the Product Development Department, was pleased with his department's performance on the last quarter's projects. It had managed to complete all projects under budget, virtually assuring Bill of a fat bonus, just in time to help with this year's Christmas purchases.

Situation 3

A: "Harvey, don't worry about the fact that your department is producing at only 70 percent capacity. Increasing your output would simply pile up inventory in front of the next production department. That would be costly for the organization as a whole. Sometimes, one department must reduce its performance so that the performance of the entire organization can improve."

B: "Susan, I am concerned about the fact that your department's performance measures have really dropped over the past quarter. Labor usage variances are unfavorable, and I also see that your machine utilization rates are down. Now, I know you are not a bottleneck department, but I get a lot of flack when my managers' efficiency ratings drop."

Situation 4

A: Colby was muttering to himself. He had just received last quarter's budgetary performance report. Once again, he had managed to spend more than budgeted for both materials and labor. The real question now was how to improve his performance for the next quarter.

B: Great! Cycle time had been reduced, and at the same time, the number of defective products had been cut by 35 percent. Cutting the number of defects reduced production costs by more than planned. Trends were favorable for all three performance measures.

Situation 5

A: Cambry was furious. An across-the-board budget cut! "How can they expect me to provide the computer services required on less money? Management is convinced that costs are out of control, but I would like to know where—at least in my department!"

B: A careful study of the Accounts Payable Department revealed that 80 percent of an accounts payable clerk's time was spent resolving discrepancies between the purchase order, receiving document, and supplier's invoice. Other activities, such as recording and preparing checks, consumed only 20 percent of the clerk's time. A redesign of the procurement process eliminated virtually all discrepancies and produced significant cost savings.

Situation 6

A: Five years ago, the management of Breeann Products commissioned an outside engineering consulting firm to conduct a time-and-motion study so that labor efficiency standards could be developed and used in production. These labor efficiency standards are still in use today and are viewed by management as an important indicator of productive efficiency.

B: Janet was quite satisfied with this quarter's labor performance. Compared with the same quarter of last year, labor productivity had increased by 23 percent. Most of the increase was due to a new assembly approach suggested by production line workers. She was also pleased to see that materials productivity had increased. The increase in materials productivity was attributed to reducing scrap because of improved quality.

Situation 7

A: "The system, not people at work stations, is what converts materials into products. Therefore, process efficiency is more important than labor efficiency—but we also must pay particular attention to those who use the products we produce, whether inside or outside the firm."

B: "I was quite happy to see a revenue increase of 15 percent over last year, especially when the budget called for a 10 percent increase. However, after reading the recent copy of our trade journal, I now wonder whether we are doing so well. I found out the market expanded by 30 percent, and our leading competitor increased its sales by 40 percent."

5-3

Implementation of Activity-Based Management
LO1

Jane Erickson, manager of an electronics division, was not pleased with the results that had recently been reported concerning the division's activity-based management implementation project. For one thing, the project had taken eight months longer than projected and had exceeded the budget by nearly 35 percent. But even more vexatious was the fact that after all was said and done, about three-fourths of the plants were reporting that the activity-based product costs were not much different for most of the products than those of the old costing system. Plant managers were indicating that they were continuing to use the old costs as they were easier to compute and understand. Yet, at the same time, they were complaining that they were having a hard time meeting the bids of competitors. Reliable sources were also revealing that the division's product costs were higher than many competitors'. This outcome perplexed plant managers because their control system still continued to report favorable materials and labor efficiency variances. They complained that ABM had failed to produce any significant improvement in cost performance.

Jane decided to tour several of the plants and talk with the plant managers. After the tour, she realized that her managers did not understand the concept of non-value-added costs nor did they have a good grasp of the concept of kaizen costing.

No efforts were being made to carefully consider the activity information that had been produced. One typical plant manager threw up his hands and said: "This is too much data. Why should I care about all this detail? I do not see how this can help me improve my plant's performance. They tell me that inspection is not a necessary activity and does not add value. I simply can't believe that inspecting isn't value-added and necessary. If we did not inspect, we would be making and sending more bad products to customers."

Required

Explain why Jane's division is having problems with its ABM implementation.

5-4

Functional-Based versus Activity-Based or Strategic-Based Responsibility Accounting; Ethical Issues; Incentives
LO1

David Christensen, plant manager, was given the charge to produce 120,000 bolts used in the manufacture of small twin-engine aircraft. Directed by his divisional manager to give the bolt production priority over other jobs, he had two weeks to produce the units. Meeting the delivery date was crucial for renewal of a major contract with a large airplane manufacturer. Each bolt requires 20 minutes of direct labor and five ounces of metal. After producing a batch of bolts, each bolt is subjected to a stress test. Those that pass are placed in a carton, which is stamped "Inspected by inspector no. ____" (the inspector's identification number is inserted). Defective units are discarded, having no salvage value. Because of the nature of the process, rework is not possible.

At the end of the first week, the plant had produced 60,000 acceptable units and used 24,000 direct labor hours—4,000 hours more than the standard allowed. Furthermore, a total of 65,000 bolts had been produced, and 5,000 had been rejected, creating an unfavorable materials usage variance of 25,000 ounces. David knew that a performance report would be prepared when the 120,000 bolts were completed. This report would compare the labor and materials used with that allowed. Any variance in excess of 5 percent of standard would be investigated. David expected the same or worse performance for the coming week and was worried about a poor performance rating for himself. Accordingly, at the beginning of the second week, David moved his inspectors to the production line (all inspectors had production experience). However, for reporting purposes, the production hours provided by inspectors would not be counted as part of direct labor. They would still appear as a separate budget item on the performance report. Additionally, David instructed the inspectors to pack the completed bolts in the cartons and stamp them as inspected. One inspector objected; David reassigned the inspector temporarily to materials handling and gave an inspection stamp with a fabricated identification number to a line worker who was willing to stamp the cartons of bolts as inspected.

Required

1. Explain why David stopped inspections on the bolts and reassigned inspectors to production and materials handling. Discuss the ethical ramifications of this decision.
2. What features in the functional-based responsibility accounting system provided the incentive(s) for David to take the actions described? Would an activity-based or strategic-based responsibility accounting system have provided incentives that discourage this kind of behavior? Explain.
3. What likely effect would David's actions have on the quality of the bolts? Was the decision justified by the need to obtain a renewal of the contract, particularly if the plant returns to a normal inspection routine after the rush order is completed? Do you have any suggestions about the quality approach taken by this company? Explain why activity-based responsibility accounting might play a useful role in this setting.

5-5

Root Cause (Driver Analysis)
LO2

For the following two activities, ask a series of "why" questions (with your answers) that reveal the root cause. Once the root cause is identified, use a "how" question to reveal how the activity can be improved (with your answer).

Activity 1: Daily cleaning of a puddle of oil near production machinery.
Activity 2: Providing customers with sales allowances.

5-6

Non-Value-Added Activities: Non-Value-Added Cost
LO2

Whitley Company has 20 clerks that work in its Accounts Payable Department. A study revealed the following activities and the relative time demanded by each activity:

Activities	Percentage of Clerical Time
Comparing purchase orders and receiving orders and invoices	15%
Resolving discrepancies among the three documents	70
Preparing checks for suppliers	10
Making journal entries and mailing checks	5

The average salary of a clerk is $30,000.

Required

Classify the four activities as value-added or non-value-added, and calculate the clerical cost of each activity. For non-value-added activities, state why they are non-value-added.

5-7

Root Cause (Driver) Analysis
LO2

Refer to **Exercise 5-6.**

Required

Suppose that clerical error—either Whitley's or the supplier's—is the common root cause of the non-value-added activities. For each non-value-added activity, ask a series of "why" questions that identify clerical error as the activity's root cause.

5-8

Process Improvement/ Innovation
LO1, LO2

Refer to **Exercise 5-7.** Suppose that clerical error is the common root cause of the non-value-added activities. Paying bills is a subprocess that belongs to the procurement process. The procurement process is made up of three subprocesses: purchasing, receiving, and paying bills.

Required

1. What is the definition of a process? Identify the common objective for the procurement process. Repeat for each subprocess.
2. Now, suppose that Whitley decides to attack the root cause of the non-value-added activities of the bill-paying process by improving the skills of its purchasing and receiving clerks. As a result, the number of discrepancies found drops by 30 percent. Discuss the potential effect this initiative might have on the bill-paying process. Does this initiative represent process improvement or process innovation? Explain.

5-9

Process Improvement/Innov ation
LO1, LO2

Refer to **Exercise 5-8.** Suppose that Whitley attacks the root cause of the non-value-added activities by establishing a totally different approach to procurement called electronic data interchange (EDI). EDI gives suppliers access to Whitley's online database that reveals Honley's production schedule. By knowing Whitley's production schedule, suppliers can deliver the parts and supplies needed just in time for their use. When the parts are shipped, an electronic message is sent from the supplier to Whitley that the shipment is en route. When the order arrives, a bar code is scanned with an electronic wand initiating payment for the goods. EDI involves no paper, no purchase orders, no receiving orders, and no invoices.

Required

Discuss the potential effects of this solution on Whitley's bill-paying process. Is this process innovation or process improvement? Explain.

5-10

Calculation of Value- and Non-Value-Added Costs; Unused Capacity LO2, LO3

EXCEL

Six independent situations follow.

A. A manual insertion process takes 30 minutes and eight pounds of material to produce a product. Automating the insertion process requires 15 minutes of machine time and 7.5 pounds of material. The cost per labor hour is $12, the cost per machine hour is $8, and the cost per pound of materials is $10.
B. With its original design, a gear requires eight hours of setup time. By redesigning the gear so that the number of different grooves needed is reduced by 50 percent, the setup time is reduced by 75 percent. The cost per setup hour is $50.
C. A product currently requires six moves. By redesigning the manufacturing layout, the number of moves can be reduced from six to zero. The cost per move is $20.
D. Inspection time for a plant is 16,000 hours per year. The cost of inspection consists of salaries of eight inspectors, totaling $320,000. Inspection also uses supplies costing $5 per inspection hour. The company eliminated most defective components by eliminating low-quality suppliers. The number of production errors was reduced dramatically by installing a system of statistical process control. Further quality improvements were realized by redesigning the products, making them easier to manufacture. The net effect was to achieve a close to zero defect state and eliminate the need for any inspection activity.
E. Each unit of a product requires six components. The average number of components is 6.5 due to component failure, requiring rework and extra components. By developing relations with the right suppliers and increasing the quality of the purchased component, the average number of components can be reduced to six components per unit. The cost per component is $500.
F. A plant produces 100 different electronic products. Each product requires an average of eight components that are purchased externally. The components are different for each part. By redesigning the products, it is possible to produce the 100 products so that they all have four components in common. This will reduce the demand for purchasing, receiving, and paying bills. Estimated savings from the reduced demand are $900,000 per year.

Required

Provide the following information for each of the six preceding situations.

1. An estimate of the non-value-added cost caused by each activity.
2. The root cause(s) of the activity cost (such as plant layout, process design, and product design).
3. The cost reduction measure: activity elimination, activity reduction, activity sharing, or activity selection.

5-11

Calculation of Value-Added and Non-Value-Added Costs; Activity Volume and Unused Capacity Variances LO3

Snow Technology produces transmissions for snowmobiles. Because of competitive pressures, the company was making an effort to reduce costs. As part of this effort, management implemented an activity-based management system and began focusing its attention on processes and activities. Purchasing was among the processes (activities) that were carefully studied. The study revealed that the number of purchase orders was a good driver for purchasing costs. During the last year, the company incurred fixed purchasing costs of $252,000 (salaries of six employees). These fixed costs provide a capacity of processing 28,800 orders (4,800 per employee at practical capacity). Management decided that the value-added standard number of purchase orders is 14,400. The actual orders processed in the most recent period were 27,600.

EXCEL

Required

1. Calculate the activity volume and unused capacity variances for the purchasing activity. Explain what each variance means.
2. Prepare a report that presents value-added, non-value-added, and actual costs for purchasing. Explain why highlighting the non-value-added costs is important.
3. Explain why purchasing would be viewed as a value-added activity. List all possible reasons. Also, list some possible reasons that explain why the demand for purchasing is more than the value-added standard.
4. Assume that management is able to improve the purchasing activity and reduce the demand for purchasing from 27,600 orders to 21,600 orders. What actions should now be taken regarding activity capacity management?

5-12

Cost Report; Value- and Non-Value-Added Costs
LO3

Willson Company has developed value-added standards for four activities: purchasing parts, assembling parts, administering parts, and inspecting parts. The activities, the activity driver, the standard and actual quantities, and the price standards follow for 2005:

Activities	Activity Driver	*SQ*	*AQ*	*SP*
Purchasing parts	Orders	1,500	2,100	$300
Assembling parts	Labor hours	180,000	199,500	12
Administering parts	Number of parts	18,000	25,800	110
Inspecting parts	Inspection hours	0	75,000	15

The actual prices paid per unit of each activity driver were equal to the standard prices.

Required

1. Prepare a cost report that lists the value-added costs, non-value-added costs, and actual costs for each activity.
2. Which activities are non-value-added? Explain why. Explain why value-added activities can have non-value-added costs.

5-13

Trend Report; Non-Value-Added Costs
LO3

Refer to **Exercise 5-12.** Suppose that Willson Company used an activity analysis program during 2006 in an effort to reduce non-value-added costs. The value-added standards, actual quantities, and prices for 2006 follow:

Activities	Activity Driver	*SQ*	*AQ*	*SP*
Purchasing parts	Orders	1,500	1,800	$300
Assembling parts	Labor hours	180,000	186,000	12
Administering parts	Number of parts	18,000	24,000	110
Inspecting parts	Inspection hours	0	45,000	15

Required

1. Prepare a cost trend report that compares the non-value-added costs for 2005 with those of 2006.
2. Comment on the value of a trend report.

5-14

Activity Analysis; Activity Drivers; Driver Analysis; and Behavioral Effects LO2, LO3

Kenzie Sorensen, controller of Riqueza Company, has been helping an outside consulting group install an activity-based cost management system. This new accounting system is designed to support the company's efforts to become more competitive (by creating a competitive advantage). For the past two weeks, she has been identifying activities, associating workers with activities, and assessing the time and resources consumed by individual activities. Now, she and the consulting group have entered into the fourth phase of activity analysis: assessing value content. At this stage, Kenzie and the consultants also plan to identify drivers for assigning costs to cost objects. Furthermore, as a preliminary step to improving activity efficiency, they decided to identify potential root causes of activity costs. Kenzie's assignment for today is to assess the value content of five activities, choose a suitable activity driver, and identify the possible root causes of the activities. Following are the five activities she is investigating along with possible activity drivers:

Activity	Possible Activity Drivers
Setting up equipment	Setup time, number of setups
Creating scrap*	Pounds of scrap, number of defective units
Welding subassemblies	Welding hours, subassemblies welded
Materials handling	Number of moves, distance moved
Inspecting parts	Hours of inspection, number of defective parts

*Scrap is defined as a bad product or subassembly that cannot be reworked and so must be discarded.

Kenzie ran a regression analysis for each potential activity driver, using the method of least squares, to estimate the variable- and fixed-cost components. In all five cases, costs were highly correlated with the potential drivers. Thus, all drivers appeared to be good candidates for assigning costs to products. The company plans to reward production managers for reducing product costs.

Required

1. For each activity, assess the value content, and classify each activity as value- or non-value-added (justify the classification). Identify some possible root causes of each activity, and describe how this knowledge can be used to improve activity management. For purposes of discussion, assume that the value-added activities are not performed with perfect efficiency.
2. Describe the behavior that each activity driver will encourage, and evaluate the suitability of that behavior for the company's objective of creating a sustainable competitive advantage.

5-15

Kaizen Costing LO3

Paulan Motors Division had been given the charge to reduce the delivery time of its tractor motors from three days to one day. To help achieve this goal, engineering and production workers had made the commitment to reduce setup times. Current setup times were 15 hours. Setup cost was $100 per setup hour. For the first quarter, engineering developed a new process design that it believed would reduce the setup time from 15 hours to 10 hours. After implementing the design, the actual setup time dropped from 15 to 9 hours, one hour more than expected. In the second quarter, production workers suggested a new setup procedure. Engineering's evaluation of the suggestion was positive, and it projected that the new approach would save an additional hour of setup time. Setup labor was trained to perform new setup procedures. The actual reduction in setup time based on the suggested changes was 2.5 hours.

Required

1. What kaizen setup standard would be used at the beginning of each quarter?
2. Describe the kaizen subcycle using the two quarters of data provided by Paulan.

3. Describe the maintenance subcycle using the two quarters of data provided by Paulan.
4. How much non-value-added cost was eliminated by the end of two quarters?
5. How does kaizen costing differ from standard costing?

5-16

Customer-Driven Costs
LO4

Carbon Company has two classes of customers: JIT firms and non-JIT firms. The JIT customer places small, frequent orders, and the non-JIT customer tends to place larger, less frequent orders. Both types of customer are buying the same product. Carbon charges a manufacturing cost plus 25 percent for a given order. The 25 percent markup is set large enough to cover nonmanufacturing costs and provide a reasonable return for Carbon. Both customer types generated the same sales in units, so Carbon's management had assumed that the customer support costs were about the same and priced the goods the same for each customer. Carbon recently received some complaints from some of the non-JIT customers. Several of these customers are threatening to take their business to other suppliers who allegedly charge less. For example, one customer said that he could buy the same 5,000 units from a competitor for $3 per unit less than Carbon's price. This customer wanted a price concession.

Willis Johnson, a recently hired cost accountant, suggested that the problem may have to do with unfair cost assignments and suggested that customer costs be assigned to each customer category using activity-based costing. He collected the following information about customer-related activities and costs for the most recent quarter:

	JIT Customers	Non-JIT Customers
Sales orders	400	40
Sales calls	40	40
Service calls	200	100
Average order size	500	$5,000
Manufacturing cost/unit	$ 100	$ 100
Customer costs:		
Processing sales orders	$1,760,000	
Selling goods	640,000	
Servicing goods	600,000	
Total	$3,000,000	

Required

1. Calculate the total revenues per customer category and assign the customer costs to each customer type using revenues as the allocation base.
2. Calculate the customer cost per customer type using activity-based costing assignments. Discuss the merits of offering the non-JIT customers a $3 price decrease.
3. Assume that the JIT customers are simply imposing the frequent orders on Carbon Company. The JIT customers and Carbon have never formally discussed the supply of goods on a just-in-time basis. The sales pattern has simply evolved over time. As an independent consultant, what would you suggest to Carbon's management?

5-17

Supplier Costing
LO4

EXCEL

Lumus Company manufactures refrigerators. Lumus produces all the parts necessary for its product except for one electronic component, which is purchased from two local suppliers: Vance, Inc., and Foy Company. Both suppliers are reliable and seldom deliver late; however, Vance sells the component for $23.50 per unit while Foy sells the same component for $21.50. Lumus purchases 80 percent of its components from Foy because of its lower price. The total annual demand is 2,000,000 components.

Larry Hartley, Vance's vice president of sales, recently met with Jill Linsenmeyer, Lumus's purchasing manager, and urged her to purchase more of its units, arguing that Vance's component is of much higher quality and so should prove to be less costly than its competitor's lower-quality component. Larry offered to supply Vance with all the components needed and asked for a long-term contract. With a five-year contract for 1,600,000 or more units, Vance will sell the component for $22.50 per unit with a contractual provision for an annual product-specific inflationary adjustment. Jill is intrigued by the offer and wonders if the higher-quality component actually does cost less than the lower-quality Foy component. To help assess the cost effect of the two components, the following data were collected for supplier-related activities and suppliers:

I. Activity data

	Activity Cost
Inspecting components (sampling only)	$ 240,000
Reworking products (due to failed component)	760,500
Warranty work (due to failed component)	$4,800,000

II. Supplier data

	Vance	Foy
Unit purchase price	$23.50	$21.50
Units purchased	400,000	1,600,000
Sampling hours*	40	1,960
Rework hours	90	1,410
Warranty hours	400	7,600

*Sampling inspection for Vance's product has been reduced because the reject rate is so low.

Required

1. Calculate the cost per component for each supplier, taking into consideration the costs of the supplier-related activities and using the current prices and sales volume. What should Jill Linsenmeyer do? Explain.
2. Suppose that Lumus loses $1,000,000 in sales per year because of the reputation effect of defective units attributable to failed components. Choose one of the drivers already listed, and assign the cost of lost sales to each supplier. By how much would this change the cost of each supplier's component?

Problems

5-18

ABM Implementation, Activity Analysis, Activity Drivers, Driver Analysis, Behavioral Effects
LO1, LO2

Joseph Fox, controller of Thorpe Company, has been in charge of a project to install an activity-based cost management system. This new system is designed to support the company's efforts to become more competitive. For the past six weeks, he and the project committee members have been identifying and defining activities, associating workers with activities, and assessing the time and resources consumed by individual activities. Now, he and the project committee are focusing on three additional implementation issues: (1) identifying activity drivers, (2) assessing value content, and (3) identifying cost drivers (root causes). Joseph has assigned a committee member the responsibilities of assessing the value content of five activities, choosing a suitable activity driver for each activity, and identifying the possible root causes of the activities. Following are the five activities with possible activity drivers:

Activity	Possible Activity Drivers
Setting up equipment	Setup time, number of setups
Performing warranty work	Warranty hours, number of defective units
Welding subassemblies	Welding hours, subassemblies welded
Moving materials	Number of moves, distance moved
Inspecting components	Hours of inspection, number of defective components

The committee member ran a regression analysis for each potential activity driver, using the method of least squares to estimate the variable- and fixed-cost components. In all five cases, costs were highly correlated with the potential drivers. Thus, all drivers appeared to be good candidates for assigning costs to products. The company plans to reward production managers for reducing product costs.

Required

1. What is the difference between an activity driver and a cost driver? In answering the question, describe the purpose of each type of driver.
2. For each activity, assess the value content and classify each activity as value-added or non-value-added (justify the classification). Identify some possible root causes of each activity, and describe how this knowledge can be used to improve activity performance. For purposes of discussion, assume that the value-added activities are not performed with perfect efficiency.
3. Describe the behavior that each activity driver will encourage, and evaluate the suitability of that behavior for the company's objective of becoming more competitive.

5-19

Activity-Based Management; Non-Value-Added Costs
LO1, LO2, LO3

Danna Martin, president of Mays Electronics, was concerned about the end-of-the-year marketing report that she had just received. According to Larry Savage, marketing manager, a price decrease for the coming year was again needed to maintain the company's annual sales volume of integrated circuit boards (CBs). This would make a bad situation worse. The current selling price of $18 per unit was producing a $2-per-unit profit—half the customary $4-per-unit profit. Foreign competitors kept reducing their prices. To match the latest reduction would reduce the price from $18 to $14. This would put the price below the cost to produce and sell it. How could these firms sell for such a low price? Determined to find out if there were problems with the company's operations, Danna decided to hire a consultant to evaluate the way in which the CBs were produced and sold. After two weeks, the consultant had identified the following activities and costs:

Batch-level activities:	
Setting up equipment	$ 125,000
Materials handling	180,000
Inspecting products	122,000
Product-sustaining activities:	
Engineering support	120,000
Handling customer complaints	100,000
Filling warranties	170,000
Storing goods	80,000
Expediting goods	75,000
Unit-level activities:	
Using materials	500,000
Using power	48,000
Manual insertion labor[a]	250,000
Other direct labor	150,000
Total costs	$1,920,000[b]

[a]Diodes, resistors, and integrated circuits are inserted manually into the circuit board.
[b]This total cost produces a unit cost of $16 for last year's sales volume.

The consultant indicated that some preliminary activity analysis showed that per-unit costs could be reduced by at least $7. Since the marketing manager had said that the market share (sales volume) for the boards could be increased by 50 percent if the price could be reduced to $12, Danna became quite excited.

Required

1. What is activity-based management? What phases of activity analysis were provided by the consultant? What else remains to be done?
2. Identify as many non-value-added costs as possible. Compute the cost savings per unit that would be realized if these costs were eliminated. Was the consultant correct in his preliminary cost reduction assessment? Discuss actions that the company can take to reduce or eliminate the non-value-added activities.
3. Assume that further activity analysis revealed the following: switching to automated insertion would save $60,000 of engineering support and $90,000 of direct labor. Now, what is the total potential cost reduction per unit available from activity analysis? With these additional reductions, can Mays maintain current sales? Increase sales by 50 percent? What form of activity analysis is this: reduction, sharing, elimination, or selection?
4. Calculate income based on current sales, prices, and costs. Now, calculate the income using a $14 price and a $12 price, assuming that the maximum cost reduction possible is achieved (including Requirement 3's reduction). What price should be selected?

5-20

Value-Added and Kaizen Standards; Non-Value-Added Costs; Volume Variance; Unused Capacity
LO3

John Thomas, vice president of Mallett Company (a producer of a variety of plastic products), has been supervising the implementation of an activity-based cost management system. One of John's objectives is to improve process efficiency by improving the activities that define the processes. To illustrate the potential of the new system to the president, John has decided to focus on two processes: production and customer service.

Within each process, one activity will be selected for improvement: materials usage for production and sustaining engineering for customer service. (Sustaining engineers are responsible for redesigning products based on customer needs and feedback.) Value-added standards are identified for each activity. For materials usage, the value-added standard calls for six pounds per unit of output. (Although the plastic products differ in shape and function, their size—as measured by weight—is uniform.) The value-added standard is based on the elimination of all waste due to defective molds. The standard price of materials is $5 per pound. For sustaining engineering, the standard is 58 percent of current practical activity capacity. This standard is based on the fact that about 42 percent of the complaints have to do with design features that could have been avoided or anticipated by the company.

Current (at the end of 2008) practical capacity is defined by the following requirements: 6,000 engineering hours for each product group that has been on the market or in development for five years or less, and 2,400 hours per product group of more than five years. Four product groups have less than five years' experience, and 10 product groups have more. There are 24 engineers, each paid a salary of $60,000. Each engineer can provide 2,000 hours of service per year. No other significant costs are incurred for the engineering activity.

Actual materials usage for 2008 was 25 percent above the level called for by the value-added standard; engineering usage was 46,000 hours. A total of 80,000 units of output was produced. John and the operational managers have selected some improvement measures that promise to reduce non-value-added activity usage by 40 percent in 2006. Selected actual results achieved for 2009 are as follows:

Units produced	80,000
Materials used	584,800
Engineering hours	35,400

The actual prices paid for materials and engineering hours are identical to the standard or budgeted prices.

Required

1. For 2008, calculate the non-value-added usage and costs for materials usage and sustaining engineering. Also, calculate the cost of unused capacity for the engineering activity.
2. Using the targeted reduction, establish kaizen standards for materials and engineering (for 2009).
3. Using the kaizen standards prepared in Requirement 2, compute the 2009 usage variances, expressed in both physical and financial measures, for materials and engineering (for engineering, compare actual resource usage with the kaizen standard). Comment on the company's ability to achieve its targeted reductions. In particular, discuss what measures the company must take to capture any realized reductions in resource usage.

5-21

Benchmarking and Non-Value-Added Costs
LO2, LO3

Muebles Products manufactures a line of high-quality recliners in two plants, one in Lincoln and the other in Santa Clara. Each plant is set up as a profit center. During the past year, both plants sold the regular model for $720. Sales volume averages 20,000 units per year in each plant. Recently, the Santa Clara plant reduced the price of the regular model to $640. Discussion with the Santa Clara manager revealed that the price reduction was possible because the plant had reduced its manufacturing and selling costs by decreasing "non-value-added costs." The Santa Clara plant's manufacturing and selling costs for the regular chair were $560 per unit. The Santa Clara manager offered to lend the Lincoln plant his cost accounting manager to help it achieve similar results. The Lincoln plant manager readily agreed, knowing that his plant must keep pace—not only with the Santa Clara plant but also with competitors. A local competitor had also reduced its price on a similar model, and Lincoln's marketing manager had indicated that the price must be matched or sales would drop dramatically. In fact, the marketing manager suggested that if the price were dropped to $624 by the end of the year, the plant could expand its share of the market by 20 percent. The plant manager agreed but insisted that the current profit per unit must be maintained, and he wants to know if the plant can at least match the $560-per-unit cost of the Santa Clara plant. He also wants to know if the plant can achieve the cost reduction using the approach of the Santa Clara plant.

The plant controller and the Santa Clara cost accounting manager have assembled the following data for the most recent year. The actual cost of inputs, their value-added (ideal) quantity levels, and the actual quantity levels are provided (for production of 20,000 units). Assume there is no difference between actual prices of activity units and standard prices.

	SQ	**AQ**	**Actual Cost**
Materials (lb.)	380,000	400,000	$ 8,400,000
Labor (hr.)	91,200	96,000	1,200,000
Setups (hr.)	—	6,400	480,000
Material handling (moves)	—	16,000	1,120,000
Warranties (number repaired)	—	16,000	1,600,000
Total			$12,800,000

Required

1. Calculate the non-value-added cost per unit. Assuming that non-value-added costs can be reduced to zero, can the Lincoln plant match the Santa Clara plant's per-unit cost? Can expanding market share be achieved? What actions would you take if you were the plant manager?
2. Describe the role benchmarking played in the efforts of the Lincoln plant to protect and improve its competitive position.

5-22

ABM, Kaizen Costing
LO2, LO3

Elparte, Inc., supplies carburetors for a large automobile manufacturing company. The auto company has recently requested that Elparte decrease its delivery time. Elparte made a commitment to reduce the lead time for delivery from eight days to two days. To help achieve this goal, engineering and production workers had made the commitment to reduce time for the setup activity (other activities such as moving materials and rework were also being examined simultaneously). Current setup times were 12 hours. Setup cost was $300 per setup hour. For the first quarter, engineering developed a new process design that it believed would reduce the setup time from 12 hours to 8 hours. After implementing the design, the actual setup time dropped from 12 hours to 9 hours. In the second quarter, production workers suggested a new setup procedure. Engineering gave the suggestion a positive evaluation, and they projected that the new approach would save an additional five hours of setup time. Setup labor was trained to perform the new setup procedures. The actual reduction in setup time based on the suggested changes was six hours.

Required

1. What kaizen setup standard would be used at the beginning of each quarter?
2. Describe the kaizen subcycle using the two quarters of data provided by Elparte.
3. Describe the maintenance subcycle using the two quarters of data provided by Elparte.
4. How much non-value-added cost was eliminated by the end of two quarters? Discuss the role of kaizen costing in activity-based management.
5. Explain why kaizen costing is compatible with activity-based responsibility accounting while standard costing is compatible with financial-based responsibility accounting.

5-23

Customers as a Cost Object
LO4

EXCEL

Oaklawn National Bank has requested an analysis of checking account profitability by customer type. Customers are categorized according to the size of their account: low balances, medium balances, and high balances. The activities associated with the three different customer categories and their associated annual costs are given below.

Opening and closing accounts	$ 200,000
Issuing monthly statements	300,000
Processing transactions	2,050,000
Customer inquiries	400,000
Providing ATM services	1,120,000
Total cost	$4,070,000

Additional data concerning the usage of the activities by the various customers are also provided:

	Account Balance		
	Low	**Medium**	**High**
Number of accounts opened/closed	15,000	3,000	2,000
Number of statements issued	450,000	100,000	50,000
Processing transactions	18,000,000	2,000,000	500,000

Number of telephone minutes	1,000,000	600,000	400,000
Number of ATM transactions	1,350,000	200,000	50,000
Number of checking accounts	38,000	8,000	4,000

Required

1. Calculate the cost per account per year by dividing the total cost of processing and maintaining checking accounts by the total number of accounts. What is the average fee per month that the bank should charge to cover the costs incurred because of checking accounts?
2. Calculate the cost per account by customer category using activity rates.
3. Currently, the bank offers free checking to all its customers. The interest revenues average $90 per account; however, the interest revenues earned per account by category are $80, $100, and $165 for the low- medium- and high-balance accounts, respectively. Calculate the average profit per account (average revenue less average cost from Requirement 1). Now calculate the profit per account using the revenue per customer type and the unit cost per customer type calculated in Requirement 2.
4. After the analysis in Requirement 3, a vice president recommended eliminating the free checking feature for low-balance customers. The bank president expressed reluctance to do so, arguing that the low-balance customers more than made up for the loss through cross sales. He presented a survey that showed that 50 percent of the customers would switch banks if a checking fee were imposed. Explain how you could verify the president's argument using activity-based costing.

5-24

ABC and Customer-Driven Costs
LO4

Sorensen Manufacturing produces several types of bolts used in aircrafts. The bolts are produced in batches according to customer orders. Although there are a variety of bolts, they can be grouped into three product families. Because the product families are used in different kinds of aircraft, customers also can be grouped into three categories, corresponding to the product family they purchase. The number of units sold to each customer class is the same. The selling prices for the three product families range from $0.50 to $0.80 per unit. Historically, the costs of order entry, processing, and handling were expensed and not traced to individual customer groups. These costs are not trivial and totaled $4,500,000 for the most recent year. Furthermore, these costs had been increasing over time. Recently, the company started emphasizing a cost reduction strategy; however, any cost reduction decisions had to contribute to the creation of a competitive advantage.

Because of the magnitude and growth of order-filling costs, management decided to explore the causes of these costs. They discovered that order-filling costs were driven by the number of customer orders processed. Further investigation revealed the following cost behavior for the order-filling activity:

Step-fixed cost component: $50,000 per step (2,000 orders define a step)*
Variable cost component: $20 per order

*Sorensen currently has sufficient steps to process 100,000 orders.

The expected customer orders for the year total 100,000. The expected usage of the order-filling activity and the average size of an order by customer category follow:

	Category I	Category II	Category III
Number of orders	50,000	30,000	20,000
Average order size	600	1,000	1,500

As a result of the cost behavior analysis, the marketing manager recommended the imposition of a charge per customer order. The president of the company concurred. The charge was implemented by adding the cost per order to the price of each order (computed using the projected ordering costs and expected orders). This ordering cost was then reduced as the size of the order increased and eliminated as the order size reached 2,000 units (the marketing manager indicated that any penalties imposed for orders greater than this size would lose sales from some of the smaller customers). Within a short period of communicating this new price information to customers, the average order size for all three product families increased to 2,000 units.

Required

1. Sorensen traditionally has expensed order-filling costs. What is the most likely reason for this practice?
2. Calculate the cost per order for each customer category.
3. Calculate the reduction in order-filling costs produced by the change in pricing strategy (assume that resource spending is reduced as much as possible and that the total units sold remains unchanged). Explain how exploiting customer activity information produced this cost reduction. Are there any other internal activities that might benefit from this pricing strategy?

5-25

Activity-Based Supplier Costing
LO4

EXCEL

Bevil, Inc., manufactures tractors for agricultural usage. Bevil purchases the engines needed for its tractors from two sources: Johnson Engines and Watson Company. The Johnson engine is the more expensive of the two sources and has a price of $1,000. The Watson engine is $900 per unit. Bevil produces and sells 88,000 tractors. Of the 88,000 engines needed for the tractors, 16,000 are purchased from Johnson Engines and 72,000 are purchased from Watson Company. The production manager, Jamie Murray, prefers the Johnson engine. However, Jan Booth, purchasing manager, maintains that the price difference is too great to buy more than the 16,000 units currently purchased. Booth also wants to maintain a significant connection with the Johnson source just in case the less expensive source cannot supply the needed quantities. Even though Jamie understands the price argument, he is convinced that the quality of the Johnson engine is worth the price difference.

Frank Wallace, the controller, has decided to use activity costing to resolve the issue. The following data have been collected:

I. Activity Cost Data

Replacing engines[a]	$3,200,000
Expediting orders[b]	4,000,000
Warranty work[c]	7,200,000

[a]All units are tested after assembly, and some are rejected because of engine failure. The failed engines are removed and replaced, with the supplier replacing any failed engine. The replaced engine is retested before being sold. Engine failure often causes collateral damage, and other parts often need to be replaced.
[b]Due to late or failed delivery of engines.
[c]Repair work is for units under warranty and almost invariably is due to engine failure. Repair usually means replacing the engine. This cost plus labor, transportation, and other costs make warranty work very expensive.

II. Supplier Data

	Watson	Johnson
Engines replaced (by source)	3,960	40
Late or failed shipments	396	4
Warranty repairs (by source)	4,880	120

Required

1. Calculate the activity-based supplier cost per engine (acquisition cost plus supplier-related activity costs). Which of the two suppliers is the low-cost supplier?

Explain why this is a better measure of engine cost than the usual purchase costs assigned to the engines.

2. Consider the supplier cost information obtained in Requirement 1. Suppose further that Johnson can only supply a total of 40,000 units. What actions would you advise Bevil to undertake with its suppliers?

Managerial Decision Case

5-26

Ethical Considerations
LO1

Tim Ireland, controller of Roberts Electronics Division, was having lunch with Jimmy Jones, chief design engineer. Tim and Jimmy were good friends, having belonged to the same fraternity during their college days. The luncheon, however, was more business than pleasure.

Jimmy: Well, Tim, you said this morning that you have something important to tell me. I hope this isn't too serious. I don't want my weekend ruined.

Tim: Well, the matter is important. You know that at the beginning of this year, I was given the charge to estimate postpurchase costs for new products. This is not an easy task.

Jimmy: Yeah, I know. That's why I had our department supply you with engineering specs on the new products—stuff like expected component life.

Tim: This new product you've been developing has a problem. According to your reports, there are two components that will wear out within about 14 months. According to your test runs, the product starts producing at subpar performance during the 13th month.

Jimmy: Long enough to get us past the 12-month warranty. So why worry? There are no warranty costs for us to deal with.

Tim: Yes, but the customer then must incur substantial repair costs. And the product will have to be repaired once again before its useful life is ended. The estimated repair costs, when added to the normal life-cycle costs, put the whole-life cost above the target cost. According to the new guidelines, we are going to have to scrap this new product—at least using its current design. Perhaps you can find a new design that avoids the use of these two components—or find ways that they won't be so stressed so that they last much longer.

Jimmy: Listen, Tim. I don't have the time or the budget to redesign this product. I have to come under budget and meet the targeted production date, or I'll have the divisional manager down my throat. Besides, you know that I'm up for the engineering management position at headquarters. If this project goes well, then it'll give me what I need to edge out my competitors. If I do the redesign, my opportunity for the job is gone. Help me out on this. You know how much this opportunity means to me.

Tim: I don't know what I can do. I have to file the whole-life cost report, and I'm required to supply supporting documentation from marketing and engineering.

Jimmy: Well, that's easy to solve. Linda, the engineer who ran the tests on this product, owes me a favor. I'll get her to redo the tests so that the data produce a 24-month reliability period for the components. That should cut your estimated repair costs in half. Would that be enough to meet the targeted whole-life costs?

Tim: Yes, but . . .

Jimmy: Hey, don't worry. If I tell Linda that I'll push her for chief divisional engineer, she'll cooperate. No sweat. This is a one-time thing. How about it? Are you a player?

Required

1. What pressures does Tim have to comply with Jimmy's request? Do you think he should comply? Would you, if you were Tim? If not, how would you handle the situation?
2. Assume that Tim cooperates with Jimmy and covers up the design deficiency. What standards of ethical conduct for management accountants were violated? (See the IMA code described in Chapter 1.)
3. Suppose that Tim refuses to cooperate. Jimmy then gets Linda to rerun the tests anyway, with the new, more optimistic results. He then approaches Tim with the tests and says that he is sending a copy of the latest results to the divisional manager. Jimmy says he will challenge any redesign recommendations that Tim recommends. What should Tim do?

Research Assignment

5-27

Cybercase
LO4

The objective of benchmarking is to improve performance by identifying, understanding, and adopting outstanding best practices from others. If this process is carried out inside the organization, then it is called internal benchmarking. It is not uncommon for one facility within an organization to have better practices than another. Unfortunately, it is unusual for these better practices to naturally spread throughout the organization. The American Productivity & Quality Center (APQC) has conducted a study to understand what prevents the transfer of practices within a company. It also has made some recommendations concerning internal benchmarking.

Required

Access http://www.apqc.org and other Internet resources to answer the following:

1. Why is internal benchmarking an attractive option for an organization?
2. Why do companies want to engage in internal benchmarking?
3. What are some of the organizational obstacles relating to internal benchmarking?
4. Identify some recommendations that will make internal transfers of best practices more effective.
5. Internal benchmarking is a prominent example of what is called knowledge management or knowledge sharing. Use the APQC site and other Internet resources to define knowledge management (or knowledge sharing). Now access and describe Ernst & Young's knowledge sharing service called "Ernie."

© Getty Images

PART 3

Product and Service Costing

Chapter 6: Job-Order and Process Costing

Chapter 7: Support-Department Cost Allocation; Appendix: Joint Cost Allocation

chapter 6

Job-Order and Process Costing

learning objectives

After studying this chapter, you should be able to:

1. Describe the basic characteristics of and the differences between job-order costing and process costing, and identify the types of firms that would use each method.
2. Describe the cost flows associated with job-order costing.
3. Describe the cost flows associated with process costing.
4. Define equivalent units, and explain their role in process costing.
5. Prepare a departmental production report using the weighted average method.
6. Explain how process costing is affected by nonuniform application of manufacturing inputs and the existence of multiple processing departments.
7. (Appendix A) Complete a departmental production report using the FIFO method.
8. (Appendix B) Prepare the journal entries associated with job-order and process costing.

Scenario

Healthblend

Brianna Gibson, owner of Healthblend Nutritional Supplements, was reviewing last year's income statement. Net income for the year was up 30 percent; Brianna was pleased. Ten years earlier, she had begun producing herbal and nutritional formulas in her basement. Now, the company had grown into a multimillion-dollar business. Even so, Brianna felt that she could not afford to be complacent. She pondered two recent conversations.

The day before, Brianna had called on the manager of a retail store located in a metropolitan athletic club. The manager told her that some athletes and body builders were looking for personalized nutritional supplements. No such formulas were available on the market. He felt it would be easy to make up the supplements, since each used many of the same ingredients, simply in different proportions. Brianna was intrigued by the idea. Her niece, Delia, was an accomplished marathoner and believed fervently in the value of protein-based nutritional supplements. Could this be an opportunity for Delia to go into business for herself? With Brianna's manufacturing expertise and Delia's knowledge of nutrition, a new company might be profitable.

Later in the day, the owner of a health-food store mentioned that some other suppliers had dropped competing lines because they were no longer profitable. He asked Brianna if all of her products were profitable or if she simply offered the full range as a marketing strategy. She admitted that she did not know whether each product was profitable—in fact, she didn't even know the manufacturing cost of each individual product. She only knew that overall profits are high.

Upon reflection, Brianna decided that knowing individual product costs would be useful for decisions regarding production methods, prices, and product mix. In addition, if Delia took on the new opportunity, she would need help setting up the accounting system. So, Brianna contacted Judith Mansfield, a local CPA, for help. After several visits by Judith and her staff, Brianna received the following preliminary report:

Dear Ms. Gibson:

As you know, your current accounting system does not collect the necessary data for costing out individual products. You currently have three major product lines: mineral, herb, and vitamin. Each product, regardless of the type, passes through three processes: picking, encapsulating, and bottling. In picking, the ingredients are measured, sifted, and blended. In encapsulating, the powdered mix from the first process is put into capsules. The capsules are then transferred to the bottling department where they are bottled, and the bottles are labeled and fitted with safety seals and lids.

Each bottle contains 50 capsules. The cost of materials among the three product lines differs, but within a product line, the cost of materials for different products does not vary significantly. The layout of the plant is structured so that all three product lines are produced simultaneously; thus, there are three different picking departments, one for each major product line.

Based on this, we recommend that you accumulate costs of manufacturing by process for a given period of time and measure the output for that same period. By dividing the costs accumulated for the period by the output for the period, a good measure of individual product cost can be obtained. This cost system will require minimal additional bookkeeping.

If Delia decides to go forward with the new company, I would be happy to work with her to develop an appropriate costing system.

Questions to Think About

1. Why do you suppose that Brianna did not originally implement an accounting system that would give individual product costs?
2. Using a separate work-in-process account for each producing department, describe the flow of costs through Healthblend's plant.
3. What types of managerial decisions would be facilitated by having unit product cost information?
4. How would Delia's cost accounting system differ from that of Healthblend?

Characteristics of the Job-Order and Process Environment

Objective 1

Describe the basic characteristics of and the differences between job-order costing and process costing, and identify the types of firms that would use each method.

Companies keep track of total and unit costs for a number of reasons, including compiling financial statements, determining profitability, and making decisions (for example, what price to charge). The accounting system to be used depends on the types of products or services produced. Manufacturing and service firms can be divided into two major types: job-order firms, which produce unique products or services; and process firms, which produce relatively homogeneous products or services.

Job-Order Production and Costing

Firms operating in job-order industries produce a wide variety of services or products that are quite distinct from each other. Customized or built-to-order products fit into this category, as do services that vary from customer to customer. Common job-order processes include printing, construction, furniture making, automobile repair, and medical services.

Job-order systems may be used to produce goods for inventory that are subsequently sold in the general market. Often, however, a job is associated with a particular customer order. The key feature of job-order costing is that the cost of one job differs from that of another job and must be kept track of separately.

For job-order production systems, costs are accumulated by job. A **job** is one distinct unit or set of units. For example, a job may consist of a remodeling project for the Ruiz family or building a set of 12 tables for the children's reading room of the local library. This approach to assigning costs is called a **job-order costing system**. In a job-order firm, collecting costs by job provides vital information for management. For example, prices are frequently based on costs in a job-order environment. This would be the case for the Healthblend custom formula supplements. The materials in each formula would be different, as would the amount of labor and equipment needed (some formulas would be mixed and packaged, other would be ground and then pressed into tablets or encapsulated).

Process Production and Costing

Firms in process industries mass produce large quantities of similar or homogeneous products. Examples of process manufacturers include food, cement, petroleum, and chemical firms. One gallon of paint is the same as another gallon. The important point is that the cost of one unit of a product is identical to the cost of another. Service firms can also use a process-costing approach. For example, check-clearing departments of banks incur a uniform cost to clear a check, no matter the size of the check or the name of the payee.

Process costing works well whenever relatively homogeneous products pass through a series of processes and receive similar amounts of manufacturing costs. Large manufacturing plants, such as chemical, food, and tire manufacturers, use process costing. In the opening scenario, the consultant for Healthblend Nutritional Supplements studied Healthblend's traditional therapeutic formulas and found that a large number of similar products pass through an identical set of processes. Since each product within a product line passing through the three processes receives similar "doses" of materials, labor, and overhead, there was no need to accumulate costs by batches (a job-order costing system). Instead, costs could be accumulated by process.

The fundamental point is that the cost accounting system should be designed to fit the nature of operations. Job-order and process costing systems fit pure job and pure process production environments. There are many settings, however, in which blends of the two costing systems may be suitable. By studying the pure forms of job-order and process costing, we can develop the ability to understand and use any hybrid form.

Process firms accumulate production costs by process or department for a given period of time. Process output for that period of time is measured. Then, unit costs are computed by dividing the process costs for the given period by the output of the period. This approach to cost accumulation is known as a **process-costing system**. Exhibit 6-1 summarizes and contrasts the characteristics of job-order and process costing.

Cost Flows Associated with Job-Order Costing

Objective 2

Describe the cost flows associated with job-order costing.

Now let's consider the calculation of unit costs under job-order costing. While the variety of product cost definitions discussed in Chapter 2 applies to both job-order and process costing, we will use the traditional product-costing definition to illustrate job-order costing procedures.

Calculating Unit Cost with Job-Order Costing

Product costs consist of direct materials, direct labor, and overhead. In a job-order environment, predetermined overhead rates are always used, since the completion of a job rarely coincides with the completion of a fiscal year. Therefore, normal costing is used, and the unit cost of a job is simply the total cost of materials used on the job, labor worked on the job, and overhead assigned using one or more activity drivers. Although the concept is simple, the practical reality of the computation can be somewhat more complex, because of the record keeping involved. Let's look at a simple example.

Brianna's niece, Delia, was delighted by the opportunity to produce customized nutritional supplements. She named her company PNP for Personalized Nutritional Products, and rented factory space from Healthblend. In the first month of operation, Delia obtains two orders: the first is for 200 24-ounce jars of a powdered supplement from the retail store attached to the athletic club. Named SupliShake-001, the powder is designed to be mixed with water or milk to provide pre-workout energy. The second job is for 100 bottles of LigaStrong-001, herbal capsules designed to strengthen ligaments. Delia agrees to provide these orders at a price of cost plus 50 percent.

Let's look at the computation of unit cost for Delia's first order. SupliShake-001 will require direct materials (whey protein, fructose, cocoa, herbs and vitamins, and flavorings), direct labor (drying and grinding herbs, mixing, bottling), and overhead. Assume that overhead is assigned using a single unit-level driver, direct labor hours. Suppose that the materials cost \$1,780 and the direct labor costs \$300 (20 hours at \$15 per hour). If the predetermined overhead rate is \$12 per direct labor hour, then

Job-Order Costing	Process Costing
1. Wide variety of distinct products	1. Homogeneous products
2. Costs accumulated by job	2. Costs accumulated by process or department
3. Unit cost computed by dividing total job costs by units produced on that job	3. Unit cost computed by dividing process costs of the period by the units produced in the period

Exhibit 6-1 Comparison of Job-Order and Process Costing

the overhead applied to this job is $240 (20 hours at $12 per hour). The total cost of the job is $2,320, and the unit cost is $11.60 per bottle, computed as follows:

Direct materials	$1,780
Direct labor	300
Applied overhead	240
Total cost	$2,320
÷ number of units	÷ 200
Unit cost	$ 11.60

Since cost is so closely linked to price in this case, it is easy to see that Delia will charge the health food store $3,480 (cost of $2,320 plus 50 percent of $2,320), or $17.40 per jar.

This is a simplified example of how Delia would arrive at the total cost of a single job. But how did she know that actual materials cost $1,780, or that actual direct labor for this particular job came to $300? In order to determine those figures, Delia would need to keep track of costs using a variety of source documents. These source documents are described in the next section.

Job-Order Cost Sheet

Every time a new job is started, a job-order cost sheet is prepared. The previous computation for the SupliShake-001 job, which lists the total cost of materials, labor, and overhead for a single job, is the simplest example of a job-order cost

Managers Decide

Cost Control Helps New Products Succeed

iRobot, Inc., is an engineering contractor based in Massachusetts. Founded in the late 1980s, iRobot's mission statement is to build "cool stuff" while making money and changing the world for the better. The founders were accustomed to the academic environment of MIT's Artificial Intelligence Lab. They worked for large companies or governments that wanted them "to do something they [the clients] found interesting but only wanted one of. . . . It was like being an artist working on commission." Contracts included diverse projects like "a crab-walking minesweeper for the Department of Defense, [and] a rugged oil-well-repair bot for Halliburton." Clearly, job-order costing was appropriate for these projects.

In the mid-1990s, iRobot pitched an idea for a storytelling machine to toy maker Hasbro, Inc. The machine, a plastic-molded tableau with little characters surrounding a child's book, could actually act out the story, with dialogue and gestures. It was "unbelievably cool." Unfortunately, it was also unbelievably costly—total direct materials alone cost $3,000. Clearly, this toy was not destined for Toys "R" Us with a $19.95 price point. Hasbro turned thumbs down on the project. The result was that iRobot CEO Colin Angle began to pay close attention to cost control, and by 2000, he had a good understanding of the cost control needed for consumer products. His company developed the roomba, a small, disk-shaped vacuum cleaner. Currently in production, the roomba reflects iRobot's shift, for this type of project, from "high-cost prototype design to every-penny-counts mass production." Before, the total bid cost of the project was important, but mass production requires attention to every component's cost. ■

Source: Leigh Buchanan, "Death to Cool: How an R&D Boutique that Made Only Elite, Sexy Products Became a Big-Time Mass Marketer of the Mundane," *Inc.* (July 2003): 82–87 and 104, http://www.irobot.com

sheet. The **job-order cost sheet** is prepared for every job; it is subsidiary to the work-in-process account and is the primary document for accumulating all costs related to a particular job. Exhibit 6-2 illustrates a simple job-order cost sheet.

Some companies may find that the customer's name is sufficient to identify a job. For example, a construction company may identify its custom houses as the "Smith residence" or the "Malkovich residence." As more and more jobs are produced, a company will usually find it most convenient to number them. Thus, you will see Job 13, Job 22, and Job 44, etc. Perhaps the job number starts with the year, so that the first job of 2008 is 2008-1, the second is 2008-2, and so on. The key point is that each job is unique and must have a uniquely identifiable name. This name, or job-order number, heads the job-order cost sheet.

Work in Process consists of all incomplete work. In a job-order system, this would be all of the unfinished jobs. The balance in Work in Process at the end of the month would be the total of all the job-order cost sheets for the incomplete jobs.

In a manual accounting system, the job-order cost sheet is a document. In an automated accounting system, the cost sheet usually corresponds to a record in a work-in-process master file. The collection of all job-order cost sheets defines a **work-in-process file**. In a manual system, the file would be located in a filing cabinet, whereas in an automated system, it is stored electronically on magnetic tape or hard disk. In either system, the file of job-order cost sheets serves as a subsidiary work-in-process ledger.

Both manual and automated systems require the same kind of data in order to accumulate costs and track the progress of a job. A job-order costing system must have the ability to identify the quantity of direct materials, direct labor, and overhead consumed by each job. In other words, documentation and procedures are needed to associate the manufacturing inputs used by a job with the job itself. This need is satisfied through the use of materials requisitions for direct materials, time tickets for direct labor, and source documents for other activity drivers that might be used in applying overhead.

Other source documents are used to record costs that are tracked on the job-order cost sheet. For example, **materials requisition forms** are used to assign direct materials costs to each job. Exhibit 6-3 shows an example of a materials requisition form. Labor **time tickets** are used to track the hours worked by direct labor on each job. Exhibit 6-4 shows an example of a job time ticket.

If a company uses activity-based costing, it must keep track of more than one activity driver (for example, machine hours, number of purchase orders, number of setups, etc.) and post the actual amounts of each to the job-order cost sheets. If the amount of the driver is already accounted for (e.g., number of purchase orders), no new source document is needed. If that is not the case, a new source document

PNP
Job-Order Cost Sheet

Job Name: SupliShake-001
Date Started: January 3, 2008
Date Completed: January 29, 2008

Direct materials	$ 1,780
Direct labor	300
Applied overhead	240
Total cost	$ 2,320
÷ number of units	÷ 200
Unit cost	$ 11.60

Exhibit 6-2 Job-Order Cost Sheet

Material Requisition Number 12

Date: January 11, 2008
Department: PNP
Job: SupliShake-001

Description	Quantity	Cost/Unit	Total Cost
Whey protein powder	500 lbs	$1.20	$600

Exhibit 6-3 Materials Requisition Form

Job Time Ticket Number 8

Employee Number: 4
Name: Ed Wilson
Date: Jan. 12, 2008

Start Time	Stop Time	Total Time	Hourly Rate	Amount	Department
8:00	10:00	2	$15	$30	Picking
10:00	11:00	1	15	15	Bottling
11:00	12:00	1	15	15	PNP
1:00	5:00	4	15	60	Bottling

Exhibit 6-4 Job Time Ticket

must be developed. For example, a source document that will track the machine hours used by each job can be modeled on job time tickets.

ETHICS

In a job-order firm, where price is so often based on cost, it is critically important to keep careful track of the costs of a job. Ethical issues arise when a firm adds costs from one job to the job-order sheet of another job. The first job is undercosted and underpriced while the second job is overcosted and overpriced. Customers rely on the professionalism and honesty of the job-order firm in record keeping.

All completed job-order cost sheets of a firm serve as a subsidiary ledger for the finished goods inventory. Adding the totals of all completed job-order cost sheets gives the cost of finished goods inventory at any point in time. As finished goods are sold and shipped, the cost records are pulled (or deleted) from the finished goods inventory file. These records then form the basis for calculating a period's cost of goods sold. We will examine the flow of costs through these accounts next.

The Flow of Costs through the Accounts

When we talk about cost flow, we are talking about the way we account for costs from the point at which they are incurred to the point at which they are recognized as an expense on the income statement. The principal interest in a job-order costing system is the flow of manufacturing costs. Thus, we describe the way the three manufacturing cost elements—direct materials, direct labor, and overhead—flow through Work-in-Process, into Finished Goods, and, finally, into Cost of Goods Sold.

Let's continue to use the simplified job-shop environment provided by PNP. To start the business, Delia rented a back room in the Healthblend factory and bought the necessary production equipment. Recall that she finalized two orders for January: one for 200 jars of SupliShake-001, and a second for 100 bottles of LigaStrong-001. Both orders will be sold for manufacturing costs plus 50 percent. Delia created two job-order cost sheets, one for each order. The first job-order cost sheet is for the SupliShake-001; the second is for the LigaStrong-001.

Accounting for Materials Since operations have just begun, there are no beginning inventories. To produce the nutritional powder and capsules in January and have a supply of materials on hand at the beginning of February, Delia purchases, on account, $3,500 of raw materials (herbs, whey protein, flavorings, capsules, boxes, etc.). Physically, the materials are kept in the materials storeroom. In the accounting records, the Materials and Accounts Payable accounts are each increased by $3,500. Materials is an inventory account that appears on the balance sheet under Current Assets. It is also the controlling account for all materials. Any purchase increases the materials account.

© PR Newswire/GlaxoSmithKline Consumer Healthcare

Direct materials include not only the powdered ingredients and the flavoring, but also the jar, lid, and label.

When Delia needs materials for a job, they are removed from the storeroom. The cost of the materials is removed from the materials account and added to the work-in-process account. Of course, in a job-order environment, the materials requisitioned must be "tagged" with the appropriate job name. Suppose that Delia needs $1,780 of materials for SupliShake-001 and $1,300 for LigaStrong-001. Then, the job-order cost sheet for SupliShake-001would show $1,780 for direct materials, and the job-order cost sheet for LigaStrong-001 would show $1,300 for direct materials. Exhibit 6-5 summarizes the materials cost flows into these two jobs.

We just saw that the materials account increased by $3,500 due to purchases and decreased by $3,080 as materials were withdrawn for use in production. The balance in the materials account after these two transactions is $420. This is calculated by taking the beginning balance of zero in the materials account, adding $3,500 of purchases, and subtracting $3,080 of materials used in production. These transactions are shown in Exhibit 6-5.

Accounting for Direct Labor Cost Since two jobs were in progress during January, Delia must determine both the total number of direct labor hours worked, and the time worked on each job. SupliShake-001 required 20 hours of labor at an average wage rate of $15 per hour, for a total direct labor cost of $300. For LigaStrong-001, the total was $450, based on 30 hours of labor at an average hourly wage of $15. These amounts are posted to each job's cost sheet. The summary of the labor cost flows is given in Exhibit 6-6. Notice that the direct labor costs assigned to the two jobs exactly equal the total labor costs assigned to Work in Process. Remember that the labor cost flows reflect only direct labor cost. Indirect labor is assigned as part of overhead.

Materials Account	
Beginning balance	0
Purchases	$3,500
Direct materials used	3,080
Ending balance	$420

Job-Order Cost Sheet Job: SupliShake-001		Job-Order Cost Sheet Job: LigaStrong-001	
Direct materials	$1,780	Direct materials	$1,300
Direct labor		Direct labor	
Applied overhead		Applied overhead	
Total cost		Total cost	
Number of units	÷ 200	Number of units	÷ 100
Unit cost		Unit cost	

Exhibit 6-5 Summary of Materials Cost Flows

Wages Payable	
Direct labor hours	50
x Wage rate	x $15
Total direct labor	$750

Job-Order Cost Sheet Job: SupliShake-001		Job-Order Cost Sheet Job: LigaStrong-001	
Direct materials	$1,780	Direct materials	$1,300
Direct labor	300	Direct labor	450
Applied overhead		Applied overhead	
Total cost		Total cost	
Number of units	÷ 200	Number of units	÷ 100
Unit cost		Unit cost	

Exhibit 6-6 Summary of Direct Labor Cost Flows

More accounts are involved in this transaction than meet the eye in Exhibit 6-6. Accounting for labor cost is a complex process, since the company must keep track of FICA, Medicare, federal and state unemployment taxes, vacation time, and so on. We will concentrate on the concept that direct labor adds to the cost of the product or service and not on the details of the various labor-related accounts.

Accounting for Overhead In normal costing, actual overhead costs are never assigned directly to jobs. Overhead is applied to each individual job using a predetermined rate or rates. Overhead can be applied using a single plantwide rate, or departmental rates, or activity rates. Actual overhead costs incurred must be accounted for as well, but on an overall (not job-specific) basis.

Suppose that total estimated overhead costs for Delia's project total $14,400. This includes depreciation on equipment, rent payments for her use of the factory, her share of utilities for the factory, and liability insurance. Assume Delia has budgeted direct labor hours of 1,200 for the year. Accordingly, the predetermined overhead rate is:

$$\text{Overhead rate} = \$14{,}400/1{,}200 = \$12 \text{ per DLH}$$

For SupliShake-001, with a total of 20 hours worked, the amount of *applied overhead cost* posted to the job-order cost sheet is $240 ($12 × 20). For LigaStrong-001, the applied overhead cost is $360 ($12 × 30). Since direct labor hours are already being collected to assign direct labor costs to jobs, overhead assignment would not demand any additional data collection. In normal costing, only applied overhead ever enters the work-in-process account.

To illustrate how actual overhead costs are recorded, assume that Delia incurred the following indirect costs for January:

Rent payment	$400
Utilities	50
Equipment depreciation	100
Insurance	65
Total overhead costs	$615

It is important to understand that the actual overhead costs never enter the work-in-process account. The usual procedure is to record actual overhead to the overhead control account. Then, at the end of the period, actual overhead is reconciled with applied overhead, and any variance is closed to the appropriate accounts. Typically, the overhead variance is relatively small (immaterial), so it is closed to Cost of Goods Sold. That is, an overapplied overhead variance means that too much overhead was applied, and Cost of Goods Sold must be reduced by that amount. Similarly, an underapplied overhead variance means that too little overhead was applied, and Cost of Goods Sold must be increased by that amount.

By the end of January, actual overhead incurred is $615, while applied overhead is $600. Therefore, there is an overhead variance of $15 ($615 × $600) that is underapplied for the month of January.

The flow of overhead costs is summarized in Exhibit 6-7. Notice that the total overhead applied from all jobs is entered in the work-in-process account.

Let's recap. The cost of a job includes direct materials, direct labor, and applied overhead. Each of these resources is entered on the job-order cost sheet. Work in Process, at any point in time, is the total of the costs on all open job-order cost sheets.

Accounting for Finished Goods When a job is completed, the direct materials, direct labor, and applied overhead amounts are totaled to yield the manufacturing cost of the job. This job cost sheet is then transferred to a finished goods file. Simultaneously, the costs of the completed job are transferred from the work-in-process

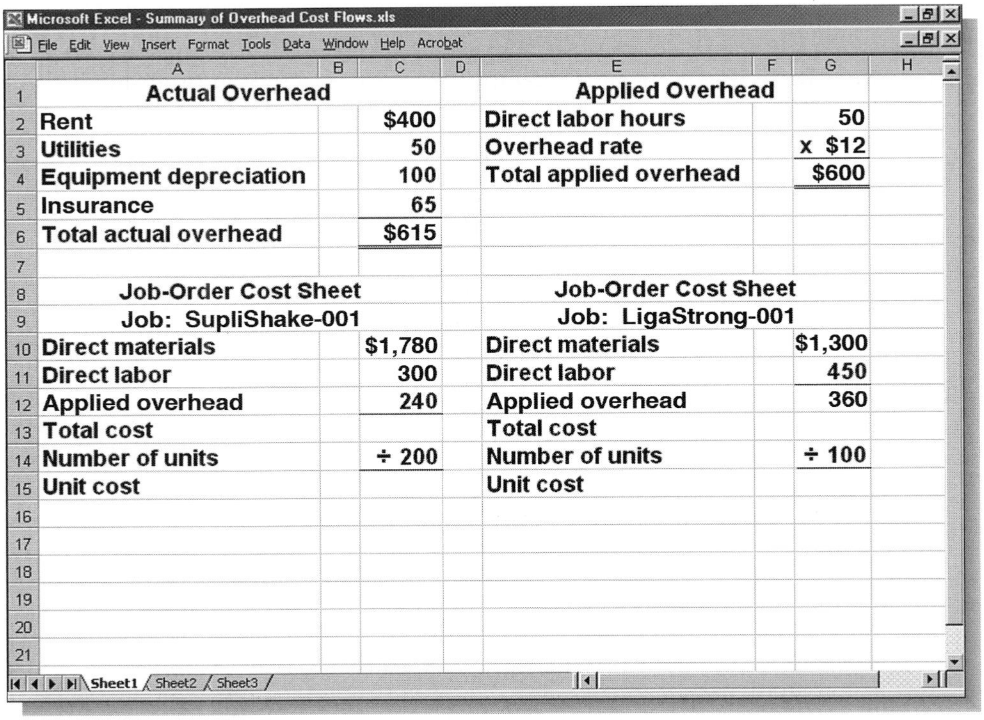

Microsoft Excel - Summary of Overhead Cost Flows.xls

	A	B	C	D	E	F	G	H
1	Actual Overhead				Applied Overhead			
2	Rent		$400		Direct labor hours		50	
3	Utilities		50		Overhead rate		x $12	
4	Equipment depreciation		100		Total applied overhead		$600	
5	Insurance		65					
6	Total actual overhead		$615					
7								
8	Job-Order Cost Sheet				Job-Order Cost Sheet			
9	Job: SupliShake-001				Job: LigaStrong-001			
10	Direct materials		$1,780		Direct materials		$1,300	
11	Direct labor		300		Direct labor		450	
12	Applied overhead		240		Applied overhead		360	
13	Total cost				Total cost			
14	Number of units		÷ 200		Number of units		÷ 100	
15	Unit cost				Unit cost			

Exhibit 6-7 Summary of Overhead Cost Flows

account to the finished goods account. For example, assume that the jars of SupliShake-001 were completed in January with the completed cost sheet shown in Exhibit 6-8. Since they are completed, the total manufacturing costs of $2,320 must be transferred from the work-in-process account to the finished goods account. A summary of the cost flows occurring when a job is finished is shown in Exhibit 6-8.

The completion of a job is an important step in the flow of manufacturing costs. The cost of the completed job must be removed from work in process, added to finished goods, and, eventually, added to the cost of goods sold expense on the income statement. To ensure accuracy in computing these costs, a cost of goods manufactured statement is prepared. The schedule of the cost of goods manufactured presented in Exhibit 6-9 summarizes the production activity of PNP for January. It is important to note that applied overhead is used to arrive at the cost of goods manufactured. Both work-in-process and finished goods inventories are carried at normal cost rather than actual cost.

Notice that ending work in process is $2,110. Where did we obtain this figure? Of the two jobs, the SupliShake-001 was finished and transferred to finished goods. The bottles of LigaStrong-001 are still in process, however, and the manufacturing costs assigned thus far are direct materials, $1,300; direct labor, $450; and applied overhead, $360. The total of these costs gives the cost of ending work in process. You may want to check these figures against the job-order cost sheet for LigaStrong-001 shown in Exhibit 6-8.

Accounting for Cost of Goods Sold In a job-order firm, units can be produced for a particular customer or they can be produced with the expectation of selling the units later. If a job is produced specially for a customer and then shipped to the customer, the cost of the finished job becomes the cost of goods sold. When the jars of SupliShake-001 are completed, then, recognize that Cost of Goods Sold increases by $2,320 while Work in Process decreases by the same amount (the job is

Microsoft Excel - Summary of Finished Goods Cost Flows.xls

Job-Order Cost Sheet			**Job-Order Cost Sheet**	
Job: SupliShake-001			**Job: LigaStrong-001**	
Direct materials	$1,780		Direct materials	$1,300
Direct labor	300		Direct labor	450
Applied overhead	240		Applied overhead	360
Total cost	$2,320		Total cost	$2,110
Number of units	÷ 200		Number of units	÷ 100
Unit cost	$11.60		Unit cost	
Finished Goods Account				
SupliShake-001	$2,320			

Exhibit 6-8 Summary of Finished Goods Cost Flows*

*There is no reason to show the unit cost of the bottles of LigaStrong-001, since they are still in process.

PNP
Schedule of Cost of Goods Manufactured
For the Month Ended January 31, 2008

Direct materials:		
Beginning materials inventory	$ 0	
Purchases of materials	3,500	
Total materials available	$3,500	
Ending materials	420	
Total materials used		$3,080
Direct labor		750
Overhead:		
Rent		$ 400
Utilities	50	
Depreciation on equipment	100	
Insurance	65	
	$ 615	
Less: Underapplied overhead	15	
Applied overhead		600
Current manufacturing costs		$4,430
Add: Beginning work in process		0
Total manufacturing costs		$4,430
Less: Ending work in process		2,110
Cost of goods manufactured		$2,320

Exhibit 6-9 Schedule of Cost of Goods Manufactured

no longer incomplete—so its costs cannot stay in Work in Process). Then, the sale is recognized by increasing both Sales Revenue and Accounts Receivable by $3,480 (cost plus 50 percent of cost or $2,320 + $1,160).

Exhibit 6-10 presents a schedule of cost of goods for PNP for January. Typically, the overhead variance is not material and, therefore, is closed to Cost of Goods Sold. The cost of goods sold before an adjustment for an overhead variance is called the **normal cost of goods sold**. After the adjustment for the period's overhead variance takes place, the result is called the **adjusted cost of goods sold**. The adjusted cost of goods sold appears as an expense on the income statement.

Typically, the closing of the overhead variance to the cost of goods sold account is not done until the end of the year. Variances are expected each month because of nonuniform production and nonuniform actual overhead costs. As the year unfolds, these monthly variances often offset each other so that the year-end variance is small. Nonetheless, to illustrate how the year-end overhead variance would be treated, we will close out the overhead variance experienced by PNP in January.

Notice that there are two cost of goods sold figures in Exhibit 6-10. The first is the normal cost of goods sold and is equal to actual direct materials, actual direct labor, and applied overhead for the jobs that were sold. The second figure is adjusted cost of goods sold. The adjusted cost of goods sold is equal to the normal cost of goods sold plus or minus the overhead variance. In this case, overhead has been underapplied (actual overhead of $615 is $15 higher than the applied overhead of $600), so this amount is added to the normal cost of goods sold. If the overhead variance shows overapplied overhead, then that amount would be subtracted from normal cost of goods sold.

Suppose that the SupliShake-001 had not been ordered by a customer but had been produced with the expectation that it could be sold through a subsequent marketing effort. Then, all 200 units might not be sold at the same time. Assume that on January 31, there were 150 jars sold. In this case, the cost of goods sold figure is the unit cost times the number of units sold ($11.60 × 150, or $1,740). The unit cost figure is found on the cost sheet in Exhibit 6-8.

Manufacturing costs, however, are not the only costs experienced by a firm. Nonmanufacturing costs are also incurred. A description of how we account for these costs follows.

Accounting for Nonmanufacturing Costs

Costs associated with selling and general administrative activities are classified as nonmanufacturing costs. These costs are period costs and are not assigned to the product; they are not part of the manufacturing cost flows.

Assume PNP had the following additional transactions in January:

Advertising circulars	$275
Sales commissions	125
Office supplies	200
Depreciation, office equipment	150

Statement of Cost of Goods Sold

Beginning finished goods inventory	$ 0
Cost of goods manufactured	2,320
Goods available for sale	$2,320
Less: Ending finished goods inventory	0
Normal cost of goods sold	$2,320
Add: Underapplied overhead	15
Adjusted cost of goods sold	$2,335

Exhibit 6-10 Statement of Cost of Goods Sold

PNP Income Statement For the Month Ended January 31, 2008		
Sales		$3,480
Less: Cost of goods sold		2,335
Gross margin		$1,145
Less selling and administrative expenses:		
Selling expenses	$400	
Administrative expenses	350	750
Operating income		$ 395

Exhibit 6-11 Income Statement

The first two transactions fall in the category of selling expense, and the last two into the category of administrative expense. So, the selling expense control account would increase by $400 ($275 + $125), and the administrative expense control account would increase by $350 ($200 + $150).

Controlling accounts accumulate all of the selling and administrative expenses for a period. At the end of the period, all of these costs flow to the period's income statement. An income statement for PNP is shown in Exhibit 6-11.

With the preparation of the income statement, the flow of costs through the manufacturing, selling, and administrative expense accounts is complete. A more detailed look at the actual accounting for these cost flows is undertaken in the appendix to this chapter.

The Process Environment and Cost Flows

Objective 3

Describe the cost flows associated with process costing.

Consider the consultant's memo in the opening scenario. Healthblend's products pass through three processes, each centered in a producing department. In the Picking Department, direct labor selects the appropriate herbs, vitamins, minerals, and inert materials (typically, some binder such as cornstarch) for the product to be manufactured. Then, the materials are measured and combined in a mixer to blend them thoroughly. When the mix is complete, the resulting mixture is sent to the Encapsulating Department where the vitamin, mineral, or herb blend is loaded into a machine that fills one-half of a gelatin capsule. The filled half is matched to another half of the capsule, and a safety seal is applied. This process is entirely mechanized. Overhead in this department consists of depreciation on and maintenance of machinery, supervision, fringe benefits, light, and power. In the final step, filled capsules are transferred to the Bottling Department, loaded into a hopper, and automatically counted into bottles. Filled bottles are mechanically capped, and direct labor then manually packs the correct number of bottles into boxes to ship to retail outlets.

Now, let's look at Healthblend from an accounting perspective. Suppose that Healthblend has only one Picking

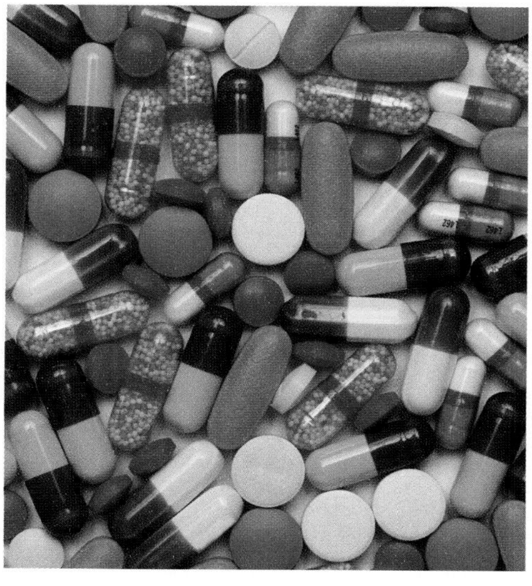

© Getty Images/PhotoDisc

The capsules shown here go through an encapsulating process, just like that of Healthblend. The tablets, however, require a different process—tableting—in which the powdered materials are pressed into tablets. While the direct materials of the capsules and tablets may be the same, the costs of the two processes can be quite different.

Department through which all three major product lines pass. Since the product lines differ significantly in the cost of their material inputs, accumulating material costs by process no longer makes any sense. More accurate product costing can be achieved by accumulating material costs by batch. In this case, labor and overhead could still be accumulated by process, but raw materials would be assigned to batches using a job-order costing approach. Note, however, that even with this change, process costing could still be used for the Encapsulating Department and the Bottling Department. In these two departments, each product receives the same amount of material, labor, and overhead.

This example illustrates that some manufacturing settings may need to use a blend of job-order and process costing. Using job-order procedures to assign material costs to products and a process approach to assign conversion costs is known as **operation costing**. Other blends are possible as well. The example also shows that it is possible to use more than one form of costing within the same firm. This is the case if Healthblend uses operation costing for the Picking Department and process costing for the other two departments.

Types of Process Manufacturing

In a process firm, units typically pass through a series of manufacturing or producing departments; in each department or process, an operation brings a product one step closer to completion. In each department, materials, labor, and overhead may be needed. Upon completion of a particular process, the partially completed goods are transferred to the next department. After passing through the final department, the goods are completed and transferred to the warehouse.

Production at Healthblend Nutritional Supplements is an example of sequential processing. In **sequential processing**, units must pass through one process before they can be worked on in later processes. At Healthblend, materials must be picked, then those materials are passed along to Encapsulating, where they are placed into capsules. Finally, the completed capsules are passed to the Bottling Department, where they are put into bottles.

Another processing pattern is **parallel processing**, in which two or more sequential processes are required to produce a finished good. Partially completed units (for example, two subcomponents) can be worked on simultaneously in different processes and then brought together in a final process for completion. For example, the manufacture of hard drives for personal computers may have two series of processes. In the first series, write-heads and cartridge disk drives are produced, assembled, and tested. In a second series of processes, printed circuit boards are produced and tested. These two major subcomponents then come together for assembly in the final process. Notice that the two series of subprocesses can occur independently of (or parallel to) each other.

Other forms of parallel processes also exist. However, regardless of which processing pattern exists within a firm, all units produced share a common property. Since units are homogeneous and subjected to the same operations for a given process, each unit produced in a period should receive the same unit cost. Understanding how unit costs are computed requires an understanding of the manufacturing cost flows that take place in a process-costing firm.

How Costs Flow Through the Accounts in Process Costing

The manufacturing cost flows for a process-costing system are generally the same as those for a job-order costing system. As raw materials are purchased, the cost of these materials flows into a materials inventory account. Similarly, materials, direct labor, and applied overhead costs flow into a work-in-process account. When goods are completed, their cost is transferred from Work in Process to Finished Goods.

Finally, as goods are sold, the cost of the finished goods is transferred to the cost of goods sold account.

Although job-order and process cost flows are generally similar, some differences do exist. In process costing, each producing department has its own work-in-process account. As goods are completed in one department, they are transferred to the next department. Exhibit 6-12 illustrates this process for Healthblend. Notice that a product (let's say multivitamins) starts out in the Picking Department, where the proper amounts of vitamins, minerals, and inert materials are mixed. Picking direct labor and applied overhead are recognized and added to the picking work-in-process account. When the mixture is properly blended, it is transferred to the Encapsulating Department, where capsules are filled. The filled capsules are transferred out to the Bottling Department. In Bottling, the capsules are bottled, and the bottles are packaged. The important point is that as the product is transferred from one department to another, so are all of the costs attached to the product. By the end of the process, all manufacturing costs end up in the final department (here, Bottling) with the final product.

The costs transferred from a prior process to a subsequent process (for example, from Encapsulating to Bottling) are referred to as **transferred-in costs**. These transferred-in costs are (from the viewpoint of the subsequent process) a type of materials cost. Now let's see how the cost of direct materials, direct labor, and applied overhead are accounted for in each processing department's Work in Process account.

Accumulating Costs in the Production Report

In process costing, costs are accumulated by department for a period of time. The **production report** is the document that summarizes the manufacturing activity that takes place in a process department for a given period of time. A production report contains information on costs transferred in from prior departments as well as costs added in the department such as direct materials, direct labor, and overhead; it is subsidiary to the work-in-process account, just as the job-order cost sheet is subsidiary to the work-in-process account in a job-order costing system.

A production report provides information about the physical units processed in a department as well as the manufacturing costs associated with them. Thus, a production

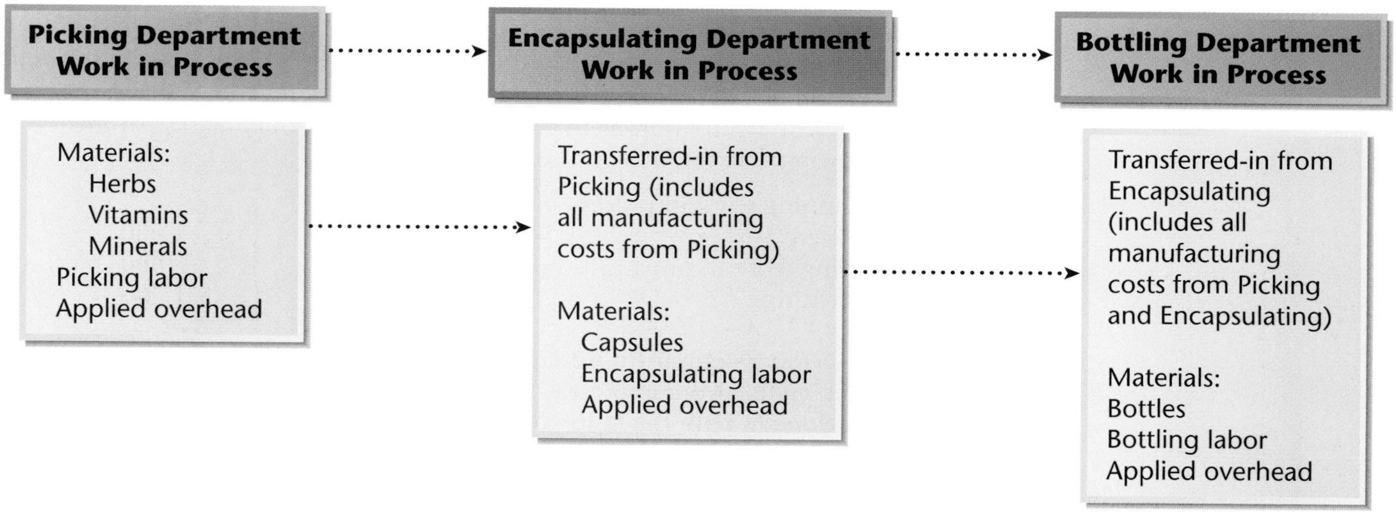

Exhibit 6-12 Flow of Manufacturing Costs Through the Accounts of a Process-Costing Firm

report is divided into a unit information section and a cost information section. The unit information section has two major subdivisions: (1) units to account for and (2) units accounted for. Similarly, the cost information section has two major subdivisions: (1) costs to account for and (2) costs accounted for. A production report traces the flow of units through a department, identifies the costs charged to the department, shows the computation of unit costs, and reveals the disposition of the department's costs for the reporting period.

Traditional manufacturing firms may have significant beginning and ending work-in-process inventories. It is the presence of these inventories that leads to much of the complication surrounding process costing. These complications are due to several factors: the presence of beginning and ending work-in-process inventories; different approaches to the treatment of beginning inventory cost; and nonuniform application of manufacturing costs. We will discuss the treatment of these complicating factors in the following sections.

The Impact of Work-in-Process Inventories on Process Costing

Objective 4

Define equivalent units, and explain their role in process costing.

The computation of a unit cost for the work performed during a period is a key part of the production report. This unit cost is needed both to compute the cost of goods transferred out of a department and to value ending work-in-process inventory.[1] Conceptually, this is easy—just divide total cost by the number of units produced. However, the presence of work-in-process inventories causes problems. First, defining a unit of production can be difficult, given that some units produced during a period are complete, while those in ending inventory are not. This is handled through the concept of equivalent units of production. Second, how should the costs of beginning work in process be treated? Should they be pooled with current period costs or separated and transferred out first? Two methods have been developed to handle this problem: the weighted average method and the FIFO method.

Equivalent Units of Production

By definition, ending work in process is not complete. Thus, a unit completed and transferred out during the period is not identical (or equivalent) to one in ending work-in-process inventory, and the cost attached to each unit should not be the same. In computing the unit cost, the output of the period must be defined.

To illustrate the output problem of process costing, assume that Department A had the following data for October:

Units in beginning work in process	—
Units completed	1,000
Units in ending work in process (25 percent complete)	600
Total manufacturing costs	$11,500

What is October's output? If we say 1,000 units, we ignore the effort expended on the units in ending work in process. Furthermore, the manufacturing costs incurred in October belong to both the units completed and to the partially completed units in ending work in process. On the other hand, if we say 1,600 units, we ignore the fact that the 600 units in ending work in process are only partially completed. Out-

1 While both manufacturing and service firms can use process costing, typically only manufacturing firms encounter the problems connected with the valuation of ending inventories of work in process and finished goods. As a result, much of the material in this section concerns process manufacturing.

put must be measured to reflect the effort expended on both completed and partially completed units.

The solution is to calculate equivalent units of output. **Equivalent units of output** are the complete units that could have been produced given the total amount of manufacturing effort expended for the period under consideration. Determining equivalent units of output for transferred-out units is easy; a unit would not be transferred out unless it were complete. Every transferred-out unit is an equivalent unit. Units remaining in ending work-in-process inventory, however, are not complete. Someone in production must "eyeball" ending work in process to estimate its degree of completion. In the example, the 600 units in ending work in process are 25 percent complete; this is *equivalent* to 150 fully completed units (600 × 25%). The equivalent units for October would be the 1,000 completed units plus 150 equivalent units in ending work in process, a total of 1,150 units of output. Exhibit 6-13 illustrates the concept of equivalent units of production.

Knowing the output for a period and the manufacturing costs for the department for that period ($11,500 in this example), we can see that the unit cost is $10 ($11,500/1,150). The unit cost is used to assign a cost of $10,000 ($10 × 1,000) to the 1,000 units transferred out and a cost of $1,500 ($10 × 150) to the 600 units in ending work in process. Note that the unit cost is $10 per equivalent unit. Thus, when valuing ending work in process, the $10 unit cost is multiplied by the equivalent units, not the actual number of partially completed units.

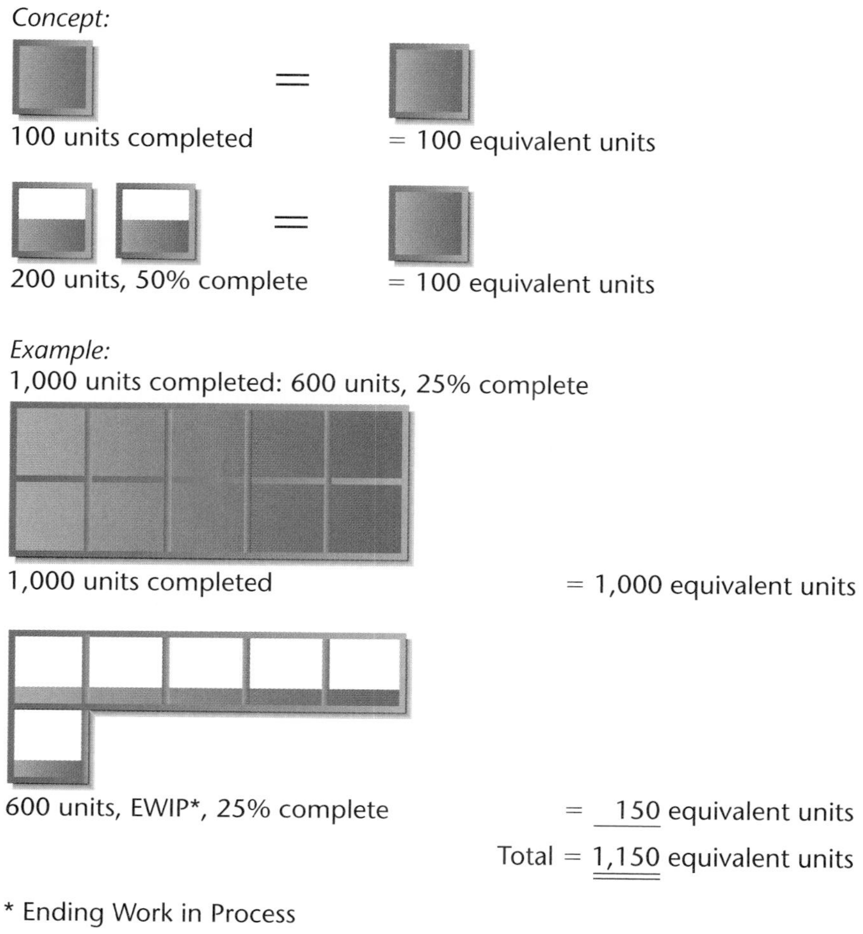

Exhibit 6-13 Equivalent Units of Production

Two Methods of Treating Beginning Work-in-Process Inventory

The presence of beginning work-in-process inventories also complicates the computation of the unit cost. The work done on these partially completed units represents prior-period work at prior-period cost. In computing a current-period unit cost for a department, two approaches have evolved for dealing with the prior-period output and prior-period costs found in beginning work in process: the weighted average method and the first-in, first-out (FIFO) method. Basically, the **weighted average costing method** combines beginning inventory costs with current-period costs to compute unit cost. In essence, the costs are pooled, and only one average unit cost is computed and applied to both units transferred out and units remaining in ending inventory.

The **FIFO costing method**, on the other hand, separates units in beginning inventory from those produced during the current period. It is assumed that units from beginning inventory are completed first and transferred out along with all of the prior-period costs as well as the current-period costs necessary to complete those units. Then, current-period production is started and completed (and transferred out with only current costs) or left incomplete as ending work-in-process inventory.

If product costs do not change from period to period, or if there is no beginning work-in-process inventory, the FIFO and weighted average methods yield the same results. The weighted average method is discussed in more detail in the next section. Further discussion of the FIFO method is found in Appendix A.

Weighted Average Costing

Objective 5

Prepare a departmental production report using the weighted average method.

The weighted average costing method treats beginning inventory costs and the accompanying equivalent output as if they belong to the current period. This is done for costs by adding the manufacturing costs in beginning work in process to the manufacturing costs incurred during the current period. The total cost is treated as if it were the current period's total manufacturing cost. Similarly, beginning inventory output and current-period output are merged in the calculation of equivalent units. Under the weighted average method, equivalent units of output are computed by adding units completed to equivalent units in ending work in process. Notice that the equivalent units in beginning work in process are included in the computation. Consequently, these units are counted as part of the current period's equivalent units of output.

Five Steps in Preparing a Production Report

The production report summarizes cost and manufacturing activity for a producing department for a given period of time. The production report is subsidiary to the work-in-process account for a department. The general pattern is described by the following five steps:

1. Physical units flow analysis
2. Calculation of equivalent units
3. Computation of unit cost
4. Valuation of inventories (goods transferred out and ending work in process)
5. Cost reconciliation

Both the weighted average and FIFO approaches follow the same general pattern for costing out production. In the ensuing discussion, we will follow the five steps previously listed. Doing so gives some structure to the method of accounting for process costs and makes it easier to learn and remember.

Example of the Weighted Average Method

To illustrate the weighted average method, let's use cost and production data for Healthblend's Picking Department for July (assume that units are measured in gallons):

Production:	
Units in process, July 1, 75% complete	20,000
Units completed and transferred out	50,000
Units in process, July 31, 25% complete	10,000
Costs:	
Work in process, July 1	$ 3,525
Costs added during July	10,125

Using the data for the Picking Department, Exhibit 6-14 illustrates the use of the weighted average method to allocate manufacturing costs to units transferred out and to units remaining in ending work in process. Notice that costs from beginning work in process (BWIP) are pooled with costs added to production during July. These total pooled costs ($13,650) are averaged and assigned to units transferred out and to units in ending work in process (EWIP). On the units' side, we concentrate on the degree of completion of all units at the end of the period. We are not concerned with the percentage of completion of beginning work-in-process inventory. We care only about whether or not these units are complete by the end of July. Thus, equivalent units are computed by pooling manufacturing efforts from June and July.

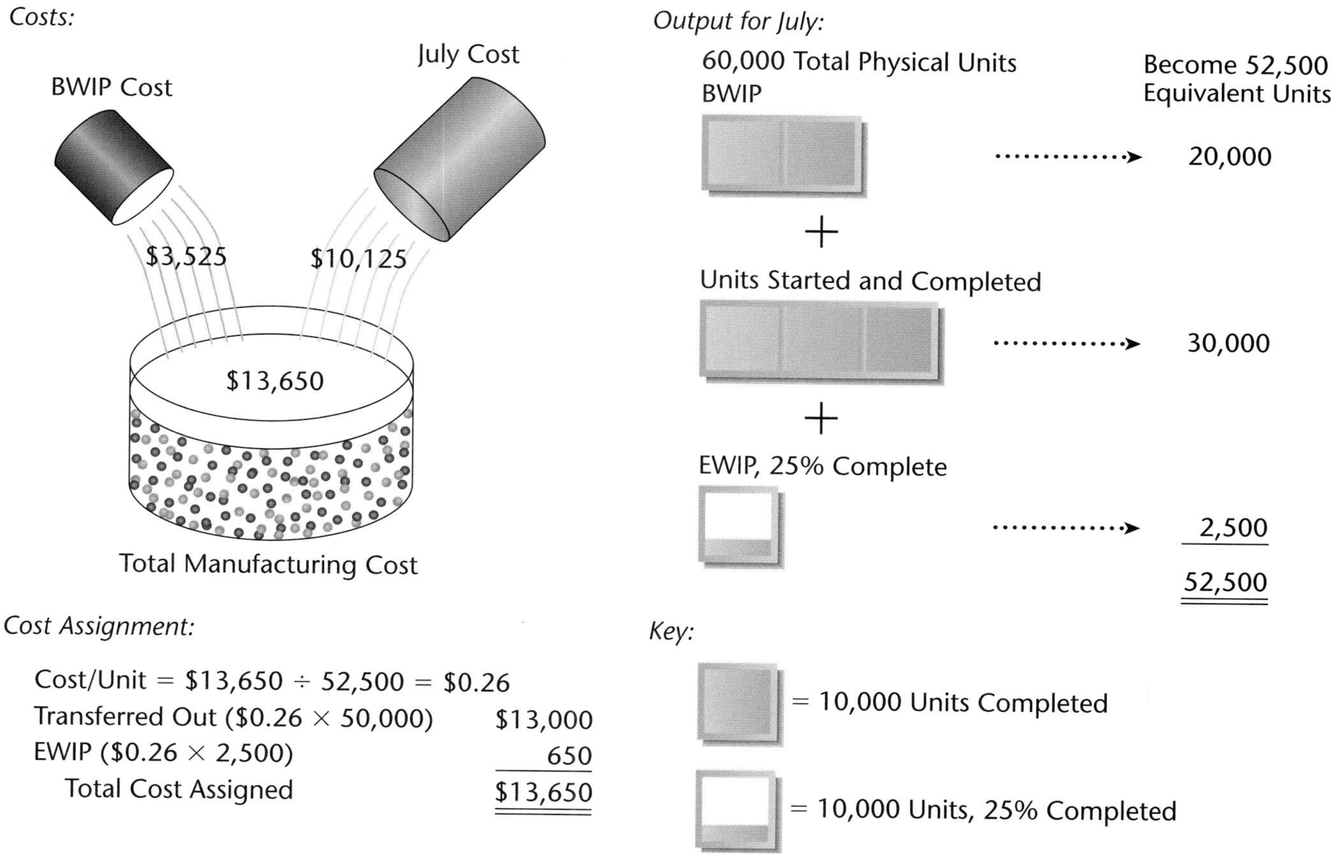

Exhibit 6-14 Weighted Average Method

Let's take a closer look at the July production in Healthblend's Picking Department by focusing on the five steps of the weighted average method.

Step 1: Physical Units Flow Analysis The purpose of step 1 is to trace the physical units of production. Physical units are not equivalent units; they are units that may be in any stage of completion. We can see in Exhibit 6-14 that there are 60,000 physical units.[2] In this example, 20,000 are from beginning inventory. Another 40,000 were started in July. From those 40,000, only 10,000 remain in ending inventory, 25 percent complete. The analysis of physical flow of units is usually accomplished by preparing a **physical flow schedule** like the one shown in Exhibit 6-13. To construct the schedule from the information given in the example, two calculations are needed. First, units started and completed in this period are obtained by subtracting the units in beginning work in process from the total units completed. Next, the units started are obtained by adding the units started and completed to the units in ending work in process. Notice that the "total units to account for" must equal the "total units accounted for." The physical flow schedule in Exhibit 6-15 is important because it contains the information needed to calculate equivalent units (step 2).

Step 2: Calculation of Equivalent Units Given the information in the physical flow schedule, the weighted average equivalent units for July can be calculated. This calculation is shown in Exhibit 6-16. Notice that July's output equals 52,500 units: 50,000 units completed and transferred out and 2,500 equivalent units from ending inventory (10,000 × 25%). What about beginning inventory? There were 20,000 units in beginning inventory, 75 percent complete. These units are included in the 50,000 units completed and transferred out during the month. Thus, beginning inventory units are treated as if they were started and completed during the current period.

Units to account for:		
Units in beginning work in process (75 percent complete) . . .		20,000
Units started during the period		40,000
Total units to account for		60,000
Units accounted for:		
Units completed and transferred out:		
Started and completed	30,000	
From beginning work in process	20,000	50,000
Units in ending work in process (25 percent complete)		10,000
Total units accounted for		60,000

Exhibit 6-15 Physical Flow Schedule

Units completed	50,000
Add: Units in ending work in process × Fraction complete	
(10,000 units × 25%)	2,500
Equivalent units of output	52,500

Exhibit 6-16 Equivalent Units of Production: Weighted Average Method

2 In Exhibit 6-14, every box represents 10,000 units. The key point to remember is that a unit may be in any stage of completion. We can see that output for July consists of six boxes: two for beginning work in process, three for units started and completed, and one for ending work in process. Hence, there are 60,000 physical units to account for.

Step 3: Computation of Unit Cost In addition to July's output, July manufacturing costs are needed to compute a unit cost. The weighted average method rolls back and includes the manufacturing costs associated with the units in beginning work in process. Thus, the total manufacturing cost for July is defined as $13,650 ($3,525 + $10,125).

Given the manufacturing costs for July and the output for the month, the unit cost can be calculated and used to determine the cost of goods transferred out and the cost of ending work in process. For July, the weighted average method gives the following unit cost:

Unit cost = $13,650/52,500 = $0.26 per equivalent unit

Step 4: Valuation of Inventories Using the unit cost of $0.26, the cost of goods transferred to the Encapsulating Department is $13,000 (50,000 units × $0.26 per unit), and the cost of ending work in process is $650 (2,500 equivalent units × $0.26 per unit). Notice that units completed (from step 1), equivalent units in ending work in process (from step 2), and the unit cost (from step 3) were all needed to value both goods transferred out and ending work in process.

Step 5: Cost Reconciliation The total manufacturing costs assigned to inventories are as follows:

Goods transferred out	$13,000
Goods in ending work in process	650
Total costs accounted for	$13,650

The manufacturing costs to account for are also $13,650.

Beginning work in process	$ 3,525
Incurred during the period	10,125
Total costs to account for	$13,650

Thus, the costs to account for are exactly assigned to inventories, and we have the necessary **cost reconciliation**. Remember, the total costs assigned to goods transferred out and to ending work in process must agree with the total costs in beginning work in process and the manufacturing costs incurred during the current period.

Production Report Steps 1 through 5 provide all of the information needed to prepare a production report for the Picking Department for July. This report is given in Exhibit 6-17.

Evaluation of the Weighted Average Method

The major benefit of the weighted average method is simplicity. By treating units in beginning work in process as belonging to the current period, all equivalent units belong to the same category when it comes to calculating unit costs. Thus, unit cost computations are simplified. The main disadvantage of this method is reduced accuracy in computing unit costs for current-period output and for units in beginning work in process. If the unit cost in a process is relatively stable from one period to the next, the weighted average method is reasonably accurate. However, if the price of manufacturing inputs increases significantly from one period to the next, the unit cost of current output is understated, and the unit cost of beginning work-in-process units is overstated. If greater accuracy in computing unit costs is desired, a company should use the FIFO method to determine unit costs.

Healthblend Nutritional Supplements Picking Department Production Report for July 2008 (Weighted Average Method)

Unit Information

Physical Flow			
Units to account for:		Units accounted for:	
Units in beginning work in process	20,000	Units completed	50,000
Units started	40,000	Units in ending work in process	10,000
Total units to account for	60,000	Total units accounted for	60,000
Equivalent Units			
Units completed	50,000		
Units in ending work in process	2,500		
Total equivalent units	52,500		

Cost Information

Costs to account for:	
Beginning work in process	$ 3,525
Incurred during the period	10,125
Total costs to account for	$13,650
Cost per equivalent unit	$ 0.26

	Transferred Out	Ending Work in Process	Total
Costs accounted for:			
Goods transferred out ($0.26 × 50,000)	$13,000	—	$13,000
Goods in ending work in process ($0.26 × 2,500)	—	$650	650
Total costs accounted for	$13,000	$650	$13,650

Exhibit 6-17 Production Report—Weighted Average Method (July 2008)

Multiple Inputs and Multiple Departments

Objective 6

Explain how process costing is affected by nonuniform application of manufacturing inputs and the existence of multiple processing departments.

Accounting for production under process costing is complicated by nonuniform application of manufacturing inputs and the presence of multiple processing departments. How process-costing methods address these complications will now be discussed.

Nonuniform Application of Manufacturing Inputs

Up to this point, we have assumed that work in process being 60 percent complete meant that 60 percent of direct materials, direct labor, and overhead needed to complete the process have been used and that another 40 percent are needed to finish the units. In other words, we have assumed that manufacturing inputs are applied uniformly as the manufacturing process unfolds.

Assuming uniform application of conversion costs (direct labor and overhead) is not unreasonable. Direct labor input is usually needed throughout the process, and overhead is normally assigned on the basis of direct labor hours. Direct materials, on the other hand, are not as likely to be applied uniformly. In many instances, materials are added at either the beginning or the end of the process.

The costs of the Bottling Department include the cost of the bottles and caps and the direct labor and the overhead associated with the bottling process.

© Getty Images/PhotoDisc

For example, look at the differences in Healthblend's three departments. In the Picking and Encapsulating departments, all materials are added at the beginning of the process. However, in the Bottling Department, materials are added both at the beginning (filled capsules and bottles) and at the end (bottle caps and boxes).

Work in process in the Picking Department that is 50 percent complete with respect to conversion inputs would be 100 percent complete with respect to the material inputs. But work in process in Bottling that is 50 percent complete with respect to conversion would be 100 percent complete with respect to bottles and transferred-in capsules, but zero percent complete with respect to bottle caps and boxes.

Different percentage completion figures for manufacturing inputs require the calculation of equivalent unit for each category of manufacturing input. Thus, there are equivalent units calculated for each category of materials and for the conversion costs. The conversion costs category can be broken down into direct labor and overhead, if desired, but if direct labor and overhead are applied uniformly this serves no useful purpose.

To illustrate, assume the Picking Department of Healthblend has the following data for September:

Production:	
Units in process, September 1, 50% complete*	10,000
Units completed and transferred out	60,000
Units in process, September 30, 40% complete*	20,000

*With respect to conversion costs

Costs:	
Work in process, September 1:	
Materials	$1,600
Conversion costs	200
Total	$1,800
Current costs:	
Materials	$12,000
Conversion costs	3,200
Total	$15,200

Assuming that Healthblend uses the weighted average method for process costing, the effect of nonuniform application of manufacturing inputs is easily illustrated. Exhibit 6-18 illustrates step 1, creating the physical flow schedule. Accounting for the flow of physical units is not affected by the nonuniform application of manufacturing inputs because physical units may be in any stage of completion.

Nonuniform application of inputs, however, does affect the computation of equivalent units (step 2). Exhibit 6-19 illustrates this computation. Notice that two categories of input are used to calculate equivalent units. Since all materials are added at the beginning of the process, all units are 100 percent complete with respect to materials. Thus, there are 20,000 equivalent units of materials in ending work in process. However, since only 40 percent of the conversion costs have been applied, there are only 8,000 (20,000 × 40%) conversion equivalent units in ending work in process.

Units to account for:		
Units in beginning work in process		10,000
Units started during September		70,000
Total units to account for		80,000
Units accounted for:		
Units completed and transferred out:		
Started and completed	50,000	
From beginning work in process	10,000	60,000
Units in ending work in process (40 percent complete)		20,000
Total units accounted for		80,000

Exhibit 6.18 Physical Flow Schedule: Nonuniform Inputs

	Materials	Conversion
Units completed	60,000	60,000
Add: Units in ending work in process × Fraction complete:		
20,000 × 100%	20,000	—
20,000 × 40%	—	8,000
Equivalent units of output	80,000	68,000

Exhibit 6.19 Calculation of Equivalent Units: Nonuniform Application

When different categories of equivalent units exist, a unit cost for each category must be computed. The cost per completed unit (step 3) is the sum of these individual unit costs. The computations for the example are as follows:

$$\begin{aligned}\text{Unit materials cost} &= (\$1{,}600 + \$12{,}000)/80{,}000 \\ &= \$0.17 \\ \text{Unit conversion cost} &= (\$200 + \$3{,}200)/68{,}000 \\ &= \$0.05 \\ \text{Total unit cost} &= \text{Unit materials cost} + \text{Unit conversion cost} \\ &= \$0.17 + \$0.05 \\ &= \$0.22 \text{ per completed unit}\end{aligned}$$

Cost of the units transferred out (step 4) is accomplished by multiplying the unit cost by the number of units completed:

$$\text{Cost of goods transferred out} = \$0.22 \times 60{,}000 = \$13{,}200$$

Costing out ending work in process is done by obtaining the cost of each manufacturing input and then summing these individual input costs. For this example, it requires adding the cost of the materials in ending work in process to the conversion costs in ending work in process.

The cost of materials is the unit materials cost multiplied by the materials equivalent units in ending work in process. Similarly, the conversion costs in ending work in process is the unit conversion cost times the conversion equivalent units. Thus, the cost of ending work in process is as follows:

Materials: $0.17 × 20,000	$3,400
Conversion: $0.05 × 8,000	400
Total cost	$3,800

Step 5 reconciles the costs to ensure that the computations are correct.

Costs to account for:	
Beginning work in process	$ 1,800
Incurred during the period	15,200
Total costs to account for	$17,000
Cost per equivalent unit	$ 0.22

Costs accounted for:	
Goods transferred out	$13,200
Goods in ending work in process	3,800
Total costs accounted for	$17,000

Using the information generated from the five steps, a production report can be prepared (see Exhibit 6-20). As the example has shown, applying manufacturing inputs at different stages of a process poses no serious problems. However, the effort required to compute the costs has increased.

Healthblend Nutritional Supplements Picking Department
Production Report for September 2008
(Weighted Average Method)

Unit Information

Units to account for:		Units accounted for:	
Units in beginning work in process	10,000	Units completed	60,000
Units started during the period	70,000	Units in ending work in process	20,000
Total units to account for	80,000	Total units accounted for	80,000

	Equivalent Units	
	Materials	**Conversion**
Units completed	60,000	60,000
Units in ending work in process	20,000	8,000
Total equivalent units	80,000	68,000

Cost Information

	Materials	**Conversion**	**Total**
Costs to account for:			
Beginning work in process	$ 1,600	$ 200	$ 1,800
Incurred during the period	12,000	3,200	15,200
Total costs to account for	$13,600	$3,400	$17,000
Cost per equivalent unit	$ 0.17	$ 0.05	$ 0.22

	Transferred Out	**Ending Work in Process**	**Total**
Costs accounted for:			
Goods transferred out ($0.22 × 60,000)	$13,200	—	$13,200
Goods in ending work in process:			
Materials ($0.17 × 20,000)	—	$3,400	3,400
Conversion ($0.05 × 8,000)	—	400	400
Total costs accounted for	$13,200	$3,800	$17,000

Exhibit 6-20 Production Report—Weighted Average Method

Multiple Departments

In process manufacturing, some departments receive partially completed goods from prior departments. The usual approach is to treat transferred-in goods as a separate materials category when calculating equivalent units.

In dealing with transferred-in goods, two important points should be remembered. First, the cost of this material is the cost of the goods transferred out as computed in the prior department. Second, the units started in the subsequent department correspond to the units transferred out from the prior department (assuming that there is a one-to-one relationship between the output measures of both departments).

For example, let's consider the month of September for Healthblend and restrict our attention to the transferred-in category. Assume that the Encapsulating Department had 15,000 units in beginning inventory (with transferred-in costs of $3,000) and completed 70,000 units during the month. Further, the Picking Department completed and transferred out 60,000 units at a cost of $13,200 in September. In constructing a physical flow schedule for the Encapsulating Department, its dependence on the Picking Department must be considered:

Units to account for:	
Units in beginning work in process	15,000
Units transferred in during September	60,000
Total units to account for	75,000
Units accounted for:	
Units completed and transferred out:	
Started and completed	55,000
From beginning work in process	15,000
Units in ending work in process	5,000
Total units accounted for	75,000

Equivalent units for the transferred-in category are calculated as follows (ignoring other input categories):

Transferred in:	
Units completed	70,000
Add: Units in ending work in process × Fraction complete (5,000 × 100%)*	5,000
Equivalent units of output	75,000

*Remember that the ending work in process is 100 percent complete with respect to transferred-in costs, not to all costs of the Encapsulating Department.

To compute the unit cost, we add the cost of the units transferred in from Picking in September to the transferred-in costs in beginning work in process and divide by transferred-in equivalent units:

$$\begin{aligned}\text{Unit cost (transferred-in category)} &= (\$13{,}200 + \$3{,}000)/75{,}000\\ &= \$16{,}200/75{,}000\\ &= \$0.216\end{aligned}$$

The only additional complication introduced in the analysis for a subsequent department is the presence of the transferred-in category. As has just been shown, dealing with this category is similar to handling any other category. However, it must be remembered that the current cost of this special type of material is the cost of the units transferred in from the prior process and that the units transferred in are the units started.

Appendix A: Production Report—FIFO Costing

Objective 7

Complete a departmental production report using the FIFO method.

Under the FIFO costing method, the equivalent units and manufacturing costs in beginning work in process are excluded from the current-period unit cost calculation. This method recognizes that the work and costs carried over from the prior period legitimately belong to that period.

Differences between the FIFO and Weighted Average Methods

If changes occur in the prices of the manufacturing inputs from one period to the next, then FIFO produces a more accurate (that is, more current) unit cost than does the weighted average method. A more accurate unit cost means better cost control, better pricing decisions, and so on. Keep in mind that if the period is as short as a week or a month, however, the unit costs calculated under the two methods are not likely to differ much. In that case, the FIFO method has little, if anything, to offer over the weighted average method. Perhaps for this reason, many firms use the weighted average method.

Since FIFO excludes prior-period work and costs, we need to create two categories of completed units. The FIFO method assumes that units in beginning work in process are completed first, before any new units are started. Thus, one category of completed units is beginning work-in-process units. The second category is for those units started and completed during the current period.

For example, assume that a department had 20,000 units in beginning work in process and completed and transferred out a total of 50,000 units. Of the 50,000 completed units, 20,000 are the units initially found in work in process. The remaining 30,000 were started and completed during the current period.

These two categories of completed units are needed in the FIFO method so that each category can be costed correctly. For the units started and completed, the unit cost is obtained by dividing total current manufacturing costs by the current-period equivalent output. However, for the beginning work-in-process units, the total associated manufacturing costs are the sum of the prior-period costs plus the costs incurred in the current period to finish the units. As can be seen in Exhibit 6-21, costs from the current period and from beginning inventory are not pooled. Instead, current-period costs are added to beginning inventory costs in order to complete the units on hand at the start of the period.

Example of the FIFO Method

The computations in Exhibit 6-21 are based on the same Healthblend data used for the weighted average method when we assumed uniform use of manufacturing inputs (Exhibit 6-14). Using the same data highlights the differences between the two methods. The five steps to cost out production follow.

Production:	
Units in process, July 1, 75% complete	20,000
Units completed and transferred out	50,000
Units in process, July 31, 25% complete	10,000
Costs:	
Work in process, July 1	$ 3,525
Costs added during the month	10,125

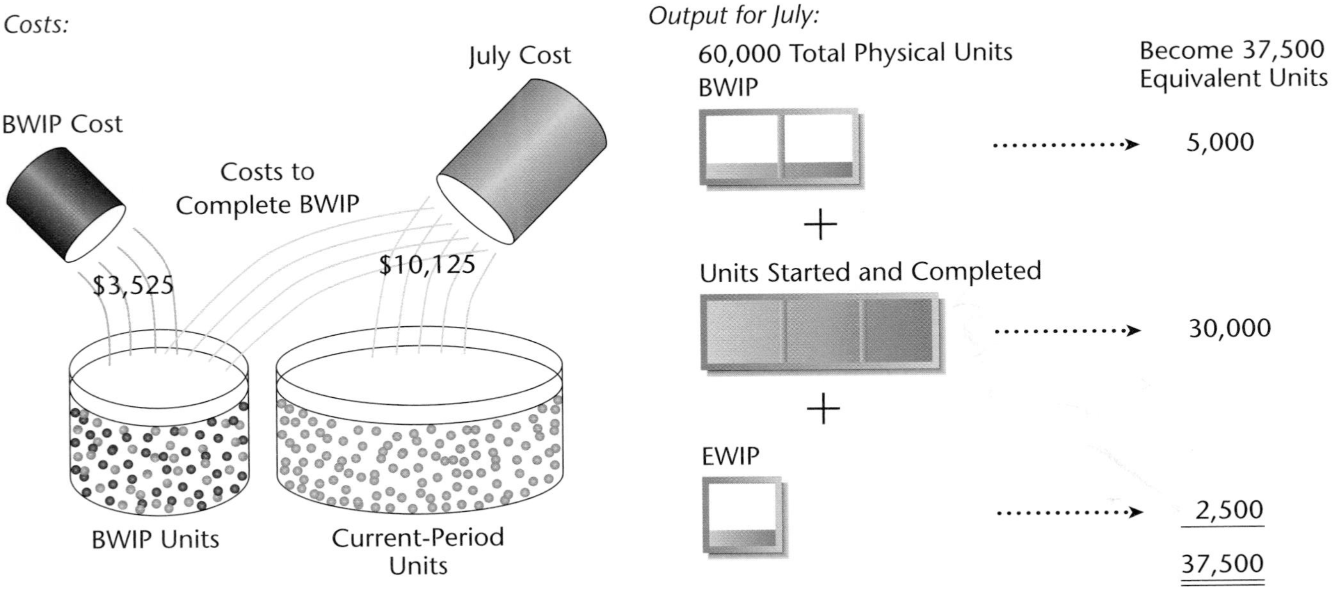

Cost Assignment:

Unit Cost = $10,125 ÷ 37,500 = $0.27

Transferred Out:	
From BWIP	$ 3,525
Complete BWIP ($0.27 × 5,000)	1,350
Started and Completed in July ($0.27 × 30,000)	8,100
Total	$12,975
EWIP ($0.27 × 2,500)	675
Total Cost Assigned	$13,650

Key:

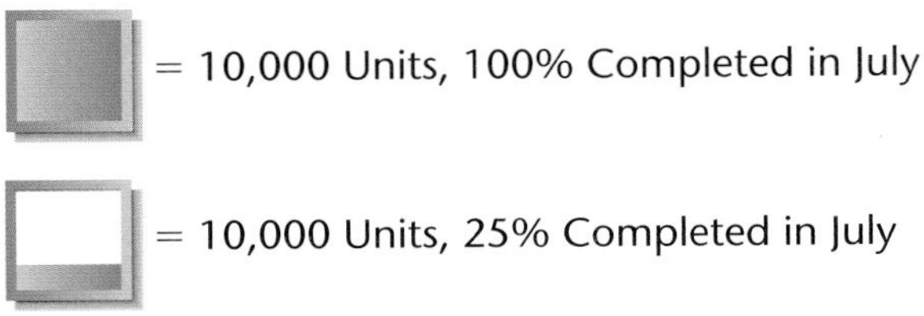

Exhibit 6-21 FIFO Method

Step 1: Physical Units Flow Analysis The purpose of step 1 is to trace the physical units of production. As with the weighted average method, in the FIFO method, a physical flow schedule is prepared. This schedule, shown in Exhibit 6-22, is identical for both methods.

Step 2: Calculation of Equivalent Units Exhibit 6-23 illustrates the calculation of equivalent units under the FIFO method. From the equivalent unit computation in Exhibit 6-23, one difference between weighted average and FIFO becomes immediately apparent. Under FIFO, the equivalent units in beginning work in process (work done in the prior period) are not counted as part of the total equivalent work. Only the equivalent work to be completed this period is counted. The equivalent work to be completed for the units from the prior period is computed by multiplying the number of units in beginning work in process by the percentage of work remaining. Since in this example the percentage of work done in the prior period is 75 percent, the percentage left to be completed this period is 25 percent, or an equivalent of 5,000 additional units of work.

The effect of excluding prior-period effort is to produce the current-period equivalent output. Recall that under the weighted average method, 52,500 equivalent units were computed for this month. Under FIFO, only 37,500 units are calculated for the

Units to account for:		
Units in beginning work in process (75 percent complete)		20,000
Units started during the period		40,000
Total units to account for		60,000
Units accounted for:		
Units completed:		
Started and completed	30,000	
From beginning work in process	20,000	50,000
Units in ending work in process (25 percent complete)	10,000	
Total units accounted for		60,000

Exhibit 6-22 Physical Flow Schedule

Units started and completed	30,000
Add: Units in beginning work in process × Fraction to be completed (20,000 × 25%)	5,000
Add: Units in ending work in process × Fraction complete (10,000 × 25%)	2,500
Equivalent units of output	37,500

Exhibit 6-23 Equivalent Units of Production: FIFO Method

same month. These 37,500 units represent current-period output. The difference, of course, is explained by the fact that the weighted average method rolls back and counts the 15,000 equivalent units of prior-period work (20,000 units BWIP × 75%) as belonging to this period.

Step 3: Computation of Unit Cost The additional manufacturing costs incurred in the current period are $10,125. Thus, the current-period unit manufacturing cost is $10,125/37,500, or $0.27. Notice that the costs of beginning inventory are excluded from this calculation. Only current-period manufacturing costs are used.

Step 4: Valuation of Inventories Since all equivalent units in ending work in process are current-period units, the cost of ending work in process is simply $0.27 × 2,500, or $675. However, when it comes to valuing goods transferred out, another difference emerges between the weighted average method and FIFO.

Under weighted average, the cost of goods transferred out is simply the unit cost times the units completed. Under FIFO, however, there are two sources of completed units: 20,000 units from beginning inventory and 30,000 units started and completed. The cost of the 30,000 units that were started and completed in the current period and transferred out is $8,100 ($0.27 × 30,000). For these units, the use of the current-period unit cost is entirely appropriate.

However, the cost of the beginning work-in-process units that were transferred out is another matter. These units started the period with $3,525 of manufacturing costs already incurred and 15,000 units of equivalent output already completed. To finish these units, the equivalent of 5,000 units were needed. The cost of finishing the units in beginning work in process is $1,350 ($0.27 × 5,000). Adding this $1,350 to the $3,525 in cost carried over from the prior period gives a total manufacturing cost for these units of $4,875. The unit cost of these 20,000 units, then, is about $0.244 ($4,875/20,000).

Step 5: Cost Reconciliation With the completion of step 5, the production report can be prepared. This report is shown in Exhibit 6-24. The total costs assigned to production are as follows:

Goods transferred out:	
Units in beginning work in process	$ 4,875
Units started and completed	8,100
Goods in ending work in process	675
Total costs accounted for	$13,650

The total manufacturing costs to account for during the period are:

Beginning work in process	$ 3,525
Incurred during the period	10,125
Total costs to account for	$13,650

Healthblend Nutritional Supplements Picking Department
Production Report for July 2008
(FIFO Method)

Unit Information

Units to account for:	
Units in beginning work in process	20,000
Units started during the period	40,000
Total units to account for	60,000

	Physical Flow	Equivalent Units
Units accounted for:		
Units started and completed	30,000	30,000
Units completed from beginning work in process	20,000	5,000
Units in ending work in process	10,000	2,500
Total units accounted for	60,000	37,500

Cost Information

Costs to account for:	
Beginning work in process	$ 3,525
Incurred during the period	10,125
Total costs to account for	$13,650
Cost per equivalent unit	$ 0.27

	Transferred Out	Ending Work in Process	Total
Costs accounted for:			
Units in beginning work in process:			
From prior period	$ 3,525	—	$ 3,525
From current period ($0.27 × 5,000)	1,350	—	1,350
Units started and completed ($0.27 × 30,000)	8,100	—	8,100
Goods in ending work in process ($0.27 × 2,500)	—	$675	675
Total costs accounted for	$12,975	$675	$13,650

Exhibit 6-24 Production Report—FIFO Method

Often the total costs accounted for do not precisely equal the costs to account for due to rounding error. An easy way to bring the amounts into balance is to adjust the cost of goods transferred out by the amount of the rounding error.

Appendix B: Journal Entries Associated with Job-Order and Process Costing

Objective 8

Prepare the journal entries associated with job-order and process costing.

We have looked at the flow of costs through the accounts in both the job-order and process costing systems, but how are the transactions actually entered into the accounting system? This is done by making journal entries and posting them to the accounts.

Journal Entries Associated with Job-Order Costing

Let's summarize the various transactions that occurred during the month of January for PNP.

1. Materials costing $3,500 were purchased on account.
2. Materials costing $3,280 were requisitioned for use in production.
3. Direct labor costing $750 was recognized as a liability in the wages payable account.
4. Overhead was applied to production at the rate of 12 per direct labor hour. A total of 50 direct labor hours were worked.
5. Actual overhead costs of $615 were incurred.
6. The SupliShake-001 job was completed and transferred to finished goods.
7. The SupliShake-001 job was sold at cost plus 50 percent.
8. Underapplied overhead was closed to cost of goods sold.

The journal entries for each of the above transactions are as follows:

1.	Materials	3,500	
	Accounts Payable		3,500
2.	Work in Process	3,280	
	Materials		3,280
3.	Work in Process	750	
	Wages Payable		750
4.	Work in Process	600	
	Overhead Control		600
5.	Overhead Control	615	
	Rent Payable		400
	Utilities Payable		50
	Accumulated Depreciation		100
	Insurance Payable		65
6.	Finished Goods	2,320	
	Work in Process		2,320
7.	Cost of Goods Sold	2,320	
	Finished Goods		2,320
	Accounts Receivable	3,480	
	Sales Revenue		3,480
8.	Cost of Goods Sold	15	
	Overhead Control		15

Let's look more closely at each of the above journal entries. Journal entry (1) shows that the purchase of materials increases the materials account as well as the accounts payable account. In other words, the company has increased both assets (materials on hand) and liabilities (through Accounts Payable).

Entry (2) shows the transfer from the materials storeroom to the factory floor. In other words, the materials are no longer awaiting requisition, they are being used. Therefore, the work-in-process account goes up, but the materials account goes down.

Entry (3) recognizes the contribution of direct labor. The amount of direct labor wages is added to Work in Process and also to the liability account, Wages Payable.

Entry (4) recognizes the application of overhead to the jobs. Since 50 hours of direct labor were worked, and the overhead rate is $12 per direct labor hour, then $600 has been applied to overhead. Notice that this overhead application increases the work-in-process account and is credited to Overhead Control.

Entry (5) shows that the actual overhead incurred is debited to Overhead Control. The credit is to the various payable accounts.

Entry (6) shows the transfer of the SupliShake-001 job from Work in Process to Finished Goods. We find the appropriate cost by referring to the job-order cost sheet in Exhibit 6-8.

Entry (7) consists of two journal entries. First, we recognize the cost of SupliShake-001 by debiting Cost of Goods Sold for the cost and crediting Finished

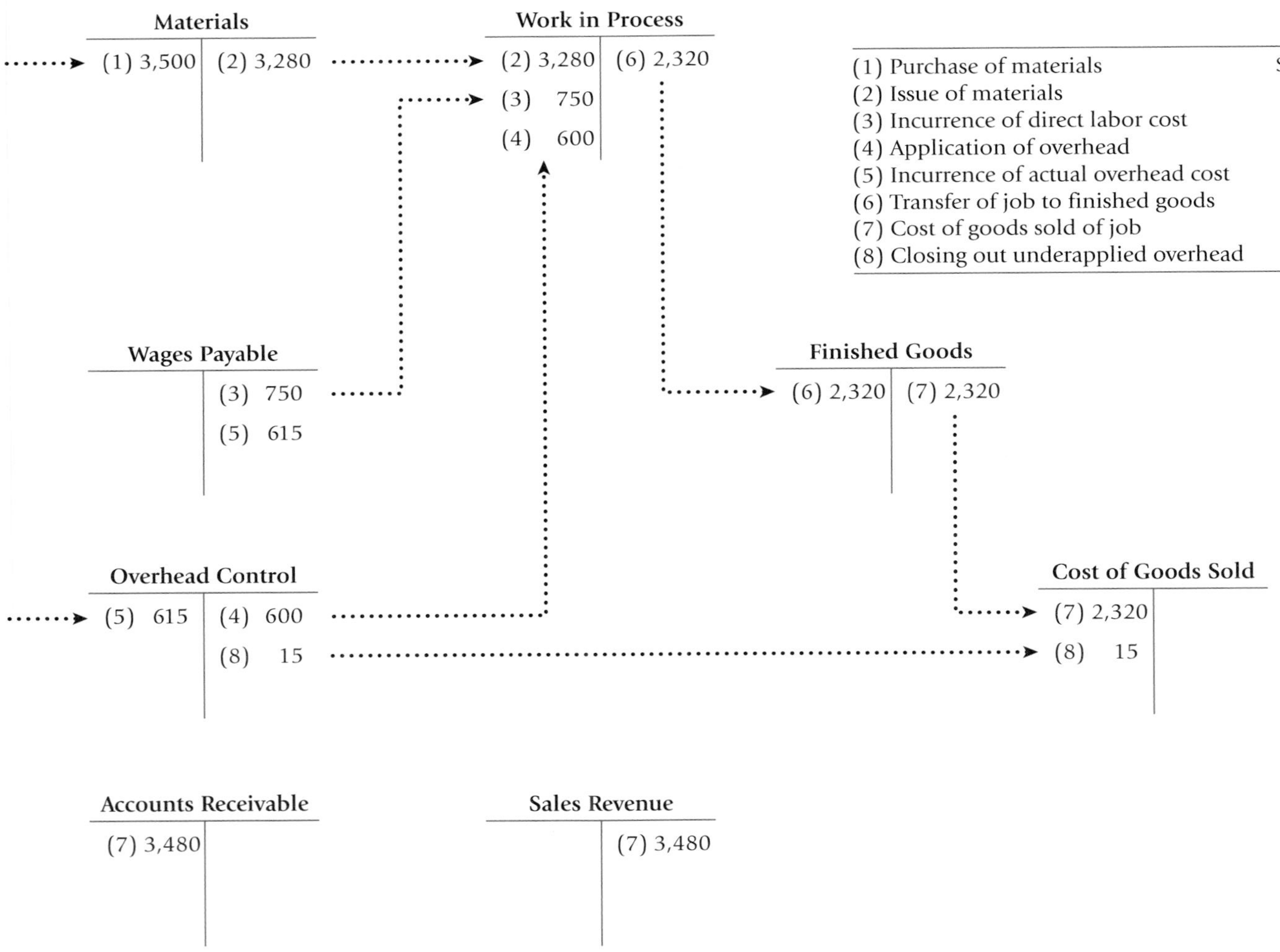

(1) Purchase of materials	$3,500
(2) Issue of materials	3,280
(3) Incurrence of direct labor cost	750
(4) Application of overhead	600
(5) Incurrence of actual overhead cost	615
(6) Transfer of job to finished goods	2,320
(7) Cost of goods sold of job	2,320
(8) Closing out underapplied overhead	15

Exhibit 6-25 Posting of Journal Entries to the Accounts

Goods. This entry mirrors the physical movement of the order out of the warehouse and to the customer. The second entry shows the sales price. It is very important here to separate the cost of the job from the sale. This always requires two entries.

Finally, we check the overhead control account. It has a debit balance of $15, indicating that the overhead variance is $15 underapplied. To bring the balance to zero, then, Overhead Control must be credited $15 and Cost of Goods Sold debited $15. Exhibit 6-25 summarizes these journal entries and posts them to the appropriate accounts.

Journal Entries Associated with Process Costing

The journal entries for process costing generally parallel those described in a job-order costing system. In fact, the entries to record the purchase of materials, the transfer of product from Finished Goods to Cost of Goods Sold, and the sale of product are identical in form to the corresponding entries in job-order costing. It is the Work in Process accounts that differ due to the multiple accounts that a process costing firm may have.

Suppose that Healthblend decides to produce 2,000 bottles of multivitamins with the following costs:

	Picking Department	Encapsulating Department	Bottling Department
Direct materials	$1,700	$1,000	$800
Direct labor	50	60	300
Applied overhead	450	500	600

The journal entries for the direct materials, direct labor, and applied overhead for this example are as follows:

1.	Work in Process—Picking	1,700	
	Materials		1,700
2.	Work in Process—Encapsulating	1,000	
	Materials		1,000
3.	Work in Process—Bottling	800	
	Materials		800
4.	Work in Process—Picking	50	
	Wages Payable		50
5.	Work in Process—Encapsulating	60	
	Wages Payable		60
6.	Work in Process—Bottling	300	
	Wages Payable		300
7.	Work in Process—Picking	450	
	Overhead Control		450
8.	Work in Process—Encapsulating	500	
	Overhead Control		500
9.	Work in Process—Bottling	600	
	Overhead Control		600

But what about the transfer of completed units from one department to the next? When the multivitamin mixture is transferred to the Encapsulating Department from the Picking Department, it takes $2,200 of cost along with it ($1,700 materials + $50 wages payable + $450 overhead control). This $2,200 is a transferred-in cost to the Encapsulating Department, and it is treated as another type of direct materials cost. (You could think of the Encapsulating Department as "buying" the mixture from the Picking Department.) Then, Encapsulating adds $1,560 of cost from its process and transfers completed capsules plus $3,760 of cost ($2,200 from Picking and $1,560 added in Encapsulating) to the Bottling Department. Again, Bottling treats the $3,760 of transferred-in cost as a direct materials cost and adds its own cost of $1,700 ($800 + $300 + $600) to come up with a total cost of $5,460. The completed bottles of multivitamins are transferred to the finished goods warehouse along with the $5,460 of manufacturing cost. If there were 2,000 bottles manufactured, each would have a manufacturing cost of $2.73 ($5,460/2,000).

When the mixture is transferred from Picking to Encapsulating, the following journal entry would occur:

10.	Work in Process—Encapsulating	2,200	
	Work in Process—Picking		2,200

Similarly, the journal entry to record the transferred-in costs from Encapsulating to Bottling would be:

11.	Work in Process—Bottling	3,760	
	Work in Process—Encapsulating		3,760

Finally, when the completed multivitamins leave the Bottling Department for the finished goods warehouse, the following entry would be made:

12.	Finished Goods	5,460	
	Work in Process—Bottling		5,460

Exhibit 6-26 summarizes these journal entries and posts them to the appropriate accounts.

WIP—Picking		WIP—Encapsulating		WIP—Bottling		Finished Goods	
(1) 1,700		(2) 1,000		(3) 600			
(4) 50		(5) 60		(6) 300			
(7) 450		(8) 500		(9) 600			
	(10) 2,200 ······➤	(10) 2,200	(11) 3,760 ······➤	(11) 3,760			
					(12) 5,460 ······➤	(12) 5,460	

Exhibit 6-26 Posting of Journal Entries to the Accounts

Summary of Learning Objectives

1. Describe the basic characteristics of and the differences between job-order costing and process costing, and identify the types of firms that would use each method.

Job-order costing and process costing are two major cost assignment systems. Job-order costing is used in firms that produce a wide variety of heterogeneous (unique) products. Process costing is used by firms that mass produce a homogeneous product.

2. Describe the cost flows associated with job-order costing.

In job-order costing, the key document or record for accumulating manufacturing costs is the job-order cost sheet. Materials requisition forms (for direct materials), time tickets (for direct labor), and source documents for manufacturing activities are the source documents needed to assign manufacturing costs to jobs. The cost of each job is accumulated on the job-order cost sheet. The total job cost consists of actual direct materials, actual direct labor, and overhead applied using a predetermined rate (or rates). The balance in Work in Process consists of the balances of all incomplete jobs. When a job is finished, its cost is transferred from Work in Process to Finished Goods, and then, when sold, to Cost of Goods Sold.

3. Describe the cost flows associated with process costing.

Cost flows under process costing are similar to those under job-order costing. Raw materials are purchased and debited to the raw materials account. Direct materials used in production, direct labor, and applied overhead are charged to the work-in-process account. In a production process with several processes, there is a work-in-process account for each department or process. Goods completed in one department are transferred out to the next department. When units are completed in the final department or process, their cost is credited to Work in Process and debited to Finished Goods.

4. Define equivalent units, and explain their role in process costing.

Equivalent units of production are the complete units that could have been produced given the total amount of manufacturing effort expended during the period. The number of physical units is multiplied by the percentage of completion to calculate equivalent units. Two approaches have evolved for dealing with beginning work-in-process inventory costs. The weighted average costing method combines beginning inventory costs with current-period costs to compute unit costs. The FIFO costing method separates units in beginning inventory from those produced during the current period.

5. Prepare a departmental production report using the weighted average method.

The production report summarizes the manufacturing activity occurring in a department for a given period. It discloses information concerning the physical flow of units, equivalent units, unit costs, and the disposition of the manufacturing costs associated with the period.

6. Explain how process costing is affected by nonuniform application of manufacturing inputs and the existence of multiple processing departments.

Nonuniform application of productive inputs requires the determination of separate percentage of completion figures for each input. This, in turn, requires the computation of separate equivalent units and unit costs. When a company has more than one processing department, the output of one department becomes the material of a succeeding department. The usual method is to handle the transferred-in units and costs as another form of material.

7. (Appendix A) Complete a departmental production report using the FIFO method.

A production report prepared according to the FIFO method separates the cost of beginning work in process from the cost of the current period. Beginning work in process is assumed to be completed and transferred out first. Costs from beginning work in process are not pooled with the current-period costs in computing unit cost. Additionally, equivalent units of production exclude work done in the prior period.

8. (Appendix B) Prepare the journal entries associated with job-order and process costing.

In job-order costing, materials and direct labor are charged to the work-in-process account (Materials and Wages Payable are credited, respectively). Overhead costs are assigned to Work in Process using a predetermined rate. Actual overhead costs are accumulated in the overhead control account. The cost of completed units is credited to Work in Process and debited to Finished Goods. When goods are sold, the cost is debited to Cost of Goods Sold and credited to Finished Goods. In process costing, there is a different Work in Process account for each department or process. When units are completed in one department, their total cost is charged to the Work in Process account of the next department (and the WIP of the first department is credited).

Key Terms

Adjusted cost of goods sold, 224
Cost reconciliation, 233
Equivalent units of output, 229
FIFO costing method, 230
Job, 214
Job-order cost sheet, 217
Job-order costing system, 214
Materials requisition form, 217
Normal cost of goods sold, 224
Operation costing, 226
Parallel processing, 226
Physical flow schedule, 232
Process-costing system, 215
Production report, 227
Sequential processing, 226
Time ticket, 217
Transferred-in costs, 227
Weighted average costing method, 230
Work-in-process file, 217

Review Problems

1. Job Cost Using Plantwide and Departmental Overhead Rates

Timter Company uses a normal job-order costing system. The company has two departments through which most jobs pass. Selected budgeted and actual data for the past year follow:

	Department A	Department B
Budgeted overhead	$100,000	$500,000
Actual overhead	$110,000	$520,000
Expected activity (direct labor hours)	50,000	10,000
Expected machine hours	10,000	50,000
Actual direct labor hours	51,000	9,000
Actual machine hours	10,500	52,000

During the year, several jobs were completed. Data pertaining to one such job, Job #10, follow:

Direct materials	$20,000
Direct labor cost:	
Department A (5,000 hours @ $6 per hr.)	$30,000
Department B (1,000 hours @ $6 per hr.)	$6,000
Machine hours used:	
Department A	100
Department B	1,200
Units produced	10,000

Timter Company uses a plantwide predetermined overhead rate to assign overhead to jobs. Direct labor hours (DLH) are used to compute the predetermined overhead rate.

Required

1. Compute the predetermined overhead rate.
2. Using the predetermined rate, compute the per-unit manufacturing cost for Job #10.
3. Recalculate the unit manufacturing cost for Job #10 using departmental overhead rates. Use direct labor hours for Department A and machine hours for Department B. Explain why this approach provides a more accurate unit cost.

Solution

1. The predetermined overhead rate is $600,000/60,000 = $10 per DLH. Add the budgeted overhead for the two departments and divide by the total expected direct labor hours (DLH = 50,000 + 10,000).

2.

Direct materials	$ 20,000
Direct labor	36,000
Overhead ($10 × 6,000 DLH)	60,000
Total manufacturing costs	$116,000
Unit cost ($116,000/10,000)	$ 11.60

3. The predetermined rate for Department A is $100,000/50,000 = $2 per DLH. The predetermined rate for Department B is $500,000/50,000 = $10 per MHr.

Direct materials	$20,000
Direct labor	36,000
Overhead:	
Department A ($2 × 5,000)	10,000
Department B ($10 × 1,200)	12,000
Total manufacturing costs	$78,000
Unit cost ($78,000/10,000)	$ 7.80

Overhead assignment using departmental rates is more accurate because there is a higher correlation with the overhead assigned and the overhead consumed. Notice that Job #10 spends most of its time in Department A, the less overhead-intensive of the two departments. Departmental rates reflect this differential time and consumption better than plantwide rates do.

2. Calculation of Work in Process and Cost of Goods Sold with Multiple Jobs

Greenthumb Landscape Design designs landscape plans and plants the material for clients. On April 1, there were three jobs in process, Jobs #68, #69, and #70. During April, two more jobs were started, Jobs #71 and #72. By April 30, Jobs #69, #70, and #72 were completed. The following data were gathered:

	Job #68	Job #69	Job #70	Job #71	Job #72
4/1 Balance	$540	$1,230	$990	$ 0	$ 0
Direct materials	700	560	75	3,500	2,750
Direct labor	500	600	90	2,500	2,000

Overhead is applied at the rate of 120 percent of direct labor cost. Jobs are sold at cost plus 40 percent. Operating expenses for April totaled $3,670.

Required

1. Prepare job-order cost sheets for each job as of April 30.
2. Calculate the ending balance in Work in Process (as of April 30) and Cost of Goods Sold for April.
3. Construct an income statement for Greenthumb Landscape Design for the month of April.

Solution

1.

	Job #68	Job #69	Job #70	Job #71	Job #72
4/1 Balance	$ 540	$1,230	$ 990	$ 0	$ 0
Direct materials	700	560	75	3,500	2,750
Direct labor	500	600	90	2,500	2,000
Applied overhead	600	720	108	3,000	2,400
Totals	$2,340	$ 3,110	$1,263	$9,000	$7,150

2. Ending balance in Work in Process = Job #68 + Job #71
= $2,340 + $9,000
= $11,340

Cost of Goods Sold for April = Job #69 + Job #70 + Job #72
= $3,110 + $1,263 + $7,150
= $11,523

3.

Greenthumb Landscape Design
Income Statement
For the Month Ended April 30, 20XX

Sales*	$16,132
Cost of goods sold	11,523
Gross margin	$ 4,609
Less: Operating expenses	3,670
Operating income	$ 939

*Sales (rounded to the nearest dollar) = $11,523 + 0.40($11,523) = $16,132

3. Process Costing

Payson Company, which uses the weighted average method, produces a product that passes through two departments: Mixing and Cooking. In the Mixing Department, all materials are added at the beginning of the process. All other manufacturing inputs are added uniformly. The following information pertains to the Mixing Department for February:

a. Beginning work in process (BWIP), February 1: 100,000 pounds, 40 percent complete with respect to conversion costs. The costs assigned to this work are as follows:

Materials	$20,000
Labor	10,000
Overhead	30,000

b. Ending work in process (EWIP), February 28: 50,000 pounds, 60 percent complete with respect to conversion costs.

c. Units completed and transferred out: 370,000 pounds. The following costs were added during the month:

Materials	$211,000
Labor	100,000
Overhead	270,000

Required

1. Prepare a physical flow schedule.
2. Prepare a schedule of equivalent units.
3. Compute the cost per equivalent unit.
4. Compute the cost of goods transferred out and the cost of ending work in process.
5. Prepare a cost reconciliation.

Solution

1. Physical flow schedule:

Units to account for:		
Units in BWIP		100,000
Units started		320,000
Total units to account for		420,000
Units accounted for:		
Units completed and transferred out:		
Started and completed	270,000	
From BWIP	100,000	370,000
Units in EWIP		50,000
Total units accounted for		420,000

2. Schedule of equivalent units:

	Materials	Conversion
Units completed	370,000	370,000
Units in EWIP × Fraction complete:		
Materials (50,000 × 100%)	50,000	—
Conversion (50,000 × 60%)	—	30,000
Equivalent units of output	420,000	400,000

3. Cost per equivalent unit:

Materials unit cost = ($20,000 + $211,000)/420,000 = $0.550
Conversion unit cost = ($40,000 + $370,000)/400,000 = $1.025
Total unit cost = $1.575 per equivalent unit

4. Cost of goods transferred out and cost of ending work in process:

Cost of goods transferred out = $1.575 × 370,000
= $582,750
Cost of ending work in process = ($0.55 × 50,000) + ($1.025 × 30,000)
= $58,250

5. Cost reconciliation:

Costs to account for:	
Beginning work in process	$ 60,000
Incurred during the period	581,000
Total costs to account for	$641,000
Costs accounted for:	
Goods transferred out	$582,750
Work in process	58,250
Total costs accounted for	$641,000

Questions for Writing and Discussion

1. Explain the differences between job-order costing and process costing.
2. Why are the accounting requirements for job-order costing more demanding than those for process costing?
3. Give some examples of service firms that might use job-order costing, and explain why they use it.
4. Suppose that you and a friend decide to set up a lawnmowing service next summer. Describe the source documents that you would need to account for your activities.
5. How is job-order costing related to profitability analysis? To pricing?
6. What is the role of materials requisition forms in a job-order costing system? Time tickets? Predetermined overhead rates?
7. Distinguish between sequential processing and parallel processing.
8. What are equivalent units? Why are they needed in a process-costing system?
9. Under the weighted average method, how are prior-period costs and output treated? How are they treated under the FIFO method?
10. Under what conditions will the weighted average and the FIFO methods give essentially the same results?
11. How is the equivalent unit calculation affected when materials are added at the beginning or end of the process rather than uniformly throughout the process?
12. Explain why transferred-in costs are a special type of material for the Receiving Department.
13. What journal entry would be made as goods are transferred out from one department to another department? From the final department to the warehouse?
14. Describe the five steps in accounting for the manufacturing activity of a processing department, and explain how they interrelate.
15. In assigning costs to goods transferred out, how do the weighted average and FIFO methods differ?
16. How would process costing for services differ from process costing for manufactured goods?

Exercises

6-1

Job-Order vs. Process
LO1

Identify each of the following types of businesses as either job-order or process.

a. Paint manufacturing
b. Auto manufacturing
c. Toy manufacturing
d. Custom cabinet making
e. Airplane manufacturing (e.g., 767s)
f. Personal computer assembly
g. Furniture making
h. Custom furniture making
i. Dental services
j. Hospital services
k. Paper manufacturing
l. Auto repair
m. Architectural services
n. Landscape design services
o. Light bulb manufacturing

6-2

Job-Order vs. Process
LO1

For each of the following types of industries, give an example of a firm that would use job-order costing. Then, give an example of a firm that would use process costing.

1. Auto manufacturing
2. Dental services
3. Auto repair
4. Costume making

6-3

Costing Jobs
LO2

Rossiter, Inc., designs and builds projects for individual customers. On August 1, there were two jobs in process: Job #614 with a beginning balance of $10,200; and Job 615 with a beginning balance of $9,670. Rossiter applies overhead at the rate of 60 percent of direct labor cost.

During August, Jobs #616 and #617 were started. Data on August costs for all jobs are as follows:

	Job #614	Job #615	Job #616	Job #617
DM	$4,200	$9500	$1,000	$3,150
DL	1,800	4,000	150	800

Job #615 was completed on August 22, and the client was billed at cost plus 40 percent. All other jobs remained in process.

Required

1. Prepare job-order cost sheets for each job as of the end of August.
2. Calculate the balance in Work in Process on August 31.
3. What is the price of Job #614?

6-4

Costing Jobs
LO2

Zarabi Company builds internal conveyor equipment to client specifications. The October 1 balance of Job #265 was $30,330; the October balance of Job #266 was $62,170.

During October, Jobs #267 and #268 were started. Data on October costs for all jobs are as follows:

	Job #265	Job #266	Job #267	Job #268
DM	$13,000	$ 7,000	$3,500	$4,750
DL	15,000	12,000	1,900	7,000

Job #265 was completed on October 28, and the client was billed at cost plus 30 percent. All other jobs remained in process. Overhead is applied at the rate of 75% of direct labor cost.

Required

1. Calculate the overhead applied to each job during the month of October.
2. Prepare job-order cost sheets for each job as of the end of October.
3. Calculate the balance in Work in Process on October 31.
4. What is the price of Job #265?

6-5

Job Cost
LO2

Jordan Levis, owner of AudioSupreme, sells and installs audio components and home theater systems. She just completed the installation of speakers and audio wiring in ten houses being built by Dream Homes, Inc. The job required materials costing $3,400 and 50 direct labor hours at $10 per hour. Overhead is applied on the basis of direct labor hours at a rate of $4 per hour.

Required

1. What is the total cost of the job? The unit cost?
2. If Jordan charges a price that is one-and-one-half times cost, what price is charged for each home?
3. What type of information would Jordan want to keep track of on a simple labor time ticket?

6-6

Balance of Work in Process and Finished Goods, Cost of Goods Sold
LO2

Ballenger Company uses job-order costing. At the end of the month, the following information was gathered:

Job #	Total Cost	Completed?	Sold?
901	$650	yes	no
902	400	no	no
903	550	yes	no
904	695	yes	yes
905	860	yes	no
906	750	no	no
907	180	yes	yes
908	700	no	no
909	905	no	no
910	803	yes	no

The beginning balance of Finished Goods was zero.

Required

1. Calculate the balance in Work in Process at the end of the month.
2. Calculate the balance in Finished Goods at the end of the month.
3. Calculate Cost of Goods Sold for the month.

6-7

ABC and Job-Order Costing
LO2

Bosserman Company, a job-order costing firm, worked on three jobs in July. Data are as follows:

	Job #70	Job #71	Job #72
Balance, 7/1	$25,000	$0	$0
Direct materials	$12,900	$9,900	$35,350
Direct labor	$20,000	$6,500	$13,000
Machine hours	250	200	1,200
Material moves	50	10	200
Purchase orders	10	40	10

ABC is used to apply overhead to jobs. The power rate is $2 per machine hour; the materials handling rate is $25 per move; and the purchasing rate is $40 per purchase order. By July 31, Jobs #70 and #71 were completed, and Job #70 was sold. Job #72 remained in process. On July 1, the balance in Finished Goods was zero.

Required

1. Prepare job-order cost sheets for each job showing all costs through July 31.
2. Calculate the balance in Work in Process on July 31.
3. Calculate the balance in Finished Goods on July 31.
4. Calculate Cost of Goods Sold for July.

6-8

Income Statement for the Job-Order Costing Firm
LO2

Refer to **Exercise 6-7.** Bosserman prices its jobs at cost plus 40 percent. During July, variable marketing expenses were 10 percent of sales, fixed marketing expenses were $4,100, and administrative expenses were $3,900.

Required

Prepare an income statement for Bosserman Company for the month of July.

6-9

Appendix Exercise: Job Cost, Journal Entries
LO2, LO8

Barrymore Costume Company, located in New York City, sews costumes for plays and musicals. Barrymore considers itself primarily a service firm, as it never produces costumes without a preexisting order and purchases materials only to the specifications of the particular job. Any finished goods ending inventory is temporary and is "zeroed out" as soon as the show producer pays for the order. Overhead is applied on the basis of direct labor cost. During the first quarter of 2006, the following activity took place in each of the accounts listed below.

Work in Process

	Debit	Credit
Bal.	17,000	245,000
DL	80,000	
OH	140,000	
DM	40,000	
Bal.	32,000	

Finished Goods

	Debit	Credit
Bal.	40,000	210,000
	245,000	
Bal.	75,000	

Overhead Control

Debit		Credit
138,500		140,000
	Bal.	1,500

Cost of Goods Sold

Debit	Credit
210,000	

Job #32 was the only job in process at the end of the first quarter. A total of 1,000 direct labor hours at $10 per hour were charged to Job #32.

Required

1. Assuming that overhead is applied on the basis of direct labor cost, what was the overhead rate used during the first quarter of 2006?

2. What was the applied overhead for the first quarter? The actual overhead? The under- or overapplied overhead?
3. What was the cost of goods manufactured for the quarter?
4. Assume that the overhead variance is closed to Cost of Goods Sold. Prepare the journal entry to close out the overhead control account. What is the adjusted balance in Cost of Goods Sold?
5. For Job #32, identify the costs incurred for direct materials, direct labor, and overhead.

6-10

Appendix Exercise: Overhead Application; Journal Entries; Job Cost
LO2, LO8

At the beginning of the year, Paxton Company budgeted overhead of $180,000 and 20,000 direct labor hours. During the year, Job #K456 was completed with the following information: direct materials cost, $4,140; direct labor cost, $4,000. The average wage for Paxton Company is $10 per hour.

By the end of the year, a total of 21,000 direct labor hours had actually been worked, and Paxton Company incurred the following actual overhead costs for the year:

Equipment lease	$ 5,000
Depreciation on building	20,000
Indirect labor	101,300
Utilities	18,000
Other overhead	45,000

Required

1. Calculate the overhead rate for the year.
2. Calculate the total cost of Job #K456.
3. Prepare the journal entries to record actual overhead and to apply overhead to production for the year.
4. Is overhead over- or underapplied? By how much?
5. Assuming that the normal cost of goods sold for the year is $740,000, what is the adjusted cost of goods sold?

6-11

Basic Cost Flows
LO3

Leikam Company produces dress slacks in three departments: Cutting, Sewing, and Packaging. During the month, the three departments recorded the following costs:

	Cutting Department	Sewing Department	Packaging Department
Direct materials	$5,400	$ 900	$225
Direct labor	150	1,800	900
Applied overhead	750	3,600	900

Six hundred pairs of slacks were completed during the month. There is no beginning or ending work in process in any department.

Required

1. Prepare a schedule showing, for each department, the cost of direct materials, direct labor, applied overhead, products transferred in from a prior department, and total manufacturing cost.
2. (a) Calculate the cost transferred from Cutting to Sewing.
   (b) Calculate the cost transferred from Sewing to Packaging.
   (c) Calculate the cost transferred from Packaging to Finished Goods.
3. What is the total unit cost of a pair of slacks?

6-12

Equivalent Units
LO4

Department F had the following data for August:

Units in beginning work in process	—
Units completed	600
Units in ending work in process (20% complete)	300

Required

1. Calculate equivalent units of production in ending work-in-process inventory.
2. Calculate total equivalent units of production for Department F for August.

6-13

Physical Flow, Equivalent Units
LO4, LO6

Rade Company manufactures a product that passes through two processes. For the month of April, the first department had beginning work in process of 14,000 units. Ending work in process had 8,500 units, 25 percent complete with respect to conversion costs. During April, Rade started 40,000 units in process.

Required

1. Prepare a physical flow schedule.
2. Compute equivalent units for materials and for conversion cost.

6-14

Weighted Average Method; Nonuniform Inputs, Cost of Units Transferred Out and Ending Work in Process
LO4, LO5, LO6

Calmore, Inc., manufactures products that pass through two or more processes. Calmore uses the weighted average method to compute unit costs. During May, equivalent units were computed as follows:

	Materials	Conversion
Units completed	45,000	45,000
Units in ending work in process × Fraction complete:		
8,000 × 0%	—	—
8,000 × 60%	—	4,800
Equivalent units of output	45,000	49,800

The unit cost was computed as follows:

Materials	$1.30
Conversion	0.50
Total	$1.80

Required

1. Determine the cost of ending work in process and the cost of the goods transferred out.
2. If possible, prepare a physical flow schedule.

6-15

Nonuniform Inputs, Equivalent Units
LO4, LO6

Shaw Company produces a product that passes through two departments. Data for December on Department 1 included: beginning work in process was zero; ending work in process had 3,600 units, 50 percent complete with respect to conversion costs; and 6,480 units were started. Materials are added at the beginning of the process in Department 1.

Data for December on Department 2 included: beginning work in process was 1,200 units, 20 percent complete with respect to conversion costs; and 600 units were in ending work in process, 40 percent complete with respect to conversion costs. All materials are added at the end of the process in Department 2.

Required

1. For Department 1 for December, calculate the following:
   a. Number of units transferred to Department 2.
   b. Equivalent units of production for materials and for conversion costs.
2. For Department 2 for December, calculate the following:
   a. Number of units transferred out to Finished Goods.
   b. Equivalent units of production for materials and for conversion costs.

6-16

Steps in Preparing a Cost of Production Report
LO5

EXCEL

Cocolots, Inc., manufactures chocolate syrup in three departments: Cooking, Mixing, and Bottling. Cocolots uses the weighted average method. The following are cost and production data for the Mixing Department for June (assume that units are measured in gallons):

Production:	
Units in process, June 1, 60% complete	60,000
Units completed and transferred out	240,000
Units in process, June 30, 20% complete	40,000
Costs:	
Work in process, June 1	$ 390,600
Costs added during June	1,171,800

Required

1. Prepare a physical flow analysis for the Mixing Department for the month of June.
2. Calculate equivalent units of production for the Mixing Department for the month of June.
3. Calculate unit cost for the Mixing Department for the month of June.
4. Calculate the cost of units transferred out and the cost of ending work-in-process inventory.
5. Prepare a cost reconciliation for the Mixing Department for the month of June.

6-17

Cost of Production Report
LO5

Refer to **Exercise 6-16.** Prepare a cost of production report for the Mixing Department for the month of June.

6-18

Equivalent Units—Weighted Average Method
LO4

The following data are for four independent process-costing departments:

	A	B	C	D
Beginning inventory	3,200	1,000	0	30,000
Percent completion	30%	40%	0%	75%
Units started	17,000	23,000	40,000	40,000
Ending inventory	4,000	0	9,000	10,000
Percent completion	25%	0%	10%	25%

Required

Compute the equivalent units of production for each of the above departments using the weighted average method.

6-19

Appendix Exercise: Equivalent Units—FIFO Method
LO4, LO7

Using the data from **Exercise 6-18**, compute the equivalent units of production for each of the four departments using the FIFO method.

6-20

Nonuniform Inputs
LO5, LO6

Terry Linens, Inc., manufactures bed and bath linens. The Bath Linens Department sews terry cloth into towels of various sizes. Terry uses the weighted average method. All materials are added at the beginning of the process. The following data are for the Bath Linens Department for August:

Production:	
Units in process, August 1, 25 percent complete*	10,000
Units completed and transferred out	60,000
Units in process, August 31, 60 percent complete*	20,000
Costs:	
Work in process, August 1:	
Materials	$ 49,000
Conversion costs	2,625
Total	$ 51,625
Current costs:	
Materials	$351,000
Conversion costs	78,735
Total	$429,735

*With respect to conversion costs

Required

1. Prepare a physical flow schedule for the Bath Linens Department for August.
2. Calculate equivalent units of production for the Bath Linens Department for August.
3. Calculate unit cost for materials, for conversion, and in total for the Bath Linens Department for August.
4. Calculate the cost of units transferred out and the cost of ending work in process.
5. Prepare a cost reconciliation for the Bath Linens Department for August.

6-21

Cost of Production Report; Nonuniform Inputs LO5, LO6

Refer to **Exercise 6-20**. Prepare a cost of production report for the Bath Linens Department for August using the weighted average method.

EXCEL

6-22

Weighted Average Method; FIFO; Single-Department Analysis; Multiple Cost Categories
LO4, LO5, LO7

Kimbeth Manufacturing Company uses a process-costing system to manufacture Dust Density Sensots for the mining industry. The following information pertains to operations for the month of May 2008.

	Units
Beginning work in process, May 1	16,000
Started in production during May	100,000
Completed production during May	92,000
Ending work in process, May 31	24,000

Beginning work in process was 60 percent complete for materials and 20 percent complete for conversion costs. Ending work in process was 90 percent complete for materials and 40 percent complete for conversion costs.

CMA

Costs pertaining to May are as follows:

a. Beginning work in process: materials, $54,560; direct labor, $20,320; and overhead, $15,240.
b. Costs incurred during May: materials, $468,000; direct labor, $182,880; and overhead, $390,160.

Choose the *best* answer for each of the following multiple-choice questions. **(CMA adapted)**

1. Using the FIFO method, the equivalent units for materials are
   a. 97,600 units.
   b. 104,000 units.
   c. 107,200 units.
   d. 108,000 units.
   e. 113,600 units.
2. Using the FIFO method, the equivalent units for conversion costs are
   a. 85,600 units.
   b. 88,800 units.
   c. 95,200 units.
   d. 98,400 units.
   e. 101,600 units.
3. Using the FIFO method, the equivalent unit cost of materials is
   a. $4.12.
   b. $4.50.
   c. $4.60.
   d. $4.80.
   e. $5.46.
4. Using the FIFO method, the equivalent unit conversion cost is
   a. $5.65.
   b. $5.82.
   c. $6.00.
   d. $6.20.
   e. $6.62.
5. Using the FIFO method, the total cost of units in ending work in process at May 31, 2008, is
   a. $153,072.
   b. $154,800.
   c. $155,328.
   d. $156,960.
   e. $159,648.
6. Using the weighted average method, the equivalent unit cost of materials for May is
   a. $4.12.
   b. $4.50.
   c. $4.60.
   d. $5.03.
   e. $5.46.

7. Using the weighted average method, the equivalent unit conversion cost for May is
   a. $5.65.
   b. $5.83.
   c. $5.99.
   d. $6.41.
   e. $6.62.

8. Using the weighted average method, the total cost of units in ending work in process at May 31, 2008, is
   a. $86,400.
   b. $153,960.
   c. $154,800.
   d. $155,328.
   e. $156,864.

6-23

Appendix Exercise: FIFO Equivalent Units; Unit Cost
LO7

EXCEL

Nogaleen Company manufactures a liquid diet product in three departments. Data for Blending, the first department, follow:

Production:	
Units in process, August 1, 75 percent complete	120,000
Units completed and transferred out	400,000
Units in process, August 31, 30 percent complete	90,000
Costs:	
Work in process, August 1	$ 340,600
Costs added during August	1,516,500

Nogaleen uses FIFO costing.

Required

1. Prepare a physical flow schedule for the Blending Department for August.
2. Calculate equivalent units of production for the Blending Department for August.
3. Calculate unit cost for materials, conversion, and in total for August.
4. Calculate the cost of units transferred out and the cost of ending work in process.
5. Prepare a cost reconciliation for the Blending Department.

6-24

Appendix Exercise: FIFO Cost of Production Report
LO7

Refer to **Exercise 6-23**. Prepare a cost of production report for the Blending Department of Nogaleen Company for the month of August.

6-25

Appendix Problem: Unit Cost; Ending Work in Process; Journal Entries
LO2, LO8

During August, Pamell, Inc., worked on two jobs. Data relating to these two jobs follow:

	Job #64	Job #65
Units in each order	50	100
Units sold	50	—
Materials requisitioned	$1,240	$985
Direct labor hours	410	583
Direct labor cost	$6,150	$8,745

Overhead is assigned on the basis of direct labor hours at a rate of $12. During August, Job #64 was completed and transferred to Finished Goods. Job #65 was the only unfinished job at the end of the month.

Required

1. Calculate the per-unit cost of Job #64.
2. Compute the ending balance in the work-in-process account.
3. Prepare the journal entries reflecting the completion and sale on account of Job #64. The selling price is 160 percent of cost.

Problems

6-26

Calculating Ending Work in Process; Income Statement
LO2

Tara Aldrin installs outdoor water gardens. On June 1, Tara had three jobs in process, for the Fazels, Myrons, and Pattons, with the following costs:

	Fazel	Myron	Patton
Direct materials	$ 560	$ 270	$1,200
Direct labor	900	700	1,000
Applied overhead	270	210	300
Total	$1,730	$1,180	$2,500

During the month of June, two more jobs were started, the Raider and Willis houses. Materials and labor costs incurred by each job in June are as follows:

	Materials	Direct Labor
Fazel	$600	$1,200
Myron	350	980
Patton	260	650
Raider	780	1,350
Willis	725	900

The Fazel and Myron jobs were completed and billed by June 30.

Required

1. If overhead is applied on the basis of direct labor dollars, what is the overhead rate?
2. Prepare simple job-order cost sheets for each of the five jobs in process during June.
3. What is the ending balance of Work in Process on June 30? What is the cost of jobs sold in June? (Round your answers to the nearest dollar.)
4. Suppose that Tara prices her jobs at cost plus 40 percent. In addition, during June, marketing and administrative costs of $1,200 were incurred. Prepare an income statement for the month of June.

6-27

Activity-Based Costing and Overhead Rates; Unit Costs
LO2

Lacy Company manufactures specialty tools to customer order. Budgeted overhead for the coming year is as follows:

Purchasing	$30,000	Engineering	$20,000
Setups	15,000	Other	25,000

Previously, Jennifer Langston, Lacy Company's controller, had applied overhead on the basis of machine hours. Expected machine hours for the coming year are 10,000. Jennifer has been reading about activity-based costing, and she wonders whether or not it might offer some advantages to her company. She decided that appropriate drivers for overhead activities are purchase orders for purchasing, number of setups for setup cost, engineering hours for engineering cost, and machine hours for other. Budgeted amounts for these drivers are 5,000 purchase orders, 1,000 setups, and 500 engineering hours.

Jennifer has been asked to prepare bids for two jobs with the following information:

	Job 1	Job 2
Direct materials	$4,500	$8,600
Direct labor	$1,000	$2,000
Number of purchase orders	15	20
Number of setups	2	3
Number of engineering hours	25	10
Number of machine hours	200	200

The typical bid price includes a 30 percent markup over full manufacturing cost.

Required

1. Calculate a plantwide rate for Lacy Company based on machine hours. What is the bid price of each job using this rate?
2. Calculate activity rates for the four overhead activities. What is the bid price of each job using these rates?
3. Which bids are more accurate? Why?

6-28

Appendix Problem: Journal Entries; T-Accounts
LO2, LO8

Lowder, Inc., builds custom conveyor systems for warehouses and distribution centers. During the month of July, the following occurred:

a. Materials were purchased on account for $44,200.
b. Materials totaling $27,000 were requisitioned for use in production—$12,500 for Job #703 and the remainder for Job #704.
c. Direct labor payroll for the month was $28,200, with an average wage of $15 per hour. Job #703 required 780 direct labor hours; Job #704 required 1,100 direct labor hours.
d. Actual overhead of $19,950 was incurred and paid.
e. Overhead is charged to production at the rate of $10 per direct labor hour.
f. Job #703 was completed and transferred to finished goods.
g. Job #704, which was started during July, remained in process at the end of the month.
h. Job #700, which had been completed in May, was sold on account for cost plus 40 percent.

Beginning balances as of July 1 were as follows:

Materials	$ 6,070
Work in Process (for Job #703)	13,000
Finished Goods (for Job #700)	6,240

Required

1. Prepare the journal entries for events (a) through (e) above.
2. Prepare simple job-order cost sheets for Jobs #703 and #704.
3. Prepare the journal entries for events (f) and (h) above.
4. Calculate the ending balances of:

a. Materials
b. Work in Process
c. Finished Goods

6-29

Appendix Problem: Journal Entries; Job Costs
LO2, LO8

The following transactions occurred during the month of April for Kearney Company.

a. Materials costing $3,000 were purchased on account.
b. Materials totaling $1,700 were requisitioned for use in production, $500 for Job #443 and the remainder for Job #444.
c. During the month, direct laborers worked 50 hours on Job #443 and 100 hours on Job #444. Direct laborers are paid at the rate of $8 per hour.
d. Overhead is applied using a plantwide rate of $7.50 per direct labor hour.
e. Actual overhead for the month was $1,230 and was paid in cash.
f. Job #443 was completed and transferred to Finished Goods.
g. Job #442, which had been completed and transferred to Finished Goods in March, was sold on account for cost ($2,000) plus 25 percent.

Required

1. Prepare journal entries for transactions (a) through (e).
2. Prepare job-order cost sheets for Jobs #443 and #444. Prepare journal entries for transactions (f) and (g).
3. Prepare a schedule of cost of goods manufactured for April. Assume that the beginning balance in the materials account was $1,400 and the beginning balance in the work-in-process account was zero.

6-30

Weighted Average Method; Cost of Production Report
LO5

Debroux Company produces a product that passes through an assembly process and a finishing process. All manufacturing costs are added uniformly for both processes. The following information was obtained for the Assembly Department for February:

a. Work in process, February 1, had 12,000 units (60 percent complete) and the following costs:

Direct materials	$93,128
Direct labor	32,432
Overhead applied	17,200

b. During February, a total of 34,600 units were completed and transferred to the Finishing Department, and the following costs were added to production:

Direct materials	$133,760
Direct labor	140,640
Overhead applied	58,752

c. On February 28, there were 5,400 partially completed units in process. These units were 70 percent complete.

Required

Prepare a production report for the Assembly Department for February using the weighted average method of costing. The report should disclose the physical flow of units, equivalent units, and unit costs and should track the disposition of manufacturing costs.

6-31

Appendix Problem: FIFO Method; Cost of Production Report
LO7

EXCEL

Refer to the data in **Problem 6-30.**

Required

Prepare a production report for the Assembly Department for February using the FIFO method of costing. The report should contain the same schedules described in Problem 6-30. (*Hint:* Carry the unit cost computation to four decimal places.)

6-32

Weighted Average Method; Single-Department Analysis; Three Cost Categories
LO4, LO5, LO6

Tyrone Company produces a variety of stationery products. One product, sealing wax sticks, passes through two processes: blending and molding. The weighted average method is used to account for the costs of production. Two ingredients, paraffin and pigment, are added at the beginning of the blending process and heated and mixed for several hours. After blending, the resulting product is sent to the Molding Department, where it is poured into molds and cooled. The following information relates to the blending process for August:

a. Work in process, August 1, had 20,000 pounds, 20 percent complete with respect to conversion costs. Costs associated with partially completed units were:

Paraffin	$120,000
Pigment	100,000
Direct labor	30,000
Overhead applied	10,000

b. Work in process, August 31, had 30,000 pounds, 70 percent complete with respect to conversion costs.

c. Units completed and transferred out totaled 500,000 pounds. Costs added during the month were:

Paraffin	$3,060,000
Pigment	2,550,000
Direct labor	3,877,500
Overhead applied	1,292,500

Required

1. Prepare the following: (a) a physical flow schedule and (b) an equivalent unit schedule with cost categories for paraffin, pigment, and conversion costs.
2. Calculate the unit cost for each cost category.
3. Compute the cost of ending work in process and the cost of goods transferred out.
4. Prepare a cost reconciliation.

6-33

Appendix Problem: FIFO Method; Single Department Analysis; Transferred-in Goods
LO7

EXCEL

Grace Sauces, Inc., manufactures a steak sauce that passes through several processes. During the first quarter of the year, the Mixing Department received 180,000 quarts of liquid from the Cooking Department (transferred in at $230,400). Upon receiving the liquid, the Mixing Department adds spices and allows blending to take place for 45 minutes. The product is then passed on to the Bottling Department.

There were 144,000 quarts in process at the beginning of the quarter, 75 percent complete with respect to conversion costs. The costs attached to the beginning inventory were as follows:

Transferred in	$45,600
Powder	6,432
Conversion costs	14,400

Costs added by the Mixing Department during the first quarter were

Powder	$33,500
Conversion costs	72,640

There were 31,500 quarts in ending inventory, 20 percent complete with respect to conversion costs.

Required

Prepare a production report using the FIFO method. Follow the five steps outlined in the chapter in preparing the report. Carry out unit costs to three decimal places. Round to the nearest dollar in the production report.

6-34

Weighted Average Method; Transferred-in Goods
LO3, LO4

Refer to **Problem 6-33.**

Required

Prepare a production report for the Mixing Department using the weighted average method.

6-35

Weighted Average Method; Journal Entries; Two-Department Analysis
LO5, LO8

Seacrest Company uses a process-costing system. The company manufactures a product that is processed in two departments: Department A and Department B. In Department A, materials are added at the beginning of the process; in Department B, additional materials are added at the end of the process. In both departments, conversion costs are incurred uniformly throughout the process. As work is completed, it is transferred out. The following table summarizes the production activity and costs for November:

	Department A	Department B
Beginning inventories:		
Physical units	5,000	8,000
Costs:		
Transferred in	—	$ 45,320
Direct materials	$ 10,000	—
Conversion costs	$ 6,900	$ 16,800
Current production:		
Units started	25,000	?
Units transferred out	28,000	33,000
Costs:		
Transferred in	—	?
Direct materials	$57,800	$ 37,950
Conversion costs	$95,220	$128,100
Percentage completion:		
Beginning inventory	40%	50%
Ending inventory	80%	50%

Required

1. Using the weighted average method, prepare the following for Department A:
   a. A physical flow schedule
   b. An equivalent unit calculation
   c. Calculation of unit costs
   d. Cost of ending work in process and cost of goods transferred out
   e. A cost reconciliation

2. Prepare journal entries that show the flow of manufacturing costs for Department A.
3. Repeat Requirements 1 and 2 for Department B.

6-36

Appendix Problem: FIFO Method; Two-Department Analysis; Journal Entries
LO5, LO7, LO8

Refer to the data in **Problem 6-35.**

Required

Repeat the requirements in **Problem 6-35** using the FIFO method. (*Hint:* Carry unit costs to three decimal places.)

6-37

Weighted Average Method; Multiple-Department Analysis
LO5 LO6

Strathmore, Inc., manufactures educational toys using a weighted average, process-costing system. Plastic is molded into the appropriate shapes in the Molding Department. Molded components are transferred to the Assembly Department where the toys are assembled and additional materials (for example, fasteners and decals) are applied. Completed toys are then transferred to the Packaging Department where each toy is boxed.

Strathmore showed the following data on toy production for February:

	Molding	Assembly	Packaging
Beginning inventory:			
Units	500	—	150
Prior department	—	—	$ 1,959.00
Materials	$2,500.00	—	$ 375.00
Conversion costs	$1,050.00	—	$ 225.00
Started or transferred in:			
Units	1,000	?	?
February costs:			
Prior department	—	$14,950.00	$11,754.00
Materials	$5,000.00	$487.60	$ 2,407.50
Conversion costs	$7,660.00	$ 1,166.00	$ 2,977.50
Ending inventory in units	200	400	—

Beginning and ending work in process for the three departments showed the following degree of completion:

	Molding	Assembly	Packaging
Degree of completion:			
Beginning work in process, materials	100%	—	100%
Beginning work in process, conversion costs	30	—	50
Ending work in process, materials	100	40%	—
Ending work in process, conversion costs	20	40	—

Required

1. Prepare a physical flow schedule for February for the following:
   a. Molding Department
   b. Assembly Department
   c. Packaging Department
2. Compute equivalent units of production for direct materials and for conversion costs for the following:
   a. Molding Department
   b. Assembly Department
   c. Packaging Department

3. Complete the following unit cost chart:

	Molding	Assembly	Packaging
Unit prior department cost*			
Unit materials cost			
Unit conversion cost			
Total unit cost			

*Cost transferred in from prior department

4. Determine the cost of ending work in process and the cost of goods transferred out for each of the three departments.
5. Reconcile the costs for each department.

6-38

Appendix Problem: FIFO Method; Multiple-Department Analysis
LO5, LO7

Refer to the data in **Problem 6-37.**

Required

Repeat Requirements 2 through 5 using the FIFO method. (*Hint:* Carry unit costs to three decimal places.)

Managerial Decision Case

6-39

Production Report; Ethical Issues
LO5

Consider the following conversation between Gary Means, manager of a division that produces industrial machinery, and his controller, Donna Simpson, a CMA and CPA:

Gary: Donna, we have a real problem. Our operating cash is too low, and we are in desperate need of a loan. As you know, our financial position is marginal, and we need to show as much income as possible—and our assets need bolstering as well.

Donna: I understand the problem, but I don't see what can be done at this point. This is the last week of the fiscal year, and it looks like we'll report income just slightly above breakeven.

Gary: I know all this. What we need is some creative accounting. I have an idea that might help us, and I wanted to see if you would go along with it. We have 200 partially finished machines in process, about 20 percent complete. That compares with the 1,000 units that we completed and sold during the year. When you computed the per-unit cost, you used 1,040 equivalent units, giving us a manufacturing cost of $1,500 per unit. That per-unit cost gives us cost of goods sold equal to $1.5 million and ending work in process worth $60,000. The presence of the work in process gives us a chance to improve our financial position. If we report the units in work in process as 80 percent complete, this will increase our equivalent units to 1,160. This, in turn, will decrease our unit cost to about $1,345 and cost of goods sold to $1.345 million. The value of our work in process will increase to $215,200. With those financial stats, the loan would be a cinch.

Donna: Gary, I don't know. What you're suggesting is risky. It wouldn't take much auditing skill to catch this one.

Gary: You don't have to worry about that. The auditors won't be here for at least six to eight more weeks. By that time, we can have those partially completed units completed and sold. I can bury the labor cost by having some of our more loyal workers work overtime for some bonuses. The overtime will never be reported. And, as you know, bonuses come out of the corporate budget and are assigned to overhead—next year's overhead. Donna, this will work. If we look good and get the loan to boot, corporate headquarters will treat us well. If we don't do this, we could lose our jobs.

Required

1. Should Donna agree to Gary's proposal? Why or why not? To assist in deciding, review the standards in the Statement of Ethical Professional Practice for management accountants described in Chapter 1. Do any apply?
2. Assume that Donna refuses to cooperate and that Gary accepts this decision and drops the matter. Does Donna have any obligation to report the divisional manager's behavior to a superior? Explain.
3. Assume that Donna refuses to cooperate; however, Gary insists that the changes be made. Now what should she do? What would you do?
4. Suppose that Donna is age 63 and that the prospects for employment elsewhere are bleak. Assume again that Gary insists that the changes be made. Donna also knows that Gary's supervisor, the owner of the company, is his father-in-law. Under these circumstances, would your recommendations for Donna differ? If you were Donna, what would you do?

Research Assignment

6-40

Research Assignment
LO1, LO2

Interview an accountant who works for a service organization that uses job-order costing. For a small firm, you may need to talk to an owner/manager. Examples are a funeral home, insurance firm, repair shop, medical clinic, and dental clinic. Write a paper describing the job-order costing system used by the firm. Some of the questions that the paper should address are

a. What service(s) does the firm offer?
b. What document or procedure do you use to collect the costs of the services performed for each customer?
c. How do you assign the cost of direct labor to each job?
d. How do you assign overhead to individual jobs?
e. How do you assign the cost of direct materials to each job?
f. How do you determine what to charge each customer?
g. How do you account for a completed job?

State how the service firm you investigated adapted the job-order accounting procedures described in the chapter to its particular circumstances. Were the differences justified? If so, explain why. Also, offer any suggestions you might have for improving the approach that you observed.

6-41

Cybercase
LO1, LO4

Go to the Web site for **Crayola, Inc.**, accessible via the chapter web links at the Interactive Study Center on www.thomsonedu.com/accounting/hansen. There is a "factory tour" that you can take. Take the factory tours for crayons and for markers. List the departments for each product. Verbally trace the flow of costs through each department to come up with a listing of total manufacturing costs for each of the finished products.

chapter 7

Support-Department Cost Allocation

learning objectives

After studying this chapter, you should be able to:

1. Describe the difference between support departments and producing departments.
2. Calculate single and multiple charging rates for a support department.
3. Allocate support-department costs to producing departments using the direct, sequential, and reciprocal methods.
4. Compute departmental overhead rates.
5. (Appendix) Describe the allocation of joint costs to products.

Scenario

Hamilton and Barry, a large regional public accounting firm, consists of three major departments: Audit, Tax, and Management Advisory Services (MAS). Six months previously, the firm had set up an in-house Photocopying Department. While the cost was slightly higher than that charged by independent photocopying shops, the partners believed that the added convenience and security were worth it.

Even though the Photocopying Department was running smoothly, one of the departments, MAS, was not pleased. The head of MAS was incensed with the $0.12 charge per page to use the in-house services. He had taken some of his department's work to KopyKats, the photocopying shop around the corner. In fact, he threatened to go as far as boycotting the Photocopying Department until the charges came down. As a result, Jan McClintock, managing partner of Hamilton and Barry, decided to investigate.

Jan's first step was to talk with the head of the Photocopying Department. There she learned that the $0.12 per copy charge was based on peak usage of the equipment. In their firm, peak usage occurred in April when the Tax Department ran most of their copies. The equipment was purchased for peak usage—not average usage—and thus the charge was higher than at an outside firm that might have more even usage throughout the year. Jan decided to revisit the issue of setting charges, and to investigate the possibility of a dual charging system.

Questions to Think About

1. Why do you think that the photocopying charges amount to $0.12 per page? List the types of costs incurred for photocopying, and divide them into fixed and variable categories.

2. Jan mentioned the security and convenience of in-house photocopying. How do you think the firm might weigh these factors in deciding whether or not the cost of in-house copying is "worth it"?

3. Since the firm as a whole has decided to have an in-house copying department, why are copying costs charged to the individual departments? What purpose does the practice of developing support-department charging rates serve?

The earlier chapters have focused on product costs and the way that they are assigned to products. The complexity of many modern firms leads the accountant to focus particularly on the assignment of overhead. In Chapter 4, we learned that there are a variety of ways to assign overhead: plantwide rates, departmental rates, and activity-based costing. In this chapter, we further explain the way that support-department costs are assigned to producing departments for the calculation of departmental overhead rates.

Allocation is simply a means of dividing a pool of costs and assigning it to various subunits. It is important to realize that allocation does not affect the total cost. Total cost is neither reduced nor increased by allocation. However, the amounts of cost assigned to the subunits can be affected by the allocation procedure chosen. Because cost allocation can affect bid prices, the profitability of individual products, and the behavior of managers, it is an important topic.

An Overview of Cost Allocation

Objective 1

Describe the difference between support departments and producing departments.

Mutually beneficial costs, which occur when the same resource is used in the output of two or more services or products, are **common costs**. While these common costs may pertain to periods of time, individual responsibilities, sales territories, and classes of customers, this chapter will concentrate on the costs common to departments and to products. For example, the wages paid to security guards at a factory are a common cost of all of the different products manufactured there. The benefits of security are applicable to each product, yet the assignment of security cost to the individual products is an arbitrary process. The way that common costs are assigned to departments, and then to units of product or service, is the topic of this chapter.

Types of Departments

In the functional model of the firm, cost objects are departments. There are two categories of departments: producing departments and support departments. **Producing departments** are directly responsible for creating the products or services sold to customers. In the opening scenario's public accounting firm, examples of producing departments are auditing, tax, and management advisory services. In a manufacturing setting, producing departments are those that work directly on the products being manufactured (for example, grinding and assembly). **Support departments** provide essential support services for producing departments. These departments are indirectly connected with an organization's services or products. Examples include maintenance, grounds, engineering, housekeeping, personnel, and storage. Of course, the Photocopying Department of Hamilton and Barry is a support department.

Once the producing and support departments have been identified, the overhead costs incurred by each department can be determined. Note that this involves tracing costs to the departments, not allocating costs, because the costs are directly associated with the individual department. A factory cafeteria, for example, would have food costs, salaries of cooks and servers, depreciation on dishwashers and stoves, and supplies (e.g., napkins and plastic forks). Overhead directly associated with a producing department, such as assembly in a furniture-making plant, would include utilities (if measured in that department), supervisory salaries, and depreciation of equipment used in that department. Overhead that cannot be easily assigned to a producing or support department is assigned to a catchall department such as general factory. General factory might include depreciation on the factory building, rental of a Santa Claus suit for the factory Christmas party, the cost of restriping the parking lot, the plant manager's salary, and telephone service. In this way, all costs are assigned to a department.

Exhibit 7-1 shows how a furniture-manufacturing firm and a bank (an example of a service firm) can be divided into producing and support departments. The furniture-manufacturing plant may be departmentalized into two producing departments (Assembly and Finishing) and four support departments (Materials Storeroom, Cafeteria, Maintenance, and General Factory). The bank might be departmentalized into three producing departments (Auto Loans, Commercial Lending, and Personal Banking) and three support departments (Drive-Thru, Data Processing, and Bank Administration). Overhead costs are traced to each department. Note that every overhead cost must be assigned to one, and only one, department.

Allocating Costs from Departments to Products

Once the company has been departmentalized and all overhead costs have been traced to the individual departments, support-department costs are assigned to producing departments, and overhead rates are developed to cost products.

Let's consider why this is done. Suppose that only the overhead directly traced to producing departments was assigned to products passing through those departments. The costs of the support departments would not be assigned to products since, by definition, products never pass through support departments. But we know that the costs of providing support services are part of the total product costs and must be assigned to the products. So, support-department costs must be allocated to producing departments.

Manufacturing Firm: Furniture Maker

Producing Departments	Support Departments
Assembly: Supervisory salaries Small tools Indirect materials Depreciation of machinery Finishing: Sandpaper Depreciation of sanders and buffers	Materials storeroom: Clerk's salary Depreciation of forklift Cafeteria: Food Cooks' salaries Depreciation of stoves Maintenance: Janitors' salaries Cleaning supplies Machine oil and lubricants General factory: Depreciation of building Security and utilities

Service Firm: Bank

Producing Departments	Support Departments
Auto loans: Loan processors' salaries Forms and supplies Commercial lending: Lending officers' salaries Depreciation of office equipment Bankruptcy prediction software Personal banking: Supplies and postage for statements	Drive-thru: Tellers' salaries Depreciation of equipment Data processing: Personnel salaries Software Depreciation of hardware Bank administration: Salary of CEO Receptionist's salary Telephone costs Depreciation of bank vault

Exhibit 7-1 Examples of Departmentalization for a Manufacturing Firm and a Service Firm

Departmental overhead rates are necessary because there are multiple products being worked on in each producing department. If there were only one product within a producing department, all the service costs allocated to that department would belong to that product. Recall that a predetermined overhead rate is computed by taking total estimated overhead for a department and dividing it by an estimate of an appropriate base. Now we see that a producing department's overhead consists of two parts: overhead directly traced to a producing department and overhead allocated to the producing department from the support departments. A support department cannot have an overhead rate that assigns overhead costs to units produced because it does not make a salable product. That is, products do not pass through support departments. The nature of support departments is to service producing departments, not the products that pass through the producing departments. For example, maintenance personnel repair and maintain the equipment in the Assembly Department, not the furniture that is assembled in that department. Exhibit 7-2 summarizes the steps involved.

Types of Allocation Bases

Producing departments require support services; therefore, the costs of support departments are caused by the activities of the producing departments. **Causal factors** are variables or activities within a producing department that provoke the incurrence of support service costs. In choosing a basis for allocating support-department costs, every effort should be made to identify appropriate causal factors (cost drivers). Using causal factors results in more accurate product costs. Furthermore, if the causal factors are known, managers can better control the consumption of support services.

To illustrate the types of cost drivers that can be used, consider the following three support departments: Power, Personnel, and Materials Handling. For power costs, a logical allocation base is kilowatt-hours, which can be measured by separate meters for each department. If separate meters do not exist, perhaps machine hours used by each department would provide a good proxy, or driver. For personnel costs, both the number of producing-department employees and the labor turnover (for example, number of new hires) are possible cost drivers. For materials handling, the number of material moves, the hours of material handling used, and the quantity of material moved are all possible cost drivers. Exhibit 7-3 lists some possible cost drivers that can be used to allocate support-department costs. When competing cost drivers exist, managers need to decide which one provides the most convincing relationship.

While the use of a causal factor to allocate common cost is the best, sometimes an easily measured causal factor cannot be found. In that case, the accountant looks for a good proxy. For example, the common cost of plant depreciation may be allocated to producing departments on the basis of square footage. Square footage does

1. Departmentalize the firm.
2. Classify each department as a support department or a producing department.
3. Trace all overhead costs in the firm to a support department or producing department.
4. Allocate support-department costs to the producing departments.
5. Calculate predetermined overhead rates for the producing departments.
6. Allocate overhead costs to the units of individual products through the predetermined overhead rates.

Exhibit 7-2 Steps in Allocating Support-Department Costs to Producing Departments

Accounting:	Payroll:
Number of transactions	Number of employees
Cafeteria:	Personnel:
Number of employees	Number of employees
Data processing:	Number of firings or layoffs
Number of lines entered	Number of new hires
Number of hours of service	Direct labor cost
Engineering:	Power:
Number of change orders	Kilowatt-hours
Number of hours	Machine hours
Maintenance:	Purchasing:
Machine hours	Number of orders
Maintenance hours	Cost of orders
Materials storeroom:	Shipping:
Number of material moves	Number of orders
Pounds of material moved	
Number of different parts	

Exhibit 7-3 Examples of Possible Cost Drivers for Support Departments

not cause depreciation; however, it can be argued that the number of square feet a department occupies is a good proxy for the services provided to it by the factory building. The choice of a good proxy to guide allocation is dependent upon the company's objectives for allocation.

Objectives of Allocation

A number of important objectives are associated with the allocation of support-department costs to producing departments and ultimately to specific products. The following major objectives have been identified by the IMA:[1]

1. To obtain a mutually agreeable price.
2. To compute product-line profitability.
3. To predict the economic effects of planning and control.
4. To value inventory.
5. To motivate managers.

Competitive pricing requires an understanding of costs. Only by knowing the costs of each service or product can the firm create meaningful bids. If costs are not accurately allocated, the costs of some services could be overstated, resulting in bids that are too high and a loss of potential business. Alternatively, if the costs are understated, bids could be too low, producing losses on these services.

Closely allied to pricing is profitability. Multiproduct companies need to be sure that all products are profitable and that the overall profitability of the firm is not disguising the poor performance of individual products.

By assessing the profitability of various services, a manager may evaluate the mix of services offered by the firm. From this evaluation, it may be decided to drop some services, reallocate resources from one service to another, reprice certain services, or exercise greater cost control in some areas. These steps would meet the IMA's planning and control objective. Of course, accurate costs are important to determining profit.

1 Statements of Management Accounting (Statement 4B), Allocation of Service and Administrative Costs (Montvale, N.J.: NAA, 1985). The NAA is now known as the Institute of Management Accountants (IMA).

For manufacturing organizations, inventory valuation can be important. Rules of financial reporting (GAAP)[2] require that direct manufacturing costs and all indirect manufacturing costs be assigned to the products produced. Inventories and cost of goods sold must include direct materials, direct labor, and all manufacturing overhead.

Allocations can be used to motivate managers. If the costs of support departments are not allocated to producing departments, managers may treat these services as if they were free. In reality, of course, the marginal cost of a service is greater than zero. By allocating the costs and holding managers of producing departments responsible for the economic performance of their units, the organization ensures that managers will use a service until the marginal benefit of the service equals its marginal cost. Thus, allocating service costs helps each producing department select the correct level of service consumption.

There are other behavioral benefits. Allocating support-department costs to producing departments encourages managers of those departments to monitor the performance of support departments. Since the costs of the support departments affect the economic performance of their own departments, those managers have an incentive to control service costs through means other than simple usage of the service. We can see this happening in the opening scenario as Gary compared the cost of in-house copying with external copy companies. If a support department is not as cost effective as an outside source, perhaps the company should discontinue supplying the service internally. For example, many university libraries are moving toward the use of outside contractors for photocopying services. They have found that these contractors are more cost efficient and provide a higher level of service to library users than did the previous method of using professional librarians to make change, keep the copy machines supplied with paper, fix paper jams, and so on. This possibility of comparison should result in a more efficient internal support department. Monitoring by managers of producing departments will also encourage managers of support departments to be more sensitive to the needs of the producing departments.

Clearly, then, there are good reasons for allocating support-department costs. The validity of these reasons, however, depends on the accuracy and fairness of the cost assignments made. Because support-department cost allocation feeds into overall producing department costs, and these costs are often used to determine profitability and departmental performance, the method of cost allocation can be of real interest to producing department managers. Ethically, the accountant should attempt to choose fair allocation methods. That means that, to the extent possible, the allocation base should be causally related to the cost under consideration. In addition, changing the allocation base can result in different dollar allocations. It is important to ensure that any changes are made for valid reasons, not in order to simply pump up profit margins to increase the price charged (see Problem 7-32 for an example of this), or to help a manager friend to obtain a larger bonus than he or she has earned.

Many college libraries outsource activities such as photocopying. This ensures that professional librarians can concentrate on their primary tasks of ordering and organizing books, and helping users.

ETHICS

2 Generally accepted accounting principles.

In determining how to allocate support-department costs, the guideline of cost-benefit must be considered. In other words, the costs of implementing a particular allocation scheme must be compared to the benefits to be derived. As a result, companies try to use easily measured and understood bases for allocation.

Allocating One Department's Costs to Another Department

Objective 2

Calculate single and multiple charging rates for a support department.

Frequently, the costs of a support department are allocated to other departments through the use of a charging rate. In this case, we focus on the allocation of one department's costs to other departments. For example, a company's Data-Processing Department may serve various other departments. The cost of operating the Data-Processing Department is then allocated to the user departments.

A Single Charging Rate

Some companies prefer to develop a single charging rate. Let's return to the case of Hamilton and Barry, the public accounting firm from the opening scenario. Recall that the firm developed an in-house Photocopying Department to serve its three producing departments (Audit, Tax, and Management Advisory Services, or MAS). The costs of the Photocopying Department include fixed costs of $26,190 per year (salaries and machine rental) and variable costs of $0.023 per page copied (paper and toner). Estimated usage (in pages) by the three producing departments is as follows:

Audit Department	94,500
Tax Department	67,500
MAS Department	108,000
Total	270,000

If a single charging rate is used, the fixed costs of $26,190 will be combined with estimated variable costs of $6,210 (270,000 × $0.023). Total costs of $32,400 are divided by the estimated 270,000 pages to be copied to yield a rate of $0.12 per page.

The amount charged to the producing departments is solely a function of the number of pages copied. Suppose that the actual usage is Audit, 92,000 pages; Tax, 65,000 pages; and MAS, 115,000 pages. The total Photocopying Department charges would be as shown.

	Number of Pages	×	Charge per Page	=	Total Charges
Audit	92,000		$0.12		$ 11,040
Tax	65,000		0.12		7,800
MAS	115,000		0.12		13,800
Total	272,000				$32,640

Notice that the use of a single rate results in the fixed cost being treated as if it were variable. In fact, to the producing departments, photocopying is strictly variable. Did the Photocopying Department need $32,640 to copy 272,000 pages? No, it needed only $32,446 [$26,190 + (272,000 × $0.023)]. The extra amount charged is due to the treatment of a fixed cost in a variable manner.[3] In the next section, we see how multiple charging rates can eliminate this problem.

3 Note that the Photocopying Department would have charged out less than the cost needed if the number of pages copied had been less than the budgeted number of pages. You might calculate the total cost charged for a total of 268,000 pages ($0.12 × 268,000 = $32,160) and compare it with the cost incurred of $32,354 [$26,190 + ($0.023 × 268,000)].

Multiple Charging Rates

Sometimes a single charging rate masks the variety of causal factors that lead to a support department's total costs. The Hamilton and Barry Photocopying Department is a good example. We saw that a single charging rate was based on the number of pages copied. Then, it looked like every page copied cost $0.12. But this is not true. A large portion of the costs of the Photocopying Department are fixed; they are not caused by the number of pages copied. Recall that $26,190 per year is spent on wages and rental of the photocopier. Why is this cost incurred? A talk with the photocopying company representative quickly yields the information that the size of the machine rented depends not on the number of pages copied per year, but on monthly peak usage. When Hamilton and Barry established the Photocopying Department, it must have surveyed the Audit, Tax, and MAS departments to determine each one's highest monthly usage. Let's assume that the Audit and MAS departments have fairly even copying needs throughout the year. In other words, these two departments anticipate needing 202,500 (94,500 + 108,000) copies per year and will average 16,875 per month. Since no one month is higher than the other, peak monthly usage for these two departments is also 16,875 copies. The Tax Department, however, anticipates a different pattern. Of its 67,500 budgeted yearly copies, it expects to need one-third, or 22,500 copies, in the month of April. Therefore, the peak usage in one month is expected to be 39,375 copies. It is this usage for which the size of the Photocopying Department is designed.

Now, we can develop two charging rates for the Photocopying Department. One is the variable rate for toner and paper. This is simply $0.023 per page. Of course, the causal factor is number of pages copied. The second rate is for the fixed cost of equipment rental and wages. This is assigned to the producing departments based on their planned peak usage.

	Peak Number of Pages	Proportion of Peak Usage	Total Fixed Costs	Amount Allocated to Each Department
Audit	7,875	0.20	$26,190	$ 5,238
Tax	22,500	0.57	26,190	14,928
MAS	9,000	0.23	26,190	6,024
Total	39,375			$26,190

The amount charged to the producing departments is now a function of both the number of pages copied and of the anticipated peak usage. Suppose that the actual usage is Audit, 92,000 pages; Tax, 65,000 pages; and MAS, 115,000 pages. The total Photocopying Department charges would be as shown.

	Number of Pages × $0.023	+	Fixed Cost Allocation	=	Total Charges
Audit	$2,116		$ 5,238		$ 7,354
Tax	1,495		14,928		16,423
MAS	2,645		6,024		8,669
Total	$6,256		$26,190		$32,446

Notice that the allocation of Photocopying Department costs is very different when the two charging rates are used. In this case, the Tax Department absorbs a larger proportion of the cost, because its peak usage is responsible for the size of the department. Notice, too, that the amount charged of $32,446 is very close to the actual cost of running the department. With the two charging rates, each one based on a strong causal factor, the allocation of cost to the using departments is clearly based on the amount of cost that they actually cause the support department.

Could there be more than two charging rates? Definitely. However, as a company breaks down support-department resources and causal factors more finely, it may be approaching activity-based costing. The extra precision of charging rates must be balanced against the cost of determining and applying those rates. As always, the company must consider costs and benefits.

Budgeted versus Actual Usage

When we allocate support-department costs to the producing departments, should we allocate actual or budgeted costs? The answer is budgeted costs. There are two basic reasons for allocating support-department costs. One is to cost units produced. In this case, the budgeted support-department costs are allocated to producing departments as a preliminary step in forming the overhead rate. Recall that the overhead rate is calculated at the beginning of the period, when actual costs are not known. Thus, budgeted costs must be used. The second usage of allocated support-department costs is for performance evaluation. In this case, too, budgeted support-department costs are allocated to producing departments.

Managers of support and producing departments usually are held accountable for the performance of their units. Their ability to control costs is an important factor in their performance evaluation. This ability is usually measured by comparing actual costs with planned or budgeted costs. If actual costs exceed budgeted costs, the department may be operating inefficiently, with the difference between the two costs the measure of that inefficiency. Similarly, if actual costs are less than budgeted costs, the unit may be operating efficiently.

A general principle of performance evaluation is that managers should not be held responsible for costs or activities over which they have no control. Since managers of producing departments have significant input regarding the level of service consumed, they should be held responsible for their share of service costs. This statement, however, has an important qualification: A department's evaluation should not be affected by the degree of efficiency achieved by another department.

This qualifying statement has an important implication for the allocation of support-department costs. Actual costs of a support department should not be allocated to producing departments, because they include efficiencies or inefficiencies achieved by the support department. Managers of producing departments have no control over the degree of efficiency achieved by a support-department manager. By allocating budgeted costs instead of actual costs, no inefficiencies or efficiencies are transferred from one department to another.

Whether budgeted usage or actual usage is used depends on the purpose of the allocation. For product costing, the allocation is done at the beginning of the year on the basis of budgeted usage so that a predetermined overhead rate can be computed. If the purpose is performance evaluation, however, the allocation is done at the end of the period and is based on actual usage. The use of cost information for performance evaluation is covered in more detail in Chapter 9, which covers "standard costing."

Let's return to our photocopying example. Recall that annual budgeted fixed costs were $26,190 and the budgeted variable cost per page was $0.023. The three producing departments—Audit, Tax, and MAS—estimated usage at 94,500 copies, 67,500 copies, and 108,000 copies, respectively. Given these data, the costs allocated to each department at the beginning of the year using a single charging rate are shown in Exhibit 7-4.

When the allocation is done for the purpose of budgeting the producing departments' costs, then, of course, the budgeted support-department costs are used. The photocopying costs allocated to each department would be added to other producing department costs, including those directly traceable to each department plus other support-department allocations, to compute each department's anticipated spending. In a manufacturing plant, the allocation of budgeted support-department

	Number of Copies	×	Total Rate	=	Allocated Cost
Audit	94,500		$0.12		$ 11,340
Tax	67,500		0.12		8,100
MAS	108,000		0.12		12,960
Total	270,000				$32,400

Exhibit 7-4 Use of Budgeted Data for Product Costing

costs to the producing departments would precede the calculation of the predetermined overhead rate.

During the year, each producing department would also be responsible for actual charges incurred based on the actual number of pages copied. Going back to the actual usage assumed previously, a second allocation is now made to measure the actual performance of each department against its budget. The actual photocopying costs allocated to each department for performance evaluation purposes are shown in Exhibit 7-5.

	Number of Copies	×	Total Rate	=	Allocated Cost
Audit	92,000		$0.12		$ 11,040
Tax	65,000		0.12		7,800
MAS	115,000		0.12		13,800
Total	272,000				$32,640

Exhibit 7-5 Use of Actual Data for Performance Evaluation Purposes

Choosing a Support-Department Cost Allocation Method

Objective 3

Allocate support-department costs to producing departments using the direct, sequential, and reciprocal methods.

So far, we have considered cost allocation from a single support department to several producing departments. We used the direct method of support department cost allocation, in which support-department costs are allocated only to producing departments. This was appropriate in the earlier example because no other support departments existed, and there was no possibility of interaction among support departments. Many companies do have multiple support departments, and they frequently interact. For example, in a factory, personnel and cafeteria serve each other and other support departments as well as the producing departments.

© Getty Images/PhotoDisc

Company cafeterias are support departments. All of the costs you can identify here are direct costs of the cafeteria, and will be allocated to the producing departments on the basis of (for example) number of employees.

Ignoring these interactions and allocating service costs directly to producing departments may produce unfair and inaccurate cost assignments. For example, Power, although a support department, may use 30 percent of the services of the Maintenance Department. The maintenance costs caused by the Power Department belong to the Power Department. By not assigning these costs to the Power Department, its costs are understated.

In effect, some of the costs caused by power are "hidden" in the Maintenance Department, because maintenance costs would be lower if the Power Department did not exist. As a result, a producing department that is a heavy user of power and an average or below-average user of maintenance may then receive, under the direct method, a cost allocation that is understated.

In determining which support-department cost allocation method to use, companies must determine the extent of support-department interaction. In addition, they must weigh the costs and benefits associated with three methods of allocating costs. In the next three sections, the direct, sequential, and reciprocal methods are described and illustrated.

Direct Method of Allocation

When companies allocate support-department costs only to the producing departments, they are using the **direct method** of allocation. The direct method is the simplest and most straightforward way to allocate support-department costs. Variable service costs are allocated directly to producing departments in proportion to each department's usage of the service. Fixed costs are also allocated directly to the producing department, but in proportion to the producing department's normal or practical capacity.

Exhibit 7-6 illustrates the lack of support-department reciprocity on cost allocation using the direct method. In Exhibit 7-6, we see that using the direct method, support-department cost is allocated to producing departments only. No cost from one support department is allocated to another support department. Thus, no support-department interaction is recognized.

Suppose there are two support departments, Power and Maintenance, and two producing departments, Grinding and Assembly, each with a "bucket" of directly traceable overhead cost.
Objective: Distribute all maintenance and power costs to Grinding and Assembly using the direct method.

Direct method—Allocate maintenance and power costs only to Grinding and Assembly.

After allocation—Zero cost in maintenance and power; all overhead cost is in Grinding and Assembly.

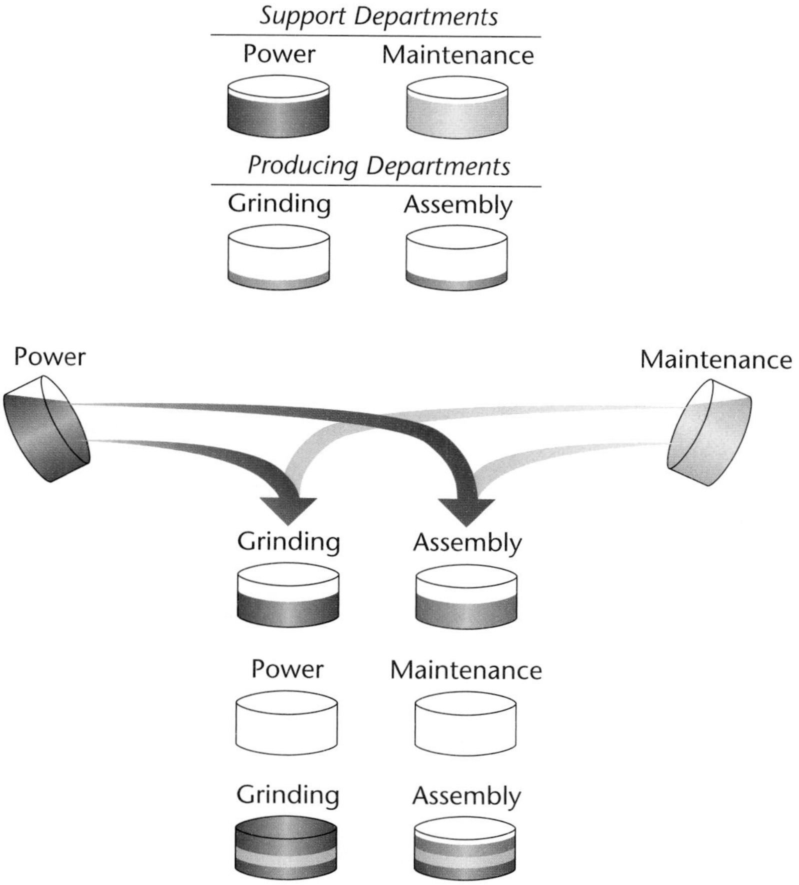

Exhibit 7-6 Allocation of Support-Department Costs to Producing Department: Direct Method

To illustrate the direct method, consider the data in Exhibit 7-7 that show the budgeted activity and budgeted costs of two support departments and two producing departments. Assume that the causal factor for power costs is kilowatt-hours and that the causal factor for maintenance costs is maintenance hours. These causal factors are used as the bases for allocation. In the direct method, only the kilowatt-hours and the maintenance hours in the producing departments are used to compute the allocation ratios. The direct method allocation ratios and the support-department cost allocations based on the data given in Exhibit 7-7 are shown in Exhibit 7-8. (To simplify the illustration, no distinction is made between fixed and variable costs.)

Sequential Method of Allocation

The **sequential (or step) method** of allocation recognizes that interactions among the support departments occur. However, the sequential method does not fully recognize support-department interaction. Cost allocations are performed in step-down fashion, following a predetermined ranking procedure. Usually, the sequence is defined by ranking the support departments in order of the amount of service rendered,

	Support Departments		Producing Departments	
	Power	Maintenance	Grinding	Assembly
Direct costs*	$250,000	$160,000	$100,000	$60,000
Normal activity:				
Kilowatt-hours	—	200,000	600,000	200,000
Maintenance hours	1,000	—	4,500	4,500

*For a producing department, direct costs refer only to overhead costs that are directly traceable to the department.

Exhibit 7-7 Data for Illustrating Allocation Methods

Step 1—Calculate Allocation Ratios

	Grinding	Assembly
Power: $\frac{600,000}{(600,000 + 200,000)}$	0.75	—
$\frac{200,000}{(600,000 + 200,000)}$	—	0.25
Maintenance: $\frac{4,500}{(4,500 + 4,500)}$	0.50	—
Maintenance: $\frac{4,500}{(4,500 + 4,500)}$	—	0.50

Step 2—Allocate Support-Department Costs Using the Allocation Ratios

	Support Departments		Producing Departments	
	Power	Maintenance	Grinding	Assembly
Direct costs	$ 250,000	$ 160,000	$100,000	$ 60,000
Power[a]	(250,000)	—	187,500	62,500
Maintenance[b]	—	(160,000)	80,000	80,000
	$ 0	$ 0	$367,500	$202,500

[a]Allocation of power based on allocation ratios from Step 1: 0.75 × 250,000; 0.25 × $250,000.
[b]Allocation of maintenance based on allocation ratios from Step 1: 0.50 × $160,000; 0.50 × $160,000.

Exhibit 7-8 Direct Allocation Illustrated

from the greatest to the least. Degree of service is usually measured by the direct costs of each support department; the department with the highest cost is seen as rendering the greatest service.

Exhibit 7-9 illustrates the sequential method. First, the support departments are ranked, usually in accordance with direct costs; here, Power is first, then Maintenance. Next, power costs are allocated to Maintenance and the two producing departments. Then, the costs of maintenance are allocated only to producing departments.

The costs of the support department rendering the greatest service are allocated first. They are distributed to all support departments below it in the sequence and to all producing departments. Then, the costs of the support department next in sequence are similarly allocated, and so on. In the sequential method, once a support department's costs are allocated, it never receives a subsequent allocation from another support department. In other words, costs of a support department are

Suppose there are two support departments, Power and Maintenance, and two producing departments, Grinding and Assembly, each with a "bucket" of directly traceable overhead cost.

Objective: Distribute all maintenance and power costs to Grinding and Assembly using the sequential method.

Step 1: Rank service departments—#1 Power, #2 Maintenance.

Step 2: Distribute power to Maintenance, Grinding, and Assembly.

Then, distribute maintenance to Grinding and Assembly.

After allocation—Zero cost in Maintenance and Power; all overhead cost is in Grinding and Assembly.

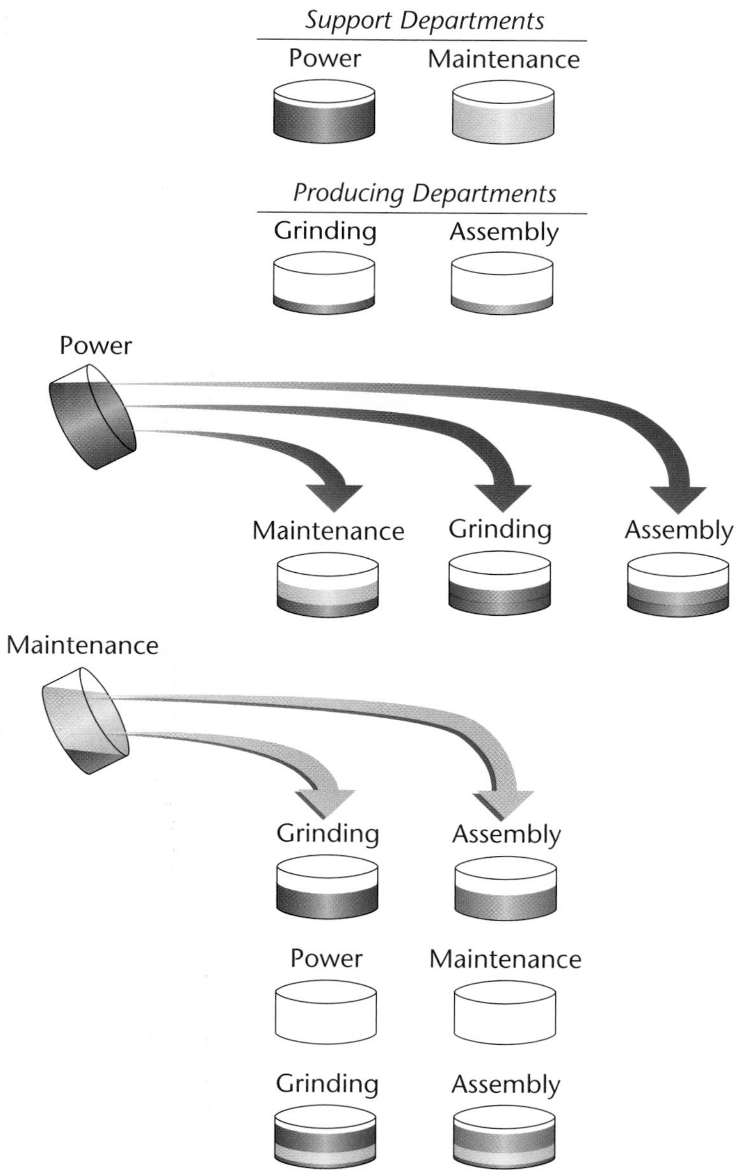

Exhibit 7-9 Allocation of Support-Department Costs to Producing Department: Sequential Method

never allocated to support departments above it in the sequence. Also, note that the costs allocated from a support department are its direct costs plus any costs it receives in allocations from other support departments. The direct costs of a department, of course, are those that are directly traceable to the department.

To illustrate the sequential method, consider the data provided in Exhibit 7-7. Using cost as a measure of service, the support department rendering more service is Power. Thus, its costs will be allocated first, followed by those for Maintenance.

The allocations obtained with the sequential method are shown in Exhibit 7-10. The first step is to compute the allocation ratios. Note that the allocation ratios for the Maintenance Department ignore the usage by the Power Department, since its costs cannot be allocated to a support department above it in the allocation sequence. The second step is to allocate the support-department costs using the allocation ratios computed in the first step. Notice that $50,000 of the Power Department's costs are allocated to the Maintenance Department. This reflects the fact that the Maintenance Department uses 20 percent of the Power Department's output. As a result, the cost of operating the Maintenance Department increases from $160,000 to $210,000. Also, notice that when the costs of the Maintenance Department are allocated, no costs are allocated back to the Power Department, even though it uses 1,000 hours of the output of the Maintenance Department.

The sequential method is more accurate than the direct method because it recognizes some interactions among the support departments. It does not recognize all interactions, however; no maintenance costs were assigned to the Power Department even though it used 10 percent of the Maintenance Department's output. The reciprocal method corrects this deficiency.

Step 1—Calculate Allocation Ratios

		Maintenance	Grinding	Assembly
Power:	$\frac{200,000}{(200,000 + 600,000 + 200,000)}$	0.20	—	—
	$\frac{600,000}{(200,000 + 600,000 + 200,000)}$	—	0.60	—
	$\frac{200,000}{(200,000 + 600,000 + 200,000)}$	—	—	0.20
Maintenance:	$\frac{4,500}{(4,500 + 4,500)}$	—	0.50	—
Maintenance:	$\frac{4,500}{(4,500 + 4,500)}$	—	—	0.50

Step 2—Allocate Support-Department Costs Using the Allocation Ratios

	Support Departments		Producing Departments	
	Power	Maintenance	Grinding	Assembly
Direct costs	$ 250,000	$ 160,000	$100,000	$ 60,000
Power[a]	(250,000)	50,000	150,000	50,000
Maintenance[b]	—	(210,000)	105,000	105,000
	$ 0	$ 0	$355,000	$215,000

[a]Allocation of power based on allocation ratios from Step 1: 0.20 × $250,000; 0.60 × $250,000; 0.20 × $250,000.

[b]Allocation of maintenance costs based on allocation ratios from Step 1: 0.50 × $210,000; 0.50 × $210,000.

Exhibit 7-10 Sequential Allocation Illustrated

Managers Decide

Medicare Recognizes the Importance of Support Department Cost Allocation

Since 1966, Medicare has required all health care providers to allocate the costs of service departments to revenue producing departments. The Medicare cost report requires that health care providers use the step-down (sequential) method or the double-apportionment method (which is a two-stage variation of the step-down method) to calculate operating costs for patient care departments. Health care organizations rarely use the direct method because service departments provide many services to other departments and because the direct method is not allowed on Medicare cost reports. The Medicare guideline for the step-down method requires that the order of the sequence be from the service center that renders the greatest service to the least. The magnitude of service is determined by the number of other centers served. If two centers render service to an equal number of centers, then the center with the greatest amount of expense is allocated first. ■

Source: Provider Reimbursement Manual: Part I, Chapter 23, http://www.cms.hhs.gov, accessed March 2006.

Reciprocal Method of Allocation

The **reciprocal method** of allocation recognizes all interactions among support departments. Under the reciprocal method, one support department's use by another figures in determining the total cost of each support department, where the total cost reflects interactions among the support departments. Then, the new total of support-department costs is allocated to the producing departments. This method fully accounts for support-department interaction.

Total Cost of Support Departments To determine the total cost of a support department so that it reflects interactions with other support departments, a system of simultaneous linear equations must be solved. Each equation, which is a cost equation for a support department, is defined as the sum of the department's direct costs plus the proportion of service received from other support departments:

$$\text{Total cost} = \text{Direct costs} + \text{Allocated costs}$$

This method is best described using an example, employing the same data used to illustrate the direct and sequential methods (see Exhibit 7-11). The allocation ratios needed for the simultaneous equations are interpreted as follows: Maintenance receives 20 percent of Power's output; Power receives 10 percent of Maintenance's output. Now, let P equal the total cost of the Power Department and M equal the total cost of the Maintenance Department. As previously indicated, the total cost of a support department is the sum of its direct costs plus the proportion of service received from other support departments. Using the data and allocation ratios from Exhibit 7-11, the cost equation for each support department can be expressed as follows:

$$\begin{aligned} P &= \text{Direct costs} + \text{Share of Maintenance's costs} && (7.1)\\ &= \$250{,}000 + 0.1M \text{ (Power's cost equation)} \\ M &= \text{Direct costs} + \text{Share of Power's costs} && (7.2)\\ &= \$160{,}000 + 0.2P \text{ (Maintenance's cost equation)} \end{aligned}$$

The direct-cost components of each equation are taken from Exhibit 7-11, as are the allocation ratios.

	Support Departments		Producing Departments	
	Power	Maintenance	Grinding	Assembly
Direct costs:*	$250	$160	$100,000	$60,000
Normal activity:				
Kilowatt-hours	—	200,000	600,000	200,000
Maintenance hours	1,000	—	4,500	4,500
	Proportion of Output Used by Department			
	Power	Maintenance	Grinding	Assembly
Allocation ratios:				
Power	—	0.20	0.60	0.20
Maintenance	0.10	—	0.45	0.45

*For a producing department, direct costs are defined as overhead costs that are directly traceable to the department.

Exhibit 7-11 Data for Illustrating Reciprocal Method

The Power cost equation (Equation 7.1) and the Maintenance cost equation (Equation 7.2) can be solved simultaneously to yield the total cost for each support department. Substituting Equation 7.1 into Equation 7.2 gives the following:

$$\begin{aligned} M &= \$160{,}000 + 0.2(\$250{,}000 + 0.1M) \\ M &= \$160{,}000 + \$50{,}000 + 0.02M \\ 0.98M &= \$210{,}000 \\ M &= \$214{,}286 \end{aligned}$$

Substituting this value for M into Equation 7.1 yields the total cost for Power:

$$\begin{aligned} P &= \$250{,}000 + 0.1(\$214{,}286) \\ &= \$250{,}000 + \$21{,}429 \\ &= \$271{,}429 \end{aligned}$$

After the equations are solved, the total costs of each support department are known. These total costs, in contrast to the direct or sequential methods, reflect all interactions between the two support departments.

Allocation to Producing Departments Once the total costs of each support department are known, the allocations to the producing departments can be made. These allocations, based on the proportion of output used by each producing department, are shown in Exhibit 7-12. Notice that the total costs allocated to the producing departments (from Power and Maintenance) equal $410,000, the total direct costs of the two support departments ($250,000 + $160,000). (Actually, the total allocated costs equal $410,001, but the difference is due to a rounding error.)

Comparison of the Three Methods

Exhibit 7-13 gives the cost allocations from the Power and Maintenance departments to the Grinding and Assembly departments using the three support-department cost allocation methods. How different are the results? Does it really matter which method is used? Depending on the degree of interaction among the support departments, the three allocation methods can give radically different results. In this particular example, the direct method allocated $12,500 more to the Grinding Department (and $12,500 less to the Assembly Department) than the sequential method did. Surely, the manager of the Assembly Department would prefer the direct method,

Allocate Support-Department Costs Using the Allocation Ratios (Exhibit 7-11) and the Total Support-Department Costs from Reciprocal Method Equations

	Support Departments		Producing Departments	
	Power	Maintenance	Grinding	Assembly
Direct costs	$ 250,000	$ 160,000	$ 100,000	$ 60,000
Power[a]	(271,429)	54,286	162,857	54,286
Maintenance[b]	21,429	(214,286)	96,429	96,429
	$ 0	$ 0	$359,286	$210,715

[a]Power: 0.20 × $271,429; 0.60 × $271,429; 0.20 × $271,429.
[b]Maintenance: 0.10 × $214,286; 0.45 × $214,286; 0.45 × $214,286.

Exhibit 7-12 Reciprocal Allocation Illustrated

and the manager of the Grinding Department would prefer the sequential method. Because allocation methods do affect the cost responsibilities of managers, it is important for the accountant to understand the consequences of the different methods and to have good reasons for the eventual choice.

It is important to keep a cost-benefit perspective in choosing an allocation method. The accountant must weigh the advantages of better allocation against the increased cost of using a more theoretically preferred method, such as the reciprocal method. For example, about 20 years ago, the controller for the **IBM** Poughkeepsie plant decided that the reciprocal method of cost allocation would do a better job of allocating support-department costs. He identified more than 700 support departments and solved the system of equations using a computer. Computationally, he had no problems. However, the producing-department managers did not understand the reciprocal method. They were sure that extra cost was being allocated to their departments; they just were not sure how. After months of meetings with the line managers, the controller threw in the towel and returned to the sequential method—which everyone did understand.

Another factor in allocating support-department cost is the rapid change in technology. Many firms currently find that support-department cost allocation is useful for them. However, the move toward activity-based costing and just-in-time manufacturing can virtually eliminate the need for support-department cost allocation. In the case of a JIT factory with manufacturing cells, much of the service (for example, maintenance, material handling, and setups) is performed by cell workers. (Recall that a manufacturing cell is a "factory within a factory" that is devoted to the production of one product from start to finish.) Allocation is not necessary.

	Direct Method		Sequential Method		Reciprocal Method	
	Grinding	Assembly	Grinding	Assembly	Grinding	Assembly
Direct costs	$100,000	$ 60,000	$100,000	$ 60,000	$100,000	$ 60,000
Allocated from power	187,500	62,500	150,000	50,000	162,857	54,286
Allocated from maintenance	80,000	80,000	105,000	105,000	96,429	96,429
Total cost	$367,500	$202,500	$355,000	$215,000	$359,286	$210,715

Exhibit 7-13 Comparison of Support-Department Cost Allocations Using the Direct, Sequential, and Reciprocal Methods

Departmental Overhead Rates and Product Costing

Objective 4

Compute departmental overhead rates.

Upon allocating all support costs to producing departments, an overhead rate can be computed for each department. This rate is computed by adding the allocated support costs to the overhead costs that are directly traceable to the producing department and dividing this total by some measure of activity, such as direct labor hours or machine hours.

For example, from Exhibit 7-10, the total overhead costs for the Grinding Department after allocation of support costs are $355,000. Assume that machine hours are the base for assigning overhead costs to products passing through the Grinding Department and that the normal level of activity is 71,000 machine hours. The overhead rate for the Grinding Department is computed as follows:

Overhead rate = $355,000/71,000 machine hours = $5 per machine hour

Similarly, assume that the Assembly Department uses direct labor hours to assign its overhead. With a normal level of activity of 107,500 direct labor hours, the overhead rate for the Assembly Department is as follows:

Overhead rate = $215,000/107,500 direct labor hours = $2 per direct labor hour

Using these rates, the product's unit cost can be determined. To illustrate, suppose a product requires two machine hours of grinding per unit produced and one hour of assembly. The overhead cost assigned to one unit of this product would be $12 [(2 × $5) + (1 × $2)]. If the same product uses $15 of materials and $6 of labor (totaled from Grinding and Assembly), then its total unit cost is $33 ($12 + $15 + $6).

One might wonder, however, just how accurate this $33 cost is. Is this really what it costs to produce the product in question? Since materials and labor are directly traceable to products, the accuracy of product costs depends largely on the accuracy of the assignment of overhead costs. This, in turn, depends on the degree of correlation between the factors used to allocate service costs to departments and the factors used to allocate the department's overhead costs to the products. For example, if power costs are highly correlated with kilowatt-hours and machine hours are highly correlated with a product's consumption of the Grinding Department's overhead costs, then we can have some confidence that the $5 overhead rate accurately assigns costs to individual products. However, if either the allocation of service costs to the Grinding Department or the use of machine hours is faulty—or both are faulty—then product costs will be distorted. The same reasoning can be applied to the Assembly Department. To ensure accurate product costs, great care should be used in identifying and using causal factors for both stages of overhead assignment.

Proper allocation of the costs of oil and gas pipelines is necessary to appropriately charge pipeline users for the cost of the service.

Appendix: Joint Cost Allocation

Objective 5

Describe the allocation of joint costs to products.

When two or more products are produced simultaneously by the same process up to a "split-off" point, they are called **joint products**. The **split-off point** is the point at which the joint products become separate and identifiable. For example, oil and natural gas are joint products. When a company drills for oil, it gets natural gas as well. The costs of exploration, acquisition of mineral rights, and drilling are incurred to the initial split-off point. Such costs are necessary to bring crude oil and natural gas out of the ground, and they are common costs to both products. Of course, some joint products may require processing beyond the split-off point. For example, crude oil can be processed further into aviation fuel, gasoline, kerosine, naptha, and other petrochemicals. The key point is that the direct materials, direct labor, and overhead costs incurred up to the initial split-off point are joint costs that can be allocated to the final product only in some arbitrary manner. Exhibit 7-14 depicts the joint production process.

Accounting for Joint Product Costs

The accounting for overall joint costs of production (direct materials, direct labor, and overhead) is no different from the accounting for product costs in general. It is the *allocation* of joint costs to the individual products that is the source of difficulty. The allocation must be done for income tax and financial reporting purposes—to value inventory carried on the balance sheet and to determine income. Thus, an allocation method must be found that, though arbitrary, allocates the costs on as reasonable a basis as possible. Because judgment is involved, equally competent accountants can arrive at different costs for the same product. There are a variety of methods for allocating joint costs. These methods include the physical units method, the sales-value-at-split-off method, and the net realizable value method.

Physical Units Method Under the **physical units method**, joint costs are distributed to products on the basis of some physical measure. These physical measures may be expressed in units such as pounds, tons, gallons, board feet, atomic weight, or heat units.

Computationally, the physical units method allocates to each joint product the same proportion of joint cost as the underlying proportion of units. So, if a joint process yields 300 pounds of Product A and 700 pounds of Product B, Product A receives 30 percent of the joint cost and Product B receives 70 percent. An alternative computation is to divide total joint costs by total output to find an average unit cost. The average unit cost is then multiplied by the number of units of each product. Although the method is not wholly satisfactory, it has a measure of logic behind it. Since all products are manufactured by the same process, it is impossible to say that one costs more per unit to produce than the other.

For example, suppose that a sawmill processes logs into four grades of lumber totaling 3,000,000 board feet as follows.

Exhibit 7-14 Joint Production Process

First and second	450,000
No. 1 common	1,200,000
No. 2 common	600,000
No. 3 common	750,000
Total	3,000,000

Total joint cost is $186,000. Using the physical units method, how much joint cost is allocated to each grade of lumber? First, we find the proportion of the total units for each grade; then, we assign each grade its proportion of joint cost.

	Units	Percent of Units	Joint Cost Allocation
First and second	450,000	0.15	$ 27,900
No. 1 common	1,200,000	0.40	74,400
No. 2 common	600,000	0.20	37,200
No. 3 common	750,000	0.25	46,500
Totals	3,000,000		$186,000

The physical units method presumes that each unit of material in the final product costs just as much to produce as any other. This is especially true where the dominant element can be traced to the product.

Sales-Value-at-Split-Off Method The **sales-value-at-split-off method** allocates joint cost based on each product's proportionate share of sales value at the split-off point. Under this method, the higher the market value, the greater the share of joint cost charged against the product. As long as the prices at split-off are stable, or the fluctuations in prices of the various products are synchronized (not necessarily in amount, but in the rate of change), their respective allocated costs remain constant.

Using the same example of lumber mill costs given in the preceding discussion of the physical units method, the joint cost of $186,000 is distributed to the various grades on the basis of their market value at split-off.

	Units	Price at Split-off	Sales Value at Split-off	Percent	Allocated Joint Cost
First and second	450,000	$300	$135,000	0.2699	$ 50,201
No. 1 common	1,200,000	200	240,000	0.4799	89,261
No. 2 common	600,000	121	72,600	0.1452	27,007
No. 3 common	750,000	70	52,500	0.1050	19,530
Totals	3,000,000		$500,100		$185,999*

*Does not sum to $186,000 due to rounding.

Note that the joint cost is allocated in proportion to sales value at the split-off point. No. 1 common, for example, is valued at $240,000 at split-off, and that amount is 47.99 percent of the total sales value. Therefore, 47.99 percent of total joint cost is assigned to the No. 1 common grade.

Net Realizable Value Method When market value is used to allocate joint costs, we are talking about market value *at the split-off point.* However, on occasion, there is no ready market price for the individual products at the split-off point. In this case, the net realizable value method can be used. First, we obtain a **hypothetical sales value** for each joint product by subtracting all separable (or further) processing costs from the eventual market value. This approximates the sales value at split-off. Then, the **net realizable value method** can be used to prorate the joint costs based on each product's share of hypothetical sales value.

Suppose that a company manufactures two products, Alpha and Beta, from a joint process. One production run costs $5,750 and results in 1,000 gallons of Alpha and 3,000 gallons of Beta. Neither product is salable at split-off, but must be further processed such that the separable cost for Alpha is $1 per gallon and for Beta is $2 per gallon. The eventual market price for Alpha is $5 and for Beta, $4. Joint cost allocation using the net realizable value method is as follows:

	Price	Further Processing Cost	Hypothetical Market Price	Number of Units	Hypothetical Market Value	Allocated Joint Cost
Alpha	$5	$1	$4	1,000	$ 4,000	$2,300
Beta	4	2	2	3,000	6,000	3,450
					$10,000	$5,750

Note that joint cost is allocated on the basis of each product's share of hypothetical market value. Thus, Alpha receives 40 percent of the joint cost ($2,300) because it accounts for 40 percent of the hypothetical market value. The net realizable value method is particularly useful when one or more products cannot be sold at the split-off point but must be processed further.

By-Products Joint production processes result in the output of two or more products which are produced simultaneously. Joint or main products have relatively significant sales value. **By-products** have relatively less significant sales value. Typically, by-products are not allocated any of the joint product costs. Instead, by-product sales may be listed as "Other income" on the income statement, or they may be treated as a credit to Work In Process of the main product(s).

Summary of Learning Objectives

1. Describe the difference between support departments and producing departments.

Producing departments create the products or services that the firm is in business to manufacture and sell. Support departments provide support for the producing departments but do not create a salable product themselves. Because support departments exist to support a variety of producing departments, the costs of the support departments are common to all producing departments.

The reasons for support-department cost allocation include inventory valuation, product-line profitability, pricing, and planning and control. Allocation can also be used to encourage favorable managerial behavior.

2. Calculate single and multiple charging rates for a support department.

When the costs of one support department are allocated to other departments, a charging rate must be developed. A single rate combines variable and fixed costs of the support department to generate a charging rate.

When multiple rates are used, a separate rate is computed for each type of resource based on a causal factor. Then, actual usage of each type of causal factor is multiplied by the appropriate rate to get the amount of support-department cost to be allocated.

Budgeted, not actual, costs should be allocated so that the efficiencies or inefficiencies of the support departments themselves are not passed on to the producing departments.

3. Allocate support-department costs to producing departments using the direct, sequential, and reciprocal methods.

Three methods can be used to allocate support costs to producing departments: the direct method, the sequential method, and the reciprocal method. They differ in the degree of support-department interaction considered. By considering support-department interactions, more accurate product costing is achieved. The result can be improved planning, control, and decision making. Two methods of allocation recognize interactions among support departments: the sequential (or step) method and the reciprocal method. These methods allocate service costs among some (or all) interacting support departments before allocating costs to the producing departments.

4. Compute departmental overhead rates.
Departmental overhead rates are calculated by adding direct departmental overhead costs to those costs allocated from the support departments and dividing the sum by the budgeted departmental base.

5. (Appendix) Describe the allocation of joint costs to products.
Joint production processes result in the output of two or more products which are produced simultaneously. Joint or main products have relatively significant sales value. By-products have relatively less sales value. Joint costs must be allocated to the individual products for purposes of financial reporting. Several methods have been developed to allocate joint costs, including the physical units method, the sales-value-at-split-off method, and the net realizable value method. Typically, by-products are not allocated any of the joint product costs. Instead, by-product sales are listed as "Other income" on the income statement, or they are treated as a credit to Work In Process of the main product(s).

Key Terms

By-product, 291
Causal factors, 274
Common costs, 272
Direct method, 281
Hypothetical sales value, 290
Joint product, 289
Net realizable value method, 291
Physical units method, 289
Producing departments, 272
Reciprocal method, 285
Sales-value-at-split-off method, 290
Sequential (or step) method, 282
Split-off point, 289
Support departments, 272

Review Problems

1. Allocation of Support-Department Costs Using the Direct, Sequential, and Reciprocal Methods

Antioch Manufacturing produces machine parts on a job-order basis. Most business is obtained through bidding. Most firms competing with Antioch bid full cost plus a 20 percent markup. Recently, with the expectation of gaining more sales, Antioch reduced its markup from 25 percent to 20 percent. The company operates two support departments and two producing departments. The budgeted costs and the normal activity levels for each department follow.

	Support Departments		Producing Departments	
	A	B	C	D
Overhead costs	$100,000	$200,000	$100,000	$50,000
Number of employees	8	7	30	30
Maintenance hours	2,000	200	6,400	1,600
Machine hours	—	—	10,000	1,000
Labor hours	—	—	1,000	10,000

The direct costs of Department A are allocated on the basis of employees, while those of Department B are based on maintenance hours. Departmental overhead rates are used to assign costs to products. Department C uses machine hours, and Department D uses labor hours.

The firm is preparing to bid on a job (Job K) that requires three machine hours per unit produced in Department C and no time in Department D. The expected prime costs (direct materials and direct labor) per unit are $67.

Required

1. Allocate the support costs to the producing departments using the direct method.
2. What will the bid be for Job K if the direct method of allocation is used?
3. Allocate the support costs to the producing departments using the sequential method.
4. What will the bid be for Job K if the sequential method is used?
5. Allocate the support costs to the producing departments using the reciprocal method.
6. What will the bid be for Job K if the reciprocal method is used?

Solution

1.

	Support Departments		Producing Departments	
	A	**B**	**C**	**D**
Direct costs	$100,000	$200,000	$100,000	$ 50,000
Department A	(100,000)	—	50,000[a]	50,000[a]
Department B	—	(200,000)	160,000[b]	40,000[c]
Total	$ 0	$ 0	$310,000	$140,000

[a]$50,000 = (30/60) × $100,000
[b]$160,000 = (6,400/8,000) × $200,000
[c]$40,000 = (1,600/8,000) × $200,000

2. Department C: Overhead rate = $310,000/10,000 = $31 per machine hour. Product cost and bid price:

Prime cost	$ 67
Overhead (3 × $31)	93
Total unit cost	$160
Bid price ($160 × 1.2)	$192

3.

	Support Departments		Producing Departments	
	A	**B**	**C**	**D**
Direct costs	$100,000	$200,000	$ 100,000	$ 50,000
Department B	40,000[a]	(200,000)	128,000[b]	32,000[c]
Department A	(140,000)	—	70,000[d]	70,000[d]
Total	$ 0	$ 0	$298,000	$152,000

[a]$40,000 = (2,000/10,000) × $200,000
[b]$128,000 = (6,400/10,000) × $200,000
[c]$32,000 = (1,600/10,000) × $200,000
[d]$70,000 = (30/60) × $140,000

4. Department C: Overhead rate = $298,000/10,000 = $29.80 per machine hour. Product cost and bid price:

Prime cost	$ 67.00
Overhead (3 × $29.80)	89.40
Total unit cost	$156.40
Bid price ($156.40 × 1.2)	$187.68

5. Allocation ratios:

	Proportion of Output Used by Department			
	A	B	C	D
A	—	0.1045	0.4478	0.4478
B	0.2000	—	0.6400	0.1600

$A = \$100{,}000 + 0.2000B$
$B = \$200{,}000 + 0.1045A$

$$\begin{aligned} A &= \$100{,}000 + 0.2(\$200{,}000 + 0.1045A) \\ A &= \$100{,}000 + \$40{,}000 + 0.0209A \\ 0.9791A &= \$140{,}000 \\ A &= \$142{,}988 \\ B &= \$200{,}000 + 0.1045(\$142{,}988) \\ B &= \$214{,}942 \end{aligned}$$

6.

	Support Departments		Producing Departments	
	A	B	C	D
Direct costs	$100,000	$200,000	$100,000	$ 50,000
Department B	42,988	(214,942)	137,563	34,391
Department A	(143,002)	14,942	64,030	64,030
Total	$ (14)	$ 0	$301,593	$148,421

The ($14) remaining in Department A is the result of a rounding error.

7. Department C: Overhead rate = $301,593/10,000 = $30.16 per machine hour.

Product cost and bid price:

Prime cost	$ 67.00
Overhead (3 × $30.16)	90.48
Total unit cost	$157.48
Bid price ($157.48 × 1.2)	$188.98

2. Allocating Joint Product Costs

Sanders Pharmaceutical Company purchases a material that is then processed to yield three chemicals: anarol, estyl, and betryl. In June, Sanders purchased 10,000 gallons of the material at a cost of $250,000, and the company incurred joint conversion costs of $70,000. June sales and production information are as follows:

	Gallons Produced	Price at Split-Off	Further Processing Cost per Gallon	Eventual Sales Price
Anarol	2,000	$55	—	—
Estyl	3,000	40	—	—
Betryl	5,000	30	$5	$60

Anarol and estyl are sold to other pharmaceutical companies at the split-off point. Betryl can be sold at the split-off point or processed further and packaged for sale as an asthma medication.

Required:

Allocate the joint costs to the three products using the

1. physical units method
2. sales-value-at-split-off method
3. net realizable value method

Solution

1. Total joint cost to be allocated = $250,000 + $70,000 = $320,000

Physical Units Method:

	Gallons Produced	Percent of Gallons Produced	×	Joint Cost	=	Joint Cost Allocation
Anarol	2,000	(2,000/10,000) = 0.20		$320,000		$ 64,000
Estyl	3,000	(3,000/10,000) = 0.30		320,000		96,000
Betryl	5,000	(5,000/10,000) = 0.50		320,000		160,000
Total	10,000					$320,000

2. Sales-Value-at-Split-Off Method:

	Gallons Produced	Price at Split-Off	Revenue at Split-Off	Percent of Revenue	×	Joint Cost	Joint Cost Allocation
Anarol	2,000	$55	$110,000	0.28947		$320,000	$ 92,630
Estyl	3,000	40	120,000	0.31579		320,000	101,053
Betryl	5,000	30	150,000	0.39474		320,000	126,317
Total			$380,000				$320,000

3. Net Realizable Value Method:

Step 1: Determine hypothetical sales revenue.

	Eventual Price	−	Further Processing Cost per Gallon	+	Hypothetical Sales Price	×	Gallons	+	Hypothetical Revenue
Anarol	$55		—		$55		2,000		$ 110,000
Estyl	40		—		40		3,000		120,000
Betryl	60		$5		55		5,000		275,000
Total									$505,000

Step 2: Allocate joint cost as a proportion of hypothetical sales revenue.

	Hypothetical Sales Revenue	Percent	×	Joint Cost	=	Joint Cost Allocation
Anarol	$ 110,000	0.21782		$320,000		$ 69,702
Estyl	120,000	0.23762		320,000		76,039*
Betryl	275,000	0.54456*		320,000		174,259
Total margin	$505,000					$320,000

*Rounded up.

Questions for Writing and Discussion

1. Describe the two-stage allocation process for assigning support-department costs to products in a functional manufacturing environment.
2. Explain how allocating support-department costs can be helpful in pricing decisions.
3. Why must support-department costs be assigned to products for purposes of inventory valuation?
4. Explain how allocation of support-department costs is useful for planning and control.
5. Assume that a company has decided not to allocate any support-department costs to producing departments. Describe the likely behavior of the managers of the producing departments. Would this be good or bad? Explain why allocation would correct this type of behavior.
6. Explain how allocating support-department costs will encourage support departments to operate more efficiently.
7. Why is it important to identify and use causal factors to allocate support-department costs?
8. Identify some possible causal factors for the following support departments:
   a. Cafeteria
   b. Custodial Services
   c. Laundry
   d. Receiving, Shipping, and Storage
   e. Maintenance
   f. Personnel
   g. Accounting
9. Explain why it is better to allocate budgeted support-department costs rather than actual support-department costs.
10. Explain the difference between the direct method and the sequential method.
11. The reciprocal method of allocation is more accurate than either the direct or sequential methods. Do you agree? Explain.
12. What is a joint cost? How does it relate to by-products?
13. How do joint costs differ from other common costs?

Exercises

7-1

Classifying Manufacturing Departments as Producing or Support
LO1

Classify each of the following departments in a factory as a producing department or a support department.

a. Payroll
b. Quality Control
c. Cooking
d. Packaging
e. Data Processing
f. Engineering
g. Drilling
h. Cutting
i. Power
j. Equipment Maintenance
k. Finishing
l. Landscaping
m. Blending
n. General Factory
o. Timekeeping

7-2

Classifying Service Firm Departments as Producing or Support
LO1

Classify each of the following departments in a hospital as a producing department or a support department.

a. Janitorial Staff
b. Laundry
c. Courier (runner goes from floor to floor, picking up and delivering interdepartmental mail and delivering patient specimens to the lab)
d. Landscaping

e. Payroll
f. Operating Rooms
g. Laboratory
h. Medical Records
i. Admitting
j. Radiology
k. Pediatrics
l. Data Processing
m. Supplies
n. Purchasing
o. Billing

7-3

Identifying Causal Factors
LO1

For the following support departments, identify one or more causal factors that might be useful for support-department cost allocation purposes.

a. Supervision
b. Data Processing
c. Quality Control
d. Purchasing
e. Receiving
f. Shipping
g. Vending (stocking snack machines throughout the plant)
h. Grounds
i. Building Depreciation
j. Power and Light
k. Employee Benefits
l. Housekeeping
m. Equipment Repair
n. Heating and Cooling

7-4

Single Charging Rate
LO2

Stewart Larson manages five apartment houses in a college town. A local attorney agreed to provide legal services on an as-needed basis for $80 per hour. Based on the past two years' experience, Stewart and the attorney estimated that 100 hours would be needed annually for help with matters such as the wording of leases or the pursuit of a court claim against a nonpaying tenant.

Stewart wanted to charge the apartment building owners for legal assistance by levying a monthly charge. However, he had no good idea of how many hours each owner would use. Deciding that the number of units in each apartment house would be a good proxy for use of legal services, Stewart determined that a single charging rate based on number of units would be reasonable. The number of units for each apartment building is as follows:

The Roost	130
Magnolia House	70
Oak Park	120
Wisteria Lane	50
Elm Street	30
Total	400

By the end of the first year, the actual usage of legal hours was: The Roost, 35; Magnolia House, 10; Oak Park, 45; Wisteria Lane, 15; and Elm Street, 25.

Required

1. Calculate a charging rate for legal services based on number of apartment units.
2. What was the total amount charged by the attorney to Stewart Larson by the end of the first year? What was the amount charged to each of the apartment owners

using the charging rate computed in Requirement 1? How much would have been charged to each apartment owner if actual usage of legal hours had been the basis?

3. Which base is better for charging legal services—number of units or number of hours of legal service? Why?

7-5

Single Charging Rate LO2, LO3

EXCEL

Agador Auto Dealers has three producing departments: New Car Sales, Used Car Sales, and Service. The Service Department provides service to both outside customers and to the New and Used Car departments. Agador charges the New and Used Car departments for their use of the Service Department. It seems fair to charge each department for the cost of actual direct materials used (e.g., oil and engine parts) and to develop a single charging rate for direct labor and overhead.

Assume the following budgeted amounts for the Service Department for the year:

Direct labor hours	24,000
Direct labor cost	$320,000
Overhead cost	$400,000

Actual materials and direct labor hours (DLH) incurred by the Service Department during the year are:

	Materials	Actual DLH
New Car Sales Department	$ 3,100	1,000
Used Car Sales Department	7,860	4,700
Service Department—outside customers	86,300	19,400
Total	$97,260	25,100

Required

1. Calculate the single charging rate per hour of labor.
2. Suppose that the Used Car Sales Department gets a 2001 Ford Ranger as a trade-in that needs general maintenance and some transmission work. The Service Department spends twelve hours working on the car and uses $517 of parts. Calculate the charge to the Used Car Sales Department by the Service Department.
3. Calculate the total costs charged by the Service Department to each of the producing departments for the year.

7-6

Single Charging Rate LO2

Pollard Company charges all of its departments and manufacturing cells for the use of machine maintenance services. Budgeted maintenance costs for the year are $193,200, and budgeted maintenance hours are 4,200. By the end of the year, total actual maintenance hours equal 4,110, and actual costs are $190,060.

Required

1. Calculate the billing rate for machine maintenance.
2. If the small motor cell used 370 maintenance hours during the year, what was the cell charged for maintenance services?
3. Were the departments and cells (taken as a whole) over- or undercharged for the actual costs of machine maintenance, and by how much?

7-7

Multiple Charging Rates LO2

Refer to **Exercise 7-6**. Several departments complained that they were being overcharged for maintenance. The manager of the Assembly Department said, "I can't understand why my department was charged $460 for maintenance last month. We had one guy in for just a little over a day. What's going on?"

The controller for the plant reviewed the charge to the Assembly Department for the previous month and verified that it was correct. Then, he took a closer look at the costs of the Maintenance Department. Originally, the Maintenance Department did primarily routine cleaning and oiling of machinery. However, in the past few years, many of the manufacturing cells acquired complex computer-controlled machinery that requires technical support and diagnostic equipment. The budgeted cost of the department can be broken down into $48,000 for salaries and supplies for routine maintenance and the remainder for salaries and depreciation on equipment for the more technical equipment maintenance. Budgeted hours of routine maintenance are 2,000, with 2,200 hours for the more technical maintenance.

Required

1. Explain how the controller verified the accuracy of the $460 charged to the Assembly Department.
2. Calculate two charging rates for the Maintenance Department: a rate for routine maintenance based on hours needed for routine maintenance; and a rate for technical maintenance based on hours needed for technical maintenance. Assuming that the Assembly Department needed only routine maintenance last month, what would the charge have been under the dual rate system?
3. What does this experience suggest for the determination of charging rates for support departments?

7-8

Allocating Support-Department Cost Using the Direct Method
LO3

Schroeder Company manufactures a product in a factory that has two producing departments, Cutting and Sewing, and two support departments, S1 and S2. The activity driver for S1 is number of employees, and the activity driver for S2 is number of maintenance hours. The following data pertain to Schroeder Company:

	Support Departments		Producing Departments		
	S1	**S2**	**Cutting**	**Sewing**	
Direct costs	$200,000	$140,000	$122,000	$90,500	
Normal activity:					
Number of employees	—	50	120	80	200 total
Maintenance hours	1,200	—	15,000	5,000	20,000 total

Required

1. Calculate the allocation ratios to be used under the direct method for Departments S1 and S2. (Each support department will have two allocation ratios—one for cutting and the other for sewing.)
2. Allocate the support-department costs to the producing departments using the direct method.

7-9

Allocating Support-Department Costs Using the Sequential Method
LO3

Refer to **Exercise 7-8.** Under the sequential method, the Department S1 costs are allocated first.

Required

1. Calculate the allocation ratios to be used under the sequential method for S1 and S2. Carry your calculations out to two digits. (S1 will have three allocation ratios—one each for S2, Cutting, and Sewing. S2 will have two allocation ratios—one for each producing department.)
2. Allocate the support-department costs to the producing departments using the sequential method.

7-10

Allocating Support-Department Costs Using the Reciprocal Method
LO3

Refer to **Exercise 7-8**.

Required

1. Calculate the allocation ratios to be used under the reciprocal method for S1 and S2. Carry your calculations out to four digits. (S1 will have three allocation ratios—one each for S2, Cutting, and Sewing. S2 will have three allocation ratios—one each for S1, Cutting, and Sewing.)
2. Develop a cost equation for each support department, and solve for the total support-department costs.
3. Based on the calculations in Requirement 1, allocate the support-department costs to the producing departments using the reciprocal method.

7-11

Computing Departmental Overhead Rates and Product Cost
LO4

Sweet Creations Bakery, Inc., has two producing departments: Baking and Decorating. In the Baking Department, ingredients are mixed, poured into the appropriate pans, and baked. In the Decorating Department, baked goods are iced and decorated (if necessary). At the beginning of the year, the following budgeted information was provided:

	Baking	Decorating
Machine hours	6,250	1,000
Direct labor hours	1,000	6,000
Total overhead	$150,000	$42,000

Overhead in the Baking Department is based on the number of machine hours; overhead in the Decorating Department is based on the number of direct labor hours.

Required

1. Calculate overhead rates for each producing department.
2. Suppose that direct materials cost $55 per batch of 100 loaves, and direct labor costs $42 per batch of 100 loaves. One batch of bread requires two hours in the Baking Department and no time in the Decorating Department. What is the unit cost of one loaf of bread?
3. Cara Dearman ordered a five-tier cake for her wedding. It will require one hour in the Baking Department and 8 hours in the Decorating Department. Direct materials are estimated at $20, and direct labor cost is estimated at $50. What is the cost of the Dearman wedding cake? If the cake is priced at 300 percent of cost (the markup covers transportation to the reception venue, setting up the cake, and profit), what is the price of the wedding cake?

7-12

Direct Method and Overhead Rates
LO3, LO4

Golden Company manufactures pottery in two producing departments: Shaping and Firing. Three support departments support the production departments: Power, General Factory, and Human Resources. Budgeted data on the five departments follow:

	Support Departments			Producing Departments	
	Power	Gen. Factory	HR	Shaping	Firing
Direct overhead costs	$90,000	$167,000	$84,000	$72,000	$230,000
Kilowatt-hours	—	13,000	25,000	20,000	80,000
Square feet	2,000	—	6,000	24,000	8,000
Direct labor hours	—	—	—	10,000	4,000

Power is allocated on the basis of kilowatt-hours, General Factory is allocated on the basis of square footage, and Human Resources is allocated on the basis of direct labor hours. The company does not break overhead into fixed and variable components.

Required

1. Allocate the overhead costs to the producing departments using the direct method. (Round allocation ratios to two decimal places.)
2. Using direct labor hours, compute departmental overhead rates.

7-13

Sequential Method and Overhead Rates
LO3, LO4

Refer to the data in **Exercise 7-12**. The company has decided to use the sequential method of allocation instead of the direct method.

Required

1. Allocate the overhead costs to the producing departments using the sequential method. (Round allocation ratios to two decimal places.)
2. Using direct labor hours, compute departmental overhead rates.

7-14

Appendix Exercise: Physical Units Method
LO5

Alomar Company manufactures four products from a joint production process: andol, incol, ordol, and exsol. The joint costs for one batch equal $100,000.

At the split-off point, a batch yields 1,000 andol, 1,500 incol, 2,500 ordol, and 3,000 exsol. All products are sold at the split-off point: andol sells for $20 per unit; incol sells for $75 per unit; ordol sells for $64 per unit, and exsol sells for $22.50 per unit.

Required

Allocate the joint costs using the physical units method.

7-15

Appendix Exercise: Sales-Value-at-Split-Off Method
LO5

Refer to **Exercise 7-14** and allocate the joint costs using the sales-value-at-split-off method.

7-16

Appendix Exercise: Net Realizable Value Method
LO5

Presley, Inc., produces two products, ups and downs, in a single process. The joint costs of this process were $42,000, and 39,000 units of ups and 21,000 units of downs were produced. Separable processing costs beyond the split-off point were as follows: ups, $18,000; downs, $5,780. Ups sell for $2.00 per unit; downs sell for $2.18 per unit.

Required

1. Allocate the $42,000 joint costs using the estimated net realizable value method.
2. Suppose that ups could be sold at the split-off point for $1.80 per unit. Should Presley sell ups at split-off or process them further? Show supporting computations.

7-17

Reciprocal Method and Overhead Rates
LO3, LO4

Homard Company produces boxes of juice drinks in two producing departments (Mixing and Packaging) and two support departments (Human Resources and Power). The following budgeted data pertain to these four departments:

	Support Departments		Producing Departments	
	Human Resources	Power	Mixing	Packaging
Overhead	$110,000	$150,000	$100,000	$280,000
Payroll	—	$90,000	$105,000	$105,000
Kilowatt-hours	5,000	—	15,000	45,000
Direct labor hours	—	—	20,000	30,000

Costs of the Human Resources Department are allocated on the basis of payroll, and costs of the Power Department are allocated on the basis of kilowatt-hours.

Required

1. Allocate the overhead costs of the support departments to the producing departments using the reciprocal method.
2. Using direct labor hours, compute departmental overhead rates (to the nearest penny).

7-18

Direct Method and Overhead Rates
LO3, LO4

Refer to the data in **Exercise 7-17**. The company has decided to simplify its method of allocating service costs by switching to the direct method.

Required

1. Allocate the costs of the support departments to the producing departments using the direct method.
2. Using direct labor hours, compute departmental overhead rates (to the nearest penny). Which rate do you consider more accurate—the one using the reciprocal method or the one using the direct method? Explain.

7-19

Sequential Method and Overhead Rates
LO3, LO4

Refer to the data in **Exercise 7-17.**

Required

1. Allocate the costs of the support departments using the sequential method. Allocate Human Resources first, then Power.
2. Using direct labor hours, compute departmental overhead rates (to the nearest penny). Explain why these rates are generally more accurate than those computed using the direct method.

7-20

Reciprocal Method
LO3

Trinity Medical Clinic has two support departments and two revenue-producing departments. The controller for the clinic has decided to use the reciprocal method to allocate the costs of the support departments (A and B) to the producing departments (C and D). She has prepared the following cost equations for the two support departments. *A* equals the total cost for the first support department, and *B* equals the total cost for the second support department.

$$A = \$35{,}000 + 0.3B$$
$$B = \$40{,}000 + 0.2A$$

Before the controller was able to complete the allocation, she had to leave to take care of an emergency. In addition to these equations, she left a hastily scribbled note indicating that Department C uses 20 percent of A's output and 40 percent of B's output.

Required

Allocate the costs of the two support departments to each of the two producing departments using the reciprocal method.

7-21

Direct Method; Overhead Rates; Unit Cost
LO3, LO4

Goodson Company has two support departments—Human Resources and General Factory—and two producing departments—Grinding and Assembly. Budgeted data for each follow:

	Human Resources	General Factory	Grinding	Assembly
Direct costs	$70,000	$230,000	$63,900	$39,500
Square feet	4,000	—	2,000	6,000
Direct labor hours	600	11,000	20,000	80,000
Machine hours	—	1,000	4,000	1,000

Human Resources is allocated on the basis of direct labor hours; General Factory is allocated on the basis of square footage.

EXCEL

Required

1. Allocate overhead costs to the producing departments using the direct method.
2. Calculate departmental overhead rates, using machine hours for Grinding and direct labor hours for Assembly.
3. If a unit has prime costs of $123 and spends one hour in Grinding and 12 hours in Assembly, what is the unit cost?

7-22

Sequential Method; Overhead Rates; Unit Cost
LO3, LO4

Refer to the data in **Exercise 7-21**.

Required

1. Allocate the costs of the support departments using the sequential method.
2. Calculate departmental overhead rates, using machine hours for Grinding and direct labor hours for Assembly.
3. If a unit has prime costs of $123 and spends one hour in Grinding and 12 hours in Assembly, what is the unit cost?

EXCEL

7-23

Reciprocal Method; Overhead Rates; Unit Cost
LO3, LO4

Refer to the data in **Exercise 7-21**.

Required

1. Allocate the costs of the support departments using the reciprocal method.
2. Calculate departmental overhead rates, using machine hours for Grinding and direct labor hours for Assembly.
3. If a unit has prime costs of $123 and spends one hour in Grinding and 12 hours in Assembly, what is the unit cost?

7-24

Appendix Exercise: Physical Units Method and Sales-Value-at-Split-Off Method
LO5

McGraw Company manufactures three products from a joint production process: alphas, betas, and gammas. The joint costs for one batch are as follows:

Direct materials	$68,800
Direct labor	28,000
Overhead	28,200

At the split-off point, a batch yields 12,500 alphas, 17,500 betas, and 20,000 gammas. All products are sold at the split-off point: alpha sells for $20 per unit; beta sells for $50 per unit, and gamma sells for $18 per unit.

Required

1. Allocate the joint costs using the physical units method.
2. Allocate the joint costs using the sales-value-at-split-off method.

Problems

7-25

Comparison of Methods of Allocation LO3

EXCEL

MedServices, Inc., is divided into two operating departments: Laboratory and Tissue Pathology. The company allocates delivery and accounting costs to each operating department. Delivery costs include the costs of a fleet of vans and drivers that drive throughout the state each day to clinics and doctors' offices to pick up specimens and deliver them to the centrally located laboratory and tissue pathology offices. Delivery costs are allocated on the basis of number of samples. Accounting costs are allocated on the basis of the number of transactions processed. No effort is made to separate fixed and variable costs; however, only budgeted costs are allocated. Allocations for the coming year are based on the following data:

	Support Departments		Operating Departments	
	Delivery	Accounting	Laboratory	Tissue Pathology
Overhead costs	$240,000	$270,000	$345,000	$456,000
Number of samples	—	—	70,200	46,800
Transactions processed	2,000	200	24,700	13,300

Required

1. Allocate the support-department costs using the direct method.
2. Allocate the support-department costs using the sequential method.

7-26

Comparison of Methods of Allocation LO3, LO4

Bender Automotive Works, Inc., manufactures a variety of front-end assemblies for automobiles. A front-end assembly is the unified front of an automobile and includes the headlamps, fender, and surrounding metal/plastic. Bender has two producing departments: Drilling and Assembly. Usually, the front-end assemblies are ordered in batches of 100.

Two support departments provide support for Bender's operating units: Maintenance and Power. Budgeted data for the coming quarter follow. The company does not separate fixed and variable costs.

	Support Departments		Producing Departments	
	Maintenance	Power	Drilling	Assembly
Overhead costs	$320,000	$400,000	$163,000	$90,000
Machine hours	—	22,500	30,000	7,500
Kilowatt-hours	40,000	—	36,000	324,000
Direct labor hours	—	—	5,000	40,000

The predetermined overhead rate for Drilling is computed on the basis of machine hours; direct labor hours are used for Assembly.

Recently, a truck manufacturer requested a bid on a three-year contract that would supply front-end assemblies to a nearby factory. The prime costs for a batch of 100 front-end assemblies are $1,817. It takes two machine hours to produce a batch in the Drilling Department and 50 direct labor hours to assemble the 100 front-end assemblies in the Assembly Department.

Bender's policy is to bid full manufacturing cost plus 15 percent.

Required

1. Prepare bids for Bender Automotive Works, Inc., using each of the following allocation methods:

a. Direct method
b. Reciprocal method

2. Which method more accurately reflects the cost of producing the front-end assemblies? Why?

7-27

Comparison of Ranking of Support Departments Using the Sequential Method
LO3, LO4

Refer to the data in **Problem 7-26**.

Required

1. Prepare bids for Bender Automotive Works, Inc., using each of the following allocation methods:

   a. Sequential method, allocating Maintenance first, then Power.
   b. Sequential method, allocating Power first, then Maintenance.

2. Was there a difference in the bids calculated in Requirement 1? Why or why not?

7-28

Reciprocal Method; Cost of Operating a Support Department
LO3, LO4

Petro-Chem, Inc., is a small company that acquires high-grade crude oil from low-volume production wells owned by individuals and small partnerships. The crude oil is processed in a single refinery into Two Oil, Six Oil, and impure distillates. Petro-Chem does not have the technology or capacity to process these products further and sells most of its output each month to major refineries. There were no beginning finished goods or work-in-process inventories on November 1. The production costs and output of Petro-Chem for November are as follows:

Crude oil acquired and placed into production	$5,000,000
Direct labor and related costs	2,000,000
Manufacturing overhead	3,000,000

Production and sales:

Two Oil, 300,000 barrels produced; 80,000 barrels sold at $20 each.
Six Oil, 240,000 barrels produced; 120,000 barrels sold at $30 each.
Distillates, 120,000 barrels produced and sold at $15 per barrel.

Required

1. Calculate the amount of joint production cost that Petro-Chem would allocate to each of the three joint products by using the physical units method. (Carry out the ratio calculation to four decimal places.)
2. Calculate the amount of joint production cost that Petro-Chem would allocate to each of the three joint products by using the relative sales value method.

7-29

Sequential and Direct Methods
LO3, LO4

Lilly Candies has three producing departments—Mixing, Cooking, and Packaging—and five support departments. The following is the basic information on all departments (bases represent practical annual levels):

	Number of Items Processed	Number of Employees	Square Feet Occupied	Machine Hours	Labor Hours
Cafeteria	300	5	5,000	—	—
Personnel	1,000	10	7,000	—	—
Custodial Services	200	7	2,000	—	—
Maintenance	2,500	15	16,000	—	—
Cost Accounting	—	13	5,000	—	—
Mixing	2,800	20	40,000	4,000	30,000
Cooking	2,700	10	30,000	10,000	20,000
Packaging	3,000	20	20,000	6,000	50,000
Total	12,500	100	125,000	20,000	100,000

The budgeted overhead costs for the departments are as follows for the coming year:

	Fixed	Variable	Total
Cafeteria	$ 20,000	$ 40,000	$ 60,000
Personnel	70,000	20,000	90,000
Custodial Services	80,000	—	80,000
Maintenance	100,000	100,000	200,000
Cost Accounting	130,000	16,500	146,500
Mixing	120,000	20,000	140,000
Cooking	60,000	10,000	70,000
Packaging	25,000	40,000	65,000

Required

1. Allocate the support-department costs to the producing departments using the direct method.
2. Compute a predetermined fixed overhead rate and a predetermined variable overhead rate. Assume that overhead is applied using direct labor hours for Mixing and Packaging and machine hours for Cooking.
3. Allocate the support-department costs to the producing departments using the sequential method. (*Hint:* Allocate fixed costs in order of descending magnitude of direct fixed costs. Allocate variable costs in order of descending magnitude of direct variable costs.)
4. Compute predetermined fixed and variable overhead rates based on Requirement 3. Overhead is applied using direct labor hours for Mixing and Packaging and machine hours for Cooking.
5. Assume that the prime costs for a batch of chocolate bars total $60,000. The batch requires 1,000 direct labor hours in Mixing, 1,500 machine hours in Cooking, and 5,000 direct labor hours in Packaging. Assume that the selling price is equal to full manufacturing cost plus 30 percent. Compute the selling price of the batch assuming that costs are allocated using the direct method. Repeat using the sequential method. Comment on the implications of using different allocation methods, assuming that a markup of 30 percent is typical for the industry. Which allocation method do you think should be used?

7-30

Fixed and Variable Cost Allocation
LO3

Golden Oaks is a chain of assisted-living apartments for retired people who cannot live completely alone, yet do not need 24-hour nursing services. The chain has grown from one apartment complex in 1998 to five complexes located in Texas and Louisiana. In 2006, the owner of the company decided to set up a centralized purchasing department to purchase food and other supplies and to coordinate inventory decisions. The Purchasing Department was opened in January 2006 by renting space adjacent to corporate headquarters in Shreveport, Louisiana. Each apartment complex has been supplied with personal computers and modems by which to transfer information to central purchasing on a daily basis.

The Purchasing Department has budgeted fixed costs of $70,000 per year. Variable costs are budgeted at $18 per purchase order. Actual costs in 2006 equaled budgeted costs. Further information is as follows:

	Actual Revenues		Actual Purchase Orders
	2005	2006	Used in 2006
Baton Rouge	$ 675,000	$ 781,000	1,475
Kilgore	720,000	750,000	1,188
Longview	900,000	912,000	500
Paris	1,125,000	1,098,000	525
Shreveport	1,080,000	1,100,000	562

Required

1. Suppose the total costs of the Purchasing Department are allocated on the basis of 2006 revenues. How much will be allocated to each apartment complex?
2. Suppose that Golden Oaks views 2005 revenue figures as a proxy for budgeted capacity of the apartment complexes. Thus, fixed Purchasing Department costs are allocated on the basis of 2005 revenues, and variable costs are allocated according to 2006 usage multiplied by the variable rate. How much Purchasing Department cost will be allocated to each apartment complex?
3. Comment on the two allocation schemes. Which is better? Explain.

7-31

Plantwide Overhead Rate versus Departmental Rates; Effects on Pricing Decisions
LO3, LO4

Alden Peterson, marketing manager for Retlief Company, had been puzzled by the outcome of two recent bids. The company's policy was to bid 150 percent of the full manufacturing cost. One job (labeled Job SS) had been turned down by a prospective customer, who had indicated that the proposed price was $3 per unit higher than the winning bid. A second job (Job TT) had been accepted by a customer, who was amazed that Retlief could offer such favorable terms. This customer revealed that Retlief's price was $43 per unit lower than the next-lowest bid.

Alden knew that Retlief Company was more than competitive in terms of cost control. Accordingly, he suspected that the problem was related to cost assignment procedures. Upon investigating, Alden was told that the company used a plantwide overhead rate based on direct labor hours. The rate was computed at the beginning of the year using budgeted data. Selected budgeted data follow:

	Department A	Department B	Total
Overhead	$500,000	$2,000,000	$2,500,000
Direct labor hours	200,000	50,000	250,000
Machine hours	20,000	120,000	140,000

The above information led to a plantwide overhead rate of $10 per direct labor hour. In addition, the following specific manufacturing data on Job SS and Job TT were given.

	Job SS		
	Department A	Department B	Total
Direct labor hours	5,000	1,000	6,000
Machine hours	200	500	700
Prime costs	$100,000	$20,000	$120,000
Units produced	14,400	14,400	14,400

	Job TT		
	Department A	Department B	Total
Direct labor hours	400	600	1,000
Machine hours	200	3,000	3,200
Prime costs	$10,000	$40,000	$50,000
Units produced	1,500	1,500	1,500

This information led to the original bid prices of $18.75 per unit for Job SS and $60 per unit for Job TT.

Then, Alden discovered that the overhead costs in Department B were higher than those of Department A because Department B has more equipment, higher maintenance, higher power consumption, higher depreciation, and higher setup costs. So he tried reworking the two bids by using departmental overhead rates. Department A's overhead rate was $2.50 per direct labor hour; Department B's overhead rate was $16.67 per machine hour. These rates resulted in unit prices of $14.67 for Job SS and $101.01 for Job TT.

Alden still was not satisfied, however. He did some reading on overhead allocation methods and learned that proper support-department cost allocation can lead to more accurate product costs. He decided to create four support departments and recalculate departmental overhead rates. Information on departmental costs and related items follows:

	Maintenance	Power	Setups	General Factory	Dept. A	Dept. B
Overhead	$500,000	$225,000	$150,000	$625,000	$200,000	$800,000
Maintenance hours	—	1,500	500	—	1,000	7,000
Kilowatt-hours	4,500	—	—	15,000	10,000	50,000
Direct labor hours	10,000	12,000	6,000	8,000	200,000	50,000
Number of setups	—	—	—	—	40	160
Square feet	25,000	40,000	5,000	15,000	35,360	94,640

The following allocation bases (cost drivers) seemed reasonable:

Support Department	Allocation Base
Maintenance	Maintenance hours
Power	Kilowatt-hours
Setups	Number of setups
General Factory	Square feet

Required

1. Using the direct method, verify the original departmental overhead rates.
2. Using the sequential method, allocate support-department costs to the producing departments. Calculate departmental overhead rates using direct labor hours for Department A and machine hours for Department B. What would the bids for Job SS and Job TT have been if these overhead rates had been in effect?
3. Which method of overhead cost assignment would you recommend to Alden? Why?
4. Suppose that the best competing bid was $4.10 lower than the original bid price (based on a plantwide rate). Does this affect your recommendation in Requirement 3? Explain.

Managerial Decision Cases

7-32

Allocation; Pricing; Ethical Behavior
LO1, LO2

Emma Hanks, manager of a division that produces valves and castings on a special-order basis, was excited about an order received from a new customer. The customer, a personal friend of Bob Johnson, Emma's supervisor, had placed an order for 10,000 valves. The customer agreed to pay full manufacturing cost plus 25 percent. The order was timely since business was sluggish, and Emma had some concerns about her division's ability to meet its targeted profits. Even with the order, the division would likely fall short in meeting the target by at least $50,000. After examining the cost sheet for the order, however, Emma thought she saw a way to increase the profitability of the job. She reached for the phone to call her division controller, Lenny Cabot, CMA.

A few minutes later, Lenny met Emma in her office. Emma explained her plan to increase the profitability of the valve job. As currently written, the cost sheet reflected an allocation of maintenance costs to the Grinding Department based on maintenance hours used. In fact, sixty percent of maintenance costs were allocated to Grinding on that basis. But suppose that machine hours were used as the allocation base instead of maintenance hours? Then the allocation ratio would increase from 60 percent to 80 percent. This change would result in an increase of $10 per unit of the job. With the 25 percent markup, the revenues on that job would jump by $12.50 per unit—increasing the profitability of the division by $125,000. At that point, Emma asked Lenny to change the allocation base from maintenance hours worked to machine hours.

Lenny protested briefly, pointing out that considerable time had been spent assessing the causal relationships. He and the management team found that maintenance hours reflected the consumption of maintenance cost much better than machine hours. He worried that the change would not result in a fair cost assignment. Finally, he reminded Emma that maintenance hours had been used as the allocation base for maintenance cost for several years.

Emma brushed aside Lenny's protests, saying that allocations are arbitrary anyway. She pointed out that changing the allocation base for this new job would increase its profitability and allow their division to meet targeted profit goals for the year. Their ability to get the capital they needed to expand the business depended meeting profit goals, as did their likelihood of receiving year-end bonuses. She also reminded him that the new customer had a prosperous business and could easily afford to pay somewhat more for this order.

Required

1. Evaluate Emma's position. Do you agree with her reasoning? Explain. What should Emma do?
2. If you were the controller, what would you do? Do any of the standards for ethical conduct for management accountants apply to the controller (see Chapter 1)? Explain.
3. Suppose Lenny refused to change the allocation scheme. Emma then issued the following ultimatum: "Either change the allocation or look for another job!" Lenny then made an appointment with Bob Johnson and disclosed the entire affair. Bob, however, was not sympathetic. He advised Lenny to do as Emma had requested, arguing that the request represented good business sense. Now what should Lenny do?
4. Refer to Requirement 3. Lenny decided that he cannot comply with the request to change the allocation scheme. Appeals to higher-level officials have been in vain. Angered, Lenny submitted his resignation and called the new customer affected by the cost reassignment. In his phone conversation, Lenny revealed Emma's plan to increase the job's costs in order to improve the division's profits. The new customer expressed her gratitude and promptly canceled her order for 10,000 valves. Evaluate Lenny's actions. Should he have informed the customer about Emma's intent? Explain.

7-33

Direct Method; Settlement of a Contract Dispute LO3, LO4

A state government agency contracted with FlyRite Helicopters to provide helicopter services on a requirements contract. After six months, FlyRite discovered that the agency's original estimates of the number of flying hours needed were grossly overstated. FlyRite Helicopters is now making a claim against the state agency for defective specifications. The state has been advised by its legal advisers that its chances in court on this claim would not be strong, and, therefore, an out-of-court settlement is in order. As a result of the legal advice, the state agency has hired a local CPA firm to analyze the claim and prepare a recommendation for an equitable settlement.

The particulars on which the original bid was based follow. The contract was for three different types of helicopters and had a duration of one year. Thus, the data reflect the original annual expectations. Also, the costs and activity pertain only to the contract.

	Aircraft Type		
	Hughes 500D	206B Jet Ranger	206L-1 Long Ranger
Flying hours	1,200	1,600	900
Direct costs:			
Fixed:			
Insurance	$32,245	$28,200	$55,870
Lease payments	31,000	36,000	90,000
Pilot salaries	30,000	30,000	30,000
Variable:			
Fuel	$24,648	$30,336	$22,752
Minor servicing	6,000	8,000	4,500
Lease	—	—	72,000

In addition to the direct costs, the following indirect costs were expected:

	Fixed Costs	Variable Costs
Maintenance	$ 26,000	$246,667
Hangar rent	18,000	—
General administrative	110,000	—

Maintenance and general administrative costs are allocated to each helicopter on the basis of flying hours; hangar rent is allocated on the basis of the number of helicopters. The company has one of each type of aircraft.

During the first six months of the contract, the actual flying hours were as follows:

Aircraft Type	Flying Hours
500D	299
206B	160
206L-1	204

The state agency's revised projection of total flying hours for the year is given below.

Aircraft Type	Flying Hours
500D	450
206B	600
206L-1	800

Required

1. Assume that FlyRite won the contract with a bid of cost plus 15 percent, where cost refers to cost per flying hour. Compute the original bid price per flying hour for each type of helicopter. Next, compute the original expected profit of the contract.
2. Compute the profit (or loss) earned by FlyRite for the first six months of activity. Assume that the planned costs were equal to the actual costs. Also, assume that 50 percent of the fixed costs for the year have been incurred. Compute the profit that FlyRite should have earned during the first six months, assuming that 50 percent of the hours originally projected (for each aircraft type) had been flown.
3. Compute the profit (or loss) that the contract would provide FlyRite assuming the original price per flying hour and using the state agency's revised projection of hours needed.
4. Assume that the state has agreed to pay what is necessary so that FlyRite receives the profit originally expected in the contract. This will be accomplished by revising the price paid per flying hour based on the revised estimates of flying hours. What is the new price per flying hour?

Research Assignments

7-34

Research Assignment LO1, LO2

Contact the controller of a local hospital, and arrange an interview. Ask the hospital controller the following questions, and write up the responses:

a. How many support departments do you have in the hospital? Will you describe several for me?
b. How many different revenue-producing departments are there in the hospital? Will you describe several for me?
c. How do you assign support-department costs to revenue-producing departments?
d. How many different products are there in the hospital?
e. How do you assign the costs of the support departments to individual products?
f. How many different products are costed in your hospital?
g. How do you determine the cost of a particular product?

7-35

Cybercase LO1

Browse through the websites of one or more major financial services companies, such as those listed below. Their websites are provided in the chapter web links at the Interactive Study Center on http://www.thomsonedu.com/accounting/hansen.

Fidelity
Merrill Lynch
Prudential
Allstate Insurance
Citibank
KPMG
Ernst and Young
Deloitte

Then, identify as many producing departments as possible. Are any support departments listed? Why or why not? (*Hint:* Consider the purpose of the website and who is expected to use it.)

© Getty Images

PART 4

Planning and Control

Chapter 8: Budgeting for Planning and Control

Chapter 9: Standard Costing: A Managerial Control Tool

Chapter 10: Segmented Reporting, Investment Center Evaluation, and Transfer Pricing

chapter 8

Budgeting for Planning and Control

learning objectives

After studying this chapter, you should be able to:

1. Discuss budgeting and its role in planning, control, and decision making.
2. Define and prepare a *master budget,* identify its major components, and outline the interrelationships of its various components.
3. Describe flexible budgeting, and list the features that a budgetary system should have to encourage managers to engage in goal-congruent behavior.
4. Explain how activity-based budgeting works.

Scenario

By virtually all measures, Dr. Roger Jones was a successful dentist. Annual revenues from his practice of more than $750,000 provided him with a salary of $150,000. Additionally, years ago, he had invested in a very popular local Mexican food restaurant, Texas Rex, Inc., of which he had become sole owner. Because of its reputation and appeal, Texas Rex had developed a line of clothing with the dinosaur logo. The income from the restaurant and its clothing line was much more than what his professional practice was providing.

In fact, Dr. Jones's dental practice was constantly receiving infusions of money from his Texas Rex income. For example, the practice often struggled to meet payroll taxes and pay its suppliers from its own internally generated funds. Recently, Texas Rex funds were used to pay one supplier more than $200,000.

Weary of the constant demands of his practice on the Texas Rex funds, Dr. Jones was determined to get to the root of his practice's financial difficulties. He called Lawson, Johnson, and Smith, a local CPA firm, and requested help to determine the cause of his recurring financial difficulties. John Smith, a partner in the CPA firm, spent a week examining the records of the practice and extensively interviewing Dr. Jones. He delivered the following report:

Dear Dr. Jones:

The cause of your current financial difficulties is the absence of proper planning and control. Currently, many spending decisions are made arbitrarily and without considering affordability. Because of this, resources are often committed beyond the capabilities of the practice.

The following examples illustrate some of the decisions that have contributed to your financial troubles:

1. *Salary increases.* You have granted 5 percent increases each year whether or not the business could successfully absorb these increases.
2. *Cash withdrawals.* For the past five years, you have withdrawn approximately $1,000 in cash per month. These withdrawals have been treated as a loan from the corporation to you, the president of the corporation.
3. *Equipment purchases.* During the past five years, the corporation has acquired a van, a video recorder, a refrigerator, a microwave, and an in-house stereo system. Some items were purchased for cash, and some are still being paid for in installments. None of them was essential to the mission of your corporation.

These decisions, and others like them, have adversely affected the financial status of your dental practice. To solve your practice's financial problems, I recommend the installation of a formal budgetary system. A comprehensive financial plan is needed so that you know where you are going and what you are capable of doing.

Sincerely, John Smith, CPA

Questions to Think About

1. Why did Dr. Jones fire his bookkeeper? Were his practice's financial problems her fault? Why or why not?
2. How would a formal budgeting system help Dr. Jones get out of his financial difficulties?
3. Many small businesses do not budget, reasoning that they are small enough to mentally keep track of all revenues and expenditures. Comment on this idea.
4. Do you budget? Explain why you do or do not.

Description of Budgeting

Objective 1

Discuss budgeting and its role in planning, control, and decision making.

All businesses should prepare budgets; all large businesses do. As the scenario for Dr. Jones shows, budgeting is vital for small businesses, too. Every for-profit and not-for-profit entity can benefit from the planning and control provided by budgets.

Budgeting and Planning and Control

Planning and control are inextricably linked. Planning is looking ahead to see what actions should be taken to realize particular goals. Control is looking backward, determining what actually happened and comparing it with the previously planned outcomes. This comparison can then be used to adjust the budget, looking forward once more. Exhibit 8-1 illustrates the cycle of planning, results, and control.

A key component of planning, **budgets** are financial plans for the future; they identify objectives and the actions needed to achieve them. Before a budget is prepared, an organization should develop a strategic plan. The **strategic plan** identifies strategies for future activities and operations, generally covering at least five years. The organization can translate the overall strategy into long-term and short-term

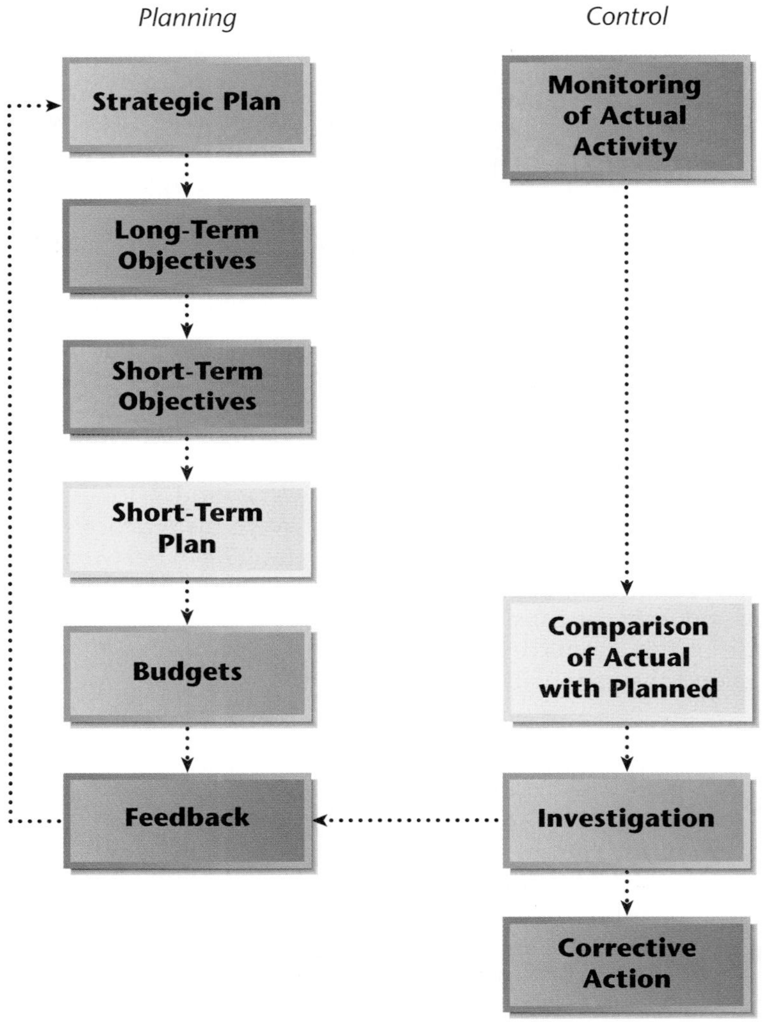

Exhibit 8-1 Planning, Control, and Budgets

objectives. These objectives form the basis of the budget. There should be a tight linkage between the budget and the strategic plan. This linkage helps management to ensure that all attention is not focused on the short run. This is important because budgets, as one-period plans, are short run in nature.

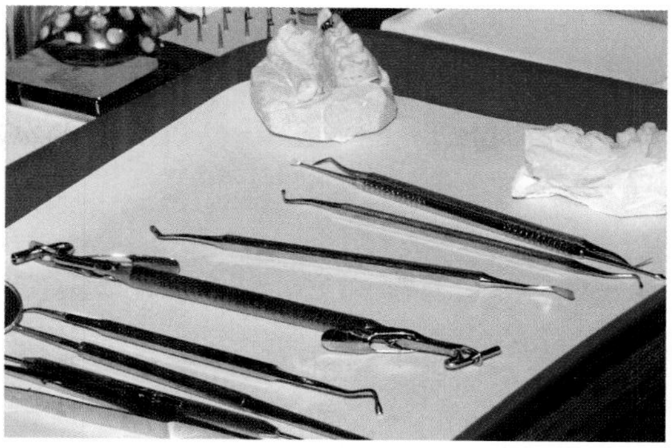
© Getty Images/PhotoDisc

Services, such as dental practices, also benefit from carefully prepared financial plans.

To illustrate the planning process, let's revisit the opening scenario and relate it to Exhibit 8-1. Assume that Dr. Jones's strategic plan is to increase the size and profitability of his business by building a reputation for quality and timely service. A key element in achieving this strategy is the addition of a dental laboratory to his building so that crowns, bridges, and dentures can be made in-house. This is his long-term objective. In order to add the laboratory, he needs additional money. His financial status dictates that the capital must be obtained by increasing revenues. After some careful calculation, Dr. Jones concludes that annual revenues must be increased by 10 percent; this is a short-term objective.

How are these long-term and short-term objectives to be achieved? Suppose that Dr. Jones finds that his fees for fillings and crowns are below the average in his community and decides that the 10 percent increase can be achieved by increasing these fees. He now has a short-term plan. A sales budget would outline the quantity of fillings and crowns expected for the coming year, the new per-unit fee, and the total fees expected. Thus, the sales budget becomes the concrete plan of action needed to achieve the 10 percent increase in revenues. As the year unfolds, Dr. Jones can compare the actual revenues received with the budgeted revenues (monitoring and comparing). If actual revenues are less than planned, he should figure out why (investigation). Then, he can act to remedy the shortfall, such as working longer hours or increasing fees for other dental services (corrective action). The reasons for the shortfall may also lead to changes in future plans (feedback).

Advantages of Budgeting

A budgetary system gives an organization several advantages.

1. It forces managers to plan.
2. It provides information that can be used to improve decision making.
3. It provides a standard for performance evaluation.
4. It improves communication and coordination.

Budgeting forces management to plan for the future. It encourages managers to develop an overall direction for the organization, foresee problems, and develop future policies.

Budgets improve decision making. For example, if Dr. Jones had known the expected revenues and the costs of supplies, lab fees, utilities, salaries, and so on, he might have lowered the rate of salary increases, avoided borrowing money from the corporation, and limited the purchase of nonessential equipment. These better decisions, in turn, might have prevented the problems that arose and resulted in a better financial status for both the business and Dr. Jones.

Budgets set standards that can control the use of a company's resources and motivate employees. A vital part of the budgetary system, **control** is achieved by comparing actual results with budgeted results on a periodic basis (for example, monthly). A large difference between actual and planned results is feedback revealing that the system is out of control. Steps should be taken to find out why, and then to correct the situation. For example, if Dr. Jones knows how much amalgam should be used in a filling and what the cost should be, he can evaluate his use of this resource. If more amalgam is being used than expected, Dr. Jones may discover that he is often careless in its use and that extra care will produce savings. The same principle applies to other resources used by the corporation. In total, the savings could be significant.

Budgets also serve to communicate and coordinate. Budgets formally communicate the plans of the organization to each employee. Accordingly, all employees can be aware of their role in achieving those objectives. Since budgets for the various areas and activities of the organization must all work together to achieve organizational objectives, coordination is promoted. Managers can see the needs of other areas and are encouraged to subordinate their individual interests to those of the organization. The role of communication and coordination becomes more significant as an organization increases in size.

Preparing the Master Budget

Objective 2

Define and prepare a *master budget,* identify its major components, and outline the interrelationships of its various components.

The **master budget** is the comprehensive financial plan for the organization as a whole. Typically, the master budget is for a one-year period corresponding to the fiscal year of the company. Yearly budgets are broken down into quarterly and monthly budgets. The use of smaller time periods allows managers to compare actual data with budgeted data more frequently, so problems may be noticed and solved sooner.

Some organizations have developed a continuous budgeting philosophy. A **continuous budget** is a moving 12-month budget. As a month expires in the budget, an additional month in the future is added so that the company always

Managers Decide

Continuous Budgeting

The concept of continuous budgeting is driven by the need to make dynamic adjustments to budgets. Firms operate in continuously changing environments and the ability to reflect changes in the budgets based on changes in the environment is critical. Budgeting and planning software facilitates this flexibility requirement. For example, Huntsman Corporation, a chemical company, uses budgeting and forecasting software to meet the demands of external and internal users for various snapshots of the future. The company uses rolling monthly forecasts to recalibrate results for the balance of the year. Huntsman's director of corporate finance indicated that prices of raw materials (such as those for ethylene and crude oil) can change quickly, noting that the most recent three months may be quite different from what you thought they'd be four months ago. The controller of Childrens Hospital Los Angeles (CHLA) made a similar observation. CHLA uses budgeting and planning software to run various budgetary scenarios, such as assessing the impact of new Blue Cross rates on units throughout the hospital. ■

Source: Tim Reason, "Partial Clearing: Budgeting Software Isn't the Key to Corporate Finance Reform, but It Can Help CFOs Manage Expectations in a Sinking Economy," *CFO: Magazine for Senior Financial Executives,* December 2002 (available online at www.CFO.com using "Browse Back Issues").

has a 12-month plan on hand. Proponents of continuous budgeting maintain that it forces managers to plan ahead constantly.

Directing and Coordinating

Most organizations prepare the master budget for the coming year during the last four or five months of the current year. The **budget committee** reviews the budget, provides policy guidelines and budgetary goals, resolves differences that arise as the budget is prepared, approves the final budget, and monitors the actual performance of the organization as the year unfolds. The president of the organization appoints the members of the committee, who are usually the president, vice presidents, and the controller. The controller usually serves as the **budget director**, the person responsible for directing and coordinating the organization's overall budgeting process.

Major Components of the Master Budget

A master budget can be divided into operating and financial budgets. **Operating budgets** describe the income-generating activities of a firm: sales, production, and finished goods inventories. The ultimate outcome of the operating budgets is a pro forma or budgeted income statement. **Financial budgets** detail the inflows and outflows of cash and the overall financial position. Planned cash inflows and outflows appear in the cash budget. The expected financial position at the end of the budget period is shown in a budgeted, or pro forma, balance sheet. Since many of the financing activities are not known until the operating budgets are known, the operating budget is prepared first.

Preparing the Operating Budget

The operating budget consists of a budgeted income statement accompanied by the following supporting schedules:

1. Sales budget
2. Production budget
3. Direct materials purchases budget
4. Direct labor budget
5. Overhead budget
6. Selling and administrative expenses budget
7. Ending finished goods inventory budget
8. Cost of goods sold budget

To illustrate the master-budgeting process, let's look at the clothing line of Dr. Jones's restaurant, Texas Rex, Inc., a trendy restaurant in the Southwest. The restaurant sells T-shirts with the Texas Rex logo (a dinosaur who engages in a variety of adventures while eating the Mexican food for which the restaurant is known). The operating budget and its various schedules are illustrated using the Texas Rex clothing manufacturing plant.

Sales Budget The **sales budget** is the projection approved by the budget committee that describes expected sales in units and dollars. Because the sales budget is the basis for all of the other operating budgets and most of the financial budgets, it is important that the sales budget be as accurate as possible.

The first step in creating a sales budget is to develop the sales forecast. This is usually the responsibility of the Marketing Department. One approach to forecasting sales is the *bottom-up approach,* which requires individual salespeople to submit sales predictions. These are aggregated to form a total sales forecast. The accuracy of this sales forecast may be improved by considering other factors such as the general economic climate, competition, advertising, pricing policies, and so on. Some companies supplement the bottom-up approach with other, more formal approaches, such as time-series analysis, correlation analysis, and econometric modeling.

The sales forecast is merely the initial estimate. The sales forecast is presented to the budget committee for consideration. The budget committee may decide that the forecast is too pessimistic or too optimistic and revise it appropriately. For example, if the budget committee decides that the forecast is too pessimistic and not in harmony with the strategic plan of the organization, it may recommend specific actions to increase sales beyond the forecast level, such as increasing promotional activities and hiring additional salespeople.

Schedule 1 illustrates the sales budget for Texas Rex's standard T-shirt line. For simplicity, we assume that Texas Rex has only one product: a standard, short-sleeved T-shirt with the Texas Rex logo screen printed on the back. (For a multiple-product firm, the sales budget reflects sales for each product in units and sales dollars.)

Schedule 1
Texas Rex, Inc.
Sales Budget
For the Year Ended December 31, 2008

	Quarter				
	1	**2**	**3**	**4**	**Year**
Units	1,000	1,200	1,500	2,000	5,700
Unit selling price	× $10	× $10	× $10	× $10	× $10
Budgeted sales	$10,000	$12,000	$15,000	$20,000	$57,000

Notice that the sales budget reveals that Texas Rex's sales fluctuate seasonally. Most sales take place in the summer and fall quarters. This is due to the popularity of the T-shirts in the summer and the sales promotions that Texas Rex puts on for "back to school" and Christmas.

Production Budget The **production budget** describes how many units must be produced in order to meet sales needs and satisfy ending inventory requirements. From Schedule 1, we know how many T-shirts are needed to satisfy sales demand for each quarter and for the year. If there were no beginning or ending inventories, the T-shirts to be produced would exactly equal the units to be sold. This would be the case in a JIT (just-in-time manufacturing) firm. However, many manufacturing firms use inventories as a buffer against uncertainties in demand or production. Assume that company policy requires 20 percent of the next quarter's sales in ending inventory, and that beginning inventory of T-shirts for the first quarter of the year was 180.

To compute the units to be produced, both unit sales and units of beginning and ending finished goods inventory are needed:

$$\text{Units to be produced} = \text{Expected unit sales} + \text{Units in ending inventory} - \text{Units in beginning inventory}$$

The formula is the basis for the production budget in Schedule 2. Let's go through the first column of Schedule 2, the production needs for the first quarter. We see that Texas Rex anticipates sales of 1,000 T-shirts. In addition, the company wants 240 T-shirts in ending inventory at the end of the first quarter (0.20 × 1,200). Thus, 1,240 T-shirts are needed during the first quarter. Where will these 1,240 T-shirts come from? Beginning inventory can provide 180 of them, leaving 1,060 T-shirts to be produced during the first quarter. Notice that the production budget is expressed in terms of units.

Schedule 2
Texas Rex, Inc.
Production Budget
For the Year Ended December 31, 2008

	Quarter 1	2	3	4	Year
Sales (Schedule 1)	1,000	1,200	1,500	2,000	5,700
Desired ending inventory	240	300	400	200*	200
Total needs	1,240	1,500	1,900	2,200	5,900
Less: Beginning inventory	(180)	(240)	(300)	(400)	(180)
Units to be produced	1,060	1,260	1,600	1,800	5,720

*Assume that sales for the first quarter of 2009 are estimated at 1,000 units.

Two important points should be noted. First, the beginning inventory for one quarter is always equal to the ending inventory of the previous quarter. For Quarter 2, the beginning inventory is 240 T-shirts, which is identical to the desired ending inventory of Quarter 1. Second, the column for the year is not simply the addition of the amounts for the four quarters. Notice that the desired ending inventory for the year is 200 T-shirts which is, of course, equal to the desired ending inventory for the fourth quarter. The beginning inventory for the year is 180 T-shirts, which is the beginning inventory for the first quarter.

Direct Materials Purchases Budget After the production schedule is completed, the budgets for direct materials, direct labor, and overhead can be prepared. The **direct materials purchases budget** tells the amount and cost of raw materials to be purchased in each time period; it depends on the expected use of materials in production and the raw materials inventory needs of the firm. The company needs to prepare a separate direct materials purchases budget for every type of raw material used.

The amount of direct materials needed for production depends on the number of units to be produced. For simplicity, suppose that Texas Rex's logo T-shirts require two types of raw material: plain T-shirts costing $3 each and ink (for the screen printing) costing $0.20 per ounce. On a per-unit basis, the factory needs one plain T-shirt and five ounces of ink for each logo T-shirt that it produces. Then, if Texas Rex wants to produce 1,060 T-shirts in the first quarter, it will need 1,060 plain T-shirts and 5,300 ounces of ink (5 ounces × 1,060 T-shirts). Once expected usage is computed, the purchases (in units) can be computed as follows:

Purchases = Direct materials needed for production + Desired direct materials in ending inventory − Direct materials in beginning inventory

The quantity of direct materials in inventory is determined by the firm's inventory policy. Texas Rex's policy is to have 10 percent of the following month's production needs in ending inventory. Let's assume that the factory had 58 plain T-shirts and 390 ounces of ink on hand on January 1.

The two direct materials purchases budgets for Texas Rex are presented in Schedule 3. Notice how similar the direct materials purchases budget is to the production budget. Let's go through the first quarter of Schedule 3, starting with the plain T-shirts. It takes one plain T-shirt for every logo tee, so the 1,060 logo T-shirts to be produced are multiplied by one to obtain the number of plain T-shirts needed for production. Then, the desired ending inventory of 126 (10 percent of the next quarter's production needs) is added. We see that 1,186 plain T-shirts are needed during the first quarter. Of this total, 58 are already in beginning inventory, meaning the remaining 1,128 must be purchased. Multiplying the 1,128 plain T-shirts by the cost of $3 each gives Texas Rex the $3,384 expected cost of plain T-shirt purchases for the first quarter of the year.

Schedule 3
Texas Rex, Inc.
Direct Materials Purchases Budget
For the Year Ended December 31, 2008

	Quarter				
Plain T-shirts:	**1**	**2**	**3**	**4**	**Year**
Units to be produced (Schedule 2)	1,060	1,260	1,600	1,800	5,720
Direct materials per unit	× 1	× 1	× 1	× 1	× 1
Production needs	1,060	1,260	1,600	1,800	5,720
Desired ending inventory	126	160	180	106*	106
Total needs	1,186	1,420	1,780	1,906	5,826
Less: Beginning inventory	(58)	(126)	(160)	(180)	(58)
Direct materials to be purchased	1,128	1,294	1,620	1,726	5,768
Cost per plain T-shirt	× $3	× $3	× $3	× $3	× $3
Total purchase cost plain T-shirts	$3,384	$3,882	$4,860	$5,178	$17,304

	Quarter				
Ink:	**1**	**2**	**3**	**4**	**Year**
Units to be produced (Schedule 2)	1,060	1,260	1,600	1,800	5,720
Direct materials per unit	× 5	× 5	× 5	× 5	× 5
Production needs	5,300	6,300	8,000	9,000	28,600
Desired ending inventory	630	800	900	530*	530
Total needs	5,930	7,100	8,900	9,530	29,130
Less: Beginning inventory	(390)	(630)	(800)	(900)	(390)
Direct materials to be purchased	5,540	6,470	8,100	8,630	28,740
Cost per ounce	× $0.20	× $0.20	× $0.20	× $0.20	× $0.20
Total purchase cost of ink	$1,108	$1,294	$1,620	$1,726	$ 5,748
Total direct materials purchase cost	$4,492	$5,176	$6,480	$6,904	$23,052

*We do not know production for the first quarter of 2007 because we do not know sales for the second quarter of 2007. Therefore, the desired ending inventories of 106 plain T-shirts and 530 ounces of ink are given simply to complete this example.

The second section of the direct materials purchases budget is for ink. Again, let's go through the first quarter. It takes five ounces of ink for every logo tee, so the 1,060 logo T-shirts to be produced are multiplied by five to obtain the 5,300 ounces of ink needed for production. Then, the desired ending inventory of 630 ounces (10 percent of the next quarter's production needs) is added. We see that 5,930 ounces of ink are needed during the first quarter. Of this total, 390 ounces are already in beginning inventory, meaning the remaining 5,540 ounces must be purchased. Multiplying the 5,540 ounces of ink by the cost of $0.20 per ounce gives Texas Rex the $1,108 expected cost of ink purchases for the first quarter of the year.

The total direct materials purchases of $4,492 for the first quarter is the sum of the $3,384 plain T-shirt purchases and the $1,108 ink purchases. Of course, there would be a separate direct materials purchases budget for each type of raw material in a firm.

Direct Labor Budget The **direct labor budget** shows the total direct labor hours needed and the associated cost for the number of units in the production budget. As with direct materials, the budgeted hours of direct labor are determined by the relationship between labor and output. For example, if a batch of 100 logo T-shirts requires 12 direct labor hours, then the direct labor time per logo T-shirt is 0.12 hour.

Given the direct labor used per unit of output and the units to be produced from the production budget, the direct labor budget is computed as shown in

Schedule 4. In the direct labor budget, the wage rate ($10 per hour in this example) is the average wage paid the direct laborers associated with the production of the T-shirts. Since it is an average, it allows for the possibility of differing wage rates paid to individual laborers.

Schedule 4
Texas Rex, Inc.
Direct Labor Budget
For the Year Ended December 31, 2008

	Quarter				
	1	2	3	4	Year
Units to be produced (Schedule 2)	1,060	1,260	1,600	1,800	5,720
Direct labor time per unit (hr.)	× 0.12	× 0.12	× 0.12	× 0.12	× 0.12
Total hours needed	127.2	151.2	192	216	686.4
Average wage per hour	× $10	× $10	× $10	× $10	× $10
Total direct labor cost	$1,272	$1,512	$1,920	$2,160	$6,864

Overhead Budget The **overhead budget** shows the expected cost of all indirect manufacturing items. Unlike direct materials and direct labor, there is no readily identifiable input-output relationship for overhead items. Instead, there are a series of activities and related drivers. Experience can be used as a guide to determine how these overhead activities vary with their drivers. Individual items that will vary are identified (for example, supplies and utilities), and the amount that is expected to be spent for each item per unit of activity is estimated. Individual rates are then totaled to obtain a variable overhead rate. For our example, let's assume that two overhead cost pools are created, one for overhead activities that vary with direct labor hours and one for all other activities, which are fixed. The variable overhead rate is $5 per direct labor hour; fixed overhead is budgeted at $6,580 ($1,645 per quarter). Using this information and the budgeted direct labor hours from the direct labor budget (Schedule 4), the overhead budget in Schedule 5 is prepared.

Schedule 5
Texas Rex, Inc.
Overhead Budget
For the Year Ended December 31, 2008

	Quarter				
	1	2	3	4	Year
Budgeted direct labor hours (Schedule 4)	127.2	151.2	192.0	216.0	686.4
Variable overhead rate	× $5	× $5	× $5	× $5	× $5
Budgeted variable overhead	$ 636	$ 756	$ 960	$1,080	$ 3,432
Budgeted fixed overhead*	1,645	1,645	1,645	1,645	6,580
Total overhead	$2,281	$2,401	$2,605	$2,725	$10,012

*Includes $540 of depreciation in each quarter.

Ending Finished Goods Inventory Budget The **ending finished goods inventory budget** supplies information needed for the balance sheet and also serves as an important input for the preparation of the cost of goods sold budget. To prepare this budget, the unit cost of producing each logo T-shirt must be calculated using information from Schedules 3, 4, and 5. The unit cost of a logo T-shirt and the cost of the planned ending inventory are shown in Schedule 6.

Schedule 6
Texas Rex, Inc.
Ending Finished Goods Inventory Budget
For the Year Ended December 31, 2008

Unit-cost computation:	
Direct materials ($3 + $1)	$4.00
Direct labor (0.12 hr. @ $10)	1.20
Overhead:	
Variable (0.12 hr. @ $5)	0.60
Fixed (0.12 hr. @ $9.59)*	1.15**
Total unit cost	$6.95

*Budgeted fixed overhead (Schedule 5)/Budgeted direct labor hours (Schedule 4) = $6,580/686.4 = $9.59**
**Rounded

	Units	Unit Cost	Total
Finished goods: Logo T-shirts	200	$6.95	$1,390

Cost of Goods Sold Budget Assuming that the beginning finished goods inventory is valued at $1,251, the budgeted cost of goods sold schedule can be prepared using Schedules 3, 4, 5, and 6. The **cost of goods sold budget** reveals the expected cost of the goods to be sold. The cost of goods sold schedule (Schedule 7) is the last schedule needed before the budgeted income statement can be prepared.

Schedule 7
Texas Rex, Inc.
Cost of Goods Sold Budget
For the Year Ended December 31, 2008

Direct materials used (Schedule 3)*	$22,880
Direct labor used (Schedule 4)	6,864
Overhead (Schedule 5)	10,012
Budgeted manufacturing costs	$39,756
Beginning finished goods	1,251
Goods available for sale	$41,007
Less: Ending finished goods (Schedule 6)	(1,390)
Budgeted cost of goods sold	$39,617

*Production needs = (5,720 plain T-shirts × $3) + (28,600 oz. ink × $0.20)

Selling and Administrative Expenses Budget The next budget to be prepared, the **selling and administrative expenses budget**, outlines planned expenditures for nonmanufacturing activities. As with overhead, selling and administrative expenses can be broken down into fixed and variable components. Such items as sales commissions, freight, and supplies vary with sales activity. The selling and administrative expenses budget is illustrated in Schedule 8.

Budgeted Income Statement With the completion of the budgeted cost of goods sold schedule and the budgeted selling and administrative expenses budget, Texas Rex has all the operating budgets needed to prepare an estimate of operating income. This budgeted income statement is shown in Schedule 9. The eight schedules already prepared, along with the budgeted operating income statement, define the operating budget for Texas Rex.

Operating income is *not* equivalent to the net income of a firm. To yield net income, interest expense and taxes must be subtracted from operating income. The

Schedule 8
Texas Rex, Inc.
Selling and Administrative Expenses Budget
For the Year Ended December 31, 2008

	Quarter				
	1	**2**	**3**	**4**	**Year**
Planned sales in units (Schedule 1)	1,000	1,200	1,500	2,000	5,700
Variable selling and administrative expenses per unit	× $0.10	× $0.10	× $0.10	× 0.10	× $0.10
Total variable expenses	$ 100	$ 120	$ 150	$ 200	$ 570
Fixed selling and administrative expenses:					
Salaries	$ 1,220	$ 1,220	$ 1,720	$1,220	$ 5,380
Utilities	50	50	50	50	200
Advertising	100	200	300	500	1,100
Depreciation	150	150	150	150	600
Insurance	200	200	200	200	800
Total fixed expenses	$ 1,720	$ 1,820	$ 2,420	$2,120	$ 8,080
Total selling and administrative expenses	$ 1,820	$ 1,940	$ 2,570	$2,320	$ 8,650

interest expense deduction is taken from the cash budget shown in Schedule 10. The taxes owed depend on the current tax laws.

Schedule 9
Texas Rex, Inc.
Budgeted Income Statement
For the Year Ended December 31, 2008

Sales (Schedule 1)	$ 57,000
Less: Cost of goods sold (Schedule 7)	(39,617)
Gross margin	$ 17,383
Less: Selling and administrative expenses (Schedule 8)	(8,650)
Operating income	$ 8,733
Less: Interest expense (Schedule 10)	(60)
Income before income taxes	$ 8,673
Less: Income taxes (Schedule 10)	(2,550)
Net income	$ 6,123

Preparing the Financial Budget

The remaining budgets found in the master budget are the financial budgets. The usual financial budgets prepared are:

1. The cash budget
2. The budgeted balance sheet
3. The budget for capital expenditures

The master budget also contains a plan for acquiring long-term assets—assets that have a time horizon that extends beyond the one-year operating period. Some of these assets may be purchased during the coming year; plans to purchase others may be detailed for future periods. This part of the master budget is typically referred to as the *capital budget.* Decision making for capital expenditures is considered in Chapter 13. Accordingly, only the cash budget and the budgeted balance sheet will be illustrated here.

Cash Budget Knowledge of cash flows is critical to managing a business. Often a business is successful in producing and selling a product but fails because of timing problems associated with cash inflows and outflows. By knowing when cash deficiencies and surpluses are likely to occur, a manager can plan to borrow cash when needed and to repay the loans during periods of excess cash. Bank loan officers use a company's **cash budget** to document the need for cash, as well as the ability to repay. Because cash flow is the lifeblood of an organization, the cash budget is one of the most important budgets in the master budget. The cash budget is illustrated in Exhibit 8-2.

Cash flow is the lifeblood of an organization.

© Getty Images/PhotoDisc

Cash available consists of the beginning cash balance and the expected cash receipts. Expected cash receipts include all sources of cash for the period being considered. The principal source of cash is from sales. Because a significant proportion of sales is usually on account, a major task of an organization is to determine the pattern of collection for its accounts receivable. If a company has been in business for a while, it can use its experience in creating an accounts receivable aging schedule. In other words, the company can determine, on average, what percentages of its accounts receivable are paid in the months following sales. For example, assume a company, Patton Hardware, has the following accounts receivable payment experience:

Percent paid in the month of sale	30%
Percent paid in the month after the sale	60
Percent paid in the second month after the sale	10

If Patton sells $100,000 worth of goods on account in the month of May, then it would expect to receive $30,000 cash from May credit sales in the month of May, $60,000 cash from May credit sales in June, and $10,000 from May credit sales in July. (Notice that Patton expects to receive all of its accounts receivable. This is not typical. If a company experiences, let's say, 3 percent uncollectible accounts, then this 3 percent of sales is ignored for the purpose of cash budgeting—because no cash is received from customers who default.)

The cash disbursements section lists all planned cash outlays for the period. All expenses not resulting in a cash outlay are excluded from the list (depreciation, for

Beginning cash balance	xxx
Add: Cash receipts	xxx
Cash available	xxx
Less: Cash disbursements	xxx
Less: Minimum cash balance	xxx
Cash surplus (deficiency)	xxx
Add: Cash from loans	xxx
Less: Loan repayments	xxx
Add: Minimum cash balance	xxx
Ending cash balance	xxx

Exhibit 8-2 The Cash Budget

example, is never included in the disbursements section). A disbursement that is typically not included in this section is interest on short-term borrowing. This interest expenditure is reserved for the section on loan repayments.

The cash excess or deficiency line compares the cash available with the cash needed. Cash needed is the total cash disbursements plus the minimum cash balance required by company policy. The minimum cash balance is simply the lowest amount of cash on hand that the firm finds acceptable. Consider your own checking account. You probably try to keep at least some cash in the account, perhaps because by having a minimum balance you avoid service charges, or because a minimum balance allows you to make an unplanned purchase. Similarly, companies also require minimum cash balances. The amount varies from firm to firm and is determined by each company's particular needs and policies. If the total cash available is less than the cash needed, a deficiency exists. In such a case, a short-term loan will be needed. On the other hand, with a cash excess (cash available is greater than the firm's cash needs), the firm has the ability to repay loans and perhaps make some temporary investments.

The final section of the cash budget consists of borrowings and repayments. If there is a deficiency, this section shows the necessary amount to be borrowed. When excess cash is available, this section shows planned repayments, including interest expense.

The last line of the cash budget is the planned ending cash balance. Remember that the minimum cash balance was subtracted to find the cash excess or deficiency. However, the minimum cash balance is not a disbursement, so it must be added back to yield the planned ending balance.

To illustrate the cash budget, assume the following for Texas Rex:

a. A $1,000 minimum cash balance is required for the end of each quarter. Money can be borrowed and repaid in multiples of $1,000. Interest is 12 percent per year. Interest payments are made only for the amount of the principal being repaid. All borrowing takes place at the beginning of a quarter, and all repayment takes place at the end of a quarter.
b. One-quarter of all sales are for cash, 90 percent of credit sales are collected in the quarter of sale, and the remaining 10 percent are collected in the following quarter. The sales for the fourth quarter of 2005 were $18,000.
c. Purchases of direct materials are made on account; 80 percent of purchases are paid for in the quarter of purchase. The remaining 20 percent are paid for in the following quarter. The purchases for the fourth quarter of 2005 were $5,000.
d. Budgeted depreciation is $540 per quarter for overhead and $150 per quarter for selling and administrative expenses (see Schedules 5 and 8).
e. The capital budget for 2008 revealed plans to purchase additional screen printing equipment. The cash outlay for the equipment, $6,500, will take place in the first quarter. The company plans to finance the acquisition of the equipment with operating cash, supplementing it with short-term loans as necessary.
f. Corporate income taxes are approximately $2,550 and will be paid at the end of the fourth quarter (Schedule 9).
g. Beginning cash balance equals $5,200.
h. All amounts in the budget are rounded to the nearest dollar.

Given this information, the cash budget for Texas Rex is shown in Schedule 10 (all figures are rounded to the nearest dollar). Much of the information needed to prepare the cash budget comes from the operating budgets. In fact, Schedules 1, 3, 4, 5, and 8 contain important input. However, these schedules by themselves do not supply all of the needed information. The collection pattern for revenues and the payment pattern for direct materials must be known before the cash flow for sales and purchases on credit can be found.

Schedule 10
Texas Rex, Inc.
Cash Budget
For the Year Ended December 31, 2008

	Quarter 1	Quarter 2	Quarter 3	Quarter 4	Year	Source[a]
Beginning cash balance	$ 5,200	$ 1,023	$ 1,611	$ 3,762	$ 5,200	g
Collections:						
Cash sales	2,500	3,000	3,750	5,000	14,250	b, 1
Credit sales:						
Current quarter	6,750	8,100	10,125	13,500	38,475	b, 1
Prior quarter	1,350	750	900	1,125	4,125	b, 1
Total cash available	$ 15,800	$ 12,873	$ 16,386	$ 23,387	$ 62,050	
Less disbursements:						
Direct materials:						
Current quarter	$ (3,594)	$ (4,141)	$ (5,184)	$ (5,523)	$(18,442)	c, 3
Prior quarter	(1,000)	(898)	(1,035)	(1,296)	(4,229)	c, 3
Direct labor	(1,272)	(1,512)	(1,920)	(2,160)	(6,864)	4
Overhead	(1,741)	(1,861)	(2,065)	(2,185)	(7,852)	d, 5
Selling and administrative	(1,670)	(1,790)	(2,420)	(2,170)	(8,050)	d, 8
Income taxes	—	—	—	(2,550)	(2,550)	f, 9
Equipment	(6,500)	—	—	—	(6,500)	e
Total disbursements	$(15,777)	$(10,202)	$(12,624)	$(15,884)	$(54,487)	
Minimum cash balance	(1,000)	(1,000)	(1,000)	(1,000)	(1,000)	a
Total cash needs	$(16,777)	$(11,202)	$(13,624)	$(16,884)	$(55,487)	
Excess (deficiency) of cash available over needs	$ (977)	$ 1,671	$ 2,762	$ 6,503	$ 6,563	
Financing:						
Borrowings	1,000	—	—	—	1,000	a
Repayments	—	(1,000)	—	—	(1,000)	a
Interest[b]	—	(60)	—	—	(60)	a
Total financing	$ 1,000	$ (1,060)			$ (1,060)	
Ending cash balance[c]	$ 1,023	$ 1,611	$ 3,762	$ 6,503	$ 6,503	

[a]Letters refer to the information on page 327. Numbers refer to schedules already developed.
[b]Interest payment is 6/12 × 0.12 × $1,000. Since borrowings occur at the beginning of the quarter and repayments at the end of the quarter, the principal repayment takes place after six months.
[c]Total cash available minus total disbursements plus (or minus) total financing.

Exhibit 8-3 displays the pattern of cash inflows from both cash and credit sales. Let's look at the cash receipts for the first quarter of 2008. Cash sales during the quarter are budgeted for $2,500 (0.25 × $10,000; Schedule 1). Collections on account for the first quarter relate to credit sales made during the last quarter of the previous year and the first quarter of 2008. Quarter 4, 2007, credit sales equaled $13,500 (0.75 × $18,000) and $1,350 of those sales (0.10 × $13,500) remain to be collected in Quarter 1, 2008. Quarter 1, 2008, credit sales are budgeted at $7,500, and 90 percent will be collected in that quarter. Therefore, $6,750 will be collected on account for credit sales made in that quarter. Similar computations are made for the remaining quarters.

Similar computations are done for purchases. In both cases, patterns of collection and payment are needed in addition to the information supplied by the schedules. Additionally, all noncash expenses, such as depreciation, need to be removed from the total amounts reported in the expense budgets. Thus, the budgeted expenses in Schedules 5 and 8 were reduced by the budgeted depreciation for each quarter. Overhead expenses in Schedule 5 were reduced by depreciation of $540 per quarter.

Source	Quarter 1	Quarter 2	Quarter 3	Quarter 4
Cash sales	$ 2,500	$ 3,000	$ 3,750	$ 5,000
Received on account from:				
Quarter 4, 2007	1,350			
Quarter 1, 2008	6,750	750		
Quarter 2, 2008		8,100	900	
Quarter 3, 2008			10,125	1,125
Quarter 4, 2008				13,500
Total cash receipts	$10,600	$11,850	$14,775	$19,625

Exhibit 8-3 Texas Rex's Cash Receipts Pattern for 2008

Balance Sheet December 31, 2007 Assets		
Current assets:		
Cash	$ 5,200	
Accounts receivable	1,350	
Materials inventory	252	
Finished goods inventory	1,251	
Total current assets		$ 8,053
Property, plant, and equipment:		
Land	$ 1,100	
Building and equipment	30,000	
Accumulated depreciation	(5,000)	
Total property, plant, and equipment		26,100
Total assets		$34,153
Liabilities and Owners' Equity		
Current liabilities:		
Accounts payable		$ 1,000
Owners' equity:		
Retained earnings	$33,153	
Total owners' equity		33,153
Total liabilities and owners' equity		$34,153

Exhibit 8-4 Texas Rex, Inc., Balance Sheet—December 31, 2007

Selling and administrative expenses were reduced by $150 per quarter. The net amounts are what appear in the cash budget.

The cash budget shown in Schedule 10 underscores the importance of breaking down the annual budget into smaller time periods. The cash budget for the year gives the impression that sufficient operating cash will be available to finance the acquisition of the new equipment. Quarterly information, however, shows the need for short-term borrowing ($1,000) because of both the acquisition of the new equipment and the timing of the firm's cash flows. Most firms prepare monthly cash budgets, and some even prepare weekly and daily budgets.

Another significant piece of information emerges from Texas Rex's cash budget. By the end of the third quarter, the firm has more cash ($3,762) than necessary to meet operating needs. The management of Texas Rex should consider investing the excess cash in an interest-bearing account. Once plans are finalized for use of the excess cash, the cash budget should be revised to reflect those plans. Budgeting is a dynamic process. As the budget is developed, new information becomes available, and better plans can be formulated.

Budgeted Balance Sheet The budgeted balance sheet depends on information contained in the current balance sheet and in the other budgets in the master budget. The budgeted balance sheet for December 31, 2008, is given in Schedule 11. The balance sheet for December 31, 2007, is given in Exhibit 8-4. Explanations for the budgeted figures follow the schedule.

As we have described the individual budgets that make up the master budget, the interdependencies of the component budgets have become apparent. A diagram displaying these interrelationships is shown in Exhibit 8-5.

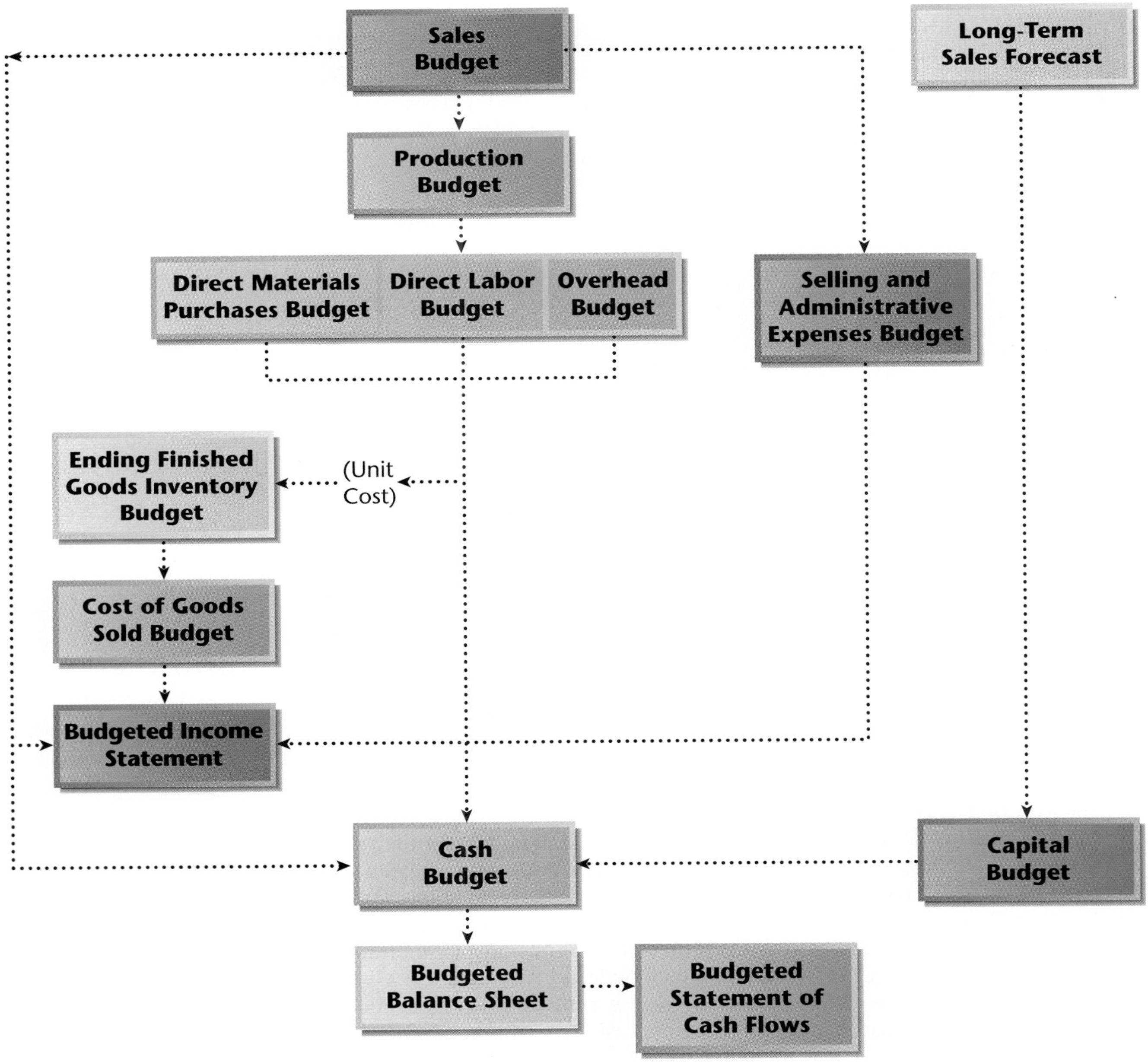

Exhibit 8-5 The Master Budget and Its Interrelationships

Schedule 11
Texas Rex, Inc.
Budgeted Balance Sheet
December 31, 2008

Assets

Current assets:		
Cash	$ 7,503[a]	
Accounts receivable	1,500[b]	
Materials inventory	,424[c]	
Finished goods inventory	1,390[d]	
Total current assets		$ 10,817
Property, plant, and equipment:		
Land	$ 1,100[e]	
Building and equipment	36,500[f]	
Accumulated depreciation	(7,760)[g]	
Total property, plant, and equipment		29,840
Total assets		$40,657

Liabilities and Owners' Equity

Current liabilities:		
Accounts payable		$ 1,381[h]
Owners' equity:		
Retained earnings	$39,276[i]	
Total owners' equity		39,276
Total liabilities and owners' equity		$40,657

[a]Ending balance from Schedule 10.
[b]Ten percent of fourth-quarter credit sales (0.75 × $20,000)—see Schedules 1 and 10.
[c]From Schedule 3 [(106 × $3) + (530 × $0.20)].
[d]From Schedule 6.
[e]From the December 31, 2007, balance sheet.
[f]December 31, 2007, balance ($30,000) plus new equipment acquisition of $6,500 (see the 2007 ending balance sheet and Schedule 10).
[g]From the December 31, 2007, balance sheet, Schedule 5, and Schedule 8 ($5,000 + $2,160 + $600).
[h]Twenty percent of fourth-quarter purchases (0.20 × $6,904)—see Schedules 3 and 10.
[i]$33,153 + $6,123 (December 31, 2007, balance plus net income from Schedule 9).

Using Budgets for Performance Evaluation

Objective 3

Describe flexible budgeting, and list the features that a budgetary system should have to encourage managers to engage in goal-congruent behavior.

Budgets are useful control measures. To be used in performance evaluation, however, two major considerations must be addressed. The first is to determine how budgeted amounts should be compared with actual results. The second consideration involves the impact of budgets on human behavior.

Static Budgets versus Flexible Budgets

Budgets can be used for both planning and control. In planning, companies prepare a master budget based on their best estimate of the level of sales to be achieved in the coming year. However, typically, the actual level of activity does not equal the budgeted level. As a result, budgeted amounts cannot be compared with actual results. Therefore, companies may also prepare flexible budgets to be used for performance evaluation.

Static Budgets The master budget developed for Texas Rex is an example of a static budget. A **static budget** is a budget for a particular level of activity. For Texas Rex, budgets were developed based on expected annual sales of 5,700 T-shirts.

Because static budgets depend on a particular level of activity, they are not very useful when it comes to preparing performance reports.

To illustrate, suppose that Texas Rex's first-quarter sales were greater than expected; a total of 1,100 T-shirts were sold instead of the 1,000 budgeted in Schedule 1. Because of increased sales activity, production was increased over the planned level. Instead of producing 1,060 units (Schedule 2), Texas Rex produced 1,200 units.

A performance report comparing the actual production costs for the first quarter with the original planned production costs is given in Exhibit 8-6. In contrast to Schedule 5, budgeted amounts for individual overhead items are provided. Thus, the individual budgeted amounts for each overhead item are new information (except for depreciation). Usually, this information would be detailed in an overhead budget.

According to the report, there were unfavorable variances for direct materials, direct labor, supplies, and power. However, there is something fundamentally wrong with the report. Actual costs for production of 1,200 T-shirts are being compared with planned costs for production of 1,060. Because direct materials, direct labor, and variable overhead are variable costs, we would expect them to be greater at a higher level of production. Thus, even if cost control were perfect for the production of 1,200 units, unfavorable variances would be produced for at least some of the variable costs. To create a meaningful performance report, actual costs and expected costs must be compared at the *same* level of activity. Since actual output often differs from planned output, some method is needed to compute what the costs should have been for the actual output level.

Flexible Budgets The budget that enables a firm to compute expected costs for a range of activity levels is called a **flexible budget**. The key to flexible budgeting is knowledge of fixed and variable costs. There are two types of flexible budgeting:

1. Budgeting for the *expected* level of activity. This type of flexible budget can help managers deal with uncertainty by allowing them to see the expected outcomes for a range of activity levels. It can be used to generate financial results for a number of plausible scenarios.
2. Budgeting for the *actual* level of activity. This type of flexible budget is used after the fact to compute what costs should have been for the actual level of activity. Those expected costs are then compared with the actual costs in order to assess performance.

	Actual	Budgeted	Variance
Units produced	1,200	1,060	140 F[a]
Direct materials cost	$4,830	$4,240[b]	$590 U[c]
Direct labor cost	1,440	1,272[d]	168 U
Overhead:[e]			
Variable:			
Supplies	535	477	58 U
Power	170	159	11 U
Fixed:			
Supervision	1,055	1,105	(50) F
Depreciation	540	540	0
Total	$8,570	$7,793	$777 U

[a]F means the variance is favorable.
[b]This is from Schedule 3 [(1,060 × $3) + (1,060 × 5 × $0.20)].
[c]U means the variance is unfavorable.
[d]This is from Schedule 4.
[e]Schedule 5 provides the aggregate amount of budgeted overhead (for example, the aggregate variable overhead is 0.12 × 1,060 × $5 = $636, and the total budgeted fixed overhead is $1,645).

Exhibit 8-6 Performance Report Quarterly Production Costs

Flexible budgeting is the key to providing the frequent feedback that managers need to exercise control and effectively carry out the plans of an organization.

Let's prepare the first type of flexible budget for Texas Rex. Suppose that management wants to know the cost of producing 1,000 T-shirts, 1,200 T-shirts, and 1,400 T-shirts. To compute the expected cost for these different levels of output, we need to know the cost behavior pattern of each item in the budget. That is, we need to know the variable cost per unit and the fixed cost for the time period. From Schedule 6, we know the variable costs for direct materials ($4 per T-shirt), direct labor ($1.20 per T-shirt), and variable overhead ($0.60 per T-shirt). To increase the detail of the flexible budget, let's assume that these are variable costs per unit for supplies ($0.45) and power ($0.15). These two individual variable overhead amounts sum to $0.60. From Schedule 5, we also know that fixed overhead is budgeted at $1,645 per quarter. Exhibit 8-7 displays a flexible budget for production costs at these three levels of activity.

Notice in Exhibit 8-7 that total budgeted production costs increase as the production level increases. Budgeted costs change because total variable costs go up as output increases. Because of this, flexible budgets are sometimes referred to as **variable budgets**. Since Texas Rex has a mix of variable and fixed costs, the overall cost of producing one T-shirt *goes down* as production *goes up*. This makes sense. As production increases, there are more units over which to spread those fixed costs.

Flexible budgets are powerful control tools because they allow management to compute what the costs should have been for the level of output that actually occurred. Exhibit 8-7 reveals what the costs should have been for the actual level of activity (1,200 units). Now we can provide management with a useful performance report, one that compares actual and budgeted costs for the actual level of activity. This is the second type of flexible budget, and this report is given in Exhibit 8-8.

The revised performance report in Exhibit 8-8 paints a much different picture from the one in Exhibit 8-6. Now we can see that all of the variances are fairly small. Had they been larger, management would have searched for the cause and tried to correct the problems.

A difference between the actual amount and the flexible budget amount is the **flexible budget variance**. The flexible budget provides a measure of the efficiency of a manager. In other words, given the level of production achieved, how well did the manager control costs? To measure whether or not a manager accomplishes his or her goals, the static budget is used. The static budget represented certain goals that the firm wanted to achieve. A manager is effective if the goals described by the static budget are achieved or exceeded. In the Texas Rex example, production volume

Production costs	Variable Cost per Unit	Range of Production (units) 1,000	1,200	1,400
Variable:				
Direct materials	$4.00	$4,000	$4,800	$5,600
Direct labor	1.20	1,200	1,440	1,680
Variable overhead:				
Supplies	0.45	450	540	630
Power	0.15	150	180	210
Total variable costs	$5.80	$5,800	$6,960	$8,120
Fixed overhead:				
Supervision		$1,105	$1,105	$1,105
Depreciation		540	540	540
Total fixed costs		$1,645	$1,645	$1,645
Total production costs		$7,445	$8,605	$9,765

Exhibit 8-7 Flexible Production Budget

	Actual	Budget*	Variance
Units produced	1,200	1,200	—
Production costs:			
Direct materials	$4,830	$4,800	$30 U
Direct labor	1,440	1,440	0
Variable overhead:			
Supplies	535	540	(5) F
Power	170	180	(10) F
Total variable costs	$6,975	$6,960	$ 15 U
Fixed overhead:			
Supervision	$1,055	$1,105	$ (50) F
Depreciation	540	540	0
Total fixed costs	$1,595	$1,645	$ (50) F
Total production costs	$8,570	$8,605	$ 35 F

*From Exhibit 8-7.

Exhibit 8-8 Actual versus Flexible Performance Report: Quarterly Production Costs

was 140 units greater than the original budgeted amount; the manager exceeded the original budgeted goal. Therefore, the effectiveness of the manager is not in question.

The Behavioral Dimension of Budgeting

Budgets are often used to judge the performance of managers. Bonuses, salary increases, and promotions are all affected by a manager's ability to achieve or beat budgeted goals. Since a manager's financial status and career can be affected, budgets can have a significant behavioral effect. Whether that effect is positive or negative depends in large part on how budgets are used.

Managers Decide

Performance Evaluation and Flexible Budgeting

In formulating the budget for the coming year, LRL Radiology Clinic used the prior year's actual workload with its volume and mix of patients served, adjusted for changes in forecasted demand. This process produced a budget of 60,000 imaging procedures for the year (5,000 per month). At the end of the year, the budgeted costs for this level of patient load were compared with the actual costs incurred on a month-by-month basis. Significant variances were analyzed to determine the causes. For example, in the month of August, large unfavorable variances were reported for x-ray technicians and x-ray film. Investigation revealed that the variances were attributable mostly to a significant increase in the volume of imaging procedures, resulting from the closure of a competitor's clinic. Thus, the unfavorable variances occurred because the budgeted costs of a static volume were compared with the actual costs of a larger-than-expected actual output. This example emphasizes the importance of flexible budgeting to better monitor and understand the consumption of resources.

Source: Bautista, C. L., "Meeting the Challenge of Cost Containment: A Case Study Using Variance Analysis," *Journal of Health Care Finance* (Fall 1994): pp. 13–24.

Meaningful participation in the budgetary process helps managers internalize an organization's goals.

© Getty Images/PhotoDisc

Positive behavior occurs when the goals of individual managers are aligned with the goals of the organization and the manager has the drive to achieve them. The alignment of managerial and organizational goals is often referred to as **goal congruence**. If the budget is improperly administered, subordinate managers may subvert the organization's goals. **Dysfunctional behavior** is individual behavior that is in basic conflict with the goals of the organization.

An ideal budgetary system is one that achieves complete goal congruence and, simultaneously, creates a drive in managers to achieve the organization's goals in an ethical manner. While an ideal budgetary system probably does not exist, research and practice have identified some key features that promote a reasonable degree of positive behavior. These features include frequent feedback on performance, monetary and nonmonetary incentives, participative budgeting, realistic standards, controllability of costs, and multiple measures of performance.

Frequent Feedback on Performance Managers need to know how they are doing as the year unfolds. Providing them with frequent, timely performance reports allows them to know how successful their efforts have been, to take corrective actions, and to change plans as necessary.

Monetary and Nonmonetary Incentives A sound budgetary system encourages goal-congruent behavior. The means an organization uses to influence a manager to exert effort to achieve an organization's goal are called **incentives**. Traditional organizational theory assumes that individuals are primarily motivated by monetary rewards, resist work, and are inefficient and wasteful. Thus, **monetary incentives** are used to control a manager's tendency to shirk and waste resources by relating budgetary performance to salary increases, bonuses, and promotions. The threat of dismissal is the ultimate economic sanction for poor performance. In reality, individuals are motivated by more than economic factors. Individuals are also motivated by intrinsic psychological and social factors, such as the satisfaction of a job well done, recognition, responsibility, self-esteem, and the nature of the work itself. Thus, **nonmonetary incentives**, including job enrichment, increased responsibility and autonomy, nonmonetary recognition programs, and so on, can be used to enhance a budgetary control system.

Participative Budgeting Rather than imposing budgets on subordinate managers, **participative budgeting** allows subordinate managers considerable say in how the budgets are established. Typically, overall objectives are communicated to the manager, who helps develop a budget that will accomplish these objectives. Participative budgeting communicates a sense of responsibility to subordinate managers and fosters creativity. Since the subordinate manager creates the budget, it is more likely that the budget's goals will become the manager's personal goals, resulting in greater goal congruence. The increased responsibility and challenge inherent in the process provide nonmonetary incentives that lead to a higher level of performance.

Participative budgeting has three potential problems:

1. Setting standards that are either too high or too low.
2. Building slack into the budget (often referred to as padding the budget).
3. Pseudoparticipation.

Some managers may tend to set the budget either too loose or too tight. Since budgeted goals tend to become the manager's goals when participation is allowed, making this mistake in setting the budget can result in decreased performance levels. If goals are too easily achieved, a manager may lose interest, and performance may actually drop. Challenge is important to aggressive and creative individuals. Similarly, setting the budget too tight ensures failure to achieve the standards and frustrates the manager. This frustration, too, can lead to poorer performance. The trick is to get managers in a participative setting to set high, but achievable, goals.

The second problem with participative budgeting is the opportunity for managers to build slack into the budget. **Budgetary slack** (or *padding the budget*) exists when a manager deliberately underestimates revenues or overestimates costs. Either approach increases the likelihood that the manager will achieve the budget and consequently reduces the risk that the manager faces. Top management should carefully review budgets proposed by subordinate managers and provide input, where needed, in order to decrease the effects of building slack into the budget.

The third problem with participation occurs when top management assumes total control of the budgeting process, seeking only superficial participation from lower-level managers. This practice is termed **pseudoparticipation**. Top management is simply obtaining formal acceptance of the budget from subordinate managers, not seeking real input. Accordingly, none of the behavioral benefits of participation will be realized.

Realistic Standards Budgeted objectives are used to gauge performance; accordingly, they should be based on realistic conditions and expectations. Budgets should reflect operating realities such as actual levels of activity, seasonal variations, efficiencies, and general economic trends. Flexible budgets are used to ensure that budgeted costs can be realistically compared to costs for actual levels of activity. Interim budgets should reflect seasonal effects. **Toys "R" Us**, for example, would expect much higher sales in the quarter that includes Christmas than in other quarters. Budgetary cuts should be based on *planned* increases in efficiency and not simply arbitrary across-the-board reductions. Across-the-board cuts without any formal evaluation may impair the ability of some units to carry out their missions. General economic conditions also need to be considered. Budgeting for a significant increase in sales when a recession is projected is not only foolish but potentially dangerous.

Controllability of Costs Ideally, managers are held accountable only for costs that they can control. **Controllable costs** are costs whose level a manager can influence. For example, divisional managers have no power to authorize such corporate-level costs as research and development and salaries of top managers. Therefore, they should not be held accountable for the incurrence of those costs. If noncontrollable costs are put in the budgets of subordinate managers to help them understand that these costs also need to be covered, then they should be separated from controllable costs and labeled as *noncontrollable.*

Multiple Measures of Performance Often, organizations make the mistake of using budgets as their only measure of managerial performance. While financial measures of performance are important, overemphasis can lead to a form of dysfunctional behavior called *milking the firm* or *myopia*. **Myopic behavior** occurs when a manager takes actions that improve budgetary performance in the short run but bring long-run harm to the firm. For example, to meet budgeted cost objectives or profits, managers can fail to promote promotable employees or reduce expenditures for preventive maintenance, for advertising, and for new product development. Using measures that are both financial and nonfinancial and that are long term and short term can alleviate this problem. Budgetary measures by themselves are inadequate. The use of an integrated multiple-measures system known as the *Balanced Scorecard* is explored in Chapter 16.

Activity-Based Budgeting

Objective 4

Explain how activity-based budgeting works.

Companies that have implemented an activity-based cost (ABC) system may also wish to install an **activity-based budgeting system**. A budgetary system at the activity level can be a useful approach to support continuous improvement and process management. Furthermore, because activities consume resources and, thus, cause cost, activity-based budgeting may prove to be a much more powerful planning and control tool than the traditional, functional-based budgeting approach. An activity-based budgetary approach can be used to emphasize cost reduction through the elimination of wasteful activities and to improve the efficiency of necessary activities.

Static Activity Budgets

Activities cause costs by consuming resources; however, the amount of resources consumed depends on the demand for the activity's output. Thus, to build an activity-based budget, three steps are needed: (1) the activities within an organization must be identified, (2) the demand for each activity's output must be estimated, and (3) the cost of resources required to produce this level of activity must be assessed. If an organization has implemented an ABC or ABM (activity-based management) system, then step 1 will already have been accomplished. Assuming that ABC has been implemented, the major emphasis for activity-based budgeting is estimating the workload (demand) for each activity and then budgeting the resources required to sustain this workload. The workload for each activity must be set to support the sales and production activities expected for the coming period.

As with traditional budgeting, activity-based budgeting begins with sales and production budgets. Direct materials and direct labor budgets are also compatible with an ABC framework because these production inputs are directly traceable to the individual products. The major differences between functional and activity-based budgeting are found within the overhead and selling and administration expenses categories. In a functional-based approach, budgets within these categories are typically detailed by cost elements (see Exhibit 8-6 for an example of a detailed overhead budget). These cost elements are classified as variable or fixed with respect to units produced or sold. Furthermore, these budgets are usually constructed by budgeting for a cost item within a department (function) and then rolling these items up into the master overhead budget. For example, the cost of supervision in the overhead budget of Exhibit 8-6 is the sum of all the supervision costs of the various departments. Activity-based budgeting, on the other hand, identifies the overhead, selling, and administrative *activities* and then builds a budget for each activity, based on the resources needed to provide the required *activity* output levels. Costs are classified as variable or fixed with respect to the activity driver, not just to units produced or units sold.

Consider the activity of purchasing materials. The demand for purchasing is a function of the materials needed for producing the various products and services. Let the number of purchase orders be the driver for purchasing. Suppose that materials needed as expressed by the materials purchases budget create a demand for 15,000 purchase orders. To execute the purchasing activity, resources such as purchasing agents, supplies (forms, paper, stamps, envelopes, etc.), desks, computers, and office space are needed. Assuming that a clerk can process 3,000 orders per year, then five clerks are needed. Similarly, five desks, five computers, and office space for five agents are required. A budget for the purchasing activity is given below (depreciation is on the desks and computers, and occupancy is the cost of the office space).

Salaries	Depreciation	Supplies	Occupancy	Total
$200,000	$5,000	$15,000	$6,000	$226,000

Of the resources consumed by the purchasing activity, supplies is a flexible resource and, therefore, a variable cost, whereas the other resources consumed are committed resources and display a fixed cost behavior (a step-fixed cost behavior in the case of salaries and depreciation). However, there is an important difference that should be mentioned: Fixed and variable purchasing costs are defined with respect to the *number of purchase orders* and not direct labor hours or units produced or other measures of production output. The cost behavior of each activity is defined with respect to *its* output measure (which is often different from the production-based drivers used in functional-based budgeting). Knowing the output measure provides significant insight for controlling activity costs. In an activity framework, controlling costs translates into managing activities. For example, by redesigning products so that they use more common components, the number of purchase orders can be decreased. By decreasing the number of purchase orders demanded, flexible resource demand is reduced; furthermore, decreasing the number of purchase orders demanded also reduces the purchasing capacity needed, and costs will decrease. This is an example of activity-based management.

Activity Flexible Budgeting

The ability to identify changes in activity costs as activity output changes allows managers to more carefully plan and monitor activity improvements. **Activity flexible budgeting** is the prediction of what activity costs will be as activity output changes. Variance analysis within an activity framework makes it possible to improve traditional budgetary performance reporting. It also enhances the ability to manage activities.

In a functional-based approach, budgeted costs for the actual level of activity are obtained by assuming that a single unit-based driver (units of product or direct labor hours) drives all costs. A cost formula is developed for each cost item as a function of units produced or direct labor hours. Exhibit 8-7 illustrates a traditional flexible budget using units of product as the driver. Exhibit 8-9 presents a flexible budget based on direct labor hours. If, however, costs vary with respect to more than one driver and the drivers are not highly correlated with direct labor hours, then the predicted costs can be misleading.

The solution, of course, is to build flexible budget formulas for more than one driver. Cost estimation procedures (high-low method, the method of least squares, and so on) can be used to estimate and validate the cost formulas for each activity. In principle, the variable-cost component for each activity should correspond to resources acquired as needed (flexible resources), and the fixed-cost component should correspond to resources acquired in advance of usage (committed resources). This multiple-formula approach allows managers to predict more accurately what costs ought to be for different levels of activity usage, as measured by the activity output measure. These costs can then be compared with the actual costs to help

	Cost Formula		Direct Labor Hours	
	Fixed	Variable	10,000	20,000
Direct materials	—	$10	$100,000	$200,000
Direct labor	—	8	80,000	160,000
Maintenance	$ 20,000	3	50,000	80,000
Machining	15,000	1	25,000	35,000
Inspections	120,000	—	120,000	120,000
Setups	50,000	—	50,000	50,000
Purchasing	220,000	—	220,000	220,000
Total	$425,000	$22	$645,000	$865,000

Exhibit 8-9 Flexible Budget: Direct Labor Hours

assess budgetary performance. Exhibit 8-10 illustrates an activity flexible budget. Notice that the budgeted amounts for materials and labor are the same as those reported in Exhibit 8-9; they use the same activity output measure. The budgeted amounts for the other items differ significantly from the traditional amounts because the activity output measures differ.

Assume that the first activity level for each driver in Exhibit 8-10 corresponds to the actual activity usage levels. Exhibit 8-11 compares the budgeted costs for the actual activity usage levels with the actual costs. One item is on target, and the other six items are mixed. The net outcome is a favorable variance of $21,500.

	Driver: Direct Labor Hours			
	Formula		Level of Activity	
	Fixed	Variable	10,000	20,000
Direct materials	—	$10	$100,000	$200,000
Direct labor	—	8	80,000	160,000
Subtotal	$ 0	$18	$180,000	$360,000
	Driver: Machine Hours			
	Fixed	**Variable**	**8,000**	**16,000**
Maintenance	$20,000	$5.50	$64,000	$108,000
Machining	15,000	2.00	31,000	47,000
Subtotal	$35,000	$7.50	$95,000	$155,000
	Driver: Number of Setups			
	Fixed	**Variable**	**25**	**30**
Inspections	$80,000	$2,100	$132,500	$143,000
Setups	—	1,800	45,000	54,000
Subtotal	$80,000	$3,900	$177,500	$197,000
	Driver: Number of Orders			
	Fixed	**Variable**	**15,000**	**25,000**
Purchasing	$211,000	$1	$226,000	$236,000
Total			$678,500	$948,000

Exhibit 8-10 Activity Flexible Budget

	Actual Costs	Budgeted Costs	Budget Variance
Direct materials	$ 101,000	$ 100,000	$ 1,000 U
Direct labor	80,000	80,000	—
Maintenance	55,000	64,000	(9,000) F
Machining	29,000	31,000	(2,000) F
Inspections	125,500	132,500	(7,000) F
Setups	46,500	45,000	1,500 U
Purchasing	220,000	226,000	(6,000) F
Total	$657,000	$678,500	$(21,500) F

*Actual levels of drivers: 10,000 direct labor hours, 8,000 machine hours, 25 setups, and 15,000 orders.

Exhibit 8-11 Activity-Based Performance Report*

Managers Decide

Activity-Based Budgeting

In fiscal year 2001, the Small Business Administration (SBA) began to use activity-based budgeting with the objective of showing the relationship between the outputs and the resources needed. . . .The SBA begins activity-based budgeting by identifying the services that customers expect to receive from its various offices. These services constitute the outputs of the SBA. Once the outputs are identified, the SBA identifies the activities needed to produce the outputs. Since activities consume resources, it is then possible to determine the level of funding needed for the various outputs. This information is then used to decide which outputs can be produced given the funding provided. The objective is to manage resources to maximize the agency's outputs so that America's small businesses are best served. ■

Source: www.sba.gov/cfo/abb.html, accessed July 19, 2006.

The performance report in Exhibit 8-11 compares total budgeted costs for the actual level of activity with the total actual costs for each activity. It is also possible to compare the actual fixed activity costs with the budgeted fixed activity costs and the actual variable activity costs with the budgeted variable costs. For example, assume that the actual fixed inspection costs are $82,000 (due to a midyear salary adjustment, reflecting a more favorable union agreement than anticipated) and that the actual variable inspection costs are $43,500. The variable and fixed budget variances for the inspection activity are computed as follows:

Activity	Actual Cost	Budgeted Cost	Variance
Inspections:			
Fixed	$ 82,000	$ 80,000	$ 2,000 U
Variable	43,500	52,500	(9,000) F
Total	$125,500	$132,500	$(7,000) F

Breaking each variance into fixed and variable components provides more insight into the source of the variation in planned and actual expenditures. Other kinds of variance analysis are useful for activity management; however, consideration of these types of analyses was discussed in Chapter 5.

Summary of Learning Objectives

1. Discuss budgeting and its role in planning, control, and decision making.

Budgeting is the creation of a plan of action expressed in financial terms. Budgeting plays a key role in planning, control, and decision making. Budgets also serve to improve communication and coordination, a role that becomes increasingly important as organizations grow in size.

2. Define and prepare a *master budget,* identify its major components, and outline the interrelationships of its various components.

The master budget, the comprehensive financial plan of an organization, is made up of the operating and financial budgets. The operating budget is the budgeted income statement and all supporting schedules. The sales budget (Schedule 1) consists of the anticipated quantity and price of all products to be sold. The production budget (Schedule 2) gives the expected production in units to meet forecasted sales and desired ending inventory goals; expected production is supplemented by beginning inventory. The direct materials purchases budget (Schedule 3) gives the necessary purchases during the year for every type of raw material to meet production and desired ending inventory goals. The direct labor budget (Schedule 4) and overhead budget (Schedule 5) give the amounts of these resources necessary for the coming year's production. The overhead budget may be broken down into fixed and variable components to facilitate preparation of the budget. The selling and administrative expenses budget (Schedule 8) gives the forecasted costs for these functions. The finished goods inventory budget (Schedule 6) and the cost of goods sold budget (Schedule 7) detail production costs for the expected ending inventory and the units sold, respectively. The budgeted income statement (Schedule 9) outlines the net income to be realized if budgeted plans come to fruition.

The financial budget includes the cash budget, the capital expenditures budget, and the budgeted balance sheet. The cash budget (Schedule 10) is simply the beginning balance in the cash account, plus anticipated receipts, minus anticipated disbursements, plus or minus any necessary borrowing. The budgeted (or pro forma) balance sheet (Schedule 11) gives the anticipated ending balances of the asset, liability, and equity accounts if budgeted plans hold.

3. Describe flexible budgeting, and list the features that a budgetary system should have to encourage managers to engage in goal-congruent behavior.

The success of a budgetary system depends on how seriously human factors are considered. To discourage dysfunctional behavior, organizations should avoid overemphasizing budgets as a control mechanism. Other areas of performance should be evaluated in addition to budgets. Budgets can be improved as performance measures by using participative budgeting and other nonmonetary incentives, providing frequent feedback on performance, using flexible budgeting, ensuring that the budgetary objectives reflect reality, and holding managers accountable for only controllable costs.

4. Explain how activity-based budgeting works.

Activity-based budgeting identifies activities, demands for activity output, and the cost of resources needed to support the activity output demanded. The principal difference in an activity-based approach is a detailed listing of activities and their expected costs within the overhead, selling, and administrative categories. Activity-based budgeting has the potential of being more accurate than traditional budgeting because it focuses on output measures for each activity and thus allows a manager to understand cost behavior at a much more detailed level. Activity flexible budgeting is also more accurate because it uses cost formulas that depend on each activity's output measures.

Key Terms

Review Problems

1. Selected Operational Budgets

Young Products produces coat racks. The projected sales for the first quarter of the coming year and the beginning and ending inventory data are as follows:

Unit sales	100,000
Unit price	$15
Units in beginning inventory	8,000
Units in targeted ending inventory	12,000

The coat racks are molded and then painted. Each rack requires four pounds of metal, which costs $2.50 per pound. The beginning inventory of materials is 4,000 pounds. Young Products wants to have 6,000 pounds of metal in inventory at the end of the quarter. Each rack produced requires 30 minutes of direct labor time, which is billed at $9 per hour.

Required

1. Prepare a sales budget for the first quarter.
2. Prepare a production budget for the first quarter.
3. Prepare a direct materials purchases budget for the first quarter.
4. Prepare a direct labor budget for the first quarter.

Solution

1. **Young Products**
Sales Budget
For the First Quarter

Units	100,000
Unit price	× $15
Sales	$1,500,000

2. **Young Products**
Production Budget
For the First Quarter

Sales (in units)	100,000
Desired ending inventory	12,000
Total needs	112,000
Less: Beginning inventory	8,000
Units to be produced	104,000

3. **Young Products**
Direct Materials Purchases Budget
For the First Quarter

Units to be produced	104,000
Direct materials per unit (lb.)	× 4
Production needs (lb.)	416,000
Desired ending inventory (lb.)	6,000
Total needs (lb.)	422,000
Less: Beginning inventory (lb.)	4,000
Materials to be purchased (lb.)	418,000
Cost per pound	× $2.50
Total purchase cost	$1,045,000

4.

Young Products
Direct Labor Budget
For the First Quarter

Units to be produced	104,000
Labor: Hours per unit	× 0.5
Total hours needed	52,000
Cost per hour	× $9
Total direct labor cost	$468,000

2. Cash Budgeting

Rogier, Inc., expects to receive cash from sales of $45,000 in March. In addition, Rogier expects to sell property worth $3,500. Payments for materials and supplies are expected to total $10,000, direct labor payroll will be $12,500, and other expenditures are budgeted at $14,900. On March 1, the cash account balance is $1,230.

Required

1. Prepare a cash budget for Rogier, Inc., for the month of March.
2. Assume that Rogier, Inc., wanted a minimum cash balance of $15,000 and that it could borrow from the bank in multiples of $1,000 at an interest rate of 12 percent per year. What would Rogier's adjusted ending balance for March be? How much interest would Rogier owe in April assuming that the entire amount borrowed in March would be paid back?

Solution

1.

Rogier, Inc.
Cash Budget
For the Month of March

Beginning cash balance	$ 1,230
Cash sales	45,000
Sale of property	3,500
Total cash available	$49,730
Less disbursements:	
Materials and supplies	$ 10,000
Direct labor payroll	12,500
Other expenditures	14,900
Total disbursements	$37,400
Ending cash balance	$12,330

2.

Unadjusted ending balance	$12,330
Plus borrowing	3,000
Adjusted ending balance	$15,330

In April, interest owed would be $(1/12 \times 0.12 \times \$3{,}000) = \$30$.

Questions for Writing and Discussion

1. Define the term *budget.* How are budgets used in planning?
2. Define *control.* How are budgets used to control?
3. Explain how both small and large organizations can benefit from budgeting.
4. Discuss some of the reasons for budgeting.
5. What is a master budget? An operating budget? A financial budget?
6. Explain the role of a sales forecast in budgeting. What is the difference between a sales forecast and a sales budget?
7. All budgets depend on the sales budget. Is this true? Explain.
8. How do master budgets differ among manufacturing, merchandising, and service organizations?
9. Discuss the differences between static and flexible budgets. Why are flexible budgets superior to static budgets for performance reporting?
10. Explain why mixed costs must be broken down into their fixed and variable components before a flexible budget can be developed.
11. Why is goal congruence important?
12. Why is it important for a manager to receive frequent feedback on his or her performance?
13. Discuss the roles of monetary and nonmonetary incentives. Do you believe that nonmonetary incentives are needed? Why or why not?
14. What is participative budgeting? Discuss some of its advantages.
15. A budget too easily achieved will lead to diminished performance. Do you agree or disagree? Explain.
16. What is the role of top management in participative budgeting?
17. Explain why a manager has an incentive to build slack into the budget.
18. Explain how a manager can "milk the firm" to improve budgetary performance.
19. Identify performance measures other than budgets that can be used to discourage myopic behavior. Discuss how you would use these measures.
20. How important are the behavioral aspects of a budgetary control system? Explain.
21. In an era of budgetary cuts, across-the-board cuts harm good programs more than bad programs. Do you agree? What approach would you recommend? Why?
22. Explain how an activity-based budget is prepared.
23. What is the difference between an activity flexible budget and a functional-based (traditional) flexible budget?

Exercises

8-1

Budgeting Concepts
LO1

1. A budget is
   a. a long-term plan.
   b. prepared for at least two years.
   c. only a control tool.
   d. necessary only for large firms.
   e. a short-term financial plan.

2. Identify which of the following is not part of the control process:
   a. Monitoring of actual activity.
   b. Comparison of actual with planned activity.
   c. Investigating.
   d. Developing a strategic plan.
   e. Taking corrective action.

3. Which of the following is not an advantage of budgeting:
   a. It forces managers to plan.
   b. It provides information for decision making.
   c. It guarantees that an improvement in organizational efficiency.

d. It provides a standard for performance evaluation.
e. It improves communication and coordination.

4. The budget committee

a. reviews the budget.
b. resolves differences that arise as the budget is prepared.
c. approves the final budget.
d. is directed (typically) by the controller.
e. All of the above.

5. A moving, twelve-month budget, updated monthly, is

a. a waste of time and effort.
b. a continuous budget.
c. a master budget.
d. not used by industrial firms.
e. always used by firms that prepare a master budget.

8-2

Planning and Control
LO1

(A) Dr. Jones, a dentist, wants to increase the size and profitability of his business by building a reputation for quality and timely service. **(B)** To achieve this, he plans on adding a dental laboratory to his building so that crowns, bridges, and dentures can be made in-house. **(C)** To add the laboratory, he needs additional money, which he decides must be obtained by increasing revenues. After some careful calculation, Dr. Jones concludes that annual revenues must be increased by 10 percent.

(D) Dr. Jones finds that his fees for fillings and crowns are below the average in his community and decides that the 10 percent increase can be achieved by increasing these fees. **(E)** He then identifies the quantity of fillings and crowns expected for the coming year, the new per-unit fee, and the total fees expected. **(F)** As the year unfolds (on a month-by-month basis), Dr. Jones compares the actual revenues received with the budgeted revenues. For the first three months actual revenues were less than planned. **(G)** Upon investigating, he discovered that he had some reduction in the number of patients because he had also changed his available hours of operation. **(H)** He returned to his old schedule, and found out that the number of patients was restored to the original expected levels. **(I)** However, to make up the shortfall, he also increased the price of some of his other services.

Required

Match the statements following the letters with the following planning and control elements (a letter may be matched to more than one item):

1. Corrective action
2. Budgets
3. Feedback
4. Investigation
5. Short-term plan
6. Comparison of actual with planned
7. Monitoring of actual activity
8. Strategic plan
9. Short-term objectives
10. Long-term objectives

8-3

Sales Budget
LO1, LO2

Freshaire, Inc., produces two types of air fresheners: Mint Freshener and Lemon Freshener. Both products are sold in 32-ounce bottles. Mint sells for $3.00 per bottle, and Lemon sells for $3.50 per bottle. Projected sales (in bottles) for the coming four quarters are as follows:

EXCEL

	Mint	Lemon
First quarter, 2008	80,000	100,000
Second quarter, 2008	110,000	100,000
Third quarter, 2008	124,000	120,000
Fourth quarter, 2008	140,000	140,000
First quarter, 2009	90,000	110,000

The vice president of sales believes that the projected sales are realistic and can be achieved by the company.

Required

1. Prepare a sales budget for each quarter of 2008 and for the year in total. Show sales by product and in total for each time period.
2. How will Freshaire, Inc., use this sales budget?

8-4
Production Budget
LO2

Refer to **Exercise 8-3.** Freshaire, Inc., next prepared a production budget for each product. Beginning inventory of Mint Freshener on January 1 was 4,000 bottles. The company's policy is to have 10 percent of the next quarter's sales of Mint Freshener in ending inventory. Beginning inventory of Lemon Freshener on January 1 was 6,400 bottles. The company's policy is to have 20 percent of the next quarter's sales of Lemon Freshener in ending inventory.

Required
Prepare a production budget for each product by quarter and in total for the year.

8-5
Production Budget
LO2

Pescado produces tuna in cans. The sales budget for the first four months of the year is presented below.

	Unit Sales	Dollar Sales
January	200,000	$150,000
February	240,000	180,000
March	220,000	165,000
April	200,000	150,000

Company policy requires that ending inventories for each month be 35 percent of next month's sales. At the beginning of January, the inventory of tuna is 38,000 cans.

Required
Prepare a production budget for the first quarter of the year. Show the number of cans that should be produced each month as well as for the quarter in total.

8-6
Raw Materials Purchases Budget
LO2

Refer to **Exercise 8-5.** Two raw materials needed are tuna and cans. Each can of tuna requires one can and 4 ounces of tuna. Company policy requires that ending inventories of raw materials for each month be 20 percent of the next month's production needs. That policy was met on January 1.

Required
Prepare separate direct materials purchases budgets for cans and for tuna for the months of January and February (in units only).

8-7
Production Budget
LO2

Carson, Inc., produces office supplies, including pencils. Pencils are bundled in packages; each package sells for $0.50. The sales budget for the first four months of the year follows for this product.

	Unit Sales	Dollar Sales
January	200,000	$100,000
February	240,000	120,000
March	220,000	110,000
April	200,000	100,000

Company policy requires that ending inventories for each month be 15 percent of next month's sales. However, at the beginning of January, due to greater sales in December than anticipated, the beginning inventory of pencils is only 18,000 packages.

Required

Prepare a production budget for the first quarter of the year. Show the number of units that should be produced each month as well as for the quarter in total.

8-8

Direct Materials Purchases Budget
LO2

Manning Company produces a variety of labels, including iron-on name labels, which are sold to parents of camp-bound children. (The camps require campers to have their name on every article of clothing.) Each roll consists of 25 yards of paper strip with 1,000 copies of the child's name. Each yard of paper strip costs $0.30. Manning has budgeted production of the label rolls for the next four months as follows:

	Rolls in Units
March	20,000
April	60,000
May	100,000
June	12,000

Inventory policy requires that sufficient paper strip be in ending monthly inventory to satisfy 20 percent of the following month's production needs. The inventory of paper strip at the beginning of March equals exactly the amount needed to satisfy the inventory policy.

Required

Prepare a direct materials purchases budget for March, April, and May showing purchases in units and in dollars for each month and in total.

8-9

Direct Labor Budget
LO2

Refer to the production budget in **Exercise 8-8.** Each roll of labels produced requires (on average) 0.04 direct labor hour. The average cost of direct labor is $12 per hour.

Required

Prepare a direct labor budget for March, April, and May showing the hours needed and the direct labor cost for each month and in total.

8-10

Sales Budget
LO2

Swasey, Inc. manufactures six models of leaf blowers and weed eaters. Swasey's budgeting team is finalizing the sales budget for the coming year. Sales in units and dollars for last year follow:

Product	Number Sold	Price	Revenue
LB-1	16,800	$29	$ 487,200
LB-2	18,000	15	270,000
WE-6	25,200	13	327,600
WE-7	16,200	10	162,000
WE-8	2,400	22	52,800
WE-9	1,000	26	26,000
Total			$1,325,600

In looking over the previous year's sales figures, Swasey's sales budgeting team recalled the following:

a. Model LB-1 is a newer version of the leaf blower with a gasoline engine. The LB-1 is mounted on wheels, instead of being carried. This model is designed for the commercial market, and did better than expected its first year. As a result, the number of units of model LB-1 to be sold were forecast at 200 percent of the previous year's units. The price for the coming year was also increased by $1 per unit.
b. Models WE-8 and WE-9 were introduced on October 1 last year. They are lighter versions of the traditional weed eater, and designed for smaller households or condo units. Swasey estimates that demand for both models will continue at the previous year's rate.
c. A competitor has announced plans to introduce an improved version of model WE-6, Swasey's traditional weed eater. Swasey believes that the model WE-6 price must be cut 20 percent to maintain unit sales at the previous year's level.
d. It was assumed that unit sales of all other models would increase by 20 percent, prices remaining constant.

Required

Prepare a sales budget by product and in total for Swasey, Inc. for the coming year.

8-11

Production Budget; Direct Materials Purchases Budget
LO2

EXCEL

Raylene Webber, owner of Raylene's Flowers and Gifts, produces gift baskets for various special occasions. Each gift basket includes fruit and assorted small gifts (e.g., a coffee mug, deck of cards, novelty cocoa mixes, scented soap) in a basket that is wrapped in colorful cellophane. Raylene has estimated the following sales of the standard gift basket for the rest of the year and January of next year.

September	200
October	150
November	180
December	250
January	100

Raylene likes to have 10 percent of the next month's sales needs on hand at the end of each month. This requirement was met on August 31.

Materials needed for each basket are as follows:

Fruit	1 pound
Small gifts	5 items
Cellophane	3 feet (cut from the roll of cellophane)
Basket	1

The materials inventory policy is to have 5 percent of the next month's fruit needs on hand as well as 50 percent of the next month's production needs for all other materials. (The relatively low inventory amount for fruit is designed to prevent spoilage.) Materials inventory on September 1 met this company policy.

Required

1. Prepare a production budget for September, October, November, and December for gift baskets.
2. Prepare a direct materials purchases budget (in units only) for the four types of materials used in the production of gift baskets for the months of September, October, and November. (Round all answers to the nearest whole unit.)
3. Why can't you prepare a direct materials purchases budget for December?

8-12

Cash Receipts Budget
LO2

Lawrence, Inc., found that about 10 percent of its sales during the month were for cash. Lawrence has the following accounts receivable payment experience:

Percent paid in the month of sale	30%
Percent paid in the month after the sale	60%
Percent paid in the second month after the sale	7%

Lawrence's anticipated sales for the next few months are

April	$200,000
May	240,000
June	230,000
July	246,000
August	250,000

Required

1. Calculate credit sales for May, June, July, and August.
2. Prepare a cash receipts budget for July and August.

8-13

Cash Receipts Budget
LO2

Janzen, Inc., sells all of its product on account. Janzen has the following accounts receivable payment experience:

Percent paid in the month of sale	20%
Percent paid in the month after the sale	60
Percent paid in the second month after the sale	15

To encourage payment in the month of sale, Janzen gives a 2 percent cash discount. Janzen's anticipated sales for the next few months are:

April	$200,000
May	220,000
June	230,000
July	210,000
August	250,000

Required

1. Prepare a cash receipts budget for July.
2. Prepare a cash receipts budget for August.

8-14

Cash Budget
LO2

Marvel Company provided the following information relating to cash payments.

a. Marvel purchased direct materials on account in the following amounts.

June	20,000
July	25,000
August	30,000

Marvel pays 25 percent of accounts payable in the month of purchase, and the remaining 75 percent in the following month.

b. In July, direct labor cost $40,000. August direct labor cost was $50,000. The company finds that typically 90 percent of direct labor cost is paid in cash during the month, with the remainder paid in the following month.

c. August overhead amounted to $70,000, including $5,500 of depreciation.

d. Marvel took out a loan of $10,000 on May 1. Interest, due with payment of principal, accrued at the rate of 12 percent per year. The loan and all interest was repaid on August 31.

Required

Prepare a schedule of cash payments for Marvel Company for the month of August.

8-15

Cash Budget
LO2

EXCEL

The owner of a small mining supply company has requested a cash budget for June. After examining the records of the company, you find the following:

a. Cash balance on June 1 is $345.
b. Actual sales for April and May are

	April	May
Cash sales	$ 10,000	$15,000
Credit sales	25,000	25,000
Total sales	$35,000	$40,000

c. Credit sales are collected over a three-month period: 50 percent in the month of sale, 30 percent in the second month, and 15 percent in the third month. The sales collected in the third month are subject to a 1.5 percent late fee, but only half of the affected customers pay the late fee, and the owner does not think it is worth his while to try to collect from the other half. The remaining sales are uncollectible.
d. Inventory purchases average 60 percent of a month's total sales. Of those purchases, 40 percent are paid for in the month of purchase. The remaining 60 percent are paid for in the following month.
e. Salaries and wages total $8,700 a month, including a $4,500 salary paid to the owner.
f. Rent is $1,200 per month.
g. Taxes to be paid in June are $5,500.

The owner also tells you that he expects cash sales of $20,000 and credit sales of $30,000 for June. There is no minimum cash balance required. The owner of the company does not have access to short-term loans.

Required

1. Prepare a cash budget for June. Include supporting schedules for cash collections and cash payments.
2. Did the business show a negative cash balance for June? Assuming that the owner has no hope of establishing a line of credit for the business, what recommendations would you give the owner for dealing with a negative cash balance?

8-16

Performance Reporting
LO3

Zapato, Inc. produces sandals. Data for the second quarter are as follows:

Master Budget	Actual Data
Budgeted production: 1,000	Actual Production: 1,100 units
Materials: 2 leather strips @ $5	Materials cost: $11,200
Labor: 0.5 hrs @ $8.00	Labor cost: $4,400

Required

1. Prepare a performance report using a budget based on expected production.
2. Comment on the limitations of this report.

8-17

Overhead Budget; Flexible Budget
LO2, LO3

Regina Johnson, controller for Pet-Care Company, has been instructed to develop a flexible budget for overhead costs. The company produces two types of dog food. One, BasicDiet, is a standard mixture for healthy dogs. The second, SpecDiet, is a reduced-protein formulation for older dogs with health problems. The two dog foods use common raw materials in different proportions. The company expects to produce 100,000 fifty-pound bags of each product during the coming year. BasicDiet requires 0.25 direct labor hours (DLH) per bag, and SpecDiet requires 0.30. Regina has developed the following fixed and variable costs for each of the four overhead items:

Overhead Item	Fixed Cost	Variable Rate per DLH
Maintenance	$17,000	$0.40
Power		0.50
Indirect labor	26,500	1.60
Rent	18,000	

Required

1. Prepare an overhead budget for the expected activity level for the coming year.
2. Prepare an overhead budget that reflects production that is 10 percent higher than expected (for both products) and one for production that is 20 percent lower than expected.

8-18

Performance Report
LO3

Refer to the information given in **Exercise 8-17.** Assume that Pet-Care actually produced 120,000 bags of BasicDiet and 100,000 of SpecDiet. The actual overhead costs incurred were as follows:

Maintenance	$ 40,500
Power	31,700
Indirect labor	119,000
Rent	18,000

Required

1. Prepare a performance report for the current year.
2. Based on the report, would you judge any of the variances to be significant? Can you think of some possible reasons for the variances?

8-19

Participative versus Imposed Budgeting
LO3

CMA

An effective budget converts the goals and objectives of an organization into data. The budget serves as a blueprint for management's plans. The budget is also the basis for control. Management performance can be evaluated by comparing actual results with the budget.

Thus, creating the budget is essential for the successful operation of an organization. Finding the resources to implement the budget—that is, getting from a starting point to the ultimate goal—requires the extensive use of human resources. How managers perceive their roles in the process of budgeting is important to the successful use of the budget as an effective tool for planning, communicating, and controlling.

Required

1. Discuss the behavioral implications of planning and control when a company's management employs
   a. an imposed budgetary approach
   b. a participative budgetary approach
2. Communication plays an important role in the budgetary process, whether a participative or an imposed budgetary approach is used.
   a. Discuss the differences between communication flows in these two budgetary approaches.
   b. Discuss the behavioral implications associated with the communication process for each of the budgetary approaches. **(CMA adapted)**

8-20

Activity-Based Budgeting
LO4

Olsen Company has implemented an activity-based accounting system and now has decided to begin activity-based budgeting. For the inspection activity, an inspector, working 2,000 hours per year, is paid a salary of $50,000. The products are produced in batch sizes of 1,000. A sample of each batch is taken and the products in the sample are run through a series of electronic tests. On average, each batch sample requires 100 hours for testing. The testing equipment is leased at $10,000 per year and has 5,000 hours of testing capability per year. Power and other materials for the test costs $2.00 per hour.

Required

1. Suppose that Olsen budgets 50,000 units for production for the coming year. What is the budget for the inspection activity?
2. Now assume that the budget is 60,000 units. Prepare a budget for inspection for this level of activity.
3. Prepare a flexible budget formula, assuming that production is usually between 60,000 and 80,000 units. Is the flexible budget formula valid only for this range of activity? Explain.

8-21

Activity-Based Budgeting: Static and Flexible
LO4

EXCEL

Jamison, Inc., uses three forklifts to move materials from Receiving to Stores. The forklifts are also used to move materials from Stores to the production area. The forklifts are obtained through an operating lease that costs $8,000 per year per forklift. Jamison employs 10 forklift operators who receive an average salary of $40,000 per year, including benefits. Each move requires the use of a crate. The crates are used to store the parts and are emptied only when the parts are used in production. Crates are disposed of after one cycle (two moves), where a cycle is defined as Receiving to Stores to Production. Each crate costs $2.00. Fuel for a forklift costs $1.20 per gallon. A gallon of gas is used for every 20 moves. Forklifts can make three moves per hour and are available for 280 days per year, 24 hours per day (the remaining time is downtime for various reasons). Each operator works 40 hours per week and 50 weeks per year.

Required

1. Prepare an annual budget for the activity of moving materials, assuming that all of the capacity of the activity is used. Identify which resources you would treat as fixed costs and which would be viewed as variable costs.
2. Assume that the company uses only 90 percent of the activity capacity. What is the budget for this level of activity?
3. Suppose that a redesign of the plant layout reduces the demand for moving materials by 75 percent. What would be the budget for this new activity level?

Problems

8-22

Flexible Budgeting
LO3

Budgeted overhead costs for two different levels of activity follow.

	Direct Labor Hours	
	1,000	**2,000**
Maintenance	$ 10,100	$13,100
Depreciation	7,000	7,000
Supervision	16,000	16,000
Supplies	2,400	4,800
Power	1,000	2,000
Other	12,940	14,240

Required

Prepare a flexible budget for an activity level of 1,800 direct labor hours.

8-23

Cash Receipts Budget
LO2

Kendall Law Firm has found from experience that 30 percent of its services are for cash. The remaining 70 percent are on credit. An aging schedule for accounts receivable reveals the following pattern:

a. Ten percent of fees on credit are paid in the month service is rendered.
b. Seventy percent of fees on credit are paid in the month following the legal service.
c. Seventeen percent of fees on credit are paid in the second month following the legal service.
d. Three percent of fees on credit are never collected.

Fees (on credit) that have not been paid until the second month following performance of the legal service are considered overdue and are subject to a 2 percent late charge.

Kendall has developed the following forecast of fees:

May	$228,000
June	255,000
July	204,000
August	240,000
September	300,000

Required

Prepare a schedule of cash receipts for August and September.

8-24

Operating Budget; Comprehensive Analysis
LO2

EXCEL

Briggs Manufacturing produces a subassembly used in the production of jet aircraft engines. The assembly is sold to engine manufacturers and to aircraft maintenance facilities. Projected sales for the coming four months follow:

January	40,000
February	50,000
March	60,000
April	60,000

The following data pertain to production policies and manufacturing specifications followed by Briggs Manufacturing:

a. Finished goods inventory on January 1 is 32,000 units, each costing $148.71. The desired ending inventory for each month is 80 percent of the next month's sales.
b. The data on materials used are as follows:

Direct Material	Per-Unit Usage	Cost per Pound
Metal	10 lbs.	$8
Components	6	2

Inventory policy dictates that sufficient materials be on hand at the beginning of the month to produce 50 percent of that month's estimated sales. This is exactly the amount of material on hand on January 1.

c. The direct labor used per unit of output is four hours. The average direct labor cost per hour is $9.25.
d. Overhead each month is estimated using a flexible budget formula. (Activity is measured in direct labor hours.)

	Fixed-Cost Component	Variable-Cost Component
Supplies	—	$1.00
Power	—	0.50
Maintenance	$ 30,000	0.40

(continued)

	Fixed-Cost Component	Variable-Cost Component
Supervision	16,000	—
Depreciation	200,000	—
Taxes	12,000	—
Other	80,000	1.50

e. Monthly selling and administrative expenses are also estimated using a flexible budgeting formula. (Activity is measured in units sold.)

	Fixed Costs	Variable Costs
Salaries	$50,000	—
Commissions	—	$2.00
Depreciation	40,000	—
Shipping	—	1.00
Other	20,000	0.60

f. The unit selling price of the subassembly is $215.

g. All sales and purchases are for cash. The cash balance on January 1 equals $378,000. If the firm develops a cash shortage by the end of the month, sufficient cash is borrowed to cover the shortage. Any cash borrowed is repaid at the end of the quarter, as is the interest due. (Cash borrowed at the end of the quarter is repaid at the end of the following quarter.) The interest rate is 12 percent per annum. No money is owed at the beginning of January.

Required

Prepare a monthly operating budget for the first quarter with the following schedules:

1. Sales budget
2. Production budget
3. Direct materials purchases budget
4. Direct labor budget
5. Overhead budget
6. Selling and administrative expenses budget
7. Ending finished goods inventory budget
8. Cost of goods sold budget
9. Budgeted income statement (ignore income taxes)
10. Cash budget

8-25

Cash Budget; Pro Forma Balance Sheet
LO2

Ryan Richards, controller for Grange Retailers, has assembled the following data to assist in the preparation of a cash budget for the third quarter of 2008:

a. Sales:

May (actual)	$100,000
June (actual)	120,000
July (estimated)	90,000
August (estimated)	100,000
September (estimated)	135,000
October (estimated)	110,000

b. Each month, 30 percent of sales are for cash and 70 percent are on credit. The collection pattern for credit sales is 20 percent in the month of sale, 50 percent in the following month, and 30 percent in the second month following the sale.

c. Each month, the ending inventory exactly equals 50 percent of the cost of next month's sales. The markup on goods is 25 percent of cost.

d. Inventory purchases are paid for in the month following the purchase.

e. Recurring monthly expenses are as follows:

Salaries and wages	$10,000
Depreciation on plant and equipment	4,000
Utilities	1,000
Other	1,700

f. Property taxes of $15,000 are due and payable on July 15, 2008.
g. Advertising fees of $6,000 must be paid on August 20, 2008.
h. A lease on a new storage facility is scheduled to begin on September 2, 2008. Monthly payments are $5,000.
i. The company has a policy to maintain a minimum cash balance of $10,000. If necessary, it will borrow to meet its short-term needs. All borrowing is done at the beginning of the month. All payments on principal and interest are made at the end of a month. The annual interest rate is 9 percent. The company must borrow in multiples of $1,000.
j. A partially completed balance sheet as of June 30, 2008, follows. (Accounts payable is for inventory purchases only.)

Cash	$?	
Accounts receivable	?	
Inventory	?	
Plant and equipment	425,000	
Accounts payable		$?
Common stock		210,000
Retained earnings		268,750
Total	$?	$?

Required

1. Complete the balance sheet given in (j).
2. Prepare a cash budget for each month in the third quarter and for the quarter in total. (The third quarter begins on July 1.) Provide a supporting schedule of cash collections.
3. Prepare a pro forma balance sheet as of September 30, 2008.

8-26

Participative Budgeting; Not-for-Profit Setting
LO3

CMA

Scott Weidner, the controller in the division of social services for the state, recognizes the importance of the budgetary process for planning, control, and motivation. He believes that a properly implemented process of participative budgeting and management by exception will motivate his subordinates to improve productivity within their particular departments. Based upon this philosophy, Scott has implemented the following budgetary procedures:

1. An appropriation target figure is given to each department manager. This amount represents the maximum funding that each department can expect to receive in the next fiscal year.
2. Department managers develop their individual budgets within the following spending constraints as directed by the controller's staff:

   a. Requests for spending cannot exceed the appropriated target.
   b. All fixed expenditures should be included in the budget. Fixed expenditures include such items as contracts and salaries at current levels.
   c. All government projects directed by a higher authority should be included in the budget in their entirety.

3. The controller's staff consolidates the requests from the various departments into one budget for the entire division.

4. Upon final budget approval by the legislature, the controller's staff allocates the appropriation to the various departments on instructions from the division manager. However, a specified percentage of each department's appropriation is held back in anticipation of potential budget cuts and special funding needs. The amount and use of this contingency fund is left to the discretion of the division manager.
5. Each department is allowed to adjust its budget when necessary to operate within the reduced appropriation level. However, as stated in the original directive, specific projects authorized by a higher authority must remain intact.
6. The final budget is used as the basis of control for a management-by-exception form of reporting. Excessive expenditures by account for each department are highlighted on a monthly basis. Department managers are expected to account for all expenditures over budget. Fiscal responsibility is an important factor in the overall performance evaluation of department managers. Scott believes his policy of allowing the department managers to participate in the budget process and then holding them accountable for the final budget is essential, especially in times of limited resources. He further believes that the department managers will be motivated to increase the efficiency and effectiveness of their departments because they have provided input into the initial budgetary process and are required to justify any unfavorable performances.

Required

1. Discuss the advantages and limitations of participative budgeting.
2. Identify deficiencies in Scott Weidner's outline for a budgetary process. Recommend how each identified deficiency can be corrected. **(CMA adapted)**

8-27

Cash Budget
LO2

The controller of Minota Company is gathering data to prepare the cash budget for July 2008. He plans to develop the budget from the following information:

a. Of all sales, 30 percent are cash sales.
b. Of credit sales, 60 percent are collected within the month of sale. Half of the credit sales collected within the month receive a 2 percent cash discount (for accounts paid within 10 days). Twenty percent of credit sales are collected in the following month; remaining credit sales are collected the month thereafter. There are virtually no bad debts.
c. Sales for the second two quarters of the year follow. (The first three months are actual sales, and the last three months are estimated sales.)

	Sales
April	$ 460,000
May	600,000
June	1,000,000
July	1,140,000
August	1,200,000
September	1,134,000

d. The company sells all that it produces each month. The cost of raw materials equals 24 percent of each sales dollar. The company requires a monthly ending inventory equal to the coming month's production requirements. Of raw materials purchases, 50 percent are paid for in the month of purchase. The remaining 50 percent are paid for in the following month.
e. Wages total $110,000 each month and are paid in the month incurred.
f. Budgeted monthly operating expenses total $336,000, of which $50,000 is depreciation and $6,000 is expiration of prepaid insurance. (The annual premium of $72,000 is paid on January 1.)

g. Dividends of $140,000, declared on June 30, will be paid on July 15.
h. Old equipment will be sold for $25,200 on July 4.
i. On July 13, new equipment will be purchased for $168,000.
j. The company maintains a minimum cash balance of $20,000.
k. The cash balance on July 1 is $27,000.

Required

Prepare a cash budget for July. Give a supporting schedule that details the cash collections from sales.

8-28

Performance Reporting; Behavioral Considerations LO1, LO3

CMA

Berwin, Inc., is a manufacturer of small industrial tools with annual sales of approximately $3.5 million. Sales growth has been steady during the year, and there is no evidence of cyclical demand. Production has increased gradually during the year and has been evenly distributed throughout each month. The company has a sequential processing system. The four manufacturing departments—Casting, Machining, Finishing, and Packaging—are all located in the same building. Fixed overhead is assigned using a plantwide rate.

Berwin has always been able to compete with other manufacturers of small tools. However, its market has expanded only in response to product innovation. Thus, research and development are very important and have helped Berwin to expand as well as maintain demand.

Carla Viller, controller, has designed and implemented a new budget system in response to concerns voiced by George Berwin, president. Carla prepared an annual budget that has been divided into 12 equal segments; this budget can be used to assist in the timely evaluation of monthly performance. George was visibly upset upon receiving the May performance report for the Machining Department. George exclaimed, "How can they be efficient enough to produce nine extra units every working day and still miss the budget by $300 per day?" Gene Jordan, supervisor of the Machining Department, could not understand "all the red ink" when he knew that the department had operated more efficiently in May than it had in months. Gene stated, "I was expecting a pat on the back, and instead, the boss tore me apart. What's more, I don't even know why!"

Berwin, Inc.
Machining Department Performance Report
For the Month Ended May 31, 2008

	Budgeted	Actual	Variance
Volume in units	3,000	3,185	185 F
Variable manufacturing costs:			
Direct materials	$24,000	$ 24,843	$ 843 U
Direct labor	27,750	29,302	1,552 U
Variable overhead	33,300	35,035	1,735 U
Total variable costs	$85,050	$ 89,180	$4,130 U
Fixed manufacturing costs:			
Indirect labor	$ 3,300	$ 3,334	$ 34 U
Depreciation	1,500	1,500	—
Taxes	300	300	—
Insurance	240	240	—
Other	930	1,027	97 U
Total fixed costs	$ 6,270	$ 6,401	$ 131 U
Corporate costs:			
Research and development	$ 2,400	$ 3,728	$1,328 U
Selling and administrative	3,600	4,075	475 U
Total corporate costs	$ 6,000	$ 7,803	$1,803 U
Total costs	$97,320	$103,384	$6,064 U

Required

1. Review the May performance report. Use the information given in the report and elsewhere.
   a. Discuss the strengths and weaknesses of the new budgetary system.
   b. Identify the weaknesses of the performance report, and explain how it should be revised to eliminate each weakness.
2. Prepare a revised report for the Machining Department using the May data.
3. What other changes would you make to improve Berwin's budgetary system? **(CMA adapted)**

8-29

Functional versus Flexible Budgeting
LO3, LO4

Amy Bunker, production manager, was upset with the latest performance report, which indicated that she was $100,000 over budget. Given the efforts that she and her workers had made, she was confident that they had met or beat the budget. Now, she was not only upset but also genuinely puzzled over the results. Three items—direct labor, power, and setups—were over budget. The actual costs for these three items follow:

Direct labor	$ 210,000
Power	135,000
Setups	140,000
Total	$485,000

Amy knew that her operation had produced more units than originally had been budgeted, so that more power and labor had naturally been used. She also knew that the uncertainty in scheduling had led to more setups than planned. When she pointed this out to Gary Grant, the controller, he assured her that the budgeted costs had been adjusted for the increase in productive activity. Curious, Amy questioned Gary about the methods used to make the adjustment.

Gary: If the actual level of activity differs from the original planned level, we adjust the budget by using budget formulas—formulas that allow us to predict the costs for different levels of activity.

Amy: The approach sounds reasonable. However, I'm sure something is wrong here. Tell me exactly how you adjusted the costs of direct labor, power, and setups.

Gary: First, we obtain formulas for the individual items in the budget by using the method of least squares. We assume that cost variations can be explained by variations in productive activity where activity is measured by direct labor hours. Here is a list of the cost formulas for the three items you mentioned. The variable X is the number of direct labor hours.

Direct labor cost = $\$10X$
Power cost = $\$5{,}000 + \$4X$
Setup cost = $100,000

Amy: I think I see the problem. Power costs don't have a lot to do with direct labor hours. They have more to do with machine hours. As production increases, machine hours increase more rapidly than direct labor hours. Also. . . .

Gary: You know, you have a point. The coefficient of determination for power cost is only about 50 percent. That leaves a lot of unexplained cost variation. The coefficient for labor, however, is much better—it explains about 96 percent of the cost variation. Setup costs, of course, are fixed.

Amy: Well, as I was about to say, setup costs also have very little to do with direct labor hours. And I might add that they certainly are not fixed—at least not all of them. We had to do more setups than our original plan called for because of the scheduling changes. And we have to pay our people when they work extra hours. It seems like we are always paying overtime. I wonder if we simply do not have enough people for the setup activity. Also, there are supplies that are used for each setup, and these are not cheap. Did you build these extra costs of increased setup activity into your budget?

Gary: No, we assumed that setup costs were fixed. I see now that some of them could vary as the number of setups increases. Amy, let me see if I can develop some cost formulas based on better explanatory variables. I'll get back with you in a few days.

Assume that after a few days' work, Gary developed the following cost formulas, all with a coefficient of determination greater than 90 percent:

Direct labor cost = $\$10X$, where X = Direct labor hours
Power cost = $\$68,000 + 0.9Y$, where Y = Machine hours
Setup cost = $\$98,000 + \$400Z$, where Z = Number of setups

The actual measures of each of the activity drivers are as follows:

Direct labor hours	20,000
Machine hours	90,000
Number of setups	110

Required

1. Prepare a performance report for direct labor, power, and setups using the direct-labor-based formulas.
2. Prepare a performance report for direct labor, power, and setups using the multiple-cost-driver formulas that Gary developed.
3. Of the two approaches, which provides the more accurate picture of Amy's performance? Why?

8-30

Activity Flexible Budgeting
LO4

Billy Adams, controller for Westcott, Inc., prepared the following budget for manufacturing costs at two different levels of activity for 2008:

	Direct Labor Hours Level of Activity	
	50,000	**100,000**
Direct materials	$300,000	$ 600,000
Direct labor	200,000	400,000
Depreciation (plant)	100,000	100,000
Subtotal	$600,000	$1,100,000
	Machine Hours Level of Activity	
	200,000	**300,000**
Maintaining equipment	$360,000	$ 510,000
Machining	112,000	162,000
Subtotal	$472,000	$672,000
	Material Moves Level of Activity	
	20,000	**40,000**
Materials handling	$165,000	$290,000
	Number of Batches Inspected Level of Activity	
	100	**200**
Inspections	$ 125,000	$ 225,000
Total	$1,362,000	$2,287,000

During 2008, Westcott worked a total of 80,000 direct labor hours, used 250,000 machine hours, made 32,000 moves, and performed 120 batch inspections. The following actual costs were incurred:

Direct materials	$440,000
Direct labor	355,000
Depreciation	100,000
Maintenance	425,000
Machining	142,000
Materials handling	232,500
Inspections	160,000

Westcott applies overhead using rates based on direct labor hours, machine hours, number of moves, and number of batches. The second level of activity (the far right column in the preceding table) is the practical level of activity (the available activity for resources acquired in advance of usage) and is used to compute predetermined overhead pool rates.

Required

1. Prepare a performance report for Westcott's manufacturing costs in 2008.
2. Assume that one of the products produced by Westcott is budgeted to use 10,000 direct labor hours, 15,000 machine hours, and 500 moves and will be produced in five batches. A total of 10,000 units will be produced during the year. Calculate the budgeted unit manufacturing cost.
3. One of Westcott's managers said the following: "Budgeting at the activity level makes a lot of sense. It really helps us manage costs better. But the above budget really needs to provide more detailed information. For example, I know that the materials-handling activity involves the usage of forklifts and operators, and this information is lost with simply reporting the total cost of the activity for various levels of output. We have four forklifts, each capable of providing 10,000 moves per year. We lease these forklifts for five years, at $10,000 per year. Furthermore, for our two shifts, we need up to eight operators if we run all four forklifts. Each operator is paid a salary of $30,000 per year. Also, I know that fuel costs us about $0.25 per move."

   Based on these comments, explain how this additional information may help Wescott better manage its costs. Also, assuming that these are the only three items, expand the detail of the flexible budget for materials handling to reveal the cost of these three resource items for 20,000 moves and 40,000 moves, respectively. You may wish to review the concepts of flexible, committed, and discretionary resources found in Chapter 3.

8-31

Master Budget; Comprehensive Review
LO2

Optima Company is a high-technology organization that produces a mass-storage system. The design of Optima's system is unique and represents a breakthrough in the industry. The units Optima produces combine positive features of both floppy and hard disks. The company is completing its fifth year of operations and is preparing to build its master budget for the coming year (2008). The budget will detail each quarter's activity and the activity for the year in total. The master budget will be based on the following information:

a. Fourth-quarter sales for 2007 are 55,000 units.
b. Unit sales by quarter (for 2008) are projected as follows:

First quarter	65,000
Second quarter	70,000
Third quarter	75,000
Fourth quarter	90,000

The selling price is $400 per unit. All sales are credit sales. Optima collects 85 percent of all sales within the quarter in which they are realized; the other 15 percent are collected in the following quarter. There are no bad debts.

c. There is no beginning inventory of finished goods. Optima is planning the following ending finished goods inventories for each quarter:

First quarter	13,000 units
Second quarter	15,000
Third quarter	20,000
Fourth quarter	10,000

d. Each mass-storage unit uses five hours of direct labor and three units of direct materials. Laborers are paid $10 per hour, and one unit of direct materials costs $80.
e. There are 65,700 units of direct materials in beginning inventory as of January 1, 2008. At the end of each quarter, Optima plans to have 30 percent of the direct materials needed for next quarter's unit sales. Optima will end the year with the same level of direct materials found in this year's beginning inventory.
f. Optima buys direct materials on account. Half of the purchases are paid for in the quarter of acquisition, and the remaining half are paid for in the following quarter. Wages and salaries are paid on the 15th and 30th of each month.
g. Fixed overhead totals $1 million each quarter. Of this total, $350,000 represents depreciation. All other fixed expenses are paid for in cash in the quarter incurred. The fixed overhead rate is computed by dividing the year's total fixed overhead by the year's expected actual units produced.
h. Variable overhead is budgeted at $6 per direct labor hour. All variable overhead expenses are paid for in the quarter incurred.
i. Fixed selling and administrative expenses total $250,000 per quarter, including $50,000 depreciation.
j. Variable selling and administrative expenses are budgeted at $10 per unit sold. All selling and administrative expenses are paid for in the quarter incurred.
k. The balance sheet as of December 31, 2007, is as follows:

Assets	
Cash	$ 250,000
Direct materials inventory	5,256,000
Accounts receivable	3,300,000
Plant and equipment	33,500,000
Total assets	$42,306,000

Liabilities and Stockholders' Equity	
Accounts payable	$ 7,248,000*
Capital stock	27,000,000
Retained earnings	8,058,000
Total liabilities and stockholders' equity	$42,306,000

*For purchase of direct materials only.

l. Optima will pay quarterly dividends of $300,000. At the end of the fourth quarter, $2 million of equipment will be purchased.

Required

Prepare a master budget for Optima Company for each quarter of 2008 and for the year in total. The following component budgets must be included:

a. Sales budget
b. Production budget

c. Direct materials purchases budget
d. Direct labor budget
e. Overhead budget
f. Selling and administrative expenses budget
g. Ending finished goods inventory budget
h. Cost of goods sold budget
i. Cash budget
j. Pro forma income statement (using absorption costing and ignoring income taxes)
k. Pro forma balance sheet

8-32

Flexible Budgeting
LO3, LO4

CMA

Patterson Company employs flexible budgeting techniques to evaluate the performance of several of its activities. The selling expenses flexible budgets for three representative monthly activity levels follow.

Representative Monthly Flexible Budgets for Selling Expenses

Activity measures:			
Unit sales volume	400,000	425,000	450,000
Dollar sales volume	$10,000,000	$10,625,000	$11,250,000
Number of orders	4,000	4,250	4,500
Number of salespersons	72	72	72
Monthly expenses:			
Advertising and promotion	$ 1,200,000	$ 1,200,000	$ 1,200,000
Administrative salaries	57,000	57,000	57,000
Sales salaries	75,600	75,600	75,600
Sales commissions	300,000	318,750	337,500
Salesperson travel	170,000	175,000	180,000
Sales office expense	490,000	498,750	507,500
Shipping expense	675,000	712,500	750,000
Total	$ 2,967,600	$ 3,037,600	$ 3,107,600

The following assumptions were used to develop the selling expenses flexible budgets:

a. The average size of Patterson's sales force during the year was planned to be 72 people.
b. Salespersons are paid a monthly salary plus commission on gross dollar sales.
c. The travel costs are best characterized as a step-variable cost. The fixed portion is related to the number of salespersons; the variable portion tends to fluctuate with gross dollar sales.
d. Sales office expense is a mixed cost with the variable portion related to the number of orders processed.
e. Shipping expense is a mixed cost with the variable portion related to the number of units sold.

A sales force of 80 persons generated a total of 4,300 orders resulting in a sales volume of 420,000 units during November. The gross dollar sales amounted to $10.9 million. The selling expenses incurred for November were as follows:

Advertising and promotion	$1,350,000
Administrative salaries	57,000
Sales salaries	84,000
Sales commissions	327,000
Salesperson travel	185,000
Sales office expense	497,200
Shipping expense	730,000
Total	$3,230,200

Required

1. Explain why the selling expenses flexible budgets presented would not be appropriate for evaluating Patterson Company's November selling expenses; indicate how the flexible budget would have to be revised.
2. Prepare a selling expenses report for November that Patterson Company can use to evaluate its control over selling expenses. The report should have a line for each selling expense item showing the appropriate budgeted amount, the actual selling expense, and the monthly dollar variation. **(CMA adapted)**

Managerial Decision Cases

8-33

Budgetary Performance; Rewards; Ethical Behavior
LO3

Linda Ellis, division manager, is evaluated and rewarded on the basis of budgetary performance. She, her assistants, and the plant managers are all eligible to receive a bonus if actual divisional profits are between budgeted profits and 120 percent of budgeted profits. The bonuses are based on a fixed percentage of actual profits. Profits above 120 percent of budgeted profits earn a bonus at the 120 percent level. (In other words, there is an upper limit on possible bonus payments.) If the actual profits are less than budgeted profits, no bonuses are awarded. Now, consider the following actions taken by Linda:

a. Linda tends to overestimate expenses and underestimate revenues. This approach facilitates the ability of the division to attain budgeted profits. Linda believes the action is justified because it increases the likelihood of receiving bonuses and helps keep the morale of the managers high.
b. Suppose that toward the end of the fiscal year, Linda saw that the division would not achieve budgeted profits. Accordingly, she instructed the Sales Department to defer the closing of a number of sales agreements to the following fiscal year. She also decided to write off some inventory that was nearly worthless. Deferring revenues to next year and writing off the inventory in a no-bonus year increased the chances of a bonus for next year.
c. Assume that toward the end of the year, Linda saw that actual profits would likely exceed the 120 percent limit. She took actions similar to those described in (b).

Required

1. Comment on the ethics of Linda's behavior. Are her actions right or wrong? What role does the company play in encouraging her actions?
2. Suppose that you are the marketing manager for the division and you receive instructions to defer the closing of sales until the next fiscal year. What would you do?
3. Suppose that you are a plant manager and you know that your budget has been padded by the division manager. Further, suppose that the padding is common knowledge among the plant managers, who support it because it increases their ability to achieve the budget and receive a bonus. What would you do?
4. Suppose that you are the division controller and you receive instructions from the division manager to accelerate the recognition of some expenses that legitimately belong to a future period. What would you do?

8-34

Cash Budget
LO2

According to the analysis of a local consultant, the financial difficulties facing Dr. Roger Jones have been caused by the absence of proper planning and control.[1] Budgetary control is sorely needed. To assist you in preparing a plan of action that will help his dental practice regain financial stability, Dr. Jones has made available the financial information describing a typical month in the following table.

	Revenues	
	Average Fee	**Quantity**
Fillings	$ 50	90
Crowns	300	19
Root canals	170	8
Bridges	500	7
Extractions	45	30
Cleaning	25	108
X-rays	15	150

	Costs	
Salaries:		
Two dental assistants	$1,900	
Receptionist/bookkeeper	1,500	
Hygienist	1,800	
Public relations (Mrs. Jones)	1,000	
Personal salary	6,500	
Total salaries		$12,700
Benefits		1,344
Building lease		1,500
Dental supplies		1,200
Janitorial		300
Utilities		400
Phone		150
Office supplies		100
Lab fees		5,000
Loan payments		570
Interest payments		500
Miscellaneous		500
Depreciation		700
Total costs		$24,964

Benefits include Dr. Jones's share of social security and a health insurance premium for all employees. Although all revenues billed in a month are not collected, the cash flowing into the business is approximately equal to the month's billings because of collections from prior months. The dental office is open Monday through Thursday from 8:30 a.m. to 4:00 p.m. and on Friday from 8:30 a.m. to 12:30 p.m. A total of 32 hours are worked each week. Additional hours could be worked, but Dr. Jones is reluctant to do so because of other personal endeavors that he enjoys.

Dr. Jones has noted that the two dental assistants and the receptionist are not fully utilized. He estimates that they are busy about 65 to 70 percent of the time. Dr. Jones's wife spends about five hours each week on a monthly newsletter that is sent to all patients; she also maintains a birthday list and sends cards to the patients on their birthdays.

1 Review the chapter's introductory scenario for a description of the financial difficulties that Dr. Jones faces on a recurring basis.

Dr. Jones spends about $2,400 yearly on informational seminars. These seminars, targeted especially for dentists, teach them how to increase their revenues. It is from one of these seminars that Dr. Jones decided to invest in promotion and public relations (the newsletter and the birthday list).

Required

1. Prepare a monthly cash budget for Dr. Jones. Does Dr. Jones have a significant cash flow problem? How would you use the budget to show Dr. Jones why he is having financial difficulties?
2. Using the cash budget prepared in Requirement 1 and the information given in the case, recommend actions to solve Dr. Jones's financial problems. Prepare a cash budget that reflects these recommendations and demonstrates to Dr. Jones that the problems can be corrected. Do you think that Dr. Jones will accept your recommendations? Do any of the behavioral principles discussed in the chapter have a role in this type of setting? Explain.

Research Assignment

8-35

Cybercase
LO1, LO2

In a similar sense as companies, the U.S. government must prepare a budget each year. However, unlike private, for-profit companies, the budget and its details are available to the public. The entire budgetary process is established by law. The government makes available a considerable amount of information concerning the federal budget. Most of this information can be found on the Internet. Using Internet resources (e.g., consider accessing the Office of Management and Budget), answer the following questions:

1. When is the federal budget prepared?
2. Who is responsible for preparing the federal budget?
3. How is the final federal budget determined? Explain in detail how the government creates its budget.
4. What percentage of the gross domestic product (GDP) is represented by the federal budget?
5. What are the revenue sources for the federal budget? Indicate the percentage contribution of each of the major sources.
6. How does our spending as a percentage of GDP compare to that of other countries?
7. How are deficits financed?

chapter 9

Standard Costing: A Managerial Control Tool

learning objectives

After studying this chapter, you should be able to:

1. Tell how unit standards are set and why standard costing systems are adopted.
2. State the purpose of a standard cost sheet.
3. Describe the basic concepts underlying variance analysis, and explain when variances should be investigated.
4. Compute the materials and labor variances, and explain how they are used for control.
5. Calculate the variable and fixed overhead variances, and give their definitions.
6. Appendix: Prepare journal entries for materials and labor variances, and show how to account for overhead variances.

Scenario

At the start of a new year, Rosita Mendez, president of Blue-Corn Foods, Inc., liked to look back over the past year's results. She reviewed the income statement with pleasure: Sales were up and costs were down. Operating income had increased significantly over the year before. Rosita firmly believed that these improvements could be largely traced to the institution of a standard costing system early last year.

At this time last year, Rosita was also reviewing the previous year's performance, but was not happy. Sales were slipping and costs seemed out of control. Quality control had been lacking; more than once, a state government's division of weights and measures had fined Blue-Corn Foods for underfilling its bags of "Bluechitos," crispy chips made from blue corn. Rosita had gone directly to Blue-Corn Foods' controller, Mel Hamilton. Mel had confirmed her assessment of the need for closer cost and quality control. He explained that a standard cost system could go a long way toward solving the difficulties that troubled Rosita. A standard cost system determines the price and quantity standards for materials, labor, and overhead. Then, budgeted costs for labor, materials, and overhead could be established for each unit produced. Mel pointed out that a standard cost system could give an early warning of problems in filling the snack bags with the correct weight of chips. Production managers could be held responsible for meeting the established standards. Rosita agreed that a standard cost system would be a useful cost control tool, and asked Mel to set up a pilot system for the Bluechitos product line.

A year later, Rosita could see the improvements made possible by a standard cost system. The problem with underfilling bags was essentially solved. There had been a steep drop in the number of fines levied against the company. In addition, the Bluechitos line manager was delighted with the help the new price and quantity standards gave in budgeting for the coming year. In fact, that line was the first to complete its budget for the coming year. Other line managers noticed and wanted standard costs developed for their lines as well. Rosita made a note to tell Mel Hamilton to extent the standard costing system to all product lines.

Questions to Think About

1. What motivated Rosita to implement a more formal cost control system?
2. Why does a standard cost system provide more detailed control information?
3. What type of control is being exercised with the use of standards?
4. How can standards be used to control costs?

Unit Standards

Objective 1

Tell how unit standards are set and why standard costing systems are adopted.

In the preceding scenario, Rosita and Mel both recognized the need to encourage operating managers to control costs. Cost control often means the difference between success and failure or between above-average profits and lesser profits. Rosita was convinced that cost control meant that her managers had to be cost conscious, and they had to assume responsibility for this important objective. Mel suggested that the way to control costs and involve managers is through the use of a formal budgetary system.

In Chapter 8, we learned that budgets set standards that are used to control and evaluate managerial performance. However, budgets are aggregate measures of performance; they identify the revenues and costs in total that an organization should experience if plans are executed as expected. By comparing the actual costs and actual revenues with the corresponding budgeted amounts at the same level of activity, a measure of managerial efficiency emerges.

Although the process just described provides significant information for control, control can be enhanced by developing standards for unit amounts as well as for total amounts. In fact, the groundwork for unit standards already exists within the framework of flexible budgeting. For flexible budgeting to work, the budgeted variable cost per unit of input for each unit of output must be known for every item in the budget. The budgeted variable input cost per unit of output is a unit standard. Unit standards are the basis or foundation on which a flexible budget is built.

The unit standard cost for a particular input relies on quantity standards and price standards. The **quantity standards** refer to the amount of input that should be used per unit of output. The **price standards** refer to the amount that should be paid for the quantity of the input to be used. The unit standard cost can be computed by multiplying these two standards: Quantity standard × Price standard.

© PR Newswire Coca-Cola Company

Coca-Cola bottlers know exactly how much proprietary Coke syrup and carbonated water to use for each size bottle. They also know standard costs per bottle and can easily determine just how much a filled bottle should cost.

For example, a soft-drink bottling company may decide that five ounces of fructose should be used for every 16-ounce bottle of cola (the quantity standard), and the price of the fructose should be $0.05 per ounce (the price standard). The standard cost of the fructose per bottle of cola is then $0.25 (5 × $0.05). The standard cost per unit of fructose can be used to predict what the total cost of fructose should be as the activity level varies; it then becomes a flexible budget formula. Thus, if 10,000 bottles of cola are produced, the total expected cost of fructose is $2,500 ($0.25 × 10,000); if 15,000 bottles are produced, the total expected cost of fructose is $3,750 ($0.25 × 15,000).

How Standards Are Developed

Historical experience, engineering studies, and input from operating personnel are three potential sources of quantitative standards. Although historical experience may provide an initial guideline for setting standards, it should be used with caution. Often, processes are operating inefficiently; adopting input-output relationships from the past thus perpetuates these inefficiencies. Engineering studies can determine the most efficient way to operate and can provide very rigorous guidelines; however, engineered standards are often too rigorous. They may not be achievable by operating personnel. Since operating personnel are accountable for meeting the standards, they should have significant input in setting standards. The same principles governing participative budgeting pertain to setting unit standards.

Price standards are the joint responsibility of operations, purchasing, personnel, and accounting. Operations determines the quality of the inputs required;

personnel and purchasing have the responsibility of acquiring the input quality requested at the lowest price. Market forces, trade unions, and other external forces limit the range of choices for price standards. In setting price standards, purchasing must consider discounts, freight, and quality; personnel, on the other hand, must consider payroll taxes, fringe benefits, and qualifications. Accounting is responsible for recording the price standards and preparing reports that compare actual performance to the standard.

Types of Standards

Standards are generally classified as either ideal or currently attainable. **Ideal standards** demand maximum efficiency and can be achieved only if everything operates perfectly. No machine breakdowns, slack, or lack of skill (even momentary) are allowed. **Currently attainable standards** can be achieved under efficient operating conditions. Allowance is made for normal breakdowns, interruptions, less than perfect skill, and so on. These standards are demanding but achievable.

Of the two types, currently attainable standards offer the most behavioral benefits. If standards are too tight and never achievable, workers become frustrated, and performance levels decline. However, challenging but achievable standards tend to extract higher performance levels—particularly when the individuals subject to the standards have participated in their creation.

Why Standard Cost Systems Are Adopted

Two reasons for adopting a standard cost system are frequently mentioned: to improve planning and control and to facilitate product costing.

Planning and Control Standard costing systems enhance planning and control and improve performance measurement. Unit standards are a fundamental requirement for a flexible budgeting system, which is a key feature of a meaningful planning and control system. Budgetary control systems compare actual costs with budgeted costs by computing variances, the difference between the actual and planned costs for the actual level of activity. By developing unit price and quantity standards, an overall variance can be decomposed into a price variance and a usage or efficiency variance.

By performing this decomposition, a manager has more information. If the variance is unfavorable, a manager can tell whether it is attributable to discrepancies between planned prices and actual prices, to discrepancies between planned usage and actual usage, or to both. Since managers have more control over the usage of inputs than over their prices, efficiency variances provide specific signals regarding the need for corrective action and where that action should be focused. Thus, in principle, the use of efficiency variances enhances operational control. Additionally, by breaking out the price variance, over which managers potentially have less control, the system provides an improved measure of managerial efficiency.

The benefits of operational control, however, may not extend to the advanced manufacturing environment. The use of a standard cost system for operational control in an advanced manufacturing environment can produce dysfunctional behavior. For example, materials price variance reporting may encourage the purchasing department to buy in large quantities to take advantage of discounts. Yet, this may lead to holding significant inventories, something not desired by JIT firms. Thus, the detailed computation of variances—at least at the operational level—is discouraged in this new environment. Nonetheless, standards in the advanced manufacturing environment are still useful for planning, for example, in the creation of bids. Also, variances may still be computed and presented in reports to higher-level managers so that the financial dimension can be monitored.

Managers Decide

Standards Help Dairy Trim Delivery Costs

Smith Dairy is a family-owned producer of milk and milk products that operates in Ohio, Indiana, and Kentucky. A fleet of refrigerated trucks delivers its products throughout its sales region. Distribution cost is the second-highest cost in a dairy, exceeded only by production cost. Thus, operating standards are set for such things as truck speed, shifting patterns, idling times, braking intensity, temperature in transit, Department of Transporation (DOT) log compliance, and unloading rates. Low unloading rates and excessive amounts of speed, shifting, idling time, and braking can significantly increase delivery costs. Furthermore, incorrect temperatures can ruin a load of goods.

To better monitor delivery performance and improve compliance with operating standards, Smith installed onboard computers in each of its delivery trucks. These computers monitor and report on speed, shifting, and temperature in transit; and they have reduced idle time and lowered fuel costs. The computer record also legally replaces the DOT logs that drivers formerly completed manually (saving about $100,000 per year). The system has also led to improved driver safety by capturing how vehicles are operated on a real-time basis. ■

Source: Jack Mans, "High-Tech Cost Management," *Dairy Foods* (March 2000): 51–53.

Finally, it should be mentioned that there are many firms operating with conventional manufacturing systems. Standard cost systems are widely used. According to one survey, 87 percent of the firms responding used a standard cost system.[1] Furthermore, the survey revealed that significant numbers of the respondents were calculating variances at the operational level. For example, about 40 percent of the firms using a standard costing system reported labor variances for small work crews or individual workers.

Product Costing In a standard costing system, costs are assigned to products using quantity and price standards for all three manufacturing costs: direct materials, direct labor, and overhead. In contrast, a normal costing system predetermines overhead costs for the purpose of product costing but assigns direct materials and direct labor to products by using actual costs. Overhead is assigned using a budgeted rate and actual activity. At the other end of the cost assignment spectrum, an actual costing system assigns the actual costs of all three manufacturing inputs to products. Exhibit 9-1 summarizes these three cost assignment approaches. Standard product costing has several advantages over normal costing and actual costing. One, of course, is the greater capacity for control. Standard costing systems also provide readily available unit cost information that can be used for pricing decisions. This is particularly helpful for companies that do a significant amount of bidding and that are paid on a cost-plus basis.

Other simplifications are also possible. For example, if a process-costing system uses standard costing to assign product costs, there is no need to compute a unit

1 Bruce R. Gaumnitz and Felix P. Kollaritsch, "Manufacturing Variances: Current Practice and Trends," *Journal of Cost Management* (Spring 1991): pp. 58–64. Similar widespread usage is also reported by Carole B. Cheatham and Leo R. Cheatham, "Redesigning Cost Systems: Is Standard Costing Obsolete?" *Accounting Horizons* (December 1996): pp. 23–31. Furthermore, a survey of UK firms reveals that 76% of them use a standard costing system. See Colin Drury, "Standard Costing: A Technique at Variance with Modern Management," *Management Accounting* (London, November 1999): pp. 56–58.

	Manufacturing Costs		
	Direct Materials	Direct Labor	Overhead
Actual costing system	Actual	Actual	Actual
Normal costing system	Actual	Actual	Budgeted
Standard costing system	Standard	Standard	Standard

Exhibit 9-1 Cost Assignment Approaches

cost for each equivalent unit cost category. A standard unit cost would exist for each category.[2] Additionally, there is no need to distinguish between the FIFO and weighted average methods of accounting for beginning inventory costs. Usually, a standard process-costing system will follow the equivalent unit calculation of the FIFO approach. That is, current equivalent units of work are calculated. By calculating current equivalent units of work, current actual production costs can be compared with standard costs for control purposes.

Standard Product Costs

Objective 2

State the purpose of a standard cost sheet.

Standard costs can also be used in service organizations. The **IRS**, for example, could set standard processing times for different categories of returns. If the standard processing time is three minutes for a 1040EZ and the standard price of labor is $9 per hour, then the standard cost of processing a 1040EZ is $0.45 [$9 × (3/60)]. Other examples exist. The federal government is using a standard costing system for reimbursing Medicare costs. Based on several studies, illnesses have been classified into diagnostic related groups (DRGs), and the hospital costs that should be incurred for an average case identified. (The costs include patient days, food, medicine, supplies, use of equipment, and so on.) The government pays the hospital the standard cost for the DRG. If the cost of the patient's treatment is greater than the DRG allows, the hospital suffers a loss. If the cost of the patient's treatment is less than the DRG reimbursement, the hospital gains. On average, the hospital supposedly breaks even. Although service organizations can and do make use of standard costing, applications are more common in manufacturing organizations. Furthermore, the concepts are more easily illustrated in manufacturing settings.

In manufacturing firms, the **standard cost per unit** is the sum of the standard costs for direct materials, direct labor, and overhead. The **standard cost sheet** provides the details underlying the standard unit cost. To illustrate, let's develop a standard cost sheet for a 16-ounce bag of Bluechitos, the corn chips produced by Blue-Corn Foods, Inc. The production of the corn chips begins with steaming and soaking corn kernels overnight in a lime solution. This process softens the kernels so that they can be shaped into a sheet of dough. The dough is then cut into small triangular chips. Next, the chips are toasted in an oven and dropped into a deep fryer. After cooking, the chips pass under a salting device and are inspected for quality. Substandard chips are sorted and discarded; the chips passing inspection are bagged by a packaging machine. The bags of chips are manually packed into boxes for shipping.

Four materials are used to process corn chips: blue corn, lime, cooking oil, and salt. The package in which the chips are placed is also classified as a direct material. The Bluechitos line has two types of direct laborers: machine operators and inspectors (or sorters). Variable overhead is made up of three costs: gas, electricity, and

2 If you have not yet read Chapter 6 on process costing, the example illustrating the simplifications made possible by standard costing will not be as meaningful. However, the point is still relevant. Standard costing can bring useful computational savings.

Description	Standard Price	Standard Usage	Standard Cost*	Subtotal
Direct materials:				
Blue corn	$ 0.006	18 oz.	$0.108	
Cooking oil	0.031	2 oz.	0.062	
Salt	0.005	1 oz.	0.005	
Lime	0.400	0.01 oz.	0.004	
Bags	0.044	1 bag	0.044	
Total direct materials				$0.223
Direct labor:				
Inspectors	7.000	0.0070 hr.	$0.049	
Machine operators	10.000	0.0008 hr.	0.008	
Total direct labor				0.057
Overhead:				
Variable overhead	3.850	0.0078 hr.	$0.030	
Fixed overhead	32.050	0.0078 hr.	0.250**	
Total overhead				0.280
Total standard unit cost				$0.560

*Calculated by multiplying price times usage.
**Rounded

Exhibit 9-2 Standard Cost Sheet for Bluechitos

water. Both variable and fixed overhead are applied using direct labor hours. The standard cost sheet is given in Exhibit 9-2. Note that it should cost $0.56 to produce a 16-ounce bag of blue-corn chips. Also, notice that the company uses 18 ounces of corn to produce a 16-ounce bag of chips. There are two reasons for this. First, some chips are discarded during the inspection process. The company plans on a normal amount of waste. Second, the company wants to have more than 16 ounces in each bag to increase customer satisfaction with its product and avoid any further problems with fair packaging laws.

Exhibit 9-2 also reveals other important insights. The standard usage for variable and fixed overhead is tied to the direct labor standards. For variable overhead, the rate is $3.85 per direct labor hour. Since one bag of corn chips uses 0.0078 direct labor hour, the variable overhead cost assigned to a bag of corn chips is $0.03 ($3.85 × 0.0078). For fixed overhead, the rate is $32.05 per direct labor hour, making the fixed overhead cost per bag of corn chips $0.25 ($32.05 × 0.0078). Nearly half of the cost of production is fixed, indicating a capital-intensive production effort. Indeed, much of the operation is mechanized.

The standard cost sheet also reveals the quantity of each input that should be used to produce one unit of output. The unit quantity standards can be used to compute the total amount of inputs allowed for the actual output. This computation is an essential component in computing efficiency variances. A manager should be able to compute the **standard quantity of materials allowed *(SQ)*** and the **standard hours allowed *(SH)*** for the actual output. This computation must be done for every class of direct material and every class of direct labor. Assume, for example, that 100,000 bags of corn chips are produced during the first week of March. How much blue corn should have been used for the actual output of 100,000 bags? The unit quantity standard is 18 ounces of blue corn per bag (see Exhibit 9-2). For 100,000 bags, the standard quantity of blue corn allowed is computed as follows:

$$\begin{aligned} SQ &= \text{Unit quantity standard} \times \text{Actual output} \\ &= 18 \times 100{,}000 \\ &= 1{,}800{,}000 \text{ ounces} \end{aligned}$$

The computation of standard direct labor hours allowed can be illustrated using machine operators. From Exhibit 9-2, we see that the unit quantity standard is 0.0008 hour per bag produced. Thus, if 100,000 bags are produced, the standard hours allowed are as follows:

$$
\begin{aligned}
SH &= \text{Unit labor standard} \times \text{Actual output} \\
&= 0.0008 \times 100{,}000 \\
&= 80 \text{ direct labor hours}
\end{aligned}
$$

Variance Analysis: General Description

Objective 3

Describe the basic concepts underlying variance analysis, and explain when variances should be investigated.

A flexible budget can be used to identify the costs that should have been incurred for the actual level of activity. This figure is obtained by multiplying the amount of input allowed for the actual output by the standard unit price. Letting SP be the standard unit price of an input and SQ the standard quantity of inputs allowed for the actual output, the planned or budgeted input cost is $SP \times SQ$. The actual input cost is $AP \times AQ$, where AP is the actual price per unit of the input, and AQ is the actual quantity of input used.

Price and Efficiency Variances

The **total budget variance** is simply the difference between the actual cost of the input and its planned cost. For simplicity, we will refer to the total budget variance as the total variance:

$$\text{Total variance} = (AP \times AQ) - (SP \times SQ)$$

In a standard costing system, the total variance is broken down into price and usage variances. **Price (rate) variance** is the difference between the actual and standard unit price of an input multiplied by the number of inputs used: $(AP - SP)AQ$. **Usage (efficiency) variance** is the difference between the actual and standard quantity of inputs multiplied by the standard unit price of the input: $(AQ - SQ)SP$. It is easy to show that the total variance is the sum of price and usage variances:

$$
\begin{aligned}
\text{Total variance} &= \text{Price variance} + \text{Usage variance} \\
&= (AP - SP)AQ + (AQ - SQ)SP \\
&= [(AP \times AQ) - (SP \times AQ)] + [(SP \times AQ) - (SP \times SQ)] \\
&= (AP \times AQ) - (SP \times AQ) + (SP \times AQ) - (SP \times SQ) \\
&= (AP \times AQ) - (SP \times SQ)
\end{aligned}
$$

Exhibit 9-3 presents a three-pronged diagram that describes this process. Usually, the total variance is divided into price and efficiency components for direct materials and direct labor. The treatment of overhead is discussed later in the chapter.

Unfavorable (U) variances occur whenever actual prices or usage of inputs are greater than standard prices or usage. When the opposite occurs, **favorable (F) variances** are obtained. Favorable and unfavorable variances are not equivalent to good and bad variances. The terms merely indicate the relationship of the actual prices or quantities to the standard prices and quantities. Whether or not the variances are good or bad depends on why they occurred. Determining why requires managers to do some investigation.

The Decision to Investigate

Rarely will actual performance exactly meet the established standards, and management does not expect it to. Random variations around the standard are expected. Because of this, management should have in mind an acceptable range of performance. When

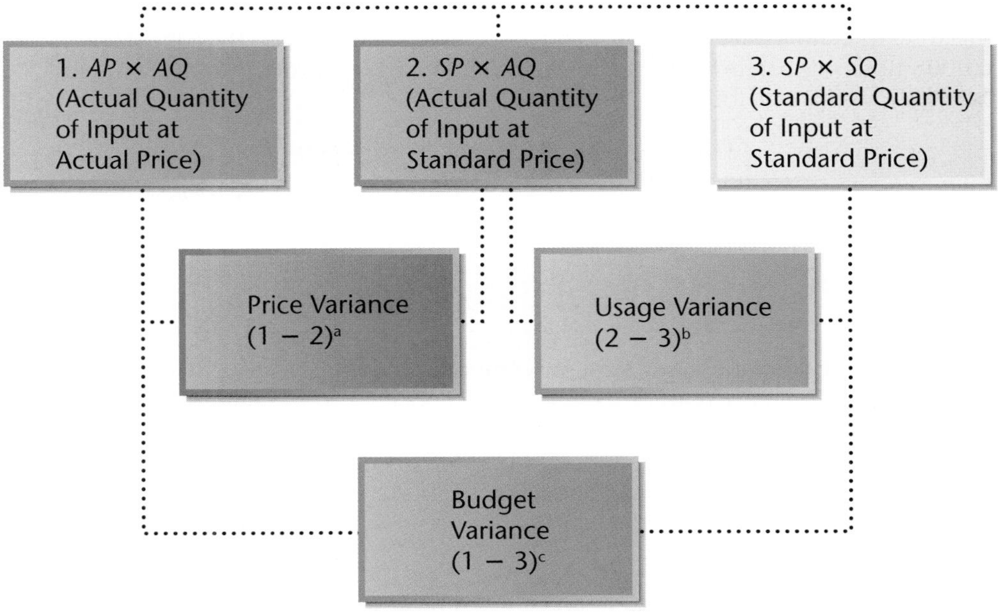

Exhibit 9-3 Variance Analysis: General Description

variances are within this range, they are assumed to be caused by random factors. When a variance falls outside this range, the deviation is likely to be caused by nonrandom factors, either factors that managers can control or factors that they cannot control. In the noncontrollable case, managers need to revise the standard.

Keeping production within standards can have ethical implications. A few examples from the pharmaceutical industry may drive home the importance of variance investigation.[3] Drugs must contain a certain amount of the active ingredient, plus or minus a small percent (for example, aspirin claiming to have five grains per tablet must really have somewhere between 90 and 110 percent of the specified amount). The FDA is responsible for ensuring the safety and efficacy of drugs manufactured at home and abroad. An anonymous letter alerted the FDA to manufacturing problems with an antibiotic produced by a Canadian firm, **Novopharm Ltd.** Basically, the drug was too strong and could potentially destroy beneficial bacteria along with the harmful bacteria. Upon investigation, the FDA found the blending process to be "out of control." The result was that the firm stopped shipping that drug until the process could be corrected. Another FDA investigation centered on **Haimen Pharmaceutical Factory** in China. There, the FDA found the samples of an antileukemia drug to be too weak. Again, large variances from standard triggered an investigation. Interestingly, the question of what to do about the company and the drug was not clear-cut. In this case, the FDA did not withdraw its approval because the drug was in short supply.

ETHICS

Now that we understand why variance investigation is important, we need to understand when to investigate. Investigating the cause of variances and taking corrective action, like all activities, have a cost associated with them. As a general principle, an investigation should be undertaken only if the anticipated benefits are greater than the expected costs. Assessing the costs and benefits of a variance investigation is not an easy task, however. A manager must consider whether a variance will recur. If so, the process may be permanently out of control, meaning that periodic savings may be achieved if corrective action is taken. But how can we tell if the

3 The examples given here are taken from an article by Christopher Drew, "Medicines from Afar Raise Safety Concerns," *New York Times* (29 October 1995): pp. A1, A16.

variance is going to recur unless an investigation is conducted? And how do we know the cost of corrective action unless the cause of the variance is known?

Because it is difficult to assess the costs and benefits of variance analysis on a case-by-case basis, many firms adopt the general guideline of investigating variances only if they fall outside of an acceptable range. They are not investigated unless they are large enough to be of concern. They must be large enough to be caused by something other than random factors and large enough (on average) to justify the costs of investigating and taking corrective action.

How do managers determine whether variances are significant? How is the acceptable range established? The acceptable range is the standard plus or minus an allowable deviation. The top and bottom measures of the allowable range are called the **control limits**. The upper control limit is the standard plus the allowable deviation, and the lower control limit is the standard minus the allowable deviation. Current practice sets the control limits subjectively: based on past experience, intuition, and judgment, management determines the allowable deviation from standard.[4] Exhibit 9-4 graphically illustrates the concept of control limits. The assumed standard is $100,000, and the allowable deviation is plus or minus $10,000. The upper limit is $110,000, and the lower limit is $90,000. Investigation occurs whenever an observation falls outside of these limits (as would be the case for the sixth observation). Trends can also be important.

The control limits are often expressed both as a percentage of the standard and as an absolute dollar amount. For example, the allowable deviation may be expressed as the lesser of 10 percent of the standard amount, or $10,000. In other words, management will not accept a deviation of more than $10,000 even if that deviation is less than 10 percent of the standard. Alternatively, even if the dollar amount is less than $10,000, an investigation is required if the deviation is more than 10 percent of the standard amount.

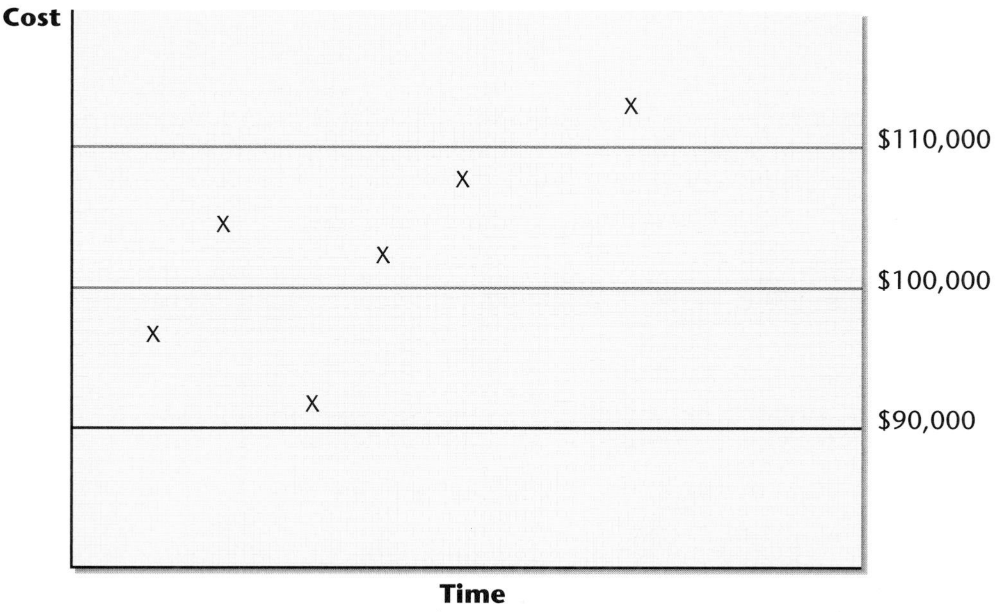

Exhibit 9-4 Control Chart

4 Gaumnitz and Kollaritsch, "Manufacturing Variances: Current Practices and Trends," report that about 45–47 percent of the firms responding to their survey use dollar or percentage control limits. Most of the remaining firms use judgment rather than any formal identification of limits.

Formal statistical procedures can also be used to set the control limits. In this way, less subjectivity is involved, and a manager can assess the likelihood of the variance being caused by random factors. At this time, the use of such formal procedures has gained little acceptance.[5]

Variance Analysis: Materials and Labor

Objective 4

Compute the materials and labor variances, and explain how they are used for control.

The total variance measures the difference between the actual costs of materials and labor and their budgeted costs for the actual level of activity. To illustrate, consider these selected data for the Bluechitos line from the first week of March:[6]

Actual production	48,500 bags of corn chips
Actual cost of corn	780,000 ounces at $0.0069 = $5,382
Actual cost of inspectors	360 hours at $7.35 = $2,646

Using these actual data and the unit standards from Exhibit 9-2, a performance report for the first week of March can be developed (see Exhibit 9-5). As has been mentioned, the total variance can be divided into price and usage variances, providing more information to the manager. We will do so in the following sections.

Direct Materials Variances

The three-pronged (columnar) or formula approaches may be used to calculate materials price and usage variances.

The Columnar Approach The columnar approach illustrated in Exhibit 9-3 can be used to calculate the materials price and usage variances. This calculation for the Bluechitos example is illustrated in Exhibit 9-6. Only the price and usage variances for corn are shown. Many find this graphical approach easier than the use of variance formulas.

Materials Price Variance: Formula Approach The materials price variance can be calculated separately. The **materials price variance *(MPV)*** measures the difference between what should have been paid for materials and what was actually paid. The formula for computing this variance is:

$$MPV = (AP \times AQ) - (SP \times AQ)$$

	Actual Costs	Budgeted Costs*	Total Variance
Corn	$5,382.00	$5,238.00	$144.00 U
Inspectors labor	2,646.00	2,376.50	269.50 U

*The standard quantities for materials and labor are computed as unit quantity standards from Exhibit 9-2:
Corn: 18 × 48,500 = 873,000 ounces
Labor: 0.007 × 48,500 = 339.5 hours
Multiplying these standard quantities by the unit standard prices given in Exhibit 9-2 produces the budgeted amounts appearing in this column:
Corn: $0.006 × 873,000 = $5,238.00
Labor: $7.00 × 339.5 = $2,376.50

Exhibit 9-5 Performance Report: Total Variances

5 According to Gaumnitz and Kollaritsch, only about 1 percent of the responding firms used formal statistical procedures.

6 To keep the example simple, only one material (corn) and one type of labor (inspectors) are illustrated. A complex analysis for the company would include all types of materials and labor.

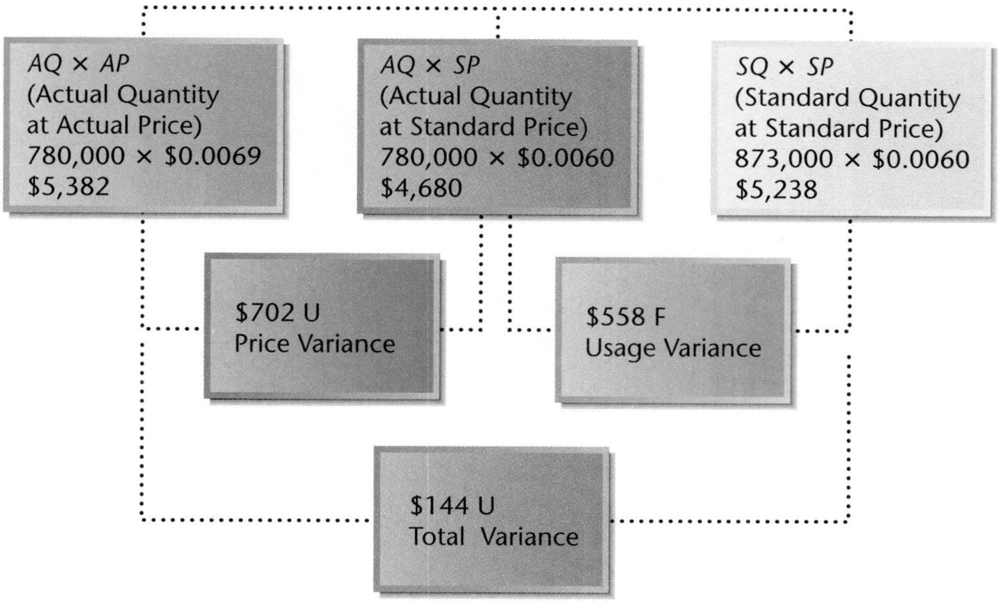

Exhibit 9-6 Material Variances: Columnar Approach

or, factoring, we have:

$$MPV = (AP - SP)AQ$$

where

$$AP = \text{The actual price per unit}$$
$$SP = \text{The standard price per unit}$$
$$AQ = \text{The actual quantity of material used}$$

Computation of the Materials Price Variance The Bluechitos line purchased and used 780,000 ounces of blue corn for the first week of March. The purchase price was \$0.0069 per ounce. Thus, *AP* is \$0.0069, *AQ* is 780,000 ounces, and *SP* (from Exhibit 9-2) is \$0.0060. Using this information, the materials price variance is computed as follows:

$$\begin{aligned} MPV &= (AP - SP)AQ \\ &= (\$0.0069 - \$0.0060)780{,}000 \\ &= \$0.0009 \times 780{,}000 \\ &= \$702 \text{ U} \end{aligned}$$

$$\text{Percent of } SP \times AQ = \$702/\$4{,}680 = 15\%$$

Responsibility for the Materials Price Variance The responsibility for controlling the materials price variance usually belongs to the purchasing agent. Admittedly, the price of materials is largely beyond his or her control; however, the price variance can be influenced by such factors as quality, quantity discounts, distance of the source from the plant, and so on. These factors are often under the control of the agent.

Using the price variance to evaluate the performance of purchasing has some limitations. Emphasis on meeting or beating the standard can produce some undesirable outcomes. For example, if the purchasing agent feels pressured to produce favorable variances, materials of lower quality than desired may be purchased or too much inventory may be acquired to take advantage of quantity discounts.

Retail stores also use variance analysis to help them control costs. Store managers can determine how much inventory is on hand and whether it will meet the needs of the new period's sales budget.

© Digital Vision

Analysis of the Materials Price Variance The first step in variance analysis is deciding whether the variance is significant or not. If it is judged insignificant, no further steps are needed. Assume that an unfavorable materials price variance of $702 is judged significant (15 percent of the standard cost). The next step is to find out why it occurred.

For the Bluechitos example, the investigation revealed that a higher-quality corn was purchased because of a shortage of the usual grade in the market. Once the reason is known, corrective action can be taken if necessary—and if possible. In this case, no corrective action is needed. The firm has no control over the supply shortage; it will simply have to wait until market conditions improve.

Timing of the Price Variance Computation The materials price variance can be computed at one of two points: (1) when the materials are purchased, or (2) when they are issued for use in production. Computing the price variance at the point of purchase is preferable. It is better to have information on variances earlier rather than later. The more timely the information, the more likely that proper managerial action can be taken. Old information is often useless information.

Materials may sit in inventory for weeks or months before they are needed in production. By the time the materials price variance is computed, signaling a problem, it may be too late to take corrective action. Or, even if corrective action is still possible, the delay may cost the company thousands of dollars. For example, suppose a new purchasing agent is unaware of the availability of a quantity discount on a material. If the materials price variance that ignores the discount is computed when a new purchase is made, the resulting unfavorable signal would lead to quick corrective action. (In this case, the action would be to use the discount for future purchases.) If the materials price variance is not computed until the material is issued to production, it may be several weeks or even months before the problem is discovered.

If the materials price variance is computed at the point of purchase, *AQ* needs to be redefined as the actual quantity of materials purchased, rather than actual materials used. Since the materials purchased may differ from the materials used, the overall materials budget variance is not necessarily the sum of the materials price variance and the materials usage variance. When the materials purchased are all used in production for the period in which the variances are calculated, the two variances will equal the total variance.

Recognizing the price variance for materials at the point of purchase also means that materials inventory is carried at standard cost. The journal entry associated with the purchase of materials for a standard cost system is illustrated in the appendix to this chapter.

Direct Materials Usage Variance: Formula Approach The **materials usage variance *(MUV)*** measures the difference between the direct materials actually used and the direct materials that should have been used for the actual output. The formula for computing this variance is:

$$MUV = (SP \times AQ) - (SP \times SQ)$$

or, factoring, we have:

$$MUV = (AQ - SQ)SP$$

where

AQ = The actual quantity of material used
SQ = The standard quantity of material allowed for the actual output
SP = The standard price per unit

Computation of the Materials Usage Variance The Bluechitos line used 780,000 ounces of blue corn to produce 48,500 bags of corn chips. Therefore, *AQ* is 780,000. From Exhibit 9-2, we see that *SP* is \$0.006 per ounce of blue corn. Although standard materials allowed (*SQ*) has already been computed in Exhibit 9-5, the details underlying the computation need to be reviewed. Recall that *SQ* is the product of the unit quantity standard and the actual units produced. From Exhibit 9-2, the unit standard is 18 ounces of blue corn for every bag of corn chips. Thus, *SQ* is 18 × 48,500, or 873,000 ounces. Therefore, the materials usage variance is computed as follows:

$$\begin{aligned} MUV &= (AQ - SQ)SP \\ &= (780{,}000 - 873{,}000)(\$0.006) \\ &= \$558 \text{ F} \end{aligned}$$

$$\text{Percent of } SQ \times SP = \$558/\$5{,}238 = 10.7\%$$

When materials are issued, the materials usage variance can be calculated. Accounting for the issuance of materials in a standard cost system is illustrated in the appendix to this chapter.

Responsibility for the Materials Usage Variance The production manager is generally responsible for materials usage. Minimizing scrap, waste, and rework are all ways in which the manager can ensure that the standard is met. However, at times, the cause of the variance is attributable to others outside the production area, as the next section shows.

As with the price variance, employing the usage variance to evaluate performance can lead to undesirable behavior. For example, a production manager feeling pressure to produce a favorable variance might allow a defective unit to be transferred to finished goods. While this avoids the problem of wasted materials, it may create customer-relations problems.

Analysis of the Materials Usage Variance Investigation revealed that the favorable materials usage variance is the result of the higher-quality corn acquired by the purchasing department. In this case, the favorable variance is essentially assignable to purchasing. Since the materials usage variance is favorable—but smaller than the unfavorable price variance—the overall result of the change in purchasing is unfavorable. In the future, management should try to resume purchasing of the normal-quality corn.

If the overall variance had been favorable, a different response would be expected. If the favorable variance were expected to persist, the higher-quality corn should be purchased regularly and the price and quantity standards revised to reflect it. As this possibility reveals, standards are not static. As improvements in production take place and conditions change, standards may need to be revised to reflect the new operating environment.

Direct Labor Variances

The rate (price) and efficiency (usage) variances for labor can be calculated using either the columnar approach of Exhibit 9-3 or a formula approach.

Columnar Approach The three-pronged calculation for inspectors at the Blue-Corn Foods plant is illustrated in Exhibit 9-7. The calculation using formulas is discussed next.

Labor Rate Variance: Formula Approach The **labor rate variance *(LRV)*** computes the difference between what was paid to direct laborers and what should have been paid:

$$LRV = (AR \times AH) - (SR \times AH)$$

or, factoring, we have:

$$LRV = (AR - SR)AH$$

where

AR = The actual hourly wage rate
SR = The standard hourly wage rate
AH = The actual direct labor hours used

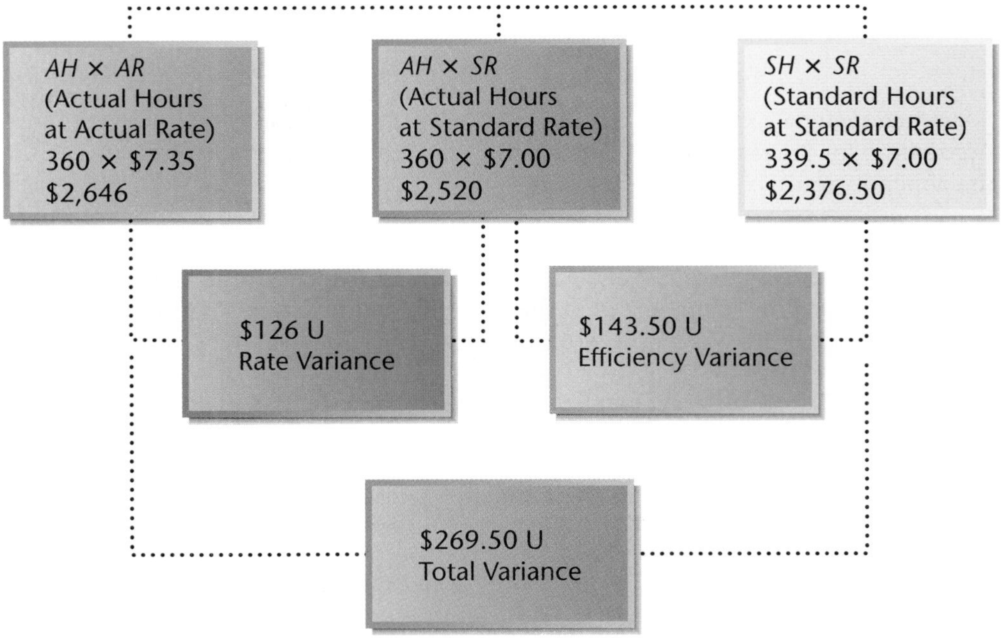

Exhibit 9-7 Labor Variances: Columnar Approach

Computation of the Labor Rate Variance Direct labor activity for the Bluechitos inspectors will be used to illustrate the computation of the labor rate variance. We know that 360 hours were used for inspection during the first week in March. The actual hourly wage paid for inspection was \$7.35. From Exhibit 9-2, the standard wage rate is \$7.00. Thus, *AH* is 360, *AR* is \$7.35, and *SR* is \$7.00. The labor rate variance is computed as follows:

$$\begin{aligned} LRV &= (AR - SR)AH \\ &= (\$7.35 - \$7.00)360 \\ &= \$0.35 \times 360 \\ &= \$126\ \text{U} \end{aligned}$$

$$\text{Percent of } SR \times AH = \$126/\$2{,}520 = 5\%$$

Responsibility for the Labor Rate Variance Labor rates are largely determined by such external forces as labor markets and union contracts. The actual wage rate rarely departs from the standard rate. When labor rate variances do occur, they usually do so because an average wage rate is used for the rate standard and because more skilled and more highly paid laborers are used for less skilled tasks. Unexpected overtime can also be the cause of a labor rate variance.

Wage rates for a particular labor activity often differ among workers because of differing levels of seniority. Rather than selecting labor rate standards reflecting those different levels, an average wage rate is often chosen. As the seniority mix changes, the average rate changes. This will give rise to a labor rate variance; it also calls for a new standard to reflect the new seniority mix. Controllability is not assignable for this cause of a labor rate variance.

However, the use of labor is controllable by the production manager. The use of more skilled workers to perform less skilled tasks (or vice versa) is a decision that a production manager consciously makes. For this reason, responsibility for the labor rate variance is generally assigned to the individuals who decide how labor will be used.

Analysis of the Labor Rate Variance Although a 5 percent variance is not likely to be judged significant, for illustrative purposes, assume that an investigation is conducted. The cause of the variance is found to be the use of more highly paid and skilled machine operators as inspectors, which occurred because two inspectors quit without formal notice. The corrective action is to hire and train two new inspectors.

Labor Efficiency Variance: Formula Approach The **labor efficiency variance (*LEV*)** measures the difference between the labor hours that were actually used and the labor hours that should have been used:

$$LEV = (AH \times SR) - (SH \times SR)$$

or, factoring, we have:

$$LEV = (AH - SH)SR$$

where

AH = The actual direct labor hours used
SH = The standard direct labor hours that should have been used
SR = The standard hourly wage rate

Computation of the Labor Efficiency Variance The Bluechitos line used 360 direct labor hours for inspection while producing 48,500 bags of corn chips. From Exhibit 9-2, the rate of 0.007 hour per bag of chips at a cost of \$7 per hour should have been used. The standard hours allowed for inspection are 339.5 (0.007

$\times$ 48,500). Thus, *AH* is 360, *SH* is 339.5, and *SR* is \$7. The labor efficiency variance is computed as follows:

$$\begin{aligned} LEV &= (AH - SH)SR \\ &= (360 - 339.5)\$7 \\ &= 20.5 \times \$7 \\ &= \$143.50\text{ U} \end{aligned}$$

$$\text{Percent of } SH \times SR = \$143.50/\$2{,}376.50 = 6\%$$

Responsibility for the Labor Efficiency Variance Generally speaking, production managers are responsible for the productive use of direct labor. However, as is true of all variances, once the cause is discovered, responsibility may be assigned elsewhere. For example, frequent breakdowns of machinery may cause interruptions and nonproductive use of labor. But the responsibility for these breakdowns may be faulty maintenance. If so, the maintenance manager should be charged with the unfavorable labor efficiency variance.

Production managers may be tempted to engage in dysfunctional behavior if too much emphasis is placed on the labor efficiency variance. For example, to avoid losing hours and prevent using additional hours because of possible rework, a production manager could deliberately transfer defective units to finished goods.

Analysis of the Labor Efficiency Variance Assume that the \$143.50 unfavorable variance was judged significant, and its cause was investigated. The investigation revealed that more shutdowns of the process occurred because the duties of the machine operators were split between machine operations and inspection. (Recall that this reassignment was necessary because two inspectors quit unexpectedly.) This resulted in more idle time for inspection. Also, the machine operators were unable to meet the standard output per hour for inspection because of their lack of experience with the sorting process. The corrective action needed to solve the problem is the same as that recommended for the unfavorable rate variance—hire and train two new inspectors.

Sum of LRV and LEV From Exhibit 9-7, we know that the total labor variance is \$269.50 unfavorable. This total variance is the sum of the unfavorable labor rate variance and the unfavorable labor efficiency variance (\$126.00 + \$143.50).

Variance Analysis: Overhead Costs

Objective 5

Calculate the variable and fixed overhead variances, and give their definitions.

For direct materials and direct labor, total variances are broken down into price and efficiency variances. The total overhead variance, the difference between applied and actual overhead, is also broken down into component variances. How many component variances are computed depends on the method of variance analysis used. We will focus on one method only. First, we will divide overhead into categories: fixed and variable. Next, we will look at component variances for each category. The total variable overhead variance is divided into two components: the variable overhead spending variance and the variable overhead efficiency variance. Similarly, the total fixed overhead variance is divided into two components: the fixed overhead spending variance and the fixed overhead volume variance.

Variable Overhead Variances

To illustrate variable overhead variances, we will examine one week of activity for Blue-Corn Foods (for the first week in March). The following data were gathered for this time period:

Variable overhead rate (standard)	\$3.85 per DLH
Actual variable overhead costs	\$1,600
Actual hours worked (machining and inspection)	400
Bags of chips produced	48,500
Hours allowed for production	378.3[a]
Applied variable overhead	\$1,456[b]

[a]0.0078 × 48,500
[b]\$3.85 × 378.3 (rounded to nearest dollar; overhead is applied using hours allowed in a standard cost system)

Total Variable Overhead Variance The total variable overhead variance is the difference between the actual and the applied variable overhead. For our example, the total variable overhead variance is computed as follows:

$$\text{Total variance} = \$1{,}600 - \$1{,}456$$
$$= \$144\ \text{U}$$

This total variance can be divided into spending and efficiency variances. This computation is illustrated using a three-pronged approach in Exhibit 9-8.

Variable Overhead Spending Variance The **variable overhead spending variance** measures the aggregate effect of differences between the actual variable overhead rate (*AVOR*) and the standard variable overhead rate (*SVOR*). The actual variable overhead rate is simply actual variable overhead divided by actual hours. For our example, this rate is \$4 per hour (\$1,600/400 hours). The formula for computing the variable overhead spending variance is:

$$\begin{aligned}\text{Variable overhead spending variance} &= (AVOR \times AH) - (SVOR \times AH)\\ &= (AVOR - SVOR)AH\\ &= (\$4.00 - \$3.85)400\\ &= \$60\ \text{U}\end{aligned}$$

Comparison to the Price Variances of Materials and Labor The variable overhead spending variance is similar but not identical to the price variances of materials and labor; there are some conceptual differences. Variable overhead is not a homogeneous input—it is made up of a large number of individual items, such as indirect materials, indirect labor, electricity, maintenance, and so on. The standard

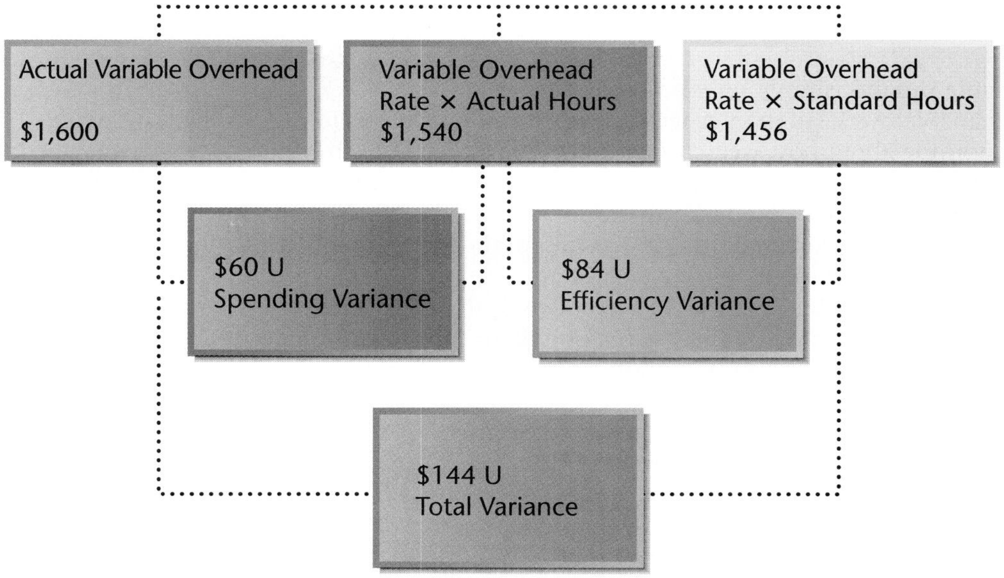

Exhibit 9-8 Variable Overhead Variances: Columnar Approach

variable overhead rate represents the weighted cost per direct labor hour that should be incurred for all variable overhead items. The difference between what should have been spent per hour and what actually was spent per hour is a type of price variance.

A variable overhead spending variance can arise because prices for individual variable overhead items have increased or decreased. Assume, for the moment, that the price changes of individual overhead items are the only cause of the spending variance. If the spending variance is unfavorable, price increases for individual variable overhead items are the cause; if the spending variance is favorable, price decreases are dominating.

If the only source of the variable overhead spending variance was price changes, then it would be completely analogous to the price variances of materials and labor. Unfortunately, the spending variance is also affected by how efficiently overhead is used. Waste or inefficiency in the use of variable overhead increases the actual variable overhead cost. This increased cost, in turn, is reflected in an increased actual variable overhead rate. Thus, even if the actual prices of the individual overhead items were equal to the budgeted or standard prices, an unfavorable variable overhead spending variance could still take place. For example, more kilowatt-hours of power may be used than should be—yet, this is not captured by any change in direct labor hours, but the effect is reflected by an increase in the total cost of power and, ultimately, the total cost of variable overhead. Similarly, efficiency can decrease the actual variable overhead cost and decrease the actual variable overhead rate. Efficient use of variable overhead items contributes to a favorable spending variance. If the waste effect dominates, the net contribution will be unfavorable; if efficiency dominates, the net contribution is favorable. Hence, the variable overhead spending variance is the result of both price and efficiency.

Responsibility for the Variable Overhead Spending Variance Many variable overhead items are affected by several responsibility centers. For example, utilities are a joint cost.[7] To the extent that consumption of variable overhead can be traced to a responsibility center, responsibility can be assigned. Consumption of indirect materials is an example of a traceable variable overhead cost.

Controllability is a prerequisite for assigning responsibility. Price changes of variable overhead items are essentially beyond the control of supervisors. If price changes are small (as they often are), the spending variance is primarily a matter of the efficient use of overhead in production, which is controllable by production supervisors. Accordingly, responsibility for the variable overhead spending variance is generally assigned to production departments.

Analysis of the Variable Overhead Spending Variance The $60 unfavorable variance simply reveals that, in the aggregate, Blue-Corn Foods spent more on variable overhead than expected. Even if the variance were insignificant, it reveals nothing about how well costs of individual variable overhead items were controlled. Control of variable overhead requires line-by-line analysis for each individual item. Exhibit 9-9 presents a performance report that supplies the line-by-line information essential for proper control of variable overhead. Assume that the numbers come from Blue-Corn's accounting records.

From Exhibit 9-9, it is clear that two of the three items present no control problems for the firm. Electricity is the only item showing an unfavorable variance; in fact, it is the cause of the overall variable overhead spending variance. If the variance is significant, an investigation may be warranted. This investigation may reveal that the power company raised the price of electricity. If so, the cause of the variance is beyond the control of the company. The correct response is to revise the budget formula to reflect the increased cost of electricity. However, if the price of electricity has

7 If a company installs meters to measure consumption of utilities for each responsibility center, responsibility can be assigned. However, the cost of assigning responsibility can sometimes exceed any potential benefit. The alternative is allocation. Unfortunately, allocation can be arbitrary, and it is often difficult to identify accurately the amount actually consumed.

Blue-Corn Foods, Inc.
Flexible Budget Performance Report
For the Week Ended March 8, 2008

	Cost Formula[a]	Actual Costs	Budget[b]	Spending Variance
Gas	$3.00	$1,190	$1,200	$ 10 F
Electricity	0.78	385	312	73 U
Water	0.07	25	28	3 F
Total cost	$3.85	$1,600	$1,540	$60 U

[a]Per direct labor hour.
[b]Computed using the cost formula and an activity level of 400 actual direct labor hours.

Exhibit 9-9 Flexible Budget Performance Report

remained unchanged, the usage of electricity is greater than expected. For example, the company may find that there were more startups and shutdowns of machinery than normal, causing an increased consumption of electricity.

Variable Overhead Efficiency Variance Variable overhead is assumed to vary as the production volume changes. Thus, variable overhead changes in proportion to changes in the direct labor hours used. The **variable overhead efficiency variance** measures the change in variable overhead consumption that occurs because of efficient (or inefficient) use of direct labor. The efficiency variance is computed using the following formula:

$$\begin{aligned}\text{Variable overhead efficiency variance} &= (AH - SH)SVOR \\ &= (400 - 378.3)\$3.85 \\ &= \$84\text{ U (rounded)}\end{aligned}$$

Responsibility for the Variable Overhead Efficiency Variance The variable overhead efficiency variance is directly related to the direct labor efficiency or usage variance. If variable overhead is truly proportional to direct labor consumption, then, like the labor usage variance, the variable overhead efficiency variance is caused by efficient or inefficient use of direct labor. If more (or fewer) direct labor hours are used than the standard calls for, the total variable overhead cost will increase (or decrease). The validity of the measure depends on how valid the relationship is between variable overhead costs and direct labor hours. In other words, do variable overhead costs really change in proportion to changes in direct labor hours? If so, responsibility for the variable overhead efficiency variance should be assigned to the individual who has responsibility for the use of direct labor: the production manager.

Analysis of the Variable Overhead Efficiency Variance The reasons for the unfavorable variable overhead efficiency variance are the same as those offered for the unfavorable labor usage variance. More hours were used than the standard called for because of excessive idle time for inspectors and because the machine operators used as substitute inspectors were inexperienced in sorting. More information concerning the effect of labor usage on variable overhead is available in a line-by-line analysis of individual variable overhead items. This can be accomplished by comparing the budget allowance for the actual hours used with the budget allowance for the standard hours allowed for each item. A performance report that makes this comparison for all variable overhead costs is shown in Exhibit 9-10.

From Exhibit 9-10, we can see that the cost of gas is affected most by inefficient use of labor. This can be explained by the need to keep the cooking oil hot (assuming gas is used for cooking) even though the cooking process is slowed down by the subsequent sorting process.

Blue-Corn Foods, Inc. Performance Report For the Week Ended March 8, 2008						
Cost	Cost Formula[a]	Budget for Actual Costs	Actual Hours	Spending Variance[b]	Budget for Standard Hours[c]	Efficiency Variance[d]
Gas	$3.00	$1,190	$1,200	$10 F	$1,135	$65 U
Electricity	0.78	385	312	73 U	295	17 U
Water	0.07	25	28	3 F	26	2 U
Total	$3.85	$1,600	$1,540	$60 U	$1,456	$84 U

[a]Per direct labor hour
[b]Spending variance = Actual costs − Budget for actual hours
[c]Computed using the cost formula and an activity level of 378.3 standard hours. Rounded to the nearest dollar.
[d]Efficiency variance = Budget for actual hours − Budget for standard hours

Exhibit 9-10 Performance Report—Variable Overhead

The column labeled "Budget for Standard Hours" gives the amount that should have been spent on variable overhead for the actual output. The total of all items in this column is the applied variable overhead, the amount assigned to production in a standard cost system. Note that in a standard cost system, variable overhead is applied using the hours allowed for the actual output (*SH*), while in normal costing, variable overhead is applied using actual hours (see Chapter 4). Although not shown in Exhibit 9-10, the difference between actual costs and this column is the total variable overhead variance (underapplied by $144). Thus, the underapplied variable overhead variance is the sum of the spending and efficiency variances.

Fixed Overhead Variances

We will again use the Blue-Corn Foods example to illustrate the computation of the fixed overhead variances. The yearly data needed for the example follow:

Budgeted or Planned Items	
Budgeted fixed overhead	$749,970
Practical activity	23,400 direct labor hours[a]
Standard fixed overhead rate	$ 32.05[b]

[a]Hours allowed to produce 3,000,000 bags of chips: 0.0078 × 3,000,000
[b]$749,970/23,400

Actual Results	
Actual production	2,750,000 bags of chips
Actual fixed overhead cost	$749,000
Standard hours allowed for actual production	21,450*

*0.0078 × 2,750,000

Total Fixed Overhead Variance The total fixed overhead variance is the difference between actual fixed overhead and applied fixed overhead, when applied fixed overhead is obtained by multiplying the standard fixed overhead rate times the standard hours allowed for the actual output. Thus, the applied fixed overhead is:

$$\begin{aligned}\text{Applied fixed overhead} &= \text{Standard fixed overhead rate} \times \text{Standard hours}\\ &= \$32.05 \times 21{,}450\\ &= \$687{,}473 \text{ (rounded)}\end{aligned}$$

The total fixed overhead variance is the difference between the actual fixed overhead and the applied fixed overhead:

$$\text{Total fixed overhead variance} = \$749{,}000 - \$687{,}473$$
$$= \$61{,}527 \text{ underapplied}$$

To help managers understand why fixed overhead was underapplied by $61,527, the total variance can be broken into two variances: the fixed overhead spending variance and the fixed overhead volume variance. The calculation of the two variances is illustrated in Exhibit 9-11.

Fixed Overhead Spending Variance The **fixed overhead spending variance** is defined as the difference between the actual fixed overhead and the budgeted fixed overhead. The spending variance is favorable because less was spent on fixed overhead items than was budgeted.

Responsibility for the Fixed Overhead Spending Variance Fixed overhead is made up of a number of individual items such as salaries, depreciation, taxes, and insurance. Many fixed overhead items—long-run investments, for instance—are not subject to change in the short run; consequently, fixed overhead costs are often beyond the immediate control of management. Since many fixed overhead costs are affected primarily by long-run decisions, and not by changes in production levels, the budget variance is usually small. For example, depreciation, salaries, taxes, and insurance costs are not likely to be much different from planned.

Analysis of the Fixed Overhead Spending Variance Because fixed overhead is made up of many individual items, a line-by-line comparison of budgeted costs with actual costs provides more information concerning the causes of the spending variance. Exhibit 9-12 provides such a report. The report reveals that the fixed overhead spending variance is essentially in line with expectations. The fixed overhead spending variances, both on a line-item basis and in the aggregate, are relatively small.

Fixed Overhead Volume Variance The **fixed overhead volume variance** is the difference between budgeted fixed overhead and applied fixed overhead. The volume variance measures the effect of the actual output differing from the output used

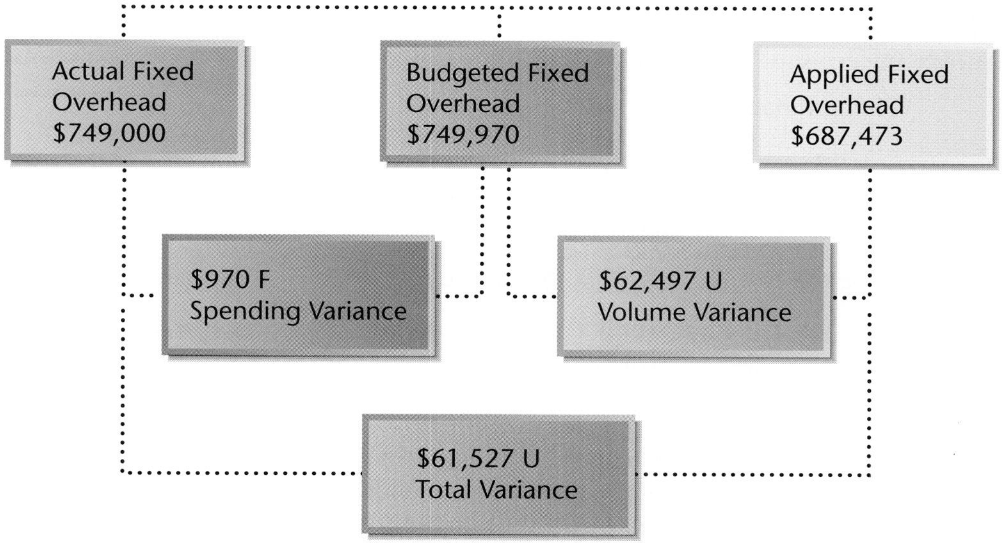

Exhibit 9-11 Fixed Overhead Variances

Blue-Corn Foods, Inc. Performance Report For the Year Ended March 8, 2008			
Fixed Overhead Items	Actual Cost	Budgeted Cost	Variance
Depreciation	$530,000	$530,000	$ 0
Salaries	159,370	159,970	600 F
Taxes	50,500	50,000	500 U
Insurance	9,130	10,000	870 F
Total fixed overhead	$749,000	$749,970	$970 F

Exhibit 9-12 Performance Report—Fixed Overhead

Standard costing helps give an early warning of potential problems. In the baking department, the quality of the chips is determined by inspection, and compared with the expected standard amounts. If all chips look evenly browned, then all is well in that department. If not, the variance can be investigated to determine the underlying cause.

© John Madere/Corbis

at the beginning of the year to compute the predetermined standard fixed overhead rate. If you think of the output used to calculate the fixed overhead rate as the activity capacity acquired and the actual output as the activity capacity used, then the volume variance is analogous to the cost of unused activity capacity described in Chapter 4. This analogy holds up well when we use practical capacity for computing the fixed overhead rate. All of the fixed overhead costs are resources spent to acquire production capacity in advance of usage.

For example, at the beginning of the year, Blue-Corn Foods has the capacity to produce 3,000,000 bags of chips, using 23,400 direct labor hours. The actual output is 2,750,000 bags. Thus, the actual output is less than expected, and only 21,450 hours are allowed for the actual output. Less capacity was used than acquired, and the cost of this unused capacity is calculated by multiplying the rate by the difference in the expected and actual capacities (measured in hours):

$$\begin{aligned}\text{Volume variance} &= \$32.05(23{,}400 - 21{,}450)\\ &= (\$32.05 \times 23{,}400) - (\$32.05 \times 21{,}450)\\ &= \$749{,}970 - \$687{,}473\\ &= \text{Budgeted fixed overhead} - \text{Applied fixed overhead}\\ &= \$62{,}497 \text{ U}\end{aligned}$$

Therefore, we can interpret the volume variance as a measure of capacity utilization.

Responsibility for the Fixed Overhead Volume Variance Assuming that volume variance measures capacity utilization implies that the general responsibility for this variance should be assigned to the production department. At times, however, investigation into the reasons for a significant volume variance may reveal the cause to be factors beyond the control of production. In this instance, specific responsibility may be assigned elsewhere. For example, if purchasing acquires a material of lower quality than usual, significant rework time may result, causing lower production and an unfavorable volume variance. In this case, responsibility for the variance rests with purchasing, not production.

Appendix: Accounting for Variances

Objective 6

Appendix: Prepare journal entries for materials and labor variances, and show how to account for overhead variances.

To illustrate recording variances, we will assume that the materials price variance is computed at the time materials are purchased. With this assumption, we can state a general rule for a firm's inventory accounts: all inventories are carried at standard cost. Actual costs are never entered into an inventory account. In recording variances, unfavorable variances are always debits, and favorable variances are always credits.

Entries for Direct Materials Variances

Materials Price Variance The entry to record the purchase of materials follows (assuming an unfavorable *MPV* and that *AQ* is materials purchased):

Materials Inventory	$SP \times AQ$	
Materials Price Variance	$(AP - SP)AQ$	
Accounts Payable		$AP \times AQ$

For example, if *AP* is $0.0069 per ounce of corn, *SP* is $0.0060 per ounce, and 780,000 ounces of corn are purchased, the entry would be:

Materials Inventory	4,680	
Materials Price Variance	702	
Accounts Payable		5,382

Notice that the raw materials are carried in the inventory account at standard cost.

Materials Usage Variance The general form for the entry to record the issuance and usage of materials, assuming a favorable *MUV*, is as follows:

Work in Process	$SQ \times SP$	
Materials Usage Variance		$(AQ - SQ)SP$
Materials Inventory		$AQ \times SP$

Here *AQ* is the materials issued and used, not necessarily equal to the materials purchased. Notice that only standard quantities and standard prices are used to assign costs to Work in Process; no actual costs enter this account.

For example, if *AQ* is 780,000 ounces of corn, *SQ* is 873,000 ounces, and *SP* is $0.006, then the entry would be as follows:

Work in Process	5,238	
Materials Usage Variance		558
Materials Inventory		4,680

Notice that the favorable usage variance appears as a credit entry.

Entries for Direct Labor Variances

Unlike the materials variances, the entry to record both types of labor variances is made simultaneously. The general form of this entry follows (assuming a favorable labor rate variance and an unfavorable labor efficiency variance).

Work in Process	$SH \times SR$	
Labor Efficiency Variance	$(AH - SH)SR$	
Labor Rate Variance		$(AR - SR)AH$
Accrued Payroll		$AH \times AR$

Again, notice that only standard hours and standard rates are used to assign costs to Work in Process. Actual prices or quantities are not used.

To give a specific example, assume that *AH* is 360 hours of inspection, *SH* is 339.5 hours, *AR* is $7.35 per hour, and *SR* is $7.00 per hour. The following journal entry would be made:

Work in Process	2,376.50	
Labor Efficiency Variance	143.50	
Labor Rate Variance	126.00	
Accrued Payroll		2,646.00

Disposition of Materials and Labor Variances

At the end of the year, the variances for materials and labor are usually closed to Cost of Goods Sold. (This practice is acceptable provided that variances are not material in amount.) Using the previous data, the entries would take the following form:

Cost of Goods Sold	971.50	
Materials Price Variance		702.00
Labor Efficiency Variance		143.50
Labor Rate Variance		126.00
Materials Usage Variance	558.00	
Cost of Goods Sold		558.00

If the variances are material, they must be prorated among various accounts. For the materials price variance, it is prorated among Materials Inventory, Work in Process, Finished Goods, and Cost of Goods Sold. The remaining materials and labor variances are prorated among Work in Process, Finished Goods, and Cost of Goods Sold. Typically, materials variances are prorated on the basis of the materials balances in each of these accounts and the labor variances on the basis of the labor balances in the accounts.

Overhead Variances

Although overhead variances can be recorded following a pattern similar to that described for labor and materials, these variances are more generally treated as part of a periodic overhead analysis. Applied overhead is accumulated in the applied accounts, and actual overhead is accumulated in the control accounts. Periodically (for example, monthly), performance reports that provide overhead variance information are prepared. At the end of the year, the applied accounts and control accounts are closed out and the variances isolated. The overhead variances are then disposed of by closing them to Cost of Goods Sold if they are not material or by prorating them among Work in Process, Finished Goods, and Cost of Goods Sold if they are material.

Summary of Learning Objectives

1. Tell how unit standards are set and why standard costing systems are adopted.

A standard cost system budgets quantities and costs on a unit basis. These unit budgets are for labor, materials, and overhead. Standard costs, therefore, are the amount that should be expended to produce a product or service. Standards are set using historical experience, engineering studies, and input from operating personnel, marketing, and accounting. Currently attainable standards are those that can be achieved under efficient operating conditions. Ideal standards are those achievable under maximum efficiency, or ideal operating conditions. Standard costing systems are adopted to improve planning and control and to facilitate product costing. By comparing actual outcomes with standards and breaking the variance into price and quantity components, detailed feedback is provided to managers. This information allows managers to exercise a greater degree of cost control than that found in a normal or an actual costing system. Decisions such as bidding are also made easier when a standard costing system is in place.

2. State the purpose of a standard cost sheet.

The standard cost sheet provides the details for the computation of the standard cost per unit. It shows the standard costs for materials, labor, and variable and fixed overhead. It also reveals the quantity of each input that should be used to produce one unit of output. Using these unit quantity standards, the standard quantity of materials allowed and the standard hours allowed can be computed for the actual output. These computations play an important role in variance analysis.

3. Describe the basic concepts underlying variance analysis, and explain when variances should be investigated.

The budget variance is the difference between actual costs and planned costs. In a standard costing system, the budget variance is broken down into price and usage variances. By breaking the budget variances into price and usage variances, managers have more ability to analyze and control the total variance. Variances should be investigated if they are material and if the benefits of corrective action are greater than the costs of investigation. Because of the difficulty of assessing cost and benefits on a case-by-case basis, many firms set up formal control limits—either a dollar amount, a percentage, or both. Others use judgment to assess the need to investigate.

4. Compute the materials and labor variances, and explain how they are used for control.

The materials price and usage variances are computed using either a three-pronged approach or formulas. The three-pronged approach for materials is illustrated in Exhibit 9-6. The materials price variance is the difference between what should have been paid for materials and what was paid (generally associated with the purchasing activity). The materials usage variance is the difference between the cost of the materials that should have been used and the amount that was used (generally associated with the production activity). When a significant variance is signaled, an investigation is undertaken to find the cause. Corrective action is taken, if possible, to put the system back in control. The labor variances are computed using either a three-pronged approach or formulas. The three-pronged approach for labor is illustrated in Exhibit 9-7. The labor rate variance is caused by the actual wage rate differing from the standard wage rate. It is the difference between the wages that were paid and those that should have been paid. The labor efficiency variance is the difference between the cost of the labor that was used and the cost of the labor that should have been used. When a significant variance is signaled, investigation is called for, and corrective action should be taken, if possible, to put the system back in control.

5. Calculate the variable and fixed overhead variances, and give their definitions.

The variable overhead spending variance is the difference between the actual variable overhead cost and the budgeted variable overhead cost for actual hours worked. Therefore, it is a budget variance, resulting from price changes and efficient or inefficient use of variable overhead inputs. The variable efficiency variance is the difference between budgeted variable overhead at actual hours and applied variable overhead. It is strictly attributable to the efficiency of labor usage and assumes that the variable overhead items are all driven by direct labor hours.

The fixed overhead spending variance is the difference between the actual fixed overhead costs and the budgeted fixed overhead costs. Hence, it is simply a budget variance. The volume variance is the difference between the budgeted fixed overhead and the applied fixed overhead. It occurs whenever the actual production volume is different from the expected production volume and, thus, is a measure of capacity utilization.

6. **Appendix: Prepare journal entries for materials and labor variances, and show how to account for overhead variances.**

Assuming that the materials price variance is computed at the point of purchase, all inventories are carried at standard cost. Actual costs are never entered into an inventory account. Accounts are created for materials price and usage variances and for labor rate and efficiency variances. Unfavorable variances are always debits; favorable variances are always credits. Overhead variances are generally not journalized. Instead, periodic overhead reports are prepared that provide overhead variance information.

Key Terms

Control limits, 375
Currently attainable standards, 369
Favorable (F) variances, 373
Fixed overhead spending variance, 387
Fixed overhead volume variance, 387
Ideal standards, 369
Labor efficiency variance (*LEV*), 381
Labor rate variance (*LRV*), 380
Materials price variance (*MPV*), 376
Materials usage variance (*MUV*), 379
Price standards, 368
Price (rate) variance, 373
Quantity standards, 368
Standard cost per unit, 371
Standard cost sheet, 371
Standard hours allowed (*SH*), 372
Standard quantity of materials allowed (*SQ*), 372
Total budget variance, 373
Unfavorable (U) variances, 373
Usage (efficiency) variance, 373
Variable overhead efficiency variance, 385
Variable overhead spending variance, 383

Review Problem

Materials, Labor, and Overhead Variances

Wangsgard Manufacturing has the following standard cost sheet for one of its products:

Direct materials (2 ft. @ $5)	$10
Direct labor (0.5 hr. @ $10)	5
Fixed overhead (0.5 hr. @ $2)*	1
Variable overhead (0.5 hr. @ $4)	2
Standard unit cost	$18

*Rate based on expected activity of 2,500 hours.

During the most recent year, the following actual results were recorded:

Production	6,000 units
Direct materials (11,750 ft. purchased and used)	$ 61,100
Direct labor (2,900 hrs.)	29,580
Fixed overhead	6,000
Variable overhead	10,500

Required

Compute the following variances:

1. Materials price and usage variances.
2. Labor rate and efficiency variances.
3. Variable overhead spending and efficiency variances.
4. Fixed overhead spending and volume variances.

Solution

1. Materials variances:

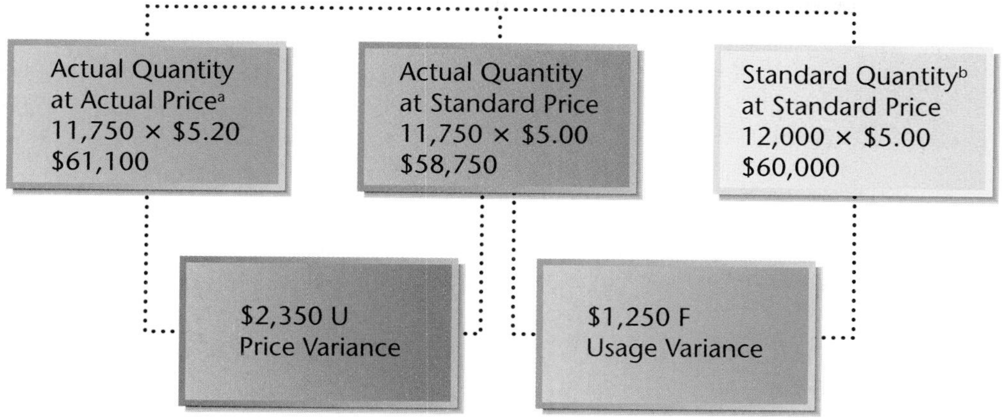

[a]$61,100/11,750 = $5.20 = Actual price
[b]2 × 6,000 = 12,000 = Standard quantity

Or, using formulas, we have:

$$\begin{aligned} MPV &= (AP - SP)AQ \\ &= (\$5.20 - \$5.00)11{,}750 \\ &= \$2{,}350\ \text{U} \\ MUV &= (AQ - SQ)SP \\ &= (11{,}750 - 12{,}000)\$5.00 \\ &= \$1{,}250\ \text{F} \end{aligned}$$

2. Labor variances:

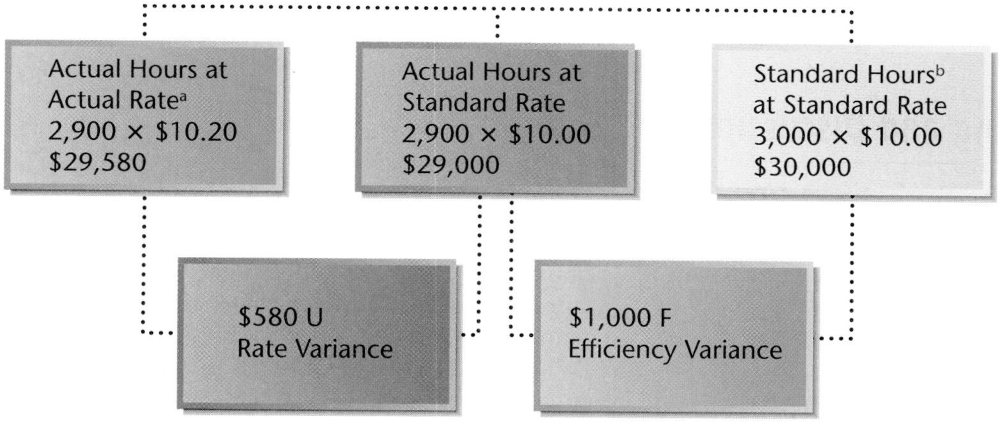

[a]$29,580/2,900 = $10.20 = Actual price
[b]0.5 × 6,000 = 3,000 = Standard hours

Or, using formulas, we have:

$$\begin{aligned} LRV &= (AR - SR)AH \\ &= (\$10.20 - \$10.00)2{,}900 \\ &= \$580\ \text{U} \\ LEV &= (AH - SH)SR \\ &= (2{,}900 - 3{,}000)\$10.00 \\ &= \$1{,}000\ \text{F} \end{aligned}$$

3. Variable overhead variances:

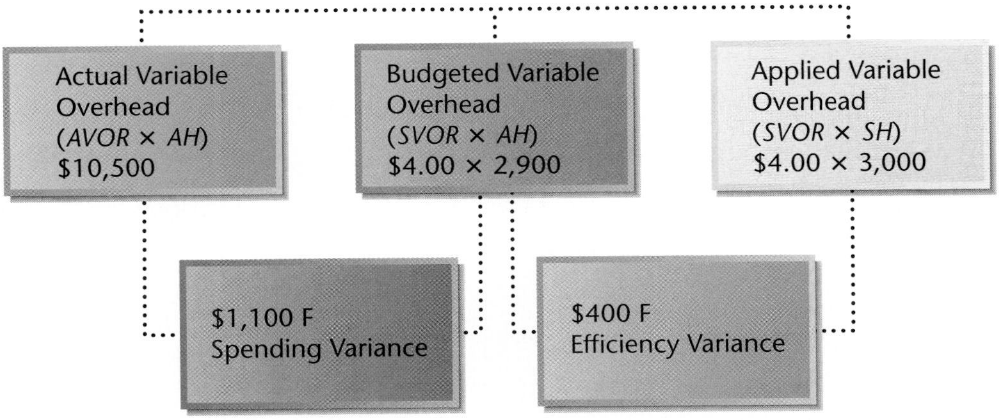

4. Fixed overhead variances:

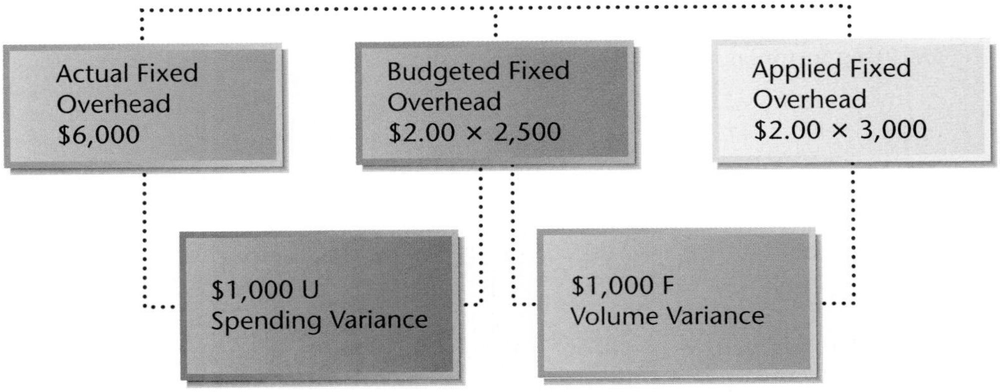

Questions for Writing and Discussion

1. Discuss the difference between budgets and standard costs.
2. Describe the relationship that unit standards have with flexible budgeting.
3. What is the quantity decision? The pricing decision?
4. Why is historical experience often a poor basis for establishing standards?
5. Should standards be set by engineering studies? Why or why not?
6. What are ideal standards? Currently attainable standards? Of the two, which is usually adopted? Why?
7. Explain why standard costing systems are adopted.
8. How does standard costing improve the control function?
9. Discuss the differences among actual costing, normal costing, and standard costing.
10. What is the purpose of a standard cost sheet?
11. The budget variance for variable production costs is broken down into quantity and price variances. Explain why the quantity variance is more useful for control purposes than the price variance.
12. When should a standard cost variance be investigated?
13. What are control limits, and how are they set?
14. Explain why the materials price variance is often computed at the point of purchase rather than at the point of issuance.
15. The materials usage variance is always the responsibility of the production supervisor. Do you agree or disagree? Why?
16. The labor rate variance is never controllable. Do you agree or disagree? Why?
17. Suggest some possible causes of an unfavorable labor efficiency variance.
18. Explain why the variable overhead spending variance is not a pure price variance.

19. The variable overhead efficiency variance has nothing to do with efficient use of variable overhead. Do you agree or disagree? Why?
20. Explain why the fixed overhead spending variance is usually very small.
21. What is the cause of an unfavorable volume variance? Does the volume variance convey any meaningful information to managers?
22. Which do you think is more important for control of fixed overhead costs: the spending variance or the volume variance? Explain.

Exercises

9-1

Setting Standards and Assigning Responsibility
LO1

Choose the *best* answer for each of the following multiple-choice questions:

1. Historical experience should be used with caution in setting standards because
   a. most companies have very poor records.
   b. ideal standards are always better than historical standards.
   c. they may not be achievable by operating personnel.
   d. they may perpetuate operating inefficiencies.
   e. None of the above.
2. Standards set by engineering studies
   a. can determine the most efficient way of operating.
   b. can provide very rigorous guidelines.
   c. may not be achievable by operating personnel.
   d. often do not allow operating personnel to have much input.
   e. All of the above.
3. To determine the standard cost per unit of output for a particular input, the manager must
   a. know the price per unit of input.
   b. know the quantity of input used per unit of output.
   c. know the total budgeted output.
   d. All of the above.
   e. Only a and b.
4. A currently attainable standard is one that
   a. relies on maximum efficiency.
   b. is based only on historical experience.
   c. can be achieved under efficient operating conditions.
   d. makes no allowances for normal breakdowns, interruptions, less than perfect skills, and so on.
   e. Both a and d.
5. An ideal standard is one that
   a. relies on maximum efficiency.
   b. is based only on historical experience.
   c. can be achieved under efficient operating conditions.
   d. makes no allowances for normal breakdowns, interruptions, less than perfect skills, and so on.
   e. Both a and d.
6. Standard costing systems are adopted
   a. to enhance operational control.
   b. to imitate most other firms.
   c. to encourage purchasing managers to take advantage of purchase discounts.
   d. so that the weighted average method can be used for process manufacturers.
   e. All of the above.

9-2

Setting Standards and Assigning Responsibility
LO1

CMA

Associated Media Graphics (AMG) is a rapidly expanding company involved in the mass reproduction of instructional materials. Ralph Boston, owner and manager of AMG, has made a concerted effort to provide a quality product at a fair price with delivery on the promised due date. Expanding sales have been attributed to this philosophy. As the business grows, however, Ralph is finding it increasingly difficult to personally supervise the operations of AMG. As a result, he is beginning to institute an organizational structure that would facilitate management control.

One recent change was to designate the operating departments as cost centers, with control over departmental operations transferred from Ralph to each departmental manager. However, quality control still reports directly to Ralph, as do the finance and accounting functions. A materials manager was hired to purchase all materials and oversee inventory handling (receiving, storage, and so on) and record keeping. The materials manager is also responsible for maintaining an adequate inventory based upon planned production levels.

The loss of personal control over the operations of AMG caused Ralph to look for a method to evaluate performance efficiently. Dave Cress, a new cost accountant, proposed the use of a standard costing system. Variances for materials, labor, and overhead could then be calculated and reported directly to Ralph.

Required

1. Assume that AMG is going to implement a standard costing system and establish standards for materials, labor, and overhead.
   a. Who should be involved in setting the standards for each cost component?
   b. What factors should be considered in establishing the standards for each cost component?
2. Describe the basis for assignment of responsibility under a standard costing system. **(CMA adapted)**

9-3

Computation of Inputs Allowed; Materials and Labor; Service Company
LO2

Garrison Company has a contract with a major computer manufacturer to do warranty repairs for computers with a given set of failure diagnostics. During the year, Garrison Company repaired 1,700 units. Garrison's materials and labor standards for performing the repairs are:

Direct materials (4 components @ $14.00)	$56
Direct labor (1.5 hr. @ $16)	24

Required

1. Compute the standard hours allowed for the repair of 1,700 units.
2. Compute the standard number of components allowed for the repair of 1,700 units.

9-4

Computation of Inputs Allowed; Materials and Labor; Service Company
LO2

Seasonal Confections, Inc., a manufacturer of candies for various seasons of the year, wants to set up a standard costing system. The controller decided to set up a standard cost card for one product line. He chose the chocolate bunny line, which operates from February through April of each year. The chocolate bunnies are 8" tall dark chocolate molded rabbits. They are very popular each Easter season. Last year, Seasonal Confections produced 40,000 dark chocolate bunnies with the following total costs:

Direct materials (340,000 oz. @ $0.30)	$102,000
Direct labor (10,000 DLH @ $9)	90,000

Required

1. Compute the direct materials allowed per bunny in ounces.
2. Compute the direct labor hours allowed per bunny in hours.
3. Set up a standard cost card for the prime cost of one chocolate bunny.

9-5

Computation of Inputs Allowed; Materials and Labor; Service Company
LO2

Refer to the data in **Exercise 9-4**. Suppose that Seasonal Confections expects to produce 47,000 dark chocolate bunnies this spring.

Required

1. Compute the standard quantity of direct materials allowed for the production of 47,000 bunnies.
2. Compute the standard hours allowed for the production of 47,000 bunnies.
3. Compute the total standard prime cost for the production of 47,000 bunnies.

9-6

Investigation of Variances
LO3

Ellerbee Cable Company uses a standard costing system to control the labor costs associated with cable installation and repair. Ellerbee uses the following rule to determine whether the labor efficiency variance should be investigated: a labor efficiency variance will be investigated when the amount exceeds the lesser of $2,100 or 5% of standard cost. The company collected reports for the past four months to provide the following information:

Month	*LEV*	Standard Labor Cost
1	$2,280 F	$45,000
2	2,000 U	50,000
3	1,900 F	48,000
4	3,050 U	60,000

Required

1. Using the rule provided, identify the cases that will be investigated.
2. Suppose investigation reveals that the cause of an unfavorable labor efficiency variance is the hiring of a number of new workers who worked more slowly while they were being trained. Who is responsible? What corrective action would likely be taken?

9-7

Investigation of Variances
LO3

Underwood Company uses the following rule to determine whether materials usage variances ought to be investigated: A materials usage variance will be investigated anytime the amount exceeds the lesser of $8,000 or 10 percent of the standard cost. Reports for the past five weeks provided the following information:

Week	*MUV*	Standard Materials Cost
1	$7,000 F	$80,000
2	7,800 U	75,000
3	6,000 F	80,000
4	9,000 U	85,000
5	7,000 U	69,000

Required

1. Using the rule provided, identify the cases that will be investigated.
2. Suppose investigation reveals that the cause of an unfavorable materials usage variance is the use of lower-quality materials than are usually used. Who is responsible? What corrective action would likely be taken?

3. Suppose investigation reveals that the cause of a significant unfavorable materials usage variance is attributable to a new approach to manufacturing that takes less labor time but causes more material waste. Examination of the labor efficiency variance reveals that it is favorable and is larger than the unfavorable materials usage variance. Who is responsible? What action should be taken?

9-8

Materials and Labor Variances
LO4

EXCEL

Sunny Juice Company produces fruit juices, sold in gallons. Recently, the company adopted the following standards for one gallon of its cranberry juice:

Direct materials (128 oz. @ \$0.046)	\$5.888
Direct labor (0.038 hr. @ \$12.00)	0.456
Standard prime cost	\$6.344

During the first week of operation, the company experienced the following actual results:

a. Gallon units produced: 52,000
b. Ounces of materials purchased: 6,420,000 ounces at \$0.047
c. No beginning or ending inventories of raw materials
d. Direct labor: 2,000 hours at \$12.50

Required

1. Compute price and usage variances for direct materials.
2. Compute the rate variance and the efficiency variance for direct labor.

9-9

Overhead Variances; Service Company
LO5

EXCEL

Chalmet, Inc., operates a delivery service for over 70 restaurants. Chalmet has a fleet of vehicles and has invested in a sophisticated computerized communications system to coordinate its deliveries. Chalmet has gathered the following data on last year's operations:

a. Deliveries made: 73,000
b. Direct labor: 52,000 delivery hours at \$8
c. Actual fixed overhead: \$710,000
d. Actual variable overhead: \$160,000

Chalmet employs a standard costing system. During the year, the following rates were used: standard fixed overhead rate, \$14 per delivery hour; standard variable overhead rate, \$3.00 per hour. The labor standard requires 0.75 hour per delivery. (These rates were based on a standard normal volume of 50,000 delivery hours.)

Required

1. Compute the variable overhead spending and efficiency variances.
2. Compute the fixed overhead spending and volume variances.

9-10

Decomposition of Budget Variances; Materials and Labor
LO4

Guerin Corporation produces leather purses. The company uses a standard costing system and has set the following standards for materials and labor:

Leather (5 strips @ \$7)	\$35
Direct labor (1.5 hrs. @ \$14)	21
Total prime cost	\$56

During the year, Guerin produced 34,000 leather purses. Actual leather purchased was 173,500 strips at \$6.82 per strip. There were no beginning or ending inventories of leather. Actual direct labor was 50,900 hours at \$13.50 per hour.

Required

1. Compute the costs of leather and direct labor that should have been incurred for the production of 34,000 leather purses.

2. Compute the total budget variances for materials and labor.
3. Break down the total variance for materials into a price variance and a usage variance.
4. Break down the total variance for labor into a rate variance and an efficiency variance.

9-11

Appendix Exercise: Materials and Labor Variances; Journal Entries
LO4, LO6

EXCEL

Zawatsky Products produces instructional aids. Among the company's products are whiteboards, which use colored markers instead of chalk. They are particularly popular for conference rooms in educational institutions and executive offices of large corporations. The standard costs of materials and labor for this product follow:

Direct materials	11 lbs. @ $7.95
Direct labor	4 hrs. @ $9.40

During the first month of the year, 20,100 boards were produced. Information concerning actual costs and usage of materials and labor follows:

Materials purchased	222,500 lbs. @ $8.05
Materials used	220,400 lbs.
Direct labor	79,900 hrs.; total cost: $759,050

Required

1. Compute the materials price and usage variances.
2. Compute the labor rate and efficiency variances.
3. Prepare journal entries for all activity relating to materials and labor for the month.

9-12

Overhead Application; Overhead Variances
LO5

EXCEL

Chef's-Best Company is planning to produce 800,000 electric mixers for the coming year. Each mixer requires one-half standard hour of labor for completion. The company uses direct labor hours to assign overhead to products. The total overhead budgeted for the coming year is $1,120,000, and the standard fixed overhead rate is $0.55 *per unit produced.* Actual results for the year follow:

Actual production (units)	786,000
Actual direct labor hours	390,000
Actual variable overhead	$695,000
Actual fixed overhead	$430,300

Required

1. Compute the applied fixed overhead.
2. Compute the fixed overhead spending and volume variances.
3. Compute the applied variable overhead.
4. Compute the variable overhead spending and efficiency variances.

9-13

Appendix Exercise: Overhead Application; Overhead Variances
LO5

Mediamet Company produces one product and uses a standard costing system. The direct labor standard indicates that three direct labor hours should be used for every unit produced. The normal production volume is 120,000 units of this product. The budgeted overhead for the coming year follows:

Fixed overhead	$864,000*
Variable overhead	1,440,000

*At normal volume.

Mediamet applies overhead on the basis of direct labor hours.

During the year, Mediamet produced 120,600 units, worked 361,800 direct labor hours, and incurred actual fixed overhead costs of $940,320 and actual variable overhead costs of $1,443,500.

Required

1. Calculate the standard fixed overhead rate and the standard variable overhead rate.
2. Compute the applied fixed overhead and the applied variable overhead. What is the total fixed overhead variance? Total variable overhead variance?
3. Break down the total fixed overhead variance into a spending variance and a volume variance. Discuss the significance of each.
4. Compute the variable overhead spending and efficiency variances. Discuss the significance of each.

9-14

Materials; Labor; and Overhead Variances
LO4, LO5

At the beginning of 2008, Krayler Company had the following standard cost sheet for one of its chemical products:

Direct materials (6 lbs. @ $6.40)	$38.40
Direct labor (1.8 hrs. @ $18.00)	32.40
Fixed overhead (1.8 hrs. @ $8.00)	14.40
Variable overhead (1.8 hrs. @ $1.50)	2.70
Standard cost per unit	$87.90

Krayler computes its overhead rates using practical volume, which is 288,000 units. The actual results for 2008 are:

a. Units produced: 280,000
b. Materials purchased: 1,684,700 pounds at $6.60
c. Materials used: 1,684,000 pounds
d. Direct labor: 515,000 hours at $18.10
e. Fixed overhead: $4,140,200
f. Variable overhead: $872,000

Required

1. Compute price and usage variances for materials.
2. Compute the labor rate and labor efficiency variances.
3. Compute the fixed overhead spending and volume variances.
4. Compute the variable overhead spending and efficiency variances.

9-15

Appendix Exercise: Journal Entries
LO6

Refer to the data in **Exercise 9-14**. Prepare journal entries for the following:

1. The purchase of raw materials
2. The issuance of raw materials to production (Work in Process)
3. The addition of labor to Work in Process
4. The addition of overhead to Work in Process
5. Closing out of materials, labor, and overhead variances to Cost of Goods Sold

9-16

Variances; Evaluation; and Behavior
LO1

Jackie Iverson was furious. She was about ready to fire Tom Rich, her purchasing agent. Just a month ago, she had given him a salary increase and a bonus for his performance. She had been especially pleased with his ability to meet or beat the price standards. But now she had found out that it was because of a huge purchase of materials. It would take months to use that inventory, and there was hardly space to store it. In the meantime, where could the other materials supplies that would be ordered and processed on a regular basis be put? Additionally, it was a lot of capital to tie up in inventory—money that could have been used to help finance the cash needs of the new product just coming on line.

Her interview with Tom had been frustrating. He was defensive, arguing that he thought that she wanted those standards met and that the means were not that important. He also pointed out that quantity purchases were the only way to meet the price standards. Otherwise, an unfavorable variance would have been realized.

Required

1. Why did Tom Rich purchase the large quantity of materials? Do you think that this behavior was the objective of the price standard? If not, what is/are the objective(s)?
2. Suppose that Tom is right and that the only way to meet the price standards is through the use of quantity discounts. Also, assume that using quantity discounts is not a desirable practice for this company. What would you do to solve this dilemma?
3. Should Tom be fired? Explain.

9-17

Materials and Labor Variances; Activity-Based Costing
LO4

T-Top Company produces single-colored T-shirts. The following standards for one T-shirt have been established:

Direct materials (0.5 yds. @ $2)	$1.00
Direct labor (0.15 hrs. @ $9.00)	1.35
Standard prime cost	$2.35

During the year, 20,700 yards of fabric were purchased and used in the production of 41,300 T-shirts. The actual prime costs were:

Direct materials	$ 38,295
Direct labor	57,226 (for 6,200 hrs.)

Required

Compute the materials and labor variances associated with the production of T-shirts last year, labeling each variance as favorable or unfavorable.

9-18

Appendix Exercise: Journal Entries
LO6

Refer to **Exercise 9-17**. Prepare journal entries for the following:

Required

1. The purchase of materials
2. The issuance of materials
3. The addition of labor to Work in Process
4. Closing of variances to Cost of Goods Sold

9-19

Incomplete Data; Variance Analysis
LO4, LO5

Layner Company uses a standard costing system. During the past quarter, the following variances were computed:

Variable overhead efficiency variance	$ 8,000 U
Labor efficiency variance	20,000 U
Labor rate variance	6,000 U

Layner applies variable overhead using a standard rate of $2 per direct labor hour allowed. Four direct labor hours are allowed per unit produced (only one type of product is manufactured). During the quarter, Layner used 20 percent more direct labor hours than should have been used.

Required

1. What were the actual direct labor hours worked? The total hours allowed?
2. What is the standard hourly rate for direct labor? The actual hourly rate?
3. How many actual units were produced?

Problems

9-20

Basics of Variance Analysis; Variable Inputs
LO3, LO4

EXCEL

Jasper Company manufactures large plastic bins for industrial usage. One of Jasper's larger customers uses model T-367. Jasper located a plant dedicated to the manufacture of model T-367 across the street from the customer's plant. To help ensure cost efficiency, a standard costing system was installed in the plant. The following standards have been established for the product's variable inputs:

	Standard Quantity	Standard Price (Rate)	Standard Cost
Direct materials	10 lbs.	$ 1.70	$17.00
Direct labor	0.60 hrs.	10.00	6.00
Variable overhead	0.60 hrs.	2.50	1.50
Total			$24.50

During the first week in January, the company had the following actual results:

Units produced	4,000
Actual labor costs	$26,500
Actual labor hours	2,500
Materials purchased and used	38,500 lbs. @ $1.72
Actual variable overhead costs	$16,500

Other information includes the following. The purchasing agent located a new source of slightly higher-quality plastic, and this material was used during the first week in January. Also, a new manufacturing process was implemented on a trial basis. The new process required a slightly higher level of skilled labor. The higher-quality material has no effect on labor utilization. However, the new manufacturing process was expected to reduce materials usage by 0.25 pound per can.

Required

1. Compute the materials price and usage variances. Assume that the 0.25 pound reduction of materials occurred as expected and that the remaining effects are all attributable to the higher-quality material. Would you recommend that the purchasing agent continue to buy this quality? Or should the usual quality be purchased? Assume that the quality of the end product is not affected significantly.
2. Compute the labor rate and efficiency variances. Assuming that the labor variances are attributable to the new manufacturing process, should it be continued or discontinued? In answering, consider the new process's materials reduction effect as well. Explain.
3. Refer to Requirement 2. Suppose that the industrial engineer argued that the new process should not be evaluated after only one week. His reasoning was that it would take at least a week for the workers to become efficient with the new approach. Suppose that the production is the same the second week and that the actual labor hours were 2,200 and the labor cost was $22,400. Should the new process be adopted? Assume the variances are attributable to the new process. Assuming production of 4,000 units per week, what would be the projected annual savings? (Include the materials reduction effect.)

9-21

Standard Cost Concepts
LO1, LO2, LO3, LO4

Match the following terms with their definitions:

1. Total budget variance
2. Labor efficiency variance
3. Ideal standards
4. Materials price variance
5. Standard cost sheet

6. Fixed overhead volume variance
7. Control limits
8. Standard hours allowed
9. Variable overhead efficiency variance
10. Currently attainable standards
11. Labor rate variance
12. Unfavorable variance
13. Materials usage variance
14. Standard quantity of materials allowed
15. Fixed overhead spending variance

a. $(AQ - SQ)SP$
b. Standard hours per unit × Units produced
c. Actual cost > Standard cost
d. Details the standard unit cost
e. Actual cost less planned cost
f. Actual fixed overhead less budgeted fixed overhead
g. Budgeted fixed overhead less applied fixed overhead
h. $(AH - SH)SR$
i. Standard materials per unit × Units produced
j. $(AR - SR)AQ$
k. Maximum efficiency
l. Attained under efficient operating conditions
m. $(AH - SH)$ × Variable overhead rate
n. $(AP - SP)AQ$
o. Allowable limits for variances

9-22

Setting Standards; Materials and Labor Variances
LO1, LO2, LO4

CMA

Osgood Company is a small manufacturer of wooden household items. Ellen Rivkin, the controller, plans to implement a standard costing system for Osgood. She has the information needed to develop standards for Osgood's products.

One of Osgood's products is a wooden cutting board. Each cutting board requires 1.25 board feet of lumber and 12 minutes of direct labor time to prepare and cut the lumber. The cutting boards are inspected after they are cut. Because the cutting boards are made of a natural material that has imperfections, one board is normally rejected for each five that are accepted (the rejected boards are totally scrapped). Four rubber foot pads are attached to each good cutting board. A total of 15 minutes of direct labor time is required to attach all four foot pads and finish each cutting board. The lumber for the cutting boards costs $3 per board foot, and each foot pad costs $0.05. Direct labor is paid at the rate of $8 per hour.

Required

1. Develop the standard costs for the direct-cost components of the cutting board. The standard cost should identify the standard quantity, standard rate, and standard cost per unit for each direct-cost component of the cutting board.
2. Identify the advantages of implementing a standard costing system.
3. Explain the role of each of the following persons in developing standards:

   a. Purchasing manager
   b. Industrial engineer
   c. Cost accountant

4. Assume that the standards have been set and that the following actual results occur during the first month under the new standard costing system:

   a. Actual good units produced: 10,000
   b. Lumber purchased: 16,000 board feet at $3.10 per foot
   c. Lumber used: 16,000 board feet

d. Rubber foot pads purchased (and used): 51,000 at $0.048 each
e. Direct labor cost: 5,550 hours at $8.05 per hour

Compute the price and usage variances for materials and the rate and efficiency variances for labor. **(CMA adapted)**

9-23

Setting a Direct Labor Standard; Learning Curve Effects; Service Company
LO1, LO2

Mantenga Company provides routine maintenance services for heavy moving and transportation vehicles. Although the vehicles vary, the maintenance services provided follow a fairly standard pattern. Recently, a potential new customer has approached the company and requested a new maintenance service for a radically different type of vehicle. New servicing equipment and some new labor skills will be needed to provide the maintenance service. The customer is placing an initial order to service 150 vehicles and has indicated that if the service is satisfactory, several additional orders of the same size will be placed every three months over the next three to five years.

Mantenga uses a standard costing system and wants to develop a set of standards for the new service. The usage standards for direct materials such as oil, lubricants, and transmission fluids were easily established. The usage standard is 25 quarts per servicing with a standard cost of $4.00 per quart. Management has also decided on standard rates for labor and overhead: the standard labor rate is $15 per hour, the standard variable overhead rate is $8 per hour, and the standard fixed overhead rate is $12 per hour. The only remaining decision is the standard for labor usage. To assist in developing this standard, the engineering department has estimated the following relationship between units serviced and average direct labor hours used:

Units Serviced	Cumulative Average Time per Unit
40	2.500 hrs.
80	2.000 hrs.
160	1.600 hrs.
320	1.280 hrs.
640	1.024 hrs.

As the workers learn more about servicing the new vehicles, they become more efficient, and the average time needed to service one unit declines. Engineering estimates that all of the learning effects will be achieved by the time 320 units are produced. No further improvement will be realized past this level.

Required

1. Assuming no further improvement in labor time per unit is possible past 320 units, explain why the cumulative average time per unit at 640 is lower than the time at 320 units.
2. What standard would you set for the per-unit usage of direct labor? Explain.
3. Using the labor standard from Requirement 2, prepare a standard cost sheet that details the standard service cost per unit.
4. Given the standard you set in Requirement 2, would you expect favorable or unfavorable labor and variable overhead efficiency variances for servicing the first 320 units? Explain.

9-24

Appendix Problem: Variance Analysis; Revision of Standards; Journal Entries
LO4, LO5, LO6

The Minot plant of Rao's Small Motor Division produces a major subassembly for motorcycles. The plant uses a standard costing system for production costing and control. The standard cost sheet for the subassembly follows:

Direct materials (7.0 lbs. @ $6.00)	$42.00
Direct labor (2 hrs. @ $12.00)	24.00
Variable overhead (2 hrs. @ $10.00)	20.00
Fixed overhead (2 hrs. @ $6.00)	12.00
Standard unit cost	$98.00

During the year, the Minot plant had the following actual production activity:

a. Production of subassemblies totaled 70,000 units.
b. A total of 465,000 pounds of materials was purchased at $5.80 per pound.
c. There were 26,400 pounds of materials in beginning inventory (carried at $6 per pound). There was no ending inventory.
d. The company used 150,000 direct labor hours at a total cost of $1,950,000.
e. Actual fixed overhead totaled $913,000.
f. Actual variable overhead totaled $1,470,000.

The Minot plant's practical activity is 75,000 units per year. Standard overhead rates are computed based on practical activity measured in standard direct labor hours.

Required

1. Compute the materials price and usage variances. Of the two materials variances, which is viewed as the most controllable? To whom would you assign responsibility for the usage variance in this case? Explain.
2. Compute the labor rate and efficiency variances. Who is usually responsible for the labor efficiency variance? What are some possible causes for this variance?
3. Compute the variable overhead spending and efficiency variances.
4. Compute the fixed overhead spending and volume variances. Interpret the volume variance. What can be done to reduce this variance?
5. Assume that the purchasing agent for the small motors plant purchased a lower-quality material from a new supplier. Would you recommend that the plant continue to use this cheaper material? If so, what standards would likely need revision to reflect this decision? Assume that the end product's quality is not significantly affected.
6. Prepare all possible journal entries.

9-25

Fixed Overhead Spending and Volume Variances; Capacity Management
LO5

Lorale Company, a producer of recreational vehicles, recently decided to begin producing a major subassembly for jet skis. The subassembly would be used by Lorale's jet ski plants and also would be sold to other producers. The decision was made to lease two large buildings in two different locations: Little Rock, Arkansas, and Athens, Georgia. The company agreed to a 10-year, renewable lease contract. The plants were of the same size, and each had 10 production lines. New equipment was purchased for each line and workers hired to operate the equipment. The company also hired production line supervisors for each plant. A supervisor is capable of directing up to two production lines per shift. Two shifts are run for each plant. The practical production capacity of each plant was 300,000 subassemblies per year. There are two standard direct labor hours allowed for each subassembly. The costs for leasing, equipment depreciation, and supervision are given below for a single plant (the costs are assumed to be the same for each plant).

Supervision (10 supervisors @ $50,000)	$ 500,000
Building lease (annual payment)	800,000
Equipment depreciation (annual)	1,100,000
Total fixed overhead costs*	$2,400,000

*For simplicity, assume these are the only fixed overhead costs.

After beginning operations, Lorale discovered that demand for the product in the region covered by the Little Rock plant was less than anticipated. At the end of the first year, only 240,000 units were sold. The Athens plant sold 300,000 units as expected. The actual fixed overhead costs at the end of the first year were $2,500,000 (for each plant).

Required

1. Calculate a fixed overhead rate based on standard direct labor hours.

2. Calculate the fixed overhead spending and volume variances for the Little Rock and Athens plants. What is the most likely cause of the spending variance? Why are the volume variances different for the two plants?
3. Suppose that from now on the sales for the Little Rock plant are expected to be no more than 240,000 units. What actions would you take to manage the capacity costs (fixed overhead costs)?
4. Calculate the fixed overhead cost per subassembly for each plant. Do they differ? Should they differ? Explain. Do activity-based costing concepts help in analyzing this issue?

9-26

Appendix Problem: Unit Costs; Multiple Products; Variance Analysis; Journal Entries; Service Setting
LO2, LO4, LO5, LO6

The Maternity Department of the city hospital has two types of patients: Normal and Cesarean. The standard quantities of labor and materials per patient day for 2008 are:

	Normal	Cesarean
Direct materials (lb.)	8	20
Nursing labor (hr.)	2	4

The standard price paid per pound of direct materials is $10. (Direct materials for this case refer to linens.) The standard rate for labor is $16. Overhead is applied on the basis of direct labor hours. Departmental overhead rates are used in the hospital. Budgeted overhead for the Maternity Department for the year follows:

Budgeted fixed overhead	$720,000
Budgeted variable overhead	960,000

The Maternity Department expects to use 24,000 nursing hours in 2008; standard overhead rates are computed using this activity level. Actual operating data for 2008 are:

a. Patient days produced: normal, 3,500; Cesarean, 7,000
b. Direct materials purchased and used: 172,000 pounds at $9.50—30,000 for normal maternity patients and 142,000 for Cesarean patients; no beginning or ending raw materials inventories
c. Nursing labor: 36,500 hours—7,200 hours for normal patients and 29,300 hours for the Cesarean patients; total cost of labor, $580,350
d. Variable overhead: $1,215,000
e. Fixed overhead: $700,000

Required

1. Prepare a standard cost sheet showing the unit cost per patient day for each type of patient.
2. Compute the materials price and usage variances for each type of patient. Prepare journal entries to record materials activity.
3. Compute the labor rate and efficiency variances. Prepare journal entries to record labor activity.
4. Compute the variances for variable and fixed overhead. Prepare journal entries to record overhead activity. All variances are closed to Cost of Services Sold.
5. Assume that you know only the total direct materials used for both patient types and the total direct nursing hours used for both products. Can you compute the total materials usage and labor efficiency variances? Explain.

9-27

Incomplete Data; Overhead Analysis
LO2, LO4, LO5

Norris Company produces telephones. To help control costs, Norris employs a standard costing system and uses a flexible budget to predict overhead costs at various levels of activity. For the most recent year, Norris used a standard overhead rate of $18 per direct labor hour. The rate was computed using practical activity. Budgeted overhead costs are $792,000 for 36,000 direct labor hours and $1,080,000 for 60,000 direct labor hours. During the past year, Norris generated the following data:

a. Actual production: 100,000 units
b. Fixed overhead volume variance: $36,000 U
c. Variable overhead efficiency variance: $24,000 F
d. Actual fixed overhead costs: $380,000
e. Actual variable overhead costs: $620,000

Required

1. Calculate the fixed overhead rate.
2. Determine the fixed overhead spending variance.
3. Determine the variable overhead spending variance.
4. Determine the standard hours allowed per unit of product.
5. Assuming the standard labor rate is $13 per hour, compute the labor efficiency variance.

9-28

Control Limits; Variance Investigation
LO3, LO4, LO5

Demismell Company produces a well-known cologne. The standard manufacturing cost of the cologne is described by the following standard cost sheet:

Direct materials:	
Liquids (4.2 oz. @ $0.25)	$1.05
Bottles (1 @ $0.05)	0.05
Direct labor (0.2 hr. @ $12.50)	2.50
Variable overhead (0.2 hr. @ $4.70)	0.94
Fixed overhead (0.2 hr. @ $1.00)	0.20
Standard cost per unit	$4.74

Management has decided to investigate only those variances that exceed the lesser of 10 percent of the standard cost for each category or $20,000.

During the past quarter, a total of 250,000 four-ounce bottles of cologne was produced. Descriptions of actual activity for the quarter follow:

a. A total of 1.15 million ounces of liquids was purchased, mixed, and processed. Evaporation was higher than expected (no inventories of liquids are maintained). The price paid per ounce averaged $0.27.
b. Exactly 250,000 bottles were used. The price paid for each bottle was $0.048.
c. Direct labor hours totaled 48,250 with a total cost of $622,425.
d. Variable overhead costs totaled $239,000.
e. Fixed overhead costs were $50,500.

Normal production volume for Demismell is 250,000 bottles per quarter. The standard overhead rates are computed using normal volume. All overhead costs are incurred uniformly throughout the year.

Required

1. Calculate the upper and lower control limits for each manufacturing cost category.
2. Compute the total materials variance, and then break it into price and usage variances. Would these variances be investigated?
3. Compute the total labor variance, and break it into rate and efficiency variances. Would these variances be investigated?
4. Compute all overhead variances. Would any of them be investigated? Would you recommend a different approach to deal with overhead? Explain.

9-29

Appendix Problem: Flexible Budget; Standard Cost Variances; T-Accounts LO4, LO5, LO6

Shumaker Company manufactures a line of high-top basketball shoes. At the beginning of the year, the following plans for production and costs were revealed:

Pairs of shoes to be produced and sold	55,000
Standard cost per unit:	
Direct materials	$15
Direct labor	12
Variable overhead	6
Fixed overhead	3
Total unit cost	$36

During the year, a total of 50,000 units was produced and sold. The following actual costs were incurred:

Direct materials	$775,000
Direct labor	590,000
Variable overhead	310,000
Fixed overhead	180,000

There were no beginning or ending inventories of materials. The materials price variance was $5,000 unfavorable. In producing the 50,000 units, 63,000 hours were worked, which was 5 percent more hours than the standard allowed for the actual output. Overhead costs are applied to production using direct labor hours.

Required

1. Using a flexible budget, prepare a performance report comparing expected costs for the actual production with actual costs.
2. Determine the following:
   a. Materials usage variance
   b. Labor rate variance
   c. Labor efficiency variance
   d. Fixed overhead spending and volume variances
   e. Variable overhead spending and efficiency variances
3. Use T-accounts to show the flow of costs through the system.

9-30

Control Limits; Variance Investigation LO3, LO4

The management of Golding Company has determined that the cost to investigate a variance produced by its standard costing system ranges from $2,000 to $3,000. If a problem is discovered, the average benefit from taking corrective action usually outweighs the cost of investigation. Past experience from the investigation of variances has revealed that corrective action is rarely needed for deviations within 8 percent of the standard cost. Golding produces a single product, which has the following standards for materials and labor:

Direct materials (8 lbs. @ $0.25)	$2
Direct labor (0.4 hr. @ $7.50)	3

Actual production for the past three months with the associated actual usage and costs for materials and labor follow. There were no beginning or ending materials inventories.

	April	May	June
Production (units)	90,000	100,000	110,000
Direct materials:			
Cost	$189,000	$218,000	$230,000
Usage (lb.)	723,000	870,000	885,000

(continued)

	April	May	June
Direct labor:			
Cost	$270,000	$323,000	$360,000
Usage (hr.)	36,000	44,000	46,000

Required

1. What upper and lower control limits would you use for materials variances? For labor variances?
2. Compute the materials and labor variances for April, May, and June. Identify those that would require investigation.
3. Let the horizontal axis be time and the vertical axis be variances measured as a percentage deviation from standard. Draw horizontal lines that identify upper and lower control limits. Plot the labor and material variances for April, May, and June. Prepare a separate graph for each type of variance. Explain how you would use these graphs (called control charts) to assist your analysis of variances.

9-31

Standard Costing; Planned Variances
LO2, LO4

CMA

As part of its cost control program, Hepler Company uses a standard costing system for all manufactured items. The standard cost for each item is established at the beginning of the fiscal year, and the standards are not revised until the beginning of the next fiscal year. Changes in costs, caused during the year by changes in material or labor inputs or by changes in the manufacturing process, are recognized as they occur by the inclusion of planned variances in Hepler's monthly operating budgets.

Following is the labor standard that was established for one of Hepler's products effective June 1, 2008, the beginning of the fiscal year:

Assembler A labor (5 hrs. @ $10)	$ 50
Assembler B labor (3 hrs. @ $11)	33
Machinist labor (2 hrs. @ $15)	30
Standard cost per 100 units	$113

The standard was based on the labor being performed by a team consisting of five persons with assembler A skills, three persons with assembler B skills, and two persons with machinist skills; this team represents the most efficient use of the company's skilled employees. The standard also assumed that the quality of materials that had been used in prior years would be available for the coming year.

For the first seven months of the fiscal year, actual manufacturing costs at Hepler have been within the standards established. However, the company has received a significant increase in orders, and there is an insufficient number of skilled workers to meet the increased production. Therefore, beginning in January, the production teams will consist of eight persons with assembler A skills, one person with assembler B skills, and one person with machinist skills. The reorganized teams will work more slowly than the normal teams; as a result, only 80 units will be produced in the same time period in which 100 units would normally be produced. Faulty work has never been a cause for units to be rejected in the final inspection process, and it is not expected to be a cause for rejection with the reorganized teams.

Furthermore, Hepler has been notified by its material supplier that lower-quality materials will be supplied beginning January 1. Normally, one unit of materials is required for each good unit produced, and no units are lost due to defective material. Hepler estimates that 10 percent of the units manufactured after January 1 will be rejected in the final inspection process due to defective material.

Required

1. Determine the number of units of lower-quality material that Hepler Company must enter into production in order to produce 54,000 good finished units.

2. How many hours of each class of labor must be used to manufacture 54,000 good finished units?
3. Determine the amount that should be included in Hepler's January operating budget for the planned labor variance caused by the reorganization of the labor teams and the lower-quality material. **(CMA adapted)**

9-32

Standard Cost Sheet; Incomplete Data; Variance Analysis
LO2, LO4, LO5

Briggs Company had recently acquired Metalica, Inc., a small manufacturing firm located in the Midwest. Unfortunately, Metalica had very poor internal controls, and a master disk with some fundamental cost data for the past year was accidentally erased. No backup existed. Kathy Shorts, an internal auditor for Briggs, was assigned to Metalica and given the task of reconstructing some of the cost records. At first, she was discouraged with the assignment, but she became excited when she discovered part of a computer printout containing some information about last year's operations. The information, pertaining to Metalica's cost accounting system, follows:

Selected Actual Results

Direct materials: 10,000 pounds purchased and used, costing $51,000
Production: 20,000 units
Labor cost: 4,400 hours, cost $34,320
Fixed overhead cost: $23,000
Variable overhead cost: $46,000

Variances

Materials price variance	$ 1,000 U
Materials usage variance	10,000 F
Labor efficiency variance	3,200 U
Variable overhead efficiency	4,000 U
Variable overhead spending	2,000 U
Underapplied fixed overhead	3,000 U
Volume variance	4,000 U

Kathy also interviewed Metalica's controller and discovered that overhead rates are based on expected actual activity. Metalica calculates two variances for variable overhead and two for fixed overhead. However, before Kathy could analyze the information she had gathered, she had to take emergency leave because of a family crisis. You have been given the task of performing the analysis described by the following requirements.

Required

1. Prepare a standard cost sheet in good form. Show fixed and variable overhead as separate items.
2. Compute the fixed overhead spending variance.
3. Compute the labor rate variance.
4. Determine the expected actual activity used to compute the predetermined fixed overhead rate.

Managerial Decision Cases

9-33

Standard Costing
LO1, LO2, LO3

Mark Wright, Inc. (MWI) is a specialty frozen-food processor located in the midwestern states. Since its founding in 1982, MWI has enjoyed a loyal clientele that is willing to pay premium prices for the high-quality frozen food it prepares from specialized recipes. In the last two years, the company has experienced rapid sales growth

CMA

in its operating region and has had many inquiries about supplying its products on a national basis. To meet this growth, MWI expanded its processing capabilities, which resulted in increased production and distribution costs. Furthermore, MWI has been encountering pricing pressure from competitors outside its normal marketing region.

Because MWI desires to continue its expansion, Jim Condon, CEO, has engaged a consulting firm to assist MWI in determining its best course of action. The consulting firm recommended instituting a standard costing system that would also facilitate a flexible budgeting system to better accommodate the changes in demand that can be expected when serving an expanding market area. Jim met with his management team and explained the consulting firm's recommendations. Jim then assigned the task of establishing standard costs to his management team. After discussing the situation with the respective staffs, the management team met to review the matter.

Jane Morgan, purchasing manager, advised that meeting expanded production would necessitate obtaining basic food supplies from other than MWI's traditional sources. This would entail increased material and shipping costs and might result in lower-quality supplies. Consequently, these increased costs would need to be made up by the processing department if current costs are to be maintained or reduced.

Stan Walters, processing manager, countered that the need to accelerate processing cycles to increase production, coupled with the possibility of receiving lower-grade supplies, could be expected to result in a slip in quality and a greater product rejection rate. Under these circumstances, per-unit labor utilization could not be maintained or reduced, and forecasting future unit labor content would become very difficult.

Tom Lopez, production engineer, advised that if the equipment is not properly maintained and thoroughly cleaned at prescribed daily intervals, the quality and unique taste of the frozen-food products would probably be affected. Jack Reid, vice president of sales, stated that if quality could not be maintained, MWI could not expect to increase sales to the levels projected.

When Jim was apprised of the problems encountered by his management team, he advised them that if agreement could not be reached on the appropriate standards, he would arrange to have them set by the consulting firm and everyone would have to live with the results.

Required

1. List the major advantages of using a standard costing system.
2. List disadvantages that can result from the use of a standard costing system.
3. Identify those who should participate in setting standards, and describe the benefits of their participation in the standard-setting process.
4. What characteristics of a standard costing system make it an effective tool for cost control?
5. What could be the consequences if Jim Condon, CEO, has the standards set by the outside consulting firm? **(CMA adapted)**

9-34

Establishment of Standards; Variance Analysis
LO1, LO2, LO4

Sabroso Chips was established in 1938 by Paul and Nancy Golding (Nancy sold her piano to help raise capital to start the business). Paul assumed responsibility for buying potatoes and selling chips to local grocers; Nancy assumed responsibility for production. Since Nancy was already known for her delicious, thin potato chips, the business prospered.

Over the past 70 years, the company has established distribution channels in 11 western states, with production facilities in Utah, New Mexico, and Colorado. In 1980, Paul and Nancy Golding both died, and their son, Edward, took control of the business. By 2008, the company was facing stiff competition from national snack-food companies. Edward was advised that the company's plants needed to gain better control over production costs. To assist in achieving this objective, he hired a consultant to install a standard costing system. To help the consultant in establishing the necessary standards, Edward sent her the following memo:

To: Diana Craig, CMA
From: Edward Golding, President, Sabroso Chips
Subject: Description and Data Relating to the Production of Our Plain Potato Chips
Date: September 28, 2008

The manufacturing process for potato chips begins when the potatoes are placed into a large vat in which they are automatically washed. After washing, the potatoes flow directly to an automatic peeler. The peeled potatoes then pass by inspectors who manually cut out deep eyes or other blemishes. After inspection, the potatoes are automatically sliced and dropped into the cooking oil. The frying process is closely monitored by an employee. After they are cooked, the chips pass under a salting device and then pass by more inspectors, who sort out the unacceptable finished chips (those that are discolored or too small). The chips then continue on the conveyor belt to a bagging machine that bags them in one-pound bags. After bagging, the bags are placed in a box and shipped. Each box holds 15 bags.

The raw potato pieces (eyes and blemishes), peelings, and rejected finished chips are sold to animal-feed producers for \$0.16 per pound. The company uses this revenue to reduce the cost of potatoes; we would like this reflected in the price standard relating to potatoes.

Sabroso Chips purchases high-quality potatoes at a cost of \$0.245 per pound. Each potato averages 4.25 ounces. Under efficient operating conditions, it takes four potatoes to produce one 16-ounce bag of plain chips. Although we label bags as containing 16 ounces, we actually place 16.3 ounces in each bag. We plan to continue this policy to ensure customer satisfaction. In addition to potatoes, other materials include the cooking oil, salt, bags, and boxes. Cooking oil costs \$0.04 per ounce, and we use 3.3 ounces of oil per bag of chips. The cost of salt is so small that we add it to overhead. Bags cost \$0.11 each and boxes \$0.52.

Our plant produces 8.8 million bags of chips per year. A recent engineering study revealed that we would need the following direct labor hours to produce this quantity if our plant operates at peak efficiency:

Raw potato inspection	3,200
Finished chip inspection	12,000
Frying monitor	6,300
Boxing	16,600
Machine operators	6,300

I'm not sure that we can achieve the level of efficiency advocated by the study. In my opinion, the plant is operating efficiently for the level of output indicated if the hours allowed are about 10 percent higher.

The hourly labor rates agreed upon with the union are:

Raw potato inspectors	\$15.20
Finished chip inspectors	10.30
Frying monitor	14.00
Boxing	11.00
Machine operators	13.00

Overhead is applied on the basis of direct labor dollars. We have found that variable overhead averages about 116 percent of our direct labor cost. Our fixed overhead is budgeted at \$1,135,216 for the coming year.

Required

1. Discuss the benefits of a standard costing system for Sabroso Chips.
2. Discuss the president's concern about using the results of the engineering study to set the labor standards. What standard would you recommend?

3. Develop a standard cost sheet for Sabroso Chips' plain potato chips.
4. Suppose that the level of production was 8.8 million bags of potato chips for the year as planned. If 9.5 million pounds of potatoes were used, compute the materials usage variance for potatoes.

9-35

Standard Costing and Ethical Behavior
LO1, LO3

Pat James, the purchasing agent for a local plant of the Oakden Electronics Division, was considering the possible purchase of a component from a new supplier. The component's purchase price, $0.90, compared favorably with the standard price of $1.10. Given the quantity that would be purchased, Pat knew that the favorable price variance would help offset an unfavorable variance for another component. By offsetting the unfavorable variance, his overall performance report would be impressive and good enough to help him qualify for the annual bonus. More importantly, a good performance rating this year would help him secure a position at division headquarters at a significant salary increase.

Purchase of the part, however, presented Pat with a dilemma. He had made inquiries regarding the reliability of the new supplier and the part's quality, and reports were basically negative. The supplier had a reputation for making the first two or three deliveries on schedule, but being unreliable from then on. Worse, the part itself was of questionable quality. The number of defective units was only slightly higher than that for other suppliers, but the life of the component was 25 percent less than what other sources provided.

If the part were purchased, no problems with deliveries would surface for several months. The problem of shorter life would cause eventual customer dissatisfaction and perhaps some loss of sales, but the part would last at least 18 months after the final product began to be used. If all went well, Pat expected to be at headquarters within six months. He saw very little personal risk associated with a decision to purchase the part from the new supplier. By the time any problems surfaced, they would belong to his successor. With this rationalization, Pat decided to purchase the component from the new supplier.

Required

1. Do you agree with Pat's decision? Why or why not? How important do you think Pat's assessment of his personal risk was in the decision? Should it be a factor?
2. Do you think that the use of standards and the practice of holding individuals accountable for their achievement played major roles in Pat's decision?
3. Review the ethical standards for management accountants in Chapter 1. Even though Pat is not a management accountant, identify the standards that might apply to his situation. Should every company adopt a set of ethical standards that apply to their employees, regardless of their specialty?

Research Assignments

9-36

Research Assignment: Usefulness of Standard Costing
LO1, LO3, LO4, LO5

The usefulness of standard costing has been challenged in recent years. Some claim that its use is an impediment to the objective of continuous improvement (an objective that many feel is vital in today's competitive environment). Write a short paper that analyzes the role and value of standard costing in today's manufacturing environment. Address the following questions:

1. What are the major criticisms of standard costing?
2. Will standard costing disappear, or is there still a role for it? If so, what is the role?

3. Given the criticisms, can you explain why its use continues to be so prevalent? Will this use eventually change?
4. What are some suggestions for redesigning the standard cost systems so that they are more relevant for advanced manufacturers?
5. How compatible are ABC and standard costing?
6. If standard costing is no longer completely suitable for some manufacturing environments, what control approaches are being used to supplement (replace?) the functional-based control model?

In preparing your paper, the following references may be useful; however, do not restrict your literature search to these references. They are simply to help you get started.

1. Mike Lucas, "Standard Costing and Its Role in Today's Manufacturing Environment," *Management Accounting* (London, April 1997): pp. 32–34.
2. Carole B. Cheatham and Leo R. Cheatham, "Redesigning Cost Systems: Is Standard Costing Obsolete?" *Accounting Horizons* (December 1996): pp. 23–31.
3. Robin Cooper and Robert S. Kaplan, "Activity-Based Systems: Measuring the Costs of Resource Usage," *Accounting Horizons* (September 1992): pp. 1–13.
4. Bruce R. Gaumnitz and Felix P. Kollaritsch, "Manufacturing Variances: Current Practice and Trends," *Journal of Cost Management* (Spring 1991): pp. 58–64.
5. Robert S. Kaplan, "Limitations of Cost Accounting in Advanced Manufacturing Environments," in *Measures for Manufacturing Excellence,* ed. Robert S. Kaplan (Boston: Harvard Business School Press, 1990).
6. Mehmet C. Kocakulah and Brian D. Crowe, "Utilizing Activity-Based Costing (ABC) to Measure Loan Portfolio Profitability in a Community Bank," Cost Management (July/August 2005): pp. 40–47.
7. Robert S. Kaplan and Steven R. Anderson, "Time-Driven Activity-Based Costing," Harvard Business Review (November 2004): pp. 1–8.

9-37

Cybercase
LO1

Standard costing concepts have been applied in the health-care industry. For example, diagnostic related groups (DRGs) are used for prospective payments for Medicare patients. Select a search engine and conduct a search to see what information you can obtain about DRGs. You might try "medicare DRGs" as a possible search topic. Use the following questions to prepare a memo regarding the results of your search:

a. What is a DRG?
b. How are DRGs established?
c. How many DRGs are used?
d. How does the DRG concept relate to the standard costing concepts discussed in the chapter? Can hospitals use DRGs to control their costs? Explain.
e. What are severity DRGs? Explain how they are connected to standard costing concepts.
f. Are private insurance firms using DRGs?

chapter 10

Segmented Reporting, Investment Center Evaluation, and Transfer Pricing

learning objectives

After studying this chapter, you should be able to:

1. Explain how and why firms choose to decentralize.
2. Explain the difference between absorption and variable costing, and prepare segmented income statements.
3. Compute and explain return on investment (ROI).
4. Compute and explain residual income and economic value added (EVA).
5. Explain the role of transfer pricing in a decentralized firm.

Scenario

Geoff Maslow had long been interested in software development for music and video players. After several years of developing software programs on his own and with friends, he created his own firm, Galactic-Media, Inc., or GMI. Geoff was president and CEO; his college friend, Luz Pacheco, served as chief financial officer and COO. Luz handled day-to-day operations and Geoff dealt with outside sales and product development. Over a 4-year period, GMI grew rapidly as its bread-and-butter program, an integrated music/video player, was adopted by college students and young professionals across the country. Employment stood at 250, with departmental managers in sales, player software design, content interface, and streaming media. The growing size of the company meant that Geoff and Luz could no longer keep hands-on control of the departments.

The latest quarterly financials showed stagnant operating income and mounting expenditures on capital. Luz worried that GMI's software developers viewed having the newest computer hardware as a perk of the job—not as a tool for doing their work. Geoff agreed, but pointed out the futility of trying to review every capital spending request. He wondered how he and Luz could get their people to have the same vision that they did.

Luz believed that it was time to decentralize the company. By making department managers responsible for the sales and expenses related to their area of operations, and by evaluating them on the basis of return on investment (ROI), they could more easily align the goals of the managers with the goals of the firm. In essence, this would encourage their managers to think and act like owners of the business instead of as employees. Since the managers would then monitor their own capital spending, day-to-day operating pressures on both Geoff and Luz would be relieved. This would allow them to work on strategy and R&D. Geoff was enthusiastic about that: He wanted to spend time developing some new types of animation that would position GMI as a strong competitor to Pixar.

Questions to Think About:

1. What does stagnant operating income mean and why do you suppose that Geoff was concerned by it?

2. Does capital spending affect the income statement? How?

3. Why do you suppose that it might be a good idea for operating managers to manage their own capital spending? How would this relieve Geoff and Luz of the need to monitor day-to-day operations?

Decentralization and Responsibility Centers

Objective 1

Explain how and why firms choose to decentralize.

In general, a company is organized along lines of responsibility. The traditional organizational chart, with its pyramid shape, illustrates the lines of responsibility flowing from the CEO down through the vice presidents to middle- and lower-level managers. As the opening scenario indicates, as organizations grow larger, these lines of responsibility become longer and more numerous. The structure becomes cumbersome. Contemporary practice is moving toward a flattened hierarchy. This structure—emphasizing teams—is consistent with decentralization. **GE Capital**, for example, is essentially a group of smaller businesses. A strong link exists between the structure of an organization and its responsibility accounting system. A **responsibility accounting system** is a system that measures the results of each responsibility center according to the information managers need to operate their centers. Ideally, the responsibility accounting system mirrors and supports the structure of an organization.

Firms with multiple responsibility centers usually choose one of two decision-making approaches to manage their diverse and complex activities: *centralized* or *decentralized*. In **centralized decision making**, decisions are made at the very top level, and lower-level managers are charged with implementing these decisions. On the other hand, **decentralized decision making** allows managers at lower levels to make and implement key decisions pertaining to their areas of responsibility. **Decentralization** is the practice of delegating decision-making authority to the lower levels of management in a company. Exhibit 10-1 illustrates the difference between centralized and decentralized companies.

Organizations range from highly centralized to strongly decentralized. Most firms fall somewhere in between, with the majority tending toward decentralization. The reasons for the popularity of decentralization and the ways in which a company may choose to decentralize are discussed next.

Reasons for Decentralization

Firms decide to decentralize for several reasons, including (1) ease of gathering and using local information; (2) focusing of central management; (3) training and moti-

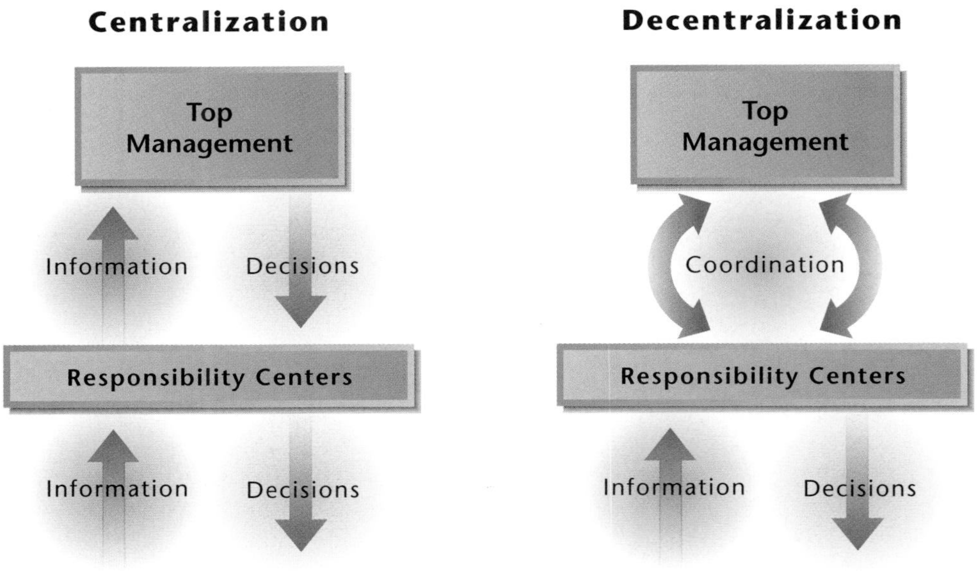

Exhibit 10-1 Centralization and Decentralization

vating of segment managers; and (4) enhanced competition, exposing segments to market forces.

Gathering and Using Local Information The quality of decisions is affected by the quality of information available. As a firm grows in size and operates in different markets and regions, central management may not understand local conditions. Lower-level managers, however, are in contact with immediate operating conditions (such as the strength and nature of local competition, the nature of the local labor force, and so on). As a result, they are often better positioned to make local decisions. For example, **McDonald's** has restaurants around the world. The tastes of people in China or France differ from those of people in the United States. So, McDonald's tailors its menu to different countries. The result is that the McDonald's in each country can differentiate to meet the needs of its local market.

Focusing of Central Management By decentralizing the operating decisions, central management is free to engage in strategic planning and decision making. The long-run survival of the organization should be of more importance to central management than day-to-day operations.

Training and Motivating of Managers Organizations always need well-trained managers to replace higher-level managers who leave to take advantage of other opportunities. What better way to prepare a future generation of higher-level managers than by providing them the opportunity to make significant decisions? These opportunities also enable top managers to evaluate local managers' capabilities. Those who make the best decisions are the ones who can be promoted.

Enhanced Competition In a highly centralized company, overall profit margins can mask inefficiencies within the various subdivisions. Large companies now find that they cannot afford to keep a noncompetitive division. One of the best ways to improve performance of a division or factory is to expose it more fully to market forces. At **Koch Industries, Inc.**, each unit is expected to act as an autonomous business unit and set prices both externally and internally. Units whose services are not required by other Koch units will die on the vine.

Divisions in the Decentralized Firm

Decentralization is usually achieved by creating units called *divisions.* One way in which divisions are differentiated is by the types of goods or services produced. For example, divisions of **PepsiCo** include **Frito-Lay**, **Gatorade**, **Quaker** brands, and **Tropicana**, as well as its flagship soft-drink division. Exhibit 10-2 shows decentralized divisions of PepsiCo. These divisions are organized on the basis of product lines. Notice that some divisions depend on other divisions. For example, PepsiCo spun off its restaurant divisions to Tricon Global Restaurants (now **Yum! Brands, Inc.**). As a result, the cola you drink at **Pizza Hut**, **Taco Bell**, and **KFC** will be Pepsi—not Coke. In a decentralized setting, some interdependencies usually exist; otherwise, a company would merely be a collection of totally separate entities.

Divisions may also be created along geographic lines. For example, **UAL, Inc.** (parent of United Airlines) has a number of regional divisions: Asia/Pacific, Caribbean, European, Latin American, and North American. The presence of divisions spanning one or more regions creates the need for performance evaluation that can take into account differences in divisional environments. A third way divisions differ is by the type of responsibility given to the divisional manager. As a firm grows, top management typically creates areas of responsibility, known as responsibility centers, and assigns subordinate managers to those areas. A **responsibility center** is a segment of the business whose manager is accountable for specified sets

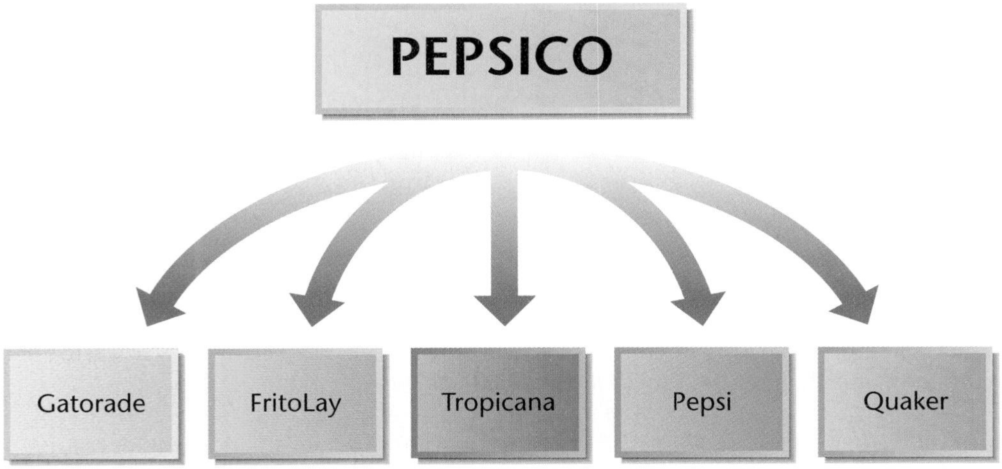

Exhibit 10-2 Decentralized Divisions

of activities. The results of each responsibility center can be measured according to the information managers need to operate their centers. The four major types of responsibility centers are as follows:

- **Cost center**—the manager is responsible only for costs
- **Revenue center**—the manager is responsible only for sales
- **Profit center**—the manager is responsible for both sales and costs
- **Investment center**—the manager is responsible for sales, costs, and capital investment

The way that responsibility centers are assigned mirrors the actual situation and the type of information available to the manager. Information is the key to appropriately holding managers responsible for outcomes. For example, a production department manager is held responsible for departmental costs but not for sales. This is because the production department manager not only directly controls some of these costs but also knows and understands them. Any difference between actual and expected costs can best be explained at this level. Exhibit 10-3 displays these centers along with the type of information they need to manage their operations. Investment centers represent the greatest degree of decentralization (followed by profit centers and finally by cost and revenue centers) because their managers have the freedom to make the greatest variety of decisions.

A production department within the factory, such as assembly or finishing, is an example of a cost center. The supervisor of a production department controls manufacturing costs but does not set a price or make marketing decisions. Therefore, the production department supervisor is evaluated on the basis of how well costs are controlled.

Inventory tracking programs fit nicely with standard costing. The materials storeroom supervisor can determine how much inventory is on hand and whether it will meet the needs of the next period's production schedule.

© Comstock Images

The marketing department manager sets the price and projected sales. Therefore, the marketing department may be evaluated as a revenue center. Direct costs of the marketing department and overall sales are the responsibility of the sales manager.

Accounting Information Used To Measure Performance				
	Capital Cost	Sales	Investment	Other
Cost center	X			
Revenue center	X	X		
Profit center	X	X		
Investment center	X	X	X	X

Exhibit 10-3 Types of Responsibility Centers and Accounting Information Used to Measure Performance

In some companies, plant managers are given the responsibility for manufacturing and marketing their products. These plant managers control both costs and revenues, putting them in control of a profit center. Operating income would be an important performance measure for profit center managers.

Finally, divisions are often cited as examples of investment centers. In addition to having control over cost and pricing decisions, divisional managers have the power to make investment decisions, such as plant closings and openings, and decisions to keep or drop a product line. As a result, both operating income and some type of return on investment are important performance measures for investment center managers.

It is important to realize that while the responsibility center manager has responsibility for only the activities of that center, decisions made by that manager can affect other responsibility centers. For example, the sales force at a floor care products firm routinely offers customers price discounts at the end of the month. Sales increase dramatically, which is good for revenue and the sales force. However, the factory is forced to institute overtime shifts to keep up with demand; this increases the costs of the factory as well as the cost per unit of product.

Managers Decide

Baseball Training Camps Qualify as Profit Centers

Manufacturing companies are not the only companies that decentralize and measure performance. Service industries also break down performance by area of business. For example, the Texas Rangers baseball team, based in Arlington, Texas, implicitly recognizes spring training as a profit center. The Rangers moved their spring training to Surprise, a suburb of Phoenix, Arizona, for the 2003 training season. That first year in Arizona, the club earned a $300,000 profit. This compares with the roughly $700,000 lost in Port Charlotte, Florida, the previous year.

What, in addition to the weather, are the benefits of training in small desert towns? Surprise invested in a $48 million spring training complex to lure the Texas Rangers and the Kansas City Royals. The complex has a 10,500-seat stadium and 12 practice diamonds.

Fans travel from across the United States and beyond to spend weeks following their favorite teams in spring training. Local communities, like Surprise, invest in state-of-the-art facilities. Tickets and concessions are major revenue sources. Less directly, increased hotel and rental car taxes fill city coffers. ■

Source: Mark Hyman, "If You Build It, They Will Train," *Business Week* (March 24, 2003): 77.

Organizing divisions as responsibility centers creates the opportunity to control the divisions through the use of responsibility accounting. Revenue center control is achieved by evaluating the efficiency and the effectiveness of divisional managers on the basis of sales revenue. Cost center control is based on control of costs and frequently employs variance analysis as described in Chapter 9. This chapter will focus on the evaluation of profit centers and investment centers.

Measuring the Performance of Profit Centers Using Variable and Absorption Income Statements

Objective 2

Explain the difference between absorption and variable costing, and prepare segmented income statements.

Profit centers are evaluated based on income statements. However, the overall income statement for the company would be of little use for this purpose. Instead, it is important to develop a segmented income statement for each profit center. Two methods of computing income have been developed, one based on variable costing and the other based on full or absorption costing. These are costing methods because they refer to the way in which product costs are determined. Recall that *product costs* are inventoried; they include direct materials, direct labor, and overhead. *Period costs,* such as selling and administrative expense, are expensed in the period incurred. The difference between variable and absorption costing hinges on the treatment of one particular cost: fixed factory overhead.

Variable costing stresses the difference between fixed and variable manufacturing costs. **Variable costing** (also called *direct costing*) assigns only variable manufacturing costs to the product; these costs include direct materials, direct labor, and variable overhead. Fixed overhead is treated as a period expense and is excluded from the product cost. The rationale for this is that fixed overhead is a cost of capacity, or staying in business. Once the period is over, any benefits provided by capacity have expired and should not be inventoried. Under variable costing, fixed overhead of a period is seen as expiring that period and is charged in total against the revenues of the period. Variable costing is also known as direct costing. However, not all variable manufacturing costs are direct product costs. For example, variable overhead, by definition, is indirect. Clearly, the more descriptive name for this method is variable costing, which is the term that will be used in this text.

Absorption costing assigns *all* manufacturing costs to the product. Direct materials, direct labor, variable overhead, and fixed overhead define the cost of a product. Thus, under absorption costing, fixed overhead is viewed as a product cost, not a period cost. Under this method, fixed overhead is assigned to the product through the use of a predetermined fixed overhead rate and is not expensed until the product is sold. In other words, fixed overhead is an inventoriable cost. Exhibit 10-4 illustrates the classification of costs as product or period costs under absorption and variable costing.

	Absorption Costing	Variable Costing
Product costs	Direct materials Direct labor Variable overhead Fixed overhead	Direct materials Direct labor Variable overhead
Period costs	Selling expenses Administrative expenses	Fixed overhead Selling expenses Administrative expenses

Exhibit 10-4 Classification of Costs as Product or Period Costs Under Absorption and Variable Costing

Generally accepted accounting principles (GAAP) require absorption costing for external reporting. The Financial Accounting Standards Board (FASB), the Internal Revenue Service (IRS), and other regulatory bodies do not accept variable costing as a product-costing method for external reporting. Yet, variable costing can supply vital cost information for decision making and control, information not supplied by absorption costing. For *internal* application, variable costing is an invaluable managerial tool.

Inventory Valuation

Inventory is valued at product or manufacturing cost. Consider the following data for Fairchild Company for last year:

Units in beginning inventory	—
Units produced	10,000
Units sold ($300 per unit)	8,000
Variable costs per unit:	
Direct materials	$ 50
Direct labor	100
Variable overhead	50
Fixed costs:	
Fixed overhead per unit produced	25
Fixed selling and administrative	100,000

These data show that there are 2,000 units in ending inventory (10,000 − 8,000). Exhibit 10-5 shows how to compute ending inventory cost under both absorption and variable costing for Fairchild Company. Notice that under absorption costing, ending inventory includes the cost of direct materials, direct labor, variable overhead, and unit fixed overhead. Under the variable costing method, ending inventory only includes the cost of direct materials, direct labor, and variable overhead. The exclusion of fixed overhead from the variable costing inventory cost results in a lower valuation of inventory than under the absorption method.

Income Statements Using Variable and Absorption Costing

Because unit product costs are the basis for cost of goods sold, the variable- and absorption-costing methods can lead to different operating income figures. The difference arises because of the amount of fixed overhead recognized as an expense under the two methods. Using the data for Fairchild Company as an example, Exhibit 10-6 shows how to develop cost of goods sold and income statements under both variable and absorption costing.

Exhibit 11-6 demonstrates that absorption-costing income is $50,000 higher than variable-costing income. This difference is due to some of the period's fixed overhead

Absorption Costing		Variable Costing	
Direct materials	$ 50	Direct materials	$ 50
Direct labor	100	Direct labor	100
Variable overhead	50	Variable overhead	50
Fixed overhead	25		
Unit product cost	$225	Unit product cost	$200
Value of ending inventory:			
= 2,000 × $225 = $450,000		= 2,000 × $200 = $400,000	

Exhibit 10-5 Fairchild Company Ending Inventory Cost Under Absorption and Variable Costing

Fairchild Company Absorption-Costing Income Statement	
Sales ($300 × 8,000)	$2,400,000
Less: Cost of goods sold*	1,800,000
Gross margin	$ 600,000
Less: Selling and administrative expenses	100,000
Operating income	$ 500,000

*Using the absorption unit product cost computed in Exhibit 10-5,
Cost of goods sold = Absorption unit product cost × Units sold = $225 × 8,000 = $1,800,000

Fairchild Company Variable-Costing Income Statement		
Sales ($300 × 8,000)		$2,400,000
Less variable expenses:		
Variable cost of goods sold**	$1,600,000	
Contribution margin		$ 800,000
Less fixed expenses:		
Fixed overhead	$ 250,000	
Fixed selling and administrative	100,000	350,000
Operating income		$ 450,000

**Using the variable unit product cost computed in Exhibit 10-5,
Cost of goods sold = Variable unit product cost × Units sold = $200 × 8,000 = $1,600,000

Exhibit 10-6 Fairchild Company Income Statements Under Absorption and Variable Costing

flowing into inventory when absorption costing is used. This occurred because less fixed overhead cost flowed into the absorption-costing cost of goods sold. In fact, only $200,000 ($25 × 8,000) of fixed overhead was included in cost of goods sold for absorption costing; the remaining $50,000 ($25 × 2,000) was added to inventory. Under variable costing, however, all of the $250,000 of fixed overhead cost for the period was added to expense on the income statement.

Notice that selling and administrative expenses are never included in product cost. They are always expensed on the income statement and never appear on the balance sheet.

Production, Sales, and Income Relationships

The relationship between variable-costing income and absorption-costing income changes as the relationship between production and sales changes. If more is sold than was produced, variable-costing income is greater than absorption-costing income. This situation is just the opposite of that for the Fairchild example. Selling more than was produced means that beginning inventory and units produced are being sold. Under absorption costing, units coming out of inventory have attached to them fixed overhead from a prior period. In addition, units produced and sold have all of the current period's fixed overhead attached. Thus, the amount of fixed overhead expensed by absorption costing is greater than the current period's fixed overhead by the amount of fixed overhead flowing out of inventory. Accordingly, variable-costing income is greater than absorption-costing income by the amount of fixed overhead flowing out of beginning inventory.

If production and sales are equal, of course, no difference exists between the two reported incomes. Since the units produced are all sold, absorption costing, like variable costing, will recognize the total fixed overhead of the period as an expense. No fixed overhead flows into or out of inventory.

The relationships between production, sales, and the two reported incomes are summarized in Exhibit 10-7. Note that if production is greater than sales, then inventory has increased. If production is less than sales, then inventory must have decreased. If production is equal to sales, then beginning inventory is equal to ending inventory.

To illustrate these relationships, consider the following example based on the operating data of Belnip, Inc., in the years 2006, 2007, and 2008.

Variable costs per unit:	
Direct materials	$4.00
Direct labor	1.50
Variable overhead (estimated and actual)	0.50
Variable selling and administrative	0.25
Estimated:	
Production volume	150,000
Fixed overhead	$150,000
Actual (each year):	
Production volume	150,000
Fixed overhead	$150,000
Fixed selling and administrative expense	$50,000
Sales price	$10 per unit

Other operating data were as follows:

	2006	2007	2008
Beginning inventory	—	—	50,000
Production	150,000	150,000	150,000
Sales	150,000	100,000	200,000
Ending inventory	—	50,000	—

Income statements prepared under absorption and variable costing are shown in Exhibit 10-8.

In 2006, the operating incomes for each method were identical. We must conclude that both methods expensed the same amount of fixed overhead. Under variable costing, we know that the period's total fixed overhead of $150,000 was expensed. Under absorption costing, the fixed overhead is unitized and becomes part of the product cost. Estimated fixed overhead was $150,000 each year. The fixed overhead rate is $1 per unit ($150,000/150,000 units produced) for all three years. The applied fixed overhead is $150,000 ($1 × 150,000) for all three years. Since the actual fixed overhead in every year is also $150,000, there is no fixed overhead variance in any year. Thus, the fixed overhead expensed for any year is simply the overhead rate times the number of units sold. For 2006, the total fixed overhead expensed under absorption costing was $150,000 ($1 × 150,000 units sold). Both methods did indeed recognize the same amount of fixed overhead expense.

	If	Then
1.	Production > Sales	Absorption net income > Variable net income
2.	Production < Sales	Absorption net income < Variable net income
3.	Production = Sales	Absorption net income = Variable net income

Exhibit 10-7 Production, Sales, and Income Relationships

Absorption-Costing Income Statements (in thousands of dollars)

	2006	2007	2008
Sales	$1,500.0	$1,000	$2,000
Less: Cost of goods sold[a]	1,050.0	700	1,400
Gross margin	$ 450.0	$ 300	$ 600
Less: Selling and administrative expenses	87.5	75	100
Operating income	$ 362.5	$ 225	$ 500

[a]Beginning inventory	—	—	$ 350
Cost of goods manufactured	$1,050	$1,050	1,050
Goods available for sale	$1,050	$1,050	$1,400
Less: Ending inventory	—	350	—
Cost of goods sold	$1,050	$ 700	$1,400

Variable-Costing Income Statements (in thousands of dollars)

	2006	2007	2008
Sales	$1,500.0	$1,000	$2,000
Less variable expenses:			
Variable cost of goods sold[a]	(900.0)	(600)	(1,200)
Variable selling and administrative[b]	(37.5)	(25)	(50)
Contribution margin	$ 562.5	$ 375	$ 750
Less fixed expenses:			
Fixed overhead	(150.0)	(150)	(150)
Fixed selling and administrative	(50.0)	(50)	(50)
Operating income	$ 362.5	$ 175	$ 550

[a]Beginning inventory	—	—	$ 300
Variable cost of goods manufactured	$900	$900	900
Goods available for sale	$900	$900	$1,200
Less: Ending inventory	—	300	—
Variable cost of goods sold	$900	$600	$1,200

[b]$0.25 per unit × Units sold

Exhibit 10-8 Absorption and Variable Costing Income Statements for Belnip, Inc.

In 2007, however, the story is different. From Exhibit 15-8, we see that the absorption-costing income was $50,000 greater than the variable-costing income ($225,000 − $175,000). The difference between the two incomes exists because there was $50,000 less fixed overhead expensed under the absorption-costing method.

Under absorption costing, each unit produced is assigned $1 of fixed overhead. Since 150,000 units were produced but only 100,000 units were sold, the remaining 50,000 units were placed in inventory. These 50,000 units carried with them $1 of fixed overhead each, for a total of $50,000. This $50,000 of the current period's fixed overhead will not be recognized as an expense until the units in inventory are sold. Thus, under absorption costing, the period's $150,000 of fixed overhead can be broken down into two categories: $100,000 is expensed and $50,000 is inventoried.

Under variable costing, however, the total fixed overhead of $150,000 is expensed since it is viewed as a period cost. Because variable costing recognizes $150,000 of fixed overhead expense and absorption costing recognizes only $100,000 of fixed overhead expense, the income reported by absorption costing is $50,000 more.

In 2008, the relationship between the two incomes reverses. The difference is now $50,000 in favor of variable costing. The favorable difference occurs because absorption costing not only recognizes $150,000 of fixed overhead expense for units produced and sold in this period but also recognizes the $50,000 of fixed overhead attached to the units in inventory that were produced in 2007 but sold in 2008. Thus, the total fixed overhead recognized as an expense is $200,000 under absorption costing versus only $150,000 under variable costing.

The key to explaining the difference between the two incomes is an analysis of the flow of fixed overhead. Variable costing always recognizes the period's total fixed overhead as an expense. Absorption costing, on the other hand, recognizes only the fixed overhead attached to the units sold. If production is different from sales, fixed overhead will flow either into or out of inventory. If the amount of fixed overhead in inventory increases, then absorption-costing income is greater than variable-costing income by the amount of the net increase. If the fixed overhead in inventory decreases, then variable-costing income is greater than absorption-costing income by the amount of the net decrease.

The change in fixed overhead in inventory is exactly equal to the difference between the two incomes. This change can be computed by multiplying the fixed overhead rate times the change in total units in the beginning and ending inventories (which is the difference between production and sales). The difference between absorption-costing operating income and variable-costing operating income can be expressed as:

$$\text{Absorption-costing income} - \text{Variable-costing income} = \text{Fixed overhead rate} \times (\text{Units produced} - \text{Units sold})$$

Exhibit 10-9 shows how this shortcut approach can be used to explain the differences.

The Treatment of Fixed Overhead in Absorption Costing

The difference between absorption and variable costing centers on the recognition of expense associated with fixed overhead. Under absorption costing, fixed overhead must be assigned to units produced. This presents two problems that we have not explicitly considered. First, how do we convert factory overhead applied on the basis of direct labor hours or machine hours into factory overhead applied to units produced? Second, what do we do when actual factory overhead does not equal applied factory overhead?

The first problem is solved relatively easily. Suppose that factory overhead is applied on the basis of direct labor hours. Further suppose that it takes 0.25 direct

	2006	2007	2008
Operating income:			
Absorption costing	$362.5	$225	$500
Variable costing	362.5	175	550
Difference	$ 0	$ 50	$ (50)
Explanation:			
Units produced	150	150	150
Units sold	150	100	200
Change in inventory	0	50	(50)
Fixed overhead rate	× $1	× $1	× $1
Difference explained*	$ 0	$ 50	$ (50)

*In 2006, absorption costing recognized only the period's fixed overhead as an expense. No fixed overhead flowed into or out of inventory. In 2007, fixed overhead of $50,000 flowed into inventory, and its recognition as an expense was deferred to a future period. In 2008, fixed overhead of $50,000 flowed out of inventory and was recognized as an expense.

Exhibit 10-9 Reconciliation of Variable and Absorption Costing (in thousands of dollars)

labor hours to produce one unit. If the fixed overhead rate is $12 per direct labor hour, then the fixed overhead per unit is $3 (0.25 × $12).

The solution to the second problem requires more thought. First, we must calculate the applied fixed overhead and assign it to units produced. Then, the total applied amount is compared to actual fixed overhead. If the over- or underapplied amount is immaterial, it is closed to Cost of Goods Sold. Any units going into ending inventory take with them the applied fixed overhead. Variable overhead (which can also be over- or underapplied) is treated in the same fashion. If the over- or underapplied amount is material, then it is allocated among ending Work in Process, Finished Goods, and Cost of Goods Sold. This complication is beyond the scope of this text.

Evaluating Profit-Center Managers

The evaluation of managers is often tied to the profitability of the units they control. How income changes from one period to the next and how actual income compares with planned income are frequently used as signals of managerial ability. To be meaningful signals, however, income should reflect managerial effort. For example, if a manager has worked hard and increased sales while holding costs in check, income should increase over the prior period, signaling success. In general terms, if income performance is expected to reflect managerial performance, then managers have the right to expect the following:

Annual or semi-annual performance reviews are often used to rate the performance of employees. During these reviews, a variety of measures related to the type of center the manager is in charge of are used to evaluate that manager's performance.

© Digital Vision

1. As sales revenue increases from one period to the next, all other things being equal, income should increase.
2. As sales revenue decreases from one period to the next, all other things being equal, income should decrease.
3. As sales revenue remains unchanged from one period to the next, all other things being equal, income should remain unchanged.

Variable costing does ensure that the above relationships hold; however, absorption costing may not. To illustrate, assume that a division has the following operating data for its first two years. (For simplicity, we assume no selling and administrative expenses.)

	2007	**2008**
Variable manufacturing costs per unit	$10	$10
Production (expected and actual units)	10,000	5,000
Units sold ($25 per unit)	5,000	10,000
Fixed overhead (estimated and actual)	$100,000	$100,000

The product cost under variable costing is $10 per unit for both years. Assuming that expected actual volume is used to compute a predetermined fixed overhead rate, the product cost under absorption costing is $20 per unit in 2007 and $30 per unit in 2008 [$10 + ($100,000/10,000) for 2007; $10 + ($100,000/5,000) for 2008].

The variable- and absorption-costing income statements are shown in Exhibit 10-10. Sales increased from 5,000 to 10,000 units. Total fixed costs, the variable manufacturing cost per unit, and the unit sales price are the same for both periods. Thus, the doubling of sales represents the only change from one period to the next. Under variable costing, income increased by $75,000 from 2007 to 2008 (from a loss of $25,000 to a profit of $50,000). However, under absorption costing, operating income decreased by $25,000 (from a profit of $25,000 to a profit of $0) despite the increase in sales!

The firm improved its sales performance from 2007 to 2008 (twice as many units were sold), fixed costs remained the same, and the unit variable cost was the same; yet, absorption costing fails to reveal this improved performance. Variable costing, on the other hand, produces an increase in income corresponding to the improved sales performance. If you were the manager, which income approach would you prefer?

Segmented Income Statements Using Variable Costing

Variable costing is useful in preparing segmented income statements because it gives useful information on variable and fixed expenses. A **segment** is a subunit of a company of sufficient importance to warrant the production of performance reports. Segments can be divisions, departments, product lines, customer classes, and so on. In segmented income statements, however, fixed expenses are broken down into two categories: *direct fixed expenses* and *common fixed expenses.* This additional subdivision highlights controllable versus noncontrollable costs and enhances the manager's ability to evaluate each segment's contribution to overall firm performance.

Direct fixed expenses are fixed expenses that are directly traceable to a segment. These are sometimes referred to as *avoidable fixed expenses* or *traceable fixed expenses* because they vanish if the segment is eliminated. For example, if the segments were sales regions, a direct fixed expense for each region would be the rent for the sales office, salary of the sales manager of each region, and so on. If one region were to be eliminated, then those fixed expenses would disappear.

Variable-Costing Income Statement

	2007	2008
Sales	$125,000	$250,000
Less variable expenses:		
Variable cost of goods sold[a]	50,000	100,000
Contribution margin	$ 75,000	$150,000
Less fixed expenses:		
Fixed overhead	100,000	100,000
Operating income (loss)	$ (25,000)	$ 50,000

Absorption-Costing Income Statement

	2007	2008
Sales	$125,000	$250,000
Less cost of goods sold[b]	100,000	250,000
Operating income (loss)	$ 25,000	$ 0

[a]$10 × 5,000 in 2007 and $10 × 10,000 in 2008

[b]	2007	2008
Beginning inventory	$ —	$100,000
Cost of goods manufactured	200,000	150,000
Goods available for sale	$200,000	$250,000
Less: Ending inventory	100,000	—
Cost of goods sold	$100,000	$250,000

Exhibit 10-10 Variable- and Absorption-Costing Income Statements

Common fixed expenses are jointly caused by two or more segments. These expenses persist even if one of the segments to which they are common is eliminated. For example, depreciation on the corporate headquarters building, the salary of the CEO, and the cost of printing and distributing the annual report to shareholders are common fixed expenses for **Walt Disney Company**. If Walt Disney Company were to sell a theme park or open a new one, then those common expenses would not be affected.

For example, Audiomatronics produces both MP3 players and DVD players. Audiomatronics provided the following information for the coming year:

	MP3 Players	DVD Players
Sales	$400,000	$290,000
Variable cost of goods sold	200,000	150,000
Direct fixed overhead	30,000	20,000

A sales commission of 5 percent of sales is paid for each of the two product lines. Direct fixed selling and administrative expense was estimated to be $10,000 for the MP3 line and $15,000 for the DVD line.

Common fixed overhead for the factory was estimated to be $100,000; common selling and administrative expense was estimated to be $20,000. Exhibit 10-11 shows a segmented income statement where the segments are product lines.

Notice that Exhibit 10-11 shows that both MP3 players and DVD players have large positive contribution margins ($180,000 for MP3 players and $125,500 for DVD players). Both products are providing revenue above variable costs that can be used to help cover the firm's fixed costs. However, some of the firm's fixed costs are caused by the segments themselves. Thus, the real measure of the profit contribution of each segment is what is left over after these direct fixed costs are covered.

The profit contribution each segment makes toward covering a firm's common fixed costs is called the **segment margin**. A segment should at least be able to cover both its own variable costs and direct fixed costs. A negative segment margin drags down the firm's total profit, making it time to consider dropping the product. Ignoring any effect a segment may have on the sales of other segments, the segment margin measures the change in a firm's profits that would occur if the segment were eliminated.

Audiomatronics, Inc.
Segmented Income Statement
For the Coming Year

	MP3 Players	DVD Players	Total
Sales	$ 400,000	$ 290,000	$ 690,000
Variable cost of goods sold	(200,000)	(150,000)	(350,000)
Variable selling expense	(20,000)	(14,500)	(34,500)
Contribution margin	$ 180,000	$ 125,500	$ 305,500
Less direct fixed expenses:			
Direct fixed overhead	(30,000)	(20,000)	(50,000)
Direct selling and administrative	(10,000)	(15,000)	(25,000)
Segment margin	$ 140,000	$ 90,500	$ 230,500
Less common fixed expenses:			
Common fixed overhead			(100,000)
Common selling and administrative			(20,000)
Net income			$ 110,500

Exhibit 10-11 Segmented Income Statement

Segmented income statements using variable costing have one feature in addition to the variable-costing income statements already shown. The division of overall fixed expenses into two subcategories, direct fixed expenses and common fixed expenses, gives additional information to the manager. This additional subdivision highlights controllable versus noncontrollable costs and enhances the manager's ability to evaluate each segment's contribution to overall firm performance.

Since direct fixed expenses can be traced to an individual segment (a product line in this example), they are caused by the existence of the segment itself. If the segment, or product line, is eliminated, these fixed expenses will vanish. This gives the manager a truer picture of segment profitability.

Common fixed expenses, on the other hand, relate to two or more segments. If one of the segments to which they are common is eliminated, the common fixed expense still exists—and at the same level as before. In the Audiomatronics example, factory depreciation and the salary of the factory supervisor are common fixed expenses. Elimination of one product line would not eliminate the factory and its associated depreciation. Similarly, the factory supervisor would still be needed to oversee the production of the other product line.

Fixed costs that are direct for one segment may be indirect, or common, for another. For example, suppose that the stereo product line is segmented into two sales territories. In that case, the depreciation on the equipment used to produce stereos is common to both territories but directly traceable to the product segment itself.

Measuring the Performance of Investment Centers Using ROI

Objective 3

Compute and explain return on investment (ROI).

Typically, investment centers are evaluated on the basis of return on investment. Other measures, such as residual income and economic value added, are discussed in the following section.

Return on Investment

Divisions that are investment centers will have an income statement and a balance sheet. So, could those divisions be ranked on the basis of net income? Suppose, for example, that a company has two divisions—Alpha and Beta. Alpha's net income is $100,000, and Beta's is $200,000. Did Beta perform better than Alpha? What if Alpha used an investment of $500,000 to produce the contribution of $100,000, while Beta used an investment of $2 million to produce the $200,000 contribution? Does your response change? Clearly, relating the reported operating profits to the assets used to produce them is a more meaningful measure of performance.

One way to relate operating profits to assets employed is to compute the **return on investment (ROI)**, which is the profit earned per dollar of investment. ROI is the most common measure of performance for an investment center. It can be defined as follows:

$$\text{ROI} = \text{Operating income/Average operating assets}$$

Operating income refers to earnings before interest and taxes. **Operating assets** are all assets acquired to generate operating income, including cash, receivables, inventories, land, buildings, and equipment. The figure for average operating assets is computed as follows:

$$\text{Average operating assets} = (\text{Beginning net book value} + \text{Ending net book value})/2$$

Opinions vary regarding how long-term assets (plant and equipment) should be valued (for example, gross book value versus net book value or historical cost versus current cost). Many firms use historical cost and net book value. There is no one correct way to calculate ROI. The important thing is to be sure that one method is applied consistently over time. This allows the company to compare the ROIs among divisions and over time.

Going back to our example, Alpha's ROI is 0.20 ($100,000/$500,000), while Beta's ROI is only 0.10 ($200,000/$2,000,000). The formula for ROI is quick and easy to use. However, breaking down ROI into margin and turnover ratios gives additional information.

Margin and Turnover

A second way to calculate ROI is to separate the formula (Operating income/Average operating assets) into margin and turnover.

$$\text{ROI} = \text{Margin} \times \text{Turnover}$$
$$= \frac{\text{Operating income}}{\text{Sales}} \times \frac{\text{Sales}}{\text{Average operating assets}}$$

Notice that "Sales" in the above formula can be cancelled out to yield the original ROI formula of Operating income/Average operating assets.

Margin is the ratio of operating income to sales. It tells how many cents of operating income result from each dollar of sales; it expresses the portion of sales that is available for interest, taxes, and profit. **Turnover** is a different measure; it is found by dividing sales by average operating assets. Turnover tells how many dollars of sales result from every dollar invested in operating assets; it shows how productively assets are being used to generate sales.

Suppose, for example, that Celimar Company earned operating income last year as shown in the following income statement:

Sales	$480,000
Cost of goods sold	222,000
Gross margin	$258,000
Selling and administrative expense	210,000
Operating income	$ 48,000

At the beginning of the year, the net book value of operating assets was $277,000. At the end of the year, the net book value of operating assets was $323,000. Then:

$$\begin{aligned}\text{Average operating assets} &= (\text{Beginning assets} + \text{Ending assets})/2\\ &= (\$277{,}000 + \$323{,}000)/2\\ &= \$300{,}000\end{aligned}$$

$$\begin{aligned}\text{Margin} &= \text{Operating income/Sales} = \$48{,}000/\$480{,}000 = 0.10 \text{ or } 10 \text{ percent}\\ \text{Turnover} &= \text{Sales/Average operating assets} = \$480{,}000/\$300{,}000 = 1.6\\ \text{ROI} &= \text{Margin} \times \text{Turnover} = 0.10 \times 1.6 = 0.16 \text{ or } 16 \text{ percent}\end{aligned}$$

Alternatively,

$$\text{ROI} = \text{Operating income/Average operating assets} = \$48{,}000/\$300{,}000$$

While both approaches yield the same ROI, the calculation of margin and turnover gives a manager valuable information. To illustrate this additional information, consider the data presented in Exhibit 10-12. The Electronics Division improved its ROI from 18 percent in year 1 to 20 percent in year 2. The Medical Supplies Division's ROI, however, dropped from 18 to 15 percent. Computing the margin and turnover ratios for each division gives a better picture of what caused the change in rates. These ratios are also presented in Exhibit 10-12.

Notice that the margins for both divisions dropped from year 1 to year 2. In fact, the divisions experienced the *same* percentage of decline (16.67 percent). A

Information for Electronics and Medical Supplies Divisions	Electronics Division	Medical Supplies Division
Year 1:		
Sales	$30,000,000	$117,000,000
Operating income	1,800,000	3,510,000
Average operating assets	10,000,000	19,500,000
ROI[a]	18%	18%
Year 2:		
Sales	$40,000,000	$117,000,000
Operating income	2,000,000	2,925,000
Average operating assets	10,000,000	19,500,000
ROI[a]	20%	15%

Margin and Turnover Comparisons	Electronics Division		Medical Supplies Division	
	Year 1	Year 2	Year 1	Year 2
Margin[b]	6.0%	5.0%	3.0%	2.5%
Turnover[c]	× 3.0	× 4.0	× 6.0	× 6.0
ROI	18.0%	20.0%	18.0%	15.0%

[a]Operating income divided by average operating assets.
[b]Operating income divided by sales.
[c]Sales divided by average operating assets.

Exhibit 10-12 Comparison of Divisional Performance Using ROI

declining margin could be explained by increasing expenses, by competitive pressures (forcing a decrease in selling prices), or both.

In spite of the declining margin, the Electronics Division was able to increase its rate of return. The reason is that the increase in turnover more than compensated for the decline in margin. One explanation for the increased turnover could be a deliberate policy to reduce inventories. (Notice that the average assets employed remained the same for the Electronics Division even though sales increased by $10 million.)

The experience of the Medical Supplies Division was less favorable. Because its turnover rate remained unchanged, its ROI dropped. This division, unlike the Electronics Division, could not overcome the decline in margin.

Advantages of ROI

At least three positive results stem from the use of ROI:

1. It encourages managers to focus on the relationship among sales, expenses, and investment, as should be the case for a manager of an investment center.
2. It encourages managers to focus on cost efficiency.
3. It encourages managers to focus on operating asset efficiency.

These advantages are illustrated by the following three scenarios:

Focus on ROI Relationships Della Barnes, manager of the Plastics Division, is mulling over a suggestion from her marketing vice president to increase the advertising budget by $100,000. The marketing vice president is confident that this increase will boost sales by $200,000. Della realizes that the increased sales will also raise expenses. She finds that the increased variable cost will be $80,000. The division will also need to purchase additional machinery to handle the increased production. The equipment will cost $50,000 and will add $10,000 of depreciation expense. As a result, the proposal will add $10,000 ($200,000 − $80,000 − $10,000 − $100,000) to operating income. Currently, the division has sales of $2 million, total expenses of $1,850,000, and net operating income of $150,000. Operating assets equal $1 million.

	Without Increased Advertising	With Increased Advertising
Sales	$2,000,000	$2,200,000
Less: Expenses	1,850,000	2,040,000
Operating income	$ 150,000	$ 160,000
Operating assets	$1,000,000	$1,050,000

ROI:
$150,000/$1,000,000 = 0.15, or 15 percent
$160,000/$1,050,000 = 0.1524, or 15.24 percent

The ROI without the additional advertising is 15 percent; the ROI with the additional advertising and $50,000 investment in assets is 15.24 percent. Since ROI is increased by the proposal, Della decides to authorize the increased advertising. In effect, the current ROI, without the proposal, is the "hurdle rate." This term is frequently used to indicate the minimum ROI necessary to accept an investment.

Focus on Cost Efficiency Kyle Chugg, manager of Turner's Battery Division, groaned as he reviewed the projections for the last half of the current fiscal year. The recession was hurting his division's performance. Adding the projected operating income of $200,000 to the actual operating income of the first half produced expected annual earnings of $425,000. Kyle then divided the expected operating income by the division's average operating assets to obtain an expected ROI of 12.15 percent. "This is awful," muttered Kyle. "Last year our ROI was 16 percent. And I'm looking at a couple more bad years before business returns to normal. Something has to be done to improve our performance."

The automotive supplies industry is highly competitive, and divisions work to keep costs and investment in assets down in order to keep return on investments at a reasonable level.

© Getty Images/PhotoDisc

Kyle directed all operating managers to identify and eliminate non-value-added activities. As a result, lower-level managers found ways to reduce costs by $150,000 for the remaining half of the year. This reduction increased the annual operating income from $425,000 to $575,000, increasing ROI from 12.15 percent to 16.43 percent as a result. Interestingly, Kyle found that some of the reductions could be maintained after business returned to normal.

Focus on Operating Asset Efficiency The Electronic Storage Division prospered during its early years. In the beginning, the division developed portable external disk drives for storing data; sales and return on investment were extraordinarily high. However, during the past several years, competitors had developed competing technology, and the division's ROI had plunged from 30 to 15 percent. Cost cutting had helped initially, but the fat had all been removed, making further improvements from cost reductions impossible. Moreover, any increase in sales was unlikely—competition was too stiff. The divisional manager searched for some way to increase the ROI by at least 3 to 5 percent. Only by raising the ROI so that it compared favorably to that of the other divisions could the division expect to receive additional capital for research and development.

The divisional manager initiated an intensive program to reduce operating assets. Most of the gains were made in the area of inventory reductions; however, one plant was closed because of a long-term reduction in market share. By installing a just-in-time purchasing and manufacturing system, the division was able to reduce its asset base without threatening its remaining market share. Finally, the reduction in operating assets meant that operating costs could be decreased still further. The end result was a 50 percent increase in the division's ROI, from 15 percent to more than 22 percent.

Disadvantages of the ROI Measure

Overemphasis on ROI can produce myopic behavior. Two negative aspects associated with ROI are frequently mentioned:

1. It can produce a narrow focus on divisional profitability at the expense of profitability for the overall firm.
2. It encourages managers to focus on the short run at the expense of the long run.

These disadvantages are illustrated by the following two scenarios:

Narrow Focus on Divisional Profitability A Cleaning Products Division has the opportunity to invest in two projects for the coming year. The outlay required for each investment, the dollar returns, and the ROI are as follows:

	Project I	Project II
Investment	$10,000,000	$4,000,000
Operating income	1,300,000	640,000
ROI	13%	16%

The division currently earns ROI of 15 percent, with operating assets of $50 million and operating income on current investments of $7.5 million. The division has approval to request up to $15 million in new investment capital. Corporate headquarters requires that all investments earn at least 10 percent (this rate represents the corporation's cost of acquiring the capital). Any capital not used by a division is invested by headquarters, and it earns exactly 10 percent.

The divisional manager has four alternatives: (1) invest in Project I, (2) invest in Project II, (3) invest in both Projects I and II, or (4) invest in neither project. The divisional ROI was computed for each alternative.

	Alternatives			
	Select Only Project I	Select Only Project II	Select Both Projects	Select Neither Project
Operating income	$ 8,800,000	$ 8,140,000	$ 9,440,000	$ 7,500,000
Operating assets	$60,000,000	$54,000,000	$64,000,000	$50,000,000
ROI	14.67%	15.07%	14.75%	15.00%

The divisional manager chose to invest only in Project II, since it would boost ROI from 15.00 percent to 15.07 percent.

While the manager's choice maximized divisional ROI, it actually cost the company profit. If Project I had been selected, the company would have earned \$1.3 million. By not selecting Project I, the \$10 million in capital is invested at 10 percent, earning only \$1 million (0.10 × \$10,000,000). The single-minded focus on divisional ROI, then, cost the company \$300,000 in profits (\$1,300,000 − \$1,000,000).

Encourages Short-Run Optimization Ruth Lunsford, manager of a Small Tools Division, was displeased with her division's performance during the first three quarters. Given the expected income for the fourth quarter, the ROI for the year would be 13 percent, at least two percentage points below where she had hoped to be. Such an ROI might not be strong enough to justify the early promotion she wanted. With only three months left, drastic action was needed. Increasing sales for the last quarter was unlikely. Most sales were booked at least two to three months in advance. Emphasizing extra sales activity would benefit next year's performance. What was needed were some ways to improve this year's performance.

After careful thought, Ruth decided to take the following actions:

1. Lay off five of the highest-paid salespeople.
2. Cut the advertising budget for the fourth quarter by 50 percent.
3. Delay all promotions within the division for three months.
4. Reduce the preventive maintenance budget by 75 percent.
5. Use cheaper raw materials for fourth-quarter production.

In the aggregate, these steps would reduce expenses, increase income, and raise the ROI to about 15.2 percent.

While Ruth's actions increase the profits and ROI in the short run, they have some long-run negative consequences. Laying off the highest-paid (and possibly the best) salespeople may harm the division's future sales-generating capabilities. Future sales could also be hurt by cutting back on advertising and using cheaper raw materials. Delaying promotions could hurt employee morale, which could, in turn, lower productivity and future sales. Finally, reducing preventive maintenance will likely increase downtime and decrease the life of the productive equipment.

Measuring the Performance of Investment Centers Using Residual Income and Economic Value Added

Objective 4

Compute and explain residual income and economic value added (EVA).

To compensate for the tendency of ROI to discourage investments that are profitable for the company but that lower a division's ROI, some companies have adopted alternative performance measures such as residual income. Economic value added is an alternate way to calculate residual income and is being used in a number of companies.

Residual Income

Residual income is the difference between operating income and the minimum dollar return required on a company's operating assets:

$$\text{Residual income} = \text{Operating income} - (\text{Minimum rate of return} \times \text{Average operating assets})$$

Let's return to the example of Celimar Company. Exhibit 10-13 shows how residual income would be calculated, assuming that Celimar requires a minimum rate of return of 12 percent.

The minimum rate of return is set by the company and is the same as the hurdle rate mentioned in the section on ROI. If residual income is greater than zero,

Celimar Company
Income Statement
For the Past Year

Sales	$480,000
Cost of goods sold	222,000
Gross margin	$258,000
Selling and administrative expense	210,000
Operating income	$ 48,000
January 1 net book value of operating assets	$277,000
December 31 net book value of operating assets	$323,000

Residual income = Operating income − (Minimum rate of return × Average operating assets)
= $48,000 − (0.12 × $300,000)
= $48,000 − $36,000
= $12,000

Exhibit 10-13 Calculation of Residual Income

then the division is earning more than the minimum required rate of return (or hurdle rate). If residual income is less than zero, then the division is earning less than the minimum required rate of return. Finally, if residual income is just equal to zero, then the division is earning precisely the minimum required rate of return.

Advantage of Residual Income Recall that the manager of the Cleaning Products Division rejected Project I because it would have reduced divisional ROI; however, that decision cost the company $300,000 in profits. The use of residual income as the performance measure would have prevented this loss. The residual income for each project is computed as follows:

Project I

Residual income = Operating income − (Minimum rate of return × Average operating assets)
= $1,300,000 − (0.10 × $10,000,000)
= $1,300,000 − $1,000,000
= $300,000

Project II

Residual income = $640,000 − (0.10 × $4,000,000)
= $640,000 − $400,000
= $240,000

Notice that both projects have positive residual income. For comparative purposes, the divisional residual income for each of the four alternatives identified follows:

	Alternatives			
	Select Only Project I	Select Only Project II	Select Both Projects	Select Neither Project
Operating assets	$60,000,000	$54,000,000	$64,000,000	$50,000,000
Operating income	$8,800,000	$ 8,140,000	$ 9,440,000	$ 7,500,000
Minimum return*	6,000,000	5,400,000	6,400,000	5,000,000
Residual income	$ 2,800,000	$ 2,740,000	$ 3,040,000	$ 2,500,000

*0.10 × Operating assets.

As shown above, selecting both projects produces the greatest increase in residual income. The use of residual income encourages managers to accept any project that earns above the minimum rate.

Disadvantages of Residual Income Residual income, like ROI, can encourage a short-run orientation. If Ruth Lunsford were being evaluated on the basis of residual income, she could have taken the same actions.

Another problem with residual income is that, unlike ROI, it is an absolute measure of profitability. Thus, direct comparison of the performance of two different investment centers becomes difficult, since the level of investment may differ. For example, consider the residual income computations for Division A and Division B, where the minimum required rate of return is 8 percent.

	Division A	Division B
Average operating assets	$15,000,000	$2,500,000
Operating income	$ 1,500,000	$ 300,000
Minimum return[a]	(1,200,000)	(200,000)
Residual income	$ 300,000	$ 100,000
Residual return[b]	2%	4%

[a]0.08 × Operating assets.
[b]Residual income divided by operating assets.

It is tempting to claim that Division A is outperforming Division B since its residual income is three times higher. Notice, however, that Division A is considerably larger than Division B and has six times as many assets. One possible way to correct this disadvantage is to compute both return on investment and residual income and use both measures for performance evaluation. ROI could then be used for interdivisional comparisons.

Economic Value Added (EVA)

A specific way of calculating residual income is *economic value added.* **Economic value added (EVA)**[1] is net income (operating income minus taxes) minus the total annual cost of capital. Basically, EVA is residual income with the cost of capital equal to the actual cost of capital for the firm (as opposed to some minimum rate of return desired by the company for other reasons). It is said that if EVA is positive, then the company is creating wealth; if EVA is negative, then the company is destroying wealth. Consider the old saying, "It takes money to make money." EVA helps the company to determine whether the money it makes is more than the money it takes to make it. Over the long term, only those companies creating capital, or wealth, can survive.

As a form of residual income, EVA is a dollar figure, not a percentage rate of return. However, it does bear a resemblance to rates of return such as ROI because it links net income (return) to capital employed. The key feature of EVA is its emphasis on *after-tax* operating profit and the *actual* cost of capital. Residual income, on the other hand, uses a minimum expected rate of return. Investors like EVA because it relates profit to the amount of resources needed to achieve it. A number of companies have been evaluated on the basis of EVA. In 2003, for example, economic value added for **General Electric** was $5,983 million, for **Wal-Mart Stores** it was $2,928 million, and for **Merck & Co.** it was $3,872 million.[2] Among large companies showing negative EVA were **IBM** at $8,032 million, **Verizon Communications** at

1 EVA was developed by Stern Stewart & Company. More information can be found on the firm's website at http://www.sternstewart.com/evaabout/whatis.php.

2 Stephen Taub, "MVPs of MVA," *CFO Magazine* (July 1, 2003), http://www.cfo.com/article.cfm/3009758.

$5,612 million, and **Disney Company** at $2,072 million. Smaller companies also differed in terms of their economic value added. **Pixar**'s was positive at $31 million while **JetBlue Airways Corp.** came in with a negative $15 million.

Calculating EVA EVA is net income, or *after-tax operating income,* minus the dollar cost of capital employed. The dollar cost of capital employed is the actual percentage cost of capital[3] multiplied by the total capital employed. The equation for EVA is expressed as follows:

EVA = After-tax operating income − (Actual percentage cost of capital × Total capital employed)

Exhibit 10-14 shows how to calculate EVA.

Behavioral Aspects of EVA A number of companies have discovered that EVA helps to encourage the right kind of behavior from their divisions in a way that emphasis on operating income alone cannot. The underlying reason is EVA's reliance on the true cost of capital. In many companies, the responsibility for investment decisions rests with corporate management. As a result, the cost of capital is considered a corporate expense. If a division builds inventories and investment, the cost of financing that investment is passed along to the overall income statement and does not show up as a reduction from the division's operating income. The result is to make investment seem free to the divisions, and of course, they want more.

Transfer Pricing

Objective 5

Explain the role of transfer pricing in a decentralized firm.

In many decentralized organizations, the output of one division is used as the input of another. This raises an accounting issue. How is the transferred good valued? When divisions are treated as responsibility centers, they are evaluated on the basis

Celimar Company earned net income last year as shown in the following income statement:

Sales	$480,000
Cost of goods sold	222,000
Gross margin	$258,000
Selling and administrative expense	210,000
Operating income	$ 48,000
Less: Income taxes (@ 30%)	14,400
Net income	$ 33,600

Total capital employed equaled $300,000. Celimar Company's actual cost of capital is 10 percent.

EVA = After-tax operating income − (Actual percentage cost of capital × Total capital employed)
= $33,600 − (0.10 × $300,000)
= $33,600 − $30,000
= $3,600

Exhibit 10-14 How to Calculate EVA

3 The computation of a company's actual cost of capital is reserved for later accounting courses.

Managers Decide

Quaker Oats Uses EVA to Reduce Costs

Quaker Oats, a division of PepsiCo, is a strong believer in the value of EVA. Prior to 1991, Quaker Oats evaluated its business segments on the basis of quarterly profits. In order to keep quarterly earnings on an upward march, segment managers offered sharp discounts on products at the end of each quarter. This resulted in huge orders from retailers and sharp surges in production at Quaker's plants at the end of each 3-month period. This practice is called *trade loading* because it "loads up the trade" (retail stores) with product. It is not inexpensive, however, because trade loading requires massive amounts of capital—e.g., working capital, inventories, and warehouses—to store the quarterly spikes in output. Quaker's plant in Danville, Illinois, produces snack foods and breakfast cereals. Before EVA, the Danville plant ran well below capacity throughout the early part of the quarter. Purchasing, however, bought huge quantities of boxes, plastic wrappers, granola, and chocolate chips. The buildup in raw materials purchases was in anticipation of the production surge of the last six weeks of the quarter. As the products were finished, Quaker packed 15 warehouses with finished goods. All costs associated with inventories were absorbed by corporate headquarters. As a result, these costs appeared to be free to the plant managers, who were encouraged to build even higher inventories. The advent of EVA and the cancellation of trade loading led to a smoothing of production throughout the quarter, higher overall production (and sales), and lower inventories. Quaker's Danville plant reduced inventories from $15 million to $9 million. Quaker has closed one-third of its 15 warehouses, saving $6 million annually in salaries and capital costs. ■

Source: Shawn Tully, "The Real Key to Creating Wealth," *Fortune* (September 20, 1993): pp. 38–50.

of operating income, return on investment, and residual income or EVA. As a result, the value of the transferred good is revenue to the selling division and cost to the buying division. This value, or internal price, is called the *transfer price.* In other words, a **transfer price** is the price charged for a component by the selling division to the buying division of the same company. Transfer pricing is a complex issue. The impact of transfer prices on divisions and the company as a whole, as well as methods of setting transfer prices, will be explored in the following sections.

Impact of Transfer Pricing on Divisions and the Firm as a Whole

When one division of a company sells to another division, both divisions as well as the company as a whole are affected. The price charged for the transferred good affects the costs of the buying division and the revenues of the selling division. Thus, the profits of both divisions, as well as the evaluation and compensation of their managers, are affected by the transfer price. Since profit-based performance measures of the two divisions are affected (for example, ROI and residual income), transfer pricing can often be a very emotionally charged issue. Exhibit 10-15 illustrates the effect of the transfer price on two divisions of ABC, Inc. Division A produces a component and sells it to another division of the same company, Division C. The $30 transfer price is revenue to Division A; clearly, Division A wants the price to be as high as possible. Conversely, the $30 transfer price is cost to Division C, just like the cost of any raw material. Division C prefers as low a transfer price as possible.

ABC, Inc.	
Division A	**Division C**
Produces component and transfers it to C for transfer price of $30 per unit	Purchases component from A at transfer price of $30 per unit and uses it in production of final product
Transfer price = $30 per unit	Transfer price = $30 per unit
Revenue to A	Cost to C
Increases net income	Decreases net income
Increases ROI	Decreases ROI
Transfer price revenue = Transfer price cost Zero dollar impact on ABC, Inc.	

Exhibit 10-15 Impact of Transfer Price on Transferring Divisions and the Company as a Whole

While the actual transfer price nets out for the company as a whole, transfer pricing can affect the level of profits earned by the multinational company through corporate income taxes and other legal requirements set by the countries in which the various divisions operate. For example, if the selling division operates in a low-tax country and the buying division operates in a high-tax country, the transfer price may be set quite high. Then, the profits would accrue to the division in the low-tax country and the cost would be assigned to the division in the high-tax country. This has the result of reducing overall corporate income taxes. The international transfer pricing situation is examined in detail in more advanced courses.

Transfer Pricing Policies

Recall that a decentralized company allows much more authority for decision making at lower management levels. It would be counterproductive for the decentralized company to then decide on the actual transfer prices between two divisions. As a result, top management sets the transfer pricing policy, but the divisions still decided whether to transfer or not. For example, top management at Verybig, Inc., may set the corporate transfer pricing policy at full manufacturing cost. Then, if Mediumbig Division wants to transfer a product to Somewhatbig Division, the transfer price would be the product cost. However, neither division is forced to transfer the product internally. The transfer pricing policy says only that *if* the product is transferred, it must be at cost.

In establishing a transfer pricing policy, the views of both the selling division and the buying division must be considered. The **opportunity cost approach** achieves this goal by identifying the minimum price that a selling division would be willing to accept and the maximum price that the buying division would be willing to pay. These minimum and maximum prices correspond to the opportunity costs of transferring internally. They are defined for each division as follows:

1. The **minimum transfer price** is the transfer price that would leave the selling division no worse off if the good were sold to an internal division than if the good were sold to an external party. This is sometimes referred to as the "floor" of the bargaining range.
2. The **maximum transfer price** is the transfer price that would leave the buying division no worse off if an input were purchased from an internal division than if the same good were purchased externally. This is sometimes referred to as the "ceiling" of the bargaining range.

The opportunity cost approach guides divisions in determining when internal transfers should occur. Specifically, the good should be transferred internally whenever the opportunity cost (minimum price) of the selling division is less than the opportunity cost (maximum price) of the buying division. By its very definition, this approach ensures that neither divisional manager is worse off by transferring internally. But what is meant by indifferent or no worse off? In practical terms, this means that total divisional profits are not decreased by the internal transfer.

Several transfer pricing policies are used in practice. These transfer pricing policies include market price, cost-based transfer prices, and negotiated transfer prices.

Market Price

If there is a competitive outside market for the transferred product, then the best transfer price is the market price. In such a case, divisional managers' actions will simultaneously optimize divisional profits and firmwide profits. Furthermore, no division can benefit at the expense of another. In this setting, top management will not be tempted to intervene.

Suppose that the Furniture Division of a corporation produces hide-a-beds. The Mattress Division of that same corporation produces mattresses, including a mattress model that fits into the hide-a-bed. If mattresses are transferred from the Mattress division to the Furniture Division, a transfer pricing opportunity exists. In this case, the Mattress Division is the selling division, and the Furniture Division is the buying division. Suppose that the mattresses can be sold to outside buyers at $50 each; this $50 is the market price. Clearly, the Mattress Division would not sell the mattresses to the Furniture Division for less than $50 each. Just as clearly, the Furniture Division would not pay more than $50 for the mattresses. The transfer price is easily set at the market price.

The market price, if available, is the best approach to transfer pricing. Since the selling division can sell all that it produces at the market price, transferring internally at a lower price would make the division worse off. Similarly, the buying division can always acquire the good at the market price, so it would be unwilling to pay more for an internally transferred good.

Will the two divisions transfer at the market price? It really does not matter, since the divisions and the company as a whole will be as well off whether or not the transfer takes place internally. However, if the transfer is to occur, it will be at the market price.

Cost-Based Transfer Prices

Frequently, there is no good outside market price. This may occur because the transferred product uses patented designs owned by the parent company. Then, a company may use a cost-based transfer pricing approach. For example, suppose that the mattress company uses a high-density foam padding in the hide-a-bed mattress and that outside companies do not produce this type of mattress in the appropriate size. If the company has set a cost-based transfer pricing policy, then the Mattress Division will charge the full cost of producing the mattress. (Recall that full cost includes the cost of direct materials, direct labor, variable overhead, and a portion of fixed overhead.) Suppose that the full cost of the mattress is as follows:

Direct materials	$15
Direct labor	5
Variable overhead	3
Fixed overhead	5
Full cost	$28

Thus, the transfer price is $28 per mattress. This amount will be paid to the Mattress Division by the Furniture Division. Notice that this transfer price does not allow for any profit for the selling division (here, the Mattress Division). The Mattress Division may well try to scale back production of the hide-a-bed mattress and increase production of mattresses available for sale to outside parties. To reduce this desire, top management may define cost as "cost plus." In this case, suppose that the company allows transfer pricing at cost plus 10 percent. Then, the transfer price is $30.80 ($28 + (0.10 × $28)).

If the policy is cost-based transfer pricing, will the transfer take place? That depends. Suppose that the Furniture Division wants to purchase lower-quality mattresses in the external market for $25 each. Then no transfer will occur. Similarly, suppose that the Mattress Division is producing at capacity and can sell the special mattresses for $40 each. The Mattress Division will refuse to transfer any mattresses to the Furniture Division, and instead, will sell all it can produce to outside parties.

Negotiated Transfer Prices

Finally, top management may allow the selling and buying division managers to negotiate a transfer price. This approach is particularly useful in cases with market imperfections, such as the ability of an in-house division to avoid selling and distribution costs. Then, the cost saved can be shared by the two divisions.

Using the example of the Mattress and Furniture divisions, suppose that the hide-a-bed mattress typically sells for $50 and has full product cost of $28. Normally, a sales commission of $5 is paid to the salesperson, but that cost will not be incurred for any internal transfers. Now, a bargaining range exists. That range goes from the minimum transfer price to the maximum.

In the example, the minimum transfer price is $45 ($50 market price less the $5 selling commission that can be avoided on internal sales). The maximum transfer price is $50 (the outside market price that the Furniture Division would have to pay if the mattresses were bought externally). What is the actual transfer price? That depends on the negotiating skills of the Mattress and Furniture Divisions' managers. Any transfer price between $45 and $50 is possible.

Summary of Learning Objectives

1. Explain how and why firms choose to decentralize.

To increase overall efficiency, many companies choose to decentralize. The essence of decentralization is decision-making freedom. In a decentralized organization, lower-level managers make and implement decisions, whereas in a centralized organization, lower-level managers are responsible only for implementing decisions. Reasons for decentralization are numerous. Companies decentralize because local managers can make better decisions using local information. Local managers can also provide a more timely response to changing conditions. Additionally, decentralization for large, diversified companies is necessary because of cognitive limitations—it is impossible for any one central manager to be fully knowledgeable about all products and markets. Other reasons include training and motivating local managers and freeing top management from day-to-day operating conditions so that they can spend time on more long-range activities, such as strategic planning.

A decentralized company sets up responsibility centers. The four types of responsibility centers are cost centers, revenue centers, profit centers, and investment centers. The actual results for each responsibility center can be compared with expected results.

2. Explain the difference between absorption and variable costing, and prepare segmented income statements.

Variable and absorption costing differ in their treatment of fixed factory overhead. Variable costing treats fixed factory overhead as a period expense. Thus, unit production cost under variable costing consists of direct materials, direct labor, and variable factory overhead. Absorption costing treats fixed factory overhead as a product cost. Thus, unit production cost under absorption costing consists of direct materials, direct labor, variable factory overhead, and a share of fixed factory overhead.

A variable-costing income statement divides expenses according to cost behavior. First, variable expenses of manufacturing, marketing, and administration are subtracted from sales to yield the contribution margin. Then, all fixed expenses are subtracted from the contribution margin to yield variable-costing net income. An absorption-costing income statement divides expenses according to function. First, the cost of goods sold is subtracted from sales to yield gross profit (or gross margin). Then, selling and administrative expenses are subtracted from gross profit to yield absorption-costing net income. A segmented income statement allows management to properly evaluate each segment's contribution to overall firm performance.

3. Compute and explain return on investment (ROI).

ROI is the ratio of operating income to average operating assets. This ratio can be broken down into two components: margin (the ratio of operating income to sales) and turnover (the ratio of sales to average operating assets). Residual income is the difference between income and the minimum rate of return required by a company times the capital employed. EVA is very similar to residual income, but after-tax income and the actual percentage cost of capital are used in the computation.

Return on investment is the most common measure of performance for managers of decentralized units. Return on investment encourages managers to focus on improving their divisions' profitability by improving sales, controlling costs, and using assets efficiently. Unfortunately, the measure can also encourage managers to increase ROI by sacrificing the long run for short-run benefits (for example, encouraging managers to forego investments that are profitable for the firm but that would lower the divisional ROI).

4. Compute and explain residual income and economic value added (EVA).

Residual income is operating income minus some minimum percentage cost of capital times capital employed. Positive residual income means that the division is earning more than the minimum cost of capital. Negative residual income means that the division is earning less than the minimum cost of capital. Residual income precisely equal to zero indicates that the division is earning precisely the minimum cost of capital.

Economic value added is after-tax operating profit minus the total annual cost of capital. If EVA is positive, then the company is creating wealth. If it is negative, then the company is destroying capital. EVA is a dollar figure, not a percentage rate of return. The key feature of EVA is its emphasis on *after-tax* operating profit and the *actual* cost of capital. Investors like EVA because it relates profit to the amount of resources needed to achieve it.

Decentralized firms may encourage goal congruence by constructing management compensation programs that reward managers for taking actions that benefit the firm. Possible reward systems include cash compensation and noncash benefits.

5. Explain the role of transfer pricing in a decentralized firm.

When one division of a company produces a product that can be used in production by another division, transfer pricing exists. The transfer price is revenue to the selling division and cost to the buying division; thus, the price charged for the intermediate good affects the operating income of both divisions. Since both divisions are evaluated on their profitability, the price charged for the intermediate good can be a point of serious contention. Three transfer pricing policies are generally used: market price, cost-based transfer price, and negotiated transfer price.

Key Terms

Review Problems

1. Absorption and Variable Costing; Segmented Income Statements

Fine Leathers Company produces a lady's wallet and a man's wallet. Selected data for the past year follow:

	Lady's Wallets	Man's Wallets
Production (units)	100,000	200,000
Sales (units)	90,000	210,000
Selling price	$5.50	$4.50
Direct labor hours	50,000	80,000
Manufacturing costs:		
Direct materials	$ 75,000	$100,000
Direct labor	250,000	400,000
Variable overhead	20,000	24,000
Fixed overhead:		
Direct	50,000	40,000
Common[a]	20,000	20,000
Nonmanufacturing costs:		
Variable selling	30,000	60,000
Direct fixed selling	35,000	40,000
Common fixed selling[b]	25,000	25,000

[a] Common overhead totals $40,000 and is divided equally between the two products.
[b] Common fixed selling costs total $50,000 and are divided equally between the two products.

Budgeted fixed overhead for the year, $130,000, equaled the actual fixed overhead. Fixed overhead is assigned to products using a plantwide rate based on expected direct labor hours, which were 130,000. The company had 10,000 man's wallets in inventory at the beginning of the year. These wallets had the same unit cost as the man's wallets produced during the year.

Required

1. Compute the unit cost for the lady's and man's wallets using the variable-costing method. Compute the unit cost using absorption costing.
2. Prepare an income statement using absorption costing.
3. Prepare an income statement using variable costing.
4. Reconcile the difference between the two income statements.
5. Prepare a segmented income statement using products as segments.

Solution

1. The unit cost for the lady's wallet is as follows:

Direct materials ($75,000/100,000)	$0.75
Direct labor ($250,000/100,000)	2.50
Variable overhead ($20,000/100,000)	0.20
Variable cost per unit	$3.45
Fixed overhead [(50,000 × $1.00)/100,000]	0.50
Absorption cost per unit	$3.95

The unit cost for the man's wallet is as follows:

Direct materials ($100,000/200,000)	$0.50
Direct labor ($400,000/200,000)	2.00
Variable overhead ($24,000/200,000)	0.12

Variable cost per unit	$2.62
Fixed overhead [(80,000 × $1.00)/200,000]	0.40
Absorption cost per unit	$3.02

Notice that the only difference between the two unit costs is the assignment of the fixed overhead cost. Notice also that the fixed overhead unit cost is assigned using the predetermined fixed overhead rate ($130,000/130,000 hours = $1 per hour). For example, the lady's wallets used 50,000 direct labor hours and so receive $1 × 50,000, or $50,000, of fixed overhead. This total, when divided by the units produced, gives the $0.50 per-unit fixed overhead cost. Finally, observe that variable nonmanufacturing costs are not part of the unit cost under variable costing. For both approaches, only manufacturing costs are used to compute the unit costs.

2. The income statement under absorption costing is as follows:

Sales [($5.50 × 90,000) + ($4.50 × 210,000)]	$1,440,000
Less: Cost of goods sold [($3.95 × 90,000) + ($3.02 × 210,000)]	989,700
Gross margin	$ 450,300
Less: Selling expenses*	215,000
Operating income	$ 235,300

*The sum of selling expenses for both products.

3. The income statement under variable costing is as follows:

Sales [($5.50 × 90,000) + ($4.50 × 210,000)]	$1,440,000
Less variable expenses:	
Variable cost of goods sold	
[($3.45 × 90,000) + ($2.62 × 210,000)]	(860,700)
Variable selling expenses	(90,000)
Contribution margin	$ 489,300
Less fixed expenses:	
Fixed overhead	(130,000)
Fixed selling	(125,000)
Operating income	$ 234,300

4. Reconciliation is as follows:

$$I_A - I_V = \$235{,}300 - \$234{,}300 = \$1{,}000$$

Thus, variable-costing income is $1,000 less than absorption-costing income. This difference can be explained by the net change of fixed overhead found in inventory under absorption costing.

Lady's wallets:	
Units produced	100,000
Units sold	90,000
Increase in inventory	10,000
Unit fixed overhead	× $0.50
Increase in fixed overhead	$ 5,000
Man's wallets:	
Units produced	200,000
Units sold	210,000
Decrease in inventory	(10,000)
Unit fixed overhead	× $0.40
Decrease in fixed overhead	$ (4,000)

The net change is a $1,000 ($5,000 − $4,000) increase in fixed overhead in inventories. Thus, under absorption costing, there is a net flow of $1,000 of the current period's fixed overhead into inventory. Since variable costing recognized all of the current period's fixed overhead as an expense, variable-costing income should be $1,000 lower than absorption costing, as it is.

5. Segmented income statement:

	Lady's Wallets	Man's Wallets	Total
Sales	$495,000	$ 945,000	$1,440,000
Less variable expenses:			
Variable cost of goods sold	(310,500)	(550,200)	(860,700)
Variable selling expenses	(30,000)	(60,000)	(90,000)
Contribution margin	$154,500	$ 334,800	$ 489,300
Less direct fixed expenses:			
Direct fixed overhead	(50,000)	(40,000)	(90,000)
Direct selling expenses	(35,000)	(40,000)	(75,000)
Segment margin	$ 69,500	$ 254,800	$ 324,300
Less common fixed expenses:			
Common fixed overhead			(40,000)
Common selling expenses			(50,000)
Operating income			$ 234,300

2. Weighted Average Cost of Capital and EVA

El Suezo, Inc., had after-tax operating income last year of $600,000. Two sources of financing were used by the company: $2.5 million of mortgage bonds paying 8 percent interest and $10 million in common stock, which was considered to be no more or less risky than other stocks. The rate of return on long-term government bonds is 6 percent. El Suezo pays a marginal tax rate of 40 percent. Total capital employed is $5.3 million.

Required

1. What is the weighted cost of capital for El Suezo?
2. Calculate EVA for El Suezo.

Solution

1. After-tax cost of the mortgage bonds:

   $= [(1 - 0.4)(0.08)] = 0.048$

   Cost of the common stock:

   = Return on long-term government bonds + Average premium
   = 6% + 6%
   = 12%

	Amount	Percent	After-Tax Cost	= Weighted Cost
Mortgage bonds	$ 2,500,000	0.20	0.048	0.0096
Common stock	10,000,000	0.80	0.120	0.0960
Total	$12,500,000			
Weighted average cost of capital				0.1056

2. Cost of capital = $5,300,000 × 0.1056 = $559,680

After-tax operating income	$600,000
Less: Cost of capital	559,680
EVA	$ 40,320

3. Transfer Pricing

The Components Division produces a part that is used by the Goods Division. The cost of manufacturing the part follows:

Direct materials	$10
Direct labor	2
Variable overhead	3
Fixed overhead*	5
Total cost	$20

*Based on a practical volume of 200,000 parts.

Other costs incurred by the Components Division are as follows:

Fixed selling and administrative	$500,000
Variable selling (per unit)	1

The part usually sells for between $28 and $30 in the external market. Currently, the Components Division is selling it to external customers for $29. The division is capable of producing 200,000 units of the part per year; however, because of a weak economy, only 150,000 parts are expected to be sold during the coming year. The variable selling expenses are avoidable if the part is sold internally.

The Goods Division has been buying the same part from an external supplier for $28. It expects to use 50,000 units of the part during the coming year. The manager of the Goods Division has offered to buy 50,000 units from the Components Division for $18 per unit.

Required

1. Determine the minimum transfer price that the Components Division would accept.
2. Determine the maximum transfer price that the manager of the Goods Division would pay.
3. Should an internal transfer take place? Why or why not? If you were the manager of the Components Division, would you sell the 50,000 components for $18 each? Explain.
4. Suppose that the average operating assets of the Components Division total $10 million. Compute the ROI for the coming year, assuming that the 50,000 units are transferred to the Goods Division for $21 each.

Solution

1. The minimum transfer price is $15. The Components Division has idle capacity and so must cover only its incremental costs, which are the variable manufacturing costs. (Fixed costs are the same whether or not the internal transfer occurs; the variable selling expenses are avoidable.)
2. The maximum transfer price is $28. The Goods Division would not pay more for the part than it has to pay an external supplier.
3. Yes, an internal transfer ought to occur; the opportunity cost of the selling division is less than the opportunity cost of the buying division. The Components Division would earn an additional $150,000 profit ($3 × 50,000). The

total joint benefit, however, is $650,000 ($13 × 50,000). The manager of the Components Division should attempt to negotiate a more favorable outcome for that division.

4. Income statement:

Sales [($29 × 150,000) ($21 × 50,000)]	$ 5,400,000
Less: Variable cost of goods sold ($15 × 200,000)	(3,000,000)
Less: Variable selling expenses ($1 × 150,000)	(150,000)
Contribution margin	$ 2,250,000
Less: Fixed overhead ($5 × 200,000)	(1,000,000)
Less: Fixed selling and administrative	(500,000)
Operating income	$ 750,000

ROI = Operating income/Average operating assets
= $750,000/$10,000,000
= 0.075

Questions for Writing and Discussion

1. Discuss the differences between centralized and decentralized decision making.
2. What is decentralization?
3. Explain why firms choose to decentralize.
4. What is the one difference between the way costs are assigned under variable and absorption costing?
5. If production is greater than sales, why is absorption-costing income greater than variable-costing income?
6. The fixed overhead expense recognized on an income statement was $100,000. The fixed overhead for the period was $80,000. Was the income statement prepared using absorption costing or variable costing? Explain.
7. Why is variable costing better than absorption costing for the evaluation of segment performance?
8. Why is variable costing better than absorption costing for planning and controlling costs?
9. What is the difference between a direct fixed cost and a common fixed cost? Why is this difference important?
10. What is the difference between contribution margin and segment margin?
11. Explain how income under absorption costing can increase from one period to the next even though selling prices and costs have remained the same.
12. Explain how the treatment of customer groups as segments can be useful to a firm.
13. What are margin and turnover? Explain how these concepts can improve the evaluation of an investment center.
14. What are the three benefits of ROI? Explain how each can lead to improved profitability.
15. What are two disadvantages of ROI? Explain how each can lead to decreased profitability.
16. What is EVA?
17. What problems do owners face in encouraging goal congruence of managers?
18. What is a transfer price?
19. Explain how transfer prices can impact performance measures, firmwide profits, and the decision to decentralize decision making.
20. Explain the opportunity cost approach to transfer pricing.
21. If the minimum transfer price of the selling division is less than the maximum transfer price of the buying division, the intermediate product should be transferred internally. Do you agree or disagree? Explain.
22. If an outside, perfectly competitive market exists for the intermediate product, what should the transfer price be? Why?
23. Discuss the advantages and disadvantages of negotiated transfer prices.
24. Identify three cost-based transfer prices. What are the disadvantages of cost-based transfer prices? When might it be appropriate to use cost-based transfer prices?

Exercises

10-1

Types of Responsibility Centers
LO1

Matching. For each type of responsibility center in column A, choose the performance measure in column B that would most likely be used to evaluate performance.

Column A	Column B
Cost center	Sales
Profit center	Total cost
Revenue center	Operating Income
Investment center	Return on Investment

10-2

Unit Costs; Inventory Valuation; Variable and Absorption Costing
LO2

Witherspoon Company produced 20,000 units during its first year of operations and sold 19,350 units. The company chose practical activity—at 20,000 units—to compute its predetermined overhead rate. Manufacturing costs are as follows:

Direct materials	$120,600
Direct labor	90,000
Expected and actual variable overhead	26,400
Expected and actual fixed overhead	68,000

Required

1. Calculate the unit cost and the cost of finished goods inventory under absorption costing.
2. Calculate the unit cost and the cost of finished goods inventory under variable costing.
3. What is the dollar amount that would be used to report the cost of finished goods inventory to external parties. Why?

10-3

Income Statements; Variable and Absorption Costing
LO2

EXCEL

The following information pertains to Lextel, Inc., for 2008:

Beginning inventory in units	—
Units produced	25,000
Units sold	23,000
Ending inventory in units	2,000
Variable costs per unit:	
Direct materials	$ 8.00
Direct labor	3.00
Variable overhead	1.80
Variable selling expenses	4.00
Fixed costs per year:	
Fixed overhead	$107,500
Fixed selling and administrative	26,800

There are no work-in-process inventories. Normal activity is 25,000 units. Expected and actual overhead costs are the same.

Required

1. Without preparing an income statement, indicate what the difference will be between variable-costing income and absorption-costing income.
2. Assume the selling price per unit is $26. Prepare an income statement (a) using variable costing and (b) using absorption costing.

10-4

Segmented Income Statement; Product-Line Analysis
LO2

EXCEL

Cocino Company produces blenders and coffeemakers. During the past year, the company produced and sold 100,000 blenders and 25,000 coffeemakers. Fixed costs for Cocino totaled $250,000, of which $90,000 can be avoided if the blenders are not produced and $45,000 can be avoided if the coffee makers are not produced. Revenue and variable cost information follow:

	Blenders	Coffee Makers
Variable expenses per appliance	$20	$43
Selling price per appliance	22	45

Required

1. Prepare product-line income statements. Segregate direct and common fixed costs.
2. What would the effect be on Cocino's profit if the coffeemaker line is dropped? The blender line?
3. What would the effect be on firm profits if an additional 10,000 blenders could be produced (using existing capacity) and sold for $20.50 on a special-order basis? Existing sales would be unaffected by the special order.

10-5

Unit Cost; Inventory Valuation; Absorption and Variable Costing; Contribution Margin
LO2

Kellen Company manufactures stackable plastic cubes that are used for storage in dorm rooms. In August 2008, Kellen began producing multicolored cubes. During the month of August, 9,000 were produced, and 8,800 were sold at $7.50 each. The following costs were incurred:

Direct materials	$10,800
Direct labor	6,750
Variable overhead	5,850
Fixed overhead	27,900

A selling commission of 10 percent of sales price was paid. Administrative expenses, all fixed, amounted to $23,000.

Required

1. Calculate the unit cost and the cost of ending inventory under absorption costing.
2. Calculate the unit cost and the cost of ending inventory under variable costing.
3. What is the contribution margin per unit?
4. Kellen believes that multicolored cubes will really take off after one year of sales. Management thinks August 2009 sales will be twice as high as August 2008 sales. Costs are estimated to remain unchanged. What is the planned operating income for Kellen for August 2009? Did you use variable or absorption costing to determine it?

10-6

Margin; Turnover; ROI
LO3

Classen Company had sales of $50,000, expenses of $48,000, and operating assets of $10,000.

Required

1. Compute the operating income.
2. Compute the margin and turnover ratios.
3. Compute the ROI.

10-7

Margin; Turnover; ROI; Average Operating Assets
LO3

Seere Company provided the following income statement for last year.

Sales	$240,000
Less: Variable expenses	195,000
Contribution margin	$ 45,000
Less: Fixed expenses	37,800
Operating income	$ 7,200

At the beginning of last year, Seere had $78,650 in operating assets. At the end of the year, Seere had $81,350 in operating assets.

Required

1. Compute average operating assets.
2. Compute the margin and turnover ratios for last year. Compute ROI.

10-8

ROI and Investment Decisions
LO3

Cheryl Manners, division manager of Radiotech, Inc., was debating the merits of a new product—a weather radio that would put out a warning if the county in which the listener lived was under a severe thunderstorm or tornado alert.

The budgeted income of the division was $480,000 with operating assets of $8,000,000. The proposed investment would add income of $270,000 and would require an additional investment in equipment of $1,500,000.

Required

1. Compute the ROI of:
   a. the division if the radio project is not undertaken
   b. the radio project alone
   c. the division if the radio project is undertaken
2. Do you suppose that Cheryl will decide to invest in the new radio? Why or why not?

10-9

Weighted Average Cost of Capital; EVA
LO4

Schipper Company had after-tax operating income last year of $115,000. Two sources of financing were used by the company: $1.3 million of mortgage bonds paying 8 percent interest and $700,000 in common stock, which was considered to be no more or less risky than other stocks. The rate of return on long-term government bonds is 6 percent. Schipper Company pays a marginal tax rate of 30 percent. Total capital employed is $1.5 million.

Required

1. What is the after-tax cost of the mortgage bonds?
2. What is the after-tax cost of the common stock?
3. What is the weighted average cost of capital for Schipper?
4. What is the dollar cost of capital for Schipper?
5. Calculate EVA for Schipper. Is Schipper creating wealth or not?

10-10

Weighted Average Cost of Capital; EVA
LO4

EXCEL

Refer to **Exercise 10-9.** Assume that Schipper Company has the same data as before, but that Schipper Company now pays a marginal tax rate of 40 percent.

Required

1. What is the after-tax cost of the mortgage bonds?
2. What is the after-tax cost of the common stock?
3. What is the weighted average cost of capital for Schipper?
4. What is the dollar cost of capital for Schipper?
5. Calculate EVA for Schipper. Is Schipper creating wealth or not?

10-11

Residual Income
LO3, LO4

The manager of a division that produces electronic audio products is considering the opportunity to invest in two independent projects. The first is a portable MP3 player. The second is a voice recorder designed as a module for visor or palm PDAs. Without the investments, the division will have average assets for the coming year of $18 million and expected operating income of $2.7 million. The expected operating incomes and the outlay required for each investment are as follows:

	MP3 Player	Voice Recorder
Operating income	$116,000	$105,000
Outlay	800,000	750,000

Corporate headquarters has made available up to $2 million of capital for this division. Any funds not invested by the division will be retained by headquarters and invested to earn the company's minimum required rate, 12%.

Required

1. Compute the residual income for each of the opportunities.
2. Compute the divisional residual income for each of the following four alternatives:
   a. The MP3 player is added.
   b. The voice recorder is added.
   c. Both investments are added.
   d. Neither investment is made; the status quo is maintained.

   Assuming that divisional managers are evaluated and rewarded on the basis of residual income, which alternative do you think the divisional manager will choose?
3. Compute the ROI for each investment.
4. Compute the divisional ROI for each of the following four alternatives:
   a. The MP3 player is added.
   b. The voice recorder is added.
   c. Both investments are added.
   d. Neither investment is made; the status quo is maintained.

   Assuming that divisional managers are evaluated and rewarded on the basis of ROI performance, which alternative do you think the divisional manager will choose?

10-12

Residual Income and ROI
LO3, LO4

Consider the following data for two divisions of the same company:

	North Woods	Midwest
Sales	$3,000,000	$10,000,000
Average operating assets	1,000,000	3,000,000
Operating income	140,000	330,000
Minimum required return	8%	8%

Required

1. Compute residual income for each division.
2. Compute ROI for each division.

10-13

Transfer Pricing
LO5

Jesper, Inc., has a number of divisions including a Furniture Division and a Motel Division. The Motel Division owns and operates a line of budget motels located along major highways. Each year, the Motel Division purchases furniture for the motel rooms. Currently, it purchases a basic dresser from an outside supplier for $42. Carrie Burnside, manager of the Furniture Division, has approached George

EXCEL

Sanchez, manager of the Motel Division, about selling dressers to the Motel Division. Carrie has researched the dresser costs and determined the following costs:

Direct materials	$ 8
Direct labor	4
Variable overhead	3
Fixed overhead	12
Total manufacturing cost	$27

Currently, the Furniture Division has capacity to produce 75,000 dressers but is only producing 60,000. The Motel Division needs 10,000 dressers per year.

Required

1. What is the maximum transfer price? The minimum transfer price? Should the transfer occur?
2. Suppose that Carrie and George agree on a transfer price of $30. What is the benefit to each division? What is the benefit to the company as a whole?
3. Suppose that the Furniture Division were operating at capacity. What would be the maximum transfer price? The minimum transfer price? Should the transfer take place in this case? Why or why not?

10-14

Transfer Pricing; Outside Market with Full Capacity
LO5

Kimer Company's Small Motor Division produces a variety of small motors that are used in various household and office appliances. Kimer's Kitchen Products Division manufactures appliances such as blenders, juicers, coffee grinders, and so on. The most frequently used motor is Model A28, which can be purchased from a number of outside suppliers for $2.30 each. The manager of the Kitchen Products Division has approached the manager of the Small Motor Division and offered to buy 150,000 Model A28 small motors. The Small Motor Division currently is producing at capacity and produces and sells 200,000 Model A28 motors to outside customers for $2.30 each.

Required

1. What is the minimum transfer price for the Small Motor Division? What is the maximum transfer price for the Kitchen Products Division? Is it important that transfers take place internally? If transfers do take place, what should the transfer price be?
2. Now assume that the Small Motor Division incurs selling costs of $0.20 per motor that could be avoided if the motors are sold internally. Identify the minimum transfer price for the Small Motor Division and the maximum transfer price for the Kitchen Products Division. Should internal transfers take place? If so, what is the benefit to the firm as a whole?
3. Suppose you are the manager of the Small Motor Division. Selling costs of $0.20 per motor are avoidable if they are sold internally. Would you accept an offer of $2.20 from the manager of the other division? How much better off (or worse off) would your division be if this price is accepted?

10-15

Transfer Pricing; Idle Capacity
LO5

The Paper Division of Edu-Tech, Inc., produces photographic paper that can be sold externally or internally to Edu-Tech's School Photography Division. Sales and cost data per package of photographic paper follow:

Unit selling price	$3.95
Unit variable product cost	$2.25
Unit product fixed cost*	$1.20
Practical capacity	500,000 units

*$600,000/500,000

During the coming year, the Paper Division expects to sell 350,000 packages of photographic paper. The School Photography Division currently plans to buy 150,000 packages of this paper on the outside market for $3.95 each. Penelope Montenegro, manager of the Paper Division, has approached Tom Holmes, manager of the School Photography Division, and offered to sell the 150,000 packages of paper for $3.75 each. Penelope explained to Tom that she can avoid selling costs of $0.40 per package and that she would split the savings by offering a $0.20 discount on the usual price.

Required

1. What is the minimum transfer price that the Paper Division would be willing to accept? What is the maximum transfer price that the School Photography Division would be willing to pay? Should an internal transfer take place? What would be the benefit (or loss) to the firm as a whole if the internal transfer takes place?
2. Suppose Tom knows that the Paper Division has idle capacity. Do you think that he would agree to the transfer price of $3.75? Suppose he counters with an offer to pay $3.20. If you were Penelope, would you be interested in this price? Explain with supporting computations.
3. Suppose that Edu-Tech, Inc.'s policy is that all internal transfers take place at full manufacturing cost. What would the transfer price be? Would the transfer take place?

10-16

Margin; Turnover; ROI
LO3

Calculate the missing data for each of these four independent companies:

	A	B	C	D
Revenue	$10,000	$45,000	$200,000	?
Expenses	$ 7,800	?	$188,000	?
Operating income	$ 2,200	$18,000	?	?
Assets	$20,000	?	$100,000	$9,600
Margin	?%	40%	?%	6.25%
Turnover	?	0.3125	?	2.00
ROI	?%	?%	?%	?%

10-17

Margin; Turnover; ROI
LO4

Refer to **Exercise 10-16.** Assume that the required rate of return for each company is 12%. Calculate the residual income for each company.

Problems

10-18

Income Statements and Firm Performance: Variable and Absorption Costing
LO2

EXCEL

Diaz Company had the following operating data for its first two years of operations:

Variable costs per unit:	
Direct materials	$ 4.00
Direct labor	2.00
Variable overhead	1.50
Fixed costs per year:	
Overhead	$120,000
Selling and administrative	163,800

Diaz produced 30,000 units in the first year and sold 26,000. In the second year, it produced 26,000 units and sold 30,000 units. The selling price per unit each year was $22. Diaz uses an actual cost system for product costing.

Required

1. Prepare income statements for both years using absorption costing. Has firm performance, as measured by income, improved or declined from Year 1 to Year 2?
2. Prepare income statements for both years using variable costing. Has firm performance, as measured by income, improved or declined from Year 1 to Year 2?
3. Calculate the fixed overhead rate for Year 1.
4. Calculate the Year 1 value of ending inventory under absorption costing and under variable costing.

10-19

Absorption Costing; Variable Costing; Reconciliation with Fixed Overhead Variance
LO2

Ziemble Company uses a predetermined overhead rate based on normal capacity expressed in units of output. Normal capacity is 75,000 units, and the expected fixed overhead cost for the year is $300,000.

During the year, Ziemble produced 74,000 units and sold 72,000 units. There was no beginning finished goods inventory. The variable-costing income statement for the year follows:

Sales (72,000 units @ $21)	$1,512,000
Less variable costs:	
Variable cost of goods sold	(756,000)
Variable selling expenses	(360,000)
Contribution margin	$ 396,000
Less fixed costs:	
Fixed overhead	(300,000)
Fixed selling and administrative	(84,000)
Operating income	$ 12,000

Any under- or overapplied overhead is closed to Cost of Goods Sold. Variable cost of goods sold is already adjusted for any variable overhead variance.

Required

1. Ziemble Company needs an income statement based on absorption costing for external reporting. Using the information provided, prepare this statement.
2. Explain the difference between the income reported by variable costing and by absorption costing.

10-20

Product Line Analysis with Complementary Effects
LO2

FunTime Company produces three lines of greeting cards: scented, musical, and regular. Segmented income statements for the past year are as follows:

	Scented	Musical	Regular	Total
Sales	$10,000	$15,000	$25,000	$50,000
Less: Variable expenses	7,000	12,000	12,500	31,500
Contribution margin	$ 3,000	$ 3,000	$12,500	$18,500
Less: Direct fixed expenses	4,000	5,000	3,000	12,000
Segment margin	$(1,000)	$ (2,000)	$ 9,500	$ 6,500
Less: Common fixed expenses				7,500
Operating income (loss)				$ (1,000)

Kathy Bunker, president of FunTime, is concerned about the financial performance of her firm and is seriously considering dropping both the scented and musical product lines. However, before making a final decision, she consults Jim Dorn, FunTime's vice president of marketing.

Required

1. Jim believes that by increasing advertising by $1,000 ($250 for the scented line and $750 for the musical line), sales of those two lines would increase by 30 percent. If you were Kathy, how would you react to this information?
2. Jim warns Kathy that eliminating the scented and musical lines would lower the sales of the regular line by 20 percent. Given this information, would it be profitable to eliminate the scented and musical lines?
3. Suppose that eliminating either line reduces sales of the regular cards by 10 percent. Would a combination of increased advertising (the option described in Requirement 1) and eliminating one of the lines be beneficial? Identify the best combination for the firm.

10-21

Absorption Costing; Variable Costing; Income Statements; Inventory Valuations; Income Reconciliation
LO2

Grehan Company produces and sells wooden pallets that are used in moving and stacking materials. The operating costs for the past year were as follows:

Variable costs per unit:	
Direct materials	$3.60
Direct labor	2.00
Variable overhead	0.40
Variable selling expenses	0.30
Fixed costs per year:	
Fixed overhead	$180,000
Fixed selling and administrative	70,000

During the year, Grehan produced 200,000 wooden pallets and sold 207,000 at $10 each. Grehan had 9,300 pallets in beginning finished goods inventory; costs have not changed from last year to this year. An actual costing system is used for product costing.

Required

1. What per-unit inventory cost will be reported on Grehan's balance sheet at the end of the year? What will be the reported income?
2. What would the per-unit inventory cost be under variable costing? Does this differ from the unit cost computed in Requirement 1? Why? What would income be using variable costing?
3. Reconcile the difference between the variable-costing and absorption-costing income figures.
4. Suppose that Grehan Company had sold 196,700 pallets during the year. What is the absorption-costing income? What is the variable-costing income?
5. Reconcile the difference between the variable-costing and absorption-costing income figures in requirement 4.

10-22

ROI for Multiple Investments; EVA
LO3, LO4

The manager of a division that produces add-on products for the automobile industry has just been presented the opportunity to invest in two independent projects. The first is an air conditioner for the back seats of vans and minivans. The second is a turbocharger. Without the investments, the division will have average assets for the coming year of $28.9 million and after-tax income of $3.179 million. The outlay required for each investment and the expected operating incomes are as follows:

	Air Conditioner	Turbocharger
After-tax operating income	$ 67,500	$89,700
Outlay	750,000	690,000

Corporate headquarters will borrow up to $1.5 million for the automotive add-on division for further investments. The amount borrowed will be through unsecured bonds at a rate of 12 percent. The marginal tax rate is 25 percent.

Required

1. Compute the ROI for each investment project.
2. Compute the budgeted divisional ROI for each of the following four alternatives:
   a. The air conditioner investment is made.
   b. The turbocharger investment is made.
   c. Both investments are made.
   d. Neither additional investment is made.

   Assuming that divisional managers are evaluated and rewarded on the basis of ROI performance, which alternative do you think the divisional manager will choose?
3. Suppose that the borrowing must be for the entire $1.5 million. Calculate the EVA of the two investments taken as a package. Based on EVA, are the investments profitable?

10-23

ROI Calculations with Varying Assumptions
LO3

White Mountain Products is a division of Parker Textiles, Inc. During the coming year, it expects to earn an operating income of $310,000 based on sales of $3.45 million; without any new investments, the division will have average net operating assets of $3 million. The division is considering a capital investment project—adding machinery to produce gaiters (tubular coverings that extend from the ankle of a ski boot to just below the knee to keep snow out of the boot)—that requires an additional investment of $600,000 and increases operating income by $57,500 (sales would increase by $575,000). If made, the investment would increase beginning net operating assets by $600,000 and ending net operating assets by $400,000. Assume that the minimum rate of return required by the company is 7 percent.

Required

1. Compute the ROI for the division without the investment.
2. Compute the margin and turnover ratios without the investment. Show that the product of the margin and turnover ratios equals the ROI computed in Requirement 1.
3. Compute the ROI for the division with the new investment. Do you think the divisional manager will approve the investment?
4. Compute the margin and turnover ratios for the division with the new investment. Compare these with the old ratios.
5. Assume that a JIT purchasing and manufacturing system is installed, reducing average operating assets by $800,000. Compute the ROI with and without the investment under this new scenario. Now do you think the divisional manager will accept the new investment? Should he accept it? Explain your answer.
6. Refer to Requirement 5. Compute the margin and turnover ratios without the investment.

10-24

ROI; Margin; Turnover
LO3

Ready Electronics is facing stiff competition from imported goods. Its operating income margin has been declining steadily for the past several years; the company has been forced to lower prices so that it can maintain its market share. The operating results for the past three years are as follows:

	Year 1	Year 2	Year 3
Sales	$10,000,000	$ 9,500,000	$ 9,000,000
Operating income	1,200,000	1,045,000	945,000
Average assets	15,000,000	15,000,000	15,000,000

For the coming year, Ready's president plans to install a JIT purchasing and manufacturing system. She estimates that inventories will be reduced by 70 percent during the first year of operations, producing a 20 percent reduction in the average operating assets of the company, which would remain unchanged without the JIT system. She also estimates that sales and operating income will be restored to Year 1 levels because of simultaneous reductions in operating expenses and selling prices. Lower selling prices will allow Ready to expand its market share.

Required

1. Compute the ROI, margin, and turnover for Years 1, 2, and 3.
2. Suppose that in Year 4 the sales and operating income were achieved as expected but inventories remained at the same level as in Year 3. Compute the expected ROI, margin, and turnover. Explain why the ROI increased over the Year 3 level.
3. Suppose that the sales and operating income for Year 4 remained the same as in Year 3 but inventory reductions were achieved as projected. Compute the ROI, margin, and turnover. Explain why the ROI exceeded the Year 3 level.
4. Assume that all expectations for Year 4 were realized. Compute the expected ROI, margin, and turnover. Explain why the ROI increased over the Year 3 level.

10-25

Weighted Average Cost of Capital; EVA
LO4

Donegal, Inc., has decided to use EVA to evaluate its performance. Last year, Donegal had after-tax operating income of $350,000. Two sources of financing were used by the company: $3 million of mortgage bonds paying 6 percent interest and $9 million in common stock, which was considered to be relatively more risky than other stocks, and had a risk premium of 8 percent. The rate on long-term treasury bonds is 3 percent. Donegal, Inc., has $4,000,000 in operating assets and pays a marginal tax rate of 40 percent.

Required

1. Calculate the weighted average cost of capital for Donegal, Inc.
2. Calculate EVA for Donegal. Is Donegal creating wealth or not?

Now suppose that Donegal, Inc., is considering borrowing $2,000,000 in unsecured bonds at a rate of 9 percent. The money will be used to purchase additional operating assets of $1,000,000 (making total operating assets of $5,000,000). This added investment will enable the company to manufacture products that are budgeted to increase after-tax operating income by $80,000. (Total after-tax operating income will be $430,000.)

3. Calculate the new weighted average cost of capital for Donegal, Inc.
4. Calculate the EVA for Donegal, Inc., including the new products. Is the new investment a good idea?

10-26

Full Cost Plus Pricing and Negotiation
LO5

Technovia, Inc., has two divisions: Auxiliary Components and Audio Systems. Divisional managers are encouraged to maximize return on investment and EVA. Managers are essentially free to determine whether goods will be transferred internally and what internal transfer prices will be. Headquarters has directed that all internal prices be expressed on a full cost plus basis. The markup in the full-cost pricing arrangement, however, is left to the discretion of the divisional managers. Recently, the two divisional managers met to discuss a pricing agreement for a subwoofer that would be sold with a personal computer system. Production of the subwoofers is at capacity. Subwoofers can be sold for $31 to outside customers. The Audio Systems Division can also buy the subwoofer from external sources for the same price; however, the manager of this division is hoping to obtain a price concession by buying internally. The full cost of manufacturing the subwoofer is $20. If the manager of the Auxiliary Components Division sells the subwoofer internally, selling and distribution costs of $5 can be avoided. The volume of business would be 250,000 units per year, well within the capacity of the producing division.

After some discussion, the two managers agreed on a full cost plus pricing scheme that would be reviewed annually. Any increase in the outside selling price would be added to the transfer price by simply increasing the markup by an appropriate amount. Any major changes in the factors that led to the agreement could initiate a new round of negotiation; otherwise, the full cost plus arrangement would continue in force for subsequent years.

Required

1. Calculate the minimum and maximum transfer prices.
2. Assume that the transfer price agreed upon between the two managers is halfway between the minimum and maximum transfer prices. Calculate the full cost plus transfer price that would represent this transfer price.
3. Refer to Requirement 2. Assume that in the following year, the outside price of subwoofers increases to $32. What is the new full cost plus transfer price?
4. Assume that two years after the initial agreement, the market for subwoofers has softened considerably, causing excess capacity for the Auxiliary Components Division. Would you expect a renegotiation of the full cost plus pricing arrangement for the coming year? Explain.

10-27

Transfer Pricing with Idle Capacity
LO5

GreenWorld, Inc., is a nursery products firm. It has three divisions that grow and sell plants: the Western Division, the Southern Division, and the Canadian Division. Recently, the Southern Division of GreenWorld acquired a plastics factory that manufactures green plastic pots. These pots can be sold both externally and internally. Company policy permits each manager to decide whether to buy or sell internally. Each divisional manager is evaluated on the basis of return on investment and EVA.

The Western Division had bought its plastic pots in lots of 100 from a variety of vendors. The average price paid was $75 per box of 100 pots. However, the acquisition made Rosario Sanchez-Ruiz, manager of the Western Division, wonder whether a more favorable price could be arranged. She decided to approach Lorne Matthews, manager of the Southern Division, to see if he wanted to offer a better price for an internal transfer. She suggested a transfer of 3,500 boxes at $70 per box.

Lorne gathered the following information regarding the cost of a box of 100 pots:

Direct materials	$35
Direct labor	8
Variable overhead	10
Fixed overhead*	10
Total unit cost	$63
Selling price	$75
Production capacity	20,000 boxes

*Fixed overhead is based on $200,000/20,000 boxes.

Required

1. Suppose that the plastics factory is producing at capacity and can sell all that it produces to outside customers. How should Lorne respond to Rosario's request for a lower transfer price?
2. Now assume that the plastics factory is currently selling 16,000 boxes. What are the minimum and maximum transfer prices? Should Lorne consider the transfer at $70 per box?
3. Suppose that GreenWorld's policy is that all transfer prices be set at full cost plus 20 percent. Would the transfer take place? Why or why not?

10-28

Setting Transfer Prices—Market Price versus Full Cost
LO5

Lansing Electronics, Inc., manufactures a variety of printers, scanners, and fax machines in its two divisions: the PSF Division and the Components Division. The Components Division produces electronic components that can be used by the PSF Division. All the components this division produces can be sold to outside customers; however, from the beginning, nearly 90 percent of its output has been used internally. The current policy requires that all internal transfers of components be transferred at full cost.

Recently, Cam DeVonn, the chief executive officer of Lansing Electronics, decided to investigate the transfer pricing policy. He was concerned that the current method of pricing internal transfers might force decisions by divisional managers that would be suboptimal for the firm. As part of his inquiry, he gathered some information concerning Part Y34, used by the Receiver Division in its production of a basic scanner, Model SC67.

The PSF Division sells 40,000 units of Model SC67 each year at a unit price of $42. Given current market conditions, this is the maximum price that the division can charge for Model SC67. The cost of manufacturing the scanner follows:

Part Y34	$ 6.50
Direct materials	12.50
Direct labor	3.00
Variable overhead	1.00
Fixed overhead	15.00
Total unit cost	$38.00

The scanner is produced efficiently, and no further reduction in manufacturing costs is possible.

The manager of the Components Division indicated that she could sell 40,000 units (the division's capacity for this part) of Part Y34 to outside buyers at $12 per unit. The PSF Division could also buy the part for $12 from external suppliers. The Components Division manager supplied the following details on the manufacturing cost of the component:

Direct materials	$2.50
Direct labor	0.50
Variable overhead	1.00
Fixed overhead	2.50
Total unit cost	$6.50

Required

1. Compute the firmwide contribution margin associated with Part Y34 and Model SC67. Also, compute the contribution margin earned by each division.
2. Suppose that Cam DeVonn abolishes the current transfer pricing policy and gives divisions autonomy in setting transfer prices. Can you predict what transfer price the manager of the Components Division will set? What should the minimum transfer price for this part be? The maximum transfer price?
3. Given the new transfer pricing policy, predict how this will affect the production decision for Model SC67. How many units of Part Y34 will the manager of the PSF Division purchase, either internally or externally?
4. Given the new transfer price set by the Components Division and your answer to Requirement 3, how many units of Part Y34 will be sold externally?
5. Given your answers to Requirements 3 and 4, compute the firmwide contribution margin. What has happened? Was Cam's decision to grant additional decentralization good or bad? Why?

10-29

Variable Costing; Targeted Income
LO2

CMA

Madengrad Company manufactures a single electronic product called Precisionmix. This unit is a batch-density monitoring device attached to large industrial mixing machines used in flour, rubber, petroleum, and chemical manufacturing. Precisionmix sells for $900 per unit. The following variable costs are incurred to produce each Precisionmix device:

Direct materials	$240
Direct labor	180
Variable overhead	105
Variable product cost	$525
Selling expense	75
Total variable cost	$600

Madengrad's annual fixed costs are $6,600,000. Except for an operating loss incurred in the year of incorporation, the firm has been profitable over the last five years. Madengrad is forecasting sales of 21,500 units for next year and has budgeted production at that level.

Required

1. Prepare a pro forma variable-costing income statement for Madengrad Company for next year.
2. Madengrad has just learned of a significant change in production technology that will cause a 10 percent increase in total annual fixed costs and a 20 percent unit labor cost increase as a result of higher-skilled direct labor. However, this change permits the replacement of a costly imported component with a domestic component. The effect is to reduce unit materials costs and variable overhead costs by 25 percent. No change in selling price is forecast. Prepare a variable-costing income statement for Madengrad Company for next year assuming it invests in the new production technology. **(CMA adapted)**

10-30

Types of Responsibility Centers
LO1

Consider each of the following scenarios.

A. Terrin Belson, plant manager for the laser printer factory of Compugear, Inc., brushed his hair back and sighed. December had been a bad month; two machines had broken down, and some direct laborers (all on salary) were idled for part of the month. Materials prices increased, and insurance premiums on the factory increased. No way out of it—costs were going up. He hoped that the marketing VP would be able to push through some price increases, but that really wasn't his department.
B. Joanna Pauly was delighted to see that her ROI figures had increased for the third straight year. She was sure that her campaign to lower costs and use machinery more efficiently (enabling her factories to sell several older machines) was the reason. Joanna planned to take full credit for the improvements at her semiannual performance review.
C. Gil Rodriguez, sales manager for CompuGear, was not pleased with a memo from headquarters detailing the recent cost increases for the laser printer line. Headquarters suggested raising prices. "Great," thought Gil, "An increase in price will kill sales—and revenue will go down. Why can't the plant shape up and cut costs like every other company in America is doing? Why turn this into my problem?"
D. Susan Whitehorse looked at the quarterly profit/loss statement with disgust. Revenue was down and cost was up—what a combination! Then, she had an idea. If she cut back on maintenance of equipment and let a product engineer go, expenses would decrease—perhaps enough to reverse the trend in operating income.

E. Shonna Abbakian had just been hired to improve the fortunes of the Southern Division of ABC, Inc. She met with top staff and hammered out a three-year plan to improve the situation. A centerpiece of the plan is the retiring of obsolete equipment and the purchasing of state-of-the-art, computer-assisted machinery. The new machinery would take time for the workers to learn to use, but once that was done, waste would be virtually eliminated.

Required

For each of the above independent scenarios, indicate the type of responsibility center involved (cost, revenue, profit, or investment) and the accounting numbers on which performance evaluation is likely based.

Managerial Decision Cases

10-31

Performance Evaluation; Absorption Costing Compared with Variable Costing LO1, LO2

Kathy Wise is manager of a new medical supplies division. She has just finished her second year and had been visiting with the company's vice-president of operations. In the first year, the operating income for the division had shown a substantial increase over the prior year. Her second year saw an even greater increase. The vice-president was extremely pleased and promised Kathy a $15,000 bonus if the division showed a similar increase in profit for the upcoming year. Kathy was elated. She was completely confident that the goal could be met. Sales contracts were already well ahead of last year's performance, and she knew that there would be no increases in costs. At the end of the third year, Kathy received the following data regarding operations for the first three years:

	Year 1	Year 2	Year 3
Production	10,000	11,000	9,000
Sales (in units)	8,000	10,000	12,000
Unit selling price	$ 10	$ 10	$ 10
Unit costs:			
Fixed overhead*	$ 2.90	$ 3.00	$ 3.00
Variable overhead	1.00	1.00	1.00
Direct materials	1.90	2.00	2.00
Direct labor	1.00	1.00	1.00
Variable selling	0.40	0.50	0.50
Actual fixed overhead	$29,000	$30,000	$30,000
Other fixed costs	$ 9,000	$10,000	$10,000

*The predetermined fixed overhead rate is based on expected actual units of production and expected fixed overhead. Expected production each year was 10,000 units. Any under- or overapplied fixed overhead is closed to Cost of Goods Sold.

Yearly Income Statements

	Year 1	Year 2	Year 3
Sales revenue	$80,000	$100,000	$120,000
Less: Cost of goods sold*	54,400	67,000	86,600
Gross margin	$25,600	$ 33,000	$ 33,400
Less: Selling and administrative	12,200	15,000	16,000
Operating income	$13,400	$ 18,000	$ 17,400

*Assumes a LIFO inventory flow.

Recall that Kathy was pleased with the operating data, but she was dismayed and perplexed by the income statements. Instead of seeing a significant increase in income for the third year, she saw a small decrease. Kathy's initial reaction was that the Accounting Department had made an error.

Required

1. Explain to Kathy why she lost her $15,000 bonus.
2. Prepare variable-costing income statements for each of the three years. Reconcile the differences between the absorption-costing and variable-costing incomes.
3. If you were the vice president of Kathy's company, which income statement (variable costing or absorption costing) would you prefer to use for evaluating Kathy's performance? Why?

10-32

Transfer Pricing
LO5

CMA

PortCo Products is a divisionalized furniture manufacturer. The divisions are autonomous segments, with each being responsible for its own sales, costs of operations, working capital management, and equipment acquisition. Each division serves a different market in the furniture industry. Because the markets and products of the divisions are so different, there have never been any transfers between divisions.

The Commercial Division manufactures equipment and furniture that is purchased by the restaurant industry. The division plans to introduce a new line of counter and chair units that feature a cushioned seat for the counter chairs. John Kline, the divisional manager, has discussed the manufacture of the cushioned seat with Russ Fiegel of the Office Division. They both believe a cushioned seat currently made by the Office Division for use on its deluxe office stool could be modified for use on the new counter chair. Consequently, John has asked Russ for a price for 100 unit lots of the cushioned seat. The following conversation took place about the price to be charged for the cushioned seats.

Russ: John, we can make the necessary modifications to the cushioned seat easily. The materials used in your seat are slightly different and should cost about 10 percent more than those used in our deluxe office stool. However, the labor time (0.5 DLH) should be the same because the seat fabrication operation basically is the same. I would price the seat at our regular rate—full cost plus 30 percent markup.

John: That's higher than I expected, Russ. I was thinking that a good price would be your variable manufacturing costs. After all, your capacity costs will be incurred regardless of this job.

Russ: John, I'm at capacity. By making the cushion seats for you, I'll have to cut my production of deluxe office stools. Of course, I can increase my production of economy office stools. The labor time freed by not having to fabricate the frame or assemble the deluxe stool can be shifted to the frame fabrication and assembly of the economy office stool. Fortunately, I can switch my labor force between these two models of stools without any loss of efficiency. As you know, overtime is not a feasible alternative in our community. I'd like to sell it to you at variable cost, but I have excess demand for both products. I don't mind changing my product mix to the economy model if I get a good return on the seats I make for you. Here are my standard costs for the two stools and a schedule of my manufacturing overhead.

Office Division
Standard Costs and Prices

	Deluxe Office Stool	Economy Office Stool
Materials, framing	$ 8.15	$ 9.76
Cushioned seat, padding	2.40	—
Vinyl	4.00	—

(continued)

	Deluxe Office Stool	Economy Office Stool
Molded seat (purchased)	—	6.00
Direct labor:		
1.5 DLH @ $7.50	11.25	
0.8 DLH @ $7.50		6.00
Manufacturing overhead:		
1.5 DLH @ $12.80	19.20	
0.8 DLH @ $12.80		10.24
Total standard cost	$45.00	$32.00
Selling price (30% markup)	$58.50	$41.60

Office Division
Manufacturing Overhead Budget

Overhead Item	Nature	Amount
Supplies	Variable—at current market prices	$ 420,000
Indirect labor	Variable	375,000
Supervision	Nonvariable	250,000
Power	Use varies with activity; rates are fixed	180,000
Heat and light	Nonvariable—light is fixed regardless of production while heat/air conditioning varies with fuel charges	140,000
Property taxes and insurance	Nonvariable—any change in amounts/rates is independent of production	200,000
Depreciation	Fixed dollar total	1,700,000
Employee benefits	20% of supervision, direct and indirect labor	575,000
Total overhead		$3,840,000
Capacity in DLH		300,000
Overhead rate/DLH		$ 12.80

John: I guess I see your point, Russ, but I don't want to price myself out of the market. Maybe we should talk to corporate management to see if it can give us any guidance.

Required

1. John Kline and Russ Fiegel did ask PortCo's corporate management for guidance on an appropriate transfer price. Corporate management suggested that they consider using a transfer price based upon variable manufacturing cost plus opportunity cost. Calculate a transfer price for the cushioned seat based upon variable manufacturing cost plus opportunity cost.
2. Which alternative transfer pricing system—full cost, variable manufacturing cost, or variable manufacturing cost plus opportunity cost—would be best as the underlying concept for an intracompany transfer pricing policy? Explain your answer. **(CMA adapted)**

10-33

Ethical Issues; Absorption Costing; Performance Measurement
LO1, LO2

Ruth Swazey, divisional controller and CMA, was upset by a recent memo she received from the divisional manager, Paul Chesser. Ruth was scheduled to present the division's financial performance at headquarters in one week. In the memo, Paul had given Ruth some instructions for this upcoming report. In particular, she had been told to emphasize the significant improvement in the division's profits over last year. Ruth, however, didn't believe that there was any real underlying improvement in the division's performance and was reluctant to say otherwise. She knew that the increase in profits was because of Paul's conscious decision to produce for inventory.

In an earlier meeting, Paul had convinced his plant managers to produce more than they knew they could sell. He argued that by deferring some of this period's fixed costs, reported profits would jump. He pointed out two significant benefits. First, by increasing profits, the division could exceed the minimum level needed so that all the managers would qualify for the annual bonus. Second, by meeting the budgeted profit level, the division would be better able to compete for much-needed capital. Ruth had objected but had been overruled. The most persuasive counterargument was that the increase in inventory could be liquidated in the coming year as the economy improved. Ruth, however, considered this event unlikely. From past experience, she knew that it would take at least two years of improved market demand before the productive capacity of the division was exceeded.

Required

1. Discuss the behavior of Paul Chesser, the divisional manager. Was the decision to produce for inventory an ethical one?
2. What should Ruth Swazey do? Should she comply with the directive to emphasize the increase in profits? If not, what options does she have?
3. In Chapter 1, ethical standards for management accountants were listed. Identify any standards that apply in this situation.

10-34

ROI and EVA; Ethical Considerations LO3

Jason Kemp was torn between conflicting emotions. On the one hand, things were going very well. He had just completed six months as the assistant financial manager in the Electronics Division of Med-Products, Inc. The pay was good, he enjoyed his coworkers, and he felt that he was part of a team that was making a difference in American health care. On the other hand, his latest assignment was causing some sleepless nights. Mel Cravens, his boss, had asked him to "refine" the figures on the division's latest project—a portable imaging device code-named ZM. The original estimates called for investment of $15.6 million and projected annual operating income of $1.87 million. Med-Products required an ROI of at least 15 percent for new project approval; so far, ZM's rate of return was nowhere near that hurdle rate. Mel encouraged him to show increased sales and decreased expenses in order to get the projected operating income above $2.34 million. Jason asked for a meeting with Mel to voice his concerns.

Jason: Mel, I've gone over the figures for the new project and can't find any way to get the operating income above $1.9 million. The sales people have given me the most likely revenue figures, and production feels that the expense figures are solid.

Mel: Jason, those figures are just projections. Sales doesn't really know what the revenue will be. In fact, when I talked with Sue Harris, our sales vice president, she said that sales could range from $1.5 million to $2.5 million. Use the higher figure. I'm sure this product will justify our confidence in it!

Jason: I know the range of sales was that broad, but Sue felt that the $2.5 million estimate was pretty unlikely. She thought that during the first five years or so the ZM sales would stay in the lower end of the range.

Mel: Again, Sue doesn't know for sure. She's just estimating. Let's go with the higher estimate. We really need this product to expand our line and to give our division a chance to qualify for sales-based bonuses. If ZM sells at all, our revenue will go up and we'll all share in the bonus pool!

Jason: I don't know, Mel. I feel pretty bad signing off on ROI projections that I have so little confidence in.

Mel: (frustrated) Look, Jason, just prepare the report. I'll back you up.

Required

1. What is the ROI of project ZM based on the initial estimates? What would ROI be if the operating income rose to $2.34 million?
2. Do you agree that Jason has an ethical dilemma? Explain. Is there any way that Mel could ethically justify raising the sales estimates and/or lowering expense estimates?
3. What do you think Jason should do? Explain.

Research Assignment

10-35

Research Assignment
LO4

Every year, *Fortune* and *Business Week* review current trends in executive compensation. Research this issue in the library, using these two magazines as a starting point, and write a three- to five-page paper on executive compensation. Be sure to give specific examples of the ways in which companies reward executives and the ways in which compensation is tied to performance.

10-36

Cybercase
LO1, LO2, LO3

Choose one or more of the following companies and access their websites in the chapter web links at the Interactive Study Center on http://www.thomsonedu.com/accounting/hansen.

- **General Mills**
- **PepsiCo**
- **United Airlines**
- **John Deere**
- **Wyeth**

Identify the types of segments for which it would be useful for the company to have income information. Now, check the company's annual report. Is the income statement reported by segment? Do the segments match your earlier identification? Why or why not? Next, check the format of the income statement given in the annual report. Is it an absorption- or variable-costing income statement?

© Getty Images

PART 5

Managerial Decision Making

chapter 11

Cost-Volume-Profit Analysis: A Managerial Planning Tool

learning objectives

After studying this chapter, you should be able to:

1. Determine the number of units that must be sold to break even or to earn a targeted profit.
2. Calculate the amount of revenue required to break even or to earn a targeted profit.
3. Apply cost-volume-profit analysis in a multiple-product setting.
4. Prepare a profit-volume graph and a cost-volume-profit graph, and explain the meaning of each.
5. Explain the impact of risk, uncertainty, and changing variables on cost-volume-profit analysis.
6. Discuss the impact of activity-based costing on cost-volume-profit analysis.

Scenario

For years, Janet McFarland's friends and family raved about her homemade jellies and salsas. Janet traditionally canned several gallons of salsa, ladled it into decorative pint jars, wrapped them, and sent them as gifts. Her friends said, "You ought to sell this stuff—you'd make a fortune!" So, Janet decided to give it a try.

First, she decided to concentrate on one product, a green cactus salsa that had gotten rave reviews. She scouted sources of jars, lids, and labels. In addition, Janet got in touch with her local agricultural extension office and learned a considerable amount about laws regulating food sales. One source of surprise was that she was required to obtain an expert confirmation of the ingredients in her salsa. Usually, Janet added a little of this and a little of that until it tasted right. She found out that this casual approach would not work. Foods were required to be labeled with the name of each ingredient in order of amount. Suddenly, it mattered whether ancho or poblano chilis were used and in what proportion. Janet needed a standardized recipe. She located a professional food chemist to analyze the recipe and certify the proportion of ingredients.

Janet traveled to a number of grocery stores and gift shops in the area. Several were willing to stock her product on consignment, placing a few jars by the cash register; others guaranteed shelf space but required a shelf charge for it. She figured that traveling to the stores, checking on sales and stock, and visiting prospective customers would take about one day a week. Before starting production, Janet consulted with her family accountant, Bob Ryan.

Janet outlined her business plan. Since her product was new on the market, she thought a price of $4.50 would be reasonable. Bob took the proposed price and the costs she had estimated, and did some quick break-even analysis. Then he looked up and gave Janet the bad news; at a price of $4.50 per jar, she would lose money. Even worse, increasing the quantity sold would just make the loss larger. As a friend and business advisor, Bob decided to help Janet reconsider her proposed methods of making the salsa, to see if the variable costs could be reduced. If she could not find a way to get her variable costs below price, her business could never succeed.

Questions to Think About

1. What kinds of variable and fixed costs do you think Janet will incur?
2. Given Bob's initial assessment that the variable costs are higher than the price, what is wrong with Janet's thought that selling more is the way to go?
3. How important is break-even analysis to a firm? Do you suppose that large companies do break-even analysis as well as small companies?
4. Why is the concept of breaking even important? Doesn't Janet want to make a profit?
5. Janet doesn't know what price to charge. How could she get a better idea?

Cost-volume-profit analysis (CVP analysis) is a powerful tool for planning and decision making. Because CVP analysis emphasizes the interrelationships of costs, quantity sold, and price, it brings together all of the financial information of the firm. CVP analysis can be a valuable tool to identify the extent and magnitude of the economic trouble a division is facing and to help pinpoint the necessary solution. For example, **Microsoft**'s Xbox 360 was sold for a retail price of $399 during its late-2005 debut. However, that price did not allow a profit. In fact, Microsoft lost about $126 per unit. Didn't they know that? Yes, it was a deliberate business strategy to sell the console at a loss, but to make a profit on the software—the games.[1]

CVP analysis can address many other issues as well, such as the number of units that must be sold to break even, the impact of a given reduction in fixed costs on the break-even point, and the impact of an increase in price on profit. Additionally, CVP analysis allows managers to do sensitivity analysis by examining the impact of various price or cost levels on profit.

While this chapter deals with the mechanics and terminology of CVP analysis, you should keep in mind that CVP analysis is an integral part of financial planning and decision making. Every accountant and manager should be thoroughly conversant with its concepts, not just the mechanics.

Break-Even Point in Units

Objective 1

Determine the number of units that must be sold to break even or to earn a targeted profit.

Since we are interested in how revenues, expenses, and profits behave as volume changes, it is natural to begin by finding the firm's break-even point in units sold. The **break-even point** is the point where total revenue equals total cost, the point of zero profit. To find the break-even point in units, we focus on operating income. We will first discuss the way to find the break-even point and then see how our approach can be expanded to determine the number of units that must be sold to earn a targeted profit.

The firm's initial decision in implementing a units-sold approach to CVP analysis is the determination of just what a unit is. For manufacturing firms, the answer is obvious. **Procter & Gamble** may define a unit as a bar of Ivory soap; Janet McFarland (from the opening scenario) would define a unit as a jar of salsa. Service firms face a more difficult choice. **Southwest Air Lines** may define a unit as a passenger mile or as a one-way trip.

A second decision centers on the separation of costs into fixed and variable components. CVP analysis focuses on the factors that effect a change in the components of profit. Because we are looking at CVP analysis in terms of units sold, we need to determine the fixed and variable components of cost and revenue with respect to units. (This assumption will be relaxed when we incorporate activity-based costing into CVP analysis.) It is important to realize that we are focusing on the firm as a whole. Therefore, the costs we are talking about are all costs of the company—manufacturing, marketing, and administrative. Thus, when we say variable cost, we mean all costs that increase as more units are sold, including direct materials, direct labor, variable overhead, and variable selling and administrative costs. Similarly, fixed cost includes fixed overhead and fixed selling and administrative expenses.

Using Operating Income in CVP Analysis

The income statement is a useful tool for organizing the firm's costs into fixed and variable categories. The income statement can be expressed as a narrative equation:

$$\text{Operating income} = \text{Sales revenues} - \text{Variable expenses} - \text{Fixed expenses}$$

1 Arik Hesseldahl, "Microsoft's Red-Ink Game," *Business Week Online* (November 22, 2005), http://businessweek.com/technology/content/nov2005/tc20051122_410710.htm, accessed March 31, 2006.

Managers Decide

CVP Analysis Important to Ford

CVP analysis can be a valuable tool to identify the extent and magnitude of the economic trouble a company is facing and to help pinpoint the necessary solution. Ford Motor Company's North American automobile business had been profitable in 2003 and 2004. But the next two years saw increasing materials and energy costs and plunging market share. The division was well below the break-even point. To reverse the slide, Ford announced a restructuring plan that would make extensive cuts in both variable and fixed costs. For example, North American manufacturing capacity is to be reduced by 26 percent (1.2 million vehicles); 14 manufacturing plants are to be closed and up to 30,000 employees laid off; and reductions are to be made in the number of salaried employees and corporate officials. On the revenue side, the company plans to adjust its sales mix by increasing the number of hybrid gas-electric vehicles. These hybrids, with their higher prices, will include the Ford Five Hundred, Mercury Montego, Ford Edge, and Lincoln MKX. If the plan works as expected, Ford's North American operations are expected to return to profitability by 2008. ■

Sources: Bill Vlasic, "Ford to Shut Wixom and 13 Other Plants," *Detroit News* (January 23, 2006), http://www.detnews.com/apps/pbcs.dll/article?AID=/20060123/AUTO01/601230407; "Ford Statement on Restructuring," *Detroit News* (January 23, 2006), http://www.detnews.com/apps/pbcs.dll/article?AID=/20060123/AUTO01/601230419, accessed March 31, 2006.

Note that we are using the term *operating income* to denote income or profit before income taxes. **Operating income** includes only revenues and expenses from the firm's normal operations. **Net income** is operating income minus income taxes.

Once we have a measure of units sold, we can expand the operating-income equation by expressing sales revenues and variable expenses in terms of unit dollar amounts and number of units. Specifically, sales revenue is expressed as the unit selling price times the number of units sold, and total variable costs are the unit variable cost times the number of units sold. With these expressions, the operating-income equation becomes:

$$\text{Operating income} = (\text{Price} \times \text{Number of units sold}) - (\text{Variable cost per unit} \times \text{Number of units sold}) - \text{Total fixed cost}$$

Suppose you were asked how many units must be sold in order to break even, or earn a zero profit. You could answer that question by setting operating income to zero and then solving the operating-income equation for the number of units.

Let's use the following example to solve for the break-even point in units. Assume that Whittier Company manufactures a mulching lawn mower. For the coming year, the controller has prepared the following projected income statement:

Sales (1,000 units @ $400)	$400,000
Less: Variable expenses	325,000
Contribution margin	$ 75,000
Less: Fixed expenses	45,000
Operating income	$ 30,000

We see that for Whittier Company, the price is $400 each, and the variable cost per unit is $325 ($325,000/1,000 units). Fixed cost is $45,000. At the break-even point, then, the operating-income equation would take the following form:

$$
\begin{aligned}
0 &= (\$400 \times \text{Units}) - (\$325 \times \text{Units}) - \$45{,}000 \\
0 &= (\$75 \times \text{Units}) - \$45{,}000 \\
\$75 \times \text{Units} &= \$45{,}000 \\
\text{Units} &= 600
\end{aligned}
$$

Therefore, Whittier must sell 600 lawn mowers to just cover all fixed and variable expenses. A good way to check this answer is to formulate an income statement based on 600 units sold.

Sales (600 units @ $400)	$240,000
Less: Variable expenses	195,000
Contribution margin	$ 45,000
Less: Fixed expenses	45,000
Operating income	$ 0

Indeed, selling 600 units does yield a zero profit.

An important advantage of the operating-income approach is that all further CVP equations are derived from the variable-costing income statement. As a result, you can solve any CVP problem by using this approach.

Shortcut to Calculating Break-Even Units

Apple understands the importance of contribution margin in setting prices for its iTunes unit. While iTunes does not contribute much to profit, it does cover expenses and allows Apple to focus on the iPod.

© PR Newswire APPLE COMPUTER, INC.

We can more quickly calculate break-even units by focusing on the contribution margin. The **contribution margin** is sales revenue minus total variable cost. At breakeven, the contribution margin equals the fixed expenses. For example, **Apple**'s iTunes charges $0.99 to download a song. Its variable costs, including payments to the record companies and others, total approximately $0.95. This means that iTunes earns a contribution margin of $0.04 for every song purchased and downloaded. The low contribution margin per unit, which must cover all fixed costs, means that iTunes is virtually a break-even business.[2]

If we substitute the unit contribution margin for price minus unit variable cost in the operating-income equation and solve for the number of units, we obtain the following fundamental break-even equation:

$$\text{Number of units} = \text{Fixed cost}/\text{Unit contribution margin}$$

Using Whittier Company as an example, we can see that the contribution margin per unit can be computed in one of two ways. One way is to divide the total contribution margin by the units sold for a result of $75 per unit ($75,000/1,000). A second way is to compute price minus variable cost per unit. Doing so yields the same result, $75 per unit ($400 − $325). To calculate the break-even number of units for Whittier Company, use the fundamental break-even equation as follows:

$$
\begin{aligned}
\text{Number of units} &= \$45{,}000/(\$400 - \$325) \\
&= \$45{,}000/\$75 \\
&= 600
\end{aligned}
$$

Of course, the answer is identical to that computed using the income statement.

2 Roger O. Crockett, "Major Hangups Over the iPod Phone," *Business Week Online* (March 24, 2005), http://yahoo.businessweek.com/technology/content/mar2005/tc20050324_7462_tc024.htm, accessed March 31, 2006.

Unit Sales Needed to Achieve Targeted Profit

While the break-even point is useful information, most firms would like to earn operating income greater than zero. CVP analysis gives us a way to determine how many units must be sold to earn a particular targeted income. Targeted operating income can be expressed as a dollar amount (for example, $20,000) or as a percentage of sales revenue (for example, 15 percent of revenue). Both the operating-income approach and the contribution margin approach can be easily adjusted to allow for targeted income.

Targeted Income as a Dollar Amount Assume that Whittier Company wants to earn operating income of $60,000. How many mulching lawn mowers must be sold to achieve this result? Let's use the income statement to find out:

$$\begin{aligned} \$60{,}000 &= (\$400 \times \text{Units}) - (\$325 \times \text{Units}) - \$45{,}000 \\ \$105{,}000 &= \$75 \times \text{Units} \\ \text{Units} &= 1{,}400 \end{aligned}$$

If, instead, we use the fundamental break-even equation, we simply add targeted profit of $60,000 to the fixed cost and solve for the number of units:

$$\begin{aligned} \text{Units} &= (\$45{,}000 + \$60{,}000)/(\$400 - \$325) \\ \text{Units} &= \$105{,}000/\$75 \\ \text{Units} &= 1{,}400 \end{aligned}$$

Whittier must sell 1,400 lawn mowers to earn a before-tax profit of $60,000. The following income statement verifies this outcome:

Sales (1,400 units @ $400)	$560,000
Less: Variable expenses	455,000
Contribution margin	$105,000
Less: Fixed expenses	45,000
Operating income	$ 60,000

Another way to check this number of units is to use the break-even point. As just shown, Whittier must sell 1,400 lawn mowers, or 800 more than the break-even volume of 600 units, to earn a profit of $60,000. The contribution margin per lawn mower is $75. Multiplying $75 by the 800 lawn mowers above breakeven produces the profit of $60,000 ($75 × 800). This outcome demonstrates that contribution margin per unit for each unit above breakeven is equivalent to profit per unit. Since the break-even point had already been computed, the number of lawn mowers to be sold to yield a $60,000 operating income could have been calculated by dividing the unit contribution margin into the target profit and adding the resulting amount to the break-even volume.

In general, assuming that fixed costs remain the same, the impact on a firm's profits resulting from a change in the number of units sold can be assessed by multiplying the unit contribution margin by the change in units sold. For example, if 1,500 lawn mowers instead of 1,400 are sold, how much more profit will be earned? The change in units sold is an increase of 100 lawn mowers, and the unit contribution margin is $75. Thus, profits will increase by $7,500 ($75 × 100).

Targeted Income as a Percent of Sales Revenue Assume that Whittier Company wants to know the number of lawn mowers that must be sold in order to earn a profit equal to 15 percent of sales revenue. Sales revenue is price multiplied by the quantity sold. Thus, the targeted operating income is 15 percent of price times quantity. Using the income statement (which is simpler in this case), we have the following:

$$
\begin{aligned}
0.15(\$400)(\text{Units}) &= (\$400 \times \text{Units}) - (\$325 \times \text{Units}) - \$45{,}000 \\
\$60 \times \text{Units} &= (\$400 \times \text{Units}) - (\$325 \times \text{Units}) - \$45{,}000 \\
\$60 \times \text{Units} &= (\$75 \times \text{Units}) - \$45{,}000 \\
\$15 \times \text{Units} &= \$45{,}000 \\
\text{Units} &= 3{,}000
\end{aligned}
$$

Does a volume of 3,000 lawn mowers achieve a profit equal to 15 percent of sales revenue? For 3,000 lawn mowers, the total revenue is $1.2 million ($400 × 3,000). The profit can be computed without preparing a formal income statement. Remember that above breakeven, the contribution margin per unit is the profit per unit. The break-even volume is 600 lawn mowers. If 3,000 lawn mowers are sold, then 2,400 (3,000 − 600) lawn mowers above the break-even point are sold. The before-tax profit, therefore, is $180,000 ($75 × 2,400), which is 15 percent of sales ($180,000/$1,200,000).

After-Tax Profit Targets When calculating the break-even point, income taxes play no role. This is because the taxes paid on zero income are zero. However, when the company needs to know how many units to sell to earn a particular net income, some additional consideration is needed. Recall that net income is operating income after income taxes and that our targeted income figure was expressed in before-tax terms. As a result, when the income target is expressed as net income, we must add back the income taxes to get operating income.

In general, income taxes are computed as a percentage of income. The after-tax profit is computed by subtracting the tax from the operating income (or before-tax profit).

$$
\begin{aligned}
\text{Net income} &= \text{Operating income} - \text{Income taxes} \\
&= \text{Operating income} - (\text{Tax rate} \times \text{Operating income}) \\
&= \text{Operating income } (1 - \text{Tax rate})
\end{aligned}
$$

or

$$\text{Operating income} = \text{Net income}/(1 - \text{Tax rate})$$

Thus, to convert the after-tax profit to before-tax profit, simply divide the after-tax profit by (1 × Tax rate).

Suppose that Whittier Company wants to achieve net income of $48,750 and its tax rate is 35 percent. To convert the after-tax profit target into a before-tax profit target, complete the following steps:

$$
\begin{aligned}
\$48{,}750 &= \text{Operating income} - (0.35 \times \text{Operating income}) \\
\$48{,}750 &= 0.65\ (\text{Operating income}) \\
\$75{,}000 &= \text{Operating income}
\end{aligned}
$$

In other words, with an income tax rate of 35 percent, Whittier Company must earn $75,000 before income taxes to have $48,750 after income taxes.[3] With this conversion, we can now calculate the number of units that must be sold:

$$
\begin{aligned}
\text{Units} &= (\$45{,}000 + \$75{,}000)/\$75 \\
\text{Units} &= \$120{,}000/\$75 \\
\text{Units} &= 1{,}600
\end{aligned}
$$

Let's check this answer by preparing an income statement based on sales of 1,600 lawn mowers.

Sales (1,600 @ $400)	$640,000
Less: Variable expenses	520,000
Contribution margin	$120,000
Less: Fixed costs	45,000
Operating income	$ 75,000
Less: Income taxes (35% tax rate)	26,250
Net income	$ 48,750

3 To practice the after-tax to before-tax conversion, calculate how much before-tax income Whittier would need to have $48,750 after-tax income if the tax rate were 40 percent. [Answer: $81,250]

Break-Even Point in Sales Dollars

Objective 2

Calculate the amount of revenue required to break even or to earn a targeted profit.

In some cases when using CVP analysis, managers may prefer to use sales revenues as the measure of sales activity instead of units sold. A units-sold measure can be converted to a sales revenue measure simply by multiplying the unit selling price by the units sold. For example, the break-even point for Whittier Company was computed at 600 mulching lawn mowers. Since the selling price for each lawn mower is \$400, the break-even volume in sales revenue is \$240,000 (\$400 × 600).

Any answer expressed in units sold can be easily converted to one expressed in sales revenues, but the answer can be computed more directly by developing a separate formula for the sales revenue case. In this case, the important variable is sales dollars, so both the revenue and the variable costs must be expressed in dollars instead of units. Since sales revenue is always expressed in dollars, measuring that variable is no problem. Let's look more closely at variable costs and see how they can be expressed in terms of sales dollars.

© Getty Images/PhotoDisc

The manufacturer of this riding mower had both variable and fixed costs. These had to be considered in determining the number of units to produce and the price to charge.

To calculate the break-even point in sales dollars, variable costs are defined as a percentage of sales rather than as an amount per unit sold. For example, suppose that price is \$10, and variable cost is \$6. Of course, the remainder is contribution margin of \$4 (\$10 − \$6). If 10 units are sold, total variable costs are \$60 (\$6 × 10 units). Alternatively, since each unit sold earns \$10 of revenue and has \$6 of variable cost, we could say that 60 percent of each dollar of revenue earned is attributable to variable cost (\$6/\$10). Thus, focusing on sales revenue, we would expect total variable costs of \$60 for revenues of \$100 (0.60 × \$100).

The **variable cost ratio** (in this example, 60 percent) is the proportion of each sales dollar that must be used to cover variable costs. The variable cost ratio can be computed by using either total data or unit data. Of course, the percentage of sales dollars remaining after variable costs are covered is the contribution margin ratio. The **contribution margin ratio** is the proportion of each sales dollar available to cover fixed costs and provide for profit. So if the variable cost ratio is 60 percent of sales, then the contribution margin ratio must be the remaining 40 percent of sales. It makes sense that the complement of the variable cost ratio is the contribution margin ratio. After all, the proportion of the sales dollar left after variable costs are covered should be the contribution margin component.

Just as the variable cost ratio can be computed using total or unit figures, the contribution margin ratio, forty percent in our exhibit, can also be computed in these two ways. That is, one can divide the total contribution margin by total sales (\$40/\$100), or one can use the unit contribution margin divided by price (\$4/\$10). Naturally, if the variable cost ratio is known, it can be subtracted from 1 to yield the contribution margin ratio (1 − 0.60 = 0.40).

Where do fixed costs fit into this? Since the contribution margin is revenue remaining after variable costs are covered, it must be the revenue available to cover fixed costs and contribute to profit. There are three possibilities: fixed cost can equal contribution margin; fixed cost can be less than contribution margin; or fixed cost can be greater than contribution margin. If fixed cost equals contribution margin, then operating income, or profit, is zero and the company is at breakeven. If fixed cost is less than contribution margin, the company earns a profit (or positive operating income). Finally, if fixed cost is greater than contribution margin, the company faces an operating loss.

Now let's turn to a couple of examples based on Whittier Company to illustrate the sales-revenue approach. Restated below is Whittier Company's variable-costing income statement for 1,000 lawn mowers.

	Dollars	Percent of Sales
Sales	$400,000	100.00%
Less: Variable costs	325,000	81.25
Contribution margin	$ 75,000	18.75%
Less: Fixed costs	45,000	
Operating income	$ 30,000	

Notice that sales revenue, variable costs, and contribution margin have been expressed as a percent of sales. The variable cost ratio is 0.8125 ($325,000/$400,000); the contribution margin ratio is 0.1875 (computed either as 1 − 0.8125 or as $75,000/$400,000). Fixed costs are $45,000. Given the information in this income statement, how much sales revenue must Whittier earn to break even?

$$\begin{aligned}\text{Operating income} &= \text{Sales} - \text{Variable costs} - \text{Fixed costs}\\ 0 &= \text{Sales} - (\text{Variable cost ratio} \times \text{Sales}) - \text{Fixed costs}\\ 0 &= \text{Sales}\ (1 - \text{Variable cost ratio}) - \text{Fixed costs}\\ 0 &= \text{Sales}\ (1 - 0.8125) - \$45{,}000\\ \text{Sales}\ (0.1875) &= \$45{,}000\\ \text{Sales} &= \$240{,}000\end{aligned}$$

Thus, Whittier must earn revenues totaling $240,000 in order to break even. (You might want to check this answer by preparing an income statement based on revenue of $240,000 and verifying that it yields zero profit.) Note that (1 − 0.8125) is the contribution margin ratio. We can skip a couple of steps by recognizing that *Sales − (Variable cost ratio × Sales)* is equal to *Sales × Contribution margin ratio.*

What about the fundamental break-even equation used to determine the break-even point in units? We can use that approach here as well. Recall that the formula for the break-even point in units is:

$$\text{Break-even units} = \text{Fixed cost}/(\text{Price} - \text{Unit variable cost})$$

If we multiply both sides of this equation by price, the left-hand side will equal sales revenue at breakeven:

$$\begin{aligned}\text{Break-even units} \times \text{Price} &= \text{Price} \times [\text{Fixed cost}/(\text{Price} - \text{Unit variable cost})]\\ \text{Break-even sales} &= \text{Fixed cost} \times [(\text{Price}/(\text{Price} - \text{Unit variable cost})]\\ \text{Break-even sales} &= \text{Fixed cost} \times (\text{Price}/\text{Contribution margin})\\ \text{Break-even sales} &= \text{Fixed cost}/\text{Contribution margin ratio}\end{aligned}$$

Again using Whittier Company data, the break-even sales dollars would be computed as ($45,000/0.1875), or $240,000. Same answer, just a slightly different approach.

Profit Targets and Sales Revenue

Consider the following question: How much sales revenue must Whittier generate to earn a before-tax profit of $60,000? (This question is similar to the one we asked earlier in terms of units, but it phrases the question directly in terms of sales revenue.) To answer the question, add the targeted operating income of $60,000 to the $45,000 of fixed cost and divide by the contribution margin ratio:

$$\begin{aligned}\text{Sales} &= (\$45{,}000 + \$60{,}000)/0.1875\\ &= \$105{,}000/0.1875\\ &= \$560{,}000\end{aligned}$$

Whittier must earn revenues equal to $560,000 to achieve a profit target of $60,000. Since breakeven is $240,000, additional sales of $320,000 ($560,000 − $240,000) must be earned above breakeven. Notice that multiplying the contribution margin ratio by revenues above breakeven yields the profit of $60,000 (0.1875 × $320,000). Above breakeven, the contribution margin ratio is a profit ratio; therefore, it represents the proportion of each sales dollar assignable to profit. For this example, every sales dollar earned above breakeven increases profits by $0.1875.

In general, assuming that fixed costs remain unchanged, the contribution margin ratio can be used to find the profit impact of a change in sales revenue. To obtain the total change in profits from a change in revenues, simply multiply the contribution margin ratio times the change in sales. For example, if sales revenues are $540,000 instead of $560,000, how will the expected profits be affected? A decrease in sales revenues of $20,000 will cause a decrease in profits of $3,750 (0.1875 × $20,000).

Comparison of the Two Approaches

For a single-product setting, converting the break-even point in units to breakeven in sales revenue is simply a matter of multiplying the unit sales price by the units sold. Then why bother with a separate formula for the sales revenue approach? There are two reasons. First, the formula for the sales revenue allows us to directly solve for revenue if that is what is desired. Second, the sales revenue approach is much simpler to use in a multiple-product setting, as we will see in the next section.

Multiple-Product Analysis

Objective 3

Apply cost-volume-profit analysis in a multiple-product setting.

Cost-volume-profit analysis is fairly simple in the single-product setting. However, most firms produce and sell a number of products or services. Even though the conceptual complexity of CVP analysis does increase with multiple products, the operation is reasonably straightforward. Let's see how we can adapt the formulas used in a single-product setting to the multiple-product setting by expanding the Whittier Company example.

Whittier Company has decided to offer two models of lawn mowers: a mulching mower to sell for $400 and a riding mower to sell for $800. The Marketing Department is convinced that 1,200 mulching mowers and 800 riding mowers can be sold during the coming year. The controller has prepared the following projected income statement based on the sales forecast:

	Mulching Mower	Riding Mower	Total
Sales	$480,000	$640,000	$1,120,000
Less: Variable expenses	390,000	480,000	870,000
Contribution margin	$ 90,000	$160,000	$ 250,000
Less: Direct fixed expenses	30,000	40,000	70,000
Product margin	$ 60,000	$120,000	$ 180,000
Less: Common fixed expenses			26,250
Operating income			$ 153,750

Note that the controller has separated direct fixed expenses from common fixed expenses. The **direct fixed expenses** are those fixed costs that can be traced to each product and would be avoided if the product did not exist. The common fixed expenses are the fixed costs that are not traceable to the products and would remain even if one of the products was eliminated.

Break-Even Point in Units

The owner of Whittier is somewhat apprehensive about adding a new product line and wants to know how many of each model must be sold to break even. If you were given the responsibility of answering this question, how would you respond?

One possible response is to use the equation we developed earlier in which fixed costs were divided by the contribution margin. This equation presents some immediate problems, however. It was developed for a single-product analysis. For two products, there are two unit contribution margins. The mulching mower has a contribution margin per unit of \$75 (\$400 − \$325), and the riding mower has one of \$200 (\$800 − \$600).[4]

One possible solution is to apply the analysis separately to each product line. It is possible to obtain individual break-even points when income is defined as product margin. Breakeven for the mulching mower is as follows:

$$\begin{aligned}\text{Mulching mower break-even units} &= \text{Fixed cost/(Price} - \text{Unit variable cost)}\\ &= \$30{,}000/\$75\\ &= 400 \text{ units}\end{aligned}$$

Breakeven for the riding mower can be computed as well:

$$\begin{aligned}\text{Riding mower break-even units} &= \text{Fixed cost/(Price} - \text{Unit variable cost)}\\ &= \$40{,}000/\$200\\ &= 200 \text{ units}\end{aligned}$$

Thus, 400 mulching mowers and 200 riding mowers must be sold to achieve a break-even product margin. But a break-even product margin covers only direct fixed costs; the common fixed costs remain to be covered. Selling these numbers of lawn mowers would result in a loss equal to the common fixed costs. No break-even point for the firm as a whole has yet been identified. Somehow, the common fixed costs must be factored into the analysis.

Allocating the common fixed costs to each product line before computing a break-even point may resolve this difficulty. The problem with this approach is that allocation of the common fixed costs is arbitrary. Thus, no meaningful break-even volume is readily apparent.

Another possible solution is to convert the multiple-product problem into a single-product problem. If this can be done, then all of the single-product CVP methodology can be applied directly. The key to this conversion is to identify the expected sales mix, in units, of the products being marketed. **Sales mix** is the relative combination of products being sold by a firm.

Determining the Sales Mix The sales mix can be measured in units sold or in proportion of revenue. For example, if Whittier plans on selling 1,200 mulching mowers and 800 riding mowers, then the sales mix in units is 1,200:800. Usually, the sales mix is reduced to the smallest possible whole numbers. Thus, the relative mix, 1,200:800, can be reduced to 12:8 and further to 3:2. That is, for every three mulching mowers sold, two riding mowers are sold.

Alternatively, the sales mix can be represented by the percent of total revenue contributed by each product. In that case, the mulching mower revenue is \$480,000 (\$400 × 1,200), and the riding mower revenue is \$640,000 (\$800 × 800). The mulching mower accounts for 42.86 percent of total revenue, and the riding mower accounts for the remaining 57.14 percent. It may seem as though the two sales mixes are different. The sales mix in units is 3:2; that is, of every five mowers sold,

4 The variable cost per unit is derived from the income statement. For the riding mower, total variable costs are \$480,000, based on sales of 800 units. This yields a per-unit variable cost of \$600 (\$480,000/800). A similar computation produces the per-unit variable cost for the mulching mower.

60 percent are mulching mowers and 40 percent are riding mowers. However, the revenue-based sales mix is 42.86 percent for the mulching mowers. What is the difference? The sales mix in revenue takes the sales mix in units and weights it by price. Therefore, even though the underlying proportion of mowers sold remains 3:2, the lower-priced mulching mowers are weighted less heavily when price is factored in. For CVP analysis, we must use the sales mix expressed in units.

A number of different sales mixes can be used to define the break-even volume. For example, a sales mix of 2:1 will define a break-even point of 550 mulching mowers and 275 riding mowers. The total contribution margin produced by this mix is $96,250 [($75 × 550) + ($200 × 275)]. Similarly, if 350 mulching mowers and 350 riding mowers are sold (corresponding to a 1:1 sales mix), the total contribution margin is also $96,250 [($75 × 350) + ($200 × 350)]. Since total fixed costs are $96,250, both sales mixes define break-even points. Fortunately, every sales mix need not be considered. Can Whittier really expect a sales mix of 2:1 or 1:1? For every two mulching mowers sold, does Whittier expect to sell a riding mower? Or for every mulching mower, can Whittier really sell one riding mower?

According to Whittier's marketing study, a sales mix of 3:2 can be expected. This is the ratio that should be used; others can be ignored. The sales mix that is expected to prevail should be used for CVP analysis.

Sales Mix and CVP Analysis Defining a particular sales mix allows us to convert a multiple-product problem into a single-product CVP format. Since Whittier expects to sell three mulching mowers for every two riding mowers, it can define the single product it sells as a package containing three mulching mowers and two riding mowers. By defining the product as a package, the multiple-product problem is converted into a single-product one. To use the approach of break-even point in units, the package selling price and variable cost per package must be known. To compute these package values, the sales mix, the individual product prices, and the individual variable costs are needed. Given the individual product data found in the projected income statement, the package values can be computed as follows:

Product	Unit Variable Price	Unit Contribution Cost	Sales Margin	Package Unit Contribution Mix	Margin
Mulching	$400	$325	$ 75	3	$225[a]
Riding	800	600	200	2	400[b]
Package total					$625

[a]This is found by multiplying the number of units in the package (3) by the unit contribution margin ($75).
[b]This is found by multiplying the number of units in the package (2) by the unit contribution margin ($200).

Given the package contribution margin, the fundamental break-even equation can be used to determine the number of packages that need to be sold to break even. From Whittier's projected income statement, we know that the total fixed costs for the Company are $96,250. Thus, the break-even point is:

Break-even packages = Fixed cost/Package contribution margin
= $96,250/$625
= 154 packages

Whittier must sell 462 mulching mowers (3 × 154) and 308 riding mowers (2 × 154) to break even. An income statement verifying this solution is presented in Exhibit 11-1.

For a given sales mix, CVP analysis can be used as if the firm were selling a single product. However, actions that change the prices of individual products can affect the sales mix because consumers may buy relatively more or less of the product. Keep in mind that a new sales mix will affect the units of each product that

	Mulching Mower	Riding Mower	Total
Sales	$184,800	$246,400	$431,200
Less: Variable expenses	150,150	184,800	334,950
Contribution margin	$ 34,650	$ 61,600	$ 96,250
Less: Direct fixed expenses	30,000	40,000	70,000
Segment margin	$ 4,650	$ 21,600	$ 26,250
Less: Common fixed expenses			26,250
Operating income			$ 0

Exhibit 11-1 Income Statement: Break-Even Solution

need to be sold in order to achieve a desired profit target. If the sales mix for the coming period is uncertain, it may be necessary to look at several different mixes. In this way, a manager can gain some insight into the possible outcomes facing the firm.

The complexity of the approach of break-even point in units increases dramatically as the number of products increases. Imagine performing this analysis for a firm with several hundred products. This observation seems more overwhelming than it actually is. Computers can easily handle a problem with so much data. Furthermore, many firms simplify the problem by analyzing product groups rather than individual products. Another way to handle the increased complexity is to switch from the units-sold to the sales-revenue approach. This approach can accomplish a multiple-product CVP analysis using only the summary data found in an organization's income statement. The computational requirements are much simpler.

Sales Dollars Approach

To illustrate the break-even point in sales dollars, the same examples will be used. However, the only information needed is the projected income statement for Whittier Company as a whole.

Sales	$1,120,000
Less: Variable costs	870,000
Contribution margin	$ 250,000
Less: Fixed costs	96,250
Operating income	$ 153,750

Notice that this income statement corresponds to the total column of the more detailed income statement examined previously. The projected income statement rests on the assumption that 1,200 mulching mowers and 800 riding mowers will be sold (a 3:2 sales mix). The break-even point in sales revenue also rests on the expected sales mix. (As with the units-sold approach, a different sales mix will produce different results.)

With the income statement, the usual CVP questions can be addressed. For example, how much sales revenue must be earned to break even? To answer this question, we divide the total fixed cost of $96,250 by the contribution margin ratio of 0.2232 ($250,000/$1,120,000):[5]

Break-even sales = Fixed cost/Contribution margin ratio
= $96,250/0.2232
= $431,228

5 Because of rounding error in the contribution margin ratio, the sales volume is slightly overstated. The correct answer is $431,200 [obtained by multiplying the package selling price by the packages needed to break even: ($2,800 × 154)].

The break-even point in sales dollars implicitly uses the assumed sales mix but avoids the requirement of building a package contribution margin. No knowledge of individual product data is needed. The computational effort is similar to that used in the single-product setting. Moreover, the answer is still expressed in sales revenue. Unlike the break-even point in units, the answer to CVP questions using sales dollars is still expressed in a single summary measure. The sales revenue approach, however, does sacrifice information concerning individual product performance.

Graphical Representation of CVP Relationships

Objective 4

Prepare a profit-volume graph and a cost-volume-profit graph, and explain the meaning of each.

It may further our understanding of CVP relationships to see them portrayed visually. A graphical representation can help managers see the difference between variable cost and revenue. It may also help them understand quickly what impact an increase or decrease in sales will have on the break-even point. Two basic graphs, the *profit-volume graph* and the *cost-volume-profit graph*, are presented here.

The Profit-Volume Graph

A **profit-volume graph** visually portrays the relationship between profits and sales volume. The profit-volume graph is the graph of the operating-income equation [Operating income = (Price × Units) − (Unit variable cost × Units) − Fixed cost]. In this graph, operating income is the dependent variable, and units is the independent variable. Usually, values of the independent variable are measured along the horizontal axis and values of the dependent variable along the vertical axis.

To make this discussion more concrete, a simple set of data will be used. Assume that Tyson Company produces a single product with the following cost and price data:

Total fixed costs	$100
Variable cost per unit	5
Selling price per unit	10

Using these data, operating income can be expressed as follows:

$$\begin{aligned}\text{Operating income} &= (\$10 \times \text{Units}) - (\$5 \times \text{Units}) - \$100 \\ &= (\$5 \times \text{Units}) - \$100\end{aligned}$$

We can graph this relationship by plotting units along the horizontal axis and operating income (or loss) along the vertical axis. Two points are needed to graph a linear equation. While any two points will do, the two points often chosen are those that correspond to zero sales volume and zero profits. When units sold are zero, Tyson experiences an operating loss of $100 (or a profit of −$100). The point corresponding to zero sales volume, therefore, is (0, −$100). In other words, when no sales take place, the company suffers a loss equal to its total fixed costs. When operating income is zero, the units sold are equal to 20. The point corresponding to zero profits (breakeven) is (20, $0). These two points, plotted in Exhibit 11-2, define the profit-volume graph shown there.

The graph in Exhibit 11-2 can be used to assess Tyson's profit (or loss) at any level of sales activity. For example, the profit associated with the sale of 40 units can be read from the graph by (1) drawing a vertical line from the horizontal axis to the profit line and (2) drawing a horizontal line from the profit line to the vertical axis. As illustrated in Exhibit 16-4, the profit associated with sales of 40 units is $100. The profit-volume graph, while easy to interpret, fails to reveal how costs change as sales volume changes. An alternative approach to graphing can provide this detail.

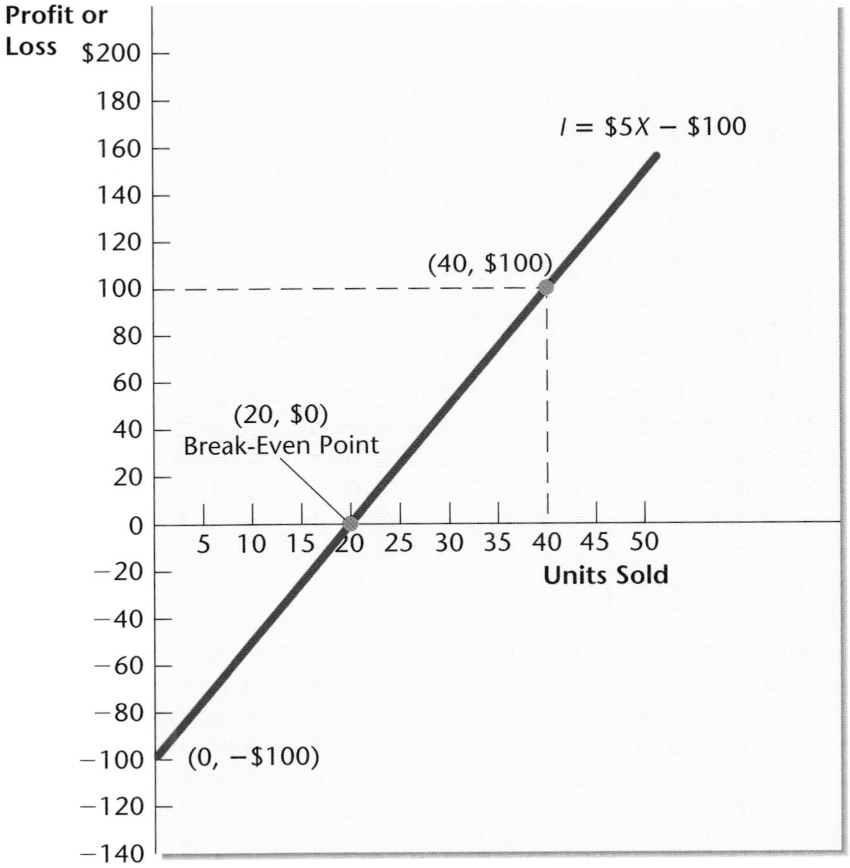

Exhibit 11-2 Profit-Volume Graph

The Cost-Volume-Profit Graph

The **cost-volume-profit graph** depicts the relationships among cost, volume, and profits. To obtain the more detailed relationships, it is necessary to graph two separate lines: the total revenue line and the total cost line. These two lines are represented, respectively, by the following two equations:

$$\text{Revenue} = \text{Price} \times \text{Units}$$
$$\text{Total cost} = (\text{Unit variable cost} \times \text{Units}) + \text{Fixed cost}$$

Using the Tyson Company example, the revenue and cost equations are as follows:

$$\text{Revenue} = \$10 \times \text{Units}$$
$$\text{Total cost} = (\$5 \times \text{Units}) + \$100$$

To portray both equations in the same graph, the vertical axis is measured in dollars and the horizontal axis in units sold.

Two points are needed to graph each equation. We will use the x-coordinates as in the profit-volume graph. For the revenue equation, setting number of units equal to 0 results in revenue of $0; setting number of units equal to 20 results in revenue of $200. Therefore, the two points for the revenue equation are (0, $0) and (20, $200). For the cost equation, units sold of 0 and units sold of 20 produce the points (0, $100) and (20, $200). The graph of each equation appears in Exhibit 11-3.

Notice that the total revenue line begins at the origin and rises with a slope equal to the selling price per unit (a slope of 10). The total cost line intercepts the vertical axis at a point equal to total fixed costs and rises with a slope equal to the

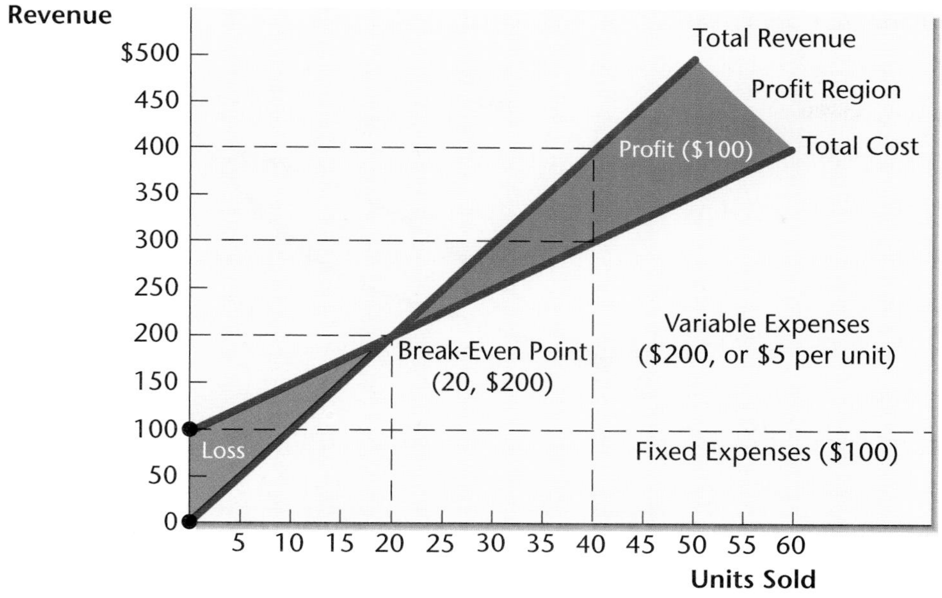

Exhibit 11-3 Cost-Volume-Profit Graph

variable cost per unit (a slope of 5). When the total revenue line lies below the total cost line, a loss region is defined. Similarly, when the total revenue line lies above the total cost line, a profit region is defined. The point where the total revenue line and the total cost line intersect is the break-even point. To break even, Tyson Company must sell 20 units and, thus, receive $200 total revenues.

Now let's compare the information available from the CVP graph with that available from the profit-volume graph. To do so, consider the sale of 40 units. Recall that the profit-volume graph revealed that this produced profits of $100. Examine Exhibit 11-3 again. The CVP graph also shows profits of $100, but it reveals more as well. The CVP graph discloses that total revenues of $400 and total costs of $300 are associated with the sale of 40 units. Furthermore, the total costs can be broken down into fixed costs of $100 and variable costs of $200. The CVP graph provides revenue and cost information not provided by the profit-volume graph. Unlike the profit-volume graph, some computation is needed to determine the profit associated with a given sales volume. Nonetheless, because of the greater information content, managers are likely to find the CVP graph a more useful tool.

Assumptions of Cost-Volume-Profit Analysis

The profit-volume and cost-volume-profit graphs just illustrated rely on some important assumptions. Some of these assumptions are as follows:

1. The analysis assumes a linear revenue function and a linear cost function.
2. The analysis assumes that price, total fixed costs, and unit variable costs can be accurately identified and remain constant over the relevant range.
3. The analysis assumes that what is produced is sold.
4. For multiple-product analysis, the sales mix is assumed to be known.
5. The selling prices and costs are assumed to be known with certainty.

Linear Functions The first assumption, linear cost and revenue functions, deserves additional consideration. Let's take a look at the underlying revenue and total cost functions identified in economics. In Exhibit 11-4, Panel A portrays the

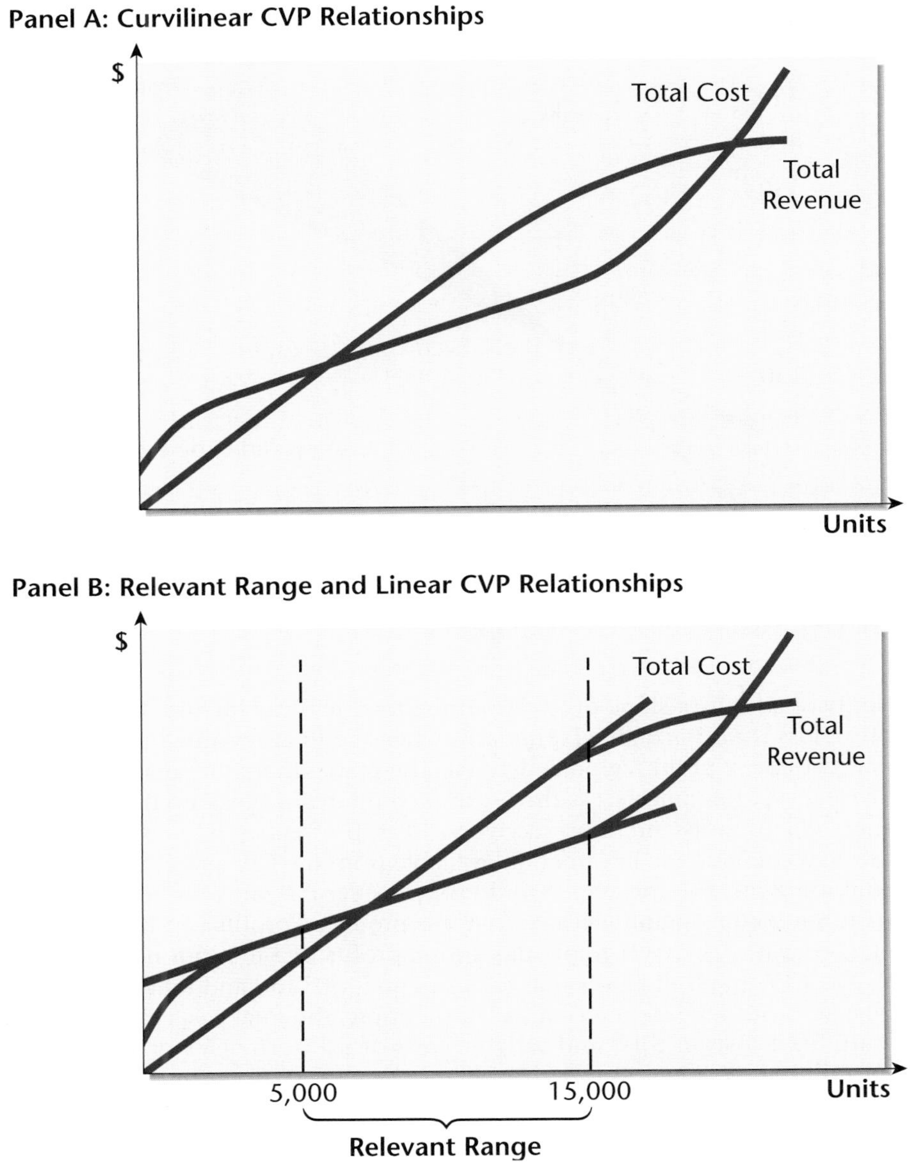

Exhibit 11-4 The Relevant Range

curvilinear revenue and cost functions. We see that as quantity sold increases, revenue also increases, but eventually begins to rise less steeply than before. This is explained quite simply by the need to decrease price as many more units are sold. The total cost function is more complicated, rising steeply at first, then leveling off somewhat (as increasing returns to scale develop), and then rising steeply again (as decreasing returns to scale develop). How can we deal with these complicated relationships?

Relevant Range Fortunately, we do not need to consider all possible ranges of production and sales for a firm. Remember that CVP analysis is a short-run decision-making tool. (We know that it is short run in orientation because some costs are fixed.) It is only necessary for us to determine the current operating range, or **relevant range**, for which the linear cost and revenue relationships are valid. In Exhibit 11-4, Panel B illustrates a relevant range from 5,000 to 15,000 units. Note that the cost and revenue relationships are roughly linear in this range, allowing us to use our linear CVP equations. Of course, if the relevant range changes, different fixed and variable costs and different prices must be used.

The second assumption is linked to the definition of relevant range. Once a relevant range has been identified, then the cost and price relationships are assumed to be known and constant.

Production Equal to Sales The third assumption is that what is produced is sold. There is no change in inventory over the period. That inventory has no impact on break-even analysis makes sense. Break-even analysis is a short-run decision-making technique; we are looking to cover all costs of a particular period of time. Inventory embodies costs of a previous period and is not considered.

Constant Sales Mix In single-product analysis, the sales mix is obviously constant—one product accounts for 100 percent of sales. Multiple-product break-even analysis requires a constant sales mix. However, it is virtually impossible to predict with certainty the sales mix. Typically, this constraint is handled in practice through sensitivity analysis. By using the capabilities of spreadsheet analysis, the sensitivity of variables to a variety of sales mixes can be readily assessed.

Prices and Costs Known with Certainty In actuality, firms seldom know prices, variable costs, and fixed costs with certainty. A change in one variable usually affects the value of others. Often there is a probability distribution to contend with. Furthermore, there are formal ways of explicitly building uncertainty into the CVP model. These issues are explored in the next section.

Changes in the CVP Variables

Objective 5

Explain the impact of risk, uncertainty, and changing variables on cost-volume-profit analysis.

Because firms operate in a dynamic world, they must be aware of changes in prices, variable costs, and fixed costs. They must also account for the effect of risk and uncertainty. In this section we look at the effect of changes in price, unit contribution margin, and fixed cost on the break-even point. We also look at ways managers can handle risk and uncertainty within the CVP framework.

Suppose that Whittier Company recently conducted a market study of the mulching lawn mower that revealed three different alternatives:

1. *Alternative 1:* If advertising expenditures increase by \$8,000, sales will increase from 1,600 units to 1,725 units.
2. *Alternative 2:* A price decrease from \$400 to \$375 per lawn mower will increase sales from 1,600 units to 1,900 units.
3. *Alternative 3:* Decreasing price to \$375 and increasing advertising expenditures by \$8,000 will increase sales from 1,600 units to 2,600 units.

Should Whittier maintain its current price and advertising policies, or should it select one of the three alternatives described by the marketing study?

Consider the first alternative. What is the effect on profits if advertising costs increase by \$8,000 and sales increase by 125 units? This question can be answered without using the equations but by employing the contribution margin per unit. We know that the unit contribution margin is \$75. Since units sold increase by 125, the incremental increase in total contribution margin is \$9,375 (\$75 × 125 units). However, since fixed costs increase by \$8,000, the incremental increase in profits is only \$1,375 (\$9,375 − \$8,000). Exhibit 11-5 summarizes the effects of the first alternative. Notice that we need to look only at the incremental increase in total contribution margin and fixed expenses to compute the increase in total profits.

	Before the Increased Advertising	With the Increased Advertising
Units sold	1,600	1,725
Unit contribution margin	× $75	× $75
Total contribution margin	$120,000	$129,375
Less: Fixed expenses	45,000	53,000
Profit	$ 75,000	$ 76,375

	Difference in Profit
Change in sales volume	125
Unit contribution margin	× $75
Change in contribution margin	$9,375
Less: Change in fixed expenses	8,000
Increase in profit	$1,375

Exhibit 11-5 Summary of the Effects of Alternative 1

For the second alternative, fixed expenses do not increase. Thus, it is possible to answer the question by looking only at the effect on total contribution margin. For the current price of $400, the contribution margin per unit is $75. If 1,600 units are sold, the total contribution margin is $120,000 ($75 × 1,600). If the price is dropped to $375, then the contribution margin drops to $50 per unit ($375 − $325). If 1,900 units are sold at the new price, then the new total contribution margin is $95,000 ($50 × 1,900). Dropping the price results in a profit decline of $25,000 ($120,000 − $95,000). The effects of the second alternative are summarized in Exhibit 11-6.

The third alternative calls for a decrease in the unit selling price and an increase in advertising costs. Like the first alternative, the profit impact can be assessed by looking at the incremental effects on contribution margin and fixed expenses. The incremental profit change can be found by (1) computing the incremental change in total contribution margin, (2) computing the incremental change in fixed expenses, and (3) adding the two results.

As shown, the current total contribution margin (for 1,600 units sold) is $120,000. Since the new unit contribution margin is $50, the new total contribution margin is $130,000 ($50 × 2,600 units). Thus, the incremental increase in total contribution

	Before the Proposed Price Decrease	With the Proposed Price Decrease
Units sold	1,600	1,900
Unit contribution margin	× $75	× $50
Total contribution margin	$120,000	$95,000
Less: Fixed expenses	45,000	45,000
Profit	$ 75,000	$50,000

	Difference in Profit
Change in contribution margin ($95,000 − $120,000)	$(25,000)
Less: Change in fixed expenses	—
Decrease in profit	$(25,000)

Exhibit 11-6 Summary of the Effects of Alternative 2

margin is $10,000 ($130,000 − $120,000). However, to achieve this incremental increase in contribution margin, an incremental increase of $8,000 in fixed costs is needed. The net effect is an incremental increase in profits of $2,000. The effects of the third alternative are summarized in Exhibit 11-7.

Of the three alternatives identified by the marketing study, the one that promises the most benefit is the third. It increases total profits by $2,000. The first alternative increases profits by only $1,375, and the second actually decreases profits by $25,000.

These examples are all based on a units-sold approach. However, we could just as easily have applied a sales revenue approach. The answers would be the same.

Introducing Risk and Uncertainty

An important assumption of CVP analysis is that prices and costs are known with certainty. This is seldom the case. Risk and uncertainty are a part of business decision making and must be dealt with somehow. Formally, risk differs from uncertainty in that under risk the probability distributions of the variables are known; under uncertainty, they are not known. For our purposes, however, the terms will be used interchangeably.

How do managers deal with risk and uncertainty? A variety of methods can be used. First, of course, management must realize the uncertain nature of future prices, costs, and quantities. Next, managers move from consideration of a break-even point to what might be called a "break-even band." In other words, given the uncertain nature of the data, perhaps a firm might break even when 1,800 to 2,000 units are sold instead of the point estimate of 1,900 units. Further, managers may engage in sensitivity or what-if analysis. In this instance, a computer spreadsheet is helpful, as managers set up the break-even (or targeted profit) relationships and then check to see the impact that varying costs and prices have on quantity sold. Two concepts useful to management are *margin of safety* and *operating leverage.* Both of these may be considered measures of risk. Each requires knowledge of fixed and variable costs.

Margin of Safety The **margin of safety** is the units sold or expected to be sold or the revenue earned or expected to be earned above the break-even volume. For example, if the break-even volume for a company is 200 units and the company is currently selling 500 units, the margin of safety is 300 units (500 − 200). The margin of safety can be expressed in sales revenue as well. If the break-even volume is $200,000 and current revenues are $350,000, then the margin of safety is $150,000.

	Before the Proposed Price and Advertising Changes	With the Proposed Price Decrease and Advertising Increase
Units sold	1,600	2,600
Unit contribution margin	× $75	× $50
Total contribution margin	$120,000	$130,000
Less: Fixed expenses	45,000	53,000
Profit	$ 75,000	$ 77,000

	Difference in Profit
Change in contribution margin ($130,000 − $120,000)	$10,000
Less: Change in fixed expenses ($53,000 − $45,000)	8,000
Increase in profit	$ 2,000

Exhibit 11-7 Summary of the Effects of Alternative 3

The margin of safety can be viewed as a crude measure of risk. There are always events, unknown when plans are made, that can lower sales below the original expected level. If a firm's margin of safety is large given the expected sales for the coming year, the risk of suffering losses should sales take a downward turn is less than if the margin of safety is small. Managers who face a low margin of safety may wish to consider actions to increase sales or decrease costs. These steps will increase the margin of safety and lower the risk of incurring losses.

Operating Leverage In physics, a lever is a simple machine used to multiply force. Basically, the lever multiplies the effort applied to create more work. The larger the load moved by a given amount of effort, the greater is the mechanical advantage. In financial terms, operating leverage is concerned with the relative mix of fixed costs and variable costs in an organization. It is sometimes possible to trade off fixed costs for variable costs. As variable costs decrease, the unit contribution margin increases, making the contribution of each unit sold that much greater. In such a case, fluctuations in sales have an increased effect on profitability. Thus, firms that have realized lower variable costs by increasing the proportion of fixed costs will benefit with greater increases in profits as sales increase than will firms with a lower proportion of fixed costs. Fixed costs are being used as leverage to increase profits. Unfortunately, it is also true that firms with a higher operating leverage will experience greater reductions in profits as sales decrease. Therefore, **operating leverage** is the use of fixed costs to extract higher percentage changes in profits as sales activity changes.

The greater the degree of operating leverage, the more that changes in sales activity will affect profits. Because of this phenomenon, the mix of costs that an organization chooses can have a considerable influence on its operating risk and profit level.

The **degree of operating leverage (DOL)** can be measured for a given level of sales by taking the ratio of contribution margin to profit, as follows:

Degree of operating leverage = Contribution margin/Profit

If fixed costs are used to lower variable costs such that contribution margin increases and profit decreases, then the degree of operating leverage increases—signaling an increase in risk.

To illustrate the utility of these concepts, consider a firm that is planning to add a new product line. In adding the line, the firm can choose to rely heavily on automation or on labor. If the firm chooses to emphasize automation rather than labor, fixed costs will be higher, and unit variable costs will be lower. Relevant data for a sales level of 10,000 units follow:

	Automated System	Manual System
Sales	$1,000,000	$1,000,000
Less: Variable costs	500,000	800,000
Contribution margin	$ 500,000	$ 200,000
Less: Fixed costs	375,000	100,000
Operating income	$ 125,000	$ 100,000
Unit selling price	$ 100	$ 100
Unit variable cost	50	80
Unit contribution margin	50	20

The degree of operating leverage for the automated system is 4.0 ($500,000/$125,000). The degree of operating leverage for the manual system is 2.0 ($200,000/$100,000). What happens to profit in each system if sales increase by 40 percent? We can generate the following income statements to see.

	Automated System	Manual System
Sales	$1,400,000	$1,400,000
Less: Variable costs	700,000	1,120,000
Contribution margin	$ 700,000	$ 280,000
Less: Fixed costs	375,000	100,000
Operating income	$ 325,000	$ 180,000

Profits for the automated system would increase by $200,000 ($325,000 − $125,000) for a 160 percent increase. In the manual system, profits increase by only $80,000 ($180,000 − $100,000) for an 80 percent increase. The automated system has a greater percentage increase because it has a higher degree of operating leverage.

In choosing between the two systems, the effect of operating leverage is a valuable piece of information. As the 40 percent increase in sales illustrates, this effect can bring a significant benefit to the firm. However, the effect is a two-edged sword. As sales decrease, the automated system will also show much higher percentage decreases. Moreover, the increased operating leverage is available under the automated system because of the presence of increased fixed costs. The break-even point for the automated system is 7,500 units ($375,000/$50), whereas the break-even point for the manual system is 5,000 units ($100,000/$20). Thus, the automated system has greater operating risk. The increased risk, of course, provides a potentially higher profit level (as long as units sold exceed 9,167).[6]

In choosing between the automated and the manual systems, the manager must assess the likelihood that sales will exceed 9,167 units. If, after careful study, there is a strong belief that sales will easily exceed this level, the choice is obvious: the automated system. On the other hand, if sales are unlikely to exceed 9,167 units, the manual system is preferable. Exhibit 11.8 summarizes the relative differences between the manual and the automated systems in terms of some of the CVP concepts.

Sensitivity Analysis and CVP

The pervasiveness of personal computers and spreadsheets has placed *sensitivity analysis* within reach of most managers. An important tool, **sensitivity analysis** is a "what if" technique that examines the impact of changes in underlying assumptions on an answer. It is relatively simple to input data on prices, variable costs, fixed costs, and sales mix and to set up formulas to calculate break-even points

	Manual System	Automated System
Price	Same	Same
Variable cost	Relatively Higher	Relatively Lower
Fixed cost	Relatively Lower	Relatively Higher
Contribution margin	Relatively Lower	Relatively Higher
Break-even point	Relatively Lower	Relatively Higher
Margin of safety	Relatively Higher	Relatively Lower
Degree of operating leverage	Relatively Lower	Relatively Higher
Down-side risk	Relatively Lower	Relatively Higher
Up-side potential	Relatively Lower	Relatively Higher

Exhibit 11-8 Differences between Manual and Automated Systems

6 This benchmark is computed by setting the profit equations of the two systems equal and solving for x: $\$50x - \$375,000 = \$20x - \$100,000$; $x = 9,167$.

and expected profits. Then, the data can be varied as desired to see how changes impact the expected profit.

In the preceding example on operating leverage, a company analyzed the impact on profit of using an automated versus a manual system. The computations were essentially done by hand, and too much variation is cumbersome. Using the power of a computer, it would be an easy matter to change the sales price in $1 increments between $75 and $125, with related assumptions about quantity sold. At the same time, variable and fixed costs could be adjusted. For example, suppose that the automated system has fixed costs of $375,000 but that those costs could easily double in the first year and come back down in the second and third years as bugs are worked out of the system and workers learn to use it. Again, the spreadsheet can effortlessly handle the many computations.

Remember that spreadsheet results are only as good as the data used to generate them. Generating the data is the most difficult job in CVP analysis. That job is determining the data to be entered in the first place. The accountant must be cognizant of the cost and price distributions of the firm, as well as of the impact of changing economic conditions on these variables. The fact that variables are seldom known with certainty is no excuse for ignoring the impact of uncertainty on CVP analysis. Fortunately, sensitivity analysis can also give managers a feel for the degree to which a poorly forecast variable will affect an answer. That is also an advantage.

ETHICS

Finally, we must note that the CVP results are only one input into business decisions. There are many other factors that may bear on decisions to choose one type of process over another, for example, or whether or not to delete certain costs. Businesses and nonprofit entities often face trade-offs involving safety. Ethical concerns also have an important place in CVP analysis. One possibility is that cost of potential problems can be estimated and included in the CVP results. Often, however, the costs and probabilities are not known with sufficient certainty. In that case, these factors are included in the ultimate decision-making process. Chapter 12, on tactical decision making, covers this topic in more detail.

CVP Analysis and Activity-Based Costing

Objective 6

Discuss the impact of activity-based costing on cost-volume-profit analysis.

Conventional CVP analysis assumes that all costs of the firm can be divided into two categories: those that vary with sales volume (variable costs) and those that do not (fixed costs). Further, costs are assumed to be a linear function of sales volume. However, many companies now realize that this fixed versus variable distinction is too simplistic. For example, major airlines including **Delta**, **Continental**, **Northwest**, and **American Airlines** have a first-class section. Passengers who fly in that section enjoy roomier seats, hot meals, and free drinks. Economy-class passengers, of course, make the trip in smaller seats crammed into the rear section of the aircraft. They often pay for meals and certainly pay for alcoholic drinks. So while the average cost for the airline may be about $0.105 per seat mile,[7] that cost must be somewhat higher for the first-class passengers, and somewhat lower for the economy-class passengers.

© Digital Vision

Modern airlines use CVP analysis in deciding whether to add a new route or to expand the number of flights on existing routes.

7 David Grossman, "Why Business Travelers Will Always Pay More to Fly," *USA Today*, February 6, 2006, http://www.usatoday.com/travel/columnist/grossman/2006-02-06-grossman_x.htm, accessed March 31, 2006.

In an activity-based costing (ABC) system, costs are divided into unit- and non-unit-based categories. Activity-based costing admits that some costs vary with units produced and some costs do not. However, while activity-based costing acknowledges that non-unit-based costs are fixed with respect to production volume changes, it also argues that many non-unit-based costs vary with respect to other activity drivers.

The use of activity-based costing does not mean that CVP analysis is less useful. In fact, it becomes more useful since it provides more accurate insights concerning cost behavior. These insights produce better decisions. CVP analysis within an activity-based framework, however, must be modified. To illustrate, assume that a company's costs can be explained by three variables: a unit-level activity driver, units sold; a batch-level activity driver, number of setups; and a product-level activity driver, engineering hours. The ABC cost equation can then be expressed as follows:

$$\text{Total cost} = \text{Fixed cost} + (\text{Unit variable cost} \times \text{Number of units}) + (\text{Setup cost} \times \text{Number of setups}) + (\text{Engineering cost} \times \text{Number of engineering hours})$$

Operating income, as before, is total revenue minus total cost. This is expressed as follows:

$$\text{Operating income} = \text{Total revenue} - [\text{Fixed cost} + (\text{Unit variable cost} \times \text{Number of units}) + (\text{Setup cost} \times \text{Number of setups}) + (\text{Engineering cost} \times \text{Number of engineering hours})]$$

Let's use the contribution margin approach to calculate the break-even point in units. At breakeven, operating income is zero, and the number of units that must be sold to achieve breakeven is as follows:

$$\text{Break-even units} = [\text{Fixed cost} + (\text{Setup cost} \times \text{Number of setups}) + (\text{Engineering cost} \times \text{Number of engineering hours})]/(\text{Price} - \text{Unit variable cost})$$

A comparison of the ABC break-even point with the conventional break-even point reveals two significant differences. First, the fixed costs differ. Some costs previously identified as being fixed may actually vary with non-unit cost drivers—in this case, setups and engineering hours. Second, the numerator of the ABC break-even equation has two non-unit-variable cost terms: one for batch-related activities and one for product-sustaining activities.

Example Comparing Conventional and ABC Analysis

To make this discussion more concrete, a comparison of conventional cost-volume-profit analysis with activity-based costing is useful. Let's assume that a company wants to compute the units that must be sold to earn a before-tax income of $20,000. The analysis is based on the following data:

Activity Driver	Unit Variable Cost	Level of Activity Driver
Units sold	$10	—
Setups	1,000	20
Engineering hours	30	1,000
Other data:		
Total fixed costs (conventional)		$100,000
Total fixed costs (ABC)		50,000
Unit selling price		20

Using CVP analysis, the units that must be sold to earn a before-tax profit of \$20,000 are computed as follows:

$$\begin{aligned}\text{Number of units} &= (\text{Targeted income} + \text{Conventional fixed cost})/\\&\quad(\text{Price} - \text{Unit variable cost})\\&= (\$20{,}000 + \$100{,}000)/(\$20 - \$10)\\&= \$120{,}000/\$10\\&= 12{,}000 \text{ units}\end{aligned}$$

Using the ABC equation, the units that must be sold to earn an operating income of \$20,000 are computed as follows:

$$\begin{aligned}\text{Number of units} = {} & [\text{Targeted income} + \text{ABC fixed cost} + (\text{Setup cost}\\& \times \text{Number of setups}) + (\text{Engineering cost}\\& \times \text{Number of engineering hours})]/(\text{Price} - \text{Unit variable cost})\end{aligned}$$

$$\begin{aligned}\text{Number of units} &= [\$20{,}000 + \$50{,}000 + (\$1{,}000 \times 20)\\&\quad + (\$30 \times 1{,}000)]/(\$20 - \$10)\\&= 12{,}000 \text{ units}\end{aligned}$$

The number of units that must be sold is identical under both approaches. The reason is simple. The total fixed cost pool under conventional costing consists of non-unit-based variable costs plus costs that are fixed regardless of the activity driver. ABC breaks out the non-unit-based variable costs. These costs are associated with certain levels of each activity driver. For the batch-level activity driver, the level is 20 setups. For the product-level variable, the level is 1,000 engineering hours. As long as the levels of activity for the non-unit-based cost drivers remain the same, then the results for the conventional and ABC computations will be the same. But these levels can change, and because of this, the information provided by the two approaches can differ significantly. The ABC equation for CVP analysis is a richer representation of the underlying cost behavior and can provide important strategic insights. To see this, let's use the same data and look at a different application.

Strategic Implications: Conventional CVP Analysis versus ABC Analysis

Suppose that after the conventional CVP analysis, marketing indicates that selling 12,000 units is not possible. In fact, only 10,000 units can be sold. The president of the company then directs the product design engineers to find a way to reduce the cost of making the product. The engineers also have been told that the conventional cost equation, with fixed costs of \$100,000 and a unit variable cost of \$10, holds. The variable cost of \$10 per unit consists of the following: direct labor, \$4; direct materials, \$5; and variable overhead, \$1. To comply with the request to reduce the break-even point, engineering produces a new design that requires less labor. The new design reduces the direct labor cost by \$2 per unit. The design would not affect materials or variable overhead. Thus, the new variable cost is \$8 per unit, and the break-even point is as follows:

$$\begin{aligned}\text{Number of units} &= \text{Fixed cost}/(\text{Price} - \text{Unit variable cost})\\&= \$100{,}000/(\$20 - \$8)\\&= 8{,}333 \text{ units}\end{aligned}$$

The projected income if 10,000 units are sold is computed as follows:

Sales (\$20 × 10,000)	\$200,000
Less: Variable expenses (\$8 × 10,000)	80,000
Contribution margin	\$120,000
Less: Fixed expenses	100,000
Operating income	\$ 20,000

Excited, the president approves the new design. A year later, the president discovers that the expected increase in income did not materialize. In fact, a loss is realized. Why? The answer is provided by an ABC approach to CVP analysis.

The original ABC cost relationship for the example follows:

$$\text{Total cost} = \$50{,}000 + (\$10 \times \text{Units}) + (\$1{,}000 \times \text{Setups}) + (\$30 \times \text{Engineering hours})$$

Suppose that the new design requires a more complex setup, increasing the cost per setup from $1,000 to $1,600. Also suppose that the new design, because of increased technical content, requires a 40 percent increase in engineering support (from 1,000 hours to 1,400 hours). The new cost equation, including the reduction in unit-level variable costs, follows:

$$\text{Total cost} = \$50{,}000 + (\$8 \times \text{Units}) + (\$1{,}600 \times \text{Setups}) + (\$30 \times \text{Engineering hours})$$

The break-even point, setting operating income equal to zero and using the ABC equation, is calculated as follows (assume that 20 setups are still performed):

$$\begin{aligned}\text{Number of units} &= [\$50{,}000 + (\$1{,}600 \times 20) + (\$30 \times 1{,}400)]/(\$20 - \$8)\\ &= \$124{,}000/\$12\\ &= 10{,}333 \text{ units}\end{aligned}$$

And, the operating income for 10,000 units is computed as follows (recall that a maximum of 10,000 units can be sold):

Sales ($20 × 10,000)		$200,000
Less: Unit-based variable expenses ($8 × 10,000)		80,000
Contribution margin		$120,000
Less non-unit-based variable expenses:		
Setups ($1,600 × 20)	$32,000	
Engineering support ($30 × 1,400)	42,000	74,000
Traceable margin		$ 46,000
Less: Fixed expenses		50,000
Operating (loss)		$ (4,000)

How could the engineers have been so off target? Didn't they know that the new design would increase setup cost and engineering support? Yes and no. They were probably aware of the increases in these two variables, but the conventional cost equation diverted attention from figuring out just how much impact changes in those variables would have. The information conveyed by the conventional equation to the engineers gave the impression that any reduction in labor cost—not affecting materials or variable overhead—would reduce total costs, since changes in the level of labor activity would not affect the fixed costs. The ABC equation, however, indicates that a reduction in labor input that adversely affects setup activity or engineering support might be undesirable. By providing more insight, better design decisions can be made. Providing ABC cost information to the design engineers would probably have led them down a different path—one that would have been more advantageous to the company.

CVP Analysis and JIT

If a firm has adopted JIT (just-in-time manufacturing), the variable cost per unit sold is reduced, and fixed costs are increased. Direct labor, for example, is now viewed as fixed instead of variable. Direct materials, on the other hand, is still a unit-based variable cost. In fact, the emphasis on total quality and long-term purchasing makes the assumption that direct materials cost is strictly proportional to units produced even more true (because waste, scrap, and quantity discounts are eliminated). Other unit-based variable costs, such as power and sales commissions, also persist. Additionally, the batch-level variable is gone (in JIT, the batch is one unit). Thus, the cost equation for JIT can be expressed as follows:

$$\text{Total cost} = \text{Fixed cost} + (\text{Unit variable cost} \times \text{Number of units}) + (\text{Engineering cost} \times \text{Number of engineering hours})$$

Since its application is a special case of the ABC equation, no example will be given.

Summary of Learning Objectives

1. Determine the number of units that must be sold to break even or to earn a targeted profit.

In a single-product setting, the break-even point can be computed in units by dividing the total fixed costs by the contribution margin per unit. In essence, sufficient units must be sold to just cover all fixed and variable costs of the firm.

2. Calculate the amount of revenue required to break even or to earn a targeted profit.

Break-even revenue is computed by dividing the total fixed costs by the contribution margin ratio. Targeted profit is added to fixed costs in determining the amount of revenue needed to yield the targeted profit.

3. Apply cost-volume-profit analysis in a multiple-product setting.

Multiple-product analysis requires that an assumption be made concerning the expected sales mix. Given a particular sales mix, a multiple-product problem can be converted into a single-product analysis. However, it should be remembered that the answers change as the sales mix changes. If the sales mix changes in a multiple-product firm, the break-even point will also change. In general, increases in the sales of high contribution margin products will decrease the break-even point, while increases in the sales of low contribution margin products will increase the break-even point.

4. Prepare a profit-volume graph and a cost-volume-profit graph, and explain the meaning of each.

CVP is based on several assumptions that must be considered in applying it to business problems. The analysis assumes linear revenue and cost functions, no finished goods ending inventories, and a constant sales mix. CVP analysis also assumes that selling prices and fixed and variable costs are known with certainty. These assumptions form the basis for simple graphical analysis using the profit-volume graph and the cost-volume-profit graph.

5. Explain the impact of risk, uncertainty, and changing variables on cost-volume-profit analysis.

Measures of risk and uncertainty, such as the margin of safety and operating leverage, can be used to give managers more insight into CVP answers. Sensitivity analysis gives still more insight into the effect of changes in underlying variables on CVP relationships.

6. Discuss the impact of activity-based costing on cost-volume-profit analysis.

CVP can be used with activity-based costing, but the analysis must be modified. In effect, under ABC, a type of sensitivity analysis is used. Fixed costs are separated from a variety of costs that vary with particular cost drivers. At this stage, it is easiest to organize variable costs as unit-level, batch-level, and product-level. Then, the impact of decisions on batches and products can be examined within the CVP framework.

The subject of cost-volume-profit analysis naturally lends itself to the use of numerous equations. Some of the more common equations used in this chapter are summarized in Exhibit 11-9.

Key Terms

1. Sales revenue = Price × Units
2. Operating income = (Price × Units) − (Unit variable cost × Units) − Fixed cost
3. Break-even point in units = Fixed cost/(Price − Unit variable cost)
4. Contribution margin ratio = Contribution margin/Sales
   or
   = (Price − Unit variable cost)/Price
5. Variable cost ratio = Total variable cost/Sales
   or
   = Unit variable cost/Price
6. Break-even point in sales dollars = Fixed cost/Contribution margin ratio
   or
   = Fixed cost/(1 − Variable cost ratio)
7. Margin of safety = Sales − Break-even sales
8. Degree of operating leverage = Total contribution margin/Profit
9. Percentage change in profits = Degree of operating leverage × Percent change in sales
10. Income taxes = Income tax rate × Operating income
11. After-tax income = Operating income − (Income tax rate × Operating income)
12. Before-tax income = After-tax income/(1 − Income tax rate)
13. ABC total cost = Fixed cost + (Unit variable cost × Number of units) + (Batch-level cost × Batch driver) + (Product-level cost × Product driver)
14. ABC break-even units = [Fixed cost + (Batch-level cost × Batch driver) + (Product-level cost × Product driver)]/(Price − Unit variable cost)

Exhibit 11-9 Summary of Important Equations

Review Problems

1. Break-Even Analysis

Cutlass Company's projected profit for the coming year is as follows:

	Total	Per Unit
Sales	$200,000	$20
Less: Variable expenses	120,000	12
Contribution margin	$ 80,000	$ 8
Less: Fixed expenses	64,000	
Operating income	$ 16,000	

Required

1. Compute the break-even point in units.
2. How many units must be sold to earn a profit of $30,000?
3. Compute the contribution margin ratio. Using that ratio, compute the additional profit that Cutlass would earn if sales were $25,000 more than expected.
4. Suppose Cutlass would like to earn operating income equal to 20 percent of sales revenue. How many units must be sold for this goal to be realized? Prepare an income statement to prove your answer.
5. For the projected level of sales, compute the margin of safety.

Solution

1. The break-even point is computed as follows:

Units = Fixed cost/(Price − Unit variable cost)
= $64,000/($20 − $12)
= $64,000/$8
= 8,000 units

2. The number of units that must be sold to earn a profit of $30,000 is calculated as follows:

Units = ($64,000 + $30,000)/$8
= $94,000/$8
= 11,750 units

3. The contribution margin ratio is $8/$20 = 0.40. With additional sales of $25,000, the additional profit would be 0.40 × $25,000 = $10,000.
4. To find the number of units sold for a profit equal to 20 percent of sales, let target income equal (0.20)(Price × Units), and solve for units.

Operating income = (Price × Units) − (Unit variable cost × Units) − Fixed cost
(0.2)($20)Units = $20(Units) − $12(Units) − $64,000
$4(Units) = $64,000
Units = 16,000

The income statement is as follows:

Sales (16,000 × $20)	$320,000
Less: Variable expenses (16,000 × $12)	192,000
Contribution margin	$128,000
Less: Fixed expenses	64,000
Operating income	$ 64,000

Operating income/Sales = $64,000/$320,000 = 0.20, or 20 percent.

5. The margin of safety is 10,000 − 8,000 = 2,000 units, or $40,000 in sales revenues.

2. Break-Even Analysis with ABC

Dory Manufacturing Company produces T-shirts screen-printed with the logos of various sports teams. Each shirt is priced at $10. Costs are as follows:

Activity Driver	Unit Variable Cost	Level of Activity Driver
Units sold	$ 5	—
Setups	$450	80
Engineering hours	20	500
Other data:		
Total fixed costs (conventional)	$96,000	
Total fixed costs (ABC)	50,000	

Required

1. Compute the break-even point in units using conventional analysis.
2. Compute the break-even point in units using ABC analysis.
3. Suppose that Dory could reduce the setup cost by $150 per setup and the number of engineering hours needed to 425. How many units must be sold to break even in this case?

Solution

1. Break-even units = Fixed cost/(Price − Unit variable cost)
= $96,000/($10 − $5)
= 19,200 units
2. Break-even units = [Fixed cost + (Setups × Setup cost) + (Engineering hours × Engineering cost)]/(Price − Unit variable cost)
= [$50,000 + ($450 × 80) + ($20 × 500)]/($10 − $5)
= $96,000/$5
= 19,200 units

3. Break-even units $= [\$50{,}000 + (\$300 \times 80) + (\$20 \times 425)]/(\$10 - \$5)$
$= \$82{,}500/\$5$
$= 16{,}500$ units

Questions for Writing and Discussion

1. Explain how CVP analysis can be used for managerial planning.
2. Describe the difference between the units-sold approach to CVP analysis and the sales-revenue approach.
3. Define the term *break-even point.*
4. Explain why contribution margin per unit becomes profit per unit above the break-even point.
5. If the contribution margin per unit is $7 and the break-even point is 10,000 units, how much profit will a firm make if 15,000 units are sold?
6. What is the variable cost ratio? The contribution margin ratio? How are the two ratios related?
7. Suppose a firm has fixed costs of $20,000 and a contribution margin ratio of 0.4. How much sales revenue must the firm have in order to break even?
8. Suppose a firm with a contribution margin ratio of 0.30 increased its advertising expenses by $10,000 and found that sales increased by $30,000. Was it a good decision to increase advertising expenses?
9. Define the term *sales mix,* and give an example to support your definition.
10. Explain how CVP analysis developed for single products can be used in a multiple-product setting.
11. Assume that a firm has two products—A and B. Last year, 2,000 units of A and 1,000 units of B were sold. The same sales mix is expected for the coming year. Total fixed expenses are $30,000, and the unit contribution margins are $10 for A and $5 for B. How many units of A and how many units of B must be sold to break even?
12. Wilson Company has a contribution margin ratio of 0.60. The break-even point is $100,000. During the year, Wilson earned total revenues of $200,000. What was Wilson's profit?
13. Explain how a change in sales mix can change a company's break-even point.
14. Define the term *margin of safety.* Explain how it can be used as a crude measure of operating risk.
15. Explain what is meant by the term *operating leverage.* What impact does increased leverage have on risk?
16. How can sensitivity analysis be used in conjunction with CVP analysis?
17. Why does the activity-based costing approach to CVP analysis offer more insight than the conventional approach?
18. How does JIT affect the firm's cost equation? CVP analysis?

Exercises

11-1

Basic Break-Even Calculations
LO1

Adams Company sells a product for $14. Unit costs are as follows:

Direct materials	$3.90
Direct labor	1.40
Variable overhead	2.10
Variable selling expenses	1.00

Total fixed overhead is $44,000 per year, and total fixed selling and administrative expenses are $47,280.

Required

Calculate each of the following:

1. Variable cost per unit
2. Contribution margin
3. Contribution margin ratio
4. Variable cost ratio
5. Total fixed cost
6. Break-even units

11-2

Break-Even in Units
LO1

Sokolov Company sells a product for $12. Unit costs are as follows:

Direct materials	$1.90
Direct labor	2.85
Variable overhead	1.25
Variable selling expenses	2.00

Total fixed overhead is $44,000 per year, and total fixed selling and administrative expenses are $37,900.

Required

1. Calculate the contribution margin per unit
2. Calculate the break-even units.
3. How many units must Sokolov produce and sell to earn operating income of $9,000?
4. Prepare an income statement for your answer in requirement 3.

11-3

Breakeven in Units
LO1

The controller of Lohrey Company prepared the following projected income statement:

Sales (15,000 units @ $8)	$120,000
Less: Variable costs	75,000
Contribution margin	$ 45,000
Less: Fixed costs	37,500
Operating income	$ 7,500

Required

1. Calculate the break-even number of units.
2. Prepare an income statement for Lohrey at breakeven.
3. How many units must Lohrey sell to earn operating income equal to $9,900?

11-4

Contribution Margin Ratio; Variable Cost Ratio; Breakeven in Sales Revenue
LO2

Refer to **Exercise 16-3** for data.

Required

1. What is the contribution margin per unit for Lohrey Company? What is the contribution margin ratio?
2. What is the variable cost ratio for Lohrey Company?
3. Calculate the break-even revenue.
4. How much revenue must Lohrey make to earn operating income equal to $9,900?

11-5

Units Sold to Break Even and to Find Targeted Income
LO1

Ingo Company produces and sells disposable foil baking pans to retailers for $3.20 per pan. The variable costs per pan are as follows:

Direct materials	$0.77
Direct labor	0.71
Variable overhead	0.60
Selling	0.32

Fixed manufacturing costs total $151,650 per year. Administrative costs (all fixed) total $28,350.

Required

1. Compute the number of pans that must be sold for Ingo to break even.
2. How many pans must be sold for Ingo to earn a before-tax profit of $12,600?
3. What is the unit variable cost? What is the unit variable manufacturing cost? Which is used in cost-volume-profit analysis, and why?

11-6

After-Tax Target Income
LO1

Refer to **Exercise 11-5**.

Required

1. Assuming a tax rate of 40 percent, how many pans must be sold to earn an after-tax profit of $25,200?
2. Now, assuming a tax rate of 30 percent, how many pans must be sold to earn after-tax income of $25,200?
3. Now, assuming a tax rate of 50 percent, how many pans must be sold to earn after-tax income of $25,200?

11-7

Break-Even Revenue, Target Revenue, Break-Even Units, Target Units
LO1, LO2

Pacheco Company sells a product for $15. Units costs are as follows:

Direct materials	$3.90
Direct labor	1.40
Variable overhead	2.10

Total fixed overhead is $52,000 per year. Variable selling expenses are $1.60 per unit sold; fixed selling and administrative expenses are $37,950.

Required

1. Calculate the contribution margin ratio
2. Calculate the break-even revenue.
3. Calculate the revenue needed to earn $18,000.
4. Calculate the break-even units, rounded to the nearest unit.
5. Calculate the units needed to earn $18,000, rounded to the nearest unit.

11-8

Multiple-Product Breakeven; Break-Even Sales Revenue; Margin of Safety
LO2, LO3, LO5

EXCEL

Switzer Company produces and sells two types of yoga-training products: how-to videotapes and a basic equipment set (blocks, strap, and small pillows). Last year, Switzer sold 10,000 videos and 5,000 equipment sets. Information on the two products is as follows:

	Video	Equipment Set
Price	$12.00	$15.00
Variable cost per unit	4.00	6.00

Total fixed costs are $70,000.

Required

1. What is the sales mix of videos and equipment sets?
2. Compute the break-even quantity of each product.
3. Prepare an income statement for Switzer for last year. What is the overall contribution margin ratio? The overall break-even sales revenue?

11-9

Multiple-Product Breakeven; Break-Even Sales Revenue; Margin of Safety
LO2, LO3, LO5

Refer to **Exercise 11-8**. Suppose that in the coming year, Switzer plans to produce an extra-thick yoga mat for sale to health clubs. The company estimates that 20,000 mats can be sold at a price of $18 and variable cost per unit of $13. Fixed costs must be increased by $48,350 (making total fixed costs $118,350). Assume that anticipated sales of the other products, as well as their prices and variable costs, remain the same.

Required

1. What is the sales mix of videos, equipment sets, and yoga mats?
2. Compute the break-even quantity of each product.
3. Prepare a budgeted income statement for Switzer for the coming year. What is the overall contribution margin ratio? The overall break-even sales revenue?

11-10

Break-Even Units, Break-Even Revenue, Margin of Safety
LO1, LO2, LO5

Cherron Company budgeted the following per-unit information for the coming year:

Price	$24.00
Direct materials	5.60
Direct labor	7.50
Variable overhead	2.90
Variable selling expense	2.00

Total fixed expense was $75,000. In the coming year, Cherron Company expects to sell 14,000 units.

Required

1. Calculate the break-even units and the break-even sales revenue.
2. Calculate the margin of safety in sales dollars.
3. Calculate the margin of safety in units.

11-11

CVP and Profit-Volume Graphs
LO4

Lotts Company produces and sells one product. The selling price is $10, and the unit variable cost is $6. Total fixed costs are $10,000.

Required

1. Prepare a CVP graph with "Units Sold" as the horizontal axis and "Dollars" as the vertical axis. Label the break-even point on the horizontal axis.
2. Prepare CVP graphs for each of the following independent scenarios:
   a. Fixed costs increase by $5,000.
   b. Unit variable cost increases to $7.
   c. Unit selling price increases to $12.
   d. Assume that fixed costs increase by $5,000 and unit variable cost is $7.
3. Prepare a profit-volume graph using the original data. Repeat, following the scenarios in Requirement 2.
4. Which of the two graphs do you think provides more information? Why?

11-12

Operating Leverage
LO5

EXCEL

Income statements for two different companies in the same industry are as follows:

	Darius	Xerxes
Sales	$500,000	$500,000
Less: Variable costs	400,000	200,000
Contribution margin	$100,000	$300,000
Less: Fixed costs	50,000	250,000
Operating income	$ 50,000	$ 50,000

Required

1. Compute the degree of operating leverage for each company.
2. Compute the break-even point for each company. Explain why the break-even point for Xerxes is higher.
3. Suppose that both companies experience a 50 percent increase in revenues. Compute the percentage change in profits for each company. Explain why the percentage increase in Xerxes's profits is so much larger than that of Darius.

11-13

Break-Even in Units
LO1, LO5

The controller of Hannibal Company prepared the following projected income statement:

Sales (5,000 units @ $15)	$75,000
Less: Variable costs	60,000
Contribution margin	$15,000
Less: Fixed costs	10,350
Operating income	$ 4,650

Required

1. Calculate the break-even number of units.
2. Calculate the break-even sales revenue.
3. Calculate the margin of safety in units.
4. Calculate the margin of safety in sales dollars.

11-14

CVP; Margin of Safety
LO2, LO5

Aeveen Company had revenues of $930,000 last year with total variable costs of $399,900 and fixed costs of $307,800.

Required

1. What is the variable cost ratio for Aeveen? What is the contribution margin ratio?
2. What is the break-even point in sales revenue?
3. What was the margin of safety for Aeveen last year?
4. Aeveen is considering starting a multimedia advertising campaign that is supposed to increase sales by $7,500 per year. The campaign will cost $5,000. Is the advertising campaign a good idea? Explain.

11-15

CVP
LO1, LO2, LO5

Solve the following independent problems.

Required

1. Sarah Company's break-even point is 1,500 units. Variable cost per unit is $300; total fixed costs are $120,000 per year. What price does Sarah charge?
2. Jesper Company charges a price of $3.50; total fixed costs are $160,000 per year; and the break-even point is 128,000 units. What is the variable cost per unit?
3. Aisha Company sold 35,000 units last year at a price of $40. Variable cost per unit was $30. The margin of safety was 300 units. What was the total fixed cost?

11-16

Contribution Margin; CVP; Margin of Safety
LO1, LO2, LO5

EXCEL

Candyland, Inc., produces a particularly rich praline fudge. Each 10-ounce box sells for $5.60. Variable unit costs are as follows:

Pecans	$0.70
Sugar	0.35
Butter	1.85
Other ingredients	0.34
Box, packing material	0.76
Selling commission	0.20

Fixed overhead cost is $32,300 per year. Fixed selling and administrative costs are $12,500 per year. Candyland sold 35,000 boxes last year.

Required

1. What is the contribution margin per unit for a box of praline fudge? What is the contribution margin ratio?
2. How many boxes must be sold to break even? What is the break-even sales revenue?
3. What was Candyland's operating income last year?
4. What was the margin of safety?

5. Suppose that Candyland, Inc., raises the price to $6.20 per box but anticipates a sales drop to 31,500 boxes. What will the new break-even point in units be? Should Candyland raise the price? Explain.

11-17

Sales Revenue Approach; Variable Cost Ratio; Contribution Margin Ratio; Margin of Safety
LO2, LO5

Skelly Company's controller prepared the following budgeted income statement for the coming year:

Sales	$315,000
Less: Variable expenses	126,000
Contribution margin	$189,000
Less: Fixed expenses	63,000
Profit before taxes	$126,000
Less: Taxes	37,800
Profit after taxes	$ 88,200

Required

1. What is Skelly's variable cost ratio? What is its contribution margin ratio?
2. Suppose Skelly's actual revenues are $46,000 more than budgeted. By how much will before-tax profits increase? Give the answer without preparing a new income statement.
3. How much sales revenue must Skelly earn to break even? What is the expected margin of safety?
4. How much sales revenue must Skelly generate to earn a before-tax profit of $90,000?
5. How much sales revenue must Skelly generate to earn an after-tax profit of $56,000? Prepare a contribution income statement to verify the accuracy of your answer.

11-18

Changes in Break-Even Points with Changes in Unit Prices
LO1, LO2

The income statement for Fellows, Inc., is as follows:

Sales	$650,000
Less: Variable expenses	240,000
Contribution margin	$ 410,000
Less: Fixed expenses	295,200
Operating income	$ 114,800

Fellows produces and sells a single product. The income statement is based on sales of 100,000 units.

Required

1. Compute the break-even point in units and in revenues.
2. Suppose that the selling price increases by 10 percent. Will the break-even point increase or decrease? Recompute it.
3. Ignoring the price increase in Requirement 2, suppose that the variable cost per unit increases by $0.35. Will the break-even point increase or decrease? Recompute it.
4. Can you predict whether the break-even point increases or decreases if both the selling price and the unit variable cost increase? Recompute the break-even point incorporating both of the changes in Requirements 2 and 3.
5. Assume that total fixed costs increase by $50,000. (Assume no other changes from the original data.) Will the break-even point increase or decrease? Recompute it.

Problems

11-19

CVP Analysis with Target Profits LO1, LO2

Tom Flannery has developed a new recipe for fried chicken and plans to open a take-out restaurant in Oklahoma City. His father-in-law has agreed to invest $500,000 in the operation provided Tom can convince him that profits will be at least 20 percent of sales revenues. Tom estimated that total fixed expenses would be $24,000 per year and that variable expenses would be approximately 40 percent of sales revenue.

Required

1. How much sales revenue must be earned to produce profits equal to 20 percent of sales revenue? Prepare a contribution income statement to verify your answer.
2. If Tom plans on selling 12-piece buckets of chicken for $10 each, how many buckets must he sell to earn a profit equal to 20 percent of sales? Twenty-five percent of sales? Prepare a contribution income statement to verify the second answer.
3. Suppose Tom's father-in-law meant that the after-tax profit had to be 20 percent of sales revenue. Under this assumption, how much sales revenue must be generated by Tom's chicken business? (Assume that the tax rate is 40 percent.)

11-20

Basic CVP Concepts LO1, LO2, LO5

Zacarello Company produces a single product. The projected income statement for the coming year is as follows:

Sales (50,000 units @ $50)	$2,500,000
Less: Variable costs	1,440,000
Contribution margin	$1,060,000
Less: Fixed costs	816,412
Operating income	$ 243,588

Required

1. Compute the unit contribution margin and the units that must be sold to break even. Suppose that 30,000 units are sold above breakeven. What is the profit?
2. Compute the contribution margin ratio and the break-even point in dollars. Suppose that revenues are $200,000 more than expected. What would the total profit be?
3. Compute the margin of safety.
4. Compute the operating leverage. Compute the new profit level if sales are 20 percent higher than expected.
5. How many units must be sold to earn a profit equal to 10 percent of sales?
6. Assume that the tax rate is 40 percent. How many units must be sold to earn an after-tax profit of $180,000?

11-21

Basic CVP Concepts LO1, LO2, LO5

Graham Company produces a variety of chemicals. One division makes reagents for laboratories. The division's projected income statement for the coming year is as follows:

Sales (110,000 units @ $25)	$2,750,000
Less: Variable expenses	1,925,000
Contribution margin	$ 825,000
Less: Fixed expenses	495,000
Operating income	$ 330,000

Required

1. Compute the contribution margin per unit, and calculate the break-even point in units (round to the nearest unit). Calculate the contribution margin ratio and the break-even sales revenue.
2. The divisional manager has decided to increase the advertising budget by $40,000. This will increase sales revenues by $400,000. By how much will operating income increase or decrease as a result of this action?
3. Suppose sales revenues exceed the estimated amount on the income statement by $315,000. Without preparing a new income statement, by how much are profits underestimated?
4. Refer to the original data. How many units must be sold to earn an after-tax profit of $360,000? Assume a tax rate of 40 percent.
5. Compute the margin of safety based on the original income statement.
6. Compute the operating leverage based on the original income statement. If sales revenues are 20 percent greater than expected, what is the percentage increase in profits?

11-22

Multiple-Product Analysis; Changes in Sales Mix
LO3

EXCEL

Gosnell Company produces two products: squares and circles. The projected income for the coming year, segmented by product line, follows:

	Squares	Circles	Total
Sales	$300,000	$2,500,000	$2,800,000
Less: Variable expenses	100,000	500,000	600,000
Contribution margin	$200,000	$2,000,000	$2,200,000
Less: Direct fixed expenses	28,000	1,500,000	1,528,000
Product margin	$172,000	$ 500,000	$ 672,000
Less: Common fixed expenses			100,000
Operating income			$ 572,000

The selling prices are $30 for squares and $50 for circles.

Required

1. Compute the number of units of each product that must be sold for Gosnell Company to break even.
2. Compute the revenue that must be earned to produce an operating income of 10 percent of sales revenues.
3. Assume that the marketing manager changes the sales mix of the two products so that the ratio is three squares to five circles. Repeat Requirements 1 and 2.
4. Refer to the original data. Suppose that Gosnell can increase the sales of squares with increased advertising. The extra advertising would cost an additional $45,000, and some of the potential purchasers of circles would switch to squares. In total, sales of squares would increase by 15,000 units, and sales of circles would decrease by 5,000 units. Would Gosnell be better off with this strategy?

11-23

CVP Analysis with Multiple Products
LO3

EXCEL

Gernon Company produces scientific and business calculators. For the coming year, Gernon expects to sell 20,000 scientific calculators and 100,000 business calculators. A segmented income statement for the two products follows:

	Scientific	Business	Total
Sales	$500,000	$2,000,000	$2,500,000
Less: Variable costs	240,000	900,000	1,140,000
Contribution margin	$260,000	$1,100,000	$1,360,000
Less: Direct fixed costs	120,000	960,000	1,080,000

(continued)

Segment margin	$140,000	$ 140,000	$ 280,000
Less: Common fixed costs			145,000
Operating income			$ 135,000

Required

1. Compute the number of scientific calculators and the number of business calculators that must be sold to break even.
2. Using information from only the "Total" column of the income statement, compute the sales revenue that must be generated for the company to break even.

11-24

CVP Equation; Basic Concepts; Solving for Unknowns
LO1, LO2

Tressa Company produces combination shampoos and conditioners in individual-use bottles for hotels. Each bottle sells for $0.36. The variable costs for each bottle (materials, labor, and overhead) total $0.27. The total fixed costs are $54,000. During the most recent year, 830,000 bottles were sold. The president of Tressa, not fully satisfied with the profit performance of the shampoo, was considering the following options to increase profitability: (1) increase promotional spending; (2) increase the quality of the ingredients and, simultaneously, increase the selling price; (3) increase the selling price; and (4) combinations of the three.

Required

1. The sales manager is confident that an advertising campaign could increase sales volume by 50 percent. If the company president's goal is to increase this year's profits by 50 percent over last year's, what is the maximum amount that can be spent on advertising?
2. Assume that the company has a plan to imprint the name of the purchasing hotel on each bottle. This will increase variable costs to $0.30. How much must the selling price be increased to maintain the same break-even point?
3. The company has decided to increase its selling price to $0.40. The sales volume drops from 830,000 to 700,000 bottles. Was the decision to increase the price a good one? Compute the sales volume that would be needed at the new price for the company to earn the same profit as last year.

11-25

Basics of the Sales Revenue Approach
LO2, LO5

Fitzgibbons Company produces plastic mailboxes. The projected income statement for the coming year follows:

Sales	$840,600
Less: Variable costs	353,052
Contribution margin	$487,548
Less: Fixed costs	250,000
Operating income	$237,548

Required

1. Compute the contribution margin ratio for the mailboxes.
2. How much revenue must Fitzgibbons earn in order to break even?
3. What volume of sales must be earned if Fitzgibbons wants to earn an after-tax income equal to 8 percent of sales? Assume that the tax rate is 34 percent.
4. What is the effect on the contribution margin ratio if the unit selling price and unit variable cost each increase by 10 percent?
5. Suppose that management has decided to give a 3 percent commission on all sales. The projected income statement does not reflect this commission. Recompute the contribution margin ratio assuming that the commission will be paid. What effect does this have on the break-even point?

6. If the commission is paid as described in Requirement 5, management expects sales revenues to increase by $80,000. Is it a sound decision to implement the commission? Support your answer with appropriate computations.

11-26

CVP with Multiple Products; Sales Mix Changes; Changes in Fixed and Variable Costs
LO3

Artistic Woodcrafting, Inc., began in 2002 as a one-person cabinet-making operation. Employees were added as the business expanded. By 2005, sales volume totaled $850,000. Volume for the first five months of 2006 totaled $600,000, and sales were expected to be $1.6 million for the entire year. Unfortunately, the cabinet business in the region where Artistic Woodcrafting is located is highly competitive. More than 200 cabinet shops are all competing for the same business.

Artistic currently offers two different quality grades of cabinets: Grade I and Grade II, with Grade I being the higher quality. The average unit selling prices, unit variable costs, and direct fixed costs are as follows:

	Unit Price	Unit Variable Cost	Direct Fixed Cost
Grade I	$3,400	$2,686	$95,000
Grade II	1,600	1,328	95,000

Common fixed costs (fixed costs not traceable to either cabinet) are $35,000. Currently, for every three Grade I cabinets sold, seven Grade II cabinets are sold.

Required

1. Calculate the Grade I and Grade II cabinets that are expected to be sold during 2006.
2. Calculate the number of Grade I and Grade II cabinets that must be sold for the company to break even.
3. Artistic Woodcrafting can buy computer-controlled machines that will make doors, drawers, and frames. If the machines are purchased, the variable costs for each type of cabinet will decrease by 9 percent, but common fixed costs will increase by $44,000. Compute the effect on operating income in 2006, and also calculate the new break-even point. Assume the machines are purchased at the beginning of the sixth month. Fixed costs for the company are incurred uniformly throughout the year.
4. Refer to the original data. Artistic Woodcrafting is considering adding a retail outlet. This will increase common fixed costs by $70,000 per year. As a result of adding the retail outlet, the additional publicity and emphasis on quality will allow the firm to change the sales mix to 1:1. The retail outlet is also expected to increase sales by 30 percent. Assume that the outlet is opened at the beginning of the sixth month. Calculate the effect on the company's expected profits for 2006, and calculate the new break-even point. Assume that fixed costs are incurred uniformly throughout the year.

11-27

Multiple Products; Break-Even Analysis; Operating Leverage
LO3, LO5

Carlyle Lighting Products produces two different types of lamps, a floor lamp and a desk lamp. Floor lamps sell for $30 and desk lamps for $20. The projected income statement for the coming year follows:

Sales	$600,000
Less: Variable costs	400,000
Contribution margin	$200,000
Less: Fixed costs	150,000
Operating income	$ 50,000

The owner of Carlyle estimates that 60 percent of the sales revenues will be produced by floor lamps with the remaining 40 percent by desk lamps. Floor lamps are also responsible for 60 percent of the variable expenses. Of the fixed expenses, one-third are common to both products, and one-half are directly traceable to the floor lamp product line.

Required

1. Compute the sales revenue that must be earned for Carlyle to break even.
2. Compute the number of floor lamps and desk lamps that must be sold for Carlyle to break even.
3. Compute the degree of operating leverage for Carlyle Lighting Products. Now, assume that the actual revenues will be 40 percent higher than the projected revenues. By what percentage will profits increase with this change in sales volume?

11-28

CVP; Margin of Safety
LO1, LO2, LO5

Victoria Company produces a single product. Last year's income statement is as follows:

Sales (29,000 units @ $42)	$1,218,000
Less: Variable costs	812,000
Contribution margin	$ 406,000
Less: Fixed costs	300,000
Operating income	$ 106,000

Required

1. Compute the break-even point in units and sales dollars.
2. What was the margin of safety for Victoria Company last year?
3. Suppose that Victoria Company is considering an investment in new technology that will increase fixed costs by $250,000 per year but will lower variable costs to 45 percent of sales. Units sold will remain unchanged. Prepare a budgeted income statement assuming that Victoria makes this investment. What is the new break-even point in units and sales dollars, assuming that the investment is made?

11-29

Multiplant Breakeven
LO3

CMA

The PTO Division of the Galva Manufacturing Company produces power take-off units for the farm equipment business. The PTO Division, headquartered in Peoria, has a newly renovated plant in Peoria and an older, less automated plant in Moline. Both plants produce the same power take-off units for farm tractors that are sold to most domestic and foreign tractor manufacturers.

The PTO Division expects to produce and sell 192,000 power take-off units during the coming year. The divisional production manager has the following data available regarding the unit costs, unit prices, and production capacities for the two plants.

	Peoria		Moline	
Selling price		$150.00		$150.00
Variable manufacturing costs	$72.00		$88.00	
Fixed manufacturing costs	30.00		15.00	
Commission (5 percent)	7.50		7.50	
General and administrative expenses	25.50		21.00	
Total unit cost		135.00		131.50
Unit profit		$ 15.00		$ 18.50
Production rate per day		400 units		320 units

All fixed costs are based on a normal year of 240 working days. When the number of working days exceeds 240, variable manufacturing costs increase by $3 per unit in Peoria and $8 per unit in Moline. Capacity for each plant is 300 working days.

Galva Manufacturing charges each of its plants a per-unit fee for administrative services such as payroll, general accounting, and purchasing, because Galva considers these services to be a function of the work performed at the plants. For each of the plants, a fee of $6.50 per unit represents the variable portion of the general and administrative expenses.

Wishing to maximize the higher unit profit at Moline, PTO's production manager has decided to manufacture 96,000 units at each plant. This production plan results in Moline's operating at capacity and Peoria's operating at its normal volume. Galva's corporate controller is not happy with this plan; he wonders if it might be better to produce relatively more at the automated plant in Peoria.

Required

1. Determine the annual break-even units for each of PTO's plants.
2. Calculate the operating income that would result from the divisional production manager's plan to produce 96,000 units at each plant.
3. Calculate the operating income that would result from sales of 192,000 power take-off units if 120,000 of them were produced at the Peoria plant and the remainder at the Moline plant. **(CMA adapted)**

11-30

CVP Analysis and Assumptions
LO2, LO5

CMA

Marston Corporation manufactures pharmaceutical products that are sold through a network of sales agents located in the United States and Canada. The agents are currently paid an 18 percent commission on sales; this percentage was used when Marston prepared the following pro forma income statement for the fiscal year ended June 30, 2008.

Marston Corporation
Pro Forma Income Statement
For the Year Ended June 30, 2008
($000 omitted)

Sales		$26,000
Cost of goods sold:		
Variable	$11,700	
Fixed	2,870	14,570
Gross margin		$11,430
Selling and admin. expenses:		
Commissions	$ 4,680	
Fixed advertising expenses	750	
Fixed administrative expenses	1,850	7,280
Operating income		$ 4,150
Fixed interest expense		650
Income before income taxes		$ 3,500
Income taxes (40 percent)		1,400
Net income		$ 2,100

Since the completion of this statement, Marston has learned that its agents are requiring an increase in the commission rate to 23 percent for the upcoming year. As a result, Marston's president has decided to investigate the possibility of hiring its own sales staff in place of the network of sales agents. He has asked Tom Ross, Marston's controller, to gather information on the costs associated with this change.

Tom estimates that Marston will have to hire eight salespeople to cover the current market area, and the annual payroll cost of each of these employees will average $80,000, including fringe benefit expenses. Travel and entertainment expenses are expected to total $600,000 for the year, and the annual cost of hiring a sales manager and sales secretary will be $150,000. In addition to their salaries, the eight salespeople will each earn commissions at the rate of 10 percent on the first $2 million in sales and 15 percent on all sales over $2 million. For planning purposes, Tom expects that all eight salespeople will exceed the $2 million mark and that sales will be at the level previously projected. Tom believes that Marston should also increase its advertising budget by $500,000.

Required

1. Calculate Marston Corporation's break-even point in sales dollars for the fiscal year ended June 30, 2008, if the company hires its own sales force and increases its advertising costs.
2. If Marston Corporation continues to sell through its network of sales agents and pays the higher commission rate, determine the estimated volume in sales dollars for the fiscal year ended June 30, 2008, that would be required to generate the same net income as that projected in the pro forma income statement presented.
3. Describe the general assumptions underlying break-even analysis that might limit its usefulness in this case. **(CMA adapted)**

Managerial Decision Cases

11-31

Ethics and a CVP Application
LO1

Danna Lumus, the marketing manager for a division that produces a variety of paper products, was considering the divisional manager's request for a sales forecast for a new line of paper napkins. The divisional manager was gathering data so that he could choose between two different production processes. The first process would have a variable cost of $10 per case produced and fixed costs of $100,000. The second process would have a variable cost of $6 per case and fixed costs of $200,000. The selling price would be $30 per case. Danna had just completed a marketing analysis that projected annual sales of 30,000 cases.

Danna was reluctant to report the 30,000 cases forecast to the divisional manager. She knew that the first process was labor-intensive, whereas the second was largely automated with little labor and no requirement for an additional production supervisor. If the first process were chosen, Jerry Johnson, a good friend, would be appointed as the line supervisor. If the second process were chosen, Jerry and an entire line of laborers would be laid off. After some consideration, Danna revised the projected sales downward to 22,000 cases.

She believed that the revision downward was justified. Since it would lead the divisional manager to choose the manual system, it showed a sensitivity to the needs of current employees—a sensitivity that she was afraid her divisional manager did not possess. He was too focused on quantitative factors in his decision making and usually ignored the qualitative aspects.

Required

1. Compute the break-even point for each process.
2. Compute the sales volume for which the two processes are equally profitable. Identify the range of sales for which the manual process is more profitable than the automated process. Identify the range of sales for which the automated process is more profitable than the manual process. Why did the divisional manager want the sales forecast?
3. Discuss Danna's decision to alter the sales forecast. Do you agree with it? Did she act ethically? Was her decision justified since it helped a number of employees retain their employment? Should the impact on employees be factored into decisions? In fact, is it unethical not to consider the impact of decisions on employees?

4. Even though Danna is not a management accountant, do any of the ethical standards for management accountants listed in Chapter 1 apply? Explain.

11-32

Service Organization; Multiple Products; Breakeven; Pricing and Scheduling Decisions
LO1, LO2, LO3

Utah Metropolitan Ballet is located in Salt Lake City. The company is housed in the Capitol Theater, one of three buildings that make up the Bicentennial Arts Center in downtown Salt Lake City. The ballet company features five different ballets per year. For the upcoming season, the five ballets to be performed are *The Dream, Petrushka, The Nutcracker, Sleeping Beauty,* and *Bugaku.*

The president and general manager has tentatively scheduled the following number of performances for each ballet for the coming season:

Dream	5
Petrushka	5
Nutcracker	20
Sleeping Beauty	10
Bugaku	5

To produce each ballet, costs must be incurred for costumes, props, rehearsals, royalties, guest artist fees, choreography, salaries of production staff, music, and wardrobe. These costs are fixed for a particular ballet regardless of the number of performances. The direct fixed costs follow for each ballet.

Dream	*Petrushka*	*Nutcracker*	*Sleeping Beauty*	*Bugaku*
$275,500	$145,500	$70,500	$345,000	$155,500

Other fixed costs are incurred as follows:

Advertising	$ 80,000
Insurance	15,000
Administrative salaries	222,000
Office rental, phone, and so on	84,000
Total	$401,000

For each performance of each ballet, the following costs are also incurred:

Utah symphony	$3,800
Auditorium rental	700
Dancers' payroll	4,000
Total	$8,500

The auditorium in which the ballet is presented has 1,854 seats, which are classified as A, B, and C. The best viewing ranges from A seats to C seats. Information concerning the different types of seat follows:

	A Seats	B Seats	C Seats
Quantity	114	756	984
Price	$35	$25	$15
Percentage sold for each performance:*			
Nutcracker	100	100	100
All others	100	80	75

*Based on experience, the same percentages are expected for the coming season.

Required

1. Compute the expected revenues from the performances that have been tentatively scheduled. Prepare a variable-costing income statement for each ballet.
2. Calculate the number of performances of each ballet required to produce the revenues needed to cover each ballet's direct fixed costs.

3. Calculate the number of performances of each ballet required for the company as a whole to break even. If you were the president and general manager, how would you alter the tentative schedule of performances?
4. Suppose that it is possible to offer a matinee of the popular *Nutcracker.* Seats would sell for $5 less than in the evening, and the rental of the auditorium would be $200 less. The president and general manager believes that five matinee performances are feasible and that 80 percent of each type of seat can be sold. What effect will the matinee have on the company's profitability? On the overall break-even point?
5. Suppose that no additional evening performances can be offered beyond those tentatively scheduled. Assume that the company will offer five matinee performances of *The Nutcracker.* Also, the company expects to receive $60,000 in government grants and contributions from supporters of the fine arts. Will the company break even? If not, what actions would you take to bring revenues in line with costs? Assume that no additional performances of *The Nutcracker* are feasible.

Research Assignment

11-33

Cybercase
LO1, LO3

Consider two competing products, **FedEx** overnight delivery of a letter and the **U.S. Postal Service** overnight express mail of a letter. Access both organizations' websites in the chapter web links at the Interactive Study Center on http://www.thomsonedu.com/accounting/hansen, and gather information about these services and the types of costs that are probably incurred. Write a brief paper listing the fixed and variable costs of each and their impact on the break-even point for these services. Do you think that the relative prices charged bear a relationship to the contribution margin? Do you suppose that the sales mix for each organization has a bearing on pricing and the break-even point?

chapter 12

Tactical Decision Making

learning objectives

After studying this chapter, you should be able to:

1. Describe the tactical decision-making model.
2. Explain how the activity resource usage model is used in assessing relevance.
3. Apply tactical decision-making concepts in a variety of business situations.
4. Choose the optimal product mix when faced with one constrained resource.
5. Explain the impact of cost on pricing decisions.
6. Appendix: Use linear programming to find the optimal solution to a problem of multiple constrained resources.

Scenario

TIDWELL

Tidwell Products, Inc.,[1] manufactures potentiometers, devices that adjust electrical resistance. Potentiometers are used in switches and knobs, for example, to control the volume on a radio or to raise or lower the lights using a dimmer switch. Currently, all parts necessary for the assembly of the products are produced internally. The firm, in operation for five years, has a single plant located in Wichita, Kansas. The facilities for the manufacture of potentiometers are leased, with five years remaining on the lease. All equipment is owned by the company. Because of increases in demand, production has been expanded significantly over the five years of operation, straining the capacity of the leased facilities. Currently, the company needs more warehousing and office space, as well as more space for the production of plastic moldings. The current output of these moldings, used to make potentiometers, needs to be expanded to accommodate the increased demand for the main product.

Leo Tidwell, owner and president of Tidwell Products, asked his vice president of marketing, John Tidwell, and his vice president of finance, Linda Thayn, to brainstorm ways to solve their capacity problem. Two proposals had been suggested and rejected. The first was to build the company's own plant. Leo believed it was too risky to invest the capital necessary to build a plant at this stage of the company's development. The second proposal involved a combination of leasing a larger facility and subleasing the current plant. This was rejected due to the difficulty of finding a tenant to sublease. After that, John was assigned the task of exploring the possibility of leasing a second facility comparable to the current one. Linda was assigned the task of identifying other possible solutions. Two weeks later, both reported back.

After some careful research, John concluded that the idea of leasing an additional plant was not a very good one. Tidwell's current level of production did not justify another plant. In fact, John predicted it would take at least five years before the company needed be concerned about expanding into another facility comparable to their current one. He believed that sales would grow modestly over the next five years, and that all that growth could be absorbed by the current production capacity. The large increases in demand that had been experienced the past five years were not likely to be repeated.

Linda had identified two feasible alternatives. One was to rent an additional building to be used for warehousing. By transferring warehousing needs to the new building, Tidwell could free up internal space for offices and for expanding the production of plastic moldings. She located a building within two miles of the plant that could be used. It has the capacity to handle both current needs and the modest growth that John predicted. The second alternative centered on outsourcing the production of some of their components. She pointed out that the market has been flooded with two components, shafts and bushings, that Tidwell currently makes. Prices have decreased significantly. They might be better off buying shafts and bushings instead of making them. Ceasing internal production of shafts and bushings would free up the space they needed.

Leo liked both of those alternatives. He asked Linda, as financial chief, to prepare a report that detailed the costs affecting the decision. He anticipated making a decision quickly.

Questions to Think About

1. Describe the decision to be made by Tidwell. Is it a strategic or tactical decision?
2. What costs do you think Leo is referring to in the last paragraph of the scenario? Give examples.
3. Assume Tidwell Products accepts Linda's first alternative. Are there any noncost factors that should be considered? What about her second alternative?

1 This scenario is based on the experiences of a real company. The names have been changed to preserve confidentiality.

One of the major roles of the management information system is supplying cost and revenue data that serve as the basis for user actions. Although a variety of user actions are possible, one of the more important actions that can be taken by users is tactical decision making. How cost and revenue data can be used to make tactical decisions is the focus of this chapter.

Tactical Decision Making

Objective 1

Describe the tactical decision-making model.

Tactical decision making consists of choosing among alternatives with an immediate or limited end in view. Accepting a special order for less than the normal selling price to utilize idle capacity and increase this year's profits is an example. Thus, some tactical decisions tend to be *short-run* in nature; however, it should be emphasized that short-run decisions often have long-run consequences. Consider a second example. Suppose that a company is considering producing a component instead of buying it from suppliers. The immediate objective may be to lower the cost of making the main product. Yet, this tactical decision may be a small part of the overall strategy of establishing a cost leadership position for the firm. Thus, tactical decisions are often *small-scale actions* that serve a larger purpose.

The overall objective of **strategic decision making** is to select among alternative strategies so that a long-term competitive advantage is established. Tactical decision making should support this overall objective, even if the immediate objective is short-run (accepting a one-time order to increase profits) or small-scale (making instead of buying a component). Thus, *sound* tactical decision making means that the decisions made not only achieve the limited objective but also serve a larger purpose. In fact, no tactical decision should be made that does not serve the overall strategic goals of an organization. A good example of a company that has made tactical decisions that are in accordance with its strategic goals is **Hyatt Hotels Corporation**.[2] In the early 1990s, steep costs jeopardized a number of Hyatt's management contracts. It was necessary to reduce the cost structure fast. However, Hyatt attacked only the costs that guests did not particularly care about (for example, turndown service, in which the bedcovers are turned down at night and a mint is left on the pillow). Services that were important to business travelers, whom Hyatt courted, were expanded (for example, in-room fax machines).

Hotels must be careful to make tactical decisions that are in keeping with their image and strategic goals.

© Kevin Fleming/Corbis

2 Richard A. Melcher, "Why Hyatt Is Toning Down the Glitz," *Business Week* (27 February 1995): pp. 92, 94.

Model for Making Tactical Decisions

How does a company go about making good tactical decisions? We can describe a general approach to making tactical decisions. The six[3] steps describing the recommended decision-making process are as follows:

1. Recognize and define the problem.
2. Identify alternatives as possible solutions to the problem; eliminate alternatives that are clearly not feasible.
3. Identify the costs and benefits associated with each feasible alternative. Classify costs and benefits as relevant or irrelevant, and eliminate irrelevant ones from consideration.
4. Total the relevant costs and benefits for each alternative.
5. Assess qualitative factors.
6. Select the alternative with the greatest overall benefit.

These six steps define a simple decision model. A **decision model** is a set of procedures that, if followed, will lead to a decision. Exhibit 12-1 depicts the sequence of steps to be followed.

Step 1	Define the problem.	Increase capacity for warehousing and production.	
Step 2	Identify the alternatives.	1. Build new facility. 2. Lease larger facility; sublease current facility. 3. Lease additional facility. 4. Lease warehouse space. 5. Buy shafts and bushings; free up needed space.	
Step 3	Identify costs and benefits associated with each feasible alternative.	Alternative 4:	
		Variable production costs	$345,000
		Warehouse lease	135,000
		Alternative 5:	
		Purchase price	460,000
Step 4	Total relevant costs and benefits for each feasible alternative.	Alternative 4	480,000
		Alternative 5	460,000
		Differential cost	$ 20,000
Step 5	Assess qualitative factors.	1. Quality of external supplier 2. Reliability of external supplier 3. Price stability 4. Labor relations and community image	
Step 6	Make the decision.	Continue to produce shafts and bushings internally; lease warehouse.	

Exhibit 12-1 Tactical Decision-Making Model for Tidwell Products' Space Problem

3 The decision-making model described here has six steps. There is nothing special about this particular listing. You may find it more useful to break down the steps into eight or 10 segments. Alternatively, you may find it useful to aggregate them into a shorter list. For example, you could use a three-step model: (1) identify the decision; (2) identify alternatives and their associated relevant costs; and (3) make the decision. The key point is to find a comfortable way for you to remember the important steps in the decision-making model.

Step 1: Define the Problem The first step is to recognize and define a specific problem. For example, the members of Tidwell's management team all recognized the need for additional space for warehousing, offices, and the production of plastic moldings. The amount of space needed, the reasons for the need, and how the additional space would be used are all important dimensions of the problem. However, the central question is *how* to acquire the additional space.

Step 2: Identify the Alternatives Step 2 is to list and consider possible solutions. Tidwell Products identified the following possible solutions:

1. Build its own facility with sufficient capacity to handle current and immediately foreseeable needs.
2. Lease a larger facility and sublease its current facility.
3. Lease an additional, similar facility.
4. Lease an additional building that would be used for warehousing only, thereby freeing up space for expanded production.
5. Buy shafts and bushings externally and use the space made available (previously used for producing these parts) to solve the space problem.

As part of this step, Tidwell must eliminate alternatives that are not feasible. The first alternative was eliminated because it carried too much risk for the company. The second alternative was rejected because subleasing was not a viable option. The third alternative was eliminated because it went too far in solving the space problem and, presumably, was too expensive. The fourth and fifth alternatives were feasible; they were within the cost and risk constraints and solved the space needs of the company. Notice that Leo linked the tactical decision (find more space) to the company's overall growth strategy by rejecting alternatives that involved too much risk at this stage of the company's development.

Step 3: Identify the Costs and Benefits Associated with Each Feasible Alternative In Step 3, the costs and benefits associated with each feasible alternative are identified. At this point, clearly irrelevant costs can be eliminated from consideration.[4] The management accountant is responsible for gathering necessary data.

Assume that Tidwell Products determines that the costs of making the shafts and bushings include the following:

Direct materials	$130,000
Direct labor	150,000
Variable overhead	65,000
Total variable production costs	$345,000

In addition, a warehouse must be leased to solve the space problem if Tidwell continues to manufacture the shafts and bushings internally. An appropriate warehouse has been located for $135,000 per year. The second alternative is to purchase the shafts and bushings externally and use the freed-up production space. An outside supplier has offered to supply sufficient products for $460,000 per year.

It should be mentioned that when the cash flow patterns become complicated for competing alternatives, it becomes difficult to produce a stream of equal cash flows for each alternative. In such a case, more sophisticated procedures can and should be used for the analysis. These procedures are discussed in the next chapter, which deals with the long-run investment decisions referred to as *capital expenditure decisions.*

4 It is fine to include irrelevant costs and benefits in the analysis as long as they are included for all alternatives. The reason we usually do not is that focusing only on the relevant costs and benefits reduces the amount of data to be collected.

Step 4: Total the Relevant Costs and Benefits for Each Feasible Alternative We now see that Alternative 4—continue producing internally and lease more space—costs $480,000, while Alternative 5—purchase outside and use internal space—costs $460,000. The comparison follows:

Alternative 4	
Variable costs of production	$345,000
Warehouse lease	135,000
Total	$480,000

Alternative 5	
Purchase price	$460,000

The differential cost is $20,000 in favor of Alternative 5.

Step 5: Assess the Qualitative Factors While the costs and revenues associated with the alternatives are important, they do not tell the whole story. Qualitative factors can significantly affect the manager's decision. Qualitative factors are simply those factors that are hard to put a number on. For example, in the make-or-buy decision facing Tidwell Products, Leo Tidwell likely would be concerned with such qualitative considerations as the quality of the shafts and bushings purchased externally, the reliability of supply sources, the expected stability of prices over the next several years, labor relations, community image, and so on. To illustrate the possible impact of qualitative factors on the make-or-buy decision, consider the first two factors: quality and reliability of supply.

If the quality of shafts and bushings is significantly less when purchased externally from what is available internally, the quantitative advantage from purchasing may be more fictitious than real. Settling for lower-quality materials may reduce the

Managers Decide

A Comfortable ER Contributes to Hospital's Health

Many of us base our impression of hospital emergency rooms on the long-running television drama *ER.* Its emergency room is crowded and functional; the décor runs to green and white (with occasional splashes of red). Where do the patient's family and friends wait? Who knows—they are typically relegated to some cramped, uncomfortable waiting area. Some hospitals, however, have taken steps to improve the ambience of the ER waiting area.

St. Vincent's Hospital in New York City worked with a furniture design company to install warm colors and lighting in its ER waiting area. The objective was to create a "warm glow." Charlotte, North Carolina's Presbyterian Hospital just opened a pediatric ER with beach murals on the ceilings and video games for kids. The waiting room attached to the ER at Emory Crawford Long Hospital resembles an upscale hotel lobby, with contemporary décor and comfortable armchairs.

Why the new emphasis on improved ER waiting areas? Hospitals have found that many patients' first contact with their hospital is through the emergency room. If that contact was brusque and unpleasant, patients and their families look elsewhere for a hospital to perform elective surgery or more extensive medical procedures. Since the vast majority of ER patients have health insurance, a poor experience in the ER can negatively affect the bottom line for the hospital's more profitable departments.

Source: Peter Landers, "Hospital Chic: The ER's Makeover," *Wall Street Journal* (July 8, 2003): pp. D1, D3.

quality of the potentiometers, thus harming sales. Because of this, Tidwell Products may choose to continue to produce the parts internally.

Similarly, if supply sources are not reliable, production schedules could be interrupted, and customer orders could arrive late. These factors can increase labor costs and overhead and hurt sales. Again, depending on the perceived trade-offs, Tidwell Products may decide that producing the parts internally is better than purchasing them, even if relevant cost analysis gives the initial advantage to purchasing.

How should qualitative factors be handled in the decision-making process? First, they must be identified. Secondly, the decision maker should try to quantify them. Often, qualitative factors are simply more difficult to quantify—not impossible. For example, possible unreliability of the outside supplier might be quantified as the probable number of days late multiplied by the labor cost of downtime in Tidwell's plant. Finally, truly qualitative factors, such as the impact of late orders on customer relations, must be taken into consideration in the final step of the decision-making model—the selection of the alternative with the greatest overall benefit.

Step 6: Make the Decision Once all relevant costs and benefits for each alternative have been assessed and the qualitative factors weighed, a decision can be made. What did Leo decide for Tidwell Products? Given the relatively small difference in costs of the two alternatives and the weight Tidwell Products assigns to ensuring quality and full employment, the decision was made to make the shafts and bushings internally and lease the warehouse.

Relevant Costs Defined

The tactical decision-making approach just described emphasized the importance of identifying and using relevant costs. But how do we identify and define the costs that affect the decision? **Relevant costs** are future costs that differ across alternatives. All decisions relate to the future; accordingly, only future costs can be relevant to decisions. However, to be relevant, a cost must not only be a future cost but must also differ from one alternative to another. If a future cost is the same for more than one alternative, it has no effect on the decision. Such a cost is an *irrelevant* cost. The ability to identify relevant and irrelevant costs is an important decision-making skill.

Relevant Costs Illustrated To illustrate the concept of relevant costs, consider Tidwell's make-or-buy alternatives. We saw that the cost of direct labor used to produce shafts and bushings is $150,000 per year (based on normal volume). Should this cost be a factor in the decision? Is the direct labor cost a future cost that differs across the two alternatives? It is certainly a future cost. To produce the shafts and bushings for another year requires the services of direct laborers, who must be paid. But does it differ across the two alternatives? If shafts and bushings are purchased from an external supplier, no internal production is needed. The services of the direct laborers can be eliminated, reducing the direct labor cost for shafts and bushings under this alternative to zero. Thus, the cost of direct labor differs across alternatives ($150,000 for the make alternative and $0 for the buy alternative). It is, therefore, a relevant cost.

Implicit in this analysis is the use of a past cost to estimate a future cost. The most recent cost of direct labor for normal activity was $150,000. This past cost was used as the estimate of next year's cost. Although past costs are never relevant, they are often used to predict what future costs will be.

Illustration of an Irrelevant Past Cost Tidwell Products uses machinery to manufacture shafts and bushings. This machinery was purchased five years ago and is being depreciated at an annual rate of $125,000. Is this $125,000 a relevant cost? In other words, is depreciation a future cost that differs across the two alternatives?

Depreciation represents an allocation of a cost already incurred. It is a **sunk cost**, a cost that cannot be affected by any future action. Although we allocate this sunk cost to future periods and call that allocation depreciation, none of the original cost is avoidable. Sunk costs are past costs. They are always the same across alternatives and are, therefore, always irrelevant.

In choosing between the two alternatives, the original cost of the machinery used to produce shafts and bushings and its associated depreciation are not factors. However, it should be noted that salvage value of the machinery (what Tidwell could receive for selling the machinery now) would be relevant and would be included as a benefit of purchasing from outside suppliers. To simplify our example, we are assuming that the salvage value of the machinery is zero.

Illustration of an Irrelevant Future Cost Assume that the cost to lease the entire factory, $340,000, is allocated to different production departments including the department that produces shafts and bushings, which receives $12,000 of the cost. Is this $12,000 cost relevant to the make-or-buy decision facing Tidwell?

The lease payment is a future cost since it must be paid during each of the next five years. But does the cost differ across the make-and-buy alternatives? Whatever option Tidwell chooses, the factory lease payment must be made—it is the same across both alternatives. The amount of the payment allocated to the remaining departments may change if production of shafts and bushings is stopped, but the level of the total payment is unaffected by the decision. It is, therefore, an irrelevant cost.

The example illustrates the importance of identifying allocations of common fixed costs. Allocations of common fixed costs can be safely classified as irrelevant since any choice usually does not affect the level of cost. The only effect may be a reallocation of those common fixed costs to fewer cost objects or segments.

We can now look at all three cost examples for the production of shafts and bushings to see which are relevant in deciding whether or not to continue production. Of the three, only direct labor cost is relevant, since it is the only one that occurs if production continues but stops if production stops.

	Cost to Make	− Cost Not to Make	= Differential Cost
Direct labor	$150,000	—	$150,000
Depreciation	125,000	$125,000	—
Allocated lease	12,000	12,000	—
	$287,000	$137,000	$150,000

The same concepts apply to benefits. One alternative may produce an amount of future benefits different from another alternative (for example, differences in future revenues). If future benefits differ across alternatives, then they are relevant and should be included in the analysis.

Ethics in Tactical Decision Making

In tactical decision making, ethical concerns revolve around the way in which decisions are implemented and the possible sacrifice of long-run objectives for short-run gain. Relevant costs are used in making tactical decisions—decisions that have an immediate view or limited objective in mind. However, decision makers should always maintain an ethical framework. Reaching objectives is important, but how you get there is perhaps more important. Unfortunately, many managers have the opposite view. Part of the reason for the problem is the extreme pressure to perform that many managers feel. Often the individual who is not a top performer may be laid off or demoted. Under such conditions, the temptation is often great to engage in questionable behavior today and let the future take care of itself.

For example, laying off employees to increase profits in the short run could loosely qualify as a tactical decision. However, if the only benefit is an increase in short-run profits and there is no evidence that the decision supports the longer-term strategic objectives of the firm, then the decision can be questioned. In fact, the workload may not decrease at all, but the number of people available to carry out the work has decreased. Pressure then may be exerted by managers on the remaining employees to work unreasonable amounts of overtime. Is this right?

All companies should have a clear mission and goals. For example, if marketing enthusiastically touts the product's high quality and reliability, while engineering and production are busily reducing the quality of the materials and reliability of the design, problems are sure to surface. Customers will see this inconsistency as an ethical lapse.

ETHICS

Debates about what is right and what is wrong can be endless. As was pointed out in Chapter 1, ethical standards have been developed to provide guidance for individuals. Additionally, many companies are hiring full-time ethics officers. Often, these officers set up hotlines so that employees can call and register complaints or ask about the propriety of certain actions. However, some ethical problems can be avoided simply by using common sense and not focusing solely on the short term at the expense of the long term. Consider two examples of cost cutting at **Ford Motor Company**. Recently, Ford decided to delete the rubber molding on the side of the Sable, saving about $100 per car. Years earlier, Ford saved approximately $7 per car by installing thin-walled gas tanks on the Pinto. Which decision do you think has ethical ramifications?

Relevance, Cost Behavior, and the Activity Resource Usage Model

Objective 2

Explain how the activity resource usage model is used in assessing relevance.

Tidwell Products' space problem was a very simple example of tactical decision making. Most tactical decisions require more complicated analysis—in particular, they require more extensive consideration of cost behavior. Earlier work on relevant costing emphasized the importance of variable versus fixed costs. Usually, variable costs were relevant, and fixed costs were not. For example, the variable costs of production were relevant to the Tidwell Products' make-or-buy decision. The depreciation expense and factory lease were not relevant. However, activity-based costing allows us to go further as we consider variable costs with respect to both unit- and non-unit-based cost drivers.

The key point is that changes in supply and demand for activity resources must be considered when assessing relevance. If changes in demand and supply for resources across alternatives bring about changes in resource spending, then the changes in resource spending are the relevant costs that should be used in assessing the relative desirability of the two alternatives.

Recall from Chapter 3 that the activity resource usage model reminds us to consider both flexible and committed resources. These categories can help us to identify relevant costs and, thus, facilitate relevant cost analysis.

Flexible Resources

Resources that can be easily purchased in the amount needed and at the time of use are called **flexible resources**. For example, electricity used to run stoves that boil fruit in the production of jelly is a resource acquired as used and needed. Thus, for this resource category, if the demand for an activity changes across alternatives, then resource spending will change and the cost of the activity is relevant to the decision. This type of resource spending is typically referred to as a variable cost. The key point is that the amount of resource demanded by the firm equals the amount of resource supplied.

Now, suppose that the jelly producer is asked by a customer to produce a special order of jelly for promotional purposes. The jelly producer must consider the following two alternatives: (1) accept a special, one-time order or (2) reject the special order. If accepting the order increases the demand for kilowatt-hours (electricity's cost driver), then the cost of electricity will differ across alternatives. Thus, electricity is relevant to the decision.

Committed Resources

Committed resources are purchased before they are used. Therefore, there may or may not be unused capacity that will affect tactical decision making. We will consider two types of committed resources: those that can be altered in the short run and those that provide capacity for multiple periods.

Committed Resources for the Short Run Some committed resources are acquired in advance of usage through implicit contracting; they are usually acquired in lumpy amounts. (Graphically, we usually think of this cost as being step-variable or step-fixed.) This category often represents resource spending associated with an organization's salaried and hourly employees. The implicit understanding is that the organization will maintain employment levels even though there may be temporary downturns in the quantity of an activity used. This means that an activity may have unused capacity available. Thus, an increase in demand for an activity across alternatives may not mean that the activity cost will increase (because all the increased demand is absorbed by the unused activity capacity). For example, assume a company has five manufacturing engineers that supply a capacity of 10,000 engineering hours (2,000 hours each). The cost of this activity capacity is $250,000, or $25 per hour. Suppose that this year the company expects to use only 9,000 engineering hours for its normal business. This means that the engineering activity has 1,000 hours of unused capacity. In deciding to reject or accept a special order that requires 500 engineering hours, the cost of engineering would be irrelevant. The order can be filled using unused engineering capacity, and the resource spending is the same for each alternative ($250,000 will be spent whether the order is accepted or not).

However, if a change in demand across activities produces a change in resource supply, then the activity cost will change and, thus, be relevant to the decision. A change in resource supply means a change in resource spending and, consequently, a change in activity cost. A change in resource spending can occur in one of two ways: (1) the demand for the resource exceeds the supply (increasing resource spending) or (2) the demand for the resource drops permanently and supply exceeds demand enough so that activity capacity can be reduced (decreasing resource spending).

To illustrate the first change, consider once again the engineering activity and the special-order decision. Suppose that the special order requires 1,500 engineering hours. This exceeds the resource supply. To meet the demand, the organization would need to hire a sixth engineer or perhaps use a consulting engineer. Either way, resource spending increases if the order is accepted; thus, the cost of engineering is now a relevant cost.

To illustrate the second type of change, suppose that the company's manager is considering purchasing a component used for production instead of making it. Assume the same facts about engineering capacity: 10,000 hours available and 9,000 used. If the component is purchased, then the demand for engineering hours will drop from 9,000 to 7,000. This is a permanent reduction because engineering support will no longer be needed for manufacturing the component. Unused capacity is now 3,000 hours—2,000 permanent and 1,000 temporary. Furthermore, since engineering capacity is acquired in chunks of 2,000, the company can reduce activity capacity and resource spending by laying off one engineer or reassigning the engineer to another plant where the services are in demand. Either way, the resource supply is reduced to 8,000 hours. If an engineer's salary is $50,000, then engineering cost would differ by $50,000 across the make-or-buy alternatives. This cost is then relevant to the decision. However, if the demand for the engineering activity drops by less than 2,000 hours, the increase in unused capacity is not enough to reduce resource supply and resource spending; in this case, the cost of the engineering activity would not be relevant.

Committed Resources for Multiple Periods Often, resources are acquired in advance for multiple periods, before the resource demands are known. Leasing or buying a building is an example. Buying multiperiod activity capacity is often done by paying cash up front. In this case, an annual expense may be recognized, but no additional resource spending is needed. Up-front resource spending is a sunk cost and, thus, is never relevant. Periodic resource spending, such as leasing, is essentially independent of resource usage. Even if a permanent reduction of activity usage is experienced, it is difficult to reduce resource spending because of formal, contractual commitments.

For example, assume a company leases a plant for $100,000 per year for 10 years. The plant is capable of producing 20,000 units of a product—the level expected when the plant was leased. After five years, suppose that the demand for the product drops and the plant needs to produce only 15,000 units each year. The lease payment of $100,000 still must be paid each year, even though production activity has decreased. Now, suppose that demand increases beyond the 20,000-unit capability. In this case, the company may consider acquiring or leasing an additional plant. Here, resource spending could change across alternatives. The decision, however, to acquire long-term activity capacity is not in the realm of tactical decision making. This is not a short-term or small-scale decision. Decisions involving multiperiod capabilities are called capital investment decisions and are discussed in Chapter 18.

Thus, for the multiperiod resource category, changes in activity demands across alternatives rarely affect resource spending and are, therefore, not usually relevant for tactical decision making. When resource spending does change, it means assessing the prospect of a multiperiod commitment, which is properly treated using capital investment decision models. A good example of the rising importance of resources requiring multiperiod commitments is the technology required for design. **Black & Decker Corporation**'s design budget in North America reached $1 million in 1995 (up from $300,000 in 1990). Companies are trying to turn this expense back into the category of a resource acquired in advance (short-term) by outsourcing much of the design work.[5] Exhibit 12-2 summarizes the activity resource usage model's role in assessing relevancy.

Illustrative Examples of Relevant Cost Applications

Objective 3

Apply tactical decision-making concepts in a variety of business situations.

Relevant costing is of value in solving many different types of problems. Traditionally, these applications include decisions to make or buy a component, to keep or drop a segment or product line, to accept a special order at less than the usual price, and to process a joint product further or sell it at the split-off point. Though by no means an exhaustive list, many of the same decision-making principles apply to a variety of problems.

Make-or-Buy Decisions

Managers are often faced with the decision of whether to make or buy components used in manufacturing. Indeed, management periodically should evaluate past decisions concerning production. Conditions upon which prior decisions were based

5 Bruce Nussbaum, "Is In-House Design on the Way Out?" *Business Week* (25 September 1995): p. 130.

Resource Category	Demand and Supply Relationships	Relevance
Flexible Resources	Supply = Demand	
	a. Demand Changes	a. Relevant
	b. Demand Constant	b. Not Relevant
Committed Resources (Short Term)	Supply − Demand = Unused Capacity	
	a. Demand Increase < Unused Capacity	a. Not Relevant
	b. Demand Increase > Unused Capacity	b. Relevant
	c. Demand Decrease (Permanent)	
	1. Activity Capacity Reduced	1. Relevant
	2. Activity Capacity Unchanged	2. Not Relevant
Committed Resources (Multiperiod Capacity)	Supply − Demand = Unused Capacity	
	a. Demand Increase < Unused Capacity	a. Not Relevant
	b. Demand Decrease (Permanent)	b. Not Relevant
	c. Demand Increase > Unused Capacity	c. Capital Decision

Exhibit 12-2 Activity Resource Usage Model and Assessing Relevance

may have changed, and as a result, a different approach may be required. Periodic evaluations, of course, are not the only source of these **make-or-buy decisions**. Frequently, as with Tidwell Products, the decision is motivated by an indirectly related, underlying problem.

To illustrate more fully the cost analysis of a make-or-buy problem, assume that Swasey Manufacturing currently produces an electronic component used in one of its printers. In one year, Swasey will switch production to another type of printer, and the electronic component will not be used. However, for the coming year, Swasey must produce 10,000 of these parts to support the production requirements for the old printer.

Swasey has been approached by a potential supplier of the component. The supplier will build the electronic component to Swasey's specifications for $4.75 per unit. The offer sounds very attractive since the full manufacturing cost per unit is $8.20. Should Swasey Manufacturing make or buy the component?

The problem and the feasible alternatives are both readily identifiable. Since the horizon for the decision is only one period, there is no need to be concerned about periodically recurring costs. Relevant costing is particularly useful for short-run analysis. We simply need to identify the relevant costs, total them, and make a choice (assuming no overriding qualitative concerns).

First, let's look at the costs associated with the production of these 10,000 parts. The full absorption cost is computed as follows:

	Total Cost	Unit Cost
Rental of equipment	$12,000	$1.20
Equipment depreciation	2,000	0.20
Direct materials	10,000	1.00
Direct labor	20,000	2.00
Variable overhead	8,000	0.80
General fixed overhead	30,000	3.00
Total	$82,000	$8.20

Most of the equipment is rented. However, one specialized piece of machinery had to be custom-made and was purchased. Rental equipment can be returned at any time without penalty; the company is charged only for the time the equipment is held. The specialized machinery will not be fully depreciated at the end of the year; however, the company plans to scrap it since it cannot be sold. The company recently purchased sufficient materials for 5,000 components. No alternative use for the materials exists. Variable overhead is applied to the electronic component at $0.40 per direct labor dollar. General fixed overhead for the plant totals $1 million. General fixed overhead is assigned to products based on the space occupied by each product. The manufacturing facilities for the component under consideration occupy 6,000 of the plant's 200,000 square feet. Thus, general fixed overhead of $30,000 is allocated to the electronic component (0.03 × $1,000,000).

Of these cost items, depreciation can be eliminated; it is a sunk cost. Since the direct materials already purchased have no alternative use, half of the cost of total direct materials is also a sunk cost. General overhead is not relevant either. The $30,000 is an allocation of a common fixed cost that will continue even if the component is purchased externally.

All other costs are relevant. The cost of renting the equipment is relevant since it will not be needed if the part is bought externally. Similarly, direct labor, the remaining 5,000 units of direct materials, and variable overhead are all relevant; they would not be incurred if the component is bought externally.

Now, let's focus on the purchase of the component. Of course, the purchase cost is relevant. If the component is made, this cost would not be incurred. Are there any other costs associated with an outside purchase? A check with the receiving dock elicited the information that the receiving and inspecting crew was at capacity. An additional purchase of this magnitude would require hiring an additional half-time employee for the year at a cost of $8,500. The Purchasing Department had sufficient excess capacity to handle the purchase of the component; thus, no additional cost would be incurred there.

A listing of the total relevant costs for each alternative follows:

	Alternatives		Differential
	Make	**Buy**	**Cost to Make**
Rental of equipment	$12,000	—	$ 12,000
Direct materials	5,000	—	5,000
Direct labor	20,000	—	20,000
Variable overhead	8,000	—	8,000
Purchase cost	—	$47,500	(47,500)
Receiving Department labor	—	8,500	(8,500)
Total relevant cost	$45,000	$56,000	$(11,000)

The analysis shows that making the product is $11,000 cheaper than buying it. The offer of the supplier should be rejected.

The same analysis can be done on a unit-cost basis. Once the relevant costs are identified, relevant unit costs can be compared. For this example, these costs are $4.50 ($45,000/10,000) for the make alternative and $5.60 ($56,000/10,000) for the buy alternative.

Keep-or-Drop Decisions

Often, a manager needs to determine whether or not a segment, such as a product line, should be kept or dropped. Segmented reports prepared on a variable-costing basis provide valuable information for these **keep-or-drop decisions**. Both the segment's contribution margin and its segment margin are useful in evaluating the performance of segments. However, while segmented reports provide useful information for keep-or-drop decisions, relevant costing describes how the information should be used to arrive at a decision.

To illustrate, consider Norton Materials, Inc., which produces concrete blocks, bricks, and roofing tile. The controller has prepared the following estimated income statement for 2008 (in thousands of dollars):

	Blocks	Bricks	Tile	Total
Sales revenue	$500	$800	$150	$1,450
Less: Variable expenses	250	480	140	870
Contribution margin	$250	$320	$ 10	$ 580
Less direct fixed expenses:				
Advertising	$ 10	$ 10	$ 10	$ 30
Salaries	37	40	35	112
Depreciation	53	40	10	103
Total	$100	$ 90	$ 55	$ 245
Segment margin	$150	$230	$(45)	$ 335
Less: Common fixed expenses				125
Operating income				$ 210

The projected performance of the roofing tile line shows a negative segment margin. This would represent the third consecutive year of poor performance for that line. The president of Norton Materials, Tom Blackburn—concerned about this poor performance—is trying to decide whether to drop or keep the roofing tile line.

His first reaction is to take steps to increase the sales revenue of roofing tiles. He is considering an aggressive sales promotion coupled with an increase in the selling price. The marketing manager thinks that this approach would be fruitless, however; the market is saturated and the level of competition too keen to hold out any hope for increasing the firm's market share. An increase in the selling price would almost certainly result in a decrease in sales revenue.

Increasing the product line's profitability through cost cutting is not feasible either. Costs were cut the past two years to reduce the loss to its present anticipated level. Any further reductions would lower the quality of the product and adversely affect sales.

With no hope for improving the profit performance of the line beyond its projected level, Tom has decided to drop it. He reasons that the firm will lose a total of $10,000 in contribution margin but save $45,000 by dismissing the line's supervisor and eliminating its advertising budget. (The depreciation cost of $10,000 is not relevant since it represents an allocation of a sunk cost.) Thus, dropping the product line has a $35,000 advantage over keeping it. Before finalizing the decision, Tom decided to notify the marketing manager and the production supervisor. The following memo was sent to both individuals:

Memo

TO: Karen Gutierrez, Marketing, and Larry Olsen, Production
FROM: Tom Blackburn, President
SUBJECT: Tentative Decision Concerning the Production of Roofing Tiles
DATE: March 14, 2008

Since there is no realistic expectation of improving the profitability of the roofing tile line, I have reluctantly decided to discontinue its production. I realize that this decision will have a negative impact on the community since our workforce will need to be reduced. I am also sympathetic to the disruption this may cause in the personal lives of many employees.

However, we must be prepared to take actions that are in the best interests of the firm. By eliminating the roofing tile line, we can improve the firm's cash position by $35,000 per year. To support this decision, I am including the following analysis (focusing only on the tile segment), in thousands of dollars:

	Keep	Drop	Differential Amount to Keep
Sales	$150	$—	$150
Less: Variable expenses	140	—	140
Contribution margin	$ 10	$—	$ 10
Less: Advertising	(10)	—	(10)
Cost of supervision	(35)	—	(35)
Total relevant benefit (loss)	$(35)	$ 0	$(35)

I have included only future costs and benefits that differ across the two alternatives. Depreciation on the tile equipment is not relevant since it is simply an allocation of a sunk cost. Also, the level of common fixed costs is unchanged regardless of whether we keep or drop the tile line.

At this point, I view the decision as tentative and welcome any response. Perhaps I am overlooking something that would affect the decision. Please respond as soon as possible.

Keep-or-Drop with Complementary Effects In response to the memo, the marketing manager wrote that dropping the roofing tile line would lower sales of blocks by 10 percent and of bricks by 8 percent. She explained that many customers buy roofing tile at the same time they purchase blocks or bricks. Some will go elsewhere if they cannot buy both products at the same location.

Shortly after receiving this response, Tom Blackburn decided to repeat the analysis, factoring in the effect that dropping the tile line would have on the sales of the other two lines. He decided to use total firm sales and total costs for each alternative. As before, depreciation and common fixed costs were excluded from the analysis on the basis of irrelevancy.

Dropping the product line reduces total sales by $264,000: $50,000 (0.10 × $500,000) for blocks, $64,000 (0.08 × $800,000) for bricks, and $150,000 for roofing tiles. Similarly, total variable expenses are reduced by $203,400: $25,000 (0.10 × $250,000) for blocks, $38,400 (0.08 × $480,000) for bricks, and $140,000 for tiles. Thus, total contribution margin is reduced by $60,600 ($264,000 − $203,400). Since dropping the tile line saves only $45,000 in supervision costs and advertising, the net effect is a disadvantage of $15,600 ($45,000 − $60,600). The following is a summary of the analysis using the new information (in thousands):

	Keep	Drop	Differential Amount to Keep
Sales	$1,450	$1,186.0	$264.0
Less: Variable expenses	870	666.6	203.4
Contribution margin	$ 580	$ 519.4	$ 60.6
Less: Advertising	(30)	(20.0)	(10.0)
Cost of supervision	(112)	(77.0)	(35.0)
Total	$ 438	$ 422.4	$ 15.6

Tom was pleased to find the outcome favoring production of the roofing tile. The unpleasant task of dismissing some of his workforce was no longer necessary. However, just as he was preparing to write a second memo announcing his new decision, he received Larry Olsen's written response to his first memo.

Keep-or-Drop with Alternative Use of Facilities The production supervisor's response was somewhat different. He agreed that roofing tile should be eliminated but suggested that it be replaced with the production of floor tile. He gave assurances that existing machinery could be converted to produce this new product with little or no cost. He had also contacted the marketing manager about the marketability of floor tile and included this assessment in his response.

The marketing manager saw the market for floor tile as stronger and less competitive than that for roofing tile. However, the other two lines would still lose sales at the same rate; producing floor tile would not change that result. The following estimated financial statement for floor tile was also submitted (in thousands of dollars):

Sales	$100
Less: Variable expenses	40
Contribution margin	$ 60
Less: Direct fixed expenses	55
Segment margin	$ 5

Tom Blackburn was now faced with a third alternative: replacing the roofing tile with floor tile. Should the roofing tile line be kept, or should it be dropped and replaced with the floor tile?

From his prior analysis, Tom knows that dropping the roofing tile decreases the firm's contribution margin by $60,600. Producing the floor tile will generate $60,000 more in contribution margin according to the estimate. Dropping the roofing tile line and replacing it with floor tile, then, will cause a $600 net decrease in total contribution margin ($60,600 – $60,000). The same outcome can be developed by directly comparing the relevant benefits and costs of the two alternatives (dollars expressed in thousands).

	Keep	Drop and Replace	Differential Amount to Keep
Sales	$1,450	$1,286.0[a]	$164.0
Less: Variable expenses	870	706.6[b]	163.4
Contribution margin	$ 580	$ 579.4	$ 0.6

[a]$1,450 – $150 – $50 – $64 + $100
[b]$870 – $140 – $25 – $38.4 + $40

The Norton Materials example again illustrates the tactical decision-making process. First, a problem was identified and defined (the poor performance of the roofing tile product line). Next, possible solutions were listed, and those that were not feasible were eliminated. For example, increasing sales or further decreasing costs were both rejected as feasible solutions. Three feasible solutions were examined: (1) keeping the product line, (2) dropping it, and (3) dropping the product line and replacing it with another product. An analysis of the costs and benefits of the feasible alternatives led to the selection of the preferred alternative (keeping the product line).

The example provides some insights beyond the simple application of the decision model. The initial analysis, which focused on two feasible alternatives, led to a tentative decision to drop the product line. Additional information provided by the marketing manager led to a reversal of the first decision. Before that decision could be implemented, the manager was made aware of a third feasible alternative which required additional analysis.

Often, managers do not have all the information necessary to make the best decision. They also may not be able to identify all feasible solutions. Managers benefit from gathering all the information available before finalizing a decision. They should attempt to identify as many feasible solutions as possible. As the example clearly illustrates, limited information can result in poor decisions. If the set of feasible solutions is too narrow, the best solution may never be selected simply because the manager has not thought of it. Managers can benefit from obtaining input from others who are familiar with the problem. By so doing, both the set of information and the set of feasible solutions can be expanded. The result is improved decision making.

Special-Order Decisions

Price discrimination laws require that firms sell identical products at the same price to competing customers in the same market. These restrictions do not apply to competitive bids or to noncompeting customers. Bid prices can vary to customers in the same market, and firms often have the opportunity to consider special orders from potential customers in markets not ordinarily served. **Special-order decisions** focus on whether a specially priced order should be accepted or rejected. These orders often can be attractive, especially when the firm is operating below its maximum productive capacity.

Suppose, for example, that an ice cream company is operating at 80 percent of its productive capacity. The company has a capacity of 20 million half-gallon units. The company produces only premium ice cream. The total costs associated with producing and selling 16 million units are as follows (in thousands of dollars):

	Total Cost	Unit Cost
Variable costs:		
Dairy ingredients	$ 11,200	$ 0.70
Sugar	1,600	0.10
Flavoring	2,400	0.15
Direct labor	4,000	0.25
Packaging	3,200	0.20
Commissions	320	0.02
Distribution	480	0.03
Other	800	0.05
Total variable costs	$24,000	$ 1.50
Fixed costs:		
Salaries	$ 960	$0.060
Depreciation	320	0.020
Utilities	80	0.005
Taxes	32	0.002
Other	160	0.010
Total fixed costs	$ 1,552	$0.097
Total costs	$25,552	$1.597
Wholesale selling price	$32,000	$2.00

An ice cream distributor from a geographic region not normally served by the company has offered to buy two million units at $1.55 per unit, provided its own label can be attached to the product. The distributor has also agreed to pay the transportation costs. Since the distributor approached the company directly, there is no sales commission. As the manager of the ice cream company, would you accept or reject this order?

The offer of $1.55 is well below the normal selling price of $2.00; in fact, it is even below the total unit cost. Even so, accepting the order may be profitable. The company does have idle capacity, and the order will not displace other units being produced to sell at the normal price. Additionally, many of the costs are not relevant; fixed costs will continue regardless of whether the order is accepted or rejected.

If the order is accepted, a benefit of $1.55 per unit will be realized that otherwise wouldn't be. However, all of the variable costs except for distribution ($0.03) and commissions ($0.02) also will be incurred, producing a cost of $1.45 per unit. The net benefit is $0.10 ($1.55 − $1.45) per unit. The relevant cost analysis can be summarized as follows:

	Accept	Reject	Differential Benefit to Accept
Revenues	$ 3,100,000	$—	$ 3,100,000
Dairy ingredients	(1,400,000)	—	(1,400,000)
Sugar	(200,000)	—	(200,000)
Flavoring	(300,000)	—	(300,000)
Direct labor	(500,000)	—	(500,000)
Packaging	(400,000)	—	(400,000)
Other	(100,000)	—	(100,000)
Profit	$ 200,000	$ 0	$ 200,000

We see that for this company, accepting the special order will increase profits by $200,000 ($0.10 × 2,000,000).

Decisions to Sell or Process Further

Joint products have common processes and costs of production up to a split-off point. At that point, they become distinguishable. For example, certain minerals such as copper and gold may both be found in a given ore. The ore must be mined, crushed, and treated before the copper and gold are separated. The point of separation is called the **split-off point**. The costs of mining, crushing, and treatment are common to both products.

Often, joint products are sold at the split-off point. Sometimes, it is more profitable to process a joint product further, beyond the split-off point, prior to selling it. Determining whether to **sell or process further** is an important decision that a manager must make.

To illustrate, consider Appletime Corporation. Appletime is a large corporate farm that specializes in growing apples. Each plot produces approximately one ton of apples. The trees in each plot must be sprayed, fertilized, watered, and pruned.

These apples are a joint product to the purchaser. Large, unblemished apples are sold to grocery stores. Small, misshapen apples are canned as pie filling or applesauce.

When the apples are ripened, workers are hired to pick them. The apples are then transported to a warehouse, where they are washed and sorted. The approximate cost of all these activities (including processing) is $300 per ton per year.

Apples are sorted into three grades (A, B, and C) determined by size and blemishes. Large apples without blemishes (bruises, cuts, wormholes, and so on) are sorted into one bin and classified as Grade A. Small apples without blemishes are sorted into a second bin and classified as Grade B. All remaining apples are placed in a third bin and classified as Grade C. Every ton of apples produces 800 pounds of Grade A, 600 pounds of Grade B, and 600 pounds of Grade C.

Grade A apples are sold to large supermarkets for $0.40 per pound. Grade B apples are packaged in 5-pound bags and sold to supermarkets for $1.30 per bag. (The cost of each bag is $0.05.) Grade C apples are processed further and made into applesauce. The sauce is sold in 16-ounce cans for $0.75 each. The cost of processing is $0.10 per pound of apples. The final output is 500 sixteen-ounce cans. Exhibit 12-3 summarizes the process.

A large supermarket chain recently requested that Appletime supply 16-ounce cans of apple pie filling for which the chain was willing to pay $0.90 per can. Appletime determined that the Grade B apples would be suitable for this purpose and estimated that it would cost $0.20 per pound to process the apples into pie filling. The output would be 500 sixteen-ounce cans.

In deciding whether to sell Grade B apples at split-off or to process them further and sell them as pie filling, the common costs of spraying, pruning, and so on are not relevant. The company must pay the $300 per ton for these activities regardless of whether it sells at split-off or processes further. However, the revenues earned at split-off are likely to differ from the revenues that would be received if the Grade B apples are sold as pie filling. Therefore, revenues are a relevant consideration. Similarly, the processing costs occur only if further processing takes place. Hence, processing costs are relevant.

Since there are 600 pounds of Grade B apples at split-off, Appletime sells 120 five-pound bags at a net per-unit price of $1.25 ($1.30 – $0.05). Thus, the total net revenues at split-off are $150 ($1.25 × 120). If the apples are processed into pie

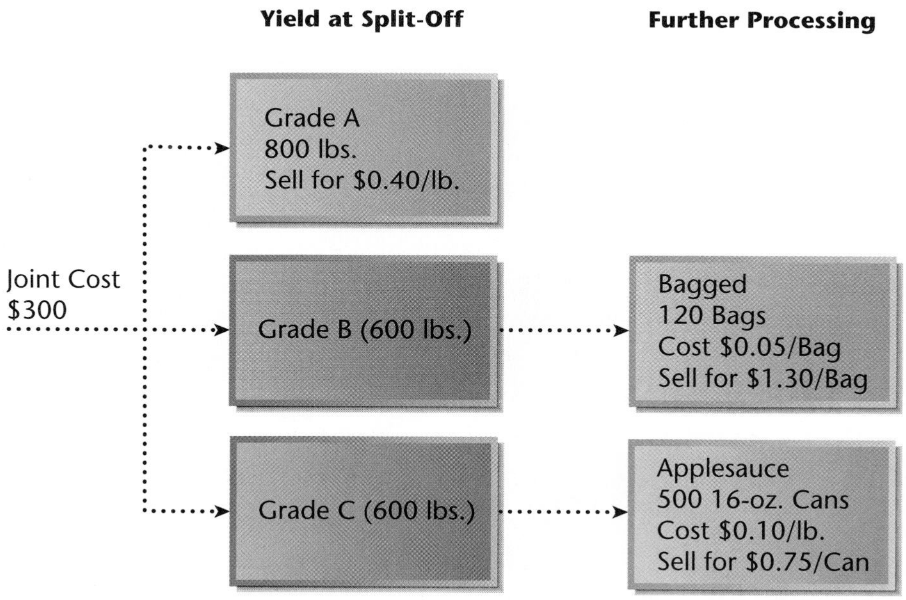

Exhibit 12-3 Appletime's Joint Process

filling, then the total revenues are \$450 (\$0.90 × 500). Therefore, the incremental revenues from processing further are \$300 (\$450 − \$150). The incremental costs of processing are \$120 (\$0.20 × 600 pounds). Since revenues increase by \$300 and costs by only \$120, the net benefit of processing further is \$180. Thus, Appletime should process the Grade B apples into pie filling. The analysis is summarized as follows:

	Process Further	Sell	Differential Amount to Process Further
Revenues	\$450	\$150	\$300
Processing cost	120	—	120
Total	\$330	\$150	\$180

Product Mix Decisions

Objective 4

Choose the optimal product mix when faced with one constrained resource.

In the preceding example, of every 2,000 pounds of apples harvested, 800 were Grade A, 600 were Grade B, and 600 were Grade C. Although the relative amounts of each type of apple can be influenced to some extent by the procedures followed in spraying, watering, fertilizing, and so on, the mix of apples is largely beyond Appletime's control. However, many organizations have total discretion in choosing their product mix. Moreover, decisions about product mix can have a significant impact on an organization's profitability.

Each mix represents an alternative that carries with it an associated profit level. A manager should choose the alternative that maximizes total profits. Since fixed costs do not vary with activity level, the total fixed costs of a firm would be the same for all possible mixes and, therefore, are not relevant to the decision. Thus, a manager needs to choose the alternative that maximizes total contribution margin.

Assume, for example, that Jorgenson Company produces two types of gears: X and Y, with unit contribution margins of \$25 and \$10, respectively. If the firm possesses unlimited resources and the demand for each product is unlimited, then the product mix decision is simple—produce an infinite number of each product. Unfortunately, every firm faces limited resources and limited demand for each product. These limitations are called **constraints**. A manager must choose the optimal mix given the constraints found within the firm.

Assuming that Jorgenson can sell all that is produced, some may argue that only Gear X should be produced and sold—it has the larger contribution margin. However, this solution is not necessarily the best. The selection of the optimal mix can be significantly affected by the relationships of the constrained resources to the individual products. These relationships affect the quantity of each product that can be produced and, consequently, the total contribution margin that can be earned. This point is most vividly illustrated when one is faced with a single resource constraint.

One Constrained Resource

Assume that each gear must be notched by a special machine. The firm owns eight machines that together provide 40,000 hours of machine time per year. Gear X requires two hours of machine time, and Gear Y requires 0.5 hour of machine time. Assuming no other constraints, what is the optimal mix of gears? Since each unit of Gear X requires two hours of machine time, a total of 20,000 units can be produced per year (40,000/2). At \$25 per unit, Jorgenson can earn a total contribution margin of \$500,000. On the other hand, Gear Y requires only 0.5 hour of machine time per unit; therefore, 80,000 (40,000/0.5) gears can be produced. At \$10 per unit, the total contribution margin is \$800,000. Producing only Gear Y yields a higher profit level than producing only Gear X—even though the unit contribution margin for X is 2.5 times larger than that for Y.

The contribution margin per unit of each product is not the critical concern. The contribution margin per unit of scarce resource is the deciding factor. The product yielding the highest contribution margin per machine hour should be selected. Gear X earns $12.50 per machine hour ($25/2), but Gear Y earns $20 per machine hour ($10/0.5). Thus, the optimal mix is 80,000 units of Gear Y and none of Gear X.

Multiple Constrained Resources

The presence of only one constrained resource is unrealistic. All organizations face multiple constraints: limitations of materials, limitations of labor inputs, limited demand for each product, and so on. The solution of the product mix problem in the presence of multiple constraints is considerably more complicated and requires the use of a specialized mathematical technique known as *linear programming,* which is defined and illustrated in the appendix at the end of this chapter.

Pricing

Objective 5

Explain the impact of cost on pricing decisions.

One of the more difficult decisions faced by a company is pricing. This section examines the impact of cost on price and the role of the accountant in gathering the needed information.

Cost-Based Pricing

Demand is one side of the pricing equation; supply is the other side. Since revenue must cover cost for the firm to make a profit, many companies start with cost to determine price. That is, they calculate product cost and add the desired profit. The mechanics of this approach are straightforward. Usually, there is some cost base and a markup. The **markup** is a percentage applied to the base cost; it includes desired profit and any costs not included in the base cost. Companies that bid for jobs routinely base bid price on cost.

Consider Elvin Company, owned and operated by Clare Elvin, which assembles and installs computers to customer specifications. Costs of the components and other direct materials are easy to trace. Direct labor cost is similarly easy to trace to each job. Assemblers receive, on average, $15 per hour. Last year, Elvin's total direct labor cost was $140,000. Overhead, consisting of utilities, small tools, building space, and so on, amounted to $84,000. Elvin Company's income statement for last year is as follows:

Revenues		$856,500
Cost of goods sold:		
Direct materials	$489,750	
Direct labor	140,000	
Overhead	84,000	713,750
Gross profit		$142,750
Selling and administrative expenses		25,000
Operating income		$ 117,750

Suppose that Clare wants to earn about the same amount of profit on each job as was earned last year. She could calculate a markup on cost of goods sold by summing selling and administrative expenses and operating income and then dividing by cost of goods sold:

$$\begin{aligned}\text{Markup on COGS} &= (\text{Selling and administrative expenses} \\ &\quad + \text{Operating income})/\text{COGS} \\ &= (\$25{,}000 + \$117{,}750)/\$713{,}750 \\ &= 0.20\end{aligned}$$

The markup on cost of goods sold is 20 percent. Notice that the 20 percent markup covers both profit and selling and administrative expenses. The markup is not pure profit.

The markup can be calculated using a variety of bases. Clearly, for Elvin Company, the cost of purchased materials is the largest component. Last year, the markup on direct materials amounted to 46.4 percent of all other costs and profit:

$$\begin{aligned}\text{Markup on direct materials} &= (\text{Direct labor} + \text{Overhead} + \text{Selling and} \\ &\quad \text{administrative expenses} + \text{Operating income})/ \\ &\quad \text{Direct materials} \\ &= (\$140{,}000 + \$84{,}000 + \$25{,}000 + \\ &\quad \$117{,}750)/\$489{,}750 \\ &= 0.749\end{aligned}$$

A markup percentage of 74.9 percent of direct materials cost would also yield the same amount of profit, assuming the level of operations and other expenses remained stable. The choice of base and markup percentage generally rests on convenience. If Clare finds that the labor varies in rough proportion to the cost of direct materials (for example, more expensive components take more time to set up) and that the cost of materials is easier to track than the cost of goods sold, then direct materials might be the better base.

To see how the markup can be used in bidding, suppose that Clare has the opportunity to bid on a job for a local insurance company. The job requires Elvin Company to assemble 100 computers according to certain specifications. She estimates the following costs:

Direct materials (computer components, software, cables)	$ 100,000
Direct labor (100 × 6 hours × $15)	9,000
Overhead (60 percent of direct labor cost)	5,400
Estimated cost of goods sold	$ 114,400
Plus 20 percent markup on COGS	22,880
Bid price	$137,280

Thus, Elvin Company's initial bid price is $137,280. Note that this is the first pass at a bid. Clare can adjust the bid based on her knowledge of competition for the job and other factors. The markup is a guideline, not an absolute rule.

If Elvin Company bids every job at cost plus 20 percent, is it guaranteed a profit? No, not at all. If very few jobs are won, the entire markup will go toward selling and administrative expenses, the costs not explicitly included in the bidding calculations.

Markup pricing is often used by retail stores, and their typical markup is 100 percent of cost. Thus, if a sweater is purchased by Graham Department Store for $24, the retail price marked is $48 [$24 + (1.00 × $24)]. Of course, the 100 percent markup is not pure profit—it goes toward the salaries of the clerks, payment for space and equipment (cash registers, furniture, and fixtures), utilities, advertising, and so on. A major advantage of markup pricing is that standard markups are easy to apply. Consider the difficulty of setting a price for every piece of merchandise in a hardware or department store. It is much simpler to apply a uniform markup to cost and then adjust prices as needed if demand is less than anticipated.

Target Costing and Pricing

We just examined the way in which companies use cost to determine price. Now, let's work backward and see how price can determine cost. **Target costing** is a method of determining the cost of a product or service based on the price (target price) that customers are willing to pay. This is also referred to as *price-driven costing.*

Most American companies, and nearly all European firms, set the price of a new product as the sum of the costs and the desired profit. The rationale is that the company must earn sufficient revenues to cover all costs and yield a profit. Peter Drucker writes, "This is true but irrelevant: Customers do not see it as their job to ensure manufacturers a profit. The only sound way to price is to start out with what the market is willing to pay."[6]

Target costing is a method of working backward from price to find cost. The marketing department determines what characteristics and price for a product are most acceptable to consumers; then, it is the job of the company's engineers to design and develop the product such that cost and profit can be covered by that price. Japanese firms have been doing this for years; American companies are beginning to use target costing. For example, Montclair Paper Mill applied target costing to solve the problem of continuing losses on every ton of paper sold. Management believed the problem was in the pricing of the product, not its manufacture. They instituted a program to reduce per ton paper costs by 60%, by reducing the cost of fiber input, increasing the yield per machine, and reducing conversion costs. The resultant cost decrease to the target cost resulted in a dramatic turnaround.[7]

Let's return to the Elvin Company example. Suppose Clare finds that the insurance company will not consider any bid over $100,000. Her cost-based bid was $137,280. Is she out of the running? No, not if she can tailor her bid to the customer's desired price. Recall that the original bid called for $100,000 of direct materials and $9,000 of direct labor. Clearly, adjusting the materials will yield the greatest savings. Working with the customer specifications, Clare must determine whether or not a less expensive set of components will achieve the insurance company objectives. Suppose that the insurance company has specified sufficient hard-disk space on each drive to accommodate particular software and that the minimum required is 800 megabytes. Clare's original bid specified 3 GB hard drives. If she reduces the hard-disk space to 1.5 GBs and uses a marginally slower drive, she could save $25,000. Substituting a slightly more expensive monitor (a $20 increase), which does not require the installation of screen-saver software, would result in saving $30 per computer on software and 15 minutes of direct labor time (at $15 per hour) to install it. The net reduction is $13.75 [($30 + $3.75) – $20] for each of the 100 computers. So far, Clare has developed the following costs:

Direct materials ($100,000 − $25,000)	$75,000
Direct labor (100 × 5.75 hours × $15)	8,625
Total prime cost	$83,625

Recall that Elvin Company applies overhead at the rate of 60 percent of direct labor cost. However, Clare must think carefully about this job. Perhaps somewhat less overhead will be incurred because purchasing is reduced (no need to purchase screen-saver software) and testing is reduced (the smaller hard drives require fewer hours of testing). Perhaps overhead for this job will amount to $4,313 (50 percent of direct labor). That would make the cost of the job $87,938 ($4,313 + $83,625).

Still, not all costs have been covered. There is the administrative cost and desired profit. If the standard markup of 20 percent is applied, the bid would be $105,526. This is still too high. Now, Clare must determine if further cuts are possi-

6 Peter Drucker, "The Five Deadly Business Sins," *Wall Street Journal* (21 October 1993): p. A22.

7 Taken from J. K. Shank and J. Fisher (1999), "Target Costing as a Strategic Tool," *Sloan Management Review,* Cambridge, Vol. 41, p. 73–82.

ble or if she wants to decrease desired profit and administrative expenses. As you can see, target costing is an iterative process. Clare will go through the cycle until she either achieves the target cost or determines that she cannot do so. Note, however, that given the customer's price ceiling, Clare now has a chance of winning the bid.

A further issue might cause concern. Is there anything ethically wrong with changing the components from the initial bid to the target-costed bid? No, the new components meet customer specifications and are clearly described in the bid. In fact, Clare's initial bid was overspecified. If the customer wants a Chevrolet, the bidder need not provide a Rolls-Royce, especially at Chevrolet prices. However, if in Clare's professional opinion the insurance company should upgrade its specifications, she could point that out. For example, if she knows that the insurance company's word-processing program is due for an upgrade that will take more hard-disk space, she could inform the company of that and encourage an increase in specified disk space.

Target costing involves much more up-front work than cost-based pricing. However, let's not forget the additional work that must be done if the cost-based price turns out to be higher than what customers will accept. Then the arduous task of bringing costs into line to support a lower price, or the opportunity cost of missing the market altogether, begins. For example, the U.S. consumer electronics market is virtually nonexistent because cost-based pricing led to increasingly higher prices. Japanese (and later Korean) firms practicing target costing offered lower prices and won the market.

Target costing can be used most effectively in the design and development stage of the product life cycle. At that point, the features of the product, as well as its costs, are still fairly easy to adjust.

Legal Aspects of Pricing

Customers and costs are important economic determinants of price. The U.S. government also has an important impact on pricing. The basic principle behind much pricing regulation is that competition is good and should be encouraged. Therefore, collusion by companies to set prices and the deliberate attempt to drive competitors out of business are prohibited. In general, cost is an important justification for price.

Predatory Pricing The practice of setting prices below cost for the purpose of injuring competitors and eliminating competition is called **predatory pricing**. It is important to note that pricing below cost is not necessarily predatory pricing. Companies frequently price an item below cost—loss leaders or weekly specials in a grocery store, for example. State laws on predatory pricing create a patchwork of legal definitions. Twenty-two states have laws against predatory pricing, each state differing somewhat in definition and rules. Oklahoma, for example, requires retailers to sell products at a price at least 6.75 percent above cost, unless the store is having a sale or matching a competitor's price. A 1937 Arkansas law forbids companies from selling or advertising "any article or product . . . at less than the cost thereof to the vendor . . . for the purpose of injuring competitors and destroying competition."

An example of the application of state predatory pricing laws is the lawsuit filed by three Conway, Arkansas, drugstores against **Wal-Mart**.[8] The druggists contended that Wal-Mart engaged in predatory pricing by selling more than 100 products below cost. One difficulty is showing exactly what cost is. Wal-Mart has low overhead and phenomenal buying power. Suppliers are regularly required to shave prices to win Wal-Mart's business. Smaller concerns cannot win such price breaks. Thus, the fact that Wal-Mart prices products below competitors' costs does not necessarily mean that those products are priced below Wal-Mart's cost. (Although in this case, the CEO of Wal-Mart did concede that Wal-Mart on occasion prices products below its own cost.)

8 Wal-Mart lost the suit in October 1993 and won the case on appeal.

A key legal point is that the below-cost price must be for the purpose of driving out competitors. Usually, this is a difficult point to prove. In general, states follow federal law in predatory pricing cases, and the federal law makes it difficult to prove predatory pricing since price competition is so highly valued.

Predatory pricing on the international market is called **dumping** and occurs when companies sell below cost in other countries. For years, U.S. automobile manufacturers have accused Japanese companies of dumping. Companies found guilty of dumping products in the United States are subject to trade restrictions and stiff tariffs—which act to increase the price of the good. The defense against a charge of dumping is demonstrating that the price is indeed above or equal to cost.

Price Discrimination Perhaps the most potent weapon against price discrimination in the United States is the 1936 Robinson-Patman Act.[9] **Price discrimination** refers to the charging of different prices to different customers for essentially the same product. Note that services and intangibles are not covered by this act. The Robinson-Patman Act states that it is unlawful "to discriminate in price between purchasers of commodities of like grade and quality . . . where the effect of such discrimination may be substantially to lessen competition, to tend to create a monopoly in any line of commerce, or to injure, destroy, or prevent competition with any person who either grants or knowingly receives the benefit of such discrimination, or with customers of either of them." A key feature is that only manufacturers or suppliers are covered by the act. Importantly, the Robinson-Patman Act does allow price discrimination under certain specified conditions: (1) if the competitive situation demands it and (2) if costs can justify the lower price. Clearly, this second condition is important for the accountant, as a lower price offered to one customer must be justified by identifiable cost savings. Additionally, the amount of the discount must be at least equaled by the amount of cost saved.

What about quantity discounts—are they permissible under Robinson-Patman? Consider quantity discounts offered by **Morton Salt** (now **Morton International, Inc.**) during the 1940s. Less-than-carload shipments were priced at $1.60 per case delivered. Carload shipments were priced at $1.50 per case, and extra discounts of $0.10 and an additional $0.05 were given for purchases of 5,000 cases and 50,000 cases, respectively, if purchased within a 12-month period. The Supreme Court, in a 1948 decision, found that Morton Salt had violated the Robinson-Patman Act because so few buyers qualified for the quantity discount; at the time, only five large chain stores had purchases high enough to qualify for the lowest price of $1.35 per case. While Morton Salt argued that the discounts were available to all purchasers, the Court noted that for all practical purposes, small wholesalers and retail grocers could not qualify for the discounts. A key point here is that so few purchasers were eligible for the discount that competition was lessened. So while the act states that quantity discounts can be given, they must not appreciably lessen competition.

Freight is considered part of the price for purposes of the Robinson-Patman Act. If a company requires the customer to pay freight charges, then there is no problem. However, price discrimination may occur if the price charged includes delivery. Suppose the firm charges a uniform delivery price. Then, customers located next to the firm pay the same price as customers located 1,000 miles away. Because the cost of delivering to nearby customers is much less than delivering to far-off customers, the nearby customers are paying "phantom freight."

The burden of proof for firms accused of violating the Robinson-Patman Act is on the firms. The cost justification argument must be buttressed by substantial cost data. Proving a cost justification is an absolute defense; however, the expense of preparing evidence and the FTC's restrictive interpretations of the defense have made

9 This section relies on two sources: William A. Rutter, *Antitrust*, 3rd ed. (Gardena, CA: Gilbert Law Summaries, 1972): pp. 57–64; and William A. Baldwin, *Market Power, Competition, and Antitrust Policy* (Homewood, IL: Richard D. Irwin, Inc., 1987): pp. 430–435.

it a seldom-used choice in the past. Now, the availability of large databases, the development of activity-based costing, and powerful computing make it a more palatable alternative. Still, problems remain. Cost allocations make such determinations particularly thorny. In justifying quantity discounts to larger companies, a company might keep track of sales calls, differences in time and labor required to make small and large deliveries, and so on.

In computing a cost differential, the company must create classes of customers based on the average costs of selling to those customers and then charge all customers in each group a cost-justifiable price.

Fairness and Pricing

Community standards of fairness have an important effect on prices. For example, should toy stores raise the price of sleds the morning after a heavy snowfall? They could, but generally they do not. Their customers believe that a price increase at such a time would be taking unfair advantage. Whether we characterize the store's reluctance to raise prices in this situation as fairness or as an act in the long-term best interests of the company, the result is the same.

© Getty Images/PhotoDisc

An early snowfall may mean that sleds are in short supply. Even so, most stores opt to ensure long-term customer goodwill by not raising the price above the normal level.

Price gouging is said to occur when firms with market power price products "too high." How high is too high? Surely, cost is a consideration. Any time price just covers cost, gouging does not occur. This is why so many firms go to considerable trouble to explain their cost structure and point out costs consumers may not realize exist. Pharmaceutical companies, for example, emphasize the research and development costs associated with new drugs. When a high price is clearly not supported by cost, buyers take offense. For example, after Hurricane Katrina in 2005, some landlords sharply raised rents on undamaged properties, even evicting some low-income tenants. Gulf Coast residents faced with those increases were outraged that some property owners would take advantage of the disaster to profiteer.[10]

It is easy to see that cost as a justification for price underlies community standards of fairness. Ethics are founded on a sense of fairness. So, unethical behavior in pricing is related to taking unfair advantage of customers. Cost-related price increases are the best defense against customer rebellion.

Appendix: Linear Programming

Objective 6

Use linear programming to find the optimal solution to a problem of multiple constrained resources.

Linear programming is a method that searches among possible solutions until it finds the optimal solution. The theory of linear programming permits many solutions to be ignored. In fact, all but a finite number of solutions are eliminated by the theory with the search then limited to the resulting finite set.

To illustrate how linear programming can be used to solve a problem of multiple constrained resources, we will use the earlier example of the product mix for Jorgenson Company. Assume that there are demand constraints for both Gear X and Gear Y. For Gear X, no more than 15,000 units can be sold; for Gear Y, no more than 40,000 units can be sold. As before, the objective is to maximize Jorgenson's total contribution margin subject to the constraints the company faces.

10 CBS News story at http://tinyurl.com/jj2zx ; *Baton Rouge Advocate,* http://tinyurl.com/h3uhn

The objective can be expressed mathematically. Let X and Y be the number of units produced and sold of Gear X and Gear Y, respectively. Since the unit contribution margins are \$25 and \$10 for X and Y, respectively, the total contribution margin (Z) can be expressed as:

$$Z = \$25X + \$10Y \tag{10.1}$$

Equation 10.1 is called the objective function. The **objective function** is the function to be optimized. In this case, the objective is to maximize the total contribution margin.

Jorgenson also has three constraints. One is the limited machine hours available for production, and the other two reflect the demand limitations for each product. Consider the machine-hour constraint first. Two machine hours are used for each unit of Gear X, and 0.5 machine hour is used for each unit of Gear Y. Thus, the total machine hours used can be expressed as $2X + 0.5Y$. The maximum of 40,000 machine hours available can be expressed mathematically as follows:

$$2X + 0.5Y \leq 40{,}000 \tag{10.2}$$

The two demand constraint limitations can also be expressed mathematically:

$$X \leq 15{,}000 \tag{10.3}$$
$$Y \leq 40{,}000 \tag{10.4}$$

Jorgenson's problem is to select the number of units of X and Y that maximize total contribution margin subject to the constraints in Equations 10.2, 10.3, and 10.4. This problem can be expressed in the following way, which is the standard formulation for a linear programming problem (often referred to as a *linear programming model*):

$$\text{Max. } Z = \$25X + \$10Y$$

subject to

$$\begin{aligned} 2X + 0.5Y &\leq 40{,}000 \\ X &\leq 15{,}000 \\ Y &\leq 40{,}000 \\ X &\geq \$\ 0 \\ Y &\geq 0 \end{aligned}$$

The last two constraints are called *nonnegativity constraints* and simply reflect the reality that negative quantities of a product cannot be produced. All constraints, taken together, are referred to as the **constraint set**.

A **feasible solution** is a solution that satisfies the constraints in the linear programming model. The collection of all feasible solutions is called the **feasible set of solutions**. For example, producing and selling 10,000 units of Gear X and 20,000 units of Gear Y would be a feasible solution and a member of the feasible set. This product mix uses 30,000 machine hours [(2 × 10,000) + (0.5 × 20,000)], which is under the limit for machine hours. Additionally, the company can sell the indicated amounts since they do not exceed the demand constraints for each product. If this mix is selected, the company would earn a contribution margin totaling \$450,000 [(\$25 × 10,000) + (\$10 × 20,000)].

However, the mix of 10,000 units of X and 20,000 units of Y is not the best mix. One better solution would be to produce and sell 12,000 units of X and 30,000 units of Y. This mix uses 39,000 machine hours [(2 × 12,000) + (0.5 × 30,000)] and produces a total contribution margin of \$600,000 [(\$25 × 12,000) + (\$10 × 30,000)]. This feasible solution is better than the first because it produces \$150,000 more in profits. However, even better feasible solutions exist. The objective is to identify the best. The best feasible solution—the one that maximizes the total contribution margin—is called the **optimal solution**.

When there are only two products, the optimal solution can be identified by graphing. Since solving the problem by graphing provides considerable insight into the way linear programming problems are solved, the Jorgenson problem will be solved in this way.

Four steps are followed in solving the problem graphically.

1. Graph each constraint.
2. Identify the feasible set of solutions.
3. Identify all corner-point values in the feasible set.
4. Select the corner point that yields the largest value for the objective function.

The graph of each constraint for the Jorgenson problem is shown in Exhibit 12-4. The nonnegativity constraints put the graph in the first quadrant. The other constraints are graphed by assuming that equality holds. Since each constraint is a linear equation, the graph is obtained by identifying two points on the line, plotting those points, and connecting them.

A feasible area for each constraint (except for the nonnegativity constraints) is determined by everything that lies below (or to the left) of the resulting line. The *feasible set* or *region* is the intersection of each constraint's feasible area. The feasible set is shown by the figure *ABCDE;* it includes the boundary of the figure.

There are five corner points: *A, B, C, D,* and *E.* Their values, obtained directly from the graph, are (0,0) for *A,* (15,0) for *B,* (15,20) for *C,* (10,40) for *D,* and (0,40) for *E.* The impact of these values on the objective function is as follows (expressed in thousands):

Corner Point	X-value	Y-value	Z = \$25X + \$10Y
A	0	0	\$ 0
B	15	0	375
C	15	20	575
D	10	40	650*
E	0	40	400

*Optimal solution

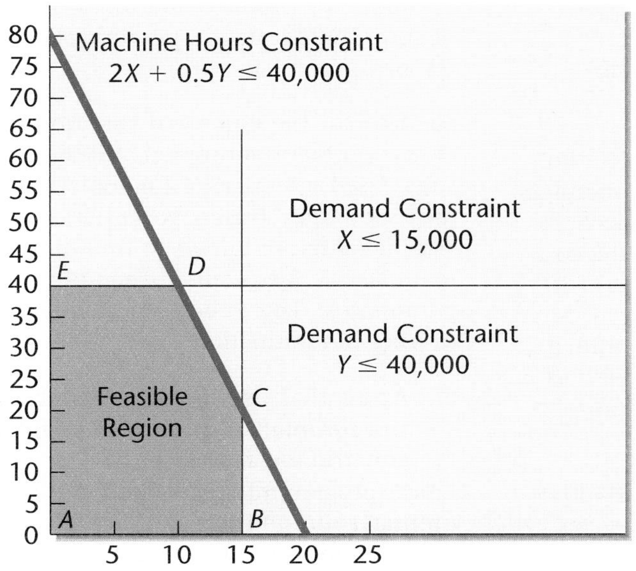

Exhibit 12-4 Graphical Solution (coordinates represent thousands)

The optimal solution calls for producing and selling 10,000 units of Gear X and 40,000 units of Gear Y. No other feasible solution will produce a larger contribution margin. It has been shown in the literature on linear programming that the optimal solution will always be one of the corner points. Thus, once the graph is drawn and the corner points identified, finding the solution is simply a matter of computing the value of each corner point and selecting the one with the greatest value.

Graphical solutions are not practical with more than two or three products. Fortunately, an algorithm called the **simplex method** can be used to solve larger linear programming problems. This algorithm has been coded and is available for use on computers to solve these larger problems.

The linear programming model is an important tool for making product mix decisions, though it requires very little independent managerial decision making. The mix decision is made by the linear programming model itself. Assuming that the linear programming model is a reasonable representation of reality, the main role for management is to ensure that accurate data are used as input to the model. This includes the ability to recognize the irrelevancy of fixed costs and the ability to assess the accounting and technological inputs accurately (for example, the unit selling prices, the unit costs, and the amount of resource consumed by each product as it is produced).

Summary of Learning Objectives

1. Describe the tactical decision-making model.
The decision-making model described in this chapter consists of six steps: recognizing and defining the problem, identifying alternatives, determining the costs and benefits of each alternative, comparing relevant costs and benefits for each alternative, assessing qualitative factors, and making the decision. In using cost analysis to choose among alternatives, managers should take steps to ensure that all important feasible alternatives are being considered.

2. Explain how the activity resource usage model is used in assessing relevancy.
The activity resource usage model breaks costs into two groups: flexible resources and committed resources. Flexible resources are acquired as used and needed; supply equals demand. If demand changes, the cost is relevant. Committed resources are acquired in advance; therefore, they may have unused capacity. The cost may or may not be relevant. If committed resources have sufficient unused capacity, their cost is not relevant. If there is not sufficient excess capacity, the additional cost is relevant.

3. Apply tactical decision-making concepts in a variety of business situations.
Several examples illustrating the application of the relevant costing model were given within the chapter. Applications were illustrated for make-or-buy decisions, keep-or-drop decisions, special-order decisions, and sell-or-process-further decisions. Product mix decisions were also discussed. The list of applications is by no means exhaustive but was given to illustrate the scope and power of relevant costing analysis.

4. Choose the optimal product mix when faced with one constrained resource.
In dealing with a resource constraint, it is important to phrase the product contribution margin in terms of contribution margin per unit of constrained resource.

5. Explain the impact of cost on pricing decisions.
Costs are important inputs into the pricing decision. Cost-based pricing uses a markup based on a subset of costs. Target costing works backward from a price acceptable to consumers to find the cost necessary to manufacture the product. The Robinson-Patman Act permits cost data to be used as an absolute defense in price discrimination cases.

6. Appendix: Use linear programming to find the optimal solution to a problem of multiple constrained resources.
Linear programming is a method that locates the optimal solution in a set of feasible solutions. The graphical method may be used with two products. When more than two products are involved, the simplex method is used.

Key Terms

Committed resources, 523
Constraint set, 540
Constraints, 533
Decision model, 517
Dumping, 538
Feasible set of solutions, 540
Feasible solution, 540
Flexible resources, 522
Joint products, 531
Keep-or-drop decisions, 526
Linear programming, 539
Make-or-buy decisions, 525
Markup, 534
Objective function, 540
Optimal solution, 540
Predatory pricing, 537
Price discrimination, 538
Price gouging, 539
Relevant costs, 520
Sell or process further, 531
Simplex method, 542
Special-order decisions, 530
Split-off point, 531
Strategic decision making, 516
Sunk cost, 520
Tactical decision making, 516
Target costing, 536

Review Problem

Special-Order Decision

Rianne Company produces a light fixture with the following unit cost:

Direct materials	$2
Direct labor	1
Variable overhead	3
Fixed overhead	2
Unit cost	$8

The production capacity is 300,000 units per year. Because of a depressed housing market, the company expects to produce only 180,000 fixtures for the coming year. The company also has fixed selling costs totaling $500,000 per year and variable selling costs of $1 per unit sold. The fixtures normally sell for $12 each.

At the beginning of the year, a customer from a geographic region outside the area normally served by the company offered to buy 100,000 fixtures for $7 each. The customer also offered to pay all transportation costs. Since there would be no sales commissions involved, this order would not have any variable selling costs.

Required

Should the company accept the order? Provide both qualitative and quantitative justification for your decision. Assume that no other orders are expected beyond the regular business and the special order.

Solution

The company is faced with a problem of idle capacity. Accepting the special order would bring production up to near capacity. Two options are available: accept or reject the order. If the order is accepted, then the company could avoid laying off employees and would enhance and maintain its community image. However, the order is considerably below the normal selling price of $12. Because the price is so low, the company needs to assess the potential impact of the sale on its regular customers and on the profitability of the firm. Considering the fact that the customer is located in a region not usually served by the company, the likelihood of an adverse impact on regular business is not high. Thus, the qualitative factors seem to favor acceptance.

The only remaining consideration is the profitability of the special order. To assess profitability, the firm should identify the relevant costs and benefits of each alternative. This analysis is as follows:

	Accept	Reject
Revenues	$ 700,000	$—
Direct materials	(200,000)	—
Direct labor	(100,000)	—
Variable overhead	(300,000)	—
Total benefits	$ 100,000	$ 0

Accepting the order would increase profits by $100,000. (The fixed overhead and selling costs are all irrelevant since they are the same across both alternatives.) *Conclusion:* The order should be accepted since both qualitative and quantitative factors favor it.

Questions for Writing and Discussion

1. What is the difference between tactical and strategic decisions?
2. Explain why depreciation on an existing asset is always irrelevant.
3. Give an example of a future cost that is not relevant.
4. Explain why relevant costs need to be expressed on a periodically recurring basis.
5. Relevant costs always determine which alternative should be chosen. Do you agree or disagree? Explain.
6. Give an example of a fixed cost that is relevant.
7. What is the difference, if any, between a relevant cost and a differential cost?
8. When, if ever, is depreciation a relevant cost?
9. What role do past costs play in relevant costing decisions?
10. Can direct materials ever be irrelevant in a make-or-buy decision? Explain.
11. Discuss the importance of complementary effects in a keep-or-drop decision.
12. What are some ways a manager can expand his or her knowledge of the feasible set of alternatives?
13. Should joint costs be considered in a sell-or-process-further decision? Explain.
14. Suppose that a product can be sold at split-off for $5,000 or processed further at a cost of $1,000 and then sold for $6,400. Should the product be processed further?
15. Why are fixed costs never relevant in a product mix decision?
16. Suppose that a firm produces two products. Should the firm always place the most emphasis on the product with the largest contribution margin per unit? Explain.
17. Why would a firm ever offer a price on a product that is below its full cost?
18. When can a firm legally offer different prices for the same product?
19. Discuss the purpose of linear programming.
20. What is an objective function? A constraint? A constraint set?
21. What is a feasible solution? A feasible set of solutions?
22. Explain the procedures for graphically solving a linear programming problem. What solution method is usually used when the problem includes more than two or three products?

Exercises

12-1

Model for Making Tactical Decisions
LO1

The model for making tactical decisions that was described in your text has six steps. These steps are listed, out of order, below. Put the steps in the correct order, starting with the step that should be taken first.

A. Select the alternative with the greatest overall benefit.
B. Identify the costs and benefits associated with each feasible alternative.
C. Assess qualitative factors.
D. Recognize and define the problem.

E. Identify alternatives as possible solutions to the problem.
F. Total the relevant costs and benefits for each alternative.

12-2

Flexible versus Committed Resources
LO2

Consider each of the following independent situations.

A. The Purchasing Department has five purchasing agents that work full time and are paid a salary of $35,000 per year. Each purchase order takes about 90 minutes, and requires approximately $5 of forms and supplies. Each order also requires, on average, about 45 minutes of telephone or Internet time to check with potential suppliers. The company pays a flat monthly rate for telephone and Internet services. The depreciation on office equipment for the Purchasing Department is $3,000 per month.
B. El Munchies, a taco stand near the college, hires counter staff at the rate of $7.50 per hour. Each staff member knows that the hours vary each week depending on the amount of business that El Munchies expects. Food is purchased from a restaurant supplier on an "as needed" basis; there is about 4 days of perishable goods inventory on hand, and a month's worth of nonperishable goods (e.g., napkins, paper cups) in inventory. Utilities are paid on a monthly basis for the previous month's usage. El Munchies has a three-year lease on the building and parking lot. Each month, the restaurant buys newspaper and radio advertising for the coming month.
C. Jared Benning runs a lawn mowing service during the summers to help pay for his college expenses. Jared bought a power mower (it runs on gasoline and must have its oil changed monthly due to the volume of lawns mowed) and a gas-powered weed eater for trimming along the edges. Jared buys a season's worth of lawn mower oil at the beginning of summer because he can get a discount if he buys in bulk. From time to time, Jared has a commitment elsewhere. When that happens, a friend of his mows the yards that day; he and the friend have agree on a per yard fee for this. Jared owns a used pickup truck and uses it to haul his equipment from job to job.

Required

Classify the resources in each of the above situations as flexible or committed. If the resource is committed, determine whether it is committed for the short term or committed for multiple periods.

12-3

Make-or-Buy Decision
LO3

Chesbrough, Inc., makes many of the components of its main product in-house. Recently, Berham Electronics offered to supply one component, K-25, at a price of $6.50 each. Chesbrough uses 20,000 units of component K-25 each year. The absorption cost per unit of this component is as follows:

Direct materials	$2.95
Direct labor	0.40
Variable overhead	1.80
Fixed overhead	4.00
Total	$9.15

The fixed overhead is an allocated expense; none of it would be eliminated if production of component K-25 stopped.

Required

1. What are the alternatives facing Chesbrough, Inc., with respect to production of component K-25?
2. List the relevant costs for each alternative. Suppose that Chesbrough, Inc., purchases K-25 from Berham Electronics. By how much will operating income increase or decrease?

12-4

Make-or-Buy Decision
LO3

Refer to **Exercise 12-3**. Now suppose that $1.85 of the fixed overhead for component K-25 is the cost of leasing special equipment used to make K-25. If production of K-25 stops, then the leased machinery can be returned immediately at no further cost.

Required

1. What are the relevant costs for each alternative?
2. If Chesbrough, Inc., purchases K-25 from Berham Electronics, by how much will operating income increase or decrease?

12-5

Keep-or-Drop Decision
LO3

Garringer Company makes two products, regulars and seasonals. Information on costs associated with each product line is as follows:

	Regulars	Seasonals
Sales revenue	$135,000	$15,000
Less: Variable expenses	50,000	8,600
Contribution margin	$ 85,000	$ 6,400
Less:		
Direct fixed expenses	3,000	1,200
Common fixed expenses	54,000	6,000
Operating income	$ 28,000	$ (800)

The direct fixed expenses are advertising and selling costs that are incurred by the particular product line. The common fixed expenses are allocated to the two product lines on the basis of sales revenue. Total common fixed expenses would not change if a product line were dropped.

Required

1. Develop a segmented income statement, by product and in total for Garringer Company. Be sure to show the segment margin for each product.
2. By how much would operating income increase or decrease if the seasonals were dropped?

12-6

Keep-or-Drop Decision
LO3

Yavapei Company produces three products: A, B, and C. A segmented income statement, with amounts given in thousands, follows:

	A	B	C	Total
Sales revenue	$1,800	$1,600	$210	$ 3,610
Less: Variable expenses	1,350	1,000	140	2,490
Contribution margin	$ 450	$ 600	$ 70	$1,120
Less: Direct fixed expenses	150	300	80	530
Segment margin	$ 300	$ 600	$(10)	$ 590
Less: Common fixed expenses				340
Operating income				$ 250

Direct fixed expenses include depreciation on equipment dedicated to the product lines of $20,000 for A, $120,000 for B, and $25,000 for C. None of the product line equipment can be sold, and would have to be disposed of if the product line were dropped.

Required

1. What impact on profit would result from dropping Product C?
2. Suppose that 10 percent of the customers for Product B choose to buy from Yavapei because it offers a full range of products, including Product C. If C were

no longer available from Yavapei, these customers would go elsewhere to purchase B. Now what is the impact on profit if Product C is dropped?

12-7

Special-Order Decision; Flexible and Committed Resources
LO2, LO3

Thomson Company has been approached by a new customer with an offer to purchase 34,000 units of Thomson's product at a price of $24 each. The new customer is geographically separated from Thomson's other customers, and there would be no effect on existing sales. Thomson normally produces 400,000 units but plans to produce and sell only 360,000 in the coming year. The normal sales price is $30 per unit. Unit cost information is as follows:

Direct materials	$ 8.00
Direct labor	10.00
Variable overhead	4.00
Fixed overhead	3.40
Total	$25.40

If Thomson accepts the order, no fixed manufacturing activities will be affected because there is sufficient excess capacity.

Required

1. Should Thomson accept the special order? By how much will profit increase or decrease if the order is accepted?
2. Suppose that Thomson's distribution center at the warehouse is operating at full capacity and would need to add capacity costing $6,000 for every 5,000 units to be packed and shipped. Should Thomson accept the special order? By how much will profit increase or decrease if the order is accepted?

12-8

Special-Order Decision
LO2, LO3

After several years producing and selling at capacity (50,000 units), Melton Company faced a year with projected sales and production of 38,000 units. A potential customer offered to purchase 7,000 units at a price of $18 each. The normal sales price is $30 each. Unit cost information is as follows:

Direct materials	$ 9.00
Direct labor	6.50
Variable overhead	2.00
Fixed overhead	3.75
Total	$21.25

Melton also pays a sales commission of $1.75. The commission would have to be paid on this order.

Required

1. Should Melton accept the special order? By how much will profit increase or decrease if the order is accepted?
2. Suppose that Melton does not have to pay the sales commission on the special order. Should Melton accept the special order? By how much will profit increase or decrease if the order is accepted?

12-9

Sell or Process Further; Basic Analysis
LO1, LO2, LO3

EXCEL

Danelle, Inc., produces four products (Alpha, Beta, Gamma, and Delta) from a common input. The joint costs for a typical quarter follow:

Direct materials	$128,000
Direct labor	56,000
Overhead	80,000

The revenues from each product are as follows: Alpha, $130,000; Beta, $93,000; Gamma, $30,000; and Delta, $40,000.

Management is considering processing Delta beyond the split-off point, which would increase the sales value of Delta to $73,700. However, to process Delta further means that the company must rent some special equipment costing $15,400 per quarter. Additional materials and labor also needed would cost $8,500 per quarter.

Required

1. What is the operating profit earned by the four products for one quarter?
2. Should the division process Product Delta further or sell it at split-off? What is the effect of the decision on quarterly operating profit?

12-10

Product Mix Decision; Single Constraint
LO4

Norton Company produces two products (Juno and Hera) that use the same material input. Juno uses two pounds of the material for every unit produced, and Hera uses five pounds. Currently, Norton has 16,000 pounds of the material in inventory. All of the material is imported. For the coming year, Norton plans to import an additional 8,000 pounds to produce 2,000 units of Juno and 4,000 units of Hera. The unit contribution margin is $30 for Juno and $60 for Hera.

Norton Company has received word that the source of the material has been shut down by embargo. Consequently, the company will not be able to import the 8,000 pounds it planned to use in the coming year's production. No other source of the material exists.

Required

1. Compute the total contribution margin that the company would earn if it could manufacture 2,000 units of Juno and 4,000 units of Hera.
2. Determine the optimal usage of the company's inventory of 16,000 pounds of the material. Compute the total contribution margin for the product mix that you recommend.

12-11

Product Mix Decision; Single Constraint
LO4

Sealing Company manufactures three types of floppy disk storage units. Each of the three types requires the use of a special machine that has a total operating capacity of 15,000 hours per year. Information on the three types of storage units is as follows:

	Basic	Standard	Deluxe
Selling price	$9.00	$30.00	$35.00
Variable cost	$6.00	$20.00	$10.00
Machine hours required	0.10	0.50	0.75

Sealing Company's marketing director has assessed demand for the three types of storage units and believes that the firm can sell as many units as it can produce.

Required

1. How many of each type of unit should be produced and sold to maximize the company's contribution margin? What is the total contribution margin for your selection?
2. Now, suppose that Sealing Company believes that it can sell no more than 12,000 of the deluxe model but up to 50,000 each of the basic and standard models at the selling prices estimated. What product mix would you recommend, and what would the total contribution margin be?

12-12

Cost-Based Pricing Decision
LO5

Colin Silverman, owner of Silverman Cabinets, Inc., is preparing a bid on a job that requires $800 of direct materials, $1,600 of direct labor, and $3,200 of overhead. Colin normally applies a standard markup based on cost of goods sold to arrive at an initial bid price. He then adjusts the price as necessary in light of other factors (for example, competitive pressure). Last year's income statement is as follows:

Sales	$206,349
Cost of goods sold	144,300
Gross margin	$ 62,049
Selling and administrative expenses	46,300
Operating income	$ 15,749

EXCEL

Required

1. Calculate the markup Colin will use.
2. What is Colin's initial bid price?

12-13

Cost-Based Pricing Decision
LO5

Last year, Bagger Company had sales revenue of $1,250,000, direct materials of $240,000, direct labor of $310,700, and overhead of $449,300. Bagger calculates sales price using a markup on cost of goods sold.

Required

1. Calculate the markup Bagger will use.
2. If a job has manufacturing cost of $43,000, what is Bagger's price?

12-14

Product Mix Decision with One Constrained Resource
LO4

Orly Company produces two models of an industrial product that require the use of a laser-operated drilling machine. The laser-operated drilling machines owned by the firm provide a total of 12,000 hours per year. Model A-4 requires six hours of machine time, and Model M-3 requires three hours of machine time. Model A-4 has a contribution margin of $24 per unit, and Model M-3 has a contribution margin of $15.

Required

1. Calculate the optimal number of units of each model that should be produced, assuming that an unlimited number of each model can be sold.
2. Calculate the optimal number of units of each model that should be produced, assuming that no more than 2,500 units of each model can be sold.

12-15

Product Mix Decision with One Constrained Resource
LO4

O'Connor Company produces two models of machine housings that require the use of a special lathe. The six lathes owned by the firm provide a total of 12,000 hours per year. Model 14-D requires four hours of machine time, and Model 33-P requires two hours of machine time. Model 14-D has a contribution margin of $12 per unit, and Model 33-P has a contribution margin of $10.

Required

1. Calculate the optimal number of units of each model that should be produced, assuming that an unlimited number of each model can be sold.
2. Calculate the optimal number of units of each model that should be produced, assuming that no more than 5,000 units of each model can be sold.

12-16

Appendix: Linear Programming Decision
LO6

Refer to **Exercise 12-15**. Assume that no more than 2,000 units of Model 14-D can be sold and that no more than 5,000 units of Model 33-P can be sold.

Required

1. Formulate the linear programming problem faced by O'Connor Company. To do so, you must derive mathematical expressions for the objective function and for the lathe constraints.
2. Solve the linear programming problem using the graphical approach.
3. Compute the total contribution margin produced by the optimal mix developed in Requirement 2.

12-17

Appendix: Product Mix; Multiple Constraints
LO6

Zanbrow Company produces two products that use the same material input. Product A uses two pounds of the material for every unit produced, and Product B uses five pounds. Currently, Zanbrow has 6,000 pounds of the material in inventory and will not be able to obtain more for the coming year. The maximum demand (sales) for A is estimated at 1,000 units, and for B it is estimated at 2,000 units. The detail of each product's unit contribution margin follows:

	Product A	Product B
Selling price	$81	$139
Less variable expenses:		
Direct materials	(20)	(50)
Direct labor	(21)	(14)
Variable overhead	(10)	(15)
Contribution margin	$30	$60

Assume that Product A uses three direct labor hours for every unit produced and that Product B uses two hours. A total of 6,000 direct labor hours is available for the coming year.

Required

1. Formulate the linear programming problem faced by Zanbrow Company. To do so, you must derive mathematical expressions for the objective function and for the material and labor constraints.
2. Solve the linear programming problem using the graphical approach.
3. Compute the total contribution margin produced by the optimal mix developed in Requirement 2.

12-18

Keep-or-Buy Decision; Sunk Costs
LO1, LO3

Heath Wilburt purchased a previously owned, two-year-old Chevrolet Silverado short-bed pickup truck for $10,200. Since purchasing the car, he has spent the following amounts on parts and labor:

New stereo system	$1,200
Trick paint	400
New tires	800
Total	$2,400

Unfortunately, the new stereo doesn't completely drown out the sounds of a grinding transmission. Apparently, the Silverado needs a considerable amount of work to make it reliable transportation. Heath estimates that the needed repairs include the following:

Transmission overhaul	$2,400
Water pump	400
Master cylinder work	1,700
Total	$4,500

In a visit to a used car dealer, Heath has found a one-year-old Dodge Ram pickup truck in mint condition for $12,300. Heath has advertised and found that he can sell the Silverado for only $9,400, and that is assuming that the truck still runs with its engine problems. If he buys the Dodge Ram, he will pay cash, but he would need to sell the Silverado.

Required

1. In trying to decide whether to restore the Silverado or buy the Dodge Ram, Heath is distressed because he already has spent $12,600 on the Silverado. The investment seems too much to give up. How would you react to his concern?

2. Assuming that Heath would be equally happy with the Silverado or the Dodge Ram, should he buy the newer pickup, or should he restore the Silverado?

12-19

Make-or-Buy Decision
LO1, LO2, LO3

EXCEL

Sherwood Company is currently manufacturing part Z911, producing 40,000 units annually. The part is used in the production of several products made by Sherwood. The cost per unit for Z911 is as follows:

Direct materials	$ 9.00
Direct labor	3.00
Variable overhead	2.50
Fixed overhead	4.00
Total	$18.50

Of the total fixed overhead assigned to Z911, $88,000 is direct fixed overhead (the lease of production machinery and salary of a production line supervisor—neither of which will be needed if the line is dropped). The remaining fixed overhead is common fixed overhead. An outside supplier has offered to sell the part to Sherwood for $16. There is no alternative use for the facilities currently used to produce the part.

Required

1. Should Sherwood Company make or buy part Z911?
2. What is the most Sherwood would be willing to pay an outside supplier?
3. If Sherwood bought the part, by how much would income increase or decrease?

12-20

Make-or-Buy Decision
LO1, LO2, LO3

EXCEL

Refer to **Exercise 12-19**. Now suppose that all of the fixed overhead is common fixed overhead.

Required

1. Should Sherwood Company make or buy part Z911?
2. What is the most Sherwood would be willing to pay an outside supplier?
3. If Sherwood bought the part, by how much would income increase or decrease?

Problems

12-21

Model for Making Tactical Decisions
LO1

Austin Porter is a sophomore at a small Midwestern university—SMWU. He is considering whether or not to continue at this university or to transfer to one with a nationally recognized engineering program. Austin's decision-making process included the following:

A. He surfed the Internet to check out the sites of a number of colleges and universities with engineering programs.
B. Austin wrote to five of the universities to obtain information on their engineering colleges, tuition and room and board costs, likelihood of his being accepted, and so on.
C. Austin compared costs of the five other schools to the cost of his present school. He totaled the balance in his checking and savings accounts, estimated the earnings from his work-study job, and asked his parents whether or not they would be able to help him out.
D. Austin's high-school sweetheart had a long heart-to-heart talk with him about their future—specifically, that there might be no future if he left town.
E. Austin thought that while he enjoyed his present college, its engineering program did not have the national reputation that would enable him to get a good job on

either the East or West coast. Working for a large company on the coast was an important dream of his.

F. Austin's major advisor agreed that a school with a national reputation would make job hunting easier. However, he reminded Austin that small-college graduates had occasionally gotten the kind of jobs Austin wanted.

G. Austin had a number of good friends at the small college, and they were encouraging him to stay.

H. A friend of Austin's from high school returned for a long weekend. She went to a prestigious university and told Austin of the fun and opportunities available at her school. She encouraged Austin to check out the possibilities elsewhere.

I. A friendly professor outside of Austin's major area ran into him at the student union. She listened to his thinking and reminded him that a degree from a small college would easily get him into a good graduate program. Perhaps he ought to consider postponing the job hunt until a master's degree was in hand.

J. Two of the three prestigious universities accepted Austin and offered him financial aid. The third one rejected his application.

K. Austin made his decision.

Required

Classify the above events as one of the six steps of the model for making tactical decisions described in your text.

12-22

Make-or–Buy Decision; Qualitative Considerations LO2, LO3

Powell Dentistry Services operates in a large metropolitan area. Currently, Powell has its own dental laboratory to produce porcelain and gold crowns. The unit costs to produce the crowns are as follows:

	Porcelain	Gold
Direct materials	$ 80	$165
Direct labor	27	27
Variable overhead	8	8
Fixed overhead	22	22
Total	$137	$222

Fixed overhead is detailed as follows:

Salary (supervisor)	$26,000
Depreciation	5,000
Rent (lab facility)	32,000

Overhead is applied on the basis of direct labor hours. These rates were computed using 5,500 direct labor hours.

A local dental laboratory has offered to supply Powell all the crowns it needs. Its price is $130 for porcelain crowns and $200 for gold crowns; however, the offer is conditional on supplying both types of crowns—it will not supply just one type for the price indicated. If the offer is accepted, the equipment used by Powell's laboratory would be scrapped (it is old and has no market value), and the lab facility would be closed. Powell uses 3,000 porcelain crowns and 800 gold crowns per year.

Required

1. Should Powell continue to make its own crowns, or should they be purchased from the external supplier? What is the dollar effect of purchasing?
2. What qualitative factors should Powell consider in making this decision?
3. Suppose that the lab facility is owned rather than rented and that the $32,000 is depreciation rather than rent. What effect does this have on the analysis in Requirement 1?

4. Refer to the original data. Assume that the volume of crowns used is 4,000 porcelain and 600 gold. Should Powell make or buy the crowns? Explain the outcome.

12-23

Sell or Process Further
LO3

Primack Pharmaceutical Corporation buys three chemicals that are processed to produce two types of analgesics used as ingredients for popular over-the-counter drugs. The purchased chemicals are blended for two to three hours and then heated for 15 minutes. The results of the process are two separate analgesics, rhinime and stercol, which are sent to a drying room until their moisture content is reduced to 6 to 8 percent. For every 1,300 pounds of chemicals used, 600 pounds of rhinime and 600 pounds of stercol are produced. After drying, rhinime and stercol are sold to companies that process them into their final form. The selling prices are $15 per pound for rhinime and $37 per pound for stercol. The costs to produce 600 pounds of each analgesic are as follows:

Chemicals	$9,360
Direct labor	8,200
Overhead	19,900

The analgesics are packaged in 20-pound bags and shipped. The cost of each bag is $1.30. Shipping costs $0.15 per pound.

Primack could process rhinime further by grinding it into a fine powder and then molding the powder into tablets. The tablets can be sold directly to retail drug stores as a generic brand. If this route is taken, the revenue received per bottle of tablets would be $5.00, with 10 bottles produced from every pound of rhinime. The costs of grinding and tableting total $2.50 per pound of rhinime. Bottles cost $0.50 each. Bottles are shipped in boxes that hold 25 at a shipping cost of $1.70 per box.

Required

1. Should Primack sell rhinime at split-off, or should rhinime be processed and sold as tablets?
2. If Primack normally sells 265,000 pounds of rhinime per year, what will be the difference in profits if rhinime is processed further?

12-24

Keep-or-Drop Decision
LO3

EXCEL

AudioMart is a retailer of radios, stereos, and televisions. The store carries two portable sound systems that have radios, tape players, and speakers. System A, of slightly higher quality than System B, costs $20 more. With rare exceptions, the store also sells a headset when a system is sold. The headset can be used with either system. Variable-costing income statements for the three products follow:

	System A	System B	Headset
Sales	$45,000	$ 32,500	$8,000
Less: Variable expenses	20,000	25,500	3,200
Contribution margin	$25,000	$ 7,000	$4,800
Less: Fixed costs*	10,000	18,000	2,700
Operating income	$15,000	$(11,000)	$2,100

* This includes common fixed costs totaling $18,000, allocated to each product in proportion to its revenues.

The owner of the store is concerned about the profit performance of System B and is considering dropping it. If the product is dropped, sales of System A will increase by 30 percent, and sales of headsets will drop by 25 percent.

Required

1. Prepare segmented income statements for the three products using a better format.
2. Prepare segmented income statements for System A and the headsets assuming that System B is dropped. Should B be dropped?

3. Suppose that a third system, System C, with a similar quality to System B, could be acquired. Assume that with C the sales of A would remain unchanged; however, C would produce only 80 percent of the revenues of B, and sales of the headsets would drop by 10 percent. The contribution margin ratio of C is 50 percent, and its direct fixed costs would be identical to those of B. Should System B be dropped and replaced with System C?

12-25

Accept or Reject a Special Order
LO2, LO3

Steve Murningham, manager of an electronics division, was considering an offer by Pat Sellers, manager of a sister division. Pat's division was operating below capacity and had just been given an opportunity to produce 8,000 units of one of its products for a customer in a market not normally served. The opportunity involves a product that uses an electrical component produced by Steve's division. Each unit that Pat's department produces requires two of the components. However, the price the customer is willing to pay is well below the price usually charged; to make a reasonable profit on the order, Pat needs a price concession from Steve's division. Pat had offered to pay full manufacturing cost for the parts. So that Steve would know that everything was aboveboard, Pat had supplied the following unit-cost and price information concerning the special order, excluding the cost of the electrical component:

Selling price	$ 32
Less costs:	
Direct materials	(17)
Direct labor	(7)
Variable overhead	(2)
Fixed overhead	(3)
Operating profit	$ 3

The normal selling price of the electrical component is $2.30 per unit. Its full manufacturing cost is $1.85 ($1.05 variable and $0.80 fixed). Pat had argued that paying $2.30 per component would wipe out the operating profit and result in her division showing a loss. Steve was interested in the offer because his division was also operating below capacity (the order would not use all the excess capacity).

Required

1. Should Steve accept the order at a selling price of $1.85 per unit? By how much will his division's profits be changed if the order is accepted? By how much will the profits of Pat's division change if Steve agrees to supply the part at full cost?
2. Suppose that Steve offers to supply the component at $2. In offering the price, Steve says that it is a firm offer not subject to negotiation. Should Pat accept this price and produce the special order? If Pat accepts the price, what is the change in profits for Steve's division?
3. Assume that Steve's division is operating at full capacity and that Steve refuses to supply the part for less than the full price. Should Pat still accept the special order? Explain.

12-26

Keep or Drop a Division
LO2, LO3

Jan Shumard, president and general manager of Danbury Company, was concerned about the future of one of the company's largest divisions. The division's most recent quarterly income statement follows:

Sales	$3,751,500
Less: Cost of goods sold	2,722,400
Gross profit	$1,029,100
Less: Selling and administrative expenses	1,100,000
Operating (loss)	$ (70,900)

Jan is giving serious consideration to shutting down the division since this is the ninth consecutive quarter that it has shown a loss. To help him in his decision, the following additional information has been gathered:

- The division produces one product at a selling price of $100 to outside parties.
- The division sells 50 percent of its output to another division within the company for $83 per unit (full manufacturing cost plus 25 percent). The internal price is set by company policy. If the division is shut down, the user division would buy the part externally for $100 per unit.
- The fixed overhead assigned per unit is $20.
- There is no alternative use for the facilities if shut down. The facilities and equipment would be sold and the proceeds invested to produce an annuity of $100,000 per year.
- Of the fixed selling and administrative expenses, 30 percent represent allocated expenses from corporate headquarters.
- Variable selling expenses are $5 per unit sold for units sold externally. These expenses are avoided for internal sales. No variable administrative expenses are incurred.

Required

1. Prepare an income statement that more accurately reflects the division's profit performance.
2. Should the president shut down the division? What would be the effect on the company's profits if the division was closed?

12-27

Appendix: Product Mix Decision; Single and Multiple Constraints; Basics of Linear Programming
LO4, LO6

Paper Products, Inc., produces table napkins and facial tissues. The manufacturing process is highly mechanized; both products are produced by the same machinery by using different settings. For the coming period, 200,000 machine hours are available. Management is trying to decide on the quantities of each product to produce. The following data are available (for napkins, one unit is one package of napkins; for facial tissues, one unit is one box of tissues):

	Napkins	Tissues
Machine hours per unit	1.00	0.50
Unit selling price	$2.50	$3.00
Unit variable cost	$1.50	$2.25

Required

1. Determine the units of each product that should be produced in order to maximize profits.
2. Because of market conditions, the company can sell no more than 150,000 packages of napkins and 300,000 boxes of facial tissues. Do the following:
   a. Formulate the problem as a linear programming problem.
   b. Determine the optimal mix using a graph.
   c. Compute the maximum profit given the optimal mix.

12-28

Appendix: Product Mix Decisions
LO4, LO6

CMA

Calen Company manufactures and sells three products in a factory of three departments. Both labor and machine time are applied to the products as they pass through each department. The nature of the machine processing and of the labor skills required in each department is such that neither machines nor labor can be switched from one department to another.

Calen's management is attempting to plan its production schedule for the next several months. The planning is complicated by the fact that labor shortages exist in the community and some machines will be down several months for repairs.

Following is information regarding available machine and labor time by department and the machine hours and direct labor hours required per unit of product. These data should be valid for at least the next six months:

		Department		
Monthly Capacity		**1**	**2**	**3**
Labor hours available		3,700	4,500	2,750
Machine hours available		3,000	3,100	2,700
Product	**Input per Unit Produced**			
401	Labor hours	2	3	3
	Machine hours	1	1	2
402	Labor hours	1	2	—
	Machine hours	1	1	—
403	Labor hours	2	2	2
	Machine hours	2	2	1

The sales division believes that the monthly demand for the next six months will be as follows:

Product	Units Sold
401	500
402	400
403	1,000

Inventory levels will not be increased or decreased during the next six months. The unit cost and price data for each product are as follows:

	Product		
	401	**402**	**403**
Unit costs:			
Direct material	$ 7	$ 13	$ 17
Direct labor	66	38	51
Variable overhead	27	20	25
Fixed overhead	15	10	32
Variable selling	3	2	4
Total unit cost	$ 118	$ 83	$129
Unit selling price	$196	$123	$167

Required

1. Calculate the monthly requirement for machine hours and direct labor hours for producing Products 401, 402, and 403 to determine whether the factory can meet the monthly sales demand.
2. Determine the quantities of 401, 402, and 403 that should be produced monthly to maximize profits. Prepare a schedule that shows the contribution to profits of your product mix.
3. Assume that the machine hours available in Department 3 are 1,500 instead of 2,700. Calculate the optimal monthly product mix using the graphing approach to linear programming. Prepare a schedule that shows the contribution to profits from this optimal mix. **(CMA adapted)**

12-29

Make-or-Buy Decision
LO2, LO3

Henderson Company produces two products, A and B. The segmented income statement for a typical quarter follows:

	Product A	Product B	Total
Sales	$150,000	$80,000	$230,000
Less: Variable expenses	80,000	46,000	126,000
Contribution margin	$ 70,000	$34,000	$104,000
Less: Direct fixed expenses*	20,000	38,000	58,000
Segment margin	$ 50,000	$(4,000)	$ 46,000
Less: Common fixed expenses			30,000
Operating income			$ 16,000

* Includes depreciation.

Product A uses a subassembly that is purchased from an external supplier for $25 per unit. Each quarter, 2,000 subassemblies are purchased. All units produced are sold, and there are no ending inventories of subassemblies. Henderson is considering making the subassembly rather than buying it. Unit variable manufacturing costs are as follows:

Direct materials	$2
Direct labor	3
Variable overhead	2

Two alternatives exist to supply the productive capacity:

1. Lease the needed space and equipment at a cost of $27,000 per quarter for the space and $10,000 per quarter for a supervisor. No other fixed expenses are incurred.
2. Drop Product B. The equipment could be adapted with virtually no cost and the existing space utilized to produce the subassembly. The direct fixed expenses, including supervision, would be $38,000, $8,000 of which is depreciation on equipment. If Product B is dropped, the sales of Product A will not be affected.

Required

1. Should Henderson Company make or buy the subassembly? If it makes the subassembly, which alternative should be chosen? Explain and provide supporting computations.
2. Suppose that dropping B will decrease sales of A by 6 percent. What effect does this have on the decision?
3. Assume that dropping B decreases sales of A by 6 percent and that 2,800 subassemblies are required per quarter. As before, assume that there are no ending inventories of subassemblies and that all units produced are sold. Assume also that the per-unit sales price and variable costs are the same as in Requirement 1. Include the leasing alternative in your consideration. Now, what is the correct decision?

12-30

Make-or-Buy Decision
LO2, LO3

CMA

Sportway, Inc., is a wholesale distributor supplying a wide range of moderately priced sporting equipment to large chain stores. About 60 percent of Sportway's products are purchased from other companies, while the remaining products are manufactured by Sportway. The company's Plastics Department is currently manufacturing molded fishing tackle boxes. Sportway is able to manufacture and sell 8,000 tackle boxes annually, making full use of its direct labor capacity at available workstations. Following are the selling price and costs associated with Sportway's tackle boxes.

Selling price per box		$86.00
Costs per box:		
Molded plastic	$ 8.00	
Hinges, latches, handle	9.00	
Direct labor ($15/hour)	18.75	
Manufacturing overhead	12.50	
Selling and administrative expenses	17.00	65.25
Profit per box		$20.75

Because Sportway believes it could sell 12,000 tackle boxes if it had sufficient manufacturing capacity, the company has looked into the possibility of purchasing the tackle boxes for distribution. Maple Products, a steady supplier of quality products, would be able to provide up to 9,000 tackle boxes per year at a price of $68 per box delivered to Sportway's facility.

Bart Johnson, Sportway's product manager, has suggested that the company could make better use of its Plastics Department by manufacturing skateboards. To support his position, Bart has a market study that indicates an expanding market for skateboards and a need for additional suppliers. He believes that Sportway could expect to sell 17,500 skateboards annually at a price of $45 per skateboard. Bart's estimate of the costs to manufacture the skateboards follows:

Selling price per skateboard		$45.00
Costs per skateboard:		
Molded plastic	$5.50	
Wheels, hardware	7.00	
Direct labor ($15/hour)	7.50	
Manufacturing overhead	5.00	
Selling and administrative expenses	9.00	34.00
Profit per skateboard		$11.00

In the Plastics Department, Sportway uses direct labor hours as the application base for manufacturing overhead. Included in the manufacturing overhead for the current year is $50,000 of factory-wide, fixed manufacturing overhead that has been allocated to the Plastics Department. For each unit of product that Sportway sells, regardless of whether the product has been purchased or is manufactured by Sportway, an allocated $6 fixed overhead cost per unit for distribution is included in the selling and administrative expenses for all products. Total selling and administrative expenses for the purchased tackle boxes would be $10 per unit.

Required

1. Prepare an analysis based on the data presented that will show which product or products Sportway, Inc., should manufacture and/or purchase in order to maximize the company's profitability. It should also show the associated financial impact. Support your answer with appropriate calculations.
2. Discuss some qualitative factors that might affect Sportway's decision. (**CMA adapted**)

Managerial Decision Cases

12-31

Make-or-Buy Decision: Ethical Considerations
LO1, LO2, LO3

Pamela McDonald, CMA and controller for Murray Manufacturing, Inc., was having lunch with Roger Branch, manager of the company's Power Department. Over the past six months, Pamela and Roger had developed a romantic relationship and were making plans for marriage. To keep company gossip at a minimum, Pamela and Roger had kept the relationship very quiet, and no one in the company was aware of it.

The topic of the luncheon conversation centered on a decision concerning the company's Power Department that Larry Johnson, president of the company, was about to make.

Pamela: Roger, in our last executive meeting, we were told that a local utility company offered to supply power and quoted a price per kilowatt-hour that they said would hold for the next three years. They even offered to enter into a contractual agreement with us.

Roger: This is news to me. Is the bid price a threat to my area? Can they sell us power cheaper than we make it? And why wasn't I informed about this matter? I should have some input. This burns me. I think I should give Larry a call this afternoon and lodge a strong complaint.

Pamela: Calm down, Roger. The last thing I want you to do is call Larry. Larry made us all promise to keep this whole deal quiet until a decision had been made. He did not want you involved because he wanted to make an unbiased decision. You know that the company is struggling somewhat, and they are looking for ways to save money.

Roger: Yeah, but at my expense? And at the expense of my department's workers? At my age, I doubt that I could find a job that pays as well and has the same benefits. How much of a threat is this offer?

Pamela: Jack Lacy, my assistant controller, prepared an analysis while I was on vacation. It showed that internal production is cheaper than buying, but not by much. Larry asked me to review the findings and submit a final recommendation for next Wednesday's meeting. I've reviewed Jack's analysis, and it's faulty. He overlooked the interactions of your department with other service departments. When these are considered, the analysis is overwhelmingly in favor of purchasing the power. The savings are about $300,000 per year.

Roger: If Larry hears that, my department's gone. Pam, you can't let this happen. I'm three years away from having a vested retirement. And my workers—they have home mortgages, kids in college, families to support. No, it's not right. Pam, just tell him that your assistant's analysis is on target. He'll never know the difference.

Pamela: Roger, what you're suggesting doesn't sound right either. Would it be ethical for me to fail to disclose this information?

Roger: Ethical? Do you think it's right to lay off employees that have been loyal, faithful workers simply to fatten the pockets of the owners of this company? The Murrays already are so rich that they don't know what to do with their money. I think that it's even more unethical to penalize me and my workers. Why should we have to bear the consequences of some bad marketing decisions? Anyway, the effects of those decisions are about gone, and the company should be back to normal within a year or so.

Pamela: You may be right. Perhaps the well-being of you and your workers is more important than saving $300,000 for the Murrays.

Required

1. Should Pamela have told Roger about the impending decision concerning the Power Department? In revealing this information, did Pamela violate any of the ethical standards described in Chapter 1?
2. Should Pamela provide Larry with the correct data concerning the Power Department? Or should she protect its workers? What would you do if you were Pamela?

12-32

Centralize versus Decentralize
LO1, LO2, LO3

Central University, a Midwestern university with approximately 13,000 students, was in the middle of a budget crisis. For the third consecutive year, state appropriations for higher education remained essentially unchanged (the university is currently in the academic year 2007–2008). Yet utilities, social security benefits, insurance, and other operating expenses have increased. Moreover, the faculty were becoming restless, and some members had begun to leave for other, higher-paying opportunities.

The president and the academic vice president had announced their intention to eliminate some academic programs and to reduce others. The savings that result would be used to cover the increase in operating expenses and for raises for the remaining faculty. Needless to say, the possible dismissal of tenured faculty aroused a great deal of concern throughout the university.

With this background, the president and academic vice president called a meeting of all department heads and deans to discuss the budget for the coming year. As the budget was presented, the academic vice president noted that Continuing Education, a separate, centralized unit, had accumulated a deficit of $504,000 over the past several years, which must be eliminated during the coming fiscal year. The vice president noted that allocating the deficit equally among the seven colleges would create a hardship on some of the colleges, wiping out all of their operating budget except for salaries.

After some discussion of alternative ways to allocate the deficit, the head of the Accounting Department suggested an alternative solution: decentralize Continuing Education, allowing each college to assume responsibility for its own continuing education programs. In this way, the overhead of a centralized continuing education program could be avoided.

The academic vice president responded that the suggestion would be considered, but it was received with little enthusiasm. The vice president observed that Continuing Education was now generating more revenues than costs—and that the trend was favorable.

A week later, at a meeting of the deans' council, the vice president reviewed the role of Continuing Education. He pointed out that only the dean of Continuing Education held tenure. If Continuing Education were decentralized, her salary ($50,000) would continue; however, she would return to her academic department, and the university would save $20,000 of instructional wages since fewer temporary faculty would be needed in her department. All other employees in the unit were classified as staff. Continuing Education had responsibility for all noncredit offerings. Additionally, it had nominal responsibility for credit courses offered in the evening on campus and for credit courses offered off-campus. However, all scheduling and staffing of these evening and off-campus courses were done by the heads of the academic departments. What courses were offered and who staffed them had to be approved by the head of each department. According to the vice president, one of the main contributions of the Continuing Education Department to the evening and off-campus programs is advertising. He estimated that $30,000 per year is being spent.

After reviewing this information, the vice president made available the following information pertaining to the department's performance for the past several years (the 2007–2008 data were projections). He once again defended keeping a centralized department, emphasizing the favorable trend revealed by the accounting data. (All numbers are expressed in thousands.)

	2004–05	**2005–06**	**2006–07**	**2007–08**
Tuition revenues:				
Off-campus	$300	$ 400	$ 400	$ 410
Evening	—[a]	525	907	1,000
Noncredit	135	305	338	375
Total	$435	$1,230	$1,645	$1,785
Operating costs:				
Administration	$132	$ 160	$ 112	$ 112
Off-campus:				
Direct[b]	230	270	270	260
Indirect	350	410	525	440

(continued)

	2004–05	2005–06	2006–07	2007–08
Evening	(—)[a]	220	420	525
Noncredit	135	305	338	375
Total	$ 847	$1,365	$1,665	$1,712
Income (loss)	$(412)	$ (135)	$ (20)	$ 73

[a]In 2004–05, the department had no responsibility for evening courses. Beginning in 2005, it was given the responsibility to pay for any costs of instruction incurred when temporary or adjunct faculty were hired to teach evening courses. Tuition revenues earned by evening courses also began to be assigned to the department at the same time.
[b]Instructors' wages.

The dean of the College of Business was unimpressed by the favorable trend identified by the academic vice president. The dean maintained that decentralization still would be in the best interests of the university. He argued that although decentralization would not fully solve the deficit, it would provide a sizable contribution each year to the operating budgets for each of the seven colleges.

The academic vice president disagreed vehemently. He was convinced that Continuing Education was now earning its own way and would continue to produce additional resources for the university.

Required

You have been asked by the president of Central University to assess which alternative—centralization or decentralization—is in the best interest of the school. The president is willing to decentralize provided that significant savings can be produced and the mission of Continuing Education will still be carried out. Prepare a memo to the president that details your analysis and reasoning and recommends one of the two alternatives. Provide both qualitative and quantitative reasoning in the memo.

Research Assignments

12-33

Research Assignment
LO1, LO2, LO5

"Dumping" is an accusation that is often made against foreign companies. Japanese automobile companies, for example, have been accused of this practice.

Required

Go to the library and find out the following:

1. What is dumping?
2. Why do international trade agreements usually prohibit dumping? Do you agree that its prohibition is good for the U.S. consumer? Explain.
3. Explain how the relevant costing principles learned in this chapter relate to dumping.
4. Provide several examples of companies accused of dumping. See if you can determine the outcome of an accusation made against one company. Why do you suppose that international companies pursue dumping even though it is prohibited? What are the ethical implications?

12-34

Cybercase
LO1, LO3

Several of the websites for major airlines contain news of current special fares and flights. A decision to run a brief "fare special" is an example of a tactical decision. Check one or more of these websites for recent examples of fare specials and write a brief paper discussing the types of cost and revenue information that would go into making this type of tactical decision.

chapter 13

Capital Investment Decisions

learning objectives

After studying this chapter, you should be able to:

1. Explain what a capital investment decision is, and distinguish between independent and mutually exclusive capital investment decisions.
2. Compute the payback period and accounting rate of return for a proposed investment, and explain their roles in capital investment decisions.
3. Use net present value analysis for capital investment decisions involving independent projects.
4. Use the internal rate of return to assess the acceptability of independent projects.
5. Discuss the role and value of postaudits.
6. Explain why NPV is better than IRR for capital investment decisions involving mutually exclusive projects.
7. Convert gross cash flows to after-tax cash flows.
8. Describe capital investment in the advanced manufacturing environment.

Scenario

Allen Manesfield, Jenny Winters, and John Jacobsen have been discussing a persistent and irritating production problem. The three are employed by Honley Medical, which specializes in the production of medical products and has three divisions: the IV Products Division, the Critical Care Monitoring Division, and the Specialty Products Division. Allen, Jenny, and John are associated with the IV Products Division—Allen as the senior production engineer, Jenny as the marketing manager, and John as the divisional controller. The three constitute the division's capital acquisitions committee, with Allen serving as the chair.

The IV Products Division produces intravenous needles (IVs) of five different sizes. During one stage of the manufacturing process, the needle is inserted into a plastic hub and bonded using epoxy glue. According to Jenny, the epoxy glue was causing the division all kinds of problems. In many cases, the epoxy wasn't bonding correctly. The rejects were high, and the division was receiving a large number of complaints from its customers. Corrective action was needed to avoid losing sales.

One possibility was to use induction welding in lieu of epoxy bonding. In induction welding, the needles are inserted into the plastic hub, and an RF generator is used to heat the needles. The RF generator works on the same principle as a microwave oven. As the needles get hot, the plastic melts, and the needles are bonded. Switching to induction welding would require an investment in RF generators and the associated tooling. But induction welding promised to reduce the cost of direct materials, eliminating the need to buy and use epoxy. Savings of direct labor costs were also predicted because the welding process is much more automated. Adding to these savings were the avoidance of daily clean-up costs and the reduction in rejects.

Several questions in the committee arose concerning this capital acquisition decision: Would the investment increase the value of the firm? Would it earn at least the rate of return required by the company? How long would it take the firm to recover the investment given the predicted savings? After discussion and analysis, the committee concluded that the investment was justified based on the savings associated with the new system. Using the predicted savings, the committee presented headquarters with a formal *net present value analysis* showing that the welding system was economically superior to the epoxy system and an analysis confirming that the expected return was greater than the division's cost of capital. Based on these analyses, headquarters approved the purchase of the new system.

Questions to Think About

1. What role, if any, should qualitative factors play in capital budgeting decisions?
2. How do we measure the financial benefits of long-term investments?
3. Why are cash flows important for assessing the financial merits of an investment?
4. What role do taxes and inflation play in assessing cash flows?
5. Should the cash flows of intangible factors be estimated?

Types of Capital Investment Decisions

Objective 1

Explain what a capital investment decision is, and distinguish between independent and mutually exclusive capital investment decisions.

Honley Medical was faced with the opportunity (or need) to invest in an induction welding system that represented a long-term commitment. New production systems, new plants, new equipment, and new product development are examples of long-term-commitment assets and projects. Usually, many alternatives are available. For example, an organization may be faced with the decision whether to invest or not invest in a new plant, or whether to invest in a flexible manufacturing system or continue with an existing traditional manufacturing system. In Honley's case, the alternatives being considered were the epoxy-bonding approach or induction welding. These long-range decisions are examples of *capital investment decisions.*

Capital investment decisions are concerned with the process of planning, setting goals and priorities, arranging financing, and using certain criteria to select long-term assets. Because capital investment decisions place large amounts of resources at risk for long periods of time and simultaneously affect the future development of the firm, they are among the most important decisions managers make. Every organization has limited resources, which should be used to maintain or enhance its long-run profitability. Poor capital investment decisions can be disastrous. For example, a failure to invest in automated manufacturing when other competitors do so may result in significant losses in market share because of the inability to compete on the basis of quality, cost, and delivery time. Competitors with more modern facilities may produce more output at lower cost and higher quality. Thus, making the right capital investment decisions is absolutely essential for long-term survival.

Risk, cash flows, and the effect on profitability are factors that must be considered when long-term assets are acquired.

The process of making capital investment decisions is often referred to as **capital budgeting**. Two types of capital budgeting projects will be considered: *independent projects* and *mutually exclusive projects.* **Independent projects** are projects that, if accepted or rejected, do not affect the cash flows of other projects. For example, a decision by **General Motors** to build a new plant for production of the Cadillac line is not affected by its decision to build a new plant for the production of its Saturn line. They are independent capital investment decisions. The second type of capital budgeting project requires a firm to choose among competing alternatives that provide the same basic service. Acceptance of one option precludes the acceptance of another. Thus, **mutually exclusive projects** are those projects that, if accepted, preclude the acceptance of all other competing projects. For example, some time ago, **Monsanto**'s Fibers Division decided to automate its Pensacola, Florida, plant. Thus, Monsanto was faced with the choice of continuing with its existing manual production operation or replacing it with an automated system. In all likelihood, part of the company's deliberation concerned different types of automated systems. If three different automated systems were being considered, this would produce four

alternatives—the current system plus the three potential new systems. Once one system is chosen, the other three are excluded; they are mutually exclusive.

Notice that one of the competing alternatives in the Monsanto example is that of maintaining the status quo (the manual system). This emphasizes the fact that new investments replacing existing investments must prove to be economically superior. Of course, at times, replacement of the old system is mandatory and not discretionary if the firm wishes to remain in business (for example, equipment in the old system may be worn out, making the old system not a viable alternative). In such a situation, going out of business could be a feasible alternative, especially if none of the new investment alternatives is profitable.

Capital investment decisions often are concerned with investments in long-term capital assets. With the exception of land, these assets depreciate over their lives, and the original investment is used up as the assets are employed. In general terms, a sound capital investment will earn back its original capital outlay over its life and, at the same time, provide a reasonable return on the original investment. Thus, one task of a manager is to decide whether or not a capital investment will earn back its original outlay and provide a reasonable return. By making this assessment, a manager can decide on the acceptability of independent projects and compare competing projects on the basis of their economic merits.

But what is meant by reasonable return? It is generally agreed that any new project must cover the opportunity cost of the funds invested. For example, if a company takes money from a money market fund that is earning 6 percent and invests it in a new project, then the project must provide at least a 6 percent return (the return that could have been earned had the money been left in the money market fund). Of course, in reality, funds for investment often come from different sources—each representing a different opportunity cost. The return that must be earned is a blend of the opportunity costs of the different sources. Thus, if a company uses two sources of funds, one with an opportunity cost of 4 percent and the other with an opportunity cost of 6 percent, then the return that must be earned is somewhere between 4 and 6 percent, depending on the relative amounts used from each source. Furthermore, it is usually assumed that managers should select projects that promise to maximize the wealth of the owners of the firm.

To make a capital investment decision, a manager must estimate the quantity and timing of cash flows, assess the risk of the investment, and consider the impact of the project on the firm's profits. One of the most difficult tasks is to estimate the cash flows. Projections must be made years into the future, and forecasting is far from a perfect science. Obviously, as the accuracy of cash-flow forecasts increases, the reliability of the decision improves. In making projections, managers must identify and quantify the benefits associated with the proposed project(s). For example, an automated cash deposit system can produce the following benefits (relative to a manual system): bank charge reductions, productivity gains, forms cost reduction, greater data integrity, lower training costs, and savings in time required to audit and do bank/cash reconciliations. The dollar value of these benefits must be assessed. Although forecasting future cash flows is a critical part of the capital investment process, forecasting methods will not be considered here. Consequently, cash flows are assumed to be known; the focus will be on making capital investment decisions given these cash flows.

Managers must set goals and priorities for capital investments. They also must identify some basic criteria for the acceptance or rejection of proposed investments. In this chapter, we will study four basic methods to guide managers in accepting or rejecting potential investments. The methods include both nondiscounting and discounting decision approaches (two methods are discussed for each approach). The discounting methods are applied to investment decisions involving both independent and mutually exclusive projects.

Nondiscounting Models

Objective 2

Compute the payback period and accounting rate of return for a proposed investment, and explain their roles in capital investment decisions.

The basic capital investment decision models can be classified into two major categories: *nondiscounting models* and *discounting models.* **Nondiscounting models** ignore the time value of money, whereas **discounting models** explicitly consider it. Although many accounting theorists disparage the nondiscounting models because they ignore the time value of money, many firms continue to use these models in making capital investment decisions. However, the use of discounting models has increased over the years, and few firms use only one model—indeed, firms seem to use both types.[1] The payback period, in particular, seems to be the most widely used nondiscounting method while the accounting rate of return is employed much less. The use of both types of models suggests that both categories supply useful information to managers as they struggle to make a capital investment decision.

Payback Period

One type of nondiscounting model is the *payback period.* The **payback period** is the time required for a firm to recover its original investment. For example, assume that Honley Medical invests in new RV generators costing $1,000,000. The net cash flows (cash inflows less cash outflows) generated by the equipment are $500,000 per year. Thus, the payback period is two years ($1,000,000/$500,000). When the cash flows of a project are assumed to be even, the following formula can be used to compute its payback period:

$$\text{Payback period} = \text{Original investment/Annual cash flows}$$

If, however, the cash flows are uneven, the payback period is computed by adding the annual cash flows until such time as the original investment is recovered. If a fraction of a year is needed, it is assumed that cash flows occur evenly within each year. For example, suppose that the investment in RV generators is $1,000,000 and has a life of five years with the following expected annual cash flows: $300,000, $400,000, $500,000, $600,000, and $700,000. The payback period for the project is 2.6 years, computed as follows: $300,000 (1 year) + $400,000 (1 year) + $300,000 (0.6 year). In the third year, when only $300,000 is needed and $500,000 is available, the amount of time required to earn the $300,000 is found by dividing the amount needed by the annual cash flow ($300,000/$500,000). Exhibit 13-1 summarizes this analysis.

One way to use the payback period is to set a maximum payback period for all projects and to reject any project that exceeds this level. Why would a firm use the payback period in this way? Some analysts suggest that the payback period can be used as a rough measure of risk, with the notion that the longer it takes for a project to pay for itself, the riskier it is. Also, firms with riskier cash flows could require a shorter payback period than normal. Additionally, firms with liquidity problems would be more interested in projects with quick paybacks. Another critical concern is obsolescence. In some industries, the risk of obsolescence is high; firms within these industries would be interested in recovering funds rapidly.

Another reason, less beneficial to the firm, may also be at work. Many managers in a position to make capital investment decisions may choose investments with

1 From the mid-1950s to 1988, surveys reveal, the use of discounting models as the primary evaluation method for capital projects went from about 9 to 80 percent. More recent surveys of firms in the United States and Canada revealed that over 90 percent of the firms used a discounting method. See A. A. Robichek and J. G. McDonald, "Financial Planning in Transition, Long Range Planning Service," Report No. 268 (Menlo Park, CA: Stanford Research Institute, January 1966); Janet D. Payne and Will Carrington Heath, "Comparative Practice in the U.S. and Canada: Capital Budgeting and Risk Assessment," *Financial Practice and Education* (Spring/Summer 1999): Vol. 9, Issue 1, pp. 16–25; and Patricia A. Ryan and Glenn P. Ryan, "Capital Budgeting Practices of the Fortune 1000: How Have Things Changed?" *Journal of Business and Management* (Fall 2002): pp. 355–364.

Year	Unrecovered Investment (beginning of year)	Annual Cash Flow
1	$1,000,000	$300,000
2	700,000	400,000
3	300,000*	500,000
4	—	600,000
5	—	700,000

*At the beginning of Year 3, $300,000 is needed to recover the investment. Since a net cash flow of $500,000 is expected, only 0.6 year ($300,000/$500,000) is needed to recover the $300,000. Thus, the payback is 2.6 years (2.0 + 0.6).

Exhibit 13-1 Honley Medical Payback Analysis: Uneven Cash Flows

quick payback periods out of self-interest. If a manager's performance is measured using such short-run criteria as annual net income, he or she may choose projects with quick paybacks to show improved net income as quickly as possible. Consider that divisional managers often are responsible for making capital investment decisions and are evaluated on divisional profit. The tenure of divisional managers, however, is typically short—three to five years would be average. Consequently, the incentive is for such managers to shy away from investments that promise healthy long-run returns but relatively meager returns in the short run. These problems can be eliminated by corporate budgeting policies and a budget review committee.

The payback period can be used to choose among competing alternatives. Under this approach, the investment with the shortest payback period is preferred over investments with longer payback periods. However, this use of the payback period is less defensible because this measure suffers from two major deficiencies: (1) it ignores the performance of the investments beyond the payback period, and (2) it ignores the time value of money.

These two significant deficiencies are easily illustrated. For example, the engineering department of Honley Medical's Specialty Products Division is considering two different types of computer-aided-design (CAD) systems: CAD-A and CAD-B. Each system requires an initial outlay of $150,000, has a five-year life, and displays the following annual cash flows:

Investment	Year 1	Year 2	Year 3	Year 4	Year 5
CAD-A	$90,000	$ 60,000	$50,000	$50,000	$50,000
CAD-B	40,000	110,000	25,000	25,000	25,000

Both investments have payback periods of two years. Thus, if a manager uses the payback period to choose among competing investments, the two investments would be equally desirable. In reality, however, the CAD-A system should be preferred over the CAD-B system for two reasons. First, the CAD-A system provides a much larger dollar return for the years beyond the payback period ($150,000 versus $75,000). Second, the CAD-A system returns $90,000 in the first year, while B returns only $40,000. The extra $50,000 that the CAD-A system provides in the first year could be put to productive use, such as investing it in another project. It is better to have a dollar now than one year from now, because the dollar on hand can be invested to provide a return one year from now.

In summary, the payback period provides information to managers that can be used as follows:

1. To help control the risks associated with the uncertainty of future cash flows.
2. To help minimize the impact of an investment on a firm's liquidity problems.

3. To help control the risk of obsolescence.
4. To help control the effect of the investment on performance measures.

However, the method suffers significant deficiencies: it ignores a project's total profitability and the time value of money. While the computation of the payback period may be useful to a manager, to rely on it solely for a capital investment decision would be foolish.

Accounting Rate of Return

The *accounting rate of return* is the second commonly used nondiscounting model. The **accounting rate of return** measures the return on a project in terms of income, as opposed to using a project's cash flow. The accounting rate of return is computed by the following formula:

Accounting rate of return = Average income/Original investment or average investment

Income is not equivalent to cash flows because of accruals and deferrals used in its computation. The average income of a project is obtained by adding the net income for each year of the project and then dividing this total by the number of years. Average net income for a project can be approximated by subtracting average depreciation from average cash flow. Assuming that all revenues earned in a period are collected and that depreciation is the only noncash expense, the approximation is exact.

Investment can be defined as the original investment or as the average investment. Letting I equal original investment, S equal salvage value, and assuming that investment is uniformly consumed, average investment is defined as follows:[2]

$$\text{Average investment} = (I + S)/2$$

To illustrate the computation of the accounting rate of return, consider an investment by Honley Medical's IV Division in special tooling that requires an initial outlay of $100,000. The life of the investment is five years with the following cash flows: $30,000, $30,000, $40,000, $30,000, and $50,000. Assume that the tooling has no salvage value after the five years and that all revenues earned within a year are collected in that year. The total cash flow for the five years is $180,000, making the average cash flow $36,000 ($180,000/5). Average depreciation is $20,000 ($100,000/5). The average net income is the difference between these two figures: $16,000 ($36,000 − $20,000). Using the average net income and original investment, the accounting rate of return is 16 percent ($16,000/$100,000). If average investment is used instead of original investment, then the accounting rate of return would be 32 percent ($16,000/$50,000).

Often debt contracts require that a firm maintain certain financial accounting ratios, which can be affected by the income reported and by the level of long-term assets. Accordingly, the accounting rate of return may be used as a screening measure to ensure that any new investment will not adversely affect these ratios. Additionally, because bonuses to managers are often based on accounting income or return on assets, they may have a personal interest in seeing that any new investment contributes significantly to net income. A manager seeking to maximize personal income will select investments that return the highest net income per dollar invested.

Unlike the payback period, the accounting rate of return does consider a project's profitability; like the payback period, it ignores the time value of money. Ignoring the time value of money is a critical deficiency in this method as well; it can lead a manager to choose investments that do not maximize profits. It is because the

2 The average investment formula is derived using the definition of the average value of a function and requires the use of calculus.

Managers Decide

Capital Budgeting and Small Firms

A survey of small firms (those with sales less than $5 million and fewer than 1,000 employees) revealed that in the 1990s the payback method was the dominant method of investment selection. Of the firms surveyed, 42.7 percent used the payback method as the primary method of investment analysis, whereas 27.6 percent of the firms used a method that specifically considered the time value of money as their primary method. Interestingly, 22.4 percent used the accounting rate of return as their primary method of investment analysis. The reason offered for this payback outcome is also interesting. It has been suggested that the widespread use of the payback method among small firms is because of the financial pressures put on the small business owner by financial institutions that are providing the capital. The emphasis is on how quickly a loan can be paid back by an investment and not on how profitable the investment is. ■

Source: S. Block, "Capital Budgeting Techniques Used by Small Business Firms in the 1990s," *Engineering Economist* (Summer 1997): Vol. 42, Issue 4, pp. 355–365.

payback period and the accounting rate of return ignore the time value of money that they are referred to as *nondiscounting models.* Discounting models use **discounted cash flows**, which are future cash flows expressed in terms of their present value. The use of discounting models requires an understanding of the present value concepts. Present value concepts are reviewed in Appendix A at the end of this chapter. You should review these concepts and make sure that you understand them before studying capital investment discount models. Present value tables (Exhibits 13B-1 and 13B-2) are presented in Appendix B at the end of this chapter. These tables are referred to and used throughout the rest of the chapter.

Discounting Models: The Net Present Value Method

Objective 3

Use net present value analysis for capital investment decisions involving independent projects.

Discounting models explicitly consider the time value of money and therefore incorporate the concept of discounting cash inflows and outflows. Two discounting models will be considered: *net present value* (NPV) and *internal rate of return* (IRR). The net present value method will be discussed first; the internal rate of return method is discussed in the following section.

NPV Defined

Net present value is the difference between the present value of the cash inflows and outflows associated with a project:

$$\begin{aligned} NPV &= [\Sigma\, CF_t/(1+i)^t - I] \\ &= [\Sigma\, CF_t df_t] - I \\ &= P - I \end{aligned} \qquad (13.1)$$

where

I = The present value of the project's cost (usually the initial outlay)
CF_t = The cash inflow to be received in period t, with $t = 1 \ldots n$
n = The useful life of the project

i = The required rate of return
t = The time period
P = The present value of the project's future cash inflows
$df_t = 1/(1 + i)^t$, the discount factor

Net present value measures the profitability of an investment. If the NPV is positive, it measures the increase in wealth. For a firm, this means that the size of a positive NPV measures the increase in the value of the firm resulting from an investment. To use the NPV method, a *required rate of return* must be defined. The **required rate of return** is the minimum acceptable rate of return. It is also referred to as the *discount rate,* the *hurdle rate,* and the *cost of capital.*

If the net present value is positive, it signals that (1) the initial investment has been recovered, (2) the required rate of return has been recovered, and (3) a return in excess of (1) and (2) has been received. Thus, if NPV is greater than zero, the investment is profitable and, therefore, is acceptable. If NPV equals zero, the decision maker will find acceptance or rejection of the investment equal because the investment will earn exactly the required rate of return. Finally, if NPV is less than zero, the investment should be rejected. In this case, it is earning less than the required rate of return.

An Example Illustrating Net Present Value

Honley Medical's Specialty Products Division has developed a new home blood pressure (BP) instrument that it believes is superior to anything on the market. The marketing manager is excited about the new product's prospects after completing a detailed market study that revealed expected annual cash revenues of $300,000. The BP instruments have a projected product life cycle of five years. Equipment to produce the instruments would cost $320,000. After five years, that equipment can be sold for $40,000. In addition to equipment, working capital is expected to increase by $40,000 because of increases in inventories and receivables. The firm expects to recover the investment in working capital at the end of the project's life. Annual cash operating expenses are estimated at $180,000. Assuming that the required rate of return is 12 percent, should Honley Medical manufacture the new BP instruments?

In order to answer the question, two steps must be taken: (1) the cash flows for each year must be identified and (2) the NPV must be computed using the cash flows from Step 1. The solution to the problem is given in Exhibit 13-2. Notice that Step 2 offers two approaches for computing NPV. Step 2A computes NPV by using discount factors from Exhibit 13B-1. Step 2B simplifies the computation by using a single discount factor from Exhibit 13B-2 for the even cash flows occurring in Years 1 through 4.

Internal Rate of Return

Objective 4

Use the internal rate of return to assess the acceptability of independent projects.

Another discounting model is the *internal rate of return* (IRR) method. The **internal rate of return** is defined as the interest rate that sets the present value of a project's cash inflows equal to the present value of the project's cost. In other words, it is the interest rate that sets the project's NPV at zero. The following equation can be used to determine a project's IRR:

$$I = \Sigma\, CF_t/(1 + I)^t \quad (13.2)$$

where $t = 1 \ldots n$

The right-hand side of Equation 13.2 is the present value of future cash flows, and the left-hand side is the investment. I, CF_t, and t are known. Thus, the IRR (the

Step 1. Cash-Flow Identification

Year	Item	Cash Flow
0	Equipment	$(320,000)
	Working capital	(40,000)
	Total	$(360,000)
1–4	Revenues	$ 300,000
	Operating expenses	(180,000)
	Total	$ 120,000
5	Revenues	$ 300,000
	Operating expenses	(180,000)
	Salvage	40,000
	Recovery of working capital	40,000
	Total	$ 200,000

Step 2A. NPV Analysis

Year	Cash Flow[a]	Discount Factor[b]	Present Value
0	$(360,000)	1.000	$(360,000)
1	120,000	0.893	107,160
2	120,000	0.797	95,640
3	120,000	0.712	85,440
4	120,000	0.636	76,320
5	200,000	0.567	113,400
Net present value			$ 117,960

Step 2B. NPV Analysis

Year	Cash Flow[a]	Discount Factor[b]	Present Value
0	$(360,000)	1.000	$(360,000)
1–4	120,000	3.037	364,440
5	200,000	0.567	113,400
Net present value			$ 117,840[c]

[a]From Step 1.
[b]From Exhibit 13B-1.
[c]This differs from the computation in Step 2A because of rounding.

Exhibit 13-2 Honley Medical Specialty Products Division Cash Flows and NPV Analysis

interest rate, *i*, in the equation) can be found using trial and error. Once the IRR for a project is computed, it is compared with the firm's required rate of return. If the IRR is greater than the required rate, the project is deemed acceptable; if the IRR is equal to the required rate of return, acceptance or rejection of the investment is equal; if the IRR is less than the required rate of return, the project is rejected.

The internal rate of return is the most widely used of the capital investment techniques. One reason for its popularity may be that it is a rate of return, a concept that managers are comfortable with using. Another possibility is that managers may believe (in most cases, incorrectly) that the IRR is the true or actual compounded rate of return being earned by the initial investment. Whatever the reasons for its popularity, a basic understanding of the IRR is necessary.

Example: Multiple-Period Setting with Uniform Cash Flows

To illustrate the computation of the IRR in a multiple-period setting, consider Honley Medical's Speciality Products Division. The division has the opportunity to invest

$1,200,000 in a new ultrasound system product that will produce net cash inflows of $499,500 at the end of each year for the next three years. The IRR is the interest rate that equates the present value of the three equal receipts of $499,500 to the investment of $1,200,000. Since the series of cash flows is uniform, a single discount factor from Exhibit 13B-2 can be used to compute the present value of the annuity. Letting *df* be this discount factor and *CF* be the annual cash flow, Equation 13.2 assumes the following form:

$$I = CF(df)$$

Solving for *df*, we obtain:

$$\begin{aligned} df &= I/CF \\ &= \text{Investment/Annual cash flow} \end{aligned}$$

Once the discount factor is computed, go to Exhibit 13B-2 and find the row corresponding to the life of the project, then move across that row until the computed discount factor is found. The interest rate corresponding to this discount factor is the IRR.

For example, the discount factor for the hospital's investment is 2.402 ($1,200,000/$499,550). Since the life of the investment is three years, we must find the third row in Exhibit 13B-2 and then move across this row until we encounter 2.402. The interest rate corresponding to 2.402 is 12 percent, which is the IRR.

Exhibit 13B-2 does not provide discount factors for every possible interest rate. To illustrate, assume that the annual cash inflows expected by the hospital are $510,000 instead of $499,500. The new discount factor is 2.353 ($1,200,000/$510,000). Going once again to the third row in Exhibit 13B-2, we find that the discount factor—and thus the IRR—lies between 12 and 14 percent. It is possible to approximate the IRR by interpolation (interpolation approximates the actual IRR by assuming that the IRR is the same proportionate distance between 12 percent and 14 percent as the actual discount factor of 2.353 is between the tabled discount factors); however, for our purposes, we will simply identify the range for the IRR as indicated by the tabled values. In practice, business calculators or spreadsheet programs can provide the values of IRR without the use of tables such as Exhibit 13B-2.

Multiple-Period Setting: Uneven Cash Flows

If the cash flows are not uniform, then Equation 13.2 must be used. For a multiple-period setting, Equation 13.2 can be solved by trial and error or by using a business calculator or a spreadsheet program. To illustrate solution by trial and error, assume that a $10,000 investment in a PC system produces clerical savings of $6,000 for the first year and $7,200 for the second year. The IRR is the interest rate that sets the present value of these two cash inflows equal to $10,000:

$$\begin{aligned} P &= [\$6{,}000/(1 + i)] + [\$7{,}200/(1 + i)^2] \\ &= \$10{,}000 \end{aligned}$$

To solve this equation by trial and error, start by selecting a possible value for *i*. Given this first guess, the present value of the future cash flows is computed and then compared with the initial investment. If the present value is greater than the initial investment, the interest rate is too low; if the present value is less than the initial investment, the interest rate is too high. The next guess is adjusted accordingly.

Assume that the first guess is 18 percent. Using *i* equal to 0.18, Exhibit 13B-1 yields discount factors of 0.847 for the first year and 0.718 for the second year. These discount factors produce the following present value for the two cash inflows:

$$\begin{aligned} P &= (0.847 \times \$6{,}000) + (0.718 \times \$7{,}200) \\ &= \$10{,}252 \end{aligned}$$

Managers Decide

Ethics and Choosing Among Competing Proposals

Frequently, hospitals are asked to approve capital expenditures in excess of available funds. The usual financial criteria for selection among competing capital projects is sound but not sufficient. An ethical analysis of proposed projects allows both economic and moral ends to be balanced. Nonprofit hospitals, for example, should actively promote outcomes that benefit others. They must provide sufficient community benefit to justify their tax-exempt status. Furthermore, capital expenditure decisions should avoid doing harm to others. Decisions that provide personal or institutional value but bring harm to the community should be avoided. Additionally, when choosing among competing proposals, those that align with the values of the organization should be favored over those that have less alignment. Finally, resource allocations should be fair and impartial. Both economic and noneconomic factors need to be considered so that the outcome is prudent and just. ■

Source: Paul B. Hofmann, "Allocating Limited Capital Resources," *Healthcare Executive* (Mar/Apr 2000): Vol. 15, Issue 2, pp. 53–55.

Since P is greater than $10,000, the interest rate selected is too low. A higher guess is needed. If the next guess is 20 percent, we obtain the following:

$$\begin{aligned} P &= (0.833 \times \$6{,}000) + (0.694 \times \$7{,}200) \\ &= \$9{,}995 \end{aligned}$$

Since this value is reasonably close to $10,000, we can say that the IRR is 20 percent. (The IRR is, in fact, exactly 20 percent; the present value is slightly less than the investment because of rounding errors in the discount factors found in Exhibit 13B-1.)

Postaudit of Capital Projects

Objective 5

Discuss the role and value of postaudits.

A key element in the capital investment process is a follow-up analysis of a capital project once it is implemented. This analysis is called a *postaudit.* A **postaudit** compares the actual benefits with the estimated benefits and actual operating costs with estimated operating costs; it evaluates the overall outcome of the investment and proposes corrective action if needed. The following case illustrates the usefulness of a postaudit activity.

Capital investment decisions, which may seem good at first, may need adjustments once implemented.

Honley Medical Company: An Illustrative Application

© Getty Images/PhotoDisc

In the opening scenario, the capital acquisitions committee of Honley Medical's IV Products Division projected cash savings for an investment in an RF generator system for bonding needles into plastic hubs. Recall that Allen Manesfield (senior production engineer), Jenny Winters (marketing manager), and John Jacobsen (division controller) were the committee members. Savings were projected and NPV and IRR analyses were carried out using the projected savings. Based on the analyses, the project was approved. But how did the investment do? What problems were encountered? What adjustments were needed? The following conversation between Allen and Jenny one year after the investment provides answers to these questions and other useful insights.

One Year Later

Jenny: Allen, I'm quite pleased with induction welding for bonding needles. In the year since the new process was implemented, we've had virtually no complaints from our customers. The needles are firmly bonded.

Allen: I wish that positive experience were true for all other areas as well. Unfortunately, implementing the process has uncovered some rather sticky and expensive problems that I simply didn't anticipate. The Internal Audit Department recently completed a postaudit of the project, and now my feet are being held to the fire.

Jenny: That's too bad. What's the problem?

Allen: You mean problems. Let me list a few for you. One is that the RF generators interfered with the operation of other equipment. To eliminate this interference, we had to install filtering equipment. But that's not all. We also discovered that the average maintenance person doesn't know how to maintain the new equipment. Now, we are faced with the need to initiate a training program to upgrade the skills of our maintenance people. Upgrading skills also implies higher wages. Although the RF bonding process is less messy, it is also more complex. The manufacturing people complained to the internal auditors about that. They maintain that a simple process, even if messy, is to be preferred—especially now that demand for the product is increasing by leaps and bounds.

Jenny: What did the internal auditors conclude?

Allen: They observed that many of the predicted savings did take place, but that some significant costs were not foreseen. Because of some of the unforeseen problems, they have recommended that I look carefully at the possibility of moving back to using epoxy. They indicated that NPV analysis using actual data appears to favor that process. With production expanding, the acquisition of additional RF generators and filtering equipment plus the necessary training is simply not as attractive as returning to epoxy bonding. This conclusion is reinforced by the fact that the epoxy process is simpler than RF bonding and by the auditors' suggestion that the mixing of the epoxy be automated, avoiding the quality problem we had in the first place.

Jenny: Well, Allen, we can't really blame ourselves. We had a real problem—there were a lot of customer complaints and a lot of rejects. We took action to solve these problems. It's difficult to foresee all the problems and hidden costs of a new process.

Allen: Unfortunately, the internal auditors don't totally agree. In fact, neither do I. I probably jumped too quickly. In the future, I intend to think through new projects more carefully.

Benefits of a Postaudit

In the case of the RF bonding decision, some of the estimated capital investment benefits did materialize: complaints from customers decreased, rejects were fewer, and direct labor and materials costs decreased. However, the investment was greater than expected because filtering equipment was needed, and actual operating costs were much higher because of the increased maintenance cost and the increased complexity of the process. Overall, the internal auditors concluded that the investment was a poor decision. The corrective action they recommended was to abandon the new process and return to epoxy bonding.[3]

Firms that perform postaudits of capital projects experience a number of benefits. First, by evaluating profitability, postaudits ensure that resources are used wisely. If the project is doing well, it may call for additional funds and additional attention. If the project is not doing well, corrective action may be needed to improve performance or abandon the project.

A second benefit of the postaudit is its impact on the behavior of managers. If managers are held accountable for the results of a capital investment decision, they are more likely to make such decisions in the best interests of the firm. Additionally, postaudits supply feedback to managers that should help improve future decision making. Consider Allen's reaction to the postaudit of the RF bonding process. Certainly, we would expect him to be more careful and more thorough in making future investment recommendations. In the future, Allen will probably consider more than one alternative, such as automating the mixing of the epoxy. Also, for those alternatives being considered, he will probably be especially alert to the possibility of hidden costs, such as increased training requirements for a new process.

The case also reveals that the postaudit was performed by the internal audit staff. Generally, more objective results are obtainable if the postaudit is done by an independent party. Since considerable effort is expended to ensure as much independence as possible for the internal audit staff, that group is usually the best choice for this task.

Postaudits, however, are costly. Moreover, even though they may provide significant benefits, they have other limitations. Most obvious is the fact that the assumptions driving the original analysis may often be invalidated by changes in the actual operating environment. Accountability must be qualified to some extent by the impossibility of foreseeing every possible eventuality.

Mutually Exclusive Projects

Objective 6

Explain why NPV is better than IRR for capital investment decisions involving mutually exclusive projects.

Up to this point, we have focused on independent projects. Many capital investment decisions deal with mutually exclusive projects. How NPV analysis and IRR are used to choose among competing projects is an interesting question. An even more interesting question to consider is whether NPV and IRR differ in their ability to help managers make wealth-maximizing decisions in the presence of competing alternatives. For example, we already know that the nondiscounting models can produce erroneous choices because they ignore the time value of money. Because of this deficiency, the discounting models are judged superior. Similarly, it can be shown that the NPV model is generally preferred to the IRR model when choosing among mutually exclusive alternatives.

NPV Compared with IRR

NPV and IRR both yield the same decision for independent projects. For example, if the NPV is greater than zero, then the IRR is also greater than the required rate of return; both models signal the correct decision. However, for competing projects, the two methods can produce different results. Intuitively, we believe that, for mutually exclusive projects, the project with the highest NPV or the highest IRR should be chosen. Since it is possible for the two methods to produce different rankings of mutually exclusive projects, the method that consistently reveals the wealth-maximizing project is preferred.

3 Honley Medical did abandon inductive welding and returned to epoxy bonding, which was improved by automating the mix. The simplicity of the process was a major qualitative factor in deciding to return to the old, but improved, process.

NPV differs from IRR in two major ways. First, NPV assumes that each cash inflow received is reinvested at the required rate of return, whereas the IRR method assumes that each cash inflow is reinvested at the computed IRR. Reinvesting at the required rate of return is more realistic and produces more reliable results when comparing mutually exclusive projects. Second, the NPV method measures profitability in absolute terms, whereas the IRR method measures it in relative terms. NPV measures the amount by which the value of the firm changes.

Since NPV measures the impact that competing projects have on the value of the firm, choosing the project with the largest NPV is consistent with maximizing the wealth of shareholders. On the other hand, IRR does not consistently result in choices that maximize wealth. IRR, as a relative measure of profitability, has the virtue of measuring accurately the rate of return of funds that remain internally invested. However, maximizing IRR will not necessarily maximize the wealth of firm owners because it cannot, by nature, consider the absolute dollar contributions of projects. In the final analysis, what counts are the total dollars earned—the absolute profits—not the relative profits. Accordingly, NPV, not IRR, should be used for choosing among competing, mutually exclusive projects or competing projects when capital funds are limited.

An independent project is acceptable if its NPV is positive. For mutually exclusive projects, the project with the largest NPV is chosen. Three steps are involved in selecting the best project from several competing projects: (1) assessing the cash-flow pattern for each project, (2) computing the NPV for each project, and (3) identifying the project with the greatest NPV. To illustrate NPV analysis for competing projects, an example is provided.

Example: Mutually Exclusive Projects

Honley Medical has committed to improve its environmental performance. One environmental project identified a manufacturing process as being the source of both liquid and gaseous residues. After six months of research activity, the Engineering Department announced that it is possible to redesign the process to prevent the production of contaminating residues. Two different process designs are being considered that prevent the production of contaminants. Both process designs are more expensive to operate than the current process; however, because the designs prevent production of contaminants, significant annual benefits are created. These benefits stem from eliminating the need to operate and maintain expensive pollution control equipment, treat and dispose of toxic liquid wastes, and pay the annual fines for exceeding allowable contaminant releases. Increased sales to environmentally conscious customers are also factored into the benefit estimates. Design B is more elaborate than Design A and will require a heavier investment and greater annual operating costs; however, it will also generate greater annual benefits. The projected annual benefits, incremental annual operating costs (over current process), capital outlays (each design requires some new production equipment), and project life for each design follow:

	Design A	Design B
Annual revenues	$179,460	$239,280
Annual operating costs	119,460	169,280
Equipment (purchased before Year 1)	180,000	210,000
Project life	5 years	5 years

All cash flows are expressed on an after-tax basis. Honley Medical must decide which design to choose. Assume that the cost of capital for the company is 12 percent.

Design A requires an initial outlay of $180,000 and has a net annual cash inflow of $60,000 (revenues of $179,460 minus costs of $119,460). Design B, with an initial outlay of $210,000, has a net annual cash inflow of $70,000 ($239,280 − $169,280). With this information, the cash-flow pattern for each project can be described and the NPV computed. These are shown in Exhibit 13-3. Based on NPV analysis, Design B is more profitable; it has the larger NPV. Accordingly, the company should select Design B over Design A.

Interestingly, Designs A and B have identical internal rates of return. As Exhibit 13-3 illustrates, both designs have a discount factor of 3.000. From Exhibit 13B-2, it is easily seen that a discount factor of 3.000 and a life of five years yields an IRR of

Cash-Flow Pattern

Year	Design A	Design B
0	$(180,000)	$(210,000)
1	60,000	70,000
2	60,000	70,000
3	60,000	70,000
4	60,000	70,000
5	60,000	70,000

Design A: NPV Analysis

Year	Cash Flow	Discount Factor[a]	Present Value
0	$(180,000)	1.000	$(180,000)
1–5	60,000	3.605	216,300
Net present value			$ 36,300

IRR Analysis

$$\text{Discount factor} = \frac{\text{Initial investment}}{\text{Annual cash flow}}$$

$$= \frac{\$180,000}{\$\ 60,000}$$

$$= 3.000$$

From Exhibit 13B-2, *df* = 3.000 for five years implies that IRR = 20%.

Design B: NPV Analysis

Year	Cash Flow	Discount Factor[a]	Present Value
0	$(210,000)	1.000	$(210,000)
1–5	70,000	3.605	252,350
Net present value			$ 42,350

IRR Analysis

$$\text{Discount factor} = \frac{\text{Initial investment}}{\text{Annual cash flow}}$$

$$= \frac{\$210,000}{\$\ 70,000}$$

$$= 3.000$$

From Exhibit 13B-2, *df* = 3.000 for five years implies that IRR = 20%.

[a]From Exhibit 13B-2.

Exhibit 13-3 Honley Medical's Environmental Project Cash-Flow Pattern and NPV Analysis: Designs A and B

Managers Decide

Changes in Capital Budgeting Practices

Many surveys over four decades have indicated that the financial managers of large firms prefer the internal rate of return and the payback method to the net present value method. However, a recent survey of Fortune 1000 firms revealed that the net present value method is now the most widely used method for investment analysis. For NPV, 85.1 percent of the respondents used this method always (49.8 percent) or frequently (35.3 percent). For IRR, 76.7 percent of the respondents used this method always (44.6 percent) or frequently (32.2 percent). These results also suggest that many firms use both discounting methods. For the payback method, 52.6 percent of the respondents used the method always (19.4 percent) or frequently (33.2 percent). The accounting rate of return was the lowest of the four, with only 14.7 percent using the method always (5.2 percent) or frequently (9.5 percent). ■

Source: P. A. Ryan and G. P. Ryan, "Capital budgeting practices of the Fortune 1000: How have things changed?" *Journal of Business and Management* (Fall 2002): pp. 355–365.

about 20 percent. Even though both projects have an IRR of 20 percent, the firm should not consider the two designs to be equally desirable. The analysis demonstrates that Design B produces a larger NPV and, therefore, will increase the value of the firm more than Design A. Design B should be chosen. This illustrates the conceptual superiority of NPV over IRR for analysis of competing projects.

Computation and Adjustment of Cash Flows

Objective 7

Convert gross cash flows to after-tax cash flows.

An important step in capital investment analysis is determining the cash-flow pattern for each project being considered. In fact, the computation of cash flows may be the most critical step in the capital investment process. Erroneous estimates may result in erroneous decisions, regardless of the sophistication of the decision models being used. Two steps are needed to compute cash flows: (1) forecasting revenues, expenses, and capital outlays; and (2) adjusting these gross cash flows for inflation and income tax effects. Of the two steps, the more challenging is the first. Forecasting cash flows is technically demanding, and its methodology is typically studied in marketing research, management science, and statistics courses. Once gross cash flows are estimated, they should be adjusted for significant inflationary effects. Finally, straightforward applications of tax law can then be used to compute the after-tax flows. At this level of study, we assume that gross cash flows forecasts are available and focus on adjusting forecasted cash flows to improve their accuracy and utility in capital expenditure analysis.

Adjusting Forecasts for Inflation

In the United States, inflation has been relatively modest, and the need to adjust cash flows may not be as critical. Even so, about 47 percent of the Fortune 100 firms use inflation adjusted cash flows.[4] Inflation can be very high in other countries, however, and for firms that operate in the international environment, the effect on

4 Patricia A. Ryan and Glenn P. Ryan, "Capital Budgeting Practices of the Fortune 1000: How Have Things Changed?" *Journal of Business and Management* (Fall 2002): pp. 355–364.

capital investment decisions can be dramatic. Venezuela, for example, has experienced double-digit inflation rates for years. Thus, it is important to know how to adjust the capital budgeting models for inflationary effects—particularly given the fact that many U.S. firms make capital investment decisions within many different national environments. In an inflationary environment, financial markets react by increasing the cost of capital to reflect inflation. Thus, the **cost of capital** is composed of two elements:

1. The real rate
2. The inflationary element (investors demand a premium to compensate for the loss in general purchasing power of the dollar or local currency)

Since the required rate of return (which should be the cost of capital) used in capital investment analysis reflects an inflationary component at the time NPV analysis is performed, inflation must also be considered in predicting the operating cash flows. If the operating cash flows are not adjusted to account for inflation, an erroneous decision may result. In adjusting predicted cash flows, specific price change indexes should be used if possible. If that is not possible, a general price index can be used.

Note, however, that the cash inflows due to the tax effects of depreciation need not be adjusted for inflation as long as the national tax law requires that depreciation be based on the *original* dollar investment. In this case, depreciation deductions should not be increased for inflation.

To illustrate, assume that a subsidiary of Honley Medical operating in Venezuela is considering a project that requires an investment of 5,000,000 bolivares and is expected to produce annual cash inflows of 2,900,000 bolivares for the coming two years. The required rate of return is 20 percent, which includes an inflationary component. The general inflation rate in Venezuela is expected to average 15 percent for the next two years. Net present value analysis with and without the adjustment of predicted cash flows for inflation is given in Exhibit 13-4. As the analysis shows, *not* adjusting predicted cash flows for inflation leads to a decision to reject the project, whereas adjusting for inflation leads to a decision to accept it. Thus, failure to adjust the predicted cash flows for inflationary effects can lead to an incorrect conclusion.

Without Inflationary Adjustment

Year	Cash Flow	Discount Factor[a]	Present Value
0	Bs.(5,000,000)	1.000	Bs.(5,000,000)
1–2	2,900,000	1.528	4,431,200
Net present value			Bs. (568,800)

With Inflationary Adjustment

Year	Cash Flow[b]	Discount Factor[c]	Present Value
0	Bs.(5,000,000)	1.000	Bs.(5,000,000)
1	3,335,000	0.833	2,778,055
2	3,835,250	0.694	2,661,664
Net present value			Bs. 439,719

[a]From Exhibit 13B-2.
[b]3,335,000 bolivares = 1.15 × 2,900,000 bolivares (adjustment for one year of inflation); 3,835,250 bolivares = 1.15 × 1.15 × 2,900,000 bolivares (adjustment for two years of inflation).
[c]From Exhibit 13B-1.
Note: All cash flows are expressed in bolivares.

Exhibit 13-4 The Effects of Inflation of Capital Investment

Conversion of Gross Cash Flows to After-Tax Cash Flows

Assuming that inflation-adjusted gross cash flows are predicted with the desired degree of accuracy, the analyst must adjust these cash flows for taxes. To analyze tax effects, cash flows are usually broken into two categories: (1) the initial cash outflows needed to acquire the assets of the project and (2) the cash inflows produced over the life of the project. Cash outflows and cash inflows adjusted for tax effects are called net cash outflows and inflows. Net cash flows include provisions for revenues, operating expenses, depreciation, and relevant tax implications. They are the proper inputs for capital investment decisions.

After-Tax Cash Flows: Year 0 The net cash outflow in Year 0 (the initial out-of-pocket outlay) is simply the difference between the initial cost of the project and any cash inflows directly associated with it. The gross cost of the project includes such things as the cost of land, the cost of equipment (including transportation and installation), taxes on gains from the sale of assets, and increases in working capital. Cash inflows occurring at the time of acquisition include tax savings from the sale of assets, cash from the sale of assets, and other tax benefits such as tax credits.

Under current tax law, all costs relating to the acquisition of assets other than land must be capitalized and written off over the useful life of the assets (the write-off is achieved through depreciation). Depreciation is deducted from revenues in computing taxable income during each year of the asset's life; however, at the point of acquisition, no depreciation expense is computed. Thus, depreciation is not relevant at Year 0. The principal tax implications at the point of acquisition are related to recognition of gains and losses on the sale of existing assets and to the recognition of any investment tax credits.

Gains on the sale of assets produce additional taxes and, accordingly, reduce the cash proceeds received from the sale of old assets. Losses, on the other hand, are non-cash expenses that reduce taxable income, producing tax savings; consequently, the cash proceeds from the sale of an old asset are increased by the amount of the tax savings.

Adjusting cash inflows and outflows for tax effects requires knowledge of current corporate tax rates. Currently, most corporations face a federal tax rate of 35 percent. State corporate tax rates vary by state. For purposes of analysis, we will assume that 40 percent is the combined rate for state and federal income taxes.

Let's look at an example. Currently, Honley Medical's Critical Care Monitoring Division uses two types of numerically controlled machines (CNC-11 and CNC-12) to produce one of its heart monitoring products. Recent technological advances have created a single CNC machine that can replace them. Management wants to know the net investment needed to acquire the new machine. If the new machine is acquired, the old equipment will be sold.

Disposition of Old Machines

Model	Book Value	Sale Price
CNC-11	$200,000	$260,000
CNC-12	500,000	400,000

Acquisition of New CNC

Purchase cost	$2,500,000
Freight	20,000
Installation	200,000
Additional working capital	180,000
Total	$2,900,000

The net investment can be determined by computing the net proceeds from the sale of the old machines and subtracting those proceeds from the cost of the new machine. The net proceeds are determined by computing the tax consequences of the sale and adjusting the gross receipts accordingly.

The tax consequences can be assessed by subtracting the book value from the selling price. If the difference is positive, the firm has experienced a gain and will owe taxes. Money received from the sale will be reduced by the amount of taxes owed. On the other hand, if the difference is negative, a loss is experienced—a noncash loss. However, this noncash loss does have cash implications. It can be deducted from revenues and, as a consequence, can shield revenues from being taxed; accordingly, taxes will be saved. Thus, a loss produces a cash inflow equal to the taxes saved.

To illustrate, consider the tax effects of selling CNC-11 and CNC-12 illustrated in Exhibit 13-5. By selling the two machines, Honley Medical receives the following net proceeds:

Sale price, CNC-11	$260,000
Sale price, CNC-12	400,000
Tax savings	16,000
Net proceeds	$676,000

Given these net proceeds, the net investment can be computed as follows:

Total cost of new machine	$2,900,000
Less: Net proceeds of old machines	676,000
Net investment (cash outflow)	$2,224,000

After-Tax Cash Flows: Life of the Project In addition to determining the initial out-of-pocket outlay, managers must also estimate the annual after-tax cash flows expected over the life of the project. If the project generates revenue, the principal source of cash flows is from operations. Operating cash inflows can be assessed from the project's income statement. The annual after-tax cash flows are the sum of the project's after-tax profits and its noncash expenses. In terms of a simple formula, this computation can be represented as follows:

$$\text{After-tax cash flows} = \text{After-tax net income} + \text{Noncash expenses}$$
$$CF = NI + NC$$

where CF = After-tax cash flows
NI = After-tax net income
NC = Noncash expenses

The most prominent examples of noncash expenses are depreciation and losses. At first glance, it may seem odd that after-tax cash flows are computed using noncash expenses. Noncash expenses are not cash flows, but they do generate cash flows by reducing taxes. Shielding revenues from taxation creates actual cash savings. The use

Asset	Gain (loss)
CNC-11[a]	$ 60,000
CNC-12[b]	(100,000)
Net gain (loss)	$ (40,000)
Tax rate	× 0.40
Tax savings	$ (16,000)

[a]The sales price minus book value is $260,000 − $200,000.
[b]The sales price minus book value is $400,000 − $500,000.

Exhibit 13-5 Tax Effects of the Sale of CNC-11 and CNC-12 of the income statement to determine after-tax cash flows is illustrated in the following example. The example is also used to show how noncash expenses can increase cash inflows by saving taxes.

The Specialty Products Division of Honley Medical plans to make a new product that requires new equipment costing $800,000. The new product is expected to increase the firm's annual revenues by $600,000 for each of the next four years. Materials, labor, and other cash operating expenses will be $250,000 per year. The equipment has a life of four years and will be depreciated on a straight-line basis. The machine will have no salvage value at the end of four years. The income statement for a typical year of the project follows:

Revenues	$ 600,000
Less:	
Cash operating expenses	(250,000)
Depreciation	(200,000)
Income before income taxes	$ 150,000
Income taxes (@ 40%)	60,000
Net income	$ 90,000

Cash flow from the income statement is computed as follows:

$$\begin{aligned} CF &= NI + NC \\ &= \$90{,}000 + \$200{,}000 \\ &= \$290{,}000 \end{aligned}$$

The income statement approach to determine operating cash flows can be decomposed to assess the after-tax, cash-flow effects of each individual category on the income statement. The decomposition approach calculates the operating cash flows by computing the after-tax cash flows for each item of the income statement:

$$\begin{aligned} CF = {} & [(1 - \text{Tax rate}) \times \text{Revenues}] - [(1 - \text{Tax rate}) \times \text{Cash expenses}] \\ & + [(\text{Tax rate}) \times \text{Noncash Expenses}] \end{aligned}$$

The first term, (1 − Tax rate) × Revenues, gives the after-tax cash inflows from cash revenues. For our example, the cash revenue is projected to be $600,000. The firm, therefore, can expect to keep $360,000 of the revenues received: (1 − Tax rate) × Revenues = 0.60 × $600,000 = $360,000. The after-tax revenue is the actual amount of after-tax cash available from the sales activity of the firm.

The second term, (1 − Tax rate) × Cash expenses, is the after-tax cash outflows from cash operating expenses. Because cash expenses can be deducted from revenues to arrive at taxable income, the effect is to shield revenues from taxation. The consequence of this shielding is to save taxes and to reduce the actual cash outflow associated with a given expenditure. In our example, the firm has cash operating expenses of $250,000. The actual cash outflow is not $250,000 but $150,000 (0.60 × $250,000). The cash outlay for operating expenses is reduced by $100,000 because of tax savings. To see this, assume that operating expenses are the only expenses and that the firm has revenues of $600,000. If operating expenses are not tax deductible, then the tax owed is $240,000 (0.40 × $600,000). If the operating expenses are deductible for tax purposes, then the taxable income is $350,000 ($600,000 − $250,000), and the tax owed is $140,000 (0.40 × $350,000). Because the deductibility of operating expenses saves $100,000 in taxes, the actual outlay for that expenditure is reduced by $100,000.

The third term, (Tax rate) × Noncash expenses, is the cash inflow from the tax savings produced by the noncash expenses. Noncash expenses, such as depreciation, also shield revenues from taxation. The depreciation shields $200,000 of revenues from being taxed and thus saves $80,000 (0.40 × $200,000) in taxes.

The sum of the three items follows:

After-tax revenues	$ 360,000
After-tax cash expenses	(150,000)

Depreciation tax shield	80,000
Operating cash flows	$290,000

The decomposition approach yields the same outcome as the income statement approach. For convenience, the three decomposition terms are summarized in Exhibit 13-6.

One feature of decomposition is the ability to compute after-tax cash flows in a spreadsheet format. This format highlights the cash-flow effects of individual items and facilitates the use of spreadsheet software packages. The spreadsheet format is achieved by creating four columns, one for each of the three cash-flow categories and one for the total after-tax cash flows, which is the sum of the first three. This format is illustrated in Exhibit 13-7 for our example. Recall that cash revenues were $600,000 per year for four years, annual cash expenses were $250,000, and annual depreciation was $200,000.

A second feature of decomposition is the ability to compute the after-tax cash effects on an item-by-item basis. For example, suppose that a firm is considering a project and is uncertain as to which method of depreciation should be used. By computing the tax savings produced under each depreciation method, a firm can quickly assess which method is most desirable.

For tax purposes, all depreciable business assets other than real estate are referred to as *personal property,* which is classified into one of six classes. Each class specifies the life of the assets that must be used for figuring depreciation. This life must be used even if the actual expected life is different from the class life; the class lives are set for purposes of recognizing depreciation and usually will be shorter than the actual life. Most equipment, machinery, and office furniture are classified as *seven-year assets.* Light trucks, automobiles, and computer equipment are classified as *five-year assets.* Most small tools are classified as *three-year assets.* Because the majority of personal property can be put into one of these categories, we will restrict our attention to them.

The taxpayer can use either the straight-line method or the **modified accelerated cost recovery system (MACRS)** to compute annual depreciation. Current law defines MACRS as the double-declining-balance method.[5] In computing depreciation, no consideration of salvage value is required. However, under either method, a **half-year**

After-tax cash revenues = (1 − Tax rate) × Cash revenues
After-tax cash expenses = (1 − Tax rate) × Cash expenses
Tax savings, noncash expenses = Tax rate × Noncash expenses

Exhibit 13-6 Computation of Operating Cash Flows: Decomposition Terms

Year	$(1 - t)R$[a]	$-(1 - t)C$[b]	tNC[c]	CF
1	$360,000	$(150,000)	$80,000	$290,000
2	360,000	(150,000)	80,000	290,000
3	360,000	(150,000)	80,000	290,000
4	360,000	(150,000)	80,000	290,000

[a] R = Revenues; t = tax rate; $(1 - t)R = (1 - 0.40)\$600,000 = \$360,000$
[b] C = Cash expenses; $-(1 - t)C = -(1 - 0.40)\$250,000 - (\$150,000)$
[c] NC = Noncash expenses; $tNC = 0.40(\$200,000) = \$80,000$

Exhibit 13-7 Illustration of the Spreadsheet Approach

5 The tax law also allows the 150 percent declining-balance method; however, we will focus on only the straight-line method and the double-declining version of MACRS.

convention applies.[6] This convention assumes that a newly acquired asset is in service for one-half of its first taxable year of service, regardless of the date that use of it actually began. When the asset reaches the end of its life, the other half year of depreciation can be claimed in the following year. If an asset is disposed of before the end of its class life, the half-year convention allows half the depreciation for that year.

For example, assume that Honley Medical purchases an automobile on March 1, 2008. The automobile costs $20,000, and the firm elects the straight-line method. Automobiles are five-year assets (for tax purposes). The annual depreciation is $4,000 for a five-year period ($20,000/5). However, using the half-year convention, the firm can deduct only $2,000 for 2008, half of the straight-line amount (0.5 × $4,000). The remaining half is deducted in the sixth year (or the year of disposal, if earlier):

Year	Depreciation Deduction
2008	$2,000 (half-year amount)
2009	4,000
2010	4,000
2011	4,000
2012	4,000
2013	2,000 (half-year amount)

Assume that the asset is disposed of in April 2010. In this case, only $2,000 of depreciation can be claimed for 2010 (early disposal rule).

If the double-declining-balance method is selected, the amount of depreciation claimed in the first year is twice that of the straight-line method. Under this method, the amount of depreciation claimed becomes progressively smaller until eventually it is exceeded by that claimed under the straight-line method. When this happens, the straight-line method is used to finish depreciating the asset. Exhibit 13-8 provides a table of depreciation rates for the double-declining-balance method for assets belonging to the three-year, five-year, and seven-year classes. The rates shown in this table incorporate the half-year convention and, therefore, are the MACRS depreciation rates.

Both the straight-line method and the double-declining-balance method yield the same total amount of depreciation over the life of the asset. Both methods also produce the same total tax savings (assuming the same tax rate over the life of the asset). However, since the depreciation claimed in the early years of a project is greater using the double-declining-balance method, the tax savings are also greater during those years. Considering the time value of money, it is preferable to have the tax savings earlier than later. Thus, firms should prefer the MACRS method of depreciation over the straight-line method. This conclusion is illustrated by the following example.

Year	Three-Year Assets	Five-Year Assets	Seven-Year Assets
1	33.33%	20.00%	14.29%
2	44.45	32.00	24.49
3	14.81	19.20	17.49
4	7.41	11.52	12.49
5		11.52	8.93
6		5.76	8.92
7		—	8.93
8		—	4.46

Exhibit 13-8 MACRS Depreciation Rates

6 The tax law requires a mid-quarter convention if more than 40 percent of personal property is placed in service during the last three months of the year. We will not illustrate this possible scenario.

Honley Medical is considering the purchase of computer equipment for $20,000. The tax guidelines require that the cost of the equipment be depreciated over five years. However, tax guidelines also permit the depreciation to be computed using either method. Of course, the firm should choose the double-declining-balance method because it brings the greater benefit.

From decomposition, we know that the cash inflows caused by shielding can be computed by multiplying the tax rate times the amount depreciated ($t \times NC$). The cash flows produced by each depreciation method and their present value, assuming a discount rate of 10 percent, are given in Exhibit 13-9. As can be seen, the present value of the tax savings from using MACRS is greater than that using straight-line depreciation.

Capital Investment: The Advanced Manufacturing Environment

Objective 8

Describe capital investment in the advanced manufacturing environment.

In the advanced manufacturing environment, long-term investments are generally concerned with the automation of manufacturing. Before any commitment to automation is made, however, a company should first make the most efficient use of existing technology. Many benefits can be realized by redesigning and simplifying the current manufacturing process. An example often given to support this thesis is automation of material handling. Automation of this operation can cost millions—and it is usually unnecessary because greater efficiency can be achieved by eliminating inventories and simplifying material transfers through the implementation of a JIT (just-in-time) system.

Once the benefits from redesign and simplification are achieved, however, it becomes apparent where automation can generate additional benefits. Many companies can improve their competitive positions by adding such features as robotics, flexible

Straight-Line Method

Year	Depreciation	Tax Rate	Tax Savings	Discount Factor	Present Value
1	$2,000	0.40	$ 800.00	0.909	$ 727.20
2	4,000	0.40	1,600.00	0.826	1,321.60
3	4,000	0.40	1,600.00	0.751	1,201.60
4	4,000	0.40	1,600.00	0.683	1,092.80
5	4,000	0.40	1,600.00	0.621	993.60
6	2,000	0.40	800.00	0.564	451.20
Net present value					$5,788.00

MACRS Method

Year	Depreciation*	Tax Rate	Tax Savings	Discount Factor	Present Value
1	$4,000	0.40	$1,600.00	0.909	$1,454.40
2	6,400	0.40	2,560.00	0.826	2,114.56
3	3,840	0.40	1,536.00	0.751	1,153.54
4	2,304	0.40	921.60	0.683	629.45
5	2,304	0.40	921.60	0.621	572.31
6	1,152	0.40	460.80	0.564	259.89
Net present value					$6,184.15

*This is computed by multiplying the five-year rates in Exhibit 18-8 by $20,000. For example, depreciation for Year 1 is 0.20 × $20,000.

Exhibit 13-9 Value of Accelerated Methods Illustrated

Investment in advanced technology requires consideration of both financial and nonfinancial criteria.

© Getty Images/PhotoDisc

manufacturing systems, and completely integrated manufacturing systems. Moreover, cheaper microchips have brought down the cost of automation and, simultaneously, have increased the power and accuracy of machine tools. These new machines can turn out components that vary less than a micron from specifications. They have also cut cycle time dramatically. **Huffman Corporation**, for example, sold a machine in 2001 that produced surgical instruments in 11 minutes, compared with the machines in 1994 that took 222 minutes.[7]

Although discounted cash-flow analysis (using net present value and internal rate of return) remains preeminent in capital investment decisions, the new manufacturing environment demands that more attention be paid to the inputs used in discounted cash-flow models. How investment is defined, how operating cash flows are estimated, how salvage value is treated, and how the discount rate is chosen all must be more carefully specified.

There is also another important dimension. Contemporary investment management involves both *financial* and *nonfinancial* criteria. It is critical that the investment management process be linked with the company's strategies. Analysis in advanced manufacturing technology should consider the contributions made to support such strategies as product enhancement, diversification, and risk reduction. For example, advanced technology may contribute to product enhancement by allowing a firm more flexibility in responding to fluctuating demands. Improving quality is also a product enhancement feature. Some of these product enhancement features may be possible to quantify. For example, it may be possible to estimate the cost savings attributable to improved quality. Other factors may be more difficult to quantify. Assessing the cost savings or increased revenues from increased flexibility may be quite difficult. Yet, the increased flexibility may be as critical for the company as the improved quality. Thus, consideration of nonfinancial factors is also important to the investment management process. Nonetheless, every possible effort should be made to quantify the factors affecting the investment decision.

How Investment Differs

Investment in automated manufacturing processes is much more complex than investment in the standard manufacturing equipment of the past. For standard equipment, the direct costs of acquisition represent virtually the entire investment. For automated manufacturing, the direct costs can represent as little as 50 or 60 percent of the total investment; software, engineering, training, and implementation are a significant percentage of the total costs. Thus, great care must be exercised to assess the actual cost of an automated system. It is easy to overlook the peripheral costs, which can be substantial.

How Estimates of Operating Cash Flows Differ

Estimates of operating cash flows from investments in standard equipment have typically relied on directly identifiable tangible benefits, such as direct savings from labor, power, and scrap. Direct labor savings have often been used as the main justification for automating. Intangible benefits and indirect savings were ignored as they often are in traditional capital investment analysis.

In the decision to automate, however, the intangible and indirect benefits can be material and critical to the viability of the project. Greater quality, more reliability,

7 See Steve Liesman, "High-Tech Devices Speed Manufacturing, and May Play Larger Role in Economy," *Wall Street Journal Interactive Edition* (February 15, 2001).

reduced lead time, improved customer satisfaction, and an enhanced ability to maintain market share are all important intangible benefits of an advanced manufacturing system. Reduction of labor in support areas such as production scheduling and stores are indirect benefits. More effort is needed to measure these intangible and indirect benefits in order to assess more accurately the potential value of investments. Automated systems can produce large savings in terms of reduced waste, lower inventories, increased quality, and reduced indirect labor. Productivity can easily increase by 50 percent or more (consider Huffman's surgical instrument machines).

An example can be used to illustrate the importance of considering intangible and indirect benefits. The Critical Monitoring Division of Honley Medical is evaluating a potential investment in a flexible manufacturing system (FMS). The choice facing the division is to continue producing with its traditional equipment, expected to last 10 years, or to switch to the new system, which is also expected to have a useful life of 10 years. The division's discount rate is 12 percent. The data pertaining to the investment are presented in Exhibit 13-10. Using these data, the net present value of the proposed system can be computed as follows:

Present value ($4,000,000 × 5.65*)	$22,600,000
Investment	18,000,000
Net present value	$ 4,600,000

*This is the discount factor for an interest rate of 12 percent and a life of 10 years (see Exhibit 13B-2).

The net present value is positive and large in magnitude, and it clearly signals the acceptability of the FMS. This outcome, however, is strongly dependent on explicit recognition of both intangible and indirect benefits. If those benefits are eliminated, then the direct savings total $2.2 million, and the NPV is negative:

Present value ($2,200,000 × 5.65)	$ 12,430,000
Investment	18,000,000
Net present value	$ (5,570,000)

	FMS	Status Quo
Investment (current outlay):		
Direct costs	$ 10,000,000	—
Software, engineering	8,000,000	—
Total current outlay	$18,000,000	—
Net after-tax cash flows	$ 5,000,000	$1,000,000
Less: After-tax cash flows for status quo	1,000,000	n/a
Incremental benefit*	$ 4,000,000	n/a

*Incremental Benefit Explained		
Direct benefits:		
Direct labor	$1,500,000	
Scrap reduction	500,000	
Setups	200,000	$2,200,000
Intangible benefits (quality savings):		
Rework	$ 200,000	
Warranties	400,000	
Maintenance of competitive position	1,000,000	1,600,000
Indirect benefits:		
Production scheduling	$ 110,000	
Payroll	90,000	200,000
Total		$4,000,000

Exhibit 13-10 Investment Data; Direct, Intangible, and Indirect Benefits

The rise of activity-based costing has made identifying indirect benefits easier with the use of cost drivers. Once they are identified, they can be included in the analysis if they are material.

Examination of Exhibit 13-10 reveals the importance of intangible benefits. One of the most important intangible benefits is maintaining or improving a firm's competitive position. A key question is what will happen to the cash flows of the firm if the investment is not made. That is, if the company chooses to forgo an investment in technologically advanced equipment, will it be able to continue to compete with other firms on the basis of quality, delivery, and cost? (The question becomes especially relevant if competitors choose to invest in advanced equipment.) If the competitive position deteriorates, the company's current cash flows will decrease.

If cash flows will decrease if the investment is not made, this decrease should show up as an incremental benefit for the advanced technology. In Exhibit 13-10, the company estimates this competitive benefit as $1,000,000. Estimating this benefit requires some serious strategic planning and analysis, but its effect can be critical. If this benefit had been ignored or overlooked, then the net present value would have been negative, and the investment alternative rejected:

Present value ($3,000,000 × 5.65)	$ 16,950,000
Investment	18,000,000
Net present value	$ (1,050,000)

Salvage Value

Terminal or salvage value has often been ignored in investment decisions. The usual reason offered is the difficulty of estimating it. Because of this uncertainty, the effect of salvage value has often been ignored or heavily discounted. This approach may be unwise, however, because salvage value could make the difference between investing or not investing. Given the highly competitive environment, companies cannot afford to make incorrect decisions.

A much better approach to deal with uncertainty is to use sensitivity analysis. **Sensitivity analysis** changes the assumptions on which the capital investment analysis relies and assesses the effect on the cash-flow pattern. Sensitivity analysis is often referred to as **what-if analysis**. For example, this approach is used to address such questions as what is the effect on the decision to invest in a project if the cash receipts are 5 percent less than projected? 5 percent more? Although sensitivity analysis is computationally demanding if done manually, it can be done rapidly and easily using computers and spreadsheet software packages such as Lotus, Excel, and QuattroPro. In fact, these packages can also be used to carry out the NPV and IRR computations that have been illustrated manually throughout the chapter. They have built-in NPV and IRR functions that greatly facilitate the computational requirements.

To illustrate the potential effect of terminal value, assume that the after-tax annual operating cash flows of the project shown in Exhibit 13-10 are $3.1 million instead of $4 million. The net present value without salvage value is as follows:

Present value ($3,100,000 × 5.65)	$17,515,000
Investment	18,000,000
Net present value	$ (485,000)

Without the terminal value, the project would be rejected. The net present value with salvage value of $2 million, however, is a positive result, meaning that the investment should be made:

Present value ($3,100,000 × 5.65)	$ 17,515,000
Present value ($2,000,000 × 0.322*)	644,000
Investment	(18,000,000)
Net present value	$ 159,000

*This is the discount factor, assuming 12 percent and 10 years (Exhibit 13B-1).

But what if the salvage value is less than expected? Suppose that the worst possible outcome is a salvage value of $1,600,000? What is the effect on the decision? The NPV can be recomputed under this new scenario:

Present value ($3,100,000 × 5.65)	$ 17,515,000
Present value ($1,600,000 × 0.322)	515,200
Investment	(18,000,000)
Net present value	$ 30,200

Thus, under a pessimistic scenario, the NPV is still positive. This illustrates how sensitivity analysis can be used to deal with the uncertainty surrounding salvage value. It can also be used for other cash-flow variables.

Discount Rates

Being overly conservative with discount rates can prove even more damaging. In theory, if future cash flows are known with certainty, the correct discount rate is a firm's cost of capital. In practice, future cash flows are uncertain, and managers often choose a discount rate higher than the cost of capital to deal with that uncertainty. If the rate chosen is excessively high, it will bias the selection process toward short-term investments.

To illustrate the effect of an excessive discount rate, consider the project in Exhibit 13-10 once again. Assume that the correct discount rate is 12 percent but that the firm uses 18 percent. The net present value using an 18 percent discount rate is calculated as follows:

Present value ($4,000,000 × 4.494*)	$17,976,000
Investment	18,000,000
Net present value	$ (24,000)

*This is the discount rate for 18 percent and 10 years (Exhibit 13B-2).

The project would be rejected. With a higher discount rate, the discount factor decreases in magnitude much more rapidly than the discount factor for a lower rate (compare the discount factor for 12 percent, 5.65, with the factor for 18 percent, 4.494). The effect of a higher discount rate is to place more weight on earlier cash flows and less weight on later cash flows, which favors short-term over long-term investments. This outcome makes it more difficult for automated manufacturing systems to appear as viable projects since the cash returns required to justify the investment are received over a longer period of time.

Appendix A: Present Value Concepts

An important feature of money is that it can be invested and can earn interest. A dollar today is not the same as a dollar tomorrow. This fundamental principle is the backbone of discounting methods. Discounting methods rely on the relationships between current and future dollars. Thus, to use discounting methods, we must understand these relationships.

Future Value

Suppose a bank advertises a 4 percent annual interest rate. If a customer invests $100, he or she would receive, after one year, the original $100 plus $4 interest {[$100 + (0.04)($100)] = (1 + 0.04)$100 = (1.04)($100) = $104}. This result can be expressed by the following equation, where F is the future amount, P is the initial or current outlay, and i is the interest rate:

$$F = P(1 + i) \tag{13A.1}$$

For the example, $F = \$100(1 + 0.04) = \$100(1.04) = \$104$.

Now suppose that the same bank offers a 5 percent rate if the customer leaves the original deposit, plus any interest, on deposit for a total of two years. How much will the customer receive at the end of two years? Again, assume that a customer invests $100. Using Equation 13A.1, the customer will earn $105 at the end of Year 1 [$F = \$100(1 + 0.05) = (\$100 \times 1.05) = \$105$]. If this amount is left in the account for a second year, Equation 13A.1 is used again with P now assumed to be $105. At the end of the second year, then, the total is $110.25 [$F = \$105(1 + 0.05) = (\$105 \times 1.05) = \$110.25$]. In the second year, interest is earned on both the original deposit and the interest earned in the first year. The earning of interest on interest is referred to as **compounding of interest**. The value that will accumulate by the end of an investment's life, assuming a specified compound return, is the **future value**. The future value of the $100 deposit in the second example is $110.25.

A more direct way to compute the future value is possible. Since the first application of Equation 13A.1 can be expressed as $F = \$105 = \$100(1.05)$, the second application can be expressed as $F = \$105(1.05) = \$100(1.05)(1.05) = \$100(1.05)^2 = P(1 + i)^2$. This suggests the following formula for computing amounts for n periods into the future:

$$F = P(1 + i)^n \qquad (13A.2)$$

Present Value

Often, a manager needs to compute not the future value but the amount that must be invested now in order to yield some given future value. The amount that must be invested now to produce the future value is known as the **present value** of the future amount. For example, how much must be invested now in order to yield $363 two years from now, assuming that the interest rate is 10 percent? Or put another way, what is the present value of $363 to be received two years from now?

In this example, the future value, the years, and the interest rate are all known; we want to know the current outlay that will produce that future amount. In Equation 13A.2, the variable representing the current outlay (the present value of F) is P. Thus, to compute the present value of a future outlay, all we need to do is solve Equation 13A.2 for P:

$$P = F/(1 + i)^n \qquad (13A.3)$$

Using Equation 13A.3, we can compute the present value of $363:

$$\begin{aligned} P &= \$363/(1 + 0.1)^2 \\ &= \$363/1.21 \\ &= \$300 \end{aligned}$$

The present value, $300, is what the future amount of $363 is worth today. All other things being equal, having $300 today is the same as having $363 two years from now. Put another way, if a firm requires a 10 percent rate of return, the most the firm would be willing to pay today is $300 for any investment that yields $363 two years from now.

The process of computing the present value of future cash flows is often referred to as **discounting**; thus, we say that we have discounted the future value of $363 to its present value of $300. The interest rate used to discount the future cash flow is the **discount rate**. The expression $F/(1 + i)^n$ in Equation 13A.3 is the **discount factor**. By letting the discount factor, called df, equal $1/(1 + i)^n$, Equation 13A.3 can be expressed as $P = F(df)$. To simplify the computation of present value, a table of discount factors is given for various combinations of i and n (see Exhibit 13B-1 in Appendix B). For example, the discount factor for $i = 10$ percent and $n = 2$ is 0.826

(simply go to the 10 percent column of the table and move down to the second row). With the discount factor, the present value of $363 is computed as follows:

$$\begin{aligned} P &= F(df) \\ &= \$363 \times 0.826 \\ &= \$300 \text{ (rounded)} \end{aligned}$$

Present Value of an Uneven Series of Cash Flows

Exhibit 13B-1 can be used to compute the present value of any future cash flow or series of future cash flows. A series of future cash flows is called an **annuity**. The present value of an annuity is found by computing the present value of each future cash flow and then summing these values. For example, suppose that an investment is expected to produce the following annual cash flows: $110, $121, and $133.10. Assuming a discount rate of 10 percent, the present value of this series of cash flows is computed in Exhibit 13A-1.

Present Value of a Uniform Series of Cash Flows

If the series of cash flows is even, the computation of the annuity's present value is simplified. Assume, for example, that an investment is expected to return $100 per year for three years. Using Exhibit 13B-1 and assuming a discount rate of 10 percent, the present value of the annuity is computed in Exhibit 13A-2.

As with the uneven series of cash flows, the present value in Exhibit 13A-2 was computed by calculating the present value of each cash flow separately and then summing them. However, in the case of an annuity displaying uniform cash flows, the computations can be reduced from three to one as described in the footnote to the exhibit. The sum of the individual discount factors can be thought of as a discount factor for an annuity of uniform cash flows. A table of discount factors that can be used for an annuity of uniform cash flows is available in Exhibit 13B-2.

Year	Cash Flow	Discount Factor*	Present Value
1	$110.00	0.909	$ 100.00
2	121.00	0.826	100.00
3	133.10	0.751	100.00
			$300.00

*Rounded

Exhibit 13A-1 Present Value of an Uneven Series of Cash Flows

Year	Cash Flow*	Discount Factor	Present Value
1	$100	0.909	$ 90.90
2	100	0.826	82.60
3	100	0.751	75.10
		2.486	$248.60

*The annual cash flow of $100 can be multiplied by the sum of the discount factors (2.486) to obtain the present value of the uniform series ($248.60).

Exhibit 13A-2 Present Value of Uniform Series of Cash Flows

Periods	2%	4%	6%	8%	10%	12%	14%	16%	18%	20%	22%	24%	26%	28%	30%	32%	40%
1	0.980	0.962	0.943	0.926	0.909	0.893	0.877	0.862	0.847	0.833	0.820	0.806	0.794	0.781	0.769	0.758	0.714
2	0.961	0.925	0.890	0.857	0.826	0.797	0.769	0.743	0.718	0.694	0.672	0.650	0.630	0.610	0.592	0.574	0.510
3	0.942	0.889	0.840	0.794	0.751	0.712	0.675	0.641	0.609	0.579	0.551	0.524	0.500	0.477	0.455	0.435	0.364
4	0.924	0.855	0.792	0.735	0.683	0.636	0.592	0.552	0.516	0.482	0.451	0.423	0.397	0.373	0.350	0.329	0.260
5	0.906	0.822	0.747	0.681	0.621	0.567	0.519	0.476	0.437	0.402	0.370	0.341	0.315	0.291	0.269	0.250	0.186
6	0.888	0.790	0.705	0.630	0.564	0.507	0.456	0.410	0.370	0.335	0.303	0.275	0.250	0.227	0.207	0.189	0.133
7	0.871	0.760	0.665	0.583	0.513	0.452	0.400	0.354	0.314	0.279	0.249	0.222	0.198	0.178	0.159	0.143	0.095
8	0.853	0.731	0.627	0.540	0.467	0.404	0.351	0.305	0.266	0.233	0.204	0.179	0.157	0.139	0.123	0.108	0.068
9	0.837	0.703	0.592	0.500	0.424	0.361	0.308	0.263	0.225	0.194	0.167	0.144	0.125	0.108	0.094	0.082	0.048
10	0.820	0.676	0.558	0.463	0.386	0.322	0.270	0.227	0.191	0.162	0.137	0.116	0.099	0.085	0.073	0.062	0.035
11	0.804	0.650	0.527	0.429	0.350	0.287	0.237	0.195	0.162	0.135	0.112	0.094	0.079	0.066	0.056	0.047	0.025
12	0.788	0.625	0.497	0.397	0.319	0.257	0.208	0.168	0.137	0.112	0.092	0.076	0.062	0.052	0.043	0.036	0.018
13	0.773	0.601	0.469	0.368	0.290	0.229	0.182	0.145	0.116	0.093	0.075	0.061	0.050	0.040	0.033	0.027	0.013
14	0.758	0.577	0.442	0.340	0.263	0.205	0.160	0.125	0.099	0.078	0.062	0.049	0.039	0.032	0.025	0.021	0.009
15	0.743	0.555	0.417	0.315	0.239	0.183	0.140	0.108	0.084	0.065	0.051	0.040	0.031	0.025	0.020	0.016	0.006
16	0.728	0.534	0.394	0.292	0.218	0.163	0.123	0.093	0.071	0.054	0.042	0.032	0.025	0.019	0.015	0.012	0.005
17	0.714	0.513	0.371	0.270	0.198	0.146	0.108	0.080	0.060	0.045	0.034	0.026	0.020	0.015	0.012	0.009	0.003
18	0.700	0.494	0.350	0.250	0.180	0.130	0.095	0.069	0.051	0.038	0.028	0.021	0.016	0.012	0.009	0.007	0.002
19	0.686	0.475	0.331	0.232	0.164	0.116	0.083	0.060	0.043	0.031	0.023	0.017	0.012	0.009	0.007	0.005	0.002
20	0.673	0.456	0.312	0.215	0.149	0.104	0.073	0.051	0.037	0.026	0.019	0.014	0.010	0.007	0.005	0.004	0.001
21	0.660	0.439	0.294	0.199	0.135	0.093	0.064	0.044	0.031	0.022	0.015	0.011	0.008	0.006	0.004	0.003	0.001
22	0.647	0.422	0.278	0.184	0.123	0.083	0.056	0.038	0.026	0.018	0.013	0.009	0.006	0.004	0.003	0.002	0.001
23	0.634	0.406	0.262	0.170	0.112	0.074	0.049	0.033	0.022	0.015	0.010	0.007	0.005	0.003	0.002	0.002	0.000
24	0.622	0.390	0.247	0.158	0.102	0.066	0.043	0.028	0.019	0.013	0.008	0.006	0.004	0.003	0.002	0.001	0.000
25	0.610	0.375	0.233	0.146	0.092	0.059	0.038	0.024	0.016	0.010	0.007	0.005	0.003	0.002	0.001	0.001	0.000
26	0.598	0.361	0.220	0.135	0.084	0.053	0.033	0.021	0.014	0.009	0.006	0.004	0.002	0.002	0.001	0.001	0.000
27	0.586	0.347	0.207	0.125	0.076	0.047	0.029	0.018	0.011	0.007	0.005	0.003	0.002	0.001	0.001	0.001	0.000
28	0.574	0.333	0.196	0.116	0.069	0.042	0.026	0.016	0.010	0.006	0.004	0.002	0.002	0.001	0.001	0.000	0.000
29	0.563	0.321	0.185	0.107	0.063	0.037	0.022	0.014	0.008	0.005	0.003	0.002	0.001	0.001	0.000	0.000	0.000
30	0.552	0.308	0.174	0.099	0.057	0.033	0.020	0.012	0.007	0.004	0.003	0.002	0.001	0.001	0.000	0.000	0.000

$^*P_n = \frac{A}{(1 + I)^n}$

Exhibit 13B-1 Present Value of $1*

Periods	2%	4%	6%	8%	10%	12%	14%	16%	18%	20%	22%	24%	26%	28%	30%	32%	40%
1	0.980	0.962	0.943	0.926	0.909	0.893	0.877	0.862	0.847	0.833	0.820	0.806	0.794	0.781	0.769	0.758	0.714
2	1.942	1.886	1.833	1.783	1.736	1.690	1.647	1.605	1.566	1.528	1.492	1.457	1.424	1.392	1.361	1.331	1.224
3	2.884	2.775	2.673	2.577	2.487	2.402	2.322	2.246	2.174	2.106	2.042	1.981	1.923	1.868	1.816	1.766	1.589
4	3.808	3.630	3.465	3.312	3.170	3.037	2.914	2.798	2.690	2.589	2.494	2.404	2.320	2.241	2.166	2.096	1.849
5	4.713	4.452	4.212	3.993	3.791	3.605	3.433	3.274	3.127	2.991	2.864	2.745	2.635	2.532	2.436	2.345	2.035
6	5.601	5.242	4.917	4.623	4.355	4.111	3.889	3.685	3.498	3.326	3.167	3.020	2.885	2.759	2.643	2.534	2.168
7	6.472	6.002	5.582	5.206	4.868	4.564	4.288	4.039	3.812	3.605	3.416	3.242	3.083	2.937	2.802	2.677	2.263
8	7.325	6.733	6.210	5.747	5.335	4.968	4.639	4.344	4.078	3.837	3.619	3.421	3.241	3.076	2.925	2.786	2.331
9	8.162	7.435	6.802	6.247	5.759	5.328	4.946	4.607	4.303	4.031	3.876	3.566	3.366	3.184	3.019	2.868	2.379
10	8.983	8.111	7.360	6.710	6.145	5.650	5.216	4.833	4.494	4.192	3.923	3.682	3.465	3.269	3.092	2.930	2.414
11	9.787	8.760	7.887	7.139	6.495	5.938	5.453	5.029	4.656	4.327	4.035	3.776	3.543	3.335	3.147	2.978	2.438
12	10.575	9.385	8.384	7.536	6.814	6.194	5.660	5.197	4.793	4.439	4.127	3.851	3.606	3.387	3.190	3.013	2.456
13	11.348	9.986	8.853	7.904	7.103	6.424	5.842	5.342	4.910	4.533	4.203	3.912	3.656	3.427	3.223	3.040	2.469
14	12.106	10.563	9.295	8.244	7.367	6.628	6.002	5.468	5.008	4.611	4.265	3.962	3.695	3.459	3.249	3.061	2.478
15	12.849	11.118	9.712	8.559	7.606	6.811	6.142	5.575	5.092	4.675	4.315	4.001	3.726	3.483	3.268	3.076	2.484
16	13.578	11.652	10.106	8.851	7.824	6.974	6.265	5.668	5.162	4.730	4.357	4.033	3.751	3.503	3.283	3.088	2.489
17	14.292	12.166	10.477	9.122	8.022	7.120	6.373	5.749	5.222	4.775	4.391	4.059	3.771	3.518	3.295	3.097	2.492
18	14.992	12.659	10.828	9.372	8.201	7.250	6.467	5.818	5.273	4.812	4.419	4.080	3.786	3.529	3.304	3.104	2.494
19	15.678	13.134	11.158	9.604	8.365	7.366	6.550	5.877	5.316	4.843	4.442	4.097	3.799	3.539	3.311	3.109	2.496
20	16.351	13.590	11.470	9.818	8.514	7.469	6.623	5.929	5.353	4.870	4.460	4.110	3.808	3.546	3.316	3.113	2.497
21	17.011	14.029	11.764	10.017	8.649	7.562	6.687	5.973	5.384	4.891	4.476	4.121	3.816	3.551	3.320	3.116	2.498
22	17.658	14.451	12.042	10.201	8.772	7.645	6.743	6.011	5.410	4.909	4.488	4.130	3.822	3.556	3.323	3.118	2.498
23	13.292	14.857	12.303	10.371	8.883	7.718	6.792	6.044	5.432	4.925	4.499	4.137	3.827	3.559	3.325	3.120	2.499
24	13.914	15.247	12.550	10.529	8.985	7.784	6.835	6.073	5.451	4.937	4.507	4.143	3.831	3.562	3.327	3.121	2.499
25	19.523	15.622	12.783	10.675	9.077	7.843	6.873	6.097	5.467	4.948	4.514	4.147	3.834	3.564	3.329	3.122	2.499
26	20.121	15.983	13.003	10.810	9.161	7.896	6.906	6.118	5.480	4.956	4.520	4.151	3.837	3.566	3.330	3.123	2.500
27	20.707	16.330	13.211	10.935	9.237	7.943	6.935	6.136	5.492	4.964	4.524	4.154	3.839	3.567	3.331	3.123	2.500
28	21.281	16.663	13.406	11.051	9.307	7.984	6.961	6.152	5.502	4.970	4.528	4.157	3.840	3.568	3.331	3.124	2.500
29	21.844	16.984	13.591	11.158	9.370	8.022	6.983	6.166	5.510	4.975	4.531	4.159	3.841	3.569	3.332	3.124	2.500
30	22.396	17.292	13.765	11.258	9.427	8.055	7.003	6.177	5.517	4.979	4.534	4.160	3.842	3.569	3.332	3.124	2.500

$^*P_n = \left(\frac{1}{i}\right)\left[\frac{1-1}{(1+i)^n}\right]$

Exhibit 13B.2 Present Value of an Annuity of $1 in Arrears*

Summary of Learning Objectives

1. Explain what a capital investment decision is, and distinguish between independent and mutually exclusive capital investment decisions.

Capital investment decisions are concerned with the acquisition of long-term assets and usually involve a significant outlay of funds. There are two types of capital investment projects: independent and mutually exclusive. Independent projects are projects that, if accepted or rejected, do not affect the cash flows of other projects. Mutually exclusive projects are those projects that, if accepted, preclude the acceptance of all other competing projects.

2. Compute the payback period and accounting rate of return for a proposed investment, and explain their roles in capital investment decisions.

Managers make capital investment decisions by using formal models to decide whether to accept or reject proposed projects. These decision models are classified as nondiscounting and discounting, depending on whether they address the question of the time value of money. There are two nondiscounting models: the payback period and the accounting rate of return.

The payback period is the time required for a firm to recover its initial investment. For even cash flows, it is calculated by dividing the investment by the annual cash flow. For uneven cash flows, the cash flows are summed until the investment is recovered. If only a fraction of a year is needed, then it is assumed that the cash flows occur evenly within each year. The payback period ignores the time value of money and the profitability of projects because it does not consider the cash inflows available beyond the payback period. However, it does supply some useful information. The payback period is useful in assessing and controlling risk, minimizing the impact of an investment on a firm's liquidity, and controlling the risk of obsolescence.

The accounting rate of return is computed by dividing the average income expected from an investment by either the original or average investment. Unlike the payback period, it does consider the profitability of a project; however, it ignores the time value of money. The payback period may be useful to managers for screening new investments to ensure that certain accounting ratios are not adversely affected (specifically accounting ratios that may be monitored to ensure compliance with debt covenants).

3. Use net present value analysis for capital investment decisions involving independent projects.

NPV is the difference between the present value of future cash flows and the initial investment outlay. To use the model, a required rate of return must be identified (usually the cost of capital). The NPV method uses the required rate of return to compute the present value of a project's cash inflows and outflows. If the present value of the inflows is greater than the present value of the outflows, the net present value is greater than zero, and the project is profitable; if the NPV is less than zero, the project is not profitable and should be rejected.

4. Use the internal rate of return to assess the acceptability of independent projects.

The IRR is computed by finding the interest rate that equates the present value of a project's cash inflows with the present value of its cash outflows. If the IRR is greater than the required rate of return (cost of capital), the project is acceptable; if the IRR is less than the required rate of return, the project should be rejected.

5. Discuss the role and value of postaudits.

Postauditing of capital projects is an important step in capital investment. Postaudits evaluate the actual performance of a project in relation to its expected performance. A postaudit may lead to corrective action to improve the performance of the project or to abandon it. Postaudits also serve as an incentive for managers to make capital investment decisions prudently.

6. Explain why NPV is better than IRR for capital investment decisions involving mutually exclusive projects.

In evaluating mutually exclusive or competing projects, managers have a choice of using NPV or IRR. When choosing among competing projects, the NPV model correctly identifies the best investment alternative. IRR, at times, may choose an inferior project. Thus, since NPV always provides the correct signal, it should be used.

7. Convert gross cash flows to after-tax cash flows.

Accurate and reliable cash-flow forecasts are absolutely critical for capital budgeting analyses. Managers should assume responsibility for the accuracy of cash-flow projections. All cash flows in a capital investment analysis should be after-tax cash flows. There are two different, but equivalent, ways to compute after-tax cash flows: the income statement method and the decomposition method. Although depreciation is not a cash flow, it does have cash-flow implications because tax laws allow depreciation to be deducted in computing taxable income. Straight-line and double-declining-balance depreciation both produce the same total depreciation deductions over the life of the depreciated asset. Because the latter method accelerates depreciation, however, it would be preferred.

8. Describe capital investment in the advanced manufacturing environment.

Capital investment in the advanced manufacturing environment is affected by the way in which inputs are determined. Much greater attention must be paid to the investment outlays because peripheral items can require substantial resources. Furthermore, in assessing benefits, intangible items such as quality and maintaining competitive position can be deciding factors. Choice of the required rate of return is also critical. The tendency of firms to use required rates of return that are much greater than the cost of capital should be discontinued. Also, since the salvage value of an automated system can be considerable, it should be estimated and included in the analysis.

Key Terms

Accounting rate of return, 568
Annuity, 591
Capital budgeting, 564
Capital investment decisions, 564
Compounding of interest, 590
Cost of capital, 579
Discount factor, 590
Discount rate, 590
Discounted cash flows, 569
Discounting, 590
Discounting models, 566
Future value, 590
Half-year convention, 583
Independent projects, 564
Internal rate of return, 570
Modified accelerated cost recovery system (MACRS), 583
Mutually exclusive projects, 564
Net present value, 569
Nondiscounting models, 566
Payback period, 566
Postaudit, 573
Present value, 590
Required rate of return, 570
Sensitivity analysis, 588
What-if analysis, 588

Review Problems

1. Basics of Capital Investment (Ignore Taxes for this Exercise.)

Kenn Day, manager of Day Laboratory, is investigating the possibility of acquiring some new test equipment. To acquire the equipment requires an initial outlay of \$300,000. To raise the capital, Kenn will sell stock valued at \$200,000 (the stock pays dividends of \$24,000 per year) and borrow \$100,000. The loan for \$100,000 would carry an interest rate of 6 percent. Kenn figures that his weighted average cost of capital is 10 percent $[(2/3 \times 0.12) + (1/3 \times 0.06)]$. This weighted cost of capital is the discount rate that will be used for capital investment decisions.

Kenn estimates that the new test equipment will produce a cash inflow of \$50,000 per year. Kenn expects the equipment to last for 20 years.

Required

1. Compute the payback period.
2. Assuming that depreciation is \$14,000 per year, compute the accounting rate of return (on total investment).
3. Compute the NPV of the test equipment.
4. Compute the IRR of the test equipment.
5. Should Kenn buy the equipment?

Solution

1. The payback period is \$300,000/\$50,000, or six years.
2. The accounting rate of return is (\$50,000 − \$14,000)/\$300,000, or 12 percent.
3. From Exhibit 13B-2, the discount factor for an annuity with *i* at 10 percent and *n* at 20 years is 8.514. Thus, the NPV is (8.514 × \$50,000) − \$300,000, or \$125,700.
4. The discount factor associated with the IRR is 6.00 (\$300,000/\$50,000). From Exhibit 13B-2, the IRR is between 14 and 16 percent (using the row corresponding to period 20).
5. Since the NPV is positive and the IRR is greater than Kenn's cost of capital, the test equipment is a sound investment. This, of course, assumes that the cash flow projections are accurate.

2. Capital Investment with Competing Projects (with Tax Effects)

Weins Postal Service (WPS) has decided to acquire a new delivery truck. The choice has been narrowed to two models. The following information has been gathered for each model:

	Custom	Deluxe
Acquisition cost	\$20,000	\$25,000
Annual operating costs	\$ 3,500	\$ 2,000
Depreciation method	MACRS	MACRS
Expected salvage value	\$ 5,000	\$ 8,000

WPS's cost of capital is 14 percent. The company plans to use the truck for five years and then sell it for its salvage value. Assume the combined state and federal income tax rate is 40 percent.

Required

1. Compute the after-tax operating cash flows for each model.
2. Compute the NPV for each model, and make a recommendation.

Solution

1. For light trucks, MACRS guidelines allow a five-year life. Using the rates from Exhibit 13-8, depreciation is calculated for each model:

Year	Custom	Deluxe
1	\$ 4,000	\$ 5,000
2	6,400	8,000
3	3,840	4,800
4	2,304	2,880
5	1,152*	1,440*
Total	\$17,696	\$22,120

*Only half the depreciation is allowed in the year of disposal.

The after-tax operating cash flows are computed using the spreadsheet format:

		Custom			
Year	$(1 - t)R$	$-(1 - t)C$	tNC	Other	CF
1	n/a	\$(2,100)	\$1,600		\$ (500)
2	n/a	(2,100)	2,560		460

(Continued)

3	n/a	(2,100)	1,536		(564)
4	n/a	(2,100)	922		(1,178)
5	1,618[a]	(2,100)	461	$2,304[b]	2,283

[a]Salvage value ($5,000) − Book value ($20,000 − $17,696 = $2,304) = $2,696; 0.60 × $2,696 = $1,618
[b]Recovery of capital = Book value = $2,304. Capital recovered is not taxed—only the gain on sale of the asset. Footnote (a) illustrates how the gain is treated. The nontaxable item requires an additional column for the spreadsheet analysis.

Deluxe

Year	(1 − *t*)R	−(1 − *t*)C	*t*NC	Other	*CF*
1	n/a	$(1,200)	$2,000		$ 800
2	n/a	(1,200)	3,200		2,000
3	n/a	(1,200)	1,920		720
4	n/a	(1,200)	1,152		(48)
5	$3,072[a]	(1,200)	576	$2,880[b]	5,328

[a]Salvage value ($8,000) − Book value ($25,000 − $22,120 = $2,880) = $5,120; 0.60 × $5,120 = $3,072
[b]Recovery of capital = Book value = $2,880. Capital recovered is not taxed—only the gain on sale of the asset. Footnote (a) illustrates how the gain is treated. The nontaxable item requires an additional column for the spreadsheet analysis.

2. NPV computation:

Custom

Year	Cash Flow	Discount Factor	Present Value
0	$(20,000)	1.000	$(20,000)
1	(500)	0.877	(439)
2	460	0.769	354
3	(564)	0.675	(381)
4	(1,178)	0.592	(697)
5	2,283	0.519	1,185
	Net present value		$(19,978)

Deluxe

Year	Cash Flow	Discount Factor	Present Value
0	$(25,000)	1.000	$(25,000)
1	800	0.877	702
2	2,000	0.769	1,538
3	720	0.675	486
4	(48)	0.592	(28)
5	5,328	0.519	2,765
	Net present value		$(19,537)

The deluxe model should be chosen since it has the larger NPV, indicating that it is the less costly of the two trucks. Note also that the net present values are negative and that we are choosing the least costly investment.

Questions for Writing and Discussion

1. Explain the difference between independent projects and mutually exclusive projects.
2. Explain why the timing and quantity of cash flows are important in capital investment decisions.
3. The time value of money is ignored by the payback period and the accounting rate of return. Explain why this is a major deficiency in these two models.
4. What is the payback period? Compute the payback period for an investment requiring an initial outlay of $80,000 with expected annual cash inflows of $30,000.
5. Name and discuss three possible reasons that the payback period is used to help make capital investment decisions.
6. What is the accounting rate of return? Compute

the accounting rate of return for an investment that requires an initial outlay of $300,000 and promises an average net income of $100,000.

7. The net present value is the same as the profit of a project expressed in present dollars. Do you agree or disagree? Explain.
8. Explain the relationship between NPV and a firm's value.
9. What is the cost of capital? What role does it play in capital investment decisions?
10. What is the role that the required rate of return plays in the NPV model? In the IRR model?
11. Explain how the NPV is used to determine whether a project should be accepted or rejected.
12. The IRR is the true or actual rate of return being earned by the project. Do you agree or disagree? Discuss.
13. Explain what a postaudit is and how it can provide useful input for future capital investment decisions, especially those involving advanced technology.
14. Explain why NPV is generally preferred over IRR when choosing among competing or mutually exclusive projects. Why would managers continue to use IRR to choose among mutually exclusive projects?
15. Suppose that a firm must choose between two mutually exclusive projects, both of which have negative NPVs. Explain how a firm can legitimately choose among two such projects.
16. Why is it important to have accurate projections of cash flows for potential capital investments?
17. Describe why it is important for a manager to conduct a careful review of the assumptions and methods used in forecasting cash flows.
18. What are the principal tax implications that should be considered in Year 0?
19. Explain why the MACRS method of recognizing depreciation is better than the straight-line method.
20. What is the half-year convention? What is the effect of this convention on the length of time it actually takes to write off the cost of a depreciable asset?
21. Explain the important factors to consider for capital investment in the advanced manufacturing environment.
22. Explain what sensitivity analysis is. How can it help in capital budgeting decisions?

Exercises

13-1

Basic Concepts
LO1 through LO8

1. Capital investments should
   a. earn back their original capital outlay.
   b. only be analyzed using the accounting rate of return.
   c. always produce an increase in market share.
   d. always be done using a payback criterion.
   e. None of the above.
2. To make a capital investment decision, a manager must
   a. estimate the quantity and timing of cash flows.
   b. assess the risk of the investment.
   c. consider the impact of the investment on the firm's profits.
   d. select investments with a positive NPV.
   e. All of the above.
3. Mutually exclusive capital budgeting projects are those that
   a. if accepted or rejected do not affect the cash flows of other projects.
   b. if accepted will produce a negative NPV.
   c. if accepted preclude the acceptance of all other competing projects.
   d. if rejected preclude the acceptance of all other competing projects.
   e. if rejected imply that all other competing projects have a positive NPV.
4. An investment of $1,000 produces a net annual cash inflow of $500 for each of five years. What is the payback period?
   a. Two years
   b. One-half year
   c. Unacceptable

d. $2,500
e. Can't be determined.

5. An investment of $1,000 produces a net cash inflow of $600 in the first year and $2,000 in the second year. What is the payback period?

   a. 1.67 years
   b. 0.50 years
   c. 2.00 years
   d. 1.20 years
   e. Can't be determined.

6. The payback period suffers from which of the following deficiencies?

   a. It is a rough measure of the uncertainty of future cash flows.
   b. It helps control the risk of obsolescence.
   c. It ignores the time value of money.
   d. It ignores the financial performance of a project beyond the payback period.
   e. Both c and d.

7. The accounting rate of return has one specific advantage not possessed by the payback period:

   a. It considers the time value of money.
   b. It measures the value added by a project.
   c. It considers the profitability of a project beyond the payback period.
   d. It is more widely accepted by financial managers.
   e. It is always an accurate measure of profitability.

8. An investment of $1,000 provides an average net income of $220 with zero salvage value. Depreciation is $20 per year. The accounting rate of return using the original investment is

   a. 44 percent.
   b. 22 percent.
   c. 20 percent.
   d. 40 percent.
   e. None of the above.

9. If the net present value is positive, it signals that the

   a. initial investment has been recovered.
   b. required rate of return has been earned.
   c. value of the firm has increased.
   d. All of the above.
   e. Only a and b.

10. Net present value measures

    a. the profitability of an investment.
    b. the change in wealth.
    c. the change in firm value.
    d. the difference in present value of cash inflows and outflows.
    e. All of the above.

11. The net present value is calculated using

    a. accounting income.
    b. the required rate of return.
    c. the internal rate of return.
    d. the future value of cash flows.
    e. None of the above.

12. Using NPV, a project is rejected if

    a. it is equal to zero.
    b. it is positive.
    c. it is negative.
    d. it is less than the hurdle rate.
    e. it is greater than the cost of capital.

13. If the present value of future cash flows is $1,200 for an investment that requires an outlay of $1,000,the NPV is

    a. $200.
    b. $1,000.
    c. $1,200.
    d. $2,200.
    e. Can't be determined.

14. Assume an investment of $1,000 produces a future cash flow of $1,000. The discount factor for this future cash flow is 0.89. The NPV is

    a. $0.
    b. $110.
    c. $2,000.
    d. $911.
    e. None of the above.

15. Which of the following is *not* true regarding the IRR?

    a. The IRR is the interest rate that sets the present value of a project's cash inflows equal to the present value of the project's cost.
    b. The IRR is the interest rate that sets the NPV = 0.
    c. The IRR is the most reliable of the capital budgeting methods.
    d. If the IRR is greater than the required rate of return, then the project is acceptable.
    e. The popularity of IRR may be attributable to the fact that it is a rate of return, a concept that managers are comfortable with using.

16. Using IRR, a project is rejected if

    a. the IRR is less than the required rate of return.
    b. the IRR is equal to the required rate of return.
    c. the IRR is greater than the cost of capital.
    d. the IRR is greater than the required rate of return.
    e. the IRR produces a NPV = 0.

17. A postaudit

    a. is a follow-up analysis of a capital project, once implemented.
    b. compares the actual benefits with the estimated benefits.
    c. evaluates the overall outcome of the investment.
    d. proposes corrective action, if needed.
    e. All of the above.

18. Postaudits of capital projects are useful because

    a. they are not very costly.
    b. they help ensure that resources are used wisely.
    c. the assumptions underlying the original analyses are often invalidated. by changes in the actual working environment.
    d. They have no significant limitations.
    e. All of the above.

19. For competing projects, NPV is preferred to IRR because
    a. maximizing IRR may not maximize the wealth of the owners.
    b. in the final analysis, total dollars earned, not relative profitability, are what count.
    c. choosing the project with the largest NPV maximizes the wealth of the shareholders.
    d. assuming that cash flows are reinvested at the required rate of return is more realistic than assuming that cash flows are reinvested at the computed IRR.
    e. All of the above.
20. Assume there are two competing projects: A and B. Project A has a NPV of $1,000 and an IRR of 15 percent; Project B has a NPV of $800 and an IRR of 20 percent. Which of the following is true?
    a. It is not possible to use NPV or IRR to choose between the two projects.
    b. Project B should be chosen because it has a higher IRR.
    c. Project A should be chosen because it has a higher NPV.
    d. Neither project should be chosen.
    e. None of the above.

13-2

Payback Period
LO1, LO2

Each of the following parts is independent. Assume all cash flows are after-tax cash flows.

1. Kaylin Hansen has just invested $200,000 in a book and video store. She expects to receive a cash income of $60,000 per year from the investment. What is the payback period for Kaylin?
2. Kambry Day has just invested $500,000 in a new biomedical technology. She expects to receive the following cash flows over the next five years: $125,000, $175,000, $250,000, $150,000, and $100,000. What is the payback period?
3. Emily Nabors invested in a project that has a payback period of 3 years. The project brings in $120,000 per year. How much did Emily invest in the project?
4. Joseph Booth invested $250,000 in a project that pays him an even amount per year for five years. The payback period is 2.5 years. How much cash does Joseph receive each year?

13-3

Accounting Rate of Return
LO1, LO2

Each of the following parts is independent. Assume all cash flows are after-tax cash flows.

1. Cameron Company is considering the purchase of new equipment that will speed up the process for extracting copper. The equipment will cost $1,500,000 and have a life of five years with no expected salvage value. The expected cash flows associated with the project follow:

Year	Cash Revenues	Cash Expenses
1	$2,500,000	$2,000,000
2	2,500,000	2,000,000
3	2,500,000	2,000,000
4	2,500,000	2,000,000
5	2,500,000	2,000,000

   Compute the equipment's accounting rate of return.
2. Merlene Jensen is considering investing in one of the following two projects. Either project will require an investment of $20,000. The expected revenues less cash expenses for the two projects follow. Assume each project is depreciable.

Year	Project A	Project B
1	$ 6,000	$6,000
2	8,000	8,000
3	10,000	12,000
4	20,000	6,000
5	20,000	6,000

Which project should be chosen based on the accounting rate of return?

3. Suppose that a project has an accounting rate of return = 25% (based on average investment) and that the average net income of the project is $100,000. How much did the company invest in the project?
4. Suppose that a project has an accounting rate of return = 50% and that the investment is $200,000. What is the average income earned by the project?

13-4

NPV
LO1, LO3

Each of the following parts is independent. Assume all cash flows are after-tax cash flows.

1. Modinero Bank is considering the purchase of a new automated teller system. The cash benefits will be $240,000 per year. The system costs $1,360,000 and will last 10 years. Compute the NPV assuming a discount rate of 12 percent. Should the bank buy the new automated teller system?
2. Brandon Smith is interested in investing in some tools and equipment so that he can do independent remodeling. The cost of the tools and equipment is $30,000. He estimates that the return from owning his own equipment will be $9,000 per year. The tools and equipment will last six years. Assuming a required rate of return of 8 percent, calculate the NPV of the investment. Should he invest?
3. Golman Company calculated the NPV of a project and found it to be $3,550. The project's life was estimated to be six years. The required rate of return used for the NPV calculation was 10 percent. The project was expected to produce annual after-tax cash flows of $10,000. What was the required investment for the project?

13-5

IRR
LO1, LO4

1. Collins Company is considering the purchase of new equipment that will speed up the process for producing hard disk drives. The equipment will cost $1,563,500 and have a life of five years with no expected salvage value. The expected cash flows associated with the project follow:

Year	Cash Revenues	Cash Expenses
1	$1,500,000	$1,000,000
2	1,500,000	1,000,000
3	1,500,000	1,000,000
4	1,500,000	1,000,000
5	1,500,000	1,000,000

Calculate the IRR. Should the new equipment be purchased?

2. Pamela Barker is evaluating an investment in an information system that will save $100,000 per year. She estimates that the system will last 10 years. The system will cost $521,600. Her company's cost of capital is 10 percent. Calculate the project's internal rate of return. Should she acquire the new system?
3. Somerset Enterprises just announced that a new plant would be built in Wilmington, Delaware. Somerset told its shareholders that the plant has an expected life of 15 years and an expected IRR equal to 24 percent. The cost of building the plant is expected to be $2,400,000. What is the expected annual cash flow from the plant?

13-6

NPV and Competing Projects
LO1, LO6

EXCEL

Murrie Medical Clinic is investigating the possibility of investing in new blood analysis equipment. Two local manufacturers of this equipment are being considered as sources of the equipment. After-tax cash inflows for the two competing projects are as follows:

Year	Larson Equipment	Lawton Equipment
1	$120,000	$ 20,000
2	100,000	20,000
3	80,000	120,000
4	40,000	160,000
5	20,000	180,000

Both projects require an initial investment of $200,000. In both cases, assume the equipment has a life of five years with no salvage value.

Required

1. Assuming a discount rate of 12 percent, compute the net present value of each piece of equipment.
2. A third option has surfaced for equipment purchased from an out-of-state supplier. The cost is also $200,000 but this equipment will produce even cash flows over its five-year life. What must the minimum annual cash flow be for this equipment to be selected over the other two? Assume a 12 percent discount rate.

13-7

Payback; Accounting Rate of Return; NPV; IRR
LO1, LO2, LO3, LO4

Wheeler Company wants to buy a numerically controlled (NC) machine to be used in producing specially machined parts for manufacturers of trenching machines. The outlay required is $800,000. The NC equipment will last five years with no expected salvage value. The expected after-tax cash flows associated with the project follow:

Year	Cash Revenues	Cash Expenses
1	$1,300,000	$1,000,000
2	1,300,000	1,000,000
3	1,300,000	1,000,000
4	1,300,000	1,000,000
5	1,300,000	1,000,000

Required

1. Compute the payback period for the NC equipment.
2. Compute the NC equipment's accounting rate of return.
3. Compute the investment's net present value, assuming a required rate of return of 10 percent.
4. Compute the investment's internal rate of return.

13-8

Payback; Accounting Rate of Return; Present Value; NPV; IRR
LO1, LO2, LO3, LO4

The first two parts are related; the last three are independent of all other parts. Assume all cash flows are after-tax cash flows.

1. Randy Willis is considering investing in one of the following two projects. Either project will require an investment of $10,000. The expected cash flows for the two projects follow. Assume each project is depreciable.

Year	Project A	Project B
1	$ 3,000	$3,000
2	4,000	4,000
3	5,000	6,000
4	10,000	3,000
5	10,000	3,000

What is the payback period for each project? If rapid payback is important, which project should be chosen? Which would you choose?
2. Calculate the accounting rate of return for each project in Requirement 1 (the expected cash flows are the difference between cash revenues and cash expenses). Which project should be chosen based on the accounting rate of return?
3. Wilma Golding is retiring and has the option to take her retirement as a lump sum of $225,000 or to receive $24,000 per year for 20 years. Wilma's required rate of return is 8 percent. Assuming she will live for another 20 years, should she take the lump sum or the annuity?
4. David Booth is interested in investing in some tools and equipment so that he can do independent dry walling. The cost of the tools and equipment is $20,000. He estimates that the return from owning his own equipment will be $6,000 per year. The tools and equipment will last six years. Assuming a required rate of return of 8 percent, calculate the NPV of the investment. Should he invest?
5. Patsy Folson is evaluating what appears to be an attractive opportunity. She is currently the owner of a small manufacturing company and has the opportunity to acquire another small company's equipment that would provide production of a part currently purchased externally. She estimates that the savings from internal production would be $25,000 per year. She estimates that the equipment would last 10 years. The owner is asking $130,400 for the equipment. Her company's cost of capital is 10 percent. Calculate the project's internal rate of return. Should she acquire the equipment?

13-9

NPV; Basic Concepts
LO3

Gerry Company is considering an investment that requires an outlay of $200,000 and promises an after-tax cash inflow one year from now of $231,000. The company's cost of capital is 10 percent.

Required

1. Break the $231,000 future cash inflow into three components: (a) the return of the original investment, (b) the cost of capital, and (c) the profit earned on the investment. Now compute the present value of the profit earned on the investment.
2. Compute the NPV of the investment. Compare this with the present value of the profit computed in Requirement 1. What does this tell you about the meaning of NPV?

13-10

Cost of Capital; NPV
LO3

EXCEL

Bradshaw Company's Product Engineering Department has developed a new product that has a three-year life cycle. Production of the product requires development of a new process that requires a current $200,000 capital outlay. The $200,000 will be raised by issuing $120,000 of bonds and by selling new stock for $80,000. The $120,000 in bonds will have net (after-tax) interest payments of $6,000 at the end of each of the three years, with the principal being repaid at the end of Year 3. The stock issue carries with it an expectation of a 17.5 percent return, expressed in the form of dividends at the end of each year ($14,000 in dividends is expected for each of the next three years). The sources of capital for this investment represent the same proportion and costs that the company typically has. Finally, the project will produce after-tax cash inflows of $100,000 per year for the next three years.

Required

1. Compute the cost of capital for the project. (*Hint:* The cost of capital is a weighted average of the two sources of capital where the weights are the proportion of capital from each source.)
2. Compute the NPV for the project. Explain why it is not necessary to subtract the interest payments and the dividend payments and appreciation from the inflow of $40,000 in carrying out this computation.

13-11

Solving for Unknowns
LO3, LO4

Solve each of the following independent cases (assume all cash flows are after-tax cash flows):

1. Thomas Company is investing $120,000 in a project that will yield a uniform series of cash inflows over the next four years. If the internal rate of return is 14 percent, how much cash inflow per year can be expected?
2. Video Repair has decided to invest in some new electronic equipment. The equipment will have a three-year life and will produce a uniform series of cash savings. The net present value of the equipment is $1,750 using a discount rate of 8 percent. The internal rate of return is 12 percent. Determine the investment and the amount of cash savings realized each year.
3. A new lathe costing $60,096 will produce savings of $12,000 per year. How many years must the lathe last if an IRR of 18 percent is realized?
4. The NPV of a project is $3,927. The project has a life of four years and produces the following cash flows:

Year 1	$10,000	Year 3	15,000
Year 2	12,000	Year 4	?

The cost of the project is two times the cash flow produced in Year 4. The discount rate is 10 percent. Find the cost of the project and the cash flow for Year 4.

13-12

NPV versus IRR
LO6

A company is thinking about two different modifications to its current manufacturing process. The after-tax cash flows associated with the two investments follow:

Year	Project I	Project II
0	$(100,000)	$(100,000)
1	—	63,857
2	134,560	63,857

The company's cost of capital is 10 percent.

Required

1. Compute the NPV and the IRR for each investment.
2. Explain why the project with the larger NPV is the correct choice for the company.

13-13

Computation of After-Tax Cash Flows
LO7

Brandt Gardner, a financial analyst for DBJ, Inc., is evaluating the possibility of investing in two independent projects. One project entails the acquisition of two trenchers for laying cable, and the other is the acquisition of two forklifts for the warehouse. The expected annual operating revenues and expenses follow for each project:

Project A (investment in trenchers):	
Revenues	$ 270,000
Cash expenses	(135,000)
Depreciation	(45,000)
Income before income taxes	$ 90,000
Income taxes	36,000
Net income	$ 54,000
Project B (acquisition of two forklifts):	
Cash expenses	$90,000
Depreciation	15,000

Required

Compute the after-tax cash flows of each project. The tax rate is 40 percent and includes federal and state assessments.

13-14

MACRS; NPV
LO7

A company is planning to buy a set of special tools for its manufacturing operation. The cost of the tools is $12,000. The tools have a three-year life and qualify for the use of the three-year MACRS. The tax rate is 40 percent; the cost of capital is 12 percent.

Required

1. Calculate the present value of the tax depreciation shield, assuming that straight-line depreciation with a half-year life is used.
2. Calculate the present value of the tax depreciation shield, assuming that MACRS is used.
3. What is the benefit of using MACRS?

13-15

Lease or Buy
LO6, LO7

EXCEL

Megan Anderson, owner of a small company, has decided that she needs to have regular access to a car for local errands and occasional business trips. Megan is trying to decide between buying or leasing the car. The purchase cost is $30,000. The annual operating costs are estimated at $5,000. If the car is leased, a five-year lease will be acquired. The lease requires a refundable deposit of $1,000 and annual lease payments of $8,000. Operating costs, in addition to the lease payment, total $4,500 per year. The company's cost of capital is 10 percent, and its tax rate is 40 percent. If the car is purchased, MACRS depreciation will be used. (There is no expected salvage value.)

Required

Using NPV analysis, determine whether the car should be leased or purchased. Assume MACRS depreciation is used for tax purposes.

13-16

Discount Rates; Automated Manufacturing
LO8

A company is considering two competing investments. The first is for a standard piece of production equipment; the second is for some computer-aided manufacturing (CAM) equipment. The investment and after-tax operating cash flows follow:

Year	Standard Equipment	CAM
0	$(500,000)	$(2,000,000)
1	300,000	100,000
2	200,000	200,000
3	100,000	300,000
4	100,000	400,000
5	100,000	400,000
6	100,000	400,000
7	100,000	500,000
8	100,000	1,000,000
9	100,000	1,000,000
10	100,000	1,000,000

The company uses a discount rate of 18 percent for all of its investments. The company's cost of capital is 10 percent.

Required

1. Calculate the net present value for each investment using a discount rate of 18 percent.
2. Calculate the net present value for each investment using a discount rate of 10 percent.
3. Which rate should the company use to compute the net present value? Explain.

13-17

Quality; Market Share; Automated Manufacturing Environment
LO8

Refer to **Exercise 13-16**. Assume that the company's cost of capital is 14 percent.

Required

1. Calculate the NPV of each alternative using the 14 percent rate.

2. Now, assume that if the standard equipment is purchased, the competitive position of the firm will deteriorate because of lower quality (relative to competitors who did automate). Marketing estimates that the loss in market share will decrease the projected net cash inflows by 50 percent for Years 3 through 10. Recalculate the NPV of the standard equipment given this outcome. What is the decision now? Discuss the importance of assessing the effect of intangible benefits.

Problems

13-18

Basic NPV Analysis
LO2, LO3, LO4, LO6

CMA

Nathan Skousen joined Sycamore Corporation four months ago and has been assisting Jake Murray, the controller, in evaluating capital projects. Shortly, Skousen will be making his first presentation to the management committee responsible for selecting capital projects, and he has been working diligently to ensure that his analysis is correct. The management committee will be considering the following two mutually exclusive projects at this meeting. Both projects require the same initial investment and have the same project lives. Skousen has used several capital budgeting methods to evaluate each project.

	Project A	Project B
Accounting rate of return	34%	26%
Internal rate of return	16%	19%
Net present value	$2.6 million	$3.5 million
Payback period	4 years	5 years

After completing his analysis, Skousen discussed the results with Murray. Skousen believes that Project B is superior to Project A and intends to recommend Project B to the management committee. Murray replied, "I agree with you that Project B appears to be the better choice; however, the group will select Project A as they have been encouraged by the head of the committee to make their decision based on the accounting rate of return. Since none of the other calculations are negative, that 34 percent accounting rate of return will sway their thinking."

Skousen was discouraged by Murray's remarks. He contemplated leaving the accounting rate of return calculation out of the analysis he presented to the committee but realized that was not a good solution as the committee would surely request it.

Required

1. For each of the four capital budgeting methods used by Nathan Skousen to evaluate the two projects at Sycamore Corporation, explain the merits and limitations of each method.
2. Explain why both Nathan Skousen and Jake Murray believe that Project B is superior to Project A.
3. Identify three qualitative considerations that generally should be considered in capital budgeting evaluations. **(CMA adapted)**

13-19

Basic NPV Analysis
LO1, LO3

CMA

Camus Blalack, process engineer, knew that the acceptance of a new process design would depend on its economic feasibility. The new process was designed to improve environmental performance. The process design required new equipment and an infusion of working capital. The equipment would cost $300,000, and its cash operating expenses would total $60,000 per year. The equipment would last for seven years but would need a major overhaul costing $30,000 at the end of the fifth year. At the end of seven years, the equipment would be sold for $24,000. An increase in working capital totaling $30,000 would also be needed at the beginning. This would be recovered at the end of the seven years.

On the benefit side, Camus estimated that the new process would save $135,000 per year in environmental costs (fines and cleanup costs avoided). The cost of capital is 10 percent.

Required

1. Prepare a schedule of cash flows for the proposed project. Assume there are no income taxes.
2. Compute the NPV of the project. Should the new process design be accepted? **(CMA adapted)**

13-20

NPV Analysis
LO1, LO3

Carbon Communications Company is considering the production and marketing of a communications system that will increase the efficiency of messaging for small businesses or branch offices of large companies. Each unit hooked into the system is assigned a mailbox number, which can be matched to a telephone extension number, providing access to messages 24 hours a day. Up to 20 units can be hooked into the system, allowing the delivery of the same message to as many as 20 people. Personal codes can be used to make messages confidential. Furthermore, messages can be reviewed, recorded, canceled, replied to, or deleted all during the same phone call. Indicators wired to the telephone blink whenever new messages are present.

To produce this system, a $1.1 million investment in new equipment is required. The equipment would last 10 years but would need major maintenance costing $100,000 at the end of its sixth year. The salvage value of the equipment at the end of 10 years is estimated to be $40,000. If this new system is produced, working capital must also be increased by $50,000. This capital will be restored at the end of the product's life cycle, estimated to be 10 years. Revenues from the sale of the product are estimated at $1.5 million per year; cash operating expenses are estimated at $1.26 million per year.

Required

1. Prepare a schedule of cash flows for the proposed project. Assume there are no income taxes.
2. Assuming that Carbon's cost of capital is 12 percent, compute the project's NPV. Should the system be produced?

13-21

Basic IRR Analysis
LO1, LO4

Lindsey Thompson, owner of Leshow Company, was approached by a local dealer in air conditioning units. The dealer proposed replacing Leshow's old cooling system with a modern, more efficient system. The cost of the new system was quoted at $96,660, but it would save $20,000 per year in energy costs. The estimated life of the new system is 10 years, with no salvage value expected. Excited over the possibility of saving $20,000 per year and having a more reliable unit, Lindsey requested an analysis of the project's economic viability. All capital projects are required to earn at least the firm's cost of capital, which is 10 percent. There are no income taxes.

Required

1. Calculate the project's internal rate of return. Should the company acquire the new cooling system?
2. Suppose that energy savings are less than claimed. Calculate the minimum annual cash savings that must be realized for the project to earn a rate equal to the firm's cost of capital.
3. Suppose that the life of the new system is overestimated by two years. Repeat Requirements 1 and 2 under this assumption.
4. Explain the implications of the answers from Requirements 1, 2, and 3.

13-22

IRR; Uncertainty; Sensitivity Analysis LO1, LO3

CMA

Bristol Engineering, Inc., manufactures electronic components for the automotive and computer industries, as well as producing a variety of small electronic appliances that are distributed through wholesalers. The company's Research and Development Department has developed an electronic device that management believes could be modified and marketed as an electronic game.

The following information for the new product was developed from the best estimates of the marketing and production managers.

Annual sales volume	1,000,000 units
Selling price	$10 per unit
Out-of-pocket variable costs	$4 per unit
Out-of-pocket fixed costs	$2,000,000 per year
Investment required	$12,000,000
Project life	5 years

At the end of the five-year useful life, there will be no residual value.

Bristol Engineering uses the internal rate of return (IRR) method and a hurdle rate of 14 percent based on the company's cost of capital to evaluate capital investment proposals.

The toy and game industry is a new market for Bristol Engineering, and management is concerned about the reliability of the estimates. The controller has proposed applying sensitivity analysis to selected factors and is investigating some alternatives. Ignore income taxes in calculating the annual cash flows and the IRR.

Required

1. Using the best estimates, calculate the IRR for the investment proposal.
2. Compute the IRR for each of the following assumptions. Treat each item independently of the others.
   a. 10 percent reduction in the per-unit selling price.
   b. 10 percent reduction in annual sales in units.
   c. 10 percent reduction in the per-unit variable cost.
3. Briefly explain the purpose and limitation of sensitivity analysis as applied to capital budgeting. **(CMA adapted)**

13-23

NPV; Uncertainty LO1, LO3

Eden Airlines is interested in acquiring a new airplane to service a new route. The route would be from Dallas to El Paso. The airplane would fly one round-trip daily except for scheduled maintenance days. There are 15 maintenance days scheduled each year. The seating capacity of the airplane is 150. Flights are expected to be fully booked. The average revenue per passenger per flight (one-way) is $200. Annual operating costs of the airplane follow:

Fuel	$1,400,000
Flight personnel	500,000
Food and beverages	100,000
Maintenance	400,000
Other	100,000
Total	$2,500,000

The airplane will cost $100,000,000 and has an expected life of 20 years. The company requires a 14 percent return. Assume there are no income taxes.

Required

1. Calculate the NPV for the airplane. Should the company buy it?
2. In discussing the proposal, the marketing manager for the airline believes that the assumption of 100 percent booking is unrealistic. He believes that the booking

rate will be somewhere between 70 percent and 90 percent, with the most likely rate being 80 percent. Recalculate the NPV using an 80 percent seating capacity. Should the airplane be purchased?

3. Calculate the average seating rate that would be needed so that NPV = 0.
4. Suppose that the price per passenger could be increased by 10 percent without any effect on demand. What is the average seating rate needed to achieve an NPV = 0? Should the company buy the airplane?

13-24

Review of Basic Capital Budgeting Procedures
LO1, LO2, LO3, LO4

EXCEL

Dr. Whitley Avard, plastic surgeon, had just returned from a conference in which she learned of a new surgical procedure for removing wrinkles around eyes in half the usual time. Given her patient-load pressures, Dr. Avard was anxious to try out the new technique. By decreasing the time spent on eye treatments or procedures, she could perform more services within a work period and thus increase her total revenues. Unfortunately, in order to implement the new procedure, some special equipment costing $74,000 was needed. The equipment had an expected life of four years, with a salvage value of $6,000. Dr. Avard estimated that her cash revenues would increase by the following amounts:

Year	Revenue Increases
1	$19,800
2	27,000
3	32,400
4	32,400

She also expected additional cash expenses amounting to $3,000 per year. The cost of capital is 12 percent. Assume there are no income taxes.

Required

1. Compute the payback period for the new equipment.
2. Compute the accounting rate of return using both original investment and average investment.
3. Compute the NPV and IRR for the project. Should Dr. Avard purchase the new equipment? Should she be concerned about payback or the accounting rate of return in making this decision?
4. Before finalizing her decision, Dr. Avard decided to call two plastic surgeons who had been using the new procedure for the past six months. The conversations revealed a somewhat less glowing report than she had received at the conference. The new procedure reduced the time required by about 25 percent rather than the advertised 50 percent. Dr. Avard estimated that the net operating cash flows of the procedure would be cut by one-third because of the extra time and cost involved (salvage value would be unaffected). Using this information, recompute the NPV of the project. What would you now recommend?

13-25

Replacement Decision; Basic NPV Analysis
LO1, LO6, LO7

Madison Company is considering replacing its existing mainframe computer with a new model manufactured by a different company. The existing computer was acquired three years ago, has a remaining life of five years, and will have a salvage value of $10,000. The book value is $200,000. Straight-line depreciation with a half-life convention is being used for tax purposes. The computer's cash operating costs, including software, personnel, and other supplies, total $100,000 per year.

The new computer has an initial cost of $500,000 and will have cash operating costs of $50,000 per year. The new computer will have a life of five years and a salvage value of $100,000 at the end of the fifth year. MACRS depreciation will be used for tax purposes. If the new computer is purchased, the old one will be sold for $50,000. The company needs to decide whether to keep the old computer or buy the new one. The cost of capital is 12 percent. The tax rate is 40 percent.

Required

Compute the NPV of each alternative. Should the company keep the old computer, or buy the new one?

13-26

Lease versus Buy
LO1, LO6, LO7

Trasky Company is trying to decide whether it should purchase or lease a new automated machine to be used in the production of a new product. If purchased, the new machine would cost $100,000 and would be used for 10 years. The salvage value at the end of 10 years is estimated at $20,000. The machine would be depreciated using MACRS over a seven-year period. The annual maintenance and operating costs would be $20,000. Annual revenues are estimated at $55,000.

If the machine is leased, the company would need to pay annual lease payments of $20,700. The first lease payment and a deposit of $5,000 are due immediately. The last lease payment is paid at the beginning of Year 10. The deposit is refundable at the end of the tenth year. In addition, under a normal contract, the company must pay for all maintenance and operating costs, although the leasing company does offer a service contract that will provide annual maintenance (on leased machines only). The contract must be paid up front and costs $30,000. Trasky estimates that the contract will reduce its annual maintenance and operating costs by $10,000. Trasky's cost of capital is 14 percent. The tax rate is 40 percent.

Required

1. Prepare schedules showing the after-tax cash flows for each alternative. (Prepare schedules for the lease alternative with and without the service contract; assume that the service contract is amortized on a straight-line basis for 10 years.) Include all revenues and costs associated with each alternative.
2. Compute the NPV for each alternative assuming that Trasky does not purchase the service contract. Should the machine be purchased or leased? For this analysis, was it necessary to include all of the costs and revenues for each alternative? Explain.
3. Compute the NPV for the lease alternative assuming that the service contract is purchased. Does this change your decision about leasing? What revenues and costs could be excluded without affecting the conclusion?

13-27

Competing Environmental Management Investments; NPV; Basic Analysis
LO1, LO6, LO7

Shane Sorensen, the CEO for Fobbs Manufacturing, was wondering which of two pollution control systems he ought to choose. The company's current production process produced a gaseous and a liquid residue. A recent state law mandated that emissions of these residues be reduced to levels considerably below current performance. Failure to reduce the emissions would invoke stiff fines and possible closure of the operating plant. Fortunately, the new law provided a transition period, and Shane had used the time wisely. His engineers had developed two separate proposals. The first proposal involved the acquisition of scrubbers for gaseous emissions and a treatment facility to remove the liquid residues. The second proposal was more radical. It entailed the redesign of the manufacturing process and the acquisition of new production equipment to support this new design. The new process would solve the environmental problem by avoiding the production of residues.

Although the equipment for each proposal normally would qualify as seven-year property, the state managed to obtain an agreement with the federal government to allow any pollution abatement equipment to qualify as five-year property. State tax law follows federal guidelines. Both proposals qualify for the five-year property benefit.

Shane's marketing vice president has projected an increase in revenues because of favorable environmental performance publicity. This increase is the result of selling more of Fobbs's products to environmentally conscious customers. However, because the second approach is "greener," the vice president believes that the revenue increase will be greater. Cost and other data relating to the two proposals are given below.

	Scrubbers and Treatment	Process Redesign
Initial outlay	$25,000,000	$50,000,000
Incremental revenues	5,000,000	15,000,000
Incremental cash expenses	12,000,000	5,000,000

The expected life for each investment's equipment is six years. The expected salvage value is $1,000,000 for scrubbers and treatment equipment and $1,500,000 for process redesign equipment. The combined federal and state tax rate is 40 percent. The cost of capital is 10 percent.

Required

1. Compute the NPV of each proposal and make a recommendation to Shane.
2. The environmental manager observes that the scrubbers and treatment facility enable the company to just meet state emission standards. She feels that the standards will likely increase within three years. If so, this would entail a modification at the end of three years costing an additional $4 million. Also, she is concerned that continued liquid residue releases—even those meeting state standards—could push a local lake into a hazardous state by the end of three years. If so, this could prompt political action requiring the company to clean up the lake. Cleanup costs would range between $20,000,000 and $30,000,000. Analyze and discuss the effect this new information has on the two alternatives. If you have read the chapter on environmental cost management (Chapter 16), describe how the concept of ecoefficiency applies to this setting.

13-28

Capital Investment; Advanced Manufacturing Environment
LO7, LO8

"I know that it's the thing to do," insisted Kathy Shorts, vice-president of finance for Coalville Manufacturing. "If we are going to be competitive, we need to build this completely automated plant."

"I'm not so sure," replied Steve Thomas, CEO of Coalville. "The savings from labor reductions and increased productivity are only $4 million per year. The price tag for this factory—and it's a small one—is $45 million. That gives a payback period of more than eleven years. That's a long time to put the company's money at risk."

"Yeah, but you're overlooking the savings that we'll get from the increase in quality," interjected John Simpson, production manager. "With this system, we can decrease our waste and our rework time significantly. Those savings are worth another million dollars per year."

"Another million will only cut the payback to about nine years," retorted Steve. "Ron, you're the marketing manager—do you have any insights?"

"Well, there are other factors to consider, such as service quality and market share," said Ron Brewer. "I think that increasing our product quality and improving our delivery service will make us a lot more competitive. I know for a fact that two of our competitors have decided against automation. That'll give us a shot at their customers, provided our product is of higher quality and we can deliver it faster. I estimate that it'll increase our net cash benefits by another $2.4 million."

"Wow! Now that's impressive," Steve exclaimed, nearly convinced. "The payback is now getting down to a reasonable level."

"I agree," said Kathy, "but we do need to be sure that it's a sound investment. I know that estimates for construction of the facility have gone as high as $48 million. I also know that the expected residual value, after the 20 years of service we expect to get, is $5 million. I think I had better see if this project can cover our 14 percent cost of capital."

"Now wait a minute, Kathy," Steve demanded. "You know that I usually insist on a 20 percent rate of return, especially for a project of this magnitude."

Required

1. Compute the NPV of the project using the original savings and investment figures. Do the calculation for discount rates of 14 percent and 20 percent. Include salvage value in the computation.
2. Compute the NPV of the project using the additional benefits noted by the production and marketing managers. Also, use the original cost estimate of $45 million. Again, do the calculation for both possible discount rates.
3. Compute the NPV of the project using all estimates of cash flows, including the possible initial outlay of $49.8 million. Do the calculation using discount rates of 14 percent and 20 percent.
4. If you were making the decision, what would you do? Explain.

13-29

Postaudit; Sensitivity Analysis
LO5, LO6, LO7

Newmarge Products, Inc., is evaluating a new design for one of its manufacturing processes. The new design will eliminate the production of a toxic solid residue. The initial cost of the system is estimated at $860,000 and includes computerized equipment, software, and installation. There is no expected salvage value. The new system has a useful life of eight years and is projected to produce cash operating savings of $270,000 per year over the old system (reducing labor costs and costs of processing and disposing of toxic waste). In addition to the operating savings, the new system will produce a depreciation tax shield absent under the old system. Straight-line depreciation (with half-year convention) will be used for tax purposes. The tax rate is 40 percent, and the cost of capital is 16 percent.

Required

1. Compute the NPV of the new system. Use the proper class life for depreciation.
2. One year after implementation, the internal audit staff noted the following about the new system: (1) the cost of acquiring the system was $60,000 more than expected due to higher installation costs, and (2) the annual cost savings were $20,000 less than expected because more labor cost was needed than anticipated. Using the changes in expected costs and benefits, compute the NPV as if this information had been available one year ago. Did the company make the right decision?
3. Upon receiving the results mentioned in the postaudit, the marketing manager indicated in a memo to the Internal Auditing Department that revenues had increased by $100,000 per year because of increased purchases by environmentally sensitive customers. Describe the effect this has on the analysis in Requirement 2.
4. Why is a postaudit beneficial to a firm?

13-30

Advanced Manufacturing Environment
LO7, LO8

Pearson Manufacturing, Inc., produces microwave ovens, electric ranges, and freezers. Because of increasing competition, Pearson is considering making an investment in a computer-aided manufacturing (CAM) system. The microwave plant has been selected for initial evaluation. The CAM system for the microwave line would replace an existing system (purchased one year ago for $6 million). Although the existing system will be fully depreciated in nine years, it is expected to last another 10 years. The CAM system would also have a useful life of 10 years.

The existing system is capable of producing 100,000 microwave units per year. Sales and production data using the existing system are provided by the Accounting Department:

Sales per year (units)	100,000
Selling price	$300
Costs per unit:	
Direct materials	80
Direct labor	90
Volume-related overhead	20
Direct fixed overhead	40*

*These are all cash expenses with the exception of depreciation, which is $6 per unit. The existing equipment is being depreciated using straight-line with no salvage value considered. The CAM system will cost $34 million to purchase plus an estimated $20 million in software and implementation. (Assume that all investment outlays occur at the beginning of the first year.) If the CAM equipment is purchased, the old equipment can be sold for $3 million.

The CAM system will require fewer parts for production and will produce with less waste. Because of this, the direct materials cost per unit will be reduced by 25 percent. Automation will also require fewer support activities and, as a consequence, volume-related overhead will be reduced by $5 per unit and direct fixed overhead (other than depreciation) by $17 per unit. Direct labor is reduced by 66 $^{2}/_{3}$ percent. Assume, for simplicity, that the new investment will be depreciated on a pure straight-line basis for tax purposes with no salvage value. Ignore the half-life convention.

The firm's cost of capital is 12 percent, but management chooses to use 18 percent as the required rate of return for evaluation of investments. The tax rate is 40 percent.

Required

1. Compute the net present value for the old system and the CAM system. Which system would the company choose?
2. Repeat the net present value analysis of Requirement 1 using 12 percent as the discount rate.
3. Upon seeing the projected sales for the old system, the marketing manager commented: "Sales of 100,000 units per year cannot be maintained in the current competitive environment for more than one year unless we buy the CAM system. The CAM system will allow us to compete on the basis of quality and lead time. If we keep the old system, our sales will drop by 10,000 units per year." Repeat the net present value analysis using this new information and a 12 percent discount rate.
4. An industrial engineer for Pearson noticed that salvage value for the CAM equipment had not been included in the analysis. He estimated that the equipment could be sold for $4 million at the end of 10 years. He also estimated that the equipment of the old system would have no salvage value at the end of 10 years. Repeat the net present value analysis using this information, the information in Requirement 3, and a 12 percent discount rate.
5. Given the outcomes of the previous four requirements, comment on the importance of providing accurate inputs for assessing investments in CAM systems.

13-31

Inflation and Capital Investment LO6, LO7

Thayn Thompson, divisional manager, has been pushing headquarters to grant approval for the installation of a new flexible manufacturing system. Finally, in the last executive meeting, Thayn was told that if he could show how the new system would increase the firm's value, it would be approved. Thayn gathered the following information:

	Old System	Flexible System
Initial investment	—	$1,250,000
Annual operating costs	$350,000	$ 95,000
Annual depreciation	$100,000	?
Tax rate*	34%	34%

(Continued)

Cost of capital	12%	12%
Expected life	10 years	10 years
Salvage value	none	none

*In order to locate its operations in the state, the company was exempted from state income taxes for 20 years. Since the company has only operated in the state for 10 years, the state tax rate could be ignored in the analysis.

With the exception of the cost of capital, this information ignores the rate of inflation, which has been 4 percent per year and is expected to continue at this level for the next decade.

Required

1. Compute the NPV for each system.
2. Compute the NPV for each system adjusting the future cash flows for the rate of inflation.
3. Comment on the importance of adjusting cash flows for inflationary effects.

Managerial Decision Cases

13-32

Capital Investment and Ethical Behavior
LO3

Manny Carson, CMA and controller of Wakeman Enterprises, had been given permission to acquire a new computer and software for the company's accounting system. The capital investment analysis had shown an NPV of $100,000; however, the initial estimates of acquisition and installation costs had been made on the basis of tentative costs without any formal bids. Manny now has two formal bids, one that would allow the firm to meet or beat the original projected NPV and one that would reduce the projected NPV by $50,000. The second bid involves a system that would increase both the initial cost and the operating cost.

Normally, Manny would take the first bid without hesitation. However, Todd Downing, the owner of the firm presenting the second bid, was a close friend. Manny had called Todd and explained the situation, offering Todd an opportunity to alter his bid and win the job. Todd thanked Manny and then made a counteroffer.

Todd: Listen, Manny, this job at the original price is the key to a successful year for me. The revenues will help me gain approval for the loan I need for renovation and expansion. If I don't get that loan, I see hard times ahead. The financial stats for loan approval are so marginal that reducing the bid price may blow my chances.

Manny: Losing the bid altogether would be even worse, don't you think?

Todd: True. However, I have a suggestion. If you grant me the job, I will have the capability of adding personnel. I know that your son is looking for a job, and I can offer him a good salary and a promising future. Additionally, I'll be able to take you and your wife on that vacation to Hawaii that we have been talking about.

Manny: Well, you have a point. My son is having an awful time finding a job, and he has a wife and three kids to support. My wife is tired of having them live with us. She and I could use a vacation. I doubt that the other bidder would make any fuss if we turned it down. Its offices are out of state, after all.

Todd: Out of state? All the more reason to turn it down. Given the state's economy, it seems almost criminal to take business outside. Those are the kind of business decisions that cause problems for people like your son.

Required

Evaluate the ethical behavior of Manny. Should Manny have called Todd in the first place? What if Todd had agreed to meet the lower bid price—would there have been any problems? Identify the standards of ethical conduct (listed in Chapter 1) that Manny may be violating, if any.

13-33

Payback; NPV; IRR; Effects of Differences in Sales on Project Viability LO2, LO3, LO4

Shaftel Ready Mix is a processor and supplier of concrete, aggregate, and rock products. The company operates in the intermountain western United States. Currently, Shaftel has 14 cement-processing plants and a labor force of more than 375 employees. With the exception of cement powder, all materials (for example, aggregates and sand) are produced internally by the company. The demand for concrete and aggregates has been growing steadily nationally, and in the West, the growth rate has been above the national average. Because of this growth, Shaftel has more than tripled its gross revenues over the past 10 years.

Of the intermountain states, Arizona has been experiencing the most growth. Processing plants have been added over the past several years, and the company is considering the addition of yet another plant to be located in Scottsdale. A major advantage of another plant in Arizona is the ability to operate year round, a feature not found in less temperate states such as Utah and Wyoming.

In setting up the new plant, land would have to be purchased and a small building constructed. Equipment and furniture would not need to be purchased; these items would be transferred from a plant that had been opened in Wyoming during the oil-boom period and closed a few years after the end of that boom. However, the equipment needs some repair and modifications before it can be used. It has a book value of $200,000, and the furniture has a book value of $30,000. Neither has any outside market value. Other costs, such as the installation of a silo, well, electrical hookups, and so on, will be incurred. No salvage value is expected. The summary of the initial investment costs by category is as follows:

Land	$ 20,000
Building	135,000
Equipment:	
Book value	200,000
Modifications	20,000
Furniture (book value)	30,000
Silo	20,000
Well	80,000
Electrical hookups	27,000
General setup	50,000
Total	$582,000

Estimates concerning the operation of the Scottsdale plant follow:

Life of plant and equipment	10 years
Expected annual sales (in cubic yards of cement)	35,000
Selling price (per cubic yard of cement)	$45.00
Variable costs (per cubic yard of cement):	
Cement	$12.94
Sand/gravel	6.42
Fly ash	1.13
Admixture	1.53
Driver labor	3.24
Mechanics	1.43
Plant operations (batching and cleanup)	1.39
Loader operator	0.50
Truck parts	1.75
Fuel	1.48
Other	3.27
Total variable costs	$35.08

(Continued)

Fixed costs (annual):	
Salaries	$135,000
Insurance	75,000
Telephone	5,000
Depreciation	58,200*
Utilities	25,000
Total fixed costs	$298,200

*Straight-line depreciation is calculated using all initial investment costs over a ten-year period assuming no salvage value.

After reviewing these data, Karl Flemming, vice president of operations, argued against the proposed plant. Karl was concerned because the plant would earn significantly less than the normal 8.3 percent return on sales. All other plants in the company were earning between 7.5 and 8.5 percent on sales. Karl also noted that it would take more than five years to recover the total initial outlay of $582,000. In the past, the company had always insisted that payback be no more than four years. The company's cost of capital is 10 percent. Assume there are no income taxes.

Required

1. Prepare a variable-costing income statement for the proposed plant. Compute the ratio of net income to sales. Is Karl correct that the return on sales is significantly lower than the company average?
2. Compute the payback period for the proposed plant. Is Karl right that the payback period is greater than four years? Explain. Suppose that you were told that the equipment being transferred from Wyoming could be sold for its book value. Would this affect your answer?
3. Compute the NPV and the IRR for the proposed plant. Would your answer be affected if you were told that the furniture and equipment could be sold for their book values? If so, repeat the analysis with this effect considered.
4. Compute the cubic yards of cement that must be sold for the new plant to break even. Using this break-even volume, compute the NPV and the IRR. Would the investment be acceptable? If so, explain why an investment that promises to do nothing more than break even can be viewed as acceptable.
5. Compute the volume of cement that must be sold for the IRR to equal the firm's cost of capital. Using this volume, compute the firm's expected annual income. Explain this result.

13-34

Cash Flows; NPV; Choice of Discount Rate; Advanced Manufacturing Environment
LO1, LO6, LO7, LO8

Charles Bradshaw, president and owner of Wellington Metal Works, had just returned from a trip to Europe.[1] While there, he had toured several plants using robotic manufacturing. Seeing the efficiency and success of these companies, Charles became convinced that robotic manufacturing is the wave of the future and that Wellington could gain a competitive advantage by adopting the new technology.

Based on this vision, Charles requested an analysis detailing the costs and benefits of robotic manufacturing for the material handling and merchandising equipment group. This group of products consists of such items as cooler shelving, stocking carts, and bakery racks. The products are sold directly to supermarkets.

A committee, consisting of the controller, the marketing manager, and the production manager, was given the responsibility of preparing the analysis. As a starting point, the controller provided the following information on expected revenues and expenses for the existing manual system:

1 This case is based, in part, on David A. Greenberg, "Robotics: One Small Company's Experience," in *Cost Accounting for the 90's* (Montvale, NJ: National Association of Accountants, 1986): pp. 57–63.

		Percentage of Sales
Sales	$400,000	100%
Less: Variable expenses[a]	228,000	57
Contribution margin	$172,000	43
Less: Fixed expenses[b]	92,000	23
Income before income taxes	$ 80,000	20

[a]Variable cost detail (as a percentage of sales):
Direct materials, 16%
Direct labor, 20%
Variable overhead, 9%
Variable selling, 12%
[b]Of the total, $20,000 is depreciation; the rest is cash expenses.

Given the current competitive environment, the marketing manager thought that this level of profitability would likely not change for the next decade.

After some investigation into various robotic equipment, the committee settled on an Aide 900 system, a robot that has the capability to weld stainless steel or aluminum. It is capable of being programmed to adjust the path, angle, and speed of the torch. The production manager was excited about the robotic system because it would eliminate the need to hire welders, which was so attractive because the market for welders seemed perpetually tight. By reducing the dependence on welders, better production scheduling and fewer late deliveries would result. Moreover, the robot's production rate is four times that of a person.

It was also discovered that robotic welding is superior in quality to manual welding. As a consequence, some of the costs of poor quality could be reduced. By providing better-quality products and avoiding late deliveries, the marketing manager was convinced that the company would have such a competitive edge that it would increase sales by 50 percent for the affected product group by the end of the fourth year. The marketing manager provided the following projections for the next 10 years, the useful life of the robotic equipment:

	Year 1	Year 2	Year 3	Years 4–10
Sales	$400,000	$450,000	$500,000	$600,000

Currently, the company employs four welders, who work 40 hours per week and 50 weeks per year at an average wage of $10 per hour. If the robot is acquired, it will need one operator who will be paid $10 per hour.

Because of improved quality, the robotic system will also reduce the cost of direct materials by 25 percent, the cost of variable overhead by 33.33 percent, and variable selling expenses by 10 percent. All of these reductions will take place immediately after the robotic system is in place and operating. Fixed costs will be increased by the depreciation associated with the robot. The robot will be depreciated using MACRS. (The manual system uses straight-line depreciation without a half-year convention and has a current book value of $200,000.) If the robotic system is acquired, the old system will be sold for $40,000.

The robotic system requires the following initial investment:

Purchase price	$380,000
Installation	70,000
Training	30,000
Engineering	40,000

At the end of 10 years, the robot will have a salvage value of $20,000. Assume that the company's cost of capital is 12 percent. The tax rate is 34 percent.

Required

1. Prepare a schedule of after-tax cash flows for the manual and robotic systems.

2. Using the schedule of cash flows computed in Requirement 1, compute the NPV for each system. Should the company invest in the robotic system?
3. In practice, many financial officers tend to use a higher discount rate than is justified by what the firm's cost of capital is. For example, a firm may use a discount rate of 20 percent when its cost of capital is or could be 12 percent. Offer some reasons for this practice. Assume that the annual after-tax cash benefit of adopting the robotic system is $80,000 per year more than the manual system. The initial outlay for the robotic system is $340,000. Compute the NPV using 12 percent and 20 percent. Would the robotic system be acquired if 20 percent is used? Could this conservative approach have a negative impact on a firm's ability to stay competitive?

Research Assignments

13-35

Cybercase
LO1, LO5, LO6

Most private-sector organizations as well as state governments develop separate budgets for capital expenditures. At present, the federal budget makes no distinction between capital outlays and operating expenses. There are some who argue that the lack of a federal capital budget encourages bad decisions. Since a $20 million outlay for a building is treated in the same way as $20 million spent on operating expenses, there may be a bias toward leasing rather than buying a building. Furthermore, the amount spent on capital goods versus consumption goods does have a bearing on economic growth. Yet the federal government continues to follow a unified budgeting approach.

Required

Search the Internet to obtain the pros and cons of federal capital budgeting. Prepare a brief summary of the various arguments that favor the establishment of a federal capital budget. Additionally, prepare a brief summary of the arguments that favor the continuation of the current unified approach. Explain which side of the debate you would support and why.

13-36

Capital Budgeting and the Environment
LO1, LO8

Pollution prevention projects are similar to investments in automated technology in the sense that more attention should be paid to the inputs used in discounted cash flow models. How this is done or should be done is a challenging question. How much attention that firms actually pay to environmental costs is also an interesting issue. The Environmental Protection Agency (EPA) has information on both of these questions/issues.

Required

1. Go to the EPA website in the chapter web links at the Interactive Study Guide on http://www.thomsonedu.com/accounting/hansen, and find the page on educational resources. Within the EPA's website, search for "capital budgeting." You should then gain access to the report: "Environmental Cost Accounting for Capital Budgeting: A Benchmark Survey of Management Accountants." Describe the results of this survey on capital budgeting and environmental costs that was conducted in collaboration with the Institute of Management Accountants.
2. Now, go to http://www.p2pays.org/ref/01/00047/6-03.htm. This document discusses the P2/Finance software developed by the Tellus Institute. Describe what this software is and what it does. Comment on the objectives of the software relative to the capital budgeting approach advocated for the advanced manufacturing environment. Now conduct a search of the internet using P2/Finance software as the search topic. Is there evidence of the software being used?

chapter 14

Inventory Management

learning objectives

After studying this chapter, you should be able to:

1. Describe the traditional inventory management model.
2. Discuss JIT inventory management.
3. Explain the theory of constraints, and tell how it can be used to manage inventory.

Scenario

SWASEY

For 20 years, Swasey Trenchers had been a leader in the field of trenching equipment. Over the past five years, however, the company had lost 20 percent of its market share. Competitors were offering a higher-quality product at a lower price and with better delivery performance. Sam Yeager, president and owner of Swasey Trenchers, Inc., looked into the problem and felt that the solution was automation. He was prepared to sink millions into that approach, convinced that automating would improve quality, lower manufacturing costs, and cut down the lead time for production. Because so much money was involved, he hired a well-respected industry consultant, Shirley Williams, to tell him how to automate and exactly what type of equipment to buy.

Shirley studied the situation at Swasey and compared operating conditions with those of others in the same industry. Her recommendation surprised Sam Yeager. She advised him not to automate, but to simplify the company's purchasing and manufacturing by installing a just-in-time system and to use the theory of constraints to structure improvements.

Shirley noted that case after case had shown that 80 percent of the competitive benefits from automation can be achieved by implementing JIT—and at a significantly decreased cost. Another company in the same line of business was having a difficult time competing. It needed 24 weeks to produce one of its products from start to finish, while a Japanese competitor produced and delivered the same product in six weeks. After installing a JIT system, the firm was able to produce the trencher in only 20 days. In some cases, however, the theory of constraints offers even more benefits. An electronic division of **Ford** used JIT to reduce its lead time from 10.6 to 8.5 days. But after one year of using the theory of constraints, lead time was reduced to 2.2 days, and then to less than two shifts. When **Boeing** used the theory of constraints, it managed to reduce its lead time by 75 percent.

Reducing lead time could lead to other benefits. Methods like JIT purchasing and manufacturing and the theory of constraints can reduce inventories—materials, work in process, and finished goods—to much lower levels. Firms often tie up 40 percent or more of their assets in inventory. That's a lot of nonproductive capital. Decreasing lead time allows a company to reduce its inventories, freeing up a lot of capital to be used elsewhere. Other inventory-related costs are also avoided, and reducing or avoiding these costs can make a company more competitive.

Shirley advised Sam to implement JIT. When that is accomplished, he would be better able to see where automation might be of the most benefit. The strategy is to simplify, automate, integrate, and continuously seek ways of improving.

Questions to Think About

1. Why do firms carry inventory?
2. What are inventory costs?
3. What can be done to minimize inventory costs?
4. How does JIT reduce inventories?
5. What are the weaknesses of JIT?
6. How does using the theory of constraints reduce inventories?
7. Why is effective management of inventory so important?

Traditional Inventory Management

Objective 1

Describe the traditional inventory management model.

Companies find that they must manage levels of inventory to establish a long-term competitive advantage. Quality, product engineering, prices, overtime, excess capacity, ability to respond to customers (due-date performance), lead times, and overall profitability are all affected by inventory levels. In general, firms with higher inventory levels than their competitors tend to be in a worse competitive position. Inventory management policy has become a competitive weapon.

How inventory policy can be used to establish a competitive advantage is the focus of this chapter. We start by reviewing the traditional inventory management model that has been the mainstay of American firms for decades. Learning the basics of this model and its underlying conceptual foundation will help us understand where it can still be appropriately applied. Understanding traditional inventory management also provides the necessary background for grasping the advantages of inventory management methods that are used in the advanced manufacturing environment such as JIT and the theory of constraints.

Inventory Costs

In a world of certainty—a world in which the demand for a product or material is known with certainty for a given period of time (usually a year)—two major costs are associated with inventory. If the inventory is a material or good purchased from an outside source, then these inventory-related costs are known as *ordering costs* and *carrying costs*. If the material or good is produced internally, then the costs are called *setup costs* and *carrying costs*.

Ordering costs are the costs of placing and receiving an order. Examples include the costs of processing an order (clerical costs and documents), the cost of insurance for shipment, and unloading costs.

Setup costs are the costs of preparing equipment and facilities so they can be used to produce a particular product or component. Examples are wages of idled production workers, the cost of idled production facilities (lost income), and the costs of test runs (labor, materials, and overhead).

Carrying costs are the costs of carrying inventory. Examples include insurance, inventory taxes, obsolescence, the opportunity cost of funds tied up in inventory, handling costs, and storage space.

Ordering costs and setup costs are similar in nature—both represent costs that must be incurred to acquire inventory. They differ only in the nature of the prerequisite activity (filling out and placing an order versus configuring equipment and facilities). Thus, in the discussion that follows, any reference to ordering costs can be viewed as a reference to setup costs.

If demand is not known with certainty, a third category of inventory costs—called *stockout costs*—exists. **Stockout costs** are the costs of not having a product available when demanded by a customer. Examples are lost sales (both current and future), the costs of expediting (increased transportation charges, overtime, and so on), and the costs of interrupted production.

Traditional Reasons for Holding Inventory

Maximizing profits requires that inventory-related costs be minimized. But minimizing carrying costs favors ordering or producing in small lot sizes, whereas minimizing ordering costs favors large, infrequent orders (minimization of setup costs favors long, infrequent production runs). Thus, minimizing carrying costs encourages small

Managers Decide

iPod Shortage Forces Apple to Get Creative

December 2004 was a difficult time for many consumers on the hunt for the more popular Apple iPod models. The strong demand throughout the year apparently didn't give Apple management a clear enough indication of the demand during the critically important Christmas season. The iPod accounts for approximately 25 percent of total Apple sales, and the shortages of certain models (especially the variously colored iPod minis) hurt not only iPod sales but the sales of other Apple products as well.

To cope with the unexpected surge in demand, Apple managers had to deal with manufacturing and distribution constraints. At least one factory is located in Asia, meaning that the lead time for shipment of production in that facility is longer due to the increased transportation time. Marketing managers also implemented strategies to deal with consumer disappointment—including encouraging consumers to check Apple retail stores for the product, or substituting other iPod models for the ones most prone to shortages. Also getting into the act was eBay, which created an iPod category on its site. Consumers able to purchase a popular model in one part of the country offered to sell to bidding consumers in other parts of the county. ■

Source: Nick Wingfield, "Out of Tune: IPod Shortage Rocks Apple," *Wall Street Journal* (December 16, 2004), http://online.wsj.com/article/SB110314977967901339.html?mod=home_whats_news_us.

or no inventories, and minimizing ordering or setup costs encourages larger inventories. The need to balance these two sets of costs so that the total cost of carrying and ordering can be minimized is one reason organizations choose to carry inventory.

Dealing with uncertainty in demand is a second major reason for holding inventory. Even if the ordering or setup costs were negligible, organizations would still carry inventory because of stockout costs. If the demand for materials or products is greater than expected, inventory can serve as a buffer, giving organizations the ability to meet delivery dates (thus keeping customers satisfied). Although balancing conflicting costs and dealing with uncertainty are the two most frequently cited reasons for carrying inventories, other reasons also exist.

Inventories of parts and raw materials are often viewed as necessary because of supply uncertainties. That is, inventory buffers of parts and materials are needed to keep production flowing in case of late deliveries or no deliveries (strikes, bad weather, and bankruptcy are examples of uncertain events that can cause an interruption in supply). Unreliable production processes may also create a demand for producing extra inventory. For example, a company may decide to produce more units than needed to meet demand because the production process usually yields a large number of nonconforming units. Similarly, buffers of inventories may be required to continue supplying customers or processes with goods even if a process goes down because of a failed machine. Finally, organizations may acquire larger inventories than normal to take advantage of quantity discounts or to avoid anticipated price increases. Exhibit 14-1 summarizes the reasons typically offered for carrying inventory. It's important to realize that these are reasons that are given to *justify* carrying inventories. A host of other reasons can be offered that *encourage* the carrying of inventories. For example, performance measures such as measures of machine and labor efficiency may promote the buildup of inventories.

1. To balance ordering or setup costs and carrying costs.
2. To satisfy customer demand (for example, meet delivery dates).
3. To avoid shutting down manufacturing facilities because of
   a. machine failure
   b. defective parts
   c. unavailable parts
   d. late delivery of parts
4. To buffer against unreliable production processes.
5. To take advantage of discounts.
6. To hedge against future price increases.

Exhibit 14-1 Traditional Reasons for Carrying Inventory

Economic Order Quantity: The Traditional Inventory Model

In developing an inventory policy, two basic questions must be addressed:

1. How much should be ordered (or produced)?
2. When should the order be placed (or the setup done)?

The first question needs to be addressed before the second can be answered.

Order Quantity and Total Ordering and Carrying Costs Assume that demand is known. In choosing an order quantity or a lot size for production, managers need to be concerned only with ordering (or setup) and carrying costs. The total ordering (or setup) and carrying costs can be described by the following equation:

$$\begin{aligned} TC &= PD/Q + CQ/2 \\ &= \text{Ordering cost} + \text{Carrying cost} \end{aligned} \tag{14.1}$$

where TC = The total ordering (or setup) and carrying costs
P = The cost of placing and receiving an order (or the cost of setting up a production run)
D = The known annual demand
Q = The number of units ordered each time an order is placed (or the lot size for production)
C = The cost of carrying one unit of stock for one year

The cost of carrying inventory can be computed for any organization that carries inventories, including retail, service, and manufacturing organizations. Of course, the inventory cost model using setup costs and lot size as inputs pertains only to those organizations that produce their own inventories (parts or finished goods). To illustrate the application for a service organization, assume that the following values apply for a part used in the repair of refrigerators (the part is purchased from external suppliers):

$$\begin{aligned} D &= 10{,}000 \text{ units} \\ Q &= 1{,}000 \text{ units} \\ P &= \$25 \text{ per order} \\ C &= \$2 \text{ per unit} \end{aligned}$$

Dividing D by Q produces the number of orders per year, which is 10 (10,000/1,000). Multiplying the number of orders per year by the cost of placing and receiving an order ($D/Q \times P$) yields the total ordering cost of \$250 ($10 \times \$25$).

The total carrying cost for the year is given by $CQ/2$; this expression is equivalent to multiplying the average inventory on hand ($Q/2$) by the carrying cost per unit (C). For an order of 1,000 units with a carrying cost of \$2 per unit, the average inventory is 500 (1,000/2), and the carrying cost for the year is \$1,000 (500 × \$2). (Assuming average inventory to be $Q/2$ is equivalent to assuming that inventory is consumed uniformly.)

Applying Equation 14.1, the total cost is \$1,250 (\$250 + \$1,000). An order quantity of 1,000 with a total cost of \$1,250, however, may not be the best choice. Some other order quantity may produce a lower total cost. The objective is to find the order quantity that minimizes the total cost. This order quantity is called the **economic order quantity (EOQ)**. The EOQ model is an example of a *push inventory system*. In a push system, the acquisition of inventory is initiated in anticipation of future demand—not in reaction to present demand. Fundamental to the analysis is the assessment of D, the future demand.

Computing EOQ

Since EOQ is the quantity that minimizes Equation 14.1, a formula for computing this quantity is easily derived:[1]

$$Q = EOQ = \sqrt{2PD/C} \quad (14.2)$$

Using the data from the preceding example, the EOQ can be computed using Equation 14.2:

$$\begin{aligned} EOQ &= \sqrt{(2 \times \$25 \times 10{,}000)/\$2} \\ &= \sqrt{250{,}000} \\ &= 500 \end{aligned}$$

Substituting 500 as the value of Q into Equation 14.1 yields a total cost of \$1,000. The number of orders placed would be 20 (10,000/500); thus, the total ordering cost is \$500 (20 × \$25). The average inventory is 250 (500/2), with a total carrying cost of \$500 (250 × \$2). Notice that the carrying cost equals the ordering cost. This is always true for the simple EOQ model described by Equation 14.2. Also, notice that an order quantity of 500 is less costly than an order quantity of 1,000 (\$1,000 versus \$1,250).

Reorder Point

The EOQ answers the question of how much to order (or produce). Knowing when to place an order (or setup for production) is also an essential part of any inventory policy. The **reorder point** is the point in time when a new order should be placed (or setup started). It is a function of the EOQ, the lead time, and the rate at which inventory is depleted. **Lead time** is the time required to receive the economic order quantity once an order is placed or a setup is initiated.

To avoid stockout costs and to minimize carrying costs, an order should be placed so that it arrives just as the last item in inventory is used. Knowing the rate of usage and lead time allows us to compute the reorder point (ROP) that accomplishes these objectives:

$$\text{ROP} = \text{Rate of usage} \times \text{Lead time} \quad (14.3)$$

To illustrate Equation 14.3, we will continue to use the refrigerator part example. Assume that the producer uses 50 parts per day and that the lead time is four days. If so, an order should be placed when the inventory level of the refrigerator part drops to 200 units (4 × 50). Exhibit 14-2 provides a graphical illustration.

1 $d(TC)/dQ = C/Q - PD/Q2 = 0$, which implies $Q^2 = 2PD/C$ and $Q = (2PD/C)^{1/2}$.

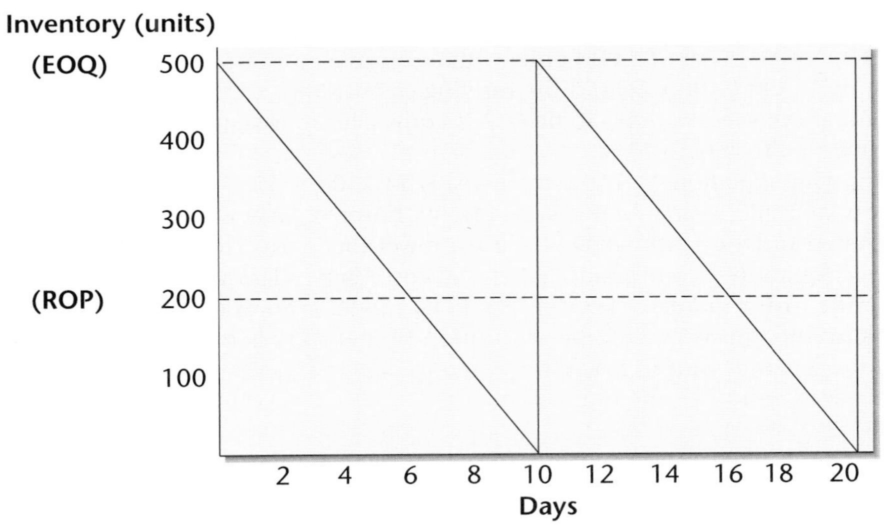

Exhibit 14-2 The Reorder Point

Note that the inventory is depleted just as the order arrives and that the quantity on hand jumps back up to the EOQ level.

Demand Uncertainty and the Reorder Point If the demand for the part or product is not known with certainty, the possibility of stockout exists. For example, if the refrigerator part was used at a rate of 60 parts a day instead of 50, the firm would use 200 parts after three and one-third days. Since the new order would not arrive until the end of the fourth day, repair activity requiring this part would be idled for two-thirds of a day. To avoid this problem, organizations often choose to carry safety stock. **Safety stock** is extra inventory carried to serve as insurance against fluctuations in demand. Safety stock is computed by multiplying the lead time by the difference between the maximum rate of usage and the average rate of usage. For example, if the maximum usage of the refrigerator part is 60 units per day, the average usage is 50 units per day, and the lead time is four days, the safety stock is computed as follows:

Maximum usage	60
Average usage	50
Difference	10
Lead time	×4
Safety stock	40

With the presence of safety stock, the reorder point is computed as follows:

$$\text{ROP} = (\text{Average rate of usage} \times \text{Lead time}) + \text{Safety stock} \quad (14.4)$$

For the refrigerator part example, the reorder point with safety stock is computed as follows:

$$\begin{aligned}\text{ROP} &= (50 \times 4) + 40 \\ &= 240 \text{ units}\end{aligned}$$

Thus, an order is automatically placed whenever the inventory level drops to 240 units. Notice that the reorder point can also be computed by multiplying the *maximum daily usage* by the lead time. Many students take this shortcut and it gives the correct answer. Managers, however, may find knowing the full reorder point equation more useful, because it reminds them that any changes in the average daily usage, lead time, and safety stock will change the reorder point.

A Manufacturing Example The service repair setting involved the purchase of inventory. The same concepts can be applied to settings where inventory is manufactured. To illustrate, consider Benson Company, a large manufacturer of farm implements with several plants throughout the nation. Each plant produces all subassemblies necessary to assemble a particular farm implement. One large plant in the Midwest produces plows. The manager of this midwestern plant is trying to determine the size of the production runs for the blade fabrication area. He is convinced that the current lot size is too large and wants to identify the quantity that should be produced to minimize the sum of the carrying and setup costs. He also wants to avoid stockouts since any stockout would shut down the Assembly Department.

To help the manager in his decision, the controller has supplied the following information:

Average demand for blades	320 per day
Maximum demand for blades	340 per day
Annual demand for blades	80,000
Unit carrying cost	$5
Setup cost	$12,500
Lead time	20 days

Based on this information, the economic order quantity and the reorder point are computed in Exhibit 14-3. As the computation illustrates, the blades should be produced in batches of 20,000, and a new setup should be started when the supply of blades drops to 6,800.

EOQ and Inventory Management

The traditional approach to managing inventory has been referred to as a *just-in-case system.*[2] In some settings, a just-in-case inventory system is entirely appropriate. For example, hospitals need inventories of medicines, drugs, and other critical supplies on hand at all times so that life-threatening situations can be handled. Using an economic order coupled with safety stock would seem eminently sensible in such an environment. Relying on a critical drug to arrive just in time to save a heart attack victim is simply not practical. Furthermore, many smaller retail stores, manufacturers, and services may not have the buying power to command alternative inventory management systems such as just-in-time purchasing.

As the plow blade example illustrates (Exhibit 14-3), the EOQ model is very useful in identifying the optimal trade-off between inventory carrying costs and setup costs. It also is useful in helping to deal with uncertainty by using safety stock. The historical importance of the EOQ model in many American industries can be better appreciated by understanding the nature of the traditional manufacturing environment. This environment has been characterized by the mass production of a few standardized products that typically have a very high setup cost. The production of the plow blades fits this pattern. The high setup cost encouraged a large batch size: 20,000 units. The annual demand of 80,000 units can be satisfied using only four batches. Thus, production runs for these firms tended to be quite long. Furthermore, diversity was viewed as being costly and was avoided. Producing variations of the product can be quite expensive, especially since additional, special features would usually demand even more expensive and frequent setups—the reason for the standardized products.

2 Eliyahu M. Goldratt and Robert E. Fox, *The Race* (Croton-on-Hudson, NY: North River Press, 1986).

$$EOQ = \sqrt{\frac{2PD}{C}}$$

$$= \sqrt{\frac{2 \times 80{,}000 \times 12{,}500}{5}}$$

$$= \sqrt{400{,}000{,}000}$$

$$= 20{,}000 \text{ blades}$$

Maximum usage	340
Average usage	320
Difference	20
Lead time	×20
Total safety stock	400

Reorder point = (Average usage × Lead time) + Safety stock
= (320 × 20) + 400
= 6,800 units

Exhibit 14-3 EOQ and Reorder Point Illustrated

JIT Inventory Management

Objective 2

Discuss JIT inventory management.

The manufacturing environment for many of these traditional, large-batch, high-setup-cost firms has changed dramatically in the past 10 to 20 years. For one thing, the competitive markets are no longer defined by national boundaries. Advances in transportation and communication have contributed significantly to the creation of global competition. Advances in technology have contributed to shorter life cycles for products, and product diversity has increased. Foreign firms offering higher-quality, lower-cost products with *specialized features* have created tremendous pressures for our domestic large-batch, high-setup-cost firms to increase both quality and product diversity while simultaneously reducing total costs. These competitive pressures have led many firms to abandon the EOQ model in favor of a *just-in-time* approach to manufacturing and purchasing.

Just-in-time manufacturng is a demand-pull system that requires goods to be pulled through the system by present demand rather than pushed through the system on a fixed schedule based on anticipated demand. Many fast-food restaurants, like **McDonald's**, use a pull system to control their finished goods inventory. When a customer orders a hamburger, it is taken from the rack. When the number of hamburgers gets too low, the cooks make new hamburgers. Customer demand pulls the materials through the system. This same principle is used in manufacturing settings. Each operation produces only what is necessary to satisfy the demand of the succeeding operation. The material or subassembly arrives just in time for production to occur so that demand can be met. Thus, complementary to and part of the total JIT system is the concept of *JIT purchasing*. **JIT purchasing** requires suppliers to deliver parts and materials just in time for production. Supplier linkages are vital. Supply of parts must be linked to production, which is linked to demand. In a survey among manufacturers in the United States, 85 percent say that some or most materials, parts, and components are supplied to them on a JIT basis.[3] Thus, JIT inventory systems now appear to be extensively used.

3 John McClenahen and Jill Jusco, "JIT Inventory Systems Hold Appeal," *Industry Week* (May 7, 2001): Vol. 250, Issue 7, pp. 11–13.

Fast food restaurants manage inventory very carefully. They keep little inventory of perishable food, but larger inventories of paper products and condiments.

JIT has two strategic objectives: to increase profits and to improve a firm's competitive position. These two objectives are achieved by controlling costs (enabling better price competition and increased profits), improving delivery performance, and improving quality. JIT offers increased cost efficiency and simultaneously has the flexibility to respond to customer demands for better quality and more variety. JIT manufacturing and purchasing represent the continual pursuit of productivity through the elimination of waste. Clearly, JIT is much more than an inventory management system. Inventories, however, are particularly viewed as representing waste. They tie up resources such as cash, space, and labor. They also conceal inefficiencies in production and increase the complexity of a firm's information system. Thus, even though JIT focuses on more than inventory management, control of inventory is an important ancillary benefit. First, we will provide an overview of the overall features of a JIT system. Next, the inventory management features of JIT will be explored in more detail.

Basic Features of JIT

Plant Layout The type and efficiency of plant layout is managed differently under JIT manufacturing. In traditional job and batch manufacturing, products are moved from one group of identical machines to another. Typically, machines with identical functions are located together in an area referred to as a department or process. Workers who specialize in the operation of a specific machine are located in each department. JIT replaces this traditional plant layout with a pattern of *manufacturing cells.* **Manufacturing cells** contain machines that are grouped in families, usually in a semicircle. The machines are arranged so that they can be used to perform a variety of operations in sequence. Each cell is set up to produce a particular product or product family. Products move from one machine to another from start to finish. Workers are assigned to cells and are trained to operate all machines within the cell. Thus, labor in a JIT environment is multiskilled, not specialized. Each manufacturing cell is essentially a minifactory, and cells are often referred to as a factory within a factory. Exhibit 14-4 compares JIT's plant layout with the traditional pattern.

Cell structure usually produces reduced lead times and lower manufacturing costs. The cellular manufacturing design can also affect plant size and number of

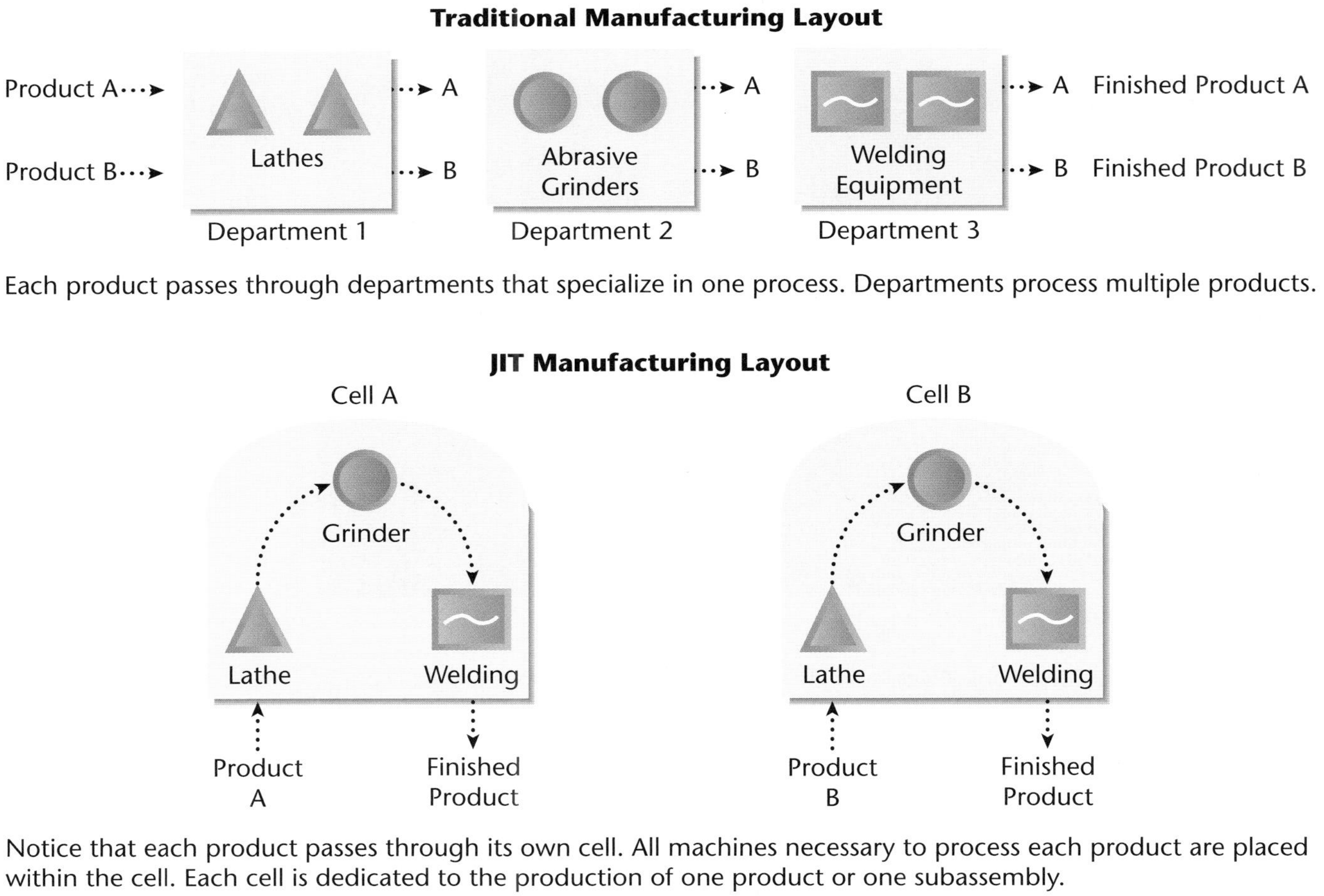

Exhibit 14-4 Plant Layout Pattern: Traditional versus JIT

plants because it typically requires less space. **Compaq Computer Corp.**, for example, cut its space requirement by 23 percent and increased output per square foot by 16 percent at its Scotland plant. Space savings like this can reduce the demand to build new plants and will affect the size of new plants when they are needed.

Grouping and Empowerment of Employees Another major structural difference between JIT and traditional organizations relates to the grouping and responsibilities of employees. As just indicated, each cell is viewed as a minifactory. Thus, each cell requires easy and quick access to support services, which means that centralized service departments must be scaled down and their personnel reassigned to work directly with manufacturing cells. Consequently, service personnel, such as manufacturing and quality engineers, are often assigned to cells.

Training cell workers to perform multiple tasks also has the effect of relocating support services to the cell. In addition to direct production work, cell workers may perform setup duties, move partially completed goods from station to station within the cell, perform preventive maintenance and minor repairs, conduct quality inspections, and perform janitorial tasks. This multiple-task capability is directly related to the pull-through production approach. Producing on demand means that production workers (formerly direct laborers) may often have "free" time. This nonproduction time can be used to perform selected support activities.

Cell workers are also given a greater degree of participation in the management of the organization. Worker input is sought and used to improve production processes. Workers at **Saturn** and **Southwest Airlines** and other JIT organizations are often involved in interviewing and hiring other employees, sometimes even including prospective bosses. The reason? If the "chemistry is right," then the workforce will be more efficient and will work together better. Managers act more as facilitators than as supervisors.

Total Quality Control JIT necessarily carries with it a much stronger emphasis on managing quality. A defective part brings production to a grinding halt. Poor quality simply cannot be tolerated in a manufacturing environment that operates without inventories. Simply put, JIT cannot be implemented without a commitment to total quality control (TQC). TQC is essentially a never-ending quest for perfect quality, the striving for a defect-free product design and manufacturing process.

Traceability of Overhead Costs A costing system uses three methods to assign costs to individual products: direct tracing, driver tracing, and allocation. Of the three methods, direct tracing is the most accurate and, thus, is preferred over the other two methods. In a departmental structure, many different products may be subjected to a process located in a single department (for example, grinding). After completion of the process, the products are then transferred to other processes located in different departments (for example, assembly, painting, and so on). Because more than one product is processed in a department, the costs of that department are shared by all products passing through it and, therefore, must be assigned to products using activity drivers (and occasionally allocation). In a JIT environment, many overhead costs assigned to products using either driver tracing or allocation are now directly traceable to products. Cellular manufacturing, multiskilled labor, and decentralized service activities are the major features of JIT responsible for this change in traceability. Exhibit 14-5 compares the traceability of some selected costs in a traditional manufacturing environment with their traceability in the JIT environment (assuming single-product cells). Comparisons are based on the three cost assignment methods.

Inventory Effects JIT typically reduces inventories to very low levels. The pursuit of insignificant levels of inventories is vital to the success of JIT. This idea of pursuing insignificant inventories, however, necessarily challenges the traditional reasons for holding inventories (see Exhibit 14-1). These reasons are no longer viewed as valid. According to the traditional view, inventories solve some underlying problem related to each of the reasons listed in Exhibit 14-1. For example, the problem of resolving the conflict between ordering or setup costs and carrying costs is solved by selecting an inventory level that minimizes the sum of these costs. If demand is

Manufacturing Cost	Traditional Environment	JIT Environment
Direct labor	Direct tracing	Direct tracing
Direct materials	Direct tracing	Direct tracing
Material handling	Driver tracing	Direct tracing
Repairs and maintenance	Driver tracing	Direct tracing
Energy	Driver tracing	Direct tracing
Operating supplies	Driver tracing	Direct tracing
Supervision (department)	Allocation	Direct tracing
Insurance and taxes	Allocation	Allocation
Plant depreciation	Allocation	Allocation
Equipment depreciation	Driver tracing	Direct tracing
Custodial services	Allocation	Direct tracing
Cafeteria services	Driver tracing	Driver tracing

Exhibit 14-5 Product Cost Assignment: Traditional versus JIT Manufacturing

JIT	Traditional
1. Pull-through system	1. Push-through system
2. Insignificant inventories	2. Significant inventories
3. Small supplier base	3. Large supplier base
4. Long-term supplier contracts	4. Short-term supplier contracts
5. Cellular structure	5. Departmental structure
6. Multiskilled labor	6. Specialized labor
7. Decentralized services	7. Centralized services
8. High employee involvement	8. Low employee involvement
9. Facilitating management style	9. Supervisory management style
10. Total quality control	10. Acceptable quality level
11. Direct tracing dominates (product costing)	11. Driver tracing dominates (product costing)

Exhibit 14-6 Comparison of JIT with Traditional Manufacturing

greater than expected or if production is reduced by breakdowns and production inefficiencies, then inventories serve as buffers, providing products to customers that may otherwise not have been available. Similarly, inventories can prevent shutdowns caused by late deliveries of materials, defective parts, and failures of machines used to produce subassemblies. Finally, inventories are often the solution to the problem of buying the best materials for the least cost through the use of quantity discounts.

JIT refuses to use inventories as the solution to these problems. In fact, inventories are viewed as wasteful and as a deterrent to a firm's ability to compete in the marketplace. High inventories signal the existence of problems that need to be addressed and often mean poor quality, long lead times, and poor due-date performance (among other things). JIT inventory management offers alternative solutions that do not require high inventories. The major differences between a JIT manufacturing environment and a traditional manufacturing environment are summarized in Exhibit 14-6. We now turn to examining the detailed inventory management differences between the two systems.

Setup and Carrying Costs: The JIT Approach

JIT takes a radically different approach to minimizing total carrying and setup costs. The traditional approach accepts the existence of setup costs and then finds the order quantity that best balances the two categories of costs. JIT, on the other hand, does not accept setup costs (or ordering costs) as a given; rather, JIT attempts to drive these costs to zero. If setup costs and ordering costs become insignificant, the only remaining cost to minimize is carrying costs, which is accomplished by reducing inventories to very low levels. This approach explains the push for zero inventories in a JIT system.

Long-Term Contracts, Continuous Replenishment, Electronic Data Interchange, and JIT II Ordering costs are reduced by developing close relationships with suppliers. Negotiating long-term contracts for the supply of outside materials will obviously reduce the number of orders and the associated ordering costs. Retailers have found a way to reduce ordering costs by adopting an arrangement known as *continuous replenishment.* With **continuous replenishment**, a manufacturer assumes the inventory management function for the retailer. The manufacturer tells the retailer when and how much stock to reorder. The retailer reviews the recommendation and approves the order if it makes sense. Wal-Mart and Procter & Gamble, for example, use this arrangement.[4] The arrangement has reduced invento-

4 Michael Hammer and James Champy, *Reengineering the Corporation* (HarperBusiness, New York, 1993).

ries for **Wal-Mart** and has also reduced stockout problems. In addition, Procter & Gamble's goods are often sold before Wal-Mart has to pay for them. For its part, **Procter & Gamble** has become a preferred supplier, has more and better shelf space, and also has less demand uncertainty. The ability to project demand better allows Procter & Gamble to produce and deliver continuously in smaller lots—a goal of JIT manufacturing. Similar arrangements can be made between manufacturers and suppliers.

The process of continuous replenishment is facilitated by *electronic data interchange.* **Electronic data interchange (EDI)** is an early form of e-commerce that essentially is an automated method of transmitting information from computer to computer. In the beginning, value-added networks (VANs) were required to transmit this information. In 1998, about 95 percent of EDI transactions moved over VANs. However, Internet communications alternatives are expected to reduce this VAN usage for EDI to less than 50 percent.[5]

Although EDI is used for many different types of business-to-business transactions, our focus is on its usage for inventory management. For example, EDI allows suppliers access to a buyer's online database. By knowing the buyer's production schedule (in the case of a manufacturer), the supplier can deliver the parts where they are needed just in time for their use. EDI involves no paper—no purchase orders or invoices. The supplier uses the production schedule, which is in the database, to determine its own production and delivery schedules. When the parts are shipped, an electronic message is sent from the supplier to the buyer that a shipment is en route. When the parts arrive, a bar code is scanned with an electronic wand and this initiates payment for the goods. Clearly, EDI requires a close working arrangement between the supplier and the buyer—they almost operate as one company rather than two separate companies.

JIT II[6] purchasing carries the JIT partnership arrangement to an even higher level. The JIT II relationship has the supplier's sales representative working on site (on a full-time basis) at the customer's facility while being paid by the supplier. This supplier employee is referred to as an in-plant representative. By being on site 100 percent of the time, the in-plant representative provides continuous supplier support. The in-plant representative attends the customer's production planning meetings, has authority to place orders on behalf of the customer, and can resolve any purchasing problems (such as order revisions and order delays). The relationship reduces the administrative costs of both parties and greatly facilitates the use of JIT purchasing. The mutual arrangement is often cemented by open-ended, long-term contracts referred to as *evergreen contracts.* Evergreen contracts have no end date, do not require rebidding, and thus reduce the demand risk for the supplier. In exchange for reduced uncertainty in demand for its products, the supplier bears some of the purchasing costs of the customer because it pays the salary of the in-plant representative. Examples of companies using JIT II are **Bose**, **IBM**, **Intel**, **Honeywell**, and **AT&T**.

Inventory Management and Ethical Dilemmas

ETHICS

The technology for tracking and managing inventory has grown increasingly sophisticated. Radio Frequency Identification (RFID) tags implanted in a product or its packaging can be used to track individual units of a product. For example, Wal-Mart has tested photographic "smart shelves." Smart shelves have a hidden camera that snaps pictures of consumers who remove an RFID-tagged item from the shelf. Later, as the consumer checks out, the RFID tag triggers another photo—this time, of the consumer buying the item. Company officials match the photos of everyone removing

5 Ken Vollmer, "The Internet Will Determine the Future of EDI," *InternetWeek* (July 23, 2001): Issue 870, pp. 23–24.

6 JIT II is a service mark of Bose Corporation.

the item from the shelf with a photo of the purchase. No second photo? Then the item may have been shoplifted. The objective was to decrease shoplifting by customers and/or employees. However, the hidden camera nature of the process—which was not disclosed to consumers by Wal-Mart—outraged consumer groups.[7]

Reducing Setup Times Reducing setup times requires a company to search for new, more efficient ways to accomplish setup. Fortunately, experience has indicated that dramatic reductions in setup times can be achieved. A classical example is that of **Harley-Davidson**. Upon adopting a JIT system, Harley-Davidson reduced setup times by more than 75 percent on the machines evaluated.[8] In some cases, Harley-Davidson was able to reduce the setup times from hours to minutes. Other companies have experienced similar results. Generally, setup times can be reduced by at least 75 percent.

Due-Date Performance: The JIT Solution

Due-date performance is a measure of a firm's ability to respond to customer needs. In the past, finished goods inventories have been used to ensure that a firm is able to meet a requested delivery date. JIT solves the problem of due-date performance not by building inventory but by dramatically reducing lead times. Shorter lead times increase a firm's ability to meet requested delivery dates and to respond quickly to the demands of the market. Thus, the firm's competitiveness is improved. JIT cuts lead times by reducing setup times, improving quality, and using cellular manufacturing. Most companies experience at least a 90 percent reduction in lead times when they implement JIT.

Avoidance of Shutdown and Process Reliability: The JIT Approach

Most shutdowns occur for one of three reasons: machine failure, defective material or subassembly, and unavailability of a material or subassembly. Holding inventories is one traditional solution to all three problems. Those espousing the JIT approach claim that inventories do not solve the problems but cover up or hide them. JIT proponents use the analogy of rocks in a lake. The rocks represent the three problems, and the water represents inventories. If the lake is deep (inventories are high), then the rocks are never exposed, and managers can pretend they do not exist. By reducing inventories to zero, the rocks are exposed and can no longer be ignored. JIT solves the three problems by emphasizing total preventive maintenance and total quality control and by building the right kind of relationship with suppliers.

Total Preventive Maintenance Zero machine failures is the goal of **total preventive maintenance**. By paying more attention to preventive maintenance, most machine breakdowns can be avoided. This objective is easier to attain in a JIT environment because of the interdisciplinary labor philosophy. It is common for a cell worker to be trained in maintenance of the machines he or she operates. Because of the pull-through nature of JIT, it is also normal for a cell worker to have idle manufacturing time. Some of this time, then, can be used productively by involving the cell workers in preventive maintenance.

Total Quality Control The problem of defective parts is solved by striving for zero defects. Because JIT manufacturing does not rely on inventories to replace defective parts or materials, the emphasis on quality for both internally produced and externally purchased materials increases significantly. It is not unusual for the

7 Source: Dennis and Sally Bacchetta, "Informed Consent: Ethical Considerations of RFID" (Jan. 10, 2006), http://www.bestelectronicstores.info/electronicstores-insight-Informed+Consent+Ethical+Considerations+of+RFID-section-1-id-86.html

8 Gene Schwind, "Man Arrives Just-In-Time to Save Harley-Davidson," *Material Handling Engineering* (August 1984): pp. 28–35.

number of rejected parts to be reduced by 75 to 90 percent. Decreasing defective parts also diminishes the justification for inventories based on unreliable processes.

The Kanban System To ensure that parts or materials are available when needed, the **Kanban system** is employed. This is an information system that controls production through the use of markers or cards. The Kanban system is responsible for ensuring that the necessary products (or parts) are produced (or acquired) in the necessary quantities at the necessary time. It is the heart of the JIT inventory management system.

A Kanban system uses cards or markers, which are plastic, cardboard, or metal plates measuring four inches by eight inches. The Kanban is usually placed in a vinyl sack and attached to the part or a container holding the needed parts.

A basic Kanban system uses three cards: a *withdrawal Kanban,* a *production Kanban,* and a *vendor Kanban.* The first two control the movement of work among the manufacturing processes, while the third controls movement of parts between the processes and outside suppliers. A **withdrawal Kanban** specifies the quantity that a subsequent process should withdraw from the preceding process. A **production Kanban** specifies the quantity that the preceding process should produce. **Vendor Kanbans** are used to notify suppliers to deliver more parts; they also specify when the parts are needed. The three Kanbans are illustrated in Exhibits 14-7, 14-8, and 14-9, respectively.

Item No.	**15670T07**	Preceding Process
Item Name	**Circuit Board**	**CB Assembly**
Computer Type	**TR6547 PC**	
Box Capacity	**8**	Subsequent Process
Box Type	**C**	**Final Assembly**

Exhibit 14-7 Withdrawal Kanban

Item No.	**15670T07**	Process
Item Name	**Circuit Board**	**CB Assembly**
Computer Type	**TR6547 PC**	
Box Capacity	**8**	
Box Type	**C**	

Exhibit 14-8 Production Kanban

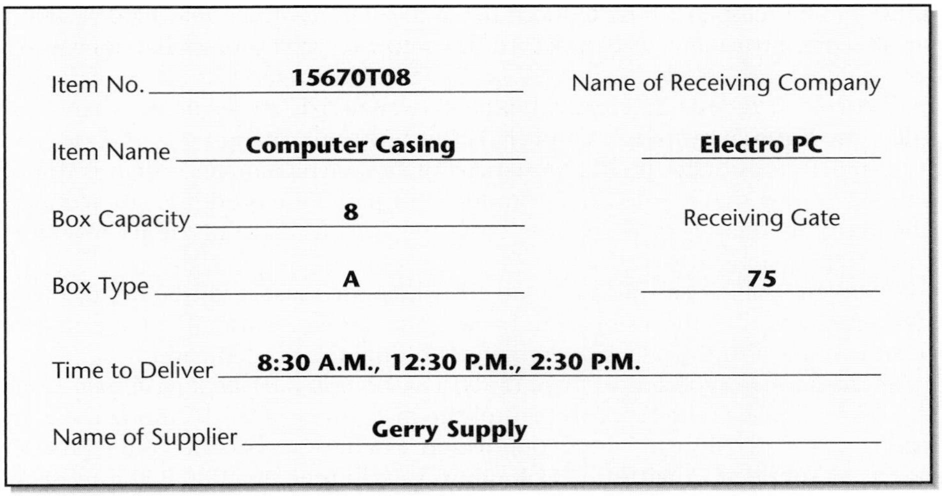
Item No. 15670T08
Item Name Computer Casing
Box Capacity 8
Box Type A
Name of Receiving Company Electro PC
Receiving Gate 75
Time to Deliver 8:30 A.M., 12:30 P.M., 2:30 P.M.
Name of Supplier Gerry Supply

Exhibit 14-9 Vendor Kanban

How Kanban cards are used to control the work flow can be illustrated with a simple example. Assume that two processes are needed to manufacture a product. The first process (CB Assembly) builds and tests printed circuit boards (using a U-shaped manufacturing cell). The second process (Final Assembly) puts eight circuit boards into a subassembly purchased from an outside supplier. The final product is a personal computer.

Exhibit 14-10 provides the plant layout corresponding to the manufacture of the personal computers. Refer to the exhibit as the steps involved in using Kanbans are outlined.

Consider first the movement of work between the two processing areas. Assume that eight circuit boards are placed in a container and that one such container is located

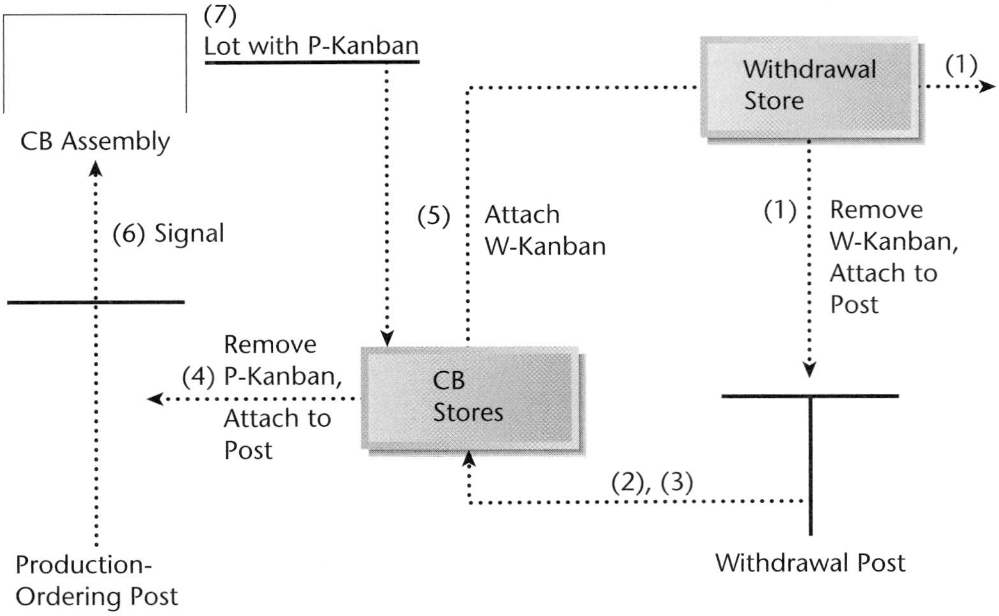

Exhibit 14-10 Kanban Process

in the CB stores area. Attached to this container is a production Kanban (P-Kanban). A second container with eight circuit boards is located near the Final Assembly line (the withdrawal store) with a withdrawal Kanban (W-Kanban). Now, assume that the production schedule calls for the immediate assembly of a computer.

The Kanban setups can be described as follows:

1. A worker from the Final Assembly line goes to the withdrawal store, removes a container of eight circuit boards, and places them into production. The worker also removes the withdrawal Kanban and places it on the withdrawal post.
2. The withdrawal Kanban on the post signals that the Final Assembly unit needs an additional eight circuit boards to restock the withdrawal store.
3. A worker from Final Assembly (or a material handler called a carrier) removes the withdrawal Kanban from the post and carries it to the CB stores.
4. At the CB stores area, the carrier removes the production Kanban from the container of eight circuit boards and places it on the production-ordering post.
5. The carrier next attaches the withdrawal Kanban to the container of parts and carries the container to the Final Assembly area. Assembly of the next computer can begin.
6. The production Kanban on the production-ordering post signals the workers of the CB assembly to begin producing another lot of circuit boards. The production Kanban is removed and accompanies the units as they are produced.
7. When the lot of eight circuit boards is completed, the units are placed in a container in the CB stores area with the production Kanban attached. The cycle is then repeated.

The use of Kanbans ensures that the subsequent process (Final Assembly) withdraws the circuit boards from the preceding process (CB Assembly) in the necessary quantity at the appropriate time. The Kanban system also controls the preceding process by allowing it to produce only the quantities withdrawn by the subsequent process. In this way, inventories are kept at a minimum, and the components arrive just in time to be used.

Essentially, the same steps are followed for a purchased subassembly. The only difference is the use of a vendor Kanban in place of a production Kanban. A vendor Kanban on a vendor post signals to the supplier that another order is needed. As with the circuit boards, the subassemblies must be delivered just in time for use. A JIT purchasing system requires the supplier to deliver small quantities on a frequent basis. These deliveries could be weekly, daily, or even several times a day. This calls for a close working relationship with suppliers. Long-term contractual agreements tend to ensure supply of materials.

Discounts and Price Increases: JIT Purchasing versus Holding Inventories

Traditionally, inventories are carried so that a firm can take advantage of quantity discounts and hedge against future price increases of the items purchased. The objective is to lower the cost of inventory. JIT achieves the same objective without carrying inventories. The JIT solution is to negotiate long-term contracts with a few chosen suppliers located as close to the production facility as possible and to establish more extensive supplier involvement. Suppliers are not selected on the basis of price alone. Performance—the quality of the component and the ability to deliver as needed—and commitment to JIT purchasing are vital considerations. Other benefits of long-term contracts exist. They stipulate prices and acceptable quality levels. Long-term contracts also reduce dramatically the number of orders placed, which helps to drive down the ordering cost. Another effect of JIT purchasing is to lower the cost of purchased parts (it is not unusual for reductions to be between 5 and 20 percent).

JIT's Limitations

JIT is not an approach that can be purchased and plugged in with immediate results. Its implementation should be more of an evolutionary process than a revolutionary process. Patience is needed. JIT is often referred to as a program of simplification—yet it is not necessarily simple or easy to implement. Time is required, for example, to build sound relationships with suppliers. Insisting on immediate changes in delivery times and quality may not be realistic and may cause confrontations between a company and its suppliers. Partnership, not coercion, should be the basis of supplier relationships. To achieve the benefits that are associated with JIT purchasing, a company may be tempted to redefine unilaterally its supplier relationships. Unilaterally redefining supplier relationships by extracting concessions and dictating terms may create supplier resentment and actually cause suppliers to retaliate. In the long run, suppliers may seek new markets, find ways to charge higher prices (than would exist with a preferred supplier arrangement), or seek regulatory relief. These actions could destroy many of the JIT benefits extracted by the impatient company.

Workers might also be affected by JIT. Sharp reductions in inventory buffers may cause a regimented workflow and high levels of stress among production workers. A deliberate pace of inventory reduction could be needed to allow workers to develop a sense of autonomy and to encourage their participation in broader improvement efforts. Forced and dramatic reductions in inventories may indeed reveal problems—but might cause even more problems such as lost sales and stressed workers. If the workers perceive that JIT will simply squeeze more out of them, then JIT efforts will likely be doomed. Perhaps a better strategy for JIT implementation is one where inventory reductions follow the process improvements that JIT offers. Implementing JIT is not easy, and it requires careful and thorough planning and preparation. Companies should expect some struggle and frustration.

The most glaring deficiency of JIT is the absence of inventory to buffer production interruptions. Current sales are constantly being threatened by an unexpected interruption in production. In fact, if a problem occurs, JIT's approach consists of trying to find and solve the problem before any further production activity occurs. Retailers who use JIT tactics also face the possibility of shortages. (JIT retailers order what they need now—not what they expect to sell. The idea is to flow goods through the channel as late as possible, keeping inventories low and decreasing the need for markdowns.) If demand increases well beyond the retailer's supply of inventory, the

The JIT approach can cause problems when there are sudden spikes in demand. If these tools are popular items (at Christmas, say), then stores may be wise to begin stocking up on inventory throughout the fall.

© PR Newswire SEARS, ROEBUCK AND CO.

retailer may be unable to make order adjustments quickly enough to avoid lost sales and irritated customers. Yet, in spite of the downside, retailers seem to be strongly committed to JIT. Apparently, losing sales on surprise hits is less costly than the cost of carrying high levels of inventory.

The JIT manufacturing company is also willing to place current sales at risk to achieve assurance of future sales. This assurance comes from higher quality, quicker response time, and less operating costs. Even so, firms must recognize that a sale lost today is a sale lost forever. Installing a JIT system so that it operates with very little interruption is not a short-run project. Thus, losing sales is a real cost of installing a JIT system.

An alternative, and perhaps complementary, approach is the theory of constraints (TOC). In principle, TOC can be used in conjunction with JIT manufacturing; after all, JIT manufacturing environments also have constraints. Furthermore, the TOC approach has the very appealing quality of protecting current sales while also striving to increase future sales by increasing quality, lowering response time, and decreasing operating costs.

Theory of Constraints

Objective 3

Explain the theory of constraints, and tell how it can be used to manage inventory.

Every firm faces limited resources and limited demand for each product. These limitations are called **constraints**. The theory of constraints recognizes that the performance of any organization is limited by its constraints. The theory of constraints then develops a specific approach to manage constraints to support the objective of continuous improvement. According to TOC, if performance is to be improved, an organization must identify its constraints, exploit the constraints in the short run, and in the long run, find ways to overcome the constraints.

Basic Concepts

TOC focuses on three measures of organizational performance: *throughput, inventory,* and *operating expenses.* **Throughput** is the rate at which an organization generates money through sales.[9] In operational terms, throughput is the difference between sales revenue and unit-level variable costs such as materials and power. Direct labor is typically viewed as a fixed unit-level expense and is not usually included in the definition. With this understanding, throughput corresponds to contribution margin. **Inventory** is all the money the organization spends in turning materials into throughput. **Operating expenses** are defined as all the money the organization spends in turning inventories into throughput. Based on these three measures, the objectives of management can be expressed as increasing throughput, minimizing inventory, and decreasing operating expenses.

By increasing throughput, minimizing inventory, and decreasing operating expenses, three financial measures of performance will be affected: net income and return on investment will increase, and cash flow will improve. Increasing throughput and decreasing operating expenses have always been emphasized as key elements in improving the three financial measures of performance. The role of minimizing inventory, however, in achieving these improvements has been traditionally regarded as less important than throughput and operating expenses.

The theory of constraints, like JIT, assigns inventory management a much more prominent role than the traditional viewpoint. TOC recognizes that lowering inventory decreases carrying costs and, thus, decreases operating expenses and improves net income. TOC, however, argues that lowering inventory helps produce a competitive edge by having better products, lower prices, and faster responses to customer needs.

9 This follows the definition given by Eliyahu M. Goldratt and Robert E. Fox in *The Race.* Other definitions and basic concepts of the theory of constraints are also based upon the developments of Goldratt and Fox.

Better Products Better products mean higher quality. It also means that the company is able to improve products and provide these improved products quickly to the market. The relationship between low inventories and quality has been described in the JIT section. Essentially, low inventories allow defects to be detected more quickly and the cause of the problem to be assessed. Improving products is also a key competitive element. New or improved products need to reach the market quickly—before competitors can provide similar features. This goal is facilitated by low inventories. Low inventories allow new product changes to be introduced more quickly because the company has fewer old products (in stock or in process) that would need to be scrapped or sold before the new product is introduced.

Lower Prices High inventories mean more productive capacity is needed and, thus, more investment in equipment and space. Since lead time and high work-in-process inventories are usually correlated, high inventories may often be the cause of overtime. Overtime, of course, increases operating expenses and lowers profitability. Lower inventories reduce carrying costs, per-unit investment costs, and other operating expenses such as overtime and special shipping charges. By lowering investment and operating costs, the unit margin of each product is increased, providing more flexibility in pricing decisions. Lower prices are possible or higher product margins if competitive conditions do not require prices to be lowered.

Responsiveness Delivering goods on time and producing goods with shorter lead times than the market dictates are important competitive tools. On-time delivery of goods is related to a firm's ability to forecast the time required to produce and deliver goods. If a firm has higher inventories than its competitors, then the firm's production lead time is higher than the industry's forecast horizon. High inventories may obscure the actual time required to produce and fill an order. Lower inventories allow actual lead times to be more carefully observed, and more accurate delivery dates can be provided. Shortening lead times is also crucial; doing so is equivalent to lowering work-in-process inventories. A company carrying 10 days of work-in-process inventories has an average production lead time of 10 days. If the company can reduce lead time from 10 to five days, then the company should now be carrying only five days of work-in-process inventories.

As lead times are reduced, it is also possible to reduce finished goods inventories. For example, if the lead time for a product is 10 days and the market requires delivery on demand, then firms must carry, on average, 10 days of finished goods inventory (plus some safety stock to cover demand uncertainty). Suppose that the firm is able to reduce lead time to five days. In this case, finished goods inventory should also be reduced to five days. Thus, the level of inventories signals the organization's ability to respond. High levels relative to those of competitors translate into a competitive disadvantage. In other words, TOC emphasizes reduction of inventories by reducing lead times.

TOC Steps

The theory of constraints uses five steps to achieve its goal of improving organizational performance:

1. Identify the organization's constraint(s).
2. Exploit the binding constraint(s).
3. Subordinate everything else to the decisions made in Step 2.
4. Elevate the binding constraint(s).
5. Repeat the process.

Step 1: Identify the Organization's Constraint(s) Constraints can be classified as external or internal. **External constraints** are limiting factors imposed on the firm from external sources (such as market demand). **Internal constraints** are limiting factors found within the firm (such as machine-time availability). Although resources and demands may be limited, certain product mixes may not meet all the demand or use all of the resources available to be used. Constraints whose limited resources are not fully used by a product mix are **loose constraints**. **Binding constraints** are those constraints whose available resources are fully utilized. Internal and external constraints are identified. The optimal product mix is identified as the mix that maximizes throughput subject to all the organization's constraints. The optimal mix reveals how much of each constrained resource is used and which of the organization's constraints are binding.

Decisions about product mix can have a significant impact on an organization's profitability. Each mix represents an alternative that carries with it an associated profit level. A manager should choose the alternative that maximizes total profits. The usual approach is to assume that only unit-based variable costs are relevant to the product mix decision. Thus, assuming that nonunit-level costs are the same for different mixes of products, the optimal mix is one that maximizes total contribution margin.

A manager must choose the optimal mix given the constraints faced by the firm. Assume, for example, that Confer Company produces two types of machine parts: X and Y, with unit contribution margins of $300 and $600, respectively. Assuming that Confer can sell all that is produced, some may argue that only Part Y should be produced and sold because it has the larger contribution margin. However, this solution is not necessarily the best. The selection of the optimal mix can be significantly affected by the relationships of the constrained resources to the individual products. These relationships affect the quantity of each product that can be produced and, consequently, the total contribution margin that can be earned. This point is most vividly illustrated with one binding internal resource constraint.

One Binding Internal Constraint Assume that each part must be drilled by a special machine. The firm owns three machines that together provide 120 drilling hours per week. Part X requires one hour of drilling, and Part Y requires three hours of drilling. Assuming no other binding constraints, what is the optimal mix of parts? Since each unit of X requires one hour of drilling, a total of 120 units of X can be produced per week (120/1). At $300 per unit, Confer can earn a total contribution margin of $36,000 per week. On the other hand, Y requires three hours of drilling per unit; therefore, 40 (120/3) parts can be produced. At $600 per unit, the total contribution margin is $24,000 per week. Producing only X yields a higher profit level than producing only Y—even though the unit contribution margin for Y is two times larger than that for X.

The contribution margin per unit of each product is not the critical concern. The contribution margin per unit of scarce resource is the deciding factor. The product yielding the highest contribution margin per drilling hour should be selected. Part X earns $300 per machine hour ($300/1), while Part Y earns only $200 per machine hour ($600/3). Thus, the optimal mix is 120 units of Part X and none of Part Y, producing a total contribution margin of $36,000 per week. Notice that the mix uses up all 120 machine hours and so the machine-hour constraint is binding.

Internal Binding Constraint and External Binding Constraint The contribution margin per unit of scarce resource can also be used to identify the optimal product mix when an external binding constraint exists. For example, assume the same internal constraint of 120 drilling hours, but also assume that Confer can sell at most 30 units of Part X and 100 units of Part Y. The internal constraint allows Confer to produce 120 units of Part X, but this is no longer a feasible choice because only 30 units of X can be sold. Thus, we now have a binding external constraint, one that affects the earlier decision to produce and sell only Part X. Since the contribution per unit of scarce resource (machine hour) is $300 for Part X and $200 for Part Y, it still makes sense to produce as much of X as possible before producing any of Y. Confer should first produce 30 units of X, using 30 machine hours. This leaves 90 machine hours, allowing the production of 30 units of Y. The optimal mix is now 30 units of X and

30 units of Y, producing a total contribution margin of $27,000 per week [($300 × 30) + ($600 × 30)].

Step 2: Exploit the Binding Constraint(s) One way to make the best use of binding constraints is to ensure that the optimal product mix is produced. Making the best use of binding constraints, however, is more extensive than simply ensuring production of the optimal mix. This step is the heart of TOC's philosophy of short-run constraint management and is directly related to TOC's goal of reducing inventories and improving performance.

In most organizations, there are only a few binding resource constraints. The major binding constraint is defined as the *drummer*. Assume, for example, that there is only one internal binding constraint. By default, this constraint becomes the drummer. The drummer constraint's production rate sets the production rate for the entire plant. Downstream processes fed by the drummer constraint are naturally forced to follow its rate of production. Scheduling for downstream processes is easy. Once a part is finished at the drummer process, the next process begins its operation. Similarly, each subsequent operation begins when the prior operation is finished. Upstream processes that feed the drummer constraint are *scheduled* to produce at the same rate as the drummer constraint. Scheduling at the drummer rate prevents the production of excessive upstream work-in-process inventories.

For upstream scheduling, TOC uses two additional features in managing constraints to lower inventory levels and improve organizational performance: *buffers* and *ropes*. First, an inventory buffer is established in front of the major binding constraint. The inventory buffer is referred to as the *time buffer*. A **time buffer** is the inventory needed to keep the constrained resource busy for a specified time interval. The purpose of a time buffer is to protect the throughput of the organization from any disruption that can be overcome within the specified time interval. For example, if it takes one day to overcome most interruptions that occur upstream from the drummer constraint, then a two-day buffer should be sufficient to protect throughput from any interruptions. Thus, in scheduling, the operation immediately preceding the drummer constraint should produce the parts needed by the drummer resource two days in advance of their planned usage. Any other preceding operations are scheduled backward in time to produce so that their parts arrive just in time for subsequent operations.

Ropes are actions taken to tie the rate at which material is released into the plant (at the first operation) to the production rate of the constrained resource. The objective of a rope is to ensure that the work-in-process inventory will not exceed the level needed for the time buffer. Thus, the drummer rate is used to limit the rate of material release and effectively controls the rate at which the first operation produces. The rate of the first operation then controls the rates of subsequent operations. The TOC inventory system is often called the **drum-buffer-rope (DBR) system**. Exhibit 14-11 illustrates the DBR structure for a general setting.

© Getty Images/PhotoDisc

If this worker is not part of the binding constraint, his production output need not (and under the drum-buffer-rope system should not) be at his maximum. Instead, the factory may need to find other uses for his necessary idle time.

The Confer Company example can be expanded to provide a specific illustration of the DBR system. Assume that there are three sequential processes: grinding, drilling, and polishing. Each of these processes has a limited amount of resources. Demand for each type of machine part produced is also limited (30 for Part X and 100 for Part Y as

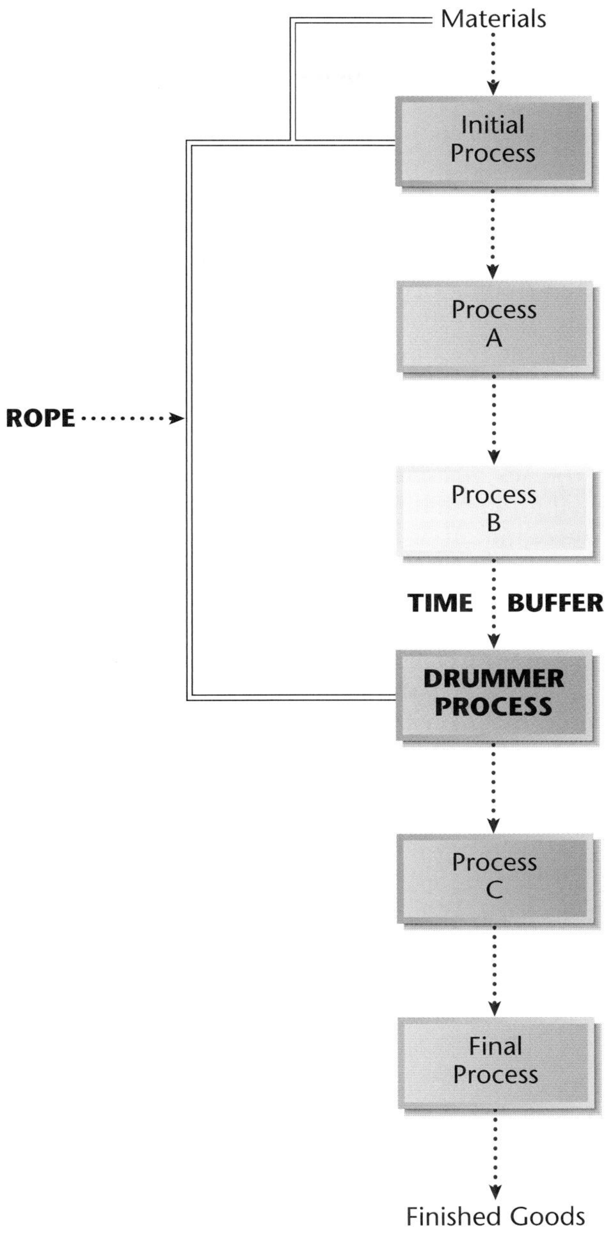

Exhibit 14-11 Drum-Buffer-Rope System: General Description

indicated earlier). Assume that the only internal binding constraint is drilling and that the optimal mix consists of 30 units of Part X and 30 units of Part Y (per week). This is the most that the drilling process can handle. The other two processes represent loose constraints and so are capable of producing more per week of each part than the optimal mix calls for. Since the drilling process feeds the polishing process, we can define the drilling constraint as the drummer for the plant. Assume that the demand for each part is uniformly spread out over the week. This means that the production rate should be six per day of each part (for a five-day workweek). A two-day time buffer would require 24 completed parts from the grinding process: 12 for Part X and 12 for Part Y. To ensure that the time buffer does not increase at a rate greater than six per day for each part, materials should be released to the grinding process such that only six of each part can be produced each day (this is the rope—tying the release of materials to the production rate of the drummer constraint). Exhibit 14-12 summarizes the specific DBR details for the Confer Company.

Step 3: Subordinate Everything Else to the Decisions Made in Step 2

The drummer constraint essentially sets the capacity for the entire plant. All remaining departments should be subordinated to the needs of the drummer constraint. This principle requires many companies to change the way they view things. For example, the use of efficiency measures at the departmental level may no longer be appropriate. Consider the Confer Company once again. Encouraging maximum productive efficiency for the Grinding Department would produce excess work-in-process inventories. For example, assume that the capacity of the Grinding Department is 80 units per week. Assuming the two-day buffer is in place, the Grinding Department would add 20 units per week to the buffer in front of the Drilling Department. Over a period of a year, the potential exists for building very large work-in-process inventories (1,000 units of the two parts would be added to the buffer over a 50-week period). Polishing, of course, must produce at the rate of drilling because it follows drilling in the sequential production process. Thus, the only concern for polishing is that it can handle the output of drilling.

Step 4: Elevate the Binding Constraint(s) Once actions have been taken to make the best possible use of the existing constraints, the next step is to embark on a program of continuous improvement by reducing the limitations that the binding constraint(s) have on the organization's performance.

Suppose, for example, that Confer Company adds a half shift for the Drilling Department, increasing the drilling hours from 120 to 180 per week. With 60 addi-

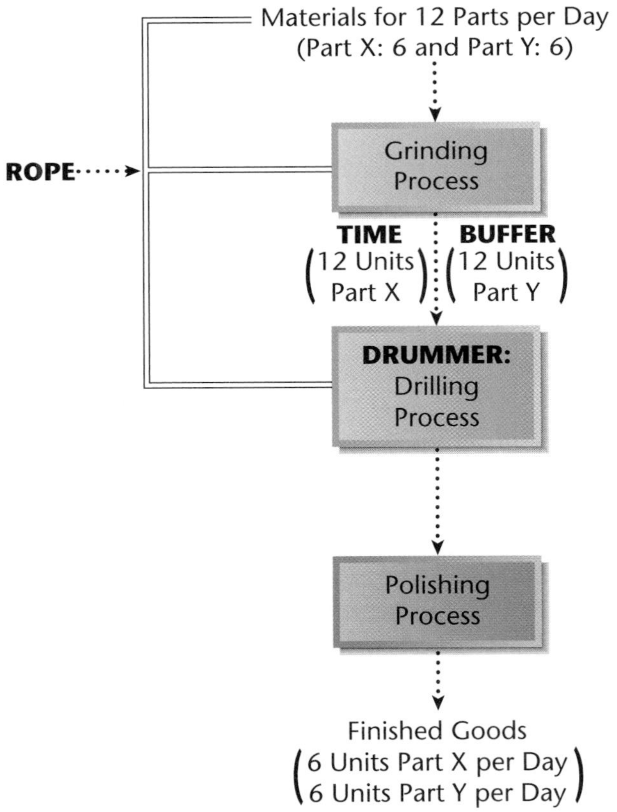

Exhibit 14-12 Drum-Buffer-Rope: Confer Company

tional drilling hours, Confer can increase production of Part Y from 30 to 50 units, an additional 20 units per week [recall that Part Y uses three hours per unit, yielding the 20 additional units (60/3)]. Since Part Y has a unit contribution margin of $600, this will increase throughput by $12,000 per week ($600 × 20), assuming that grinding and polishing can handle an increase of 20 units of Y per week. We know, for example, that grinding has 80 hours per week available and that X and Y each use one hour of grinding. Currently, 60 hours are being used. An increase of 20 units is possible.

Now, assume that polishing has 160 hours available and that Part X uses two hours per unit and Part Y, one hour per unit. For the current mix (30 of X and 30 of Y), 90 hours are being used. To increase production of Y by 20 units, 20 more hours are needed—which is certainly possible. Thus, moving from a mix of 30 units of X and 30 units of Y to a mix of 30 of X and 50 of Y is possible. Is the half shift worth it? This question is answered by comparing the cost of adding the half shift with the increased throughput of $12,000 per week. If the cost of adding the half shift is $50 per hour, then the incremental cost is $3,000 per week, and the decision to add the half shift is a good one.

Step 5: Repeat the Process Eventually, the drilling resource constraint will be elevated to a point where the constraint is no longer binding. Suppose, for example, that the company adds a full shift for the drilling operation, increasing the resource availability to 240 hours. Both the drilling and polishing constraints are capable of producing more of Part Y, but the grinding process cannot (grinding can produce a maximum of 80 units per week of any combination of X and Y). Thus, the new drummer constraint is grinding. Once the new drummer constraint is identified, then the TOC process is repeated. The objective is to continually improve performance by managing constraints.

Summary of Learning Objectives

1. Describe the traditional inventory management model.

The traditional approach uses inventories to manage the trade-offs between ordering (setup) costs and carrying costs. The optimal trade-off defines the economic order quantity. Other reasons for inventories are also offered: due-date performance, avoiding shutdowns (protecting sales), hedging against future price increases, and taking advantage of discounts. JIT and TOC, on the other hand, argue that inventories are costly and are used to cover up fundamental problems that need to be corrected so that the organization can become more competitive.

2. Discuss JIT inventory management.

JIT uses long-term contracts, continuous replenishment, and EDI to reduce (eliminate) ordering costs. Engineering efforts are made to reduce setup times drastically. Once ordering costs and setup costs are reduced to minimal levels, then it is possible to reduce carrying costs by reducing inventory levels. JIT carries small buffers in front of each operation and uses a Kanban system to regulate production. Production is tied to market demand. If an interruption occurs, throughput tends to be lost because of the small buffers. Yet, future throughput tends to increase because efforts are made to improve such things as quality, productivity, and lead time.

3. Explain the theory of constraints, and tell how it can be used to manage inventory.

TOC identifies an organization's constraints and exploits them so that throughput is maximized and inventories and operating costs are minimized. Identifying the optimal mix is part of this process. The major binding constraint is identified and is used to set the productive rate for the plant. Release of raw materials into the first process (operation) is regulated by the drummer constraint. A time buffer is located in front of critical constraints. This time buffer is sized so that it protects throughput from any interruptions. As in JIT, the interruptions are used to locate and correct the problem. However, unlike JIT, the time buffer serves to protect throughput. Furthermore, because buffers are located only in front of critical constraints, TOC may actually produce smaller inventories than JIT.

Key Terms

Review Problems

1. Inventory Costs, EOQ, Reorder Point

A local TV repair shop uses 36,000 units of a part each year (an average of 100 units per working day). It costs \$20 to place and receive an order. The shop orders in lots of 400 units. It costs \$4 to carry one unit per year in inventory.

Required

1. Calculate the total annual ordering cost.
2. Calculate the total annual carrying cost.
3. Calculate the total annual inventory cost.
4. Calculate the EOQ.
5. Calculate the total annual inventory cost using the EOQ inventory policy.
6. How much is saved per year using the EOQ versus an order size of 400 units?
7. Compute the reorder point, assuming the lead time is three days.
8. Suppose that the usage of the part can be as much as 110 units per day. Calculate the safety stock and the new reorder point.

Solution

1. Ordering cost $= PD/Q$
$= \$20 \times 36{,}000/400$
$= \$1{,}800$
2. Carrying cost $= CQ/2$
$= \$4 \times 400/2$
$= \$800$
3. Total cost = Ordering cost + Carrying cost
$= \$1{,}800 + \$800$
$= \$2{,}600$
4. $\text{EOQ} = \sqrt{2PD/C}$
$= \sqrt{(2 \times 20 \times 36{,}000/4)}$
$= \sqrt{360{,}000}$
$= 600$
5. Cost $= (PD/Q) + (CQ/2)$
$= (\$20 \times 36{,}000/600) + (\$4 \times 600/2)$
$= \$1{,}200 + \$1{,}200$
$= \$2{,}400$

6. Savings = \$2,600 − \$2,400 = \$200
7. ROP = 100 × 3 = 300 units
8. Safety stock = (110 − 100)3 = 30 units
   ROP = 110 × 3 = 330 units or 300 + 30 = 330 units

2. Optimal Mix

Two types of gears are produced: A and B. Gear A has a unit contribution margin of \$200, and Gear B has a unit contribution margin of \$400. Gear A uses two hours of grinding time, and Gear B uses five hours of grinding time. There are 200 hours of grinding time available per week. This is the only constraint.

Required

1. Is the grinding constraint an internal constraint or an external constraint?
2. Determine the optimal mix. What is the total contribution margin?
3. Suppose that there is an additional demand constraint: market conditions will allow the sale of only 80 units of each gear. Now, what is the optimal mix? The total contribution margin?

Solution

1. It's an internal constraint.
2. Gear A: \$200/2 = \$100 per grinding hour
   Gear B: \$400/5 = \$80 per grinding hour
   Since Gear A earns more contribution margin per unit of scarce resource than Gear B, only Gear A should be produced and sold (this is based on the fact that we can sell all we want of each product).

   Optimal mix: Gear A = 100 units* and Gear B= 0
   *200/2 = 100 units of A can be produced per week
   Total contribution margin = \$200 × 100 = \$20,000 per week

3. Now, we should sell 80 units of Gear A using 160 hours (2 × 80) and eight units of Gear B (40/5). Total contribution margin = (80 × \$200) + (8 × \$400) = \$19,200 per week.

3. Drummers and Inventory Management Systems

Traditional and JIT inventory management systems also have drummers—factors that determine the production rate of the plant. For a just-in-case system, the drummer is the excess capacity of the first operation. For JIT, the drummer is market demand.

Required

1. Explain why the drummer of a just-in-case system is identified as excess capacity of the first operation.
2. Explain how market demand drives the JIT production system.
3. Explain how a drummer constraint is used in the TOC approach to inventory management.
4. What are the advantages and disadvantages of the three types of drummers?

Solution

1. In a traditional inventory system, local efficiency measures encourage the manager of the first operation to keep the department's workers busy. Thus, materials are released to satisfy this objective. This practice is justified because the inventory may be needed just in case demand is greater than expected, or just in case the first operation has downtime or other problems.

2. In a JIT system, when the final operation delivers its goods to a customer, a backward-rippling effect triggers the release of materials into the factory. First, the last process removes the buffer inventory from the withdrawal store, and this leads to a P-Kanban being placed on the production post of the preceding operation. This operation then begins production, withdrawing parts it needs from its withdrawal store, leading to a P-Kanban being placed on the production post of its preceding operation. This process repeats itself—all the way back to the first operation.
3. A drummer constraint sets the production rate of the factory to match its own production rate. This is automatically true for succeeding operations. For preceding operations, the rate is controlled by tying the drummer constraint's rate of production to that of the first operation. A time buffer is also set in front of the drummer constraint to protect throughput in the event of interruptions.
4. The excess capacity drummer typically will build excess inventories. This serves to protect current throughput. However, it ties up a lot of capital and tends to cover up problems such as poor quality, bad delivery performance, and inefficient production. Because it is costly and covers up certain critical productive problems, the just-in-case approach may be a threat to future throughput by damaging a firm's competitive position. JIT reduces inventories dramatically—using only small buffers in front of each operation as a means to regulate production flow and signal when production should occur. JIT has the significant advantage of uncovering problems and eventually correcting them. However, discovering problems usually means that current throughput will be lost while problems are being corrected. Future throughput tends to be protected because the firm is taking actions to improve its operations. TOC uses time buffers in front of the critical constraints. These buffers are large enough to keep the critical constraints operating while other operations may be down. Once the problem is corrected, the other resource constraints usually have sufficient excess capacity to catch up. Thus, current throughput is protected. Furthermore, future throughput is protected because TOC uses the same approach as JIT—namely, uncovering and correcting problems. TOC can be viewed as an improvement on JIT methods—correcting the lost throughput problem while maintaining the other JIT features.

Questions for Writing and Discussion

1. What are ordering costs? Provide examples.
2. What are setup costs? Illustrate with examples.
3. What are carrying costs? Illustrate with examples.
4. What are stockout costs?
5. Explain why, in the traditional view of inventory, carrying costs increase as ordering costs decrease.
6. Discuss the traditional reasons for carrying inventory.
7. What is the economic order quantity?
8. Suppose that a material has a lead time of three days and that the average usage of the material is 12 units per day. What is the reorder point? If the maximum usage is 15 units per day, what is the safety stock?
9. Explain how safety stock is used to deal with demand uncertainty.
10. What approach does JIT take to minimize total inventory costs?
11. What is JIT manufacturing? List five ways in which JIT manufacturing differs from traditional manufacturing.
12. What are manufacturing cells? Explain how they differ from production departments.
13. Explain why some indirect manufacturing costs in traditional manufacturing become direct costs in JIT manufacturing. Give some examples of costs that change in this way.
14. Explain how long-term contractual relationships with suppliers can reduce the acquisition cost of materials.
15. What is EDI, and what relationship does it have to continuous replenishment?

16. One reason for inventory is to prevent shutdowns. How does the JIT approach to inventory management deal with this potential problem?
17. Explain how the Kanban system helps reduce inventories.
18. What is a constraint? An internal constraint? An external constraint?
19. What are loose constraints? Binding constraints?
20. Define and discuss the three measures of organizational performance used by the theory of constraints.
21. Explain how lowering inventory produces better products, lower prices, and better responsiveness to customer needs.
22. What are the five steps that TOC uses to improve organizational performance?
23. What is a drum-buffer-rope system?

Exercises

14-1

Ordering and Carrying Costs
LO1

Balfour Company uses 30,000 subassemblies in production each year. The cost of placing an order is $600. The cost of holding one unit of inventory for one year is $4. Currently, Balfour places 50 orders of 6,000 subassemblies per year.

Required

1. Compute the annual ordering cost.
2. Compute the annual carrying cost.
3. Compute the total cost of Balfour's current inventory policy.

14-2

Economic Order Quantity
LO1

Shellar Company is a wholesaler. Shellar purchases 800,000 units of product X each year for sale to retailers. The cost of placing an order is $40. The cost of holding one unit of inventory for one year is $4.

Required

1. Compute the economic order quantity.
2. How many orders would Shellar place under the EOQ policy?
3. Compute the annual ordering cost for the EOQ.
4. Compute the annual carrying cost for the EOQ.
5. Compute the total inventory-related cost at the EOQ.
6. Previously, Shellar had been purchasing 8,000 units of product X per order. What is the ordering cost per year under the previous policy? The annual carrying cost? How much money does using the EOQ policy save the company over the policy of purchasing 8,000 units per order?

14-3

Economic Order Quantity
LO1

EXCEL

Ramaswathy, Inc., makes 6,250 units of a specialty product each year. The cost of setting up the equipment to produce one batch is $100, and the carrying cost for one unit is $5.

Required

1. Compute the economic order quantity for setting up to make one batch.
2. Compute the annual setup cost for the EOQ. (*Note:* Do not round the number of setups per year to a whole number. Instead, consider that the annual setup cost is the average annual setup cost.)
3. Compute the annual carrying cost for the EOQ.

14-4

Reorder Point
LO1

Jelsen Company sells educational toys. One raw material that it orders is plastic. The plastic is melted and placed in molds to be used for the production of various toys. Information pertaining to the plastic raw material is as follows:

EXCEL

Economic order quantity	120,000 pounds
Average daily usage	8,000 pounds
Maximum daily usage	12,000 pounds
Lead time	3 days

Required

1. What is the reorder point assuming no safety stock is carried?
2. What is the reorder point assuming that safety stock is carried?

14-5

Safety Stock
LO1

Quadrex Company produces a component used in its production of cell phones. The time to set up and produce a batch of the components is four days. The average daily usage is 2,000 components, and the maximum daily usage is 2,350 components.

Required

1. Compute the reorder point assuming that safety stock is carried by Quadrex. How much safety stock does the company carry?
2. Now suppose that the average daily usage of 2,000 components is also the maximum daily usage. However, the setup time is four days on average, but could take a maximum of five days. Compute the reorder point assuming that safety stock is carried by Quadrex. How much safety stock does the company carry?

14-6

EOQ with Setup Costs; Reorder Point; Production Scheduling
LO1

Shields Manufacturing produces two different types of engines: one for riding lawn mowers and one for jet skis. To produce the different engines, equipment must be set up. Each setup configuration corresponds to a particular type of engine. The setup cost per batch of engines is $4,000 for the lawn mower engine and $7,200 for the jet ski engine. The cost of carrying lawn mower engines in inventory is $2 per engine per year. The cost of carrying jet ski engines is $3 per engine per year. During the coming year, the company expects to produce 324,000 lawn mower engines and 750,000 jet ski engines. The company hopes to sell an average of 1,296 lawn mower engines per workday and an average of 1,500 jet ski engines per workday. It takes Shields two days to set up the equipment for production of either engine. Once set up, Shields can produce 4,000 engines per workday. There are 250 workdays available per year. The lead time for lawn mower engines is 11 days and for jet ski engines is 12 days.

Required

1. Compute the number of lawn mower engines that should be produced per setup to minimize total setup and carrying costs for this product.
2. Compute the total setup and carrying costs associated with the economic order quantity for lawn mower engines.
3. What is the reorder point for lawn mower engines?
4. Repeat Requirements 1 through 3 for the jet ski engines.
5. Using the economic-order batch size, is it possible for Shields to produce the amount that can be sold of each engine? Does scheduling have a role here? Explain. Is this a push- or pull-system approach to inventory management? Explain.

14-7

EOQ; Setup Cost and Setup Time
LO1, LO2

Refer to **Exercise 14-6**. Suppose that Shields was able to reduce the setup time from 2 days to 0.5 day and that, as a consequence, setup costs are reduced to one-fourth of their current level (for both products). Engineering predicts that within one year, setup time and costs can be further reduced (from 0.5 day to 0.05 day and costs to $100).

Required

1. Calculate the EOQ for lawn mower engines for the new setup time (0.5 days). Repeat for the projected setup time and costs.
2. How is reducing the setup time to 0.05 days (and setup costs to $100) associated with JIT?

14-8

Reasons for Carrying Inventory
LO1, LO2, LO3

The following reasons have been offered for holding inventories:

1. To balance ordering or setup costs and carrying costs.
2. To satisfy customer demand (for example, meet delivery dates).
3. To avoid shutting down manufacturing facilities because of
   a. machine failure
   b. defective parts
   c. unavailable parts
   d. late delivery of parts
4. To buffer against unreliable production processes.
5. To take advantage of discounts.
6. To hedge against future price increases.

Required

1. Explain how the JIT approach responds to each of these reasons and, consequently, argues for insignificant levels of inventories.
2. The theory of constraints (TOC) criticizes the JIT approach to inventory management, arguing that it fails to protect throughput. Explain what this means, and describe how TOC addresses this issue.

14-9

Kanban Cards
LO2

Explain the use of each of the following cards in the Kanban system:

1. The withdrawal Kanban
2. The production Kanban
3. The vendor Kanban

14-10

JIT Limitations
LO2

Many companies have viewed JIT as a panacea—a knight in shining armor, which promises rescue from sluggish profits, poor quality, and productive inefficiency. It is often lauded for its beneficial effects on employee morale and self-esteem. Yet, JIT may also cause a company to struggle and may produce a good deal of frustration. In some cases, JIT appears to deliver less than its reputation seems to call for.

Required

Discuss some of the limitations and problems that companies may encounter when implementing a JIT system.

14-11

Various Topics
LO2

Choose the *best* answer for each of the following multiple-choice questions:

1. Which of the following *best* describes a JIT system?
   a. It is a demand-pull system.
   b. It requires suppliers to deliver parts and materials just in time for production.
   c. It emphasizes total quality management.
   d. It increases the number of costs that are directly traceable to a product.
   e. All of the above.
2. A JIT system is characterized by
   a. a small supplier base.
   b. departmental structure.

c. centralized services.
d. specialized labor.
e. None of the above.

3. In a JIT system, which of the following costs would typically be assigned to a product using direct tracing?

a. Plant depreciation
b. Salary of the plant supervisor
c. Landscaping
d. Material handling
e. Cafeteria services

4. An in-house representative is a(n)

a. purchasing employee who works on site at the supplier plant.
b. employee of the supplier who works on site at the customer facility and whose salary is paid for by the customer.
c. employee of the supplier who works on site at the customer facility and whose salary is paid for by the supplier.
d. supplier employee who is empowered by the customer to make purchases on behalf of the customer.
e. Both c and d.

5. A marker or card that controls movement of work among the manufacturing processes is referred to as a

a. withdrawal Kanban.
b. vendor Kanban.
c. production Kanban.
d. production-ordering post.
e. kaizen Kanban.

14-12

JIT; Traceability of Costs; Product Costing Accuracy
LO2

Weider Manufacturing Company changed to a JIT production system by setting up manufacturing cells dedicated to the production of a single product. The manufacturing costs assigned to one electronic component before and after installing JIT are shown below. In both the pre- and post-JIT setting, 200,000 units of the component are manufactured. The post-JIT manufacturing cell for this component has all machinery necessary for the component's production. Cell workers do all direct and indirect labor for the cell, including cellclean up at the end of each day. There is a submeter that measures electricity usage by the cell.

	Before	**After**
Direct materials	$ 60,000	$ 60,000
Direct labor	40,000	50,000
Maintenance	50,000	30,000
Electricity	10,000	8,000
Depreciation	12,500	10,000
Material handling	8,000	4,000
Engineering	9,500	8,000
Setups	15,000	8,400
Building and grounds	11,800	12,400
Supplies	4,000	3,000
Supervision (plant)	8,200	8,200
Cell supervision	0	30,000
Departmental supervision	18,000	0
Total	$262,000	$238,000

Required

1. Compute the unit cost of the product before and after JIT. Explain why the JIT unit cost is more accurate.
2. Identify the costs in the JIT environment that are directly traceable to the electronic component. Classify the remaining costs as those that must be traced using drivers or allocated if truly indirect.

14-13

Product Mix Decisions; Single Constraint; Two Constraints
LO3

Gallard Company has specialized machinery that can produce two types of metal housings. The machinery has a total operating capacity of 40,000 hours per year. Information on each of the two housings follows:

	Model A	Model B
Selling price	$20.00	$35.00
Unit variable cost	$15.00	$15.00

Each unit of model A requires one-half hour of machine time; each unit of model B requires 2.5 hours of machine time. The marketing manager has determined that the company can sell all that it can produce of each of the two products.

Required

1. How many of each product should be sold to maximize total contribution margin? What is the total contribution margin for this product mix?
2. Suppose that Gallard can sell no more than 50,000 units of each type at the prices indicated. How many units of each type of rod should be produced? What would be the total contribution margin for this product mix?

14-14

Product Mix Decisions; Single Constraint; Two Constraints
LO3

Jorgenson Company produces two types of gears, X and Y, with unit contribution margins of $25 and $10, respectively. Each gear must be notched by a special machine. The firm owns five machines that together provide 10,000 hours of machine time per year. Gear X requires two hours of machine time, and Gear Y requires 0.5 hours of machine time. There are no other constraints.

Required

1. What is the contribution margin per hour of machine time for each gear?
2. What is the optimal mix of gears, assuming that the company can sell all that it can produce of each of the two products? What is the total contribution margin earned for this optimal mix?
3. Now assume that a maximum of 15,000 units of each gear can be sold. What is the optimal mix of gears? What is the total contribution margin earned for this optimal mix?

14-15

Product Mix Decisions; Single Constraint, Two Constraints
LO3

EXCEL

Perkins Company has the capability of producing three types of rods used in the manufacture of different kinds of hydraulic cylinders. All three rods can be shaped and cut on the same machine. Perkins owns one of these machines, which has a total operating capacity of 30,000 hours per year. Information on each of the three rods follows:

	Type I	Type II	Type III
Selling price	$40.00	$60.00	$75.00
Unit variable cost	$25.00	$38.00	$60.00
Machine hours required	0.50	0.80	1.50

The marketing manager has determined that the company can sell all that it can produce of each of the three products.

Required

1. How many of each product should be sold to maximize total contribution margin? What is the total contribution margin for this product mix?
2. Suppose that Perkins can sell no more than 20,000 units of each type at the prices indicated. How many units of each type of rod should be produced? What would be the total contribution margin for this product mix?

14-16

Drum-Buffer-Rope System
LO3

Goicoechea, Inc., manufactures two models of bows: regular and deluxe. It sells all it can produce. Bows are produced in three processes: laminating, molding, and finishing. In laminating, limbs are created by laminating layers of wood. In molding, the limbs are heat treated, under pressure, to form a strong, resilient limb. In finishing, any protruding glue is removed, and the limbs are cleaned with acetone, dried, and sprayed with final finishes. Recently, Goicoechea implemented a TOC approach for its Waco, Texas, plant. One binding constraint was identified, and the optimal product mix was determined. The following diagram reflects the TOC outcome.

Required

1. What is the daily production rate? Which process sets this rate?
2. How many days of buffer inventory is Goicoechea carrying? How is this time buffer determined?
3. Explain what the letters A, B, and C represent. Discuss each of their roles in the TOC system.

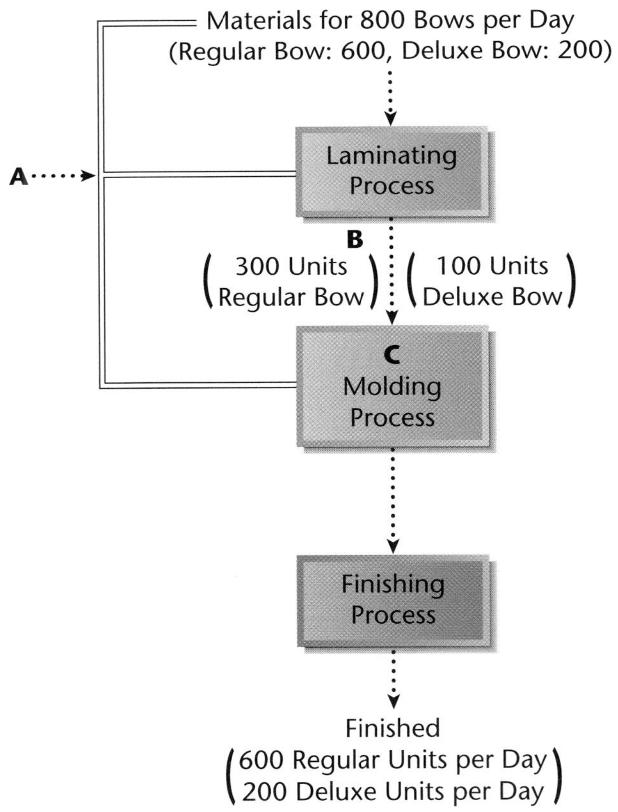

Problems

14-17

EOQ and Reorder Point
LO1

Italia Pizzeria is a popular pizza restaurant near a college campus. Brandon Thayn, an accounting student, works for Italia Pizzeria. After several months at the restaurant, Brandon began to analyze the efficiency of the business, particularly inventory practices. He noticed that the owner had more than 50 items regularly carried in inventory. Of these items, the most expensive to buy and carry was cheese. Cheese was ordered in blocks at $17.50 per block. Annual usage totals 14,000 blocks.

Upon questioning the owner, Brandon discovered that the owner did not use any formal model for ordering cheese. It took five days to receive a new order when placed, which was done whenever the inventory of cheese dropped to 200 blocks. The size of the order was usually 400 blocks. The cost of carrying one block of cheese is 10 percent of its purchase price. It costs $40 to place and receive an order.

Italia Pizzeria stays open seven days a week and operates 50 weeks a year. The restaurant closes for the last two weeks of December.

Required

1. Compute the total cost of ordering and carrying the cheese inventory under the current policy.
2. Compute the total cost of ordering and carrying cheese if the restaurant were to change to the economic order quantity. How much would the restaurant save per year by switching policies?
3. If the restaurant uses the economic order quantity, when should it place an order? (Assume that the amount of cheese used per day is the same throughout the year.) How does this compare with the current reorder policy?
4. Suppose that storage space allows a maximum of 600 blocks of cheese. Discuss the inventory policy that should be followed with this restriction.
5. Suppose that the maximum storage is 600 blocks of cheese and that cheese can be held for a maximum of 10 days. The owner will not hold cheese any longer in order to ensure the right flavor and quality. Under these conditions, evaluate the owner's current inventory policy.

14-18

EOQ; Safety Stock
LO1

EXCEL

The emergency room of the Wyandotte County Medical Center uses an EOQ model to order supplies. Lately, several physicians have complained about the availability of a particular medication to treat patients suffering from heart attacks. During the past three months, emergency room physicians, on occasion, have had to use a substitute medication—one that is known to be less effective. Because of the problem, the supply officer has decided to review the current inventory policy. The following data have been gathered:

Cost of placing and receiving an order	$ 100
Cost of carrying one package	$5.50
Average usage per day	30 vials
Maximum usage per day	35 vials
Lead time for an order	4 days
Annual demand	10,571 vials

The emergency room currently does not carry any safety stock. The emergency room operates 365 days each year.

Required

1. Compute the economic order quantity and the reorder point. What is the total ordering and carrying cost for the emergency room's current inventory policy?

2. Assume that the emergency room has decided to carry safety stock for the indicated medication. Compute how much should be carried to ensure no stockouts. Compute the total ordering and carrying cost for this policy. Will the reorder point change? If so, what is the new reorder point?

14-19

EOQ; Safety Stock; Setup Costs LO1, LO2

Geneva Company produces safety goggles for coal miners. Goggles are produced in batches according to model and size. Although the setup and production time varies for each model, the smallest lead time is six days. The most popular model, Model SG4, takes two days for setup, and the production rate is 750 units per day. The expected annual demand for the model is 36,000 units. Demand for the model, however, can reach 45,000 units. The cost of carrying one SG4 unit is $3 per unit. The setup cost is $6,000. Geneva chooses its batch size based on the economic order quantity criterion. Expected annual demand is used to compute the EOQ.

Recently, Geneva has encountered some stiff competition—especially from foreign sources. Some of the foreign competitors have been able to produce and deliver the goggles to retailers in half the time it takes Geneva to produce. For example, a large retailer recently requested a delivery of 12,000 Model SG4 goggles with the stipulation that they be delivered within seven working days. Geneva had 3,000 units of SG4 in stock. It informed the potential customer that it could deliver 3,000 units immediately and the other 9,000 units in about 14 working days—with the possibility of interim partial orders being delivered. The customer declined the offer indicating that the total order had to be delivered within seven working days so that its stores could take advantage of some special local conditions. The customer expressed regret and indicated that it would accept the order from another competitor who could satisfy the time requirements.

Required

1. Calculate the optimal batch size for Model SG4 using the EOQ model. Was Geneva's response to the customer right? Would it take the time indicated to produce the number of units wanted by the customer? Explain with supporting computations.
2. Upon learning of the lost order, the marketing manager grumbled about Geneva's inventory policy. "We lost the order because we didn't have sufficient inventory. We need to carry more units in inventory to deal with unexpected orders like these." Do you agree? How much additional inventory would have been needed to meet customer requirements? In the future, should Geneva carry more inventory? Can you think of other solutions?
3. Fenton Gray, the head of industrial engineering, reacted differently to the lost order. "Our problem is more complex than insufficient inventory. I know that our foreign competitors carry much less inventory than we do. What we need to do is decrease the lead time. I have been studying this problem, and my staff has found a way to reduce setup time for Model SG4 from two days to 1.5 hours. Using this new procedure, setup cost can be reduced to about $94. Also, by rearranging the plant layout for this product—creating what are called manufacturing cells—we can increase the production rate from 750 units per day to about 2,000 units per day. This is done simply by eliminating a lot of move time and waiting time—both non-value-added activities."

   Assume that the engineer's estimates are on target. Compute the new optimal batch size (using the EOQ formula). What is the new lead time? Given this new information, would Geneva have been able to meet the customer's time requirements? Assume that there are eight hours available in each workday.
4. Suppose that the setup time and cost are reduced to 0.5 hours and $10, respectively. What is the batch size now? As setup time approaches zero and the setup cost becomes negligible, what does this imply? Assume for example that it takes five minutes to set up and costs about $0.864 per setup.

14-20

Reorder Point with Demand Uncertainty (assumes knowledge of basic statistics)
LO1

CMA

The Old Orchard Battery Distributor Company supplies automotive batteries to retail auto parts stores in several midwestern states. The company is developing an EOQ system to assist in the management of its battery inventory. The EOQ demand distribution and purchase lead time for each type of battery have been determined.

David Kellogg, the owner of Old Orchard, has asked Marvin Rollins, his materials manager, for assistance in determining a reorder point for each type of battery. Kellogg would like the reorder points set high enough to minimize stockouts, thereby maximizing customer service. Rollins can demonstrate a reorder point calculation by using the demand data on the RJ47 battery shown below. Rollins recalls that a product's reorder point is equal to its demand during the purchase lead time plus a safety stock.

RJ47 Demand During Lead Time	RJ47 Demand Probability
100	0.03
200	0.05
300	0.20
400	0.40
500	0.25
600	0.07

The purchase lead time for the battery is six weeks.

Required

1. For the RJ47 battery:
   a. Calculate the expected demand during the lead time.
   b. Calculate the reorder point given David Kellogg's desire to minimize stockouts.
2. Without prejudice to your answer in Requirement 1, assume that the reorder point is 400. What is the probability of a stockout? **(CMA adapted)**

14-21

JIT System
LO2

Kelifo Electric Vehicle Company (Kevco) manufactures electric golf carts, electric all-terrain vehicles, and electric senior citizen mobility scooters. Each of the three products has two or three models; a total of eight models are produced. Because of the somewhat erratic product demand and the lead time needed for the setup for a model changeover, Kevco has been increasing its material and finished goods inventories. Work-in-process inventories are relatively low and have consistent costs from one month to the next.

During the last five years, Kevco has experienced increased inventory costs, decreasing profit margins, and customer complaints concerning the long lead time to fill sales orders. Kevco's president, Lou Watts, has grown concerned and has been discussing ways to change these deteriorating conditions with his production, marketing, and accounting staff.

For the past few months, this top management group has been looking at how a JIT manufacturing system utilizing a Kanban concept could be used at Kevco. The team has assembled data and information that indicates that Kevco could change its production process from one of production push to demand pull by rearranging its production floor into manufacturing cells that would be dedicated to one of three products produced. Slight modifications to the equipment in the cell would be needed for a changeover from one model to another. Cell production teams would be responsible for cell performance, maintenance on machines and equipment, solving production problems, and training. The management team is aware of, and has visited, other equipment manufacturing companies that have been quite successful in utilizing demand pull and cell manufacturing techniques.

Required

1. Discuss the effect on Kevco's planning and operating processes if Kevco implements a demand pull production system.
2. Identify and describe at least five benefits to Kevco that should result from the demand pull approach.
3. Discuss the behavioral effects of the proposed change at Kevco to team participation in planning and production.

14-22

Kanban System; EDI
LO2

Packer Company produces a product that requires two processes. In the first process, a subassembly is produced (Subassembly A); in the second process, this subassembly and a subassembly purchased from outside (Subassembly B) are assembled to produce the final product. For simplicity, assume that the assembly of one unit takes the same time as the production of Subassembly A. Subassembly A is placed in a container and sent to an area called the subassembly stores (SB stores) area. A production Kanban is attached to this container. A second container, also with one subassembly, is located near the assembly line (called the withdrawal store). This container has attached to it a withdrawal Kanban.

Required

1. Explain how withdrawal and production Kanban cards are used to control the work flow between the two processes. How does this approach minimize inventories?
2. Explain how vendor Kanban cards can be used to control the flow of the purchased subassembly. What implications does this have for supplier relationships? What role, if any, do continuous replenishment and EDI play in this process?

14-23

Product Mix Decision; Single and Multiple Constraints
LO3

Curtis Remedies, Inc., produces two herbal mixes: ImmuneBoost and MentaGrowth. ImmuneBoost has more ingredients and requires more machine time for grinding and mixing. The manufacturing process is highly mechanized; both products are produced by the same equipment by using different settings. For the coming period, 640,000 machine hours are available. Management is trying to decide on the quantities of each product to produce (in bottles of 30 pills). The following data are available:

	ImmuneBoost	MentaGrowth
Machine hours per unit	1.60	0.80
Unit selling price	$4.00	$4.80
Unit variable cost	$2.40	$3.60

Required

1. Determine the units of each product that should be produced in order to maximize profits. What is the total contribution margin earned by this optimal mix?
2. Because of market conditions, the company can sell no more than 400,000 bottles of ImmuneBoost and 480,000 bottles of MentaGrowth. Now, what is the optimal mix? Total contribution margin?

14-24

Optimal Product Mix
LO3

CMA

Wilson Company manufactures and sells three components in a factory of three departments. The components are used as replacement parts in jet aircraft. After machining in each department, the components are subjected to stress tests. The nature of the machine processing and of the labor skills required for stress testing is such that neither machines nor test labor can be switched from one department to another. Wilson's management is attempting to plan its production schedule for the next several months. The planning is complicated by the fact that labor shortages exist in the community and some machines will be down several months for repairs.

Following is information regarding available machine and test time by department and the machine hours and test hours required for each component. These data are valid for at least the next six months.

	Department		
Monthly Capacity	**A**	**B**	**C**
Test hours available	7,400	9,000	5,500
Machine hours available	6,000	6,200	5,400

		Department		
Component	**Input per Unit Produced**	**A**	**B**	**C**
12-L	Test hours	2	3	3
	Machine hours	1	1	2
14-M	Test hours	1	2	—
	Machine hours	1	1	—
40-S	Test hours	2	2	2
	Machine hours	2	2	1

The monthly demand for the next six months will be as follows:

Component	**Units Sold**
12-L	1,000
14-M	800
40-S	2,000

Inventory levels will not be increased or decreased during the next six months. The unit cost and price data for each component are as follows:

	Component		
	12-L	**14-M**	**40-S**
Unit costs:			
Direct materials	$ 14	$ 26	$ 34
Test labor	66	38	51
Variable overhead	27	20	25
Fixed overhead	15	10	32
Variable selling	3	2	4
Total unit cost	$125	$ 96	$146
Unit selling price	$203	$136	$184

Required

1. Calculate the monthly requirement for machine hours and test hours for producing Components 12-L, 14-M, and 40-S to determine whether the factory can meet the monthly sales demand.
2. Determine the quantities of each component that should be produced monthly to maximize profits. Prepare a schedule that shows the contribution to profits of your product mix. **(CMA adapted)**

14-25

Identifying and Exploiting Constraints; Constraint Elevation
LO3

Copeland Company produces two metal parts used in industrial equipment (Part A and Part B). The company has three processes: molding, grinding, and finishing. In molding, molds are created, and molten metal is poured into the shell. Grinding removes the gates that allowed the molten metal to flow into the mold's cavities. In finishing, rough edges caused by the grinders are removed by small, handheld pneumatic tools. In molding, the setup time is one hour. The other two processes have no setup time required. The demand for Part A is 600 units per day, and the demand for Part B is 1,000 units per day. The minutes required per unit for each product follow:

	Minutes Required per Unit of Product		
Product	**Molding**	**Grinding**	**Finishing**
Part A	10	20	30
Part B	20	30	40

The company operates one 8-hour shift. The molding process employs 48 workers (who each work 8 hours). Two hours of their time, however, is used for setups (assuming both products are produced). The grinding process has sufficient equipment and workers to provide 48,000 grinding minutes per shift.

The Finishing Department is labor-intensive and employs 140 workers, who each work 8 hours per day. The only significant unit-level variable costs are materials and power. For Part A, the variable cost per unit is $80 and for Part B, it is $100. Selling prices for A and B are $180 and $220, respectively. Copeland's policy is to use two setups per day: an initial setup to produce all that is scheduled for A and a second setup (changeover) to produce all that is scheduled for B. The amount scheduled does not necessarily correspond to each product's daily demand.

Required

1. Calculate the time (in minutes) needed each day to meet the daily market demand for Part A and Part B. What is the major internal constraint facing Copeland Company?
2. Describe how Copeland should exploit its major binding constraint. Specifically, identify the product mix that will maximize daily throughput.
3. Assume that manufacturing engineering has found a way to reduce the molding setup time from one hour to 10 minutes. Explain how this affects the product mix and daily throughput.

14-26

Theory of Constraints; Internal Constraints
LO3

Young Company produces two subassemblies used by aircraft manufacturers: Sub A and Sub B. Sub A is made up of two components, one manufactured internally and one purchased from external suppliers. Sub B is made up of three components, one manufactured internally and two purchased from suppliers. The company has two processes: fabrication and assembly. In fabrication, the internally produced components are made. Each component takes 20 minutes to produce. In assembly, it takes 30 minutes to assemble the components for Sub A and 40 minutes to assemble the components for Sub B. Young Company operates one shift per day. Each process employs 100 workers who each work eight hours per day.

Sub A earns a unit contribution margin of $20, and Sub B earns a unit contribution margin of $24 (calculated as the difference between revenue and the cost of materials and energy). Young can sell all that it produces of either part. There are no other constraints. Young can add a second shift of either process. Although a second shift would work eight hours, there is no mandate that it employ the same number of workers. The labor cost per hour for fabrication is $8, and the labor cost per hour for assembly is $7.

Required

1. Identify the constraints facing Young. How many binding constraints are possible? What is Young's optimal product mix? What daily contribution margin is produced by this mix?
2. What is the drummer constraint? How much excess capacity does the other constraint have? Assume that a 1.5-day buffer inventory is needed to deal with any production interruptions. Describe the drummer-buffer-rope concept using the Young data to illustrate the process.
3. Explain why the use of local labor efficiency measures will not work in Young's TOC environment.

4. Suppose Young decides to elevate the binding constraint by adding a second shift of 50 workers (for assembly only). Would elevation of Young's binding constraint improve its system performance? Explain with supporting computations.

14-27

TOC; Internal and External Constraints
LO3

EXCEL

Zaramar Manufacturing produces two types of hydraulic cylinders (small and large). Both cylinders pass through four processes: cutting, welding, polishing, and painting. With the exception of polishing, each of the processes employs 20 workers who work eight hours each day. Polishing employs 26 workers. The small cylinder sells for $80 per unit, and the large cylinder sells for $110 per unit. Materials is the only unit-level variable expense. The materials cost for the small cylinder is $40 per unit, and the materials cost for the large cylinder is $50 per unit. Zaramar's accounting system has provided the following additional information about its operations and products:

Resource Name	Resource Available	Small Cylinder Resource Usage*	Large Cylinder Resource Usage*
Cutting labor	9,600 minutes	30 minutes	20 minutes
Welding labor	9,600 minutes	30 minutes	60 minutes
Polishing labor	12,480 minutes	30 minutes	30 minutes
Painting labor	9,600 minutes	20 minutes	30 minutes
Market demand:			
Small cylinder	200 per day	1 unit	—
Large cylinder	100 per day	—	1 unit

*Per unit

Zaramar's management has determined that any production interruptions can be corrected within two days.

Required

1. Assuming that Zaramar can meet daily market demand, compute the potential daily profit. Now, compute the minutes needed for each process to meet the daily market demand. Can Zaramar meet daily market demand? If not, where is the bottleneck?
2. Determine the optimal mix and the maximum daily contribution margin (throughput).
3. Explain how a DBR system would work for Zaramar.
4. Suppose that the Engineering Department has proposed a process design change that will increase the polishing time for the small cylinder from 30 to 46 minutes per unit and decrease its welding time from 30 to 20 minutes per unit. The cost of process redesign would be $20,000. Evaluate this proposed change. What step in the TOC process does this proposal represent?

Managerial Decision Case

14-28

Ethical Issues
LO2

Mac Ericson and Tammy Ferguson met at an IMA conference two months ago and began dating. Mac is the controller for Longley Enterprises, and Tammy is a marketing manager for Sharp Products. Longley is a major supplier for Piura Products, a competitor of Sharp's. Longley has entered into a long-term agreement to supply certain materials to Piura. Piura has been developing a JIT purchasing and manufacturing system. As part of its development, Piura and Longley have established EDI capabilities. The following conversation took place during a luncheon engagement:

Tammy: Mac, I understand that you have EDI connections with Piura. Is that right?

Mac: Sure. It's part of the partners-in-profits arrangement that we have worked so hard to get. It's working real well. Knowing Piura's production schedule helps us stabilize our own schedule. It has actually cut some of our overhead costs. It has also decreased Piura's costs. I estimate that we both have decreased production costs by about 7 to 10 percent.

Tammy: That's interesting. You know, I have a real chance of getting promoted to VP of marketing. . . .

Mac: Hey, that's great. When will you know?

Tammy: It all depends on this deal that I am trying to cut with Balboa—if I win the contract, then I think I have it. My main problem is with Piura. If I knew what its production schedule was, I could get a pretty good idea as to how long it would take it to deliver. I could then make sure that we beat its delivery offer—even if we had to work overtime and do all kinds of expediting. I know that our delivery speed is very, very important to Balboa. Our quality is as good as Piura's, but it tends to beat us on delivery time. My boss would love to kick Piura. It has beat us too many times recently. I am wondering if you would be willing to help me out.

Mac: Tammy, you know that I would help if I could, but Piura's production schedule is confidential information. If word got out that I had leaked that kind of stuff to you, I would be history.

Tammy: Well, no one would ever know. Besides, I have already had a chat with Tom Anderson, our CEO. Our VP of finance is retiring. He knows about you and your capabilities. I think he would be willing to hire you—especially if he knew that you helped swing this Balboa deal. You could increase your salary by 40 percent.

Mac: I don't know. I have my doubts about the propriety of all this. It might look kind of funny if I take over as VP of finance not long after Piura loses the Balboa deal. But a VP position and a big salary increase are tempting. It's unlikely that I'll ever have a shot at the VP position in my company.

Tammy: Think it over. If you are interested, I'll arrange a dinner with Tom Anderson. He said he'd like to meet you. He knows a little about this. I'm sure that he has the ability to keep it quiet. I don't think there is much risk.

Required

1. Based on this information, has Mac violated any of the IMA standards of ethical conduct? Explain.
2. Suppose that Mac decides to provide information in exchange for the VP position. What IMA standards would he violate?

Research Assignment

14-29

Cybercase
LO3

The theory of constraints is a method for bringing about continuous improvement (the five TOC steps are a continuous improvement loop). In effect, TOC addresses three questions: (1) what to change, (2) what to change to, and (3) how to cause the change. The answers to these questions have to do with what is called the "Thinking Process." Six specific thinking process tools are suggested: the current reality tree, the evaporative cloud, the future reality tree, the negative branches, the prerequisite tree, and the transition tree. Supporters of TOC claim that the method can bring about significant improvements in lead time, inventory, and financial performance. Furthermore, some advocate changing to what is called "constraint accounting." These issues create some significant opportunities for TOC-related Internet research.

Required

1. Search the Internet, and find definitions of the thinking process and the indicated thinking process tools.
2. Search the Internet, and find examples of three companies that have successfully used the theory of constraints. List some of the benefits achieved by these companies. Is TOC more than an inventory management method?
3. Search the Internet, and find information on constraint accounting. What is constraint accounting? Is it an alternative to activity- and functional-based accounting? Explain.

PART 6

Special Topics

chapter 15

Quality Costs and Productivity: Measurement, Reporting, and Control

learning objectives

After studying this chapter, you should be able to:

1. Identify and describe the four types of quality costs.

2. Prepare a quality cost report, and differentiate between acceptable quality level and the view espoused by total quality control.

3. Tell why quality cost information is needed, and show how it is used.

4. Explain what productivity is, and calculate the impact of productivity changes on profits.

Scenario

Russell Walsh, president of Ladd Lighting Corporation, had just returned from a quality and productivity seminar, excited and encouraged by what he had heard. He immediately called a meeting with Sarah Burke, the company's production quality manager, and Dennis Schmitt, the company's controller and financial vice president. At the beginning of the meeting, he passed out the following notes that he had taken during the quality and productivity seminar (the notes included some comments about actions Russell felt that Ladd needed to take):

Notes and Comments:
Quality and Productivity Seminar
Orlando, Florida

- **Competitive Advantage.** A company can become more competitive by increasing productivity and improving quality (something that Ladd needs desperately given the trend in profits over the past several years).
- **Quality and Cost Relationships.** Fundamental principle: Improving quality decreases quality costs. Most quality-related costs are incurred because of poor quality.
- **Examples of Success.**
    - **The Ritz-Carlton Hotel Company, L.L.C.**, a two-time winner (in 1992 and 1999) of the Malcolm Baldrige National Quality Award in the service category, has more than doubled its pre-tax return on investments and earnings since 1995.[1]
    - **Sunny Fresh Foods**, another two-time winner (1999 and 2005) of the Malcolm Baldrige Award in the small business category, reports that its return on gross investment tripled over the five-year period ending in 1999, while its operating profits increased an average of 25 percent per year over the same period. Since 1999, revenues have almost doubled and market share has increased.[1]
    - **Tennant Company**, a manufacturer of industrial floor maintenance products, had some remarkable success attributable to its quality-improvement efforts. When its quality-improvement program began, Tennant estimated that its cost of doing things wrong was as high as 17 percent of sales. Within a six-year period, this cost had dropped to 8 percent of sales. Based on annual sales of $136 million, savings from improved quality totaled $12.24 million.[2]
- **Philip Crosby's Four Absolutes of Quality Management:**[3]
    - The Definition of Quality Is Conformance to Requirements, Not Goodness
    - The System for Causing Quality Is Prevention, Not Appraisal
    - The Performance Standard Is Zero Defects, Not "Close Enough"
    - The Measurement of Quality Is the Price of Nonconformance, Not Indexes
- **Cost of Quality System (COQ).** Measuring and reporting quality costs allows managers to identify potential areas for improvement and to assess results of improvement activities. Ladd needs a solid, reliable quality cost reporting system for its development and operation and to help with quality-improvement decisions. We also need to monitor and control the programs that we implement. Following the model of other companies, the controller's office will be responsible for collecting and reporting quality costs.

Questions to Think About

1. Why has measurement of productivity and quality become so important?
2. What are quality costs?
3. How can improving quality reduce quality costs?
4. What kinds of quality cost reports should be prepared by the Accounting Department?
5. What is meant by "productivity"?

1 For a detailed profile of each company, visit the chapter web links at the Interactive Study Center on http://www.thomsonedu.com/accounting/hansen.
2 Lawrence Carr and Thomas Tyson, "Planning Quality Cost Expenditures," *Management Accounting* (October 1992): pp. 52–56.
3 Philip B. Crosby, "Quality Management: The Real Thing," http://www.wppl.org/wphistory/PhilipCrosby/grant.htm, accessed March 31, 2006.

Measuring the Costs of Quality

Objective 1

Identify and describe the four types of quality costs.

By attending a productivity seminar, Russell Walsh discovered that paying more attention to quality can increase profitability. Quality improvement can increase profitability in two ways: (1) by increasing customer demand and (2) by decreasing costs. In a tightly competitive market, increased demand and cost savings can mean the difference between surviving and thriving. The U.S. government has recognized the importance of quality in today's economy. One indication is the creation in 1987 of the Malcolm Baldrige National Quality Award.[4] The Baldrige award was created to recognize U.S. companies that excel in quality management and achievement. The award categories include manufacturing, small business, service, educational, and health entities. Since no more than two awards are given per category, they are difficult to achieve and highly sought after. For example, winners in 2005 include **Sunny Fresh Foods, Inc.** (manufacturing category); **DynMcDermott Petroleum Operations** (service category); **Jenks Public Schools**, Jenks, Oklahoma (education); and **Bronson Methodist Hospital**, Kalamazoo, Michigan (health care). Winners in earlier years include **Karlee Company, Inc.**; **Operations Management International, Inc.**; **Los Alamos National Bank**; **STMicroelectronics, Inc.**; **Region Americas**; **BI**; **The Ritz-Carlton Hotel Company, L.L.C.**; **Sunny Fresh Foods**; **Boeing Airlift** and **Tanker Programs**; **Solar Turbines Incorporated**; and **Texas Nameplate Company, Inc.**

The costs of quality can be substantial and a source of significant savings. Studies indicate that costs of quality for American companies are typically 20 to 30 percent of sales.[5] Yet, quality experts maintain that the optimal quality costs level should be about 2 to 3 percent of sales. This difference between actual and optimal figures represents a veritable gold mine of opportunity. Improving quality can produce significant improvements in profitability and overall efficiency. For example, Xerox's quality improvement program produced annual savings of $53 million, $77 million, $60 million, and $20 million over a four-year period.[6]

Quality has become an important competitive dimension for both service and manufacturing organizations as well as large and small businesses. Quality is an integrating theme for all organizations. Foreign firms' ability to sell higher-quality products at lower prices has cost several U.S. firms their market share. In an effort to combat this stiff competition, many U.S. firms have increasingly paid more attention to quality and productivity, especially given the potential to reduce costs and improve product quality simultaneously. The emphasis on quality has been in process for such a sufficient period of time that some now believe that quality has shifted from a source of strategic advantage to a competitive necessity.[7]

As companies implement quality-improvement programs, a need arises to monitor and report on the progress of these programs. Managers need to know what quality costs are and how they are changing over time. Reporting and measuring quality performance are absolutely essential to the success of an ongoing quality-improvement program. A fundamental prerequisite for this reporting is measuring the costs of quality. But an operational definition of quality is needed to measure those costs.

Quality Defined

The typical dictionary definition of quality refers to the "degree or grade of excellence"; in this sense, quality is a relative measure of goodness. Defining quality as

4 The Malcolm Baldrige National Quality Award was created by Public Law 100–107 in 1987. The first awards were given in 1988.

5 Michael R. Ostrenga, "Return on Investment Through the Costs of Quality," *Journal of Cost Management* (Summer 1991): pp. 37–44.

6 Crosby, P. B. *Quality Is Free* (New York: A Mentor Book, 1980).

7 Robert S. Kaplan and David P. Norton, *The Balanced Scorecard* (Boston: Harvard Business Press, 1996): pp. 87–88.

goodness is so general that it offers no operational content. How do we build an operational definition? The answer is, "Adopt a customer focus." Operationally, a **quality product or service** is one that meets or exceeds customer expectations. In effect, quality is customer satisfaction. But what is meant by "customer expectations"? Customer expectations can be described by quality attributes or by what are often referred to as "dimensions of quality."[8] Thus, a quality product or service is one that meets or exceeds customer expectations on the following eight dimensions:

1. Performance
2. Aesthetics
3. Serviceability
4. Features
5. Reliability
6. Durability
7. Quality of conformance
8. Fitness for use

The first four dimensions describe important quality attributes but are difficult to measure. **Performance** refers to how consistently and how well a product functions. For services, the inseparability principle means that the service is performed in the presence of the customer. Thus, the performance dimension for services can be further defined by the attributes of responsiveness, assurance, and empathy. *Responsiveness* is simply the willingness to help customers and provide prompt, consistent service. *Assurance* refers to the knowledge and courtesy of employees and their ability to convey trust and confidence. *Empathy* means providing caring, individualized attention to customers. **Aesthetics** is concerned with the appearance of tangible products (for example, style and beauty) as well as the appearance of the facilities, equipment, personnel, and communication materials associated with services. **Serviceability** measures the ease of maintaining and/or repairing the product. **Features (quality of design)** refer to characteristics of a product that differentiate between functionally similar products. For example, the function of automobiles is to provide transportation. Yet, one auto may have a four-cylinder engine, a manual transmission, vinyl seats, room to seat four passengers comfortably, and front disk brakes; another may have a six-cylinder engine, an automatic transmission, leather seats, room to seat six passengers comfortably, and antilock brakes. Similarly, first-class air travel and economy air travel reflect different design qualities. First-class air travel, for example, offers more leg room, better meals, and more luxurious seats. Obviously, in both cases, the product features are different. Higher design quality is usually reflected in higher manufacturing costs and in higher selling prices. Quality of design helps a company determine its market. A market exists for both the four-cylinder and the six-cylinder cars as well as for both economy air travel and first-class air travel.

Reliability is the probability that the product or service will perform its intended function for a specified length of time. **Durability** is defined as the length of time a product functions. **Quality of conformance** is a measure of how a product meets its specifications. For example, the specifications for a machined part may be a drilled hole that is three inches in diameter, plus or minus 1/8 inch. Parts falling within this range are defined as conforming parts. **Fitness for use** is the suitability of the product for carrying out its advertised functions. If there is a fundamental design flaw, the product may fail in the field even if it conforms to its specifications. Product recalls are frequently the result of fitness-for-use failures.

Improving quality, then, means improving one or more of the eight quality dimensions while maintaining performance on the remaining dimensions. Providing

8 These dimensions are based on Edwin S. Schecter, *Managing for World Class Quality* (Milwaukee: ASQC Quality Press, 1992); and Leonard L. Berry and A. Parasurman, *Marketing Services: Competing Through Quality* (New York: Free Press, Macmillan, 1991): p. 16.

a higher-quality product than a competitor means outperforming the competitor on at least one dimension while matching performance on the remaining dimensions. Although all eight dimensions are important and can affect customer satisfaction, the quality attributes that are measurable tend to receive more emphasis. Conformance, in particular, is strongly emphasized. In fact, many quality experts believe that "quality is conformance" is the best operational definition. There is some logic to this position. Product specifications should explicitly consider such things as reliability, durability, fitness for use and performance. Implicitly, a conforming product is reliable, durable, and fit for use and performs well. The product should be produced as the design specifies it; specifications should be met. Conformance is the basis for defining what is meant by a nonconforming, or *defective,* product.

A **defective product** is one that does not conform to specifications. **Zero defects** means that all products conform to specifications. But what is meant by "conforming to specifications"? The *traditional view* of conformance assumes that there is an acceptable range of values for each specification or quality characteristic. A target value is defined, and upper and lower limits are set that describe acceptable product variation for a given quality characteristic. Any unit that falls within the limits is deemed nondefective. For example, losing or gaining zero minutes per month may be the target value for a watch, and any watch that keeps time correctly within a range of plus or minus two minutes per month is judged acceptable. On the other hand, the *robust quality view* of conformance emphasizes fitness for use. *Robustness* means hitting the target value every time. In this view, there is no range in which variation is acceptable. A nondefective watch in the robust setting would be one that does not gain or lose any minutes during the month. Since evidence exists that product variation can be costly, the robust quality definition of conformance is superior to the traditional definition.

To be labeled nondefective, a product must perform as expected.

Costs of Quality Defined

Quality-linked activities are those activities performed because poor quality may or does exist. The costs of performing these activities are referred to as costs of quality. Thus, the **costs of quality** are the costs that exist because poor quality may or does exist. This definition implies that quality costs are associated with two subcategories of quality-related activities: *control activities* and *failure activities.* **Control activities** are performed by an organization to prevent or detect poor quality (because poor quality may exist). Thus, control activities are made up of prevention and appraisal activities. **Control costs** are the costs of performing control activities. **Failure activities** are performed by an organization or its customers in response to poor quality (poor quality does exist). If the response to poor quality occurs before delivery of a bad (nonconforming, unreliable, not durable, and so on) product to a customer, the activities are classified as internal failure activities; otherwise, they are classified as external failure activities. **Failure costs** are the costs incurred by an organization because failure activities are performed. Notice that the definitions of failure activities and failure costs imply that customer response to poor quality can impose costs on an organization. The definitions of quality-related activities also imply four categories of quality costs: (1) prevention costs, (2) appraisal costs, (3) internal failure costs, and (4) external failure costs.

Prevention costs are incurred to prevent poor quality in the products or services being produced. As prevention costs increase, we would expect the costs of failure to decrease. Examples of prevention costs are quality engineering, quality training programs, quality planning, quality reporting, supplier evaluation and selection, quality audits, quality circles, field trials, and design reviews.

Appraisal costs are incurred to determine whether products and services are conforming to their requirements or customer needs. Examples include inspecting and testing materials, packaging inspection, supervising appraisal activities, product acceptance, process acceptance, measurement (inspection and test) equipment, and outside endorsements. Two of these terms require further explanation.

Product acceptance involves sampling from batches of finished goods to determine whether they meet an acceptable quality level; if so, the goods are accepted. *Process acceptance* involves sampling goods while in process to see if the process is in control and producing nondefective goods; if not, the process is shut down until corrective action can be taken. The main objective of the appraisal function is to prevent nonconforming goods from being shipped to customers.

Internal failure costs are incurred when products and services do not conform to specifications or customer needs. Detecting nonconformance occurs before the product is shipped or delivered to outside parties. These are the failures detected by appraisal activities. Examples of internal failure costs are scrap, rework, downtime (due to defects), reinspection, retesting, and design changes. These costs disappear if no defects exist.

External failure costs are incurred when products and services fail to conform to requirements or satisfy customer needs after being delivered to customers. Of all the costs of quality, this category can be the most devastating. Costs of recalls, for example, can run into the hundreds of millions. Other examples include lost sales because of poor product performance and returns and allowances because of poor quality, warranties, repairs, product liability, customer dissatisfaction, lost market share, and complaint adjustment. External failure costs, like internal failure costs, disappear if no defects exist.

Measuring Quality Costs

Quality costs can also be classified as *observable* or *hidden.* **Observable quality costs** are those that are available from an organization's accounting records. **Hidden quality costs** are opportunity costs resulting from poor quality. (Opportunity costs are not usually recognized in accounting records.) Consider, for example, all the examples of quality costs listed in the prior section. With the exception of lost sales, customer dissatisfaction, and lost market share, all the quality costs are observable and should be available from the accounting records. Note also that the hidden costs are all in the external failure category. These hidden quality costs can be significant and should be estimated. Although estimating hidden quality costs is not easy, three methods have been suggested: (1) the multiplier method, (2) the market research method, and (3) the Taguchi quality loss function.

The Multiplier Method The multiplier method assumes that the total failure cost is simply some multiple of measured failure costs:

$$\text{Total external failure cost} = k(\text{Measured external failure costs})$$

where k is the multiplier effect. The value of k is based on experience. For example, **Westinghouse Electric** reports a value of k between 3 and 4.[9] Thus, if the measured external failure costs are $2 million, the actual external failure costs are between $6 million and $8 million. Including hidden costs in assessing the amount of external failure costs allows management to determine more accurately the level of resource

9 T. L. Albright and P. R. Roth, "The Measurement of Quality Costs: An Alternative Paradigm," *Accounting Horizons* (June 1992): pp. 15–27.

spending for prevention and appraisal activities. Specifically, with an increase in failure costs, we would expect management to increase its investment in control costs.

The Market Research Method Formal market research methods are used to assess the effect poor quality has on sales and market share. Customer surveys and interviews with members of a company's sales force can provide significant insight into the magnitude of a company's hidden costs. Market research results can be used to project future profit losses attributable to poor quality.

The Taguchi Quality Loss Function The traditional zero defects definition assumes that hidden quality costs exist only for units that fall outside the upper and lower specification limits. The **Taguchi loss function** assumes that any variation from the target value of a quality characteristic causes hidden quality costs. Furthermore, the hidden quality costs increase quadratically as the actual value deviates from the target value. The Taguchi quality loss function, illustrated in Exhibit 15-1, can be described by the following equation:

$$L(y) = k(y - T)^2 \tag{15.1}$$

where

k = A proportionality constant dependent upon the organization's external failure cost structure
y = Actual value of quality characteristic
T = Target value of quality characteristic
L = Quality loss

Exhibit 15-1 demonstrates that the quality cost is zero at the target value and increases symmetrically, at an increasing rate, as the actual value varies from the

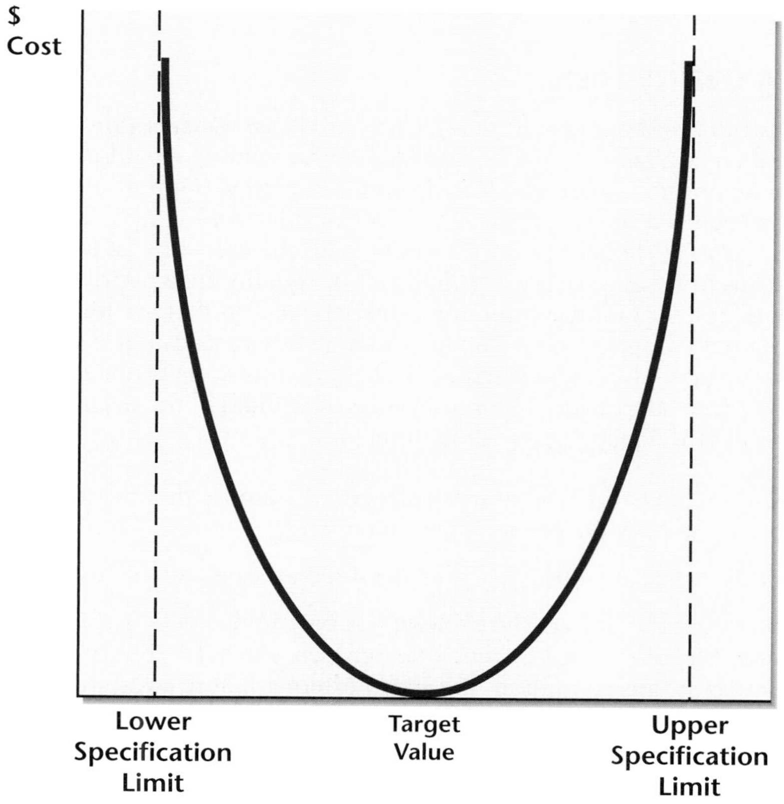

Exhibit 15-1 The Taguchi Quality Loss Function

target value. Assume, for example, that k = \$400 and T = 10 inches in diameter. Exhibit 15-2 illustrates the computation of the quality loss for four units. Notice that the cost quadruples when the deviation from the target doubles (from units 2 to 3). Notice also that the average deviation squared and the average loss per unit can be computed. These averages can be used to compute the total expected hidden quality costs for a product. If, for example, the total units produced are 2,000 and the average squared deviation is 0.025, then the expected cost per unit is \$10 (0.025 × \$400), and the total expected loss for the 2,000 units would be \$20,000 (\$10 × 2,000).

To apply the Taguchi loss function, you must estimate k. The value for k is computed by dividing the estimated cost at one of the specification limits by the squared deviation of the limit from the target value:

$$k = c/d^2$$

where

c = Loss at the lower or upper specification limit
d = Distance of limit from target value

This means that we still must estimate the loss for a given deviation from the target value. Either of the first two methods, the multiplier method or the market research method, may be used to help in this estimation (a one-time assessment need). Once k is known, the hidden quality costs can be estimated for any level of variation from the target value.

Reporting Quality Cost Information

Objective 2

Prepare a quality cost report, and differentiate between acceptable quality level and the view espoused by total quality control.

A quality cost reporting system is essential to an organization serious about improving and controlling quality costs. The first and simplest step in creating such a system is assessing current actual quality costs. A detailed listing of actual quality costs by category can provide two important insights. First, it reveals the magnitude of the quality costs in each category, allowing managers to assess their financial impact. Second, it shows the distribution of quality costs by category, allowing managers to assess the relative importance of each category.

Quality Cost Reports

The financial significance of quality costs can be assessed more easily by expressing these costs as a percentage of actual sales. Exhibit 15-3, for example, reports Ladd Lighting Corporation's quality costs as representing almost 15 percent of sales for fiscal 2008. Given the rule of thumb that quality costs should be no more than about 2.5 percent, Ladd Lighting has ample opportunity to improve profits by decreasing quality costs. Understand, however, that reduction in costs should come through

Unit	Actual Diameter (y)	$y - T$	$(y - T)2$	$k(y - T)2$
1	9.9	−0.10	0.010	\$ 4.00
2	10.1	0.10	0.010	4.00
3	10.2	0.20	0.040	16.00
4	9.8	−0.20	0.040	16.00
Total			0.100	\$40.00
Average			0.025	\$ 10.00

Exhibit 15-2 Quality Loss Computation Illustrated

Ladd Lighting Corporation Quality Cost Report for the Year Ended March 31, 2008			
	Quality Costs		Percentage (%) of Sales[a]
Prevention costs:			
Quality training	$350,000		
Reliability engineering	800,000	$1,150,000	5.18%
Appraisal costs:			
Materials inspection	$200,000		
Product acceptance	100,000		
Process acceptance	380,000	680,000	3.06
Internal failure costs:			
Scrap	$500,000		
Rework	350,000	850,000	3.82
External failure costs:			
Customer complaints	$250,000		
Warranty	250,000		
Repair	150,000	650,000	2.93
Total quality costs		$3,330,000	14.99%[b]

[a]Actual sales of $22,200,000.
[b]$3,330,000/$22,200,000 = 15%; difference is rounding error.

Exhibit 15-3 Quality Cost Report

improvement of quality. Reduction of quality costs without any effort to improve quality could prove to be a disastrous strategy.

Additional insight concerning the relative distribution of quality costs can be realized by construction of a pie chart. Exhibit 15-4 provides such a chart, using the quality costs reported in Exhibit 15-3. Notice that failure costs account for about 45% of the total quality costs. When quality costs are reduced to about 2.5% of sales, failure costs represent about 15–20% of the total costs, or about 0.5% of sales. Managers, of course, have the responsibility of assessing the optimal level of quality

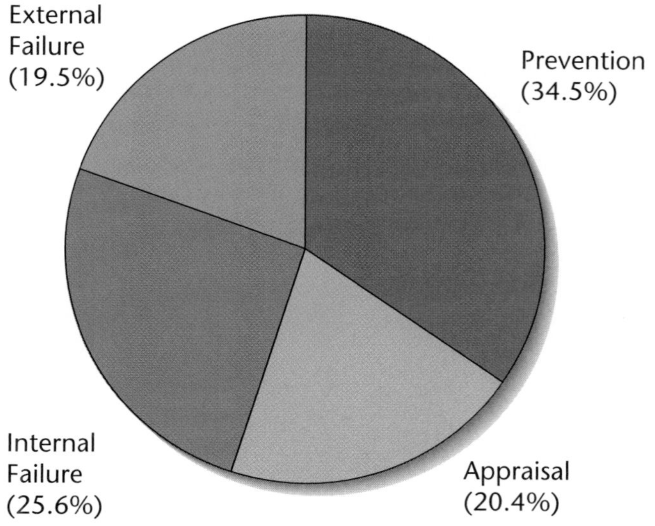

Exhibit 15-4 Relative Distribution of Quality Costs

Managers Decide

Why Quality Costs Are Not Reported

In a survey of members of the Quality Management Division of the American Society for Quality, only 65.9% of the responding firms tracked quality costs in a systematic way. The respondents who did not track quality costs gave these reasons, in order of frequency:

1. Lack of management support or interest in tracking such costs
2. Company's economic condition (start-up company, lean with little overhead, too small, etc.)
3. Lack of knowledge of how to track quality costs (from management on down)
4. Lack of adequate accounting and information technology capabilities to track quality costs
5. Management did not see any benefit from tracking quality costs and had other higher priorities ■

Source: Victor E. Sower and Ross Quarles, "Cost of Quality: Why More Organizations Do Not Use It Effectively," Annual Quality Congress (June 2003): Vol. 57, pp. 625–637.

and determining the relative amount that should be spent in each category. There are two views concerning optimal quality costs: the traditional view, calling for an *acceptable quality level,* and the contemporary view, referred to as *total quality control.* Each view offers managers insights about how quality costs ought to be managed.

Quality Cost Function: Acceptable Quality View

The acceptable quality view assumes that there is a trade-off between control costs and failure costs. As control costs increase, failure costs should decrease. As long as the decrease in failure costs is greater than the corresponding increase in control costs, a company should continue increasing its efforts to prevent or detect nonconforming units. Eventually, a point is reached at which any additional increase in this effort costs more than the corresponding reduction in failure costs. This point represents the minimum level of total quality costs. It is the optimal balance between control costs and failure costs and defines what is known as the **acceptable quality level (AQL)**. This theoretical relationship is illustrated in Exhibit 15-5.

In Exhibit 15-5, two cost functions are assumed: one for control costs and one for failure costs. It is also assumed that the percentage of defective units increases as the amount spent on prevention and appraisal activities decreases; failure costs, on the other hand, increase as the number of defective units increases. From the total quality cost function, we see that total quality costs decrease as quality improves up to a point. After that, no further improvement is possible. An optimal level of defective units is identified, and the company works to achieve this level. This level of allowable defective units is the *acceptable quality level.*

Quality Cost Function: Zero-Defects View

The AQL viewpoint is based on a traditional defective product definition. In the classic sense, a product is defective if it falls outside the tolerance limits for a quality characteristic. Under this view, failure costs are incurred only if the product fails to conform to specifications and an optimal trade-off exists between failure and control costs. The AQL view permitted and, in fact, encouraged the production of a given number of defective units. This model prevailed in the quality control world until the late 1970s, when the AQL model was challenged by the *zero-defects model.* Essentially,

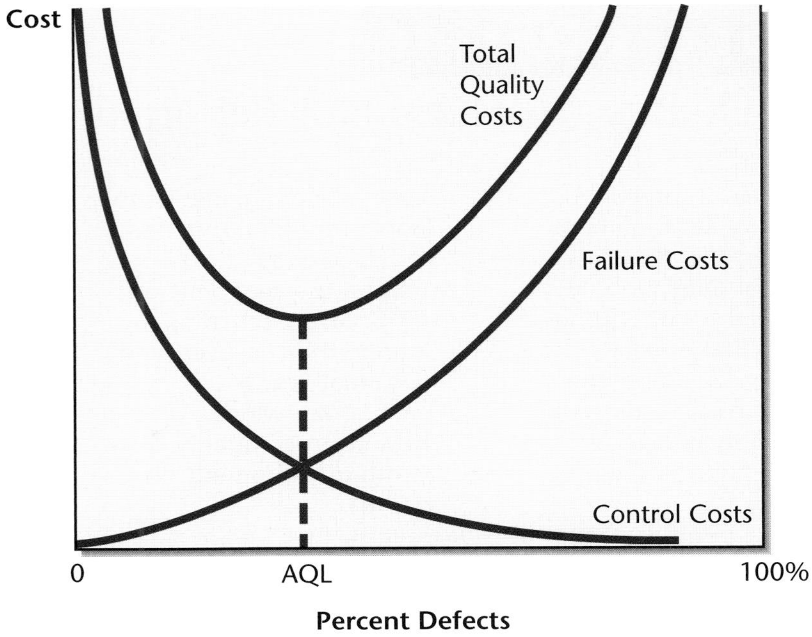

Exhibit 15-5 AQL Quality Cost Graph

the zero-defects model made the claim that it was cost-beneficial to reduce nonconforming units to zero. Firms producing increasingly fewer nonconforming units became more competitive relative to firms that continued the traditional AQL model. In the mid-1980s, the zero-defects model was taken one step further by the *robust quality model,* which challenged the definition of a defective unit. According to the robust view, a loss is experienced from producing products that vary from a target value, and the greater the distance from the target value, the greater the loss. Furthermore, the loss is incurred even if the deviation is within the specification limits. In other words, variation from the ideal is costly, and specification limits serve no useful purpose and, in fact, may be deceptive. The zero-defects model understates the quality costs and likewise the potential for savings from even greater efforts to improve quality (remember the multiplication factor of Westinghouse Electric). Thus, the robust quality model tightened the definition of a defective unit, refined our view of quality costs, and intensified the quality race.

For firms operating in an intensely competitive environment, quality can offer an important competitive advantage. If the robust quality view is correct, then firms can capitalize on it, decreasing the number of defective units (robustly defined) while simultaneously decreasing their total quality costs. This is what appears to be happening for those firms that are striving to achieve a robust zero-defect state (i.e., a state with zero tolerance) for their products. The optimal level for quality costs is where products are produced that meet their target values. The quest to find ways to achieve the target value creates a dynamic quality world, as opposed to the static quality world of AQL.

Dynamic Nature of Quality Costs The discovery that trade-offs among quality cost categories can be managed differently from what is implied by the relationships portrayed in Exhibit 15-5 is analogous to the discovery that inventory cost trade-offs can be managed differently from what the traditional inventory model (EOQ) implied. Essentially, what happens is that as firms increase their prevention and appraisal costs and reduce their failure costs, they discover that they can then cut back on the prevention and appraisal costs. What initially appeared to be a trade-off turns out to be a permanent reduction in costs for all quality cost categories. Exhibit 15-6 displays

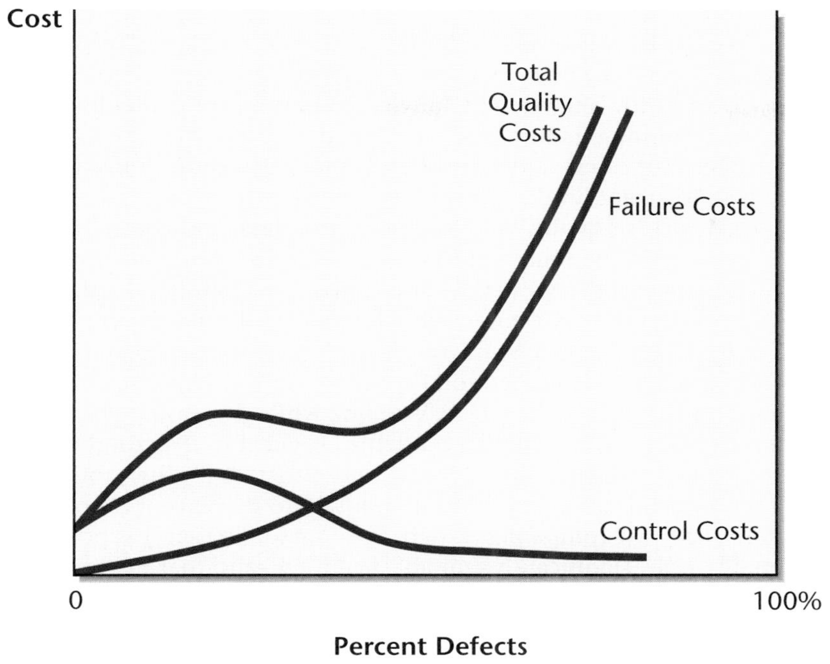

Exhibit 15-6 Contemporary Quality Cost Graph

the changes in quality cost relationships. Though it shows a total quality cost function consistent with the quality cost relationships described, there are some key differences. First, control costs do not increase without limit as a robust zero-defect state is approached. Second, control costs may increase and then decrease as the robust state is approached. Third, failure costs can be driven to zero.

Suppose, for example, that a firm has decided to improve the quality of its material inputs through the implementation of a supplier selection program. The objective is to identify and use suppliers who are willing to meet certain quality standards. As the firm works to implement this program, additional costs may be incurred (for example, review of suppliers, communication with suppliers, contract negotiations, and so on). And, initially, other prevention and appraisal costs may continue at their current levels. However, once the program is fully implemented and evidence surfaces that the failure costs are being reduced (for example, less rework, fewer customer complaints, and fewer repairs), then the company may decide to cut back on inspections of incoming materials, reduce the level of product acceptance activities, and so on. The net effect is a reduction in all quality cost categories. And quality has increased!

This example is consistent with the strategy to reduce quality costs recommended by the American Society for Quality Control:

> The strategy for reducing quality costs is quite simple: (1) take direct attack on failure costs in an attempt to drive them to zero; (2) invest in the "right" prevention activities to bring about improvement; (3) reduce appraisal costs according to results achieved; and (4) continuously evaluate and redirect prevention efforts to gain further improvement. This strategy is based on the premise that:
>
> - For each failure there is a root cause.
> - Causes are preventable.
> - Prevention is always cheaper.[10]

10 Jack Campanellam, ed., *Principles of Quality Costs* (Milwaukee: ASQC Quality Press, 1990): p. 12.

This ability to reduce total quality costs dramatically in all categories is borne out by real-world experiences. **Tennant**, for example, over an eight-year period, reduced its costs of quality from 17 percent of sales to 2.5 percent of sales and, at the same time, significantly altered the relative distribution of the quality cost categories. At the very beginning, failure costs accounted for 50 percent of the total costs of quality (8.5 percent of sales) and control costs of 50 percent (8.5 percent of sales). When the 2.5 percent level was achieved, failure costs accounted for only 15 percent of the total costs of quality (0.375 percent of sales), and control costs had increased to 85 percent of the total (2.125 percent of sales). Tennant increased quality, reduced quality costs in every category and in total, and shifted the distribution of quality costs to the control categories, with the greatest emphasis on prevention. This outcome argues strongly against the traditional quality cost model portrayed in Exhibit 15-5. According to this model, total quality costs can be decreased only by trading off control and failure costs (increasing one while decreasing the other). Further support for the total quality control model is provided by **Westinghouse Electric**. Similar to Tennant, Westinghouse Electric found that its profits continued to improve until its control costs accounted for about 70 to 80 percent of total quality costs.[11] Based on these two companies' experiences, we know that it is possible to reduce total quality costs significantly—in all categories—and that the process radically alters the relative distribution of the quality cost categories.

Activity-Based Management and Optimal Quality Costs

Activity-based management classifies activities as value-added and non-value-added and keeps only those that add value. This principle can be applied to quality-related activities. Appraisal and failure activities and their associated costs are non-value-added and should be eliminated. Prevention activities—performed efficiently—can be classified as value-added and should be retained. Initially, however, prevention activities may not be performed efficiently, and activity reduction and activity selec-

Managers Decide

Incentives to Improve Quality

Texas Nameplate Company, Inc. (TNC), is a small, privately held family business that manufactures custom nameplates (identification tags and labels that display usage information) and is a 1998 and 2004 winner of the Malcolm Baldrige Quality Award. One of the decisions made by management is to guarantee the delivery of products on time and free of defects or to supply them free of charge. Between 1998 and 2004, defects, as a percentage of sales, dropped from 1.4 percent to 0.5 percent, well below the industrial average of 2 percent; the company also reduced its production cycle time from 14 days to eight days. TNC uses two incentive programs to encourage defect-free and on-time production: gainsharing and JETS (Just Earning Time and Saving Resources). Gainsharing pays employees a portion of the savings attributable to reducing the number of defective units. JETS provides employees time off with pay when they finish their production ahead of schedule. ■

Source: National Institute of Standards and Technology, Baldrige National Quality Program Award Winners, http://www.nist.gov/public_affairs/Texas_Nameplate_PDF_final.pdf, accessed April 1, 2006.

11 These factual observations are based on those reported by Lawrence P. Carr and Thomas Tyson, "Planning Quality Cost Expenditures," *Management Accounting* (October 1992): pp. 52–56.

tion (and perhaps even activity sharing) can be used to achieve the desired value-added state. **Grede Foundries Inc.** of Milwaukee, the world's largest foundry company, has been tracking all four categories of quality costs for more than 15 years. However, it does not report prevention costs as part of its final cost-of-quality figures because it does not want its managers reducing quality costs by cutting prevention activities. It feels strongly that spending money on prevention activities pays off. For example, it has found that a 1 percent reduction in scrap reduces external defects by about 5 percent.[12]

Once the activities are identified for each category, resource drivers can be used to improve cost assignments to the individual activities. Root (cost) drivers can also be identified, especially for failure activities, and used to help managers understand what is causing the costs of the activities. This information can then be used to select ways of reducing quality costs to the level demonstrated in Exhibit 15-6. In effect, activity-based management supports the robust zero-defect view of quality costs. There is no optimal trade-off between control and failure costs; the latter are non-value-added costs and should be reduced to zero. Some control activities are non-value-added and should be eliminated. Other control activities are value-added but may be performed inefficiently, and the costs caused by the inefficiency are non-value-added. Thus, costs for these categories may also be reduced to lower levels.

Trend Analysis

Quality cost reports reveal the magnitude of quality costs and their distribution among the four categories, thus revealing opportunities for improvement. Once quality improvement measures are undertaken, it is important to determine whether quality costs are being reduced as planned. Quality cost reports will not reveal whether or not improvement has occurred. It would be useful to have a picture of how the quality-improvement program has been doing since its inception. Is the multiple-period trend—the overall change in quality costs—moving in the right direction? Are significant quality gains being made each period? Answers to these questions can be given by providing a trend chart or graph that tracks the change in quality costs through time. Such a graph is called a **multiple-period quality trend report**. By plotting quality costs as a percentage of sales against time, the overall trend in the quality program can be assessed. The first year plotted is the year prior to the implementation of the quality-improvement program. Assume that one of Ladd's plants has experienced the following:

	Quality Costs	Actual Sales	Costs as a Percentage (%) of Sales
2004	$440,000	$2,200,000	20.0%
2005	423,000	2,350,000	18.0
2006	412,500	2,750,000	15.0
2007	392,000	2,800,000	14.0
2008	280,000	2,800,000	10.0

Letting 2004 be year 0, 2005 be year 1, and so on, the trend graph is shown in Exhibit 15-7. Years of time are plotted on the horizontal axis and percentages of sales on the vertical axis. The ultimate quality cost objective of 3 percent, the target percentage, is represented as a horizontal line on the graph.

The graph reveals that there has been a steady downward trend in quality costs expressed as a percentage of sales. The graph also reveals that there is still ample room for improvement toward the long-run target percentage.

12 Nancy Chase, "Counting Costs, Reaping Returns," *Quality Magazine* (October 1998), an online article accessible via the chapter web links at the Interactive Study Center on http://www.thomsonedu.com/accounting/hansen.

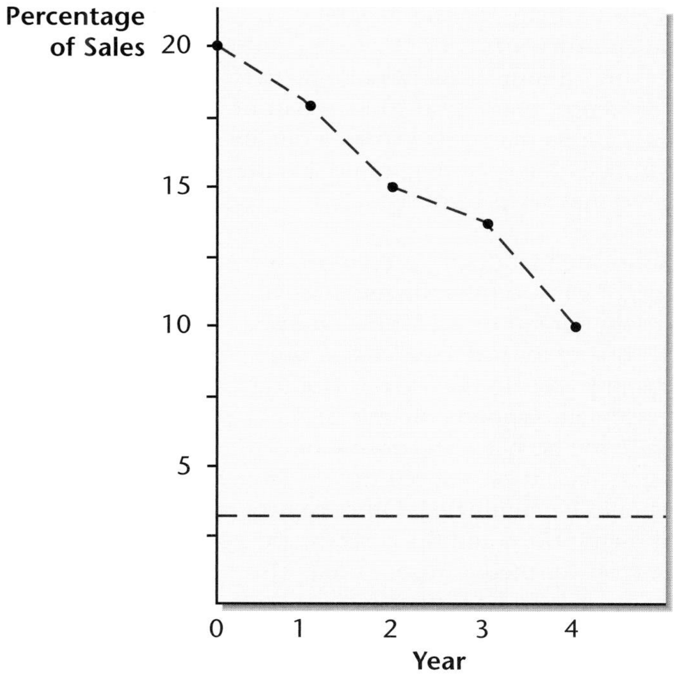

Exhibit 15-7 Multiple-Period Trend Graph: Total Quality Costs

Additional insight can be provided by plotting the trend for each individual quality category. Assume that each category is expressed as a percentage of sales for the same period of time.

	Prevention	Appraisal	Internal Failure	External Failure
2004	2.0%	2.0%	6.0%	10.0%
2005	3.0	2.4	4.0	8.6
2006	3.0	3.0	3.0	6.0
2007	4.0	3.0	2.5	4.5
2008	4.1	2.4	2.0	1.5

The graph showing the trend for each category is displayed in Exhibit 15-8. We can see that the company has had dramatic success in reducing external and internal failures. More money is being spent on prevention (the amount has doubled as a percentage). Appraisal costs have increased and then decreased. Note also that the relative distribution of costs has changed. In 2004, failure costs were 80 percent of the total quality costs (0.16/0.20). In 2008, they are 35 percent of the total (0.035/0.10). The potential to reduce quality costs also affects the way decisions are made. The usefulness of quality cost information for decision making and planning should not be underestimated.

Using Quality Cost Information

Objective 3

Tell why quality cost information is needed, and show how it is used.

The principal objective of reporting quality costs is to improve and facilitate managerial planning, control, and decision making. For example, in deciding to implement a supplier selection program to improve the quality of material inputs, a manager will need an assessment of current quality costs by item and by category, an assessment of the additional costs associated with the program, and an assessment

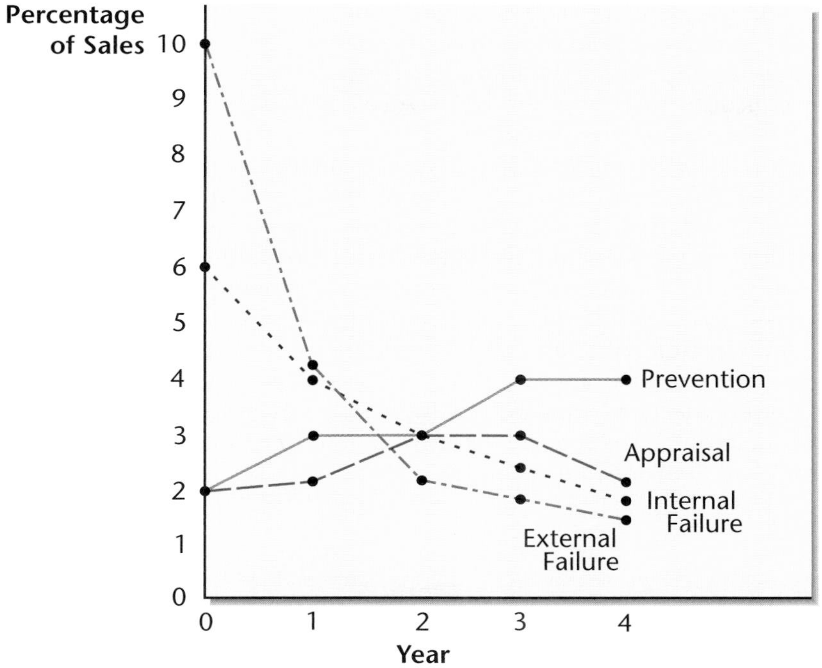

Exhibit 15-8 Multiple-Period Trend Graph: Individual Quality Cost Categories

of the projected savings by item and by category. When the costs and savings will occur must also be projected. Once these cash effects are projected, a capital budgeting analysis can be done to assess the merits of the proposed program. If the outcome is favorable and the program is initiated, then it becomes important to monitor the program through fairly standard performance reporting.

Using quality cost information for quality program implementation decisions and for evaluating the effectiveness of these programs, once implemented, is just one potential use of a quality cost system. Other important uses can also be identified. The following scenarios illustrate the utility of quality cost information for a strategic pricing decision and profitability analysis of a new product design.

© Digital Vision

Quality cost information can be used to improve new product designs.

Scenario A: Strategic Pricing

Leola Wise, the marketing manager, muttered to herself as she reviewed the latest market share data for the company's low-priced electronic measurement instruments. Once again the share had dropped! Japanese firms were continuing to put pressure on this product line. Anticipating this outcome, Leola had begun preparing a brief to support a significant price decrease for this line of products. A price decrease of $3 was needed to recapture the lost market share. The new price less the desired profit per unit produced a target cost that was less than the current actual cost of producing and selling the lower-level instruments. To continue producing this line, cost reductions would need to be made. A cost reduction strategy was needed to reestablish its competitive position.

In the last executive meeting, the discussion focused on how to achieve cost reductions. Ben Blackburn, the chief engineer, indicated that process redesign could offer about half the needed cost reduction. Leola suggested that the company adopt a total quality control position and work to reduce the cost of the lower-level instruments by decreasing quality costs. To determine the potential magnitude of the cost reductions, she asked Earl Simpson, the controller, what the quality costs were for the lower-level instruments. Earl admitted that the costs were not tracked separately. For example, the cost of scrap was buried in the work-in-process account. He did promise, however, to have some estimates of the costs—perhaps not complete—by the end of the month. The report for the lower-level instruments (in the form of a memo from Earl Simpson) follows:

Memo

TO: Leola Wise
FROM: Earl Simpson
SUBJECT: Quality Costs

Leola, I have assembled some data that may be useful to you. As requested, I have provided some estimates of the quality costs associated with this line. I have not included any costs of lost sales due to nonconforming products, as you are probably in a better position to assess this effect.

Quality costs (estimated):	
Inspection of raw materials	$ 200,000
Scrap	800,000
Rejects	500,000
Rework	400,000
Product inspection	300,000
Warranty work	1,000,000
Total estimate	$3,200,000

Upon receiving the memo, Leola immediately called the Quality Control Department and arranged a meeting with the manager, Art Smith. Art had already begun planning the implementation of a new quality program that he believed would reduce quality costs by 50 percent within 18 months. With this information and using a volume of 1,000,000 units, Leola calculated that a 50 percent reduction in the quality costs associated with the lower-level instruments would reduce costs by about $1.60 per unit ($1,600,000/1,000,000). This would make up slightly more than half of the $3 reduction in selling price that would be needed (the reduction is 15 percent of $20). Based on this outcome, Leola decided to implement the price reduction in three phases: a $1 reduction immediately, a $1 reduction in six months, and the final reduction of $1 in 12 months. This phased reduction would likely prevent any further erosion of market share and would start increasing it sometime into the second phase. By phasing in the price reductions, it would give the Quality Control Department time to reduce costs so that any big losses could be avoided.

Scenario A illustrates that both quality cost information and the implementation of a total quality control program contributed to a significant strategic decision. It also shows that improving quality is not a panacea. The reductions are not large enough to bear the full price reduction. Other productivity gains, such as those promised by engineering, will be needed to ensure the long-range viability of the product line.

Scenario B: New Product Analysis

Tara Anderson, the marketing manager, and Brittany Fox, the design engineer, were both unhappy. They had been certain that their proposal for a new product was going to be approved. Instead, they received the following report from the controller's office.

Report: New Product Analysis, Project #675

ESTIMATED PRODUCT LIFE CYCLE: 2 years
PROJECTED SALES POTENTIAL: 50,000 units (life cycle)
PROJECTED LIFE-CYCLE INCOME STATEMENT:

Sales (50,000 @ $60)	$3,000,000
Cost of inputs:	
Materials	800,000
Labor	400,000
Scrap	150,000
Inspection	350,000
Repair work	200,000
Product development	500,000
Selling	300,000
Life-cycle income	$ 300,000

DECISION: Reject
REASON(S): Life-cycle income is less than the company-required 18 percent return on sales.

"You know," Tara remarked, "I can't quite believe this report. Why don't we ask Bob how he came up with these figures."

"I agree," responded Brittany. "I'll arrange a meeting for tomorrow. I'll ask him to provide more detail than just the aggregate figures shown on the report."

The next day, the following conversation was recorded. Tara and Brittany had just completed a review of the detailed cost projections supplied by Bob Brown, the assistant controller.

Brittany: Bob, I would like to know why there is a $3-per-unit scrap cost. And the inspection costs—they seem high. Can you explain these costs?

Bob: Sure. It's based on the scrap cost that we track for existing, similar products. Also, as you know, we have a 10 percent destructive-sampling requirement for these types of products.

Brittany: Well, I think you have overlooked the new design features of this new product. Its design virtually eliminates any waste—especially when you consider that the product will be made on a numerically controlled machine.

Tara: Also, this $2-per-unit charge for repair work should be eliminated. The new design that Brittany is proposing solves the failure problems we have had with related products. It also means that the $100,000 of fixed costs associated with the repair activity can be eliminated. Furthermore, because of the new design, destructive sampling is not required and we need one less inspector than you have budgeted.

Bob: Brittany, how certain are you that this new design will eliminate some of these quality problems?

Brittany: I'm absolutely positive. The early prototypes did exactly as we expected. The results of those tests are included in the proposal. You must not have read the prototype results.

Bob: Right. I didn't. Eliminating scrap reduces the unit-level variable cost by $3 per unit. I also see where the repair and inspection activities are overcosted. We need only one inspector costing $50,000. And eliminating the repair activity saves $200,000. That means the projected life-cycle profits are $650,000 more than I have projected, which in turn means the return on sales is more than 30 percent.

Scenario B illustrates the importance of further classifying quality costs by behavior. The scenario also reinforces the importance of identifying and reporting quality costs separately. The new product was designed to reduce its quality costs, and only by knowing the quality costs assigned could Brittany and Tara have discovered the error in the life-cycle income analysis.

Reporting quality costs so that they can be used for decision making is just one objective of a good quality-costing system. Another objective is controlling quality costs—a factor critical in helping expected outcomes of decisions come to fruition. The pricing decision of Scenario A, for example, depended on the plan to reduce quality costs.

Productivity: Measurement and Control

Objective 4

Explain what productivity is, and calculate the impact of productivity changes on profits.

Productivity is concerned with producing output efficiently, and it specifically addresses the relationship of output and the inputs used to produce the output. Usually, different combinations or mixes of inputs can be used to produce a given level of output. **Total productive efficiency** is the point at which two conditions are satisfied: (1) for any mix of inputs that will produce a given output, no more of any one input is used than necessary to produce the output and (2) given the mixes that satisfy the first condition, the least costly mix is chosen. The first condition is driven by technical relationships and, therefore, is referred to as **technical efficiency**. Viewing activities as inputs, the first condition requires eliminating all non-value-added activities and performing value-added activities with the minimal quantities needed to produce the given output. The second condition is driven by relative input price relationships and, therefore, is referred to as **input trade-off efficiency**. Input prices determine the relative proportions of each input that should be used. Deviation from these fixed proportions creates input trade-off inefficiency.

Productivity improvement programs attempt to move toward a state of total productive efficiency. Technical improvements in productivity can be achieved by using less input to produce the same output or by producing more output using the same inputs or more output with relatively less inputs. For example, in 1992, **Lantech**, a wrapping-machine producer, produced eight wrapping machines per day with 50 workers, an average of 0.16 machine per worker. By 1998, the output had increased

13 Melissa Larson, "Are You Ready for Kaizen," *Quality Magazine* (June 1998), an online article accessible via the chapter web links at the Inateractive Study Center on http://www.thomson.edu.com/accounting/hansen.

to 14 machines per day using 20 workers—an average of 0.7 machine per worker. By 1992 productivity standards, about 87.5 workers would have been needed to produce 14 machines. Thus, output increased, and fewer workers were needed.[13]

Exhibit 15-9 illustrates the three ways to achieve an improvement in technical efficiency. The output is tons of steel, and the inputs are labor (number of workers) and capital (dollars invested in automated equipment). Notice that the relative proportions of the inputs are held constant so that all productivity improvement is attributable to improving technical efficiency.

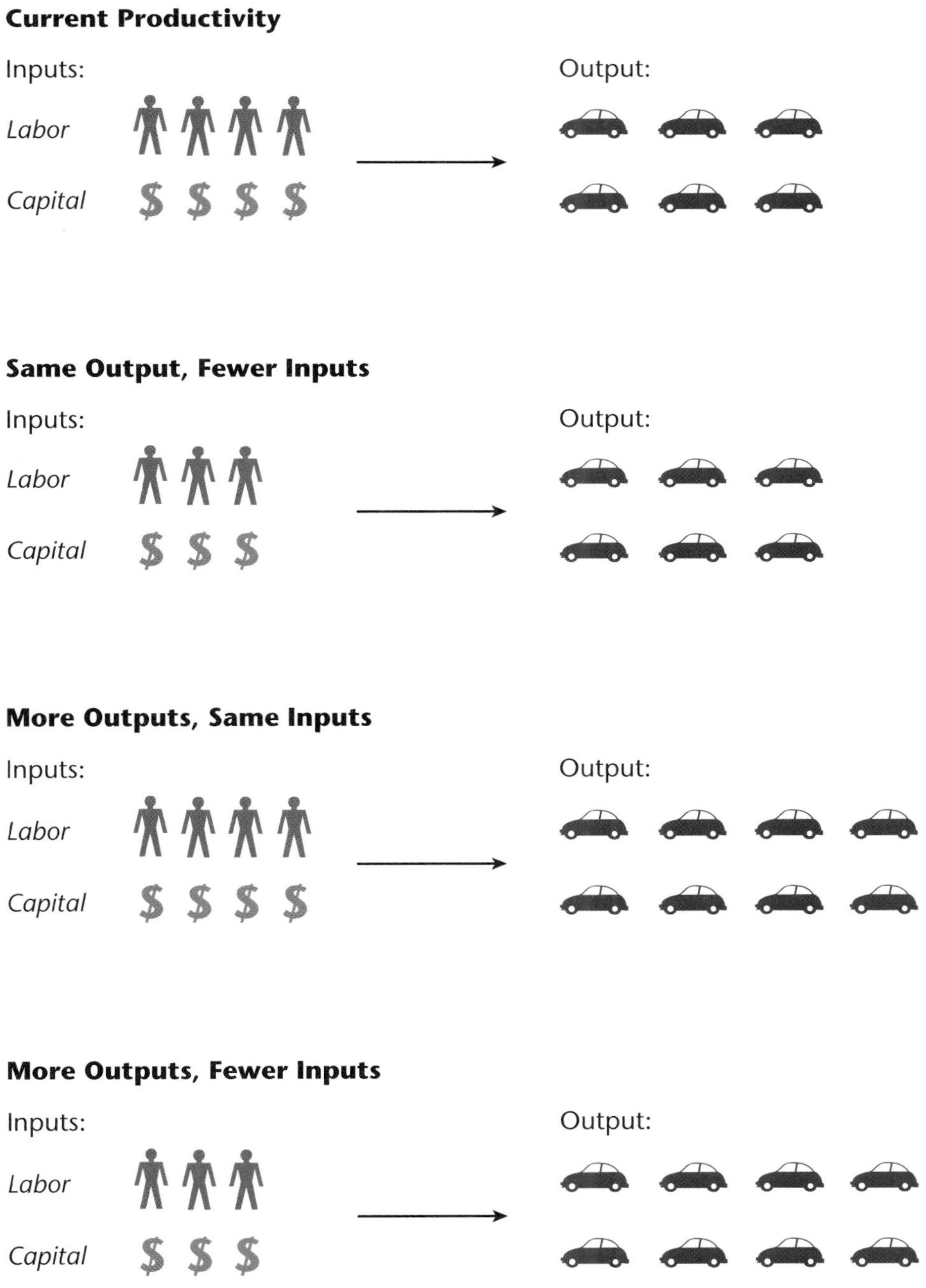

Exhibit 15-9 Technical Efficiency

Productivity improvement can also be achieved by trading off more costly inputs for less costly inputs. Exhibit 15-10 illustrates the possibility of improving productivity by increasing input trade-off efficiency. Although improving technical efficiency is what most people think of when improving productivity is mentioned, input trade-off efficiency can offer significant opportunities for increasing overall economic efficiency. Choosing the right combination of inputs can be as critical as choosing the right quantity of inputs. Notice in Exhibit 15-10 that input Combination I produces the same output as input Combination II—but that the cost is $5 million less. Total measures of productivity are usually a combination of changes in technical and input trade-off efficiency.

Partial Productivity Measurement

Productivity measurement is simply a quantitative assessment of productivity changes. The objective is to assess whether productive efficiency has increased or decreased. Productivity measurement can be actual or prospective. *Actual productivity* measurement allows managers to assess, monitor, and control changes. *Prospective* measurement is forward looking, and it serves as an input for strategic decision making. Specifically, prospective measurement allows managers to compare relative benefits of different input combinations, choosing the inputs and input mix that provide the greatest benefit. Productivity measures can be developed for each input separately or for all inputs jointly. Measuring productivity for one input at a time is called **partial productivity measurement**.

Partial Productivity Measurement Defined

Productivity of a single input is typically measured by calculating the ratio of the output to the input:

Productivity ratio = Output/Input

Because the productivity of only one input is being measured, the measure is called a *partial productivity measure.* If both output and input are measured in physical quantities, then we have an **operational productivity measure**. If output or input is expressed in dollars, then we have a **financial productivity measure**. Assume, for example, that in 2007, one of Ladd Lighting's plants produced 120,000 dining

Technically Efficient Combination I:
Total Cost of Inputs = $20,000,000

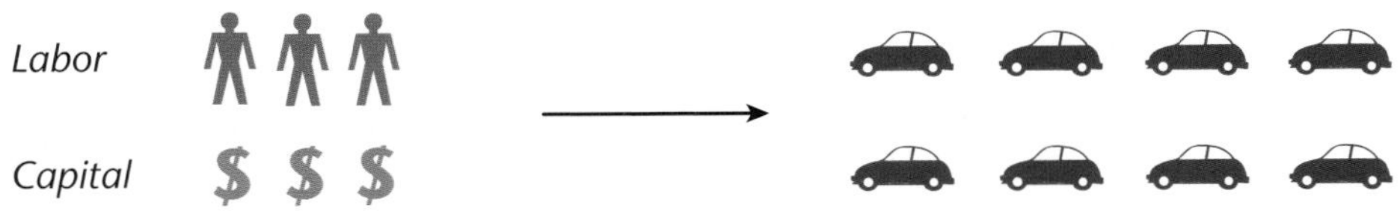

Technically Efficient Combination II:
Total Cost of Inputs = $25,000,000

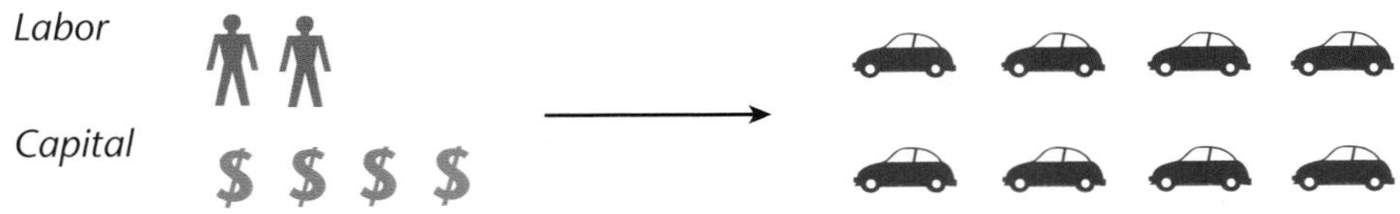

Exhibit 15-10 Input Trade-off Efficiency

room chandeliers for building wholesalers and used 40,000 hours of labor. The labor productivity ratio is three chandeliers per hour (120,000/40,000). This is an operational measure, since the units are expressed in physical terms. If the selling price of each unit is $50 and the cost of labor is $12 per hour, then output and input can be expressed in dollars. The labor productivity ratio, expressed in financial terms, is $12.50 of revenue per dollar of labor cost ($6,000,000/$480,000).

Partial Measures and Measuring Changes in Productive Efficiency

The labor productivity ratio of three chandeliers per hour measures the 2007 productivity experience of Ladd Lighting. By itself, the ratio conveys little information about productive efficiency or whether the company's productivity has improved or declined. It is possible, however, to make a statement about increasing or decreasing productivity efficiency by measuring changes in productivity. To do so, the actual current productivity measure is compared with the productivity measure of a prior period. This prior period is referred to as the **base period** and sets the benchmark, or standard, for measuring changes in productive efficiency. The prior period can be any period desired. It could, for example, be the preceding year, the preceding week, or even the period during which the last batch of products was produced. For strategic evaluations, the base period usually chosen is an earlier year. For operational control, the base period tends to be close to the current period—such as the preceding batch of products or the preceding week.

To illustrate, assume that 2007 is the base period and the labor productivity standard, therefore, is three chandeliers per hour. Further assume that late in 2007, Ladd decided to try a new procedure for producing and assembling the motors with the expectation that the new procedure would use less labor. In 2008, there were 150,000 chandeliers produced, using 37,500 hours of labor. The labor productivity ratio for 2008 is four units per hour (150,000/37,500). The change in productivity is a one-unit per hour increase in productivity (from three units per hour in 2007 to four units per hour in 2008). The *change* is a significant improvement in labor productivity and provides evidence supporting the efficacy of the new process.

Advantages of Partial Measures Partial measures allow managers to focus on the use of a particular input. Operating partial measures have the advantage of being easily interpreted by all within the organization and are therefore easy to use for assessing the productivity performance of operating personnel. Laborers, for instance, can relate to units produced per hour or units produced per pound of material. Thus, partial operational measures provide feedback that operating personnel can relate to and understand—measures that deal with the specific inputs over which they have control. This increases the likelihood that they will be accepted by operating personnel. Furthermore, for operational control, the standards for performance are often very short term. For example, standards can be the productivity ratios of prior batches of goods. Using this standard, productivity trends within the year can be tracked.

Disadvantages of Partial Measures Partial measures, used in isolation, can be misleading. A decline in the productivity of one input may be necessary to increase the productivity of another. Such a trade-off is desirable if overall costs decline, but the effect would be missed by using either partial measure. For example, changing a process so that direct laborers take less time to assemble a product may increase scrap and waste while leaving total output unchanged. Labor productivity has increased, but productive use of materials has declined. If the increase in the cost of waste and scrap outweighs the savings of the decreased labor, overall productivity has declined.

Two important conclusions can be drawn from this example. First, the possible existence of trade-offs mandates a total measure of productivity for assessing the merits of productivity decisions. Only by looking at the total productivity effect of all inputs can managers accurately draw any conclusions about overall productivity performance. Second, because of the possibility of trade-offs, a total measure of productivity must assess the aggregate financial consequences and, therefore, should be a financial measure.

Total Productivity Measurement

Measuring productivity for all inputs at once is called **total productivity measurement**. In practice, it may not be necessary to measure the effect of all inputs. Many firms measure the productivity of only those factors that are thought to be relevant indicators of organizational performance and success. Thus, in practical terms, total productivity measurement can be defined as focusing on a limited number of inputs, which, in total, indicate organizational success. In either case, total productivity measurement requires the development of a multifactor measurement approach. A common multifactor approach suggested in the productivity literature (but rarely found in practice) is the use of aggregate productivity indices. Aggregate indices are complex and difficult to interpret and have not been generally accepted. Two approaches that have gained some acceptance are *profile measurement* and *profit-linked productivity measurement.*

Profile Productivity Measurement Producing a product involves numerous critical inputs such as labor, materials, capital, and energy. **Profile measurement** provides a series or a vector of separate and distinct partial operational measures. Profiles can be compared over time to provide information about productivity changes. To illustrate the profile approach, we will use only two inputs: labor and materials. Let's return to the Ladd Lighting example. As before, Ladd implements a new production and assembly process in 2008. Only now let's assume that the new process affects both labor and materials. Initially, let's look at the case for which the productivity of both inputs moves in the same direction. The following data for 2007 and 2008 are available:

	2007	2008
Number of chandeliers produced	120,000	150,000
Labor hours used	40,000	37,500
Materials used (lbs.)	1,200,000	1,428,571

Exhibit 15-11 provides productivity ratio profiles for each year. The 2007 profile is (3, 0.100), and the 2008 profile is (4, 0.105). Comparing profiles for the two years, we can see that productivity increased for both labor and materials (from 3 to 4 for labor and from 0.100 to 0.105 for materials). The profile comparison provides enough

	Partial Productivity Ratios	
	2007 Profile[a]	2008 Profile[b]
Labor productivity ratio	3.000	4.000
Materials productivity ratio	0.100	0.105

[a]Labor: 120,000/40,000; materials: 120,000/1,200,000
[b]Labor: 150,000/37,500; materials: 150,000/1,428,571

Exhibit 15-11 Productivity Measurement: Profile Analysis with No Trade-offs—Ladd Lighting Corporation information so that a manager can conclude that the new assembly process has definitely improved overall productivity. The value of this improvement, however, is not revealed by the ratios.

As just shown, profile analysis can provide managers with useful insights about changes in productivity. However, comparing productivity profiles will not always reveal the nature of the overall change in productive efficiency. In some cases, profile analysis will not provide any clear indication of whether a productivity change is good or bad.

To illustrate this, let's revise the Ladd Lighting data to allow for trade-offs among the two inputs. Assume that all the data are the same except for materials used in 2008. Let the materials used in 2008 be 1,700,000 pounds. Using this revised number, the productivity profiles for 2007 and 2008 are presented in Exhibit 15-12. The productivity profile for 2007 is still (3, 0.100), but the profile for 2008 has changed to (4, 0.088). Comparing productivity profiles now provides a mixed signal. Productivity for labor has increased from 3 to 4, but productivity for materials has decreased from 0.100 to 0.088. The new process has caused a trade-off in the productivity in the two measures. Furthermore, while a profile analysis reveals that the trade-off exists, it does not reveal whether it is good or bad. If the economic effect of the productivity changes is positive, then the trade-off is good; otherwise, it must be viewed as bad. Valuing the trade-offs would allow us to assess the economic effect of the decision to change the assembly process. Furthermore, by valuing the productivity changes, we obtain a total measure of productivity.

Profit-Linked Productivity Measurement Assessing the effects of productivity changes on current profits is one way to value productivity changes. Profits change from the base period to the current period. Some of that profit change is attributable to productivity changes. Measuring the amount of profit change attributable to productivity change is defined as **profit-linked productivity measurement**.

Assessing the effect of productivity changes on current-period profits will help managers understand the economic importance of productivity changes. Linking productivity changes to profits is described by the following rule:

> Profit-Linkage Rule: For the current period, calculate the cost of the inputs that would have been used in the absence of any productivity change, and compare this cost with the cost of the inputs actually used. The difference in costs is the amount by which profits changed due to productivity changes.

To apply the linkage rule, the inputs that would have been used for the current period in the absence of a productivity change must be calculated. Let *PQ* represent this productivity-neutral quantity of input. To determine *PQ* for a particular input, divide the current-period output by the input's base-period productivity ratio:

$$PQ = \text{Current output/Base-period productivity ratio}$$

	Productivity Profile	
	2007[a]	2008[b]
Labor productivity ratio	3.000	4.000
Materials productivity ratio	0.100	0.088

[a]Labor: 120,000/40,000; materials: 120,000/1,200,000
[b]Labor: 150,000/37,500; materials: 150,000/1,700,000

Exhibit 15-12 Productivity Measurement: Profile Analysis with Trade-offs—Ladd Lighting Corporation

To illustrate the application of the profit-linked rule, let's return to the Ladd example with input trade-offs. To these data, we must add some cost information. The expanded Ladd data follow:

	2007	2008
Number of motors produced	120,000	150,000
Labor hours used	40,000	37,500
Materials used (lbs.)	1,200,000	1,700,000
Unit selling price (motors)	$50	$48
Wages per labor hour	$ 11	$12
Cost per pound of material	$ 2	$ 3

Current output (2008) is 150,000 motors. From Exhibit 15-12, we know that the base-period productivity ratios are 3 and 0.100 for labor and materials, respectively. Using this information, the productivity-neutral quantity for each input is computed as follows:

$$PQ \text{ (labor)} = 150{,}000/3 = 50{,}000 \text{ hrs.}$$
$$PQ \text{ (materials)} = 150{,}000/0.100 = 1{,}500{,}000 \text{ lbs.}$$

For our example, *PQ* gives labor and materials inputs that would have been used in 2008, assuming no productivity change. What the cost would have been is computed by multiplying each individual input quantity (*PQ*) by its current price (*P*) and totaling:

Cost of labor (50,000 × $12)	$ 600,000
Cost of materials: (1,500,000 × $3)	4,500,000
Total PQ cost	$5,100,000

The actual cost of inputs is obtained by multiplying the actual quantity (*AQ*) by current input price (*P*) for each input and totaling:

Cost of labor (37,500 × $12)	$ 450,000
Cost of materials (1,700,000 × $3)	5,100,000
Total current cost	$5,550,000

Finally, the productivity effect on profits is computed by subtracting the total current cost from the total *PQ* cost.

$$\begin{aligned} \text{Profit-linked effect} &= \text{Total } PQ \text{ cost} - \text{Total current cost} \\ &= \$5{,}100{,}000 - \$5{,}550{,}000 \\ &= \$450{,}000 \text{ decrease in profits} \end{aligned}$$

The calculation of the profit-linked effect is summarized in Exhibit 15-13. The summary in Exhibit 15-13 reveals that the net effect of the process change was unfavorable. Profits declined by $450,000 because of the productivity changes. Notice also that profit-linked productivity effects can be assigned to individual inputs. The increase in labor productivity creates a $150,000 increase in profits; however, the drop in materials productivity caused a $600,000 decrease in profits. Most of the profit decrease came from an increase in materials usage—apparently, waste, scrap, and spoiled units are much greater with the new process. Thus, the profit-linked measure provides partial measurement effects as well as a total measurement effect. The total profit-linked productivity measure is the sum of the individual partial measures. This property makes the profit-linked measure ideal for assessing trade-offs. A much clearer picture of the effects of the changes in productivity emerges. Unless waste and scrap can be brought under better control, the company ought to return to the old assembly process. Of course, it is possible that the learning effects of the new process are not yet fully captured and further improvements in

	(1)	(2)	(3)	(4)	(2) − (4)
Input	*PQ**	$PQ \times P$	*AQ*	$AQ \times P$	$(PQ \times P) - (AQ \times P)$
Labor	50,000	$ 600,000	37,500	$ 450,000	$ 150,000
Materials	1,500,000	4,500,000	1,700,000	5,100,000	(600,000)
Total		$5,100,000		$5,550,000	$(450,000)

*Labor: 150,000/3; materials: 150,000/0.10

Exhibit 15-13 Profit-Linked Productivity Measurement—Ladd Lighting Corporation

labor productivity might be observed. As labor becomes more proficient at the new process, it is possible that the material usage could also decrease.

Price-Recovery Component

The profit-linked measure computes the amount of profit change from the base period to the current period attributable to productivity changes. This generally will not be equal to the total profit change between the two periods. The difference between the total profit change and the profit-linked productivity change is called the **price-recovery component**. This component is the change in revenue less a change in the cost of inputs, assuming no productivity changes. Therefore, it measures the ability of revenue changes to cover changes in the cost of inputs, assuming no productivity change. To calculate the price-recovery component, we first need to compute the change in profits for each period:

	2008	2007	Difference
Revenues[a]	$7,200,000	$6,000,000	$ 1,200,000
Less cost of inputs[b]	5,550,000	2,840,000	2,710,000
Profit	$1,650,000	$3,160,000	$(1,510,000)

[a]$48 × 150,000; $50 × 120,000
[b]($12 × 37,500) + ($3 × 1,700,000); ($11 × 40,000) + ($2 × 1,200,000)

$$\begin{aligned}\text{Price recovery} &= \text{Profit change} - \text{Profit-linked productivity change}\\ &= (\$1{,}510{,}000) - (\$450{,}000)\\ &= (\$1{,}060{,}000)\end{aligned}$$

The increase in revenues would not have been sufficient to recover the increase in the cost of the inputs. The decrease in productivity simply aggravated the price-recovery problem. Note, however, that increases in productivity can be used to offset price-recovery losses.

Quality and Productivity

Improving quality may improve productivity, and vice versa. For example, if rework is reduced by producing fewer defective units, less labor and fewer materials are used to produce the same output. Reducing the number of defective units improves quality; reducing the amount of inputs used improves productivity.

Since most quality improvements reduce the amount of resources used to produce and sell an organization's output, they will improve productivity. Thus, quality improvements generally will be reflected in productivity measures. However, there are other ways to improve productivity. A firm may produce a good with little or no defects but still have an inefficient process.

For example, consider a good that passes through two 5-minute processes. (Assume the good is produced free of defects.) One unit, then, requires 10 minutes to pass through both processes. Currently, units are produced in batches of 1,200. Process 1 produces 1,200 units; then, the batch is conveyed by forklift to another location, where the units pass through Process 2. For each process, a total of 6,000 minutes, or 100 hours, is needed to produce a batch. The 1,200 finished units, then, require a total of 200 hours (100 hours for each process) plus conveyance time; assume that to be 15 minutes.

By redesigning the manufacturing process, efficiency can be improved. Suppose that the second process is located close enough to the first process so that as soon as a unit is completed by the first process, it is passed to the second process. In this way, the first and second processes can be working at the same time. The second process no longer has to wait for the production of 1,200 units plus conveyance time before it can begin operation. The total time to produce 1,200 units now is 6,000 minutes plus the waiting time for the first unit (five minutes). Thus, production of 1,200 units has been reduced from 200 hours and 15 minutes to 100 hours and five minutes. More output can be produced with fewer inputs (time).

Gainsharing

Gainsharing is providing to a company's entire workforce cash incentives that are keyed to quality and productivity gains. For example, suppose a company has a target of reducing the number of defective units by 10 percent during the next quarter for a particular plant. If the goal is achieved, the company estimates that $1,000,000 will be saved (through avoiding such things as reworks and warranty repairs). Gainsharing provides an incentive by offering a bonus to the employees equal to a percentage of the cost savings, say 20 percent.

Ford Motor Company, for example, has proposed overhauling its compensation program for its top 5,000 executives, implementing a new compensation program that replaces profit-driven bonus structures with performance-based measures such as overall product quality. The size of the bonus pool can grow or shrink depend-

Gain sharing allows employees to receive cash for productivity and quality improvements.

© Getty Images/PhotoDisc

Managers Decide

Ethics and Quality Cost Management

The management of Medrad, Inc., a manufacturer of medical devices that enhance the imaging of the human body, has identified five goals that guide decision making at all levels. One of these goals is to improve quality and productivity. In a strategic planning session, management sets one-year and five-year targets for specific objectives that relate to each goal, including the goal of improving quality and productivity. Medrad has consistently achieved the targets. Moreover, achieving these targets is done within an industry that is heavily regulated. The progress must be realized within a legal and ethical framework. Medrad has an ethical Code of Conduct that defines ethical behavior for the various transactions and interactions that occur within the company. Training in the code is part of the new employee orientation. This training is continued with a quarterly Code of Conduct Challenge sent by email to all employees. Medrad also maintains an anonymous ethical hotline, a business ethics committee, and a legal advisory board. ■

Source: National Institute of Standards and Technology, Baldrige National Quality Program Award Winners, http://www.nist.gov/public_affairs/baldrige2003/Medrad_3.3.04.pdf, accessed April 1, 2006.

ing on how well productivity and quality targets are met. **Sun Microsystems** provides another example.[14] Bonuses are tied to customer loyalty and customer quality indices. Sun Microsystems has found that such quality measures as late deliveries and software defects have declined steadily, while customer loyalty measures have increased. Pay-for-performance plans allowing employees to share in the benefits seem to create additional interest and commitment. Interestingly, these gainsharing plans are entirely complementary, and perhaps even essential, to an integrated measurement system such as the *Balanced Scorecard* discussed in Chapter 17.

Summary of Learning Objectives

1. Identify and describe the four types of quality costs.

To understand quality costs, it is first necessary to understand what is meant by quality. There are two types of quality: quality of design and quality of conformance. Quality of design concerns quality differences that arise for products with the same function but different specifications. Quality of conformance, on the other hand, concerns meeting the specifications required by the product. Quality costs are incurred when products fail to meet design specifications (and are, therefore, associated with quality of conformance). Quality costs are divided into four categories: prevention, appraisal, internal failure, and external failure. Prevention costs are those incurred to prevent poor quality. Appraisal costs are those incurred to detect poor quality. Internal failure costs are those incurred when products fail to conform to requirements and this lack of conformity is discovered before an external sale. External failure costs are those incurred when products fail to conform to requirements after an external sale is made.

2. Prepare a quality cost report, and differentiate between acceptable quality level and the view espoused by total quality control.

A quality cost report is prepared by listing costs for each item within each of the four major quality cost categories (see Exhibit 15-3). There are two views concerning the optimal distribution of quality costs: the AQL view and the zero-defects view. The AQL view holds that there is a trade-off between costs of failure and prevention and appraisal costs. This trade-off produces an optimal level of performance called

14 Both examples are from Melissa Larson, "Betting Your Bonus on Quality," *Quality Magazine* (May 1998), an online article accessible via the chapter web links at the Interactive Study Center on http://www.thomsonedu.com/accounting/hansen.

the acceptable quality level. AQL is the level at which the number of defects allowed minimizes total quality costs. The zero-defects view, on the other hand, espouses total quality control. Total quality control maintains that the conflict between failure and appraisal and prevention costs is more conjecture than real. The actual optimal level of defects is the zero-defect level; companies should be striving to achieve this level of quality. Although quality costs do not vanish at this level, they are much lower than the optimal level envisioned by the AQL view.

3. Tell why quality cost information is needed, and show how it is used.

Quality cost information is needed to help managers control quality performance and to serve as input for decision making. It can be used to evaluate the overall performance of quality-improvement programs and to help improve a variety of managerial decisions, for example, strategic pricing and new product analysis. Perhaps the most important observation is that quality cost information is fundamental to a company's pursuit of continuous improvement. Quality is one of the major competitive dimensions for world-class competitors.

4. Explain what productivity is, and calculate the impact of productivity changes on profits.

Productivity concerns how efficiently inputs are used to produce the output. Partial measures of productivity evaluate the efficient use of single inputs. Total measures of productivity assess efficiency for all inputs. Profit-linked productivity effects are calculated by using the linkage rule. Essentially, the profit effect is computed by taking the difference between the cost of the inputs that would have been used without any productivity change and the cost of the actual inputs used. Because of the possibility of input trade-offs, it is essential to value productivity changes. Only in this way can the effect of productivity changes be properly assessed. Finally, gainsharing can be used as an incentive for managers and workers to look for ways to increase quality and productivity.

Key Terms

Acceptable quality level (AQL), 665
Aesthetics, 659
Appraisal costs, 661
Base period, 677
Control activities, 660
Control costs, 660
Costs of quality, 660
Defective product, 660
Durability, 659
External failure costs, 661
Failure activities, 660
Failure costs, 660
Features (quality of design), 659
Financial productivity measure, 676
Fitness for use, 659
Gainsharing, 682
Hidden quality costs, 661
Input trade-off efficiency, 674
Internal failure costs, 661
Multiple-period quality trend report, 669
Observable quality costs, 661
Operational productivity measure, 676
Partial productivity measurement, 676
Performance, 659
Prevention costs, 661
Price-recovery component, 681
Productivity, 674
Productivity measurement, 676
Profile measurement, 678
Profit-linked productivity measurement, 679
Quality of conformance, 659
Quality product or service, 659
Reliability, 659
Serviceability, 659
Taguchi loss function, 662
Technical efficiency, 674
Total productive efficiency, 674
Total productivity measurement, 678
Zero defects, 660

Review Problems

1. Quality

At the beginning of 2008, Kare Company initiated a quality-improvement program. Considerable effort was expended to reduce the number of defective units produced. By the end of the year, reports from the production manager revealed that scrap and rework had both decreased. The president of the company was pleased to hear of the success but wanted some assessment of the financial impact of the improvements. To make this assessment, the following financial data were collected for the preceding and current years:

	2007	2008
Sales	$10,000,000	$10,000,000
Scrap	400,000	300,000
Rework	600,000	400,000
Product inspection	100,000	125,000
Product warranty	800,000	600,000
Quality training	40,000	80,000
Materials inspection	60,000	40,000

Required

1. Classify the costs as prevention, appraisal, internal failure, or external failure.
2. Compute quality cost as a percentage of sales for each of the two years. By how much has profit increased because of quality improvements? Assuming that quality costs can be reduced to 2.5 percent of sales, how much additional profit is available through quality improvements (assume that sales revenues will remain the same)?
3. Prepare a quality cost report for 2008.

Solution

1. Appraisal costs: product inspection and materials inspection; prevention costs: quality training; internal failure costs: scrap and rework; external failure costs: product warranty.
2. For 2008—total quality costs: $2,000,000; percentage of sales: 20 percent ($2,000,000/$10,000,000). For 2008—total quality costs: $1,545,000; percentage of sales: 15.45 percent ($1,545,000/$10,000,000). Profit has increased by $455,000. If quality costs drop to 2.5 percent of sales, another $1,295,000 of profit improvement is possible ($1,545,000 − $250,000).
3. **Kare Company**
   Quality Cost Report
   For the Year Ended 2008

	Quality Costs		Percentage (%) of Sales
Prevention costs:			
Quality training	$ 80,000	$ 80,000	0.80%
Appraisal costs:			
Product inspection	$125,000		
Materials inspection	40,000	165,000	1.65
Internal failure costs:			
Scrap	$300,000		
Rework	400,000	700,000	7.00
External failure costs:			
Product warranty	$600,000	600,000	6.00
Total quality costs		$1,545,000	15.45%

2. Productivity

Bearing Company made some changes at the end of 2007 that it hoped would favorably affect the efficiency of its input usage. Now, at the end of 2008, the president of the company wants an assessment of the changes in the company's productivity. The data needed for the assessment follow:

	2007	2008
Output	5,000	6,000
Output prices	$10	$10
Materials (lbs.)	4,000	4,200
Materials unit price	$ 3	$ 4
Labor (hrs.)	2,500	2,400
Labor rate per hour	$ 8	$ 8
Power (kwh)	1,000	1,500
Price per kwh	$ 2	$ 3

Required

1. Compute the partial operational measures for each input for both 2007 and 2008. What can be said about productivity improvement?
2. Prepare an income statement for each year, and calculate the total change in profits.
3. Calculate the profit-linked productivity measure for 2008. What can be said about the productivity program?
4. Calculate the price-recovery component. What does this tell you?

Solution

1. Partial measures:

	2007	2008
Materials	5,000/4,000 = 1.25	6,000/4,200 = 1.43*
Labor	5,000/2,500 = 2.00	6,000/2,400 = 2.50
Power	5,000/1,000 = 5.00	6,000/1,500 = 4.00

*Rounded.

Productive efficiency has increased for materials and labor and decreased for power. The outcome is mixed, and no statement about overall productivity improvement can be made without valuing the trade-off.

2. Income statements:

	2007	2008
Sales	$50,000	$60,000
Less: Cost of inputs	34,000	40,500
Income	$16,000	$19,500

Total change in profits: $19,500 − $16,000 = $3,500 increase

3. Profit-linked measurement:

	(1)	(2)	(3)	(4)	(2) − (4)
Input	PQ*	$PQ \times P$	AQ	$AQ \times P$	$(PQ \times P) - (AQ \times P)$
Materials	4,800	$19,200	4,200	$16,800	$2,400
Labor	3,000	24,000	2,400	19,200	4,800
Power	1,200	3,600	1,500	4,500	(900)
		$46,800		$40,500	$6,300

*Materials: 6,000/1.25; labor: 6,000/2; power: 6,000/5

The value of the increases in efficiency for materials and labor more than offsets the increased usage of power. Thus, the productivity program should be labeled successful.

4. Price recovery:

$$\begin{aligned}\text{Price-recovery component} &= \text{Profit change} - \text{Profit-linked productivity change}\\ &= \$3{,}500 - \$6{,}300\\ &= (\$2{,}800)\end{aligned}$$

This says that without the productivity improvement, profits would have declined by $2,800. The $10,000 increase in revenues would not have offset the increase in the cost of inputs. From the solution to Requirement 3, the cost of inputs without a productivity increase would have been $46,800 (column 2). The increase in the input cost without productivity would have been $46,800 − $34,000 = $12,800. This is $2,800 more than the increase in revenues. Only because of the productivity increase did the firm show an increase in profitability.

Questions for Writing and Discussion

1. Explain what is meant by "quality."
2. What is reliability? Durability?
3. What is quality of conformance?
4. Explain the difference between the traditional view of conformance and the robust view.
5. Why are quality costs the costs of doing things wrong?
6. Identify and discuss the four kinds of quality costs.
7. Explain why external failure costs can be more devastating to a firm than internal failure costs.
8. What are hidden quality costs? Provide an example.
9. What are the three methods for estimating hidden quality costs?
10. Discuss the value of a quality cost report.
11. What is the difference between the AQL model and the zero-defects model?
12. What are the differences between the zero-defects model and the robust quality model?
13. Explain the purpose of multiple-period trend analysis for quality costs.
14. Define total productive efficiency.
15. Explain the difference between partial and total measures of productivity.
16. Discuss the advantages and disadvantages of partial measures of productivity.
17. How can a manager measure productivity improvement?
18. What is profit-linked productivity measurement?
19. Explain why profit-linked productivity measurement is important.
20. What is the price-recovery component?
21. Can productivity improvements be achieved without improving quality? Explain.
22. Why is it important for managers to be concerned with both productivity and quality?
23. What are the differences between quality and productivity? Similarities?
24. What is gainsharing?

Exercises

15-1

Quality Costs; Miscellaneous Topics
LO1

Choose the *best* answer for each of the following multiple-choice questions:

1. A quality product is one that meets or exceeds customer expectations by:

   a. consistently functioning well.
   b. functioning for an acceptable length of time.
   c. meeting its specifications.
   d. being easy to maintain and repair.
   e. All of the above.

2. Conforming to specifications means that the specifications of a product
   a. fall within an acceptable range of values.
   b. exactly meet their targeted values.
   c. include all essential aspects except serviceability.
   d. are strictly controlled by quality audits.
   e. Both a and b, depending on whether the traditional view or the robust view of conformance is being emphasized.
3. Control costs are
   a. costs incurred after bad products are sent to customers.
   b. costs incurred to prevent/detect defective products.
   c. costs incurred to correct defective units before they are sent to customers.
   d. costs incurred to control product liability suits.
   e. All of the above.
4. The costs associated with quality reporting are
   a. prevention costs.
   b. appraisal costs.
   c. internal failure costs.
   d. external failure costs.
   e. None of the above.
5. The costs associated with retesting are
   a. prevention costs.
   b. appraisal costs.
   c. internal failure costs.
   d. external failure costs.
   e. None of the above.
6. The costs associated with packaging inspection are
   a. prevention costs.
   b. appraisal costs.
   c. internal failure costs.
   d. external failure costs.
   e. None of the above.
7. The costs associated with complaint adjustment are
   a. prevention costs.
   b. appraisal costs.
   c. internal failure costs.
   d. external failure costs.
   e. None of the above.
8. Quality costs that are opportunity costs and do not appear in a company's accounting records are
   a. not possible.
   b. hidden quality costs.
   c. total external failure costs.
   d. observable quality costs.
   e. only external failure costs.
9. If the total external failure cost is \$1,200,000 and the multiplier effect is 4, then the quality costs found in the firm's accounting records would be:
   a. impossible to assess.
   b. \$1,200,000.

c. $4,800,000.
d. $300,000.
e. None of the above.

10. Identify which of the following is a quality prevention cost:
    a. Quality planning
    b. Supplier evaluation and selection
    c. Quality audits
    d. Field trials
    e. All of the above
11. Identify which of the following is an appraisal cost (quality):
    a. Design reviews
    b. Quality reporting
    c. Manager of a packaging inspection team
    d. Warranties
    e. Retesting
12. Identify which of the following is an internal failure cost (quality):
    a. Supplier evaluation and selection
    b. Scrapped units
    c. Packaging inspection
    d. Product liability
    e. Complaint adjustment
13. Identify which of the following is an external failure cost (quality):
    a. Lost market share
    b. Retesting
    c. Rework
    d. Design reviews
    e. All of the above
14. For the Taguchi Loss function, $k = \$500$ and the average squared deviation is 0.05. If 1,000 units are produced, the total expected loss (hidden cost) would be:
    a. $500
    b. $500,000
    c. $50
    d. $25,000
    e. $25

15-2

Quality Cost Classification
LO1

Classify the following quality activities as prevention costs, appraisal costs, internal failure costs, or external failure costs.

1. Customers do not want second-class products. However, if they are sent slightly defective products, they may be willing to keep them provided they are given a price reduction.
2. Components from suppliers are carefully inspected.
3. Workers sand and stain a piece of wood, and then it warps. The piece of wood is then discarded as useless.
4. An automobile company recalls a model to repair a defective transmission.
5. A tire manufacturer is sued for deaths caused by a defective tire.
6. Design verification and review are used to evaluate the quality of new products.
7. New personnel are trained in quality circle methods.
8. Work stoppage to correct process malfunction (discovered using statistical process control procedures).

9. Packaging and shipping for returned products.
10. Reinspection of rework.
11. A defective product is replaced with a good one.
12. An internal audit is done to ensure that quality policies are being followed.
13. A product is redesigned to reduce the number of worker mistakes leading to a defective product.
14. Purchase orders are corrected to reflect the correct items and quantities.
15. Adjustments are made to accounts receivable to compensate for returned goods and price concessions.
16. New products are tested to ensure they function as intended.
17. Field service personnel sent to repair products on site.
18. Software corrected for defects.
19. Suppliers are evaluated to assess their capability of providing nondefective components.
20. Subassemblies are inspected.
21. Processing of customer complaints.
22. Prototype inspection and testing.
23. A worker accidentally drills a hole in a steel plate, and it must be welded shut for the plate to be useful.

15-3

Estimating Hidden Quality Costs
LO1

Bednar Company has developed the following information:

Measured external failure cost	$10,000,000
Multiplier effect (from the Multiplier Method)	4
Multiplier effect (Taguchi parameter)	$80
Average squared deviation (Taguchi)	12.5
Units produced	45,000

Required

1. Estimate the total hidden quality costs using the multiplier method.
2. Estimate the total hidden quality costs using the Taguchi quality loss function.

15-4

Quality Cost Report
LO2

During 2007 and 2008, Wilmington Company reported sales of $6,000,000 per year. Wilmington listed the following quality costs for the past two years. Assume that all changes in the quality costs are due to a quality-improvement program.

	2007	2008
Design review	$ 150,000	$ 300,000
Recalls	200,000	100,000
Reinspection	100,000	50,000
Materials inspection	60,000	40,000
Quality training	40,000	100,000
Process acceptance	—	50,000
Scrap	145,000	35,000
Lost sales (estimated)	300,000	200,000
Product inspection	50,000	30,000
Returned goods	155,000	95,000
Total	$1,200,000	$1,000,000

Required

1. Prepare a quality cost report for each year (2007 and 2008). What does this report tell management?
2. Calculate the relative distribution of quality costs by category for each year. What message does this communicate to management?

15-5

Quality Cost Improvement and Profitability; Quality Cost Report
LO1, LO2, LO3

During 2007 and 2008, Norton Company reported sales of $18,000,000 per year. Norton listed the following quality costs for the past two years. Assume that all changes in the quality costs are due to a quality-improvement program.

	2007	2008
Field trials	$ 450,000	$ 900,000
Recalls	600,000	300,000
Reinspection	300,000	150,000
Packaging inspection	180,000	120,000
Quality training	120,000	300,000
Process acceptance	—	150,000
Retesting	435,000	105,000
Lost sales (estimated)	900,000	600,000
Product inspection	150,000	90,000
Complaint adjustment	465,000	285,000
Total	$3,600,000	$3,000,000

Required

1. Prepare a quality cost report for each year (2007 and 2008).
2. How much were the additional resources invested in prevention and appraisal activities (control costs) from one year to the next? What return did this investment generate? (What reduction in failure costs was achieved?)
3. The management of Norton believes that it is possible to reduce quality costs to 2.5 percent of sales. Assuming sales continue at the $18,000,000 level, calculate the additional profit potential facing Norton. Is the expectation of improving quality and reducing quality costs to 2.5 percent of sales realistic? Explain.

15-6

Quality Costs; Distribution Across Categories; Gainsharing
LO1, LO2, LO3, LO4

Lander Company had sales of $48 million in 2001. In 2008, sales had increased to $60 million. A quality-improvement program was implemented in 2001. Overall conformance quality was targeted for improvement. The quality costs for 2001 and 2008 follow. Assume any changes in quality costs are attributable to improvements in quality.

	2001	2008
Internal failure costs	$ 3,600,000	$ 180,000
External failure costs	4,800,000	120,000
Appraisal costs	2,160,000	450,000
Prevention costs	1,440,000	750,000
Total quality costs	$12,000,000	$1,500,000

Required

1. Compute the quality costs/sales ratio for each year. Is this type of improvement possible?
2. Calculate the relative distribution of quality costs by category for 2001 (quality costs by category/total quality costs). What do you think of the relative cost distribution? How do you think quality costs will be distributed as the company approaches a zero-defects state?
3. Calculate the relative distribution of costs by category for 2008. What do you think of the level and distribution of quality costs? Do you think further reductions are possible?
4. Suppose that the CEO of Lander received a bonus equal to 10 percent of the quality cost savings each year. Do you think gainsharing is a good or bad idea? What risks are there, if any, to gainsharing?

15-7

Trade-offs among Quality Cost Categories; Gainsharing
LO2, LO4

Piura Company has sales of $10 million and quality costs of $1,200,000. The company is embarking on a major quality-improvement program. During the next three years, Piura intends to attack failure costs by increasing its appraisal and prevention costs. The "right" prevention activities will be selected, and appraisal costs will be reduced according to the results achieved. For the coming year, management is considering six specific activities: quality training, process control, product inspection, supplier evaluation, redesign of two major products, and prototype testing. To encourage managers to focus on reducing non-value-added quality costs and select the right activities, a bonus pool is established relating to reduction of quality costs. The bonus pool is equal to 10 percent of the total reduction in quality costs.

Current quality costs and the costs of these six activities are given in the following table. Each activity is added sequentially so that its effect on the cost categories can be assessed. For example, after quality training is added, the control costs increase to $400,000, and the failure costs drop to $1,300,000. Even though the activities are presented sequentially, they are totally independent of each other. Thus, only beneficial activities need be selected.

	Control Costs	Failure Costs
Current quality costs*	$ 200,000	$1,800,000
Quality training	400,000	1,300,000
Process control	650,000	900,000
Product inspection	750,000	820,000
Supplier evaluation	900,000	250,000
Prototype testing	1,200,000	150,000
Engineering redesign	1,250,000	50,000

*All current control costs are appraisal costs.

Required

1. Identify the control activities that should be implemented, and calculate the total quality costs associated with this selection. Assume that an activity is selected only if it increases the bonus pool.
2. Given the activities selected in Requirement 1, calculate the following:
   a. The reduction in total quality costs.
   b. The percentage distribution for control and failure costs.
   c. The amount for this year's bonus pool.
3. Suppose that a quality engineer complained about the gainsharing incentive system. Basically, he argued that the bonus should be based only on reductions of failure and appraisal costs. In this way, investment in prevention activities would be encouraged, and failure and appraisal costs would eventually be eliminated. After eliminating the non-value-added costs, focus could then be placed on the level of prevention costs. If this approach were adopted, what activities would be selected? Do you agree with this approach? Explain.

15-8

Quality Cost Report; Taguchi Quality Loss Function
LO1, LO2

EXCEL

At the end of 2008, Emery Manufacturing began to focus on its quality costs. As a first step, it identified the following costs in its accounting records as being quality related:

	2008
Sales (50,000 units @ $60)	$3,000,000
Scrap	90,000
Rework	120,000
Training program	36,000
Consumer complaints	60,000

(Continued)

Warranty	120,000
Test labor	90,000
Inspection labor	75,000
Supplier evaluation	9,000

Required

1. Prepare a quality cost report by quality cost category.
2. Calculate the relative distribution percentages for each quality cost category. Comment on the distribution.
3. Using the Taguchi quality loss function, an average loss per unit is computed at $5. What are the hidden costs of external failure? How does this affect the relative distribution? What effect will the hidden-cost information have on a quality-improvement program?

15-9
Taguchi Quality Loss Function
LO1

Shaw Company manufactures a product that has a target value of 32 ounces. Specification limits are 32 ounces plus or minus 0.75 ounce. The value of *k* is $120. A sample of five units produced the following measures:

Unit	Measured Weight
1	32.30
2	32.75
3	32.45
4	31.75
5	31.90

During May, a total of 50,000 units was produced.

Required

1. Calculate the loss for each unit. Calculate the average loss for the sample of five.
2. Using the average loss, calculate the hidden quality costs for April.

15-10
Multiple-Year Trend Reports
LO2

The controller of Golden Company has computed quality costs as a percentage of sales for the past five years (2004 was the first year the company implemented a quality-improvement program). This information follows:

	Prevention	Appraisal	Internal Failure	External Failure	Total
2004	3%	4%	9%	13%	29%
2005	4	5	8	11	28
2006	5	6	6	8	25
2007	6	5	4	6	21
2008	7	2	1	2	12

Required

1. Prepare a trend graph for total quality costs. Comment on what the graph has to say about the success of the quality-improvement program.
2. Prepare a graph that shows the trend for each quality cost category. What does the graph indicate about the success of the quality-improvement program? Does this graph supply more insight than the total cost trend graph? What does the graph reveal about the distribution of quality costs in 2004? In 2008?

15-11
Productivity Measurement
LO4

Helix Company produces a product that uses two inputs, materials and labor. The output and inputs for the last two years are:

	2007	2008
Output	10,000	10,000
Inputs:		
Materials (lbs)	2,500	2,000
Labor (hrs)	8,000	5,000

Materials are purchased for $8 per pound and labor is paid $10 per hour.

Required

1. Calculate the partial productivity ratios for each year. Did productivity improve from 2007 to 2008?
2. Now suppose that the labor hours for 2008 were 10,000 instead of 5,000. Using partial productivity ratios, what can you say about productivity change from 2007 to 2008? Is there anyway to evaluate the change from 2007 to 2008? Explain.

15-12

Productivity Measurement; Partial Measure
LO4

Doran Company produces a product that uses two inputs, energy and labor. During the past month, 400 units of the product were produced, requiring 320 units of energy and 1,280 hours of labor. An engineering study revealed that Doran can produce the same output of 400 units using either of the following two combinations of inputs:

	Energy	Labor
Combination A	200	800
Combination B	320	500

Energy costs $18 per unit used; the cost of labor is $15 per hour.

Required

1. Calculate the output/input ratio for each input of Combination A. Does this represent a productivity improvement over the current use of inputs? What is the total dollar value of the improvement? Classify this as technical or price efficiency improvement.
2. Calculate output/input ratios for each input of Combination B. Does this represent a productivity improvement over the current use of inputs? Now compare these ratios to those of Combination A. What has happened?
3. Compute the cost of producing the 400 units of output using Combination B. Compare this to the cost using Combination A. Does moving from Combination A to Combination B represent a productivity improvement? Explain.

15-13

Interperiod Measure of Productivity; Basic Computations
LO4

EXCEL

Bradshaw, Inc., gathered the following data for its last two years of operation:

	2007	2008
Output	96,000	120,000
Power (quantity used)	12,000	12,000
Materials (quantity used)	24,000	35,000
Unit price (power)	$1.00	$2.00
Unit price (materials)	$4.00	$5.00
Unit selling price	$2.00	$2.50

Required

1. Compute the partial operational productivity ratios for each year. Did productivity improve? Explain.

2. Compute the profit-linked productivity measure. By how much did profits increase due to productivity?
3. Calculate the price-recovery component for 2008. Explain its meaning.

15-14

Productivity Measurement; Trade-offs
LO4

EXCEL

Manson Company decided to install an automated manufacturing system. The decision to automate was made because of the promise to reduce the use of material and labor inputs. After one year of operation, management wants to evaluate the productivity change. The president is particularly interested in knowing whether the trade-off between labor, materials, and capital was favorable. Data concerning output, labor, materials, and capital are provided for the year before implementation and the year after.

	Year Before	Year After
Output	200,000	240,000
Input quantities:		
Materials (lbs.)	50,000	40,000
Labor (hrs.)	10,000	4,000
Capital	$10,000	$600,000
Input prices:		
Materials	$2	$2
Labor	$5	$5
Capital	15%	15%

Required

1. Compute the partial measures for materials, labor, and capital for each year. What caused the change in labor and materials productivity?
2. Calculate the change in profits attributable to the change in productivity of the three inputs. Assuming that these are the only three inputs, evaluate the decision to automate.

15-15

Productivity Measurement; Technical and Price Efficiency Illustrated
LO4

The manager of Lawson Company was reviewing two competing proposals for the Machining Department. The fiscal year was coming to a close, and the manager wanted to make a decision concerning the proposed process changes so that they could be used, if beneficial, during the coming year. The process changes would affect the department's input usage. For the year just ended, the Accounting Department provided the following information about the inputs used to produce 250,000 units of output:

	Quantity	Unit Prices
Materials	450,000 lbs.	$ 8
Labor	200,000 hrs.	10
Energy	100,000 kwhs.	2

Each proposal offers a process design different from the one currently used. Neither proposal would cost anything to implement. Both proposals project input usage for producing 300,000 units (the expected output for the coming year).

	Proposal A	Proposal B
Materials	450,000 lbs.	500,000 lbs.
Labor	200,000 hrs.	150,000 hrs.
Energy	100,000 kwhs.	100,000 kwhs.

Input prices are expected to remain the same for the coming year.

Required

1. Compute the partial operational productivity measures for the most recently completed year and each proposal. Does either proposal improve technical efficiency? Explain. Can you make a recommendation about either proposal using only the physical measures?
2. Calculate the profit-linked productivity measure for each proposal. Which proposal offers the best outcome for the company? How does this relate to the concept of price efficiency? Explain.

15-16

Productivity and Quality
LO4

Rington Company is considering the acquisition of an automated system that would decrease the number of units scrapped because of poor quality. (This proposal is part of an ongoing effort to improve quality.) The production manager is pushing for the acquisition because he believes that productivity will be greatly enhanced—particularly when it comes to labor and material inputs. Output and input data follow. The after-acquisition data are projections.

	Current	After Acquisition
Output (units)	10,000	10,000
Output selling price	$ 40	$ 40
Input quantities:		
Materials (lbs.)	40,000	35,000
Labor (hrs.)	20,000	15,000
Capital	$20,000	$100,000
Energy (kwhs.)	10,000	25,000
Input prices:		
Materials	$ 4.00	$ 4.00
Labor	$ 9.00	$ 9.00
Capital	10.00%	10.00%
Energy	$ 2.50	$ 2.50

Required

1. Compute the partial operational productivity ratios for materials and labor under each alternative. Is the production manager right in thinking that materials and labor productivity will increase with the automated system?
2. Compute the partial operational productivity ratios for all four inputs. Does the system improve productivity?
3. Determine the amount by which profits will change if the system is adopted. Are the trade-offs among the inputs favorable? Comment on the system's ability to improve productivity.

15-17

Basics of Productivity Measurement
LO4

EXCEL

Lau Company gathered the following data for the past two years:

	Base Year	Current Year
Output	150,000	180,000
Output prices	$20	$20
Input quantities:		
Materials (lbs.)	200,000	180,000
Labor (hrs.)	50,000	90,000
Input prices:		
Materials	$ 5	$ 6
Labor	$ 8	$ 8

Required

1. Calculate the partial operational productivity measures for each year.
2. Prepare income statements for each year. Calculate the total change in income.

3. Calculate the change in profits attributable to productivity changes.
4. Calculate the price-recovery component. Explain its meaning.

Problems

15-18

Classification of Quality Costs
LO1

Classify the following quality costs as prevention, appraisal, internal failure, or external failure.

1. Design verification and review to evaluate the quality of new products.
2. Scrapping defective units.
3. Downtime (defect-related).
4. Customer complaint department.
5. Prototype inspection and testing.
6. Maintenance of inspection equipment.
7. Grinding bumps off a poorly welded steel plate.
8. Design and development of quality equipment.
9. Quality circles.
10. Correcting an improperly filled-out purchase order.
11. The cost of repairing a product under warranty.
12. Internal audit assessing the effectiveness of the quality system.
13. Replacing a component improperly inserted and damaged.
14. Machine jammed and damaged because of an incorrectly sized subassembly.
15. Packaging inspection.
16. Quality audits.
17. Complaint adjustment.
18. Setup for testing.
19. Lending engineers to help improve processes and products of suppliers.
20. Vendor certification.
21. Extra overhead costs incurred due to returned products.
22. Supervision of in-process inspection.
23. Inspection of parts purchased from suppliers.
24. Packaging and shipping repaired goods.
25. Outside laboratory evaluation of product quality.

15-19

Various Quality and Productivity Concepts
LO1, LO2, LO3, LO4

Match the following:

1. Appraisal costs	a. Activities performed because poor quality exists
2. Financial productivity measure	b. Length of time a product functions
3. Profile measurement	c. Lost sales because of poor quality
4. Durability	d. Vector of partial productivity measures
5. Input trade-off efficiency	e. Costs of detecting poor quality
6. External failure costs	f. Revenue/labor cost
7. Base period	g. Lowest cost technically efficient inputs
8. Zero defects	h. Units produced/pounds of material used
9. Operational productivity measure	i. No nonconforming products
10. Failure activities	j. Product does intended functions
11. Profit-linked productivity	k. Standard for productivity measurement
12. Fitness for use	l. Profit change due to productivity change
13. Gainsharing	m. No more input used than necessary
14. Hidden quality costs	n. Costs not recorded in accounting records
15. Technical efficiency	o. Bonus paid for productivity/quality improvements

15-20

Quality Cost Summary; Gainsharing
LO1, LO2, LO3, LO4

Danna Lummus, the president of Karlene Company, has recently returned from a conference on quality and productivity. At the conference, she learned that many American firms have made significant progress in improving quality and reducing quality costs. Many of these firms have been able to reduce quality costs from 20 to 30 percent of sales to 2 to 3 percent of sales. She was skeptical, however, about this statistic. Even if the quality gurus were right, she was sure that her company's quality costs were much lower—probably less than 5 percent. On the other hand, if she was wrong, she would be passing up an opportunity to improve profits significantly and simultaneously strengthen her competitive position. In fact, she reflected on the comment of one of the quality experts: "Quality has become a condition of entrance to the market. If the product is not good, you will quickly go out of business." The quality issue was at least worth exploring. Moreover, she decided that it may be too risky *not* to assess her company's quality performance. She knew that her company produced most of the information needed for quality cost reporting—but there never had been a need to bother with any formal quality data gathering and analysis.

This conference, however, had convinced her that a firm's profitability can increase significantly by improving quality—provided the potential for improvement exists. Thus, before committing the company to a quality-improvement program, Linda contacted her controller and requested a preliminary estimate of the total quality costs currently being incurred. She also instructed the controller to classify quality costs into four categories: prevention, appraisal, internal failure, and external failure costs. The controller has gathered the following information from the past year, 2008:

a. Sales revenue is $30,000,000; net income is $6,000,000.
b. During the year, customers returned 90,000 units needing repair. Repair cost averages $7 per unit.
c. Ten inspectors are employed, each earning an annual salary of $45,000. These 10 inspectors are involved only with final inspection (product acceptance).
d. Total scrap is 90,000 units. All scrap is quality related. The cost of scrap is about $15 per unit.
e. Each year, approximately 450,000 units are rejected in final inspection. Of these units, 80 percent can be recovered through rework. The cost of rework is $3 per unit.
f. A customer canceled an order that would have increased profits by $750,000. The customer's reason for cancellation was poor product performance. The Accounting and Marketing Departments agree that the company loses at least this much each year for the same reason.
g. The company employs eight full-time employees in its Complaint Department. Each earns $37,500 a year.
h. The company gave sales allowances totaling $375,000 due to substandard products being sent to the customer.
i. The company requires all new employees to take its three-hour quality training program. The estimated annual cost of the program is $240,000.
j. Inspection of the final product requires testing equipment. The annual cost of operating and maintaining this equipment is $360,000.

Required

1. Prepare a simple quality cost report, classifying costs by category. Comment on the quality costs/sales ratio.
2. Discuss the distribution of quality costs among the four categories. Are they properly distributed? Explain.
3. Discuss how the company can improve its overall quality and at the same time reduce total quality costs. Consider specifically the strategy advocated by the American Society for Quality Control.

4. Suppose Karlene Company decides that a five-year program will reduce quality costs to 2.5 percent of sales and that control costs will be 80 percent of total quality costs. Calculate the income increase that will occur if sales remain at $30,000,000. Also, calculate the total amount spent on control and failure costs.
5. Refer to Requirements 1 and 4. Suppose that Danna decides to create a bonus pool to allow employees to share in the benefits from quality improvements. The bonus pool is 20 percent of quality cost reductions. How much will be put in the bonus pool for the five-year period? Why establish such a pool? Suppose that Danna's quality manager suggests that the bonus be based only on reductions of appraisal and failure costs. Explain why he might suggest this modification. Do you agree?
6. For Danna's company, hidden quality costs are estimated by using a multiplier of three. What are the actual external failure costs? What methods are available for estimating hidden quality costs? What effect does this estimation have on a quality-improvement strategy? Finally, should reductions of these costs be included in the bonus pool mentioned in Requirement 5? If included, what would be the effect on the bonus pool?

15-21

Quality Costs; Pricing Decisions; Market Share
LO3

Tannert Company manufactures furniture. One of its product lines is an economy-line kitchen table. During the last year, Tannert produced and sold 100,000 units for $100 per unit. Sales of the table are on a bid basis, but Tannert has always been able to win sufficient bids using the $100 price. This year, however, Tannert was losing more than its share of bids. Concerned, Larry Franklin, owner and president of the company, called a meeting of his executive committee (Megan Johnson, marketing manager; Fred Davis, quality manager; Kevin Jones, production manager; and Helen Jackson, controller).

Larry: I don't understand why we're losing bids. Megan, do you have an explanation?

Megan: Yes, as a matter of fact. Two competitors have lowered their price to $92 per unit. That's too big a difference for most of our buyers to ignore. If we want to keep selling our 100,000 units per year, we will need to lower our price to $92. Otherwise, our sales will drop to between 20,000 and 25,000 per year.

Helen: The unit contribution margin on the table is $10. Lowering the price to $92 will cost us $8 per unit. Based on a sales volume of 100,000, we'd make $200,000 in contribution margin. If we keep the price at $100, our contribution margin would be $200,000 to $250,000. If we have to lose, let's just take the lower market share. It's better than lowering our prices.

Megan: Perhaps. But the same thing could happen to some of our other product lines. My sources tell me that these two companies are on the tail end of a major quality-improvement program—one that allows them significant savings. We need to rethink our whole competitive strategy—at least if we want to stay in business. Ideally, we should match the price reduction and work to reduce the costs to recapture the lost contribution margin.

Fred: I think I have something to offer. We are about to embark on a new quality-improvement program of our own. I have brought the following estimates of the current quality costs for this economy line. As you can see on the overhead, these costs run about 16 percent of current sales. That's excessive, and we believe that they can be reduced to about 4 percent of sales over time.

Scrap	$ 700,000
Rework	300,000
Rejects (sold as seconds to discount houses)	250,000
Returns (due to poor workmanship)	350,000
	$1,600,000

Larry: This sounds good. Fred, how long will it take you to achieve this reduction?

Fred: Because all these costs vary with sales level, I'll express their reduction rate in those terms. Our best guess is that we can reduce these costs by about 1 percent of sales per quarter. So it should take about 12 quarters, or three years, to achieve the full benefit. Keep in mind that this is with an improvement in quality.

Megan: This offers us some hope. If we meet the price immediately, we can maintain our market share. Furthermore, if we can ever reach the point of reducing the price beyond the $92 level, then we can increase our market share. I estimate that we can increase sales by about 10,000 units for every $1 of price reduction beyond the $92 level. Kevin, how much extra capacity for this line do we have?

Kevin: We can handle an extra 30,000 or 40,000 tables per year.

Required

1. Assume that Tannert immediately reduces the bid price to $92. How long will it be before the unit contribution margin is restored to $10, assuming that quality costs are reduced as expected and sales are maintained at 100,000 units per year (25,000 per quarter)?
2. Assume that Tannert holds the price at $92 until the 4 percent target is achieved. At this new level of quality costs, should the price be reduced? If so, by how much should the price be reduced, and what is the increase in contribution margin? Assume that the price can be reduced only in $1 increments.
3. Assume that Tannert immediately reduces the price to $92 and begins the quality-improvement program. Now, suppose that Tannert does not wait until the end of the three-year period before reducing prices. Instead, prices will be reduced when profitable to do so. Assume that prices can be reduced only by $1 increments. Identify when the first future price change should occur (if any).
4. Discuss the differences in viewpoints concerning the decision to decrease prices and the short-run contribution margin analysis done by Helen, the controller. Did quality cost information play an important role in the strategic decision making illustrated by the problem?

15-22

Quality Costs; Cost-Volume-Profit Analysis
LO2, LO3

At the end of 2004, Graylevy Machining hired Mary Lou Morris to manage one of its troubled divisions. Mary Lou had the reputation of turning around businesses that were having difficulty. In 2005, the division had sales of $300 million, a unit-level variable cost ratio of 0.8, and total fixed costs of $72 million. The division produced only one product, and all sales were to external customers. Seeking to solve the division's problems, Mary Lou asked for a report on quality costs for 2005 and received the following report:

	Fixed	Variable (unit-level)
Prevention	$ 2,400,000	—
Appraisal	3,600,000	$12,000,000
Internal failure	6,000,000	24,000,000
External failure	12,000,000	60,000,000
Total	$24,000,000	$96,000,000

Mary Lou was astounded at the level of expenditure on quality costs. Although she had heard of companies with quality costs that had reached as high as 60 percent of sales, she had never personally seen any greater than 20 to 30 percent of sales. This division's level of 40 percent was clearly excessive. She immediately implemented a program to improve conformance quality. By the end of 2006, the following quality costs were reported:

	Fixed	Variable (unit-level)
Prevention	$12,000,000	—
Appraisal	12,000,000	$12,000,000
Internal failure	6,000,000	12,000,000
External failure	12,000,000	42,000,000
Total	$42,000,000	$66,000,000

Revenues and other costs were unchanged for 2006.

Mary Lou projects that by 2010 the defective rate will be 0.1 percent, compared to the rate of 2 percent for 2005. She also projects that quality costs will be reduced to $6 million, distributed as follows:

	Fixed	Variable (unit-level)
Prevention	$2,400,000	—
Appraisal	2,400,000	—
Internal failure	—	$ 240,000
External failure	—	960,000
Total	$4,800,000	$1,200,000

Required

1. Calculate the break-even point in revenues for 2005. How much was the division losing?
2. Calculate the break-even point in 2006. Explain the change.
3. Calculate the break-even point in 2010, assuming that revenues and other costs have remained the same. Is it possible to reduce quality costs as dramatically as portrayed?
4. Assume that from 2005 to 2010, the division was forced to cut selling prices so that total revenues dropped to $180 million. Calculate the income (loss) that would be reported under a 2003 cost structure. Now, calculate the income (loss) that would be reported under the 2010 quality cost structure (assuming all other costs remain unchanged). Discuss the strategic significance of quality cost management.

15-23

Quality Cost Report; Quality Cost Categories
LO1, LO2

In September 2007, Olson Company received a report from an external consulting group on its quality costs. The consultants reported that the company's quality costs total about 25 percent of its sales revenues. Somewhat shocked by the magnitude of the costs, Frank Roosevelt, president of Olson Company, decided to launch a major quality-improvement program. This program was scheduled for implementation in January 2008. The program's goal was to reduce quality costs to 2.5 percent by the end of 2008 by improving overall quality.

In 2008, it was decided to reduce quality costs to 22 percent of sales revenues. Management felt that the amount of reduction was reasonable and that the goal could be realized. To improve the monitoring of the quality-improvement program, Frank directed Pamela Golding, the controller, to prepare quarterly performance reports comparing budgeted and actual quality costs. He told Pamela that improving quality should reduce quality costs by 1 percent of sales for each of the first three quarters and 2 percent in the last quarter. Sales are projected at $5 million per quarter. Based on the consulting report and the targeted reductions, Pamela prepared the budgets for the first two quarters of the year:

	Quarter 1	Quarter 2
Sales	$5,000,000	$5,000,000
Quality costs:		
Warranty	$ 300,000	$ 250,000
Scrap	150,000	125,000
Incoming materials inspection	25,000	50,000
Product acceptance	125,000	150,000
Quality planning	40,000	60,000
Field inspection	30,000	0
Retesting	50,000	40,000
Allowances	65,000	50,000
New product review	10,000	10,000
Rework	130,000	100,000
Complaint adjustment	60,000	20,000
Downtime (defective parts)	50,000	40,000
Repairs	50,000	35,000
Product liability	85,000	60,000
Quality training	30,000	70,000
Quality engineering	0	40,000
Design verification	0	20,000
Process control measurement	0	30,000
Total budgeted costs	$1,200,000	$1,150,000
Quality costs/sales ratio	24%	23%

Required

1. Assume that Olson Company reduces quality costs as indicated. What will quality costs be as a percentage of sales for the entire year? For the end of the fourth quarter? Will the company achieve its goal of reducing quality costs to 22 percent of sales?
2. Reorganize the quarterly budgets so that quality costs are grouped in one of four categories: prevention, appraisal, internal failure, or external failure (effectively, prepare a budgeted cost of quality report). Also, identify each cost as variable or fixed. (Assume that none are mixed costs.)
3. Compare the two quarterly budgets. What do they reveal about the quality-improvement plans of Olson Company?

15-24

Distribution of Quality Costs
LO2

EXCEL

Paper Products Division produces paper diapers, napkins, and paper towels. The divisional manager has decided that quality costs can be minimized by distributing quality costs evenly among the four quality categories and reducing them to no more than 5 percent of sales. He has just received the following quality cost report:

Paper Products Division
Quality Cost Report
For the Year Ended December 31, 2008

	Diapers	Napkins	Towels	Total
Prevention:				
Quality training	$ 3,000	$ 2,500	$ 2,000	$ 7,500
Quality engineering	3,500	1,000	2,500	7,000
Quality audits	—	500	1,000	1,500
Quality reporting	2,500	2,000	1,000	5,500
Total	$ 9,000	$ 6,000	$ 6,500	$ 21,500

(Continued)

	Diapers	Napkins	Towels	Total
Appraisal:				
Inspection, materials	$ 2,000	$ 3,000	$ 3,000	$ 8,000
Process acceptance	4,000	2,800	1,200	8,000
Product acceptance	2,000	1,200	2,300	5,500
Total	$ 8,000	$ 7,000	$ 6,500	$ 21,500
Internal failure:				
Scrap	$10,000	$ 3,000	$ 2,500	$ 15,500
Disposal costs	7,000	2,000	1,500	10,500
Downtime	1,000	1,500	2,500	5,000
Total	$18,000	$ 6,500	$ 6,500	$ 31,000
External failure:				
Allowances	$10,000	$ 3,000	$ 2,750	$ 15,750
Customer complaints	4,000	1,500	3,750	9,250
Product liability	1,000	—	—	1,000
Total	$15,000	$ 4,500	$ 6,500	$ 26,000
Total quality costs	$50,000	$24,000	$26,000	$100,000

Assume that all prevention costs are fixed and that the remaining quality costs are variable.

Required

1. Assume that the sales revenue for the year totaled $2 million, with sales for each product as follows: diapers, $1 million; napkins, $600,000; and towels, $400,000. Evaluate the distribution of costs for the division as a whole and for each product line. What recommendations do you have for the divisional manager?
2. Now, assume a different scenario, where total sales of $1 million have this breakdown: diapers, $500,000; napkins, $300,000; and towels, $200,000. Evaluate the distribution of costs for the division as a whole and for each product line in this case. Do you think it is possible to reduce the quality costs to 5 percent of sales for each product line and for the division as a whole and, simultaneously, achieve an equal distribution of the quality costs? What recommendations do you have?
3. Assume total sales of $1 million with this breakdown: diapers, $500,000; napkins, $180,000; and towels, $320,000. Evaluate the distribution of quality costs. What recommendations for the divisional manager do you have?
4. Discuss the value of having quality costs reported by segment.

15-25

Trend Analysis; Quality Costs
LO2

In 2004, Don Blackburn, president of Sunnydance Enterprises, received a report indicating that quality costs were 21 percent of sales. Faced with increasing pressures from imported goods, Don resolved to take measures to improve the overall quality of the company's products. After hiring a consultant, the company began, in 2005, an aggressive program of total quality control. At the end of 2008, Don requested an analysis of the progress the company had made in reducing and controlling quality costs. The Accounting Department assembled the following data:

	Sales	Prevention	Appraisal	Internal Failure	External Failure
2004	$1,000,000	$10,000	$20,000	$ 80,000	$100,000
2005	1,200,000	30,000	40,000	100,000	120,000
2006	1,400,000	60,000	50,000	60,000	80,000
2007	1,200,000	70,000	70,000	40,000	50,000
2008	1,000,000	70,000	30,000	16,000	24,000

Required

1. Compute the quality costs as a percentage of sales by category and in total for each year.
2. Explain why quality costs increased in total and as a percentage of sales in 2005, the first year of the quality-improvement program.
3. Prepare a multiple-year trend graph for quality costs, both by total costs and by category. Using the graph, assess the progress made in reducing and controlling quality costs. Does the graph provide evidence that quality has improved? Explain.

15-26

Profit-Linked Measurement; Price Recovery; Gainsharing
LO4

Hillock Company produces handcrafted wool ponchos. Virtually all the manufacturing cost consists of materials and labor. Over the past several years, profits have been declining because the cost of the two major inputs has been increasing. David Hillock, the president of the company, has indicated that the price of the sweaters cannot be increased; thus, the only way to improve or at least stabilize profits is to increase overall productivity. At the beginning of 2008, he implemented a new productivity program. To encourage greater attention to productivity, David established a bonus pool, equal to 10 percent of the productivity gains. David now wants to know how much profits have increased from the prior year because of the productivity program. In order to provide this information to the president, the following data have been gathered:

	2007	2008
Unit selling price	$80	$80
Output produced and sold	300,000	360,000
Materials used (lbs.)	600,000	600,000
Labor used (hrs.)	150,000	150,000
Unit price of materials	$20	$22
Unit price of labor	$13	$15

Required

1. Compute the partial productivity ratios for each year. Comment on the effectiveness of the productivity improvement program.
2. Compute the increase in profits attributable to increased productivity, net of gainsharing.
3. Calculate the price-recovery component, and comment on its meaning. Ignore the bonus cost in this calculation.

15-27

Productivity Measurement
LO4

In 2007, Hepworth Products, Inc., used the following input combination to produce 8,000 units of output:

Materials	17,600 lbs.
Labor	16,000 hrs.

The following combination is optimal for an output of 8,000 units (but unknown to Hepworth Products):

Materials	8,000 lbs.
Labor	32,000 hrs.

The cost of materials is $40 per pound, and the cost of labor is $10 per hour. These input prices hold for 2007 and 2008. In 2008, Carson Products again produced 8,000 units, with the following input combination:

Materials	9,600 lbs.
Labor	50,000 hrs.

Required

1. Compute the partial productivity ratios for each of the following:
   a. The actual inputs used in 2007.
   b. The actual inputs used in 2008.
   c. The optimal input combination.

   Did productivity increase in 2008—as measured by the partial ratios?
2. Compute the cost of 2007's productive inefficiency relative to the optimal input combination.
3. By how much did profits increase because of improvements in productive efficiency from 2007 to 2008?
4. How much additional improvement in profits is possible after 2008 (assuming input costs remain the same and output doesn't change)?

15-28

Productivity Measurement; Partial and Total Measures; Price Recovery
LO4

The battery division of Chalmur Company has recently engaged in a vigorous effort to increase productivity. Over the past several years, competition had intensified, indicating to the divisional manager that a significant price decrease for Chalmur's batteries was in order. Otherwise, the division would lose at least 50 percent of its market share.

To maintain its market share, Chalmur had to decrease its per-unit price by $2.50 by the end of 2006. Decreasing the price by $2.50, however, necessitated a similar increase in cost efficiency. If divisional profits dropped by $2.50 per unit, the division's continued existence would be in question. To assess the outcome of the productivity improvement program, the following data were gathered:

	2007	2008
Output	400,000	500,000
Input quantities:		
Materials (lbs.)	100,000	100,000
Labor (hrs.)	400,000	200,000
Capital	$4,000,000	$10,000,000
Energy (kwhs.)	100,000	300,000
Input prices:		
Materials	$2.00	$3.00
Labor	$8.00	$10.00
Capital	15%	10%
Energy	$2.00	$2.00

Required

1. Calculate the partial productivity ratios for each year. Can you say that productivity has improved? Explain.
2. Calculate the profit change attributable to productivity changes.
3. Calculate the cost per unit for 2007 and 2008. Was the division able to decrease its per-unit cost by at least $2.50? Comment on the relationship between competitive advantage and productive efficiency.

15-29

Quality and Productivity; Interaction; Use of Operational Measures
LO4

Andy Confer, production-line manager, had arranged a visit with Will Keating, plant manager. He had some questions about the new operational measures that were being used.

Andy: Will, my questions are more to satisfy my curiosity than anything else. At the beginning of the year, we began some new procedures that required us to work toward increasing our output per pound of material and decreasing our output per labor hour. As instructed, I've been tracking these operational measures for each batch we've produced so far this year. Here's a copy of a trend report for the first five batches of the year. Each batch had 10,000 units in it.

Batches	Materials Usage (lbs.)	Ratio	Labor Usage (hrs.)	Ratio
1	4,000	2.50	2,000	5.00
2	3,900	2.56	2,020	4.95
3	3,750	2.67	2,150	4.65
4	3,700	2.70	2,200	4.55
5	3,600	2.78	2,250	4.44

Will: Andy, this report is very encouraging. The trend is exactly what we hoped for. I'll bet we meet our goal of reaching the batch productivity measures. Let's see, the goals for this year were 3.00 units per pound for materials and 4.00 units per hour for labor. Last year's figures were 2.50 for materials and 5.00 for labor. Things are looking good. I guess tying bonuses and raises to improving these productivity stats was a good idea.

Andy: Maybe so, but I don't understand why you want to make these trade-offs between materials and labor. The materials cost only $5 per pound, and labor costs $10 per hour. It seems like you're simply increasing the cost of making this product.

Will: Actually, it may seem that way, but it's not so. There are other factors to consider. You know we've been talking quality improvement. Well, the new procedures that you are implementing are producing products that conform to the product's specification. More labor time is needed to achieve this, and as we take more time, we do waste fewer materials. But the real benefit is the reduction in our external failure costs. Every defect in a batch of 10,000 units costs us $1,000—warranty work, lost sales, a Customer Service Department, and so on. If we can reach the materials and labor productivity goals, our defects will drop from 20 per batch to five per batch.

Required

1. Discuss the advantages of using only operational measures of productivity for controlling shop-level activities.
2. Assume that the batch productivity statistics are met by the end of the year. Calculate the change in a batch's profits from the beginning of the year to the end attributable to changes in materials and labor productivity.
3. Now, assume that three inputs are to be evaluated: materials, labor, and quality. Quality is measured by the number of defects per batch. Calculate the change in a batch's profits from the beginning of the year to the end attributable to changes in productivity of all three inputs. Do you agree that quality is an input? Explain.

15-30

Productivity; Trade-offs LO4

Connie Baker, president of Fleming Chemicals, has just concluded a meeting with two of her plant managers. She told each that their product was going to have a 50 percent increase in demand next year over this year's output (which is expected to be 10,000 gallons). A major foreign source of the material had been shut down because of civil war. It would be years before the source would be available again. The result was twofold. First, the price of the material was expected to quadruple. Second, many of the less efficient competitors would leave the business, creating more demand and higher output prices—in fact, output prices would double.

In discussing the situation with her plant managers, she reminded them that the automated process now allowed them to increase the productivity of the material. By using more machine hours, evaporation could be decreased significantly (this was a recent development and would be operational by the beginning of the new fiscal year). There were, however, only two other feasible settings beyond the current setting. The current usage of inputs for the 10,000 gallon output (current setting) and the input usage for the other two settings follow. The input usage for the remaining two settings is for an output of 15,000 gallons. Inputs are measured in gallons for the material and in machine hours for the equipment.

	Current Setting	Setting A	Setting B
Input quantities:			
Materials (gals.)	25,000	15,000	30,000
Equipment (hrs.)	6,000	15,000	7,500

The current prices for this year's inputs are $3 per gallon for materials and $12 per machine hour for the equipment. The materials price will change for next year as explained, but the $12 rate for machine hours will remain the same. The chemical is currently selling for $20 per gallon. Based on separate productivity analyses, one plant manager chose Setting A, and the other chose Setting B.

The manager who chose Setting B justified his decision by noting that it was the only setting that clearly signaled an increase in both partial measures of productivity. The other manager agreed that Setting B was an improvement but that Setting A was even better.

Required

1. Calculate the partial measures of productivity for the current year and for the two settings. Which of the two settings signals an increase in productivity for both inputs?
2. Calculate the profits that will be realized under each setting for the coming year. Which setting provides the greatest profit increase?
3. Calculate the profit change for each setting attributable to productivity changes. Which setting offers the greatest productivity improvement? By how much? Explain why this happened. (*Hint:* Look at trade-offs.)

Managerial Decision Cases

15-31

Quality Cost Performance Reports
LO2

Nickles Company, a large printer, is in its fourth year of a five-year, quality-improvement program. The program began in 2004 with an internal study that revealed the quality costs being incurred. In that year, a plan was developed to lower quality costs to 10 percent of sales by the end of 2008. Sales and quality costs for each year are as follows:

	Sales Revenues	Quality Costs
2004	$10,000,000	$2,000,000
2005	10,000,000	1,800,000
2006	11,000,000	1,815,000
2007	12,000,000	1,680,000
2008*	12,000,000	1,320,000

*Budgeted figures

Quality costs by category are expressed as a percentage of sales as follows:

	Prevention	Appraisal	Internal Failure	External Failure
2004	1.0%	3.0%	7.0%	9.0%
2005	2.0	4.0	6.0	6.0
2006	2.5	4.0	5.0	5.0
2007	3.0	3.5	4.5	3.0
2008	3.5	3.5	2.0	2.0

The detail of the 2008 budget for quality costs is also provided.

Prevention costs:	
Quality planning	$ 150,000
Quality training	20,000
Quality improvement (special project)	80,000
Quality reporting	10,000
Appraisal costs:	
Proofreading	500,000
Other inspection	50,000
Failure costs:	
Correction of typos	150,000
Rework (because of customer complaints)	75,000
Plate revisions	55,000
Press downtime	100,000
Waste (because of poor work)	130,000
Total quality costs	$1,320,000

All prevention costs are fixed; all other quality costs are variable.

During 2008, the company had $12 million in sales. Actual quality costs for 2007 and 2008 are as follows:

	2007	2008
Quality planning	$140,000	$150,000
Quality training	20,000	20,000
Special project	120,000	100,000
Quality reporting	12,000	12,000
Proofreading	580,000	520,000
Other inspection	80,000	60,000
Correction of typos	200,000	165,000
Rework	131,000	76,000
Plate revisions	83,000	58,000
Press downtime	123,000	102,000
Waste	191,000	136,000

Required

1. Prepare a quality cost performance report for 2008 that compares actual 2008 quality costs with budgeted quality costs. Comment on the firm's ability to achieve its quality goals for the year.
2. Prepare a one-period quality performance report for 2008 that compares the actual costs of 2007 with the actual costs of 2008. How much did profits change because of improved quality?
3. Prepare a graph that shows the trend in total quality costs as a percentage of sales since the inception of the quality-improvement program.
4. Prepare a graph that shows the trend for all four quality cost categories for 2004 through 2008. How does this graph show management that the reduction in total quality costs is attributable to quality improvements?

15-32

Quality Performance and Ethical Behavior
LO1, LO4

Reece Manufacturing rewards its plant managers for their ability to meet budgeted quality cost reductions. The bonus is increased if the productivity goal is met or exceeded. The productivity goal is computed by multiplying the units produced by the prevailing market price and dividing this measure of output by the total cost of the inputs used. Additionally, if the plant as a whole meets the budgeted targets, the production supervisors and workers receive salary and wage increases. Matt Rasmussen, the manager of a plant in Nebraska, feels obligated to do everything he can to provide this increase to his employees. Accordingly, he has decided to take the following actions during the last quarter of the year to meet the plant's budgeted targets and increase the productivity ratio:

a. Decrease inspections of the process and final product by 50 percent and transfer inspectors temporarily to quality training programs. Matt believes this move will increase the inspectors' awareness of the importance of quality; also, decreasing inspection will produce significantly less downtime and less rework. By increasing the output and decreasing the costs of internal failure, the plant can meet the budgeted reductions for internal failure costs and, simultaneously, increase its productivity measure. Also, by showing an increase in the costs of quality training, the budgeted level for prevention costs can be met.
b. Delay replacing and repairing defective products until the beginning of the following year. While this may increase customer dissatisfaction somewhat, Matt believes that most customers expect some inconvenience. Besides, the policy of promptly dealing with dissatisfied customers could be reinstated in three months. In the meantime, the action would significantly reduce the costs of external failure, allowing the plant to meet its budgeted target.

Required

1. Evaluate Matt's ethical behavior, taking into account his concern for his employees. Is he justified in pursuing the actions described in the problem? If not, what should he do instead?
2. Assume that the company views Matt's behavior as undesirable. What can it do to discourage it?
3. Assume that Matt is a CMA and a member of the IMA (Institute of Management). Refer to the ethical code for management accountants in Chapter 1. Are any of these ethical standards violated?

Research Assignments

15-33

Library and Cyberspace Research
LO1, LO2, LO3

Listed below are some organizations that sponsor awards for firms that improve quality:

1. **National Quality Institute** (Canada)
2. **European Foundation for Quality Management**
3. **The W. Edwards Deming Institute** (Japan)

Required

Search the Internet and learn what aspects of quality these international quality organizations emphasize. Select a company from each source that has received an award two to three years prior to the current year. Write a three- to five-page memo that compares and contrasts the experiences of the companies, where—if possible—one of the three is a service company. Include in your discussion the ways in which the companies defined quality. Also, describe how quality was measured, if at all. Were benefits of improving quality mentioned? What were they? Was there any mention of quality costs? Finally, conduct a library and/or Internet search to see if there is anything written that describes how each company is doing now. As part of this analysis, determine if the quality achievements have been maintained or not, and assess whether quality continues to be emphasized.

15-34

Cybercase
LO1

Using the Internet, answer the following questions:

1. What is the Malcolm Baldrige National Quality Award?
2. Identify three companies that have received the award during the most recent award year. Describe each company and the actions they took that apparently led to their selection.
3. Go to the website of *Quality Magazine,* which can be accessed from the chapter web links at the Interactive Study Center on http://www.thomsonedu.com/accounting/hansen and, using the resources of this site, summarize three cases of companies that have improved their quality performance during the most recent year.

chapter 16

Lean Accounting, Target Costing, and the Balanced Scorecard

learning objectives

After studying this chapter, you should be able to:

1. Describe the basic features of lean manufacturing.
2. Describe lean accounting.
3. Explain the basics of life-cycle cost management and target costing.
4. Discuss the basic features of the Balanced Scorecard and its role in lean manufacturing.

Scenario

Tara Barker, president of Allen Autoparts, Inc., had just completed a review of the company's strategic plan. The plan defined the company's current state and laid out some very important future activities. The current position of the company was good; Allen was the market leader in chassis and drivetrain auto parts. Allen produces four major product lines: shock absorbers, aluminum alloy and steel wheels, brake systems, and aluminum radiators. Tara was concerned about some of the future plans because her company was facing an increasingly competitive business environment. In particular, Tara was positioning the company to enter the Chinese market for auto parts. She had recently negotiated several joint venture agreements with Chinese companies to manufacture auto parts. However, other major players were also entering the Chinese markets and Roberts would be facing competitors like Denso (Japanese), Bosch (German), and Delphi (American). It had become more evident that her company must seek better ways of making strategic business decisions and collecting accurate, reliable information to facilitate this process. Moreover, Tara was convinced that greater efficiency was needed—that operating processes needed to be streamlined, waste needed to be eliminated, and quality and delivery performance needed to be improved. A new approach was necessary for gaining employee support for the strategic positions assumed by her company. When she expressed these concerns to Sterling Anderson, the managing partner of the local office of a national consulting firm, he suggested that she consider focusing on the implementation of lean manufacturing and target costing. He also indicated that the Balanced Scorecard provided a means for translating a firm's strategy into operational objectives and measures. Wanting to know more, Tara invited Sterling to a business lunch.

During lunch, Tara learned that lean manufacturing is concerned with eliminating waste in manufacturing processes. Promised benefits included such outcomes as reduced lead times, improved quality, improved on-time deliveries, less inventory, less space, less human effort, lower costs, and increased profitability. She learned that traditional financial measurement and control approaches may not be compatible with lean manufacturing. Nonfinancial performance measures and target costing play key roles in the elimination and control of waste. The Balanced Scorecard was also an intriguing possibility.

According to Sterling, the Balanced Scorecard is an integrated performance management system that ties performance objectives and measures to a company's strategy. A significant advantage of the Balanced Scorecard is that it links performance measures to a company's strategy, and these relationships are communicated to employees. This helps them understand how their actions affect the overall strategy of the organization.

At the conclusion of the lunch, Sterling made a strong cautionary statement regarding traditional financial control: "Tara, one of the most difficult organizational problems in an organization today is the disconnection between local performance measures and organizational strategy. Most managers receive a monthly responsibility statement that shows their expenses line by line, comparing actual costs to budgeted costs. But virtually all managers complain that these reports provide very little insight for them when it comes to increasing efficiency or even knowing exactly what is wanted from higher management. This approach encourages reactive decision making and is essentially backward-looking management."

Questions to Think About

1. How does lean manufacturing change cost accounting and management?
2. What are the similarities between JIT and lean manufacturing?
3. How are products assigned costs in a lean manufacturing environment?
4. Why are processes so important to performance management?
5. Are lean manufacturing and the Balanced Scorecard compatible approaches?

Lean Manufacturing

Objective 1

Describe the basic features of lean manufacturing.

Tara Barker, president of Allen Autoparts, was deeply concerned about being competitive in a new environment. As the company prepared to enter China, it was evident that additional effort was needed to exercise better control, reduce costs, and become more efficient. The type of environment in which a firm operates can have a significant effect on the type of control and communication system chosen and implemented. Consider, for example, a firm that produces concrete pipes and blocks. The products and production processes are well defined and relatively stable. Functional skills are specialized to gain operating efficiencies. Interactions with suppliers and customers are mostly limited to arm's-length transactions. Competition tends to be local or regional as opposed to national or international. A successful firm operating in this type of environment would tend to emphasize maintaining the status quo: preservation of market share, stable growth, and continuation of efficient production.

On the other hand, a firm like Allen Autoparts, involved in producing chassis and drivetrain auto parts, operates in an environment where change is rapid. Products and processes are constantly being redesigned and improved, and stiff national and international competitors are always present. The competitive environment demands that firms offer customized products and services to diverse customer segments. This, in turn, means that firms must find cost-efficient ways of producing high-variety, low-volume product and paying more attention to linkages between the firm and its suppliers and customers. Furthermore, for many industries, product life cycles are shrinking, placing greater demands on the need for innovation. Thus, organizations operating in a dynamic, rapidly changing environment are finding that adaptation and change are essential to survival. To find ways to improve performance, firms operating in this kind of environment are forced to reevaluate how they do things. Improving performance translates into constantly searching for ways to eliminate waste and to undertake only those actions that bring value to the customer. This philosophical approach to manufacturing is often referred to as *lean manufacturing*. **Lean manufacturing** is thus an approach designed to eliminate waste and maximize customer value. It is characterized by delivering the right product, in the right quantity, with the right quality (zero-defect), at the exact time the customer needs it and at the lowest possible cost.

Lean manufacturing systems allow managers to eliminate waste, reduce costs, and become more efficient. Firms that implement lean manufacturing are pursuing a cost reduction strategy by redefining the activities performed within an organization. Cost reduction is directly related to cost leadership. Lean manufacturing adds value by reducing waste. Successful implementation of lean manufacturing has brought about significant improvements, such as better quality, increased productivity, reduced lead times, major reductions in inventories, reduced setup times, lower manufacturing costs, and increased production rates. For example, **Celestica de Monterrey, S.A. C.V.**, a company that specializes in electronics manufacturing services, implemented lean manufacturing in its Monterrey, Mexico, facility. The implementation resulted in space utilization improvements of 34 percent, reduction in setup times of 85 percent, reduction of scrap by 66 percent, and reduction of customer lead times by 71 percent.[1]

Lean manufacturing systems have also been implemented by the following companies with similar results:[2]

1 As reported at http://www.shingoprize.org/Recipients/Articles/03_05_ShingoPrizePressRelease.htm, accessed May 22, 2006.

2 Many of these companies are winners of the Shingo Prize, which recognizes successful lean manufacturing outcomes. See http://www.shingoprize.org for a list of winners for various years. The list is but a small percentage of companies that are implementing lean manufacturing systems.

Takata Seatbelts, Inc.	**Autoliv**	**Maytag**
Lockheed Martin	**Dell Computer**	**Raytheon Missile Systems**
The Boeing Company	**Littelfuse, Inc.**	**TI Group Automotive Systems**
Boston Scientific	**Steelcase, Inc.**	

In substance, lean manufacturing is the same as the *Toyota Production System* developed by Shigeo Shingo and Taaichi Ohno. *World-class manufacturing* and *just-in-time (JIT) manufacturing and purchasing* are terms that encompass many of the same methods. Lean manufacturing is similar in concept also to Ford's lean enterprise system. However, the contributions of Shingo and Ohno overcame some of the major shortcomings and flaws of the Ford system. Specifically, the Ford system did not properly value employees and also was not structured to deal with product variety. High-variety, low-volume products were not compatible with the Ford production system. Employee empowerment, team structures, cellular manufacturing, reduced setup times, and small batches all came into being in the Toyota Production System and are integral parts of a lean manufacturing system.

What is it that allows companies to achieve the results like those described for Celestica de Monterrey? Becoming lean requires lean thinking. Lean manufacturing is distinguished by the following five principles of lean thinking:[3]

- Precisely specify value by each particular product.
- Identify the "value stream" for each.
- Make value flow without interruption.
- Let the customer pull value from the producer.
- Pursue perfection.

Value by Product

Value is determined by the customer—at the very least, it is an item or feature for which the customer is willing to pay. Customer value is the difference between realization and sacrifice. Realization is what a customer receives. Sacrifice is what customers give up, including what they are willing to pay for the basic and special product features, quality, brand name, and reputation. Value thus relates to a specific product and to specific features of the product. Adding features and functions that are not wanted by the customers is a waste of time and resources. Furthermore, attempting to market features and products that customers don't want is a waste of time and resources. Assessing value is externally oriented and not internally generated. Only value-added features should be produced; non-value-added activities should be eliminated.

Value Stream

The **value stream** is made up of all activities, both value-added and non-value-added, required to bring a product group or service from its starting point (e.g., customer order or concept for a new product) to a finished product in the hands of the customer. There are several types of value streams, the most common being the *order fulfillment value stream*. The order fulfillment value stream focuses on providing current products to current customers.[4] A second type of value stream is the *new product value* stream, which focuses on developing new products for new customers. A value stream reflects all that is done—both good and bad—to bring the product to a customer. Thus, analyzing the value stream allows management to identify waste. Activities within the value stream are value-added or non-value-added. Non-value-added

3. James Womack and Daniel Jones, *Lean Thinking* (Free Press, 2003).
4 For a more complete description of the different types of value streams, see Brian Maskell and Bruce Baggaley, *Practical Lean Accounting* (New York: Productivity Press, 2004), and Francis A. Kennedy and Jim Hutzinger, "Lean Accounting: Measuring and Managing the Value Stream," *Cost Management* (Sep/Oct 2005): pp. 31–38. These two sources also recommend the matrix approach for identifying value streams illustrated in Exhibit 16-2.

activities are the source of waste. They are of two types: (1) activities avoidable in the short run and (2) activities unavoidable in the short run due to current technology or production methods. The first type is most quickly eliminated while the second type requires more time and effort. Exhibit 16-1 visually portrays an order fulfillment value stream for one of Allen Autoparts' family of aluminum wheels. This particular value stream only has one manufacturing cell; other value streams may have several cells.

A value stream may be created for every product; however, it is more common to group products that use common processes into the same value stream. Allen Autoparts, for example, must establish at least five value streams: one for each product line and one for new product development. One way to identify the value streams is to use a simple two-dimensional matrix, where the activities/processes are listed on one dimension and the products on a second dimension. Exhibit 16-2 provides a simple matrix for the four wheel models: two aluminum models and two steel models. In this case, two value streams are indicated, where each is made up of two product models (notice that products C & D have two different processes required when compared to A & B).

Once value streams are identified, then the next step is to assign people and resources to the value streams. As a rule of thumb, each value stream should have between 25 and 150 people.[5] As much as possible, the people, the machines, the manufacturing processes, and the support activities need to be dedicated to the value streams. This allows a sense of ownership and provides a means of direct accountability. It also simplifies and facilitates product costing. In a sense, the value stream is its own independent company, and the value stream team is responsible for its improvement, growth, and profitability.

Value Flow

In a traditional manufacturing setup, production is organized by function into departments and products are produced in large batches, moving from department to department. This approach requires significant move time and wait time as each batch *moves* from one department to another and *waits* for its turn if there is a batch-in-process in front of it. Often lengthy changeovers are needed to prepare the equipment to produce the next batch of goods that may have some very different

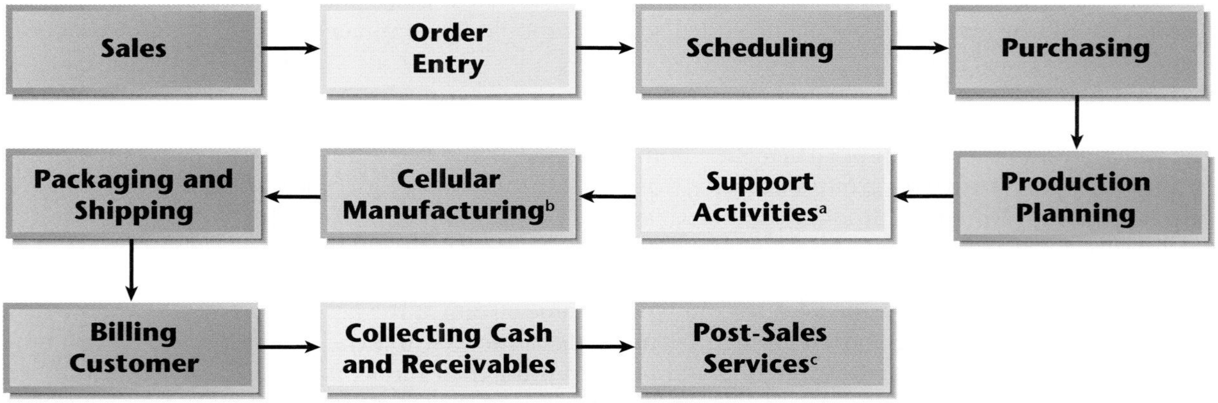

[a]Moving materials, quality management, engineering, setting up equipment, maintenance, etc.
[b]Cutting, drilling and insertion, assembly, and finishing.
[c]Customer complaints, field repairs, warranty services, etc.

Exhibit 16-1 Order-Fulfillment Value Stream—Allen AutoParts

5 Ibid.

	Production Activities: Order Fulfillment Value Stream							
Brake Model	Order Entry	Production Planning	Purchasing	Aluminum Cell[a]	Steel Cell[b]	Stress Testing[c]	Packaging & Shipping	Invoicing
A	X	X	X	X			X	X
B	X	X	X	X			X	X
C	X	X	X	X	X	X	X	X
D	X	X	X	X	X	X	X	X

[a]Casting, machining, painting, and finishing
[b]Stamping, welding, and cladding (attaching stainless steel or painted plastic components to approximate the look of chromed aluminum)
[c]To ensure that the steel wheels have the same fatigue strength as aluminum, they go through a stress test.
Models A and B would be placed in one value stream.
Models C and D would define a second value stream.

Exhibit 16-2 Matrix Approach to Identifying Value Streams

characteristics. Traditional batch production is not equipped to deal with product variety; furthermore, move and wait time are sources of waste. Batches must wait for a preceding batch and a subsequent setup *before* beginning a process. Once a batch starts a process, units are processed sequentially; as units are finished they must wait for other units in the batch to be finished before the entire batch moves to the next process. For example, if a department can process one unit every five minutes, then the first unit of a batch of 10 will be completed after five minutes but must then wait an additional 45 minutes for the remaining units to be completed before moving to the next process. Thus, there is pre-process waiting and post-process waiting. Lean manufacturing reduces wait and move time dramatically and allows the production of small batches (low volume) of differing products (high variety). The key factors in achieving these outcomes are lower setup times and cellular manufacturing.

Reduced Setup/Changeover Times With large batches, setups are infrequent and the fixed cost of a setup is spread out over many units. Typical results produce complexity in scheduling and large work in process and finished goods inventories. Reducing the time to configure equipment to produce a different type of product enables *smaller batches in greater variety* to be produced. It also decreases the time it takes to produce a unit of output, thus increasing the ability to respond to customer demand. Customers do not value changeover and therefore it represents waste. While reducing setup times is important, even more critical is the use of cellular or continuous flow manufacturing.

Cellular Manufacturing Lean manufacturing uses a series of cells to produce families of similar products. A lean manufacturing system replaces the traditional plant layout with a pattern of manufacturing cells. Cell structure is chosen over departmental structure because it reduces lead time, decreases product cost, improves quality, and increases on-time delivery. **Manufacturing cells** contain all the operations in close proximity that are needed to produce a family of products. The machines used are typically grouped in a semicircle. The reason for locating processes close to one another is to minimize move time and to keep a continuous flow between operations while maintaining zero inventory between any two operations. The cell is usually dedicated to producing products that require similar operations.

Panel A of Exhibit 16-3 shows the departmental, large-batch-orientation for one of Allen Autoparts' aluminum wheel products (Model A). The move time, wait time, and unit processing time are included. An interesting question is: How long does it take to produce a batch of 10 units in the traditional batch-production setting? Panel A addresses this question: The traditional system takes 190 minutes to produce a batch

The Assembly Department pictured here accumulates costs but does not sell final product. As a result, the department is a cost center within the factory.

of 10 units. This question is then followed by a second: How long will it take to produce the same batch of 10 units with cellular manufacturing? Panel B of Exhibit 16-3 answers this second question: For a batch of 10 units, cellular manufacturing takes only 60 minutes. Notice in the manufacturing cell that the machines are arranged so that a component or product can be produced using a sequential set of operations from start to finish. Some of the efficiencies cited earlier for Celestica de Monterrey such as reduced lead times and less space are a direct result of the cellular structure. Space savings like the 37 percent reduction that Celestica experienced can reduce the demand to build new plants and can affect the size of new plants when they are needed.

Analysis of Panel B of Exhibit 16-3 reveals some interesting outcomes. First, note that the cell can produce 12 units per hour and that the production rate is controlled by the slowest activity in the cell (referred to as the *bottleneck operation*). In this example, the slowest operation is machining and the cell's production rate is 60/5 = 12 units per hour (assuming that the cell operates at least two hours). Second, reducing the time of the non-bottleneck operations will decrease the total time required to produce the batch of 10, but it will not decrease the production rate of the cell. For example, if the time for the non-bottleneck operations is zero, then the time required to produce a batch of 10 is 50 minutes. The same

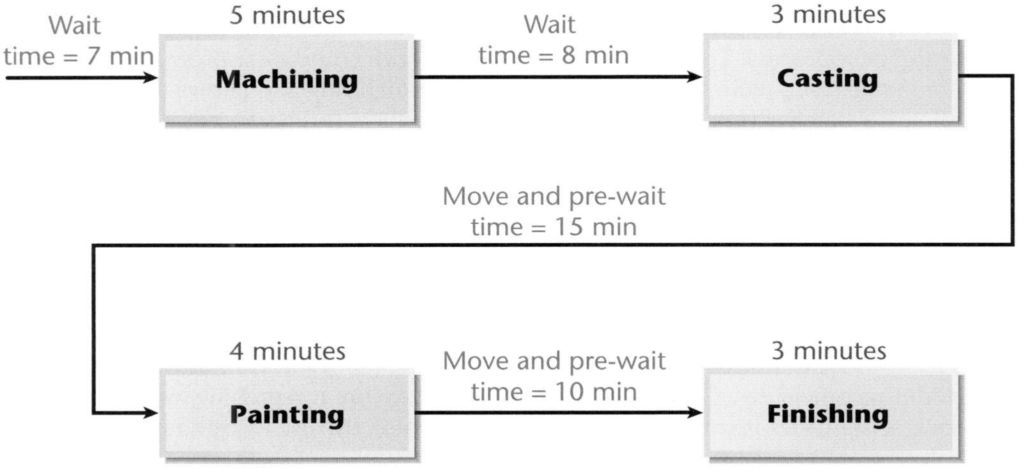

Color Code:

Blue = Value-added process time
Red = Non-value-added move and pre-process wait time

	Process Time
Machining	50 minutes
Casting	30 minutes
Painting	40 minutes
Finishing	30 minutes
Total Processing	150 minutes
Move and Wait Time	40 minutes
Total Batch Time	190 minutes

Exhibit 16-3 Panel A Current Departmental Layout—Model A Aluminum Wheel Production

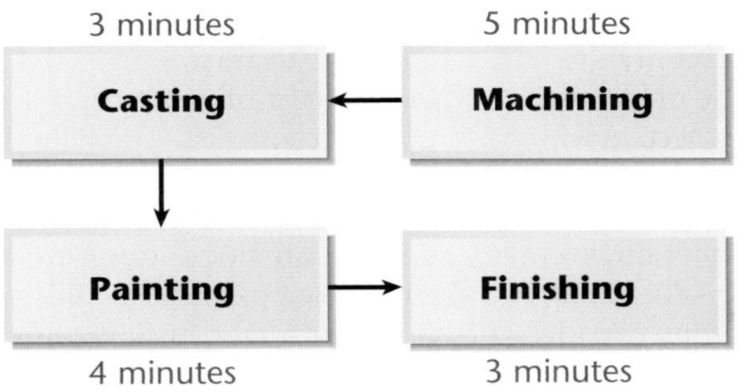

Processing Time (ten units)	Elapsed Time
First Unit	15 minutes
Second Unit	20 minutes (processing begins five minutes after the first)
—	—
—	—
Tenth Unit	60 minutes (total processing time)

Time saved over traditional manufacturing:
150 minutes − 60 minutes = 90 minutes

Note: If the cell is processing continuously, then a unit is produced every five minutes after the start-up unit (compare the elapsed times for the second and third units), and the time to produce 10 units is 50 minutes, and the time saved is 100 minutes.

Exhibit 16-3 Panel B Proposed Manufacturing Cell for Allen Autoparts (Model A)

reduction to 50 minutes can be achieved by shaving one minute off the cutting operation with the processing times of the other processes remaining the same.

Pull Value

Many firms produce for inventory and then try to sell the excess goods they have produced. Efforts are made to create demand for the excess goods—goods that customers probably do not even want. Lean manufacturing uses a *demand-pull* system. The objective of lean manufacturing is to eliminate waste by producing a product only when it is needed and only in the quantities demanded by customers. Demand pulls products through the manufacturing process. Each operation produces only what is necessary to satisfy the demand of the succeeding operation. No production takes place until a signal from a succeeding process indicates a need to produce. Parts and materials arrive just in time to be used in production. Low setup times and cellular manufacturing are the major enabling factors for producing on demand. The Kanban system described in Chapter 14 is one way to ensure that materials and products flow according to demand.

Customer demand extends back through the value chain and affects how a manufacturer deals with suppliers. Materials inventories also represent waste. Thus, managing supplier linkages is also vital to lean manufacturing. **JIT purchasing** requires suppliers to deliver parts and materials just in time to be used in production. Supply of parts must be linked to production, which is linked to demand. One effect of successful management of customer and supplier linkages is to reduce all inventories to much lower levels. Since 1980, inventories in the United States have fallen from 26 to 15 percent of the gross domestic product; furthermore, JIT purchasing is saving U.S. automakers more than $1 billion annually in inventory carrying costs.[6]

6 Art Raymond, "Is JIT Dead?" *FDM* (Jan. 2002): pp. 30–32.

Traditionally, inventories of raw materials and parts are carried so that a firm can take advantage of quantity discounts and hedge against future price increases of the items purchased. The objective is to lower the cost of inventory. JIT purchasing achieves the same objective without carrying inventories. The JIT solution is to exploit supplier linkages by negotiating long-term contracts with a few chosen suppliers located as close to the production facility as possible and by establishing more extensive supplier involvement. Suppliers are not selected on the basis of price alone. Performance—the quality of the component and the ability to deliver as needed—and commitment to JIT purchasing are vital considerations. Every effort is made to establish a partners-in-profits relationship with suppliers. Suppliers need to be convinced that their well-being is intimately tied to the well-being of the buyer.

To help reduce the uncertainty in demand for the supplier and establish the mutual confidence and trust needed in such a relationship, lean manufacturers emphasize long-term contracts that stipulate prices and acceptable quality levels. Long-term contracts also reduce dramatically the number of orders placed, which helps to drive down the ordering and receiving costs. Another effect of long-term contracting is a reduction in the cost of parts and materials—usually in the range of 5 percent to 20 percent less than what was paid in a traditional setting. The need to develop close supplier relationships often drives the supplier base down dramatically. For example, **Mercedes-Benz U.S. International**'s factory in Vance, Alabama, saved time and money by streamlining its supplier list from 1,000 to 100 primary suppliers. In exchange for annual 5 percent price cuts, the chosen suppliers have multiyear contracts (as opposed to the yearly bidding process practiced at other Mercedes plants) and can adapt off-the-shelf parts to the automaker's needs. The end result is lower costs for both Mercedes and its suppliers.[7] Suppliers also benefit, as the long-term contract ensures a reasonably stable demand for their products. A smaller supplier base typically means increased sales for the selected suppliers. Thus, both buyers and suppliers benefit, a common outcome when customer and supplier linkages are recognized and managed well. By reducing the number of suppliers and working closely with those that remain, the quality of the incoming

Managers Decide

Focus on Key Suppliers and Save

A Hackett Group study reveals that companies can save up to 5 percent of their procurement spending by reducing the number of suppliers and focusing on spending with certain key suppliers. World-class procurement organizations typically spend 27 percent less on the procurement function and operate with 38 percent fewer staff. According to the study, world-class companies have less than half the typical number of suppliers (3,408 suppliers per billion dollars of spending versus 7,805 suppliers per billion dollars of spending for the typical firm). The implications are more than simply saving procurement costs. Reducing the number of suppliers also allows a company to build stronger and more strategic relationships with its suppliers. This then translates into a gain in purchasing leverage and simultaneously lowers the cost of ongoing supplier monitoring and management. ■

Source: Staff of LogisticsToday, "Companies Can Save up to Five Percent of Their Annual Purchasing Spend by Focusing on Key Suppliers," *LogisticsToday* (Aug. 2, 2005); http://www.logisticstoday.com/diplayStory.asp?S=1&sNO=7338&MLC=GlobalSearch&OASKEY=BreakingNews, accessed May 22, 2006.

7 David Woodruff and Karen Lowry Miller, "Mercedes' Maverick in Alabama," *Business Week* (September 11, 1995): pp. 64–65.

materials can be improved significantly—a crucial outcome for the success of lean manufacturing. As the quality of incoming materials increases, some quality-related costs can be avoided or reduced. For example, the need to inspect incoming materials disappears, and rework requirements decline.

Pursue Perfection

Zero setup times, zero defects, zero inventories, zero waste, producing on demand, increasing a cell's production rates, minimizing cost, and maximizing customer value represent ideal outcomes that a lean manufacturer seeks. As the process of becoming lean begins to unfold and improvements are realized, the possibility of achieving perfection becomes more believable. The relentless and continuous pursuit of these ideals is fundamental to lean manufacturing. As the flow increases and processes begin to improve, more hidden waste tends to be exposed. The objective is to produce the highest-quality, lowest-cost products in the least amount of time. To achieve this objective, a lean manufacturer must identify and eliminate the various forms of waste.

Forms and Sources of Waste **Waste** consumes resources without adding value. Waste is anything customers do not value. Elimination of waste requires that its various forms and sources be identified. The following eight sources have been suggested as the major forms and sources of waste:

- Defective products
- Overproduction of goods not needed
- Inventories of goods awaiting further processing or consumption
- Unnecessary processing
- Unnecessary movement of people
- Unnecessary transport of goods
- Waiting
- The design of goods and services that do not meet the needs of the customer

Employee Empowerment Employee involvement is vital for identifying and eliminating all forms of waste. A major procedural difference between traditional and lean environments is the degree of participation allowed workers in the management of the organization. In a lean environment, increasing the degree of participation increases productivity and overall cost efficiency. Managers seek workers' input and use their suggestions to improve production processes. The management structure must change in response to greater employee involvement. Because workers assume greater responsibilities, fewer managers are needed, and the organizational structure becomes flatter. Flatter structures speed up and increase the quality of information exchange. The style of management needed in a lean firm also changes. Managers in a lean environment act as facilitators more than as supervisors. Their role is to develop people and their skills so that they can make value-adding contributions.

Total Quality Control Lean manufacturing necessarily carries with it a much stronger emphasis on managing quality. A defective part brings production to a grinding halt. Poor quality simply cannot be tolerated in a manufacturing environment that operates without inventories. Simply put, lean manufacturing cannot be implemented without a commitment to total quality control (TQC). TQC is essentially a never-ending quest for perfect quality: the striving for a defect-free product design and manufacturing process. Quality cost management is discussed extensively in Chapter 15.

Managers Decide

Value-Stream Mapping

Craig Cunningham, director of operations at Ontario-based Zomax Canada Co., observes that lean manufacturing is all about identifying fat in a process and cutting it out. As an example, he notes that a setup for an electronics board may require three hours, but customers do not want to pay for the time that the equipment is down—they only want to pay for what's on the board. Thus, reducing lengthy changeover times is a key part of improving flow, reducing inventories, and reducing batch size.

According to Cunningham, value-stream mapping is a good way to show what is value-added and what is not and how much time it takes to perform various activities. Value-stream mapping is simply a method of drawing out the entire manufacturing process, revealing the flow of a product and how much time it needs to move through the various steps of the value stream. Cunningham also notes that value-stream mapping can be applied to nonmanufacturing areas such as product design. This observation is supported by the experience of Rorry Harding, director of engineering at MDS Nordion in Ottawa. Using value-stream mapping, Harding was able to see the steps, times, and people involved in a design change. Using this information, the company changed the product design value stream so that the time to process a design change went from an average of 28 days to 10. ■

Source: Scott Foster, "'Value-Stream Mapping' Cuts Through Fat," *Ottawa Business Journal,* available at http://www.leanadvisors.com/Lean/articles/value_stream_mapping_article.cfm, accessed May 29, 2006.

Inventories Overproduction of goods is controlled by letting customers pull goods through the system. Inventories are lowered by cellular manufacturing, low setup times, JIT purchasing, and a demand-pull system. Inventory management is of such importance that its treatment is covered in a separate chapter, Chapter 18.

Activity-Based Management Process value analysis is the methodology for identifying and eliminating non-value-added activities. Non-value-added activities are unnecessary activities, including waiting, and thus much of the waste in a lean system is attacked using process value analysis. Process value analysis searches for the root causes of the wasteful activities and then, over time, eliminates these activities. See Chapter 5 for a detailed discussion of process value analysis.

Lean Accounting

Objective 2

Describe lean accounting.

The numerous changes in structural and procedural activities that we have described for a lean firm also change traditional cost management practices. The traditional cost management system may not work well in the lean environment. In fact, the traditional costing and operational control approaches may actually work against lean manufacturing. Standard costing variances and departmental budgetary variances will likely encourage overproduction and work against the demand-pull system needed in lean manufacturing. For example, emphasis on labor efficiency by comparing actual hours used with hours allowed for production encourages production to keep labor occupied and productive. Similarly, emphasis on departmental efficiency (e.g., machine utilization rates) will cause non-bottleneck departments to overproduce and build work-in-process inventory. Furthermore, we already know from our study of activity-based costing that in a multiple-product plant, the use of a plant-wide overhead rate can produce distorted product costs relative to focused manufacturing assignments or activity-based assignments. Distorted product costs can signal failure for lean manufacturing even when significant improvements may be occurring. To avoid obstacles and false signals, changes in both product-costing and operational control approaches are needed when moving to a value-stream-based lean manufacturing system.[8]

Focused Value Streams and Traceability of Overhead Costs

Costing systems use three methods to assign costs to individual products: direct tracing, driver tracing, and allocation. Of the three methods, the most accurate is direct tracing; thus, it is preferred over the other two methods. Assume initially that a value stream is created for each product within a plant. In a lean environment, many overhead costs assigned to products using either driver tracing or allocation are now directly traceable to products. Equipment formerly located in other departments, for example, is now reassigned to value streams, and, under the single-product value-stream structure, is dedicated to the production of a single product. In this case, depreciation is now a directly traceable product cost. Multiskilled workers and decentralized services add to the effect. Workers are assigned to the value stream and are trained to set up the equipment in the cells within the stream, maintain them, and operate them. These support functions were previously done by a different set of laborers for all product lines. Additionally, people with specialized skills (e.g., industrial engineers and production schedulers) are assigned directly to value streams. The labor cost of these employees is now directly assigned to each value stream. Typically, implementing the value-stream structure does not require an increase in the number of people needed. Lean manufacturing eliminates wasteful activities, reducing the demand for people; for example, when production planning is reduced significantly because of an efficiently functioning demand-pull system, some of those working in production planning can be cross-trained to perform value-added activities

Resources dedicated to value streams make it easier to trace costs to products.

8 Much of the material on lean accounting is based on two sources: Frances A. Kennedy and Jim Huntzinger, "Lean Accounting: Measuring and Managing the Value Stream," *Cost Management* (Sep./Oct. 2005): pp. 31–38; and Brian Maskell and Bruce Baggaley, *Practical Lean Accounting* (New York: Productivity Press, 2004).

within the value stream such as purchasing and quality control. Exhibit 16-4, a visual summary of value-stream cost assignment, shows that facility costs are assigned to each value stream. These costs are assigned using a cost per square foot (total cost/total square feet). If a value stream uses less square feet, it receives less cost. Thus, the purpose of this assignment is to motivate value stream managers to find ways to occupy less space. As space is made available, it can be used for new product lines or to accommodate increased sales. For example, suppose that the facility costs are $200,000 per year for a plant occupying 20,000 square feet. The cost per square foot is $10. If a value stream occupies 5,000 square feet, it is assigned a cost of $50,000. Should the value stream figure out how to do the same tasks with 4,000 square feet, the cost would be reduced to $40,000. Any unabsorbed facility cost would be deducted from revenue as a separate item.

Product Costing Because of multitask assignments, cross-training, and redeployment of other support personnel, most support costs are exclusive to a focused value stream and are thus assigned to a product using direct tracing. One consequence of increasing directly traceable costs is to increase the accuracy of product costing. Directly traceable costs are exclusively associated with the product and can safely be said to belong to it. Product cost is calculated by taking the costs of the period and dividing by the output. For example, suppose that the costs of the value stream are $800,000 for the month of January and the output for January is 5,000 units. The unit cost is $160 per unit ($800,000/5,000). Focused value streams are the most accurate and simple possible.

Limitations and Problems Initially, it may not be possible to assign all the people needed exclusively to a value stream. There may be some individuals working in more than one value stream. The cost of these shared workers can be assigned to individual value streams in proportion to the time spent in each stream. It is also true that even in the most ideal of circumstances, there will be some individuals

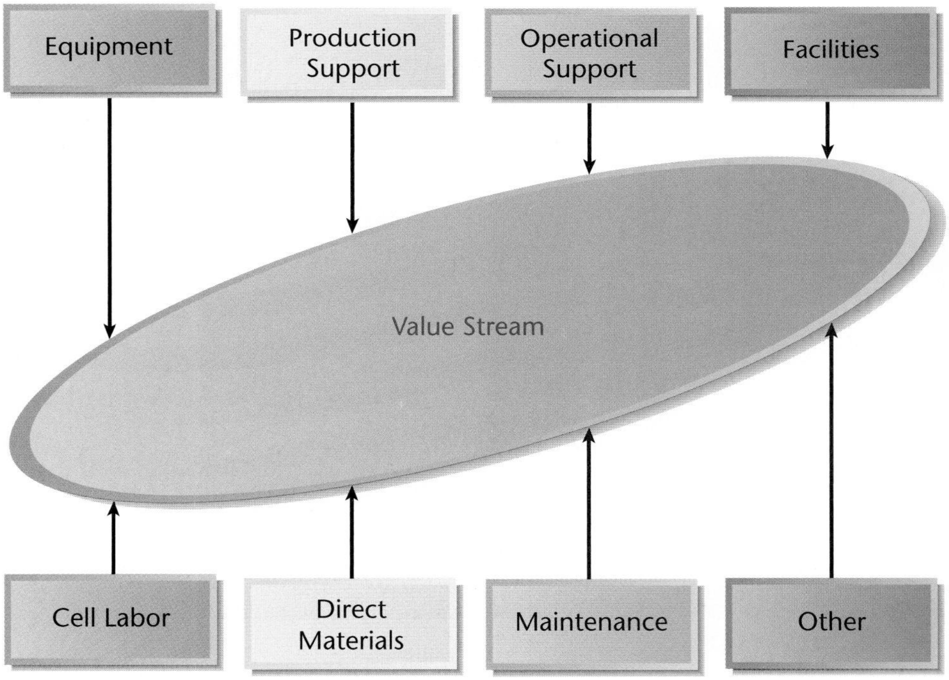

Exhibit 16-4 Value-Stream Costs

who will remain outside any particular value stream (the plant manager, for example). However, with multiple value streams, the unassigned costs are likely to be a very small percentage of the total costs. Finally, in reality, having a value stream for every product is not practical. The usual practice is to organize value streams around a family of products.

Value Stream Costing with Multiple Products

Value streams are formed around products with common processes (see Exhibit 16-2). Manufacturing cells within a value stream are thus structured to make a family of products or parts that require the same manufacturing sequence. The costs are assigned in the same way as for focused value streams. To illustrate, the actual costs for Allen Autoparts' ABS value stream are shown in Exhibit 16-5 for the week beginning April 6.

Product Costing With multiple products, product costs for value streams are calculated using an actual average cost:

Value stream product cost = Total value stream cost of period/Units shipped of period

Average costs are usually calculated weekly and are based on actual costs. For example, during the week of April 6, Allen Autoparts produced and shipped 1,000 units of Model C and 4,000 units of Model D, for a total of 5,000 units. Using the cost information from Exhibit 16-5, the average unit cost for the ABS value stream is \$120 (\$600,000/5,000). Using units shipped instead of units produced motivates managers to reduce inventories. If more units are shipped than produced, then the weekly average unit cost will decrease and inventories will reduce. If more is produced than shipped, then the unit cost will increase (because the production costs of the units produced and not shipped are added to the numerator), creating a disincentive to produce for inventory.

Some average unit cost calculations exclude materials (materials cost can be quite different between products). In this case, the average unit conversion cost is calculated. The average conversion cost for Models C and D is \$38 ([\$600,000 − \$410,000]/5,000)). The average product cost is useful provided the products are similar and consume resources in approximately the same proportions or if the product mix is relatively stable. If products are quite similar, the average product cost will approximate the individual product costs. If the mix is stable, then the trend in the average product

Allen Autoparts This Week, April 6					
	Materials	Salaries/wages	Machining	Other	Total Cost
Order Processing		\$ 12,000			\$ 12,000
Production Planning		24,000			24,000
Purchasing		18,000			18,000
Stamping	\$250,000	25,000	\$19,000	\$12,000	306,000
Welding	100,000	28,000	23,000	8,000	159,000
Cladding	60,000				60,000
Testing		7,000			7,000
Packaging and Shipping		6,000			6,000
Invoicing		8,000			8,000
Totals	\$ 410,000	\$128,000	\$42,000	\$20,000	\$600,000

Exhibit 16-5 Steel Wheel Value-Stream Costs: Models C and D

cost over time is a reasonable measure of changes in economic efficiency. If, however, the products are heterogeneous or reflect a great deal of variety through custom designing, then the average product cost is not a good measure for tracking changes in value stream efficiency; nor is there much indication of what the cost of individual products is. In this case, other product cost calculation approaches are needed—approaches that provide a much better level of accuracy.[9]

Value Stream Reporting

Costs are collected and reported by value stream. Consider a plant of Allen Autoparts that produces only four products. Within this plant are two value streams: (1) Aluminum Wheels (Models A and B) and (2) Steel Wheels (Models C and D). Exhibit 16-6 shows a profit and loss statement for the plant, for the week of April 6. (The plant had significantly increased its sales of steel wheels to auto manufacturers that were replacing low-end aluminum wheels with steel units on new models.) Costs outside the value stream (sustaining costs) are reported in a separate column. The revenues and costs reported are the actual revenues and costs for the week. To avoid distorting the current week's performance, inventory reductions are reported separately from the value-stream contributions. Adding the inventory changes also allows the income to be stated correctly for external reporting.

Decision Making

Using the average product cost for a value stream means that the individual product costs are not known. In reality, a fully specified and accurate product cost is not needed for many decisions. Waste can be eliminated at the activity and process lev-

Allen Autoparts				
	Aluminum Stream	Steel Stream	Sustaining Costs	Plant Totals
Revenues	$ 700,000	$1,500,000		$2,200,000
Material costs	(280,000)	(410,000)		(690,000)
Conversion costs	(70,000)	(190,000)		(260,000)
Value stream profit	$ 350,000	$ 900,000		$1,250,000
Value stream ROS[a]	50%	60%		
Employee costs			($40,000)	(40,000)
Other expenses			(30,000)	(30,000)
Change in inventory:				
Current less prior period				(500,000)
Plant gross profit				$ 680,000
Plant ROS				31%

[a]ROS = Return on Sales = Profit/Sales

Exhibit 16-6 Allen Autoparts—Weekly Profit & Loss Statement

9 An approach called features and characteristics costing is recommended (albeit reluctantly) by those advocating the simple average costing approach. This approach recognizes that some product components take more effort to make than others and thus cost more (differences in features and characteristics cause cost differences). An adjustment is made to the average product cost that reflects this complexity difference. The details of features and characteristics costing are covered in more advanced courses (the adjustments are not simple). One observation that deserves mention is that value streams with heterogeneous products find themselves in the same cost-distortion dilemma as plants with multiple products and plantwide overhead rates. ABC solves the distortion problem using causal tracing. ABC could, of course, be used within a value stream. The argument is that ABC is too complex and too data-intensive for a lean setting. Yet there is no compelling evidence that features and characteristics costing provides simplicity with accuracy. Further research is needed to create a simpler yet more accurate product cost for a lean accounting environment.

els without knowing product costs. We do not need detailed variances by product to signal sources of waste and potential for improvement. In fact, as already noted, standard costing variances may actually impede improvement decisions. For other decisions, the effect of the decision on the profitability of value stream may be the only information needed for certain decisions. For example, special order and make-or-buy decisions can be made at the value-stream level.

Consider a make-or-buy decision. Suppose that Allen Autoparts is currently purchasing a component used in making its wheel products and is considering making the component. The decision can be made by comparing the profitability of the value stream under the buy scenario with the profitability under the make scenario. A typical analysis would be as follows for Allen's ABS value stream:

	Buy	Make
Revenue	$1,500,000	$1,500,000
Material costs	(410,000)	(380,000)
Conversion costs	(190,000)	(200,000)
Value stream profit	$ 900,000	$ 920,000

The profitability of the value stream increases under the make alternative and so the decision would be to make the component rather than buy it.

While analysis of the effect on value-stream profitability has its merits, it also has its perils. Many of the decisions are short-term in nature and do not reflect the long-term consequences. For example, acceptance of a special order below the full cost of a product (unknown with average cost) may increase value-stream profitability because of existing unused value-stream capacity, but continued acceptance of such orders may not earn the return necessary to replace capacity that is eventually exhausted through use. Thus, other very important decisions may need individual product cost, and a lean accounting system must provide this information.[10]

Performance Measurement

Abandoning a standard cost system also removes a major operational control system, and it must be replaced. The lean control system uses a Box Scorecard that compares operational, capacity, and financial metrics with prior week performances and with a future desired state. Trends over time and the expectation of achieving some desired state in the near future are the means used to motivate constant performance improvement. Thus, the lean control approach uses a mixture of financial and nonfinancial measures for the value stream. The future desired state reflects targets for the various measures. Operational, nonfinancial measures are also used at the cell level. A typical value stream Box Scorecard is shown in Exhibit 16-7 (metrics and format can vary). Only a brief introduction to the Box Scorecard is made because the Balanced Scorecard is a more thorough and integrated approach that encompasses the concepts of a Box Scorecard.

For the operational measures, units sold per person is a partial labor productivity measure and is therefore a measure of labor *efficiency*. Dock-to-dock is the *time* it takes for a product to be manufactured from the moment the materials arrive at the receiving dock until the finished product is shipped from the shipping dock. Dock-to-dock is a cycle time measure, a concept that is more fully explored in the section on the Balanced Scorecard. First-time through is a measure of *quality* and is simply the percentage of product that made it through production without being defective and thus needing to be rejected or reworked. Capacity is labeled as *productive* (value-added), *nonproductive* (non-value-added—used but wasteful) and *available* (unused) capacity. The scorecard measures are expected to improve over time and to

10 Ibid.

be helpful in managing and bringing about improvement. For example, from the Box Scorecard in Exhibit 16-7, we see that the nonproductive capacity is targeted to go from 46 percent (current state) to 30 percent (future state), with productive capacity increasing from 20 percent to 25 percent and available capacity increasing from 34 percent to 45 percent. As waste is eliminated, the nonproductive capacity converts into available capacity. The machines, people, and other resources used for wasteful activities are now available for more productive work. For financial performance to improve, some decisions must be made with respect to the increase in available capacity. The most sensible and practical approach is to commit to use the freed-up resources to expand the business. One possibility is to add new product lines. Another possibility is to transfer the resources to other value streams that are in a high growth state with increasing resource demands. Another is to realize cost reductions by reducing headcount and eliminating resources. This latter approach is the least desirable. It makes it hard to gain the cooperation and involvement of employees with the transformation into a lean workforce if their suggestions and actions are going to lead to the loss of their jobs or the jobs of their friends and coworkers.

Life-Cycle Cost Management and the Role of Target Costing

Objective 3

Explain the basics of life-cycle cost management and target costing.

The product design stage can have a significant effect on costs to come. In fact, at least 90 percent of the costs associated with a product are committed during the development stage of the product's life cycle.[11] Thus, lean manufacturers should

	Last Week	This Week (4/6/08)	Planned Future State (6/30/08)
Operational			
Units per person	250	270	280
On-time delivery	90%	92%	97%
Dock-to-dock days	18.5	18	16
First time through	56%	58%	65%
Average product cost	$128	$120	$115
Accounts receivable days	31	30	28
Capacity			
Productive	21%	20%	25%
Nonproductive	45%	46%	30%
Available	34%	34%	45%
Financial			
Weekly sales	$1,800,000	$1,500,000	$2,000,000
Weekly material cost	$800,000	$600,000	$600,000
Weekly conversion	$400,000	$300,000	$400,000
Weekly value stream profit	$600,000	$600,000	$1,000,000
ROS	33%	40%	50%

Exhibit 16-7 Value-Stream Box Scorecard for 4/6/2008

11 John P. Campi, "Corporate Mindset: Strategic Advantage or Fatal Vision," *Journal of Cost Management* (Spring 1991): pp. 53–57; Callie Berliner and James A. Brimson (eds.), *Cost Management for Today's Advanced Manufacturing* (Boston: Harvard Business School Press, 1988). The section on life-cycle costing is based on these two sources with particular emphasis on the second source.

pay particular attention to new product development. **Product life cycle** is simply the time a product exists, from conception to abandonment. **Life-cycle costs** are all the costs associated with the product for its entire life cycle. They include development (planning, design, and testing), production (conversion activities), and logistics support (advertising, distribution, warranty, and so on). The product life cycle and the associated cost commitment curve are illustrated in Exhibit 16-8.[12]

Because total customer satisfaction has become a vital issue in the new business setting, *whole-life cost* has emerged as the central focus of life-cycle cost management. **Whole-life cost** is the life-cycle cost of a product plus its **postpurchase costs**, costs such as operation, support, maintenance, and disposal that are incurred *by the customer* after buying the product.[13] Since postpurchase costs are often an important consideration in the consumer's purchase decision, reducing these costs can provide an important competitive advantage. Notice that cost reduction, not cost control, is the emphasis. Moreover, judicious analysis and management of activities achieve cost reduction. Whole-life costing emphasizes management of the entire value chain. The **value chain** is the set of activities required to design, develop, produce, market, and service a product (or service). For a lean manufacturer, the value chain is made up of the innovation (new product) value stream and the order fulfillment value stream. Thus, **life-cycle cost management** focuses on managing value-chain activities so that a long-term competitive advantage is created. To achieve this goal, managers

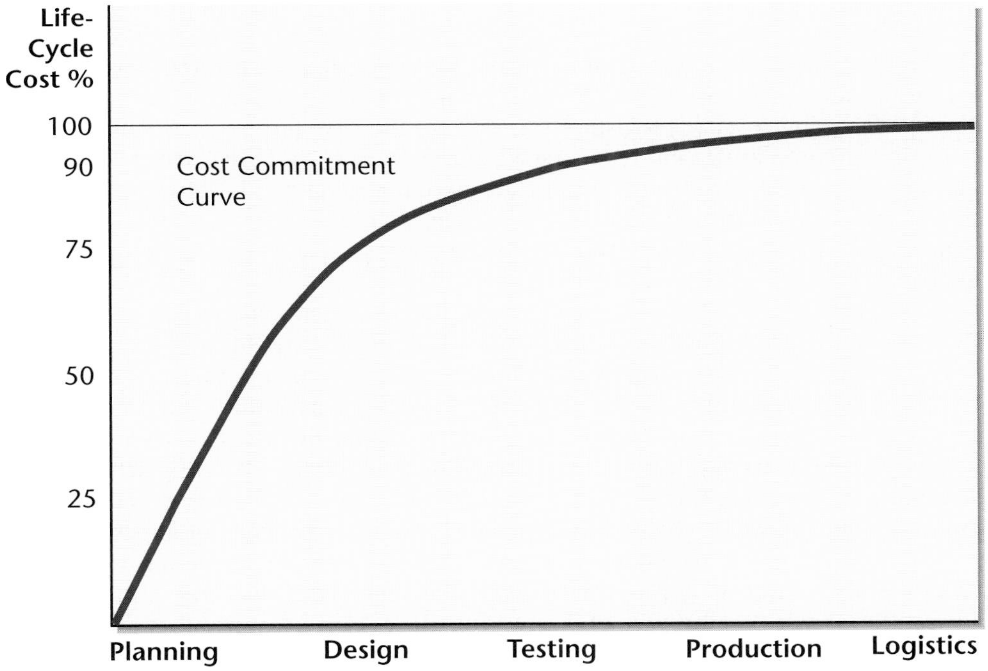

By the end of the development stage, at least 90 percent of the life-cycle costs are committed (but not incurred).

Exhibit 16-8 Life-Cycle Cost Commitment Curve

12 Life cycle can be viewed from a production or marketing perspective. We have adopted a production perspective with stages of life cycle defined by changes in the types of activities performed: development, production, and logistical. The marketing perspective, on the other hand, focuses on sales demand and has the following four stages: start-up, growth, maturity, and decline.

13 It can be argued that the whole-life cost is an alternative definition of life-cycle cost—one that includes the customer's perspective as well as the production viewpoint. For an excellent treatment of this topic, see Michael D. Shields and S. Mark Young, "Managing Product Life-Cycle Costs: An Organizational Model," *Journal of Cost Management* (Fall 1991): pp. 39–52.

must balance a product's whole-life cost, method of delivery, innovativeness, and various product attributes including performance, features offered, reliability, conformance, durability, aesthetics, and perceived quality.

Cost Reduction Since 90 percent or more of a product's costs are committed during the development stage, it makes sense to emphasize management of activities during this phase of a product's existence. Studies have shown that every dollar spent on premanufacturing activities saves \$8 to \$10 on manufacturing and postmanufacturing activities.[14] The real opportunities for cost reduction occur before manufacturing begins! Managers need to invest more in premanufacturing assets and dedicate more resources to activities in the early phases of the product life cycle so that overall whole-life costs can be reduced.

Yet, despite this observation, the traditional emphasis has been on controlling costs during the production stage (when much less can be done to influence them). Furthermore, product cost has been narrowly defined as production costs; development and logistics costs have been treated as period costs and have been virtually ignored when computing product profitability. While this practice may be acceptable for external reporting, it is not acceptable for cost management in a lean environment. In the highly competitive environment of today, lean manufacturers and world-class competitors need comprehensive product cost information. For example, little attention has been given to the effect of the customer's postpurchase costs. Reducing these costs decreases the sacrifices made by customers and thus increases customer value.

Whole-Life Product Cost From a whole-life point of view, product cost is made up of four major elements: (1) nonrecurring costs (planning, designing, and testing), (2) manufacturing costs, (3) logistic costs, and (4) the customer's postpurchase costs. Measuring, accumulating, and reporting all of a product's whole-life costs allow managers to better assess the effectiveness of life-cycle planning and build more effective and sophisticated marketing strategies. Life-cycle costing also increases their ability to make good pricing decisions and improve the assessment of product profitability.

Role of Target Costing Life-cycle cost management emphasizes cost reduction, not cost control. Thus, target costing becomes a particularly useful tool for establishing cost reduction goals. A **target cost** is the difference between the sales price needed to capture a predetermined market share and the desired per-unit profit. The sales price reflects the product specifications or functions *valued* by the customer (referred to as *product functionality*). If the target cost is less than what is currently achievable, then management must find cost reductions that move the actual cost toward the target cost. Finding those cost reductions is the principal challenge of target costing.

Three cost reduction methods are typically used: (1) reverse engineering, (2) value analysis, and (3) process improvement. Reverse engineering tears down the competitors' products with the objective of discovering more design features that create cost reductions. Value analysis attempts to assess the value placed on various product functions by customers. If the price customers are willing to pay for a particular function is less than its cost, the function is a candidate for elimination. Another possibility is to find ways to reduce the cost of providing the function, e.g., using common components. Both reverse engineering and value analysis focus on product design to achieve cost reductions and provide value to customers. The processes used to produce and market the product are also sources of potential cost reductions. Thus, redesigning processes to improve their efficiency can also contribute to achiev-

14 Michael D. Shields and S. Mark Young, "Managing Product Life-Cycle Costs: An Organizational Model," and R. I. Engwall, "Cost Management for Defense Contractors," *Cost Accounting for the 90s: Responding to Technological Change* (Montvale, N.J.: National Association of Accountants, 1988).

ing the needed cost reductions. The target-costing model is summarized in Exhibit 16-9.

A simple example can be used to illustrate the concepts described by Exhibit 16-9. Assume that a company is considering the production of a new trencher. Current product specifications and the targeted market share call for a sales price of $250,000. The required profit is $50,000 per unit. The target cost is computed as follows:

$$\text{Target cost} = \$250{,}000 - \$50{,}000$$
$$= \$200{,}000$$

It is estimated that the current product and process designs will produce a cost of $225,000 per unit. The cost reduction needed to achieve the target cost and desired profit is then $25,000 ($225,000 − $200,000). Reverse engineering of a competitor's trencher revealed a design improvement that promised to save $5,000 per unit. A marketing study of customer reactions to product functions revealed that the extra trenching speed in the new design was relatively unimportant; changing the design to reduce the trenching speed saved $10,000. The company's supplier proposed the use of a standardized component, reducing costs by another $5,000. Finally, the design team was able to change the process design and reduce the test time by 50 percent. This saved $6,000 per unit. The last change reached the threshold value, and production for the new model was approved.

Target costs are a type of currently attainable standard, but they are conceptually different from the modified standards discussed earlier. What makes them different is the motivating force. The initial modified definition of currently attainable

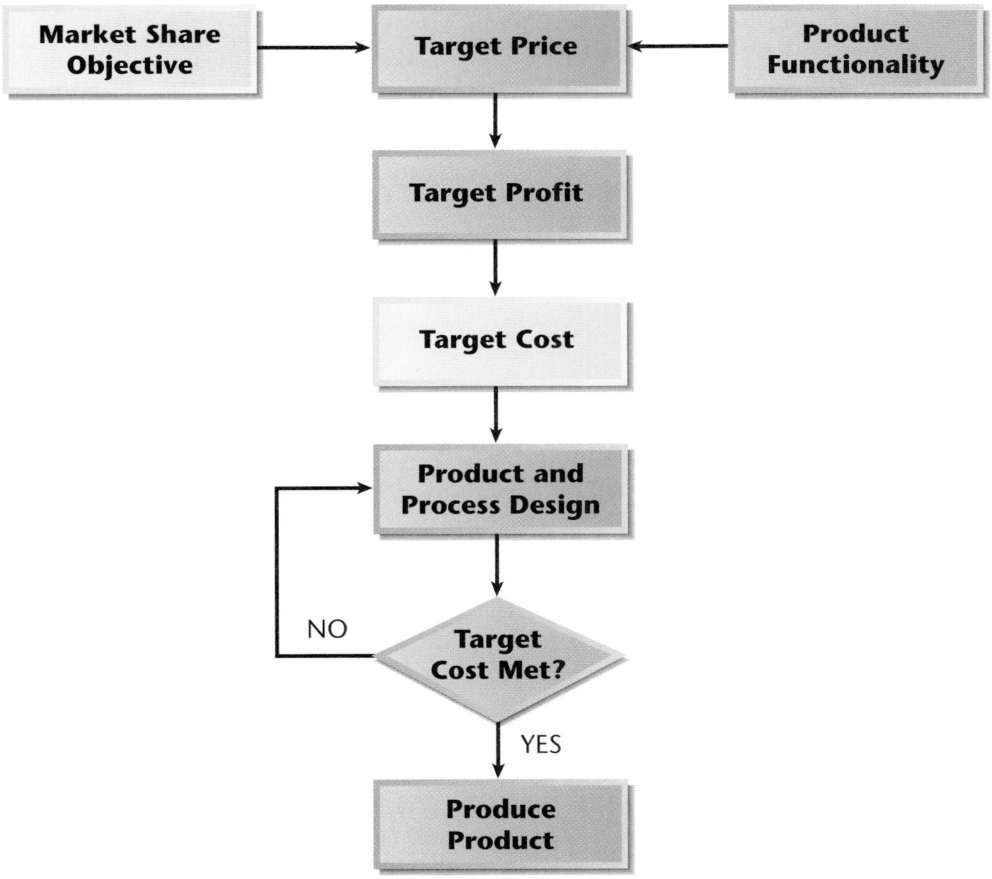

Exhibit 16-9 Target-Costing Model

Managers Decide

Target Costing Increases Value

Major-Cable, a producer of cable products, offered a low price on its specialized shielded cables to a new customer. This was Major-Cable's first sale to this machine manufacturer, which was a very large user of such cables. The offering was designed to capture this business plus similar customers. However, Major-Cable was now faced with the need to make this arrangement profitable. The customer requested the cable in 20-meter segments, but Major-Cable was accustomed to producing cable in much longer lengths. Investigation revealed that the customer wanted the 20-meter lengths so it could cut them to the specifications required by the specific machine being manufactured. As it happened, Major-Cable often produced "off-cuts"—cable too short to send to its distribution center. These shorter lengths of cable were stored in finished goods inventory in case some customer wanted a shorter length; most of the time no demand surfaced and the off-cuts were typically scrapped at year end.

Major-Cable's production manager proposed that the cable be delivered, cut to the desired lengths, just-in-time to the manufacturer. The cable would be placed in cardboard tubes or boxes instead of spools. The customer was delighted to receive the cables on a just-in-time basis and agreed to pay a higher price (the proposed JIT delivery arrangement lowered the customer's manufacturing costs). Major-Cable not only received the higher price, it reduced its own costs, as many of the cables could be taken from the off-cuts (at virtually zero cost) and the cardboard boxes were cheaper to use than spools. ■

Source: Brian H. Maskel, "Using Target Costing to Increase Value," http://www.maskell.com/FieldStories1.htm,,accessed May 29, 2006.

standards was motivated by the objective of moving toward a value-added standard generated internally by industrial engineers and production managers. Target costs, on the other hand, are externally driven, generated by an analysis of markets and competitors.

Short Life Cycles Although life-cycle cost management is important for all manufacturing firms, it is particularly important for firms that have products with short life cycles. Products must recover all life-cycle costs and provide an acceptable profit. If a firm's products have long life cycles, profit performance can be increased by such actions as redesigning, changing prices, reducing costs, and altering the product mix. In contrast, firms that have products with short life cycles usually do not have time to react in this way, and so their approach must be proactive. Thus, for short life cycles, good life-cycle planning is critical, and prices must be set properly to recover all the life-cycle costs and provide a good return. Activity-based costing can be used to encourage good life-cycle planning. By careful selection of cost drivers, design engineers can be motivated to choose cost-minimizing designs.

Life-Cycle Costing: An Example Murphy Company produces electronic products that typically have about a 27-month life cycle. At the beginning of the last quarter of 2008, a new component was proposed. Design engineering believed that the product would be ready to produce by the beginning of 2009. To produce this and other similar products, resistors had to be inserted into a circuit board. Management had discovered that the cost of the circuit board was driven by the number of

Unit Cost and Price Information	
Unit production cost	$ 6
Unit life-cycle cost	10
Unit whole-life cost	12
Budgeted unit selling price	15

Budgeted Costs				
Item	2008	2009	2010	Item Total
Development costs	$200,000	—	—	$ 200,000
Production costs	—	$240,000	$360,000	600,000
Logistics costs	—	80,000	120,000	200,000
Annual subtotal	$200,000	$320,000	$480,000	$1,000,000
Postpurchase costs*	—	80,000	120,000	200,000
Annual total	$200,000	$400,000	$600,000	$1,200,000
Units produced		40,000	60,000	

Budgeted Product Income Statements				
Year	Revenues	Costs	Annual Income	Cumulative Income
2008	—	$(200,000)	$(200,000)	$(200,000)
2009	$600,000	(320,000)	280,000	80,000
2010	900,000	(480,000)	420,000	500,000

Exhibit 16-10 Life-Cycle Costing: Budgeted Costs and Income

insertions. Knowing this, design engineering produced the new component using fewer insertions than the products in the past had employed.

The budgeted costs and profits for the product over its two-year life cycle are illustrated in Exhibit 16-10. Notice that the life-cycle unit cost is $10, compared with the conventional definition of $6 (which includes only the production costs) and the whole-life cost of $12. To be viable, of course, the product must cover all of its life-cycle costs and produce an acceptable profit (the target profit). The $15 target price can be compared with the target profit to obtain the target cost. Suppose the target profit is $6.50 per unit. Thus, the *life-cycle target cost* is $8.50. Focusing only on the $6 cost could have led to a suboptimal design and production decision. Changing the focus requires managers to move away from the traditional, financially driven definition of product cost. Conventional cost systems do not directly identify development costs with the product being developed. The whole-life cost provides even more information—information that could prove vital for the company's life-cycle strategy. For example, if competitors sell a similar product for the same price but with postpurchase costs of only $1 per unit, the company could be at a competitive disadvantage. Given this information, actions can be considered that may eliminate the disadvantage (for example, redesigning the product to lower the postpurchase costs).

Feedback on the effectiveness of life-cycle planning is also helpful. This information can help new product planning in the future as well as be useful for assessing how design decisions affect operational and support costs. Comparing actual costs with the budgeted costs can provide useful insights. Exhibit 16-11 illustrates a simple life-cycle cost performance report. As can be seen, production costs were greater than expected. Investigation revealed that costs are driven by total number of insertions, not just insertions of resistors. Further analysis also revealed that by reducing the total number of insertions, postpurchase costs could be reduced. Thus, future design work on similar products can benefit from the assessment.

Year	Item	Actual Costs	Budgeted Costs	Variance
2008	Development	$190,000	$200,000	$10,000 F
2009	Production	300,000	240,000	60,000 U
	Logistics	75,000	80,000	5,000 F
2010	Production	435,000	360,000	75,000 U
	Logistics	110,000	120,000	10,000 F

*Analysis: Production costs were higher than expected because insertions of diodes and integrated circuits also drive costs (both production and postpurchase costs). Conclusion: The design of future products should try to minimize total insertions. (Postpurchase costs are costs incurred by the customer and so would not be included in the budgeted income statements.)

Exhibit 16-11 Performance Report: Life-Cycle Costs*

The Balanced Scorecard: Basic Concepts

Objective 4

Discuss the basic features of the Balanced Scorecard and its role in lean manufacturing.

The *Balanced Scorecard* is a strategic management system that defines a strategic-based responsibility accounting system. The **Balanced Scorecard** translates an organization's mission and strategy into operational objectives and performance measures for four different perspectives: the financial perspective, the customer perspective, the internal business process perspective, and the learning and growth (infrastructure) perspective.[15] The **financial perspective** describes the economic consequences of actions taken in the other three perspectives. The **customer perspective** defines the customer and market segments in which the business unit will compete. The **internal business process perspective** describes the internal processes needed to provide value for customers and owners. Finally, the **learning and growth (infrastructure) perspective** defines the capabilities that an organization needs to create long-term growth and improvement. This last perspective is concerned with three major *enabling factors:* employee capabilities, information systems capabilities, and employee attitudes (motivation, empowerment, and alignment).

Strategy Translation

Strategy, according to the creators of the Balanced Scorecard framework, is defined as

> [C]hoosing the market and customer segments the business unit intends to serve, identifying the critical internal and business processes that the unit must excel at to deliver the value propositions to customers in the targeted market segments, and selecting the individual and organizational capabilities required for the internal, customer, and financial objectives.[16]

Strategy, then, is specifying management's desired relationships among the four perspectives. **Strategy translation**, on the other hand, means specifying objectives, measures, targets, and initiatives for each perspective. The strategy-translation process is illustrated in Exhibit 16-12. Consider, for example, the financial perspective. For the financial perspective, a company may specify an *objective* of growing revenues by introducing new products. The *performance measure* may be the percentage of revenues from the sale of new products. The *target* or *standard* for the coming year for the measure may be 20 percent (that is, 20 percent of the total revenues for the coming year must be from the sale of new products). The *initiative* describes *how* this is to be accomplished. The "how," of course, involves the other three perspectives. The

15 Robert S. Kaplan and David P. Norton, *The Balanced Scorecard* (Boston: Harvard Business School Press, 1996).
16 Robert S. Kaplan and David P. Norton, *The Balanced Scorecard*, p. 37.

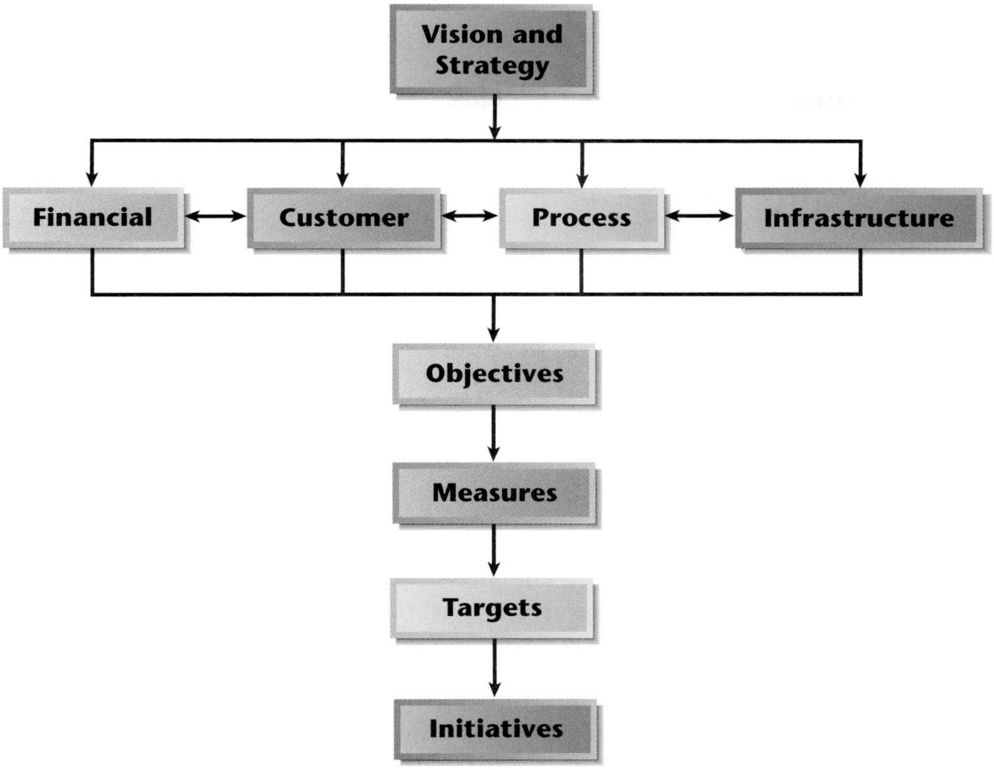

Exhibit 16-12 Strategy-Translation Process

company must now identify the customer segments, internal processes, and individual and organizational capabilities that will permit the realization of the revenue growth objective. This illustrates the fact that the financial objectives serve as the focus for the objectives, measures, and initiatives of the other three perspectives.

The Role of Performance Measures

Exhibit 16-12 illustrates quite clearly that the Balanced Scorecard is not simply a collection of critical performance measures. The performance measures are derived from a company's vision, strategy, and objectives. These measures must be balanced between *lag measures* and *lead measures,* between *objective measures* and *subjective measures,* between *financial measures* and *nonfinancial measures,* and between *external measures* and *internal measures.* **Lag measures** are outcome measures, measures of results from past efforts (e.g., customer profitability). **Lead measures (performance drivers)** are factors that drive future performance (e.g., hours of employee training). **Objective measures** are those that can be readily quantified and verified (e.g., market share), whereas **subjective measures** are less quantifiable and more judgmental in nature (e.g., employee capabilities). **Financial measures** are those expressed in monetary terms, whereas **nonfinancial measures** use nonmonetary units (e.g., cost per unit and number of dissatisfied customers). **External measures** are those that relate to *customers* and *shareholders* (e.g., customer satisfaction and return on investment). **Internal measures** are those measures that relate to the *processes* and *capabilities* that create value for customers and shareholders (e.g., process efficiency and employee satisfaction).

The performance measures must also be carefully *linked* to the organization's strategy. Doing so creates significant advantages for an organization. **Peel Memorial Hospital** implemented the Balanced Scorecard and found that patient satisfaction

The hotel industry has used the Balanced Scorecard as a tool to increase customer satisfaction.

© Digital Vision

levels increased from 89 percent to 95 percent and that staff satisfaction survey participation levels increased from 33 percent to 75 percent.[17] Other companies have had similar success—organizations such as **Hilton Hotels Corporation**, **Verizon Communications**, **Duke University Children's Hospital**, **City of Charlotte**, **NatWest Bancorp**, and **AT&T Canada LDS**. The rapid and widespread adoption of this strategic management system is a strong testimonial of its worth.

Linking Performance Measures to Strategy Balancing measures contributes to the requirement that the measures be linked to the organization's strategy. For example, balancing outcome measures with performance drivers is essential to linking with the organization's strategy. Performance drivers are the measures that make things happen and, consequently, are indicators of how the outcomes are going to be realized. Thus, they tend to be unique to a particular strategy. Outcome measures are also important because they reveal whether the strategy is being implemented successfully with the desired economic consequences. For example, if the number of defective products is decreased, does this produce a greater market share? Does this, in turn, produce more revenues and profits? These questions suggest that the most important principle of linkage is the usage of cause-and-effect relationships. In fact, a **testable strategy** can be defined as a set of linked objectives aimed at an overall goal. The testability of the strategy is achieved by restating the strategy into a set of cause-and-effect hypotheses that are expressed by a sequence of if-then statements.[18] Consider, for example, the following sequence of if-then statements that link quality training with increased profitability:

> If design engineers receive quality training, then they can redesign products to reduce the number of defective units; if the number of defective units is reduced, then customer satisfaction will increase; if customer satisfaction increases, then market share will increase; if market share increases, then sales will increase; if sales increase, then profits will increase.

The *strategy map* shown in Exhibit 16-13 illustrates the quality-improvement strategy, as described by this sequence of if-then statements. This exhibit reveals a number of interesting outcomes. First, notice how each of the four perspectives is represented. The learning and growth (infrastructure) perspective is present through the training dimension; the process perspective is represented by the redesign and manufacturing processes; the customer perspective is represented by customer satisfaction and market share; and, finally, the financial perspective is present because of revenues and profits. All four perspectives are linked through the cause-and-effect

17 Bruce W. Harber, "Working Together for Success: The Balanced Scorecard Solution at Peel Memorial Hospital." Check the chapter web links at the Interactive Study Center on http://www.thomsonedu.com/accounting/hansen for access to this online article.

18 Robert S. Kaplan and David P. Norton, *The Balanced Scorecard*, p. 149. (Kaplan and Norton describe the sequence of if-then statements only as a strategy. Calling it a testable strategy distinguishes it from the earlier, more general definition offered and, in our opinion, properly so.)

relationships hypothesized. Second, viability of the strategy is testable. Strategic feedback is available that allows managers to test the reasonableness of the strategy. Hours of training, the number of products redesigned, the number of defective units, customer satisfaction, market share, revenues, and profits are all observable measures. Thus, the claimed relationships can be checked to see if the strategy produces the expected results. If not, it could be due to one of two causes: (1) implementation problems or (2) an invalid strategy. First, it is possible that key *performance drivers* such as training and redesign of products did not achieve their targeted levels (that is, fewer hours of training and fewer products redesigned than planned). In this case, the failure to produce the targeted outcomes for defects, customer satisfaction, market share, revenues, and profits could be merely an implementation problem. On the other hand, if the targeted levels of performance drivers were achieved and the expected outcomes did not materialize, then the problem could very well lie with the strategy itself. This is an example of *double-loop feedback*. **Double-loop feedback** occurs whenever managers receive information about both the *effectiveness* of strategy implementation and the *validity* of the assumptions underlying the strategy. In a functional-based responsibility accounting system, typically only *single-loop feedback* is provided. **Single-loop feedback** emphasizes only effectiveness of implementation. In single-loop feedback, actual results deviating from planned results are a signal to take corrective action so that the plan (strategy) can be executed as intended. The validity of the assumptions underlying the plan are usually not questioned.

The Four Perspectives and Performance Measures The four perspectives define the strategy of an organization. Furthermore, the example of if-then statements illustrates that the four perspectives provide the structure or framework for developing an integrated, cohesive set of performance measures. These measures,

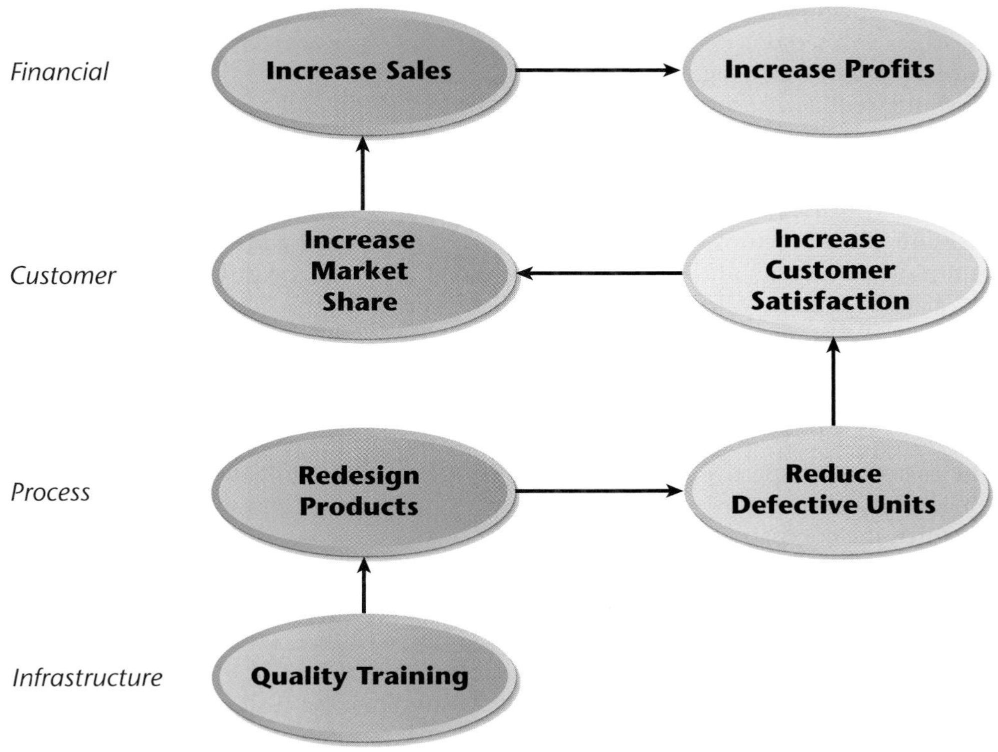

Exhibit 16-13 Testable Strategy Illustrated

once developed, become the means for articulating and communicating the strategy of the organization to its employees and managers. The measures also serve the purpose of aligning individual objectives and actions with organizational objectives and initiatives. Given the role the four perspectives play in development of performance measures, a more detailed examination of the perspectives is warranted.

The Financial Perspective

The financial perspective establishes the long- and short-term financial performance objectives. The financial perspective is concerned with the global financial consequences of the other three perspectives. Thus, the objectives and measures of the other perspectives must be linked to the financial objectives. The financial perspective has three strategic themes: revenue growth, cost reduction, and asset utilization. These themes serve as the building blocks for the development of specific operational objectives and measures.

Revenue Growth Several possible objectives are associated with revenue growth. Among these possibilities are the following: increase the number of new products, create new applications for existing products, develop new customers and markets, and adopt a new pricing strategy. Once operational objectives are known, performance measures can be designed. For example, possible measures for the above list of objectives (in the order given) are percentage of revenue from new products, percentage of revenue from new applications, percentage of revenue from new customers and market segments, and profitability by product or customer.

Cost Reduction Reductions in the cost per unit of product, per customer, or per distribution channel are examples of cost reduction objectives. The appropriate measures are obvious: the cost per unit of the particular cost object(s). Trends in these measures will tell whether the costs are being reduced or not. For these objectives, the accuracy of cost assignments is especially important. Activity-based costing can play an essential measurement role, especially for selling and administrative costs—costs not usually assigned to cost objects like customers and distribution channels.

Asset Utilization Improving asset utilization is the principal objective. Financial measures such as return on investment and economic value added are used. Since return on investment and economic value-added measures are discussed in detail in Chapter 10, they will not be discussed here. The objectives and measures for the financial perspective are summarized in Exhibit 16-14.

Customer Perspective

The customer perspective is the source of the revenue component for the financial objectives. This perspective defines and selects the customer and market segments in which the company chooses to compete.

Core Objectives and Measures Once the customers and segments are defined, then *core objectives* and *measures* are developed. **Core objectives and measures** are those that are common across all organizations. There are five key core objectives: increase market share, increase customer retention, increase customer acquisition, increase customer satisfaction, and increase customer profitability. Possible core measures for these objectives, respectively, are market share (percentage of the market),

Objectives	Measures
Revenue Growth:	
Increase the number of new products	Percentage of revenue from new products
Create new applications	Percentage of revenue from new applications
Develop new customers and markets	Percentage of revenue from new sources
Adopt a new pricing strategy	Product and customer profitability
Cost Reduction:	
Reduce unit product cost	Unit product cost
Reduce unit customer cost	Unit customer cost
Reduce distribution channel cost	Cost per distribution channel
Asset Utilization:	
Improve asset utilization	Return on investment Economic value added

Exhibit 16-14 Summary of Objectives and Measures: Financial Perspective

percentage growth of business from existing customers and percentage of repeating customers, number of new customers, ratings from customer satisfaction surveys, and individual and segment profitability. Activity-based costing is a key tool in assessing customer profitability (see Chapter 4). Notice that customer profitability is the only financial measure among the core measures. This measure, however, is critical because it emphasizes the importance of the *right* kind of customers. What good is it to have customers if they are not profitable? The obvious answer spells out the difference between being customer focused and customer obsessed.

Customer Value In addition to the core measures and objectives, measures are needed that drive the creation of *customer value* and, thus, drive the core outcomes. For example, increasing customer value builds customer loyalty (increases retention) and increases customer satisfaction. **Customer value** is the difference between realization and sacrifice, where realization is what the customer receives and sacrifice is what is given up. Realization includes such things as product functionality (features), product quality, reliability of delivery, delivery response time, image, and reputation. Sacrifice includes product price, time to learn to use the product, operating cost, maintenance cost, and disposal cost. Recall that the costs incurred by the customer *after* purchase are called postpurchase costs.

The attributes associated with the realization and sacrifice value propositions provide the basis for the objectives and measures that will lead to improving the core outcomes. The objectives for the sacrifice value proposition are the simplest: Decrease price and decrease postpurchase costs. Selling price and postpurchase costs are important measures of value creation. Decreasing postpurchase costs decreases customer sacrifice and, thus, increases customer value. Increasing customer value should favorably impact most of the core objectives. Similar favorable effects can be obtained by increasing realization. Realization objectives, for example, would include the following: improve product functionality, improve product quality, increase delivery reliability, and improve product image and reputation. Possible measures for these objectives include, respectively, feature satisfaction ratings, percentage of returns, on-time delivery percentage, and product recognition rating. Of these objectives and measures, delivery reliability will be used to illustrate how measures can affect managerial behavior, indicating the need to be careful in the choice and use of performance measures. Any of these measures would be appropriate for assessing and improving value stream performance.

Delivery reliability means that output is delivered on time. *On-time delivery* is a commonly used operational measure of reliability. To measure on-time delivery, a firm sets delivery dates and then finds on-time delivery performance by dividing the orders delivered on time by the total number of orders delivered. The goal, of course, is to achieve a ratio of 100 percent. This measure used by itself may produce undesirable behavioral consequences. Specifically, plant managers may give priority to filling orders not yet late over orders that are already late. The performance measure can encourage managers to have one very late shipment rather than several moderately late shipments! A chart measuring the age of late deliveries could help mitigate this problem. Exhibit 16-15 summarizes the objectives and measures for the customer perspective.

Process Perspective

Processes are the means for creating customer and shareholder value. Thus, the process perspective entails the identification of the processes needed to achieve the customer and financial objectives. To provide the framework needed for this perspective, a *process value chain* is defined. The **process value chain** is made up of three processes: the *innovation process,* the *operations process,* and the *postsales process.* The **innovation process** anticipates the emerging and potential needs of customers and creates new products and services to satisfy those needs. It represents what is called the *long-wave* of value creation. The **operations process** produces and delivers *existing* products and services to customers. It begins with a customer order and ends with the delivery of the product or service. It is the *short-wave* of value creation. The **postsales service process** provides critical and responsive services to customers after the product or service has been delivered.

Innovation Process: Objectives and Measures Objectives for the innovation process include the following: increase the number of new products, increase percentage of revenue from proprietary products, and decrease the time to develop new products. Associated measures are actual new products developed versus planned

Objectives	Measures
Core:	
Increase market share	Market share (percentage of market)
Increase customer retention	Percentage growth of business from existing customers
	Percentage of repeat customers
Increase customer acquisition	Number of new customers
Increase customer satisfaction	Ratings from customer surveys
Increase customer profitability	Customer profitability
Performance Value:	
Decrease price	Price
Decrease postpurchase costs	Postpurchase costs
Improve product functionality	Ratings from customer surveys
Improve product quality	Percentage of returns
Increase delivery reliability	On-time delivery percentage
	Aging schedule
Improve product image and reputation	Ratings from customer surveys

Exhibit 16-15 Summary of Objectives and Measures: Customer Perspective

products, percentage of total revenues from new products, percentage of revenues from proprietary products, and development cycle time (time to market).

Operations Process: Objectives and Measures Three operations process objectives are almost always mentioned and emphasized: increase process quality, increase process efficiency, and decrease process time. Improving quality, efficiency, and time in processes is basic to lean manufacturing. Furthermore, processes are the source of value for customers and so making sure that they are performing well on these three dimensions is critical to being competitive.

Quality. Examples of process quality measures are quality costs, output yields (good output/good input), and percentage of defective units (good output/total output). Quality costing and control are discussed extensively in Chapter 15. However, one additional quality metric should be mentioned: *first time through (FTT)*. **First time through** is a common quality metric used to measure quality in manufacturing cells and value streams and is calculated as follows:

$$\text{FTT} = (\text{Total units processed} - \text{Rejects and reworks})/\text{Total units processed}$$

FTT can be calculated for each workstation within a cell, and the overall cell FTT is the product of the workstation FTTs. Assuming three workstations:

$$\text{Cell FTT} = \text{FTT}_1 \times \text{FTT}_2 \times \text{FTT}_3$$

Thus, if FTT = 0.90 for each workstation, then the Cell FTT = $0.90 \times 0.90 \times 0.90 = 0.729$

Efficiency. Measures of process efficiency are concerned mainly with process cost and process productivity. Measuring and tracking process costs are facilitated by activity-based costing and process value analysis. These issues are explored in depth in Chapters 4 and 5. Productivity measurement is explored in Chapter 15. In a lean manufacturing environment, average cost and sales per person are typical measures of efficiency.

Time. Common process time measures are cycle time, velocity, manufacturing cycle effectiveness (MCE), takt time, and day-by-the-hour.

Cycle Time and Velocity The time to respond to a customer order is referred to as *responsiveness*. *Cycle time* and *velocity* are two operational measures of responsiveness. **Cycle time** is the length of time it takes to produce a unit of output from the time materials are received (starting point of the cycle) until the good is delivered to finished goods inventory (finishing point of the cycle). Another definition of cycle time is dock-to-dock time. Dock-to-dock time is the number of days between the time materials are received at the receiving dock and the time the finished good is shipped from the shipping dock.[19] In a lean firm, there is no finished goods inventory—goods are shipped when finished. Thus, cycle time is the time required to produce a product (time/units produced). **Velocity** is the number of units of output that can be produced in a given period of time (units produced/time).

Incentives can be used to encourage operational managers to reduce manufacturing cycle time or to increase velocity, thus improving delivery performance. A natural way to accomplish this objective is to tie product costs to cycle time and reward operational

19 Other definitions of cycles are possible; e.g., a cycle's starting point could be when the customer order is received and the finishing point when the goods are shipped to the customer. For a lean firm, the point when goods are shipped is a reasonable finishing point. Cycle time measures the time elapsed from start to finish, regardless of how the starting and finishing points are defined.

managers for reducing product costs. For example, in a lean firm, cell conversion costs can be assigned to products on the basis of the time that it takes a product to move through the cell. Using the theoretical productive time available for a period (in minutes), a value-added cost per minute can be computed.

Value-added cost per minute = Cell conversion costs/Minutes available

To obtain the conversion cost per unit, this value-added cost per minute is multiplied by the actual cycle time used to produce the units during the period. By comparing the unit cost computed using the actual cycle time with the unit cost possible using the theoretical or optimal cycle time, a manager can assess the potential for improvement. Note that the more time it takes a product to move through the cell, the greater the unit product cost. With incentives to reduce product cost, this approach to product costing encourages operational managers and cell workers to find ways to decrease cycle time or increase velocity.

An example will illustrate the concepts. Assume that a company has the following data for one of its manufacturing cells:

Theoretical velocity: 12 units per hour
Productive minutes available (per year): 400,000
Annual conversion costs: $1,600,000
Actual velocity: 10 units per hour

The actual and theoretical conversion costs per unit are shown in Exhibit 16-16. Notice from Exhibit 16-16 that the per-unit conversion cost can be reduced from $24 to $20 by decreasing cycle time from six minutes per unit to five minutes per unit (or increasing velocity from 10 units per hour to 12 units per hour). At the same time, the objective of improving delivery performance is achieved.

Manufacturing Cycle Efficiency (MCE)

Another time-based operational measure calculates manufacturing cycle efficiency (MCE) as follows:

MCE = Processing time/(Processing time + Move time + Inspection time + Waiting time)

where processing time is the time it takes to convert materials into a finished good. The other activities and their times are viewed as wasteful, and the goal is to reduce those times to zero. If this is accomplished, the value of MCE would be 1.0. As MCE

Actual Conversion Cost per Unit	
Standard cost per minute	= $1,600,000/400,000
	= $4 per minute
Actual cycle time	= 60 minutes/10 units
	= 6 minutes per unit
Actual conversion costs	= $4 × 6
	= $24 per unit
Theoretical Conversion Cost per Unit	
Theoretical cycle time	= 60 minutes/12 units
	= 5 minutes per unit
Theoretical conversion costs	= $4 × 5
	= $20 per unit

Exhibit 16-16 Conversion Cost Computations

improves (moves toward 1.0), cycle time decreases. Furthermore, since the only way MCE can improve is by decreasing waste, cost reduction must also follow.

To illustrate MCE, let's use the data from Exhibit 16-16. The actual cycle time is 6.0 minutes, and the theoretical cycle time is 5.0 minutes. Thus, the time wasted is 1.0 minute (6.0 − 5.0), and MCE is computed as follows:

$$\begin{aligned} \text{MCE} &= 5.0/6.0 \\ &= 0.83 \end{aligned}$$

Actually, this is a fairly efficient process, as measured by MCE. Many manufacturing companies have MCEs that are less than 0.05.[20]

Takt Time and Day-by-the-Hour Report **Takt time** is a Japanese term and is simply the rate at which customers demand product. For example, customer demand may require that a product be produced every 10 minutes. Thus, the required cycle time is five minutes if the firm (or value stream) is to produce on demand and minimize waste. The day-by-the-hour report provides the takt hourly quantity in one column, the actual hourly quantity produced in a second column, and the cumulative actual amount produced for the day (shift). One purpose of the report is to keep the production workers focused on producing that which is needed by the customers when they need it.

Postsales Service Process: Objectives and Measures Increasing quality, increasing efficiency, and decreasing process time are also objectives that apply to the postsales service process. Service quality, for example, can be measured by *first-pass yields,* defined as the percentage of customer requests resolved with a single service call. Efficiency can be measured by cost trends and productivity measures. Process time can be measured by cycle time, where the starting point of the cycle is defined as the receipt of a customer request and the finishing point is when the customer's problem is solved. The objectives and measures for the process perspective are summarized in Exhibit 16-17.

Objectives	Measures
Innovation:	
Increase the number of new products	Number of new products vs. planned
Increase proprietary products	Percentage revenue from proprietary products
Decrease new product development time	Time to market (from start to finish)
Operations:	
Increase process quality	Quality costs
	Output yields
	Percentage of defective units
Increase process efficiency	Unit cost trends
	Output/input(s)
Decrease process time	Cycle time and velocity
	MCE
Postsales Service:	
Increase service quality	First-pass yields
Increase service efficiency	Cost trends
	Output/input(s)
Decrease service time	Cycle time

Exhibit 16-17 Summary of Objectives and Measures: Process Perspective

20 Robert S. Kaplan and David P. Norton, *The Balanced Scorecard*, p. 117.

Learning and Growth Perspective

The learning and growth perspective is the source of the capabilities that enable the accomplishment of the other three perspectives' objectives. This perspective has three major objectives: increase employee capabilities; increase motivation, empowerment, and alignment; and increase information systems capabilities.

Employee Capabilities Three core *outcome* measurements for employee capabilities are employee satisfaction ratings, employee turnover percentages, and employee productivity (e.g., revenue per employee). Examples of lead measures or performance drivers for employee capabilities are hours of training and strategic job coverage ratios (percentage of critical job requirements filled). As new processes are created, new skills are often demanded. Training and hiring are sources of these new skills. Furthermore, the percentage of employees needed in certain key areas with the requisite skills signals the capability of the organization to meet the objectives of the other three perspectives.

Motivation, Empowerment, and Alignment Employees must not only have the necessary skills, but they must also have the freedom, motivation, and initiative to use those skills effectively. The number of suggestions per employee and the number of suggestions implemented per employee are possible measures of motivation and empowerment. Suggestions per employee provide a measure of the degree of employee involvement, whereas suggestions implemented per employee signal the quality of the employee participation. The second measure also signals to employees whether or not their suggestions are being taken seriously.

Information Systems Capabilities Increasing information system capabilities means providing more accurate and timely information to employees so that they can improve processes and effectively execute new processes. Measures should be concerned with the *strategic information availability*. For example, possible measures include percentage of processes with real-time feedback capabilities and percentage of customer-facing employees with online access to customer and product information. Exhibit 16-18 summarizes the objectives and measures for the learning and growth perspective.

Objectives	Measures
Increase employee capabilities	Employee satisfaction ratings Employee turnover percentages Employee productivity (revenue/employee) Hours of training Strategic job coverage ratio (percentage of critical job requirements filled)
Increase motivation and alignment	Suggestions per employee Suggestions implemented per employee
Increase information systems capabilities	Percentage of processes with real-time feedback capabilities Percentage of customer-facing employees with online access to customer and product information

Exhibit 16-18 Summary of Objectives and Measures: Learning and Growth Perspective

Summary of Learning Objectives

1. Describe the basic features of lean manufacturing.

Lean manufacturing has two principal objectives: eliminating waste and creating value for the customer. It is characterized by lean thinking—focusing on customer value, value streams, production flow, demand-pull, and perfection. Value is achieved by delivering the right product, in the right quantity, with the right quality (zero-defect) at the exact time the customer needs it and at the lowest possible cost. Value streams are made up of all activities, both value-added and non-value-added, required to bring a product group or service from its starting point (e.g., customer order or concept for a new product) to a finished product in the hands of the customer. Value stream analysis allows waste to be identified and eliminated. Lean manufacturing reduces wait and move time dramatically and allows the production of small batches (low volume) of differing products (high variety). The key factors in achieving these outcomes are lower setup times and cellular manufacturing. A *demand-pull* system helps eliminate waste by producing a product only when it is needed and only in the quantities demanded by customers. Zero setup times, zero defects, zero inventories, zero waste, producing on demand, increasing a cell's production rates, minimizing cost, and maximizing customer value represent ideal outcomes that a lean manufacturer seeks. Perfection is sought by the relentless pursuit of these lean manufacturing objectives.

2. Describe lean accounting.

Lean accounting is an approach designed to support and encourage lean manufacturing. To avoid obstacles and false signals, changes in both product-costing and operational control approaches are needed when moving to a value-stream-based lean manufacturing system. Average costing, value-stream cost reporting, and the heavy use of nonfinancial measures for operational control are typical lean accounting approaches. The average product cost is the total value stream cost of period divided by the units shipped of the period. Value stream costing reports the actual revenues and actual costs on a weekly basis (for each value stream). The lean control system uses a Box Scorecard that compares operational, capacity, and financial metrics with prior week performances and with a future desired state. Simplicity and compatibility are major characteristics of lean accounting.

3. Explain the basics of life-cycle cost management and target costing.

Life-cycle cost management focuses on managing value-chain activities so that a long-term competitive advantage is created. The objectives are the same as lean manufacturing: cost reduction and value creation. Target costing is a major methodology used to achieve these objectives. Three cost reduction methods are typically used: (1) reverse engineering, (2) value analysis, and (3) process improvement. Value analysis not only helps reduce costs, it also explicitly considers how value can be created for the customer.

4. Discuss the basic features of the Balanced Scorecard and its role in lean manufacturing.

The Balanced Scorecard is a strategic management system that translates the vision and strategy of an organization into operational objectives and measures. Objectives and measures are developed for each of four perspectives: the financial perspective, the customer perspective, the process perspective, and the learning and growth perspective. The objectives and measures of the four perspectives are linked by a series of cause-and-effect hypotheses. This produces a testable strategy that provides strategic feedback to managers. The Balanced Scorecard is compatible with activity-based responsibility accounting because it focuses on processes and requires the use of activity-based information to implement many of its objectives and measures.

Key Terms

Balanced Scorecard, 734
Core objectives and measures, 738
Customer perspective, 734
Customer value, 739
Cycle time, 741
Delivery reliability, 740
Double-loop feedback, 737
External measures, 735
Financial measures, 735
Financial perspective, 734
First time through, 741
Innovation process, 740
Internal business process perspective, 734
Internal measures, 735
JIT purchasing, 719
Lag measures, 735
Lead measures (performance drivers), 735
Lean manufacturing, 714
Learning and growth (infrastructure) perspective, 734

Review Problems

1. MCE, Lean Measures, and the Balanced Scorecard

Numark, Inc., manufactures a product that experiences the following activities and times:

	Hours
Processing (two departments)	42.0
Inspecting	2.8
Rework	7.0
Moving (three moves)	11.2
Waiting (for the second process)	33.6
Storage (before delivery to customer)	43.4

Required

1. Compute the MCE for this product.
2. A study lists the following root causes of the inefficiencies: poor quality components from suppliers, lack of skilled workers, and plant layout. The management of Numark immediately began to install some lean manufacturing initiatives to address the problems. First, they installed cellular manufacturing, changing the plant layout. The result was a dramatic reduction in move time and wait time. Next, they began an intensive training program to improve worker skills so that fewer defectives would be produced. They also initiated a supplier selection program, selecting and working with suppliers so that the components being delivered are of higher quality. Training and supplier selection both produced a significant reduction in defective units. Express a cost reduction strategy as a series of if-then statements that will reduce MCE and lower costs. Finally, prepare a strategy map that illustrates the causal paths. In preparing the map, use only three perspectives: learning and growth, process, and financial.
3. Is MCE a lag or a lead measure? If and when MCE acts as a lag measure, what lead measures would affect it?

Solution

1. MCE $= 42/(42 + 2.8 + 7 + 11.2 + 33.6 + 43.4)$
   $= 0.30$
2. Strategy as a series of if-then statements:
   If workers are trained and better suppliers are selected, *then* defects will decrease.
   If defects decrease, *then* rework and inspection time will decrease.
   If plant layout improves, *then* move time and wait time will decrease.

If rework, inspection time, move time, and wait time decrease, *then* storage will decrease and MCE will increase.
If storage decreases, *then* MCE will increase.
If MCE increases, *then* costs will decrease.

Strategy map

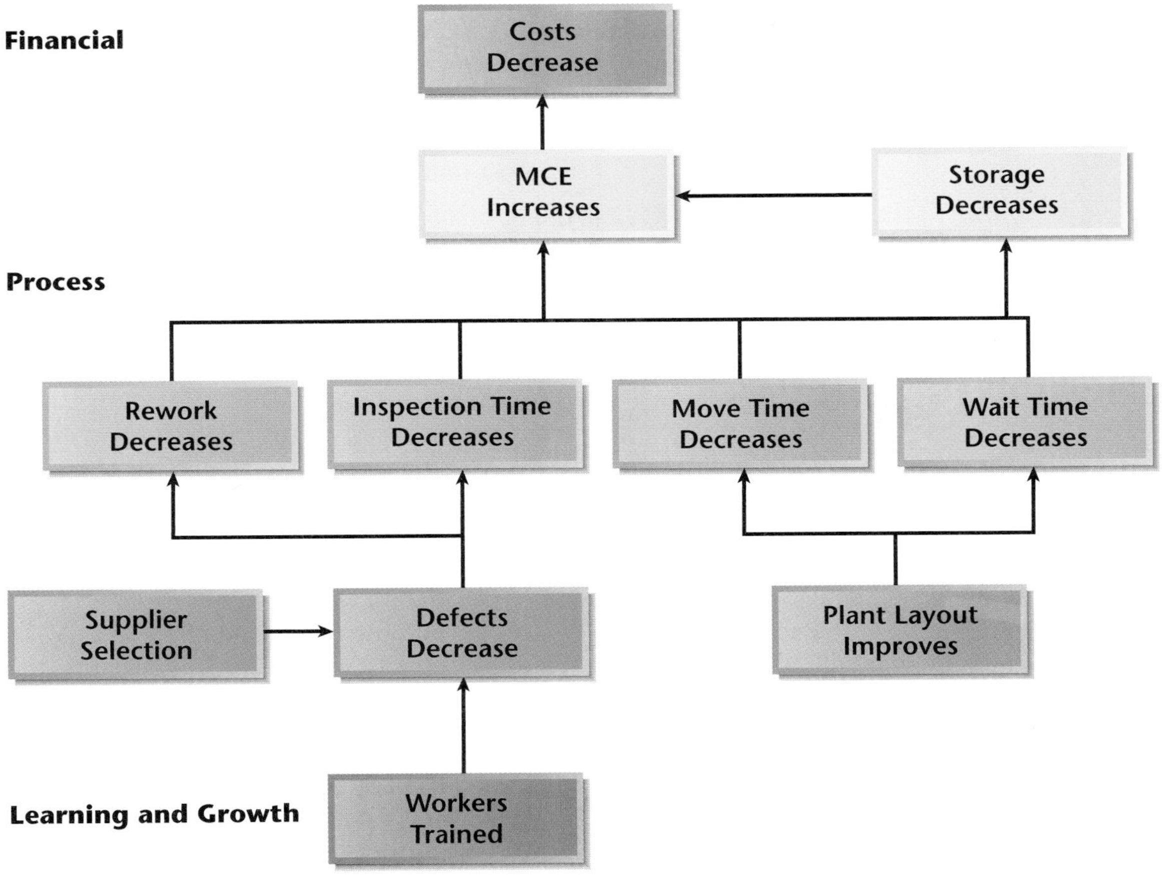

3. MCE functions as both a lag and a lead measure. To increase MCE, as indicated in Requirement 2, the process must be improved. Performance drivers or lead measures would include hours of quality training (this should reduce inspection and rework time), suggestions per employee (this could reveal ways to reduce wait time, for example), and real-time feedback capabilities (this could decrease wait and storage time). When MCE increases, then it leads or drives cost reduction.

2. Life-Cycle Cost Management and Target Costing

Silverado Parts, Inc., produces electronic products with short life cycles (of less than two years). Development has to be rapid, and the profitability of the products is tied strongly to the ability to find designs that will keep production and logistics costs low. Recently, management has also decided that postpurchase costs are important in design decisions. Last month, a proposal for a new product was presented to management. The total market was projected at 200,000 units (for the two-year period). The proposed selling price was $130 per unit. At this price, market share was expected to be 25 percent. The manufacturing and logistics costs were estimated to be $120 per unit. Development costs are $100,000. The owner of Silverado requires a $15 per unit return.

1. Calculate the target cost associated with the initial 25 percent market share. Does the initial design meet this target?
2. Now calculate the *total* life-cycle profit that the current (initial) design offers (including preproduction costs).

Solution

1.

$$\begin{aligned}\text{Target cost} &= \text{Target price} - \text{Target profit}\\ &= \$130 - \$15\\ &= \$115 \text{ per unit}\end{aligned}$$

The projected cost is $122 [$120 + ($100,000/50,000 units)], so the target is not met.

2. The projected total life-cycle profit is ($130 − $122) × 50,000 = $400,000.

Questions for Writing and Discussion

1. What is lean manufacturing?
2. What are the five principles of lean thinking?
3. Identify two types of value streams and explain how they differ.
4. How are value streams identified and created?
5. Explain how lean manufacturing is able to produce small batches (low volume products) of differing products (high variety).
6. What role does a demand-pull system have in lean manufacturing?
7. Identify eight forms and sources of waste.
8. What is a focused value stream?
9. What is the purpose of assigning facility costs to value streams, using a fixed price?
10. Why are units shipped used to calculate the value-stream product cost?
11. When will the average unit cost be useful for value streams?
12. Explain why changes in value stream profitability may be better information than individual product cost for certain decisions.
13. Explain how operational control works in a lean manufacturing firm.
14. Describe the benefits of life-cycle cost budgeting.
15. What is target costing? Describe how costs are reduced so that the target cost can be met.
16. What is the purpose of a Balanced Scorecard?
17. According to the Balanced Scorecard, what is a strategy?
18. Explain the difference between lag measures and lead measures.
19. What is a testable strategy?
20. What is meant by double-loop feedback?
21. What are the three strategic themes of the financial perspective?
22. Identify the five core objectives of the customer perspective.
23. Explain what is meant by the long-wave and the short-wave of value creation.
24. What is cycle time? Velocity?
25. What is manufacturing cycle efficiency?
26. Identify three objectives of the learning and growth perspective.

Exercises

16-1

Basic Concepts of Lean Manufacturing
LO1

Choose the *best* answer for each of the following multiple-choice questions:

1. Which of the following elements defines a lean manufacturing system?

   a. waste elimination
   b. value creation

c. cost reduction
d. continuous flow
e. All of the above.

2. Which of the following are lean thinking principles?
   a. strict control using variance analysis
   b. value streams
   c. uninterrupted value flow
   d. Both b and c.
   e. None of the above.

3. An order fulfillment value stream
   a. focuses on developing new products for new customers.
   b. focuses on providing current products to current customers.
   c. focuses on providing existing products to new customers.
   d. focuses on providing new products to existing customers.
   e. All of the above.

4. Non-value-added activities are
   a. unavoidable in the short run due to current technology or production methods.
   b. unnecessary.
   c. all avoidable in the long run.
   d. a source of waste.
   e. All of the above.

5. A value stream
   a. has only value-added activities.
   b. has both value-added and non-value-added activities.
   c. has only non-value-added activities.
   d. emphasizes standard costing controls.
   e. All of the above.

6. A value stream is usually created for
   a. heterogeneous products.
   b. products that use different processes.
   c. products that use common processes.
   d. products with the same market shares.
   e. None of the above.

7. A cell structure is chosen over a departmental structure because it
   a. reduces inventories.
   b. increases quality.
   c. reduces cost.
   d. reduces cycle time.
   e. All of the above.

8. Inventories of goods awaiting further processing or consumption are
   a. a form of waste not valued by customers.
   b. needed to ensure JIT deliveries to customers.
   c. needed to prevent stock-outs.
   d. vital for continuous flow manufacturing.
   e. None of the above.

16-2

Value-Stream Identification
LO1

Gards, Inc., formed the following matrix for its five products.

Required

Using the information in the matrix, identify the value streams.

	Production Activities/Processes							
Product Model	Order Entry	Production Planning	Subassembly 47A Cell	Basic Cell	Assembly Cell	Inspecting	Packaging & Shipping	Warranty
A		x			x	x	x	x
B		x	x		x	x	x	
C		x					x	x
D		x			x	x	x	x
E		x	x		x	x	x	

16-3

LO1: Continuous Flow versus Departmental Flow Manufacturing

PharmU, Inc., has the following departmental structure for producing a popular pain medication:

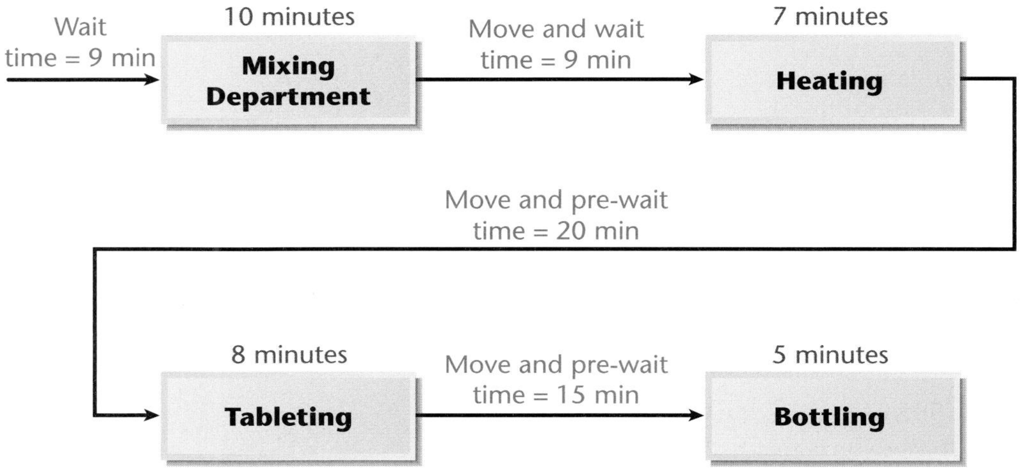

A consultant designed the following cellular manufacturing structure for the same product:

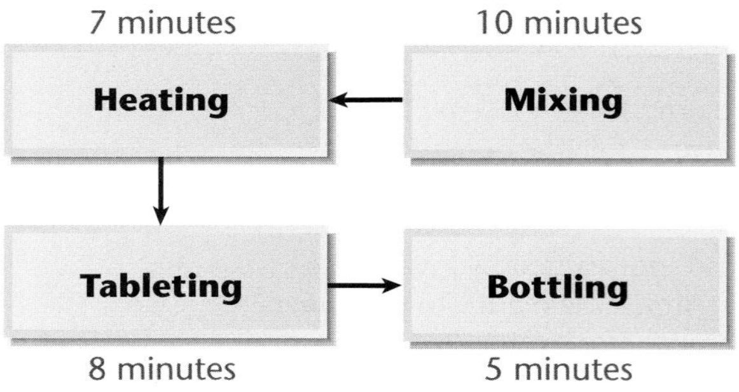

The times above the processes represent the time required to process one unit of product.

Required

1. Calculate the time required to produce a batch of 10 bottles using a batch processing departmental structure.
2. Calculate the time to process 10 units using cellular manufacturing.
3. How much manufacturing time will the cellular manufacturing structure save for a batch of 10 units?

16-4

Bottleneck Operation; Improving Production Flow
LO1

PharmU, Inc., implemented cellular manufacturing as recommended by a consultant. The production flow improved dramatically. However, the company was still faced with the need to improve its cycle time so that it could match the takt time requirement of one bottle every six minutes (ten bottles per hour). The cell structure is shown below; the times above the process represent the time required to process one unit.

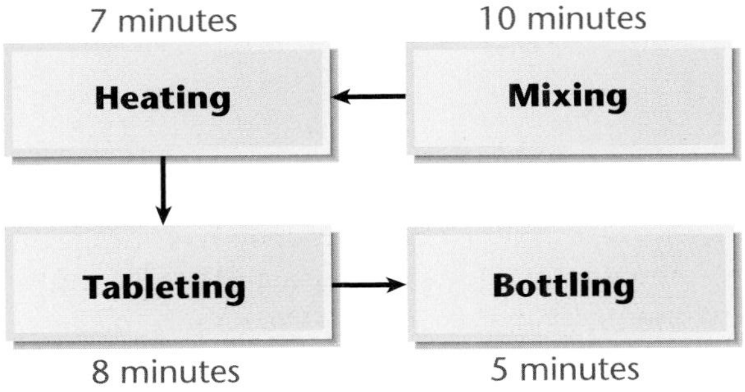

Required

1. How many units can the cell produce per hour (on a continuous running basis)?
2. How long does it take to produce one unit, assuming the cell is producing on a continuous basis?
3. What must happen for the takt time to be met so that the cell can produce one bottle every six minutes or 10 per hour, assuming the cell produces on a continuous basis?

16-5

Value Stream Costing
LO2

Wimberly, Inc. has just created five order fulfillment value streams, two focused and three that produce multiple products. The size of the plant in which the values streams are located is 100,000 square feet. The facility costs total $900,000 per year. One of the focused value streams produces a basic MP3 product. The MP3 value stream occupies 10,000 square feet. Not counting facility costs, the MP3 value stream costs total $1,800,000. There are 20,000 MP3 units produced annually. There were not sufficient quality personnel for each value stream; thus, the MP3 stream had to share a quality engineer who spends 40 percent of his time with the MP3 value stream and the other 60 percent with two other value streams. While 40 percent of the time is not sufficient time for the value streams, the contribution will be workable until other arrangements can be made. His salary is $75,000 per year. Mary Oliver, an industrial engineer, is one of two employees assigned completely to the value stream from production planning. Mary has not been with the company as long as the other production engineer. Because of the demand-pull nature of the new value stream, only one production planner is needed.

Required

1. Explain how the value stream costs of $1,800,000 were most likely assigned to the MP3 value stream. Explain how facility costs will be treated and why.
2. How many employees are likely to be located within the MP3 value stream?

3. Given that only one production planner is needed, what should the company do with its extra engineer (Mary Oliver)?
4. Calculate the unit product cost for the MP3 value stream. Comment on the accuracy of this cost and its value for monitoring value-stream performance.

16-6

Value Stream Average Costing; ABC Costs as Benchmarks
LO2

EXCEL

A value stream has three activities and two products. The units produced and shipped per week are 50 of the deluxe model (Model A) and 150 of the basic model (Model B). The resource consumption patterns are shown as follows:

	Model A	Model B	Costs of Value Stream Activities
Cell	600 minutes	1,800 minutes	$ 9,600
Engineering	15 hours	65 hours	3,400
Testing	25 hours	55 hours	3,000
Total			$16,000

Required

1. Calculate the ABC product cost for Model A and Model B.
2. Calculate the value stream average product cost. Assuming reasonable stability in the consumption patterns of the products and product mix, assess how well the products are grouped based on similarity.

16-7

Value Stream Reporting with Inventory Decrease
LO2

Shorts Manufacturing, Inc., has implemented lean manufacturing in its Kansas City plant as a pilot program. One of its value streams produces a family of small electric tools. The value stream team managers were quite excited about the results, as some of their efforts to eliminate waste were proving to be effective. During the most recent three weeks, the following data pertaining to the electric tool value stream were collected:

Week 1:
Demand = 90 units @ $40
Beginning inventory = 10 units @$20 ($5 materials and $15 conversion)
Production = 90 units using $450 of material and $1,350 of conversion cost

Week 2:
Demand = 100 units @ $40
Beginning inventory = 10 units @ $20 ($5 materials and $15 conversion)
Production = 90 units using $450 of material and $1,350 of conversion cost

Week 3:
Demand = 90 units @ $40
Beginning inventory = 0
Production = 100 units using $500 of material and $1,500 of conversion cost.

Required

1. Prepare a traditional income statement for each week.
2. Calculate the average value-stream product cost for each week. What does this cost signal, if anything?
3. Prepare a value stream income statement for each week. Assume that any increase in inventory is valued at average cost. Comment on the financial performance of the value stream and its relationship to traditional income measurement.

16-8

Box Scorecard
LO2

The following Box Scorecard was prepared for a value stream.

	Last Week	This Week (6/30/08)	Planned Future State (12/31/08)
Operational			
Units per person	100	108	115
On-time delivery	85%	90%	95%
Dock-to-dock days	12	11	9
First time through	60%	62%	70%
Average product cost	$75	$74	$70
Capacity			
Productive	25%	26%	27%
Nonproductive	65%	62%	40%
Available	10%	12%	33%
Financial			
Weekly sales	$800,000	$825,000	$1,000,000
Weekly material cost	$320,000	$330,000	$380,000
Weekly conversion cost	$280,000	$280,240	$320,000
Weekly value stream profit	$200,000	$214,760	$300,000
ROS	25%	26%	30%

Required

1. How many nonfinancial measures are used to evaluate performance? Why are nonfinancial measures used?
2. Classify the operational measures as time-based, quality-based, or efficiency-based. Discuss the significance of each category for lean manufacturing.
3. What is the role of the planned state column?
4. Discuss the capacity category and explain the meaning of each measure and its significance.
5. Discuss the relationship between the financial measures and the measures in the operational and capacity categories.

16-9

Life-Cycle Costing; Target Costing
LO3

Nabors Toys' Product Development Department was in the process of developing a new videogame player. The product life cycle is estimated at 27 months. Estimated sales over its life cycle are 1,500,000 units. For the current design, the development, production, and logistics costs for the life cycle are estimated at $180,000,000. The product specifications and the targeted market share call for a price of $150 per unit. The target profit per unit is $50. Postpurchase costs for the current design are estimated to be $36 per unit.

Required

1. What is the total life-cycle profit desired for the new model?
2. What is the projected life-cycle profit for the new model?
3. What is the target cost? How much must costs be reduced per unit and in total for this target to be met? Describe three approaches available to reduce costs so that the target cost is met.
4. Should postpurchase costs be included in life-cycle costing? In target costing? Explain.

16-10

Balanced Scorecard; Strategy Translation; Single- and Double-Loop Feedback
LO4

NBH Company, a small electronics firm, buys circuit boards and manually inserts various electronic devices into the printed circuit board. NBH sells its products to original equipment manufacturers. Profits for the last two years have been less than expected. Natalie Henson, owner of NBH, was convinced that her firm needed to adopt a revenue growth strategy to increase overall profits. To help in building a viable strategy, Natalie hired a local consultant. After a careful review, the consultant told Natalie that the main obstacle for increasing revenues was the high defect rate of her products (a 5 percent reject rate). She was told that revenues would grow if the defect rate was reduced dramatically. By decreasing the defect rate, customer satisfaction will increase. With increased customer satisfaction, NBH's market share should increase. The following suggestions were made to help ensure the success of the revenue growth strategy:

1. Improve the soldering capabilities by sending employees to an outside course.
2. Redesign the insertion process to eliminate some of the common mistakes.
3. Improve the procurement process by selecting suppliers that provide higher-quality circuit boards.

Required

1. State the revenue growth strategy using a series of cause-and-effect relationships expressed as if-then statements. It is possible to have a compound if-then statement (more than one cause for one effect).
2. Illustrate the strategy using a flow diagram like the one shown in Exhibit 16-13.
3. Explain how the revenue growth strategy can be tested. In your explanation, discuss the role of lead and lag measures, targets, and double-loop feedback.

16-11

Balanced Scorecard; Classification of Performance Measures
LO4

Listed below are a number of scorecard measures. Classify each performance measure according to the following: perspective (e.g., customer or learning and growth), financial or nonfinancial, subjective or objective, external or internal, and lead or lag. Discuss why it is sometimes difficult to classify these measures as lead or lag. Now, pick any two measures where you have difficulty explaining whether they are lead or lag, and explain when they would be lead and when they would be lag measures.

a. Number of new customers
b. Percentage of customer complaints resolved with one contact
c. Unit product cost
d. Cost per distribution channel
e. Suggestions per employee
f. Quality costs
g. Product functionality ratings (from surveys)
h. Cycle time for solving a customer problem
i. Strategic job coverage ratio
j. On-time delivery percentage
k. Percentage of revenues from new products

16-12

Cycle Time and Conversion Cost per Unit
LO4

The theoretical cycle time for a product is 15 minutes per unit. The budgeted conversion costs for the manufacturing cell are $1,350,000 per year. The total labor minutes available are 300,000. During the year, the cell was able to produce three units of the product per hour. Suppose also that production incentives exist to minimize unit product costs.

Required

1. Compute the theoretical conversion cost per unit.
2. Compute the applied conversion cost per unit (the amount of conversion cost actually assigned to the product).

3. Discuss how this approach to assigning conversion costs can improve delivery time performance.

16-13

Cycle Time and Velocity; MCE; LO4

EXCEL

A manufacturing cell has the theoretical capacity to produce 360,000 stereo speakers per quarter. The conversion cost per quarter is $720,000. There are 60,000 production hours used within the cell per quarter.

Required

1. Compute the theoretical velocity (per hour) and the theoretical cycle time (minutes per unit produced).
2. Compute the ideal amount of conversion cost that will be assigned per speaker.
3. Speaker production uses 12 minutes of move time, 10 minutes of wait time, and 18 minutes of inspection time. Compute the amount of conversion cost actually assigned to each speaker. Now calculate MCE.
4. Based on your analysis in Requirements 2 and 3, how much non-value-added time is being used? How much is it costing per speaker?

Problems

16-14

Focused Value Streams; Product Costing LO1, LO2

Sixty employees (all CPAs) of a local public accounting firm eat lunch at least twice weekly at a very popular pizza restaurant. The pizza restaurant recently began offering discounts for groups of 15 or more. Groups would be seated in a separate room, served individual bowls of salad costing $2 each, pitchers of root beer costing $3 each (each pitcher has a five-glass capacity), and medium, two-topping pizzas for $10 (ten slices each). The food would have to be ordered in advance.

Thirty of the CPAs commit to eating three slices of pizza, three glasses of root beer, and one bowl of salad (a consumption pattern of (3,3,1)). The other 30 are more hearty eaters and commit to seven slices of pizza, two glasses of root beer, and one bowl of salad (a consumption pattern of (7,2,1)). Each member of the group must pay an assessed amount for the lunch.

Required

1. Determine the total number of pizzas, pitchers of root beer, and salads that must be ordered for the 60 employees.
2. One of the CPAs offered to determine the amount that each should pay. He suggested that the easiest way is assign the average cost to each person eating in the group. Based on this suggestion, how much would each CPA pay for lunch?
3. One CPA objected to using average cost, noting that half of the CPAs are much lighter eaters than the other half. Based on the large differences in consumption behaviors, he suggested forming two groups: one for the light eaters and one for the heavier eaters. Calculate the lunch cost for each CPA for each group. Discuss the analogy to formation of focused value streams in a manufacturing environment. Calculate the cost that would be assigned using ABC. What does this tell you?

16-15

Multiple-Product Value Streams; Product Costing; Creating Available Capacity LO1, LO2

Sixty employees (all CPAs) of a local public accounting firm eat lunch at least twice weekly at a very popular pizza restaurant. The pizza restaurant recently began offering discounts for groups of 15 or more. Groups would be seated in a separate room, served individual bowls of salad costing $2 each, pitchers of root beer costing $3 each (each pitcher has a five-glass capacity), and medium, two-topping pizzas for $10 (ten slices each). The food would have to be ordered in advance.

After some detailed polling among the 60, four types of eaters were identified: two types of light eaters and two types of heavy eaters. The consumption patterns for each group are given (slices of pizza, glasses of root beer, and bowls of salad): Light Eaters (Group A): A1 = (2,2,1) and A2 = (3,3,1); Heavy Eaters (Group B): B1 = (6,3,1) and B2 = (7,2,1). There are an equal number of CPAs in each of the four groups.

Required

1. Calculate the average lunch cost for each CPA in each of the two groups, A and B. Compare this to the ABC cost assignments. Discuss the merits of grouping based on similarity. Discuss the analogy to multiple-product value streams.
2. Suppose that members of the heavy-eating group (Group B) decided that they were eating more than necessary for their health and well-being and decided to reduce their total calories. They therefore agreed to reduce consumption of pizza by one slice and consumption of root beer by one glass for each member of the group. Relative to the original order, how much extra capacity exists? If the excess capacity is eliminated by reducing the order, what is the new average cost? Suppose that the decision is to use the extra capacity to invite four guests (two of Type B1 and two of Type B2) to lunch (at the cost of the CPAs). If the original order is used as the benchmark cost, what is the extra cost of the guest program? Comment on the conceptual significance of this for manufacturing firms.

16-16

Box Scorecard; Special Order Decision LO1, LO2

Bradford Company, a manufacturer of small tools,implemented lean manufacturing at the end of 2007. The company's goal for the year was to increase the ROS to 40 percent of sales. A value stream team was established and began to work on lean improvements. During the year, the team was able to achieve significant results on several fronts. The Box Scorecard below reflects the performance measures at the beginning of the year, midyear, and end of year. Although the team members were pleased with their progress, they were disappointed in the financial results. They were still far from the targeted ROS of 40 percent. They were also puzzled as to why the improvements made did not translate into significantly improved financial performance.

	Jan. 1, 2008	June 30, 2008	Dec. 31, 2008
Operational			
Revenue per person	$15,000	$15,000	$15,000
On-time delivery	70%	90%	95%
Dock-to-dock days	15	6	5
First time through	60%	60%	90%
Average product cost	$60	$60	$59
Capacity			
Productive	40%	40%	40%
Nonproductive	50%	30%	10%
Available	10%	30%	50%
Financial			
Weekly sales	$800,000	$800,000	$800,000
Weekly material cost	$260,000	$260,000	$240,000
Weekly conversion cost	$300,000	$300,000	$300,000
Weekly value stream profit	$240,000	$240,000	$260,000
ROS	30%	30%	32.5%

Required

1. From the scorecard, what was the focus of the value-stream team for the first six months? The second six months? What are the implications of these changes?

2. Using information from the scorecard, offer an explanation for why the financial results were not as good as expected.
3. Suppose that on December 31, 2008, a potential customer offered to purchase an order of goods that would increase weekly revenues in January by $100,000 and material cost by $30,000. Using the old standard cost system, the projected conversion cost of the order would be $60,000. Would you recommend that the order be accepted or rejected? Explain.

16-17

Continuous Improvement; Balanced Scorecard; Performance Measurement
LO4

At the end of 2007, Everett Company implemented a low-cost strategy to improve its competitive position. Its objective was to become the low-cost producer in its industry and enhance its profitability. To lower costs, Everett undertook a number of lean improvement activities. Everett also adopted a Balanced Scorecard approach for its strategic performance management system. Now, after two years of operation, the president of Everett wants some assessment of the system's achievements. To help provide this assessment, the following information on one product has been gathered:

	2007	2008
Theoretical annual capacity[a]	192,000	192,000
Actual production and sales[b]	152,000	176,000
Production hours available (40 workers)	80,000	80,000
Postpurchase costs per unit	$20	$10
Scrap (pounds)	20,000	16,000
Materials used (pounds)	200,000	200,000
Actual cost per unit	$250	$200
Days of inventory	6	3
Number of defective units	9,000	4,000
Suggestions per employee	2	6
Hours of training	200	800
Selling price per unit	$300	$280
Number of new customers[c]	4,000	16,000
Market share[d]	20%	?

[a]Amount that could be produced given the available production hours.
[b]Amount that was produced given the available production hours.
[c]The increase in total sales from 2005 to 2006 all came as a result of the new customers. In 2005, the new customers were responsible for sales of 4,000 units.
[d]The total market increased by 20,000 units from 2005 to 2006.

Required

1. Compute the following measures for 2007 and 2008:
   a. Theoretical velocity and cycle time
   b. Actual velocity and cycle time
   c. Percentage change in postpurchase costs (for 2008 only)
   d. Labor productivity (output/hours)
   e. Scrap as a percentage of total materials issued
   f. Percentage change in actual product cost (for 2008 only)
   g. Percentage change in days of inventory (for 2008 only)
   h. Defective units as a percentage of total units produced
   i. New customers per unit of output
   j. Hours of training
   k. Selling price per unit (as given)
   l. Total employee suggestions
   m. Percentage of revenue from new customers
   n. Market share
   o. Percentage change in sales revenue

2. For the measures listed in Requirement 1, list likely strategic objectives and their associated measures, classified according to the four Balanced Scorecard perspectives. Evaluate the success of the strategy. Would you like any additional information to carry out this evaluation? Explain.
3. Based on the results in Requirement 2, express Everett's strategy as a series of if-then statements. What does this tell you about Balanced Scorecard measures? Identify a measure that acts both as a lead and lag measure. Now, identify a measure that acts only as a lead measure. Finally, identify a measure that acts only as a lag measure. What does this tell you?

16-18

Activity-Based Management; Non-Value-Added Costs; Target Costs
LO2, LO3

Mildred Goates, CEO of Wellington Circuits, was concerned about another price decrease for the coming year to maintain the company's annual sales volume of integrated circuit boards. The current selling price of $18 per unit was producing a $2-per-unit profit—half the customary $4-per-unit profit. To match the latest reduction by competitors would reduce the price from $18 to $14. This would put the price below the cost to produce and sell it. Determined to find a solution, Mildred had her controller gather the following information on Wellington's activities and costs:

Batch-level activities:	
Setting up equipment	$ 125,000
Materials handling	180,000
Inspecting products	122,000
Product-sustaining activities:	
Engineering support	120,000
Handling customer complaints	100,000
Filling warranties	170,000
Storing goods	80,000
Expediting goods	75,000
Unit-level activities:	
Using materials	500,000
Using power	48,000
Manual insertion labor[a]	250,000
Other direct labor	150,000
Total costs	$1,920,000[b]

[a]Diodes, resistors, and integrated circuits are inserted manually into the circuit board.
[b]This total cost produces a unit cost of $16 for last year's sales volume.

The controller expressed the belief that per-unit costs can be reduced by at least $7. Mildred was excited by this possibility, because decreasing the price to $12 would increase Wellington's market share (sales volume) for the boards by 50 percent.

Required

1. Identify as many non-value-added costs as possible. Compute the cost savings per unit that would be realized if these wasteful costs were eliminated. Was the controller correct in his preliminary cost reduction assessment? Discuss actions that the company can take to reduce or eliminate the wasteful non-value-added activities.
2. Compute the target cost required to maintain current market share, while earning a profit of $4 per unit. Now compute the target cost required to expand sales by 50 percent. How much cost reduction would be required to achieve each target?
3. Assume that further activity analysis revealed the following: switching to automated insertion would save $60,000 of engineering support and $90,000 of direct labor. Now, what is the total potential cost reduction per unit available

from activity analysis? With these additional reductions, can Wellington Circuits achieve the target cost to maintain current sales? To increase it by 50 percent?
4. Calculate income based on current sales, prices, and costs. Now, calculate the income using a $14 price and a $12 price, assuming that the maximum cost reduction possible is achieved (including Requirement 3's reduction). What price should be selected?

16-19

Target Costing; Benchmarking and Non-Value-Added Costs
LO2, LO3

EXCEL

WellCare Products manufactures a line of wheelchairs. During the past year, WellCare sold its regular model for $720. Sales volume averages 20,000 units per year. Recently, a major competitor reduced the price of its regular model to $640. WellCare's CEO was convinced that the price must be matched or sales would drop dramatically. Further research revealed that if WellCare could drop the selling price to $624 by the end of the year, the company could expand its share of the market by 20 percent. To maintain production of the product line, the current profit per unit must be maintained. The company currently produces 20,000 units per year and the CEO wants to know if the company can at least match the competitor's new price.

The plant controller and the cost accounting manager are convinced that the cost can be reduced by becoming more lean by reducing or eliminating wasteful activities. The amount of waste present in the system can be assessed by comparing the productive use of capacity (value added) with the total capacity. To help assess the waste, the actual cost of inputs, their value-added (ideal) quantity levels, and the actual quantity levels are provided (for production of 20,000 units). Assume there is no difference between actual prices of activity units and standard prices.

	SQ	AQ	Actual Cost
Materials (lb.)	380,000	400,000	$ 8,400,000
Labor (hr.)	91,200	96,000	1,200,000
Setups (hr.)	—	6,400	480,000
Material handling (moves)	—	16,000	1,120,000
Warranties (number repaired)	—	16,000	1,600,000
Total			$12,800,000

Required

1. Calculate the target cost for expanding the market share by 20 percent, assuming that the per-unit profitability is maintained as requested by the CEO.
2. Calculate the non-value-added cost per unit. Assuming that non-value-added costs can be reduced to zero, what is the per-unit cost? Can the target cost for expanding market share be achieved? What actions would you take if you were WellCare's CEO?

16-20

Life-Cycle Cost Management
LO3

EXCEL

Boyce Products manufactures products with life cycles that average three years. The first year involves product development, and the remaining two years emphasize production and sales. A budgeted life-cycle income statement developed for two proposed products follows. Each product will sell 200,000 units. The price has been set to yield a 50 percent gross margin ratio.

	Product A	Product B	Total
Sales	$4,000,000	$5,000,000	$ 9,000,000
Cost of goods sold	2,000,000	2,500,000	4,500,000
Gross margin	$2,000,000	$2,500,000	$ 4,500,000
Period expenses:			
Research and development			$(2,000,000)
Marketing			(1,150,000)
Life-cycle income			$ 1,350,000

Upon seeing the budget, Rick Moss, president of Boyce Products, called in LeeAnn Gordon, marketing manager, and Art Cummings, design engineer.

Rick: These two products are earning only a 15 percent return on sales. We need 20 percent to earn an acceptable return on our investment. Can't we raise prices?

LeeAnn: I doubt the market would bear any increase in prices. However, I will do some additional research and see what's possible. The gross profit ratio is already high. The problem appears to be with R&D. Those expenses seem higher than normal.

Art: These products are more complex than usual, and we need to have the extra resources—at least if you want to have a product that functions as we are claiming it will. Also, we are charting some new waters with the features these products are offering. Specifically, our design is intended to reduce the postpurchase costs that consumers incur, including operation, support, maintenance, and disposal. LeeAnn, if you recall, you mentioned to us a year ago that our competitors were providing products that had lower postpurchase costs. This new design is intended to make us market leaders in this area. At any rate, in the future we can probably get by on less—after we gain some experience. But it wouldn't be much less, perhaps $50,000.

Rick: That would still allow us to earn only about 15.6 percent—even after you get more proficient. Maybe we ought to stay with our more standard features.

LeeAnn: Before we abandon these new lines, perhaps we ought to look at each product individually. Maybe one could be retained. These new features will give us an edge in the market. Also, I'll bet that if he knew what was driving those costs, Art could redesign the product so that production costs could be lowered. I'm concerned that our competitors will exploit their postpurchase cost advantage. We really need to be leaders in this postpurchase area—our reputation is at stake. If we're not careful, we could begin losing market share.

Required

1. What specific improvements would you suggest to Rick to improve Boyce's life-cycle cost management system?
2. Assume that the "period" expenses are traceable to each product. Product A is responsible for 60 percent of R&D costs and 50 percent of marketing costs. Prepare a revised income statement for each product. Based on this analysis, should either product be produced?
3. Based on the revised income statements (of Requirement 2), what is the total target cost for each product? How much must production costs be reduced to make each product acceptable? Discuss how activity analysis and target costing can help achieve this outcome. Explain why this should occur now and not after the products are in production.
4. According to Art, the motivation for the new design was to reduce the postpurchase costs of the new products. Explain why whole-life cost should be the focus of life-cycle cost management.

16-21

Cycle Time; Conversion Cost per Unit; MCE
LO4

EXCEL

A manufacturing cell has the theoretical capability to produce 180,000 heaters per quarter. The conversion cost per quarter is $1,800,000. There are 60,000 production hours available within the cell per quarter.

Required

1. Compute the theoretical velocity (per hour) and the theoretical cycle time (minutes per unit produced).
2. Compute the ideal amount of conversion cost that will be assigned per heater.
3. Suppose that the actual time required to produce a heater is 30 minutes. Compute the amount of conversion cost actually assigned to each heater. Discuss how this approach to assigning conversion cost can improve delivery time.

4. Calculate MCE. How much non-value-added time is being used? How much is it costing per heater?
5. Cycle time, velocity, MCE, conversion cost per unit (theoretical conversion rate × actual conversion time), and non-value-added costs are all measures of performance for the cell process. Discuss the incentives provided by these measures.

16-22

MCE
LO2, LO4

Lemmons Company makes a product that experiences the following activities and times:

	Hours
Processing (two departments)	45.0
Inspecting	3.0
Rework	7.5
Moving (three moves)	12.0
Waiting (for the second process)	36.0
Storage (before delivery to customer)	46.5

Required

1. Compute the MCE for this product.
2. Discuss how lean improvements can help improve this efficiency measure.
3. Is this a lag or a lead measure? If lag, what would be some lead measures that would affect this measure?

16-23

Lean versus Standard-Costing-Based Measures
LO1, LO2

Continuous improvement is the governing principle of a lean accounting system. Following are several performance measures. Some of these measures would be associated with a traditional standard-costing accounting system, and some would be associated with a lean accounting system.

a. Materials price variances
b. Cycle time
c. Comparison of actual product costs with target costs
d. Materials quantity or efficiency variances
e. Comparison of actual product costs over time (trend reports)
f. Comparison of actual overhead costs, item by item, with the corresponding budgeted costs
g. Comparison of product costs with competitors' product costs
h. Percentage of on-time deliveries
i. First time through
j. Reports of value- and non-value-added costs
k. Labor efficiency variances
l. Days of inventory
m. Downtime
n. Manufacturing cycle efficiency (MCE)
o. Unused (available) capacity variance
p. Labor rate variance
q. Using a sister plant's best practices as a performance standard

Required

1. Classify each measure as lean or traditional (standard costing). If traditional, discuss the measure's limitations for a lean environment. If it is a lean measure, describe how the measure supports the objectives of lean manufacturing.
2. Classify the measures into operational (nonfinancial) and financial categories. Explain why operational measures are better for control at the shop level (production floor) than financial measures. Should any financial measures be used at the operational level?

3. Suggest some additional measures that you would like to see added to the list that would be supportive of lean objectives.

16-24

Cycle Time; Velocity; Product Costing
LO4

Silverman Company has a lean manufacturing system in place. Each manufacturing cell is dedicated to the production of a single product or major subassembly. One cell, dedicated to the production of guns, has four operations: machining, finishing, assembly, and qualifying (testing). The machining process is automated, using computers. In this process, the gun's frame, slide, and barrel are constructed. In finishing, sandblasting, buffing, and bluing are done. In assembly, the three parts of the gun are assembled along with the grip, the sight, the label, the magazine, and the clip. Finally, each firearm is tested using 20 rounds of ammunition.

For the coming year, the firearm cell has the following budgeted costs and cell time (both at theoretical capacity):

Budgeted conversion costs	$2,500,000
Budgeted raw materials	$3,000,000
Cell time	4,000 hours
Theoretical output	30,000 guns

During the year, the following actual results were obtained:

Actual conversion costs	$2,500,000
Actual materials	$2,600,000
Actual cell time	4,000 hours
Actual output	25,000 guns

Required

1. Compute the velocity (number of guns per hour) that the cell can theoretically achieve. Now compute the theoretical cycle time (number of hours or minutes per gun) that it takes to produce one gun.
2. Compute the actual velocity and the actual cycle time.
3. Compute MCE. Comment on the efficiency of the operation.
4. Compute the budgeted conversion costs per minute. Using this rate, compute the conversion costs per gun if theoretical output is achieved. Using this measure, compute the conversion costs per gun for actual output. Does this product-costing approach provide an incentive for the cell manager to reduce cycle time? Explain.

16-25

Balanced Scorecard; Non-Value-Added Activities; Strategy Translation
LO2, LO3, LO4

At the beginning of the last quarter of 2006, Microcom, Inc., a large consumer products firm, hired Leming Imai to take over one of its divisions. The division manufactured small home appliances and was struggling to survive in a very competitive market. Leming immediately requested a projected income statement for 2006. In response, the controller provided the following statement:

Sales	$25,000,000
Variable expenses	20,000,000
Contribution margin	$ 5,000,000
Fixed expenses	6,000,000
Projected loss	$ (1,000,000)

After some investigation, Leming soon realized that the products being produced had a serious problem with quality. He once again requested a special study by the controller's office to supply a report on the level of quality costs. By the middle of November, Leming received the following report from the controller:

Inspection costs, finished product	$ 400,000
Rework costs	2,000,000
Scrapped units	600,000

Warranty costs	3,000,000
Sales returns (quality-related)	1,000,000
Customer complaint department	500,000
Total estimated quality costs	$7,500,000

Leming was surprised at the level of quality costs. They represented 30 percent of sales, which was certainly excessive. He knew that to survive the division had to produce high-quality products. The number of defective units produced needed to be reduced dramatically. Thus, Leming decided to pursue a quality-driven turnaround strategy. Revenue growth and cost reduction could both be achieved if quality could be improved. By increasing revenues and decreasing costs, profitability can be increased.

After meeting with the managers of production, marketing, purchasing, and human resources, the following decisions were made, effective immediately (at the end of November 2006):

1. More will be invested in employee training. Workers will be trained to detect quality problems and empowered to make improvements. Workers will be allowed a bonus of 10 percent of any cost savings produced by their suggested improvements.
2. Two design engineers will be hired immediately, with expectations of hiring one or two more within a year. These engineers will be in charge of redesigning processes and products with the objective of improving quality. They will also be given the responsibility of working with selected suppliers to help improve the quality of their products and processes. Design engineers were considered a strategic necessity.
3. Implement a new process: evaluation and selection of suppliers. This new process has the objective of selecting a group of suppliers that are willing and capable of providing nondefective components.
4. Effective immediately, the division will begin inspecting purchased components. According to production, many of the quality problems are caused by defective components purchased from outside suppliers. Incoming inspection was viewed as a transitional activity. Once the division has developed a group of suppliers capable of delivering nondefective components, this activity will be eliminated.
5. Within three years, the goal is to produce products with a defect rate less than 0.10 percent. By reducing the defect rate to this level, marketing is confident that market share will increase by at least 50 percent (as a consequence of increased customer satisfaction). Products with better quality will help establish an improved product image and reputation, allowing the division to capture new customers and increase market share.
6. Accounting will be given the charge to install a quality information reporting system. Daily reports on operational quality data (e.g., percentage of defective units), weekly updates of trend graphs (posted throughout the division), and quarterly cost reports are the types of information required.
7. To help direct the improvements in quality activities, an aggressive continuous improvement program will be implemented. For example, for the year 2007, rework costs have a targeted future state value of 6 percent of the selling price per unit, a 25 percent reduction from the current state cost.

To ensure that the quality improvements were directed and translated into concrete financial outcomes, Leming also began to implement a Balanced Scorecard for the division. By the end of 2007, progress was being made. Sales had increased to $26,000,000, and improvements were meeting or beating expectations. For example, rework costs had dropped to $1,500,000.

At the end of 2008, two years after the turnaround quality strategy was implemented, Leming received the following quality cost report:

Quality training	$ 500,000
Supplier evaluation	230,000
Incoming inspection costs	400,000
Inspection costs, finished product	300,000
Rework costs	1,000,000
Scrapped units	200,000
Warranty costs	750,000
Sales returns (quality-related)	435,000
Customer complaint department	325,000
Total estimated quality costs	$4,140,000

Leming also received an income statement for 2008:

Sales	$30,000,000
Variable expenses	22,000,000
Contribution margin	$ 8,000,000
Fixed expenses	5,800,000
Income	$ 2,200,000

Leming was pleased with the outcomes. Revenues had grown, and costs had been reduced by at least as much as he had projected for the two-year period. Growth next year should be even greater as he was beginning to observe a favorable effect from the higher-quality products. Also, further quality cost reductions should materialize as incoming inspections were showing much higher-quality purchased components.

Required

1. Identify the strategic objectives classified by Balanced Scorecard perspectives. Next, suggest measures for each objective. Classify the measures as lead or lag measures.
2. Using the results from Requirement 1, describe Leming's strategy using a series of if-then statements. Next, prepare a visual diagram of the strategy similar to the one shown in Exhibit 16-13 (although more complex).
3. Explain how you would evaluate the success of the quality-driven turnaround strategy. What additional information would you like to have for this evaluation?
4. Explain why Leming felt that the Balanced Scorecard would increase the likelihood that the turnaround strategy would actually produce good financial outcomes.
5. The targeted future state for rework was 6 percent of sales for 2007. Was the target met? Describe the role for continuous improvement in Leming's strategy.
6. Of the quality activities listed in the 2008 report, which ones are non-value-added? By eliminating all non-value-added activities, how much further cost reduction is possible?

Managerial Decision Case

16-26

Ethical Considerations
LO1

It has been argued that ethical leadership is manifested by the long-run sustainable success of an organization.[1] According to this argument it is the ethical responsibility of an ethical leader to undertake actions that will provide sufficient profits and strength so that a company can weather difficult times when they come. Long-

1 Laura Haughey, "Five Standards of Excellence Practiced by Ethical Leaders," appearing in Marlene, Carosoli, *The Business Ethics Activity Book: 50 Exercises for Promoting Integrity at Work*, AMACOM Books, New York, NY and as an online article at http://www.workforce.com/section/09/article/23/55/60.html; accessed May 14, 2006.

range sustainability is provided by leaders who manifest five ethical leadership qualities: ethical communication, ethical quality, ethical collaboration, ethical succession planning, and ethical tenure.

Ethical communication means that leaders communicate information accurately and truthfully. Open communication is vital for long-run sustainability. Ethical quality has to do with producing quality products, quality delivery of those products, and quality customer service. Cutting waste is an essential element of this component of ethical leadership. Ethical collaboration means that ethical leaders surround themselves with sound advisors who can help identify best practices, solve problems, and resolve difficult issues that may surface. Ethical succession planning is the art of fostering and developing leadership talent within the organization so that others are available to take over the organization and run it well. Ethical tenure has to do with how long a leader should lead. Essentially, leaders should lead as long as they wish provided they are trustworthy. The goal should be serving and building the organization and not themselves.

Required

1. Long-run sustainability and ethical quality are directly associated with lean manufacturing. Do you think that it is unethical for management not to pursue lean manufacturing?
2. Evaluate each of the five qualities of ethical leadership using the standards of ethical conduct for management accountants (see Chapter 1). Identify the standards that you feel are most relevant for each leadership quality.
3. Are there any other ethical qualities that you might add to the five already identified? You may also wish to elaborate on any of the five, adding to their definition.

Research Assignment

16-27

Cybercase
LO4

The Government Performance and Results Act of 1993 requires all federal agencies to establish strategic plans and develop methods for measuring the performance of the strategic initiatives. In other words, federal agencies must implement a strategic-based responsibility accounting system. One possibility that is being explored for satisfying this mandate is the use of the Balanced Scorecard. This strategic management approach has been successfully used in the private sector. However, in governmental settings, outcomes are based on mission success rather than financial success. This fundamental difference creates a number of interesting questions:

- Can the Balanced Scorecard be adapted to fit a governmental setting?
- If so, how is it adapted (i.e., what are the changes)?
- Are there any successful applications of the Balanced Scorecard in state, local, or federal government agencies?
- What are examples of core measures? Of lead indicators?
- What are the desired characteristics of measures in the government sector?
- What are the limitations or weaknesses of this approach for this setting?

Required

Search the Internet to obtain information that will allow you to answer the above questions. You might start with the Balanced Scorecard Institute, whose website is available in the chapter web links at www.thomsonedu.com/accounting/hansen. The Balanced Scorecard Institute is a nonprofit source of information about applications of the Balanced Scorecard in government. Its mission is to serve as a web clearinghouse for government managers to exchange information, ideas, and lessons learned in building strategic management systems using the Balanced Scorecard approach.

chapter 17

Environmental Cost Management

learning objectives

After studying this chapter, you should be able to:

1. Discuss the importance of measuring environmental costs.
2. Explain how environmental costs are assigned to products and processes.
3. Describe the life-cycle cost assessment model.
4. Compare and contrast activity- and strategic-based environmental control.

Scenario

Robert Artavia, president of Thamus, Inc., had just received the results of an environmental study. The study was concerned with the installation of an effluent treatment system.[1] Thamus's largest plant was located near a river. The plant was dumping liquid residues into the river, and the amount being dumped was exceeding the levels permitted by law. These excessive levels were degrading the quality of the river's water to the point that, on occasion, fish had been killed. The effect on the fish was troublesome, but even more so was the fact that the river was an important resource for a large city. It was the source of drinking water for over a million people.

The results of the study were somewhat discouraging. While the proposed treatment system solved the effluent problem, it was an extremely expensive solution. The benefits were less than the costs, measured in current dollars. Upon further investigation, Robert discovered that the proposed solution was the cheapest of the alternatives that could be found. He also discovered that the costs and benefits were narrowly defined. The fines avoided and the costs of building and operating the system were the major inputs. Possible cleanup costs and loss of revenues because of a negative public reaction were not included because they were allegedly too difficult to estimate. Moreover, the adverse health effects were not included in the analysis.

After some thought, Robert wrote a memo to his environmental manager, chief engineer, and controller. In the memo were some direct and penetrating questions concerning Thamus and its environmental responsibilities:

- What adjustments would be needed to estimate cleanup costs and the costs associated with adverse health effects?
- Should these costs be estimated by a socially responsible firm?
- Can we gain any benefits (e.g., improved image and increased sales) by factoring these costs into our decision and then advertising the societal benefits?
- What processes and products are the sources of the contaminating effluents?
- How much of the environmental cost is traceable to each of our products?
- How much of the pollution cost is attributable to each process?
- Would eliminating a product from our product mix solve most of the problem? (There would then be no need to invest in the expensive treatment system.)
- What needs to be done to have environmental cost information integrated into our accounting system?

Questions to Think About

1. What are environmental costs?
2. Are environmental costs significant enough to track and report to management?
3. Will improving environmental performance increase or decrease total environmental costs?
4. Should environmental costs be assigned to products and processes as a separate item?
5. What is the best way to control environmental costs?
6. Should companies be concerned about environmental costs that they cause but for which they do not have financial responsibility?

1 Effluents are flows of liquid residues.

Measuring Environmental Costs

Objective 1

Discuss the importance of measuring environmental costs.

As the opening scenario illustrates, environmental performance can have a significant effect on a firm's financial position. It also reveals a need for sound environmental cost information. In reality, for many organizations, management of environmental costs is becoming a matter of high priority and intense interest. Several reasons can be offered for this increased interest, but two in particular stand out. First, in many countries, environmental regulations have increased significantly, and even more stringent regulations are expected. Often, the regulatory laws carry enormous fines or penalties, creating strong incentives for compliance. Furthermore, the costs for compliance can be significant. Thus, selecting the least costly method of compliance becomes a major objective. To satisfy this objective, compliance costs must be measured and their fundamental causes identified. Second, successful treatment of environmental concerns is becoming a significant competitive issue. Corporations are discovering that meeting sound business objectives and resolving environmental concerns are not mutually exclusive. To understand this critical observation, it is important to examine a concept known as *ecoefficiency.*

The Benefits of Ecoefficiency

Ecoefficiency essentially maintains that organizations can produce more useful goods and services while *simultaneously* reducing negative environmental impacts, resource consumption, and costs. This concept conveys at least three important messages. First, improving ecological and economic performance can and should be complementary. Second, improving environmental performance should no longer be viewed as a matter of charity and goodwill but rather as a matter of competitiveness. Third,

Managers Decide

Sustainable Growth

Interface, Inc., a producer of synthetic carpet and fabric, is committed to achieving sustainable development. Its goal is to become the first fully sustainable industrial enterprise in the world. Interface views sustainable development as a dynamic process that requires "thinking about what you do before you do it." Interface has laid out a path to sustainability that has seven fronts: 1. eliminating waste; 2. having only benign emissions (eliminating toxic substances from products, vehicles, and facilities); 3. closing the loop (redesigning processes and products so that recovered and bio-based materials can be used); 4. using resource-efficient transportation; 6. sensitizing stakeholders; and 7. redesigning commerce (creating a new business model that supports sustainability-based commerce). For example, between 1995 and 2005, Interface's waste-eliminating activities saved the company a cumulative $300 million in costs. Consider a second example. Interface's Guilford of Maine division makes fabric used to upholster cubicles. Guilford entered into an agreement to buy recycled polyester fiber that was chemically identical to virgin fiber from a soda-bottle recycling plant. Now, all the cubicle fabric is made from old soda bottles. ■

Sources: Interface, "Interface Commitments," http://www.interfacesustainability.com/commit.html, accessed May 9, 2006; Charles Fishman, "Sustainable Growth: Interface, Inc.," *Fast Company* (April 1998), available via the chapter web links at the Interactive Study Center on http://www.thomsonedu.com/accounting/hansen.

ecoefficiency is complementary to and supportive of *sustainable development.* **Sustainable development** is defined as development that meets the needs of the present without compromising the ability of future generations to meet their own needs. Although absolute sustainability may not be attainable, progress toward its achievement certainly seems to have some merit.

Ecoefficiency implies that increased efficiency comes from improving environmental performance. Incentives and causes for this increased efficiency have a number of sources. First, customers are demanding cleaner products—products that are produced without degrading the environment and whose use and disposal are environmentally friendly. Second, employees prefer to work for environmentally responsible firms, resulting in greater productivity (i.e., clean and safe working conditions attract good workers and stimulate productivity). Third, environmentally responsible firms tend to capture external benefits such as a lower cost of capital and lower insurance rates. Fourth, better environmental performance can produce significant social benefits such as benefits to human health. This, in turn, improves the company image and enhances the ability to sell its products and services. Fifth, focusing on improving environmental performance awakens within managers a need to innovate and search for new opportunities. This can lead to new markets for outputs that were formerly classified as useless residues (referred to as revalorizing by-products). Alternatively, it may mean the development of ecoefficient processes or the creation of new and more environmentally friendly products. Sixth, reducing environmental costs can maintain or create a competitive advantage. These causes and incentives for ecoefficiency are summarized in Exhibit 17-1.

The cost reduction and competitiveness incentive is particularly important. Environmental costs can be a significant percentage of total operating costs, and interestingly, many of these costs can be reduced or eliminated through effective management. Knowledge of environmental costs and their causes may lead to a redesign of a process that, as a consequence, reduces the materials used and the pollutants emitted to the environment (an interaction between the innovation and cost reduction

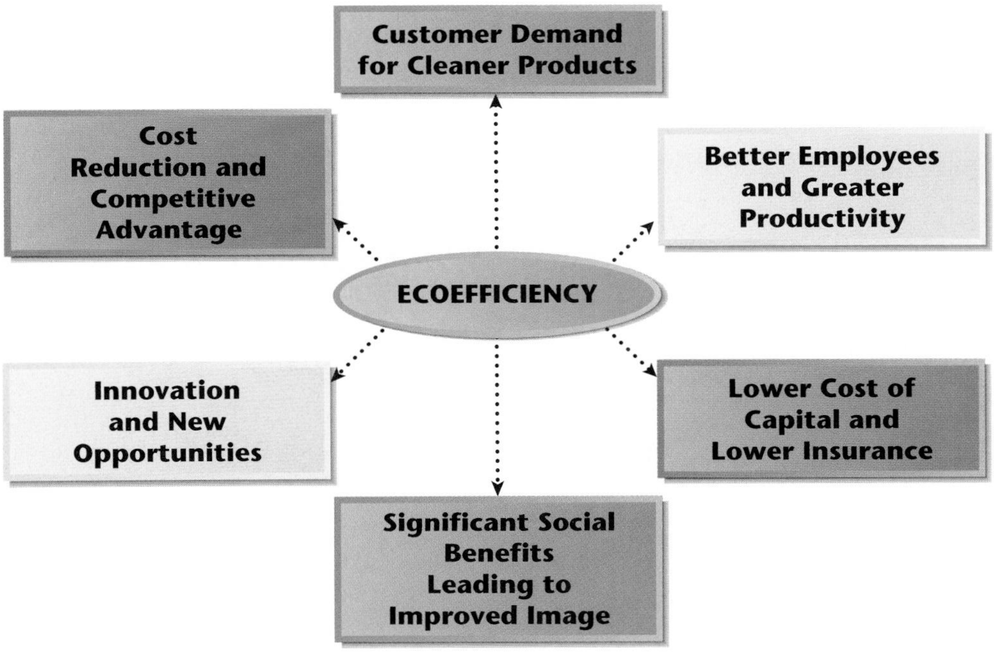

Exhibit 17-1 Causes of and Incentives for Ecoefficiency

incentives). Thus, current and future environmental costs are reduced, and the firm becomes more competitive. For example, between 1998 and 2004, **Baxter International, Inc.**, a producer of medical products, reduced toxic wastes emitted to air, water, and soil and increased recycling activity; as a consequence, the company reported cumulative environmental savings for the seven-year period of $81.9 million.[2]

Effective cost management leading to cost reduction like that described for Baxter means that environmental cost information must be provided to management. To provide this financial information, it is necessary to define, measure, classify, and assign environmental costs to processes, products, and other cost objects of interest. Environmental costs should be reported as a separate classification so managers can assess their impact on firm profitability. Furthermore, assigning environmental costs to products and processes reveals the sources of these costs and helps identify their fundamental causes so that they can be controlled.

Environmental Quality Cost Model

Before environmental cost information can be provided to management, environmental costs must be defined. Various possibilities exist; however, an appealing approach is to adopt a definition consistent with a total environmental quality model. In the total environmental quality model, the ideal state is that of zero damage to the environment (analogous to the zero-defects state of total quality management). Damage is defined as direct degradation of the environment, such as the emission of solid, liquid, or gaseous residues into the environment (e.g., water contamination and air pollution), or indirect degradation such as *unnecessary* usage of materials and energy.

Accordingly, environmental costs can be referred to as *environmental quality costs.* In a similar sense to quality costs, **environmental costs** are costs that are incurred because poor environmental quality exists or because poor environmental quality *may* exist. Thus, environmental costs are associated with the creation, detection, remediation, and prevention of environmental degradation. With this definition, environmental costs can be classified into four categories: prevention costs, detection costs, internal failure costs, and external failure costs. External failure costs, in turn, can be subdivided into realized and unrealized categories.

Environmental prevention costs are the costs of activities carried out to prevent the production of contaminants and/or waste that could cause damage to the environment. Examples of prevention activities include the following: evaluating and

Careful planning is required to prevent production of contaminants.

© Digital Vision

2 Baxter 2004 Environmental Financial Statement, available at http://www.baxter.com/about_baxter/sustainability/our_environment/performance_at_a_glance/E16_Environmental_Financial_Statement.pdf.

selecting suppliers, evaluating and selecting equipment to control pollution, designing processes and products to reduce or eliminate contaminants, training employees, studying environmental impacts, auditing environmental risks, undertaking environmental research, developing environmental management systems, recycling products, and obtaining ISO 14001 certification.[3]

Environmental detection costs are the costs of activities executed to determine if products, processes, and other activities within the firm are in compliance with appropriate environmental standards. The environmental standards and procedures that a firm seeks to follow are defined in three ways: (1) regulatory laws of governments, (2) voluntary standards (ISO 14001) developed by the International Standards Organization, and (3) environmental policies developed by management. Examples of detection activities are auditing environmental activities, inspecting products and processes (for environmental compliance), developing environmental performance measures, carrying out contamination tests, verifying supplier environmental performance, and measuring levels of contamination.

Environmental internal failure costs are costs of activities performed because contaminants and waste have been produced but not discharged into the environment. Thus, internal failure costs are incurred to eliminate and manage contaminants or waste once produced. Internal failure activities have one of two goals: (1) to ensure that the contaminants and waste produced are not released to the environment or (2) to reduce the level of contaminants released to an amount that complies with environmental standards. Examples of internal failure activities include operating equipment to minimize or eliminate pollution, treating and disposing of toxic materials, maintaining pollution equipment, licensing facilities for producing contaminants, and recycling scrap.

Environmental external failure costs are the costs of activities performed *after* discharging contaminants and waste into the environment. **Realized external failure costs** are those incurred and paid for by the firm. **Unrealized external failure costs (societal costs)** are caused by the firm but are incurred and paid for by parties outside the firm. Societal costs can be further classified as (1) those resulting from environmental degradation and (2) those associated with an adverse impact on the property or welfare of individuals. In either case, the costs are borne by others and not by the firm, even though they are caused by the firm. Of the four environmental cost categories, the external failure category is the most devastating. For example, a report by the Environmental Protection Agency (EPA) indicates that private cleanup costs, under the Comprehensive Environmental Response, Compensation, and Liability Act of 1980, have run into the tens of billions of dollars and are projected to eventually amount to several hundred billion dollars. Furthermore, cleanup costs that must be borne by taxpayers will also run in the hundreds of billions of dollars. Cleanup costs of defense wastes alone are estimated at $500 billion.[4] Examples of realized external failure activities are cleaning up a polluted lake, cleaning up oil spills, cleaning up contaminated soil, using materials and energy inefficiently, settling personal injury claims from environmentally unsound practices, settling property damage claims, restoring land to its natural state, and losing sales from a bad environmental reputation. Examples of societal costs include receiving medical care because of polluted air (individual welfare), losing a lake for recreational use because of contamination (degradation), losing employment because of contamination (individual welfare), and damaging ecosystems from solid waste disposal (degradation).

3 ISO 14001 certification is obtained when an organization installs an environmental management system that satisfies specific, privately set international standards. These standards are concerned with environmental *management* procedures and do not directly indicate acceptable levels of environmental performance. The certification, therefore, functions primarily as a signal that a firm is interested and willing to improve its environmental performance.

4 "The United States Experience with Economic Incentives for Protecting the Environment," EPA-240-R-01-001, January 2001. The report is available via the chapter web links at the Interactive Study Center on http://www.thomsonedu.com/accounting/hansen. The cost estimates reported above are in Section 3.32 of the report.

Exhibit 17-2 summarizes the four environmental cost categories and lists specific activities for each category. Within the external failure cost category, societal costs are labeled with an "S." The costs for which the firm is financially responsible are called **private costs**. All costs without the "S" label are private costs.

Environmental Cost Report

Environmental cost reporting is essential if an organization is serious about improving its environmental performance and controlling environmental costs. A good first step is a report that details the environmental costs by category. One of the results of Robert Artavia's memo with its list of questions was the establishment of an environmental cost reporting system for Thamus. Thamus discovered that reporting environmental costs by category revealed two important outcomes: (1) the impact of environmental costs on firm profitability and (2) the relative amounts expended in each category. Exhibit 17-3 provides an example of a simple environmental cost report that used by Thamus (now in its third year of reporting).

Thamus's report in Exhibit 17-3 highlights the importance of environmental costs by expressing them as a percentage of total operating costs. In this report, environmental costs are 15 percent of total operating costs, seemingly a significant amount. From a practical point of view, environmental costs will receive managerial attention only if they represent a significant amount. Although environmental managerial cost reporting is in its infancy, some evidence exists concerning this issue. After six months of investigation, **Amoco** concluded that environmental costs at its Yorktown refinery were at least 22 percent of operating costs.[5] Other evidence from

Prevention Activities Evaluating and selecting suppliers Evaluating and selecting pollution control equipment Designing processes Designing products Carrying out environmental studies Auditing environmental risks Developing environmental management systems Recycling products Obtaining ISO 14001 certification **Detection Activities** Auditing environmental activities Inspecting products and processes Developing environmental performance measures Testing for contamination Verifying supplier environmental performance Measuring contamination levels	**Internal Failure Activities** Operating pollution control equipment Treating and disposing of toxic waste Maintaining pollution equipment Licensing facilities for producing contaminants Recycling scrap **External Failure Activities** Cleaning up a polluted lake Cleaning up oil spills Cleaning up contaminated soil Settling personal injury claims (environmentally related) Restoring land to natural state Losing sales due to poor environmental reputation Using materials and energy inefficiently Receiving medical care due to polluted air (S) Losing employment because of contamination (S) Losing a lake for recreational use (S) Damaging ecosystems from solid waste disposal (S)

Exhibit 17-2 Classification of Environmental Costs by Activity

5 Daniel Baker, "Environmental Accounting's Conflicts and Dilemmas," *Management Accounting* (October 1996): pp. 46–48.

Thamus Corporation Environmental Cost Report For the Year Ended December 31, 2008			
		Environmental Costs	Percentage of Operating Costs
Prevention costs			
Training employees	$ 600,000		
Designing products	1,800,000		
Selecting equipment	400,000	$ 2,800,000	1.40%
Detection costs			
Inspecting processes	$2,400,000		
Developing measures	800,000	3,200,000	1.60
Internal failure costs			
Operating pollution equipment	$4,000,000		
Maintaining pollution equipment	2,000,000	6,000,000	3.00
External failure costs			
Cleaning up lake	$9,000,000		
Restoring land	5,000,000		
Incurring property damage claim	4,000,000	18,000,000	9.00
Totals		$30,000,000	15.00%

Exhibit 17-3 Environmental Cost Report

case studies by the **World Resources Institute** suggests that environmental costs are 20 percent or more of a firm's total operating costs.[6] It appears that environmental costs can significantly affect a firm's profitability.

The cost report also provides information relating to the relative distribution of the environmental costs. Of the total environmental costs, only 20 percent are from the prevention and detection categories. Thus, 80 percent of the environmental costs are failure costs—costs that exist because of poor environmental performance.

Reducing Environmental Costs

Fortunately, evidence exists that environmental failure costs can be reduced by investing more in prevention and detection activities. **Ford Motor Company**, for example, has made a commitment to improve its environmental performance. As part of this overall commitment, Ford has resolved to obtain ISO 14001 certification in all of its plants throughout the world. Some of its plants in Germany and England have already received this certification. In these certified plants, Ford has saved hundreds of thousands of dollars in environmental costs.[7] In the organic chemical industrial sector, studies concerned with efforts to prevent toxic waste have shown that for every dollar spent on prevention activities, about $3.49 was saved from environmental failure activities (per year).[8] For a typical project, savings were $351,000 per year, and an average of 1.6 million pounds of chemical were eliminated.[9]

It is possible that the environmental cost reduction model will behave in a very similar way to the total quality cost model. Perhaps the lowest environmental costs

6 Daryl Ditz, Janet Ranganathan, and R. Daryl Banks, *Green Ledgers: Case Studies in Corporate Environmental Accounting,* World Resources Institute (May 1995).
7 Michael Prince, "ISO Now Offering Voluntary Standards," *Business Insurance* (11 November 1996): pp. 21–23.
8 Michael E. Porter and Claus van der Linde, "Green and Competitive: Ending the Stalemate," *Harvard Business Review* (September–October 1995): pp. 120–134.
9 See also *Cutting Chemical Waste* (1985) and *Environmental Dividends: Cutting More Chemical Waste* (1991), INFORM, New York, New York. (INFORM is a not-for-profit group that conducted a study of 29 chemical companies.)

Preventing contamination is often the cheapest alternative for a company.

© Getty Images/PhotoDisc

are attainable at the *zero-damage point,* much like the zero-defects point of the total quality cost model. This point of view is certainly compatible with the notion of ecoefficiency. The idea underlying the zero-damage view is that *prevention is cheaper than the cure.* At **Phillips Petroleum**, this concept is referred to as the *rule of 1-10-100.*[10] This rule states that if a problem is solved in its own area of work, it costs $1; if the problem is solved outside the originating area but within the company, it costs $10; and if the problem is solved outside the company, it costs $100. The rule suggests that zero damage is the lowest cost point for environmental costs.

In reality, it may be that zero degradation is the low cost point for many types of contaminating activities. For example, **Numar**, a Costa Rican producer of margarines and cooking oils, managed to reduce its emission of contaminated water effluents to zero.[11] The actions taken by Numar were in response to a new environmental law that prohibited the dumping of these effluents into rivers and streams. Numar invested in a new system that treated the water and allowed it to recover usable materials and, at the same time, reuse the treated water. The annual costs of the investment, including depreciation, electricity, maintenance, and purchase of bacteria, were $116,350. Three benefits were observed. First, the amount of water required on a daily basis was reduced from 950 cubic meters to 200 cubic meters (because of the ability to recycle water). This produced savings of $391,500 per year. Second, the materials recovered from the treated water were worth $30,000 per year

Managers Decide

Reduction: A Key to Improving Environmental Performance

Interface's Guilford Maine facility found a way to achieve a significant financial return without a significant financial investment. The Guilford facility uses water in their dyeing process; consequently, considerable effort has been spent on recovering heat and recycling water. In the 1980s, a heat and water recovery system was installed. In December 2000, management decided to put effort into reducing the need for water instead of simply reclaiming energy from the volume already in use. The first effort reduced the flow of water from 60 gallons per minute (gpm) to 40 gpm. The next effort entailed installing a small brass nozzle, costing $8.50, that achieved a desired flow pattern. The nozzle reduced the flow to 21 gpm, saving over two million gallons per year (cost savings of $10,000). Interface notes that the moral of the story is to investigate "reducing" before reclaiming/recycling. ■

Source: http//www.interfacesustainability.com/dye.html as of May 9, 2006.

10 Blair W. Felmate, "Making Sustainable Development a Corporate Reality," *CMA Magazine* (March 1997): pp. 9–16.

11 Arnoldo Rodriguez, "Grupo Numar," *INCAE* (June 1997).

(cost only). Third, the company avoided stiff environmental fines and possible closure costs. Thus, the zero-degradation state for solid residues was achieved at a cost of $116,350 per year, but *benefits* of at least $421,500 were produced. The approach taken to obtain zero emissions actually increased the profitability of the firm! It is curious that a legal incentive was required for the company to seek the more efficient approach. Part of the reason can be attributed to the common view that improving environmental performance is a charitable act. It is also true that most firms do not have the necessary environmental cost information. Knowing environmental costs and how they relate to products, for example, can be a strong incentive for innovating and increasing efficiency.

An Environmental Financial Report

Ecoefficiency suggests a possible modification to environmental cost reporting. Specifically, in addition to reporting environmental costs, why not report *environmental benefits*? In a given period, there are three types of benefits: income, current savings, and cost avoidance (ongoing savings). Income refers to revenues that flow into the organization due to environmental actions such as recycling paper, finding new applications for nonhazardous waste (e.g., using wood scraps to make wood chess pieces and game boards), and increased sales due to an enhanced environmental image. Cost avoidance refers to ongoing savings produced in prior years. Current savings refer to reductions in environmental costs achieved in the current year. By comparing benefits produced with environmental costs incurred in a given period, a type of environmental financial statement is produced. Managers can use this statement to assess progress (benefits produced) and potential for progress (environmental costs). The environmental financial statement could also form part of an environmental progress report that is provided to shareholders on an annual basis. Exhibit 17-4 provides an example of an environmental financial statement. For simplicity, details of the environmental cost categories are not shown. The cost reductions shown are the sum of current savings plus avoidance of environmental costs due to prior-period environmental actions. The benefits reported reveal good progress, but the costs are still nearly three times as much as benefits, indicating that more improvements are needed.

Thamus Corporation
Environmental Financial Statement
For the Year Ended December 31, 2008

Environmental benefits	
Cost reductions, contaminants	$ 3,000,000
Cost reductions, hazardous waste disposal	4,000,000
Recycling income	2,000,000
Energy conservation cost savings	1,000,000
Packaging cost reductions	1,500,000
Total environmental benefits	$ 11,500,000
Environmental costs	
Prevention costs	$ 2,800,000
Detection costs	3,200,000
Internal failure costs	6,000,000
External failure costs	18,000,000
Total environmental costs	$30,000,000

Exhibit 17-4 Environmental Financial Statement

Assigning Environmental Costs

Objective 2

Explain how environmental costs are assigned to products and processes.

Both products and processes are sources of environmental costs. Processes that *produce* products can create solid, liquid, and gaseous residues that are subsequently introduced into the environment. These residues have the potential of degrading the environment. Residues, then, are the causes of both internal and external environmental failure costs (e.g., investing in equipment to prevent the introduction of the residues into the environment and cleaning up residues after they are allowed into the environment). Production processes are not the only source of environmental costs. Packaging is also a source of environmental costs. For example, in the United States, 30 percent of all municipal solid waste is packaging material.[12]

Products themselves can be the source of environmental costs. After a product is sold, its use and disposal by the customer can produce environmental degradation. These are examples of *environmental postpurchase costs.* Most of the time, environmental postpurchase costs are borne by society and not by the company and, thus, are societal costs. On occasion, however, environmental postpurchase costs are converted into realized external costs.

Environmental Product Costs

The environmental costs of processes that produce, market, and deliver products and the environmental postpurchase costs caused by the use and disposal of the products are examples of *environmental product costs.* **Full environmental costing** is the assignment of all environmental costs, both private and societal, to products. **Full private costing** is the assignment of only private costs to individual products. Private costing, then, would assign the environmental costs to products caused by the internal processes of the organization. Private costing is probably a good starting point for many firms. Private costs can be assigned using data created *inside* the firm. Full costs require gathering of data that are produced outside the firm from third parties. As the firm gains experience with environmental costing, it may be well advised to expand product cost assignments and implement an approach called *life-cycle cost assessment,* discussed later in the chapter.

Assigning environmental costs to products can produce valuable managerial information. For example, it may reveal that a particular product is responsible for much more toxic waste than other products. This information may lead to a more efficient and environmentally friendly alternative design for the product or its associated processes. It could also reveal that with the environmental costs correctly assigned, the product is not profitable. This could mean something as simple as dropping the product to achieve significant improvement in environmental performance and economic efficiency. Many opportunities for improvement may exist, but knowledge of the environmental product costs is the key. Moreover, it is critical that environmental costs be assigned accurately.

Functional-Based Environmental Cost Assignments

In most cost accounting systems, environmental costs are hidden within overhead. Using the environmental cost definitions and classification framework just developed, environmental costs must first be separated into an environmental cost pool. Once separated into their own pool, functional-based costing would assign these costs to individual products using unit-level drivers such as direct labor hours and machine hours. This approach may work well for a homogeneous product setting; however, Thamus, a multiple-product firm with product diversity, discovered that a functional-based assignment can produce cost distortions.

12 T. E. Graedel and B. R. Allenby, *Industrial Ecology* (Englewood Cliffs, New Jersey: Prentice Hall, 1995), p. 243.

Among the products that Thamus produces are two types of glass: Type A and Type B. There are 50,000 sheets of each type produced, and each sheet of glass requires *one-half* of a machine hour. Thamus initially used machine hours to assign environmental costs to products. In producing glass products, cadmium emissions occur. To produce cadmium emissions, a special government permit must be purchased that costs $300,000. The permit must be renewed every three years. Thus, the permit cost is $100,000 per year. The permit authorizes a certain level of cadmium emissions. If emissions exceed the allowed level, a fine is imposed. There is one unannounced inspection each quarter. The firm averages $50,000 per year in fines. Thus, the annual cost of cadmium emissions is $150,000 ($100,000 + $50,000). The environmental cost per machine hour is $3 ($150,000/50,000 machine hours). Use of this rate produces an environmental cost per unit of $1.50 for each product ($3 × 1/2 machine hour).

The accuracy of the assignment is critical. For example, what if Type A glass is responsible for all or most of the cadmium emissions? If Type A is responsible for all the emissions, then the environmental cost should be $3 per unit for Type A and $0 per unit for Type B. In this case, Type A was undercosted, and Type B was overcosted. This possibility is not imaginary. Something very similar happened with **Spectrum Glass**, a producer of specialty glass. It discovered that only one product, "Ruby Red," was responsible for all of its cadmium emissions.[13] Yet, its cost accounting system was assigning a portion of this cost to every product produced. Upon reading of the Spectrum experience, Thamus resolved to improve its environmental cost system by using activity-based costing.

Activity-Based Environmental Cost Assignments

The emergence of activity-based costing facilitates environmental costing. Tracing the environmental costs to the products responsible for those costs is a fundamental requirement of a sound environmental accounting system. Assigning costs using causal relationships is needed. This approach, of course, is exactly what ABC does.

Thamus's Cadmium Example Revisited Emitting cadmium is the environmental activity (in this case, an external failure activity). The cost of the activity is the cost of the fine and the permit fees: $150,000. Assume now that the quantity of cadmium emissions is the activity output measure, and let that quantity be 20,000 units. The activity rate is $7.50 per unit ($150,000/20,000 units). If Type A produces 20,000 units of emissions and Type B produces 0 units, then the cost assignments are as they should be: $150,000 to Type A ($7.50 × 20,000) and $0 to Type B. This ABC assignment produces a unit environmental cost of $3 for Type A ($150,000/50,000) and $0 for Type B.

All costs assigned in this example are private costs. Societal costs are also possible. If they exist, and if they can be estimated, then a fuller costing approach can be used. For example, suppose that cadmium emissions cause $150,000 per year in medical expenses for those who live in the community affected by the emissions. In this case, the cost per unit for Type A would double.

Example with Multiple Activities The cadmium example had only one activity. In reality, there will be multiple environmental activities. Each activity will be assigned costs, and activity rates will be computed. These rates are then used to assign environmental costs to products based on usage of the activity. Thamus, for example, produces two types of industrial cleaners in its Orlando plant. Exhibit 17-5 shows the assignment of environmental costs to these two products when there is a variety of activities. This cost assignment allows managers to see the relative environmental

13 Daniel Baker, "Environmental Accounting's Conflicts and Dilemmas," *Management Accounting* (October 1996): pp. 46–48.

economic impact of the two products, and to the extent that environmental costs reflect environmental damage, the unit environmental cost can also act as an index or measure of product cleanliness. The "dirtier" products can then be the focus of efforts to improve environmental performance and economic efficiency. Exhibit 17-5 reveals, for example, that Cleanser B has more environmental problems than Cleanser A. Cleanser B's environmental costs total $380,000 ($3.80 × 100,000) and are 19 percent of the total manufacturing costs. Furthermore, its environmental failure costs are $350,000, representing 92.1 percent of the total environmental costs. Cleanser A portrays a much better picture. Its environmental costs total $78,000, 8 percent of the total manufacturing costs, and the failure costs are 29.5 percent of the total environmental costs. It is evident that Cleanser B offers the most environmental and economic potential for improvement.

Life-Cycle Cost Assessment

Objective 3

Describe the life-cycle cost assessment model.

The environmental product costs may reveal a need to improve a company's *product stewardship*. **Product stewardship** is the practice of designing, manufacturing, maintaining, and recycling products to minimize adverse environmental impacts. *Life-cycle assessment* is the means for improving product stewardship. **Life-cycle assessment** identifies the environmental consequences of a product through its entire life cycle and then searches for opportunities to obtain environmental improvements. **Life-cycle cost assessment** assigns costs and benefits to the environmental consequences and improvements.

Product Life Cycle

The EPA has identified four stages in the life cycle of a product: resource extraction, product manufacture, product use, and recycling and disposal.[14] Another possible stage, not explicitly considered by the EPA guidelines, is that of product packaging. Product life cycle, including packaging, is illustrated in Exhibit 17-6. As shown, the different life-cycle stages can be under the control of someone other than the producer of the product. Note that the source of materials for the product can come through extraction (raw materials) or from recycling. If all or some of the product's components cannot be recycled, then disposal is required, and waste management becomes an issue.

Activities	Cleanser A	Cleanser B
Evaluate and select suppliers	$ 0.20	$ 0.05
Design processes (to reduce pollution)	0.10	0.10
Inspect processes (for pollution problems)	0.25	0.15
Capture and treat chlorofluorocarbons	0.05	1.00
Maintain environmental equipment	0.00	0.50
Toxic waste disposal	0.10	1.75
Excessive materials usage	0.08	0.25
Environmental cost per unit	$ 0.78	$ 3.80
Other manufacturing costs (nonenvironmental)	9.02	16.20
Unit cost	$ 9.80	$ 20.00
Units produced	100,000	$100,000

Exhibit 17-5 ABC Environmental Costing—Thamus: Orlando Plant

14 "Life-Cycle Assessment: Inventory Guidelines and Principles," EPA-600-R-92-245 (February 1993).

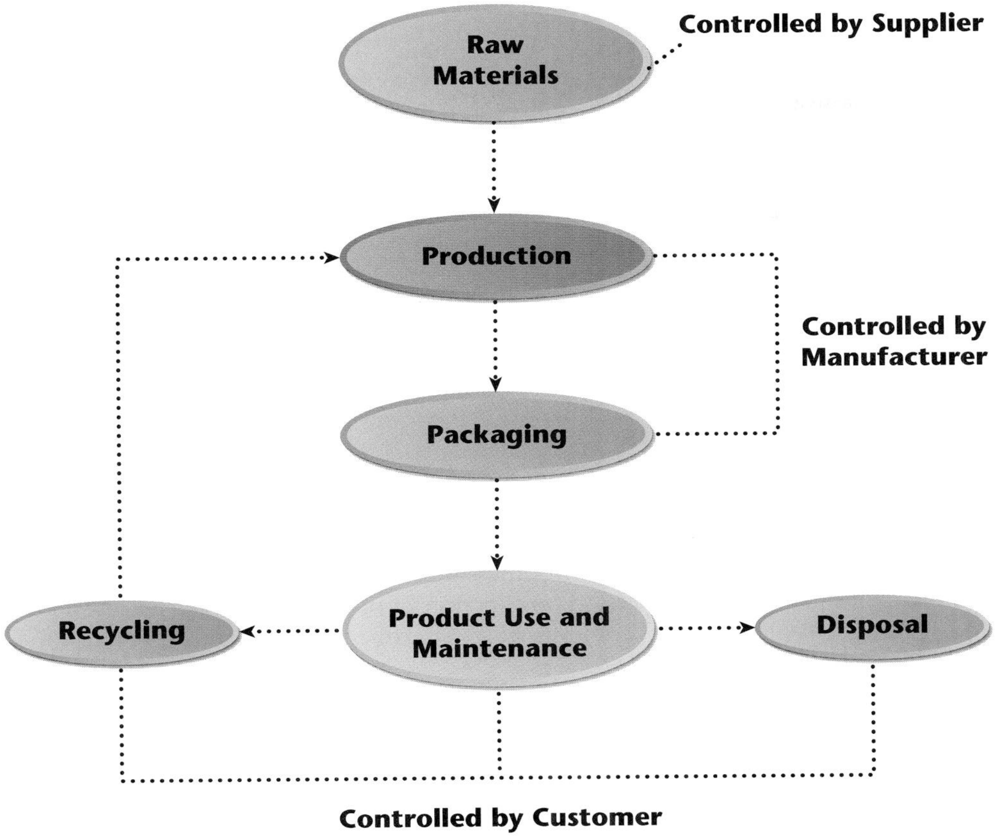

Exhibit 17-6 Product Life-Cycle Stages

The life-cycle viewpoint adopted combines supplier, manufacturer, and customer viewpoints. Both internal and external linkages are thus considered important in assessing environmental consequences of different products, the product designs, and process designs. If the cost accounting system is going to play a role in life-cycle assessment, then the most obvious step is assessing and assigning the environmental costs caused by the producer in each of the life-cycle stages. This then allows managers to compare the economic effects of competing designs. However, before discussing cost assessment, a more detailed understanding of life-cycle analysis is needed.

Assessment Stages

Life-cycle assessment is defined by three formal stages: (1) inventory analysis, (2) impact analysis, and (3) improvement analysis.[15] **Inventory analysis** specifies the types and quantities of materials and energy inputs needed and the resulting environmental releases in the form of solid, liquid, and gaseous residues. Inventory analysis spans the product's life cycle. **Impact analysis** assesses the environmental effects of competing designs and provides a relative ranking of those effects. **Improvement analysis** has the objective of reducing the environmental impacts revealed by the inventory and impact steps.

Inventory Analysis To illustrate inventory analysis, consider single-use, hot-drink cups for fast-food restaurants. A producer can choose to make the cups using either

15 T. E. Graedel and B. R. Allenby, *Industrial Ecology*, pp. 108–121.

paper or polystyrene foam. Each stage in the cup's life cycle produces certain key questions:

- What are the materials required for each type of cup?
- What are the energy requirements to produce each type?
- What kinds of effluents and emissions are produced by each?
- What is the recycle potential?
- What are the resources required for ultimate disposal?

Answering these questions defines inventory analysis. Exhibit 17-7 provides answers for the questions based on data reported in a study by Martin Hocking.[16]

Impact Analysis Impact analysis next assesses the meaning of the values provided by the inventory analysis step. For example, one advantage of paper cups is that paper is made from a renewable resource (woods and chips), while the polyfoam cup relies on petroleum, a nonrenewable resource. More careful examination, however, reveals that paper cups actually use more petroleum than polyfoam cups! The reason? Converting wood chips to pulp to paper cups uses energy. Effluents and emissions produced during the products' life cycle are also listed in Exhibit 17-7. Interestingly, the only significant environmental release for polyfoam cups is pentane, a blowing agent. On the other hand, production of paper requires extensive use of inorganic chemicals and large amounts of water effluents. Furthermore, recycling seems to favor polyfoam cups. Finally, ultimate disposal, at least in landfills, tends to favor paper cups because of their biodegradability. Yet, this advantage is called into question by recent studies indicating that biodegradable materials in anaerobic landfills remain *undegraded* over relatively long periods of time.[17] From the viewpoint of a variety of environmental impacts, perhaps polyfoam cups are better than paper cups!

Polyfoam cups may be more environmentally friendly than paper cups!

© Digital Vision

Cost Assessment Up to this point, the analysis has used only nonfinancial measures and qualitative factors. The hot-drink cup example, however, does offer the opportunity to introduce costs and discuss their value in life-cycle assessment. Life-cycle cost assessment is determining the financial consequences of the environmental impacts identified in the inventory and improvement steps of life-cycle assessment. Assessing environmental costs for the inventory stage can facilitate impact analysis. In the paper cup versus polyfoam cup example, the comparisons of operational data were fairly clean in the sense that one product's environmental impacts were almost always less than the other product's. But, even here, there are some questions that can be raised. For example, what is the cost of producing pentane emissions compared to the cost of water effluents and particulates? What are the economic benefits from recycling polyfoam cups? The advantage of assigning costs is that the total environmental costs provide an index that can be used for ranking the competing alternatives. How are costs assigned?

The answer to the cost assignment question has already been given. Materials costs are assigned through direct tracing. We can identify the amount of materials

16 M. B. Hocking, "Paper versus Polystyrene: A Complex Choice," *Science* 251 (1991): pp. 504–505.
17 T. E. Graedel and B. R. Allenby, *Industrial Ecology*, p. 149.

	Paper Cup	Polyfoam Cup
Materials usage per cup:		
Wood and bark (g)	33.0	0.0
Petroleum (g)	4.1	3.2
Finished weight (g)	10.0	11.5
Utilities per mg of material:		
Steam (kg)	9,000–12,000	5,000
Power (GJ)	3.5	0.4–0.6
Cooling water (m3)	50	154
Water effluent per mg of material:		
Volume (m3)	50–190	0.5–2.0
Suspended solids (kg)	35–60	trace
BOD (kg)	30–50	0.07
Organochlorides (kg)	5–7	0
Metal salts (kg)	1–20	20
Air emissions per mg of material:		
Chlorine (kg)	0.5	0
Sulfides (kg)	2.0	0
Particulates (kg)	5–15	0.1
Pentane (kg)	0	35–50
Recycle potential:		
Primary user	Possible	Easy
After use	Low	High
Ultimate disposal:		
Heat recovery (Mj/kg)	20	40
Mass to landfill (g)	10.1	11.5
Biodegradable	Yes	No

Exhibit 17-7 Inventory Analysis

consumed per unit and then multiply by the price paid for the materials. Energy costs and the costs of producing environmental releases are assigned through driver tracing. Thus, for existing products (or processes, if they are the cost object), we simply identify the associated environmental activities and their costs, calculate an activity rate, and assign those costs to the respective products. If some of the energy consumption and environmental releases are associated with the use of the product after purchase, then a full environmental costing analysis requires their inclusion. It is also possible to assign only private costs. Recycling and disposal are separate but important issues. Many of the costs here are societal costs, and their measurement becomes more difficult. Taking only a private costing approach is also possible for recycling and disposal.

For example, assume that the following environmental costs per unit have been determined for the two cups:

	Paper Cups	Polyfoam Cups
Materials usage	$ 0.010	$0.004
Utilities	0.012	0.003
Contaminant-related resources	0.008	0.005
Total private costs	$0.030	$0.012
Recycling benefits (societal)	(0.001)	(0.004)
Environmental cost per unit	$0.029	$0.008

The unit life-cycle costs provide a summary measure of the relative environmental impacts of the two products and serve to support the qualitative interpretations of the operational and subjective environmental data found in Exhibit 17-7.

Managers Decide

Social Responsibility and Ethical Behavior

Aviva is the sixth-largest insurance group in the world and the largest provider of insurance services in the United Kingdom. Aviva voluntarily produces a corporate social responsibility report. Corporate social responsibility is—in one sense—a type of collective ethical responsibility to customers, workforce, suppliers, and the community. According to Aviva, social responsibility is concerned with the management of performance relating to the environment, human rights, and health and safety, while maintaining adherence to rigorous standards of business conduct. Social responsibility to the environment does not mean taking action at any cost. One exception is ethics. Ethics is not something that is subject to a cost-benefit analysis—one decides to be ethical regardless of cost. Within this ethical framework, environmental performance can be improved at a pace that business can afford. For example, in 1998, Aviva committed to improving its environmental performance. At that point, the company could have changed to a 100 percent renewables-sourced electricity; however, the cost of doing so overnight was not viewed as reasonable. After eight years of effort, though, Aviva has transitioned to the state where 100 percent of its electricity in the United Kingdom is sourced from renewables. ■

Source: http://www.aviva.com/files/pdf/Aviva_ CSRreport2006.pdf as of May 17, 2006.

Improvement Analysis Assessing environmental impacts in operational and financial terms sets the stage for the final step, that of searching for ways to reduce the environmental impacts of the alternatives being considered or analyzed. It is this step that connects with the control system of an organization. Improving the environmental performance of existing products and processes is the overall objective of an environmental control system.

Strategic-Based Environmental Responsibility Accounting

Objective 4

Compare and contrast activity- and strategic-based environmental control.

The overall goal of improving environmental performance suggests that a continuous improvement framework for environmental control would be the most appropriate. In fact, an environmental perspective is a possible fifth perspective for the Balanced Scorecard framework that we discussed in Chapter 16. The creators of the Balanced Scorecard mention a specific instance in which company added an environmental perspective to their balanced scorecard.[18] If one accepts the ecoefficiency paradigm, then an environmental perspective is legitimate because improving environmental performance can be the source of a competitive advantage (the criterion for a perspective to be included). A strategic-based environmental management system provides an operational framework for improving environmental performance. For example, linking the environmental perspective to the process perspective is critical for improving environmental performance. Knowledge of root causes for environmental activities is fundamental to any process design changes needed to improve environmental performance. Thus, the Balanced Scorecard framework supplies objectives and measures that are integrated to achieve the overall goal of improving environmental performance.

18 Robert S. Kaplan and David P. Norton, *The Balanced Scorecard* (Boston: Harvard Business School, 1996): p. 35.

Environmental Perspective

We can identify at least five core objectives for the environmental perspective: (1) minimize the use of raw or virgin materials; (2) minimize the use of hazardous materials; (3) minimize energy requirements for production and use of the product; (4) minimize the release of solid, liquid, and gaseous residues; and (5) maximize opportunities to recycle.

Two environmental themes are associated with materials and energy (the first three core objectives). First, no more energy and materials should be used than absolutely necessary (conservation issue). Second, means should be sought to eliminate the usage of materials and energy that damage the environment (hazardous substance issue). Performance measures should reflect these two themes. Thus, possible measures would be total and per-unit quantities of the different types of materials and energy (e.g., pounds of toxic chemicals used), productivity measures (output/materials, output/energy), and hazardous materials (energy) costs expressed as a percentage of total materials cost.

The fourth core objective can be realized in one of two ways: (1) using technology and methods to prevent the release of residues, *once produced,* and (2) *avoiding* production of the residues by identifying fundamental causes and redesigning products and processes to eliminate the causes. Of the two methods, the second is preferred. The first method is analogous to obtaining product quality by inspection and rework (*inspecting in quality*). Experience with quality management has revealed that this approach is much more costly than *doing it right the first time.* This same outcome is likely to be true for the control of residues once produced. It makes more sense to avoid residues than it does to contain them once produced. Performance measures for this objective include pounds of toxic waste produced, cubic meters of effluents, tons of greenhouse gases produced, and percentage reduction of packaging materials.

The fifth objective emphasizes conservation of nonrenewable resources by their reuse. Recycling reduces the demand for extraction of additional raw materials. It also reduces environmental degradation by reducing the waste disposal requirements placed on end-users. Measures include pounds of materials recycled, number of different materials (the fewer, the better), number of different components (the fewer, the better for recycling), percentage of units remanufactured, and energy produced from incineration. Exhibit 17-8 summarizes the objectives and measures for the environmental perspective.

Objectives	Measures
Minimize hazardous materials	Types and quantities (total and per unit) Percentage of total materials cost Productivity measures (output/input)
Minimize raw or virgin materials	Types and quantities (total and per unit) Productivity measures (output/input)
Minimize energy requirements	Types and quantities (total and per unit) Productivity measures (output/input)
Minimize release of residues	Pounds of toxic waste produced Cubic meters of effluents Tons of greenhouse gases produced Percentage reduction of packaging materials
Maximize opportunities to recycle	Pounds of materials recycled Number of different components Percentage of units remanufactured Energy produced from incineration

Exhibit 17-8 Objectives and Measures: Environmental Perspective

The Role of Activity Management

Analysis of environmental activities is critical for a sound environmental control system. Of course, as we already know, identifying environmental activities and assessing their costs are prerequisites for activity-based environmental costing. Knowing the environmental costs and what products and processes are causing them is absolutely essential as a first step for control. Next, environmental activities must be classified as value-added and non-value-added.

Non-value-added activities are those that are not necessary if the firm is operating in an optimal environmentally efficient state. Interestingly, Porter and van der Linde claim that environmental pollution is equivalent to economic inefficiency.[19] If production of contaminants is equivalent to economic inefficiency as they claim, then all failure activities must be labeled non-value-added. Adopting an ecoefficiency paradigm implies that activities always exist that can simultaneously prevent environmental degradation and produce a state of economic efficiency better than the current state. Failure activities, of course, are not the only non-value-added activities. Many detection activities such as inspection are non-value-added as well.

Non-value-added environmental costs are the costs of non-value-added activities. These costs represent the benefits that can be captured by improving environmental performance. The key to capturing these benefits is identifying root causes for non-value-added activities and then redesigning products and processes to minimize and ultimately eliminate these non-value-added activities.

Design for the Environment This special design approach is called *design for the environment.* It touches products, processes, materials, energy, and recycling. In other words, the entire product life cycle and its effects on the environment must be considered. Manufacturing processes, for example, are the direct sources of many solid, liquid, and gaseous residues. Many of these end up being released into the environment. Often, redesign of a process can eliminate the production of such residues (the Numar case cited earlier is a good example). Product designs can also reduce environmental degradation. **Eastman Kodak**, for example, has designed its disposable cameras to facilitate recycling.[20] The disposable cameras have components that are color-coded. These components can be separated and used to build new cameras. Approximately 86 percent of each new camera is made of recycled materials. It is estimated that 5,000,000 units have been recycled since the introduction of this product, totaling about 700,000 pounds of materials.

Financial Measures Environmental improvements ought to produce significant and beneficial financial consequences. This means that the firm has achieved a favorable trade-off among failure activities and prevention activities. If ecoefficient decisions are being made, then total environmental costs should diminish as environmental performance improves. Thus, environmental cost trends are an important performance measure. One possibility is preparing a non-value-added environmental cost report for the current period and comparing these costs with the non-value-added costs of the prior period. An example of such a report is shown in Exhibit 17-9. Some care must be taken in measuring costs and trends. Cost reductions should be attributable to environmental improvements and not simply to discharging some environmental liability. Thus, external failure costs should reflect the average annual obligations resulting from current environmental efficiency. Therefore, the cost of cleaning up water pollution in 2007 is the expected annual cost assuming current environmental performance remains the same. The $900,000 cleanup cost, for example,

19 Michael E. Porter and Claus van der Linde, "Green and Competitive: Ending the Stalemate," *Harvard Business Review* (September–October 1995): pp. 120–134.

20 Joseph Fiskel, "Competitive Excellence through Environmental Excellence," *Corporate Environmental Strategy* (Summer 1997): pp. 55–61.

Non-Value-Added Environmental Activity	Year 2008	2007
Inspecting processes	$ 200,000	$ 240,000
Operating pollution equipment	350,000	400,000
Maintaining pollution equipment	200,000	200,000
Cleaning up water pollution	700,000	900,000
Property damage claim	300,000	400,000
Totals	$1,750,000	$2,140,000

Exhibit 17-9 Non-Value-Added Cost Trends: Environmental Costs

could be the annual amount that must be set aside to have the total funds necessary to execute a cleanup five years from now. As actions are taken to improve environmental performance, the amount of future cleanup may diminish, thus reducing the annual amount to $700,000. The $200,000 trend improvement, then, is attributable to improved environmental performance.

Another possibility is computing total environmental costs as a percentage of sales and tracking this value over several periods. Exhibit 17-10 illustrates such a trend graph. This graph is of particular interest because it tracks all environmental costs and not just non-value-added environmental costs. If ecoefficient decisions are being made, we should observe a reduction in total environmental costs. This implies that there is a favorable trade-off between investments in environmentally related prevention activities and reduction of environmental failure costs. The trend should be downward, as ecoefficient investments are made.

Other graphical illustrations for specific areas can also show progress made. For example, a bar graph can be used to show the total amount of a pollutant emitted on a year-by-year basis. A downward trend would be a favorable indication. Pie

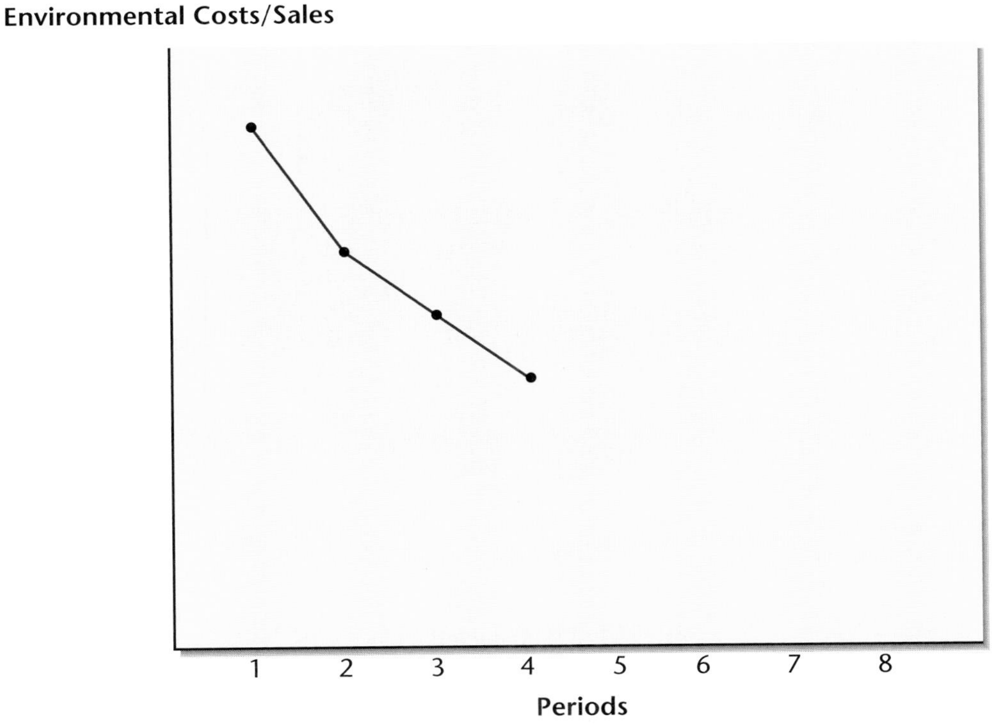

Exhibit 17-10 Environmental Cost Trend Graph

charts can be useful as well. For example, a pie chart could visually display hazardous waste management by category: percentage of waste incinerated, percentage of waste recycled/reclaimed, percentage of waste landfilled, percentage of waste treated, and percentage of waste deep-well injected. Exhibit 17-11 illustrates a bar graph analysis of CFC (chlorofluorocarbon) released over a four-year period, and Exhibit 17-12 shows a pie chart for hazardous waste management.

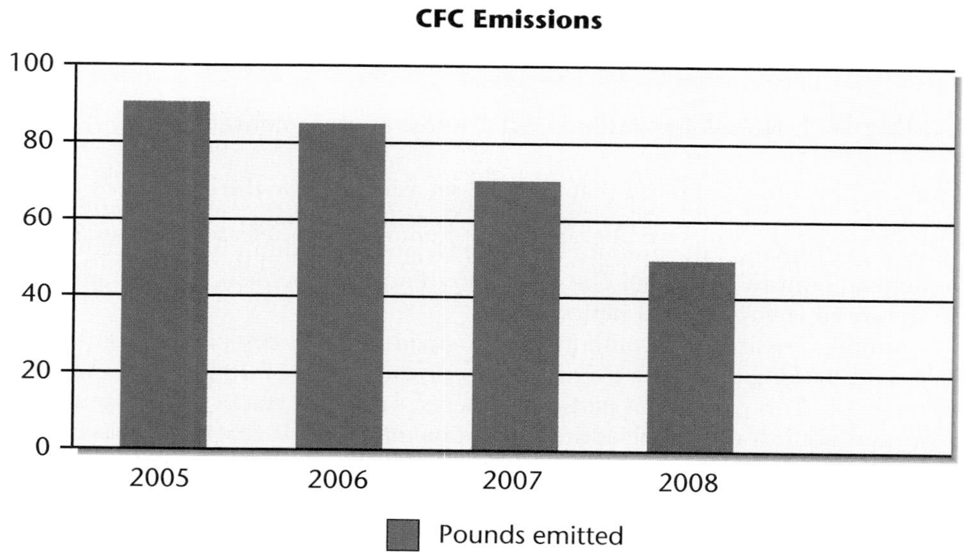

Exhibit 17-11 Bar Graph for Trend Analysis

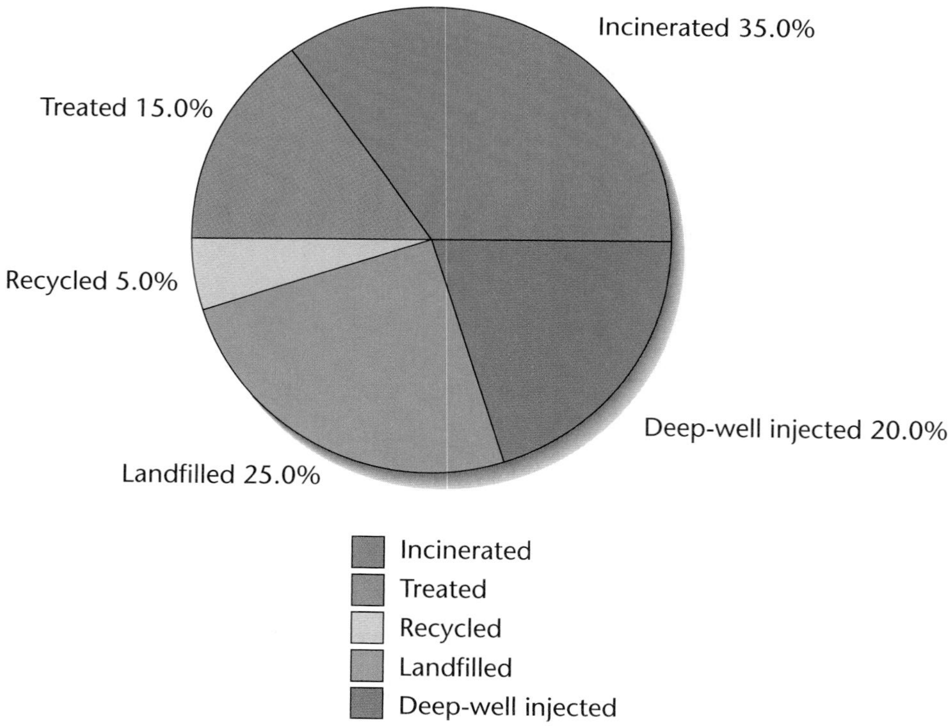

Exhibit 17-12 Hazardous Waste Pie Chart

Summary of Learning Objectives

1. Discuss the importance of measuring environmental costs.

Increasing compliance costs and the emergence of ecoefficiency have intensified the interest in environmental costing. Ecoefficiency implies that cost reductions can be achieved by increasing environmental performance. Furthermore, for many companies, environmental costs are a significant percentage of total operating costs. This fact, coupled with ecoefficiency, emphasizes the importance of defining, measuring, and reporting environmental costs. Environmental costs are those costs incurred because poor environmental quality exists or may exist. There are four categories of environmental costs: prevention, detection, internal failure, and external failure. The external failure category is divided into realized costs and unrealized costs. Realized costs are those external costs the firm has to pay. Unrealized or societal costs are caused by the firm but paid for by society. Reporting environmental costs by category reveals their importance and shows the opportunity for reducing environmental costs by improving environmental performance.

2. Explain how environmental costs are assigned to products and processes.

First, managers must decide whether they will assign only private costs or whether they want all costs to be assigned (full costing). Next, they must choose to use a functional-based approach or an activity-based approach. Under functional-based costing, an environmental cost pool is created and a rate is calculated using unit-level drivers such as direct labor hours or machine hours. Environmental costs are then assigned to each product based on their usage of direct labor hours or machine hours. This approach is probably satisfactory for those firms with little product diversity. For firms with product diversity, activity-based assignments are likely to be superior. ABC assigns costs to environmental activities and then calculates activity rates. These rates are used to assign environmental costs to products.

3. Describe the life-cycle cost assessment model.

Life-cycle cost assessment is a fundamental part of life-cycle assessment. Life-cycle cost assessment assigns costs to the environmental impacts of competing product designs. These costs are a function of the materials used, the energy consumed, and the environmental releases resulting from the manufacture of a product. Before assessing these cost assignments, it is first necessary to do an inventory analysis that details materials, energy, and environmental releases. This analysis is carried out over the life cycle of the product itself. Once completed, the financial and operational impacts can be assessed and steps taken to improve environmental performance.

4. Compare and contrast activity- and strategic-based environmental control.

Controlling environmental costs relies on a strategic-based responsibility accounting system. This system has two important features: a strategic component and an operational component. The strategic component uses the Balanced Scorecard framework. The adaptation for environmental control is the addition of a fifth perspective: the environmental perspective. The environmental perspective has five objectives relating to materials and energy usage, production and release of environmental residues, and recycling. Operational measures, such as pounds of hazardous materials and pounds of recycled materials, are developed for each objective. Activity-based management provides the operational system that produces environmental improvements. Non-value-added environmental activities and their root causes are identified. Designs for the environmental approaches are then used to eliminate these non-value-added activities. Ecoefficient improvements should produce favorable financial consequences that can be measured using trends in non-value-added environmental costs and trends in total environmental costs.

Key Terms

Ecoefficiency, 768
Environmental costs, 770
Environmental detection costs, 771
Environmental external failure costs, 771
Environmental internal failure costs, 771
Environmental prevention costs, 770
Full environmental costing, 776
Full private costing, 776
Impact analysis, 779
Improvement analysis, 779
Inventory analysis, 779
Life-cycle assessment, 778
Life-cycle cost assesssent, 778
Private costs, 772
Product stewardship, 778
Realized external failure costs, 771
Sustainable development, 769
Unrealized external failure costs (societal costs), 771

Review Problem

1. Environmental Costs

At the beginning of 2008, Kleaner Company initiated a program to improve its environmental performance. Efforts were made to reduce the production and emission of contaminating gaseous, solid, and liquid residues. By the end of the year, in an executive meeting, the environmental manager indicated that the company had made significant improvement in its environmental performance, reducing the emission of contaminating residues of all types. The president of the company was pleased with the reported success, but wanted an assessment of the financial consequences of the environmental improvements. To satisfy this request, the following financial data were collected for 2007 and 2008 (all changes in costs are a result of environmental improvements):

	2007	2008
Sales	$20,000,000	$20,000,000
Evaluating and selecting suppliers	0	600,000
Treating and disposing of toxic materials	1,200,000	800,000
Inspecting processes (environmental objective)	200,000	300,000
Land restoration (annual fund contribution)	1,600,000	1,200,000
Maintaining pollution equipment	400,000	300,000
Testing for contaminants	150,000	100,000

Required

1. Classify the costs as prevention, detection, internal failure, or external failure.
2. Prepare an environmental cost report for the most recent year where costs are expressed as a percentage of sales (instead of operating costs).

Solution

1. Prevention costs: evaluating and selecting suppliers; detection costs: testing for contaminants and inspecting processes; internal failure: maintaining pollution equipment and treating and disposing of toxic materials; and external failure: land restoration.
2. **Kleaner Company**
   Environmental Cost Report
   For the Year Ended December 31, 2008

	Environmental Costs	Percentage of Sales
Prevention costs:		
Evaluating and selecting suppliers	$ 600,000	3.00%
Detection costs:		
Inspecting processes	$ 300,000	
Testing for contaminants	100,000	
	$ 400,000	2.00
Internal failure costs:		
Treating and disposing of toxic materials	$ 800,000	
Maintaining pollution equipment	300,000	
	$1,100,000	5.50

(Continued)

External failure costs:		
Land restoration	$1,200,000	6.00
Total environmental costs	$3,300,000	16.50%

2. Assigning Environmental Costs; Life-Cycle Cost Assessment; Environmental Cost Control

Pierce Enterprises produces two types of fertilizers: Quikrichen and Longrichen. Pierce recently has received significant criticism from environmental groups, local residents, and the federal government concerning its environmental performance. Henry Hyde, president of Pierce, wants to know how the company's environmental activities affect the cost of each product. He believes that the main source of the environmental problems lies with Quikrichen but would like some evidence to support (or refute) this belief. The controller has assembled the following data to help answer this question:

	Quikrichen	Longrichen
Pounds of fertilizer produced	1,000,000	2,000,000
Engineering hours (process design)	1,500	4,500
Pounds of solid residues treated	30,000	10,000
Inspection hours (environmental)	10,000	5,000
Cleanup hours (local lake)	8,000	2,000

Additionally, the following environmental activity costs were reported:

Designing process	$150,000
Treating residues	600,000
Inspecting process	120,000
Cleaning up lake	200,000

Required

1. Calculate the environmental cost per pound of fertilizer for each product.
2. Based on the calculations in Requirement 1, which product appears to be the most environmentally harmful?
3. Would life-cycle cost assessment provide stronger evidence for the environmental suitability of each product? Explain.
4. Explain how a strategic-based responsibility accounting system can be used to help improve Pierce's performance.

Solution

1. First, calculate activity rates:

Designing process	$150,000/6,000	= $25 per engineering hour
Treating residues	$600,000/40,000	= $15 per pound of residue
Inspecting process	$120,000/15,000	= $8 per inspection hour
Cleaning up lake	$200,000/10,000	= $20 per cleanup hour

Second, use rates to assign environmental costs and calculate unit environmental costs:

	Quikrichen
$25 × 1,500	$ 37,500
$15 × 30,000	450,000
$8 × 10,000	80,000
$20 × 8,000	160,000
Total	$ 727,500
	÷1,000,000
Unit cost per pound	$ 0.7275

	Longrichen
$25 × 4,500	$ 112,500
$15 × 10,000	150,000
$8 × 5,000	40,000
$20 × 2,000	40,000
Total	$ 342,500
	÷2,000,000
Unit cost per pound	$ 0.17125

2. As measured by the environmental cost per unit, Quikrichen is the product causing the most environmental damage, confirming the president's beliefs.
3. Life-cycle assessment has three steps: inventory analysis, impact analysis, and improvement analysis. Of the three steps, the first two are concerned with identifying the materials and energy requirements, environmental releases, and the environmental effects of competing process and product designs (over the life cycle of the products). Thus, a life-cycle assessment provides a more comprehensive analysis of environmental effects than the environmental cost per unit (unless the cost per unit is a *life-cycle* environmental cost per unit).
4. The environmental perspective (from the Balanced Scorecard framework) can improve environmental performance by translating an environmental improvement strategy into operational objectives, measures, targets, and initiatives. For example, consider the five core environmental objectives. These objectives, if followed, will reduce the amounts of materials and energy used (including hazardous materials) and will also reduce residues released. Furthermore, the environmental perspective is tied to the other four perspectives of the Balanced Scorecard. Thus, it is explicitly recognized that improving environmental performance means that capabilities, processes, customers, and financial consequences must be considered.

Questions for Writing and Discussion

1. Explain why firms have an increased interest in environmental costing.
2. What is ecoefficiency?
3. What are the six incentives, or causes, for ecoefficiency?
4. What is an environmental cost?
5. What are the four categories of environmental costs? Define each category.
6. What is the difference between a realized external failure (environmental) cost and an unrealized external failure (societal) cost?
7. What does full environmental costing mean? Full private costing?
8. Explain how functional-based costing assigns environmental costs to products. What are the problems with this approach?
9. Explain how activity-based costing assigns environmental costs to products.
10. What information is communicated by the unit environmental cost of a product?
11. What is life-cycle assessment?
12. What are the environmentally important life-cycle stages of a product?
13. Define the three steps of life-cycle assessment.
14. How can life-cycle costing improve life-cycle assessment?
15. What is the justification for adding an environmental perspective to the Balanced Scorecard?
16. What are the five core objectives of the environmental perspective?
17. Why is minimizing the use of raw materials an environmental issue?
18. What are some possible performance measures for the objective of minimizing the release of residues?
19. All environmental failure activities are non-value-added activities. Do you agree or disagree? Explain.
20. What is the meaning of design for the environment? What is its role in activity-based management of environmental activities?
21. Describe the possible value of financial measures of environmental performance. Give several examples.

Exercises

17-1

Ecoefficiency and Sustainable Development LO1, LO2

Choose the *best* answer for each of the following multiple-choice questions:

1. Sustainable development means that
   a. maximum efficiency is achieved only by allowing firms to freely pollute.
   b. firm goodwill is the only way to achieve improvement in environmental performance.
   c. a company can increase economic efficiency while reducing negative environmental impacts.
   d. development meets the needs of the present without compromising the ability of future generations to meet their own needs.
   e. Both c and d.
2. Firms strive to be ecoefficient so that they
   a. can achieve a lower cost of capital.
   b. can reduce costs and become more competitive.
   c. can achieve an improved image in their markets.
   d. can find new markets for useless residues.
   e. All of the above.
3. Evaluating and selecting suppliers is an example of a(n)
   a. external failure cost.
   b. societal cost.
   c. internal failure cost.
   d. prevention cost.
   e. realized external failure cost.
4. Receiving medical care due to polluted air is an example of
   a. an unrealized external failure cost.
   b. a private cost.
   c. an internal failure cost.
   d. minimizing environmental costs.
   e. Both a and b.
5. Environmental failure costs can be reduced by investing more in
   a. pollution control equipment.
   b. processes that treat and dispose of toxic waste.
   c. land restoration projects.
   d. scrubbers.
   e. designing processes.
6. Assigning all environmental costs to products is an example of
   a. full private costing.
   b. environmental postpurchase costs.
   c. full environmental costing.
   d. life-cycle costing.
   e. product stewardship.
7. Environmental income in an environmental financial report refers to
   a. current savings from reducing the dispersion of toxic materials.
   b. revenues from environmental actions such as recycling.
   c. ongoing savings from reducing the energy intensity of goods and services.
   d. ongoing savings from reducing the material intensity of goods and services.
   e. Both b and c.

8. Cost avoidance in an environmental financial report refers to
   a. current savings from reducing the dispersion of toxic materials.
   b. ongoing savings from reducing the material intensity of goods and services.
   c. ongoing savings from reducing the energy intensity of goods and services.
   d. revenues from environmental actions such as recycling.
   e. Both b and c.
9. Select the item that represents environmental detection costs:
   a. Developing environmental performance measures
   b. Recycling products
   c. Disposing of toxic materials
   d. Carrying out contamination tests
   e. None of the above.
10. An example of an environmental internal failure cost is
    a. cleaning up oil spills.
    b. damaging ecosystems from solid waste disposal.
    c. verifying supplier environmental performance.
    d. measuring levels of contamination.
    e. none of the above.
11. An example of a societal cost is
    a. maintaining pollution equipment.
    b. recycling scrap.
    c. disposing of toxic materials.
    d. medical care due to polluted air.
    e. all of the above.
12. An example of an environmental prevention cost is
    a. restoring land to its natural state.
    b. developing environmental management systems.
    c. licensing facilities for producing contaminants.
    d. auditing environmental activities.
    e. treating toxic materials

17-2

Ecoefficiency and Sustainable Development
LO1

Two views are often expounded relative to the environment: (1) Greater production means greater pollution (economic and ecological considerations are incompatible) and (2) the state (federal and state governments) has the exclusive responsibility to solve environmental problems and see that sustainable development is supported.

Required

1. Explain why the first view is more of a myth than reality. In offering this explanation, give explicit reasons for your position.
2. What is sustainable development? Should the state have exclusive environmental responsibility for solving environmental problems and ensuring sustainable development? If not, what role should it play?

17-3

Ecoefficiency and the Environmental Quality Cost Model
LO1

One of the principal differences between the quality cost model of Chapter 15 and the environmental quality cost model described in this chapter relates to the nature of external failure costs.

Required

1. Explain how external failure costs differ between the product quality cost model and the environmental quality cost model.

2. Refer to the quality cost graph of Exhibit 15-6. Assume that this graph now portrays environmental costs (where the horizontal axis represents the degree of environmental degradation). The initial impression the graph gives is that the incentive for the firm is to move to a point of zero degradation, consistent with ecoefficiency. Now, suppose that there are no internal failure costs and that a third party (society) pays for all external failure costs. From the firm's point of view, what is its external failure cost curve? Total cost curve? What incentive does this provide for environmental degradation? Finally, does this have any implications for the role government might need to play to enable ecoefficiency to work as intended?

17-4

Classification of Environmental Costs
LO1

Classify the following environmental activities as prevention costs, detection costs, internal failure costs, or external failure costs. For external failure costs, classify the costs as societal or private. Also, label those activities that are compatible with sustainable development (SD).

1. A company takes actions to reduce the amount of scrap.
2. After its useful life, a soft-drink producer returns the activated carbon used for purifying water for its beverages to the supplier. The supplier reactivates the carbon for a second use in nonfood applications. As a consequence, many tons of material are prevented from entering landfills.
3. A water treatment system is used to treat wastewater that is then recycled through the plant, reducing the amount of water needed.
4. The inks used to print snack packages (for chips) contain heavy metals.
5. Suppliers are evaluated to verify that they are meeting mutually agreed upon environmental standards.
6. Delivery boxes are used five times and then recycled. This prevents 112 million pounds of cardboard from entering landfills and saves two million trees per year.
7. Contamination levels are measured to ensure that air emissions are less than the level permitted by law.
8. Local residents are unable to swim and boat in a lake because of pollution caused by a steel plant.
9. Processes are inspected to determine if the contaminants released are within legal limits.
10. A strip mining operation has disrupted the local ecology and caused a loss of jobs for hunting guides.
11. To reduce energy consumption, magnetic ballasts are replaced with electronic ballasts, and more efficient light bulbs and lighting sensors are installed. As a result, a total of 2.3 million kilowatt hours of electricity are saved per year.
12. Because of a legal settlement, a chemical company must spend $100,000,000 to settle claims concerning property damage resulting from contaminated soil and polluted underground water.
13. A soft-drink company uses the following practice: In all bottling plants, packages damaged during filling are collected and recycled (glass, plastic, and aluminum).
14. Products are inspected to ensure that the gaseous emissions produced during operation follow legal and company guidelines.
15. Costs are incurred for treating and disposing of toxic waste.
16. An internal audit is conducted to verify that environmental policies are being followed.

17-5

Environmental Cost Report
LO1

At the end of 2008, Lemmons Pharmaceuticals (LP) implemented an environmental quality management program. As a first step, LP identified the following costs for the year just ended in its accounting records as environmentally related:

EXCEL

	2008
Inefficient materials usage	$2,400,000
Treating and disposing of toxic waste	9,600,000
Cleanup of chemically contaminated soil	3,600,000
Testing for contamination	1,200,000
Operating pollution control equipment	1,970,000
Maintaining pollution control equipment	720,000
Performing environmental studies	240,000
Measuring contamination levels	120,000
Training (environmentally related)	150,000

Required

1. Prepare an environmental cost report by category. Assume that total operating costs are $120,000,000.
2. Calculate the relative distribution percentages for each environmental cost category (the percentage of the total environmental cost represented by each category). Comment on the distribution.
3. Suppose that the newly hired environmental manager examines the report and makes the following comment: "This report understates the total environmental costs. It fails to consider the costs that we are imposing on the local community. For example, we have polluted the river and lake so much that swimming and fishing are no longer possible. I have heard rumblings from the local citizens, and I'll bet that we will be facing a big cleanup bill in a few years."

   Assume that subsequent to the comment, engineering estimated that cleanup costs for the river and lake will amount to $12,000,000, assuming the cleanup is required within five years. To pay for the cleanup, annual contributions of $2,100,000 will be invested with the expectation that the fund will grow to $12,000,000 by the end of the fifth year. Assume, also, that the loss of recreational opportunities is costing the local community $4,800,000 per year. How would this information alter the report in Requirement 1?

17-6

Environmental Cost Assignment
LO2

EXCEL

Faraday Chemical produces two chemical products: an herbicide and an insecticide. The controller and environmental manager have identified the following environmental activities and costs associated with the two products:

	Herbicide	Insecticide
Pounds produced	12,000,000	30,000,000
Packaging materials (pounds)	3,600,000	1,800,000
Energy usage (kilowatt hours)	1,200,000	600,000
Toxin releases (pounds into air)	3,000,000	600,000
Pollution control (machine hours)	480,000	120,000
Costs of activities:		
Using packaging materials	$5,400,000	
Using energy	1,440,000	
Releasing toxins (fines)	720,000	
Operating pollution control equipment	1,680,000	

Required

1. Calculate the environmental cost per pound for each product. Which of the two appears to cause the most degradation to the environment?
2. In which environmental category would you classify excessive use of materials and energy?

3. Suppose that the toxin releases cause health problems for those who live near the chemical plant. The costs, due to missed work and medical treatments, are estimated at $3,240,000 per year. How would assignment of these costs change the unit cost? Should they be assigned?

17-7

Environmental Costing; Ecoefficiency; and Competitive Advantage LO1, LO2

EXCEL

After reviewing the data on its two chemical products (given below), the CEO of Faraday Chemical decides to launch an environmental performance improvement program.

	Herbicide	Insecticide
Pounds produced	12,000,000	30,000,000
Packaging materials (pounds)	3,600,000	1,800,000
Energy usage (kilowatt hours)	1,200,000	600,000
Toxin releases (pounds into air)	3,000,000	600,000
Pollution control (machine hours)	480,000	120,000
Costs of activities:		
Using packaging materials	$5,400,000	
Using energy	1,440,000	
Releasing toxins (fines)	720,000	
Operating pollution control equipment	1,680,000	

First, efforts were made to reduce the amount of packaging. The demand for packaging materials was reduced by 10 percent. Second, a way was found to reuse the packaging materials. Usage of packaging materials changed from one time to two times. Both changes together saved $2,970,000 in packaging costs. Third, the manufacturing processes were redesigned to produce a reduced environmental load. The new processes were able to reduce emissions by 50 percent and private emission costs by 75 percent. The new processes also reduced the demand for energy by one-third. Energy costs were also reduced by the same amount. There was no change in the demand or cost of operating pollution control equipment.

The cost of implementing the changes was $1,206,000 (salaries of $720,000 for hiring six environmental engineers and $486,000 for treating the packaging materials so they can be reused). Engineering hours used for each process are 18,000 for the herbicide process and 6,000 for the insecticide process.

Required

1. Calculate the new cost per pound for each product. Assume that the environmental reductions for each product are in the same proportions as the total reductions.
2. Calculate the net savings produced by the environmental changes for each product, in total and on a per-unit basis. Does this support the concept of ecoefficiency?
3. Classify the activities as prevention, detection, internal failure, or external failure. What does this tell you about the relationship between the various categories?
4. Describe how the environmental improvements can contribute to improving the firm's competitive position.

17-8

Life-Cycle Cost Assessment LO3

EXCEL

Lavaron Chemical Products Division produces surfactants, ingredients used in producing laundry detergents (surfactants are the components that help release soil from clothing). There are different types of surfactants possible, depending on the nature of the raw material input. One possibility, for example, is the usage of beef tallow as the primary raw material input. Another possibility is to use petrochemical stock as the primary raw material input. The primary input plus other inputs and energy sources are used to produce the surfactants. An inventory analysis produces the following data for the production of surfactants:

	Petrochemical	Tallow
Raw materials (kilograms per 1,000 kg of surfactant)	990	935
Water usage (kilograms per 1,000 kg of surfactants used)	56	560
Energy usage (kilowatt-hours per 1,000 kg of surfactants):		
For production of raw materials	60	30
Transportation	10	30
Processing (production of surfactants)	65	60
Residues (emissions per 1,000 kg of surfactants):		
Particulates (air contaminant)	5	12
Hydrocarbons (air contaminant)	40	33
Dissolved solids (liquid contaminant)	7	5
Land contamination (solid residue)	87	176

The greater water usage for tallow relates to the requirement that water must be used to produce feed for beef. The cost per kilogram of petrochemical stock is $0.40. The cost per kilogram of tallow is $0.60. Water costs $0.50 per kilogram, and energy is $1.20 per kilowatt hour. When air contaminants exceed 5 per 1,000 kilograms, pollution control equipment must be purchased and installed. The cost of acquiring and operating this equipment is $500 per five units of contaminants. Liquid contaminants are more trouble. If dumped into local streams over the life cycle, the costs are estimated to be $120 per unit of liquid contaminant. If a water treatment system is used, the cost is $60 per unit of contaminant. Finally, soil cleanup is estimated at $20 per unit of solid residue.

Required

1. Assess the relative environmental impacts of the two approaches to producing surfactants using only operational environmental measures. Which of the two approaches would you recommend? Justify your choice.
2. Use the cost information and calculate an environmental impact cost per 1,000 kg of surfactants. Which of the two approaches would you now recommend? Does the life-cycle cost approach have limitations? Explain.
3. Which parts of the life cycle described by the inventory analysis are controlled by the supplier? By the producer? What part of the inventory analysis is missing?

17-9

Life-Cycle Assessment: Packaging and Product Use; Impact Analysis
LO3

Derby Chips is an international producer of corn chips. At the end of 2006, Mary Hahn, president of Derby, appointed a task force to focus on the packaging and product use segments of its product's life cycle. Since customers consumed the contents of the package (if not consumed, the contents are biodegradable), the main concern was on the ability to conserve, recycle, and dispose of packaging materials. A new packaging proposal was being considered. A partial inventory analysis of the current packaging and the new packaging is given below.

	Current	New
Delivery boxes:		
Recycle potential	Low	High
Times used before disposal	1	5
Paper bags:		
Average package weight (ounces)	2	1.5
Ink with heavy metals	Yes	No
Ultimate disposal:		
Safe for incineration	No	Yes

Upon seeing the inventory analysis, Mary was pleased to see the apparent environmental benefits of the new packaging. However, she wanted a more detailed analysis of the impact of the new packaging. In response to this request, environmental engineers and cost accounting provided the following estimates:

Annual packages produced and sold	250,000,000
Current demand for delivery boxes	375,000,000 pounds
Recycle forecast	90% of delivery boxes used
Cost per ounce (package)	$0.025
Cost per pound (delivery boxes)	$0.75

The company's environmental engineers also indicated that in Europe and Japan, about 75 percent of the packaging will participate in waste-to-energy combustion programs for the generation of steam or electricity. In the United States, only about 25 percent of the packaging will participate in such programs. As a footnote, environmental engineering also noted that saving 300 pounds of paperboard is equivalent to saving one tree.

Required

1. Calculate the total pounds of delivery boxes saved because of the new packaging. How much does this save in dollars? How many trees are saved because of recycling and reduction in demand for boxes? Because of recycling, how many pounds of cardboard are diverted from landfills?
2. Calculate the total pounds of materials saved by reducing packaging (bag) weight. What are the dollar savings? Now assume that a design engineer has indicated that by reducing the packaging seal from the industry standard one-half inch to one-fourth inch, an additional 5 percent reduction in bag packaging can be achieved. How many pounds of materials are saved? Dollars saved?
3. Explain why the ultimate disposal qualities of packaging are important environmental considerations.
4. Why emphasize saving a material that comes from a renewable resource (trees)?

17-10

Environmental Performance Measures and Core Objectives
LO4

Identify the *core environmental objective* associated with each of the following measures.

a. Tons of greenhouse gas emissions
b. Tons of hazardous waste delivered for off-site management
c. Pounds of plastic recycled
d. British thermal units (BTUs)
e. Cars produced/pounds of steel used
f. Percentage of vehicles powered by propane gas
g. Percentage of recycled paper used (green purchasing)
h. Pounds of toxic chemical releases
i. Hazardous waste cost/total materials cost
j. Pounds of nonhazardous waste/pounds of materials issued
k. Percentage reduction in packaging materials
l. Pounds of organic chemicals in effluents sent to local river
m. Percentage of nonhazardous waste recycled

17-11

Cost Classification; Environmental Responsibility Accounting
LO1, LO4

At the beginning of 2005, Henderson Company, an international telecommunications company, embarked on an environmental improvement program. The company set a goal to have all its facilities ISO 14001 registered by 2008 (there are 30 facilities worldwide). It also adopted the Balanced Scorecard with an environmental perspective added as a fifth perspective. To communicate the environmental progress made, management decided to issue, on a voluntary basis, an annual environmental progress report. Internally, the Accounting Department issued monthly progress reports and developed a number of measures that could be reported even more frequently to assess progress. Henderson also asked an international CPA firm to prepare an auditor's report that would comment on the reasonableness and fairness of Henderson's approach to assessing and measuring environmental performance.

At the end of 2008, the controller had gathered data that would be used in preparing the environmental progress report. A sample of the data collected is given below.

Year	Number of ISO 14001 Registrations	Energy Consumption (BTUs)*	Greenhouse Gases**
2005	3	3,000	40,000
2006	9	2,950	39,000
2007	15	2,900	38,000
2008	24	2,850	36,000

* In billions (measures electricity, natural gas, and heating oil usage).
** In tons.

Required

1. What is the justification for adding an environmental perspective to the Balanced Scorecard?
2. Henderson Company decided to do the following: obtain ISO 14001 registration, prepare an annual environmental progress report, prepare internal environmental progress reports, and procure an audit of the external report. How do these decisions fit within the Balanced Scorecard framework? To what environmental cost categories do these activities belong?
3. Using the data, prepare a bar graph for each of the three environmental variables provided (registrations, energy, and greenhouse gases). Comment on the progress made on these three dimensions. To which core objectives do each of the three measures relate?

17-12

Environmental Responsibility Accounting; Cost Trends
LO4

Refer to **Exercise 17-11**. As part of its environmental cost reporting system, Henderson tracks its total environmental costs. Consider the cost and sales data given below.

Year	Total Environmental Costs	Sales Revenue
2005	$30,000,000	$250,000,000
2006	25,000,000	250,000,000
2007	22,000,000	275,000,000
2008	19,250,000	275,000,000

Required

1. Prepare a bar graph for environmental costs expressed as a percentage of sales. Assuming that environmental performance has improved, explain why environmental costs have decreased.
2. Normalize energy consumption by expressing it as a percentage of sales. Now, prepare a bar graph for energy. Comment on the progress made in reducing energy consumption. How does this compare with the conclusion that would be reached using a measure of progress that has not been normalized? Which is the best approach? Explain.

Problems

17-13

Cost Classification; Ecoefficiency; Strategic Environmental Objectives
LO1, LO4

The following items are listed in an environmental financial statement (issued as part of an environmental progress report):

Environmental benefits—savings, income, and cost avoidance:

- Ozone-depleting substances cost reductions
- Hazardous waste disposal cost reductions
- Hazardous waste materials cost reductions
- Nonhazardous waste disposal cost reductions

- Nonhazardous waste materials cost reductions
- Recycling material income
- Energy conservation cost savings
- Packaging cost reductions

Environmental costs:

- Corporate-level administrative costs
- Auditor fees
- Environmental engineering
- Facility professionals and programs
- Packaging professionals and programs for packaging reductions
- Pollution controls: operations and maintenance
- Pollution controls: depreciation
- Attorney fees for cleanup claims, notices of violations (NOVs)
- Settlements of government claims
- Waste disposal
- Environmental taxes for packaging
- Remediation/cleanup: on-site
- Remediation/cleanup: off-site

Required

1. Classify each item in the statement as prevention, detection, internal failure, or external failure. In classifying the items listed in the environmental savings category, first classify the underlying cost item (e.g., the cost of hazardous waste disposal). Next, think of how you would classify the cost of the activities that led to the cost reduction. That is, how would you classify the macroactivity *reducing hazardous waste cost disposal*?
2. For each item in the environmental benefits category, indicate a possible measure or measures and the core strategic environmental objective that would be associated with the measure. Is it possible that a measure may be associated with more than one objective? Explain.
3. Assuming ecoefficiency, what relationship over time would you expect to observe between the environmental benefits category and the environmental cost category?

17-14

Environmental Financial Reporting; Ecoefficiency; Improving Environmental Performance LO1, LO4

In 2008, Pedersen Company produced a Sustainability Report. As part of this report, an environmental financial statement was produced. In the Environmental Benefits section of the Pedersen report, three types of benefits are listed: savings, income, and cost avoidance. Consider the following data for selected items over a four-year period:

Year	Engineering Design Costs	Cost of Ozone-Depleting Substances
2005	$160,000	$2,880,000
2006	1,280,000	1,920,000
2007	640,000	1,280,000
2008	80,000	320,000

The engineering design costs were incurred to redesign the production processes and products. Redesign of the product allowed the substitution of a raw material that produced less ozone-depleting substances. Modifications in the design of the processes accomplished the same objective. Because of the improvements, the company was able to reduce the demand for pollution control equipment (with its attendant depreciation and operating costs) and avoid fines and litigation costs. All of the savings generated in a given year represent costs avoided for future years. The engineering costs are investments in design projects. Once the results of the project are realized, design costs can be reduced to lower levels. However, since some ongoing design activity is required for maintaining the system and improving it as needed, the environmental engineering cost will not be reduced lower than the $80,000 reported in 2008.

Required

1. Prepare a partial environmental financial statement, divided into benefit and cost sections for 2005, 2007, and 2008.
2. Evaluate and explain the outcomes. Does this result support or challenge ecoefficiency? Explain.

17-15

Environmental Financial Report
LO1

Avade Company, a manufacturer of cellular phones, has provided the following environmental information in its Corporate Social Responsibility Report (CSR) for 2006 and 2007; the data for 2008 comes from the preliminary draft of the 2008 CSR. In 2006, Avade committed itself to a continuous environmental improvement program, which was implemented throughout the company.

Environmental Activity	2006	2007	2008
Disposing of hazardous waste	$1,600,000	$1,200,000	$ 400,000
Measuring contaminant releases	80,000	800,000	560,000
Releasing air contaminants	4,000,000	3,200,000	2,000,000
Producing scrap (nonhazardous)	1,400,000	1,200,000	1,000,000
Operating pollution equipment	2,080,000	1,680,000	1,040,000
Designing processes and products	400,000	2,400,000	800,000
Using energy	1,440,000	1,296,000	1,152,000
Training employees (environmental)	80,000	160,000	320,000
Remediation (cleanup)	3,200,000	2,400,000	1,520,000
Inspecting processes	0	800,000	640,000

At the beginning of 2008, Avade began a new program of recycling nonhazardous scrap. The effort produced recycling income totaling $200,000. The marketing vice president and the environmental manager estimated that annual sales revenue had increased $1,600,000 since 2006 because of an improved public image relative to environmental performance. The company's Finance Department also estimated that Avade saved $640,000 in 2008 because of reduced finance and insurance costs, all attributable to improved environmental performance. All reductions in environmental costs from 2006 to 2008 are attributable to improvement efforts. Furthermore, any reductions represent ongoing savings.

Required

1. Avade has decided to prepare an environmental financial statement for 2008 for the products division. This report will be placed in the 2008 CSR. In the Cost section, classify environmental costs by category (prevention, detection, etc.). In the Benefits section, classify benefits into three categories: income, current savings, and ongoing savings.
2. Evaluate the changes in environmental performance.

17-16

Assignment of Environmental Costs
LO2

In 2006, Paula Nabors, president of Phelps, Inc., requested that environmental costs be assigned to the two major products produced by the company (two MP3 models: standard and luxury versions). She felt that knowledge of the environmental product costs would help guide the design decisions that would be necessary to improve environmental performance. The products represent two different models of MP3 (Standard and Luxury). The models use different processes and materials. To assign the costs, the following data were gathered for 2006:

Activity	Luxury Model	Standard Model	Activity Cost
Disposing of hazardous waste (tons)	240	2,160	$ 2,400
Measuring contaminant releases (transactions)	12,000	48,000	120,000
Releasing air contaminants (tons)	300	2,700	6,000,000
Producing scrap (pounds of scrap)	300,000	300,000	2,100,000
Operating pollution equipment (hours)	1,440,000	4,800,000	3,120,000
Designing processes and products (hours)	18,000	6,000	600,000
Using energy (BTUs)	7,200,000	14,400,000	2,160,000
Training employees (hours)	600	600	120,000
Remediation (labor hours)	60,000	180,000	4,800,000

During 2006, Phelps produced 2,400,000 units of the luxury model and 3,600,000 units of the standard model.

Required

1. Using the activity data, calculate the environmental cost per unit for each model. How will this information be useful?
2. Upon examining the cost data produced in Requirement 1, an environmental engineer made the following suggestions: (1) substitute a new plastic for a raw material that appeared to be the source of much of the hazardous waste (the new material actually cost less than the contaminating material it would replace) and (2) redesign the processes to reduce the amount of air contaminants produced (at a cost of $3,000,000 in 2007 and $600,000 in 2008 with annual increase of recurring costs of $200,000 to maintain the new process).

   As a result of the first suggestion, by 2008, the amount of hazardous waste produced had diminished to 600 tons, 120 tons for the Luxury Model and 480 tons for the Standard Model. The second suggestion reduced the contaminants released by 50 percent by 2008 (50 tons for the Luxury Model and 450 tons for the Standard Model). The need for pollution equipment also diminished, and the hours required for the Luxury Model and the Standard Model were reduced to 720,000 and 2,400,000, respectively. Calculate the unit cost reductions for the two models associated with the actions and outcomes described (assume the same production as in 2006). Do you think the efforts to reduce the environmental cost per unit were economically justified? Explain.

17-17

Various Concepts
LO1, LO2, LO3, LO4

Match the following items:

1. Sustainable development
2. Full environmental costing
3. Ecoefficiency
4. Inventory analysis
5. Environmental detection costs
6. Realized external failure costs
7. Product stewardship
8. Environmental internal failure costs
9. Full private costing
10. Private costs
11. Life-cycle cost assessment
12. Societal costs
13. Impact analysis
14. Improvement analysis

a. Seventy-five grams of petroleum required per unit
b. Designing, manufacturing, maintaining, and recycling products to minimize adverse environmental impacts

c. Assigning only private costs to products
d. Assigning all environmental costs to products
e. Company cleans up an oil spill
f. Assigning costs and benefits to the environmental consequences and improvements
g. Polyfoam cups are better than paper cups
h. Costs paid for by a third party
i. Not compromising the needs of future generations
j. Disposing of toxic materials
k. Measuring contamination levels
l. Reducing assessed environmental impacts
m. Simultaneously reducing environmental costs and adverse impacts
n. Environmental costs paid for by the firm

17-18

Life-Cycle Assessment LO3

EXCEL

Thomas Manufacturing produces automobile components used in automobile assembly. One of its divisions manufactures automotive front-end pieces. The division is currently considering two different designs: one using galvanized steel and the other a polymer composite. Both products are considered equally durable. The main issue being considered is the environmental effects of the designs. To help in this assessment, an inventory analysis and the associated cost information for the two designs are given below.

	Polymer	Galvanized Steel
Materials:		
Virgin materials (pounds)	8	14
Reused production scrap (pounds)	1	6
Energy:		
During production (kilowatts/pound)	15	10
During product use (pounds of petroleum used per year per unit)	66	110
Contaminants:		
Gaseous residues (pounds per unit)	0.4	0.2
Solid residues (pounds per unit)	0.6	2.0
Recycle potential:		
Incineration (pounds)	7.0	—
Quantity to landfill (pounds)	1.0	0.5
Recycled (pounds)	—	8.5
Financial information:		
Cost per pound of raw materials	$ 30.00	$ 15.00
Cost per kilowatt-hour	0.50	0.50
Cost per pound of petroleum	0.70	0.70
Cost per pound of gaseous residue	100.00	100.00
Cost per pound of solid residue	40.00	50.00
Incineration benefits per unit	2.00	—
Recyclable benefits per unit	—	20.00

Required

1. Using the operational measures, assess the environmental impact of each design. What other information would be useful?
2. Using the financial information, calculate an environmental life-cycle cost per unit. Discuss the strengths and weaknesses of this information.
3. Explain why a manager might wish to include product use and disposal information in the assessment of environmental performance. Remember, these costs

are not incurred by the company. For example, the petroleum consumption per year is a cost incurred by the end-user.
4. Based on all the above information, what recommendation would you make?

17-19

Environmental Responsibility Accounting; Balanced Scorecard
LO4

Ann Colson, president of Deerstone, Inc., a consumer products firm, has decided to follow an environmental improvement strategy. The goal is to increase profits by increasing revenues and decreasing environmental costs. Ann was convinced that revenues could be increased if she could improve the company's environmental image. Customers were demanding cleaner products, and her marketing manager had indicated that producing "greener" products would definitely lead to an increase in market share. Furthermore, Ann had recently returned from an environmental management seminar where she learned about ecoefficiency. She now believes that costs could be reduced while simultaneously improving environmental performance. She has two objectives in mind: reduce packaging and reduce production and release of contaminating residues. Ann has decided on the following actions to achieve the desired improvements:

1. Hire two environmental engineers to provide the capabilities needed to improve environmental performance. One engineer would be responsible for a new packaging design and reduction process. The other would be given responsibility to redesign products and processes with the objective of reducing the production of residues. Ann expects the actions to reduce packaging costs and pollution control costs.
2. All employees would be sent to several training seminars to learn about environmental management. They would then be empowered to make improvements in environmental performance (e.g., ways to reduce contaminants and packaging materials).
3. Once the processes and products were redesigned, she would participate in a third-party environmental certification program so that customers would be assured that the environmental improvements were valid.

Required

1. Explain why adding an environmental perspective to the Balanced Scorecard is considered to be legitimate.
2. Express the environmental improvement strategy as a series of cause-and-effect relationships in the form of if-then statements.
3. Illustrate the strategy using a flow diagram like the one shown in Exhibit 16-13 with one important modification: add an environmental perspective (the flow diagram should then illustrate five perspectives). Place the environmental perspective in between the customer and processes perspectives.

17-20

Environmental Responsibility Accounting; Trend Measurement
LO1, LO4

During the past four years, Blanding Company has made significant efforts to improve its environmental performance. Two of the strategic objectives that have received considerable attention are those of minimizing hazardous materials and minimizing release of liquid residues. Actually, there are two objectives associated with hazardous waste. First, the company wants to reduce the amount produced. Second, the company wants to shift the ways of dealing with hazardous waste from landfill and deep-well injections to such methods as incineration, treatment, and recycling. Kim Gladden, president of Blanding, also required the Accounting Department to track and report on environmental progress. Internal and external environmental progress reports were prepared. The following data pertain to the two strategic objectives that have been emphasized.

Hazardous waste objective (measured in tons):

Year	Incinerated	Treated	Recycled	Landfilled	Injected	Total
2005	2,000	2,000	1,000	35,000	10,000	50,000
2006	4,000	2,000	2,000	30,000	10,000	48,000
2007	8,000	3,000	3,000	25,000	7,000	46,000
2008	15,000	3,000	3,500	15,000	3,500	40,000

Liquid residue objective:

Year	Tons of Sulfates
2005	100
2006	92
2007	81
2008	73

The cost of landfilling hazardous waste is $50 per ton; injection is $60 per ton; incineration is $70 per ton; treatment is $100 per ton; and recycling produces a benefit of $10 per ton. Recycling, however, can be done only for a certain type of hazardous waste and only with a 70 percent successful yield. Treatment is also limited to certain types of waste. Fines, pollution control equipment, and expected cleanup costs are $4,000 per ton for the liquid residues.

Required

1. Prepare a hazardous waste bar graph that shows trends. Comment on the progress revealed.
2. Prepare a pie chart for hazardous waste for the years 2005 and 2008. Comment on the progress in reducing reliance on landfills and injections.
3. Prepare a bar graph for the liquid residues.
4. Calculate the environmental cost for hazardous waste and liquid residues in 2005 and 2008. Comment on environmental progress as measured by the financial outcomes. Is it possible that the savings are understated? Explain.

Research Assignment

17-21

Cybercase
LO1, LO2, LO4

A number of firms voluntarily disclose environmental information. Many of these firms are listed at the website for Greenbiz.com, which can be accessed via the chapter web links at the Interactive Study Center on http://www.thomsonedu.com/accounting/hansen. Among those listed are **PepsiCo**, **McDonald's**, and **Baxter**. PepsiCo reports some interesting environmental activities. Access Greenbiz.com, select a sample of these firms, and read their environmental disclosures. See how many of the following questions you can answer:

1. How much has been saved due to environmental actions? (Try Baxter.)
2. Describe the packaging reduction efforts and the resulting savings (savings can be expressed in nonfinancial terms).
3. Describe the recycling activities both for their own products as well as the materials they receive from suppliers.
4. How much reduction in contaminating residues has been reported?
5. Can you find firms that use bar graphs and pie charts to describe their environmental performance?

6. What kinds of performance measures are being used? Can you relate these to the core strategic objectives discussed in this chapter?
7. What reasons do they offer for providing environmental information?
8. How do the environmental reports compare? Select a sample of six to eight, and comment on the different approaches. Which report did you like best, and why?

17-22

Cybercase
LO2, LO4

Some might argue that environmental reporting is a form of signaling. By voluntarily disclosing environmental information, these firms are indicating that they are superior performers. Go to the Greenbiz website in Research Assignment 17-21 and select two or three firms with extensive environmental disclosures. Now, go to the Edgar database, and find firms that are in the same industry but that do not disclose environmental performance. Compare the economic performance of the firms with environmental disclosure with those with no environmental disclosure. Do you find any evidence that the environmental firms are superior performers?

chapter 18

International Issues in Management Accounting

learning objectives

After studying this chapter, you should be able to:

1. Explain the role of the management accountant in the international environment.
2. Identify the varying levels of involvement that firms can undertake in international trade.
3. List the ways management accountants can manage foreign currency risk.
4. Explain why multinational firms choose to decentralize.
5. Describe how environmental factors can affect performance evaluation in the multinational firm.
6. Discuss the role of transfer pricing in the multinational firm.
7. Discuss ethical issues that affect firms operating in the international environment.

MILLBOURNE shutter

Scenario

Jeff Millbourne is the owner/operator of Millbourne Shutter Company. Over a three-year period, he transformed his hobby of woodworking into a million-dollar business. The company makes custom shutters for homes and businesses. Millbourne Shutter Company built its reputation on the production of very high-quality shutters, using top-quality wood and building each shutter to exact specifications. The result is a shutter that works well for years. Recently, Jeff's neighbors, Lana and Evan Howell, bought a villa in France and had Millbourne design and construct shutters for it. The job was more difficult than usual, since Jeff was unable to measure the villa's windows. However, the shutters fit perfectly and were a hit in the French village. The French subcontractor who installed the shutters wanted to contract with Millbourne to make shutters for some of his other jobs. He placed an initial order for shutters at €16,230. Jeff sent the purchase order to his accountant, Rosa Perez, for help in translating the euros into dollars.

Rosa pointed out that that, at the current exchange rate of $1 equal to 0.8115 euros, the order would bring in $20,000 (€16,230/0.8115). However, she noted, the exchange rate changes from day to day. She asked how long receipt of payment would take. Jeff figured it would take about three weeks to produce that many shutters—more if it rained and painting was delayed, then two weeks to ship overseas. It could take another four weeks for Michel to send the check. Start to finish, Jeff thought it might take two and a half months.

Rosa pointed out that the time lag could mean a change in the exchange rates. If the exchange rate increased, say to 0.85 euros per dollar, the supposed $20,000 order would yield only $19,094. Of course, the reverse was also true. If the rate fell to 0.80 euros per dollar, the €16,230 could be exchanged for $20,288. Dealing in other currencies posed a new level of risk for the company—currency exchange risk.

Jeff agreed to think about the issues for a little while. He decided to go ahead with the French order, but to consider each new international order on a case-by-case basis, to ensure that the currency exchange risk did not get out of hand.

Questions to Think About

1. What do you think are the business issues that Jeff has to consider in deciding whether or not to trade overseas?

2. Rosa pointed out that exchange rates can go in two directions. If the exchange rate increases from 0.8115 euros per dollar to 0.85 euros per dollar, Jeff will get less than he expected. On the other hand, if the exchange rate decreases, he will get more than expected. Do you think that Jeff considers the two risks (increase or decrease in exchange rates) to be equal? Would he be more concerned about one than the other? Why or why not?

3. Jeff decided to consider each new international order on a case-by-case basis. What factors might influence his decisions? Think about the shipment of the shutters overseas. Are there any considerations that might differ from shipment of shutters to another state in the United States? Would there be any difference between trade with France versus trade with other countries (e.g., Russia or Iran)?

Management Accounting in the International Environment

Objective 1

Explain the role of the management accountant in the international environment.

Doing business in a global environment requires management to shift perspective. While many aspects of business remain the same, others are quite different. From his conversation with Rosa Perez, we can see that Jeff Millbourne is struggling with one of these differences—the income implications of foreign currency exchange. The company doing business in both its home country and other countries may find that credit practices that work well in the home country may cause problems in another country. Much of the difference can be related to the business environment—that is, the cultural, legal, political, and economic environments of the various countries. Just as a fish, supposedly, is not aware of water, we in the United States take our business environment for granted. We have grown accustomed to a market economy and to the concept of private property. We are also used to a legal system that enforces contracts. Our sense of ethics has grown in tandem with the underlying environment. When the environment changes, ethical problems may arise.

Where does the management accountant fit into the global business environment? Business looks to the management accountant for financial and business expertise. Good training, education, and staying abreast of changes in one's field are important to any accountant. However, the job of the management accountant in the international firm is made more challenging by the ambiguous and ever-changing nature of global business. Since much of the management accountant's job is to provide relevant information to management, staying up-to-date requires reading books and articles in a variety of business areas, including information systems, marketing, management, politics, and economics. In addition, the management accountant must be familiar with the financial accounting rules of the countries in which the firm operates.[1]

The remainder of this chapter will touch on various issues facing the multinational firm. Our focus is on the management accountant and how he or she must deal with those issues.

Levels of Involvement in International Trade

Objective 2

Identify the varying levels of involvement that firms can undertake in international trade.

A **multinational corporation (MNC)** is one that "does business in more than one country in such a volume that its well-being and growth rest in more than one country."[2] From this definition, we can see that the involvement of the MNC in international trade may take many forms. On a fairly simple level, the MNC may import materials and/or export finished products. On a more complex level, the MNC may be a large firm consisting of a parent company and a number of divisions in various countries.

In the international environment, the choice of company structure goes beyond the issue of centralized versus decentralized firm structures described in Chapter 10. While multinational companies are very often decentralized, with the subsidiaries being wholly owned by the parent firm, the many legal systems under which the firm must operate require careful consideration of company structure. Some of the choices are importing and exporting, wholly owned subsidiaries, and joint ventures.

1 For an enlightening interview with McDonald's controller—Europe, see Ramona Dzinkowski, "McDonald's Europe: Despite the Falling Euro, the Mad Cow Scare, and Other Challenges, the Fast-Food Giant Sees Continuing Opportunity in Europe," *Strategic Finance* (May 2001): pp. 25–27.

2 Yair Aharoni, "On the Definition of a Multinational Corporation," in *The Multinational Enterprise in Transition*, eds. A. Kapoor and Phillip D. Grub (Princeton, N.J.: Darwin Press, 1972): p. 4.

Importing and Exporting

A relatively simple form of multinational involvement is importing and exporting. A company may import parts for production. Similarly, a company may export finished products to foreign countries. Even such simple transactions as importing and exporting can present new risks and opportunities for companies.

Importing A company may import materials for use in production. While this transaction may seem identical to the purchase of materials from domestic suppliers, U.S. tariffs add complexity and cost. In accounting for materials, freight-in is a materials cost. An imported part may have a tariff, or duty, in addition to freight-in cost. A **tariff** is a tax on imports levied by the federal government. This tax is also a cost of materials. Companies strive to find ways to decrease tariffs. They may restrict the amount of imported materials, alter the materials by adding U.S. resources (to increase the domestic content and gain more favorable tariff status), or utilize foreign trade zones.

Foreign Trade Zones The U.S. government has set up **foreign trade zones**, which are areas near a customs port of entry that are physically on U.S. soil but are considered to be outside U.S. commerce. San Antonio, New Orleans, and the Port of Catoosa, Oklahoma, are examples of cities with foreign trade zones. Some U.S. companies have set up manufacturing plants within the foreign trade zones. Goods imported into a foreign trade zone are duty-free until they leave the zone. This has important implications for manufacturing firms that import materials. Since tariffs are not paid until the imported materials leave the zone as part of a finished product, the company can postpone payment of duty and the associated loss of working capital. Additionally, the company does not pay duty on defective materials or on inventory that has not yet been included in finished products.

An example may help to illustrate the cost advantages of operating a plant in a foreign trade zone. Suppose that Roadrunner, Inc., operates a petrochemical plant located in a foreign trade zone. The plant imports volatile materials (for example,

Imported goods, such as petrochemicals, may be shipped to the United States and then off-loaded at a Foreign Trade Zone. Doing this enables the purchaser to postpone, or even eliminate, the payment of duty.

chemicals that experience substantial evaporation loss during processing) for use in production. Wilycoyote, Inc., operates an identical plant just outside the foreign trade zone. Consider the impact on duty and related expenditures for the two plants for the purchase of $400,000 of crude oil imported from Venezuela. Both Roadrunner and Wilycoyote use the oil in chemical production. Each purchases the oil about three months before use in production, and the finished chemicals remain in inventory about five months before sale and shipment to the customer. About 30 percent of the oil is lost through evaporation during production. Duty is assessed at 6 percent of cost. Each company faces 12 percent carrying costs.

Wilycoyote pays duty, at the point of purchase, of $24,000 (0.06 × $400,000). In addition, Wilycoyote has carrying costs associated with the duty payment of 12 percent per year times the portion of the year that the oil is in materials or finished goods inventory. In this case, the months in inventory equal 8 (3 + 5). Total duty-related carrying cost is $1,920 (0.12 × 8/12 × $24,000). Total duty and duty-related carrying costs are $25,920. Roadrunner, on the other hand, pays duty at the time of sale because it is in a foreign trade zone, and imported goods do not incur duty until (or unless) they are moved out of the zone. Since 70 percent of the original imported oil remains in the final product, duty equals $16,800 (0.70 × $400,000 × 0.06). There are no carrying costs associated with the duty. A summary of the duty-related costs for the two companies follows:

	Roadrunner	**Wilycoyote**
Duty paid at purchase	$ 0	$24,000
Carrying costs of duty	0	1,920
Duty paid at sale	16,800	0
Total duty and duty-related cost	$16,800	$25,920

Clearly, Roadrunner has saved $9,120 ($25,920 − $16,800) on just one purchase of imported materials by locating in the foreign trade zone.

Foreign trade zones provide additional advantages. For example, goods that do not meet U.S. health, safety, and pollution control regulations are subject to fines. Foreign goods can be imported into foreign trade zones and modified to comply with the law without being subject to the fines. Another example of the efficient use of foreign trade zones is the assembly of high-tariff component parts into a lower-tariff finished product. In this case, the addition of domestic labor raises the domestic content of the finished product and makes the embedded foreign parts eligible for more favorable tariff treatment.[3]

The management accountant must be aware of the costs of importing materials. He or she should also be able to evaluate the potential benefits of the foreign trade zone in considering the location of satellite plants.

Exporting Exporting is the sale of a company's products in foreign countries. It is not necessary to have a production facility in the foreign country; finished products can simply be transported to the buyer. However, exporting is usually more complex than the sale of finished goods within the home country. Foreign countries have a variety of import and tariff regulations. The job of complying with the foreign rules and regulations often falls to the controller's office, just as compliance with U.S. tax regulations is an accounting function. Alternatively, a U.S. company may choose to work with an experienced distributor familiar with the legal complexities of the other countries. In some cases, the distributor is wholly owned (as is the one headed by Jeff Millbourne); in other cases, the distributor is a separate company.

3 These examples are taken from James E. Groff and John P. McCray, "Foreign Trade Zones: Opportunity for Strategic Development in the Southwest," *Journal of Business Strategies* (Spring 1992): pp. 14–26.

Treaties and Tariffs Trade treaties between countries affect the tariffs charged. For example, the North American Free Trade Agreement (NAFTA) allows importers in the United States, Mexico, and Canada to pay reduced tariffs on goods produced in the three countries. However, strict adherence to regulations is required. U.S. Customs has stepped up enforcement of NAFTA regulations by checking for valid certificates of origin on imported goods. A *certificate of origin* is a document summarizing the information enabling companies to qualify for reduced NAFTA duties. The penalties for noncompliance are steep—ranging from twice the revenue lost (in tariffs) to the domestic value of the goods. Management accountants must be aware of the customs regulations and ensure that adequate record keeping and internal control mechanisms exist.[4]

Wholly Owned Subsidiaries

A company may choose to purchase an existing foreign company, making the purchased company a wholly owned subsidiary of the parent. This strategy has the virtue of simplicity. The foreign company has established an outlet for the product and has the production and distribution facilities already set up. For example, in 1989, **Whirlpool** expanded into the European market by purchasing the appliance business of **Philips N.V.**, Europe's third-largest appliance manufacturer. This purchase gave Whirlpool immediate access to production and distribution facilities, as well as an established brand name. Even so, the approach is not inexpensive. The first three years were spent blending company cultures before the European operation could be streamlined to cut costs. Finally, more investment was necessary in marketing to replace the Philips name with Whirlpool's and to develop a marketing plan for all of Europe as opposed to the more fragmented country-by-country approach used previously.[5] Even so, success is not ensured. The European competition became more efficient and aggressive. By 1998, Whirlpool made about $10 on every $100 in sales in the United States, but only $2.30 per $100 of sales in Europe.[6]

If the laws of the country permit, an MNC can simply set up a wholly owned subsidiary or branch office in the country. In Ireland, for example, U.S. insurance and software companies have set up branch offices. **Quarterdeck Office Systems**, a part of **Symantec Corp.**, routes customer calls to its second phone-answering operation in Dublin. Scores of multilingual workers take calls from all over Europe and the United States. When it is 5:00 a.m. in California, Irish workers are well into their working day and can answer calls from customers in the U.S. eastern standard time zone. The Irish Development Authority provides generous tax and other incentives worth about a year's pay for each job created.[7]

Outsourcing of technical and professional jobs is becoming an important issue for cost-conscious U.S. firms. **Outsourcing** is the payment by a company for a business function formerly done in-house. For example, some domestic companies outsource their legal needs to outside law firms rather than hiring corporate attorneys. In the context of the MNC, outsourcing refers to the move of a business function to another country. For example, **Texas Instruments** set up an impressive software programming operation in Bangalore, in southern India. The availability of underemployed college graduates in India caused both low wage rates and high productivity. However, the underdeveloped Indian infrastructure required considerable capital investment—"Even though [Texas Instruments] had to install its own electrical generators and satellite dishes to operate efficiently, wages are low enough that work still gets done for half of what it costs in the U.S."[8]

4 "NAFTA and U.S. Customs—The Honeymoon Is Over," *Deloitte & Touche Review* (May 15, 1995): pp. 4–5.
5 Barry Rehfeld, "Where Whirlpool Flies, and Maytag Sputters," *New York Times* (January 3, 1993): p. 5.
6 Greg Steinmetz and Carl Quintanilla, "Whirlpool Expected Easy Going in Europe, and It Got a Big Shock," *Wall Street Journal* (April 10, 1998): pp. A1, A6.
7 "Your New Global Work Force," *Fortune* (December 14, 1992): pp. 52–56 and 64.
8 "Your New Global Work Force," p. 64.

Outsourcing is done by foreign firms as well. **Toyota Motor** outsourced its design needs for the Previa to California. Benefits to Toyota included the greater familiarity Californian designers have with the U.S. minivan market as well as the political advantage of having part of the Previa's development in the United States.

The management accountant must be aware of numerous costs and benefits of outsourcing that would not be available in the United States. The varying tax structures and incentives of local authorities, the overall educational level of the country, and the infrastructure all play a role in the management accountant's assessment of costs and benefits.

Joint Ventures

Sometimes, companies with the expertise needed by MNCs do not exist or are not for sale; in this case, a joint venture may work. A **joint venture** is a type of partnership in which investors co-own the enterprise. **IBM** spent much time and money on plasma display technology for portable computers until it realized that the technology was impractical because of excessive power usage. Liquid-crystal displays (LCDs) provided a possible solution, so IBM formed a joint venture with Toshiba to marry its own expertise in materials with Toshiba's superior manufacturing. IBM, **Toshiba**, and **Siemens** have also united in manufacturing memory chips. In 2001, investors from around the world teamed up to buy European telecommunications companies. **Pirelli SpA**, the Italian tire maker, and the owners of the **Benetton Group**, fashion retailers, bought a controlling interest in Italy's national phone company, **Belecom Italiz SpA**. The two purchasers believe that they can bring marketing expertise and knowledge of the consumer to the troubled telephone company.[9]

Sometimes, a joint venture is required because of restrictive laws. In China, for example, MNCs are not allowed to purchase companies or set up their own subsidiaries. Joint ventures with Chinese firms are required. Similarly, India and Thailand demand local ownership. **Loctite**, maker of Super Glue, runs joint ventures in both India and Thailand for that reason.

A special case of joint venture cooperation is the maquiladora. A **maquiladora** is a manufacturing plant, located in Mexico, which processes imported materials and re-exports them to the United States. Originally designed to encourage U.S. firms to invest in Mexico, the program has now expanded to include other foreign firms, such as **Nissan Motor** and **Sony**. Basically, the maquiladora enjoys special status in both Mexico, which grants operators an exemption from Mexican laws governing foreign ownership, and the United States, which grants exemptions from or reductions in custom duties levied on re-exported goods. Most maquiladoras are located in cities bordering the United States to take advantage of ready access to U.S. transportation and communication facilities. The Mexican advantage is low-cost, high-quality labor. The structure of the maquiladora is flexible. Mexico permits different levels of involvement. The minimal level combines low risk with low cost savings. In this case, the U.S. firm transfers materials to an existing Mexican firm and imports them back in finished form. All hiring and operating of the Mexican plant is handled by the Mexican owners. The highest level of involvement offers both high risk and high cost savings. At this level, the U.S. firm owns the Mexican subsidiary and oversees all the operations.[10]

Maquiladoras are an example of a government program to increase production that has worked well. Foreign investment has moved well beyond the border cities to a broad band of northern Mexico. Improvements in the Mexican infrastructure (for example, roads and communications) have enticed companies further into the

9 Almar Latour, "Low Stock Prices Lure Investors to Europe's Telephone Giants," *Wall Street Journal* (August 10, 2001): p. 1.

10 James E. Groff and John P. McCray, "Maquiladoras: The Mexico Option Can Reduce Your Manufacturing Cost," *Management Accounting* (January 1991): pp. 43–46.

Managers Decide

Delphi Takes Global View of Technology

Delphi, a major maker of auto parts and formerly owned by GM, is a company that thinks globally. Delphi Mexico CIO John Guevara says, "Everything we do is considered on a global basis. Just because you present an idea doesn't mean you get to keep it." An executive group composed of CIOs from three product divisions, the Mexico and European divisions, and the head of IT infrastructure planning meet regularly to discuss business-technology initiatives. They consider the basic integrity of the technology, the financial advantages proposed, and the delivery mechanisms. The council determines whether the proposed technology should be used across Delphi or just in one or two divisions, whether it should be outsourced or developed in-house, and which division's IT staff should develop it. IT location and outsourcing advantages change quickly, along with relative wage and educational advantages. In Delphi Mexico, for example, most of the staff have masters' degrees—many earned while working at Delphi. Political risk also affects the desirability of a country vis–à-vis outsourcing. ■

Source: Chris Murphy, "Crossing Borders," *Information Week* (July 7, 2003), http://www.informationweek.com/news/showArticle.jhtml?articleID=10818086

interior, lowering nonlabor costs. U.S. companies were originally drawn to the maquiladoras for the cheap labor; now, both wage rates and other benefits have risen. For example, the **GM Delphi** plant in Ciudad Juarez teaches new employees to read and write and provides low-cost mortgages. Delphi benefits by having 53 Mexican plants that have not experienced strikes for five years.[11]

U.S. firms have also found other benefits to investment in maquiladoras. For example, **Ford**'s plant in Chihuahua was built to satisfy export requirements for doing business in Mexico. Now, it supports Ford's sales to Mexico, establishing a marketing reason for the plant's presence.

No matter which structure the MNC takes, it faces issues of foreign trade. An important issue is foreign currency exchange, which is addressed in the next section.

Foreign Currency Exchange

Objective 3

List the ways management accountants can manage foreign currency risk.

When a company operates only in its home country, only one currency is used, and exchange issues never arise. However, when a company begins to operate in the international arena, it must use foreign currencies. These foreign currencies can be exchanged for the domestic currency using **exchange rates**. If the exchange rates never changed, problems would not occur. Exchange rates do change, however, often on a daily basis. Thus, a dollar that could be traded for 150 yen one day may be worth only 125 yen on another day. Currency rate fluctuations add considerably to the uncertainty of operating in the international arena.

The management accountant plays an important role in managing the company's exposure to currency risk. **Currency risk management** refers to the company's management of its transaction, economic, and translation risks due to exchange rate fluctuations. **Transaction risk** refers to the possibility that future cash transactions

11 Joel Millman, "In Mexico, a GM Worker Sprints into the Middle Class," *Wall Street Journal* (July 19, 1998): pp. B1 and B4.

will be affected by changing exchange rates. **Economic risk** refers to the possibility that a firm's present value of future cash flows will be affected by exchange rate fluctuations. **Translation (or accounting) risk** is the degree to which a firm's financial statements are exposed to exchange rate fluctuation. Let's look more closely at these three components of currency risk and ways in which the accountant can manage the company's exposure to them.

Managing Transaction Risk

Today's MNC deals in many different currencies. These currencies may be traded for one another, depending on the exchange rate in effect at the time of the trade. The **spot rate** is the exchange rate of one currency for another for immediate delivery (that is, today). Exhibit 18-1 lists a number of widely used currencies and their spot rates as of April 20, 2006. While the spot rates are surely different now, as you read this book, you can gain an idea of relative values. Changes in the spot rates can affect the value of a company's future cash transactions, posing transaction risk. Let's first get a feel for currency appreciation and depreciation before we go on to exchange gains and losses and hedging.

Currency Appreciation and Depreciation When one country's currency strengthens relative to another country's currency, **currency appreciation** occurs, and one unit of the first country's currency can buy more units of the second country's

Country (Currency Name)	US dollar equivalent	Currency per US dollar
Argentina (Peso)	0.3269	3.059
Australia (Dollar)	0.7377	1.3556
U.K. (Pound)	1.7792	0.5621
Canada (Dollar)	0.8773	1.1399
China (Renminbi)	0.124789	8.0135
Hong Kong (Dollar)	0.128955	7.7546
India (Rupee)	0.02221	45.0248
Indonesia (Rupiah)	0.000113	8880.995
Israel (Shekel)	0.2192	4.562
Japan (Yen)	0.008507	117.5503
Mexico (Peso)	0.09064	11.0327
New Zealand (Dollar)	0.6266	1.5959
Peru (New Sol)	0.3017	3.3146
Philippines (Peso)	0.01942	51.4933
Russia (Ruble)	0.03639	27.4801
Saudi Arabia (Riyal)	0.2666	3.7509
Singapore (Dollar)	0.6256	1.5985
South Korea (Won)	0.001054	948.5866
Sweden (Krona)	0.1327	7.5358
Switzerland (Franc)	0.7826	1.2778
Taiwan (Dollar)	0.03096	32.2997
Thailand (Baht)	0.02647	37.7786
U.K. (Pound)	1.7792	0.5621
Euro**	1.2323	0.8115

*Taken from the *Wall Street Journal*, April 20, 2006, http://online.wsj.com/page/mdc/2_0500-forextab-12.html?mod=2_0032

**The following countries use the Euro: Andorra, Austria, Belgium, Finland, France, Germany, Greece, Ireland, Italy, Kosovo, Luxembourg, Monaco, Montenegro, Netherlands, Portugal, San Marino, Spain, and Vatican City.

Exhibit 18-1 Spot Rates as of April 20, 2006*

currency. Conversely, **currency depreciation** means that one country's currency has become relatively weaker and buys fewer units of another currency. For example, in the summer of 1998, the Asian economic crisis meant that the dollar had strengthened against the yen and other Asian currencies. This had an impact on trade between the United States and Asia. For example, Disneyland, where Asian visitors account for about 8 percent of the total, experienced as much as a 4 percent decline in attendance due to the softening of the Asian currencies. Universal Studios Hollywood saw a decrease in attendance of about 5 percent during the summer of 1998. Why? Because while the cost of attending the theme parks and staying in hotels had not gone up, the value of the yen, ringgit, and won had gone down—making dollars much more expensive to tourists from Japan, Malaysia, and South Korea.[12]

Exchange Gains and Losses Let's examine the impact of changes in exchange rates on the sale of goods to other countries. Suppose that SuperTubs, Inc., based in Oklahoma, sells its line of whirlpool tubs at home and to foreign distributors. On January 15, Bonbain, a French distributor of luxury plumbing fixtures, orders 100 tubs at a price of $1,000 per tub, to be delivered immediately, and to be paid in euros on March 15. Has SuperTubs just made a sale of $100,000 (100 × $1,000)? The payment is to be in euros, not dollars, so we must look at the exchange rate for euros. If the exchange rate on January 15 is 0.82 euros per dollar, then Bonbain is really promising to pay 82,000 euros (0.82 × $100,000) on March 15. If the exchange rate remains at 0.82 euros per dollar on March 15, SuperTubs would receive 82,000 euros, convertible to $100,000. But suppose that the exchange rate on March 15 is 0.84 euros per dollar. Bonbain still pays 82,000 euros, but SuperTubs can convert that amount into only $97,619 (82,000/0.84), not the $100,000 it anticipated back in January when the sale was made. The difference between the two amounts, $2,381, is the loss on currency exchange. The impact of transaction risk on this example can be summarized as follows:

Receivable in dollars on January 15	$100,000
Received in dollars on March 15	97,619
Exchange loss	$ 2,381

© Richard Nowitz/Corbis

Companies buying and selling in foreign countries must be aware of currency exchange issues. Similarly, travelers are concerned with currency exchange. Adverse movement in the yen versus the dollar, for example, can make a vacation trip much more expensive than originally planned.

12 Bruce Orwall, "After Several Years of Good Times, Theme Parks Find Troubleland," *Wall Street Journal* Interactive Edition (September 21, 1998).

An **exchange loss**, then, is a loss on the exchange of one currency for another due to depreciation of the home currency.

Of course, if the euro had strengthened against the dollar, say an exchange rate of 0.80 euros per dollar, an exchange gain would occur. An **exchange gain** is the gain on the exchange of one currency for another due to appreciation of the home currency. In our example, Bonbain again pays 82,000 euros, which SuperTubs is able to convert into $102,500 (82,000/0.80). In that case, the impact of transaction risk would result in a gain:

Receivable in dollars on January 15	$100,000
Received in dollars on March 15	102,500
Exchange gain	$ 2,500

Transaction risk also affects the purchase of commodities from foreign companies. Suppose that on February 20, AmeriMon, Inc. (based in Big Timber, Montana) purchases computers from **NEC** (located in Japan) for $50,000, payable in yen on May 20. Assume the spot rate for yen is 130 per dollar on February 20. It is easy to see that AmeriMon's true payable is for 6,500,000 yen (50,000 × 130). If the spot rate for yen is 135 on May 20, it will cost AmeriMon only $48,148 (6,500,000/135) to get enough yen to pay NEC:

Liability in dollars on February 20	$50,000
Liability in dollars on May 20	48,148
Exchange gain	$ 1,852

As we can see, the more favorable May 20 spot rate has resulted in an exchange gain. Clearly, transaction risk caused by the movement of foreign currency against the dollar must be taken into account by managers as it affects the prices paid and received for goods. Suppose management does not want to be involved in gambling on exchange rates? What then? The following section on hedging explains how the accountant can manage a company's exposure to exchange gains and losses.

Hedging One way of insuring against gains and losses on foreign currency exchanges is **hedging**. Typically, a forward exchange contract is used as a hedge. The **forward contract** requires the buyer to exchange a specified amount of a currency at a specified rate (the forward rate) on a specified future date.

Let's return to our example of SuperTubs' sale of $100,000 worth of tubs to the French company. The spot rate on January 15 was 0.82 euros per dollar. SuperTubs' problem is that it does not know what the exchange rate will be on March 15. If it is more than 0.82 euros, SuperTubs will receive less than the $100,000 anticipated in accounts receivable. Of course, if the rate is less, SuperTubs will receive more. But the difficulty is in predicting short-term exchange rate movements. SuperTubs may well decide it is in the business of manufacturing and selling tubs, not in the business of betting on exchange rate fluctuations. Therefore, it will forgo the opportunity for exchange rate gains by hedging against exchange rate losses. Here is how it might work using forward contracts.

On January 15, SuperTubs purchases a contract to exchange 82,000 euros into dollars on March 15 at a forward rate of 0.825 euros. SuperTubs has agreed to sell euros for dollars. At this point, SuperTubs has locked in the exchange rate. The 0.005 difference between the spot rate of 0.82 and the forward rate of 0.825 is the premium that SuperTubs pays the exchange dealer on the transaction. Think of it as an insurance premium.

On March 15, the following transactions occur. Bonbain pays SuperTubs 82,000 euros, SuperTubs pays the exchange dealer 82,000 euros, and the exchange dealer pays SuperTubs $99,394 (82,000/0.825). The difference between the $100,000 original account receivable and the $99,394 cash paid is charged to an exchange premium expense account. Remember that in our original example, the exchange rate on March 15 is 0.84 euros per dollar. Had SuperTubs not hedged, it would have received only $97,619. Therefore, the exchange premium expense of $606 saved SuperTubs a loss of $2,381; this is a net savings of $1,775.

Receivable in dollars on January 15	$100,000
Received in dollars on March 15	99,394
Premium expense	$ 606

Of course, the hedging can also be done by agreeing to exchange dollars for a foreign currency at a future date. Recall the previous example of AmeriMon's purchase of 6,500,000 yen worth of computers. At a spot rate of 130, AmeriMon expects to pay $50,000 to satisfy its liability. AmeriMon may fear that the rate will decline, say to 125. If it does, AmeriMon will have to pay $52,000 (6,500,000/125) for the same 6,500,000 yen. A hedging transaction would resolve AmeriMon's uncertainty. Perhaps the forward rate is 128.7 yen per dollar. Then AmeriMon would purchase a forward contract to purchase 6,500,000 yen on May 20 for $50,505 (6,500,000/128.7):

Liability in dollars on February 20	$ 50,000
Payment in dollars on May 20	(50,505)
Premium expense	$ (505)

Hedging transactions can become much more complex than the foregoing examples. Companies with significant transaction exposure may choose to hedge all or part of their exposure. Hedging may also be used as a tool to manage economic risk. That use will be addressed in the following section.

Managing Economic Risk

Dealing in different currencies can introduce an economic dimension into currency exchange transactions. Recall that economic risk was defined as the impact of exchange rate fluctuations on the present value of a firm's future cash flows. The risk can affect the relative competitiveness of the firm, even if it never participates directly in international trade. Take a simple example based on the market for heavy equipment between 1981 and 1985.

Suppose that U.S. consumers can choose to purchase heavy equipment from either **Caterpillar** (based in the United States) or **Komatsu** (based in Japan). Assume the price of one type of equipment is $80,000 from both makers. However, while Caterpillar truly means $80,000, Komatsu really is interested in 10,400,000 yen, its own currency. At an exchange rate of $1 equals 130 yen, the price of $80,000 is set. Now suppose that the value of the dollar strengthens against the yen and the exchange rate becomes $1 equals 140 yen. To get the same 10,400,000 yen, Komatsu requires a price of only $74,286. The cost structures of the two firms have not changed nor has customer demand, but because of currency fluctuations, the Japanese firm has become more "competitive." Of course, as the dollar weakens, the position is reversed, and U.S. exports become relatively cheaper to foreign customers.

How does the accountant manage the company's exposure to economic risk? Most importantly, he or she must be aware of it by understanding the position of the firm in the global economy. As we can see in the Caterpillar-Komatsu example, the two firms were competitors and were linked through their customers' participation in the global marketplace. The accountant provides financial structure and communication for the firm. In preparing the master budget, for example, budgeted sales must take into account potential strengthening or weakening of the currencies of competitors' countries. Often, the controller's office is responsible for forecasting foreign exchange movements.

Hedging can provide another means of managing economic risk. For example, the **Toronto Blue Jays** baseball team receives its revenues in Canadian dollars but pays most of its expenses in U.S. dollars. In 1985, the team anticipated a loss due to unfavorable exchange rate fluctuations. To prevent this, in 1984, the team purchased forward contracts of U.S. dollars at $0.75 per Canadian dollar. The exchange rate at the end of 1984 was $0.7568 per Canadian dollar; the exchange rate dropped steadily throughout 1985 to $0.7156 by the end of the fourth quarter of 1985. The depreciation of Canada's currency, carefully hedged against through the purchase of forward contracts, resulted in a profit to the team.[13]

Managing Translation Risk

Often the parent company restates all subsidiaries' income into the home currency. This restatement can result in gain and loss opportunities on the revaluation of foreign currencies and can affect a subsidiary's financial statements and the related ROI and EVA computations.

Suppose you are a divisional manager based in Mexico. Your division earned 320,000 pesos this year, up from 200,000 pesos the year before, a hefty 60 percent increase. Now, suppose that your income is translated into dollars. If the exchange rate last year was six pesos per dollar and the exchange rate this year is 10 pesos per dollar, your net income figures translate into $33,333 income last year and $32,000 income this year. Suddenly, there is a *decrease* in income. Similar unpleasant surprises await ROI and net worth computations. The potential for gain or loss on currency revaluation is particularly relevant for countries whose currencies are volatile—and depreciating relative to the home company's currency.

Foreign currency fluctuations also cause difficulties in evaluating the local manager's adherence to company policy. **Monsanto** faced this very problem. The company noticed declining sales in some of its foreign markets. The local managers were instructed to increase promotional expenditures. However, dollar-denominated reports showed no increases. Top management continued to press local managers to carry out instructions. Local managers were frustrated by their inability to convince higher management that they had increased expenditures, since the reports showed fewer dollars being spent. Eventually, local currency statements were placed alongside dollar-denominated reports. These comparative statements clearly showed that increased expenditures had taken place.

A simple numerical example based on Monsanto's experience (but not using their figures) may illustrate the problem. Assume that Multinational, Inc., has a foreign division, FD, which has been experiencing eroding sales. Multinational directs FD managers to increase marketing expenditures. FD managers do increase marketing expenditures over the following four quarters as shown:

Quarter	Expenditures in Local Currency
1	LC 10,000
2	LC 11,000
3	LC 12,100
4	LC 13,310

As we can see, marketing expenditures have grown by 10 percent in each quarter. However, multinational managers do not see this table; instead, they see dollar-denominated reports. In order to translate local currency figures into dollars, we need the exchange rates for each quarter. Suppose that the dollar has strengthened against the local currency and the quarterly exchange rates of $1 for units of local

13 Paul V. Mannino and Ken Milani, "Budgeting for an International Business," *Management Accounting* (February 1992): pp. 36–41.

currency are 1.00, 1.20, 1.35, and 1.50, respectively. Then, FD's marketing expenditures in dollars would be as follows:

Quarter	Expenditures in Dollars
1	$10,000
2	9,167
3	8,963
4	8,873

What a difference! Not only have local managers not increased expenditures, it looks as if they have actually decreased expenditures. Only by comparing the dollar-denominated figures with those denominated in local currency can Multinational see the two effects of an increase in marketing expenditures and the strengthening of the dollar. In this case, FD's increase was hidden in currency translation.

The objective of dollar-denominated internal reports is to measure all figures on the same basis. While this strategy may work at any one point in time, it may mislead managers when comparisons are made over time. The management accountant must be aware of this source of translation risk.

Decentralization

Objective 4

Explain why multinational firms choose to decentralize.

Frequently, firms that are decentralized in the home country may exercise tighter control over foreign divisions, at least until they gain more experience with their overseas operations. Just as decentralization offers advantages for home country divisions, it also offers advantages for foreign divisions. Let's review some of those advantages.

Advantages of Decentralization in the MNC

The quality of information is better at the local level, and that can improve the quality of decisions. This is particularly true in MNCs, where far-flung divisions may be operating in a number of different countries subject to various legal systems and customs. As a result, local managers are often in a position to make better decisions. Decentralization allows an organization to take advantage of this specialized knowledge. For example, **Loctite** has local managers run their own divisions; in particular, marketing and pricing are under local control. Language is not a problem as local managers are in control. Similarly, local managers are conversant with their own laws and customs.

Local managers in the MNC are capable of a more timely response in decision making. They are able to respond quickly to customer discount demands, local government demands, and changes in the political climate.

In Chapter 10, we discussed the need for centralized managers to transmit instructions and the chance that the manager responsible for implementing the decision might misinterpret the instructions. The different languages native to managers of divisions in the MNC make this an even greater problem. MNCs address this problem in two ways. First, a decentralized structure pushes decision making down to the local manager level, eliminating the need to interpret instructions from above. Second, MNCs are learning to incorporate technology that overrides the language barrier and eases cross-border data transfers. Technology is of great help in smoothing communication difficulties between parent and subsidiary and between one subsidiary and another. Loctite's plant in Ireland uses computerized labeling on adhesives bound for Great Britain or Israel. Bar code technology "reads" the labels, eliminating the need for foreign language translation.

Just as decentralization gives the lower-level managers in the home country a chance to develop managerial skills, foreign subsidiary managers also gain valuable experience. Just as important, home country managers gain broader experience by interacting with managers of foreign divisions. The chance for learning from each other is much greater in a decentralized MNC. On and off throughout the latter half of the twentieth century, a tour of duty at a foreign subsidiary has been a part of the manager's climb to the top. Now, foreign subsidiary managers may expect to spend some time at headquarters in the home office, as well.

Creation of Divisions

The MNC has great flexibility in creating types of divisions. Divisions are often created along geographic lines. **IBM**, for example, has divisional boundaries that organize production and sales for Asia and the Far East (AFE), North America, Latin and South America, Europe, and Africa.

Product lines may afford a rationale for the creation of divisions. Many MNCs are diversified, manufacturing and selling a number of different products. The MNC may decide that the major difference is the type of product sold, not the country in which it is sold. An oil company, for example, may have an exploration division, a refining division, and a chemicals division. Each of these divisions may include plants or operations in a number of different countries.

Divisions may follow functional management lines. In the early 1970s, **Avon Products** created three regional marketing and planning centers—in New York, London, and Australia. These worked reasonably well for a while and achieved the objective of sharing expertise and training divisional managers. However, national needs and differences caused conflict. So, by the late 1980s, Avon had disbanded the regional centers and decentralized to the individual country level.[14]

The presence of divisions in more than one country creates the need for performance evaluation that can take into account differences in divisional environments. The next section examines performance evaluation in the MNC.

Measuring Performance in the Multinational Firm

Objective 5

Describe how environmental factors can affect performance evaluation in the multinational firm.

It is important for the MNC to separate the evaluation of the manager of a division from the evaluation of the division. The manager's evaluation should not include factors over which he or she exercises no control, such as currency fluctuations, taxes, and so on. Instead, managers should be evaluated on the basis of revenues and costs incurred. Once a manager is evaluated, the subsidiary financial statements can be restated to the home currency, and uncontrollable costs can be allocated.[15]

It is particularly difficult to compare the performance of a manager of a division (or subsidiary) in one country with the performance of a manager of a division in another country. Even divisions that appear to be similar in terms of production may face very different economic, social, or political forces. International environmental conditions may be very different from, and more complex than, domestic conditions.[16] Environmental variables facing local managers of divisions include economic, legal, political, social, and educational factors. Some important economic

14 Louis V. Consiglio, "Global Competitive Advantage: Lessons from Avon," Working Paper No. 1 (July 1992), Center for Applied Research, Lubin School of Business, Pace University.

15 Gerhard G. Mueller, Helen Gernon, and Gary Meek, *Accounting: An International Perspective* (Homewood, IL: Irwin, 1987).

16 Wagdy M. Abdallah, "Change the Environment or Change the System," *Management Accounting* (October 1986): pp. 33–36.

variables are inflation, foreign exchange rates, taxes, and transfer prices. Legal and political actions also have differing impacts. For example, a country may not allow cash outflows, forcing the corporation to find ways to trade for the host country's output.[17] Educational variables vary from country to country as does the sophistication of the accounting system. Sociological and cultural variables affect how the multinational firm is treated by the subsidiary's country.

The existence of differing environmental factors makes interdivisional comparison of ROI potentially misleading. Suppose a U.S.-based MNC has three divisions located in Brazil, Canada, and Spain with the following information given in millions of dollars:

	Assets	Revenues	Net Income	Margin*	Turnover*	ROI*
Brazil	$10	$ 6	$ 3	0.50	0.60	0.30
Canada	18	13	10	0.77	0.72	0.55
Spain	15	10	6	0.60	0.67	0.40

*Rounded to two decimal places

On the basis of ROI, it appears that the manager of the Canadian subsidiary did the best job, while the manager of the Brazilian subsidiary did the worst job. But is this a fair comparison? Brazil and Canada face very different legal, political, educational, and economic conditions. Inflation has been very high in South America compared with that in North America. Many South American firms have responded by adjusting reported financial amounts for inflation. Suppose, in our example, that the Canadian firm reports its assets at historical cost and the Brazilian firm adjusts its assets for inflation. If inflation, during the period the assets have been held, has averaged 100 percent (not an unreasonable assumption in a country that has faced monthly double-digit inflation rates for years), then the historical cost of the Brazilian assets would be $5 million. The calculation is as follows:

$$\begin{aligned} X + 100\%X &= \$10 \\ X + 1.00X &= \$10 \\ 2X &= \$10 \\ X &= \$5 \end{aligned}$$

If we restate the Brazilian subsidiary's assets to historical cost, then the ROI would be 60 percent (3/5 = 0.6). If this computation is used, the Brazilian subsidiary appears to be the most successful, not the least. It should be noted that accounting for inflationary effects on income and assets is very complicated and that the simple restatement just shown is not a comprehensive approach. Additionally, top management is typically aware of the existence of differential inflation rates. Still, the lack of consistency in internal reporting may obscure interdivisional comparisons, and the management accountant must be aware of this problem.

Other environmental factors can differ between countries. A minimum wage law in one country will restrict the manager's ability to affect labor costs. Another country may prevent the export of cash. Still others may have a well-educated workforce but poor infrastructure (transportation and communication facilities). All of these differing environmental factors must be taken into account when assessing managerial performance. Exhibit 18-2 lists some environmental factors that may make interdivisional comparisons misleading.

17 One MNC faced with Philippine prohibitions on taking cash out of the country decided to hold its annual meeting in Manila. All corporate costs of the meeting (for example, hotel, meals) could then be paid in pesos earned by the MNC's Philippine subsidiary. Example taken from Jeff Madura, *International Financial Management*, 2nd ed. (St. Paul, MN: West, 1989): p. 382.

Economic factors:
- Organization of central banking system
- Economic stability
- Existence of capital markets
- Currency restrictions

Political and legal factors:
- Quality, efficiency, and effectiveness of legal structure
- Effect of defense policy
- Impact of foreign policy
- Level of political unrest
- Degree of governmental control of business

Educational factors:
- Literacy rate
- Extent and degree of formal education and training systems
- Extent and degree of technical training
- Extent and quality of management development programs

Sociological factors:
- Social attitude toward industry and business
- Cultural attitude toward authority and persons in subordinate positions
- Cultural attitude toward productivity and achievement (work ethic)
- Social attitude toward material gain
- Cultural and racial diversity

Source: Adapted from Wagdy M. Abdallah, "Change the Environment or Change the System," *Management Accounting* (October 1986): pp. 33–36. Used with the permission of the Institute of Management Accountants.

Exhibit 18-2 Environmental Factors Affecting Performance Evaluation in the Multinational Firm

Political and Legal Factors Affecting Performance Evaluation

Companies doing business in foreign countries must be aware of political and legal factors that can affect them. For example, there may be restrictions on the transfer of currency outside the country. Companies have found creative ways to use the geographically restricted profits to pay for expenditures that they needed to make anyway.

The end of an international trade embargo against Vietnam encouraged U.S. consumer goods giants to invest heavily in factories in Vietnam. By 1998, for example, Tide, Lux, and Close-up were top sellers. So, were **Lever-Viso** (**Unilever's** Vietnamese joint venture) and **Procter & Gamble** happy? No, the products, while genuine, were Thai-made and smuggled into Vietnam. The reason was the devaluation of the Thai baht versus the Vietnamese dong. The Thai-manufactured goods were far cheaper than identical Vietnamese-manufactured goods. The Vietnamese companies were frustrated by the lack of enforcement by government officials against smuggling.[18]

© Getty Images/PhotoDisc

The management accountant in the MNC must be aware of more than business and finance. Political and legal systems have

18 Samantha Marshall, "Soap Smugglers Clean Up in Vietnam," *Wall Street Journal* (April 1, 1998): pp. B1 and B15.

important implications for the company. Sometimes, the political system changes quickly, throwing the company into crisis. Other times, the situation evolves more slowly. The shift in Spain's political system, from Franco's dictatorship to a democracy, is a case in point.

Management accounting has gained increased importance in Spain since the early 1980s. Part of the increased importance is due to the increase in competitive pressures. The profitability of many Spanish firms has eroded, and firms see the need for more formal mechanisms of control, such as budgeting and standard costing. A second reason is the shift from a sheltered economy and political dictatorship to a democratic society. The previous dictatorship favored external methods of control, reinforcing a coercive political and social structure. The system was isolated from the rest of Europe, with a highly regulated economy. The shift to a more democratic society and a loosening of the regulatory environment has allowed Spanish firms more freedom of action in business and has led to the need for management accounting control.[19]

Multiple Measures of Performance

Both EVA (economic value added) and ROI are important measures of managerial performance. However, they are both short-term measures. As such, the temptation exists for managers to trade off short-term benefits at the expense of the long-term well-being of the company. One way to discourage this myopic behavior is to use additional measures of performance that relate more closely to the long-term health of the division. For example, in addition to ROI and EVA, top management could look at such factors as market share, customer complaints, personnel turnover ratios, and personnel development. By letting lower-level managers know that attention to long-term factors is also vital, the tendency to overemphasize ROI or EVA should diminish.

Additionally, the use of ROI and EVA in the evaluation of managerial performance in divisions of an MNC is subject to problems beyond those faced by a decentralized company that operates in only one country. It is particularly important, then, to take a responsibility accounting approach. That is, managers should be evaluated on the basis of factors under their control. This can be facilitated by using multiple measures of performance.

Transfer Pricing and the Multinational Firm

Objective 6

Discuss the role of transfer pricing in the multinational firm.

For the multinational firm, transfer pricing must accomplish two objectives: performance evaluation and optimal determination of income taxes.

Performance Evaluation

Divisions are frequently evaluated on the basis of income and return on investment. As is the case for any transfer price, the selling division wants a high transfer price that will raise its income, and the buying division wants a low transfer price that will raise its income. But transfer prices in MNCs are frequently set by the parent company, making the use of ROI and income suspect. Because they are not under the control of divisional managers, they can no longer serve as indicators of management performance in this case.

19 Joan M. Amat Salas, "Management Accounting Systems in Spanish Firms," in the proceedings of the Second European Management Control Symposium, Volume 1.

Income Taxes and Transfer Pricing

If all countries had the same tax structure, then transfer prices would be set independently of taxes. However, as the opening scenario illustrated, this does not happen. Instead, there are high-tax countries (like the United States) and low-tax countries (such as the Cayman Islands). As a result, MNCs may use transfer pricing to shift costs to high-tax countries and shift revenues to low-tax countries.

Exhibit 18-3 illustrates this concept as two transfer prices are set. The first transfer price is $100 as title for the goods passes from the Belgian subsidiary to the reinvoicing center in Puerto Rico. Because the first transfer price is equal to full cost, profit is zero, and taxes on zero profit also equal zero. The second transfer price is set at $200 by the reinvoicing center in Puerto Rico. The transfer from Puerto Rico to the United States does result in profit, but this profit does not result in any tax because Puerto Rico has no corporate income taxes. Finally, the U.S. subsidiary sells the product to an external party at the $200 transfer price. Again, price equals cost so there is no profit on which to pay income taxes.

Consider what would have happened without the reinvoicing center. The goods would have gone directly from Belgium to the United States. If the transfer price was set at $200, the profit in Belgium would have been $100, subject to the 42 percent tax rate. Alternatively, if the transfer price set was $100, no Belgian tax would have been paid, but the U.S. subsidiary would have realized a profit of $100 and that would have been subject to the U.S. corporate income tax rate of 35 percent.

U.S.-based multinationals are subject to Internal Revenue Code Section 482 on the pricing of intercompany transactions. This section gives the IRS the authority to reallocate income and deductions among divisions if it believes that such reallocation will reduce potential tax evasion. Basically, Section 482 requires that sales be made at "arm's length." That is, the transfer price set should match the price that would be set if the transfer were being made by unrelated parties, adjusted for differences that have a measurable effect on the price. Differences include landing costs and marketing costs. Landing costs (freight, insurance, customs duties, and special taxes) can increase the allowable transfer price. Marketing costs are usually avoided for internal transfers and reduce the transfer price. The IRS allows three pricing methods that

Action	Tax Impact
Belgian subsidiary of parent company produces a component at a cost of $100 per unit. Title to the component is transferred to a reinvoicing center* in Puerto Rico at a transfer price of $100 per unit.	42% tax rate $100 revenue − $100 cost = $0 Taxes paid = $0
Reinvoicing center in Puerto Rico, also a subsidiary of parent company, transfers title of component to U.S. subsidiary of parent company at a transfer price of $200 per unit.	0% tax rate $200 revenue − $100 cost = $100 Taxes paid = $0
U.S. subsidiary sells component to external company at $200 each.	35% tax rate $200 revenue − $200 cost = $0 Taxes paid = $0

*A reinvoicing center takes title to the goods but does not physically receive them. The primary objective of a reinvoicing center is to shift profits to divisions in low-tax countries.

Exhibit 18-3 Use of Transfer Pricing to Affect Taxes Paid approximate arm's-length pricing. In order of preference, these are the *comparable uncontrolled price method,* the *resale price method,* and the *cost-plus method.*

The **comparable uncontrolled price method** essentially uses the market price. Suppose that the Belgian division of the company transfers a component to the U.S. division. If the component has a market price of $50 and shipping costs are $4, then the transfer price would be $54. If any costs are avoided as a result of internal transfer (for example, sales commissions of $5), these costs would be subtracted from the market price. In this case, the eventual transfer price would be calculated as follows:

Market price	$50
Add: Shipping	4
Less: Commissions	(5)
Transfer price	$49

The **resale price method** is equal to the sales price received by the reseller less an appropriate markup. That is, the subsidiary purchasing a good for resale sets a transfer price equal to the resale price less a gross profit percentage. Suppose our U.S. division receives a product from the French division that can be resold in the United States for $60. The U.S. division typically receives a markup of 50 percent on cost. The transfer price would be $40 ($60 = Cost + 0.5 Cost; so, cost is $40).

The **cost-plus method** is simply the cost-based transfer price. The manufacturing cost of the product is adjusted for any other expenses, such as shipping and duty. Suppose that the U.S. division produces a product that costs $25 to manufacture. It ships the product to the Brazilian division at a cost of $3. The transfer price is $28. This price can be adjusted for a markup on goods.

The determination of an arm's-length price is a difficult one. Many times, the transfer pricing situation facing a company does not "fit" any of the three preferred methods outlined. In such cases, the IRS will permit a fourth method—a transfer price negotiated between the company and the IRS. The IRS, taxpayers, and the tax court have struggled with negotiated transfer prices for years. However, this type of negotiation occurs after the fact—after income tax returns have been submitted and the company is being audited.

Recently, the IRS authorized the issuance of **advance pricing agreements (APAs)** to assist taxpaying firms in determining whether or not a proposed transfer price is acceptable to the IRS in advance of tax filing. "An APA is an agreement between the IRS and a taxpayer on the pricing method to be applied in an international transaction. It can cover transfers of intangibles (such as royalties on licenses), sales of property, provision of services, and other items. An APA is binding on both the IRS and the taxpayer for the years specified in the APA and is not made public."[20] Since the APA procedure is so new, neither the IRS nor the firms are sure of the informational requirements. Currently, the IRS may limit its advance rulings on transactions between U.S.-based companies and divisions in treaty countries, such as Australia, Canada, Japan, and the United Kingdom. For example, **Apple Computer** obtained an advance pricing agreement from the IRS on transfers of Apple products to its Australian subsidiary.[21]

Transfer pricing abuses are illegal—if they can be proved to be abuses. Many examples of both foreign and U.S. firms charging unusual transfer prices exist. The IRS successfully showed that **Toyota** had been overcharging its U.S. subsidiary for cars, trucks, and parts sold in the United States. The effect was to lower Toyota's

20 "New Intercompany Pricing Rulings Create and Eliminate Tax Uncertainty," *Deloitte & Touche Review* (March 25, 1991): p. 6.
21 Roger Y. W. Tang, "Transfer Pricing in the 1990s," *Management Accounting* (February 1992): pp. 22–26.

reported income substantially in the United States and increase income reported in Japan. The settlement reportedly approached $1 billion.[22]

The superroyalty provision of Section 482 was added in 1986 to require companies to value their intangibles more fairly. The IRS suspected that U.S. companies were transferring their intangibles (patents, copyrights, customer lists, and so on) to foreign subsidiaries at less than fair market value. For example, a U.S. pharmaceutical firm would develop a new drug and license its Puerto Rican subsidiary to produce it. The drug would then be purchased by the parent company for sale in the United States, and a royalty would be charged to the Puerto Rican subsidiary. The royalty rate, taxable income to the parent, was low, but was similar to other third-party transactions. Thus, the IRS could not challenge it. The superroyalty provision changed this situation by linking the transfer price of the intangible to the income attributable to the intangible. "A Study on Intercompany Pricing," issued in 1990, requires much stricter documentation for the pricing of intangibles.[23]

The IRS also regulates the transfer pricing of foreign companies with U.S. subsidiaries. A U.S. company that is at least 25 percent foreign owned must keep extensive documentation of arm's-length transfer pricing.

Of course, MNCs are also subject to taxation by other countries as well as the United States. Since income taxes are virtually universal, consideration of income tax effects pervades management decision making. Canada, Japan, the European Community, and South Korea have all issued transfer pricing regulations within the past 10 years.[24] This increased emphasis on transfer price justification may account for the increased use of market prices as the transfer price by MNCs. A survey of transfer pricing methods used by Fortune 500 companies in 1977 and 1990 shows that MNCs have reduced their reliance on cost-based transfer prices in favor of market-based transfer prices over the 13-year period.[25] Additionally, the most important environmental variable considered by MNCs in setting a transfer pricing policy is overall profit to the company—with overall profit including the income tax impact of intracompany transfers.

Managers may legally avoid taxes; they may not evade them. The distinction is important. Unfortunately, the difference between avoidance and evasion is less a line than a blurry gray area. While the situation depicted in Exhibit 18-3 is clearly abusive, other tax-motivated actions are not. For example, an MNC may legally decide to establish a needed research and development center within an existing subsidiary in a high-tax country since the costs are deductible. MNCs may also use tax-planning information systems that attempt to accomplish global tax minimization. This is not an easy task.

Ethics in the International Environment

Objective 7

Discuss ethical issues that affect firms operating in the international environment.

Business ethics pose difficulties in a single-country context, but they pose far more problems in a global context. Richard J. Mahoney, then-CEO of Monsanto, wrote: "As **Monsanto** becomes a global enterprise, we continually face the problem of different cultures and different cultural expectations. A service fee in one country is a bribe in another. Environmental laws can be extraordinarily strict in a country but not be enforced—and your industrial neighbors laugh at you for obeying the laws."[26] Given these difficulties, how does the modern corporation conduct business in an ethical manner? Is each country different? Is there a baseline? Some research indi-

22 "The Corporate Shell Game," *Newsweek* (April 15, 1991): pp. 48–49.
23 Alfred M. King, "The IRS's New Neutron Bomb," *Management Accounting* (December 1992): pp. 35–38.
24 Roger Y. W. Tang, "Transfer Pricing in the 1990s," *Management Accounting* (February 1992): pp. 22–26.
25 Ibid.
26 Richard J. Mahoney, "Ethics: Doing the Right Thing at Monsanto," *Management Accounting* (June 1991): p. 24.

cates that human societies do share an ethical basis. However, there are some prerequisites for the establishment of an ethical business environment. These include basic societal stability, legitimacy and accountability of government, legitimacy of private ownership and personal wealth, confidence in one's own and society's future, confidence in the ability to provide for one's family, and knowledge of how the system works and how to participate.[27]

For example, the Russian equivalent of insider trading or conflict of interest is *blat.* Blat is "an informal system of acquiring goods and services based on influence and back-door favors between acquaintances."[28] Blat is a natural extension of a culture that emphasizes personal relationships over impersonal monetary transactions. Legal contracts are still in a rudimentary phase because enforcement is weak. As a result, personal relationships, which characterize blat, are a stronger basis for business dealings.

A strong underlying system is important for enforcing contracts and provides the basis for confidence in ethical dealings. For some countries (for example, the United States and Western European countries), that system is legal with deviations punishable by law. For others (for example, Japan and countries in the Middle East), it is cultural, and deviations are punished at least as severely by loss of honor. The importance of a strong underlying social code of conduct is clearly evident in illegal business dealings. For obvious reasons, you would be loathe to contact the police or district attorney about your purchase of low-quality marijuana. Similarly in India, where foreign currency exchange is tightly controlled, the black market in currency exchange is rife with unethical conduct. If you would like to exchange dollars for rupees, you can get a markedly better rate from the black market. However, the method of exchange requires you to first hand the black marketeer your rupees and then wait a minute or two while he goes to a back room to get the dollars. Sometimes, he returns with the requisite number of dollars, sometimes not. As an Indian friend of ours said, "Then what? You can hardly go to the police!" Indians do not face this risky situation in a bank.

Other ethical problems with differing business laws exist. U.S. companies that contract with overseas firms may find themselves the target of unfavorable publicity on use of child labor. They find themselves in a quandary. Do they tell foreign companies what age worker they can hire? Our own history includes immigrant children of 10 and 12 at work in the steel mills of Bethlehem, Pennsylvania. What about incentives schemes offered to retailers to stock a particular firm's product? Indian pharmaceutical firms offer gifts and other incentives to pharmacists to obtain shelf space for their drug products. In India, the pharmacist has the ability to sell prescription drugs—whether or not they have been prescribed by a physician. Drug companies find that they must offer incentives to increase sales. In the United States, however, drugstore chains prohibit their pharmacists from accepting gifts from vendors. They believe that the practice raises ethical concerns.[29] To go back to our original question, what is a company to do when faced with conflicting sets of ethics? What if an action is legally permissible? Early in Monsanto's history, it faced the possibility of bankruptcy. John Queeny, the company's founder, was advised to "close down the plant, lay off all the workers, and then open up with new people at lower wages. 'Since when,' Mr. Queeny asked, 'do we lie to our employees?'" As a result, Monsanto holds that doing the right thing is nonnegotiable.[30] Perhaps the answer is to ask, is the action right legally? And then, is the action right morally?

27 Cynthia Scharf, "The Wild, Wild East: Everyone's a Capitalist in Russia Today, and Nobody Knows the Rules," *Business Ethics* (November/December 1992): p. 23.

28 Scharf, p. 22.

29 Daniel Pearl and Steve Stecklow, "Drug Firms' Incentives Fuel Abuse by Pharmacists in India," *Wall Street Journal* (August 16, 2001): p. 1.

30 Scharf, p. 24.

Summary of Learning Objectives

1. Explain the role of the management accountant in the international environment.

The management accountant provides financial and business expertise. The job of the management accountant in the international firm is made more challenging by the ambiguous and ever-changing nature of global business. He or she must stay up to date in a variety of business areas ranging from information systems, to marketing, to management, to politics, to economics. In addition, the management accountant must be familiar with the financial accounting rules of the countries in which his or her firm operates.

2. Identify the varying levels of involvement that firms can undertake in international trade.

Companies involved in international business may structure their activities in three major ways. They may engage in import and export activities. They may purchase wholly owned subsidiaries. They may participate in joint ventures.

3. List the ways management accountants can manage foreign currency risk.

Management accountants must be aware of the potential exposure of their firms to transaction risk, economic risk, and translation risk. They may hedge to limit exposure to these risks.

4. Explain why multinational firms choose to decentralize.

MNCs choose to decentralize for much the same reasons domestic companies choose to decentralize. The reasons are numerous. Companies decentralize because local managers can make better decisions using local information. Local managers can also provide a more timely response to changing conditions. For large, diversified companies, decentralization is necessary because it is impossible for any one central manager to be fully knowledgeable about all products and markets. Other reasons include training and motivating local managers and freeing up top management from day-to-day operating conditions so that they can spend time on more long-range activities, such as strategic planning.

5. Describe how environmental factors can affect performance evaluation in the multinational firm.

Environmental factors are those social, economic, political, legal, and cultural factors that differ from country to country and that managers cannot affect. These factors, however, do affect profits and ROI. Therefore, evaluation of the divisional manager should be separated from evaluation of the subsidiary.

6. Discuss the role of transfer pricing in the multinational firm.

When one division of a company produces a product that can be used in production by another division, transfer pricing exists. The transfer price is revenue to the selling division and cost to the buying division. As is the case with domestic companies, MNCs may use transfer prices in performance evaluation. MNCs with subsidiaries in both high- and low-tax countries may use transfer pricing to shift costs to the high-tax countries (where their deductibility will lower tax payments) and to shift revenues to low-tax countries.

7. Discuss ethical issues that affect firms operating in the international environment.

MNCs face ethical issues that do not arise for domestic companies. Other countries have business customs and laws that differ from those of the home country. The firm must determine whether a particular custom is merely a different way of doing business or a violation of its own code of ethics.

Key Terms

Review Problem

Foreign Trade Zones; Foreign Currency Exchange

Golo, Inc., has two manufacturing plants, one in Singapore and the other in San Antonio. The San Antonio plant is located in a foreign trade zone. On March 1, Golo received a large order from a Japanese customer. The order is for 10,000,000 yen to be paid on receipt of the goods, scheduled for June 1. Golo assigned this order to the San Antonio plant; however, one necessary component for the order is to be manufactured by the Singapore plant. The component will be transferred to San Antonio on April 1 using a cost-plus transfer price of $10,000 (U.S. dollars). Typically, 2 percent of the Singapore parts are defective. The U.S. tariff on the component parts is 30 percent. The carrying cost for Golo is 15 percent per year.

The following spot rates for $1 U.S. are as follows:

	Exchange Rates of $1 for	
	Yen	**Singapore Dollars**
March 1	107.00	1.60
April 1	107.50	1.55
June 1	107.60	1.50

Required

1. What is the total cost of the imported parts from Singapore to the San Antonio plant in U.S. dollars?
2. Suppose that the San Antonio plant were not located in a foreign trade zone; what would be the total cost of the imported parts from Singapore?
3. How much does Golo expect to receive from the Japanese customer in U.S. dollars using the spot rate at the time of the order?
4. How much does Golo expect to receive from the Japanese customer in U.S. dollars using the spot rate at the time of payment?
5. Suppose that on March 1, the forward rate for June 1 delivery of $1 for yen is 107.20. If Golo's policy is to hedge foreign currency transactions, what is the amount Golo expects to receive on June 1 in dollars?

Solution

1.

Transfer price	$10,000
Tariff ($9,800 × 0.3)	2,940
Total cost	$12,940

The transfer price was set in U.S. dollars, so there is no currency exchange involved for the San Antonio plant.

The San Antonio plant is in a foreign trade zone, so the 30 percent tariff is paid only on the good parts, costing $9,800 ($10,000 × 0.98).

2. If the San Antonio plant were located outside the foreign trade zone, the cost of the imported parts would be as follows:

Transfer price	$10,000
Tariff ($10,000 × 0.3)	3,000
Carrying cost of tariff*	75
Total cost	$13,075

*$3,000 × 2/12 × 0.15 = $75

3. On March 1, Golo expects to receive $93,458 (10,000,000/107).
4. On June 1, Golo expects to receive $92,937 (10,000,000/107.60).
5. If Golo hedges, the forward rate is used, and the amount to be received on June 1 is $93,284 (10,000,000/107.20).

Questions for Writing and Discussion

1. How do international issues affect the role of the management accountant?
2. What is a foreign trade zone, and what advantages does it offer U.S. companies?
3. Define outsourcing, and discuss why companies may outsource various functions.
4. What are joint ventures, and why do companies engage in them?
5. What are maquiladoras? Why have so many U.S. firms joined forces with maquiladoras?
6. What is an exchange rate for currency? What is the difference between a spot rate and a future rate?
7. What is transaction risk? Economic risk? Translation risk?
8. Define currency appreciation. What impact does currency appreciation have on a company's ability to import goods?
9. What impact does currency appreciation have on a company's ability to export its goods?
10. Mexico is considering devaluing the peso versus the dollar. You are the controller for a company considering production in Mexico through the maquiladora program. How does this news affect the decision? Now, suppose you are a local labor union leader; how do you take the news?
11. What is hedging? If a company imports materials, payable in full in 90 days in the foreign currency, why might the company want to hedge?
12. The performance of the subsidiary manager is equivalent to the performance of a subsidiary. Do you agree or disagree? Explain.
13. What environmental factors can affect divisional performance in a multinational firm?
14. What is the purpose of Internal Revenue Code Section 482? What four methods of transfer pricing are acceptable under this section?

Exercises

18-1

Preparation for Becoming a Management Accountant in an MNC
LO1

A close friend of yours is majoring in accounting and would like to work for a multinational corporation upon graduation. Your friend is unsure just what courses would help prepare for that goal and wants your advice.

Required

Advise your friend on the kind of courses that might prepare him or her for this goal.

18-2

Types of Involvement in International Trade
LO2

Match each term in Column A with its related definition in Column B.

Column A

1. ___ Maquiladora
2. ___ Import
3. ___ Joint venture
4. ___ Export
5. ___ MNC

Column B

a. A company that does business in more than one country in such volume that its well-being and growth rest in more than one country.
b. A company purchases materials or parts from another company that is located in a foreign country.
c. A company sells its product to purchasers located in foreign countries.

d. A type of partnership in which investors from one country co-own the enterprise with investors from another country.
e. A manufacturing plant located in Mexico that processes imported materials and re-exports them to the United States.

18-3

Foreign Currency Exchange
LO3

Match each term in Column A with its related definition in Column B.

Column A

1. ___ Spot rate
2. ___ Currency appreciation
3. ___ Translation risk
4. ___ Transaction risk
5. ___ Exchange rate

Column B

a. The rate at which one currency can be traded for another currency.
b. The possibility that future cash transactions will be affected by changing exchange rates.
c. A month ago, $1 U.S. was worth 8.5 Mexican pesos. Today, $1 is worth 9.0 Mexican pesos. The U.S. dollar has undergone what?
d. The degree to which a firm's financial statements are exposed to exchange rate fluctuation.
e. The exchange rate of one currency for another for immediate delivery (today).

18-4

Payment of Duty and Duty-Related Carrying Cost
LO2

EXCEL

Kamber, Inc., owns a factory located close to, but not inside, a foreign trade zone. The plant imports volatile chemicals that are used in the manufacture of chemical reagents for laboratories. Each year, Kamber imports about $14,200,000 of chemicals subject to a 30 percent tariff when shipped into the United States. About 15 percent of the imported chemicals are lost through evaporation during the manufacturing process. In addition, Kamber has a carrying cost of 10 percent per year associated with the duty payment. On average, the chemicals are held in inventory for nine months.

Required

1. How much duty is paid annually by Kamber?
2. What is the carrying cost associated with the payment of duty?

18-5

Foreign Trade Zone Cost Savings
LO2

Refer to **Exercise 18-4**. Suppose that Kamber is considering building a new plant inside a foreign trade zone to replace its chemical manufacturing plant.

Required

1. How much duty will be paid per year by the factory located inside the foreign trade zone?
2. How much in duty and duty-related carrying costs will be saved by relocating inside the foreign trade zone?

18-6

Foreign Trade Zones
LO2

Bulwar Products, Inc., imports merchandise to sell to wholesalers in the United States. Bulwar Products' controller, Shana Gillette, is reviewing a proposal for the building of a new warehouse to serve the Southeast region. She wonders if locating the new warehouse in a foreign trade zone would be of benefit to her company. Shanna estimates that the new warehouse will store imported merchandise costing about $3,750,000 per year. Inventory shrinkage at the warehouse (due to breakage and mishandling) is about 6 percent of the total. The average tariff rate on these imports is 25 percent.

Required

Will locating the warehouse in a foreign trade zone save Bulwar Products, Inc., money? If so, how much?

18-7

Exchange Gains and Losses
LO3

EXCEL

On March 1, Friedle Import-Export Company purchased merchandise from a Mexican firm costing 70,100 pesos. Payment was due, in pesos, on June 1. The exchange rates of pesos for $1 were as follows:

March 1	$1 = 10.9 pesos
June 1	$1 = 11.4 pesos

Round all answers to the nearest dollar.

Required

1. What is the liability in dollars on March 1?
2. What is the liability in dollars on June 1?
3. If Friedle pays on June 1, is there an exchange gain or loss? If so, how much is it?

18-8

Hedging
LO3

EXCEL

Refer to **Exercise 18-7**. Suppose that Friedle also sells to Mexican firms under the same terms—payment is made in pesos three months after purchase. Friedle sells merchandise to Javier, SA, on March 1, for 75,000 pesos. Payment will be made in pesos on June 1. Friedle can purchase a contract to exchange 75,000 pesos into dollars on June 1 at a forward rate of 11.1 pesos. Round all answers to the nearest dollar.

Required

1. What is the value of the receivable in dollars on March 1?
2. What is the dollar value of the amount Javier pays Friedle on June 1?
3. What is the exchange loss for Friedle if no hedging occurs?
4. If Friedle purchases the hedging contract on March 1, what is the premium expense?
5. What is the net savings to Friedle by hedging?

18-9

Currency Exchange
LO3

Basu Distributors, Inc., based in Riverside, California, is an import-export firm. On June 1, Basu purchased goods from a British company costing €600,000. Payment is due in euros on September 1. The spot rate on June 1 was 1.20 dollars per euro, and on September 1, it was 1.26 dollars per euro.

Required

1. Did the dollar strengthen or weaken against the euro during the three-month period?
2. How much would Basu have to pay for the purchase (in dollars) if it paid on June 1? How much would Basu have to pay for the purchase (in dollars) if it paid on September 1?

18-10

Exchange Gains and Losses
LO3

Refer to **Exercise 18-9**. If Basu paid for the purchase using the September 1 spot rate, what was the exchange gain or loss?

18-11

Hedging
LO3

Persephone Company engages in many foreign currency transactions. Company policy is to hedge exposure to exchange gains and losses using forward contracts. On July 1, Persephone bought merchandise from a Canadian company for 120,000

Canadian dollars, payable on September 30. Exchange rates of $1 for Canadian dollars were as follows:

Spot rate, July 1	1.30
Forward rate, September 30	1.30
Spot rate, September 30	1.35

Required

1. Did Persephone Company buy or sell Canadian dollars for future delivery?
2. According to company policy, how many U.S. dollars did Persephone pay for this purchase?

18-12

Currency Exchange Rates
LO3

Suppose you are in the market for a BMW and are considering going to Germany to purchase it, drive it around Europe for a couple of weeks, and then ship it home. The car of your choice costs €90,000. When you first looked into the possibility of buying a car in Germany, the rate of exchange was €0.84 to $1; now the exchange rate is €0.88 to $1.

Required

Has the dollar appreciated or depreciated against the euro? Would this news about the exchange rate change please or displease you? Why?

18-13

Transfer Pricing
LO6

Inter-Land, Inc., transfers a product between its U.S. division and its Danish division. The product sells for $45 in the United States. The cost of shipping to Denmark is $3.20, and Danish duty is $9. The U.S. division pays approximately $4.50 per unit for advertising and related selling expenses.

EXCEL

Required

Using the comparable uncontrolled price method, calculate the transfer price.

18-14

Transfer Pricing
LO6

The U.S. division of Inter-Land, Inc., purchases a product from the Danish division, which sells for $80 per unit in the United States. The U.S. division typically has a 25 percent markup on goods.

Required

Calculate the transfer price under the resale price method.

18-15

Divisional Performance Evaluation in the MNC
LO5

Bianca Phillips, vice president of Electronics for Consolidated, Inc., was reviewing the latest results for two divisions. The first, located in Baja California, Mexico, had posted income of $150,000 on assets of $1,500,000. The second, in Punt-on-Thames, England, showed income of $230,000 on assets of $2,000,000.

Required

1. Calculate the ROI for each division.
2. Can a meaningful comparison be made of the British division's ROI with the Mexican division's ROI? Explain.

18-16

Transfer Pricing in the MNC
LO6

Carnover, Inc., manufactures a broad line of industrial and consumer products. One of its plants is located in Madrid, Spain, and another in Singapore. The Madrid plant is operating at 85 percent capacity. Softness in the market for its main product, electric motors, has led to predictions of further softening of the market, leading perhaps to production at 65 percent capacity. If that happens, workers will have to be laid off and one wing of the factory closed. The Singapore plant manufactures heavy-duty industrial mixers that use the motors manufactured by the Madrid plant as an integral component. Demand for the mixers is strong. Price and cost information for the mixers is as follows:

Price	$2,200
Direct materials	630
Direct labor	125
Variable overhead	250
Fixed overhead	100

Fixed overhead is based on an annual budgeted amount of $3,500,000 and budgeted production of 35,000 mixers. The direct materials cost includes the cost of the motor at $200 (market price).

The Madrid plant capacity is 20,000 motors per year. Cost data are as follows:

Direct materials	$ 75
Direct labor	60
Variable overhead	60
Fixed overhead	100

Fixed overhead is based on budgeted fixed overhead of $2,000,000.

Required

1. What is the maximum transfer price the Singapore plant would accept?
2. What is the minimum transfer price the Madrid plant would accept?
3. Consider the following environmental factors:

Madrid Plant	Singapore Plant
Full employment is very important. Local government prohibits layoffs without permission (which is rarely granted). Accounting is legalistic and conservative, designed to ensure compliance with government objectives.	Cheap labor is plentiful. Accounting is based on British-American model, oriented toward decision-making investors.

How might these environmental factors affect the transfer pricing decision?

18-17

Transfer Pricing
LO6

Howell Company has a division in the United States that produces computerized thermostats for heating units. These thermostats are transferred to a division in Luxembourg. The thermostats can be (and are) sold externally in the United States for $30 each. It costs $2.35 per thermostat for shipping and $2.70 per thermostat for import duties. When the thermostats are sold externally, Howell spends $3 per thermostat for commissions and an average of $1 per thermostat for advertising.

Required

1. Which Section 482 method should be used to calculate the allowable transfer price?
2. Using the appropriate Section 482 method, calculate the transfer price.

18-18

Multiple-Choice Questions
LO2, LO3, LO4, LO5, LO6

Choose the *best* answer for each of the following multiple-choice questions:

1. Which of the following is *true* regarding foreign trade zones?

   a. They are pieces of land physically located in foreign countries that are subject to the laws of the United States.

b. They must be located near seaports.
c. Goods that enter a foreign trade zone are not subject to tariff until they leave the zone for destinations in the United States.
d. Goods sold in a foreign trade zone are not subject to U.S. income taxes.
e. All of the above.

2. A manufacturing plant located in Mexico which processes imported materials and re-exports them to the United States is called a(n)

 a. maquiladora.
 b. foreign trade zone.
 c. joint venture.
 d. exchange venture.
 e. foreign transaction.z

3. The following spot rates for $1 in terms of yen and pounds were in effect for June 1 and November 1.

	June 1	**November 1**
Japanese yen	115.0	118.0
British pound	0.699	0.650

Did the United States dollar appreciate or depreciate against these currencies between June 1 and November 1?

	Japanese yen	**British pound**
a.	appreciate	appreciate
b.	appreciate	depreciate
c.	depreciate	depreciate
d.	depreciate	appreciate
e.	Cannot tell from the information given.	

4. Translation risk

 a. is only a problem for multinational firms that translate divisional financial statements into the home currency.
 b. occurs when the dollar appreciates vis-à-vis another currency.
 c. occurs when an exchange loss is realized.
 d. can be avoided by hedging.
 e. is a problem when employees from the head office in the home country cannot speak the language(s) of their divisions in other countries.

5. The MNC may choose to decentralize

 a. to give top management greater local control of far-flung divisions.
 b. to ensure that the same policies and procedures are followed in every division.
 c. by erasing divisional lines.
 d. for the same reasons that domestic companies choose to decentralize.
 e. MNCs are never decentralized.

6. Which of the following is an environmental factor affecting performance evaluation of the divisions in the multinational firm?

 a. Economic stability
 b. Social attitude toward industry and business
 c. Literacy rates
 d. Currency restrictionse.
 e. All of the above.

7. Which of the following transfer pricing methods is approved by the United States Internal Revenue Service?
    a. Comparable uncontrolled price method
    b. Resale price method
    c. Cost-plus method
    d. Advance pricing agreement
    e. All of the above.

Problems

18-19

Decentralization in the MNC
LO4

CMA

Latest Styles Inc. (LSI) supplies a limited range of garments to several boutiques in New York. LSI produces these garments in a small factory owned and operated in Nuevo Laredo, Mexico. LSI has been more responsive to the boutiques' need for delivery of changing styles than Asian garment producers, whose shipments take 30 days. As a result, several other boutiques have approached LSI as a potential supplier. Victoria Johnson, president of LSI, has decided that expansion will be required to meet the needs of these additional boutiques.

After discussing the situation, Victoria and her executive team—Frank Corrigan, the controller, and Tom Conway, the production and shipping manager—agree that the expansion should be undertaken. Since Victoria makes most of the decisions that involve day-to-day operations and does the majority of the designing, Frank and Tom are concerned about her managing the expansion at the same time. They expressed this concern in a meeting with Victoria, who agreed that the additional workload resulting from the planned expansion would be too great for her to handle. Accordingly, she has decided to delegate some of these increased functions to Frank and Tom.

During these discussions, Victoria added that in view of the Mexican-American negotiations to establish a North American free-trade zone, she is considering even further expansion to increase the range of garments produced and also to supply boutiques in Philadelphia and Boston. Consequently, she is considering further decentralization of the business, as expanded operations in Mexico, increased product lines, and supplying two new geographical areas will require hands-on, operational management at these locations to keep up with inventory needs and differing local fashion trends. Both Frank and Tom are capable of handling these operational duties, although they will need to hire new managers to assist them in the expansion and decentralization.

Required

1. Decentralization is the extent to which power and authority are systematically delegated throughout an organization.
    a. Discuss the factors that generally determine the degree of decentralization in an organization.
    b. Describe several benefits to an organization that can generally be derived from decentralization.
    c. Discuss several disadvantages to an organization from decentralization.
2. How does NAFTA affect Victoria Johnson's decision? **(CMA adapted)**

18-20

Exporting; Maquiladoras; Foreign Trade Zones
LO2

Paladin Company manufactures plain paper fax machines in a small factory in Minnesota. Sales have increased by 50 percent in each of the past three years, as Paladin has expanded its market from the United States to Canada and Mexico. As a result, the Minnesota factory is at capacity. Beryl Adams, president of Paladin, has examined the situation and developed the following alternatives:

1. Add a permanent second shift at the plant. However, the semiskilled workers who assemble the fax machines are in short supply, and the wage rate of $15 per hour would probably have to be increased across the board to $18 per hour in order to attract sufficient workers from out of town. The total wage increase (including fringe benefits) would amount to $125,000. The heavier use of plant facilities would lead to increased plant maintenance and small tool cost.
2. Open a new plant and locate it in Mexico. Wages (including fringe benefits) would average $3.50 per hour. Investment in plant and equipment would amount to $300,000.
3. Open a new plant and locate it in a foreign trade zone, possibly in Dallas. Wages would be somewhat lower than in Minnesota, but higher than in Mexico. The advantages of postponing tariff payments on imported parts could amount to $50,000 per year.

Required

Advise Beryl of the advantages and disadvantages of each of her alternatives.

18-21

Foreign Currency Exchange; Hedging
LO3

Custom Shutters, Inc., manufactures plantation shutters according to customer order. The company has a reputation for producing excellent quality shutters that fit virtually any size or shape of window. Sales are made in all 50 states. On July 1, Custom Shutters received orders from contractors in Switzerland and Japan. Lee Mills, president and co-owner of Custom Shutters, was delighted. The Swiss order is for shutters priced at $64,000. The order is due in Geneva on September 1, with payment due in full on October 1. The Japanese order is for shutters priced at $124,000. It is due in Tokyo on August 1, with payment due in full on October 1. Both orders are to be paid in the customer's currency. The Swiss customer has a reputation in the industry for late payment, and it could take as long as six months. Lee has never received payment in foreign currency before. He had his accountant prepare the following table of exchange rates:

	Exchange Rate for $1	
	Swiss Franc	**Yen**
Spot rate	1.2360	117.70
30-Day forward rate	1.2450	117.68
90-Day forward rate	1.2590	117.70
180-Day forward rate	1.2708	117.66

Required

1. If the price of the shutters is set using the spot rate as of July 1, how many francs does Lee expect to receive on October 1? How many yen does he expect on October 1?
2. Using the number of francs and yen calculated in Requirement 1, how many dollars does Lee expect to receive on October 1? Will he receive that much? What is the value of hedging in this situation?

18-22

Transfer Pricing
LO6

The U.S. division of ABC, Inc., has excess capacity. ABC's European division, located in Lisbon, has offered to buy a component that would increase the U.S. division's utilization of capacity from 70 to 80 percent. The component has an outside market in the United States with a unit selling price of $14. The variable costs of production for the component are $7. Landing costs total $2.50 per unit, and an internal transfer avoids $1.80 per unit of variable marketing costs. The European and U.S. divisions agree on a transfer price of $10. The European division can purchase the component locally for $12.

Required

Suppose you have scheduled a meeting with an IRS representative. What arguments would you make for an advance pricing agreement that would permit the use of the $10 price?

18-23

Transfer Pricing
LO6

EXCEL

Audio-Tech, Inc., manufactures stereos and boom boxes at plants in Idaho, Minnesota, and Alabama. It also has distribution centers in Brussels, Belgium, and Montreal, Canada. The market price of the Model 655 CD^{+} stereo is $430. The unit costs are as follows:

Variable product costs	$145
Fixed factory overhead	75
Landing costs (Canada)	25
Landing costs (Belgium)	30
Avoidable marketing costs	40

Audio-Tech has set a transfer price of $430 to both the Canadian and Belgian divisions.

Required

1. Calculate the transfer price under the comparable uncontrolled price method for both the Canadian and Belgian transfers.
2. Will the IRS be concerned about the transfer price actually set by Audio-Tech?

Managerial Decision Cases

18-24

Transfer Pricing and Ethical Issues
LO6, LO7

Paterson Company,* a U.S.-based company, manufactures and sells electronic components worldwide. Virtually all its manufacturing takes place in the United States. The company has marketing divisions throughout Europe, including France. Debbie Kishimoto, manager of this division, was hired from a competitor three years ago. Debbie, recently informed of a price increase in one of the major product lines, requested a meeting with Jeff Phillips, marketing vice president. Their conversation follows.

Debbie: Jeff, I simply don't understand why the price of our main product has increased from $5 to $5.50 per unit. We negotiated an agreement earlier in the year with our manufacturing division in Philadelphia for a price of $5 for the entire year. I called the manager of that division. He said that the original price was still acceptable—that the increase was a directive from headquarters. That's why I wanted to meet with you. I need some explanations. When I was hired, I was told that pricing decisions were made by the divisions. This directive interferes with this decentralized philosophy and will lower my division's profits. Given current market conditions, there is no way we can pass on the cost increase. Profits for my division will drop at least $600,000 if this price is maintained. I think a midyear increase of this magnitude is unfair to my division.

Jeff: Under normal operating conditions, headquarters would not interfere with divisional decisions. But as a company, we are having some problems. What you just told me is exactly why the price of your product has been increased. We want the profits of all our European marketing divisions to drop.

Debbie: What do you mean that you want the profits to drop? That doesn't make any sense. Aren't we in business to make money?

*This scenario is based on the experiences of an actual firm. Names have been changed to preserve confidentiality.

Jeff: Debbie, what you lack is corporate perspective. We are in business to make money, and that's why we want European profits to decrease. Our U.S. divisions are not doing well this year. Projections show significant losses. At the same time, projections for European operations show good profitability. By increasing the cost of key products transferred to Europe—to your division, for example—we increase revenues and profits in the United States. By decreasing your profits, we avoid paying taxes in France; with losses on other U.S. operations to offset the corresponding increase in domestic profits, we avoid paying taxes in the United States as well. The net effect is a much-needed increase in our cash flow. Besides, you know how hard it is in some of these European countries to transfer out capital. This is a clean way of doing it.

Debbie: I'm not so sure that it's clean. I can't imagine the tax laws permitting this type of scheme. There is another problem, too. You know that the company's bonus plans are tied to a division's profits. This plan could cost all of the European managers a lot of money.

Jeff: Debbie, you have no reason to worry about the effect on your bonus—or on our evaluation of your performance. Corporate management has already taken steps to ensure no loss of compensation. The plan is to compute what income would have been if the old price had prevailed and base bonuses on that figure. I'll meet with the other divisional managers and explain the situation to them as well.

Debbie: The bonus adjustment seems fair, although I wonder if the reasons for the drop in profits will be remembered in a couple of years when I'm being considered for promotion. Anyway, I still have some strong ethical concerns about this. How does this scheme relate to the tax laws?

Jeff: We will be in technical compliance with the tax laws. In the United States, Section 482 of the Internal Revenue Code governs this type of transaction. The key to this law, as well as most European laws, is evidence of an arm's-length price. Since you're a distributor, we can use the resale price method to determine such a price. Essentially, the arm's-length price for the transferred good is backed into by starting with the price at which you sell the product and then adjusting that price for the markup and other legitimate differences, such as tariffs and transportation.

Debbie: If I were a French tax auditor, I would wonder why the markup dropped from last year to this year. Are we being good citizens and meeting the fiscal responsibilities imposed on us by each country in which we operate?

Jeff: Well, a French tax auditor might wonder about the drop in markup. But, the markup is still within reason, and we can make a good argument for increased costs. In fact, we've already instructed the managers of our manufacturing divisions to legitimately reassign as many costs as they can to the European product lines. So far, they have been very successful. I think our records will support the increase that you are receiving. You really do not need to be concerned with the tax authorities. Our Tax Department assures me that this has been carefully researched—it's unlikely that a tax audit will create any difficulties. It'll all be legal and above board. We've done this several times in the past with total success.

Required

1. Do you think that the tax minimization scheme described to Debbie Kishimoto is in harmony with the ethical behavior that should be displayed by top corporate executives? Why or why not? What would you do if you were Debbie?
2. Apparently, the Tax Department of Paterson Company has been strongly involved in developing the tax-minimization scheme. Assume that the accountants responsible for the decision are CMAs and members of the IMA, subject to the IMA standards of ethical conduct. Review the IMA standards for ethical conduct in

Chapter 1. Are any of these standards being violated by the accountants in Paterson's Tax Department? If so, identify them. What should these tax accountants do if requested to develop a questionable tax-minimization scheme?

18-25

Transfer Pricing; International Setting; Tax Implications
LO6

CMA

Valley Electronics Corporation is a large multinational firm involved in the manufacture and marketing of various electronic components. Recently, Rhonda Cooper, president of Valley Electronics, received some complaints from divisional managers about the company's international transfer pricing practices. Essentially, the managers believed that they had less control over how prices were set than they wished. After reviewing some of the practices, Rhonda found that three different methods were being used: (1) the comparable uncontrolled price method, (2) the resale price method, and (3) the cost-plus method. Unable to determine why there were three methods and exactly how each worked, Rhonda requested a meeting with Wayne Sill, vice president of finance. Their conversation follows.

Rhonda: Wayne, I need to respond to our divisional managers' concerns about the transfer pricing policies that we apply to goods shipped internationally. It appears that three methods are being used and that they differ across divisions.

Wayne: The three methods used are the ones allowed by Section 482 of the Internal Revenue Code. Which method is applicable depends on the operating circumstances surrounding the transfer of a particular component.

Rhonda: So the way we price these internal transfers is driven to some degree, at least, by tax laws. Interesting. Perhaps you can describe for me how each method works and what conditions dictate that we use that method.

Wayne: The basic concept underlying any transfer price we use is the notion of an arm's-length price. Ideally, an arm's-length price is the price that an unrelated party would pay for the good being transferred. The IRS allows four methods to determine the arm's-length price. We use three of those methods. The comparable uncontrolled price method is based on market price. If the good being transferred has an external market, then the transfer price should be the price paid by an unrelated party, adjusted for differences that have a measurable effect on the price.

Rhonda: What kind of differences? Give me some examples.

Wayne: Well, the market price can be adjusted for differences such as landing costs (freight, insurance, customs duties, and special taxes) and marketing costs (commissions and advertising can be avoided with internal transfers). Adding landing costs and subtracting avoidable marketing costs are allowable adjustments to the market price.

Rhonda: I see. What happens if we sell the product to a related buyer who then resells it without any further processing? Or if the transferred good has no outside market at all?

Wayne: For the resale scenario, we use the resale price method. We take the resale price realized by our marketing divisions and adjust that price for the markup percentage and any differences like the ones I mentioned for the comparable uncontrolled price method. We work back from the third-party selling price to obtain an allowable transfer price.

Rhonda: How is the markup determined?

Wayne: It corresponds to the percentage of gross profit earned by the reseller or the gross profit percentage earned by other parties who buy and resell similar products.

Rhonda: I'm beginning to understand why we have three different methods. We have divisions that fit both of the first two types. We also have some transfers that have no outside market, nor do they have any potential for resale. These goods are simply used as components of other products that are sold. Is this where cost-plus pricing is used?

Wayne: Absolutely. In this case, the transfer price is defined as the costs of production plus an appropriate gross profit percentage, with adjustments for differences such as landing costs.

Rhonda: How do we define the appropriate gross profit percentage?

Wayne: Well, it could be the gross profit percentage earned by the seller on the sale of the final product. Or, if we can obtain the information, it could be the gross profit percentage earned by another party on a similar product.

Rhonda: Seems to me that cost-plus pricing could be used for all three settings. Why don't we do that so that we have some uniformity in the way we compute transfer prices?

Wayne: There is a problem. If the requirements are met for any one of the methods, then it must be used—unless we can show that another method is more appropriate. The burden of proof is on us. I doubt that uniformity would be an acceptable justification. If the IRS audits us and determines that the transfer price does not fairly reflect profits recognized in the United States, it can reallocate corporate income for purposes of taxation.

Required

1. Assume that Valley Electronics transfers a component from a U.S. division to a German division for $11.70. The landing costs are $2.50 per unit, and the avoidable commissions and advertising total $0.50 per unit. The component has a market price within the United States of $10. Is the company complying with the comparable uncontrolled price method? Would the IRS be concerned if the transfer price is greater than the market price after adjustments? Why or why not?
2. Assume that a manufacturing division in the United States transfers a component to a marketing division for resale. The resale price is $8, the gross profit percentage (gross profit divided by sales) is 25 percent, and landing costs total $1.20 per unit. Suppose that the actual transfer price (excluding landing costs) is $4.50. Should the company continue transferring at $4.50?
3. Suppose that a U.S. division has excess capacity. A European division has offered to buy a component that would increase the U.S. division's utilization of its capacity. The component has an outside market in the United States with a unit selling price of $12. The variable costs of production for the component are $6. Landing costs total $2 per unit, and an internal transfer avoids $1.25 per unit of marketing costs. The European division can purchase the component locally for $12. Ignoring income taxes, what is the minimum price that the European division should pay for the component (including landing costs)? The maximum price? Assuming that the joint benefit is split equally, what is the transfer price? Now discuss the impact of the Internal Revenue Code Section 482 regulations on this decision. (*Hint:* Consider Wayne's closing statement.) **(CMA adapted)**

Research Assignment

18-26

Cybercase
LO2

Find five multinational companies with web pages that describe their type(s) of involvement in international trade. Find at least one joint venture. What proportion of revenues and profit stem from the overseas ventures?

Glossary

A

Absorption costing A product-costing method that assigns all manufacturing costs to a product: direct materials, direct labor, variable overhead, and fixed overhead.

Absorption-costing (full-costing) income Income computed by following a functional classification

Acceptable quality level (AQL) The optimal balance between control costs and failure costs.

Accounting rate of return A measure of the return on a project in terms of income.

Activity A basic unit of work performed within an organization. It can also be defined as an aggregation of actions within an organization useful to managers for purposes of planning, controlling, and decision making.

Activity analysis The process of identifying, describing, and evaluating the activities an organization performs.

Activity attributes Financial and nonfinancial information items that describe individual activities.

Activity-based budgeting system A budgeting system at the activity level.

Activity-based management (ABM) A system-wide, integrated approach that focuses management's attention on activities with the objective of improving customer value and the profit achieved by providing this value.

Activity-based responsibility accounting A control system defined by centering responsibility on processes and teams that uses financial and nonfinancial measures of performance.

Activity-based costing (ABC) A cost assignment approach that first uses direct and driver tracing to assign costs to activities and then uses drivers to assign costs to cost objects.

Activity-based costing (ABC) system A cost system that first traces costs to activities and then traces costs from activities to products.

Activity-based management A systemwide, integrated approach that focuses management's attention on activities with the objective of improving customer value and the resulting profit. It emphasizes activity-based costing (ABC) and process value analysis.

Activity-based management (ABM) accounting system An accounting system that emphasizes the use of activities for assigning and managing costs.

Activity capacity The number of times an activity can be performed.

Activity dictionary A list of activities described by specific attributes such as name, definition, classification as primary or secondary, and activity driver.

Activity drivers Factors that measure the consumption of activities by products and other cost objects.

Activity elimination The process of eliminating non-value-added activities.

Activity flexible budgeting The prediction of what activity costs will be as activity output changes.

Activity input The resource consumed by an activity in producing its output.

Activity output The result or product of an activity.

Activity output measure The number of times an activity is performed; the quantifiable measure of output.

Activity reduction Decreasing the time and resources required by an activity.

Activity selection The process of choosing among different sets of activities that are caused by competing strategies.

Activity sharing Increasing the efficiency of necessary activities by using economies of scale.

Activity volume variance The difference between the actual activity level acquired (practical capacity) and the value-added standard quantity of activity that should be used.

Actual costing An approach that assigns actual cost of direct materials, direct labor, and overhead to products.

Adjusted cost of goods sold The cost of goods sold after the adjustment for the period's overhead variance.

Administrative costs All costs associated with research, development, and general administration of an organization that cannot reasonably be assigned to either marketing or production.

Advance pricing agreements (APAs) Agreements between the Internal Revenue Service and a taxpayer on the acceptability of a transfer price. The agreement is private and is binding on both parties for a specified period of time.

Aesthetics A quality attribute that is concerned with the appearance of tangible products as well as the appearance of the facilities, equipment, personnel, and communication materials associated with services.

Allocation Assignment of indirect costs to cost objects.

Annuity A series of future cash flows.

Applied overhead The total overhead assigned to actual production at any point in time.

Appraisal costs Costs incurred to determine whether products and services are conforming to their requirements or customer needs.

B

Balanced Scorecard A strategic management system that defines a strategic-based responsibility accounting system.

Base period A prior period used to set the benchmark for measuring productivity changes.

Batch-level activities Activities performed each time a batch of goods is produced.

Benchmarking An approach that uses best practices as the standard for evaluating activity performance.

Best-fitting line The line that fits a set of data points best in the sense that the sum of the squared deviations of the data points from the line is the smallest.

Binding constraints Constraints whose available resources are fully utilized.

Break-even point The point where total revenue equals total cost, the point of zero profit.

Budgetary slack The process of padding the budget by overestimating costs and underestimating revenues.

Budget committee A committee responsible for reviewing the budget, providing policy guidelines and budgetary goals, resolving differences that arise as the budget is prepared, approving the final budget, and monitoring actual performance.

Budget director The individual responsible for directing and coordinating an organization's overall budgeting process.

Budgets Financial plans for the future that identify objectives and the actions needed to achieve them.

By-products Two or more products that are produced simultaneously in joint production processes.

C

Capital budgeting The process of making capital investment decisions.

Capital investment decisions The process of planning, setting goals and priorities, arranging financing, and using certain criteria to select long-term assets.

Carrying costs Costs of carrying inventory.

Cash budget A detailed plan that outlines all sources and uses of cash.

Causal factors Variables or activities within a producing department that provoke the incurrence of support services costs.

Centralized decision making When decisions are made at the top level and lower-level managers are charged with implementing these decisions.

Certified internal auditor A person who has passed a comprehensive examination designed to ensure technical competence and has two years' experience.

Certified management accountant (CMA) A person who has passed a rigorous qualifying examination, has met an experience requirement, and participates in continuing education.

Certified public accountant (CPA) A person who is permitted (by law) to serve as an external auditor and who must pass a national examination and be licensed by the state in which he or she practices.

Coefficient of correlation The square root of the coefficient of determination, which is used to express not only the degree of correlation between two variables, but also the direction of the relationship.

Coefficient of determination The percentage of variability in the dependent variable that is explained by an independent variable.

Committed fixed costs Expenses incurred for the acquisition of long-term activity capacity.

Committed resources Resources that are supplied in advance of usage; These resources may or may not have an unused capacity.

Common costs The costs of resources used in the output of two or more services or products.

Common fixed expenses Expenses jointly caused by two or more segments.

Comparable uncontrolled price method The transfer price most preferred by the Internal Revenue Service under Section 482. The comparable uncontrolled price is essentially equal to the market price.

Compounding interest The earning of interest on interest.

Constraints Mathematical expressions that express resource limitations.

Constraint set The collection of all constraints that pertain to a particular optimization problem.

Consumption ratio The proportion of each activity consumed by a product.

Continuous budget A moving 12-month budget with a future month added as the current month expires.

Continuous improvement The process of searching for ways to increase the overall efficiency and productivity of activities by reducing waste, increasing quality, and reducing costs.

Continuous replenishment A system where a manufacturer assumes the inventory management function for the retailer.

Contribution margin Sales revenue minus total variable cost.

Contribution margin ratio The proportion of each sales dollar available to cover fixed costs and provide for profit.

Control The process of comparing actual results with budgeted results on a periodic basis.

Control activities Activities performed by an organization to prevent or detect poor quality; made up of prevention and appraisal activities.

Control costs The costs of performing control activities.

Controllable costs Costs whose level a manager can influence.

Controller The chief accounting officer; supervises all accounting departments.

Control limits The maximum allowable deviation from a standard.

Controlling The managerial activity of monitoring a plan's implementation and taking corrective action as needed.

Conversion cost The sum of direct labor cost and overhead cost.

Core objectives and measures Those objectives and measures common to most organizations.

Cost The cash or cash-equivalent value sacrificed for goods and services that is expected to bring a current or future benefit to the organization.

Cost assignment The process of associating the costs, once measured, with the units produced.

Cost behavior The general term for describing whether costs change as output changes.

Cost center A division of a company that is evaluated on the basis of cost.

Cost formula The equation for a straight line; Total cost = Fixed cost + (Variable rate × Output).

Cost measurement The act of determining the dollar amounts of direct materials, direct labor, and overhead used in production.

Cost object Any item such as a product, customer, department, project, activity, and so on, for which costs are measured and assigned.

Cost of capital The cost of investment funds, usually viewed as a weighted average of the costs of funds from all sources.

Cost of goods manufactured The total cost of goods completed during the current period.

Cost of goods sold The cost of direct materials, direct labor, and overhead attached to the units sold.

Cost of goods sold budget The estimated costs for the units sold.

Costs of quality Costs that exist because poor quality may or does exist.

Cost-plus method A transfer price acceptable to the Internal Revenue Service under Section 482. The cost-plus method is simply a cost-based transfer price.

Cost reconciliation The final section of the production report that compares the costs to account for with the costs accounted for to ensure that they are equal.

Cost-volume-profit graph Graph depicting the relationships among cost, volume, and profits.

Currency appreciation When one country's currency strengthens relative to another country's currency.

Currency depreciation When one country's currency has become relatively weaker and buys fewer units of another currency.

Currency risk management A company's management of its transaction, economic, and translation exposure due to exchange rate fluctuations.

Currently attainable standards Standards that can be achieved under efficient operating conditions.

Customer perspective A Balanced Scorecard viewpoint that defines the customer and market segments in which the business will compete.

Customer value The difference between what a customer receives (customer realization) and what the customer gives up (customer sacrifice).

Cycle time The length of time required to produce one unit of a product.

D

Decentralization The practice of delegating decision-making authority to the lower levels of management in a company.

Decentralized decision making When managers at lower levels are allowed to make and implement key decisions pertaining to their areas of responsibility.

Decision making The process of choosing among competing alternatives.

Decision model A set of procedures that, if followed, will lead to a decision.

Degree of operating leverage (DOL) A measure of the sensitivity of profit changes to changes in sales volume. It measures the percentage change in profits resulting from a percentage change in sales.

Delivery reliability Output is delivered on time.

Dependent variable A variable whose value depends on the value of another variable.

Direct costs Costs that can be easily and accurately traced to a cost object.

Direct fixed expenses Those fixed costs that can be traced to each product and would be avoided if the product did not exist.

Direct labor Labor that is directly traceable to the goods or services being produced.

Direct labor budget A budget showing the total direct labor hours needed and the associated cost for the number of units in the production budget.

Direct materials Those materials that are directly traceable to the goods or services being produced.

Direct materials purchases budget Budget that details the amount and cost of raw materials to be purchased in each time period; it depends on the expected use of materials in production and the raw materials inventory needs of a firm.

Direct method A method that allocates service costs directly to producing departments. This method ignores any interactions that may exist among support departments.

Direct tracing The process of identifying and assigning costs that are exclusively and physically associated with a cost object.

Discounted cash flows Future cash flows expressed in terms of their present value.

Discount factor The factor used to convert a future cash flow to its present value.

Discounting The process of computing the present value of future cash flows.

Discounting models Capital investment models that explicitly consider the time value of money in identifying criteria for accepting or rejecting proposed projects.

Discount rate The interest rate used to discount the future cash flow.

Discretionary fixed costs Costs incurred for the acquisition of short-term activity capacity.

Double-loop feedback Information about both the effectiveness of strategy implementation and the validity of assumptions underlying the strategy.

Driver analysis The effort expended to identify those factors that are the root causes of activity costs.

Driver tracing The use of drivers to assign costs to cost objects.

Drivers Factors that cause changes in resource usage, activity usage, costs, and revenues.

Drum-buffer-rope (DBR) system The TOC inventory management system that relies on the drum beat of the major constrained resources, time buffers, and ropes to determine inventory levels.

Dumping Predatory pricing on the international market.

Dysfunctional behavior Individual behavior that is in basic conflict with the goals of the organization.

E

Ecoefficiency A view of environmental management that maintains that organizations can produce more useful goods and services while simultaneously reducing negative environmental impacts, resource consumption, and costs.

Economic order quantity (EOQ) The amount that should be ordered (or produced) to minimize the total ordering (or setup) and carrying costs.

Economic valued added (EVA) A way of calculating residual income; net income (operating income minus taxes) minus the total annual cost of capital.

Economic risk The possibility that a firm's present value of future cash flows will be affected by exchange rate fluctuations.

Electronic business (e-business) Any business transaction or information exchange that is executed using information and communication technology.

Electronic data interchange (EDI) An early form of e-commerce that is an automated method of transmitting information from computer to computer.

Employee empowerment The authorizing of operational personnel to plan, control, and make decisions without explicit authorization from middle- and higher-level management.

Ending inventory The cost of inventory on hand at the end of a period.

Environmental costs Costs that are incurred because poor environmental quality exists or because poor environmental quality may exist.

Environmental detection costs Costs of activities executed to determine if products, processes, and other activities within a firm are in compliance with appropriate environmental standards.

Environmental external failure costs Costs of activities performed after discharging contaminants and waste into the environment.

Environmental internal failure costs Cost of activities performed because contaminants and waste have been produced but not discharged into the environment.

Environmental prevention costs Costs of activities carried out to prevent the production of contaminants and/or waste that could cause damage to the environment.

Equivalent units of output The complete units that could have been produced given the total amount of manufacturing effort expended for the period under consideration.

Ethical behavior Choosing actions that are "right," "proper," and "just." Our behavior can be right or wrong, it can be proper or improper, and the decisions we make can be fair or unfair.

Exchange gain The gain on the exchange of one currency for another due to appreciation of the home currency.

Exchange loss A loss on the exchange of one currency for another due to depreciation of the home currency.

Exchange rates The rates at which foreign currency can be exchanged for domestic currency.

Expected activity capacity Expected activity output for the coming year.

Expenses Expired costs.

External constraints Limiting factors imposed on the firm from external sources.

External linkages Activity relationships between the firm and the firm's suppliers and customers.

External measures Measures that relate to customers and shareholders.

F

Facility-level activities Activities that sustain a factory's general manufacturing processes.

Failure activities Activities performed by an organization or its customers in response to poor quality.

Failure costs The costs incurred by an organization because failure activities are performed.

Favorable (F) variances Variances produced whenever the actual amounts are less than the budgeted or standard allowances.

Feasible set of solutions The collection of all feasible solutions.

Feasible solution A solution that satisfies the constraints in the linear programming model.

Features (quality of design) Characteristics of a product that differentiate functionally similar products.

Feedback Information that can be used to evaluate or correct the steps being taken to implement a plan.

Financial measures Measures expressed in monetary terms.

Financial perspective A Balanced Scorecard viewpoint that describes the financial consequences of actions taken in the other three perspectives.

Financial productivity measure A productivity measure in which inputs and outputs are expressed in dollars.

Fitness for use The suitability of a product for carrying out its advertised functions.

Flexible resources Resources that can be easily purchased in the amount needed and at the time of use.

FIFO costing method A process costing method that separates units in beginning inventory from those produced during the current period. Unit costs include only current period costs and production.

Financial accounting information system An accounting information subsystem that is primarily concerned with producing outputs for external users, using well-specified economic events as inputs and processes that meet certain rules and conventions.

Financial budget A division of the master budget that details the inflows and outflows of cash and overall financial position.

Financial (functional)-based responsibility accounting system A control system defined by centering responsibility on organizational units and individuals that expresses performance measures in financial terms.

Finished goods inventory budget Budget that supplies information needed for the balance sheet and also serves as an important input for the preparation of the cost of goods sold budget.

First time through A common quality metric used to measure quality in manufacturing and value streams.

Fixed activity rate The total committed cost divided by the total capacity available.

Fixed cost A cost that stays the same as output changes.

Fixed overhead spending variance The difference between actual fixed overhead and the budgeted fixed overhead.

Fixed overhead volume variance The difference between budgeted fixed overhead and applied fixed overhead.

Flexible budget A budget that enables a firm to compute expected costs for a range of activity levels.

Flexible budget variance The difference between the actual amount and the flexible budget amount.

Flexible resources Resources that are purchased as used and needed. There is no unused or excess capacity for these resources.

Foreign trade zone An area near a customer's port of entry that is physically on U.S. soil but considered to be outside U.S. commerce. Goods imported into foreign trade zones are duty-free until they leave the zone.

Forward contract An agreement that requires the buyer to exchange a specified amount of currency at a specified rate (the forward rate) on a specified future date.

Full environmental costing The assignment of all environmental costs, both private and societal, to products.

Full private costing The assignment of only private costs to individual products.

Functional-based costing (FBC) An approach for assigning costs of shared resources to products and other cost drivers using only production or unit-level drivers.

Functional-based management A managerial approach that attempts to control costs by assigning costs to organizational units and then holding the organizational unit manager responsible for controlling the assigned costs.

Functional-based management (FBM) accounting systems An accounting information system that emphasizes the use of functional organizational units to assign and manage costs.

Future value The value that will accumulate by the end of an investment's life, assuming a specified compound return.

G

Gainsharing Providing to a company's entire workforce cash incentives that are keyed to quality and productivity gains.

Goal congruence The alignment of managerial and organizational goals.

Goodness of fit The degree of association between cost and activity.

H

Half-year convention The assumption that a newly acquired asset is in service for one-half year of its first taxable year regardless of the date the service actually began.

Hedging A way of insuring against gains and losses on foreign currency exchange.

Heterogeneity When there is a greater chance of variation in the performance of services than in the production of products.

Hidden quality costs Opportunity costs resulting from poor quality.

High-low method A method of determining the equation of a straight line by preselecting two points (the high and low points) that will be used to compute the intercept and slope parameters.

Hypothetical sales value Eventual market value less all separable (or further) processing costs.

I

Ideal standards Standards that demand maximum efficiency and can only be achieved if everything operates perfectly.

Impact analysis A life-cycle assessment step that assesses the environmental effects of competing designs and provides a relative ranking of those effects.

Improvement analysis A life-cycle assessment step that has the objective of reducing the environmental impacts revealed by the inventory and impact steps.

Incentives The means an organization uses to influence managers to exert effort to achieve an organization's goal.

Independent projects Projects that, if accepted or rejected, do not affect the cash flow of other projects.

Independent variable A variable that measures output and explains changes in cost; its value does not depend on the value of another variable.

Indirect costs Costs that cannot be easily and accurately traced to a cost object.

Industrial value chain The linked set of value-creating activities from basic raw materials to the disposal of the final product by end-use customers.

Innovation process A process that anticipates the emerging and potential needs of customers and creates new products and services to satisfy those needs.

Input trade-off efficiency The least-cost, technically efficient mix of inputs.

Inseparability The fact that producers of services and buyers of services must usually be in direct contact for an exchange to take place.

Intangibility When buyers of services cannot see, feel, hear, or taste a service before it is bought.

Intercept parameter The fixed cost, representing the point where the cost formula intercepts the vertical axis.

Internal business process perspective A Balanced Scorecard viewpoint that describes the internal processes needed to provide value for customers and owners.

Internal constraints Limiting factors found within a firm.

Internal failure costs Costs incurred when products and services do not conform to specifications or customer needs.

Internal linkages Relationships among activities that are performed within a firm's portion of the industrial value chain (the internal value chain).

Internal measures Measures that relate to the processes and capabilities that create value for customers and shareholders.

Internal rate of return The interest rate that sets the present value of a project's cash inflows equal to the present value of the project's cost.

Internal value chain The set of activities required to design, develop, produce, market, distribute, and deliver products and services to customers.

Inventory All the money the organization spends in turning materials into throughput.

Inventory analysis A life-cycle assessment step that specifies the types and quantities of materials and energy inputs needed and the resulting environmental releases.

Investment center A division of a company that is evaluated on the basis of return on investment.

J

JIT purchasing A purchasing method that requires suppliers to deliver parts and materials just in time to be used in production.

JIT II Form of a JIT purchasing method that requires the supplier's sales representative to work on site (on a full-time basis) at the customer's facility while being paid by the supplier.

Job One distinct unit or set of units.

Job-order costing system A costing system in which costs are collected and assigned to units of production for each individual job.

Job-order cost sheet A subsidiary account to the work-in-process account on which the total costs of materials, labor, and overhead for a single job are accumulated.

Joint products Two or more products that are produced simultaneously by the same process up to a "split-off" point.

Joint venture A type of partnership in which investors co-own the enterprise.

Just-in-time manufacturing A demand-pull system that requires goods to be pulled through the system by present demand rather than pushed through the system on a fixed schedule based on anticipated demand.

K

Kaizen costing Efforts to reduce costs of existing products and processes.

Kaizen standard An interim standard that reflects the planned improvement for a coming period.

Kanban system An information system that controls production through the use of markers or cards.

Keep-or-drop decisions Relevant costing analyses that focus on keeping or dropping a segment of a business.

L

Labor efficiency variance (LEV) The difference between the labor hours that were actually used and the labor hours that should have been used.

Labor rate variance (LRV) The difference between what was paid to direct laborers and what should have been paid.

Lag measures Outcome measures of results from past efforts.

Lead measures (performance drivers) Factors that drive future performance.

Lead time The time required to receive the economic order quantity once an order is placed or a setup is initialized.

Lean manufacturing A philosophical approach designed to eliminate waste and maximize customer value that is characterized by delivering the right product, in the right quantity, with the right quality, at the exact time the customer needs it and at the lowest possible cost.

Learning and growth (infrastructure) perspective A Balanced Scorecard viewpoint that defines the capabilities that an organization needs to create long-term growth and improvement.

Life-cost management The management of value-chain activities so that a long-term competitive advantage is created.

Life-cycle assessment Identifying the environmental consequences of a product through its entire life cycle and searching for opportunities to obtain environmental improvements.

Life-cycle cost assessment A method that assigns costs and benefits to environmental consequences and improvements.

Life-cycle costs All the costs associated with a product for its entire life cycle.

Linear programming A method that searches among possible solutions until it finds the optimal solution.

Line positions Positions that have direct responsibility for the basic objectives of an organization.

Long run A period of time in which all costs are variable.

Loose constraints Constraints whose limited resources are not fully used by the product mix.

M

Make-or-buy decisions Relevant costing analyses that focus on whether a component should be made internally or purchased externally.

Management accounting information system An information system that provides information needed to satisfy specific management objectives.

Manufacturing cells Machines grouped in families, usually in a semicircle, so that they can be used to perform a variety of operations in sequence. Each cell is set up to produce a particular product or product family.

Maquiladora A manufacturing plant, located in Mexico, which processes imported materials and re-exports them to the United States.

Margin The ratio of operating income to sales.

Margin of safety The units sold or expected to be sold or the revenue earned or expected to be earned above the break-even volume.

Marketing (selling) costs The costs necessary to market, distribute, and service a product or service.

Markup A percentage applied to the base cost; it includes desired profit and any costs not included in the base cost.

Master budget The comprehensive financial plan for an organization as a whole; is typically for a one-year period corresponding to the fiscal year of a company.

Materials price variance (MPV) The difference between what should have been paid for materials and what was actually paid.

Materials requisition forms Forms used to assign direct materials costs to each job.

Materials usage variance (MUV) The difference between the direct materials actually used and the direct materials that should have been used for the actual output.

Maximum transfer price The transfer price that would leave the buying division no worse off if an input were purchased from an internal division than if the same good were purchased externally.

Method of least squares A statistical method to find a line that best fits a set of data. It is used to break out the fixed and variable components of a mixed cost.

Minimum transfer price The transfer price that would leave the selling division no worse off if the good were sold to an internal division than if the good were sold to an external party.

Mixed cost A cost that has both a fixed and a variable component.

Modified accelerated cost recovery system (MACRS) An allowable method for computing depreciation for tax purposes.

Monetary incentives The use of economic rewards to motivate managers.

Multinational corporation (MNC) A corporation for which a significant amount of business is done in more than one country.

Multiple-period quality trend report A graph that plots quality costs (as a percentage of sales) against time.

Multiple regression The use of least squares analysis to determine the parameters in a linear equation involving two or more explanatory variables.

Mutually exclusive projects Projects that, if accepted, preclude the acceptance of other competing projects.

Myopic behavior Managerial actions that improve budgetary performance in the short run but bring long-run harm to a firm.

N

Net income Operating income minus income taxes.

Net present value The difference between the present value of the cash inflows and outflows associated with a project.

Net realizable value method Method used to prorate joint costs based on each product's share of hypothetical sales value.

Nondiscounting models Capital investment models that identify criteria for accepting or rejecting projects without considering the time value of money.

Nonfinancial measures Measures expressed in nonmonetary units.

Noninventoriable (period) costs Costs that are expensed in the period in which they are incurred.

Nonmonetary incentives The use of psychological and social rewards to motivate managers.

Nonproduction costs Those costs associated with the functions of designing, developing, marketing, distribution, customer service, and general administration.

Non-unit-level activity drivers Factors that measure the consumption of non-unit-level activities by product.

Non-unit-level drivers Drivers other than production drivers that describe cause-and-effect relationships and other cost objects.

Non-value-added activity Any activity other than those that are absolutely essential to remain in business.

Non-value-added costs Costs that are caused either by non-value-added activities or the inefficient performance of value-added activities.

Normal activity capacity The average activity output for a given period.

Normal costing An approach that assigns the actual costs of direct materials and direct labor to products; however, overhead costs are assigned to products using predetermined rates.

Normal cost of goods sold The cost of goods sold before an adjustment for an overhead variance.

O

Objective function The function to be optimized, usually a profit function; thus optimization usually means maximizing profits.

Objective measures Measures that can be readily quantified and verified.

Observable quality costs Costs that are available from an organization's accounting records.

Operating assets All assets acquired to generate operating income, including cash, receivables, inventories, land, buildings, and equipment.

Operating budget A division of the master budget that describes the income-generating activities of a firm (sales, production, and finished goods inventories).

Operating expenses All the money the organization spends in turning inventories into throughput.

Operating income Only revenue and expenses from a firm's normal operations.

Operating leverage The use of fixed costs to extract higher percentage changes in profits as sales activity changes.

Operational productivity measure A measure that is expressed in physical terms.

Operation costing Using job-order procedures to assign material costs to products and a process approach to assign conversion costs.

Operations process A process that produces and delivers existing products and services to customers.

Opportunity cost The benefit given up or sacrificed when one alternative is chosen over another.

Opportunity cost approach A transfer pricing system that identifies the minimum price that a selling division would be willing to accept and the maximum price that a buying division would be willing to pay.

Optimal solution The best feasible solution—the one that maximizes the total contribution margin.

Ordering costs Costs of placing and receiving an order.

Outsourcing The payment by a company for a business function formerly done in-house.

Overapplied overhead The variance when the actual overhead is less than the applied overhead.

Overhead All production costs other than direct materials and direct labor.

Overhead budget Budget that shows the expected cost of all indirect manufacturing items.

Overhead variance The difference between the actual overhead and the applied overhead.

P

Parallel processing A processing pattern in which two or more sequential processes are required to produce a finished good.

Participative budgeting An approach to budgeting that allows managers who will be held accountable for budgetary performance to participate in the budget's development.

Partial productivity measurement A ratio that measures productivity for one input at a time.

Payback period The time required for a firm to recover its original investment.

Performance The measure of how consistently and well a product functions.

Performance reports Financial and nonfinancial feedback in the form of formal reports that compare actual data with planned data or benchmarks.

Perishability When services cannot be stored for future use by a consumer.

Physical flow schedule A schedule that reconciles units to account for with units accounted for. The physical units are not adjusted from percent of completion.

Physical units method Method of allocating joint costs under which the joint costs are distributed to products on the basis of some physical measure that may be expressed in units. Under this method, each joint product is allocated the same proportion of joint cost as the underlying proportion of units.

Planning The managerial activity involving the detailed formulation of action to achieve a particular end; it requires setting objectives and identifying methods to achieve those objectives.

Pool rate The overhead costs for a homogeneous cost pool divided by the practical capacity of the activity driver associated with the pool.

Postaudit A follow-up analysis of an investment decision, comparing actual benefits and costs with expected benefits and costs.

Postpurchase costs Costs such as operation, support, maintenance, and disposal that are incurred by the customer after buying a product.

Postsales service process A process that provides critical and responsive service to customers after the product or service has been delivered.

Practical activity capacity The maximum output that can be realized if an activity is performed efficiently.

Practical capacity The efficient level of activity performance.

Predetermined overhead rate A rate based on estimated data (Predetermined overhead rate = Budgeted (estimated) cost / Estimated activity usage).

Predatory pricing The practice of setting prices below cost for the purpose of injuring competitors and eliminating competition.

Present value The amount that must be invested now to produce the future value.

Prevention costs Costs incurred to prevent poor quality in the products or services being produced.

Price discrimination The charging of different prices to different customers for essentially the same product.

Price gouging When firms with market power price products too high.

Price (rate) variance The difference between the actual and standard unit price of an input multiplied by the number of inputs used.

Price-recovery component The difference between the total profit change and the profit-linked productivity change.

Price standards The amount that should be paid for the quantity of the input to be used.

Primary activity An activity that is consumed by a product or customer.

Prime cost The sum of direct materials cost and direct labor cost.

Private costs Costs for which a firm is financially responsible.

Process-costing system A costing system that accumulates production costs by process or by department for a given period of time.

Process creation The installation of an entirely new process with the objective of meeting customer and financial objectives.

Processes Activities with a common objective.

Process improvement Incremental and constant increases in the efficiency of an existing process.

Process innovation (business reengineering) The performance of a process in a radically new way with the objective of achieving dramatic improvements in response time, quality, and efficiency.

Process value analysis An approach that focuses on processes and activities and emphasizes systemwide performance instead of individual performance.

Process value chain The innovation, operations, and postsales service processes.

Producing departments Units within an organization responsible for producing the products or services that are sold to customers.

Product cost A cost assignment that supports a well-specified managerial objective.

Product diversity The situation present when products consume overhead activities in systematically different proportions.

Production budget Budget that describes how many units must be produced in order to meet sales needs and satisfy ending inventory requirements.

Production costs Those costs associated with the manufacture of goods or the provision of services.

Production Kanban A card or marker that specifies the quantity that the Kanban system should produce.

Production report The document that summarizes the manufacturing activity that takes place in a process department for a given period of time.

Production (unit-level) drivers Measures of consumption that are highly correlated with production output.

Productivity The efficient production of output, using the least quantity of inputs possible.

Productivity measurement A quantitative assessment of productivity changes.

Product-level (sustaining) activities Activities performed as needed to support the various products produced by a company.

Product life cycle The time a product exists, from conception to abandonment.

Product stewardship The practice of designing, manufacturing, maintaining, and recycling products to minimize adverse environmental impacts.

Profile measurement A series or vector of separate and distinct partial operational measures.

Profit center A division of a company that is evaluated on the basis of operating income or profit.

Profit-linked productivity measurement Measuring the amount of profit change attributable to productivity change.

Profit-volume graph A visual portrayal of the relationship between profits and sales volume.

Pseudoparticipation A budgetary system in which top management assumes total control of the budgeting process and seeks only superficial participation from lower-level managers.

Publicly traded company A company that issues stock traded on U.S. stock exchanges.

Q

Quality of conformance A measure of how a product meets its specifications.

Quality product or service A product or service that meets or exceeds customer expectations.

Quantity standards The amount of input that should be used per unit of output.

R

Realized external failure costs Costs incurred by and paid for by a firm.

Reciprocal method A method of allocation that simultaneously allocates service costs to all user departments. It fully accounts for support-department interaction.

Relevant costs Future costs that differ across alternatives.

Relevant range The range of output over which the assumed cost/output relationship is valid for the normal operations of a firm.

Reliability The probability that a product or service will perform its intended function for a specified length of time.

Reorder point The point in time when a new order should be placed (or setup started).

Required rate of return The minimum acceptable rate of return.

Resale price method A transfer price acceptable to the Internal Revenue Service under Section 482. The resale price method computes a transfer price equal to the sales price received by the reseller, less an appropriate markup.

Residual income The difference between operating income and the minimum dollar return required on a company's operating assets.

Resource drivers Factors that measure the consumption of resources by activities.

Responsibility accounting A system that measures the results of each responsibility center according to the information managers' need to operate their center.

Responsibility accounting system A system that measures the results of each responsibility center according to the information managers need to operate their centers.

Responsibility center A segment of the business whose manager is accountable for specified sets of activities.

Return on investment (ROI) The profit earned per dollar of investment.

Revenue center The division of a business that is evaluated on the basis of sales.

Root causes The most basic causes for an activity being performed.

Ropes Actions taken to tie the rate at which material is released into the plant (at the first operation) to the production rate of the constrained resource.

S

Safety stock Extra inventory carried to serve as insurance against fluctuations in demand.

Sales budget The projection approved by the budget committee that describes expected sales in units and dollars; it is the basis for all the other operating budgets and most financial budgets.

Sales mix The relative combination of products being sold by a firm.

Sales-value-at-split-off method Method of allocating joint costs based on each product's proportionate share of sales value at the split-off point.

Sarbanes-Oxley Act (SOX) Legislation passed in June 2002 establishing stronger government control and regulation of public companies in the United States; it applies to publicly traded companies.

Scattergraph A plot of data points.

Scatterplot method A method of determining the equation of a line by plotting the data on a graph.

Secondary activity An activity that is consumed by other primary and secondary activities.

Segment A subunit of a company of sufficient importance to warrant the production of performance reports.

Segment margin The profit contribution each segment makes toward covering a firm's common fixed costs.

Selling and administrative expenses budget Budget that outlines planned expenditures for nonmanufacturing activities.

Sell or process further Relevant costing analysis that focuses on whether a product should be processed beyond the split-off point.

Sensitivity analysis The "what if" process of altering certain key variables to assess the effect on the original outcome.

Sequential (or step) method A method that allocates service costs to user departments in a sequential manner. It gives partial consideration to interactions among support departments.

Sequential processing A processing pattern in which units must pass through one process before they can be worked on in later processes.

Serviceability The ease of maintaining and/or repairing a product.

Services Tasks or activities performed for a customer or an activity performed by a customer using an organization's products or facilities.

Setup costs Costs of preparing equipment and facilities so they can be used to produce a particular product or component.

Short run A period of time in which at least one cost is fixed.

Simplex method An algorithm that identifies the optimal solution for a linear programming problem.

Single-loop feedback Information about the effectiveness of strategy implementation.

Slope parameter The variable cost per unit of activity usage.

Special-order decisions Decisions that focus on whether a specially priced order should be accepted or rejected.

Split-off point The point at which products become distinguishable after passing through a common process.

Spot rate The exchange rate of one currency for another for immediate delivery.

Staff positions Positions that are supportive in nature and have only indirect responsibility for an organization's basic objectives.

Standard cost per unit The sum of the standard costs for direct materials, direct labor, and overhead.

Standard cost sheet A listing of the details underlying the standard unit cost.

Standard hours allowed (SH) The direct labor hours that should have been used to produce the actual output (Unit labor standard × Actual output).

Standard quantity of materials allowed (SQ) The quantity of materials that should have been used to produce the actual output (Unit materials standard × Actual output).

Static budget A budget for a particular level of activity.

Step cost A cost function in which cost is defined for ranges of activity usage.

Stockout costs Costs of not having a product available when demanded by a customer.

Strategic cost management The use of cost data to develop and identify superior strategies that will produce a sustainable competitive advantage.

Strategic decision making The process of choosing among alternative strategies with the goal of selecting one or more strategies that provide a company with a reasonable assurance of long-term growth and survival.

Strategic plan Plan that identifies strategies for future activities and operations, generally covering at least five years.

Strategy The process of choosing a business's market and customer segments, identifying its critical internal business processes, and selecting the individual and organizational capabilities needed to meet internal, customer, and financial objectives.

Strategy translation Specifying objectives, measures, targets, and initiatives for each Balanced Scorecard perspective.

Subjective measures Measures that are nonquantifiable and whose values are judgmental in nature.

Sunk cost A cost that cannot be affected by any future action.

Supplies Those materials necessary for production that do not become part of the finished product or are not used in providing a service.

Supply chain management The management of material flows beginning with suppliers and their upstream suppliers, moving to the transformation of materials into finished goods, and finishing with the distribution of finished goods to customers and their downstream customers.

Support departments Units within an organization that provide essential support services for producing departments.

Sustainable development Development that meets the needs of the present without compromising the ability of future generations to meet their own needs.

T

Tactical decision making Choosing among alternatives with an immediate or limited end in view.

Taguchi loss function A function that assumes that any variation from the target value of a quality characteristic causes hidden quality costs.

Takt time The rate at which customers demand product.

Tangible products Goods produced by converting raw materials though the use of labor and capital inputs, such as plant, land, and machinery.

Target cost The difference between the sales price needed to capture a predetermined market share and the desired per-unit profit.

Target costing A method of determining the cost of a product or service based on the price (target price) that customers are willing to pay.

Tariff A tax on imports levied by the federal government.

Technical efficiency The point at which, for any mix of inputs that will produce a given output, no more of any one input is used than is absolutely necessary.

Testable strategy A set of linked objectives aimed at an overall goal.

Theoretical activity capacity The absolute maximum activity output possible if the activity is performed perfectly.

Throughput The rate at which an organization generates money through sales.

Time buffer The inventory needed to keep the constrained resource busy for a specified time interval.

Time tickets Forms used to track the hours worked by direct labor on each job.

Total budget variance The difference between the actual cost of the input and its planned cost.

Total preventive maintenance A program of preventive maintenance that has zero machine failures as its standard.

Total product The complete range of tangible and intangible benefits that a customer receives from a purchased product.

Total productive efficiency The point at which technical and price efficiency are satisfied.

Total productivity measurement An assessment of productive efficiency for all inputs combined.

Total quality management A philosophy in which manufacturers strive to create an environment that will enable workers to manufacture perfect (zero-defect) products.

Traceability The ability to assign a cost to a cost object in an economically feasible way by means of a cause-and-effect relationship.

Tracing The actual assignment of costs to a cost object using an observable measure of resources consumed by the cost object.

Transaction risk The possibility that future cash transactions will be affected by changing exchange rates.

Transfer price The price charged for a component by the selling division to the buying division of the same company.

Transferred-in costs The costs transferred from a prior process to a subsequent process.

Translation (or accounting) risk The degree to which a firm's financial statements are exposed to exchange rate fluctuation.

Treasurer The person responsible for the finance function. Specifically, the treasurer raises capital and manages cash and investments.

Turnover Sales divided by average operating assets.

U

Underapplied overhead The variance when the actual overhead is greater than the applied overhead.

Unfavorable (U) variances Variances produced whenever the actual input amounts are greater than the budgeted or standard allowances.

Unit cost The total cost associated with the units produced divided by the number of units produced.

Unit-level activities Activities performed each time a unit is produced.

Unit-level activity drivers Factors that cause changes in cost as the units produced change.

Unrealized external failure costs (societal costs) Costs caused by a firm but that are incurred and paid for by parties outside the firm.

Unused capacity variance The difference between activity availability and activity usage.

Usage (efficiency) variance The difference between the actual and standard quantity of inputs multiplied by the standard unit price of the input.

V

Value-added activities Those activities necessary to remain in business.

Value-added costs The costs to perform value-added activities with perfect efficiency.

Value-added standard The optimal output level for an activity.

Value chain The set of activities required to design, develop, produce, market, and service a product or service.

Value stream Stream made up of all activities, both value-added and non-value-added, required to bring a group or service from its starting point to a finished product in the hands of the customer.

Variable activity rate The total cost of flexible resources divided by the capacity used.

Variable budgets (*See* **Flexible budget.**)

Variable cost A cost that, in total, varies in direct proportion to changes in output.

Variable costing A product-costing method that assigns only variable manufacturing costs to production: direct materials, direct labor, and variable overhead. Fixed overhead is treated as a period cost.

Variable cost ratio The proportion of each sales dollar that must be used to cover variable costs.

Variable overhead efficiency variance The change in variable overhead consumption that occurs because of efficient (or inefficient) use of direct labor.

Variable overhead spending variance The measure of the aggregate effect of differences between the actual variable overhead rate and the standard variable overhead rate.

Velocity The number of units of output that can be produced in a given period of time.

Vendor Kanban A card or marker that notifies suppliers to deliver more parts and specifies when parts are needed.

W

Waste Anything customers do not value; it consumes resources without adding value.

Weighted average costing method A process-costing method that combines the beginning inventory costs with current-period costs to compute unit cost. Costs and output from the current period and the previous period are averaged to compute unit costs.

What-if analysis (*See* **Sensitivity analysis.**)

Whole-life cost The life-cycle cost of a product plus its postpurchase costs.

Withdrawal Kanban A card that specifies that quantity that a subsequent process should withdraw from the preceding process.

Work in process All partially completed units found in production at a given point in time.

Work-in-process file A file that is a collection of all job cost sheets.

Z

Zero defects A quality performance standard that requires all products and services to be produced and delivered according to specifications.

Subject Index

Company Index